EVELYN ROSE MBE, the world-famous authority on Jewish food and food customs, was an internationally acclaimed food writer. For forty years she was food columnist of the *Jewish Chronicle* – the UK's largest Jewish newspaper – never missing a single issue. Renowned for her imaginative, easy-to-follow and fail-proof recipes, Evelyn also earned a devoted following in the general community through her broadcasts on radio and TV, her Master Classes in Food and Wine and her cookbooks, including *The Entertaining Cookbook* and *Weekend Cook* (with Sula Leon).

In 1989 Evelyn Rose was awarded an MBE for her services to the consumer. She held the coveted Bronze Medal of the International Wine and Food Society. For her services to her profession, she was elected one of only five Honorary Life Fellows of the Institute of Home Economics. She was the Joint National Chairman of the Guild of Food Writers.

She collaborated with her daughter Judi on *The First Time Cookbook*, and their bestselling *Mother & Daughter Jewish Cooking* went on to conquer the American market.

Evelyn Rose died in May 2003. She left behind her devoted husband Myer – always her favourite taster and adviser – sons David and Alan, Judi, and five much loved grandchildren.

Other titles by Evelyn Rose

The Entertaining Cookbook
Evelyn Rose Goes Microwave
The First-Time Cookbook (with Judi Rose)
The New Jewish Cuisine
Mother & Daughter Jewish Cooking

THE NEW COMPLETE INTERNATIONAL JEWISH COOKBOOK

EVELYN ROSE

ROBSON BOOKS

For Myer,
who after more than 40 years
is still testing – and tasting.

This edition published in 2004 by
Robson Books,
The Chrysalis Building, Bramley Road,
London W10 6SP

An imprint of The Chrysalis Books Group

British Library Cataloguing in Publication Data
A catalogue record for this title is available from the British Library.

ISBN 1 86105 732 6

Designed by Linda Wade
Line illustrations by Julie Beech

Printed in Finland by WS Bookwell

Contents

PRESERVES

COOKING FOR A CROWD

FESTIVALS

ACKNOWLEDGEMENTS

'Thus sayeth Kohelet, "There is nothing new under the sun"', and of no sphere is this aphorism from Ecclesiastes more true than the world of food and cookery. My own knowledge is only the sum of that accumulated by hundreds of generations of Jewish women who have cooked before me. All I can hope to do is to make that knowledge relevant - and accessible - to people cooking at this particular time.

So while acknowledging below the help of the very many people who have each in their own way contributed to the sum total of this book, I must also pay tribute to those women who cooked before me and who, without benefit of cookery books, established an oral tradition of superb Jewish food that has been passed down in an unbroken chain from mother to daughter - and not infrequently to son - from the beginning of our recorded history.

My first and deepest thanks go to my husband, Myer, for his untiring help and support in every aspect of my work, and also to my children, David and Andrea, Alan and Christiana, and in particular Judi, for their constant encouragement and advice.

Sula Leon, my friend and partner in Master Classes in Food and Wine, has been generous in both practical support and encouragement. My publisher, Jeremy Robson, and his co-directors, Carole Robson and Cheryll Roberts, together with my editor, Louise Dixon, have given me enthusiastic - and patient - support throughout a prolonged gestation period. My personal assistant, Diane Ward, produced the manuscript with unwavering efficiency and Lesley Levene edited it with immense skill, understanding and tact.

Dayan O. Y. Westheim of the Manchester Beth Din and Rabbi Dr Michael Hilton were generous with their advice, as was food scientist Lawrence Shields. Gordon Beech, Managing Director of Stanneylands Hotel, Wilmslow, Cheshire, gave freely of his expertise, as did his Executive Chef, Steven Kitchen, who headed the food preparation and photographic styling team of Kate Simmonds, Christine Windeler and myself. I must also thank Master Butcher Jeffrey Holland of Hymark Kosher Butchers, who showed great initiative in preparing meat and poultry to my often unusual specifications.

The following people generously shared their family recipes and experiences with me, although I take full responsibility for their present form, which took shape only after many testing sessions in the kitchen and round the dinner table: Minda Alexander; Myrtle Allen, Ballymaloe Country House Hotel, Eire, and Darina Allen, Ballymaloe Cookery School, Eire; Alexandra Baron; Ethel Bernstein; Roslyn Blain; Bayla Brandeis; Christine Brioude-Giuliani, Hotel du Vivarais, Ardèche, France; Faye Bussin; Susan Campion; Sonia Caplan; Chana Cohen, Israel; Polly Conn; Michael Cummings; Peter Dixon, White Moss House Hotel, English Lakes; Vera Ellison; Ilse J. Eton; Vera Freedman; Rose Frohwein; Barbara Goodman; Ursula Gross;

Shiphra Grosskopf; Dr Elizabeth Higham; Marion Jones, Croque en Bouche, Malvern Wells, Worcestershire; Lawrence Kay, Master Baker; Marilyn Kaye; Jill King; Ruth Kyte; Phyllis Leigh; Jose Levene; Agneta Levi; Helen Lister; Millie Livshin; Rosalyn Livshin; Mme Marlet, Normandy; Daphne Martell; Dr Basil and Olivia Messer; Rochelle Miller; Minnie Morgan; Ernest and Fay Moritz; Bertha Rayner; Eileen Rose; Pamela Rose; Dorothy Rothmer; Elaine Rubens; Carol Shields; Sybil Shields; Ruth Silman; Steffi Surkes; Anne Stonefield; and Margaret Travis.

EVELYN ROSE
Manchester, England

FOREWORD BY JUDI ROSE

Some years ago, on the cookery page of the *Jewish Chronicle* just before Pesach, a worried-looking Moses was pictured with a chef's toque on his head and a copy of an Evelyn Rose cookery book under his arm. The caption – suitably adapted from Exodus – read: 'You promised us chicken soup and knaidlach, chopped liver and gefilte fish,' said the Children of Israel. 'Instead we were given coq au vin blanc and apricot frangipane. Was it for this time that we were led out of bondage?'

My mother, pleased and tickled by this cartoon, was also defiant. She believed that tradition-inspired innovation was the way forward for Jewish food. Incorporating tastes and ingredients from other cuisines, using new technology to save time and effort, and keeping an eye on healthy, nutritious eating were not only desirable, they were essential for modern Jewish cookery.

As a result, over nearly fifty years ago Evelyn Rose almost single-handedly re-defined Anglo-Jewish cuisine. The now classic Gefilte Fish Provencal (page 57), Savoury Strudels (pages 17-18, 163-4) and Luscious Lemon Cake (page 419) were all her creations, but clearly, too much of a fusion of Jewish tradition with shifting tastes and lifestyles.

In choosing and developing her recipes, my mother also believed that each dish must have *tam* – that extra 'something' which makes it taste special, and thus worth the trouble for busy people wondering what to put on their table. She also tested and wrote her recipes time and time again to be sure that success was a certainty. This guarantee of tasty food and recipes that 'always work' is doubtless the reason why this book has been continuously in print since it was first published in 1976, and why her fans refer to it as their 'bible'.

When Evelyn Rose wrote, and later revised, *The New Complete*, she also added her zest for life, a taste for adventure and her own unique qualities: devotion to her craft, commitment to her readers and an extra ingredient of her own – a large helping of love. Within these pages, you will find all this – and more – in generous measure.

Happy cooking.

Judi Rose

JEWISH FOOD: INTRODUCTION TO THE 1976 EDITION

One can almost pinpoint the exact occasion, in the second millennium BCE, when the art of Jewish cookery was born. On that day the course of world history was changed when the matriarch Rebecca, by the judicious use of herbs and spices, gave the savour of wild venison to the insipid flesh of a young kid, and established a culinary philosophy of 'taste with economy' that has been followed by her descendants ever since.

When Rebecca made her kid casserole and her son Esau sold his birthright for a bowl of lentil soup, the everyday food of those early Jews was primitive in the extreme. Except on special occasions, the staple diet consisted of boiled vegetables such as leeks, garlic and onions, and salads of raw herbs, with boiled meat cooked only on a holiday. During the following 2,000 years, the Jews became in turn the subjects of the four civilizations in which the art of the kitchen was first evolved. When the empires of these Egyptians, Persians, Greeks and Romans had faded into history, their cooking methods survived - in the kitchens of their former subjects.

To this day Jewish housewives, during Pesach (the Feast of the Passover), make a sweetmeat of dried apricots which their ancestors learned when they were slaves in Egypt; they make a stuffed strudel with the same filling of poppy seeds and honey that was used to garnish the fattened dormice at Trimalchio's famous Roman feast; and during Shavuot (the Feast of Weeks) they bake honey and cheese cakes that are a legacy of the many years of Seleucid rule.

If these 'remembrances of foods past' were the sum total of Jewish cooking, it is doubtful that it would have survived to the present day. Jewish tradition teaches that when Moses descended from Mount Sinai he gave the waiting Jewish women the code of culinary practice by which they have conducted their kitchens ever since, and which has been responsible, to a large extent, for the unique flavour and character of their food.

In the Jewish dietary laws, there are the prohibitions: no shellfish; no pig; no carrion; no birds of prey; no thing that crawls upon its belly. Then there are the categories of permitted foods: only those fish that have fins and scales; only those beasts that chew the cud and have cloven hooves; only those birds that have been slaughtered according to the law. Then there are the cooking and serving instructions for these permitted foods: foods of animal and dairy origin not to be combined either during the cooking or the serving; dairy foods to be served after meat foods only when a specified number of hours has elapsed; meat to be purged of its blood before use.

However, it was in the Ten Commandments themselves that there appeared those instructions which have resulted in the development of some of the most typical of Jewish foods - those dishes that can be cooked one day and served the next. 'On the seventh day thou shalt do no work, neither thy maidservant nor thy manservant,' said the Law, and so Jewish housewives would spend all day Thursday, and most of Friday before dusk, making herring salads, liver pâté, soups, fruit pies, yeast cakes and, in particular, those meat and vegetable casseroles that could be left in a low oven overnight, such as Cholent and Tsimmes.

In nineteenth-century Russia, after the synagogue service on the Sabbath, the children of the household would be sent to the bakers to collect their family's dish in time for Saturday lunch. Should a child stumble and spill his dish of Cholent, then the whole village would dip into its own pots to make up a meal for the unfortunate family. A layered fruit and pastry pudding that was often cooked in this way was probably of early French origin, for it was called shalet from the medieval French word for hot, 'chauldt'.

The need to differentiate between meat and milk meals encouraged the development of many delicious dairy dishes made from velvety 'kaese', a soft cheese made from naturally soured milk. These dishes include cheese 'kreplach' (a form of ravioli), 'lokshen' and 'kaese' (noodle and cheese casserole), and the 'blintze', a paper-thin pancake, stuffed with slightly sweetened cream cheese, which is the most famous Jewish dish to be absorbed into international cuisine.

The shortage of kosher meat in the ghettos of medieval Europe forced the housewife to find ways of stretching her meagre supply. Usually, she would mince it and use it as a stuffing for a variety of different doughs and vegetables. In Russia the housewife would stuff the meat into a 'varenike' (potato dough) or a 'piroshke' (yeast dough); in Hungary she would stuff a pepper ('gefilte paprika'); in Austria she would use a strudel dough; in Poland a chicken's neck ('gefilte helzel') or a noodle dough ('kreplach').

Those Jews who lived in the Middle East stuffed carrots, aubergines (eggplants), tomatoes and even leeks, using an ingenious metal 'excavator' to remove the vegetable flesh. When meat became more plentiful, other methods of cooking it were adopted, but all were based on braising or casseroling, for kosher meat is used only a few days after it has been killed and tends to be tough when it is dry-roasted.

Some of the most interesting Jewish foods are those cooked in celebration of a festival. In biblical times, these festivals were the occasions for the family to make a pilgrimage on foot to the Temple at Jerusalem, where they would offer the first ripe fruits from their fields, as well as bread and cakes made from the new season's wheat. The delicious meal pancakes that were offered in the Temple on these occasions are still eaten at Pesach to this day.

No artificial leavening may be used in Pesach baking, so whisked sponges and meringues are the most popular confectionery. As ordinary flour may not be used, ground nuts, matzah meal and potato starch are substituted. There are coconut pyramids and almond macaroons, whisked sponges and ground-nut torten, and cinnamon balls made of ground almonds and sugar; many of these are made from recipes dating back to the Middle Ages. At the harvest festival of Sukkot (the Feast of Tabernacles) everyone makes strudels and stuffed vegetables, as symbols of the bounty of harvest time.

Perhaps the finest Jewish cooks of Western Europe were those who lived in the old Austro-Hungarian Empire. To these women, Friday was 'strudel day'; they would rise at 6 am to stretch the tissue-paper-thin dough on to a cloth laid on the kitchen table and make yard-wide tins of yeast cake, topped with cherries ('kirschen kuchen'), plums ('zwetschen kuchen') or cheese ('kaesekuchen') that would last the family until after the Sabbath on the following day.

The cooking that is done in the majority of Western Jewish households, however, owes much of its inspiration to the fish and fowl of Poland, Czechoslovakia and the states that border the Baltic Sea. In the freshwater lakes of these countries swam the carp and the bream that were used to make the famous 'gefilte fish'. Today, Western Jews use haddock, hake, cod and halibut flap to make this delicious fish dish, which has a close affinity to the quenelles de brochet of France. If you visit Israel, you will have this mixture served in a pepper and tomato sauce, or as an appetizer, formed into little balls that are fried and served with pickled cucumbers. Gefilte fish apart, the new generations of Israeli Jews have discarded many of the traditional dishes of those families who came from the colder lands of Europe, and now enjoy a far lighter diet of vegetables, dairy foods and fish, albeit spiced with many traditional dishes of the Middle East.

Food of an entirely different nature from that prepared by Western Jews is cooked by those Jews who were expelled from Spain by Ferdinand and Isabella in 1492 and settled in many of the countries bordering the Mediterranean. The cookery of the Sephardim, as they are known, is spicy and aromatic, and their cakes, flavoured with rose-water and almond oil, seem to have come straight out of the Arabian Nights. These cakes include 'gereybes', crisp shortbread 'bracelets' fastened with a split almond; 'kahks', light bread rolls topped with sesame seeds; and pastries stuffed with dates and almonds. But perhaps their most delicious concoctions are the 'kibbehs', slender cases of meal pastry moulded on the finger and then filled with minced lamb, and the cheesecakes of filo pastry (the strudel paste of the Middle East), filled with a savoury mixture of grated cheese and egg.

Today the young Jewish housewife can buy prepacked the traditional foods of the past: chicken soup in a can; gefilte fish in a jar; even the Sabbath chicken is offered to her ready-roasted in a plastic bag. The fish her ancestors learned to fry in Egypt she can buy from the refrigerated counter of the delicatessen, and the delicate noodles that her grandmother dried on a tea-towel draped over the back of the kitchen chair she can shower direct from packet to pan.

But I for one hope that what the women of Israel learned from the Egyptians, the Persians, the Greeks and the Romans will not be forgotten too easily.

INTRODUCTION TO THE 1992 EDITION

In 1974, when this book was in its original gestation period, the world of food in general, and Jewish food in particular, was a very different place from what it is at the beginning of this final decade of the century.

Families still ate together every night of the week; the microwave, with its promise of meals that can be cooked or reheated in minutes by anyone from the age of 8, was still a blip on most people's cooking horizon and late-comers' meals had to be kept hot in the oven, often with great inconvenience to the cook.

The freezer was far from being standard equipment in most kitchens and the food processor was possessed only by the adventurous few.

Air freight was just beginning to make possible a year-round season for foods such as strawberries and tomatoes, and the exotic bonanza of aubergines, avocados, celery and melons from the kibbutzim of Israel had only begun to appear on the greengrocers' shelves, in the aftermath of the Yom Kippur War.

More was still beautiful when it came to feeding the family, and chicken fat had not yet become anathema to a cholesterol-conscious generation of Jewish mothers. Fried fish was still on most households' weekly cooking agenda and meat of all kinds, usually prepared with 3 or 4 times the amount of fat used today, was still considered the mainstay of family meals.

Although the dinner party, with its kosher version of classic dishes such as Boeuf Bourgignon and Sauté de Veau Marengo, was interesting the younger households, the food most people ate was still overwhelmingly traditional - chopped liver and chicken soup in the Ashkenazi community, stuffed vegetables and savoury cheese cakes in the Sephardi one. And all over the world, and particularly in Israel, the leavening of the Jewish diet with sweet and savoury riches from communities as distant in culinary terms as Morocco and Hungary had only just begun, as the children of immigrants from these different backgrounds began to marry and absorb each other's food cultures.

Kosher convenience foods were used with a slightly guilty conscience even by working women. They felt they had to be super-mum as well, and that the provision of food from both the shopping and the cooking point of view still had to be their total responsibility. I well remember, on the days I had to be away from home, leaving more elaborate meals for the family than those I made when I was in my role as full-time wife and mother. And the very idea of offering guests a menu even partly composed of ready-to-eat foods from the deli or the supermarket was unthinkable - entertaining was still equated with long hours in the kitchen - any other way was no way to treat your guests!

Today a totally different shopping and cooking scenario has affected the Jewish and non-Jewish household alike. Stimulated by ever more glamorous television programmes and articles on every aspect of the subject in magazines and newspapers of every kind, food is a major topic of interest for men as well as women. It's significant that there is now a Guild of Food (as opposed to cookery) Writers, many of whose members constantly discourse on the subject without actually touching life at the kitchen stove!

Paradoxically, the aspirations raised by all this mouthwatering coverage have to be realized by women - and men - with less time than ever to devote to food preparation, so a vast industry has grown up to satisfy the need by offering ready-to-serve, high-quality dishes in an ever increasing variety which have been prepared in the kitchen of a factory rather than the home.

At the same time, there is a yearning - stimulated largely by the micro-portions and pallid flavours of so much of the 'nouvelle cuisine' - for the uncomplicated but supremely tasty dishes 'like mama used to make', whatever her nationality or religion.

So where does this leave the Jewish kitchen with its long-simmered dishes, so many of which were packed with what we now consider an unacceptable weighting of saturated fat and sugar - essential for life in a cold climate before the days of universal central heating but totally out of step with today's views on a healthy, well-balanced diet? And what about the concept of sweetness as a symbol of hospitality and good fortune - an intrinsic part of the celebration of so many of the festivals?

In this new edition, I have set out to meet all these challenges to the Jewish way with food so that it remains relevant for the way we live now. But while adapting the old traditions to these new food ways, I have also been very mindful of the need to strengthen the links with our past. For many of us whose family records are lost for ever, whether through war, pogrom or forced emigration, the only tangible evidence of the women from whom we are descended lies in the dishes and the folk knowledge they have passed on to us. The recipe for Haimische Pickled Cucumbers, for instance, that you will find in this book must have taken several generations to perfect, for it displays an understanding of the scientific principles that underlie the process of pickling cucumbers long before those principles had appeared in any book accessible in the Pale of Settlement, and which therefore could have been deduced only by long trial and error.

Jewish food is no stranger to innovation - how else could it have survived as a recognizable cuisine through so many vicissitudes of fortune? But while I have given methods that use our modern machines - such as the microwave and the food processor - I have also in some cases given the traditional method, because I believe it to be an important part of our culinary history.

The dishes in the book have come from a wide variety of Jewish communities - from Eastern and Western Europe, North and South America, North Africa, Israel and the other countries of the Mediterranean, and from the British Isles. Some are traditional in the sense that they have been passed down through several generations. Others, however, are even now being absorbed into Jewish food culture, because they meet the needs of the Jewish dietary or Sabbath observance laws, or are suitable for serving as symbolic foods at the different festivals. This enrichment of our cuisine has been going on for centuries and is one reason for its survival.

All the dishes for everyday and family eating have been carefully reworked to make their ingredients acceptable as part of a healthy and nutritious diet. However, dishes which are only eaten occasionally for High Days and Holy Days, for parties and celebrations, have not been modified - except perhaps for the substitution of low-fat ingredients such as yoghurt, smetana and fromage frais for the richer dairy cream - because it would damage their authenticity. In addition, there is an enormous variety of non-traditional vegetable dishes and fruit-based desserts that take advantage of the abolition of the seasons which has been made possible by the worldwide chilled-food transportation network.

In common with the general population, an ever increasing number of Jewish women now aspire to combine a work life outside the home with their domestic role within it. For these people I have listed those dishes that will fit into a busy lifestyle, as well as the modes of entertaining which happily combine the best of factory and home-made food.

For the growing number of vegetarians there is an extended chapter of dishes containing neither meat nor fish, with menus to match for the different festivals.

However, because I believe they still have an important role to play in our cuisine - both from the nutritional and from the satisfaction point of view - there are large meat and poultry sections, albeit with many lighter dishes that are grilled or roasted in contrast to the heartier casseroles. (There is also far less emphasis on frying in the fish section.) Because of its scarcity and therefore high price throughout the centuries, meat has always been prized in the Jewish kitchen. It should be remembered, however, that as early as the time of Moses the Jewish attitude to animal welfare was enshrined in the Ten Commandments, which lay down the right to a day of rest even for the ox and the ass.

Whereas the first edition of this book was heavily weighted towards the Ashkenazi kitchen, I have since read widely, consulted, eaten, cooked and now include many dishes from the Sephardi cuisine in all its many exciting manifestations. I hope this will give a more balanced picture of Jewish cuisine worldwide. For the same reasons I have greatly widened the spectrum of symbolic dishes cooked for the different festivals and the customs associated with them.

Hospitality has been considered a *mitzvah* or pious deed ever since, as recorded in Genesis, Abraham and Sarah entertained the three 'strangers within the gates' with Sarah's home-made bread even before they knew they were welcoming angels of the Lord. Fashions change but the feelings that prompt them remain the same, so I have included a large section on entertaining, not only 'within the gates' but also in the wider community, when cooking for 25 or 50 becomes the name of the game.

All the dishes conform to the Jewish dietary laws. A very large number of ingredients and prepared foods for the general market are now accepted by the rabbinical authorities. These are listed in kashrut guides, which should be consulted if in doubt.

I hope this book reflects in some measure the excitement, the variety, the flavour, the history and the love that is interwoven in what we call 'Jewish food', and that it will in some small way help to preserve it for the generations that are to come.

HOW TO USE THE RECIPES

Solid measures are first given in spoons, pounds and ounces.

Liquid measures are first given in spoons, pints or fluid ounces. Within the brackets that follow these measures, the first figure given is the metric equivalent and the second is the American equivalent measure in cups: e.g.

3 oz (75 g/⅓ cup) – solid measure
5 fl oz (150 ml/⅔ cup) – liquid measure

American equivalent ingredients or terms given in brackets: e.g.

glacé (candied) cherries
double (heavy) cream

Temperatures are first expressed as a gas number and then in degrees: e.g.

Gas No. 3 (325°F/160°C)

Length measurements are first given in inches and then in centimetres: e.g.

2 in (5 cm)

Spoon measures are level. As I find the use of millimetres to express spoon capacity unnecessarily complicated, I have used household (imperial measure) tablespoons and teaspoons throughout. (The tablespoon has a capacity of 20 ml, the teaspoon 5 ml.) As the difference in volume is so small I have assumed British and American spoons to be interchangeable but some adjustment in the quantity of seasonings may be necessary to suit individual tastes.

Butter is slightly salted, unless unsalted is specified.

Margarine is a soft variety labelled 'high in polyunsaturates', unless a block of firm margarine is specified.

Sugar is granulated unless caster (superfine), icing (confectioner's) or a variety of brown sugar is specified. There is no standardized nomenclature for brown sugar but provided some kind of soft light- or medium-brown sugar (*not* the granular demerara sugar unless specified) is used, the exact shade of brown is not important. However, unless specified, the very dark-brown molasses sugar should *not* be used as its treacly flavour and colour can overwhelm the other ingredients in a dish.

Eggs are number 3 size – approximately 2 oz (50 g) in weight. The egg size is only critical when 4 or more eggs are used in a recipe; in that case extra large (or small) eggs can upset the ratio of liquids to solids.

Flour is plain unless self-raising is specified, and white unless brown is specified. 'Special' (sometimes called 'supreme') self-raising flour is fine-milled from soft wheat and produces cakes of a very fine texture. If it is not available, a regular white self-raising flour can be used instead. American readers should use 'cake' flour, plus baking powder. 4 oz (125 g/1 cup) of plain flour plus 1 level teaspoon of baking powder = 4 oz (125 g/1 cup) of self-raising flour.

Tin and pan sizes are given for guidance only, and those of approximately the same size can be used, provided they are the same depth or deeper than specified.

Oven temperatures are given for guidance only, as different ovens vary in the distribution of heat and the time taken to complete the cooking of a particular food. This is most marked when a fan-assisted or forced-air oven is used, and here you should follow the manufacturers' instructions for cooking something similar.

The microwave timings in this book are based on a 650-watt oven manufactured before September 1991. If using a machine purchased after that date, the power output will still be shown in watts but it will have been measured according to a new internationally agreed standard IFC 705. It is advisable to contact your supplier who will be able to tell you how the wattage of your machine compares with the wattages given in this book.

When using a 600-watt machine, add 5 seconds per minute of cooking time: for example, if the recipe in the book takes 6 minutes, cook it in your machine for 6½ minutes.

When using a 500-watt machine, add 20 seconds per minute of cooking time: for example, if the recipe in the book takes 6 minutes, cook it in your machine for 8 minutes.

When using a 700-watt machine, subtract 5 seconds per minute of cooking time: for example, if the recipe in the book takes 6 minutes, cook it in your machine for 5½ minutes.

Cooking times: Minimum cooking times are always given. Any food, if underdone when checked, can be given additional time, whereas food overcooked in a microwave may be inedible: for example, fish or chicken becomes hard and dry, cakes become rubbery in texture.

Microwave-safe dishes: All cooking dishes and coverings must be selected from those materials recommended as safe to use in the microwave.

Meals in a hurry: Where appropriate, at the start of each chapter you will find a list of those dishes that can be produced speedily, with a minimum of effort.

FOOD STORAGE TIMES

The recommended storage times given in the recipes are based on certain assumptions, as listed below.

In the freezer: All foods, whether cooked or raw, are stored in airtight containers, freezer storage bags or foil packages to prevent freezer 'burn'. The exceptions are soft or fragile foods that are 'open frozen' until firm and must then be packaged in the same way.

The recommended storage time is based on the maximum period after which deterioration of flavour or texture may take place. If foods are frozen for longer than recommended, they will not be dangerous to eat but they will be past their prime.

In the refrigerator: All cooked and prepared foods are stored in airtight containers and covered with recommended clingfilm (saran-wrap) or foil to avoid dehydration and the transference of flavours and smells from one food to another. All raw fruits and vegetables are stored in plastic bags or containers, according to variety.

The recommended storage time is based on the maximum period during which the food is pleasant and *safe* to eat.

Fuller details on food storage can be found in my *Entertaining Cookbook* (Robson Books).

ADAPTING GENERAL RECIPES FOR THE JEWISH KITCHEN

Many recipes published in general cookery books, newspapers and magazines need adapting in some way before they can be used in the Jewish kitchen: they may contain non-kosher ingredients, or combine meat and dairy products in the same dish, or simply include a dairy food in a dish that is to be served as part of a meat meal.

It is then a question of finding suitable alternative ingredients that, while satisfying the requirements of the dietary laws, will not cause a radical alteration in the flavour and texture of the original dish. Here are my suggestions for overcoming the more common problems of this kind.

Butter

To ***fry meat and poultry:*** For each 1 oz (25 g/2 tbsp) butter, substitute 2 tablespoons of olive or sunflower oil or a chicken-flavoured vegetable fat.

To ***sauté vegetables*** *for a meat casserole or soup:* Substitute an equal amount of margarine or olive oil.

To ***fry or roast potatoes:*** For each 1 oz (25 g/2 tbsp) butter substitute 2 tablespoons of oil and a nut of margarine.

In a ***pudding or cake*** *for a meat meal:* Substitute an equal amount of soft margarine; in addition, use water to mix instead of milk. If only a small number of eggs is included in the recipe, substitute an extra egg for 2 fl oz (50 ml/$\frac{1}{4}$ cup) of the milk.

In ***pastry*** *for a meat meal:* For each 5 oz (150 g/$\frac{2}{3}$ cup) butter, substitute 4 oz (125 g/$\frac{1}{2}$ cup) margarine and 1 oz (25g 2 tbsp) soft white fat (shortening).

In the ***batter for dessert crêpes*** *for a meat meal:* Substitute an equal amount of melted margarine (or sunflower oil for savoury crêpes).

In a ***chicken soup or sauce:*** Substitute an equal quantity of chicken-flavoured vegetable fat or soft margarine.

To fry ***pancakes or crêpes*** *for a meat meal:* Substitute a flavourless vegetable oil.

To ***shallow-fry blintzes*** *for a meat meal:* Substitute an equal quantity of margarine and 1 tbsp flavourless oil (to prevent over-browning of the margarine).

Milk

In a ***batter*** *for crêpes, blintzes, ordinary pancakes or Yorkshire pudding to serve at a meat meal:* For each 10 fl oz (275 ml/$\frac{1}{4}$ cups) of milk, substitute 8 fl oz (225 ml/1 cup) of water plus 1 egg and 1 tablespoon of flavourless oil. The blintzes and pancakes will be lighter and thinner, and fried stuffed blintzes will be crisper, than when made with milk. Yorkshire pudding will have a crisper crust, but a less spongy inside.

In a ***sauce or soup*** *that contains chicken or meat, or to serve at a meat meal: Either* substitute kosher non-dairy pouring cream *or* substitute chicken stock, making the soup look 'creamy' by whisking in 1 egg yolk for each 5 fl oz (150 ml/⅔ cup) of liquid and heat until steaming.

Cream

To enrich a ***chicken sauce, soup or casserole:*** *Either* substitute an equal quantity of kosher non-dairy pouring cream (*not* whipping cream) *or* for each 2 or 3 tablespoons of cream thicken the sauce with 1 egg yolk. *Or* for each 5 fl oz (150 ml/⅔ cup) double (heavy) cream substitute the following **nut cream** (but do *not* allow it to boil): liquidize for 1 minute at maximum speed ½ oz (15 g/1 tbsp) of soft margarine, 5 fl oz (150 ml/⅔ cup) of water, a teaspoon of sugar and 2 oz (500 g/½ cup) of cashew nuts. Refrigerate for several hours to allow the cream to thicken.

To substitute for whipped cream in a ***cold dessert:*** *Either* for each 5 fl oz (150 ml/⅔ cup) of double (heavy) or whipping cream substitute 4 fl oz (125 ml/½ cup) of kosher non-dairy whipping cream *or,* in a jellied (gelatine) dessert, for every 5 fl oz (150 ml/⅔ cup) of double (heavy) or whipping cream substitute a meringue made by whisking 2 egg whites until stiff and then whisking in 2 teaspoons of caster (superfine) sugar – this will produce a lighter, less unctuous texture than cream. I do not think any non-dairy cream is a worthwhile substitute for Crème Chantilly (sweetened whipped cream served to accompany another dish) and it is better to do without it altogether.

Chicken Stock

In a milk soup or sauce: Substitute vegetable stock made with a cube or paste, or a chicken-flavoured *parev* stock-cube or powder.

Shellfish

In a fish cocktail or salad: Substitute an equal weight of fillets of a firm white fish such as halibut, bream or lemon sole, poached, then cut into small cubes or coarsely flaked.

In a creamed casserole or filling for pastry cases or fish pie: Substitute an equal quantity of fresh salmon, halibut or haddock, poached, then flaked or cut in 1-inch (2.5 cm) cubes.

In a deep-fried dish: Substitute an equal weight of raw fillets of lemon sole, plaice or baby halibut, cut into bite-size strips. Coat with batter or with flour, egg and breadcrumbs (as for Fried Fish in the Jewish Manner, p. 61) and fry as directed.

Smoked or Salted Meat

In a savoury flan: Substitute for bacon or ham a food with a salty tang such as black olives, smoked mackerel, smoked salmon or anchovies.

In mixed grills: Substitute an equal weight of smoked top rib for bacon.

In a salad for a meat meal: Substitute smoked turkey breast for ham.

In a meat or chicken casserole: You can substitute an equal quantity of smoked top rib for bacon. Many people do not like a smoky flavour in a hot casserole, however, and there is no reason why it should not be omitted in dishes such as Coq au Vin and Boeuf Bourguignonne.

Hindquarter Meat Cuts

If you live in a community where the 'porging' of hindquarter meat is not allowed, the following forequarter cuts can be substituted instead (kosher cuts are named first):

First-cut shoulder steak, blade steak, alki steak or bola (chuck): Use in place of braising or stewing cuts, such as round steak.
Corner or prime bola (chuck): Use for braising or pot-roasting in place of topside or silverside of beef.
Pickled brisket: Use in place of pickled silverside.
Boned and rolled wing rib (well hung): Use in place of sirloin or fillet for roasting.
Rib steaks (well hung): Use in place of rump, sirloin or point steak - 'entrecôte' steak is actually rib steak.
Minced bola (chuck): Use in place of minced beefsteak.
First-cut lamb chops and cutlets: Use in place of loin or leg chops.
Shoulder of lamb: Use in place of leg of lamb.
Boned shoulder of lamb: Use in place of boned fillet of lamb.
Boned shoulder or breast of lamb: Use in place of boned and cubed leg - for kebabs, say.
Boned-out veal shoulder chops: Use in place of leg of veal for escalopes, scallopini and schnitzel.

Checking for Kashrut

Methods of preparing prepacked and ready-prepared foods are constantly changing, as are the ingredients and additives used in them. Therefore, please consult either a recognized kashrut guide or a rabbi if you are uncertain of the status of any item listed on any packet that does not carry a recognized certificate of kashrut. (For details of how to make kosher meat and poultry at home, see pp. 133-4).

GLOSSARY

eingemacht	home-made (referring to a sweet preserve)
forspeise	tasty appetizer
hackbrattle	wooden board with sides
hackmesser	wooden-handled chopping knife
haimische,	traditional home style
der heim	former home of immigrant Jews, usually in Eastern Europe
milchik	dairy
parev	neutral - neither milk nor meat
porge	to remove blood and fat to make kosher
rebeizen	hand-grater
schmalz	fat - usually referring to chicken fat or herring: eg schmalz (matjes) herring
silicone paper	baking parchment - superior to greaseproof paper because it never requires greasing and can be used again and again, it is the choice of the professional baker

STARTERS

HORS D'OEUVRES

Hors d'oeuvres in a Hurry

To start a meal with a tasty dish has been considered an aid to appetite and digestion since Roman times. Yet while the elaborately dressed dishes exemplified by the French hors d'oeuvres were based on foods available only to the rich, in Jewish cuisine the humblest peasants in the Pale of Settlement expected to start their meal with a plate of schmaltz herring dressed with oil and vinegar, or a salad of salt herring sweetened with apple and garnished with egg. These *forspeise,* or tasty starters, are enjoyed by Jews in every country in the world, though more recently the traditional chopped liver and pickled herring have been augmented by smoked salmon and trout, as well as by vegetable ragouts and pâtés, and by the dressed avocados, aubergines (eggplants) and artichokes grown in Israel.

Pâté Plus

It is said that the Jewish poultry-breeders of Strasbourg were the first to devise pâté de foie gras. But the pâté or chopped liver of the traditional Ashkenazi Jewish Saturday lunch is an altogether more plebeian affair, invented as a means of using the giblets of the Sabbath fowl or a small amount of ox liver to make a cheap and tasty starter that could be made on Friday for lunch after the synagogue on the following day. Originally the liver was really *chopped,* using a wooden-handled chopping knife - or *hackmesser* - but it was supplanted by the mincer (and later the electric mincer) as soon as immigrant households could afford them. (Cast-iron mincers were first manufactured in the 1860s; there is one with an embossed Magen Dovid on it dating from about this time in the Prague Jewish Museum.) I first developed and published the food-processor method in the late 1970s.

CHOPPED LIVER

Serves 4 as an appetizer, 6 when spread on biscuits (crackers).
Keeps 2 days under refrigeration.
Freeze 1 month.

Calf and ox liver may both be used to make chopped liver, but the flavour is sweeter and the texture softer when calf liver is used. This, however, is only available occasionally and is also much more expensive than ox liver.

8 oz (225 g) liver
1 medium onion, peeled
2 hard-boiled eggs (simmered for 12 minutes then plunged into cold water and kept there till required)
½ level teasp salt
10 grinds of black pepper
rendered chicken fat or chicken-flavoured vegetable fat to bind (about 2 rounded tbsp)

The liver must be koshered beforehand (see 'How to Make Meat and Poultry Kosher', p. 133). Put the koshered liver into a saucepan with half the onion. Cover with cold water. Bring slowly to the boil, cover and simmer for 10 minutes over very gentle heat. Drain the liver thoroughly and discard the half-onion. Remove the outer skin from the liver.

Traditional method Put the cooked liver through the mincer using the medium cutter, together with the remaining raw half-onion, one whole egg and the white of the other. Put in a basin with the salt and pepper and add the fat to bind it together. If the mixture looks crumbly, add a little more soft fat.

Food-processor method Put the liver and onion into the bowl and process until finely chopped - about 3 seconds. Add one shelled and halved egg, the white of the other, the remaining seasonings and fat and process until blended - another 2 seconds. Scrape down sides of bowl and if mixture looks a little dry, add a further tablespoon of fat.

Turn into a shallow dish and smooth the surface flat. Refrigerate, covered with foil. Just before serving push the remaining hard-boiled egg yolk through a metal sieve on to the surface of the liver. Serve with sliced challah or matzah crackers.

CHICKEN LIVER PÂTÉ IN THE JEWISH STYLE

Serves 6-8 as a starter, 10-12 as a spread.
Keeps 5 days under refrigeration.
Freeze 1 month.

A world of taste and texture divides traditional Gehakte Leber (chopped liver), with its raw onion and coarse but comforting texture, and the smooth mildness of Chicken Liver Pâté in the Jewish Style prepared with the food processor. The onion is sautéed to caramelize it and enrich the flavour of this superb pâté. It also ensures better keeping-qualities than when raw onion is used, as in the preceding recipe. This kind of liver pâté can be made with a mincer, but to get a smooth and 'creamy' texture it should be made in a food processor.

4 hard-boiled eggs (1 for the garnish)
1 large onion, finely chopped
1 medium clove of garlic, crushed
3 oz (75 g/⅓ cup) soft margarine or 5 tbsp rendered chicken fat or chicken-flavoured vegetable fat
5-10 grinds (1 teasp) of sea salt
1 lb (450 g) ready-koshered chicken livers (or see p. 134)
20 grinds of black pepper
good pinch of ground nutmeg

Hard-boil the eggs for 10 minutes, then leave in the pan covered with cold water. Fry the onion and the garlic gently in the fat until a rich brown (this is important if the right depth of flavour is to be achieved). As the onion cooks, sprinkle it with the sea salt.

Shell 3 of the eggs and cut in half.

Put the onion and the garlic with their juices into the food processor and process until smooth, then add the remaining ingredients and process again until smooth. Taste, and add more seasonings if necessary, but remember that the flavours will intensify over the next few hours. Turn into a terrine or oval gratin dish or divide between individual cocottes. Chill, covered with clingfilm (saranwrap), preferably overnight. Refrigerate the extra egg.

One hour before serving, remove the pâté from the refrigerator and leave at room temperature. Just before serving, pass the remaining egg through a mouli or sieve and use it to decorate the top of the pâté. Serve with warm French bread or slices of challah.

CHICKEN LIVER PÂTÉ WITH MARINATED TARRAGON PEARS

Serves 8.
Dressing keeps 1 day under refrigeration if required.

If you combine a scoop of this smooth pâté with a pear marinated in a tarragon-flavoured dressing, nestling on a bed of mixed leaves, the result is stunning, both in appearance and flavour.

1 recipe Chicken Liver Pâté *(see p. 4)*
4 ripe Comice or William pears, peeled, halved and cored, or 1 large and 1 medium cans pears in fruit juice
frisée or mixed salad greens

For the dressing
1 tbsp lemon juice
1 tbsp orange juice
3 teasp Crème de Cassis (blackcurrant liqueur) or blackcurrant cordial
2 teasp raspberry vinegar or cider vinegar
5 tbsp sunflower oil
1 tbsp walnut oil
½ teasp salt
10 grinds of black pepper
1 thin sliver of fresh ginger the size of a penny, peeled and finely chopped
1 tbsp snipped fresh tarragon

The day before, make the pâté and refrigerate. Put the dressing ingredients into a screw-top jar and shake until thickened, then refrigerate.

Early the next day, put the fresh or drained canned pears in a shallow dish, shake the dressing to rethicken it, then spoon over the pears. Refrigerate again.

Half an hour before serving, arrange scoops of pâté on individual serving dishes and arrange a 'nest' of salad greens at the side. Arrange a pear-half on top and spoon over the dressing.

Delicious with challah.

A PÂTÉ OF CHICKEN LIVERS AND STUFFED OLIVES
(without egg)

Serves 6–8 as a starter.
Keeps 4 days under refrigeration.
Freeze 3 months.

This is a rich and smooth pâté in the French style which I have adapted for the Jewish kitchen. The flavour improves after 24 hours.

6 oz (175 g/¾ cup) margarine or chicken-flavoured vegetable fat
1 large onion, finely chopped
1 clove of garlic, peeled
1 teasp sea salt
20 grinds of black pepper
1 lb (450 g) chicken livers, grilled to make kosher and also to cook through *(see p. 134)*
2 bay leaves
4 tbsp medium-dry Amontillado sherry
4 oz (125 g/1 cup) green stuffed olives, sliced

For the garnish
a few olives
sprigs of parsley

Put half the fat into a frying pan and sauté the onion and the garlic over moderate heat until they turn a rich golden brown. Sprinkle with the pepper and salt, then add the livers and the bay leaves and cook, stirring frequently, until the livers have absorbed the flavours - about 3-4 minutes. Add the sherry and continue to cook until it has almost evaporated. Discard the bay leaves. Turn the contents of the pan into a food processor, together with the remaining fat, and process until it feels absolutely smooth on the tongue. Stir in the sliced olives. Taste and add more salt and pepper if necessary.

To serve as a starter, turn into 6 or 8 tiny soufflé dishes, cover with clingfilm (saranwrap) and chill, preferably overnight. Garnish just before serving with a slice of olive and a tiny sprig of parsley.

EGG AND SPRING ONION FORSPEISE (*Pâté of Egg and Onion*)

Serves 6 as a starter, 15 as a spread.
Keeps 1 day under refrigeration.

This delicious appetizer is traditionally made with a *hackmesser*. This long and tedious job was in many families performed by one of the men, using a *hackbrettle* - a wooden chopping-board with sides to prevent the ingredients getting out of hand. A mincer produces entirely the wrong texture but now it can be made just as effectively with the food processor. As the onions should still have a little 'crunch' in the, do not overprocess. Some families use a medium onion instead of the spring onions. For a dairy meal, soft butter can be used instead of the other fats.

1 bunch of spring onions (scallions), plus 4 inches (10 cm) of the green, or 1 medium onion, cut in 1-inch (2.5-cm) chunks
8 hard-boiled eggs, shelled and halved
3 rounded tbsp soft margarine or rendered chicken fat or chicken-flavoured vegetable fat
½ teasp salt
10 grinds of black pepper

Put the onions into the bowl of the food processor and pulse for 3 seconds until roughly chopped. Add all the remaining ingredients and pulse for a further 5 seconds, until finely chopped and blended together. Turn into a small gratin dish, smooth the top level and mark with a pattern using the blade of a knife. Cover with foil and chill for a least an hour before serving.

CALVES' FOOT JELLY

Serves 6-8.
Keeps 2 days under refrigeration.
Do not freeze.

This dish of meat from calves' feet, set in a savoury jelly, arouses strong emotions - some people go misty-eyed when it is mentioned, others loathe the very thought of it. Each community of European Jews has a different name for it: Fusnogge (Yiddish), Ptchia (Russian), Sulze (German). It is a perfect example of the ability of the Jewish cook to make a speciality dish from humble ingredients.

2 calves' feet (koshered), with cold water to cover them
1 large onion, peeled
1 fat clove of garlic, peeled
3 bay leaves
1 level teasp black peppercorns
2 level teasp salt
2 tbsp lemon juice (or cider vinegar if preferred)
3 hard-boiled eggs, sliced

For the garnish
lemon quarters
tomatoes and cress

It's easiest to use an oval heatproof casserole in which the cleaned feet can be laid without having to saw them up. Put in the feet, cover with cold water and bring to the boil on top of the stove. Simmer for 10 minutes, then, using a wet spoon, skim off the froth. Add the onion, garlic, bay leaves, peppercorns and salt. Cover and simmer gently for a further hour, either on top of the stove or in the oven. Skim once more, partially cover, and continue to simmer for a further $2\frac{1}{2}$–3 hours, or until the gristle and meat are coming away from the bone.

Lift out the bones and any meat attached to them and set aside. Strain the liquid into a bowl, then return to the washed pan, together with the lemon juice and the meat, cut into $\frac{3}{8}$-inch (1-cm) cubes. Bring once more to the boil, then take off the heat altogether.

To set the jelly I use a narrow French pâté dish, 9 x 5 x 3 inches (22.5 x 12.5 x 7.5 cm) in size, but a loaf tin of similar size is equally good, particularly if you wish to turn it out for slicing. Pour half the liquid into the dish, and leave in the refrigerator until it is beginning to set. Arrange a layer of the sliced hard-boiled eggs on top, and spoon over the remaining mixture, including the meat. Chill overnight in the refrigerator until firm. Slices can be cut from the dish, or the jelly can be turned out on to a platter and decorated with the cress, tomatoes and lemon wedges.

Smoked Salmon and Other Fishy Starters

The smoking and pickling of meat and fish is an art for which Jews seem to have a special talent - and taste. Smoking of meat in particular was widely practised by the Jews of Eastern Europe - the modern 'deli' is the direct descendant of the old-style European pickled and smoked meat shop - and they took that skill with them when they emigrated to America and Western Europe in the latter years of the nineteenth century.

Jews have long had a 'special relationship' with smoked salmon. The appearance on the table of such an expensive food signified a very special occasion - a wedding, a barmitzvah or a festival - when, in contrast to the cheap and simple foods of everyday life, the poor immigrant Jews could enjoy a little luxury. And the more smoked salmon that was on offer, the greater was judged the hospitality of the host. This relationship has persisted to the present day.

Today, however, this one-time luxury food can be bought in every supermarket, fresh or frozen, and in a wide range of flavours, qualities and packaging. In an ideal world, one would always choose wild Scotch smoked salmon that has not been frozen at any point in its history. But modern technology has vastly improved the taste and texture of all grades of smoked salmon, and large-scale production of farmed fish under virtually natural conditions means that, even though the price has not actually gone down, in relation to the cost of other foods smoked salmon is no longer something that needs to be reserved for special occasions. And as most fish, even the very top grades, can be bought ready-sliced, one can pick up a packet ready for immediate use, rather than have to rely, as in the past, on the carving skill of the deli-owner. However, as with most foods, the price usually reflects the quality. As the degree of smoking varies enormously - some smoked salmon has an almost kippered taste - it's worth shopping around to find the flavour you prefer. In general, salmon is much more lightly smoked and salted than in the past because, with the advent of refrigerators and freezers, the preservative qualities of the process - a combination of the effects of drying, the presence in the actual smoke of chemicals which act on the bacteria that cause spoilage and a high salt concentration - are less important than the flavour. That is why the lightly cured 'gravlax', which does not go through a smoking process, is now almost as popular as smoked salmon.

Fresh smoked salmon has a limited shelf-life so it's essential to adhere to the use-by date. Frozen salmon (provided it has not been thawed before sale - if it has, it should be treated as fresh) can be stored for up to 2 months in the domestic freezer. After that, the high fat content may cause it to develop 'off' flavours.

The finest-quality smoked salmon commands a price beyond that of the most expensive steak. But for a special occasion, it is still the ideal partner for a chilled glass of champagne, embellished with only a grind of black pepper, a squeeze of lemon and some fine-grained, thinly sliced, buttered brown bread.

There is also a lot to be said for a sandwich of smoked salmon on fresh black bread or a split soft roll (such as the plaetzels on p. 464) which has first been spread with a thin layer of smoked salmon mousse, or on an oven-fresh bagel, buttered and spread with the best cream cheese.

Allow 2 oz (50g) if served alone, or 1 oz (25g) if served as part of a mixed hors d'oeuvre.

PECAN AND SMOKED SALMON ROULADE WITH A SALAD OF MIXED LEAVES

Serves 6–8.
Salmon pâté keeps 3 days under refrigeration; the complete roulade keeps 2 days.
Freeze pâté only 1 month.

This is an elegant presentation of a superb smoked salmon pâté which makes a perfect starter for a dairy or fish dinner, or a light main course for lunch.

8 oz (225 g) best smoked salmon
4 oz (125 g/½ cup) cream cheese
2 oz (50 g/¼ cup) soft butter
1–2 tbsp lemon juice
1 tbsp creamed horseradish
15 grinds of black pepper
1 tbsp fresh snipped dill
2 oz (50 g/½ cup) finely chopped pecan nuts
2 tbsp finely chopped parsley

For the salad
1 small pack mixed salad leaves
2 tbsp nut oil vinaigrette (see p. 300)

Work the smoked salmon in a food processor with the cream cheese, butter, lemon juice and creamed horseradish until smooth. Season the mixture with black pepper and snipped dill. Turn into a basin and chill for several hours until firm.

Shape the mixture into a cylinder 2 in (5 cm) in diameter by laying it on clingfilm (saranwrap), then moulding it into a cylinder about 12 in (30 cm) long. Chill until an hour before the meal.

To serve, sprinkle the finely chopped pecan nuts and parsley evenly on a piece of foil. Carefully remove the clingfilm, then roll the roulade evenly in the nut/parsley mixture. Slice and garnish with a small salad of the leaves, which have been tossed in the vinaigrette.

SMOKED SALMON MOUSSE

Enough to fill 8 rolls or bagels, or 8 little pots as a starter.
Keeps 4 days under refrigeration.
Freeze 1 month.

This is a lightly whipped, pale-pink mixture, relatively low in fat, which can be made using less expensive fish or trimmings.

6 oz (175g) smoked salmon
large sprig of fresh dill (1 tbsp when snipped)
1 teasp lemon rind, finely grated
½ small clove of garlic, peeled, or ½ inch (1.25 cm) garlic purée

6 oz (175 g/ ¾ cup) low- or medium-fat soft cheese
5 fl oz (150 ml/⅔ cup) low-fat natural fromage frais or yoghurt

In the food processor, purée all the ingredients together until the mixture is absolutely smooth. Turn into a bowl and chill for several hours to allow the flavours to develop.

A SALAD OF SMOKED SALMON AND FUSILLI IN A LIGHTLY CURRIED SAUCE

Serves 6.
Eat the same day.

Those little curlicues that form the pasta shapes the Italians call fusilli (also sold as 'twists' or 'spirals') positively drink up a sauce or dressing, which make them the ideal basis for this elegant pink and green dish of smoked salmon and asparagus in a lightly curried dressing. Serve it with crusty granary bread as either a starter for a dinner party or a light main course for lunch. It looks particularly pretty in fairly large wine glasses lined with leaves from the heart of a 'Little Gem' lettuce; for a buffet meal it can be arranged in a shallow entrée dish. To prevent the colour bleaching out in the dressing, it's important to stir the salmon through it only an hour before serving.

8 oz (225 g) smoked salmon, cut in juliennes (narrow strips)
9 oz (250 g/3 cups) fusilli (pasta twists or spirals)
8 oz (225 g) fresh or frozen all-green asparagus

For the dressing
10 fl oz (275 ml/1¼ cups) Greek-style yoghurt or creamed smetana or 8% fromage frais or soured cream
5 fl oz (150 ml/⅔ cup) whipping cream
1 clove of garlic, crushed
1 teasp curry powder
15 grinds of black pepper
2 tbsp finely grated onion
1 tbsp capers, drained

For the garnish
a few reserved asparagus tips
paprika

Earlier in the day, mix all the dressing ingredients in a bowl and lay the smoked salmon juliennes on top. Cover and refrigerate. An hour before serving, cook the fusilli according to the packet instructions, until *al dente.* Cook the asparagus until bite-tender and cut in 1-inch (2.5-cm) pieces.

Turn the pasta in the dressing and gently toss until pasta and smoked salmon are evenly coated. Stir in the asparagus, reserving some of the tips for garnish. Leave at room temperature.

To serve, spoon the salad into the chosen dish or glasses. Garnish with the reserved asparagus tips and a light dusting of paprika.

MELON AND SMOKED SALMON KEBABS

Eat the same day.
Makes 48.
Serves 10 generously.

These make perfect taste 'ticklers' to serve with drinks in the garden before a summer lunch party.

1 medium-sized Galia or Ogen melon, well ripened
8 oz (225 g) first-quality thinly sliced smoked salmon
juice of ½ lemon
black pepper

For the garnish
a few sprigs of dill, fennel or parsley

Cut the melon in half, remove the seeds and peel completely (most easily with a serrated bread knife). Cut into neat ½-inch (1.25-cm) cubes, then put into a sieve to drain for at least half an hour (it can be refrigerated at this point for up to 12 hours).

About 45 minutes before serving, turn the cubes on to paper towels and dab as dry as possible. Sprinkle the salmon slices with black pepper and lemon juice. Cut each slice into strips ¾ inch (2 cm) wide and just long enough to encircle the cubes of melon. Wrap each strip round a cube and spear closed with a cocktail stick, then arrange on a flat dish, garnished with a sprig of herb.

PICKLED HERRINGS

Makes 12 servings.
Keeps 6 weeks under refrigeration, but becomes more acidic as time goes by.

Sometimes called 'Bismarcks' or 'rollmops'. Although these can now be bought in jars, the home-pickled variety are especially delicious, and their acidity can be varied to suit the family's taste. If salt herrings are not available, soak fresh cleaned and boned herrings in a salt-and-water brine (2 oz/50 g/¼ cup salt and 1 pint/575 ml/2½ cups water to 6 herrings) for 2 hours, then put in the spiced vinegar as directed for the salt herrings.

6 salt herrings
1 pint (575 ml/2½ cups) white vinegar, or 7 fl oz (200 ml/¾ cup plus 2 tbsp) acetic acid (33%) diluted with 14 fl oz (400 ml/2 cups) water
2 medium onions, thinly sliced
1 large unpeeled lemon, sliced
1 level tbsp pickling spice
2 bay leaves
1 dried chilli pepper
2 level tbsp brown sugar
white pepper

For the garnish
tomato
cucumber

Behead the herrings, slit the belly and remove the entrails. Put the fish in a glass casserole (so that the smell will not linger) and place under the cold-water tap. Leave the water running in a gentle trickle. After an hour, turn off the tap and let the herrings stand overnight covered in cold water. Next day, lift them out of the water and drain well. Lay them on a piece of paper, then scrape with a blunt knife to remove loose scales. Wash again under the cold-water tap and put on a board. Open the front, then turn over and press the back with the flat of the hand. Turn over again and you will find that the backbone can be lifted out easily. Remove any other loose bones. Sprinkle each herring very lightly with white pepper, add two or three thin rings of onion, then roll up from tail to head. If the herrings are very large, you may find it easier to split them lengthwise before rolling. Skewer each herring closed with a wooden cocktail stick. Put in a glass jar in alternate layers with the sliced lemon, the onion and the spices. Put the vinegar and sugar into a pan and bring to the boil. Immediately the liquid bubbles, turn off the heat and leave until it is lukewarm. Pour over the herrings. Cover and refrigerate for 4 days before using.

Serve in ½-inch (1.25-cm) slices, either speared on a cocktail stick with a drink or as an hors d'oeuvre garnished with the pickled onion slices, tomato and cucumber.

CHOPPED HERRING SALAD
(*Gehakte Herring*)

Serves 4 as an appetizer, 8 spread on biscuits (crackers).
Keeps 2 days under refrigeration.
Do not freeze.

This delicious mixture is made from herrings which are preserved by salting in wood casks between layers of rock salt. The salt herring was a staple food of the Ashkenazi Jews of

Russia and Poland. Indeed, two herrings of any kind will provide an adult man with his full daily requirement of protein.

The seasoning of chopped herrings is very much a matter of taste. You may, for instance, use fresh lemon juice instead of vinegar, and crumbled matzah crackers in place of biscuits. If you start with the balance of flavours I suggest below, you can then adjust as you wish. For chopping a *hackmesser* or *hachoir* (double-handed chopping knife) was traditionally used, with the ingredients placed on a *hackbrettle*, but today an almost identical texture can be achieved by using a food processor. Serve chopped herring as a pâté with matzah crackers, rye bread or challah, or as a topping for crackers or bread.

If you cannot get traditional salt herrings from the barrel, either use well-rinsed commercial pickled herring fillets (also known as rollmops) or soak fresh herring fillets in a salt-and-water brine (2 oz/50 g/¼ cup salt to a pint /575 ml/2½ cups water) for 2 hours, then treat as salt herring fillets.

6 salt herrings, soaked, filleted and skinned (see below)
1 medium onion, peeled and cut in 1-in (2.5-cm) chunks
2 medium (5 oz/150 g) tart cooking apples (Bramley variety if available), cored, peeled and cut in 1-in (2.5-cm) chunks
2 level tbsp ground almonds (optional)
6 large eggs, hard-boiled, shelled and cut in half (reserve 1 yolk for garnish)
2 Digestive (graham crackers) or Marie (semi-sweet) biscuits (cookies), coarsely crushed
2 teasp acetic acid (33%)
6 teasp caster (superfine) sugar
pinch of white pepper

Traditional method The day before, cut the heads off the herrings, slit the belly and remove the entrails. Place in a glass casserole and put under the cold-water tap, with the water running in a gentle trickle. After an hour, turn off the tap and leave the herrings covered in cold water overnight.

Next day, lift the herrings out of the water and drain well. Put on a board and slit the skin down the centre back; in this way it can be peeled off easily from both sides. Flatten the back of each herring with the palm of the hand, turn it over and lift out the backbone. Remove any other bones which may be sticking out.

Cut the fish up roughly, and put on a chopping board kept specially for the purpose. Add the egg, the apple and the grated onion, and chop until all the ingredients are very fine. Now sprinkle on the crushed biscuits, vinegar, sugar and pepper, mixing well. The biscuit crumbs should be sufficient to soak up excess juice. If not, add a few more. Taste and add a little more vinegar or sugar if necessary.

Food-processor method Wash and drain the herring fillets as above and bone them in the same way. Pulse the onion in the food processor until finely chopped, then remove it. Chop the apple in the same way, then remove that also. Put the chunks of herring, the halves of hard-boiled eggs, the ground almonds (if used) and the biscuits into the machine with the acetic acid and sugar. Pulse until finely chopped. Return the apple and onion to the machine, pulse briefly to blend, taste and reseason if necessary.

Pile the chopped herring into a dish about 1 inch (2.5 cm) deep, cover with clingfilm (saranwrap) and chill.

Just before serving, sieve the remaining egg yolk over the top.

SCHMALTZ (MATJES) HERRINGS

Serves 4–6.
Keeps 3 days under refrigeration.

Schmaltz herrings are prepared by lightly salting the first herrings of the season (especially plump and succulent because they have not yet developed a roe) in a brine of salt, saltpetre and sugar, using a process originated by Dutch fishermen. When in season, they make a most tasty, if thirst-making, hors d'oeuvre. A great favourite at Jewish wedding receptions, served with a chaser of schnaps, schmaltz or matjes herrings can be bought ready-filleted from many delicatessens.

6 fillets schmaltz (matjes) herrings
spring onions (scallions) or Spanish onions
tomatoes
fresh cucumber
lemon juice or wine vinegar
black pepper

Half an hour before dinner, cut the fillets into 1-inch (2.5-cm) slices and arrange in a narrow, shallow dish, surrounded by alternate slices of tomato and fresh cucumber. Over the fish squeeze just enough lemon juice or wine vinegar to moisten it and 'point up' the flavour. Sprinkle with several grinds of black pepper, and then some finely sliced spring onions or raw Spanish onions. Serve with black bread or challah. For cocktails, spear the herring portions on toothpicks.

ROAST HERRING

Serves 4.
Keeps 3 days under refrigeration.
Do not freeze.

This Lithuanian dish was often served with *eier kichel* – light, unsweetened biscuits.

2 salt herrings
2 medium onions
pinch of salt
2 level teasp sugar
pinch of pepper
1 teasp acetic acid (33%)

Put the salt herrings in water to cover and leave to soak overnight. Next day, skin, fillet and cut in small bite-sized pieces. Slice the onion into a small casserole, barely cover with water and season with the salt, sugar and pepper. Cover and cook until soft (Gas No. 3/325°F/160°C) – about 40 minutes. Add the herrings and the acetic acid. Re-cover and simmer for a further half an hour to develop the flavours. Serve with plain or buttered black bread.

SOUSED HERRINGS

Serves 6–8.
Keeps 2 days under refrigeration.

A favourite Jewish dish, quite different from the Scottish dish of the same name.

6–8 medium fresh herrings, filleted
1 medium onion, finely sliced
10 fl oz (275 ml/1¼ cups) vinegar
5 fl oz (150 ml/⅔ cup) water
few peppercorns
blade of mace
1 bay leaf
salt and pepper
1 teasp sugar
1 tbsp golden (corn) syrup

Wash and scale herrings, split lengthwise, sprinkle with salt and pepper and a little onion, then roll up from the tail with the skin side out. Pack side by side in a shallow casserole. Sprinkle with the remaining onion, then with vinegar, water and seasonings. (The liquid should just come to top of herrings but not cover them.) Sprinkle dish with sugar and then with golden syrup. Cover loosely with foil. Put in moderate oven until simmering, then reduce to Gas No. 2 (300°F/150°C) for 3 hours, or until a rich brown with liquid reduced by half. Do not allow liquid to boil, or the herrings will be hard.

A LOW-FAT TARAMASALATA

Serves 8 as part of a mixed starter, 12 as a dip or spread.
Keeps 5 days under refrigeration.
Freeze 1 month.

This recipe substitutes Greek-style yoghurt for most of the oil in the traditional recipe.

4 oz (125 g) decrusted challah
2 oz (50 g) spring onion (scallion) bulbs or shallots
4 oz (125 g/½ cup) smoked cod's roe
10 grinds of black pepper
2 teasp lemon juice
2 teasp tomato purée
3 tbsp extra virgin olive oil
8 oz (225 g/1 cup) Greek-style yoghurt

Soak the bread for 5 minutes in cold water to cover, then squeeze as dry as possible. Finely chop the onions in the food processor, then add the skinned roe (cut in 1-inch/2.5-cm chunks), the bread, black pepper, lemon juice and tomato purée and process until a smooth paste is formed. With the motor running, slowly add the oil through the feed tube. Finally, add the yoghurt and pulse in briefly until smooth and creamy. Spoon into a bowl or small terrine, cover tightly with clingfilm (saranwrap) or foil and chill for at least 12 hours. Serve with pitta bread and crudités or piled on fingers of toast.

LOW-FAT SMOKED MACKEREL MOUSSE

Makes approx 1 lb (450 g).
Keeps 3–4 days under refrigeration.
Freeze 2 months.

Smoked fish such as mackerel and herring have recently been added to that select group of foods that are both delicious to eat and positively good for your health.

Smoked mackerel is particularly succulent but it can sit a little heavily on the stomach when it is eaten 'as is'. It's much more digestible when made into a mousse with ingredients containing only a trace of fat, and with butter replaced by extra fish. I find that it's very popular served with carrot or celery-stick 'dippers' with drinks before a meal; in between it makes a marvellous 'snack' on matzah crackers or crispbread.

14 oz (400 g) (approx. 3 fillets) smoked mackerel
5 fl oz (150 ml/⅔ cup) very low-fat fromage frais
4 oz (125 g/½ cup) Quark or other very low-fat soft cheese
2 teasp horseradish relish
10 grinds of black pepper

Remove the skin from the fish and flake into a blender or food processor. Add all the remaining ingredients and blend or process until absolutely smooth. Pile into a bowl. Cover with clingfilm (saranwrap) and chill for several hours to allow it to firm up.

VARIATION

LOW-FAT SMOKED TROUT MOUSSE

Substitute the same amount of smoked trout fillets for the smoked mackerel.

MAQUEREAUX AU VIN BLANC
(*Mackerel in White Wine*)

Serves 6–8.
Keeps 4 days under refrigeration.
Do not freeze.

In the classic French recipe for this dish, Muscadet, the dry white wine produced on the west coast of France where the Loire runs into the Atlantic, is simmered with fine fat mackerel that are caught nearby. I find that any crisp dry white wine can be used, and for those who prefer a less fatty fish, trout fillets can be treated in exactly the same way.

The result – tender fillets embedded in a lightly set aspic – makes a superb cold starter for a dinner party. It's also helpful that this may be made two days ahead since the jellied stock prevents the fish drying out. And the long period of marinading in the refrigerator imparts a deliciously delicate flavour.

The classic recipe calls for half a bottle of wine, but this may be reduced, if you prefer, to a quarter bottle (7 fl oz/200 ml/¾ cup plus 2 tbsp) and the remaining liquid made up with fish stock or water.

A good, robust brown bread is called for to mop up the delicious juices.

4 x 10 oz (275 g) fresh mackerel or trout, filleted, but the bones reserved

For the poaching liquid
14 fl oz (400 ml/1¼ cups) dry white wine or combined wine and stock (see above)
5 fl oz (150 ml/⅔ cup) water
1 medium onion
1 carrot
1 unpeeled lemon
1 peeled clove of garlic
1 teasp mixed pickling spice (including a dried chilli pepper)
½ teasp salt
1 teasp sugar
sprig of dill
sprig of parsley

For the garnish
sprigs of dill

Put the fish bones and the ingredients for the poaching liquid into a 8-inch (20-cm) pan. Bring to the boil and simmer, partly covered, for 30 minutes to concentrate the flavours. Leave to cool. Cut the fillets in two lengthwise, then arrange side by side in a wide pan or heatproof casserole. Strain the poaching liquid over them and bring slowly to the boil. Allow the liquid to bubble gently for just 3 minutes, by which time the fish should have lost its raw appearance. Take off heat, cover pan and leave until the stock is cold.

Lift fillets out of the liquid, carefully strip off skin, then arrange side by side in a shallow oval dish. Bring the poaching liquid to the boil and bubble fiercely for 3 to 5 minutes, by which time it will have a good strong flavour. If it is too acid, add another teaspoonful of sugar and stir to dissolve. Spoon enough of this liquid over the fish to coat it lightly.

Any leftover stock can be frozen for later use.

Chill for at least 12 hours. Just before serving, garnish with tiny sprigs of fresh dill.

PROVENÇALE FISH SALAD

Serves 8–10 as part of a buffet, 4–6 as a starter.
Keeps 3 days under refrigeration.
Do not freeze.

A piquant fish salad which makes a delicious low-fat alternative to the more traditional fried-fish starter.

2 lb (900 g) filleted halibut or haddock
1 teasp sugar
pinch of white pepper
1½ teasp salt

For the dressing
2 tbsp chopped parsley
2 medium cloves of garlic, crushed
6 tbsp sunflower oil
2 tbsp walnut or hazelnut oil
2 tbsp fresh lemon juice

4 tbsp white wine vinegar or cider vinegar
1 teasp mild chilli powder
15 grinds of black pepper
½ teasp salt
4 rounded tbsp 8% fromage frais or 10 fl oz (275 ml/1¼ cups) soured cream
4 oz (125 g/1 cup) walnuts, coarsely chopped

Place the fish in a pan with barely enough water to cover and sugar, pepper and salt. Poach for 20 minutes, covered, on top of the stove, or 6 minutes at 100 per cent power in the microwave. Cool for 5 minutes, then lift fish out with slotted spoon. Place in a bowl and flake roughly with a fork.

In a large bowl whisk together all dressing ingredients except the cream and walnuts until thick. Fold in cream and nuts and spoon on top of fish. Toss gently together, then chill. Garnish with a pinch of paprika before serving.

Melon Hors d'oeuvres

The melon is reputed to have been developed in the gardens of the emperors of Persia and, like the grape, it takes its flavour from the soil of its birthplace. To swell and sweeten, it needs a wet winter and a hot summer - the exact climatic conditions found in the Negev desert in Israel. A few years ago Israeli agriculturists took the sweet and subtly flavoured Charentais melon and naturalized it in Kibbutz Ogen, where the conditions of soil and sun were similar to the west coast of France. Now Ogen melons and another new variety, the Galia, are produced all over the Mediterranean.

All varieties of melon must be tested for ripeness at the blossom end, which gives gently when the fruit is ripe. Canteloupe-type melons (Galia, Ogen, Charentais) also develop a glorious musky perfume. The skin of a ripe Galia will turn from green to yellow. If a melon reaches its peak before it is needed, it can be stored in the least cold part of the refrigerator for up to four days. However, it should never be served over-chilled, as this will ruin the delicate flavour.

TO SERVE WHOLE OR HALVES OF OGEN, GALIA, CANTELOUPE OR CHARENTAIS-TYPE MELONS

Allow 1 melon per person if it is the size of a grapefruit; half if it is larger.

Take a small 'cap' of rind off smaller melons. Cut larger ones in two, then take a silver off the base so the fruit will sit evenly on the plate.

Scoop out the seeds and put them, with any free juice, into a sieve over a bowl. Sweeten this juice with a little caster (superfine) sugar or granular sweetener and stir in a squeeze of lemon juice. Divide between the melons and chill for 1 hour before serving.

1-2 oz (25-50 g) raspberries or blueberries per serving can be added to the syrup.

HONEYDEW MELON WEDGES IN GINGER SAUCE

Serves 6-8.
Eat the same day.

A really superb honeydew melon needs no embellishment as the flavour is very satisfying in itself, but other less succulent fruit will benefit from the following treatment, which helps to draw out the natural juices of the fruit.

1 large ripe honeydew melon
3 tbsp caster (superfine) sugar or granular sweetener
2 teasp ground ginger

For the garnish
sweet black grapes

Cut the melon into 6 or 8 wedges and discard the seeds. Take each wedge in turn and, with a sharp serrated knife, cut between the flesh and the skin, then cut vertically into 1-inch

(2.5-cm) slices, leaving on the skin. Arrange the wedges on a serving plate in a sunburst pattern.

Mix the sugar and ginger and divide between the slices, sprinkling it in an even layer. Leave 1 hour at room temperature, then chill for ½–1 hour before serving.

Decorate with small bunches of black grapes.

MELON AND GRAPE COCKTAIL

Serves 6–8.
Keeps 1 day under refrigeration.

This can be made with either honeydew or Ogen melons. Citrus juices are used to draw out the natural juices from the other fruits.

1 large honeydew or 2 Ogen or other Canteloupe-type melons
juice of 1 large orange
juice of 1 large lemon
2–3 oz (50–75 g/¼–⅓ cup) caster (superfine) sugar (depending on the sweetness of the melon)
8 oz (225 g/1 cup) each black and green grapes

For the garnish
sprigs of mint

Cut the melon in half, remove the pips, then scoop out the flesh in balls using a melon-cutter or deep-bowled spoon. Put in a bowl. Put the orange and lemon juice with the sugar into a small pan and dissolve over gentle heat without boiling (40 seconds on 100 per cent power in the microwave). Pour over the melon. Add the grapes, but leave them on top of the mixture (if they are mixed with the juices too soon they will lose their crispness). Cover and leave in the larder or a cool place for several hours to allow the fruit juices to flow. About 1 hour before serving, mix the fruit thoroughly. Arrange in grapefruit glasses and chill. Serve garnished with sprigs of mint.

GALIA MELON AND SORBET WITH A MINTED FRUIT SAUCE

Serves 8.

This is a cool and elegant way to start a summer supper. However, the sorbet is really only worth making if you have access to a small electric sorbetière. Otherwise you will need to use the method on p. 362. The dish still looks very pretty with the minted sauce alone.

2 large, very ripe melons
3½ oz (90 g/½ cup) caster (superfine) sugar
3 tbsp lemon juice

For the sauce
juice of 2 large oranges or 6 oz (175 ml/¾ cup) freshly squeezed bottled juice
3 tbsp lemon juice
1 tbsp caster (superfine) sugar or granular sweetener
3 teasp finely chopped mint leaves

For the garnish
8 sprigs of mint

To make the sorbet, use a piece of melon weighing 1½ lb (675 g) (in the skin) - about half a large melon. Take out the seeds, scoop out the flesh and purée in a food processor or liquidizer, together with the sugar and lemon juice, until absolutely smooth. Taste and add a little more lemon juice if necessary, remembering that the sweetness will diminish in the freezer. Transfer to a sorbetière and freeze as directed for 20 minutes, then put in the freezer to complete freezing.

To make the sauce Mix the orange and lemon juice with the sugar and stir until it is dissolved. Just before serving, add the mint.

To serve, arrange scoops of sorbet on individual plates, garnish with crescents of melon and spoon over a little of the sauce. Decorate with the sprigs of mint.

Note To save time, make the scoops of sorbet ahead of time, arrange on a flat dish and freeze until required, then transfer to the plates.

Mainly Vegetables

AVOCADO

The skin may be a rich green colour or almost black, the surface dimpled or smooth, but with the exception of the knobbly skinned Haas variety, whose skin turns from green to purply black, you can really only judge the ripeness of an avocado by feel. The fruit cannot be ripened on the tree, and as the crop is exported under refrigeration, the chances are that the avocado you buy will still be hard and under-ripe. Take it home and leave it at room temperature - or in the airing cupboard for speed - for at least two days. When it is ripe enough to use, the fruit will give slightly all over if pressed between the palms. This is the best condition for eating 'on the half-shell' with a well-flavoured dressing or a stuffing of tartly flavoured citrus, fish or chicken salad replacing the stone. If, however, it is to be used for a dip or spread, then it should be very soft all over so that the flesh has a creamy consistency when it is scooped out.

Over-chilling will ruin the texture (the avocado cannot be successfully frozen whole), but if the fruit ripens too soon, it can be stored for several days in the bottom of the refrigerator. Once cut, the flesh soon oxidizes and discolours, but this can be prevented by mixing it with a lemon or mayonnaise dressing, or covering the cut surface closely with clingfilm (saranwrap).

Avocados are good news on the nutritional front because they contain no starch whatsoever and minimal sugar (so they're useful for diabetics), are easily digestible (so they're excellent for both the very young and the elderly) and are bursting with a positive alphabet of vitamins and trace elements, including vitamins A, B1, B2, C, E, K and folic acid, and 14 basic minerals including iron, copper, calcium, potassium, manganese and sodium.

To prepare Cut with a stainless-steel knife lengthwise and separate by twisting gently to take apart. To take the stone out, loosen it with a knife blade and lift out. To peel, place avocado upside down, score skin down the centre lightly and strip back or pare off. For halves, slices and cubes, cut avocado lengthwise; for rings and half moons, cut crosswise. Serve at room temperature except where chilling is specified in recipes for cold soups, desserts or moulds.

AVOCADO WITH VINAIGRETTE DRESSING

Serves 6–8.
Cut and eat the same day.
Do not freeze.

An old favourite, lifted out of the ordinary by the delicious walnut-flavoured dressing. Make the dressing several hours before dinner to allow the flavours to mature.

3–4 fat avocados

For the dressing
4 tbsp wine vinegar or cider vinegar
2 tbsp lemon juice
1 clove of garlic
2 level teasp caster (superfine) sugar or granular sweetener
1 teasp Dijon mustard
1½ tbsp chopped fresh mixed herbs – parsley, chives, tarragon, chervil
1 level teasp salt
10 grinds of black pepper
1 tbsp very finely chopped spring onion (scallion) bulb or 1 shallot
¼ teasp mild chilli powder
2 tbsp walnut oil plus 4 fl oz (125 ml/½ cup) sunflower or other flavourless oil

Put the vinegar, lemon juice and all the seasonings into a screw-top jar and shake until well blended. Then add the oils and shake again until thickened. Leave at room temperature until required. About half an hour before dinner, cut avocados in half and remove the stones. Spoon a little dressing into each cavity and spread a little more over the cut surface to prevent discoloration. Refrigerate.

Place either in special oval avocado dishes or on a bed of flat leaves. Serve the remaining dressing at the table. The flesh is scooped out with a teaspoon. Eat with brown bread and butter.

AVOCADO AUX ANCHOIS

Serves 6–8.
Avocado mixture keeps for up to 24 hours under refrigeration.
Do not freeze.

A superb blend of colours and flavours. For a dinner party starter, serve it spooned into wine glasses. For a light supper main course, arrange on individual plates or in avocado dishes, surrounded by shredded lettuce and accompanied by fresh rye bread.

3–4 ripe but still firm medium avocados
1½ x 2 oz (50 g) cans anchovies in olive oil
1 sweet red pepper

For the dressing
2 tbsp wine vinegar
1 tbsp fresh lemon juice
3 tbsp sunflower oil
1 tbsp walnut oil or extra virgin olive oil
1 clove of garlic, peeled and halved
1 teasp sugar or granular sweetener
10 grinds of black pepper
½ teasp sea salt
½ teasp Dijon mustard
3 spring onion (scallion) bulbs, finely chopped
1 tbsp chopped parsley

For the garnish
½ x 2oz (50 g) can anchovies
black olives

In a screw-top jar shake all the dressing ingredients together until slightly thickened, then pour into a mixing bowl. Halve, then peel or scoop out the avocado flesh with a dessert spoon and cut into ⅜-inch (1-cm) cubes. Add to the dressing. Halve, deseed and then cube the red pepper in the same way. Add to the avocado, together with the drained anchovies cut in ½-inch (1.25-cm) lengths. Blend gently with the dressing, cover and refrigerate for several hours. Remove the garlic halves, then serve as suggested, garnished with the anchovies and black olives.

AVOCADO STING

Serves 6–8.
Eat the same day.
Do not freeze.

An excellent dish to serve in a meat buffet, arranging the slices of avocado in a shallow gratin dish. Or the dressing can be used on the half-shell.

3–4 avocados

For the dressing

4 tbsp fresh orange juice (1 large orange)
2 tbsp fresh lime juice (1½ limes)
2 teasp cider, raspberry vinegar or white wine vinegar
1 teasp wholegrain mustard
½ teasp freshly ground coriander seed
1 teasp salt
1 teasp sugar or granular sweetener
8 grinds of black pepper
1 medium clove of garlic, peeled and crushed
5 fl oz (150 ml/⅔ cup) extra virgin olive oil
1 tbsp chopped fresh parsley or coriander

Put all the dressing ingredients in a screw-top jar and shake until thickened - 1-2 minutes - or process until thick in the food processor.

Either halve, stone and peel the avocados, cut in thick slices and spoon over some of the dressing, garnishing the dish with a few salad leaves, or use the dressing to spoon into the halved and stoned avocados.

FRESH PEACH AND AVOCADO SALAD

Serves 8.
Eat the same day.
Do not freeze.

With its delicate garnish of mint and lemon strands, this is a very pretty dish either as a dinner party starter or on a buffet table. The slightly acid fruit contrasts well with the bland flavour of the avocado.

4 small, ripe but firm avocados
4 ripe peaches or nectarines, or 2 medium mangoes
1 pack French-style salad leaves, or a mixture of frisée, watercress and lamb's lettuce

For the dressing

5 fl oz (150 ml/⅔ cup) extra virgin olive oil
4 tbsp fresh lemon juice
2 tbsp raspberry vinegar or white wine vinegar
1 teasp salt
1 teasp caster (superfine) sugar or granular sweetener
1 fat clove of garlic, crushed (optional)
2 tbsp chopped fresh mint

For the garnish

2 tbsp skinned pistachios or toasted pine kernels, coarsely chopped
fine strands of lemon peel
sprigs of mint

Several hours in advance, shake all the dressing ingredients in a screw-top jar until thickened - about 2 minutes.

Peel, halve, stone and slice the avocados. Halve, stone and slice the fruit. Arrange the avocado slices in one shallow dish and the fruit slices in another, then pour the dressing evenly over them.

To serve (may be done 1 hour in advance), arrange a bed of leaves on 8 plates, then lay the avocado and fruit decoratively on top. Dribble a little of the remaining dressing on each salad and garnish with the chopped nuts, mint and lemon peel.

ASPARAGUS

Although asparagus is flown in throughout the year from many different parts of the world, choice home-grown asparagus has but a brief - and therefore expensive - season, so it is worth taking great care with selection and preparation. It will be well repaid by the resulting exquisite flavour and texture.

Choose a bundle with thick, green-tipped stalks, firm and fresh-looking. Untie the bundle and wash it, tips down, in a bowl under cold running water, then gently scrub it with a soft brush to remove the sand which clings to the tips. Unless it is a variety whose stalks are all green, break off the woody lower 2 inches (5 cm) of the stalk - they always seem to snap at just the right place.

Scrape away the last inch (2.5 cm) of scales on the lower stem using a small sharp knife, then retie the asparagus into a bundle of even length, using soft string. If you have no asparagus pan, leave a loop of string to make it easy to lift the cooked bundle from the pan. Asparagus must be cooked *al dente* - that is, it must have a tender head with a slightly chewy stalk, so that one can almost suck the juices out of it. To achieve this, it is necessary to steam the tender heads, while boiling the tougher stalks.

The pan You can buy a special cylindrical asparagus pan, which has a perforated inner section that lifts out like a double-boiler, but for most households a percolator without the coffee container works just as well and is far cheaper to buy (for heaven's sake, though, keep it for asparagus only!).

To cook Put 6 inches (15 cm) of boiling water into the pan, add the bundle of asparagus, tips to the top, close the lid and simmer for 14 minutes. To test whether done, taste one stalk - the tip should be tender without being mushy.

The sauce While the asparagus is cooking, it is as well to get ready the sauce and the dish. The simplest sauce, and I think the best, is plain melted butter, although Hollandaise Sauce (see p. 77) is also often served.

MELTED BUTTER SAUCE

3 oz (75 g/3/4 cup) butter (preferably unsalted)
few grains of cayenne pepper
squeeze of lemon juice

Put the butter into a sauce boat and leave in a warm place (the warming oven or the side of the stove, or heat in the microwave on defrost for 40 seconds), so that the butter becomes liquid without oiling. Just before serving, add the cayenne and lemon juice.

The asparagus dish This can be as elaborate as a specially designed entrée dish with a built-in tray on which the cooked asparagus is placed to drain, or as simple as a flat platter with a linen napkin liner to absorb excess moisture - but be sure to heat it well as asparagus quickly goes cold. Lay the steaming bundle of asparagus on the dish, untie the string and serve at once. Tepid asparagus is horrid. About 6–7 fat stalks are quite sufficient for one serving, with a slice of challah for mopping up the combined juices and butter sauce. And – fingers please! That is the only way to eat asparagus.

ARTICHOKES

It is not so much the taste for artichokes that needs to be acquired as the manner of eating them! Not for inclusion in the menu of a formal banquet (unless the heart alone is served), they make the most blissful of hors d'oeuvres at a friendly family meal. Choice artichokes feel weighty in the hand and the stalk should look green and fresh. They may be stored raw for several days under refrigeration. The preparation is simple, if precise.

First, don't be tempted to cut off the stem of the artichoke before you have prepared it. Use it as a 'handle' to steady the head while you cut away the top inch of the vegetable, using a sharp bread knife and a sawing motion. Then *break* the stem off by bending it firmly down. This pulls out the stem fibres from the heart and ensures that it will be smooth and tender when cooked. The traditional way to cook artichokes is to boil them in a very large pan of salted water, partly covered for 40 to 45 minutes, or until a leaf can be easily pulled out. However, you can also wrap each one tightly in clingfilm (saranwrap) and microwave it on full power - this will take 19 minutes for 6 artichokes, 15 minutes for 4 and 10 minutes for 2. Leave them in the film to stand for 5 minutes, then unwrap and allow to stand until cool enough to handle. Leaving the large outer leaves intact (these have the fleshy base that is so delicious when eaten), take hold of the inner cone of delicate, insubstantial leaves in the centre and give it a good twist - it will come away and can then be easily lifted out. This will reveal the choke, a mass of fine filaments that can either be pulled out with the fingers or, as I find easier, carefully scooped out with a teaspoon. Now you will have revealed the delicious 'heart' of the artichoke, sitting at the bottom of a little cup that can be filled with a French dressing or Hollandaise just before serving.

I find the delicate flavour of this exotic vegetable is better appreciated at room temperature rather than chilled. However, for convenience you can do the cooking the day before, refrigerate overnight and then leave the artichokes in the kitchen for a couple of hours before serving.

A fairly tart French dressing with plenty of chopped fresh herbs makes a good contrast with the rather bland artichoke flavour (see Avocado with Vinaigrette Dressing, p. 18, for recipe). Ready-made vinaigrette dressings are vastly improved with extra fresh herbs, tarragon in particular.

When eating, start pulling off the leaves from the centre first; they will already be coated with sauce at the base. Leaves from further out can be dipped into the dressing, which soaks into the heart.

CARCIOFI TONNATO
(Fresh Artichokes Stuffed with Tuna in the Sicilian Manner)

Serves 4.
Do not freeze.

4 globe artichokes, cooked and prepared as described on pp. 20–21

half-quantity vinaigrette dressing (see p. 18)

For the filling

1 x 7 oz (200 g) can best-quality tuna
2 teasp anchovy purée
1 teasp garlic purée (or ½ clove garlic)
½ x 5 oz (150 g) jar capers
2 tbsp chopped parsley
10 grinds of black pepper
½ teasp ground sea salt
4 tbsp extra virgin olive oil

To make the filling, mix together the drained and well-mashed tuna, the anchovy and garlic purées (or crushed garlic), the drained and mashed capers, the parsley, salt and pepper. Use this mixture to fill the centre of each artichoke then sprinkle with the olive oil. Chill for several hours.

Serve with the vinaigrette for dipping the outer leaves.

IMAM BAYELDI
(*Whole Aubergines in Tomato*)

Serves 6–8.
Keeps 3 days under refrigeration.
Do not freeze.

The following recipe is how the Turks make this rich, luscious dish, though different versions are served all over the Middle East.

6–8 small, oval aubergines (eggplants)
(approx. 8 oz/225 g each)
2 large onions
3 tbsp extra virgin olive oil
whole tomatoes, drained from a 15 oz (425 g) can, chopped
2 tbsp currants
½ teasp cinnamon
½ teasp cumin
1 teasp brown sugar
½ level teasp salt
10 grinds of black pepper
1½ tbsp chopped parsley

For the sauce
4 fl oz (125 ml/½ cup) hot water
3 tbsp extra virgin olive oil
2 tbsp lemon juice
2 teasp brown sugar
1 clove of garlic, halved

Cut a deep slit lengthwise in the centre of each aubergine, sprinkle inside with salt and leave for 30 minutes. Squeeze out any black juices, rinse under the cold tap and dab dry.

Slice the onions finely, then sauté gently in the 3 tbsp oil until golden. Add the tomatoes, currants, spices, sugar, salt and pepper and simmer gently until the mixture is thick but still juicy. Add the parsley.

Cool, then use to stuff the slits in each aubergine. Arrange the aubergines side by side in a shallow casserole, slit side up and add sauce ingredients – first the water and olive oil. Then pour over the lemon juice and sprinkle with the sugar. Add the garlic.

Cover the dish and simmer very gently, either on top of the stove or in the oven, Gas No. 3 (325°F/160°C), for 1½ hours, or until quite soft and most of the liquid has been absorbed. Chill, preferably overnight.

When you are ready, lift the aubergines from the sauce, spoon a little of it over each one, and serve with bread or toast.

CHATZILIM
(*Poor Man's Caviare*)

Serves 8 as a starter, 12–14 as a dip.
Keeps 2 weeks under refrigeration.
Do not freeze.

A delicious eastern Mediterranean starter to serve like a pâté with toast and butter, or as a stuffing for tomatoes. Also known as Potljelly by Romanian Jews.

(1½ lb/675 g) aubergines (eggplants)
1 clove of garlic, crushed
1 tbsp finely chopped onion
juice of ½ lemon (2 tbsp)
3 tbsp olive oil
1 level teasp sea salt
10 grinds of black pepper
2 tbsp finely chopped parsley
1 tbsp finely chopped green pepper (optional)

For the garnish
black olives

Cut off the prickly stalk-ends of the aubergines, then prick all over with a fork (this prevents them bursting and burning the cook!). Traditionally the aubergines are grilled over charcoal, giving the dish its characteristic smoky flavour. However, unless you have a charcoal grill to hand it's much more convenient to bake them at Gas No. 8 (450°F/230°C) for 30 minutes, until they have begun to collapse and a skewer meets no resistance when the centre is pierced. If more convenient, lay them on a paper towel and cook in the microwave on 100 per cent power for 16 minutes. Leave for 1 minute, then pierce with a skewer to test as before.

Allow to cool for a few minutes, then cut in half and scoop out the flesh from the skin. Chop the remaining ingredients into it using a *hackmesser* or a large cook's knife, adding the olive oil and lemon juice last. Taste and add more lemon juice and seasonings if necessary. Put into a fairly shallow pottery dish.

Garnish with black olives and serve with challah or pitta bread.

BABA GHANOUSH (*Aubergine and Tahina Purée*)

Serves 8 as a starter, 12–14 as a dip.
Keeps 1 week under refrigeration.

1 recipe Chatzilim (see p. 22)
plus *1 extra clove of garlic*
1 extra tbsp lemon juice
4 rounded tbsp canned or bottled tahina (sesame seed paste)
pinch ofd Cayenne pepper
½ teasp ground cumin

Bake the aubergines in the same way as for the Chatzilim, but put the flesh into the food processor, together with all the remaining ingredients. Purée until creamy and smooth. Cover and chill for several hours, then turn into a dish.

CHAMPIGNONS À LA GRECQUE

Serves 6, or 8–10 when part of a mixed hors d'oeuvre.
Keeps 4 days under refrigeration.
Do not freeze.

Serve these delicately flavoured mushrooms in small, shallow dishes with a large teaspoon. Make 24 hours in advance to savour them at their best.

1½ lb (675 g/7½ cups) tiny button mushrooms
6 tbsp extra virgin olive oil
6 tbsp water
1½ tbsp lemon juice
1½ tbsp wine vinegar
1 teasp tomato purée
10 grinds of black pepper
1 teasp ground coriander
½ teasp dried Italian seasoning herbs
1 clove of garlic, crushed
1 large bay leaf
large sprig each of parsley and fresh thyme (or pinch of dry thyme)
½ teasp salt
½ teasp sugar
10 grinds black pepper

For the garnish
tiny sprigs of fresh thyme

Wipe mushrooms with a damp cloth and cut the stalks level with the caps. Put all the remaining ingredients into a pan, bring to the boil, cover and simmer for 5 minutes. Uncover, put in mushrooms, spoon liquid over them, cover and simmer for 8–10 minutes or until just tender. Remove mushrooms to a container, using a slotted spoon. Boil juice down until thick (there should be about 5 or 6 tablespoons). Strain over mushrooms, cover and chill overnight.

Serve in little saucers or individual ramekins, with plenty of country bread to mop up the delicious juices.

PEPERONI RIPIENI ALLA PIEDMONTESE *(Stuffed Peppers, Piedmont Style)*

Serves 6–8 (with another antipasto).
Keeps 2 days under refrigeration.
Do not freeze.

This is a starter in the true Italian tradition. The cooks of Imperial Rome discovered that oil, which is the main ingredient of so many antipasti, forms an effective barrier in the stomach against the too rapid absorption of alcohol. Such reasoning motivated the development of the Russian *zakuski* and the German *forspeise* – dishes that were eaten with high-alcohol drinks such as vodka, kummel and schnapps, a custom enthusiastically adopted by Jews and still to be seen at Jewish weddings and barmitzvahs.

6–8 small, squat red peppers
8 oz (225 g/4 cups) fresh brown breadcrumbs
7 tbsp extra virgin olive oil
2 oz (50 g/½ cup) grated Cheddar cheese
2 oz (50 g/½ cup) black olives, stoned and chopped
6 anchovy fillets, finely chopped, or 3 teasp anchovy purée
3 tbsp capers, drained
2 tbsp finely chopped parsley
10 grinds of black pepper
salt

Cut a thin slice off each pepper and keep it to one side. Remove the seeds, then arrange the peppers side by side in a shallow baking dish. Sauté the breadcrumbs in half the oil until crisp and golden, then put in a bowl together with the cheese, olives, anchovies, capers, parsley and black pepper. Stir well, taste and add a little salt if necessary. Divide the mixture between the peppers, then cover with the lids. To the remaining oil add 5 tbsp water, stir well and pour over the peppers. Cook uncovered in a moderate oven, Gas No. 4 (350°F/180°C), for 35–40 minutes, basting once or twice, until the peppers feel tender when pierced with a sharp knife. Serve at room temperature.

SALADE PROVENÇALE

Serves 6–8.
Eat the same day.

The hot sun of Provence produces herbs of a unique flavour and it is this particular quality that gives a special perfume to local dishes, such as the famous salad of the region – sometimes called Salade Niçoise. This combines an assortment of fresh salad vegetables with tuna and anchovies, all bathed in a wonderful herby dressing. There are no strict rules for the ingredients, but to give it substance you do need either potatoes or white haricot beans. So if you don't have everything in the list of ingredients below, just substitute what you do have – but be sure to make the wonderful dressing that helps to marry all the different flavours.

1 x 15 oz (425 g) can white haricot beans or 12 oz (350 g) cooked new potatoes, sliced
2 x 7 oz (200 g) cans best-quality tuna in oil
2 x 2 oz (50 g) cans anchovy fillets in olive oil
½ cucumber
1 each medium red and yellow peppers
4 oz (125 g/1 cup) fat black olives
8 oz (225 g) cherry tomatoes
2 hard-boiled eggs
3 'Little Gem' lettuces
8 oz (225 g) fresh or frozen green haricot beans, lightly cooked

For the dressing

4 fl oz (125 ml/½ cup) grapeseed oil or sunflower oil
1 fl oz (25 ml/2 tbsp) extra virgin olive oil or walnut oil
3 tbsp wine vinegar or cider vinegar
1 tbsp lemon juice
1 fat clove of garlic
2 teasp dry mustard
2 teasp caster (superfine) sugar or granular sweetener

1 teasp salt
15 grinds of black pepper
1 tbsp mixed chopped fresh herbs – chives, parsley, oregano, chervil

First make the dressing by putting all the ingredients in a screw-top jar and shaking vigorously for a minute or two (you will notice that the mustard helps to make a thick emulsion). Drain the white haricot beans thoroughly, then put in a small bowl with a few tablespoons of the dressing, and leave for 1 hour. If potatoes are used instead of the beans, treat in the same way.

Drain the tuna and flake it roughly. Cut the drained anchovies down the middle. Cut the cucumber in thin slices. Deseed the peppers and cut in ⅛-inch-thick (0.3-cm) strips. Leave the olives and the tomatoes whole but halve the eggs. Separate the leaves of the lettuces, rinse and dry. Arrange all these ingredients in a salad bowl or glass dish that is wide and shallow rather than deep (this helps when tossing in the dressing). Just before serving, add the green haricot beans. Toss at the table with just enough of the dressing to coat the ingredients.

Serve with crusty French bread.

ANCHOVY AND TOMATO HORS D'OEUVRE

Serves 6.
Eat the same day.
Do not freeze.

This is a simple recipe from the Charente-Maritime region of France. It needs really ripe and sweet Mediterranean-type tomatoes such as the Marmande variety.

6 large, very ripe tomatoes
1 x 2 oz (50 g) can anchovy fillets
black olives
1 salad onion, sliced as thinly as possible

For the parsley dressing
1 tbsp wine or cider vinegar or lemon juice
4 tbsp extra virgin olive oil
1 level teasp sugar or granular sweetener
½ teasp salt
½ teasp paprika
½ teasp mustard
10 grinds of black pepper
1 tbsp chopped parsley
½ clove of garlic, left whole

Shake all the dressing ingredients together in a screw-top jar, then leave for several hours in the cool. Just before serving, slice the tomatoes and remove any woody cores. Arrange 3 or 4 slices on each serving plate and criss-cross with anchovy fillets, cut in half lengthwise, filling the gaps with black olives. Top with a few shavings of onion.

Just before serving, remove the garlic, then sprinkle the hors d'oeuvre with the dressing.

Serve with fresh challah or black bread.

CHERRY TOMATO MEZZE

Serves 8–10.
Eat freshly made.

These are delicious little titbits.

20 tiny cherry tomatoes
4 oz (125 g/½ cup) feta cheese
pesto or pesto purée
toothpicks

Cut tomatoes in half and scoop out seeds with a teaspoon. Turn upside down on a double thickness of kitchen paper for 30 minutes, keeping matching halves together. Cut feta in ½-inch (1.25-cm) pieces, each about ⅓ inch (1 cm) thick.

To assemble, spread a layer of pesto on one half of a tomato, put a piece of feta on top, then top with the other half of the tomato spread with more pesto. Squeeze gently together, then secure with a toothpick.

SOUPS AND GARNISHES

Soups in a Hurry

Jewish cooks have been making soup of some kind since the beginning of our recorded history - after all, Jacob diverted the very course of our destiny when he tempted Esau with his savoury 'mess of pottage'. And it was the soups of pulses and cereals that did so much to nourish the immigrant families who could not afford enough meat in the early years of this century. It is certainly worth restating the basic concepts of soup-making in terms of our modern way of eating. Besides, home-made soup is so delicious!

To store soup All soups improve in flavour if they are allowed to mature overnight. However, they should always be stored covered, under refrigeration, and will keep sweet for up to 3 days.

To freeze soup Store in containers of plastic or glass, with an inch headroom to allow for the expansion of the liquid when frozen. Alternatively, the soup can be frozen in a plastic bag shaped to fit a container. When the liquid has frozen, lift out the bag and store in the freezer for up to 3 months.

To defrost soup In a hurry, soup can be reheated from the frozen state - most satisfactorily in the microwave. Generally, it is better to allow it to defrost in the refrigerator overnight and then pour it into the soup pan to reheat. This avoids any chance of burning, particularly with a thick soup.

Soup Stocks

Stock is quite simply a flavoured liquid from which soups and sauces are made. The more flavourful the stock, the tastier will be the soup or the sauce. In Jewish cookery, meat stocks are traditionally made by simmering the coarser parts of root vegetables with herbs and koshered bones, enriched if desired with a piece of shin beef or a portion of fowl. To extract flavour from these ingredients, the stock must be simmered very slowly for many hours, preferably in the oven. However, with a pressure cooker, one can make excellent stock in only an hour. If stock is made the day before the soup, it should be chilled in the fridge or freezer. It will then be easy to lift off any fat that has congealed on the surface overnight. Stock is an excellent way of using up odds and ends of vegetables that have a good flavour but are too coarse to use in the soup itself.

Here are some different ways to make stock for soup.

BONE STOCK

Keeps 3 days under refrigeration.
Freeze 3 months.

Koshered bones
green part of a fat leek
leaves from a head of celery
½ white turnip
½ onion
2 squashy tomatoes
1 bay leaf
10 peppercorns
large sprig of parsley
2 level teasp salt

Put the bones and the coarsely cut vegetables into a pressure cooker and cover with cold water. Add the seasonings. Pressurize for 1 hour. Alternatively, the ingredients can be put in a soup pan, brought to simmering point, then simmered on the top of the stove for 3 hours or in the oven (Gas No. 2/300°F/150°C) for the same length of time. Strain out all the vegetables. If the stock is not to be used at once, it can be either refrigerated until next day or boiled down to concentrate it, then poured into a plastic container and frozen.

Note It is not necessary to cut fresh vegetables for stock, but any leftover ends of carrot, half-onions, squashy tomatoes, etc. can be used. In fact, the coarser the vegetables, the more flavour they will add.

BEEF AND BONE STOCK

Proceed as above, but add ½-1 lb (225-450 g) shin beef to the vegetables. The cooked meat can be either served in the soup or used to make kreplach (see p. 50) or other minced-meat pastries.

COOKED BONE STOCK

The bone left from a roast rib makes excellent stock. Proceed as above. Use the stock for barley soup.

COOKED CHICKEN AND BONE STOCK

Next time you roast or braise a chicken or fowl, freeze the cooked carcass and you will have the foundation for a low-fat chicken soup that can rival in flavour one enriched in the traditional way with a piece of fat hen. To make the soup, break up the carcass so it will fit comfortably into the soup pan or pressure cooker, add a couple of sets of giblets (if available), two fat carrots and the white part of a leek (both finely sliced), a few squashy tomatoes (or 2 teaspoons of tomato purée), half a large onion and a small bunch of parsley. Add 2½ pints (1.5 1/6 cups) of cold water, a teaspoon of salt and 20 grinds of black pepper and allow the pot to simmer on the lowest possible light for 3 hours (or pressurize for 1 hour). Better still, simmer it in the oven, where it will develop an even richer flavour.

After this long, slow cooking, strain out the vegetables, bones and giblets, returning any chicken salvaged from them to the pan, then refrigerate or freeze overnight so that the fat content will solidify and can be easily removed next day. When the soup is reheated, the chicken flavour will probably need strengthening with a couple of chicken stock-cubes.

BOUILLON-CUBE STOCK

For the small family, it is probably a more economical proposition, and certainly saves on time, to use commercial bouillon-cubes, which are diluted with water according to the manufacturer's instructions. Excellent beef and chicken cubes are available in a kosher pack.

VEGETABLE STOCK

I prefer to use a commercial vegetable stock-cube or paste, as it has a more intense flavour than home-made stock.

Always check the label of a stock-cube and do not buy any which list monosodium glutamate (MSG) high on the list. This is used as a flavour reinforcer and if it is listed as a major ingredient, this suggests it is being used to hide the absence of genuine flavourings extracted from beef, chicken or vegetables.

Note If a soup requires a long cooking time – for instance, barley soup and split-pea soup – the bones and meat (if used) can be cooked simultaneously with the soup ingredients. In that case, the bones should be put into the pan, covered with the amount of water specified in the recipe, and the mixture brought to the boil. The scum from the bones should then be carefully removed with a wet spoon before the soup cereals and vegetables are added.

Rich and Clear

Clear soups depend almost entirely on the flavour from the stock or bouillon with which they are made. I like to cook them in the oven, as the heat completely surrounds the soup pan and seems to give its contents an extra depth of flavour.

TRADITIONAL CHICKEN SOUP

Serves 4–6.
Keeps 3 days under refrigeration.
Freeze 3 months.

Chicken soup is traditionally made by simmering a fowl (or part of one) in water flavoured with a variety of vegetables. However, if the fowl is to be casseroled rather than boiled, or a younger bird roasted or fried, then the soup can be made with the feet and giblets alone, and the flavour strengthened by the addition of a chicken bouillon-cube (see also Cooked Chicken and Bone Stock, p. 27). Chicken soup should always be made the day before it is served, as the flavour is incomparably better on the second day, when the pale stock will have metamorphosed into 'Jewish penicillin', the legendary golden liquid which is said to be a cure for every ill! Chicken soup is usually garnished with lokshen (vermicelli), egg noodles, knaidlach (soup dumplings), mandlen (soup nuts) or kreplach (ravioli) – see pp. 49–53.

A whole or half chicken or fowl, with the feet (if available), wings and giblets
2 teasp salt
pinch of white pepper
1 large onion
2 large carrots
leaves and top 2 in (5 cm) of 2 sticks celery
1 sprig of parsley
1 very ripe tomato
any soft eggs from inside the fowl (if used).

Put the bird, feet, wings and giblets in a large, heavy soup pan with 3 pints (1.75 l/7½ cups) water, salt and pepper. Cover and bring to the boil. Remove any froth with a large, wet metal spoon.

Peel onion and carrots, cut in half and add to the pan with celery, parsley, tomato and eggs.

Bring back to the boil, then reduce the heat so that the liquid is barely bubbling. Cover and continue to simmer for a further 3 hours, either on top of the stove or in a slow oven,

Gas No. 2 (300°F/150°C) or until the chicken feels very tender when a leg is prodded.

Strain the soup into a large bowl; reserve giblets and carrots in another container. Cover and put in the fridge overnight.

Next day, remove any congealed fat and return the soup to the pan. (If there is a thick layer of fat, it can be heated in a pan to drive off any liquid and then, when it has stopped bubbling, cooled and stored like rendered raw fat). Add the cooked giblets and the carrot (cut into small dice) and reheat slowly before serving with any of the garnishes mentioned above. Allow approximately ½ oz (15 g/¼ cup) per person of lokshen cooked according to packet directions in boiling water or the soup.

A BATCH OF CHICKEN SOUP FOR THE FREEZER

Makes about 1 gallon (4.5 l/20 cups) before concentrating.
Freeze 3 months.

It is really worthwhile to prepare and freeze a month's supply of chicken soup at one time, as all the tedious parts of the process - straining the vegetables, stripping the flesh from the carcass and the giblets, even washing up the pan - then need be done only once. You can divide the batch into convenient portions which, when required, can simply be simmered for a short time with some fresh vegetables.

To make this quantity of soup you will need a pan of 1½ gallons (6 l/30 cups) capacity, tall rather than broad, so that the base diameter is equal to that of the gas ring or hot plate of the cooker. I use an enamelled steel pan with a white enamel interior which is particularly easy to clean.

It is advisable to use at least a portion of a fowl - also called a 'boiling hen' (stewing chicken). If you do not like it plain-boiled, the cooked flesh can always be used in a pie or pilaff. But if you do not use any fowl at all, and rely solely on giblets, then you may need to add chicken stock-cubes to deepen the flavour. It is important to be generous with soup vegetables and always to include some ripe tomatoes or a little tomato purée to deepen the colour without giving the stock a taste of tomato.

3-4 sets of chicken giblets
the last wing joint previously cut from chickens before they were roasted, then frozen (if available)
any carcasses from roast birds in the freezer
1 whole or half a boiling fowl, together with the feet (if available)
3 large onions, peeled but left whole
6 carrots, each cut lengthwise into 4
leaves and top 2 in (5 cm) of the stalks from a bunch of celery
2 oz (50 g) bunch of parsley, including the stalks
4 very soft, ripe tomatoes or 1 tbsp tomato purée
1 tbsp salt
½ teasp white pepper

Put the giblets, wings, feet, broken-up cooked carcasses and fowl (if used) into the pan and cover with 8 or 9 pints (4.5 l/20 cups) of water - sufficient to come to within an inch or two of the top of the pan. Bring slowly to the boil, then remove the scum from the top with a wet metal spoon. Add all the other ingredients, bring back to the boil, cover and simmer for at least 3 hours on top of the stove, or 4 hours in the oven. (An oven set at Gas No. 2/300°F/150°C should keep the liquid at a slow bubble.)

At the end of the cooking time, lift out the giblets with a slotted spoon and put in a bowl. Lift out and discard any cooked carcasses. Remove the cooked fowl and reserve for another purpose. Place a coarse sieve over a large bowl and pour the soup through to separate it from the vegetables (which can now be discarded as all their goodness and flavour will be in the soup). Strip the meat from the giblets and wings and refrigerate until it can be added to the defatted soup next day. If freezer space is at a premium, the soup can be boiled down to half its volume. In any event, chill it overnight so that the congealed fat can be removed the next day.

Divide the defatted stock into convenient

amounts, allowing 2 pints (1.25 l/5 cups) for 4–6 servings (1 pint/575 ml/2½ cups if condensed). Divide the giblet meat between the portions, label and freeze.

When ready to use the soup Put the required amount of frozen soup into a pan and add the following:

1–2 good-quality chicken stock-cubes (the number will depend on the strength of the soup)
1 medium carrot, cut into ⅜-in (1-cm) cubes
1-in (2.5-cm) length of the white part of a leek, finely shredded
chopped parsley

Bring the soup slowly to the boil with the vegetables and simmer for 30 minutes. Stir in the parsley and serve with the desired garnish.

CURRIED CHICKEN SOUP

Serves 6–8.
Keeps 3 days under refrigeration.
Freeze 3 months.

A creamy soup with a gently curried flavour.

1 tbsp sunflower oil
1 large onion
2 large carrots
1½ tbsp mild curry powder
2½ pints (1.5 l/6¼ cups) chicken soup or stock (home-made)
several sprigs of parsley with stalks
1 bay leaf
6 oz (175 g) uncooked chicken-breast meat
4 tbsp long-grain rice
8 oz (225 g) frozen peas
salt and black pepper to taste

Gently heat the oil in a heavy soup pan, then add the finely chopped onion and carrot – both can be chopped in a food processor. Stir in the curry powder, then cover and cook gently, stirring occasionally, for about 25 minutes, or until the vegetables are tender and golden. Add the soup or stock, parsley, bay leaf, chicken breast and rice, then cover and simmer until the chicken is tender – about 20 minutes. Allow the chicken to cool in the soup, then lift out, remove skin and dice the meat finely.

Remove bay leaf and parsley from the pan, then pour the soup through a sieve into a large bowl. Put the vegetable-and-rice mixture into a blender or food processor with a cup of the liquid and process until smooth. Return this purée to the soup pan, together with the remaining liquid, the chicken and the peas. Simmer for a further 15 minutes, or until the peas are quite tender, adding salt and black pepper and a little extra curry powder if necessary.

Three Slimline Chicken Soups

The basis is a completely defatted chicken stock with a selection of diced vegetables and a very little optional vermicelli. (1 ring of vermicelli weighing ⅔ oz (20 g) has a calorie count of 72 and is sufficent for a soup giving 4 generous servings). The three soups below are delicious enough to serve to non-dieters as well. To defat the chicken stock quickly and completely, partly freeze it until the fat is solid enough to scrape off with a spoon (this takes 2–3 hours). If you like a thicker soup, you may

prefer the courgette and lettuce version below. All three soups will improve if left for at least 6 hours before serving. Reheat gently until bubbling.

All the soups serve 4. They keep 3 days under refrigeration and freeze for 3 months.

SLIMLINE CHICKEN NOODLE SOUP

2 pints (1.25 l/5 cups) chicken stock
3 oz (75 g) each of turnip, the white part of a leek, carrot and shredded yellow pepper
3 tbsp (1 ring) vermicelli
2 teasp chopped parsley

Bring the stock to the boil, add the diced vegetables and the vermicelli (if used), cover and simmer for 10 minutes. Taste and add salt and pepper if necessary.

SLIMLINE MUSHROOM AND COURGETTE SOUP

Make in exactly the same way as Slimline Chicken Noodle Soup but using these ingredients:

2 pints (1.25 l/5 cups) chicken stock
4 oz (125 g/1½ cups) very fresh mushrooms with stalk, wiped with damp cloth, then thinly sliced
1 large carrot, cut into ⅜-inch (1-cm) cubes
1 unpeeled courgette, wiped and cut into ⅜-inch (1-cm) slices
2 teasp tomato purée
2 teasp chopped parsley

SLIMLINE COURGETTE AND LETTUCE SOUP

This needs a slightly different method.

1½lb (675 g) courgettes
1 tbsp minced dried onion
2 pints (1.25 1/5 cups) chicken stock
½ teasp salt
15 grinds of black pepper
1 medium lettuce
2 teasp chopped parsley or snipped chives

Put the thinly sliced, unpeeled courgettes, onion, stock, salt and pepper into a soup pan and simmer, covered, until the courgettes are soft - 10–15 minutes. Add the shredded lettuce and let soup bubble uncovered for 3 minutes. Then blend or process until smooth. Just before serving, stir in the parsley or chives.

CELERY AND CARROT SOUP

Serves 6.
Keeps 3 days under refrigeration.
Freeze for 3 months.

A very satisfying fairly low-calorie soup with an excellent flavour.

1 fat head of celery plus the leaves
12 oz (350 g) large, mature carrots
2 pints (1.25 l/5 cups) good chicken stock
1 tbsp minced dried onion
1 large bay leaf
large sprig of parsley

Cut off ½ inch (1.25 cm) from the root end of the celery and discard it. Cut off the leaves and reserve. Wash celery in cold water, then slice as thinly as possible with the carrot - a food processor does the job especially well. Put the stock in a soup pan and add all the remaining ingredients except for the celery leaves. Bring to the boil, then simmer until the vegetables are absolutely tender - 15–20 minutes. Remove the bay leaf, then process or (for a smoother texture) liquidize until puréed. If the soup still feels fibrous, push it through a sieve or a mouli to remove the strings. Return to the pan, bring slowly to the boil and add the chopped celery leaves. Leave to stand for several hours, during which time it will thicken slightly. Serve piping hot.

BEETROOT BORSCHT

Serves 6–8.
Cooked beet juice will keep 4 days under refrigeration, the complete soup for 2 days.
Freeze 3 months.

The preparation of this much-loved soup used to entail tedious grating of all the vegetables on a *rebeizen* - hand-grater. However, nowadays not only does the food processor save time and labour, but by chopping the vegetables very finely the flavour can be extracted from them very quickly and so the soup will have a very fresh taste. Using the food processor to blend the eggs with some of the stock to thicken the soup also lessens the chance that it will curdle. It is best to make the soup one day, then cool and reheat until steaming just before serving on the next. Hot borscht is usually served with a garnish of sliced, boiled potatoes; cold borscht, with a swirl of soured cream.

2 lb (1 kg) old beets or 3 bunches of young beets
1 medium carrot, peeled
1 medium onion, peeled
2½ pints (1.5 l/6 cups) water (for dairy borscht) or meat or chicken stock (for meat borscht)
15 grinds of black pepper
2 teasp salt (if water is used)
2 tbsp sugar

To thicken
3 tbsp lemon juice or 1 teasp citric acid crystals
3 whole eggs

Have ready a 4-pint (2 l/10-cup) soup pan. Trim the beets, then peel or scrape. Cut all the vegetables into 1-inch (2.5-cm) chunks, then process in two batches until very finely chopped. Put in the pan with the water or stock, pepper, salt (if used) and sugar. Bring to the boil, cover and simmer for 20 minutes, until the vegetables are soft and the liquid is a rich, dark red.

Pour the contents through a coarse strainer into a bowl and discard the vegetables, then return the strained beet juice to the pan and leave on a low heat. Put the lemon juice and the whole eggs into the food processor and process for 5 seconds, until well mixed. With the motor running, pour two ladles of the hot beet juice through the feed tube and process for a further 3 seconds, then add to the beet juice in the pan and heat gently, whisking constantly with a batter whisk until the soup is steaming and has thickened slightly. Do not let it boil, or it will curdle. Taste and adjust the seasoning so that there is a gentle blend of sweet and sour. The soup reheats well.

For Borscht on the Rocks, see p. 46.

TOMATO RICE SOUP

Serves 4–6.
Keeps 3 days under refrigeration.
Freeze 3 months.

A simple soup, but one with a very agreeable sweet/sour flavour.

2 pints (1.25 l/5 cups) stock, made from chicken or beef bouillon-cubes, bone stock, leftover chicken soup or cooked chicken and bone stock (see recipes for Stock, pp. 26–8)
1 medium can (15 oz/425 g) chopped peeled plum tomatoes or passata (sieved tomatoes)
juice of a large lemon
2 level tbsp sugar or granular sweetener
4 level tbsp canned or tubed tomato purée
2 level tbsp short- or long-grain rice

Put the soup or stock into a soup pan and add all the remaining ingredients, pushing the tomatoes and their juice through a coarse sieve into the pan if you prefer a smooth soup. Bring the soup gently to the boil, then add the rice. Reduce the heat so that the soup barely bubbles, cover and cook very gently for half an hour or until the rice is tender (bite a grain) and has slightly thickened the soup. Taste. The soup should be slightly sweet and sour. Add a little more sugar or lemon juice if required.

TOMATO AND BASIL SOUP

Serves 6.
Keeps 3 days under refrigeration.
Freezes 3 months.

This can be made in both a dairy or a chicken version.

Basil is now imported and also grown under glass in this country right through the winter – the soup isn't worth making with the dried herb. It is equally delicious served cold.

1 oz (25 g/2 tbsp) butter plus 1 tbsp olive oil (or 3 tbsp olive oil for chicken version)

1 medium onion, chopped

1 bunch of spring onions (scallions), chopped

1 deseeded red pepper, chopped

1 large clove of garlic, chopped

1 x $1\frac{1}{4}$ lb (550 g) can of Italian plum tomatoes in juice ($1\frac{1}{2}$ medium cans)

1 heaped tbsp tomato purée

$\frac{1}{2}$ teasp sea salt

15 grinds of black pepper

1 heaped teasp brown sugar

1 vegetable or chicken stock-cube, dissolved in 15 fl oz (425 ml/2 cups) hot water

juice of 1 orange and 3 strips of the peel

2 bay leaves

handful of fresh basil leaves (approx. 1 oz/25 g)

For the garnish

chopped chives

croûtons

soured cream (for dairy version)

In a covered pan, soften the onion, spring onions and red pepper in the fat until golden, but do not allow to brown. Add the garlic, tomatoes, tomato purée, salt, pepper, sugar, stock, strips of orange peel and the bay leaves. Simmer covered for 30 minutes, stirring occasionally. Discard bay leaves, then purée the mixture in the blender or food processor and return to the pan.

Put the basil leaves into the blender with a couple of ladles of the soup mixture. Blend this liquid until the herb is finely chopped, then return to the pan. Bring to the boil then leave for several hours (or preferably overnight) for the flavours to develop.

Serve sprinkled lightly with chives. Serve the dairy version topped with soured cream. Serve the croûtons separately.

FRESH TOMATO SOUP WITH LITTLE MEATBALLS

Serves 8.
Freeze 3 months.

Deep-red plum tomatoes or the large French tomatoes that are allowed to ripen on the vine, together with the lavish use of fresh herbs, give this soup a wonderful fresh and summery flavour. However, canned tomatoes and dried herbs can be used in winter - to different effect.

As a certain amount of fat leaches out of the meatballs, it's advisable to chill the soup overnight so that this can be removed before reheating.

For the meatballs

large sprig of parsley
½ onion, cut in rough 1-inch (2.5-cm) chunks
1 egg
1 large slice of brown bread
½ teasp salt
10 grinds of black pepper
1 lb (450 g) fresh minced (ground) beef
1 tbsp matzah meal

For the soup

2 tbsp olive or sunflower oil
1 large onion, thinly sliced
1 clove of garlic, peeled and sliced
3 teasp brown sugar or granular sweetener
1½ lb (675 g) deep-red, fully ripe tomatoes, quartered, or 1 x 28 oz (800 g) can peeled plum tomatoes canned in tomato juice
2 pints (1.25 l/5 cups) hot water
3 beef stock-cubes
1 tbsp tomato purée
10 fl oz (275 ml/1¼ cups) tomato juice or juice strained from canned tomatoes
1 bay leaf
large sprig of parsley
1 teasp salt
15 grinds of black pepper
1 tbsp chopped marjoram or oregano or 1 teasp dried Italian herb seasoning

To make the meatballs Put the parsley in the food processor and process until chopped. Add the onion, egg, bread and seasonings, then process until a smooth purée is formed. Turn into a mixing bowl, then add the matzah meal and the beef. Mix thoroughly with a fork and set aside.

To make the soup Heat the oil in a large soup pan, add the sliced onion and garlic, sprinkle with the brown sugar, stir well, cover and cook for 10 minutes, until the onion is softened and golden. Add the tomatoes, re-cover and simmer until the vegetables are quite soft - about 15 minutes. Push them through a sieve or a food mill and discard the tomato skins and any onion debris that won't go through. Return this purée to the pan and add the water, stock-cubes, tomato purée, tomato juice, bay leaf, parsley, salt, pepper and Italian herb seasoning if used. Simmer very gently for 30 minutes. Discard the parsley and the bay leaf.

Meanwhile, with wetted palms, form the meat mixture into approximately 36 tiny balls about the size of a walnut, then drop them into the simmering soup, cover and cook gently for 30 minutes. Cool the soup and the meatballs, then refrigerate. Next day, skim off the solidified fat, bring slowly to the boil and, just before serving, stir in the fresh marjoram or oregano. Serve the soup with 4 or 5 meatballs per person.

Soup for a Winter's Night

In all these recipes, water plus bouillon-cubes (in proportion recommended on packet) can be substituted for stock or water plus bones.

BARLEY SOUP

Serves 4–6.
Keeps 3 days under refrigeration.
Freeze 3 months.

Scottish in origin but Jewish by adoption, this soup is especially delicious when the stock has been made from the bones from a roast rib of beef or a shoulder of lamb. If ordinary bone stock is used, a little (8 oz/225 g) shin beef will greatly improve the flavour.

2½ oz (65 g/¾ cup) pot or pearl barley
7 oz (200 g) onion, finely chopped
2 tbsp sunflower oil
8 oz (225 g) carrots, cut in ⅜-inch (1-cm) dice
3 oz (75 g) of the white part of a fat leek, finely shredded
3 pints (1.75 l/7 cups) strong meat stock
a few sprigs of parsley
1½ teasp salt
⅛ teasp white pepper
5 grinds of black pepper

Put the barley into a bowl and add boiling water to cover. Immediately turn into a sieve and rinse well under the cold tap. Sauté the onion in the oil until soft and golden. Add the remaining vegetables, together with the barley, stock, parsley and seasonings. Bring to the boil and then cover, reducing the heat until the mixture is barely bubbling. Simmer for 3 hours, by which time the barley will have thickened the soup.

HOBENE GROPEN

Serves 8 at one sitting, or 4 twice.
Keep 3 days under refrigeration.
Freeze 3 months.

This is a 'creamy' soup with a very satisfying flavour that is especially rich in the B vitamins. It is made with a variety of oats known in Jewish households as *hobene gropen* or *hubergrits,* but if you ask for it in the local health food shops, you will get better results by calling it pinhead oatmeal. In appearance it looks rather like bits of broken barley because the grains are 'kibbled' or cracked, rather than milled like other cereals. Because it is a wholegrain cereal it does need to be simmered for several hours, but the result is a wonderfully sustaining winter soup.

6 level tbsp hobene gropen *(pinhead oatmeal)*
8 oz (225 g) or more shin beef
2 level teasp salt
¼ level teasp white pepper
4 pints (2 l/10 cups) meat stock
1 large potato
1 onion
1 carrot
1 fat stalk of celery
good sprig of parsley

Put the *hobene gropen* into a small basin and cover with boiling water. Leave to settle while you add the meat, with the salt and pepper, to the stock. Bring to the boil and skim off any froth with a wet metal spoon. Add the strained *hobene gropen,* reduce the heat so that the soup is barely bubbling, then cover and simmer in this way for 1 hour. Meanwhile, cut the potato into ½-inch (1.25-cm) cubes, and dice the onion, carrot and celery into ¼-inch (0.5 cm) cubes. Add these vegetables to the soup, together with the parsley sprig. Cover again and simmer for a further 2 hours, by which time the soup should be creamy and the meat tender. Remove the sprig of parsley, taste, and add more salt and pepper if required. Sprinkle with chopped parsley and serve piping hot.

To serve on the second day, add half a cup of water and reheat gently.

CHICKEN SOUP WITH HOBENE GROPEN

Serves 4–6.
Keeps 3 days under refrigeration.
Freeze 3 months.

8 oz (225 g) onion, chopped
3 tbsp sunflower oil
4 pints (2 l/10 cups) chicken stock
6 level tbsp hobene gropen *(pinhead oatmeal)*
4 oz (125 g/½ cup) butter (lima) beans, soaked overnight in water to cover
1 teasp salt
15 grinds of black pepper
good pinch of white pepper
1 large carrot, cut in ⅜-inch (1-cm) dice

Sauté the onion in the oil until soft and golden. Add the stock and bring to the boil, then shower in the oatmeal, stirring, followed by the strained butter beans, salt and peppers. Cover and simmer for 2 hours. Add the carrot and simmer, covered, for a further hour. Taste and reseason if necessary.

HAIMISCHE WINTER SOUP

Serves 8 at one sitting or 4 twice.
Keeps 3 days under refrigeration.
Freeze 3 months.

This is the soup *par excellence* 'like Mama used to make'. Indeed, for nineteenth-century Russian and Polish peasants it was also their main dish of the day, as the pulses and cereals it contained made it extremely nourishing, while still cheap. The blend of ingredients also gives it a superb flavour and one capable of infinite variation: for example, butter (lima) beans can be substituted for haricot (dried white) beans, pot barley for pearl barley, brown lentils for red lentils. The consistency of the soup can also be easily adjusted by boiling it down or diluting it with extra stock.

8 oz (225 g/1 cup) green split peas
4 oz (125 g/½ cup) red lentils
2 level tbsp pearl barley
4 level tbsp haricot (dried white) beans
8 oz (225 g) soup meat (optional but nice)
3 pints (1.75 l/7 cups) stock, or 3 pints water and 1 soup bone
2 level teasp salt
10 grinds of black pepper
1 level teasp fines herbes
2 large carrots, diced into ⅜-in)1-cm) cubes
2 stalks celery, diced into ¾-in (2-cm) cubes
white part of a fat leek, well washed and thinly sliced
large sprig of parsley
1 large carrot, coarsely grated

The day before making the soup, put the split peas, lentils, barley and beans into a large bowl, cover with twice their depth of cold water and leave to soak and swell overnight. Next day, put the meat and the stock (or the water and bone) with the salt into a large soup pan and bring to the boil. Skim with a wet metal spoon. Tip the cereals into a fine sieve to remove any excess soaking water, then put under the cold tap and rinse thoroughly until the water that drains from them is quite clear.

Add to the soup pan with the seasonings and all the vegetables except the grated carrot. Bring back to the boil, then reduce the heat until the mixture is barely bubbling. Cover and simmer for 2 hours, then uncover and add the grated carrot. Continue to cook for a further hour, stirring the pan occasionally to make sure the soup does not stick to the base as it thickens. The soup is ready when the lentils and split peas have turned into a purée. Taste and add more seasonings if required. Remove the sprig of parsley.

Leftover soup can have a tablespoon of tomato purée added, together with half a cup of water to thin it down before reheating.

SPLIT PEA SOUP

Serves 6–8.
Keeps 3 days under refrigeration.
Freeze 3 months.

12 oz (350 g/1½ cups) green split peas
4 oz (125 g/½ cup) butter (lima) beans
2 carrots
2 stalks celery
1 onion
white part of a leek
2 tbsp sunflower oil
3 pints (1.75 l/7 cups) meat stock or equivalent made from bouillon-cubes
salt and pepper

Soak split peas and butter beans overnight in cold water to cover generously. Finely dice the carrots and the celery, chop the onion and finely slice the leek (or, for speed, all the vegetables can be finely chopped in the food processor). Put in the soup pan with the oil, cover and cook gently for 10 minutes or until the oil is absorbed. Pour on the stock and add the rinsed cereals. Simmer for 2½–3 hours, seasoning to taste.

VARIATION

MILCHIK SPLIT PEA SOUP

Use vegetable stock and sauté the vegetables in butter instead of oil.

AMERICAN LENTIL SOUP

Serves 8.
Keeps 3 days under refrigeration.
Freeze 3 months.

There's one little triangle of land in the USA where the volcanic soil, the elevation and the level of rainfall produce what are perhaps the finest lentils in the world. Their flavour is rich, almost meaty (they never become mushy, so they're ideal for salads or pilaffs) and they need no soaking at all. The colour of the raw lentils is a greeny-brown, almost khaki shade, but they cook down to make a chestnut-brown soup that positively sticks to your ribs – and so it should with all that protein and fibre. The soup thickens on standing, so it's advisable to thin it with boiling water when it's reheated.

2 medium onions
2 medium carrots
2 thick stalks celery plus a few leaves
2 cloves of garlic
3 tbsp olive oil or sunflower oil
8 oz (225 g/l cup) continental or brown lentils
3 pints (1.75 l/7 cups) chicken, beef or vegetable stock
2 bay leaves
1 teasp dried fines herbes or ½ teasp Italian seasoning herbs
15 grinds of black pepper
1½ teasp salt

Finely chop all the vegetables and the garlic (easiest in a food processor), then add to the hot oil in a gallon soup pan. Stir well, cover and allow to 'sweat' on a low light for about 20 minutes, or until the mixture is a rich gold in colour. Add all the remaining ingredients and bring to the boil, stirring well. Turn the light down very low, cover and simmer for 40 minutes, stirring occasionally to stop the soup 'catching' on the bottom of the pan. Taste a lentil to ensure that it's tender, then remove and discard the bay leaves and purée approximately half the soup in a blender or food processor. Return to the pan, stir well, and leave for several hours for the flavours to develop. Reheat slowly until piping hot.

HUNGARIAN GOULASH SOUP

Serves 6–8.
Keeps 3 days under refrigeration.
Freeze 3 months.

This deservedly famous soup is just the one to come home to on a cold winter's night. Indeed, it's almost a meal in itself, only lacking extra meat and potatoes to become a true goulash.

Paprika – the spice made from the dried and pulverized flesh of sweet red peppers – comes in no less than 6 different strengths in its native Hungary; the mild *kulonleges* is the one most similar in flavour to the kind sold in supermarkets in the UK. Should you visit Hungary, don't miss the opportunity to bring home a few packs of *kulonleges* (I'm told it translates as 'delicate and of exquisite flavour'), and you might also try *edes-nemes* (noble, sweet), *tozsa* (rose) and *csemege* (mild); unless your family have cast-iron stomachs, though, I'd keep away from *eros* – the hot one.

1 large onion
2½ tbsp sunflower oil
1½ tbsp mild paprika pepper
½ teasp wine vinegar
1 lb (450 g) shin beef, cut into ½-inch (1.25-cm) cubes
1 rounded tbsp tomato purée
1 clove of garlic, skinned
2 teasp caraway seeds
1 teasp lemon zest
½ teasp dried marjoram
hot water or stock to cover
1 lb (450 g) potatoes, peeled and cut into ½-inch (1.25-cm) cubes
2 pints (1.25 l/5 cups) meat or vegetable stock
1 teasp salt
2 teasp light brown sugar

To thicken
1 level tbsp cornflour slaked with 2 tbsp cold water

For the garnish
1 small pickled cucumber, drained and cubed, or 2 frankfurters, sliced

Sauté the finely sliced onion in the oil until soft and golden (cover for first 5 minutes). Add the paprika and stir well, then add the vinegar, meat and tomato purée and cook over moderate heat until richly browned. Meanwhile, chop together the garlic, caraway seeds, zest and marjoram, then add them to the meat and barely cover with hot water. Stir well, bring to the simmer, cover and cook for 1 hour, or until the meat is barely tender.

Add the potatoes to the meat with the stock, salt and sugar. Cover and simmer for a further 10–15 minutes, or until the potatoes are tender. Taste and reseason if necessary. Add the cornflour mixed to a cream with the cold water, then bubble for 3 minutes. Leave for several hours for the flavour to develop, then reheat together with the garnish until bubbling throughout.

CABBAGE BORSCHT

Serve 8.
Keeps 3 days under refrigeration.
Freeze 3 months.

This might be called the Jewish version of Pot au Feu, for a 2-lb (900-g) slice of brisket can be cooked in the soup, both to flavour it and to turn it into a simple main course. However, for serving simply as a meal starter, the amount of meat specified in the recipe is sufficient, though a larger quantity will of course add to the flavour (and, alas, to the cost). I give a quantity for 8 as it is really not worth making a smaller amount. Cabbage borscht improves in flavour overnight and the solidified fat can then easily be removed.

½–1-lb (225–450-g) piece of brisket
1 marrow bone (if available)
2 level teasp salt
3 pints (1.75 l/7 cups) water
1 onion, finely chopped
1 medium can (approx. 15 oz/425 g) whole peeled tomatoes in juice
4 level tbsp sugar
pinch of white pepper

1 small head of white cabbage
4 level tbsp sultanas (white raisins)
juice of 2 lemons or 2 level teasp citric or tartaric acid crystals (sour salt)

In a large soup pan put the brisket, bone, salt and water. Bring slowly to the boil, then skim the surface using a wet metal spoon. Add the onion, tomatoes, sugar and pepper. Bring to the boil, reduce the heat until the soup simmers, cover and cook for a further 2 hours, or until the meat is almost tender. Discard the bone. While the soup is cooking, finely shred the cabbage, put it into a colander and sprinkle with some coarse salt. When the meat is almost tender, pour a kettleful of boiling water over the salted cabbage to take away any undue cabbagey flavour. Drain the cabbage and add to the soup.

Simmer for a further 30 minutes, or until the cabbage is tender. Add the sultanas and the lemon juice or citric acid and simmer for 5 minutes to blend the flavours. Serve plain or with a boiled potato.

Parev Creamy Vegetable Soups

In any competition for the title of champion soup-maker, it would be hard to choose between Jewish and French cooks. But whereas our traditional soups are based mainly on cereals and pulses such as barley, beans, lentils and split peas, the French go for vegetables in a big way. And while they add extra flavour with milk and cream, we prefer to rely on a rich bone, meat or chicken stock - historically, *milchik* soups have been less favoured in the Jewish kitchen because they can be used only with dairy meals.

However, by using a blender to purée a soup of mixed vegetables, it's possible to make a *parev* version of a French-style recipe that still has a wonderfully 'creamy' texture. If any of these soups thicken on standing, thin down with a little extra vegetable stock - or milk if it is to be served before a dairy meal. To contrast with the creamy texture, garnish each plate with a few croûtons. For convenience and the minimum use of fat, crisp them in the oven when you've heated it for some other purpose (see p. 53).

WINTER CREAM OF VEGETABLE SOUP

Serves 6–8.
Keeps 3 days under refrigeration.
Freezes 3 months.

A small amount of red pepper adds zing to this simple soup.

8 oz (225 g) potato
8 oz (225 g) onion
7 oz (200 g) carrots
4 oz (125 g) white part of a leek
1 small (4 oz/125 g) red pepper
3 tbsp sunflower oil
$2\frac{1}{2}$ pints (1.5 l/$6\frac{1}{4}$ cups) vegetable stock
1 bay leaf
$\frac{1}{8}$ teasp powdered nutmeg
$\frac{1}{2}$ teasp freeze-dried fines herbes
1 teasp salt
$\frac{1}{4}$ teasp white pepper

Peel the potatoes and leave covered with cold water. Prepare the remaining vegetables according to type, then cut in roughly 1-inch (2.5-cm) chunks and chop finely in the food processor. Sweat in the oil over moderate heat for 15 minutes (keep the lid on), then uncover, stir well and add the potatoes cut in chunks, together with all the remaining ingredients. Cover and simmer for a further 20 minutes, until the potatoes are absolutely tender. Purée in 2 or 3 batches in a blender until creamy; if you prefer a little texture, use the food processor. Allow to stand for several hours, then reheat slowly just before serving.

CARROT, ORANGE AND CORIANDER SOUP

Serves 4–6.
Keeps 3 days under refrigeration.
Freeze 3 months.

1 large onion, finely sliced
2 tbsp sunflower oil
1 clove of garlic, finely chopped
2 teasp ground coriander
$1\frac{1}{2}$ lb (675 g) well-flavoured carrots, finely chopped
8 oz (225 g) potatoes, peeled and finely chopped
$2\frac{1}{2}$ pints (1.5 l/$6\frac{1}{4}$ cups) vegetable stock
peeled zest of $\frac{1}{2}$ large orange
$\frac{1}{2}$ teasp salt
$\frac{1}{4}$ teasp white pepper

Sauté the onion in the oil in a covered pan until soft and golden - about 10 minutes. Add the garlic and coriander and cook, stirring, for a further 2 minutes, then add the carrots and potatoes and stir thoroughly to mix them with the onion.

Add the stock, orange zest, salt and pepper, then cover and simmer for 20–30 minutes, until the vegetables are tender.

Purée the soup (preferably in a blender) until absolutely smooth. Leave overnight to mature in flavour.

Soups with a Difference

AUBERGINE AND CORIANDER SOUP

Serves 6.
Keeps 3 days under refrigeration.
Freeze 3 months.

The rich flavour and creamy texture of this unusual soup make it hard to believe that it contains no dairy products. Even the oil that's necessary to cook the aubergine (eggplant) is kept to an absolute minimum by roasting rather than frying the vegetables.

For a dairy meal, use the vegetable stock and, if desired, stir in 4 tablespoons of soured cream or Greek-style yoghurt just before serving.

$1\frac{1}{2}$ lb (675 g) aubergines, peeled and cut in 1-in (2.5-cm) cubes
6 tbsp olive oil
1 teasp salt
$\frac{1}{4}$ teasp white pepper
1 medium onion, finely chopped
2 medium cloves of garlic, finely chopped
1 teasp ground coriander
1 bay leaf
$1\frac{3}{4}$ pints (1 l/$4\frac{1}{2}$ cups) chicken or vegetable stock
4 tbsp medium-dry Amontillado sherry
1 tbsp chopped fresh coriander or parsley

Put the aubergine cubes in a colander or salad spinner, sprinkle generously with salt and leave for 30 minutes. Rinse off with cold water and spin or dab dry with paper towels.

Preheat the oven to Gas No. 8 (450°F/230°C). Put 3 tablespoons oil in a l-inch-deep (2.5-cm) baking tin, then add the aubergine and toss gently to coat with the oil. Sprinkle with the salt and pepper and roast for 15–20 minutes, stirring once or twice.

Meanwhile, using the remaining 3 tablespoons of oil, sauté the onion and garlic in a soup pan over moderate heat, keeping the lid on until the onion is softened and golden. Add the aubergine, sprinkle with the ground coriander and cook, stirring occasionally, for a further 5 minutes. Then add the bay leaf, stock and sherry, cover and simmer for 10 minutes. Discard the bay leaf, then purée the mixture in a blender or food processor and return to the pan. Reseason if necessary, then heat until just bubbling. Stir in the fresh coriander or parsley and serve.

BUTTERNUT SQUASH SOUP WITH GINGER AND LIME

Serves 6–8.
Keeps 3 days under refrigeration.
Freeze 3 months.

Butternut squash is shaped like an elongated pear. It has a pinky-beige skin and bright-yellow flesh, and makes a superb soup for either a dairy or a meat meal because of its creamy texture.

The garnish is optional. Some may find it a little exotic, but the combination of lime and ginger adds a superb finish for a special-occasion meal.

1 medium onion, finely chopped
2 fat cloves of garlic, peeled and chopped
1½ tbsp peeled and finely chopped fresh ginger
2 oz (50 g/¼ cup) butter or margarine
2 lb (900 g) butternut squash, peeled, seeds removed and thinly sliced
2 pints (1.25 l/5 cups) vegetable or chicken stock
2 teasp fresh lime juice
15 grinds of black pepper
½ teasp salt

For the garnish
4 tbsp sunflower oil (for frying)
3 tbsp julienne strips of peeled fresh ginger
3 teasp julienne strips of lime peel
2 tbsp toasted pine kernels

In a large soup pan sauté the onion, garlic and ginger in the butter (lid on) until the onion is soft and golden. Add the squash and stock, bring to the boil and then simmer covered for 20 minutes, or until the squash feels absolutely tender when pierced with a slim, sharp knife. Purée in a blender (preferably) or food processor until absolutely smooth, then return to the pan, and stir in the lime juice, pepper and salt. Taste for seasoning, then reheat until barely bubbling. (The soup can be refrigerated for up to 3 days at this point.)

For the garnish, sauté the ginger strips in the oil until a pale gold, then drain on crumpled paper.

To serve, divide the soup between bowls and garnish with the fried ginger, lime rind and pine kernels.

BASQUE SWEET PEPPER AND RICE SOUP

Serves 6–8.
Keeps 3 days under refrigeration.
Freeze 3 months.

This light but satisfying consommé is given extra body by the addition of a little rice.

1 very large onion
3 large carrots
2 fat cloves of garlic, peeled
3 tbsp extra virgin olive oil
3 pints (1.75 l/7 cups) beef or vegetable stock (using 4 cubes)
2 oz (50 g/⅓ cup) Basmati rice, rinsed
3 tbsp medium-dry Amontillado sherry
20 grinds of black pepper
2 each red and green peppers, halved then cut in ⅜-in (1-cm) cubes
1 teasp salt

Finely chop the onion, carrots and garlic (most easily done in a food processor), then add to the oil in a large soup pan. Cover and cook very gently for 25 minutes, stirring occasionally, until softened and golden. Add the stock, bring to the boil, then re-cover and cook for a further 20 minutes. Pour the soup through a sieve into a bowl, pressing down on the vegetables with the back of a spoon to extract all the juices. Discard the vegetables and return the liquid to the pan, together with the rice, sherry, pepper strips, salt and pepper. Simmer, partially covered, for 20 minutes, or until the rice is tender.

SPINACH AND GREEN PEA SOUP WITH FRESH MINT AND TOASTED PINE KERNELS

Serves 6–8.
Keeps 3 days under refrigeration.
Freeze 3 months.

A soup with a positive health bonus and a wonderfully satisfying taste - that's how I'd describe this deep-green soup. It would make a perfect starter to a spring dinner party. Sautéeing the onion in a little butter undoubtedly deepens the flavour, but I have made it very successfully omitting the fat completely and substituting 2 teaspoons of dried minced onion (added at the beginning) for the fresh vegetable. Another bonus for weightwatchers - it is thickened naturally by the spinach and the peas, so it doesn't need either flour or cornflour. The pine kernels add a touch of luxury, but toasted slivered almonds can be used instead. Serve the soup with warm wholemeal pitta bread (to avoid it drying up when reheated, sprinkle the surface lightly with cold water and then grill briefly until warm to the touch). Make the soup the day before it is required for maximum flavour.

1½ oz (40 g/3 tbsp) butter
1 large onion
1¼ pints (725 ml/3 cups) vegetable stock
8 oz (225 g) frozen chopped spinach
1 lb (450 g) frozen garden peas
1 teasp salt
10 grinds of black pepper
1 bunch of fresh mint or 3 teasp dried mint
1 pint (525 ml/2½ cups) semi-skimmed milk
1 oz (25 g/¼ cup) pine kernels, toasted

Gently melt the butter in a soup pan and cook the finely chopped onion, covered, until it is soft and golden - about 10 minutes. Add the stock, defrosted spinach and peas and cook, partly covered, until the peas are quite tender - about 10 minutes. Add salt and pepper and the washed mint leaves - if fresh, there should be 2 cups, loosely packed - and cook a further 5 minutes. Purée until absolutely smooth, preferably in a blender, though a food processor will serve without giving quite such a smooth texture.

Heat the milk in the soup pan until steaming, then add the vegetable purée and bring to simmering point. Leave to stand for several hours, then taste and reseason if necessary when it reaches simmering point. If it has thickened considerably, add extra water until it is the consistency of pouring cream.

Divide into soup cups, garnishing each one with a sprinkle of pine kernels.

SUPER CREAM OF MUSHROOM SOUP

Serves 6–8.
Keeps 3 days under refrigeration.
Freeze 3 months.

This is a very rich soup with a most intriguing taste. For maximum flavour, the mushrooms can be either sliced paper thin (in a food processor) or coarsely - rather than finely - chopped.

2 oz (50 g/¼ cup) butter
1 small onion, finely chopped
8 oz (225 g/3 cups) pinky mushrooms, coarsely chopped or thinly sliced
10 fl oz (275 ml/1¼ cups) water
1 vegetable stock-cube
2 level tbsp chopped parsley
1 small clove of garlic, crushed

For sauce base
2 oz (50 g/¼ cup) butter
2 oz (50 g/½ cup) flour
2 pints (1.25 l/5 cups) milk
1 teasp salt
¼ teasp nutmeg
¼ teasp white pepper
good pinch of herb salt
1 glass medium sherry (optional)
4 tbsp cream (optional)

Melt the butter in a soup pan, add the onion, cover and simmer for 5 minutes. Uncover, add the mushrooms, re-cover and cook for a further 5 minutes. Then add the water, stock-cube, parsley and garlic.

Turn into a basin. In the same pan put the butter, flour, milk, salt, nutmeg, white pepper and herb salt. Bring slowly to the boil, whisking all the time with a batter whisk or balloon whisk. Bubble for 5 minutes, then stir in the mushroom mixture. Cool, then refrigerate for several hours, or overnight, to develop the flavour. When ready to serve, bring back to the simmer. It should be the consistency of thin cream. If too thick, dilute with a little water. When steaming hot, taste, add extra seasoning if necessary and stir in the sherry and cream if they are being used.

CRÈME FORESTIÈRE

Serves 6–8.
Keeps 3 days under refrigeration.
Freeze 3 months.

A more sophisticated version for a special meal.

1 medium onion, finely sliced
2 oz (50 g/¼ cup) butter
12 oz (350 g) white part of a leek, finely sliced
12 oz (350 g/3¾ cups) mushrooms, sliced (reserve 3 oz/75 g/1 cup)
6 fl oz (175 ml/¾ cup) dry white wine
1½ pints (850 ml/3¾ cups) vegetable stock
2 medium bay leaves
1½ teasp salt
15 grinds of black pepper
¼ teasp ground nutmeg or mace
1 tbsp cornflour (cornstarch)
10 fl oz (275 ml/1¼ cups) semi-skimmed milk
3 tbsp medium dry sherry

For the garnish
5 fl oz (150 ml/⅔ cup) single cream or 8% fromage frais
1 tbsp snipped chives

Sauté the onion in the butter in a covered pan for 5 minutes, uncover and continue to cook, stirring, for a further 5 minutes, until golden. Add the leeks and mushrooms and cook, stirring, for a further 5 minutes.

Pour in the wine and bubble uncovered for 3 minutes to intensify the flavour, then add the stock and seasoning. Cover and cook for 15 minutes, until the vegetables are tender.

Purée, preferably in a blender, return to the pan and stir in the cornflour and milk, which have already been mixed to a smooth cream. Add the reserved mushrooms, finely sliced, and bring slowly to the boil. Simmer for 3 minutes, then leave to cool. Refrigerate for at least 8 hours.

To serve, stir in the sherry and reheat until barely bubbling, reseasoning if necessary. Put the cream in a small jug and stir in the chives, then put a tablespoonful on to each serving.

MOTHER'S MILCHIKE SOUP

Serves 6.
Keeps 3 days under refrigeration.
Freeze 3 months.

This soup was made to herald summer in the villages of the Pale of Settlement. It is fresh and simple, with the flavour of young vegetables.

2 oz (50 g/¼ cup) butter
1 onion, finely chopped
4 new potatoes, cubed
1 grated carrot
1-lb (450-g) pack fresh or frozen mixed special vegetables (including baby carrots and petit pois)
1½ pints (850 ml/3¾ cups) water
1 level teasp salt
pinch of pepper
1 level teasp sugar
10 fl oz (275 ml/1¼ cups) milk
1 tbsp cornflour
1 tbsp snipped chives or spring onion (scallion) tops

Melt the butter in a heavy pan and 'sweat' the onion in the covered pan until soft and golden. Add the potatoes, carrot and mixed vegetables. Cover with the water, add the salt, pepper and sugar. Simmer covered for 30 minutes, or until all the vegetables are tender. Stir in the milk mixed with the cornflour, and simmer for 3 minutes. Stir in the chives or spring onion tops.

Some families make tiny knaidlach (see p. 51) with butter instead of chicken fat and serve them in this soup.

CURRIED CREAM OF BROCCOLI SOUP

Serves 6–8.
Keeps 3 days under refrigeration.
Freeze 3 months.

To add a little substance to an informal fish supper, a beautiful pale-green soup can be made from the excellent fresh broccoli now available all the year round. If left to stand for several hours, it develops a subtly interesting flavour which belies its simple ingredients. Serve it with brown-bread croutons and a scattering of flaked almonds.

1 lb (450 g) very green broccoli
1 onion, finely chopped
1 oz (25 g/2 tbsp) butter
2 vegetable stock-cubes or 2 teasp vegetable paste
plus *1¼ pints (725 ml/3 cups) hot water*
2 level tbsp cornflour
1 pint (575 ml/2½ cups) semi-skimmed milk
1 teasp salt
10 grinds of black pepper
¼ teasp ground nutmeg
½–1 teasp curry powder
5 fl oz (150 ml/⅔ cup) whipping (light) cream

For the garnish
1 oz (25 g/¼ cup) toasted pine kernels or flaked almonds

Cut the broccoli stalks off the flowers, trim the ends and slice into ½-inch-thick (1.25-cm) chunks. Place in a soup pan with boiling water to cover, put on the lid and simmer for 5 minutes. Add the florets and boil briskly for a further 4 minutes. Drain and refresh with cold water to set the colour.

Sauté the onion in the butter in a covered pan until soft and golden. Add the broccoli and sauté quickly to absorb the butter, then blend or process until puréed, adding a little of the stock. Mix the cornflour and the milk smoothly together, then turn into the soup pan, together with the vegetable purée and stock. Bring slowly to the boil, adding the salt, pepper and spices. Simmer for 3 minutes, then leave for several hours.

To serve, add a swirl of cream to each bowl, pouring it carefully from a small jug, and garnish with toasted nuts.

NEW ENGLAND SALMON CHOWDER

Serves 6–8.
Keeps 2 days under refrigeration.
Do not freeze.

To be worthy of the name, a chowder should be so thick with fish and vegetables that it's half-way between a soup and a very superior stew. Like so many classic dishes, this had humble beginnings on the east coast of the United States, where fishermen would cook leftovers from the day's catch in a big iron pot called a *chaudière* – hence the name. A true chowder has some ingredients that are not acceptable in a Jewish kitchen, so Sula Leon and I devised this kosher – and very special – version for our Master Classes. Serve it as a light supper main dish or, in small portions, as a starter before a light luncheon of cheeses and savoury dips.

1 lb (450 g) boiling potatoes, cut in ½-inch (1-cm) cubes
½ teasp salt
sprig of parsley
1 small bay leaf

1 pint (575 ml/2½ cups) milk
bulbs from 1 bunch spring onions (green onions) or 5 oz (150 g) shallots, both finely chopped
2 oz (50 g/¼ cup) butter
3½ fl oz (90 ml/7 tbsp) dry white wine
10 oz (275 g) filleted and skinned salmon
½ teasp salt
good pinch of white pepper
1 tbsp lemon juice
1 tbsp cornflour (cornstarch) mixed to a cream with
2 tbsp top of milk or single (light) cream
3 tbsp snipped dill
10 grinds of black pepper
2 oz (50 g) smoked salmon, cut in shreds

In a medium saucepan combine the potatoes, ½ a teaspoon of salt, parsley, bay leaf and the milk and bring to the boil. Simmer for 10–12 minutes, or until potato cubes are just tender. Remove the parsley and bay leaf.

Meanwhile, in a soup pan cook the spring onions or shallots gently in the butter until soft and golden, then add the wine and bubble until only 4 tablespoons remain. Lay the salmon on top, sprinkle with the salt, white pepper and lemon juice, cover with a piece of silicone paper and a lid, and cook very gently for 6–8 minutes, or until the fish feels firm to the touch, turning once.

Transfer the salmon to a plate and cut in ½-inch (1.25-cm) chunks. Add the slaked cornflour (cornstarch) to the milk mixture and bring to the boil, then simmer for 3 minutes. Pour on to the onion mixture and then add the salmon chunks, the dill and the black pepper, adjusting the seasoning if necessary. Bring to steaming point, then leave to mature for several hours, or overnight.

Just before serving, reheat to steaming point, thin if necessary with a little more wine or milk and stir in the shreds of smoked salmon.

Chilled Soups

HIDEG MEGGYLEVES (*Hungarian Cherry Soup*)

Serves 6–8.
Keeps 3 days under refrigeration.
Soup without the cream freezes 3 months.

An odd hybrid of starter and dessert, fruit soup is made with a combination of fruits, which can include peaches, plums, cherries or nectarines. It is then slightly thickened and enriched with smetana or soured cream.

The finest variety of fruit soup, however, is Yayin Duvdivanim. This is made with Morello cherries and I enjoyed a plate of it in Budapest – its place of birth, where it is called Hideg Meggyleves.

The fresh Morello cherries that give the soup its unique flavour are rarely found in Britain, but you should be able to track down some excellent bottled ones, ready-stoned, which are actually grown in Hungary.

Serve the soup as you would a chilled borscht – as a starter in either a glass or a soup cup. It also makes splendid picnic fare kept cool in a large flask or cool-bag. The flavour is best if the soup is prepared one day ahead.

If using fresh cherries, use 1 lb (450 g) weight when stoned, increase sugar to 6 oz (175 g/¾ cup) and use 1¾ pints (1 1/4½ cups) water.

juice from cherries (should be 12 fl oz/350 ml/1½ cups)
7 fl oz (200 ml/¾ cup plus 2 tbsp) port-type wine or Kiddush wine
1½ pints (850 ml/3¾ cups) water
2 oz (50 g/¼ cup) sugar
grated rind of ½ lemon
½ teasp salt
1 stick of cinnamon
1 x 1½ lb (675 g) jar pitted Morello cherries in syrup (reserve a few for garnish)
1 tbsp cornflour mixed to a cream with 1 teasp lemon juice and 1 tbsp water
10 fl oz (275 ml/1¼ cups) soured cream

Put the strained juice, wine, water, sugar, lemon rind, salt and cinnamon stick into a soup pan, bring to the boil and bubble uncovered for 7 minutes, until the liquid is well flavoured. Add the cherries and the cornflour liquid, bring back to the boil and simmer for 3 minutes until clear. Cool until it stops steaming, then refrigerate until absolutely cold. Put the soured cream in a bowl and add a ladle or two of the cold cherry mixture, whisking until smooth. Pour this creamy liquid back into the cherry mixture and chill until just before serving. Serve cold but not icy, garnished with a few of the reserved cherries.

COLD FRUIT SOUP

Serves 6–8.
Keeps 3 days under refrigeration.
Freeze 3 months.

German Jews who summered, before the Second World War, in cottages on the shores of the Baltic made marvellous cold soups from the fruits of high summer. The choice of ingredients depends on the season, but this combination of the sweet and the tart is particularly refreshing.

8 oz (225 g/1¼ cups) stoned plums
8 oz (225 g/1¼ cups) Morello (sour red) or other tart cherries
8 oz (225 g) sliced peaches
2½ pints (1.5 l/6¼ cups) water
pinch of salt
small cinnamon stick or 1 level teasp ground cinnamon
3 oz (75 g/⅓ cup) sugar
2 tbsp cornflour (cornstarch)
5 fl oz (150 ml/⅔ cup) soured cream

In a soup pan put the stoned and sliced fruit, the water, seasoning and sugar. Simmer, covered, for 15–20 minutes or until the fruit is tender, then force through a fine sieve or blend until smooth. Mix the cornflour with a little water (or better still, sweet red wine), stir into the soup and simmer for 10 minutes, until thickened and clear. Chill well.

Serve in soup cups, topped with soured cream, as a refreshing 'starter' to a summer meal.

BORSCHT ON THE ROCKS

Serves 6–8.
Cooked beet juice keeps 4 days under refrigeration, the complete soup for 2 days.
Freeze 3 months.

A chilled glass of that heart-of-the-winter favourite, beetroot borscht, makes a superb non-alcoholic aperitif for a summer dairy lunch. If you prefer, you can serve a larger quantity in a soup cup as a cold starter for the meal – young beets give the borscht an amazing magenta colour, and teamed with a bowl of roses, it would create a delicious pink colour scheme for the table. The calories can be trimmed by substituting Greek yoghurt or fromage frais for the more traditional soured cream. Using a food processor to whisk the eggs and juice together is a good insurance against curdling. The beet juice can be frozen for 3 months, but once enriched with eggs and cream it's best to keep it refrigerated.

3 bunches of young beets (or 2 lb/900 g old beets)
1 medium onion
1 medium carrot
2¼ pints (1.5 l/6 cups) hot water plus
3 vegetable stock-cubes
15 grinds of black pepper
2 tbsp sugar or granular substitute

To thicken
3 tbsp lemon juice
3 whole eggs
5 fl oz (150 ml/⅔ cup) soured cream, Greek yoghurt or 8% fromage frais

Have ready a half-gallon soup pan. Trim the

beets, wash thoroughly and peel only if old. Peel the onion and the carrot. Cut all the vegetables into roughly 1-inch (2.5-cm) chunks, then process in two batches until very finely chopped. Put in the pan with the water, cubes, pepper and sugar or sweetener. Bring to the boil, cover and simmer for 20 minutes, until the vegetables are soft and the liquid is a rich, dark red.

Pour the contents through a coarse strainer into a bowl and discard the vegetables. Return the strained beet juice to the pan and leave on a low heat. Put the lemon juice and the whole eggs into the food processor and process for 5 seconds, until well mixed. With the motor running, pour two ladles of the hot beet juice through the feed tube and process for a further 3 seconds, then add to the beet juice in the pan and heat gently, whisking constantly with a batter whisk or balloon whisk until the soup is steaming and has thickened slightly. Do not let it boil or it will curdle. Taste and adjust the seasoning so that there is a gentle blend of sweet and sour.

Chill thoroughly. Just before serving, whisk in the cream, yoghurt or fromage frais.

SCHAV
(*Cold Sorrel Soup*)

Serves 6.
Keeps 4 days under refrigeration.
Do not freeze.

This is a form of borscht with a typical sweet and sour flavour. Sorrel grows prolifically in Russia and the Baltic States - as a child I used to help my Latvian-born grandmother search for the 'wild' herb on the local golf course. Now I grow it myself in our suburban garden.

1 lb (450 g) sorrel or spinach, or 8-oz (225-g) pack frozen leaf spinach
½ onion, finely chopped
2¼ pints (1.5 l/6 cups) water
2 level teasp salt
2 level tbsp sugar
juice of a large lemon (3 tbsp)
3 eggs
5 fl oz (150 ml/⅔ cup) soured cream

If fresh spinach or sorrel is used, rinse well until completely clear of grit. Drain and strip the leaves from the stalks, then shred the leaves finely. For both the frozen and the fresh vegetables, put the greens into a soup pan, together with the onion, water and salt. Cover and simmer for 20 minutes. Add the sugar and lemon juice and simmer for a further 10 minutes. Have the eggs well whisked in a large bowl. Pour the hot soup slowly on to the eggs. The residual heat will be sufficient to thicken the soup. Chill overnight. Serve either topped with the soured cream or blended with it.

TARATOUR
(*Herbed Yoghurt Soup*)

Serves 6.
Keeps 3 days under refrigeration.
Do not freeze.

The herbs can be from the garden or the supermarket but use them fresh rather than dried for this delicate Israeli summer soup. Prepare it and chill overnight.

10 fl oz (275 ml/1¼ cups) semi-skimmed milk
15 fl oz (425 ml/2 cups) natural yoghurt
5 fl oz (150 ml/⅔ cup) Greek-type yoghurt or smetana
1 medium cucumber
1 small bunch of radishes
2 tbsp chives
2 heaped tbsp dill leaves or 1 heaped tbsp chopped parsley
2 sprigs fresh tarragon
small bunch of young mint leaves
½ teasp salt
10 grinds of black pepper

In a large jug or lipped bowl gently stir together the milk and yoghurts (or smetana, if used). Peel the cucumber and cut into matchsticks. Trim the radishes and slice very thinly. Snip chives and dill or parsley and chop tarragon and mint. Stir all these into the yoghurt mixture, together with the salt and pepper, cover and refrigerate until well chilled. Stir before serving.

SOUPE AU CRESSON

Serves 6–8.
Keeps 2 days under refrigeration.
Freeze purée 2 months.

The slightly acid, tangy taste of watercress is especially delicious in a cold soup but equally good when hot. You *can* use less, but the four packs specified do produce a soup to remember.

3 packs (9 oz/250 g total weight) watercress (reserve 1 pack for garnish)
1½ oz (40 g/3 tbsp) butter
1 medium onion, finely chopped
white part of a fat leek, finely sliced
1 lb (450 g) potatoes, peeled and thinly sliced
2 pints (1.25 l/5 cups) vegetable stock
1 bay leaf
1½–2 teasp salt
15 grinds of black pepper
10 fl oz milk (275 ml/1¼ cups) milk
5 fl oz (150 ml/⅔ cup) soured cream (or strained Greek-style natural yoghurt)

For the garnish
leaves from reserved watercress, finely chopped
2 tbsp toasted pine kernels or flaked almonds

Wash and spin dry all the watercress, then cut off the leaves from one bunch, rewrap and refrigerate.

Melt the butter in a soup pan, add the onion and leek and sauté, covered, for 2 minutes, until soft and golden. Add the potatoes, stock, bay leaf and seasonings, bring to the boil, cover and simmer for 20 minutes, until the potatoes are tender. Add the remaining watercress, stalks as well as leaves, bring to the boil and simmer, uncovered, for 2 minutes.

Purée in a blender or food processor until absolutely smooth. Return the purée to the rinsed pan and bring slowly to simmering point, then stir in the milk, remove from the heat and leave, covered, until cool enough to refrigerate. Pour into a large bowl or jug, cover with clingfilm (saranwrap) and refrigerate for at least 12 hours.

To serve, stir in the reserved chopped watercress leaves and the cream or yoghurt, taste and add extra salt if necessary. Garnish each serving with a scattering of pine kernels or flaked almonds.

Soup Garnishes

Many people consider that what goes into the soup as garnish is the best part of the dish. Certainly, kreplach, gefilte helzel, knaidlach and piroshke are all delicacies in their own right, and, when served with a deeply flavoured soup, they combine to make what can only be described as a *mechiah*, or a very special dish. Many garnishes once made in the home kitchen can now be bought ready-made, but with the exception of lokshen (noodles), I would say that the home-made variety wins every time.

Garnishes for Meat Soups

GEFILTE HELZEL *(Stuffed Neck)*

Serves 4, but can easily be eaten by 2!
Keeps 2 days under refrigeration.

I know of no other cuisine that treats a hen's neck in this delectable way. If you intend to stuff a helzel you will need to tell the butcher, so that he can give you a fowl with the neck intact – the neck of a chicken is too small to be practicable.

This probably vies with potato kugel for the title of 'most-calorie-intensive haimische dish'.

2 oz (50 g/½ cup) plain (all-purpose) flour, minus 1 rounded tbsp (replace this with a rounded tbsp semolina or fine matzah meal – it gives the helzel a better texture)
3 level tbsp raw chicken fat, finely chopped
1 level tbsp coarsely grated raw onion
good pinch of salt
white pepper
1 fowl's neck, untorn

Mix all the stuffing ingredients together with a fork. The mixture should look slightly moist. If it is too dry add a little more fat; if too loose, a little more semolina or meal. With a coarse sewing needle and strong thread, sew up one end of the neck and fill it with the stuffing mixture. It should be only loosely packed, as it swells during cooking. Carefully sew up the other end. Rinse the stuffed neck with cold water, then pour boiling water over it to make the skin smooth. If the bird is to be boiled, cook the helzel with it in the soup pan, then brown it with the bird for half an hour in the oven. If the bird is not to be browned after boiling, the helzel can be browned in the oven by itself for half an hour, or in the roasting pan with a joint of meat.

Serve in slices with chicken soup.

HOME-MADE LOKSHEN *(Egg Noodles)*

Makes about 12 oz (350 g) dry weight.
Keeps 4 days under refrigeration.

'Lokshen' comes from the Turkish *laktsche,* which eventually passed into the Slavonic languages.

This may be counted a labour of love, but it's great fun to make and if a dough hook – or even easier, a food processor – is used, there's none of the tedious kneading our grandmothers had to do when they made this dough every Friday and left the noodles on tea-towels to dry, festooned on the back of the kitchen chair.

8 oz (225 g/2 cups) plain (all-purpose) flour
pinch of salt
2 eggs
1 tbsp plus 2 teasp lukewarm water

By machine Put the flour and salt in bowl, make a well and add eggs and water. Knead with dough hook until a smooth, non-sticky dough is formed – 3-4 minutes.
By hand Put flour and salt on a board, make a well in centre, drop in the whole eggs and water, gradually drawing in the surrounding flour with a knife. Mix with the hand until a firm dough is formed. Knead with heel of hand until like chamois leather in appearance – about 5 minutes.

With a food processor With the metal blade, process the flour, eggs and salt until thoroughly blended, then slowly add the water through the feed tube until it forms a ball that leaves the sides of the bowl clean. If the dough is too sticky (it will depend on the absorbent quality of the flour), add a little more flour. Process for a further 40 seconds to knead dough, then turn it out on to a floured board. Knead briefly with the heel of the hand to ensure that the dough looks like chamois leather – that is, very smooth and springy. Cover with a large bowl and leave to 'relax' for 20 minutes.

To shape the lokshen Divide the dough in two for easier handling. Roll each piece until it is paper-thin and you can see the board through it. It will then be about 14 inches (35 cm) square – if sufficiently kneaded, it will not stick to the board. Place a dry tea-towel on the table and dust it lightly with flour. Place the squares of dough on top and sprinkle them with flour. Leave for a further 20 minutes, or until the surface no longer feels sticky to the touch. Roll each sheet into a loose, flattened 'Swiss roll', about 3 inches (7.5 cm) in diameter, and cut it into slices each ⅛–¼ inch (0.3–0.5 cm) wide, using a sharp cook's knife, and then unroll. If you are going to cook the lokshen the same day, spread them out on the tea-towel and leave for 5 minutes. If you wish to use them later, drape the towel over the back of a trolley handle or chair, and leave them until they are dry and brittle (about an hour). Cook the lokshen in boiling soup or salted water, until bite-tender.

VARIATIONS

PLAETSCHEN

(Noodle Squares)

Cut the rolled-out dough into strips ½ inch (1.25 cm) wide. Pile the strips on top of each other and then cut into ½ inch (1.25 cm) squares. When required, boil until tender and use as a garnish for a consommé or chicken soup.

SHPAETZLEN

(Bow Knots)

Cut the rolled-out dough into strips 1 inch (2.5 cm) wide, and then into 1 inch (2.5 cm) squares. Pinch the squares with the fingers to make little bow shapes. When required, boil until tender and use as a garnish for a chicken or tomato soup.

FINGERHUETCHEN

(Thimble Noodles)

Roll out the dough, but leave to dry for only 15 minutes, then fold in half. Using a floured thimble or tiny metal cutter, cut through both layers making little circles. Drop into deep fat heated to 375°F (190°C) - when a square of bread will brown in 30 seconds - and cook for a minute or until slightly browned. Drain on paper towels, then serve hot in chicken soup.They may be reheated in a moderate oven.

KREPLACH

Makes approximately 48.
Keeps 3 days, raw or cooked, under refrigeration.
Freeze cooked 3 months.

Affectionately known as 'Jewish ravioli', these three-cornered pastries are said to symbolize the three Patiarchs, Abraham, Isaac and Jacob. Kreplach are eaten in many households on Kol Nidre, the eve of the Yom Kippur fast, as well as Shavuot (the Feast of Weeks), when they are eaten filled with cream cheese and smothered in sour cream to celebrate the giving of the dietary laws to Moses on Mount Sinai and the consequent distinction between meat and dairy foods (see also Cheese Knishes, p. 656). The meat filling for kreplach is made from shin beef which has first been cooked in water until tender, together with the same ingredients as for the bone stock (p. 27). The resulting rich stock can then be used as the basis for a soup.

1 recipe home-made Lokshen dough (see p. 49)

For the filling

½ medium onion, peeled and cut in 1-in (2.5-cm) chunks
1 lb (450 g) shin beef, cooked and cut in 1-in (2.5-cm) cubes
1 egg
½ level teasp salt
speck of white pepper

Pulse the onion and meat in the food processor until finely 'minced' - about 5 seconds. Do *not* process until pasty. Add the egg and seasoning through the feed tube and process until evenly moistened and just beginning to cling together - another 3 seconds. Or put the onion and meat through the mincer, stir in the beaten egg and seasoning and turn into a bowl.

Have ready a half-gallon (2.25 l/10-cup) pan, half-full of boiling water with 2 teaspoons of salt in it. Roll out the dough as thinly as for the lokshen but do not leave it to dry. Instead, roll it into a flattened 'Swiss roll' and cut across into pieces 2 inches (5 cm) wide, then unroll and pile these strips on top of each other and cut them into 2-inch (5-cm) squares. Put a teaspoon of the meat filling in the centre of each square, then fold over into a triangle, pressing the edges securely to seal - dampen them with water only if necessary. As each one is formed, lay it on a sheet of greaseproof paper.

Add one-third of the kreplach to the boiling water, bring back to the boil, cover and cook for 15 minutes, tasting after 10 minutes to see if they are tender. Drain and reserve. Repeat with the remaining kreplach. Reheat in the soup for 5-10 minutes. Alternatively, the *uncooked* kreplach can be left out in the kitchen until the surface is quite dry - about 2 hours (turning once or twice) - then stored in the refrigerator and cooked as required.

KNAIDLACH

Serves 6–8.
Keeps 2 days under refrigeration.
Freeze 1 month.

These are sometimes called *halkes* or matzah balls. The secret of success is to use sufficient fat to make them tender yet still firm when the spoon goes in. Provided the specified amount of fat is used, the amount of matzah meal may be increased if you prefer a firmer (though equally tender) texture. However, I must warn you that one family's perfect knaidlach is another's cannon-balls! Ground almonds greatly enhance the flavour and texture, but an equal quantity of medium matzah meal can be used instead.

2 large eggs
2 very slightly rounded tbsp rendered chicken fat, chicken-flavoured vegetable fat or soft margarine
5 tbsp warm chicken soup or water
1 teasp salt
$^1/_4$ teasp white pepper
$^1/_4$ teasp ground ginger (optional)
1 oz (25 g/$^1/_4$ cup) ground almonds
4 oz (125g/1 cup) medium matzah meal

Whisk the eggs until fluffy,then stir in the soft fat, tepid soup or water, seasonings, ground almonds and matzah meal, and mix thoroughly. The mixture should look moist and thick, but should not be quite firm enough to form into balls. If too soft, add a little more meal; if too firm, add a teaspoon or two of water. Chill for at least an hour, but overnight will do no harm. The mixture will then firm up.

Half-fill a pan with water and bring to the boil, then add 2 teaspoons of salt. Take pieces of the chilled mixture the size of large walnuts and roll between wetted palms into balls. Drop these balls into the boiling water, reduce the heat until the water is simmering, cover and simmer for 40 minutes without removing the lid. Strain from the water with a slotted spoon and drop into simmering soup.

For a small number or a special occasion, cook the knaidlach in chicken soup rather than in water. They will absorb some of the soup but with it also its delicious flavours.

Note To freeze knaidlach, open-freeze the cooked and drained knaidlach until solid - about 2 hours - then put them into plastic bags. To use, defrost for 1 hour at room temperature, then reheat in the simmering soup.

KNAIDLACH
(Made with Oil)

Serves 4–6.
Freeze 3 months.

Although it is traditional to use rendered chicken fat to make these exquisite soup dumplings, many people now prefer to use oil instead. The result is very light and tender, if perhaps less full-flavoured, knaidlach.

4 oz (125 g/1 cup) medium matzah meal
8 fl oz (225 ml/1 cup) boiling water
1 large egg, whisked until frothy
2 tbsp corn oil or sunflower oil
1 teasp salt
speck of white pepper

Put the matzah meal into a bowl and stir in the boiling water, followed by all other ingredients. Mix thoroughly, then refrigerate for 1 hour to allow the matzah meal to swell and the mixture to firm up. Have ready a large pan of boiling water containing 2 teaspoons of salt. Roll the mixture into little balls about the size of walnuts. Drop into the boiling water and then simmer uncovered for about 20 minutes, or until the knaidlach rise to the top of the pan. Drain, then put into simmering chicken soup.

MANDLEN
(Soup Nuts)

Serves 4–6.
Keeps 1 week in an airtight tin.
Freeze 3 months.

These are delicious served with chicken or tomato soup. Put a dish on the table and let everyone help themselves. Mandlen may be baked or fried, whichever you prefer.

3 oz (75 g/¾ cup) plain (all-purpose) flour
½ level teasp salt
1 large egg
2 teasp oil

Sift the flour and salt into a bowl. Make a well in the centre of the flour and drop in the egg and the oil. Gradually work in the surrounding flour to make a soft dough that you can roll between your fingers into a 'sausage'. If too stiff, add a drop more oil; if too soft, add a teaspoonful more flour. Work the dough into a ball with your hands, then divide it into 3. On a floured board, roll each piece into a pencil-thick length and cut it into ½-inch (1.25-cm) pieces.

To bake Arrange the mandlen on an oiled, flat baking sheet, leaving room for them to puff up. Bake at Gas No. 5 (375°F/190°C) for 20 minutes, or until golden brown. After 10 minutes open the oven and shake the tray, so that the mandlen will brown evenly. When quite cold, store them in an airtight tin until needed.

To fry Leave the uncooked mandlen for 30 minutes on the pastry board, for the surface to dry out a little. Pour oil to a depth of ¾ inch (2 cm) into a frying pan. After oil has been heating gently for 5 minutes, drop in one mandlen as a 'tester'. If gentle bubbles appear round it, the oil is hot enough. Put more mandlen into the oil, but do not overcrowd the pan, or the oil will become too cool. Allow them to cook at a steady bubble, turning them so that they brown on all sides. When golden brown, lift out with a slotted spoon and drain on crumpled kitchen paper. Alternatively, fry for 2–3 minutes in a deep-fryer in oil heated to 190°C (375°F).

When quite cold, store in an airtight tin. Mandlen may be frozen and then reheated when required.

To reheat, put in a small heatproof casserole and leave for 10 minutes in a moderate oven, Gas No. 4 (350°F/180°C).

QUICK MANDLEN

Makes about 30 mandlen, enough for 6–8 people.
Make fresh as required.

These are excellent to make at the last moment before a Yomtov lunch, or as a garnish for leftover chicken soup. They are crisp and puffy, but soften very quickly in soup.

2 large eggs
1 tbsp cold water
1 level teasp salt
a few grinds of black pepper
4 oz (125 g/1 cup) self-raising flour or
4 oz (125 g/1 cup) plain (all-purpose) flour and
1 level teasp baking powder

Beat the eggs, the water and the seasoning with a rotary egg beater, until the mixture is thick and frothy. Sift the flour into the egg and beat with a fork until a thick batter-like consistency is obtained - about 2 minutes. In a 9-inch (22.5-cm) frying pan, pour enough oil to come to a depth of 1/2 inch (1.25-cm). After 3 minutes of heating, drop a little of the mixture from a teaspoon. If bubbles appear round it, the oil is ready. Drop teaspoonfuls of the mixture into the oil, leaving room for them to swell. Reduce the heat until the oil is bubbling gently round each soup nut. When bubbles appear on their surface, turn the mandlen over and continue to cook until both sides are a rich brown. Drain on crumpled kitchen paper. Put in a heatproof dish and leave in the oven until required. They are not suitable for storing.

Garnish for Meat or Parev Soups

CROÛTONS

Serves 6–8.
Freeze for 3 months.

4 large slices brown or rye bread
3 tbsp sunflower or olive oil
1 teasp dried Herbes de Provence

Cut bread into 3/8-inch (1-cm) cubes and mix in a flat baking tin with oil and herbs. Bake in a moderate oven, Gas No. 4 (350°F/180°C) for 15–20 minutes, stirring once or twice so that the croûtons brown evenly.

A Garnish for Cream Soups

BUTTERED CROÛTONS

Serves 6–8.
Leftovers freeze 3 months.

The garnish for a cream soup must be light yet crisp. Use slightly stale bread to get the crispiest results.

4 thin slices bread
1 oz (25 g/2 tbsp) butter
1 tbsp oil

Cut bread into 3/8-inch (1-cm) cubes.

To fry Heat the butter and oil in a heavy frying pan. As soon as the foaming stops, put in the bread and fry gently until crisp and golden on all sides. Drain well on crumpled kitchen paper.

To bake Preheat oven to Gas No. 4 (350°F/180°C). Meanwhile, melt the butter and oil in a tray about 9 x 7 inches (22.5 x 18 cm) and 1 inch (2.5 cm) deep. Add the croûtons, shake well to coat them with the fat, then bake for 15–20 minutes, shaking once, until crisp and golden brown. Drain on crumpled paper.

Reheat briefly in the oven just before serving in little pottery dishes.

FISH AND VEGETARIAN MEALS

Kosher Fish around the World

(Courtesy of Kashrut Division, London Beth Din, and United Synagogue Publications Ltd)

UK	*France*	*Holland*	*Italy*	*Spain*
Anchovy	Anchois	Anchovis	Acciugia	Boqueron
Barbel	Barbue	Barbeel	-	-
Bass	Bar Commun	Baars	Persico, Branzino	Lubina
Bream	Breme	Brasum	-	-
Brill	Barbue	Griet	Rombo, Liscio	-
Brisling	-	-	-	-
Carp	Carpe	Karper	Carpa	-
Coalfish	-	Koolvis	-	-
Cod	Morue, Cabillaud	Kabeljauw	Merluzzo	Bacalao
Dab	Limande	Schar	-	-
Dace	-	-	-	-
Flounder	Flet	-	-	-
Grayling	Ombre	Vlagzalm	-	-
Gurnard	Grondin	Poon	Pesce Capone	-
Haddock	Aiglefin	Schelvis	-	-
Hake	Merluche	Kabeljauw	Nasello	Merluza
Halibut	Fletan	Heilbot	-	-
Herring	Hareng	Hareng	Aringa	-
John Dory	-	-	-	-
Ling	-	Leng	-	-
Mackerel	Maquereau	Makreel	Sgombro	Caballa
Mullet	Mulet	Baars	-	-
Perch	Perche	Baars	Pesce Persico	-
Pike	Brochet	Snoek	Luccio	-
Pilchard	Pilchard	-	Sardina	Sardina
Plaice	Carrelet, Plie	Schol	-	-
Pollack	Lieu Jaune	Pollak	-	-
Roach	Gardon	Blankvoorn	-	-
Saithe	-	-	-	-
Salmon	Saumon	Zalm	Salmone	Salmon
Sardine	Sardine	Sardine	Sardina	Sardina
Shad	Alose	Elft	-	-
Sild	-	-	-	-
Smelt	Eperlan	Spiering	-	-
Snoek	Snoek	Snoek	-	-
Sole	Sole	Tong	Sogliola	Lenguado
Sprat	Sprat	Sprot	Spratto	-
Tench	Tanche	Zeelt	Tinca	-
Trout	Truite	Forel	Trota	Trucha
Tuna	Thon	Tonijin	Tonno	Atun
Whitebait	Blanchaille	-	-	-
Whiting	Merlan	Wijting	Bianchetti	-

Australia

Anchovy
Baramundi
Barracouta
Barracuda
Blue Eye
Blue Grenadier
Bluefin
Bream
Carp
Cod
Coral Perch
Duckfish
Flathead
Flounder
Garfish
Groper
Haddock
Hake
Harpuka
Herring
Jewfish
John Dory
Lemon Sole
Mackerel
Morwong
Mullet
Murray Cod
Murray Perch
Murray Perth Tuna
Northern Blue Fin
Orange Roughy
Perch
Pike
Pilchard
Redfin
Salmon
Sardine
Shad
Sild
Skipjack (striped)
Snapper
Southern Blue Fin
Tailor
Terakiji
Trevally
Trout
Yellowfin
Yellowtail
Whiting

Hong Kong

Anchovy
Bigeye
Carp
Crevalle
Croaker
Giant Perch
Grey Mullet
Grouper
Japanese Sea Perch
Leopard Coral Trout
Pampano
Pilchard
Red Sea Bream
Round Herring
Sardine
Scad
Whitefish

Non Kosher Fish

(Courtesy of Kashrut Division, London Beth Din)

The following species of fish are non-kosher: abbot, allmouth, angelfish, angler, beluga, blonde, catfish, caviar, cockles, conger eel, crabs, dogfish, eelpout, eels, fiddlefish, fishing frog, flake, frog-fish, goosefish, guffer eel, huss, lumpfish, monkfish, mussels, ray, rigg, rock salmon, rockfish, roker, sea devil, sea pout, shellfish, skate, sturgeon, swordfish, thornback ray, turbot.

FISH

Fish in a Hurry

Maybe it's because Jewish housewives have been cooking fish for about 3,500 years - ever since their ancestors were slaves in Egypt - but there can be little doubt that the Jewish ways with fish are some of the most practical and tasty in the whole repertoire of cookery.

Cooking Fish in the Microwave

COOKING TIMES

The following cooking times are useful if you want to cook fish in quantities different from those given in specific recipes. They should also be helpful in converting conventional fish recipes for the microwave.

Note If stock or wine is added for flavour, allow 30 seconds extra time for each 4 fl oz (125 ml/½ cup) liquid.

THIN FILLETS

For example, small plaice or sole ½ inch (1.25 cm) thick, covered and cooked flat on a plate on 100 per cent power:

4 oz (125 g) 1 minute
6–8 oz (175–225 g) 2 minutes
12 oz–1 lb (350–450 g) 2½ minutes
1½–2 lb (675–900 g) 5 minutes

Allow to stand, covered, for 3 minutes.

THICK FILLETS

For example, haddock, cod, salmon, hake 1 inch (2.5 cm) thick, covered and cooked flat on a plate on 100 per cent power:

8 oz (225 g)   3 minutes
12 oz–1 lb (350–450 g)   4½ minutes
1½–2 lb (675–900 g)   6 minutes

Allow to stand, covered, for 3 minutes.

STEAKS OF FISH

For example, halibut, salmon, cod, haddock ¾ inch (2 cm) thick, weighing 6–7 oz (175–200 g), arranged in a circle with thinner part to centre of the dish, covered and cooked on 100 per cent power:

1 fish steak   3 minutes
2 fish steaks   4½ minutes
4 steaks   6 minutes
6 steaks   8 minutes

Allow to stand, covered, for 3 minutes.

SMALL WHOLE FISH

For example, trout weighing 8–10 oz (225–275 g), cleaned and head removed, laid side by side, tail to head, covered, steamed plain with or with enough melted butter to moisten the skin. Cook on 100 per cent power:

1 fish   3 minutes
2 fish   5 minutes
3 fish   6½ minutes
4 fish   8–9 minutes

Allow to stand, covered, for 3 minutes.

TESTING FOR DONENESS

Minimum cooking times are given. The exact time will depend on the temperature of the fish and personal taste. After the fish has been allowed to stand for 3 minutes, test to make sure the fish is opaque (rather than glassy) right through to the centre and will flake easily with a fork.

FISH IN SAUCE

To reheat, cover and cook on 80 per cent power for 5 minutes, or until steaming.

Perfect Fried Fish

In most Jewish households fried fish means cold fish, for properly prepared, it is one of the best dishes to cook on Friday for serving on the Sabbath. The frying of fish in oil (the only fat which remains palatable when cold) is a method adopted by Eastern European (Ashkenazi) Jews from those Sephardi Jews (originally from Spain and Portugal via Holland) who had lived in England since the resettlement of the Jews in 1657. Until recent years it was for British Jews the most popular method of preparing fish. However, recent nutritional advice on the need to reduce the total fat intake in the diet has relegated this method of cooking to high days and holidays, although Jewish delis still report high sales of fried fish throughout the entire year. It may be that, as with food in general, it is the home *cooking* rather than the eating of fried fish that has fallen out of favour.

Fried fish which is still palatable two days later depends on three main factors: the pan, the coating and the temperature of the oil. An open frying pan was always used in the Jewish kitchen until the advent of the controlled-temperature deep-fryer. I would not recommend any new cook to go back to the traditional open-pan method with all its attendant difficulties of temperature and smell control, not to mention the inevitable oil-spattered cooker top. However, as it is a method perfected by generations of Jewish women in communities all over the world, I believe it deserves a place in this book.

Modern Version

FRIED FILLETS OR STEAKS OF FISH IN THE JEWISH MANNER

Serves 6–8.
Keeps 2 days, lightly covered, in a cool cupboard, 3 days in the refrigerator.
Freeze 3 months.

Steaks of sole, hake, haddock, cod, halibut or large plaice should be cut ¾–1 inch (2–2.5 cm) thick. Fillets should be 1 inch (2.5 cm) thick. Fillets of plaice, sole or baby halibut should be cut from fish not less than 1½ lb (675 g) in weight.

6–8 fillets or steaks of fish
salt
1 egg
2 rounded tbsp flour
coating crumbs or matzah meal

Wash the fish under cold running water and arrange round the sides of a colander. Sprinkle lightly with cooking salt and leave to drain.

To coat the fish, have ready 3 plastic or glass containers, each slightly longer than the fillet or steak of fish. Arrange these containers side by side with beaten egg in one, plain (all-purpose) flour in the second and dried coating crumbs (the colour of oatmeal) or matzah meal in the third. (Stale challah or French bread which has been allowed to dry out completely in the bread bin or drawer can be crushed to crumbs in the food processor).

Dip the washed and drained fish into the flour, patting off any excess, then into the egg, which is spread in an even layer all over the surface of the fish with a pastry brush, then finally into the crumbs, which are patted on in an even layer. Arrange the coated fish on a tray ready for frying.

Note Chopped Fried Fish (see p. 65) does not need the flour and egg treatment, only the coating, as the matzah meal in the mixture prevents any moisture in the fish from escaping.

THE OIL

I use sunflower oil to fry fish as I think it produces a particularly crisp and digestible coating. However, any flavourless vegetable oil, such as corn or peanut oil, can be used.

If the oil smells acrid after it has been used, it has been overheated and has started to decompose and should be thrown away. So should any oil which has become dark and smelly (because it has been used many times). However, a little of this oil added to a panful of fresh oil will help the fish to brown more quickly.

TO FRY THE FISH BY THE TRADITIONAL METHOD

The ideal fish-frying pan can be made either of heavy cast aluminium, stainless steel or iron, but in each case it must have a thick base that sits evenly on the cooker. The sides should be at least 2 inches (5 cm) high to prevent the bubbling oil from spattering over the cooker. It should be at least 9–10 inches (22.5–25 cm) in diameter. After each frying session, pour the cool oil through a sieve into a screw-top glass or plastic jar. An aluminium or stainless steel pan should be washed in the usual way in hot water with detergent. An iron pan should simply be wiped clean with kitchen paper. A little new oil is added to the old oil each time fish is fried.

Heat the empty pan for 3 minutes over medium heat, then put the oil into it to a depth of 1 inch (2.5 cm) and heat steadily for 4 minutes. Then test to see that a cube of bread browns in 30 seconds or an oil thermometer registers 375°F (190°C). Lift up the fish on a slotted spoon and lower it into the hot oil. Do not overcrowd the pan, or too much cold fish put in too soon will lower the temperature drastically and the fish will be soggy. Cook the fish over medium heat with the oil bubbling steadily, until the first side is a rich brown. This will take about 4 minutes for a fillet, 5–7 minutes for a thick steak. Turn it carefully, using a slotted spoon and a fork, and cook until the second side is brown. Have ready a shallow casserole or a cooling tray covered with crumpled kitchen paper. Lift out the fish to drain. If the fillets are not stiff and crisp when they are lifted out, turn up the heat and return them to the pan for a further minute's cooking in hotter oil. Perfect fried fish should look dry and crisp. As soon as it has drained completely, lift it on to a platter and store until required.

TO FRY FISH USING A THERMOSTATICALLY CONTROLLED DEEP-FRYER

To fry steaks and fillets I prefer to remove the frying basket, as this increases the capacity of the pan. However, I keep it in when frying chopped fish balls as they seem to cook more evenly when securely held.

Pour in oil to the depth recommended by the manufacturer (usually indicated by a mark on the inside surface). Then heat the oil to the temperature recommended for frying fish (375°F/190°C).

It is essential not to crowd the pan, as too much cold fish can drastically lower the temperature of the oil and so allow the fish to absorb it before the temperature can be restored. The pan is closed and the timer set as follows:

7 minutes for fillets and chopped fish balls
8 minutes for steaks

While the fish is cooking, line a shallow casserole with crumpled paper towels or tissue paper. When the fish is cooked, lift it out with a large slotted spoon and lay it on its side round the edge of the dish so that any drops of free oil can drain away. After 5–6 minutes (just before the next batch is ready) the fish can be lifted carefully on to a serving dish.

TO STORE FRIED FISH

If the fish is to be eaten within 2 days I prefer to store it in a cool, ventilated cupboard, as it will keep crisper for longer if not exposed to a damp atmosphere.

OVEN FRIED FISH

Cooked in oil, keeps 3 days under refrigeration.
Freeze 2 months.

This is a most useful way to serve hot 'fried' fish for a large number without being tied to the cooker at the last minute or permeating the house with the odour of hot oil. It also ensures that the very minimum of oil is absorbed.

6–8 oz (175–225 g) breadcrumbs or matzah meal
6–8 fillets or steaks of any white fish
1 egg
4 tbsp oil or 2 oz (50 g/¼ cup) melted butter and 1 tbsp oil
1 teasp salt

Preheat the oven to Gas No. 6 (400°F/200°C). Put the crumbs or matzah meal in the oven to brown as it heats up, taking them out when they are well coloured.

Wash and salt the fish and leave to drain. Beat the egg with the fat and salt and put in a shallow casserole. Have ready a piece of greaseproof paper with the coating crumbs on it. Dry each piece of fish thoroughly with kitchen towelling, then brush with the egg mixture and coat with the crumbs. Arrange the coated fish side by side on flat oven baking trays (no need to grease them). Leave in a cool place until required.

Put all the fish in the oven and allow to cook, without turning, for 20–25 minutes, depending on the thickness. Serve hot.

SARDINES FRITES À LA SAUCE VERTE

Serves 6–8.
Serve hot off the pan.
Leftovers keep 1 day under refrigeration.

The crunchy whole sardines are delicious served with the slightly acid green mayonnaise. The ale promotes a particularly crisp coating. These make a delicious starter before a cold main course, or they could be served with boiled new potatoes and a salad for a light summer lunch. Allow 3 fish per serving.

18–24 fresh sardines
salt
black pepper
small can light ale
4–6 oz (125–175 g/1–1½ cups) seasoned flour

For the sauce

8 oz (225 g) fresh sorrel or spinach, or 4 oz (125 g) frozen leaf spinach
½ oz (15 g/1 tbsp) butter
1 teasp Dijon mustard
4 tbsp lemon juice
1 tbsp chopped parsley
1 tbsp chopped chervil, if available
10 fl oz (275 ml/1¼ cups) mayonnaise

Clean the fish, lightly salt and pepper the insides, pass through the ale and then the flour, patting off any excess. Deep-fry, 4 at a time, in a frying basket at 375°F (190°C) for 5 minutes, until golden brown. Drain on crumpled kitchen paper. May be kept hot for 40 minutes at Gas No. ¼ (225°F/110°C).

To make the sauce, wash the sorrel or spinach and cook in a knob of butter until limp and all free liquid has evaporated. Purée, then add all the remaining ingredients and process until smooth in food processor.

FRIED FRESH HERRINGS

Have them either filleted or gutted without being split. (Fish on the bone is more fiddly to eat but is more flavoursome.) Scrape well with a knife to remove the scales, divide large fish (about 12 oz/350 g) in 2 lengthwise. Wash, salt and leave to drain in a colander. Dip in flour and egg, but finish with a coating of medium oatmeal or porridge oats whizzed for 3 seconds in a blender, or matzah meal.

Note For each 4 herrings allow 1 beaten egg and 3 oz (75 g/1 cup) oatmeal, porridge oats or matzah meal. Fry as before. Serve warm or cold. Allow 1 large herring per person.

Gefilte Fish

Gefilte fish was originally a fish 'forcemeat' made from a variety of chopped or minced freshwater fish, which was used to stuff the skin of a carp. The whole fish was then poached in a flavoured fish stock, which jellied when it was cold.

Today we make a similar mixture but (at least in the UK and the USA) use mainly sea fish and put balls of this mixture directly in the stock to poach instead of stuffing it into the fish. These fish balls can also be fried in the same way as fish fillets or steaks, or poached in a sweet and sour tomato sauce in the Sephardi fashion (see p. 628), or in a lemon sauce (see p. 77) in the English fashion.

My mother used to tell of being sent to the fish market in Manchester in the early years of this century to carry home, with the help of her younger brothers and sisters, a stone (14 lb/6.5 kg) of fish. This would be chopped by hand, using a *hackmesser*, by the women of the house, to make gefilte fish.

Soon the hand-chopper was superseded by the hand-mincer, and then by the electric mincer. True emancipation, however, came only with the food processor, whose metal blade almost exactly duplicates the action of the hand-held chopper.

Today, in the larger cities, many fishmongers will mince fish to order. Otherwise I would strongly recommend using the food processor instead.

For those who still use a mincer, I recommend that the egg, onion and seasoning be puréed in a blender, and then the fish mixed following the method advised when using the food processor.

I find that 2 lb (900 g) is the minimum of fish worth processing, and 6 lb (2.75 kg) the maximum that can easily be handled by one person at a time. Do not process the fish longer than stated in the recipe, or you will end up with puréed rather than chopped fish balls. To get the best results, allow the matzah meal to swell in the egg and onion purée before adding to the fish. If you are short of time, the fish mix can be refrigerated overnight and then shaped and cooked or frozen the next day. I do not advise freezing the fish mix without shaping it as it takes so long to defrost.

Equal quantities of haddock and cod make a tasty and relatively economical mixture. However, when small fillets of hake are available at a reasonable price, they can be used instead - they do give the fish a superior flavour and texture.

GEFILTE FISH MIX

Keeps 3 days under refrigeration.
Freeze 3 months raw or cooked.

To make 36–40 patties or balls

3 lb (1.5 kg) hake fillet, skinned, and 3 lb (1.5 kg) haddock fillet, skinned, or 3 lb (1.5 kg) haddock fillet, skinned, and 3 lb (1.5 kg) cod fillet, skinned
3 medium onions, peeled
6 eggs
6 teasp salt
½ teasp white pepper
6 teasp sugar or granular sweetener
3 tbsp oil
6 oz (175 g/1½ cups) medium matzah meal

To make 12–14 patties or balls

1 lb (450 g) hake fillet, skinned, and 1 lb (450 g) haddock fillet, skinned, or 1 lb (450 g) haddock fillet, skinned, and 1 lb (450 g) cod fillet, skinned
1 medium onion, peeled
2 eggs
2 teasp salt
pinch of white pepper
2 teasp sugar or granular sweetener
1 tbsp oil
2 oz (50 g/½ cup) medium matzah meal

Wash and salt the fish and leave to drain. Cut the onion in 1-inch (2.5 cm) chunks and put into the food processor, together with the eggs, seasoning and oil, then process until reduced to a smooth purée. (If you wish to make the larger quantity using a processor of standard - 1½ pints (850 ml/3¾ cups - liquid capacity, you will need to do this in 2 batches, using 3 eggs and 1½ onions each time - all the seasonings can go into 1 batch to avoid complicated arithmetic!) Pour this purée into a large bowl and stir in the matzah meal, then leave to swell.

Cut the fish into 1-inch (2.5 cm) chunks and put in the processor, half-filling the bowl each time. Process for 5 seconds, until the fish is finely chopped, then add to the egg and onion purée and blend in using a large fork. Repeat until all the fish has been processed, then mix thoroughly - if preparing a large quantity, this is most easily done with the widespread fingers of one hand. The mixture should be firm enough to shape into a soft patty or ball. If it feels too 'cloggy', rinse out the processor bowl with 1 or 2 tablespoons of water and stir that in. If it feels very soft, stir in 1 or 2 tablespoons of meal. Leave for half an hour, or overnight (under refrigeration) if preferred.

To shape, dip the hands into cold water and form the mixture into patties about $2\frac{1}{2}$ inches (7 cm) long, $1\frac{1}{2}$ inches (4 cm) wide and $\frac{3}{4}$ inch (2 cm) thick, or into balls the size of a small apple. The fish can now be cooked or frozen raw.

To freeze raw Arrange the patties or balls side by side on a tray lined with greaseproof paper or foil. When the tray is full, cover with a layer of paper or foil and make another layer on top. Put the tray, uncovered, in the freezer for 2 hours or until the patties are firm to the touch. They can now be packed, 12 in a plastic bag, or they can be individually over-wrapped in clingfilm (saranwrap) to make it easy to remove a few at a time.

To defrost Lay the frozen patties side by side on a board. Leave either overnight in the refrigerator, or from 1 to 3 hours at room temperature, until they are soft all the way through.

CHOPPED FRIED FISH (FRIED GEFILTE FISH, BRITISH STYLE)

Keeps 3 days under refrigeration.
Freeze 3 months.

These delicious fluffy fishcakes with their crunchy coating can be eaten at any time of day or night. They're also superb for picnics and journeys – to my mind, they are the ultimate in 'convenience' foods. Serve them hot with baked potatoes, latkes or chips, at room temperature with a variety of salads, at any temperature with pickled cucumbers or chrane (horseradish and beetroot sauce).

Allow 1–2 patties per person.

2-lb or 6-lb quantity Gefilte Fish mix (see p. 64), shaped into patties (as described on p. 64).

To fry the patties This is most easily done in a deep-fryer, but you can use a deep frying pan (skillet). In either case, coat the patties evenly, either with fine, dry breadcrumbs (easily prepared from dry, stale challah in the food processor) or with medium matzah meal.

To use a deep-fryer Heat the oil to 375°F (190°C). Cook 4 or 5 patties at a time in the basket, allowing approximately 6–7 minutes, or until a rich golden-brown.

To use a frying pan Heat oil 1 inch (2.5 cm) deep until it is hot enough to brown a 1-inch (2.5 cm) cube of bread in 30 seconds. Gently lower in enough balls to fill the pan without overcrowding it – usually 5 or 6 in a 9-inch (22.5 cm) pan. Cook steadily over moderate heat, turning every 2 or 3 minutes, until the patties are an even brown – 7 or 8 minutes in all. In either case, drain the fish by standing it up round the sides of a dish lined with crumpled kitchen or tissue paper.

To serve hot, allow to cool for 30 minutes.

Defrosted fish can be recrispened in a moderate oven, Gas No. 4 (350°F/180°C) for 10 minutes, or crisp to the touch.

TRADITIONAL PLATTER OF GEFILTE FISH

Makes 12–14 balls.
Serves 8–10.
Keeps 3 days under refrigeration.
Freeze 3 months (freeze cooked fish balls and the stock in separate containers).

Gefilte fish can be poached in the microwave (see this page), but the flavour is undoubtedly superior if it is simmered slowly on top of the stove in the traditional way. If you freeze the dish, you will need to restore the 'jell' to the stock when you are ready to use it. To do this, pour the stock into a pan, bring to the boil and cook for 1 minute, then cool and pour it over the fish. I do think the fish has a better texture if freshly poached, however, so I usually freeze the uncooked balls, then defrost them in the refrigerator overnight and poach them as though they were newly prepared. It is as well to order the head, skin and bones in advance.

2-lb quantity Gefilte Fish mix (see p. 64)

For the stock
1 cleaned hake or haddock head
skin and bones from the fish
2 level teasp salt
water to cover the bones
1 medium onion, thinly sliced
2 medium carrots, sliced ¼ inch (0.5 cm) thick
2 level teasp sugar

The dish looks more attractive if the fish is shaped into balls rather than patties. To get the maximum flavour, first simmer the head, skin and bones of the fish with the salt and cold water to cover, for 30 minutes, then remove the skin and bones (leave in the head as this helps the stock to jell). Add the onion, carrots, sugar and balls of fish. Bring to the boil, then turn the heat low, cover the pan and simmer for 1½ hours. Uncover and simmer for a further 30 minutes to concentrate the stock. Lift out the balls and arrange them on a platter, topping each fish ball with a slice of carrot. Pour the stock through a strainer over the fish, then chill overnight before serving.

TO POACH GEFILTE FISH IN THE MICROWAVE

Serves 4–6 with 14 small patties or 7 larger ones.
Keeps 3 days under refrigeration.
Freeze raw patties 3 months.

While I do not think the flavour is quite as deep as when the fish is stewed in the traditional manner, this is a marvellous way of cooking just enough fish for one meal, using your own ready-frozen gefilte fish balls. Both the stock and the fish can be prepared in the microwave in 30 minutes. However, you will need to leave the dish overnight if you wish the sauce to jell. The fish is still delicious even if no fish skins and bones are available for the stock.

7 balls of raw Gefilte Fish (see p. 64)

For the stock
(sufficient for 2 occasions)

2 lb (900 g) fish heads, skins and bones, well washed
boiling water to cover the bones (about 1½ pints/850 ml/3¾ cups)
1 medium onion, thinly sliced
2 medium carrots, sliced ¼ inch (0.5 cm) thick
2 level teasp sugar
2 level teasp salt

Put the well-washed heads, skins and broken-up bones into a large bowl or lidded casserole, barely cover with boiling water, then cook, covered, on 100 per cent power until boiling – about 10 minutes. Uncover, skim the top, then add the remaining stock ingredients. Cover and cook on 50 per cent power for 10 minutes. Strain. Measure ½ pint (275 ml/1¼ cups) and freeze the remainder.

Arrange the fish patties on a round or oval dish, positioning them in a ring, then pour over the stock with the carrots. Cover with a lid or pierced clingfilm (saranwrap), then cook on 100 per cent power for 5 minutes. Turn each ball over, then cook on 50 per cent power for a further 7 minutes.

Leave to stand, covered, until cold, then refrigerate until required.

GEFILTE FISH PROVENÇALE

Serves 6–8.
Keeps 4 days under refrigeration.
Freeze 3 months.

The fish is poached in a delicious tomato and pepper sauce. This dish can be served either warm or chilled. It improves with keeping.

6–8 patties of raw Gefilte Fish mix *(see p. 64)*

For the sauce

1 tbsp oil
1 onion, finely chopped
1 can (15 oz/425 g) Italian tomatoes, sieved or liquidized
2 tbsp tomato ketchup
1 green or red pepper, seeded and thinly sliced
1 level teasp salt
1 level teasp brown sugar
10 grinds of black pepper
1 bay leaf
½ teasp dried Herbes de Provence

To make the sauce, heat the oil and sauté the onion until transparent, then add all the remaining ingredients and bubble until reduced to a thick coating consistency. Arrange the raw fish patties in a shallow ovenproof dish, pour over the sauce and loosely cover with foil. Bake in a slow oven, Gas No. 2 (300°F/150°C) for 1 hour, basting once or twice.

GEFILTE FISH PROVENÇALE IN THE MICROWAVE

Serves 4–6.
The cooked dish keeps 3 days under refrigeration.
Do not freeze.

A 10-inch (25-cm) round dish with a glass lid makes a perfect cooking and serving dish, or you can use an oval gratin dish covered with clingfilm (saranwrap). I like to leave the fish in the sauce for several hours to allow it to absorb the wonderful flavours. If you are using frozen raw patties, let them defrost overnight in the refrigerator, or in the microwave defrost on 30 per cent power for 14 minutes, turning the patties over once. Leave to stand for 20 minutes.

8 fish patties (total weight approx. 2 lb/900 g)

For the sauce

1 can or tube (5 oz/150 g) tomato purée or 2 rounded tbsp
10 fl oz (275 ml/1¼ cups) boiling water
2 teasp olive or sunflower oil
1 teasp onion salt
2 canned sweet red peppers, drained and cut in thin strips, or 1 large red pepper, cut in strips
1 tbsp tomato ketchup
1 bay leaf
10 grinds of black pepper
½ teasp dried Italian herbs or Herbes de Provence
1 teasp brown sugar

Whisk all the sauce ingredients together in a 2-pint (1.25 l/5 cup) microwave-safe jug or bowl until smooth. Heat the sauce, covered, on 100 per cent power for 3 minutes.

Arrange the raw patties side by side in a casserole, pour over the sauce, and cook covered on 100 per cent power for 6 minutes. Remove the lid, baste the fish with the sauce, then re-cover and cook on 50 per cent power for a further 5 minutes.

Leave covered for 10 minutes, then remove clingfilm (saranwrap) if used and refrigerate until required. Leave at room temperature for 1 hour before serving.

TERRINE OF GEFILTE FISH WITH A PINK MAYONNAISE SAUCE

Serves 10.
Keeps for 3 days under refrigeration.
Freeze 3 months.
The refrigerated sauce keeps as long as ordinary mayonnaise but does not freeze.

This stunning new presentation of an old favourite is baked in a loaf shape decorated with vegetable 'flowers'. (The decoration can be omitted if preferred.) It is simpler to prepare than the traditional balls and easy to slice at the table with a serrated knife.

For the terrine
1 lb (450 g) filleted and skinned haddock
1 lb (450 g) filleted and skinned hake
1 large (7 oz/200 g) onion, peeled
2 eggs
2 teasp salt
pinch of white pepper
2 teasp sugar
1 tbsp oil
2 tbsp cold water
2 oz (50 g/½ cup) medium matzah meal
1 oz (25 g/¼ cup) ground almonds

For the decoration
1 thin 'finger' carrot
1 small green pepper

For the sauce
5 rounded tbsp mayonnaise
2 rounded tbsp tomato ketchup
3 teasp white horseradish sauce

Prepare the gefilte fish in the usual way by mixing the puréed onion, eggs, seasoning, oil and water, and adding to the matzah meal and ground almonds. Add the minced or processed fish and mix well with a fork. Set to one side.

Preheat the oven to Gas No. 4 (350°F/180°C). Choose a loaf-shaped container made of glass, foil or tin measuring approximately 9 x 5 x 3 inches (22.5 x 12.5 x 7.5 cm), grease it with oil and line the bottom and two short sides with a strip of silicone paper. Peel the carrot and cut into thin rounds; cut the green pepper into a similar number of thin 'stalks'. Blanch the carrots in boiling water for 5 minutes (or until tender) and blanch the strips of pepper for 30 seconds. Put both into a colander and drench with cold water to set the colour, then pat dry. Arrange on the base of the container in a design.

Spoon some of the fish mix on top of this design, being careful not to disturb it and packing it down well with the back of a spoon. Pile the remainder on top, levelling the surface. Cover with a piece of silicone paper and then with foil, tucking it in round the outside. Place the terrine in a large ovenproof dish at least 2 inches (5 cm) deep and surround it with enough boiling water to come half-way up the sides. (This prevents it drying out in the oven.) Bake for 45–50 minutes, or until the surface feels spongy to gentle touch. Lift from the water bath and leave for 15 minutes. Then remove the cover, run a knife round the edges and carefully turn out on to a long dish or tray. Lift off the strip of silicone paper. Serve at room temperature.

To make the sauce, mix all the ingredients together and put in a decorative bowl. Leave for several hours to let the flavours develop.

Grilled Fish

Unlike meat, fish does not need a fierce heat as it is unnecessary to 'sear' the outside to contain the juices. Indeed, too high a heat will make the fish dry. Instead, it needs a little (preferably olive) oil or butter to keep it moist and flavoursome.

Use steaks cut ¾–1 inch (2–2.5 cm) thick, or fillets from a 1½-lb (675-g) fish. Put 1 oz (25 g/2 tbsp) butter or oil in the grill pan or in a flat, cast-iron dish just large enough to contain the fish. Put it under a gentle heat to melt without browning – the melted butter or oil should make a thin layer on the bottom of the dish. If it does not, add a little more. The minute the fat has melted, put the washed and salted fish into it, then turn the fish over. In this way both sides will be coated and thus protected by the fat. Sprinkle each piece of fish with salt and pepper and dust very lightly with flour. Grill gently but steadily without turning, allowing 10 minutes for a piece ¾-inch (2 cm) thick and 12 minutes for one that is 1 inch (2.5 cm) thick; 2 or 3 minutes before the fish is done sprinkle with a further dusting of flour or a light sprinkling of dry breadcrumbs. Baste twice with the fat and juices while the fish is cooking. When the fish is done, the fillets will be a rich golden brown. Steaks will be the same colour, and the centre bone will move easily when pulled. Serve the fish with the pan juices poured over them and thick wedges of lemon.

VARIATION

SAVOURY FISH STEAKS

Using steaks of hake, haddock or halibut, omit the second dusting with flour and instead spread each steak with a thin coating of reduced-calorie mayonnaise, then sprinkle with salt and pepper and finally with a thin layer of dry breadcrumbs. Baste with the pan juices and continue grilling for a further 3 or 4 minutes until the topping is crisp and brown.

GRILLED HERRINGS OR MACKEREL WITH APPLE SAUCE

Serves 4–5.
Leftovers and sauce will keep 4 days under refrigeration.
Sauce freezes 3 months.

Fine, fat fillets of fresh herring or mackerel grilled until the flesh is creamy and firm in texture make a wonderful mid-week family meal. The piquant sauce helps to neutralize the natural oiliness of this most nourishing of fish. As they have special seasons when they are in their prime, consult the fishmonger before you buy. The sauce is optional.

4–6 herring fillets cut from 12–14 oz (350–450 g) fish

For the sauce

nut of butter or margarine
12 oz (350 g) Bramley cooking apples
1 tbsp brown sugar or granular sweetener
2 teasp water
3 teasp bottled creamed horseradish

For the topping

2tbsp sunflower oil
1 tbsp cider vinegar or red wine vinegar
3 teasp Dijon or English ready-made mustard
2 teasp Worcestershire Sauce
1 teasp soy sauce
½ teasp sea salt
15 grinds of black pepper

First, make the sauce by melting the butter in a small pan and adding the roughly chopped apple, sugar and water. Cover and simmer until the apples fall, then beat to a purée. Stir in the creamed horseradish. (In the microwave, cook all the ingredients except the horseradish in a covered dish for 2 minutes on 100 per cent power, stir, cover and cook for a further 2 minutes, then beat to a purée and finish as above.)

Wash the fish, salt lightly and leave in a colander to drain for 10 minutes. Meanwhile, mix the topping ingredients together in a small bowl.

Lightly grease the grill pan and heat it up 3 inches (7.5 cm) from the grill for 3 minutes. Then lay the fish fillets in it side by side, skin-side down, and brush them thickly with the topping mixture. Grill for 10 minutes, until the fish is a rich brown. Serve at once, accompanied by the sauce at room temperature.

GOLDEN GRILLED FILLETS OF MACKEREL WITH A CLEMENTINE AND CUCUMBER SALAD

Serves 6.
Leftovers keep 2 days under refrigeration.

This is a fish dish to choose if you're looking for a rich taste and satisfying texture without a stratospheric price. However, because mackerel has a high oil content, though it is of excellent composition from a health point of view, it does need to be tempered by some kind of acidity - hence the popularity of gooseberry sauce as an accompaniment. In this recipe, the acidity is provided both by the delicious marinade and by the tangy citrus and cucumber salad that accompanies it. I like to serve this dish with crispy baked potatoes - they take only 30 minutes if you have a combination microwave. The fish is equally delicious served at room temperature as part of a cold buffet.

6–8 split mackerel fillets cut from 3–4 x 12–14 oz (350–400 g) (approx.) whole fish

For the marinade
2 tbsp light soy sauce
2 tbsp fresh orange juice
1 tbsp sun-dried tomato paste or 1 tbsp tomato pureé
1 tbsp finely chopped parsley
1 clove of garlic, finely chopped
2 teasp Worcestershire Sauce
2 teasp lemon juice
15 grinds of black pepper

For the salad
1½ tbsp granulated sugar or granular sweetener
1½ tbsp boiling water
3 tbsp cider vinegar
2 tbsp chopped dill
10 grinds of black pepper
1 medium cucumber
6–8 clementines

Wash and lightly salt the mackerel fillets, then lay side by side in a heatproof dish suitable for grilling. Mix together the marinade ingredients, then spoon or brush over the fish in an even layer. Allow to marinate at room temperature for 1 hour. Grill 4 inches (10 cm) from a hot grill for 9–10 minutes, or until the fish flakes easily and is firm to the touch.

To make the salad, put the sugar or sweetener in a small bowl, add the boiling water and stir until dissolved. Then stir in the vinegar, dill and black pepper. Pour over the thinly sliced cucumber and the peeled and sectioned clementines in a shallow dish and leave for at least 1 hour. Serve at the side of the fish.

Poached Fish

STOVE-TOP FISH CASSEROLE

Serves 6–8.
Leftovers keep 2 days under refrigeration.

A simple but wonderfully flavoursome dish. Any thick fillet of white fish such as hake, haddock, cod, lemon sole or plaice can be used, but my favourite (provided the price is right) is a filleted tail of North Sea hake, which is particularly creamy when cooked this way. As with all recipes for poached fish, it is essential that the liquid does no more than tremble - boiling liquid ruins the texture of the flesh. A 9-inch (22.5-cm) lidded stove-to-table sauté pan is the most convenient cooking utensil. Otherwise use a lidded frying pan and transfer to a gratin dish just before serving.

1½–2 lb (675–900 g) white fish
1 level teasp salt
½ large carrot
½ medium onion
2 oz (50 g/¼ cup) butter
speck of white pepper
1 small bay leaf

10 peppercorns (optional)
2 teasp cornflour (cornstarch)
1 small can (6 fl oz/175 ml/¾ cup) evaporated milk or 5 fl oz (150 ml/⅔ cup) single (light) cream
2 tsp chopped parsley
1 x 29 oz (825 g) can new potatoes or 2 lb (900 g) scraped new potatoes boiled until tender
1 small pack frozen peas (optional)
chopped parsley

Wash and salt the fish, then cut thick fillets such as hake into 6–8 pieces and roll up thinner fillets.

Grate the carrot and the onion finely. Heat the butter in the chosen pan and the minute it has melted, but before it starts to change colour, add the grated vegetables. Stir for 1 or 2 minutes to allow them to absorb some of the butter and begin to soften, then add the fish and turn it over so that it becomes coated with the buttery vegetables.

Now add just enough water to cover the bottom of the pan to a depth of ¼ inch (0.5 cm). Sprinkle the fish with the salt and pepper, add the bay leaf and the peppercorns at the side of the pan, cover and simmer *very* gently for 20 minutes, or until the fish looks creamy right through. Remove bay leaf and peppercorns. Put the cornflour in a bowl and stir in the evaporated milk or cream. Add to the fish and allow to bubble for 3 minutes.

Finally stir in the drained new potatoes, chopped parsley and cooked frozen peas (if used) and leave covered on a very low heat for 3 or 4 minutes.

GRATIN DE SOLE À LA CRÈME

Serves 6–8.
Do not freeze.

'Charlotte', 'Pink Fir Apple', 'Belle de Fontenay' and 'Linzer Delikatess' are not, as you might think, unusual varieties of apple; in fact they are several kinds of 'designer' new potatoes that are ideal to use for gratins of this sort as their waxy texture helps them to absorb cooking liquids without going soggy. Even if they're not named in the supermarket, you can tell them by their golden colour. In this speedy but exceptionally delicious dish, they soak up the flavoured cream so that you have a complete main course of potatoes, sauce and fish all in one dish. The oven-ready dish can be refrigerated for up to 12 hours, but be sure to leave it at room temperature for 1 hour before baking.

2 lb (900 g) waxy new potatoes
6–8 x 4 oz (125 g) fillets of lemon sole or plaice
10 fl oz (275 ml/1¼ cups) whipping cream
1½ teasp salt
¼ teasp white pepper
small bunch spring onions (scallions) with 4 inches (10 cm) of green
2 oz (50 g/¼ cup) butter
6 tbsp grated Cheddar or Gruyère cheese
butter for greasing

Scrub the potatoes, then cook in their skins until barely tender. Skin when cool if desired, then slice ⅜ inch (1 cm) thick. Wash and skin the fish, then sprinkle lightly with salt. Season the cream with the salt and pepper.

Finely chop the spring onions and gently sauté in the 2 oz butter until soft and golden.

Take a dish about 1½ inches (4 cm) deep and wide enough to hold the folded fillets in one layer and butter it well. Arrange the sliced potatoes evenly over the bottom.

Roll up each fillet and lay them in an even layer on top of the potatoes, then spoon over the seasoned cream. Scatter evenly with the grated cheese.

Place a sheet of buttered foil or silicone paper lightly on top. Bake at Gas No. 3 (325°F/160°C) for 30 minutes, until the sauce is bubbling very slightly and the fish has lost its glassy appearance. Take off the paper and grill gently for 3–4 minutes, until a rich golden brown, then serve at once.

VARIATION

Sauté 8 oz (225 g/2½ cups) sliced button mushrooms with the spring onions for 5 minutes, until any liquid has disappeared. Turn into a bowl and season with 1½ teaspoons of salt and ¼ of a teaspoon of nutmeg. Divide the mixture between the fish fillets, roll up and arrange on the potatoes as before.

POACHED FISH FILLETS IN A RICH WINE SAUCE

Serves 6–8.
Leftovers keep 1 day under refrigeration.
Freeze 1 month.

This is a sumptuous dish for a dinner party, not to be undertaken lightly. However, it can be cooked ahead then reheated (see instructions at end of recipe). The ideal fish to use is prime Dover Sole, but if this is not available, thick fillets of lemon sole, baby halibut or plaice can be used. However, it is essential to have all the fish bones and heads to make the fish stock, which adds so much to the flavour of the sauce.

5½–6½ lb (2.5–3 kg) whole Dover Sole, lemon sole, baby halibut or plaice (2½ lb/1 kg when filleted), giving 6–8 good-sized fillets or 12–16 smaller ones
bones and heads from the fish
2 tbsp finely chopped shallots or spring onion (scallion) bulbs
5 fl oz (150 ml/⅔ cup) dry white wine
5 fl oz (150 ml/⅔ cup) fish stock (see below)
a few black peppercorns
1 small bay leaf
sprig of parsley
1 oz (25 g/2 tbsp) butter for greasing the cooking dish
8 oz (225 g/2 cups) button mushrooms
nut of butter

For the sauce

10 fl oz (275 ml/1¼ cups) strained poaching liquid (see method)
1½ oz (40 g/3 tbsp) butter worked to a paste with 1 oz (25 g/¼ cup) flour
8 fl oz (225 ml/1 cup) double (heavy) cream
salt and black pepper to taste
2 heaped tbsp grated sharp cheese (mature Cheddar, for example)
nut of butter

First make the fish stock. Remove the dark skin from the fillets and put it with the fish bones and heads into a pan, cover with 2 pints (1.25 1/5 cups) of cold water and simmer, uncovered, for 30 minutes, or until the liquid is reduced to a cupful. Strain and reserve.

To poach the fish, set the oven at Gas No. 6 (400°F/200°C). Butter a baking tin or dish just large enough to hold the rolled fish in one layer and scatter the shallots on the bottom. Salt the fish lightly on both sides, then roll up (or fold in half if too thick) and lay on top. Pour in the wine and stock, scatter with the peppercorns and tuck in the bay leaf and parsley sprig. Cover with foil and cook for 20 minutes, or until the fish has lost its translucent appearance. Remove from the oven and turn the heat down to Gas No. ½ (250°F/120°C).

While the fish is cooking, slice the mushrooms thinly into a pan containing the nut of butter. Sprinkle them lightly with salt (to bring out the juices), cover and simmer for 5 minutes, then uncover and cook until the liquid has evaporated. Put on the lid and keep warm.

Lift the cooked fish out of its liquor with a slotted fish slice and drain on paper towels. Arrange the cooked mushrooms in a 10–12-inch-long (25–30-cm) gratin dish and lay the cooked fillets side by side on top. Keep warm in the oven. Measure the fish liquor into a small pan and bring to the boil, then add the creamed butter and flour mixture, a teaspoonful at a time, whisking constantly. Now whisk in the cream and bubble gently until the sauce will coat the back of the spoon. Add salt and pepper to taste, then pour the sauce evenly over the fish. Sprinkle with the cheese and dot with the butter.

To serve at once Grill gently until a rich golden brown.

To serve later Allow the dish to cool completely and cover with foil. Half an hour before it is required, reheat until bubbly round the edges (15–20 minutes in a moderate oven, 5 minutes in a microwave, covered with clingfilm/saranwrap). Then grill gently until a rich golden brown.

VARIATION

Omit the mushroom bed. Instead remove the pips from 6 oz (175 g/1 cup) muscatel grapes, then arrange in the centre of the dish, surround with the cooked fillets and coat with the sauce. Grill as described above.

Fresh Salmon and Its Sauces

It is rare indeed to find salmon cooked to perfection – the flesh silky and moist on the tongue. No matter how large the portion of fish, if it is to be served cold it should not be at simmering point for longer than 10 minutes; the cooking is continued as the fish cooks in the cooking liquor. Salmon keeps its delicate colour better if neither lemon nor vinegar is added to the cooking liquor.

TO FREEZE SALMON

Raw salmon must be of superb quality and guaranteed freshness – you should have it direct from the fishmonger – if it is to be frozen in the domestic freezer. The salmon can be frozen whole or in cuts or steaks. The viscera should be removed, but do not wash the fish. Wrap in clingfilm (saranwrap) and then in foil or a plastic bag. However, with salmon now available throughout the year from fish farms, I see no reason for freezing it (with an inevitable change in texture) other than in exceptional circumstances.

Cooked salmon does freeze but it is so much better freshly cooked that I would do so only with leftovers.

TO POACH A WHOLE SALMON

Cooked fish will keep under refrigeration for 3 days. Leftovers freeze 3 months.

Ask the fishmonger to scale the fish, clean out the viscera (without slitting the belly too far) and remove the eyes but leave on the head (if it will fit into your cooking utensil). Lay the fish on the drainer of a fish kettle and cover with cold water. To each ½ pint (275 ml/1¼ cups) water used, add 2 level teaspoons of salt and a little white pepper. Cover the fish kettle and bring the water very slowly to the boil – this should take at least half an hour. Allow to simmer for 1 minute to the pound (5 minutes minimum).

To serve the whole salmon hot Turn out the heat but leave the salmon in the covered fish kettle for half an hour. Drain on its strainer, covered with a paper towel, for 5 minutes, then skin and serve whole or in portions.

To serve the whole salmon cold Remove from the heat and leave to cool in the cooking liquor (this will take a minimum of 3 hours). Do not refrigerate if it is to be served the same day. Skin and serve in the same way as hot salmon.

TO BAKE A WHOLE SALMON IN FOIL

Cooked fish will keep under refrigeration for 3 days and will freeze for 3 months.

This is an excellent method of cooking several fish at once, or a single fish if there is no fish kettle available. You can use the method whether the fish is to be served hot or cold.

Lightly grease a sheet of foil (large enough to enclose the fish) using corn or sunflower oil if it is to be served cold, butter if it is to be served hot. Lay the fish on top and wrap securely so that no juices can escape, but do not mould the foil too close or the heat cannot circulate. Bake in a moderate oven, Gas No. 4 (350°F/180°C) for 10 minutes to the pound and 10 minutes over. A 4-lb (1.75 kg) salmon with head on will take 50 minutes, a 5-lb (2.25 kg) salmon will take 60 minutes. Leave for 15 minutes in the foil, then unwrap.

If the fish is to be served hot, test by inserting a knife into the backbone - the fish should look pale pink and creamy and come away easily when lifted. If you are serving it cold, leave it to cool in the foil; to skin and bone a whole fish, see below.

WHOLE SALMON IN THE MICROWAVE WITH A STRAWBERRY AND CUCUMBER SALAD

Serves 6–8.

This is an excellent method of cooking a medium-size fish. Whole cooked salmon can be kept for 3 days in the refrigerator, but its texture is at its peak about 2 hours after cooking. If the salmon is to be served warm, allow it to rest in the kitchen for 15–30 minutes - the delicate flavour can be obscured if the fish is too warm.

1 x 3½ lb (1.5 kg) salmon
salt
white pepper

For the salad dressing
2 level tbsp caster sugar or granulated sweetener
½ teasp salt
2 tbsp boiling water
4 tbsp white wine vinegar
1 tbsp fresh dill or mint

For the salad
1 fat cucumber
1 lb (450 g) strawberries

About 2 hours before dinner make the dressing by dissolving the sugar and salt in the boiling water, then stirring in the vinegar and finely snipped dill or chopped mint. Allow to cool. For the salad, finely slice the unpeeled cucumber and thickly slice the hulled strawberries. Reserve a few slices of both to garnish the salmon, then arrange the remainder decoratively in a shallow gratin or quiche dish. Pour over the cooled dressing.

To cook the salmon, line a 9-inch (22.5-cm) soufflé dish with clingfilm (saranwrap). Remove the head from the salmon and sprinkle the well-washed body cavity with salt and pepper. Curl the fish round in the dish, then cover with punctured clingfilm and cook on 100 per cent power for 9½ minutes. Uncover, cover the tail section with a scrap of foil to prevent it from drying out, then re-cover the fish and cook for a further 1½ minutes. Leave the fish to cool, then carefully skin and arrange on a serving dish. Decorate with the reserved strawberries and cucumber slices and serve with the salad.

TO SKIN AND BONE A WHOLE COOKED SALMON

Follow this step-by-step procedure:

1 Using a long, thin-bladed sharp knife, cut through the skin along the length of the backbone, across the tail and around the head.
2 Using the blade of the knife, peel off the skin and pull off the fins.
3 With the back of the knife, scrape away the shallow layer of brown-coloured flesh over the centre of the fish.
4 Turn the salmon over and repeat, and then cut down along the backbone.
5 Turn the knife flat, ease the fillet gently from the bone and lift off (with a large fish this may have to be done in 2 pieces).
6 At the head and tail, cut through the bone with scissors and peel the bones away. Replace the upper fillet.

By tradition the fish is coated with aspic or aspic mayonnaise. However, it is much simpler - and very effective - to cover the fish completely with thin overlapping slices of cucumber, and present on a bed of curly lettuce leaves.

WHOLE FILLETED SALMON WITH A LIME AND WATERCRESS SAUCE

Serves 8.
Keeps 2 days under refrigeration.
Freeze leftover fish and sauce for 1 month.

Perhaps the best way to combine convenience and flavour is to have a salmon both filleted and skinned, then cook it in the oven with a little wine to keep it moist and juicy - the cooking time will be less than for bone-in fish. These fish juices can then be used in a delectable sauce to serve over each portion of salmon. If you do not wish to make a sauce based on the cooking liquid, omit it altogether. Instead ask the fishmonger for the bones of the fish and lay them in between the two fillets to help keep the salmon juicy. Discard just before portioning. Serve cold.

1 x 3½–4 lb (1.5–1.75 kg) salmon or salmon trout
sea salt
white pepper
1 tbsp flavourless oil
several sprigs of fresh tarragon
2 shallots or large spring onion bulbs (scallions)
10 fl oz (275 ml/1¼ cups) fish or weak vegetable stock or dry white wine, such as Riesling

For the sauce
2 bunches very fresh watercress
poaching liquid from the fish
grated rind and juice of 1 lime
5 fl oz (150 ml/⅔ cup) each double (heavy) and soured cream or 8% fromage frais
1 teasp wholegrain mustard
½ tsp salt
10 grinds of black pepper
1 teasp sugar or granular sweetener

Preheat the oven to Gas No. 5 (375°F/190°C), and lightly oil a double piece of wide foil large enough to parcel the salmon. Lay the foil in a baking tin, place a fillet on top and season lightly with salt and white pepper. Sprinkle with a very little oil and lay the sprigs of tarragon on top. Lay the second fillet on top of the first, re-forming the fish.

Heat the shallots and wine until steaming (top of stove or microwave), then pour over and around the fish and seal it in a parcel. With your hands, gently mould it into a rounded shape like a whole fish. Bake for 30 minutes, open carefully and check that it is pale pink right through, then pour the juices through a sieve into a small pan. Rewrap the fish and leave it to go cold. Boil the fish juices down to 3 fl oz, then chill until quite cold.

To make the sauce, cut the stalks from the watercress, leaving a little bouquet in water to use as a garnish. Put the remaining leaves into the food processor, together with the chilled poaching liquid and all the remaining ingredients. Process until the watercress is finely chopped and the sauce is thick enough to coat the back of a wooden spoon. Pour into a jug and refrigerate.

To serve, portion the fish and spoon some of the sauce over each piece of fillet, then serve garnished with the reserved watercress.

VARIATION

WHOLE FILLETED SALMON WITH A DELICATE WINE AND CREAM SAUCE (SERVED WARM)

Serves 6–8.
Keeps 2 days under refrigeration.
Freeze leftover fish and sauce 1 month.

For the sauce

poaching liquid from the fish
1½ oz (40 g/3 tbsp) butter
1 oz (25 g/¼ cup) flour
5 fl oz (150 ml/⅔ cup) double (heavy) cream
5 fl oz (150 ml/⅔ soured cream or 8% fromage frais
1 tbsp fresh chopped fennel or dill

For the garnish

several sprigs fennel or dill
cooked asparagus spears

Cook the salmon as in the previous recipe, using 10 fl oz (275 ml/1¼ cups) wine as the cooking liquid. After pouring this liquid into the saucepan, turn the oven down to its lowest temperature, close the parcel again and return it to the oven. The fish can now be kept hot for up to an hour.

To make the sauce, remove the shallots from the saucepan with a slotted spoon and bring the liquid to simmering point. Cream together the butter and flour (beurre manié) and add to the liquid in the saucepan a teaspoon at a time, whisking with a small balloon whisk after each addition. Slowly stir in the creams with a wooden spoon and bubble gently until the sauce will coat the back of the spoon. Taste and reseason if necessary, then stir in the chopped herbs.

To serve, put a platter (long enough to hold the fish) to warm in the oven. Open the parcel of fish, then invert the warm platter on top and turn them over together so that the fish is in position on the dish. Discard the foil. Spoon the hot sauce over the fish. Garnish with herb sprigs and asparagus spears. Serve at once.

TO POACH A CUT OF SALMON

This will keep 3 days under refrigeration and will freeze for 3 months.

Place the washed and salted fish on a double piece of greaseproof paper or foil greased with a little oil, then fold into a parcel, securing it if necessary with loosely tied string. Put it in a pan and cover with cold water. Add 2 level teaspoons salt and a speck of pepper and bring slowly to the boil.

To serve hot Reduce the heat and allow to *simmer* (but never boil) for 6 minutes to the pound and 6 minutes extra. Lift out, drain well, unwrap and serve.

To serve cold When the water comes to the boil bubble for 3 minutes only, then remove from the heat and leave the fish in the covered pan until the liquid is cold - at least 3 hours. It can be kept in the liquid for up to 3 days under refrigeration. Skin, portion and foil-cover when required.

TO POACH SALMON STEAKS ON TOP OF THE STOVE

Lightly butter a large frying pan. Lay in the salmon steaks and add 6 fl oz (175 ml/¾ cup) of water or fish stock for 4 steaks, 12 fl oz (350 ml/1½ cups) for 8 steaks. Bring to simmering point, cover and simmer - never boil - for 10 minutes, turning the fish once.

POACHED SALMON STEAKS IN THE MICROWAVE

Serves 4.
Keeps 3 days under refrigeration.
Leftovers keep 3 months in the freezer.

4 x 6 oz (175 g) salmon steaks
5 fl oz (150 ml/⅔ cup) fish stock
squeeze of lemon juice
salt
white pepper

Arrange the washed steaks round the edge of a quiche dish, with the thin part to the centre. Pour on the stock and lemon juice and cover, then cook on 100 per cent power for 6 minutes, turning fish over after 3 minutes. Leave to stand for 5 minutes, then sprinkle lightly with salt and pepper.

EASY HOLLANDAISE SAUCE
(*Blender or Food-processor Method*)

Serves 8.
Use the same day.
Do not freeze.

This is easy in comparison with the classic method! It is essential that both the liquids and the butter are thoroughly heated before they are added to the yolks.

2 tbsp lemon juice
1 tbsp white wine vinegar
9 oz (250 g/1 cup plus 2 tbsp) butter or margarine
4 egg yolks
1 teasp caster sugar
pinch of salt

Place lemon juice and vinegar in a small pan. Melt the fat in another pan. Heat the lemon juice and vinegar until bubbling. In the blender or processor, blend egg yolks, sugar and salt for 2 seconds. When the vinegar mixture is boiling, trickle into the blender or food processor, processing all the time. Do the same with the foaming butter or margarine, trickling it in until you have a thick, smooth sauce. Keep warm, if desired, in a basin standing in a pan of warm water.

VARIATIONS

SAUCE BÉARNAISE

Stir in 2 tablespoons of chopped fresh tarragon or 2 teaspoons of the dried herb after the butter or margarine has been added.

AVOCADO HOLLANDAISE

Peel 1 small, very ripe avocado and remove the stone. Purée the flesh in the food processor or blender, then remove. There is no need to wash the bowl. Make the sauce as above, then pulse or blend in the avocado purée.

TARRAGON AND LEMON SAUCE

Serves 6–8.
Keeps 2 days under refrigeration.
Do not freeze.

A light, delicately flavoured sauce to serve with any poached fish. It's especially good with salmon.

15 fl oz (425 ml/2 cups) fish or weak vegetable stock
4 egg yolks
1 tbsp cornflour (cornstarch)
3 tbsp fresh lemon juice
8 grinds of black pepper
10 grinds sea salt
3 teasp caster sugar
1 tbsp chopped fresh tarragon

Process all the ingredients except the tarragon in the food processor for 5 seconds until thoroughly mixed. Turn into a thick-based pan and stir over medium heat until the mixture thickens and lightly coats the back of a wooden spoon. Stir in the tarragon. Leave to thicken overnight in the refrigerator. Serve at room temperature.

SALMON STEAKS IN SOURED CREAM SAUCE

Serves 6.
Keeps 1 day under refrigeration.
Do not freeze.

An unctuous partnership of silky salmon and delicate wine sauce.

6 x 6 oz (175 g) salmon steaks, ¾ inch (2 cm) thick
1 oz (25 g/2 tbsp) butter
1 level teasp salt
2 shallots or 4 spring onion bulbs (scallions) finely chopped
1 tbsp lemon juice
2 bay leaves, crumbled
4 fl oz (125 ml/½ cup) dry white wine, such as Chablis
4 fl oz (125 g/½ cup) fish stock
1 oz (25 g/2 tbsp) butter plus 1 tbsp flour for beurre manié
5 fl oz (150 ml/⅔ cup) fromage frais, soured cream or Greek-style yoghurt

For the garnish
chopped parsley

Preheat the oven to Gas No. 5 (375°F/190°C). Wash salmon steaks, then drain well. Smear 1 oz (25 g/2 tbsp) butter over the bottom and sides of a baking dish wide enough to hold the fish in one layer. Arrange the steaks in it side by side and sprinkle with salt, onions, lemon juice and bay leaves. Add the wine and fish stock. Cover with foil and bake for 15-20 minutes, basting once, until the fish flakes easily with a fork. (In a suitable dish, wide enough to hold the fish in one layer, this takes 10 minutes on top of the stove, but make sure the liquid barely bubbles.)

Meanwhile, with a fork work together the butter and flour for the beurre manié.

Lift the cooked fish out of the baking dish, then strain the cooking liquid into a small pan. Skin the fish (but leave on the bone) and return to the washed baking dish or a heatproof serving platter. Loosely cover with foil and keep warm (for up to 30 minutes) at Gas No. ¼ (225°F/110°C). Bring the fish liquor to the simmer, then add the beurre manié a teaspoon at a time, whisking all the time. Finally, stir in the fromage frais. Taste, then pour over the steaks, masking them completely. Alternatively, the sauce may be made ahead and gently reheated just before serving.

Grill for 3 minutes until golden brown. Sprinkle with parsley and serve.

Note For 8-10, use 8-10 salmon steaks and 10 fl oz (275 ml/1¼ cups) of fromage frais, soured cream or Greek-style yoghurt.

GRILLED SALMON

Serves 4-6.
Leftovers keep 2 days under refrigeration.

Grilled salmon must be served as soon as it is cooked, or the flesh may become dry and heavy.

4-6 centre steaks of salmon, ¾-1 inch (2-2.5 cm) thick
2 oz (50 g/¼ cup) butter
flour or dry breadcrumbs
juice of 1 lemon
salt
black pepper

Wash, salt and then dab dry the salmon. In the grill pan melt the butter until it stops foaming, then place each steak in it, and immediately turn over. Grill for 3 minutes only, turn and grill a further 7 minutes, until the flesh begins to shrink from the bones. At this stage you can dust the fish with a little flour or a few dry breadcrumbs, baste with the butter and turn up the heat for a further minute to brown the fish. Lift the fish on to a warm dish and add the lemon juice to the pan juices, together with a little salt and black pepper. Stir well and pour over the fish.

VARIATION

QUICK PIQUANT SAUCE

Lift the cooked fish on to a serving dish. Add 5 fl oz (150 ml/$\frac{2}{3}$ cup) soured cream or creamy (8%) fromage frais and the juice of half a lemon to the juices in the grill pan. Stir under a gentle grill until warm, then pour over the salmon.

FILLETS OF SALMON UNDER A CRUSHED PECAN CRUST

Serves 6–8.
Serve the same day.

My colleague Sula Leon and I developed this recipe for our Master Classes in Food and Wine. It has proved one of our most popular ever recipes because it combined simplicity with superb flavour and juiciness. It can also be served cold.

1½–2 lb (675–900 g) thick salmon fillet, cut into 6–8 pieces
salt
white pepper
reduced-calorie mayonnaise

For the crust
8 oz (225 g/2 cups) shelled pecans
4 tbsp snipped fresh chives
1½ oz (40 g/3 tbsp) unsalted butter, melted

In the food processor, grind the nuts until like coarse sand, then mix with the chives and melted butter in a small bowl. Lightly grease with butter a shallow tin wide enough to hold the pieces of salmon in one layer. Arrange them in this dish and season lightly with the salt and pepper, then spread the surface with a thin layer of mayonnaise and cover completely with the nut mixture, patting it on well. Leave until shortly before serving.

15 minutes before serving, put in a preheated oven, Gas No. 7 (425°F/220°C), for 8–10 minutes, or until the salmon flakes easily with a fork. Keep warm until required.

TWICE-BAKED SALMON SOUFFLÉS

Serves 6–8.
Cook and serve the same day.

These are first cooked 2 hours or so before the meal. Yes, they do collapse as they wait, but once they're put back in the oven under a coating of savoury cream 15 minutes before serving, they rise triumphantly once again. You will need the larger quantity of cream if the soufflés are turned out into individual shallow cocottes, or you can omit the cream altogether and substitute an equal quantity of a coating consistency white sauce flavoured with dill.

For the soufflés
2 oz (50 g/¼ cup) butter or margarine
2 oz (50 g/½ cup) flour
10 fl oz (275 ml/1¼ cups) milk
1 teasp salt
¼ teasp white pepper
2 teasp tomato purée
1 teasp dried tarragon
2 oz (50 g/½ cup) Gruyère cheese, grated
4 eggs, separated
7 oz (200 g) cooked salmon or 10 oz (275 g) raw fillet

For the sauce
½ teasp salt
10 grinds of black pepper
1 tbsp fresh dill, snipped, or 1 tsp dried
10–15 fl oz (275–425 ml/1¼–2 cups) whipping cream
2 oz (50 g/½ cup) Gruyère cheese, grated

Preheat the oven to Gas No. 5 (375°F/190°C). Put a roasting tin half-filled with hot water in the oven. Butter 6–8 teacups.

Put the butter or margarine, flour and milk into a heavy-based pan and whisk together over medium heat until thickened. Bubble 3 minutes, then stir in the salt, pepper, tomato purée and tarragon. Take off the heat and add the cheese. Separate the eggs, dropping yolks into the hot sauce and whisking well after each addition. Put the whites in a large bowl. Finally, stir the skinned and flaked salmon into the hot sauce.

Whisk the whites with a pinch of salt until they hold soft, glossy peaks and *stir* a quarter of the resulting mixture into the sauce to lighten it, then fold in the rest using a rubber spatula. Divide between the prepared cups, then arrange in the roasting tin and cook for 20 minutes.

Remove from the oven and the roasting tin, cool 10 minutes, then carefully loosen round the edges with a knife and turn out into individual gratin dishes or one large one. The soufflés can now be left at room temperature for up to 2 hours.

When ready to cook, preheat the oven to Gas No. 8 (450°F/230°C). Add the seasonings and herbs to the cream, then pour over and around the souffles and scatter with the cheese. Bake for 15 minutes until well risen and bubbling. Serve at once with the sauce.

SALMON KEDGEREE

Serves 4.
Keeps 2 days under refrigeration.
Do not freeze.

A delicious variation of the classic recipe, this can be served as a main course or (using margarine) as a starter for 6 before a cold-meat main course.

1 tbsp oil
1 shallot or a small bunch of spring onion bulbs (scallions), finely chopped
8 oz (225 g/1⅓ cups) long-grain rice or 7 oz (200 g) packet rice and wild rice mixed
4 tbsp dry white wine (optional)
1 pint (575 ml/2½ cups) fish stock, or 1 pint (575 ml/2½ cups) water plus 1 fish stock-cube
1 tbsp lemon juice
½ teasp salt
8 grinds of black pepper
8 oz (225 g) fresh salmon fillet, skinned
4 hard-boiled eggs
1 oz (25 g/2 tbsp) butter or margarine
1 tbsp chopped parsley
1 oz (25 g/¼ cup) flaked almonds

In an 8-inch (20-cm) lidded frying pan, heat the oil and fry the onion until soft and creamy gold in colour, then add the rice and toss over a high heat for 1 minute. Add the wine (if used) and bubble until it has almost evaporated, then add the fish stock, lemon juice, salt and pepper, and bring to the boil. Cover tightly and simmer gently for about 20 minutes, until the rice is bite-tender (taste it). Cut the salmon into ½-inch (1-cm) chunks and add to the rice, cover and cook for a further 5 minutes, stirring occasionally, over gentle heat until the fish is cooked. Stir in the chopped eggs, butter or margarine and parsley, and mix with a fork. Turn into a heatproof serving dish and sprinkle with the almonds. Just before serving, pop under a hot grill for 2 minutes until golden brown.

Halibut

GRILLED HALIBUT IN ALMOND BUTTER

Serves 4.
Leftovers keep 2 days under refrigeration.

Large halibut are rare and expensive, but the flavour of the freshly landed fish (*not* frozen) when simply grilled with butter can hardly be bettered. First-quality fresh hake, haddock and cod can also be cooked this way.

1–1½ lb (450 g–675 g) halibut, cut from centre, in ¾-in (2-cm) steaks
½ teasp salt
10 grinds of black pepper
2 oz (50 g/¼ cup) butter plus ½ oz (15 g/1 tbsp)
a little flour
1 oz (25 g/¼ cup) blanched flaked almonds
juice of ½ a lemon

Salt and pepper the fish. Melt the butter in the grill pan, put in the fish and turn to coat it. Cook for 2 minutes under moderate heat on one side, turn, sprinkle with flour and grill very gently, basting once, for 10–12 minutes, depending on thickness. Lift out on to a warm plate. Add the further ½ oz butter to the grill pan, together with the almonds. Cook under the grill until the almonds turn pale gold, then add the lemon juice and seasonings, pour over the fish and serve at once.

BAKED HALIBUT CRÉOLE

Serves 4–6.
Leftovers keep 2 days under refrigeration.
Do not freeze.

This dish has its own built-in sauce which prevents the fish from drying out in the oven. It can be prepared in the morning and then baked just before dinner.

1 oz (25 g/2 tbsp) butter
1 small onion, finely chopped
1 clove of garlic, finely chopped
4 large tomatoes, skinned and chopped (or the equivalent canned)
1 large red or yellow pepper, seeded and diced
1½–2 lb (675–900 g) halibut, cut into 4–6 steaks
good pinch of dried oregano
good pinch of mild chilli powder
1 level teasp salt
10 grinds of black pepper
4 heaped tbsp dry breadcrumbs, tossed in 2 oz (50 g/¼ cup) melted butter, mixed with 2 rounded tbsp grated mature Cheddar or Gouda cheese

Melt the butter and in it cook the onion and garlic until golden, then add the tomatoes and pepper and cook for 2–3 minutes, until the butter has been absorbed. Butter well a shallow oven-to-table casserole and arrange the steaks in it. Add the seasoning to the buttered vegetables and divide them evenly between the fish steaks. Cover with a layer of the crumb mixture. Refrigerate until half an hour before dinner. Bake in a hot oven, Gas No. 6 (400°F/200°C) for half an hour, until the fish flakes easily with a fork and the topping is golden.

SAMAK KEBAB

Serves 6–8.
Keeps 1 day under refrigeration.
Do not freeze.

For this unusual recipe I have borrowed a Turkish way of marinating cubes of fish in a spicy sauce. This has a dramatic effect on even the least exotic varieties such as cod and haddock – even frozen halibut is quite transformed. The marinade softens the texture of the fish, while the spices add extra zing. Kebabs prepared by this method are best hot off the grill or barbecue, but they're still delicious eaten at room temperature up to an hour after cooking.

2–3 lb (900 g–1.25 kg) filleted fish (halibut, sea bass, haddock or cod)
2 large onions
8 tbsp lemon juice
2 teasp ground cumin
2 fat cloves of garlic, finely chopped
1 teasp paprika
1 teasp sea salt
20 grinds of black pepper
4 tbsp olive oil

For the garnish
coarsely chopped parsley
lemon wedges
paprika

Cut the fish into 1-inch (2.5-cm) cubes and put in one layer in a shallow dish. Skin, grate and extract juice from onions, then mix together in a small basin all ingredients except olive oil. Pour this marinade over fish. Leave for at least an hour, turning 2–3 times. Thread the fish on to wooden skewers and brush all over with the olive oil. The dish can be prepared to this stage early in the day. To cook, grill for 6–8 minutes until golden, turning frequently.

To serve, arrange the coarsely chopped parsley on an oval fish platter, lay the fish on top and garnish with the lemon wedges and an extra dusting of paprika.

Trout and Its Sauces

RAINBOW TROUT

For fish to be cooked whole, choose those weighing between 8 oz (225 g) and 12 oz (350 g).

TROUT BAKED IN FOIL

Freeze 1 month, but texture may deteriorate.
This recipe keeps the fish juicy and completely fat-free.

For each person
1 x 8–12 oz (225–350 g) trout, head removed and cleaned
flavourless oil for brushing on foil
fish seasoning or fine sea salt
black pepper
1 tbsp lemon juice
1 tsp dried onion flakes (optional)

Set the oven at Gas No. 4 (350°F/180°C). Cut a piece of foil large enough to make a loose parcel around the fish. Grease it lightly with oil, lay the fish in the centre, season the inside lightly with the salt, pepper, lemon juice and onion flakes, if used. Fold up into a loose but airtight parcel. Put in the oven and allow 20 minutes for an 8 oz (225 g) trout, 25 minutes for a 12 oz (350 g) one.

To serve, leave for 5 minutes after taking from the oven and then unwrap, skin and arrange on a plate. Serve with or without the juice, as preferred. The trout can be eaten hot or cold, with lemon sections, mayonnaise or a special sauce.

VARIATION

TROUT BAKED WITH WINE AND CREAM

Before enclosing each trout in foil, spoon over it 1 tbsp each of dry white wine and whipping (light) cream, and top it with a pinch of dried tarragon or a few leaves of the fresh herb. Cook it in the same way, spooning the cream and wine mixture over the skinned fish. Serve hot.

GRILLED TROUT

Have the fish gutted and cleaned but leave head on (this keeps it moist). Brush the skin lightly with oil. Grill the fish under a moderate heat for 5–10 minutes each side, depending on the thickness (a 1½-inch/4-cm-thick fish will take 15–18 minutes in total). Test by removing a little skin and see if the fish flakes easily with a fork.

To serve, remove top skin, season with salt and pepper and sprinkle with lemon juice at the table.

FILLETS OF TROUT UNDER A CHEESE CRUST

Serves 4.
Leftovers keep 1 day under refrigeration.

This method of grilling fish fillets (plaice and lemon sole can also be used) keeps them moist and flavoursome without basting. The dish can be prepared at any time up to 12 hours in advance and then can be ready for the table in 7–8 minutes.

4 large fillets of trout, skinned
salt
white pepper
approx. 3–4 tbsp reduced-calorie mayonnaise
4 level tbsp dry breadcrumbs
4 rounded tbsp grated medium Cheddar, Edam or Gouda
1 oz (25 g/2 tbsp) melted butter

Wash the fillets and season lightly with salt and white pepper, then arrange side by side in a lightly oiled grill-proof dish that can go to the table.

Spread each fillet with a thin coating of the mayonnaise. In a bowl mix the breadcrumbs, the cheese and the melted butter, then pat on top of the fillets, covering them completely.

Grill under moderate heat for 7 minutes, until the topping is a rich golden brown and the fish flakes easily with a fork.

TROUT WITH ALMONDS COOKED IN THE MICROWAVE

Serves 4.
Keeps 2 days under refrigeration.
Freeze 1 month.

This method saves pre-heating a conventional oven. The buttered almond garnish can be omitted and the lemon juice alone poured over the fish.

4 x 8 oz (225 g) trout
4 tbsp fresh tarragon, chopped, or ½ tsp dried
½ teasp salt

For the garnish
2 oz (50 g/¼ cup) butter or margarine
2 oz (50 g/½ cup) flaked almonds
3 tbsp lemon juice
10 grinds of black pepper

Have the fish cleaned and the heads removed. Wash the body cavity, sprinkle with the herbs and salt, then lay in a shallow serving dish, side by side but head to tail. Cover and cook on 100 per cent power for 8 minutes.

Leave to stand, covered, for 5 minutes while you prepare the garnish.

In a medium bowl, melt the butter on 100 per cent power for 1½ minutes (cover with a paper towel to avoid splashing). Add the almonds and cook uncovered on 100 per cent power for 3½ minutes, until golden brown, then stir in the lemon juice and black pepper.

Uncover the fish and carefully remove the top skin, then pour over the sauce and reheat, uncovered, on 100 per cent power for 1 minute. Serve at once.

For a completely fat-free dish, omit the butter. Spread the almonds on a plate and cook on 100 per cent power for 3½ minutes, then mix with the lemon juice.

FRIED TROUT
(*Truite Meunière*)

Serves 3–4.

I rarely fry trout today, preferring the low-fat methods such as grilling and baking. However, for the occasional special meal this method does produce a wonderfully flavoursome dish.

To serve a larger number, either use 2 frying pans or cook in 2 batches.

3–4 x 8–10 oz (225–275 g) trout

To coat the fish
2 oz (50 g/½ cup) flour
1 teasp salt
speck of white pepper

To fry the fish
2 oz (50 g/½ cup) butter
2 tsp oil

You will need a large, heavy frying pan, wide enough to hold 3-4 fish side by side.

Have the fish cleaned through the gills, leaving the head intact, as this will prevent the fish from getting greasy when it is cooked.

Put the coating flour on to a square of greaseproof paper or a shallow dish as long as the fish. Wash and salt the fish, and allow them to drain in a colander for 10 minutes. Then lift them by the tail and, 1 at a time, roll them quickly in the flour, making sure each fish is coated thinly but completely. This gives a light but crisp coating. Heat the empty frying pan for 2 minutes, then put in the butter and the oil. The minute the butter starts to foam, lower in the fish side by side, making sure the underside of each fish is lying flat in the bubbling fat. Cook steadily at a gentle bubble for 5 minutes, by which time the underside should be a rich crisp brown. Carefully turn over each fish, using 2 spoons so that you do not pierce the flesh. Fry the second side for a further 5 minutes, then lift out and put side by side in a shallow entrée dish, and keep hot (for up to 30 minutes) in the oven at Gas No. 2 (300°F/150°C).

VARIATION

TRUITE AUX AMANDES (Classic Method)

When the fish are cooked, pour away any over-browned butter, wipe out the pan with kitchen paper, and put another 2 oz (50 g/$1/4$ cup) of butter into it. Allow the butter to heat and foam, then throw in a handful (about 2 oz/50 g/$1/2$ cup) of split almonds. Let them cook for 2 or 3 minutes until golden, then add the juice of a lemon and plenty of black pepper. Swirl around the pan, pour over the trout and serve at once.

TRUITE PÈRE LOUIS

Serves 3–4.

Père Louis used to serve this dish at his hotel in Montmorillon, in the heart of provincial France, where it is the custom to select the live fish from a tank, then stun, gut and cook it to order. The ideal fish for this recipe weighs between 8 and 10 oz (225–275 g). The butter and the lemon juice 'point up' the flavour of a really fine trout. Some 30 years on, I cannot improve on the original recipe.

Cook the fish as for Truite Meunière (see p. 83). Shortly before serving, make the following sauce:

2 tbsp brandy
8 fl oz (225 ml/1 cup) whipping cream
2 teasp lemon juice
salt
black pepper
2 oz (50 g/$1/2$ cup) flaked almonds

After the fish has been cooked and removed from the pan, discard all but 2 tablespoons of the buttery juices. To them add the brandy, cream and lemon juice. Bubble until of a coating consistency, season, then pour over the fish and decorate with the almonds.

Note For 6 fish, use same amount of sauce ingredients but increase cream to 10 fl oz (275 ml/1$1/4$ cups).

SESAME SAUCE FOR TROUT

Sufficient for 4 fish.

1 oz (25 g) butter or margarine
1 tbsp sesame oil
1 oz (25 g) white sesame seeds
3 tbsp fresh lemon juice
5 tbsp fish or vegetable stock
pinch of salt
speck of white pepper

In a small saucepan melt the butter or margarine and sesame oil, then add the sesame seeds and sauté gently until they are golden brown, tossing them in the pan several times. Add the remaining ingredients and bring to the boil, then simmer until the liquid is reduced by half. When the fish are cooked, transfer to individual plates and remove skin. Reheat the sauce and spoon over the fish. Serve at once.

ITALIAN ANCHOVY SAUCE FOR BAKED OR GRILLED TROUT

Sufficient for 6–8 fish.
Do not freeze.

1 x 2 oz (50 g) can anchovy fillets, well drained
2 oz (50g/¼ cup) unsalted butter
8 fl oz (225 ml/1 cup) dry white wine
2 tbsp lemon juice
2 teasp chopped parsley
10 grinds of black pepper

Rinse the anchovy fillets in cold water, then drain, dry and roughly chop. Melt the butter in a small pan, add the chopped anchovies and stir over a moderate heat until they form a smooth mixture – about 3 minutes. Add the wine and simmer for 5 minutes to concentrate the flavour. Finally, stir in the lemon juice and herbs and season with the black pepper. Add any juices from the cooked fish, then reheat and serve.

Note The sauce can be made in advance and reheated with the fish juices just before serving with the warm fish.

Fish Plus

FILLETS OF SOLE IN HERBED PASTRY ENVELOPE WITH AN AVOCADO MAYONNAISE

Serves 6–8.
Serve the same day.

A superb dinner party dish that can be made ready for the oven well before guests arrive. (Don't get the envelopes ready more than 2 hours in advance, though, or the pastry may go soggy.)

6–8 x approx. 4 oz (125 g) fillets of lemon sole, skinned
fine sea salt
6–8 x ¾ oz (20 g) slices of smoked salmon
6 tbsp chopped parsley
2 tbsp snipped dill
2 teasp finely grated lemon rind
2 x 14 oz (400 g) packets of puff pastry

For the glaze
1 egg yolk
1 tbsp cream or top of milk

Wash and dry the fish, arrange skin-side down and sprinkle lightly with the salt. Lay a slice of smoked salmon on each fillet, and roll up from the wider end.

Divide the herbs and lemon rind in 2 and work on each packet of pastry as follows. Roll out ¼ inch (0.5 cm) thick and sprinkle with a portion of herbs and lemon rind. Press the herbs and rind into the pastry using the rolling pin – if necessary roll out the pastry further so that you have a 12-inch (30-cm) square. Divide into 4 6-inch (15-cm) squares. Lay a rolled fillet of fish diagonally, seam side down, on each square, moisten edges of pastry with water, bring the 4 corners together and pinch the edges together to seal. Arrange on a moistened baking sheet. Repeat with the second packet of pastry. Chill for 15 minutes, then glaze with the yolk mixture. Bake at No. 7 (425°F/220°C) for 23–25 minutes, or until a rich brown. (May be kept hot for 20 minutes in a slow oven – Gas No. ½/250°F/120°C.)

Serve fish envelopes with a spoonful of Avocado Mayonnaise (see p. 86). This looks particularly effective if halved and emptied limes are used as containers.

AVOCADO MAYONNAISE

Serves 6–8.
Keeps 2 days under refrigeration.

1 large, very ripe avocado, peeled, stoned and cut in roughly 1-in (2.5-cm) chunks
1–2 tbsp lemon juice
5 fl oz (150 ml/$^2/_3$ cup) reduced-calorie mayonnaise
2 rounded tbsp low-fat fromage frais or Greek-style yoghurt
10 grinds of black pepper

Purée the avocado and lemon juice in the food processor, then pulse in all the remaining ingredients. Taste and add the second tablespoon of lemon juice if too bland. Chill for several hours.

SALMON KULEBIAKA WITH DILLED FROMAGE FRAIS

Makes 2 kulebiakas, each of which will give 4–5 generous portions.
Cook and serve the same day.

A superb Russian 'pie', the rich relation of the humble pirogen. The rice noodles are a substitute for *vesiga*, the dried backbone of the sturgeon, which even if it were available, would not be kosher.

14 sheets (1 x 14 oz/400 g) packet filo pastry
4–5 oz (125–150 g) butter or margarine, melted

For the filling
2 x 14 oz (400 g) fillets fresh salmon, skinned
4 fl oz (125 ml) dry white wine
3 oz (75 g/$^1/_2$ cup) millet or buckwheat
2 oz (50 g) rice noodles (Chinese vermicelli) or fine egg vermicelli
8 oz (225 g) fresh or frozen asparagus spears
4 hard-boiled eggs, finely chopped
4 tbsp fennel or dill, finely chopped
2 tbsp lemon juice
1$^1/_2$ teasp salt
20 grinds of black pepper

For the glaze
1 egg yolk, mixed with 2 teasp cold water

For the sauce
8 fl oz (225 ml/1 cup) fromage frais, soured cream or Greek-style yoghurt
2 teasp chopped fennel
salt and pepper to taste

Cut each fillet of salmon in 2 lengthwise and lay side by side in a shallow dish. Heat the wine until steaming (1$^1/_2$ minutes on 100 per cent power in the microwave), then pour over the salmon and leave until cool.

Cook the millet or buckwheat in a pan of boiling salted water until tender but not soggy - approximately 15 minutes. Rinse, drain and spread on a plate to dry. Pour boiling water over the noodles, leave 10 minutes to soften, then rinse, drain, dry with paper towels and finely chop. Trim the asparagus spears and cook until barely tender (10–12 minutes poached in water on top of the stove or 6 minutes with 3 tbsp water in the microwave).

Preheat the oven to Gas No. 5 (375°F/190°C). Mix the millet or buckwheat, rice noodles, chopped eggs, fennel and lemon juice, then highly season with the salt and pepper. Taste and add more seasonings if necessary. Divide into 2 portions.

To make each kulebiaka, use 1 portion of filling and 7 sheets of filo pastry. Cover the other 7 with a tea-towel, as this stops them drying out. Take the pastry from the packet and lay 1 sheet on a tea-towel. Brush evenly with melted butter and then repeat with 4 more sheets, buttering them all, including the top one. Spread half of the filling in a rectangle all over the top sheet, then top with 2 more sheets, buttered as before. Spread the remaining filling on the top sheet, but leave a margin of 2 inches (5 cm) all the way round. Arrange two of the pieces of salmon on the pastry so that they form a rectangle of approximately even thickness (overlap two thin ends of the fish to achieve this). Cut each piece of asparagus in half lengthwise and then across, and arrange half of them on top of the salmon. Sprinkle lightly with salt and pepper. Fold in the two short sides of the pastry to enclose the salmon, then roll up loosely into a Swiss roll.

Transfer, join down, to a greased baking sheet and paint evenly all over with the egg glaze. Make slanting cuts at 2-inch (5-cm) intervals through the top layer of pastry (this facilitates slicing later).

Repeat with the remaining ingredients to make a second kulebiaka.

Bake for 25 minutes, or until a rich golden brown. Leave for 15 minutes before slicing.

Serve plain or with the sauce, made by mixing the fromage frais or Greek yoghurt with the fennel and seasoning to taste.

FISH PIE

Serves 10, or 4–5 twice.
Leftovers keep 2 days under refrigeration.
Freeze 1 month.
This dish freezes well, so it's worth making this quantity and freezing half.
Otherwise use half-quantities for 4–5.

Cook the mixture either in 2 foil containers or 1 large dish measuring approximately 13 x 8½ x 2-inches (33 x 21 x 5 cm) - any deeper and the potatoes may over-brown before the fish sauce has heated through.

2½ lb (1.25 kg) smoked haddock fillets
1½ pints (850 ml/3¾ cups) milk
3 oz (75 g/¾ cup) plain flour
3 oz (75 g/⅓ cup) butter
3 rounded tbsp double cream or small can evaporated milk
3 teasp dry mustard
20 grinds of black pepper
good pinch of white pepper
¼ teasp mace } *or to taste*
¼ teasp mild curry powder }
3 hard-boiled eggs, coarsely chopped
4 oz (125 g/1 cup) grated cheese

For the topping
3 lb (1.5 kg) freshly boiled potatoes
approx. 4 fl oz (125 ml/½ cup) milk
3 oz (75 g/⅓ cup) butter
1 level teasp salt
speck of white pepper

Place the fish in a saucepan, cover with cold water, bring to the boil, then immediately pour off the water. Cover the fish with the milk, bring to a gentle boil, cover with a lid and simmer very gently for 10 minutes. Lift out the fish with a slotted spoon, remove the skin, and coarsely flake the flesh.

Now make the sauce with the milk. Put it into a pan with the flour and butter and start whisking it over moderate heat using a batter whisk or balloon whisk. When it's evenly thickened, you can change over to a wooden spoon, and allow it to bubble for 3 minutes. At this stage add the cream, mustard, pepper and spices. Turn off the heat and add the chopped eggs and cheese, stirring well until the cheese melts. Finally, stir in the flaked fish, then transfer into the buttered dish.

Drain the potatoes and return them to a low light. Trickle the milk down the inside of the pan and don't start whisking (preferably with an electric whisk) the potatoes until it begins to steam. Whisk in the butter, salt and pepper.

Pile the potatoes on top of the fish and make a design with a fork. For special occasions, pipe across the top.

Bake at Gas No. 5 (375°F/190°C) for 35-40 minutes, or until the top is a rich golden brown and you can just see the filling bubbling up a little at the side.

If you make smaller pies, use Gas No. 6 (400°F/200°C) for 20-25 minutes. To keep hot, simply turn the oven down to Gas No. 1 (275°F/140°C) for up to an hour.

Canned Salmon and Tuna

SALMON FRITTERS

Makes 10 large patties.
Keep 2 days under refrigeration.
Freeze 3 months.

These fritters should be thinner than chopped fried fish. They are delicious with a parsley sauce.

2 eggs
1½ lb (675 g) canned salmon, drained then skinned, boned and flaked
2 rounded tbsp mashed potatoes (instant will do)
1 small onion, grated
½ teasp salt
parsley or chervil
1 teasp grated lemon rind
1½ level tbsp matzah meal
dry coating crumbs or matzah meal

Beat the eggs to blend, then add the well-flaked fish, potato, onion, seasoning and the matzah meal. The mixture should be just firm enough to form into patties. If too soft, add a further tablespoon of meal. Leave for half an hour. With wetted hands, take spoonfuls of the mixture and form into balls, then, using a spatula, form into patties ⅜ inch (1 cm) thick. Drop into a bowl of coating crumbs or matzah meal to get a thin coating. Fry in hot oil ¾ inch (2 cm) deep in the pan, or in a deep-fryer (375°F/190°C) for 6 minutes until a rich brown on both sides. As the patties are ready, transfer them to a heatproof dish and keep them hot in a low oven until dinnertime. They are also excellent served at room temperature.

TUNA AND MUSHROOM SOUFFLÉ

Serves 4.
Eat at once.

The soufflé has got a bad name for itself as the dish that waits for no one. True, once it's ready to come out of the oven, you can't leave it standing around - it just collapses in a heap. On the credit side, though, it won't come to any harm if you get it ready for the oven in advance. Once it's in the baking dish, you've got an hour's grace before it must be baked.

This isn't a dinner party dish but an ideal main course to serve when 4 friends want to enjoy an informal meal together.

I usually put the soufflé in the oven the minute my guests arrive, then serve a starter of dips and nibbles with drinks so that we're ready to sit down just when the soufflé has had its 35 minutes in the oven.

To achieve the perfect soufflé, richly brown and well risen, it's important to *stir* some of the beaten egg white into the sauce to lighten the texture, so that the remainder can be folded in without crushing out any air.

1 oz plus 3 oz (25 g plus 75 g/¼ cup plus ¾ cup) mature Cheddar cheese
1 x 7 oz (200 g) can tuna
4 oz (125 g/1½ cups) very fresh mushrooms
2 oz (50 g/¼ cup) butter
small bunch of spring onions (scallions)
¼ teasp ground nutmeg
1½ oz (40 g/1½ tbsp) flour
8 fl oz (225 g/1 cup) semi-skimmed milk
1 teasp salt
1 teasp Dijon mustard
1 tbsp chopped parsley
4 eggs plus 1 extra white

First butter a soufflé or other round ovenproof dish of 3-pint (1.75 l/7-cup) capacity (about 8 inches/20 cm in diameter and 3 inches/7.5 cm deep) and coat it with the 1 oz (25 g/¼ cup) of cheese, finely grated.

Drain and flake the tuna, grate the 3 oz (75 g/¾ cup) of cheese and coarsely chop the mushrooms.

In a large pan, melt the butter, add the finely chopped spring onion bulbs (including 2 inches/5 cm of the green) and the mushrooms, sprinkle with the nutmeg and cook briskly for 5 minutes, until softened. Add the flour, milk, remaining seasoning and parsley, and whisk over a moderate heat until creamily thickened - it will be quite stiff, rather than sauce-like. Cook for 3 minutes, stirring constantly, then take off the heat.

Have ready a large bowl for the egg whites. Separate the 4 eggs, stirring the yolks into the sauce one at a time and dropping the whites into the bowl, then add the extra white. Stir the tuna and the cheese into the sauce and taste. It should be highly seasoned, as the beaten egg whites will dilute the flavour. Whisk the whites with a pinch of salt until they hold glossy peaks that just topple over when the beater is withdrawn. *Stir* a quarter of this mixture into the sauce, then use a rubber spatula to *fold in* the rest. Spoon into the prepared dish and smooth level. Cover with the large bowl and leave, if desired, for up to an hour.

Preheat the oven to Gas No. 6 (400°F/200°C) - the oven must be thoroughly heated. 35 minutes before you wish to serve the soufflé, put it in the oven and turn down to Gas No. 5 (375°F/190°C). Don't be tempted to take a peek. When the time is up, check that it is well risen and a rich brown on top. Serve at once with crusty bread and a cucumber and tomato salad.

VARIATION

SALMON SOUFFLÉ

Add 1 tablespoon of tomato purée to the sauce and substitute best-quality canned salmon for the tuna.

TUNA STUFFED AUBERGINES

Serves 6–8.
Keeps 1 day under refrigeration.
Do not freeze.

A good dish for a light lunch or supper.

3–4 glossy aubergines (eggplants), approx. 8 oz (225 g) each
2 tbsp oil
1 large onion, finely chopped
1 clove of garlic, crushed
1 x 15 oz (425 g) can chopped tomatoes
1 tbsp tomato purée
1 teasp dried Italian seasoning or 1 tbsp fresh chopped herbs, including basil and parsley
½ teasp salt
10 grinds of black pepper
1 teasp brown sugar
2 x 7 oz (200 g) cans tuna
2 tbsp dry breadcrumbs
1 oz (25 g/2 tbsp) melted butter or margarine
4 oz (125 g/1 cup) grated cheese

Cut the aubergines in half lengthways. Using a spoon, carefully remove the inside flesh, leaving a ½-inch (1-cm) layer of raw aubergine in the shell. Chop the flesh roughly. Heat the oil in a lidded pan or frying pan, then add the onion and chopped aubergine and cook covered until soft and golden - about 10 minutes. Add the garlic, tomatoes, purée, herbs and all the seasoning. Bring to the boil and simmer uncovered for 10 minutes, until thick and juicy.

Drain and flake the tuna, then add to the cooked mixture. Arrange the aubergine halves side by side in a lidded casserole and divide the mixture between them. Mix the crumbs and melted fat, then add the cheese. Divide this mixture between the aubergines as well. Cover and cook for 1½ hours at Gas No. 3 (325°F/160°C), or until the aubergines feel tender when pierced with a sharp knife. If the top is not a rich brown, put under the grill for 3 minutes.

TUNA FRITTATA

Serves 4–5.
Serve hot off the pan.

A good dish for an alfresco supper - tasty, sustaining and quick to prepare. Serve with a bowl of small tomatoes and good rye bread.

½ x 2 oz (200 g) can anchovy fillets
1 x 7 oz (200 g) can tuna
6 eggs
2 tbsp cold water
½ teasp dried Italian seasoning
2 teasp chopped parsley
pinch of salt
8 grinds of black pepper
1 oz (25 g/2 tbsp) butter
1 tbsp olive oil or sunflower oil

Preheat the grill. Drain the anchovies and chop into small pieces. Drain and coarsely flake the tuna. Whisk the eggs to blend with the water, then add the herbs and seasonings, followed by the anchovies and tuna. Heat the butter and oil in an 8–9 inch (20–22.5 cm) pan, then add the egg mixture and cook slowly until golden brown underneath - about 8 minutes. Then grill *gently* until set. Serve at once.

TUNA AND CORN CASSEROLE

Serves 5–6.
Keeps 1 day under refrigeration.
Do not freeze.

A useful mid-week casserole.

1 medium can 12 oz (340 g) whole-kernel corn
1 x 7 oz (200 g) can tuna
2 hard-boiled eggs
4 oz (125 g/1 cup) short-cut macaroni
1 pint (575 ml/2½ cups) milk
1 small sweet red pepper
2 oz (50 g/¼ cup) butter or margarine
1 tbsp chopped shallot or spring onion (scallion)
2 rounded tbsp flour
1 teasp salt
pinch of white pepper
1 teasp Dijon mustard
1 teasp lemon juice
2 rounded tbsp dry coating crumbs
2 rounded tbsp finely grated cheese

Drain the corn, flake the tuna and slice the eggs. Cook and drain the macaroni. Arrange in a well-buttered gratin dish about 1½ inches (3.5 cm) deep. Heat the milk until steaming, then pour into a jug. Deseed the red pepper and cut in ⅜-inch (1-cm) squares. Rinse out pan and melt butter in it. Put in the onion and red pepper and cook gently for 5 minutes, until softened but unbrowned. Add flour and bubble for 2 minutes, take off heat, add hot milk all at once and whisk until smooth. Return to the heat and bring to the boil. Add salt, pepper, mustard and lemon juice. Simmer 2 minutes, then pour over contents of casserole. Mix crumbs and cheese and sprinkle evenly on top. If freshly made, put under a gentle grill until brown and bubbly. Otherwise reheat at Gas No. 6 (400°F/200°C) for 15–20 minutes.

TAGLIATELLE AL TONNO
Tagliatelle with Tuna

Serves 4–5.
Serve at once.
Leftovers keep 1 day under refrigeration.
Do not freeze.

A smooth, full-flavoured sauce made with ready-to-hand ingredients.

1 oz (25 g) (large bunch) parsley, finely chopped
8 fresh basil leaves
7 oz (200 g) can tuna in oil
2 oz (50 g/½ cup) shelled walnut halves
finely grated rind of 1 lemon
½ clove of garlic
1 teasp Worcestershire Sauce
6 fl oz (175 ml/¾ cup) extra virgin olive oil
20 grinds of black pepper
½ teasp salt
1 lb (450 g) tagliatelle (fresh if possible)

Process the parsley and basil leaves until finely chopped. Add the drained tuna, nuts, lemon rind, garlic and Worcestershire Sauce to the bowl and process until smooth. Add the olive oil gradually with the salt and pepper. Taste and add extra seasoning if necessary. Scoop out into a little bowl.

Add 2 teaspoons of olive oil to a very large pan of boiling salt water (this stops the pasta sticking together), add the tagliatelle and cook according to the packet instructions. (Fresh pasta will take only 3 minutes, so do not overcook.) Drain well and turn into a fairly deep, hot serving dish. Add the sauce and mix with a spoon and fork until all the strands of pasta are evenly coated. Serve at once.

INSALATA DI TONNO E PATATE
(A Salad of Tuna and New Potatoes)

Serves 6–7.
Keeps 1 day under refrigeration.
Do not freeze.

A variation on the traditional Italian tuna with beans. To allow the onion to soften and the dressing to permeate the potatoes and tuna, prepare at least 12 hours in advance, though up to 2 days will do no harm.

2 lb (900 g) new potatoes
2 x 7 oz (200 g) cans tuna, well drained
1 mild onion
1 head of salad such as frisée, cos or oakleaf
tiny sprigs of parsley

For the dressing

2 fl oz (50 ml/¼ cup) extra virgin olive oil
3 fl oz (75 ml/⅓ cup) sunflower oil
2 tbsp vine vinegar
1 tbsp lemon juice
1 teasp sugar or granular sweetener
1 teasp Dijon mustard
1 teasp salt
15 grinds of black pepper
1 clove of garlic, crushed
large handful of parsley, finely chopped

Boil the potatoes in their skins and leave to cool. Skin, then thickly slice them (in halves if very small). Drain the tuna and break into large chunks. Put both into a bowl with the onion, sliced paper-thin. Shake all the dressing ingredients together in a screw-top jar until a thick emulsion is formed. Stir gently through the first mixture, adding just enough to thoroughly moisten it. Refrigerate. To serve, arrange the salad leaves round the edge of a gratin or quiche dish or a wooden salad bowl, then spoon in the salad and decorate with the parsley sprigs.

TUNA, OLIVE AND PASTA SALAD

Serves 6.
Keeps 1 day under refrigeration.
Do not freeze.

The secret of success with pasta salads is to dress them *hot* – when they can most readily absorb the spicy flavours. If the weather is warm, it's advisable to refrigerate the salad as soon as it has been mixed, but leave it at room temperature to 'loosen up' half an hour before serving.

10 oz (275 g) fusilli (pasta spirals)
2 x 7 oz (200 g) cans tuna in oil, drained and roughly flaked
4 oz (125 g/1 cup) soft cheese such as Gouda, cut in ½-inch (1.25-cm) cubes
4 oz (125 g/1 cup) black Provençale or Greek olives
bunch of spring onions (scallions), trimmed and thinly sliced
1 medium red pepper, seeded and cut in ½-inch (1.25-cm) cubes
1 medium yellow pepper, seeded and cut in ½-inch (1.25-cm) cubes

For the dressing
2 fl oz (50 ml/¼ cup) sunflower oil
3 fl oz (75 ml/⅓ cup) olive oil
2 tbsp white wine vinegar
2 tbsp lemon juice
1 fat clove of garlic, finely chopped
2 teasp caster sugar or granular sweetener
1 teasp sea salt
15 grinds of black pepper
1 tbsp chopped parsley
2 teasp each fresh chopped basil and oregano, or 1 teasp dried fines herbes or Herbes de Provence
2 teasp Dijon mustard

Put all the dressing ingredients into a screw-top jar and shake until thickened. Put to one side.

Cook the pasta until tender – 15 minutes if dried, 4 or 5 minutes if fresh. Put all the other salad ingredients into a bowl and add the pasta, then pour on enough of the dressing to coat the ingredients (you will probably need all of it). Chill for several hours before serving.

VEGETARIAN DISHES

Vegetarian Dishes in a Hurry

Avocado and Egg Pâté	(see p. 95)
French Omelette and Variations	(see p. 100)
Omelette Basquaise	(see p. 101)
Cheese and Chive Omelette Soufflé	(see p. 101)
Scrambled Eggs and Variations	(see p. 103)
Piperrada	(see p. 104)
Israeli Cheese Pancakes	(see p. 107)
Rarebits and Variations	(see p. 110)
Spaghettini al Olive Nere	(see p. 116)
Linguine with Walnut Sauce	(see p. 116)

Meat-eating has been central to Jewish cooking ever since the dietary laws given to Moses on Mount Sinai set meat apart from other food by laying down a series of detailed rules for its preparation and serving. Because this inevitably made it an expensive commodity, it was prized for its scarcity value and was often eaten only on the Sabbath and on High Days and Holy Days.

Today, however, a growing number of Jews, as is true of the general population, are making a conscious effort to eat fewer animal foods in favour of a higher proportion of the so-called 'natural' foods or 'wholefoods' - terms that embrace a wide variety of cereals, pulses, fruits and vegetables.

Most of these people are not vegetarians in the strict sense of the word, for they do eat fish and chicken and, occasionally, meat - so 'demi-vegetarians' might be an appropriate description of their eating style.

Quite apart from the ethical considerations that motivate the vegetarian movement as a whole, there are many reasons why this type of diet is enjoying such popularity. Many Jewish students find 'eating vegetarian' an acceptable way to stay within their budgets and still keep kashrut. Many young mothers believe that a diet that is less meat-centred is good for their family's health, while older people find the lighter meals are easier on their digestion. However, nutritionists now believe that limited amounts of lean meat are a useful addition to the diet, in particular as an easily available source of iron.

Nevertheless, meatless dishes, well cooked and well seasoned, do add essential variety to everyday meals, and it is in this spirit that I offer the following recipes. You will not find any 'mock' this or that traditional dish in the chapter, though it has to be said that a certain Aubergine Pâté does bear a striking resemblance both in appearance and flavour to Chopped Liver! Each of the dishes in this chapter is delicious in its own right, and will be enjoyed by omnivores, demi-vegetarians and vegetarians with, I hope, equal delight.

Note You will find a number of vegetarian cheeses available now - no longer confined to specialist shops but on supermarket shelves. These are made with vegetarian rennet and can be used in any of the recipes that follow.

Israeli-style Vegetable Pâtés

During the first years of the State of Israel, when meat was a luxury, these pâtés became popular as the kibbutz cooks transmuted European Gehakte Leber into these light yet tasty vegetarian delicacies.

Serve the pâtés in little pots or in scoops set on plates, as you would a liver pâté. They can also be used as a topping for toast fingers or as a 'dip' with scoop-shaped crisps.

KATSIS KISHUIM
(*Courgette Pâté*)

Serves 6–8 as a starter, 10 as a dip.
Keeps 3 days under refrigeration.
Do not freeze.

Light on the tongue, with a delicate but intriguing flavour - no one can guess the main ingredient without asking.

1 oz (25 g/2 tbsp) butter or margarine
1 medium onion, thinly sliced
1½ lb (675 g) courgettes, topped, tailed and thinly sliced
½ teasp sea salt
10 grinds of black pepper
pinch of Cayenne pepper (or chilli powder)
1 medium sprig of parsley
3 hard-boiled eggs, shelled and quartered

Melt the fat and sauté the onion over moderate heat until it has turned a rich gold, then add the courgettes and seasonings and toss well. When the courgettes begin to colour, cover and steam them over a low heat, shaking the pan occasionally, until they feel tender when pierced with a sharp knife - 5–6 minutes. Chop the parsley in the food processor, then add the hard-boiled egg quarters with the vegetables and juices and process until the mixture becomes a smooth pâté. Turn into a terrine or pottery bowl, cover and chill for several hours, then leave at room temperature for half an hour before serving.

CAVED KATSIS TSIMCHONI
(*Aubergine and Egg Pâté*)

Serves 8 as a starter, 12 as a dip.
Keeps 3 days under refrigeration.
Do not freeze.

Although I don't usually go for 'mock' dishes, this really does taste uncannily like a chicken liver pâté - it's the caramelized onions that give it such a satisfying 'meaty' flavour.

1½ lb (675 g) aubergines (eggplants), peeled and cut in 1-inch (2.5-cm) cubes
salt
2 medium onions, coarsely chopped
5 tbsp sunflower oil
1 oz (25 g/2 tbsp) butter or margarine
1 clove of garlic, finely chopped
5 hard-boiled eggs, shelled and halved
10 grinds of black pepper

Put the aubergine cubes into a salad spinner, sprinkling each layer with salt (1 tablespoon altogether). Leave for 30 minutes, then rinse and spin dry.

Cook the onions, covered, in the hot oil and butter over moderate heat until softened - about 8 minutes - then uncover and cook steadily until a deep golden brown. Add the aubergines and garlic, stir well, then cover and cook for 15 minutes, or until the aubergine is absolutely tender.

Tip the contents of the pan into the food processor, add the halved eggs, black pepper and ½ teaspoon of salt, then pulse until finely chopped - like a coarse liver pâté.

Turn into a terrine or oval dish and chill thoroughly until required.

AVOCADO AND EGG PÂTÉ

Serves 8 as a pâté, 12 as a dip.
Keeps 2 days under refrigeration.
Do not freeze.

Another favourite Israeli appetizer, although I first ate it on the West Coast of the USA, from where, I believe, it originates. There is a strong affinity with the traditional egg *forspeise,* but it has the added richness of avocados.

large bunch of parsley
small bunch of spring onion (scallion) bulbs
4 ripe avocados
1 tbsp lemon juice
4 hard-boiled eggs, halved
1 teasp salt
10 grinds of black pepper
1 rounded tbsp mayonnaise

Chop the parsley and the spring onions finely in the food processor. Add the peeled, stoned and roughly cubed avocados and the lemon juice, then add the eggs and seasonings. Pulse until the eggs are finely chopped. Turn into a bowl and add enough of the mayonnaise to bind the mixture into a pâté. Taste and reseason if necessary. Pile into a shallow bowl and chill until required. Serve with 'scoop' crisps or spread on fingers of challah.

Vegetable Stews, Fritters and More

CAPONATA ALLA SICILIANA

Serves 6-8.
Keeps 3 days under refrigeration.
Do not freeze.

According to the Sicilian cookery book *Sicilia e le isole in bocca,* this rich and wonderful aubergine (eggplant) stew originated in the Mafia port of Palermo. Certainly its ingredients - the aubergines and capers in particular - and the prodigal use of olive oil suggest an origin in that part of the world. But wherever it comes from, it is a magnificent dish in its own right. Serve with plenty of brown or rye country bread to mop up the delicious juices.

1 rounded tbsp salt
2 lb (900 g) fine aubergines, unpeeled but cut into ¾-inch (2-cm) cubes
7 tbsp olive oil
2 cloves of garlic, finely chopped
4 tbsp olive oil
2 medium onions, finely sliced
1 celery heart (6-8 stalks), sliced ½ inch (1.25 cm) thick
1 x 15 oz (425 g) can chopped tomatoes, well drained
8 oz (225 g/2 cups) olives, sliced from the stone
2 tbsp capers, well drained
2 tbsp granulated sugar or granular sweetener
4 tbsp white wine vinegar
15 grinds of black pepper
1 teasp dried basil

For the garnish
sprigs of fresh herbs - coriander, parsley or basil

Half fill a salad spinner with cold water, add the salt and then the aubergines, cover and leave for 30 minutes. Pour off the water, then spin dry.

Heat the 7 tablespoons of oil in a large lidded sauté pan, add the dried aubergines and the garlic, toss to coat with the fat and cover. Allow to go brown and to soften for 20 minutes, stirring 2 or 3 times. Remove with a slotted spoon.

Meanwhile, heat the 4 tablespoons of oil in an 8-inch (20-cm) pan, put in the onions, stir well, cover and cook until golden and softened. Add the celery and cook a further 5 minutes, then add all the remaining ingredients and cook, uncovered, until thick and juicy.

Stir in the sautéd aubergines, tossing carefully to mix all the ingredients thoroughly. Chill for several hours, or overnight, before serving.

PEPERONATA A LA VENETO

Serves 6–8 with another antipasto.
Keeps 3 days under refrigeration.
Do not freeze.

Again, a superb vegetable ragout based mainly on aubergines (eggplants) and peppers. This makes a wonderfully rustic starter served with tangy country-style bread.

1–1¼ lb (450–575 g) aubergines
salt
10 oz (275 g) small pickling onions or shallots, topped and tailed
4 tbsp extra virgin olive oil
1 clove of garlic
4 yellow peppers
5 fl oz (150 ml/⅔ cup) dry fruity white wine
1 x 7 oz (200 g) can tomatoes
½ tsp salt
15 grinds of black pepper

Cut the unpeeled aubergines into ¾-inch (2-cm) cubes and put in a salad spinner or colander, layering with salt (about 1 tablespoon altogether). After half an hour, rinse well, then spin or pat dry. Put the onions in a small dish, cover and cook in the microwave for 2 minutes on 100 per cent power (or blanch in boiling water for 5 minutes), then strip off the skins.

Put the oil in a wide frying pan, add the garlic (bruised with the flat of a knife), then heat until it browns. At that point the garlic can be discarded.

Add the onions and cook gently until soft and golden, then add the aubergine cubes and the peppers, seeded and cut into ¾-inch-wide (2-cm) strips. Pour over the wine, cover and cook gently for 20 minutes, then uncover, add the chopped tomatoes and cook briskly for a further few minutes, until most of the liquid has evaporated. Stir in the salt and black pepper.

Chill for 24 hours for the flavours to develop. Serve in small cocottes at room temperature with challah, rye bread or Italian ciabatta bread and a dish of black olives.

MEDITERRANEAN VEGETABLE RAGOUT

Serves 6.
Keeps 4 days under refrigeration.
Do not freeze.

This is equally delicious served hot as part of a vegetable main course, partnering baked potatoes topped with cheese, or at room temperature as a starter before a pasta main course or a cheeseboard. It's important to use an extra virgin olive oil as this gives the dish its special unctuous quality. Hot or cold, the flavour is vastly improved if it is cooked one day and served the next.

1 large aubergine (eggplant), unpeeled and cut in ½-inch (1.25-cm) slices
2 medium courgettes, unpeeled and cut in ½-inch (1.25-cm) slices
salt
4 tbsp extra virgin olive oil
1 medium onion, finely chopped
1 fat clove of garlic, finely chopped

1 each red and green pepper, seeded and cut in ½-inch (1.25-cm) strips
½ x 15 oz (425 g) can chopped tomatoes
2 rounded teasp tomato purée
1 teasp dried Italian seasoning
1 teasp brown sugar or granular sweetener
1 teasp salt
15 grinds of black pepper
1 tbsp chopped parsley
1 tbsp shredded fresh basil leaves or 1 teasp dried basil

Put the sliced aubergine and courgettes in a colander or salad spinner, sprinkle thickly with salt and leave for 30 minutes. Rinse well and dab dry. (Salting cuts down on the oil needed for frying them.)

In a heavy lidded saucepan or deep frying pan, heat the oil and fry the onion and garlic until golden. Then add the aubergine and courgettes, mix well, cover and cook until softened and golden. Add the peppers and cook (covered) for a further 5 minutes, then add all the remaining ingredients except the fresh herbs. Simmer uncovered for about 10 minutes, stirring occasionally until the vegetables are just bite-tender and the mixture is thick but still juicy. Stir in the fresh herbs.

FRICASSEE OF WOODLAND MUSHROOMS

Serves 4–6.
Keeps 2 days under refrigeration.
Do not freeze.

A simple yet succulent dish that makes an ideal introduction to the less familiar varieties of exotic mushrooms. Perhaps the prettiest is the creamy-coloured oyster mushroom, which has the same beautiful convolutions as an oyster shell, with delicate creamy gills on the underside of the cup. The least familiar is the robustly-flavoured Shitake mushroom, often referred to as the 'forest' or 'black' mushroom in Far Eastern recipes. The caps vary in colour from creamy brown to a very dark chestnut. Both of these varieties make stunning companions for the familiar buttons and cups.

Serve the fricassee plain or with the soured cream sauce as a simple supper dish or starter with plenty of granary or French bread to mop up the delicious juices.

8 oz (225 g/2½ cups) button mushrooms
4 oz (125 g/1¼ cups) Shitake mushrooms
4 oz (125 g/1¼ cups) oyster mushrooms
1 small bunch of spring onion (scallion) bulbs with 1 inch (2.5 cm) of the green
2 oz (50 g/¼ cup) butter or margarine
1 tbsp olive oil
1 medium clove of garlic
½ teasp sea salt
10 grinds of black or Szechuan pepper
2 tbsp rice wine or Amontillado sherry
5 fl oz (150 ml/⅔ cup) soured cream or creamed smetana

Cut off the last ¼ inch (0.5 cm) of the stalks from the button mushrooms and discard. Remove the tough stalks from the other varieties. Wipe the mushrooms with a damp cloth but do not peel them. Slice the spring onions into 1½-inch (4-cm) lengths, then toss in the fats over medium heat until they begin to soften – about 2–3 minutes. Add the mushrooms and the garlic (bruised with the flat of a knife but still in its skin), and toss to coat them well with the buttery juices. Continue to cook over moderate heat, shaking the pan and sprinkling with the seasonings. They will absorb the fat but don't add any more, for in 2–3 minutes it will reappear on their surface and they will begin to brown. Immediately stir in the rice wine and continue to cook until almost all the moisture has evaporated. Serve at once or, just before serving, reheat until steaming with the soured cream or smetana.

LENTIL ROAST

Serves 6.
Keeps 3 days under refrigeration.
Freeze 1 month.

This is served at King's College, Cambridge, and is made to the recipe of a former student. It is quite delicious and can be used as a main course.

11 oz (300 g/1½ cups) red lentils
1 lb (450 g) onions
4 oz (125 g/½ cup) butter or margarine
1 fat clove of garlic, crushed, or ¼ teasp garlic powder
10 fl oz (275 ml/1¼ cups) cold water
2 teasp yeast extract
9 oz (250 g/2 cups plus 1 tbsp grated Cheddar cheese
1 tsp dried Italian seasoning herbs
1 teasp salt (if necessary)
4 tbsp dried coating crumbs

The night before, put the lentils into a bowl and cover with twice their depth of cold water (alternatively, use non-soak lentils).

Next day, or when ready to make the roast, turn lentils into a sieve and run water through until it is clear. Leave them in sieve to drain. Grease a tin or casserole measuring approximately 10 x 8 x 2 inches (25 x 20 x 5 cm) and preheat the oven to Gas No. 2 (300°F/150°C).

Peel, halve and chop the onions coarsely. Melt the butter and cook the onion and garlic (if used) until golden brown. Add the water and yeast extract, then remove from the heat. Add half the cheese, the herbs and garlic powder (if used), as well as the drained lentils. Taste and add up to 1 teaspoon of salt if necessary. Mix well, then turn into the buttered tin or casserole dish. Mix the remaining cheese with the breadcrumbs and sprinkle on top. Bake for 2 hours, until crusty. Serve in squares.

FRITTELE MISTE, SALSA DI POMODORO
(*Mixed Vegetable Fritters with a Tomato Sauce*)

Serves 6–8.
Cooked fritters keep crisp in a low oven for up to an hour.
Do not freeze.

It is the beer in the batter than produces a wonderfully crisp coating for these vegetable fritters. If you prefer, use only a single type of vegetable. Serve the frittele as a starter or as a light main dish.

2 medium courgettes
2 medium aubergines (eggplants)
salt

For the batter
4 oz (125 g/1 cup) bread flour
pinch of salt
2 tbsp sunflower oil
5 fl oz (150 ml/⅔ cup) beer
1 egg white

For the sauce
1 x 14 oz (400 g) can tomatoes in juice
1 tbsp tomato purée
1 tbsp extra virgin olive oil
1 teasp light brown sugar
1 teasp sea salt
15 grinds of black pepper
1 teasp dried Italian herbs
1 bay leaf
2 teasp dried minced onion
2 fat cloves of garlic, peeled and crushed
2 tbsp chopped parsley or basil

Cut the unpeeled courgettes in diagonal slices ⅜ inch (1 cm) thick. Cut each aubergine in half lengthwise, then cut in slices in the same way. Layer the vegetables with salt in a salad spinner, then cover with water and leave for 30 minutes before draining and spinning as dry as possible.

Meanwhile, prepare the batter by processing all the ingredients except the egg white for 1 minute, then turn into a medium basin and leave.

Make the sauce by putting all the ingredients except the fresh herbs into a heavy-based pan and simmering uncovered for 15 minutes, or until almost as thick as ketchup. Stir in the fresh herbs and set aside.

Just before frying the frittele, whisk the egg white until it holds soft peaks, then fold into the batter.

Have ready a deep-fryer (or a pan one-third full of oil) heated to 350°F (180°C) - when a cube of bread will brown in 40 seconds. Turn on the oven to Gas No. 1 (275°F/140°C).

Using tongs to hold it, draw each slice of vegetable through the batter, shaking off any excess, and put into the hot oil (don't crowd the pan). Cook until golden - about 4 minutes. Drain on kitchen paper. Transfer the frittele as they cook to a shallow dish lined with kitchen paper and leave in the oven until required.

Serve with the hot Salsa di Pomodoro.

FRITTO DI FINOCCHIO CON SUGHETTO DI ACCIUGHE
(Fennel Fritters with Anchovy Sauce)

Serves 6–8.
Cooked fritters keep crisp in the oven for up to an hour.
Do not freeze.

An unusual combination of flavours.

batter as for the Frittele Miste (see p. 98)
2 large or 3 medium bulbs of fennel

For the sauce

5 fl oz (150 ml/2/3 cup) mayonnaise
6 anchovy fillets, finely chopped, or 3 teasp anchovy purée
1 tbsp spring onions (scallion), finely chopped
2 tbsp chopped parsley
pinch of salt
pinch of dry mustard
5 fl oz (150 ml/2/3 cup) Greek yoghurt or 8% fromage frais

Make the sauce several hours in advance by putting the mayonnaise into a bowl and whisking in the remaining ingredients. Cover and chill until required.

Make the batter by processing all ingredients (except the egg white) until smooth. Just before frying, fold in the stiffly whisked egg white.

Cut the fennel in half and then in thin slices, each piece held together by a segment of the stalk.

Using tongs, draw each section of fennel through the batter, shaking off any excess. Cook as described for Frittele Miste (see pp. 98–9).

All Sorts of Eggs

VARIOUS OMELETTES

The traditional Ashkenazi Jewish omelette or 'pfannkuchen' is more akin to the Spanish 'frittata' than the French rolled variety, and used to be a favourite for Sunday supper, served with fresh black bread and butter. Sephardi Jews make delicious oven-baked omelettes, while in America the omelette soufflé with cream cheese and chives is served in many households. The recipes that follow are capable of infinite variety, but with each of them I have given a different method of making omelettes to perfection.

FRENCH OMELETTE WITH MUSHROOM FILLING

Serves 2.

The French omelette is a very 'private' dish, best served to no more than 2 people at once, as larger omelettes can be tough. However, for more people it is possible to double up on the filling and then make a series of small omelettes to serve hot off the pan.

The pan is of vital importance. It should be thick-based with rounded sides (to make rolling easier), but the material is not of supreme importance, as I have made excellent omelettes in aluminium, enamelled steel and iron pans.

Cooking secrets are few To blend the yolks and the whites, beat the eggs with a large fork or small balloon whisk - a rotary whisk makes them too bubbly and spoils the cooked texture. Add this mixture to the butter when it is just changing colour from yellow to fawn. And *don't* turn the omelette - if the pan is the right size for the number of eggs, the top surface will be creamily set by the bottom heat alone.

3–4 eggs
1 teasp cold water
pinch of salt and pepper
large nut (½ oz/1 tbsp) and tiny nut of butter or margarine

For the filling

4 oz (125 g/1¼ cups) mushrooms
1 oz (25 g/2 tbsp) butter or margarine
2 level teasp flour
2 tbsp milk or 1 tbsp cream
pinch of salt and few grinds of black pepper
pinch of ground mace or nutmeg
2 tsp brandy (optional)

First, make the filling. Cut off ¼ inch (0.5 cm) from the tip of each mushroom stalk and discard. Do not peel the mushrooms but wipe with a damp paper towel. Slice each of them into 4 right through the stalk. Melt the butter in a small saucepan. Add the sliced mushrooms and toss to coat them in the butter. Leave to cook gently for 5 minutes, then stir in the flour (to take up any free butter), and add the milk or cream and the seasonings. Bring to simmering point, then leave on a very low heat.

Now make the omelette. Put an oval serving dish in the oven or under the grill to heat. Get out a 7-inch (18-cm) omelette pan - that is, a frying pan with rounded sides - and put it on the cooker. Break the eggs into a mixing bowl, add the water, salt and pepper, and beat with a fork until the yolks and whites are just blended (the mixture should not be too frothy). Turn the heat on under the empty pan and heat for 2 minutes. Have ready a fork and a flexible spatula. Put in the nut of butter, and the minute it turns from yellow to pale fawn, pour in the beaten eggs. Immediately start to tilt the pan with one hand, while you push the cooked egg towards the centre with the fork held in the other, so that the uncooked egg can flow to the side. When the top of the omelette is set but still creamy, stir the brandy (if used) into the mushroom mixture and spoon it on to one side of the omelette. Fold the omelette over and push another tiny nut of butter underneath it to glaze it. After another 15 seconds, turn the omelette over on to the serving plate. Rush to the table and eat at once!

VARIATION 1

Fry the mushrooms as above, then stir in 3 teaspoons of chopped parsley and a small crushed clove of garlic. Spoon on to the omelette as before.

VARIATION 2

Do not make a filling but instead add any of the following to the beaten eggs: 1 tablespoon of mixed herbs (any combination of chives, parsley, tarragon and chervil); 2 tablespoons of grated cheese; 2 tablespoons of tiny bread or cooked potato cubes, fried until crisp in a little oil.

AUBERGINE OMELETTE

Serves 3–4.

A delicious flat omelette, served from the pan in which it is cooked.

1 large aubergine (eggplant) cut in ½-inch (1.5-cm) cubes
salt
2 tbsp sunflower or olive oil
1 tbsp butter or margarine
2 tomatoes, peeled and diced, or 2 canned ones, well drained
1 clove of garlic, crushed
1 level tbsp chopped parsley
½ tsp dried oregano
6 eggs, whisked to blend with ½ tsp salt and 8 grinds of black pepper

Sprinkle the unpeeled aubergine cubes with coarse salt, place a weight on top, cover them and leave for half an hour. Rinse well and dry thoroughly.

Heat the oil and butter or margarine in an 8-inch (20-cm) omelette pan, then add the aubergine and sauté gently for 15 minutes until tender. Add the tomatoes and cook until juice disappears, then season with garlic and herbs. Pour on beaten eggs, stir well, then cook until set and golden brown underneath. Put briefly under the grill (broiler), then serve from the dish.

OMELETTE BASQUAISE

Serves 3–4.

2 oz (50 g/¼ cup) butter or margarine
2 teasp olive oil
1 small onion, finely chopped
1 red pepper, diced
2 mushrooms, sliced
3 canned or skinned fresh tomatoes, chopped
1 small clove of garlic, crushed
1 teasp oregano
1 teasp chopped parsley
salt and black pepper
6 eggs, beaten to blend with ½ tsp salt, 8 grinds of black pepper
2 oz (50 g/½ cup) mature Cheddar, grated

Melt the butter with the oil in an 8-inch (20-cm) omelette pan, then add the onions. Sauté gently for 5 minutes, then add the pepper, mushrooms, tomatoes, garlic and seasonings. Cover and cook for 10 minutes, until soft, then uncover, pour on the eggs and proceed as for Aubergine Omelette (see above). Just before putting under the grill (broiler), sprinkle with the grated cheese.

CHEESE AND CHIVE OMELETTE SOUFFLÉ

Serves 4–5.
Serve hot off the pan.

A satisfying omelette which is quite low in calories. For 2 servings, halve the quantities and fry in a 7-inch (18-cm) pan.

6 eggs, separated
8 oz (225 g/1 cup) low-fat soft cheese of any kind
1 tbsp chopped chives or 2 teasp finely chopped spring onions (scallions)
salt and black pepper
pinch of Cayenne pepper
pinch of mustard
1 oz (25 g/2 tbsp) butter or margarine

Have ready an 8-inch (20-cm) frying pan. Beat the yolks into the cheese, then stir in the seasonings and beat until the mixture is thick and smooth. Whisk the whites until they hold stiff but still glossy peaks. Pour the yolk mixture on to the whites and cut and fold with a rubber spatula until evenly blended. Put the fat into the frying pan, and heat until it stops foaming. Pour in the omelette mixture, smooth it level and then cook very gently for 5–6 minutes, until it has puffed on top and the underside is brown when a corner of the omelette is lifted from the pan. Grill (broil) very gently for a further 3 or 4 minutes, until well risen and golden. Cut into sections and serve at once.

BAKED OMELETTES IN THE SEPHARDI STYLE

'Eggah' (the Arabic word) to the Egyptian Jews, 'fritada' in those communities which still use Ladino (medieval Judaeo-Spanish), 'kuku' in Tunisia, these baked omelettes have a firm rather than a creamy texture and can be served warm from the oven or at room temperature. They make an excellent vegetarian main course but can also be cut into small cubes and speared on cocktail sticks to serve with drinks.

They can be served plain, with a cucumber and yoghurt salad or with minted fromage frais.

They can be frozen uncooked but ready to bake, but should be thawed and baked freshly on the day they are to be served.

TUNA EGGAH

Serves 4–5.

A very simple variation, using Lancashire and Cheddar cheeses.

3 large eggs
1 fat spring onion (scallion), finely chopped
1 x 7 oz (200 g) can tuna fish, drained and flaked
2 tbsp milk or single cream
5 oz (150 g/1¼ cup) crumbled Lancashire cheese
½ teasp salt
10 grinds of black pepper
knob of soft butter or margarine
½ teasp dried Herbes de Provence
4 tbsp grated mature Cheddar cheese

Whisk the eggs to blend, then stir in all the other ingredients except the Cheddar cheese. Turn into a well-greased gratin dish approximately 10 inches (25 cm) in diameter, and sprinkle with the cheese.

Bake at Gas No. 4 (350°F/180°C) for 30 minutes, or until firm to the touch and a rich brown on top.

BADINJAN KUKU
(*Tunisian Baked Aubergine Omelette*)

Serves 4–5.

2 medium aubergines (eggplants)
salt
3 tbsp extra virgin olive oil
1 large beef tomato, finely sliced
1 small onion, finely chopped
1 medium clove of garlic, finely chopped
2 tbsp finely chopped dill or parsley
2 tbsp raisins
pinch of ground saffron (optional)
10 grinds of black pepper
1 teasp salt
6 large eggs, beaten

Cut the aubergines into roughly 1-inch (2.5-cm) chunks, put on a large plate or in a salad spinner and sprinkle liberally with salt. After 30 minutes rinse well with cold water, drain thoroughly and dry.

Heat the oil in a large frying pan, add the well-dried aubergine chunks, the tomato, onion and garlic, and sauté gently for 5 minutes. Stir in the dill, raisins, saffron, black pepper and salt.

Preheat the oven to Gas No. 3 (325°F/160°C) and oil a gratin baking dish approximately 10 inches (25 cm) in diameter. Stir the vegetable mixture into the eggs, turn into the baking dish and cook, uncovered, for 35–40 minutes, or until firm to gentle touch.

Leave to cool before cutting.

SCRAMBLED TO PERFECTION

A perfect dish of scrambled eggs is set but still creamy, with a good liaison between the butter and the eggs. In the classic recipe, cream and extra butter are used to produce this unctuous texture, but today most people prefer to cut down on the fat. The result, though, is still excellent. See also the variation using a low-fat soft cheese, which produces a similar creamy texture.

SCRAMBLED EGGS

Serves 4–5.

6–8 eggs
4 tbsp milk or cream
1 level teasp salt
10 grinds of black pepper
1 oz (25 g/2 tbsp) butter or margarine

Optional extras

1 oz (25 g/2 tbsp) butter or margarine, or 2 tbsp creamy fromage frais

Blend the eggs with the milk (or cream) and the salt and pepper by beating them for about 30 seconds using a large fork or rotary whisk. Melt the butter in a pan approximately 7 inches (18 cm) in diameter over a low heat, then add the egg mixture and start stirring with a spoon. At first nothing will happen, but don't be tempted to turn up the heat. After 2 minutes the eggs will begin to thicken. Keep on stirring all round the sides and the bottom, lifting the pan off the heat if the mixture seems to be cooking too quickly. When the mixture looks soft and creamily set, it's ready. If you wish, now's the time to drop in either the extra butter or fromage frais. This immediately stops any further cooking and helps to achieve the creamy, rich texture that's so delectable. Serve on a hot plate with really fresh buttered black bread or on buttered brown toast.

VARIATIONS

CHIVE SCRAMBLE

Add 1 tablespoonful of scissored chives to the beaten eggs.

CHEESE SCRAMBLE

Add 4 tablespoons of grated sharp cheese to the eggs before serving – the heat of the mixture will be sufficient to melt the cheese.

MUSHROOM SCRAMBLE

Nicest are the tiny button mushrooms, cooked in a nut of butter for 2 minutes, then stirred into the scrambled eggs before serving.

Alternatively, sauté 2 oz (50 g/1 cup) thinly sliced fresh button mushrooms in the cooking butter. After 3 minutes, add the beaten egg mixture and proceed to cook as in the basic recipe.

COTTAGE CHEESE SCRAMBLE

As soon as the egg mixture begins to thicken, stir in 4 oz (125 g/½ cup) cottage cheese or other low-fat soft cheese (about 8 tablespoons) and 1 tablespoon of snipped chives (if available), and continue to cook until the mixture is the consistency of half-whipped cream. Add no further butter or cream.

LUXURY SCRAMBLED EGG (with Smoked Salmon)

Blend the eggs with a pinch of Cayenne pepper. In the 1 oz (50 g/2 tbsp) butter gently sauté 2 tablespoons of finely chopped spring onions (scallions) and 1 small yellow pepper, seeded and diced. When these vegetables have softened – about 5 minutes – add to the beaten egg mixture and proceed as in the basic recipe. Just before serving stir in 4 oz (125 g) shredded smoked salmon.

PIPERRADA
(*Spanish-style Scrambled Eggs*)

Serves 4.
Serve hot off the pan.

Though capsicums (sweet peppers) are native to Mexico and Central America, they have been a mainstay of Sephardi and Askenazi cuisine for centuries. A point of interest: weight for weight, peppers contain between 6 and 9 times the Vitamin C of tomatoes and have only 78 calories per 100 g (3½ oz) – the weight of an average pepper.

4 tbsp extra virgin olive oil
2 onions, thinly sliced
2 cloves of garlic, finely chopped
2 large, very ripe beefsteak tomatoes, halved, deseeded and sectioned
2 yellow peppers, deseeded and cut in thin strips
2 red peppers, deseeded and cut in thin strips
sea salt
pepper
6 eggs

Heat the oil in a large lidded frying pan. Add the onion and garlic and sauté, covered, until softened and golden. Add the tomatoes and peppers to the pan and simmer gently, uncovered, for 10–12 minutes, until the peppers are softened but still slightly firm. Uncover, reduce the heat and season to taste. Beat the eggs just to blend, then pour over the pepper mixture. Cook very gently for several minutes, or long enough for the eggs to begin to set but still be very creamy. Slide on to a warm serving dish.

BAKED EGGS

The French have perfected this method of cooking eggs to the extent of inventing special dishes, known as ramekins, for the purpose. But there are homelier methods that are just as tasty for family occasions.

OEUFS EN COCOTTE

For each serving
a nut of butter or margarine
2 tbsp thick cream or creamy fromage frais
1–2 eggs
salt
pepper

The cooking dish should be about 2½ inches (6 cm) in diameter and about 1½ inches (4 cm) deep, and made of glass, earthenware or heatproof porcelain. The eggs are cooked, insulated from the heat of the oven, by hot water, to stop them becoming tough.

Half fill a rectangular tin (large enough to hold all the ramekins) with boiling water and put it on a low heat on top of the stove. Use half the butter to grease the dishes and pour in half the cream. Put the dishes in the water and when the cream begins to steam - after 2 minutes - add the whole eggs, season with salt and pepper, then cover with the remaining cream and dot with the remaining butter. Transfer the tin and the dishes to the oven. Bake at Gas No. 5 (375°F/190°C) for 10 minutes, by which time the eggs will be set but shiver slightly when the dish is moved. The eggs can be kept hot out of the oven (but still in the water bath) for up to 15 minutes.

VARIATION 1

WITH HERBS AND CHEESE

First make the sauce. Into a thick-bottomed pan put 1 tablespoon of soured cream or creamy fromage frais, 4 oz (125 g/1 cup) grated cheese, 1 tablespoon sherry and 2 level tablespoons of a mixture of as many of the following chopped fresh herbs as are available: parsley, thyme, tarragon, chives, chervil. Stir over gentle heat until smooth and pale green, then season with a pinch of salt and black pepper. Use in place of cream. This mixture stores for weeks in the refrigerator.

VARIATION 2

WITH MIXED HERBS

Add 1 teaspoon of mixed chopped parsley, chives and chervil (if available) to the cream or fromage frais for each serving.

EGGS IN CORN AND CHEESE SAUCE

Serves 2.
Leftovers keep 2 days under refrigeration.
Do not freeze.

This is a very satisfying low-cost supper dish, equally convenient to make for 2, 4 or indeed 6 people. To serve 4, simply double all the ingredients except the eggs - use 6 eggs. For 6 people use 9 eggs, 1 pint (575 ml/2½ cups) of sauce and an 11 oz (300 g) can of corn.

4 eggs
½ x 7 oz (200 g) can corn with peppers

For the sauce
5 fl oz (150ml/⅔ cup) milk
1 level tbsp flour
1 oz (25 g/2 tbsp) butter or margarine
¼ tsp salt
3 or 4 shakes ground nutmeg
1 tsp Dijon or English made mustard
5 grinds of black pepper
2 tbsp single cream or evaporated milk
2 oz (50 g/½ cup) grated sharp cheese

For the topping
1 level tbsp dry breadcrumbs
1 level tbsp finely grated cheese
1 oz (25 g/2 tbsp) butter or margarine, cut in little bits

Simmer the eggs in their shells for 12 minutes, then plunge into cold water.

To make the sauce, put the cold milk, flour, butter, salt, nutmeg, mustard and pepper into a pan and whisk over gentle heat until bubbling. Bubble for 3 minutes, still stirring, then whisk in the cream or evaporated milk and the grated sharp cheese. Turn off the heat and continue to whisk until the cheese has melted, and the sauce is quite smooth.

Select a ½ pint/275 ml/1¼ cups heatproof dish about 1½ inches (4 cm) deep or use 2 individual casseroles. Butter each dish well, and cover with the drained corn. Spread about a quarter of the sauce on top, then arrange the shelled and halved hard-boiled eggs on top, cut side down. Spoon over the remaining sauce, then cover with the breadcrumbs and cheese mixed together. (If you do not have breadcrumbs available, you can use just cheese.) Dot with the butter.

Either grill (broil) very slowly for 10 minutes, until bubbly and richly brown, or put in a quick oven, Gas No. 5 (375°F/190°C) for 15 minutes, until bubbly, then grill quickly for 2–3 minutes, until the topping is a rich golden brown. Serve at once with wholemeal bread.

Dairy Dishes

Since the separation of meat and milk foods laid down in the dietary laws, Jewish cooking has always put special emphasis on dairy dishes made from butter, eggs, cream and cheese. The first cheese-making tribes in Asia Minor were idol worshippers whose food products the early Jews were forbidden to eat. So from Biblical times, the making of soft cheese from naturally soured milk became a highly developed craft in the Jewish household, reaching its high point in the nineteenth-century kitchens of Russia and Poland.

Today, cheese-making is left mainly to the commercial dairyman, but curd cheese of all kinds, as well as soured cream and milk, is still widely used in the Jewish kitchen. Indeed, Jewish dairy specialities such as cheese blintzes and cheesecake are now eaten in the general as well as the Jewish community.

SOURED CREAM

Once upon a time it was called 'smetana' (a word now reserved only for soured milk) and it was skimmed off the milk curds before they were put to drain for cheese. Today it's called 'soured (sour) cream' and its use is certainly not limited to Jewish households. Even in the commercial dairies, however, it is still made in much the same way, although to speed up the souring process (particularly with pasteurized cream) the cream is 'injected' with some of the same bacteria that the pasteurization process has destroyed. After it has been homogenized (to prevent separation), the cream is 'set', rather like yoghurt, with a lactic acid bacillus. Soured cream will keep for 7 days on the middle shelf of the refrigerator, and it can be used in almost any dish for which one would use fresh cream. Apart from its delicious flavour, it has one big advantage: although as thick as whipping cream, it contains less than half the butter-fat content. Although it will not whip by itself, it can be blended with sweet cream to give a very rich flavour and texture. One disadvantage: it separates if heated to boiling point, so it must be added to hot sauces with very great care.

SOFT WHITE CHEESE (KAESE)

Soft cheeses are generally classified by the amount of butter-fat they contain. There are two main categories: *curd cheese,* which is similar to old-fashioned home-made cheese and whose richness depends on the amount of cream that is added, and *cottage cheese,* which is a granular cheese made from skim milk, sometimes enriched with added cream.

In addition, there is a bewildering array of low-fat soft cheeses, many of which are interchangeable with whipped cream - for example, fromage frais and quark kaese. If you are watching fat intake, check the nutritional data on the packet as this can vary enormously.

HOME-MADE KAESE (*Soft Milk Cheese*)

Makes 14-16 oz (400-450 g/1¾-2 cups).
Keeps 1 week under refrigeration.
Do not freeze.

This is a useful way either to use up sour milk or to produce a delicious cheese if commercial varieties are not available. It is marginally cheaper than most commercial cheese. However, probably the best reason for making it occasionally is - tradition!

3 pints (1.75 l/7 cups) milk (Jersey milk will give the richest cheese)
1 tbsp natural yoghurt can be added to each pint of milk to help the milk to sour

A triangular cheesebag is required; this can be made from an old pillowcase, a thin tea-towel or a piece of butter muslin. Ideally, your cheesebag should have 2 sides each 18 inches (45 cm) long and the third side 12 inches (30 cm) long. Put the milk with the yoghurt into a tall jug or pottery crock. If it is ice cold, put it in the oven at the lowest temperature until it feels pleasantly warm. Take out and leave to sour for 48 hours. An ideal spot is on a ledge above a heating radiator, or in an airing cupboard. After 48 hours, the cream will have thickened and soured and the milk below will have set to a junket-like clot. Carefully skim off the cream and refrigerate until required. Put the soured milk, still in its container, to heat very gently so that the thin whey will rise to the top. This can be done either in the oven, set at its lowest heat, or on top of the stove, with the container of milk standing on an flameproof mat or wire trivet. Do not overheat, or the curds will become toughened. As soon as the whey has separated from the curds (after 15-30 minutes), remove the milk from the heat. Pour the curds and whey into the bag and tie it up with string. Hang it up where it can drip freely, with a bowl underneath to catch the drips. Allow to drip for 12 hours, or until no whey can be seen dripping from the bag. Turn out the cheese into a bowl. It is now ready to use in a cheesecake.

For table use Stir in the soured cream which has been skimmed off, and season to taste with salt and a pinch of sugar. Spoon back into the cheese bag, tie into an oval shape, cover with foil and then a weight. Leave for an hour, then carefully turn out on to a platter. If preferred, serve the cream separately and simply turn the cheese into a pottery bowl.

ISRAELI CHEESE PANCAKES

Serves 4.
Make batter and fry pancakes the same day.

Israeli food today conjures up a picture of the exotic fruit and vegetables grown so brilliantly in the Negev and exported to gourmets all over the world. But the fruits of the earth were not so abundant in the years immediately after the founding of the State. Meat and poultry in particular were in extremely short supply. It was then that milk cheese - the 'kaese' of the Eastern European Jews - became the staple protein food. This recipe was originally called 'cheese steaks' and was served like a mock cutlet. If there is less cheese available than specified, an equivalent amount of flour can be substituted. The mixture should resemble a very thick batter like a 'chremslach' mixture (see p. 623).

8 oz (225 g/1 cup) cottage or curd cheese
2 eggs
2 oz (50 g/½ cup) self-raising flour or 2 oz (50 g/½ cup) plain (all-purpose) flour and ½ level teasp baking powder
1 level teasp each of sugar and salt
2 oz (50 g/¼ cup) butter or margarine and 1 tbsp oil (or all oil) for frying
sugar and cinnamon mixed together

Put the cheese and the eggs into separate bowls. Beat the eggs with a rotary whisk until fluffy, then stir into the cheese, together with the flour and the seasonings. Put the butter and oil into a heavy frying pan over moderate heat. The minute the butter starts to foam, drop tablespoonsful of the mixture into the pan, flattening slightly with the back of the spoon. Fry gently until risen and golden brown on one side, then turn and cook until the second side is brown. Serve hot off the pan with cinnamon sugar.

The Savoury Soufflé

Unnecessary mystique surrounds the making of this superb dish, which in essence is no more than a thick, well-flavoured sauce lightened with egg whites, then baked until it is barely set - with a crunchy brown 'top hat'. The French use the almost untranslatable word *baveuse* to describe the quivery inside texture. Follow these pointers and you cannot go wrong.

The oven As a soufflé needs a steady heat all round it, always preheat the oven well in advance and at a temperature a gas mark (25°F/10°C) higher than is required. This ensures not only that the oven is thoroughly heated but also that there is a margin of safety to allow for the inevitable heat loss when the oven door is opened. If the baking tray is preheated at the same time, the soufflé will be further helped to rise (this is unnecessary with a fan-assisted oven).

The dish For a hot soufflé there is no need to extend the sides with a high band of paper - simply choose a dish deep enough to allow for expansion without explosion. Always butter this dish thoroughly, and for extra crunchiness scatter the bottom and sides with finely grated cheese (Parmesan is ideal).

The timing Some cookbooks recommend freezing the raw soufflé in advance, but I find this interferes with the rise. One can, however, complete the soufflé (bar the baking) up to 1 hour in advance. This means that it can safely wait until guests have arrived before being put in the oven. As a soufflé *must* be served as soon as it is ready, it is better for the guests to wait for it than vice versa.

The cheese It is necessary to use a cheese that will melt creamily in the oven but has a little 'bite' to its flavour. One can use a mixture of grated Gruyère and Parmesan or Cheddar. However, if it is available there is nothing to compare with Lancashire cheese, which need only be crumbled (rather than grated) into the mixture.

The extra egg white can be one you have in stock in the refrigerator or a fresh one - in the latter case, the unused egg yolk should be put in a tiny airtight plastic container, refrigerated, then used within 24 hours.

CHEESE SOUFFLÉ

Serves 4.
Eat immediately.

grated Parmesan cheese for coating dish
1½ oz (40 g/⅓ cup) flour
2 oz (50 g/¾ cup) butter or margarine
10 fl oz (275 ml/1¼ cups) milk
½ teasp salt
10 grinds of pepper
1 tsp Dijon mustard
pinch of Cayenne pepper
pinch of ground nutmeg
4 large eggs, separated, plus an extra white
good pinch of cream of tartar or salt
3 oz (75 g/¾ cup) coarsely grated, well-flavoured cheese

Butter a dish 3 inches (7.5 cm) deep and 8 inches (20 cm) in diameter and sprinkle with Parmesan cheese. Preheat the oven to Gas No. 6 (400°F/200°C) and put in a baking tin.

Put the flour, butter and cold milk into a heavy-bottomed 8-9 inch (20-22.5 cm) pan and bring gently to the boil, whisking with a batter whisk or a balloon whisk. Add the seasonings, then bubble for 3 minutes, stirring constantly with a wooden spoon. Remove from the heat. Have ready the bowl in which you intend to whisk the egg whites. Separate the eggs and drop the yolks 1 at a time into the hot sauce, stirring well after each addition, while you drop its companion white into the bowl. Add the extra white and whisk them with the cream of tartar or salt until they stand up in stiff glossy peaks when the beaters are withdrawn.

Take a quarter of the meringue and *stir* it into the sauce, followed by all but 1 tablespoon of the grated cheese. Spoon the remaining meringue on top and, using a rubber spatula, *fold* it into the sauce as gently as possible so that the mixture becomes an even colour but remains fluffy in texture. Coax it gently into the prepared dish. With the flat of a knife, make a shallow groove round the edge of the mixture, 1 inch (2.5 cm) away from the rim of the dish (this helps it to rise into a 'top hat' shape). Sprinkle with the remaining grated cheese.

At this point the soufflé can be covered with a large bowl and left to stand for up to an hour before baking.

Put on the tray in the preheated oven, then turn the oven down to Gas No. 5 (375°F/190°C). The soufflé will be ready to eat in 35 minutes, by which time the top will be a crusty brown.

VARIATION

LOVAGE SOUFFLÉ

Serves 4.

A delicious creamy soufflé with a delicate flavour of celery (from the lovage leaves). A lovage plant is easy to grow in any temperate climate. It is a perennial and will produce deliciously scented leaves each season.

Make exactly as for Cheese Soufflé but stir in 1 tablespoon of snipped chives and 3 level tablespoons of finely shredded lovage or celery leaves.

INDIVIDUAL MUSHROOM SOUFFLÉS

Serves 8.

An original starter for a dinner party. However, the mixture can also be baked in the same size dish as for the Cheese Soufflé and will then serve 4 as a main course.

grated cheese for coating dishes
1 oz (25 g/2 tbsp) butter or margarine
8 oz (225 g/4 cups) mushrooms, finely sliced
¼ medium onion or 3 shallots, very finely chopped
2 tbsp medium sherry (optional)
a squeeze of lemon juice

For the sauce
1½ oz (40 g/⅜ cup) flour
1½ oz (40 g/3 tbsp) butter or margarine
8 fl oz (225 ml/1 cup) milk
1 level teasp salt
pinch of white pepper
pinch of ground mace
2 tbsp thick cream
1 tbsp chopped parsley or snipped chives
2 oz (50 g/½ cup) well-flavoured grated cheese
4 large eggs, separated, plus an extra white

Butter 8 individual soufflé dishes (approximately 5 fl oz/150 ml/⅔ cup capacity) and coat with finely grated cheese. Set the oven at Gas No. 7 (425°F/220°C). Put in a baking tray to heat up.

Melt the butter, then add the vegetables, sherry and lemon juice. Cover and cook for 5 minutes. Uncover and allow to bubble until all the moisture has evaporated - about 3 minutes.

To make the sauce, put the flour, butter and cold milk into a pan, and whisk over gentle heat until a thick sauce is formed. Add the seasonings, bubble for 3 minutes, then take off the heat and add the cream, parsley or chives, all but 1 tablespoon of the cheese, the 4 egg yolks and the mushroom mixture. Whisk the egg whites with a pinch of salt until they hold stiff glossy peaks. *Stir* a quarter of the whites thoroughly into the sauce, then gently *fold* in the rest.

Divide the mixture between the soufflé dishes and then sprinkle with the remaining cheese. Arrange the dishes on the heated tray, then turn the heat down to Gas No. 6 (400°F/200°C) and bake for 20 minutes.

AUBERGINE, TOMATO AND CHEESE CASSEROLE

Serves 6–8.
Keeps 2 days under refrigeration.
Freeze 3 months.

A superb main dish for a vegetarian meal, accompanied by baked potatoes - the early Cyprus ones are ideal. Allow the dish to cool for 15 minutes; by then it will be easy to slice. If you freeze the cheese for 30 minutes first, it will be much easier to grate.

3 lb (1.5 kg) oval aubergines (eggplants), sliced diagonally ½ inch (1 cm) thick
3 fl oz (75 ml/⅓ cup) oil (for grilling/broiling the aubergines)
12 oz (350 g/3 cups) Edam or Mozzarella cheese, coarsely grated
4 rounded tbsp finely grated Cheddar cheese

For the sauce
2 tbsp extra virgin olive oil
2 medium onions, finely chopped
2 cloves of garlic, peeled and crushed
1 x 29 oz (825 g) can plum tomatoes, well drained or 2 x 11 oz (300 g) cans tomato and mushroom sauce
1 tbsp tomato purée
1 teasp brown sugar
2 teasp dried oregano
1 teasp dried Italian seasoning herbs
1 teasp salt
15 grinds of black pepper

Layer the aubergine slices in a colander, sprinkling each layer with coarse salt, and leave to sweat for 30 minutes. Meanwhile, set the oven at Gas No. 6 (400°F/200°C) and make the sauce. Heat the oil and sauté the onions and garlic until soft and golden. Add all the remaining ingredients and bubble gently, uncovered, stirring occasionally, for 15–20 minutes, until thick and juicy.

Wash the aubergine slices under running water to remove the salt, drain and dry either in a salad spinner or with kitchen towels. Heat the grill at the highest setting. Brush the slices on one side with oil and grill until golden brown – about 3 minutes. Turn, brush with more oil and repeat with the second side. Continue until all the slices have been grilled.

To assemble the dish, arrange a thin layer of tomato sauce on the bottom of a large gratin dish or individual dishes, then cover with a layer of aubergines, a layer of Edam cheese and a sprinkle of grated Cheddar. Repeat with the remaining ingredients, ending with the cheese layer. Bake for 35–40 minutes, until golden brown and bubbly. It is good served warm (covered and reheated if this is convenient) or at room temperature.

Rarebits

Here are some variations on the rarebit (rabbit) theme which owe everything to Lancashire and Wales and nothing to traditional Jewish food. They're delicious!

A pound (450 g/4 cups) of a tasty cheese ready-grated in the freezer is an excellent insurance against the what-on-earth-shall-we-have-for-supper syndrome which so often occurs on a Sunday.

To grate cheese successfully in a food processor, which makes short work of a tedious job, cut the cheese in chunks to fit the feed tube and freeze for 15 minutes for a hard cheese such as Cheddar, 30 minutes for a softer cheese such as Edam. This stops the cheese from becoming soggy and gumming up the works when it is heated by the friction generated in the machine.

SUPERIOR WELSH RAREBIT

With grated cheese to hand – which can be used straight from the freezer – it takes only minutes to prepare this rather superior version of Welsh Rarebit. The quantity I give will generously cover 2 large slices of toast and serve 2 as a snack. However, if a larger quantity is prepared, the cheese mixture can be kept covered in the refrigerator for up to a week.

6 oz (175 g/3 cups) Cheddar or Lancashire cheese, grated
1 level tbsp flour
2 fl oz (50 ml/¼ cup) beer, or milk if preferred
1 large egg yolk
nut of soft butter or margarine
¼ tsp chilli powder or a good pinch of Cayenne pepper
1 teasp Worcestershire sauce
½ teasp dry mustard
2 large slices of wholemeal or rye bread toast

Set aside 2 heaped tablespoons of the grated cheese and reserve. Mix the remainder with the flour in a small bowl. In a small pan bring the beer or milk to the boil over moderate heat, then add the cheese, a tablespoon at a time, stirring until smooth after each addition. When all the cheese has been stirred in, take the pan from the heat and drop in the egg yolk, the butter or margarine and the seasonings and stir well. Arrange each piece of cooled toast on a separate heatproof dish or shallow cocotte, spoon the cheese mixture evenly over each slice and sprinkle with the reserved cheese. Grill (broil) for 1 or 2 minutes, until bubbly and golden brown.

VARIATION

BUCK RAREBIT

Divide the rarebit mixture more thinly between 3–4 slices of toast. Grill (broil) as before, then top each serving with a poached egg.

CHEESE SPREAD FOR TOASTED SANDWICHES

Serves 4–6 as a snack; enough for 8 rounds of bread. Keeps 1 week under refrigeration.

A more savoury version to go in between rather than on top of slices of bread. It can, however, be treated as a rarebit (rabbit), and spread on toast fingers and then grilled.

nut of butter or margarine
2 teasp snipped chives
2 level teasp sugar or granular sweetener
2 teasp flour
pinch of salt
1 tbsp cider vinegar or white wine vinegar
4 tbsp evaporated milk or single (light) cream
4 oz (125 g/1 cup) sharp cheese, grated

Melt the nut of butter, then stir in the chives, sugar, flour, salt, vinegar and milk. Whisk over gentle heat until thickened. Take off the heat, add the cheese and stir until melted. Cool.

To use for toasted sandwiches Use 8 rounds of bread to make 4 sandwiches, spreading the bottom round with a quarter of the cheese mixture and the top round with a little made mustard. Press the 2 slices of bread together, then spread thinly but evenly on both sides with soft butter or margarine. Either toast in an electric sandwich-maker or heat an empty, heavy frying pan for 3 minutes, then put in the sandwiches. Cook slowly but steadily for 5 minutes, until bottom is golden, then turn and cook second side.

Cut each sandwich into 4 triangles and arrange on a platter with pickled onions and cucumbers as a garnish.

BALLYMALOE CHEESE FONDUE

Serve at once.

This Irish version of the traditional Swiss dish is a speciality of Myrtle Allen's lovely Ballymaloe House Hotel. The tomato chutney (bought or home-made) gives it a wonderful new flavour dimension.

For each person allow the following
1 tbsp dry white wine
½ small crushed clove of garlic
1 teasp tomato chutney (see p. 503)
1 teasp chopped parsley
3 oz (75 g) grated Cheddar cheese
½ stick French bread, cut in cubes

Put all the ingredients except the bread into a small saucepan or fondue pot. Heat, stirring until smooth and bubbling, and then serve with the bread which each diner spears on a fondue fork and dips into the pot.

Pasta Plus

A GRATIN OF PASTA, AUBERGINE AND CHEESE

Serves 4–6.
The uncooked dish can be refrigerated for up to 24 hours before cooking.

This is a very good dish that you can prepare many hours in advance and then bake just before serving. It makes a satisfying vegetarian main course or a light supper dish.

1 lb (450 g) aubergines (eggplants), unpeeled, cut in 1-inch (2.5-cm) cubes
oil for deep-frying
12 oz (350 g) penne (pasta quills), about 1½ inches (4 cm) long, ½ inch (1.25 cm) in diameter
7–8 oz (200–225 g) Mozzarella or Gouda cheese, thinly sliced

For the sauce
2 tbsp olive oil
2 cloves of garlic, crushed
2 x 14 oz (400 g) cans chopped tomatoes
1 tbsp tomato purée
1½ tsp salt
20 grinds of black pepper
2 teasp light brown sugar or granular sweetener
small bunch of basil (12–15 leaves), finely chopped, or 1 tbsp chopped parsley and 1 teasp dried basil

To ensure that the aubergines absorb the minimum of oil, deep-fry them or brush them all over with oil and grill (broil) them until they are softened and a beautiful golden brown on both sides. Drain well on kitchen paper.

To prepare the tomato sauce, in an 8-inch (20-cm) pan lightly brown the crushed garlic in the oil, then add all the remaining ingredients, excluding the fresh herbs but including the dried herb if used, and simmer uncovered for 15–20 minutes, until thickened but still juicy. Then stir in the fresh herbs.

Meanwhile, cook the pasta in a large pan of boiling salted water according to packet directions – a tablespoon of oil added to the water helps to stop it boiling over and the pasta sticking together. When the pasta is bite-tender but still firm – this will take about 10 minutes – drain thoroughly, then add to the sauce, together with the cubes of aubergine. Pour half this mixture into a lightly greased baking dish about 2 inches (5 cm) deep. Cover with half the cheese and top with the remaining pasta mixture. Finally, cover with the remaining cheese. Bake in a moderate oven, Gas No. 4 (350°F/180°C), for 15 minutes, or until the cheese has melted (it will take rather longer if the dish has been allowed to go cold). The dish can also be heated, uncovered, in the microwave at 100 per cent power for 5 minutes, or until the cheese has melted.

MUSHROOM LASAGNE

Serves 6 for supper, 8 for a buffet.
Keeps 2 days under refrigeration.
May be reheated (covered with foil).

It's their rich and nutty flavour that make mushrooms such a valuable ingredient in everything from soups to savouries. But an equally important, if hidden, asset is their food value – their protein contains more essential amino acids than that of any other vegetable food except soya beans and spinach.

So a recipe for a vegetarian pasta dish that includes 2 lb (900 g) of mushrooms (and, incidentally, a generous amount of protein-rich cheese) is very good news whether you're looking for a nourishing meatless main dish or a superlative casserole to serve for a supper party. For the best results, use either a make of lasagne that needs no precooking or fresh pasta squares which can be overlapped to form the layers mentioned in the recipe.

approx. 8 oz (225 g) fresh or no-cook packeted green or white lasagne
8 oz (225 g/2 cups) medium mature Cheddar cheese

For the sauce
2 oz (50 g/¼ cup) butter or margarine
1½ oz (40 g/6 tbsp) plain (all-purpose) flour
1½ pints (850 ml/3¾ cups) milk
pinch of white pepper
¼ tsp salt
2 egg yolks

For the mushroom mixture
2 tbsp olive oil
1 fat clove of garlic, cut in half
½ small onion, finely chopped
2 lb (900 g/10 cups) thinly sliced open-cup mushrooms
1½ teasp dried oregano
½ teasp salt
15 grinds of black pepper
2 tbsp Amontillado sherry
2 tbsp chopped parsley

To make the sauce, put the butter, flour, milk and seasonings into a heavy-based 8-inch (20-cm) saucepan and gradually bring to the boil, stirring constantly with a balloon or batter whisk. Simmer for 5 minutes to cook the flour thoroughly, then drop in the egg yolks and immediately whisk to blend them well in. Set aside.

Preheat the oven to Gas No. 6 (400°F/200°C). Lightly grease a 12 x 8 x 2 inch (30 x 20 x 5 cm) baking dish.

To make the mushroom mixture, in a large frying pan cook the garlic in the oil until it is golden brown, then discard it. In the same oil, gently sauté the onion until golden, then add the mushrooms and cook briskly for 3 or 4 minutes, until they are beginning to colour. Sprinkle with the oregano, salt and pepper and pour in the sherry. Continue to cook uncovered until the moisture has almost completely evaporated. Stir in the parsley.

To assemble the lasagne, spread a thin layer of the sauce on the base of the dish, arrange a layer of lasagne on top and cover with a third of the mushroom mixture. Spread a third of the sauce on top and (setting aside 3 tablespoons for topping) sprinkle with a third of the cheese. Repeat twice, sprinkling the top layer of sauce with the additional reserved cheese. Cover with foil and bake for 25 minutes, or until bubbly, then uncover and allow to brown for a further 10 minutes. Cool for 15 minutes before cutting into squares.

PESTO LASAGNE

Serves 6.
This may be reheated but is best served fresh.
The oven-ready dish can be refrigerated for up to 24 hours.

If you grow basil, this luxurious, wonderfully perfumed dish is for you. However, 8–10 oz (225–275 g) bottled pesto can be substituted.

12 pieces no-cook lasagne or fresh lasagne squares

For the pesto
2 medium cloves of garlic, peeled and roughly chopped
3½ oz (90 g/1 cup) fresh basil leaves
5 fl oz (150 ml/⅔ cup) virgin olive oil
1 oz (25 g/¼ cup) pine kernels, lightly toasted
2 oz (50 g/½ cup) finely grated Parmesan
8 grinds of black pepper
½ tsp coarse sea salt

For the béchamel sauce
1¼ pints (725 ml/3 cups) milk
5 fl oz (150 ml/⅔ cup) whipping cream
sprig of parsley
1 bay leaf
8 black peppercorns
¼ onion
1½ oz (40 g/3 tbsp) butter or margarine
1½ oz (40 g/6 tbsp) plain flour
1 teasp salt
good grating of nutmeg or good pinch of ground nutmeg

For the topping

2–3 tbsp fresh breadcrumbs
2–3 tbsp Parmesan (or Cheddar)
1 oz (25 g/2 tbsp) butter or margarine

To make the pesto, put all the ingredients into the food processor and process until a smooth purée, scraping the sides down once or twice.

To make the béchamel sauce, first heat the milk and cream to steaming with the parsley, bay leaf, peppercorns and onion, then cover and leave to infuse off the heat for 10 minutes. Melt the butter, stir in the flour and cook gently for 2 minutes. Strain the hot milk on to the roux with salt and nutmeg, whisking constantly with a balloon whisk, and cook, stirring until bubbly. Simmer uncovered for 5 minutes, then take off the heat. Stir in the pesto thoroughly.

Lightly butter a rectangular oven-to-table dish measuring approximately 12 x 8 x 2 inches (30 x 20 x 5 cm) and put a thin layer of sauce on the bottom. Now fit 3 layers of the pasta on top, covering each with the sauce. Mix the breadcrumbs and cheese and scatter evenly on top, then dot with the butter.

The dish can now be left for up to 24 hours or cooked as follows. Preheat the oven to Gas No. 4 (350°F/180°C). Cover the lasagne with foil and bake for 25 minutes, then uncover and cook for a further 15–20 minutes, until the top is golden brown. If necessary, finish under the grill (broiler).

Cool for 10 minutes, then serve.

TORTINO CON TAGLIATELLE

Serves 6–8.
Leftovers keep 2 days.
Reheat in microwave.
Do not freeze.

For an economical supper dish, country cooks in Liguria on the Italian Riviera often make a hearty casserole or 'Tortino' – it can best be described as a pie without pastry – using any vegetables in season. After a night out, this is a wonderful dish to come home to, as it can be made well ahead and needs only 15–20 minutes in a quick oven to emerge bubbling and crunchy. It is marvellous served with brown rolls and a green salad such as Insalata Siciliana (see p. 286). This elegant version uses slivers of smoked salmon for extra piquancy, but for vegetarians the fish can be omitted and 4 oz of a low-fat garlic and herb cream cheese added to the fromage frais instead.

approx. 12 oz (350 g) fresh green and white tagliatelle
4 oz (125 g/½ cup) unsalted butter or margarine
1 large onion, finely chopped
1 lb (450 g/5 cups) mushrooms, finely sliced
½ teasp nutmeg
salt
black pepper
8 oz (225 g) smoked salmon, cut in slivers (optional)
2 tbsp snipped dill
10 fl oz (275 ml/2 cups) creamy 8% fromage frais, smetana or Greek yoghurt
12 oz (350 g/3 cups) tasty Lancashire cheese, grated or crumbled
2 heaped tbsp dry breadcrumbs

Cook the tagliatelle in boiling salted water according to directions, then drain well. Meanwhile, sauté the onion in half the butter until soft and golden, then add the mushrooms and cook briskly until they are also beginning to brown and no free liquid remains in the pan. Season with the nutmeg, a little salt and plenty of black pepper. Mix the salmon (or garlic and herb cheese), dill and fromage frais together.

Use some of the remaining butter to lightly grease an oval gratin dish. Add the remaining butter to the hot tagliatelle and mix well, seasoning with sea salt and plenty of black pepper, then arrange in an even layer in the bottom of the dish. Spoon the mushroom and onion mixture on top and spread over that the salmon or herb-cheese mixture. Mix the cheese with the crumbs and spread evenly on top.

Cook for 15-20 minutes at Gas No. 7 (425°F/220°C), until crunchy and golden brown.

PASTA WITH A SAUCE FROM SYRACUSE

Serves 4.
Keeps up to 3 days under refrigeration.
Freeze sauce or leftover dish for 1 month.

The joy of pasta is that it takes so little time to cook, and the speed with which you can put together this delicious dish defies belief - it looks particularly inviting made with a mixture of the three colours of pasta spirals. Anchovies are always used in Sicily but if you prefer the sauce to be wholly vegetarian a tablespoon of drained capers can be added instead.

The sauce will come to no harm if it is made in advance, but it's best to mix it with the hot pasta just before serving.

12 oz (350 g) rigatoni or penne pasta (spirals or ridged short-cut macaroni)
grated cheese

For the sauce

1 lb (450 g) aubergines (eggplants), unpeeled, cut in ⅜-inch (1-cm) cubes
1 each medium red and yellow peppers
1 tbsp sunflower oil
1 tbsp olive oil
2 cloves of garlic, finely chopped
1 x 15 oz (425 g) can chopped Italian tomatoes
1 dozen fat black olives, stoned
1 can anchovies, drained and cut in ½-inch (1-cm) lengths
10 grinds of black pepper
6 leaves of fresh basil, coarsely shredded

Put the unpeeled cubes of aubergine in a salad spinner or colander and sprinkle thickly with salt. Leave for 30 minutes, then rinse well and dry. Meanwhile, grill (broil) the peppers until the skin looks charred, leave wrapped in paper towels for 5 minutes, then strip off the skin with your fingers and cut the flesh in narrow strips. In a heavy 9-inch (22.5-cm) saucepan or deep-lidded frying pan, heat the oils and sauté the aubergine (covered) for 10 minutes, then uncover and add all the remaining ingredients. Cover and simmer gently for 15 minutes, then taste and add a little salt if necessary. The sauce should be thick but juicy.

Meanwhile, cook the pasta according to the packet directions and drain well. Put the hot sauce into a bowl and, using 2 spoons, toss with the hot pasta so that every piece is coated before turning into a warm entrée dish. Serve at once with finely grated cheese.

Two Uncooked Pasta Sauces

The Italians have always insisted that there is nothing like a steaming bowl of pasta lightly laced with a savoury sauce to provide a cheap, satisfying and almost instant meal. Now nutritionists are also singing pasta's praises, for the special durum wheat that's the essential ingredient for any successful pasta dough is very high in protein, while sauces are invariably based on olive oil, rich in the monounsaturates that we're now told are essential for a healthy diet. But what about the taste factor? Pasta in itself is neutral in flavour - which is why it's so good to partner the much more assertive olive oil. But here you must be sure to use oil from the first pressing - it's invariably labelled 'extra virgin' - because no heat (which would spoil the flavour) is used in extracting it. I find for general use that the supermarket own-brands are excellent. However, as your palate begins to be more selective you may like to try oil from different countries, each of which has its own style. Keep the olive oil at room temperature but well shielded from the light (which tends to make it go rancid).

In the 2 pasta dishes which follow, the sauce is not cooked. To prepare the first, all you need is a food processor and for the second, a sharp cook's knife. But because the sauce is only at room temperature, it's essential to have the serving dish and plates very hot, so that the pasta doesn't become lukewarm when it is mixed with the sauce.

SPAGHETTINI AL OLIVE NERE (*Pasta with Black Olives*)

An almost instant meal for 2. Serve with crusty bread and a salad of mixed leaves or tomatoes. For 4, simply double all the ingredients.

5 oz (150 g) spaghettini or spaghetti (fresh or dried)
5 oz (150 g/1 cup) fat black olives
1 medium clove of garlic
1 tsp fresh oregano or marjoram, finely chopped, or $\frac{1}{4}$ tsp dried
3 tbsp extra virgin olive oil
10 grinds of black pepper
1 oz (25 g/2 tbsp) unsalted butter or margarine

First cook the pasta in boiling salted water according to directions - it must be *al dente,* with a little bite left. While it cooks, cut the olive flesh away from the stones and chop coarsely with a knife. Chop the garlic and herbs finely, then put with the olives in a small bowl. Slowly stir in the olive oil and add the pepper.

Melt the butter in a large bowl in the microwave. Drain the pasta (leaving some water clinging to it), then add to the butter in the bowl. Toss well to coat the strands and then add the olive mixture. Toss all together with a large spoon and fork.

LINGUINE WITH WALNUT SAUCE

Serves 6 (or 4; see below).
Make and eat the same day.

The many varieties of fresh (as opposed to packeted dry) pasta that you can find in the chill cabinets of most supermarkets and delicatessens need only 5 minutes or less to cook, so they make an ideal choice for a summer meal. Both tagliatelle (broad noodles) and linguine (thin spaghetti) are delicious dressed with an uncooked walnut sauce - similar to pesto but without the basil or pine kernels - which can be prepared in the same time as it takes the pasta to cook. As the sauce is cold, be sure to toss it with the pasta in a heated dish and serve it on hot plates.

This makes a delicious starter for 6 before a fish main course, or it can be the centre dish of a light supper for 4, accompanied by a green salad with a herb vinaigrette or by very ripe sliced tomatoes sprinkled with thinly scissored fresh basil, a squeeze of lemon juice, a little sea salt and black pepper and a tiny sprinkling of extra virgin olive oil. Serve with French bread (recrisped for 5 minutes in a moderate oven) or rye bread spread with a low-fat cream cheese.

12-14 oz (350-400 g) fresh linguine or green and white fresh tagliatelle (save 4 tbsp of the ccoking liquid)
3 oz (75 g/1 cup) freshly grated Parmesan or other finely grated cheese

For the sauce
4 oz (125 g/1 cup) walnuts
$\frac{1}{2}$ small clove of garlic
2 oz (50 g/$\frac{1}{4}$ cup) butter or margarine
$3\frac{1}{2}$ fl oz (100 ml/$\frac{1}{2}$ cup) fromage frais, Greek yoghurt or smetana
$\frac{1}{2}$ tsp salt
15 grinds of black pepper

In the food processor blend the walnuts, garlic, butter, fromage frais, salt and pepper very thoroughly until you have a smooth sauce. Cook the pasta and drain it lightly, adding 4 tablespoons of the cooking liquid to the sauce to thin it to coating consistency. Mix the pasta with the sauce. Add the grated Parmesan cheese and toss well together, then serve.

BEAN AND PASTA SALAD

Serves 8.
Keeps 2 days under refrigeration.

A salad made with the little corkscrews of pasta the Italians call 'fusilli' makes a very flavoursome alternative to the more familiar potato or rice salad to serve as a starter or light main course. Fusilli come in a colourful mixture of plain, tomato and spinach flavours and the best contain nothing but durum wheat semolina - the flour that makes the finest pasta - and dried and powdered vegetables. The cooked fusilli should be tossed with the dressing immediately they have been drained - this stops them sticking together - and then the complete salad needs several hours in the refrigerator to give the bland pasta time to soak up the highly seasoned dressing. Leave at room temperature for half an hour before serving.

1 small bunch of trimmed spring onions (scallions)
1 x 15 oz (425 g) can red kidney beans, well drained
12 oz (350 g) fusilli

For the dressing
4 fl oz (125 ml/½ cup) sunflower oil
1 tbsp olive oil
3 tbsp white wine vinegar or cider vinegar
1 teasp salt
1 teasp caster sugar
15 grinds of black pepper
1 rounded teasp Dijon mustard
2 tbsp chopped parsley

Set your largest pan (two-thirds full of hot water) to come to the boil - the pasta should have room to 'swim' in it. Meanwhile, make the dressing by shaking all the ingredients together in a screwtop jar until they thicken into an emulsion - after 1 or 2 minutes. Finely shred the spring onion bulbs with 4 inches (10 cm) of the green, then put in a large bowl with the well-drained beans. To cook the pasta, add a tablespoonful of salt to the boiling water, add the fusilli, bring the water back to the boil, leave the lid half on (to stop the pot boiling over) and cook for 12 minutes before testing for done-ness - the pasta should be tender when bitten but not so soft that it has become flabby.

Turn the pasta into a large colander, allow it to drain thoroughly for a couple of minutes, then add to the beans. Pour over the vinaigrette dressing and toss gently but thoroughly, preferably with a pair of wooden salad servers. Cover the bowl with clingfilm (saranwrap) and chill until 30 minutes before serving, then pile lightly into a salad bowl and leave at room temperature until required.

Strudels, Pies, Pizzas and More

ASPARAGUS STRUDEL WITH A MINTED CUCUMBER SAUCE

Serves 8 (makes 2 strudel).
Leftovers keep 1 day under refrigeration.
Do not freeze.

1 x 14 oz (400 g) packet filo pastry (12 sheets needed)
4 oz (125 g/½ cup) melted butter or margarine

For the filling
2 x 9 oz (250 g) packs frozen asparagus, thawed
2 oz (50 g/¼ cup) butter or margarine
white part of 2 young leeks, thinly sliced
1 shallot or 3 spring onion bulbs (scallions) finely chopped
8 oz (225 g/2 cups) Gruyère or Jarlsberg cheese, finely grated
3 eggs, beaten to blend
2 tbsp chopped fresh mint
2 tbsp chopped parsley
3 tbsp chopped fresh dill
2 tbsp snipped chives
1 teasp salt
20 grinds of black pepper
½ teasp paprika pepper
pinch of Cayenne pepper
1½ tbsp fresh lemon juice
2 oz (50 g/½ cup) flaked almonds, toasted (3 minutes on 100 per cent power, stirring once)

For sprinkling on the strudel
1 tbsp each sesame seeds and poppy seeds

For the Minted Cucumber Sauce
½ large cucumber, peeled and cut in ⅜ inch (1 cm) cubes
1 x 9 oz (250 g) carton 8% fromage frais or Greek yoghurt
1 medium clove of garlic, crushed
2 teasp dried mint
¼ teasp salt
8 grinds of black pepper

Lay the defrosted asparagus on a double thickness of kitchen paper to remove excess moisture, then cut in 1-inch (2.5-cm) lengths and place in a large bowl.

Melt the 2 oz butter and sauté the leeks and shallot or spring onions until soft and transparent. Add to the asparagus together with all the other filling ingredients. Mix gently but thoroughly together and adjust the seasoning if necessary.

Preheat the oven to Gas No. 5 (375°F/190°C).

To assemble each strudel, proceed as follows. Take 6 pastry sheets from the packet and lay them on top of each other, brushing each in turn with a thin layer of melted butter. Arrange half the asparagus mixture across the lower edge of the pastry layer in a long strip 3 inches (7.5 cm) wide, leaving 3 inches (7.5 cm) of pastry clear on the bottom edge and 1 inch (2.5 cm) on either side. Turn in the sides to enclose the filling, then roll up into a strudel and arrange on a greased tray. Cut through the top layer of pastry at 2-inch (5-cm) intervals.

Repeat with another 6 leaves of pastry and the remaining filling. Brush the tops and sides of each strudel with a thin layer of butter and scatter with the mixed seeds. Bake for 30–35 minutes, until a rich golden brown. Cool for 10 minutes before serving with the sauce.

To make the sauce, put the cucumber in a salad spinner, sprinkle lightly with salt and leave for 30 minutes. Rinse off the salt and spin dry (this can also be done in a colander but the cucumber will need to be dried with paper towels). Put the fromage frais into a bowl with the garlic, mint and seasonings, then stir in the cucumber. Taste and add more salt if necessary. Chill for several hours, then serve with the slices of strudel.

A STRUDEL OF STIR-FRIED VEGETABLES WITH MAYONNAISE CHANTILLY

Serves 6–8.
Leftovers keep 1 day under refrigeration.
Do not freeze.

Full of protein and vitamins.

1 x 14 oz (400 g) packet filo pastry (12 sheets needed)
4 oz (125 g/½ cup) butter or margarine

For the filling
1 oz (25 g/2 tbsp) butter or margarine
2 teasp olive or sunflower oil
1 x 1lb (450 g) pack frozen stir-fry vegetables
8 oz (225 g/2½ cups) closed-cap mushrooms, thinly sliced
4 oz (125 g) mangetout, cut in half lengthwise
2 eggs, beaten
6 oz (175 g/1½ cups) sharp Cheddar cheese, grated
½ teasp salt
10 grinds of black pepper
1 tbsp finely chopped parsley
2 tbsp sesame seeds

For the Mayonnaise Chantilly
8 oz (225 g/1 cup) Greek yoghurt, fromage frais or creamed smetana
3 rounded tbsp mild mayonnaise
1 tbsp snipped chives
pinch of salt
speck of white pepper

Preheat the oven to Gas No. 5 (375°F/190°C). To make the filling, put the butter and oil in a wok or frying pan and stir-fry all the vegetables until bite tender – about 3–4 minutes – then mix with the eggs, cheese, seasonings and parsley. Cool until the mixture stops steaming.

Overlap 2 sheets of pastry so that you have a layer 17 inches (42.5 cm) wide (you may need only 1½ sheets depending on the size). Brush lightly with melted butter, then repeat with 5 more layers, brushing each layer and stacking them on top of each other.

Spoon the cooled filling on to the edge of the pastry nearest to you, leaving a 1-inch (2.5-cm) border all round, making a mound about 3 inches (7.5 cm) across. Turn in the sides to enclose the filling, then roll up the pastry into a flattened Swiss roll. Arrange, seal side down, on a greased baking tray, then brush the top lightly with melted butter and scatter thickly with sesame seeds. Bake for 35 minutes, or until golden. Slice and serve within 30 minutes together with the sauce.

To make the sauce, stir all the ingredients together and serve at room temperature.

PETITES TARTES AU BLEU

Makes 8 x 4-inch (10-cm) tartes 1 inch (2.5 cm) deep, or 1 x 9½-inch (24-cm) tarte 1¼ inches (3 cm) deep.
Serve the filled tartes freshly baked.
Do not freeze.

Baked cases can be filled and then frozen raw. They do not need to be thawed before cooking but will need 5 minutes longer in the oven.

This makes a wonderful starter or main dish for a special lunch or supper. The creamy filling contrasts brilliantly with the sharp flavour of the cheese. The individual tartes or the wedges cut from the large quiche look very decorative garnished with small bunches of black grapes. Tiny wedges of the tarte also make delicious titbits to go with drinks.

For the pastry

9 oz (250 g/2¼ cups) plain (all-purpose) flour
pinch of salt
1½ teasp icing (confectioners') sugar
5½ oz (165 g/⅔ cup plus 1 tbsp) firm butter or margarine
4 tbsp cold water (3 tbsp if using a food processor)

For the filling

5 oz (150 g/⅔ cup) skimmed-milk cheese or other low-fat cheese
4 oz (125 g) blue cheese such as Stilton or Danish Blue, crumbled
1 oz (25g/2 tbsp) butter or margarine
3 x size 2 eggs, beaten
10 fl oz (275 ml/1¼ cups) whipping cream
15 grinds of black pepper
1 tbsp finely snipped chives

To make the pastry, by hand or by machine, mix the flour, salt and icing sugar, then rub in the fat until each particle is the size of a small pea. Sprinkle with the water to moisten the dry ingredients evenly so that they can be gathered into a dough – it should be moist enough to hold together without being sticky. Alternatively, make by the Food-processor Method (see p. 371). Flatten into a 1-inch-thick (2.5-cm) circle and chill for 30 minutes, then roll out to fit the tarte tins (using a 6-inch/15- cm plate or pan lid as a template), or the large case. Prick all over with a fork, then press a piece of foil into the larger tin only, moulding it into shape. Freeze for a further 30 minutes, then bake at Gas No. 7 (425°F/220°C) for 8 minutes, until the pastry is set and firm to the touch (the small tartes can now be removed). Remove the foil from the large tin, prick the base again and continue to bake for a further 3–5 minutes, until quite dry to the touch but only lightly browned. Set aside.

To make the filling, cream the two cheeses and the butter together in a bowl, then add the slightly beaten eggs, followed by the cream, pepper and chives. Taste and add a little salt if necessary. Divide between the tartes or the large tin, filling them to the brim. Bake at Gas No. 5 (375°F/190°C) for 30 minutes, or until golden. Serve warm 10–15 minutes after baking, or later the same day at room temperature.

May be gently reheated.

CHEESE FEUILLETÉ

Serves 6.
Raw feuilleté can be refrigerated for 1 day or frozen for 3 months.
Thaw before baking.
Serve freshly baked.

The crisp pastry layers enclose a fluffy savoury filling.

1 x 12–14 oz (350–400 g) packet of puff pastry

For the filling

6 oz (175 g/1½ cups) Cheddar cheese, grated
8 oz (225 g/1 cup) low- or medium-fat soft cheese (curd or Quark)
1 oz (25 g/¼ cup) blue cheese – eg Stilton or Danish Blue
1 egg
½ teasp paprika
1 tbsp chopped parsley
2 teasp chopped fresh marjoram or oregano
1 tbsp snipped chives

For the glaze

1 egg yolk
1 teasp water
2 teasp sesame seeds

To make the filling, put the grated Cheddar, soft cheese and blue cheese into a bowl, then beat in the whisked egg, the seasonings and the herbs.

Divide the pastry into 2 and roll each half into a rectangle measuring approximately 14 x 18 inches (35 x 45 cm). The pastry should be thin. Lay 1 rectangle on a baking tray and spread with the filling, leaving 1 inch (2.5 cm) of pastry clear all the way round. Dampen this margin with cold water, then lay the second rectangle carefully on top.

Seal the pastry all the way round by pressing down on it with the side of the hand, then flake the edges with the back of a knife blade. Make cuts through the top layer at 2-inch (5-cm) intervals to allow steam to escape. Chill until ready to bake.

Preheat the oven to Gas No. 8 (450°F/230°C). Mix the egg yolk with the water, then paint it evenly all over the top, and scatter with the sesame seeds. Bake for 15 minutes, then turn the temperature down to Gas No. 6 (400°F/200°C) for a further 15–20 minutes, by which time it should be well risen, crisp to the touch and richly browned. Serve in slices.

MUSHROOM CRESCENTS

Makes 6.
Freeze raw or cooked for 1 month.

Crunching through a croissant used to be a pleasure reserved for continental breakfasting. Then croissants crossed the Channel. Latterly the French had the novel idea of adding a filling – and hey presto, the breakfast roll became a filling snack and an acceptable Gallic fast food. And these too have made their mark in this country.

They really are quite delicious, but immensely high in calories, as a true croissant is made from flaky pastry raised with yeast, so it's positively saturated with fat.

In this recipe I've modified the traditional mixture to produce a croissant that looks the same and has the same delicious flavour, but contains only a third of the fat. Inside I've tucked a stuffing of mushrooms and cheese. Delightful when served with coffee, it also makes a tasty vegetarian meal or accompaniment to a fish meal.

For the dough

8 oz (225 g/2 cups) strong white bread flour
1 teasp sugar
1 teasp salt
1 x ¼ oz (7 g) sachet easy-blend yeast
1 oz (25 g/2 tbsp) butter or margarine
3 fl oz (75 ml/⅓ cup) hand-hot milk
1 large egg
additional ½ oz (15 g/1 tbsp) butter or margarine

For the filling

8 oz (225 g/2½ cups) fresh mushrooms, coarsely chopped
nut of butter or margarine
4 oz (125 g/1 cup) mature Cheddar cheese, grated
2 tbsp chopped parsley
½ teasp Dijon mustard
½ teasp salt
pinch of ground nutmeg

For the glaze

1 beaten egg
1 tbsp sesame seeds

To make the dough in the food processor blend the flour, sugar, salt and yeast to mix for 2 seconds. Drop in the 1 oz butter and process for 5 seconds, then add the milk and egg and process until a soft, scone-like dough is formed. If very sticky add a little extra flour. Process for 1 minute to knead the dough. Turn out on floured board and knead by hand for 30 seconds.

To mix by machine or by hand, stir the dry ingredients together in a large bowl and rub in the 1 oz butter. Mix to a soft but non-sticky dough with the milk and egg, adding a little extra flour if sticky. Turn out on floured board and knead for 3-4 minutes, until smooth and springy.

Lightly oil a large mixing bowl, put in the dough and turn it so that it is coated with the fat to prevent drying. Cover with clingfilm (saranwrap) and leave for about 40 minutes, by which time it will have doubled in size.

With a microwave this process can be hastened by microwaving the bowl of dough on 100 per cent power for 20 seconds. Leave 5 minutes, then repeat. It should double in bulk in 20 minutes.

While the dough is rising, prepare the filling. Gently sauté the mushrooms in the nut of butter for 5 minutes, then allow to bubble, uncovered, until the liquid evaporates. Cool a little, then mix with the cheese, parsley, mustard, salt and nutmeg.

MUSHROOM CRESCENTS

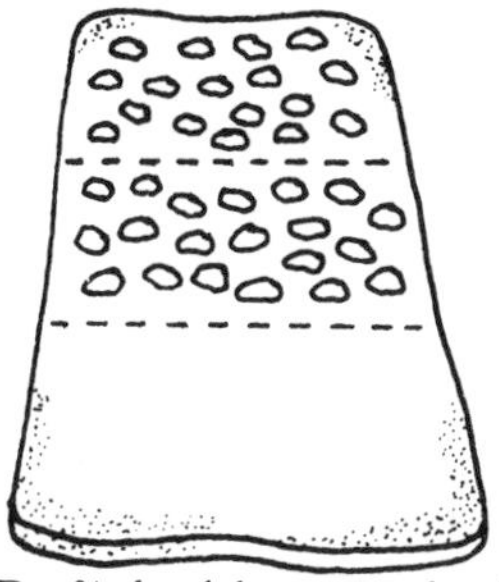

Dot ⅔rds of the rectangle of dough with the extra ½ oz (15 g/1 tbsp) butter

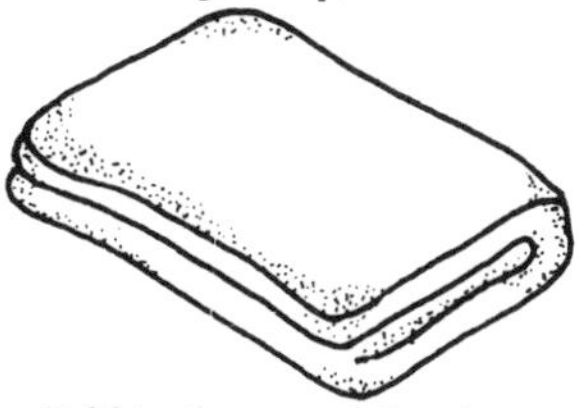

Fold in three, seal the three open sides with the side of the hand, roll into round

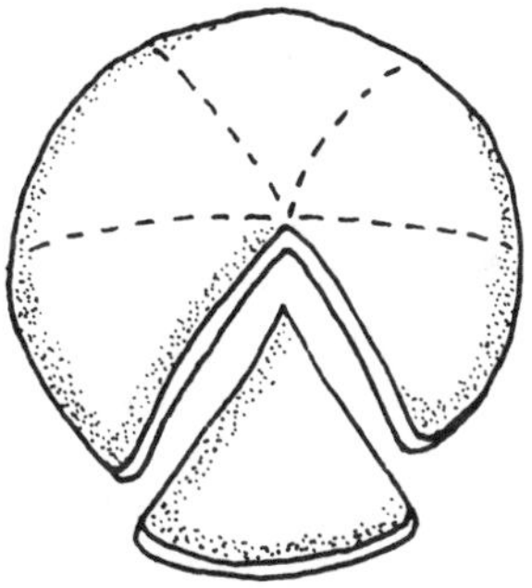

Divide dough into six triangles

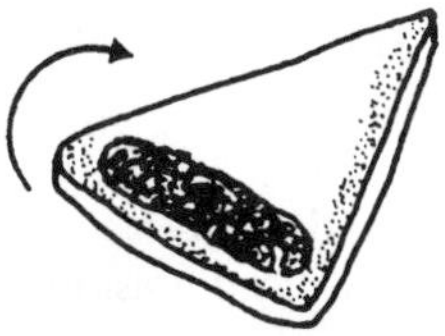

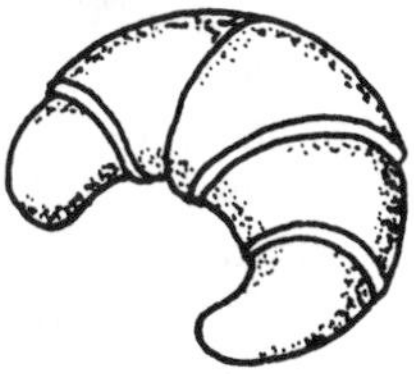

Roll up from wide end to form a crescent shape

On a floured board roll the dough into a rectangle 12 x 6 inches (30 x 15 cm). Scatter two-thirds of the dough with ½ oz (1tbsp) butter cut into tiny pieces. Fold in 3 and seal the ends. Leave for 10 minutes for the dough to relax.

Lightly flour the board and roll the dough into a 14-inch (35-cm) circle. Brush with a little beaten egg. Section and cut into 6 equal segments, then divide the filling between them, placing this at the wider end. Roll up tightly, curl in a crescent shape and place on a greased baking tray. Brush with the remaining egg and scatter with the sesame seeds. Slip tray into a large plastic bag and allow 20–30 minutes for croissants to double in size. Bake in a preheated oven, Gas No. 6 (400°F/200°C) for 15 minutes, or until golden brown. Best served warm. May be reheated.

PIZZA

Serves 4–6 (makes 2 x 11 inch/27.5 cm pizzas). Freeze 3 months.

One of the joys of eating in Israel is the enormous choice of unusual kosher cheeses, and now many of them are available in this country - generally wherever kosher delicatessen and groceries are sold.

Tal Ha Emek, the variety I use for this pizza, is a splendid melting cheese (similar to Emmenthal) and therefore ideal. If it is not available where you shop, a Lancashire cheese may be used instead.

For the dough

1 x ¼ oz (7 g) sachet easy-blend yeast or a scant 1 oz (25 g) fresh yeast
1½ teasp brown sugar
5 fl oz (150 ml/⅔ cup) hand-hot water
11 oz (300 g/2¾ cups) wholewheat, granary or white bread flour
1½ teasp salt
1 egg
2 tbsp extra virgin olive oil

For the topping

2 tbsp extra virgin olive oil
1 medium onion
1 fat clove of garlic
1 teasp brown sugar
1 teasp sea salt
20 grinds of black pepper
1 teasp dried basil
1 bay leaf
1 x 14 oz (400 g) can chopped tomatoes
1 rounded tbsp tomato purée

For the garnish

1 large red or yellow pepper
4 oz (125 g/1¼ cups) button mushrooms
1 can anchovies or 4 oz (125 g) olives
8 oz (225 g/2 cups) Tal Ha Emek or Lancashire cheese
extra virgin olive oil
dried Italian herbs

If fresh yeast is used, crumble into a mixing bowl or the food processor and add the sugar, water and a few tablespoons of the flour. Mix together until smooth, then add all the remaining ingredients and mix until a ball of dough is formed.

If easy-blend yeast is used, put the flour, salt, sugar and yeast into the bowl and mix for 30 seconds or process for 3 seconds. Add the egg, oil and hand-hot water and mix to a dough.

To knead dough, process for 1 minute with the steel blade or knead with a dough hook for 5 minutes, adding 1 or 2 extra tablespoons of flour if the dough is still sticky. Put the dough into a large, lightly oiled bowl, turn to coat with the oil, then cover the bowl with clingfilm (saranwrap). Leave in a warm room for 1 hour, by which time it will have doubled in bulk.

Meanwhile, prepare the topping. In an 8-inch (20-cm) saucepan cook the finely chopped onion and garlic in the 2 tablespoons of oil until soft and golden. Add all the remaining topping ingredients and simmer, uncovered, for around 15 minutes, until as thick as ketchup. This may also be done in 6 minutes on 100 per cent power in a glass or plastic bowl in the microwave. Discard the bay leaf and allow to cool.

When the dough has risen, divide it in 2 and roll each half into a circle 11 inches (27.5 cm) in diameter. Lay each circle on an 11-inch (27.5 cm) pizza pan or on a greased tray and turn up the edges slightly to form a shallow rim. Spread the tomato topping evenly on each pizza and garnish with thinly sliced peppers, sliced mushrooms and drained, split anchovies or olives. Finally arrange the cheese cut in thin slices all over the top. Sprinkle the surface of the pizza lightly with olive oil and scatter with Italian herb seasoning. The pizzas can now be refrigerated until ready to bake later in the day, or they can be left to rise for 20 minutes, then open-frozen before being wrapped in foil.

To cook the fresh pizzas, allow to rise at room temperature for 20 minutes while the oven is thoroughly preheated to Gas No. 8 (450°F/230°C). Bake the pizzas for 20 minutes, or until the crust around the edge is a rich golden brown. Serve at once.

To cook the frozen pizzas, bake from frozen at Gas No. 7 (425°F/220°C) in a thoroughly preheated oven for 30–35 minutes.

To bake the pizza and then freeze it, bake at Gas No. 7 (425°F/220°C). Cool, open-freeze and then package. Reheat from frozen at Gas No. 6 (400°F/200°C) for 20 minutes or thaw in package at room temperature for 2 hours, then reheat at Gas No. 6 (400°F/200°C) for 10–15 minutes.

PARTY PIZZA

Serves 10.
Freeze uncooked pastry case and sauce 3 months.
Leftover baked pizza keeps 2 days under refrigeration.

The deliciously flaky pastry contrasts with the juicy sauce.

1 recipe for Cream Cheese Flaky Pastry (see p. 402).

For the filling

2 tbsp extra virgin olive oil
1 large onion
2 level teasp sugar
2 level teasp salt
20 grinds of black pepper
½ teasp dried basil
1 fat clove of garlic, crushed
2 bay leaves
1 x 28 oz (800 g) can tomatoes
2 tbsp tomato purée
8 oz (225 g/2 cups) Cheddar cheese
1 can anchovies or 4 oz (125 g) black olives

To make the filling, heat the oil in a large saucepan, then add the chopped onion and cook gently until soft and golden. Add all the remaining ingredients except the cheese and anchovies or olives. Simmer gently for about 15 minutes, until the sauce is the consistency of ketchup.

Roll out the pastry to fit 2 x 7-inch (17.5-cm) or 1 x 11-inch (27.5-cm) loose-bottomed flan tins. Spoon the filling into the uncooked crust. Cut the cheese into matchsticks and arrange on top with the drained fillets of anchovy or the sliced olives. Bake in a hot oven, Gas No. 7 (425°F/220°C), for 15–20 minutes. Serve warm.

PETITES PISSALADIÈRES

Serves 6–8.
Freeze raw circles of dough 1 month. Serve complete pissaladières same day.

These miniature pizzas – albeit with an unmistakably French accent – make a superb vegetarian main course, with a green salad and a baked potato as plate-mates.

Don't be put off by the yeast dough. It's very easy to put together and, better news still, can be shaped and frozen, ready for the oven. The filling can also be made and refrigerated up to 2 days in advance.

For the dough

11 oz (300 g/3¾ cups) plain (all-purpose) flour
1½ teasp each salt and sugar
1 x ¼ oz (7 g) sachet easy-blend yeast or scant 1 oz (25 g) fresh yeast
1 egg
2 tbsp olive oil
5 fl oz (150 ml/⅔ cup) hand-hot water

For the topping

2 cans anchovy fillets, drained, or 8 oz (225 g/2½ cups) sliced mushrooms
2½ lb (1.25 kg) onions, peeled and very thinly sliced (use a food processor if possible)
5 tbsp olive oil (plus 1 tbsp extra if mushrooms used)
1 clove of garlic, peeled and crushed
6 sprigs of parsley
1 sprig of fresh thyme or ½ teasp dried thyme
1 small bay leaf
1 x 7 oz (200 g) can tomatoes, drained
1½ teasp salt
15 grinds of black pepper
24 black olives
little extra olive oil

To prepare the dough with easy-blend yeast, put the flour, salt, sugar and yeast into a bowl. Process for 2 seconds (or mix for 30 seconds). Now slowly add the egg, oil and hot water and process 1 minute in food processor (or knead for 5 minutes in mixer), adding further 1 oz (25 g) flour if the mixture is sticky. Turn out on floured board and knead lightly by hand (about 30 seconds), until the underside of the dough is smooth.

With fresh yeast, put it in the bowl of the processor or mixer with the sugar, lukewarm water and a few tablespoons of the flour. Process or mix until evenly blended, then add all the remaining ingredients. Process for 1 minute (or knead with dough hook for 5 minutes), until smooth and no longer sticky. Add 1 or 2 extra tablespoons of flour if dough is still sticky after kneading.

Grease a mixing bowl, put the dough in and turn over so the top is greased. Cover with clingfilm (saranwrap) and leave in a warm place until double in bulk – about 1 hour. Punch dough down and divide it into 8 pieces. Roll or press each piece of dough into a circle 5 inches (12.5 cm) in diameter with a slightly-thickened edge. Transfer the circle to greased baking sheets and use at once, cover with foil and freeze. (If not to be used next day, frozen circles can be stored on top of each other in a plastic bag or container.)

Prepare the topping while the dough is rising. If mushrooms are used, sauté for 5 minutes in 1 tablespoon of oil. Put the onions and 5 tablespoons of oil in a frying pan with the garlic and herbs. Cover and cook gently for 25 minutes. Uncover and stir in the tomatoes. Re-cover and cook slowly for a further 20 minutes, until the onions are meltingly soft and have amalgamated with the tomatoes. Add the salt and pepper. Remove the bay leaf and the herbs. Turn into a bowl and leave to cool.

To assemble the pissaladières, defrost the circles of dough overnight in the refrigerator. Set the oven at Gas No. 6 (400°F/200°C). Spread the onion mixture over the dough, arrange the anchovies or the sautéd mushrooms and the olives decoratively on top and sprinkle with a little olive oil to prevent the surface from drying out. Leave for 15 minutes, then bake for 15–20 minutes, or until the edges are golden and crisp. Serve warm.

SAVOURY PASTRY

Sufficient for 1 x 8–9-inch (20–22.5-cm) flan case.
Uncooked pastry keeps 2 days under refrigeration.
Freeze 3 months.

This is splendid for all kinds of quiches or savoury tarts.

4 oz (125 g/½ cup) butter or margarine
6 oz (175 g/1½ cups) plain (all-purpose) flour
pinch of salt
1 level teasp icing (confectioners') sugar
about 2 tbsp icy water
squeeze of lemon juice

Rub the fat into the flour with salt and sugar, until no particles larger than a small pea appear when the bowl is shaken. Mix to a firm dough with the icy water and lemon juice. Alternatively, use the Food-processor Method (see p. 371). Foil wrap and chill. Use as directed in the recipe.

BROWN HERB PASTRY

Sufficient for 1 x 9–10-inch (22.5–25-cm) flan tin.

5 oz (150 g/⅔ cup) butter or margarine
4 oz (125 g/½ cup) granary flour
4 oz (125 g/½ cup) plain (all-purpose) white flour
½ teasp salt
2 teasp icing sugar
1 teasp Herbes de Provence
1 teasp fines herbes
1 rounded tbsp chopped parsley
1 teasp dry mustard
1 egg, beaten with 1 teasp wine vinegar and 1 tbsp cold water

Rub the fat into the flours with the salt, sugar, herbs and mustard. When no particles larger than a small pea remain, mix to a firm dough with the egg mixture. Alternatively, use the Food-processor Method (see p. 371). Foil wrap and chill. Use as directed in the recipe.

SWISS CHEESE QUICHE

Serves 8.
Uncooked pastry case keeps 2 days under refrigeration.
Freeze 3 months.

A gently flavoured quiche, very quickly made.

1 recipe Savoury Pastry (see this page)

For the filling

1 large onion, finely chopped
1 oz (25 g/2 tbsp) butter or margarine
8 oz (225 g/2 cups) Gruyère or Emmental cheese, or 8 oz (225 g/2 cups) mature Gouda, grated
1 level tbsp flour
3 eggs, well beaten
8 fl oz (225 ml/1 cup) single (light) cream
salt and pepper
¼ teasp nutmeg

Sauté the onion in the butter until soft and pale gold in colour. Roll out the pastry and use it to line a 9-inch (22.5-cm) quiche dish 1 inch (2.5 cm) deep. With a fork lightly toss the cheese with the flour. Spread on the bottom of the pricked pastry shell and cover with the sautéd onions. Beat eggs and cream together and season lightly with salt and pepper. Pour over grated cheese and onions. Sprinkle surface with nutmeg.

Bake at Gas No. 6 (400°F/200°C) for 15 minutes, then reduce heat to Gas No. 3 (325°F/160°C) and continue baking for 30 minutes, until puffed and golden and firm to gentle touch.

Serve warm. May be reheated.

LANCASHIRE CHEESE TART WITH GARDEN HERBS

Makes 10 large portions, 14 smaller ones.
Keeps 2 days under refrigeration.
Freeze raw pastry and filling 3 months.

This makes a monster flan with a superb creamy texture due to the special properties of the cheese. Ask the cheesemonger for 'tasty Lancashire'.

For the pastry

1 recipe Brown Herb Pastry (see p. 125), chilled for at least 30 minutes

For the filling

5 eggs
8 fl oz (225 ml/⅔ cup) milk
5 fl oz (150 ml/⅔ cup) single (light) cream
½ level teasp salt
12 grinds of black pepper
2 level tbsp snipped chives or chopped parsley
1 lb (450 g/4 cups) crumbly Lancashire cheese or mature Cheddar cheese, grated

To make the pastry case, have ready a 12-inch (30-cm) flan tin set on a baking tray. Roll out the chilled pastry ⅛ inch (0.3 cm) thick on a floured board, and gently ease into the flan tin, trimming level with a sharp knife. Prick all over with a fork and put in the freezer for at least half an hour.

To make the filling, whisk the eggs with the milk, cream, seasonings and herbs. Crumble the cheese with the fingers and add to the egg mixture. Pour into the pastry shell.

Bake in a quick oven, Gas No. 7 (425°F/220°C), for 20 minutes, then at Gas No. 4 (350°F/180°C) for a further 30–40 minutes, until rich brown and puffed. Serve warm.

PROVENÇALE CHEESE, OLIVE AND ANCHOVY TARTE

Serves 8.
Raw and cooked pastry freeze 3 months.
Refrigerate raw pastry case 1 day, baked pastry case 3 days.

A savoury and satisfying French-style tarte. For strict vegetarians, omit the anchovies.

For the pastry

1 recipe Brown Herb Pastry (see p. 125), chilled for at least 30 minutes

For the filling

small bunch spring onion bulbs (scallions), finely sliced
1 oz (25 g/2 tbsp) butter or margarine
1 tbsp cornflour (cornstarch)
5 fl oz (150 ml/⅔ cup) single (light) cream
5 fl oz (150 ml/⅔ cup) creamy fromage frais
3 eggs, beaten to blend
1 teasp Dijon mustard
1 teasp freeze-dried Herbes de Provence
10 grinds of black pepper
6 oz (175 g/1½ cups) mature Cheddar cheese, finely grated
4 oz (125 g/1 cup) fat black olives, stoned and cut in pieces
2 x 2 oz (50 g) cans anchovies, drained and cut in small pieces

To sprinkle on the tarte

1 oz (25 g/¼ cup) finely grated cheese (Parmesan if available)

To make the case, choose a loose-bottomed quiche tin 9–10 inches (22.5–25 cm) in diameter and 1 inch (2.5 cm) deep. Roll the chilled dough on a floured board into a circle 11–12 inches (27.5–30 cm) in diameter, lift on to the rolling pin and then ease it into the tin, pressing it well into the sides. Trim off any excess, using a sharp knife. Prick the case all over with a fork, then line it with a piece of foil pressed into the shape, and covering the edges of the pastry. Freeze for at least 30 minutes, or more if convenient.

Preheat the oven to Gas No. 6 (400°F/200°C) and put a baking sheet in it to heat up at the same time. Lay the frozen case on the hot baking sheet and bake for 15 minutes, or until the pastry is firm to gentle touch. Remove the foil, prick the base again and return to the oven for a further 8 to 10 minutes, until crisp and dry. This case can now be frozen for later use or used at once.

To complete the tarte, preheat the oven to Gas No. 5 (375°F/190°C). Soften the spring onions in the butter over moderate heat for 3–4 minutes, until beginning to colour. Put the cornflour into a bowl and slowly stir in the cream and fromage frais, followed by the beaten egg and seasonings. Finally stir in the cheese, olives and anchovies (if used).

Spoon into the pastry and sprinkle with the 1 oz (25g/¼ cup) cheese. Bake for 30 minutes, or until puffed and golden and firm to gentle touch. Leave at least 15 minutes before serving.

The tarte can be reheated in a moderate oven, Gas No. 4 (350°F/180°C), until warm to the touch.

VARIATION

INDIVIDUAL TARTES

These look most effective served for a special lunch or after-theatre supper. You will need 8 loose-bottomed tarte tins, 4 inches (10 cm) in diameter and 1 inch (2.5 cm) deep. Make the pastry and filling in the same way as for the large tarte but bake the pastry 'blind' for only 12 minutes. Fill and bake at the same temperature for 25 minutes.

TOURTE FORESTIÈRE
(Mushroom Tart in a Brown Pastry Crust)

Serves 8.
Keeps 3 days under refrigeration.
The tourte will freeze for 1 month, raw pastry for 3 months.

This is a magnificent vegetarian main dish – the savoury mushroom filling is baked in a satisfying brown herb pastry crust. It's a large tourte, but leftovers keep extremely well. Brown cap mushrooms will give a particularly rich flavour.

For the pastry

1 recipe Brown Herb pastry (see p. 125), chilled for at least 30 minutes

For the filling

2 oz (50 g/¼ cup) butter
1 large onion, very finely chopped
1 small clove of garlic, crushed
1 lb (450 g/5 cups) brown cap mushrooms, very thinly sliced
12 fl oz (350 ml/1½ cups) milk
1 oz (25 g/4 tbsp) cornflour (cornstarch)
½ teasp salt
pinch of white pepper
¼ teasp ground mace (or nutmeg)
2 egg yolks, beaten
4–6 tbsp double (heavy) cream
3 tbsp Amontillado sherry
1 tbsp chopped fresh parsley or fresh coriander

For the topping

3 tbsp sesame seeds
2 tbsp grated Parmesan cheese

Shape one-third of the pastry into a 1-inch-thick (2.5-cm) block, wrap in clingfilm (saran-wrap) or foil and *freeze* for 1 hour.

Roll out the remaining pastry to fit a 9–10-inch (22.5-cm) loose-bottomed or ceramic flan tin, approximately 1½ inches (4 cm) deep. Prick all over and freeze while the filling is prepared.

To make the filling, melt the butter over gentle heat, then sauté the onion and garlic for 5 minutes, or until soft and golden. Add the mushrooms, cover and cook for a further 5 minutes, then uncover and bubble for 2–3 minutes to evaporate any free liquid. Add the milk slowly to the cornflour, mixing all the time, then pour into the pan with the seasonings and bring to the boil, stirring constantly with a wooden spoon. Simmer for 3 minutes.

In a small bowl whisk the egg yolks, cream, sherry and parsley, then add to the pan and reheat until steaming. Do not allow to boil. Leave until cold.

To assemble the tourte, preheat the oven to Gas No. 6 (400°F/200°C) and spoon the cold filling into the frozen pastry case. Grate the block of frozen pastry all over the top. Sprinkle evenly with the sesame and cheese mixture, and bake for 30 minutes, or until a rich golden brown.

Serve warm but not hot. Reheats well.

MEAT

MEAT IN JEWISH COOKERY

The classic meat dishes of Jewish cuisine include no roasts at all; rather, they are casseroles and braises, rich in flavour and meltingly tender.

Because of the dietary laws, which lay down that meat must be koshered within 3 days of slaughter, it was impossible to hang kosher meat before the days of refrigeration, so the meat was too fresh to roast well. Now, however, it is possible to tenderize the meat by hanging it in a butcher's cold room. This means that the prime cuts, such as wing rib (short rib) and shoulder of lamb, can be roasted most successfully, while the eye of the rib can be grilled or fried.

Due to the variable availability and higher price of kosher meat, minced (ground) beef has always been the main standby of the Jewish cook because of the ease with which it could be extended, either with fillers such as rice, bread or matzah meal or by using it as a filling for pastry or vegetables. In this chapter, while due attention is paid to the meat dishes of tradition, the majority of the recipes are of a more modern origin, suitable to the new conditions under which kosher meat is now marketed and cooked.

Choosing and Using Kosher Cuts of Meat

Many kosher butchers now sell meat in both fresh and frozen prepacks which name the cut and the most suitable method of cooking, so it's easier than ever now to pick what you need, even if you don't have a thorough knowledge of the subject. This applies in particular to the more 'convenient' cuts which need only to be put in the oven or under the grill (broiler) to make the kind of quick and easy family meal that was unknown a few years ago. Yet there is a huge variety of other more 'old-fashioned' cuts, such as shin or top rib, which make less expensive but extremely tasty eating, and which the butcher doesn't bother to prepack because housewives find they haven't the time to prepare them in the traditional manner. A good butcher can cut and trim even this kind of meat to make it easier to handle, however, and dishes can be made from it quite speedily using modern time-saving equipment such as the slow-cooker, the automatic oven, the pressure cooker and the microwave oven. That is why I have given below a detailed list of *all* the kosher cuts, as well as some guidance on the best ways in which to cook them.

Although the nomenclature used to describe the cuts of kosher meat may vary from town to town, as well as from one country to the next, I have tried to describe them in such a way that the part of the animal they come from can be easily identified. I have also given directions for making meat and poultry kosher.

All meats should be completely cooked before storage; partially cooking meat raises the internal temperature just enough to encourage the growth of bacteria, but not enough to kill them.

BEEF

Fresh beef is bright red when first cut, but darkens on standing.

Tender beef is usually flecked with fat, rather like marble, and is surrounded by a creamy layer of fat, which may be removed before cooking. (Fatless meat cannot be tender, however, unless cooked by moist heat, as in a casserole or braise.) The inside of the bones should be rosy, and the meat firm and moist to the touch, and very smooth.

Hanging is essential to tenderize beef that is to be roasted or grilled, although it is not necessary for more naturally tender meat such as lamb and veal. The meat should be hung in the butcher's cold store for 10–14 days at a temperature between 32° and 34°F (0°–1°C). It's a good idea to order large roasting joints well in advance so that the butcher will have time to hang the meat to your satisfaction.

Beef Cuts

Shin beef For soup. Makes a flavoursome if rather fibrous stew; the traditional cut for Hungarian Goulash. Also used for Cholent.

Brisket (a) *Thin end* For Tsimmes - used sliced, trimmed of most of the fat. (b) *Point* For covered roasting (in fat without liquid) or for pickling, or for overnight cooking in a Cholent or Dfina. Only economical in a joint weighing 3 lb (1.5 kg) or over. Meaty but fatty (middle brisket has a thinner layer of fat).

Flank Needs rolling. Cheap. Sweet when pot-roasted, but must be pressed and served cold, or it falls to bits. Also for pickling (not as tasty as brisket).

Neck Steak For mincing (grinding) or stewing - has plenty of 'body'.

Chuck or back steak Stew, mince (grind) or braise.

Shoulder steak First-cut for braising, cut in ¾-inch (2-cm) thick slices, or for stews, cut in 1-inch (2.5-cm) cubes. If hung for 10 days, it can be fried.

Blade steak Braise in slices, or pot-roast whole piece. The thin gristle running through can be nicked out before serving.

Alki or round bola (part of shoulder steak), also known as *chuck* Braise; good whether served hot or cold. Thin slices can be cut into 'fairy' steaks, which are beaten out to tenderize them and can then be fried.

Top rib Similar to flank but with more flavour. For Borscht, Cabbage Soup, Cholent, Dfina. Smoked top rib looks like 'streaky' bacon and is said to have a similar taste.

Wing rib (standing rib) For roasting; can be boned out for spit-roasting, or shortened rib on bone can be spitted - keeping bone in adds to flavour.

Lid of rib (top of back rib) Usually rolled, then roasted or spitted; excellent when cold for sandwiches. The joint weighs only 2½–3 lb (1.25–1.5 kg), so is useful for a small family.

Rib or 'entrecote' steaks Boned out and cut ¾–1 inch (2–2.5 cm) thick for grilling (broiling) or frying. Must be hung for 7–10 days.

Bola (chuck) (a) *Corner or prime bola* For braising, with plenty of vegetables. Hung bola can be dry-roasted, very slowly, loosely foil-covered for half the time, allowing 40 minutes to the pound (450 g), or it can be sliced and grilled (broiled). (b) *Slice* For braising, in tomato or wine sauce. Bola, frozen and then cut paper-thin, can be used for minute steaks.

Liver For chopping. A young beast's liver need only be grilled (broiled); an older

animal's liver should be grilled to make kosher, then simmered in salted water for half an hour. (See 'How to Make Meat and Poultry Kosher', below.)
Knuckle and shin beef For soup.
Oxtail For soup (not always available).
Minced (ground) beef Should always be frozen or cooked as soon after mincing as possible, and never kept longer than 24 hours under refrigeration, as the large surface area makes it deteriorate more quickly than other meat.

LAMB

Good lamb joints have plenty of light pinkish meat, creamy fat and very little bone.

Lamb Cuts

Neck and scrag For Scotch Broth.
First-cut chops (cutlets) There are 24 in each animal. For grilling (broiling), frying, roasting (6–8 joined together make a 'rack' or *'carré d'agneau'*; 6 first-cut cutlets from each side joined together make a 'Crown of Lamb').
Middle neck For casseroling.
Breast Casserole with spring vegetables. Boned, stuffed and rolled, it makes a good roast for a small family.
Shoulder Roast. Can be boned or rolled, or boned, pocketed and stuffed. Also used cubed for kebabs.

VEAL

Good veal is between 6 and 8 weeks old, the flesh milky rather than pink in colour.

An older animal, still too young to be classified as beef, is called a 'sterk' (it's also known as 'barley beef'). Insipid in flavour, tenderness is its only virtue.

Veal Cuts

Shank of veal For use in thick soups such as Barley Soup and Hobene Gropen. For Calves' Foot Jelly or casseroles. It must be cut with an electric saw.
Shoulder The thick part of the shoulder can be plain-roasted; the blade end is best boned out, stuffed and braised. Flavour with bay leaf, carrots and onions, and cook in a covered casserole.
Breast Have it boned and pocketed, or boned and rolled, then stuff and braise.
First-cut chops Grill (broil) or fry. Also use boned-out for escalopes.
Shoulder chops Boned-out, made kosher, frozen and sliced for schnitzel or scallopini.
Calf liver Grill (broil) to make kosher (see p. 134) for details), then smother with onions in the frying pan. Or use for Chopped Liver or pâté.

How to Make Meat and Poultry Kosher

All prepacked meat and poultry, and a very large percentage of the fresh supply available in the large centres of Jewish population, has already been made kosher under rabbinical supervision and can therefore be cooked without any further ritual preparation.

If, however, the food does have to be made kosher at home or in an institution, the following procedures should be followed exactly.

Meat and Poultry

(Including bones and giblets, but excluding liver and grilling/broiling steaks, for which special instructions are given below.) All poultry must be drawn before it is made kosher.

1 As soon as possible after the food has been delivered, put it into a deep plastic or enamel bucket and cover completely with cold water.
2 Leave it to soak for half an hour.
3 Take it out and place it on a wire or plastic draining grid, tilted so that the liquid can easily drain away. Leave it to drain for 5 minutes.

4 Thoroughly sprinkle every surface with koshering (coarse) salt. (This can be obtained from a kosher butcher or grocer.)
5 Leave for 1 hour.
6 Rinse the food 3 times in cold water, to remove all trace of salt and blood.

Meat and bones should then be well dried with a paper towel and either cooked at once or stored until required in the refrigerator or freezer.

Poultry and giblets must additionally be scalded as follows:

7 Put the bird in a bowl and pour boiling water over it from a kettle.
8 When cool enough to handle, scrape the skin of the bird with a blunt knife to remove any feathers or coarse bits of skin; remove the skin from the feet. Look inside the body cavity to make sure it is absolutely clean, and that no traces of the entrails remain. Trim off any loose skin from the giblets. Dry thoroughly, and either cook at once or store in the refrigerator or freezer.

Liver

As liver contains too much blood to be effectively made kosher by soaking and salting, the following method is used instead:

1 A thick piece of liver should be cut open; thinner slices should be cut across the surface to facilitate the removal of the blood.
2 Wash the liver thoroughly in cold water, then sprinkle it on both sides with cooking salt (koshering salt is too coarse for the purpose).
3 Place the liver on a wire grid set on a foil-lined grill (broiler) pan (both kept only for this purpose).
4 Grill (broil) gently until the liver changes colour and the surface looks dry, then turn and grill the second side in the same way. Discard the foil after use.

Alternatively, replace steps 3 and 4 by putting the salted liver in a wire basket or on a wire grid over a gas flame and cooking it in the same way, until it has changed colour on both sides. Afterwards, the wire basket or grid should be held over the flame to burn off any residue, then washed, wiped and stored. Chicken livers are made kosher in the same way.

Calf's liver can be served without further preparation, or it can be put in a frying pan and smothered with fried onions. Ox liver must be tenderized by simmering in salted water for half an hour. It can then be used for Chopped Liver.

Steaks

Steaks that are to be grilled (broiled) do not need to be soaked and salted. The grilling process draws out the blood from the meat, and this is considered to satisfy the requirements of kashrut. However, they will have been made kosher by soaking and salting in the usual manner if they have been purchased from a shop selling only ready-koshered meat.

Note All utensils used to make food kosher should be kept exclusively for that purpose. After use, they should be washed and wiped with a special cloth, then stored separately from other kitchen equipment.

On Roasting

A *roasting tin* fitted with a metal rack keeps the joint above the fat as it is cooking, so it doesn't have a chance to soak any of it up. The tin should be made of a heavy material such as *pressed* aluminium or stainless steel. (A standing rib roast does not need to be set on a rack as the curve of the rib bone will keep the joint raised above the fat.) A tin measuring 13 x 10 x 2 inches (33 x 25 x 5 cm) is a good average size and is large enough to accommodate a joint (or a chicken) weight 3–5 lb (1.5–2.5 kg).

A sliced onion strewn in the bottom of the tin half-way through the cooking period will give a rich colour and a good flavour to *gravy* made from the meat juices.

A *meat thermometer* takes the guesswork out of roasting, especially if you are particular about the degree of 'doneness' you require.

All roasts are easier to *carve* if they are left in a warm place to 'settle' after they have finished cooking. During this resting time, the juices which have been drawn to the surface of the meat by the heat of the oven will go back towards the centre of the joint and in this way are not lost when the meat is carved.

A good *carving knife* is a worthwhile investment. An electric carving knife is particularly useful for carving boned joints; otherwise use a conventional carving knife, but buy an efficient knife sharpener.

BEEF

Beef in a Hurry

Sabbath Casseroles

CHOLENT

The dish goes by several names - cholent, sholent, or shalet to mention but a few - and the ingredients, though basically meat, potatoes and fat, are capable of infinite variety according to the whim of the cook and her geographical location. But, as one Jewish cookery writer puts it, this ancient Sabbath concoction is best defined as 'any dish that has the stamina to stand up to 24 hours in the oven'. The origins of the name are believed to lie in two medieval French words, *chauld* (hot) and *lent* (slow), which exactly describes the cooking technique required.

The need for a hot dish that would conform to the laws of Sabbath observance was less pressing when the Jews lived in Palestine, though as far back as the time of the Second Temple there are records of food being kept hot for Sabbath in special vessels. But in the bitter winters of Europe, a hot dish was vital and the cholent (to give it its more usual name) became staple Sabbath fare for both the rich city Jew and his poor country cousin alike.

The cholent ritual was an important part of Jewish life in the Polish villages of the nineteenth century. Each family would mark its pot with chalk and tie it with string before sending it to be cooked in the baker's oven. It was a tragedy indeed if a child should drop the hot dish on the way home, and the whole village would give a spoonful to make up the family's meal. In those cholents, potatoes and kasha (groats) were the main ingredients, with a good meat bone to help the flavour. But the richer communities, where kosher meat was more readily available, would put in a good chunk of boneless brisket or top rib. Jews who came to Britain in the latter years of the nineteenth century continued to make their cholent just as they had done in *der heim,* putting in butter beans or barley for variety, and topping the dish with a fluffy knaidel (dumpling). They found it an ideal way of feeding their large families in the days when a joint, as we know it today, was beyond the finances of most immigrants. The cholent cooked to perfection in a coal oven, as it had done in the wood ovens of Russia and Poland.

But as gas and electricity took over in the kitchen, the days of the cholent were numbered. Tastes changed too, and what had tickled the palate on a bitter winter's day in Poland sat heavily on the Westernized stomachs of the next generation. It didn't taste the same either when cooked in a gas or electric oven at a temperature of 250°F (120°C).

The Jews who emigrated to America kept on making cholent for the first years, but they were able to buy meat more readily and the recipe soon took on a more lavish look. A typical version includes brisket, onions, butter beans (known as lima beans in the USA), barley or potatoes.

Today, the cholent tradition is carried on among communities of Orthodox Jews, using ovens and slow cookers controlled by a time switch (to accord with Sabbath law).

CHOLENT

Serves 6.
Keeps 3 days under refrigeration.
Freeze leftovers 3 months.

1 lb (450 g/2½ cups) butter (dried lima) beans
3 lb (1.75 kg) piece of boneless brisket
½ teasp salt
20 grinds of pepper
1 teasp paprika
1 teasp ginger
2 tbsp chicken fat or 2 oz (50 g/¼ cup) margarine
3 sliced onions
1 clove of garlic, crushed
1 bay leaf
6 peeled whole potatoes or 8 oz (225 g/2 cups) pearl barley

Soak the butter beans in water to cover overnight, then drain well. Rub the brisket with the salt, pepper, paprika and ginger, then brown quickly in the chicken fat or margarine, together with the onions and the garlic. Put in a deep earthenware casserole (a hot-pot or Dutch oven is ideal). Add the bay leaf, drained and soaked beans and the potatoes or barley. Cover with boiling water, put a lid on the dish and place in a quick oven, Gas No. 6 (400°F/200°C) for 30 minutes, or until the contents start to bubble. Turn the heat right down to Gas No. ½ (250°F/120°C), and leave overnight. Serve for lunch the next day. If the dish is to be served as an accompaniment, use only 8 oz (225 g/1¼ cups) butter beans, 8 oz (225 g) meat and a knuckle bone for flavour.

DFINA

La dfina (Adafina, as it's known in Gibraltar) is the Sephardic version of cholent. It was particularly prized among North African Jews, who had a saying that *un Sabbat sans dfina est comme un roi sans ville.* Until they emigrated to Israel and France in the 1960s, women in Morocco, Tunisia and Algeria would spend every Friday afternoon heating a special clay oven. Then, as the Sabbath approached, they filled a cooking pot with all the ingredients for the dfina, sealed it tightly and then surrounded it with damp cloths and a sheet of tin plate to ensure that nothing caught fire. The dfina was left overnight in the gentle heat of the oven.

There is a typical Tunisian recipe given by Suzanne Roukhamovsky in her book *Gastronomie Juive*:

> Wash plenty of sorrel, blanch it a little, squeeze well and fry it in oil. In an earthenware casserole, put some sliced beef, a blanched calf's foot, garlic, onions, salt, pepper, the fried sorrel, white haricot beans and eggs in the shell, which will be hard-boiled the next day. Moisten with water to cover, cover tightly and leave overnight in the oven.

Other recipes call for chick peas, peppers, potatoes and a 'kouclas' – a monster meatball.

ADAFINA

Serves 8.
Keeps 3 days under refrigeration.
Freeze 3 months.

This recipe comes from Gibraltar but from a family who originated in Morocco. Today it is cooked only for special holy days such as Rosh Hashanah, at least by Gibraltarians living in the West.

The different ingredients are placed in the pan in a specific order so that the degree of heat getting to them is correct - the parboiled rice is carefully wrapped to prevent it from losing its texture, then placed in the centre of the pot together with the *hamine* eggs (*ham* is Hebrew for hot). The adafina turns a glorious copper colour during the long, slow cooking.

8 oz (225 g/1 cup) dried chick peas (garbanzo beans) soaked for 24 hours in 2 pints (1.25/5 cups) cold water
3 tbsp sunflower oil or corn oil
2 large (8 oz/225 g) onions, thinly sliced
3 lb (1.5 kg) piece of brisket or top rib
2 tbsp ground paprika
6 oz (175 g/¾ cup) long-grain rice, cooked in 15 fl oz (425 ml/2 cups water seasoned with 1 teasp salt and ¼ teasp ground nutmeg
2 teasp salt
20 grinds of black pepper
1 teasp cinnamon
1 teasp allspice (piment)
1 teasp chilli powder
1 teasp brown sugar
6 oz (175 g/¾ cup) barley, rinsed in cold water then drained
1 whole head of garlic, unpeeled
8 raw eggs in their shells, well washed
8 medium potatoes, peeled
boiling water

The day before they are required, put the chick peas to soak in the cold water - they will swell to 3 times their size. Start to prepare the Adafina 1½ hours before commencement of the Sabbath (or, if for a weekday festival meal, whenever convenient the evening of the day before) - it needs at least 12 hours in the oven. You will need a 1-gallon (4.5-l/20 cup) capacity ovenproof pan or casserole.

Heat the oil gently in the pan, add the onions and fry slowly until a rich golden brown. Rub the meat with the paprika, then fry it briskly to seal on all sides. While it is browning, bring the water and seasonings for the rice to the boil in a small heavy pan. Add the rice, cover and simmer for 15 minutes until the water has been absorbed and the rice is barely tender. Wrap carefully in aluminium foil and prick all over with a fork so that the flavours can penetrate (or the rice can be wrapped in muslin/cheesecloth in the traditional way). Mix together the salt, pepper, cinnamon, allspice, chilli power and brown sugar.

Now start adding all the remaining ingredients to the pan, putting them around and on top of the meat and sprinkling each layer with some of the mixed seasonings. The eggs and the rice should be buried in the middle and the potatoes arranged on top. Add just enough boiling water to cover the potatoes, then cover the pan and bring to the boil on top of the stove. Simmer gently for 30 minutes, then transfer to a very slow oven, Gas No. ¼ (225°F/110°C) and leave untouched until lunchtime the next day.

To serve, lift the meat on to a plate - it will be meltingly tender and practically falling apart, like a French daube - and cut it into serving portions. Arrange the meat, potatoes and shelled eggs on a large platter on a bed of chick peas, barley and gravy. Serve the rice separately.

Braised Joints

BRAISED BOLA (OR CHUCK)

Serves 8–10, or 5 people twice.
Keeps 3 days under refrigeration.
Freeze leftovers 3 months.

Bola or 'chuck' comes from the shoulder of the animal. It is solid meat, with very little fat flecking the muscle, so it responds best to moist heat. It is therefore a very suitable joint to braise when it is first seared to seal it and then cooked on a bed of vegetables in a covered casserole. Braised bola is delicious either hot or cold, provided it is cooked very slowly.

3–5 lb (1.5–2.5 kg) corner of bola (chuck)
1 level teasp salt
1 level teasp dry mustard
2 level teasp flour
2 tbsp oil
2 small onions, coarsely sliced
2 stalks of celery, coarsely sliced
2 carrots, coarsely sliced
½ green pepper
salt
black pepper
2 bay leaves
2 teasp Herbes de Provence
2 tbsp chopped parsley
1 clove of garlic
1½ pints (800 ml/3¾ cups) beef stock

Set the oven at Gas No. 3 (325°F/160°C). Rub the salt, mustard and flour into the raw surface of the meat. In a heavy-based casserole, heat the oil and brown the floured meat quickly on all sides. Lift it out on to a plate. Into the same fat put the sliced onions, cooking them until soft and golden (this is important as it helps to colour the sauce). Add all the remaining vegetables and stir them well to absorb any remaining fat. Sprinkle with a little additional salt and 10 grinds of black pepper. Add the bay leaves, herbs, parsley, garlic and stock. Stir the contents of the casserole thoroughly, then replace the browned meat on the savoury vegetable bed. Put on the lid and place in the oven. When the liquid starts to bubble (after about 15 minutes) turn the oven down to Gas No. 2 (300°F/150°C) and cook for 2½–3 hours, depending on the weight of the meat. Allow 40 minutes per pound (450 g) plus 40 minutes for the piece. 10 minutes before serving, take off the lid and allow the surface of the meat to dry off.

To serve, put the meat on a hot dish. Push all the vegetables and juices through a sieve into a small pan, or process in the blender until smooth. Turn into a pan. Skim off any excess fat, heat to boiling, and simmer until well reduced and full of flavour. Season with salt and pepper and serve with the meat cut into thin slices.

BRAISED BRISKET

Serves 4–6, plus leftovers for sandwiches.
Cooked meat keeps 3 days under refrigeration.
Freeze 3 months.

One of the tastiest of kosher cuts. Leftover brisket should be forced into a basin, covered with a saucer and a 2-lb (1-kg) weight, and then refrigerated. Next day it will cut to perfection.

3 lb (1.5 kg) corner of brisket
1 tbsp sunflower oil or olive oil
1 bay leaf
6 peppercorns
2 level teasp salt
10 grinds of black pepper
6 pickling onions or shallots, peeled
3 fl oz (75 ml/⅓ cup) boiling water
2 large potatoes
2 medium carrots

Brown the meat quickly in the hot oil. Sprinkle with the seasonings. Put in a casserole surrounded with the onions and the boiling water. Cover and cook in a slow oven, Gas No. 2 (300°F/150°C) for 3 hours. 1 hour before the meat is ready, surround it with thick slices of potato and carrot. Serve the brisket cut in thick slices, together with the potatoes and carrots, in the delicious meat juices.

DAUBE MARSEILLAISE (*Beef Braised in Wine*)

Serves 8–10, or 4–5 people twice.
Keeps 3 days under refrigeration.
Freeze 3 months.

This would make a superb dish for a family dinner at Chanukkah. Cold, it cuts beautifully for a supper party.

Bola (chuck) is marinated in wine, which give it the moistness this kosher cut usually lacks.

4 lb (2 kg) corner of bola or chuck

For the marinade
peeled zest of 1 orange (without the pith)
12 peppercorns, slightly crushed with the end of a rolling pin or in a mortar
a sprig of fresh rosemary or 1 teasp of dried rosemary
2 fat bay leaves
a large sprig of parsley
½ bottle of dry red wine
1 onion, thinly sliced

For braising the beef
1 large onion
1 carrot
1 red pepper (optional)
1 sprig of parsley
1 bay leaf
2 tbsp olive oil
a little paprika pepper
salt
black pepper
2 teasp tomato purée (optional)

24 hours before you intend to cook the beef, heat the marinade ingredients to boiling point, then allow to go quite cold (I do this in the cast-iron enamelled casserole in which I intend to cook the meat). Put the joint into the marinade and leave in a cool place until cooking time. Baste the meat several times with the juices, and turn it so that the marinade can soak in.

To cook Have ready the large onion and carrot, finely sliced, the sliced red pepper (optional) and the sprig of parsley and bay leaf. Lift the meat from the marinade and dry it thoroughly using paper towels. This is essential so that it will brown. Strain the marinade into a small bowl. Wash out the casserole and in it heat the oil. Put the meat into the hot fat and cook it at a moderate sizzle, turning to brown it on all sides. Towards the end of the browning time, slip the carrot and onion under the meat and continue to cook until they are limp and brown. Dust the meat with a little paprika pepper, salt and black pepper. Add the sliced pepper (if used), then pour in the marinade. Cover and bring to the boil, then transfer to a slow oven, Gas No. 2 (300°F/150°C) and cook at a gentle simmer for 3 hours. If you like a rich, deep gravy, add 2 teaspoons of tomato purée half-way through the cooking time. When the meat is cooked - it will 'give' when pressed - lift it on to a heatproof plate, return to the oven, turn the oven down to 'warm' and deal with the gravy. This can be puréed in a blender or food processor and then reheated, or sieved and thickened with 2 teaspoons cornflour (cornstarch).

To serve, cut the meat in slices about ⅜ inch (1 cm) thick and place in overlapping rows on a flat meat plate. Pour the sauce over. Sprinkle with chopped parsley, or garnish with glazed carrots.

Minced (Ground) Beef

MEATBALLS IN THE INTERNATIONAL JEWISH KITCHEN

The use of minced fresh meat, extended with some kind of filler, which can be bread, grated potato, matzah meal, ground rice or ordinary rice, and formed into balls, is universal in the Jewish kitchen. But the recipes vary between communities.

Jews with their roots in Eastern Europe, particularly Russia, Poland and the Baltic States, make balls or patties called bitkis, which are well browned, moistened with stock or gravy, then cooked slowly with fried onions (see p. 142).

Carnatzlakh are Romanian-style meatballs with tapered ends, rolled in paprika and flour, then grilled, or stewed with fried aubergines in a sweet-and-sour tomato sauce. Koenigsberger Klops are the German-style equivalent, cooked in a thickened gravy. Kofta Keftedes eem Tahina are Sephardi-style meatballs, spiced with cumin, allspice or cinnamon and grilled under a covering of tahina (sesame seed paste). Kefta de Left are Tunisian-style meatballs, dipped in egg and flour, fried and then stewed with turnips in a tomato sauce. Koftes Abafadas are Turkish-style, slowly stewed in oil and water. Albondigas al Buyor are Salonika (Greek Sephardi) variants, stewed in a honey-and-tomato sauce (see p. 144). Kofta are Moroccan-style meatballs, simmered uncovered in a sauce flavoured with cumin, paprika, chilli pepper and lemon juice. Klopslers are Polish-style meatballs, stewed with onions.

MINCED (GROUND) BEEF

Always use best-quality minced steak with the lowest fat content available (10 per cent or less).

A meatball can vary in texture from the 'chopped meat' hamburger, which is first cousin to a steak, to the finely minced sheftalia or kofte so popular in Greece and Turkey. All, however, need a tasty, gristle-free minced (ground) meat as a foundation.

It is advisable, therefore, to shop around until you find the minced (ground) meat that suits your taste. It does not necessarily have to come from a prime joint as a cheaper one, such as neck, can often provide the 'meatiest' mince. Be sure that it has been minced fresh on the day you buy it, then use it within 24 hours as the number of cut surfaces makes it deteriorate more quickly than other meat. It does, however, freeze to perfection, both raw and cooked. Beefburgers and meatballs can also be frozen, both cooked and raw, providing a ready meal for the barbecue or the grill.

TO FREEZE BEEFBURGERS AND MEATBALLS

Open-freeze on trays for 2 hours, then pack in plastic bags.

MEAT EXTENDERS

Most people like to add some form of 'extender' to minced (ground) meat, not only because it make it go further but also because it gives a more tender texture. You can take your pick of breadcrumbs, soaked bread, grated potato, matzah meal or porridge oats. I think bread gives the lightest results.

Although it is most convenient to process the eggs, extender and seasoning in a blender or food processor, it is best to mix in the meat by hand, for if it is packed too closely, as is the tendency with an electric mixer, it is not as light in texture.

BASIC MINCED (GROUND) BEEF MIXTURE

2 slices of bread, each cut 1 inch (2.5 cm) thick
2 large eggs
½ large onion
1 large sprig of parsley (optional)
1 level teasp salt
15 grinds of black pepper
3 teasp dark soy sauce
2 lb (1 kg) raw minced (ground) beef

By hand Soak the bread in water to cover, then squeeze dry and add to the beaten eggs, grated onions, herbs (if used) and seasonings.

By blender or food processor Put the fresh herbs, unbeaten eggs, slices of soaked bread, chunks of onion and seasonings into the blender or food processor and process for 30 seconds, or until smooth.

In both cases Work together the raw meat and the egg mixture with the hands or a large fork, until smoothly blended. Leave for 30 minutes. The mixture can now be formed into patties or balls, and grilled, fried or stewed as required.

Note I have given quantities for 2 lb (1 kg) mince as it's as quick to prepare as 1 lb and any raw mix not required can be frozen.

BITKI
(*Russian-Style Meatball Casserole*)

Serves 4.
Keeps 4 days under refrigeration.
Freeze 3 months.

1 lb (450 g) basic minced (ground) beef mixture
1 tbsp flour mixed with a pinch of salt and pepper
1 tbsp sunflower oil or olive oil
1 large onion, sliced or chopped
10 fl oz (275 ml/1¼ cups) meat stock or thin leftover gravy
½ teasp salt
8 grinds of black pepper
1 small bay leaf

Wet the hands under the cold-water tap. Take large spoonfuls of the raw meat mixture and form into balls the size of small apples, then flatten slightly into patties. There should be 6. Put the seasoned flour on to a piece of paper, and dip each patty into it. Shake off any excess flour. Heat the oil in a heavy frying pan for 4 minutes, put in the meatballs and fry steadily until they are a rich brown on both sides. Remove the meat to a plate and in the same fat fry the onions until they are soft and golden, but not crispy. Add the bouillon or gravy to the pan with a further sprinkle of salt and pepper and the bay leaf. Stir the pan well to release any meat juices that may have stuck to the bottom. Arrange the patties in a shallow uncovered casserole in which they can fit side by side. Pour the gravy round them, and cook slowly, Gas No. 2 (300°F/150°C) for 45 minutes, basting occasionally. Alternatively, the meat can be put back into the frying pan, surrounded by the onions and gravy, and left to cook very gently for the same time, turning the meat once or twice.

BRAZILIAN MEATBALLS

Serves 4.
Keeps 4 days under refrigeration.
Freeze 3 months.

Another low-fat recipe.

1 lb (450 g) of Basic Minced Beef Mixture
(see p. 142)

For the sauce
1 medium onion, finely sliced, then each slice halved
1 clove of garlic, finely chopped
2 tbsp sunflower oil or olive oil
4 oz (125 g/1¼ cups) button mushrooms, sliced
1 small red and 1 small green pepper, deseeded and cut in ½-inch (1-cm) pieces
1 level tbsp runny honey
2 teasp dark soy sauce
10 grinds of black pepper
½ teasp salt
1 x 14oz (400 g) can plum tomatoes in juice
5 fl oz (150 ml/⅔ cup) meat or chicken stock

To make the meatballs Leave the mince mixture for 30 minutes, then form into small balls (the size of a golf ball) with wetted palms.

To make the sauce In an oven-to-table casserole, sauté the onion slices and the garlic in the oil until soft and golden (keeping the dish covered most of the time). Uncover and sauté the sliced mushrooms for 2 or 3 minutes, then add all the remaining sauce ingredients and stir well.

Bring this sauce to the boil, stirring, then drop in the meatballs. Spoon some sauce over them, cover and simmer either 1 hour on top of the stove or 1½ hours in a low oven, Gas No. 2 (300°F/150°C).

Serve from the casserole with rice or pasta.

IZMIR KEUFTEH
(*Smyrna Meatballs*)

Serves 6–8.
Keeps 4 days under refrigeration.
Freeze 3 months.

The meatballs are stewed in a smooth sweet-and-sour sauce. Pine kernels add greatly to this dish.

For the meat mixture
2 lb (900 g) Basic Minced Beef Mixture (see p. 142)
plus 1 teasp ground cinnamon

For the sauce
1 large onion
2 tbsp oil
2 oz (50 g/½ cup) pine kernels (optional)
1 x 5 oz (150 g) can tomato purée and 2 cans water
juice of ½ large lemon
1 level tbsp brown sugar
salt
pepper

Follow basic method for mixing minced (ground) beef, then leave to stand for half an hour.

While the minced meat is standing, cut the onion in half and then cut in very thin slices. Heat oil in deepish frying pan or casserole, add onion and cook gently for about 5 minutes until limp. Meanwhile, shape the meat into 'golf balls' and add to the pan (in 2 lots if necessary) and cook gently until golden brown. If pine kernels are used, add them and cook for 2 minutes until golden. Now add the remaining sauce ingredients and bring to the boil (the meatballs should be barely covered – if not, add a little more water). Cover and simmer for 1 hour.

Alternatively, transfer to the oven, Gas No. 3 (325°F/160°C) for 1 hour, then uncover and allow the sauce to reduce for a further 15 minutes. Just before serving, sprinkle with a rounded tablespoon of finely chopped parsley.

ROMANIAN MEATBALLS

Serves 6–8 as a main course, 10 as an entrée or for a buffet.
Keeps 4 days under refrigeration.
Freeze 3 months.

1 lb (900 g) Basic Minced Beef Mixture (see p. 142)
1½ lb (675 g) aubergines (eggplants)
4 tbsp oil
1 level tbsp salt

For the sauce

2 medium (5 oz/150 g) onions
1–2 green peppers, according to size
2 tbsp oil
1 x 29 oz/825 g) can tomatoes or 2 x 14 oz (400 g) cans
2 level tbsp brown sugar
1 level teasp citric acid or 2 tbsp lemon juice
1 level teasp salt
10 grinds of black pepper
1 crushed clove of garlic
1 level teasp dried basil
1 x 5 oz (150 g) can tomato purée

Follow basic method for mixing minced (ground) beef. Leave mixture to rest for 30 minutes, then form into 'golf balls' and arrange in the bottom of a shallow ovenproof casserole.

While meat is resting, peel aubergines, cut in ¾-inch (1.5-cm) slices, then cover with water plus 1 level tablespoon of salt. When meatballs have been formed, drain aubergines well, squeeze with the hands to extract the juices and dry thoroughly.

Peel and slice the onions very finely. Halve, deseed and then cut the peppers into ⅜-inch (1-cm) strips.

Heat the oil in a large frying pan, then cook the onion until soft and golden – about 10 minutes. Add the strips of pepper and continue to cook for another 5 minutes. Now add all the remaining sauce ingredients, stir well and bubble for 5 minutes to thicken. Pour over the meatballs, cover and leave in a low oven, Gas No. 2 (300°F/150°C) for 1½ hours. Meanwhile, fry the aubergines in 4 tablespoons of oil until golden. Keep covered for the first 10 minutes. Drain on kitchen paper, then add to the meatballs. Simmer uncovered for a further 30 minutes, until the sauce is thick but still juicy.

This dish freezes and reheats well.

ALBONDIGAS AL BUYOR
(*Greek-style Meatballs in a Sweet-and-Sour Tomato Sauce*)

Serves 4–5.
Keeps 4 days under refrigeration.
Freeze 3 months.

1 lb (450 g) Basic Minced Beef Mixture (see p. 142)
2 tbsp oil

For the sauce

1 medium (5 oz/150 g) onion, finely chopped
2 level teasp salt
10 grinds of black pepper
2 level tbsp fine dark brown sugar or 1 rounded tbsp honey
2 teasp ready-made mustard
2 teasp soy sauce
1 tbsp lemon juice
5 oz (150 g/½ cup) can tomato purée, diluted with 2 cans water

Mix and fry the meatballs as for Bitki (see p. 142).

To make the sauce, remove the fried meatballs, and in the same fat sauté the onion until golden. Add all the remaining ingredients and simmer for 5 minutes. (This sauce can also be used with grilled hamburgers.) Place meatballs in a casserole, pour over sauce and cover. Either simmer on the top of the stove for 30 minutes or bake in a slow oven, Gas No. 2 (300°F/150°C), for 45 minutes.

ALBONDIGAS MEXICAN STYLE

Serves 6–7.
Keeps 4 days under refrigeration.
Freeze 3 months.

The meatballs can be fried before adding to the sauce, but the fat content of the dish is reduced if they are simply added raw to the simmering sauce – this helps to seal the surface in a similar way.

If possible, chill the casserole overnight so that any surface fat can be removed.

For the meatballs

1½ lb (675 g) lean minced (ground) beef
2 oz (50 g/6 tbsp) raisins
1 medium onion
3 oz (75 g) brown or white bread
2 eggs
1 teasp salt
10 grinds of black pepper
2 teasp chopped fresh coriander or parsley

For the sauce

1 large onion, finely chopped
2 tbsp olive oil
1 large red pepper, deseeded and cut in ½-inch (1-cm) squares
1 fat clove of garlic, peeled and chopped
4 tbsp medium-dry Amontillado sherry
1 x 5 oz (150 g) can tomato purée
8 fl oz (225 ml/1 cup) boiling water
2 teasp red wine vinegar or cider vinegar
2 teasp ground cumin
1 teasp salt
20 grinds of black pepper
pinch of Cayenne pepper or 1 teasp mild chilli powder
1 bay leaf
2 oz stuffed green olives, sliced

For the garnish

2 oz almonds, blanched, slivered and toasted

To make the meatballs Put the meat and raisins in a large bowl. Purée all the remaining ingredients in the food processor or blender, then add to the meat mixture and stir until thoroughly mixed. Shape into ovals each about 2 inches (5 cm) long and chill while the sauce is prepared.

To make the sauce In a large lidded frying pan sauté the onion in the oil (covering the pan) until soft and golden – about 5 minutes. Uncover and add the pepper and garlic, then sauté uncovered for a further 3-4 minutes before adding all the remaining ingredients (except the olives). Stir well and bring to the boil. Add the meatballs, cover and simmer for 45 minutes, turning once. Just before serving, add the olives, sprinkle with the toasted almonds and serve with rice or pasta.

BEEFBURGERS

Serves 4–5.
Freeze raw 2 months.
Freeze cooked 1 month.

Beefburgers made only from meat can be a little tough in texture. This has an egg and a slice of bread in the mixture to lighten it and some interesting seasonings to add to the flavour.

The beefburgers can be grilled (broiled), barbecued, fried on a ridged griddle or thermal-grilled in a forced-air or fan-assisted oven.

1 egg
half an onion, cut in chunks
1 thick slice of brown bread
1 tbsp tomato ketchup
2 teasp soy sauce
1 teasp salt
10 grinds of black pepper
1 level teasp yeast extract or vegetable paste
2 lb (900 g) minced (ground) raw beef

Put all the ingredients except the meat into a food processor or blender and process until puréed. Turn into a large bowl and add the meat, mixing thoroughly together with a fork to avoid packing the meat too tightly. Form into 4 or 5 'steaks' each about ¾ inch (2 cm) thick. Grill (broil) for 5 minutes on each side until a rich brown.

SAVOURY MEATLOAF

Serves 4, twice.
Keeps 2 days under refrigeration.
Freeze 3 months.

The meatloaf, which is loosely based on the French terrine, is one of America's most useful additions to modern Jewish cuisine. The dish also has strong connections with the Polish 'klops' and the over-sized Tunisian meatball – the 'kouclas' – cooked in the centre of the Dfina (see pp. 137–8).

It's tasty, economical and equally delicious served hot from the oven with baked or mashed potato, or at room temperature with chips, latkes or salad.

For the meatloaf

1 medium (5 oz/150 g) onion, peeled and cut in 1-inch (2.5-cm) chunks
2 large slices of brown bread or 2 oz (50 g/1 cup) fresh breadcrumbs
2 eggs
2 teasp dry mustard
2 teasp tomato ketchup
1 tbsp dark soy sauce
1½ teasp salt
20 grinds of black pepper
large sprig of parsley
2 tbsp medium matzah meal or porridge oats
2lb (900 g) fresh minced (ground) beef

For the gravy

1 small onion, finely chopped
1 tbsp sunflower oil
8 fl oz (225 ml/1 cup) beef stock
2 level teasp cornflour (cornstarch)

To make the meatloaf In a blender or food processor purée all the ingredients except the matzah meal (or porridge oats) and the meat. Put in a bowl, stir in the meal (or oats), then add the minced meat and mix thoroughly with a large fork.

Turn the mixture into a 2-lb (900-g) loaf tin, 9 x 5 x 3 inches (22.5 x 12.5 x 7.5 cm), packing it down well. Turn out into a roasting tin just big enough to leave a margin round it. Put in a quick oven, Gas No. 6 (400°F/200°C), for 15 minutes, then turn down to Gas No. 4 (350°F/180°C) for a further 45 minutes.

To make the gravy While meat is cooking, fry the onion in the oil until golden brown, then stir in the beef stock mixed with the cornflour. Bring to boil, then pour over and round meatloaf 15 minutes before it is cooked.

Serve loaf in slices with gravy.

Note If meatloaf is to be served cold, there is no need for gravy.

MEXICAN RICE

Serves 4 as a main course, 6 with a meat or poultry main dish.
Keeps 3 days under refrigeration.
Freeze 3 months.

A quick and tasty one-dish main course. Leftovers can be reheated covered in the microwave or a moderate oven until piping hot.

1 medium (5 oz/150 g) onion, finely chopped
1 red pepper, diced
4 stalks of celery, diced
1 tbsp sunflower oil or olive oil
1 lb (450 g) minced (ground) beef
1 x 29 oz (825 g) can whole or chopped tomatoes in juice
2 tbsp tomato purée
1 clove of garlic, crushed
juice of ½ lemon
½ level teasp mild chilli powder
2 level teasp salt
2 level teasp sugar
10 grinds of black pepper
1 level teasp paprika

For the rice

15 fl oz (425 ml/2 cups) chicken or meat stock
6 oz (175 g/1 cup) Basmati rice, soaked in cold water for 15 minutes, then well rinsed in a sieve until the water runs clear

In a heavy frying pan or casserole gently brown the onion, red pepper and celery in the hot oil. Add the meat, cook until it loses its red colour,then cover with tomatoes, tomato purée, garlic, lemon, and seasonings. Cover and simmer on top of the stove or in the oven for 1 hour at Gas No. 3 (325°F/160°C).

To cook the rice, bring the stock to the boil, add the rice, stir until simmering, then cover and simmer for 20 minutes. Add the rice to the meat sauce and simmer uncovered for 15-20 minutes, or longer, until thick and juicy.

BEEF AND RICE, WESTERN STYLE

Serves 6 generously.
Keeps 3 days under refrigeration.
Freeze 3 months.

This is a favourite in California.

1 medium (5 oz/150 g) onion, finely chopped
4 stalks of celery, finely sliced (about 1 cupful)
½ yellow or red pepper, deseeded and finely chopped
1 tbsp oil
8 oz (225 g/1 cup) Basmati rice, soaked in cold water for 15 minutes, then well rinsed in a sieve until the water runs clear
1 lb (450 g) raw minced (ground) beef
1 x 29 oz (825 g) can peeled plum tomatoes
2 level teasp brown sugar
1 teasp salt
10 grinds of black pepper
2 teasp dark soy sauce
4 oz (125 g/1 cup) black olives, stones removed

Add the onions, celery and pepper to the hot oil in a stove-to-table casserole or lidded frying pan, cover and simmer until softened (about 7 minutes). Uncover, add the rice and cook for 2 more minutes, then add the meat and cook uncovered, breaking it up with a fork until it has lost its redness and begins to turn brown. Add the tomatoes, seasonings and olives. Bring to the boil. Cover then transfer to the oven, Gas No. 3 (325°F/160°C), and cook for 1 hour, stirring once. Leftovers can be reheated until piping hot in a covered dish in the microwave or a moderate oven.

NOODLE AND MEAT RING

Serves 4–5.
Leftovers keep 2 days under refrigeration.
Ring freezes 1 month.
Meat filling and sauce freeze 3 months.

A very satisfying, quickly made mid-week family meal. Only half the savoury mince is required. The remainder can be frozen, or 2 complete rings can be cooked.

6 oz (175 g/1½ cups) broad egg noodles or fresh tagliatelle
1 egg
1 level teasp salt
20 grinds of black pepper
1 tbsp chopped parsley

For the mince
1 tbsp oil
1 medium onion (5 oz/150 g), finely chopped
1 lb (450 g/2 cups) minced (ground) beef
1 medium-sized green or red pepper, finely diced
2 rounded tbsp tomato ketchup
2 teasp dark soy sauce
1 teasp salt
10 grinds of black pepper
1 tbsp chopped parsley
5 tbsp water

For the Pizzaiola sauce
1 x 14 oz (400 g) can chopped tomatoes
1 tbsp tomato purée
1 tbsp extra virgin olive oil
1 level teasp salt
1 level teasp sugar
10 grinds of black pepper
1 level teasp dried mixed Italian herbs
1 clove of garlic, peeled and crushed
2 tbsp chopped fresh parsley or basil

Heat the oil and cook the onion until golden, then add the meat and cook until it loses its redness and begins to turn brown, stirring all the time. Add all the remaining mince ingredients, stir well, cover and simmer for 15 minutes. If desired, divide into two portions for freezing.

Cook the noodles according to packet directions. Put in a sieve and pour cold water through, then drain well. Put into a mixing bowl and add one portion of the fresh or defrosted meat mixture and the beaten egg, salt, pepper and parsley. Turn into a greased casserole or ring mould. Cover with greaseproof paper. Bake for 40 minutes at Gas No. 4 (350°F/180°C). Turn out or serve from the dish with the Pizzaiola sauce.

To cook the ring in the microwave, turn into a lightly greased microwave-safe ring mould or casserole. Cover with clingfilm (saranwrap) and pierce a hole in it. Microwave on 75–80 per cent power for 8 minutes. Take out of oven and allow to stand for 3 minutes.

To make the sauce, simmer all the sauce ingredients together in an uncovered pan until thick but still juicy - about 10 minutes on top of the stove, 5 minutes on 100 per cent in the microwave.

MEXICAN SPICED BEEF WITH A POTATO CRUST

Serves 6–8.
Cooked meat mixture keeps 3 days under refrigeration.
Freeze 3 months.

This very superior cottage pie makes a marvellous main dish for an informal Sunday supper. The meat can be ready-cooked and in the dish (in the fridge) up to a day in advance, but the potatoes are fluffiest if mashed and spooned over just before baking. A bottle of a hearty red wine and a fresh fruit salad to follow would complete the menu.

1 large onion
2 tbsp olive oil
2 medium red peppers cut in ½-inch (1-cm) squares
2 medium cloves of garlic, peeled and chopped
1½ lb (675 g) lean minced (ground) beef
2 x 15 oz (425 g) cans chopped tomatoes in juice

2 teasp brown sugar
2 teasp ground cumin
1 teasp salt
20 grinds of black pepper
pinch of Cayenne pepper or 1 teasp mild chilli powder
1 bay leaf
3 rounded tbsp raisins
1 x 8 oz (225 g) can sweetcorn or 8 oz (225 g) pack frozen sweetcorn kernels
2 oz (50 g/½ cup) stuffed green olives, sliced

For the topping
3 lb (1.5 kg) boiling potatoes
4 tbsp margarine
2 teasp salt
2 shakes of white pepper

To make the filling In a large lidded frying pan sauté the finely chopped onion in the oil (covering the pan) until it is soft and golden - about 5 minutes. Uncover and add the pepper squares and the chopped garlic. Sauté uncovered for a further 3-4 minutes, then add the beef and cook, stirring with a fork to break it up until it loses its pink colour. Add all the remaining ingredients (except the olives), stir well, cover and simmer very slowly, stirring occasionally, for 45 minutes. Uncover and bubble until thick and juicy. Discard the bay leaf and stir in the sliced olives.

To make the topping In a large saucepan put the peeled potatoes (cut in 1-inch/2.5 cm chunks), add the salt and enough cold water to cover them by 1 inch (2.5 cm), bring to the boil and simmer for 10-15 minutes, or until tender when pierced with a pointed knife. Drain the potatoes, return to the pan, cover with a tea-towel and leave over a moderate heat for 30 seconds to evaporate any excess moisture. Add the fat to the pan with the seasonings and whisk the potatoes with a hand-held electric whisk until smooth and fluffy.

Transfer the meat mixture to a baking dish about 2 inches (5 cm) deep and cover completely with the potatoes. Bake the casserole in a preheated oven at Gas No. 6 (400°F/200°C) for 35-40 minutes, until bubbling and lightly browned.

VARIATION

PICADILLO

(*Sweet and Savoury Mexican Beef*)

Serves 4-5.
Keeps 3 days under refrigeration.
Freeze 3 months.

Make the Mexican Spiced Beef Mixture but omit the potato topping. Serve piping hot with bulgar (see p. 277) or rice, or use as a filling for warm pitta bread. The flavour deepens if left overnight.

COTTAGE PIE

Serves 4-5.
Leftovers keep 2 days under refrigeration.
Freeze 1 month.

This (together with Shepherd's Pie, p. 150) is the kind of dish the children of immigrants were taught to make at school, as part of an attempt to teach them about English culture.

2 tbsp oil
1 large onion, finely chopped
1 lb (450 g) minced shoulder steak (ground beef)
1 level tbsp flour
5 fl oz (150 ml/⅔ cup) meat stock
2 teasp tomato purée
½ teasp salt
15 grinds of black pepper
2 teasp dark soy sauce

For the potato topping
2 lb (900 g) potatoes
3 oz (75 g/⅓ cup) margarine
2 level teasp salt
¼ teasp white pepper

Grease an ovenproof dish approximately 7 x 7 x 2 inches (18 x 18 x 5 cm). Heat the oil, then add the onion and cook gently until soft and golden. Add the meat and continue to cook until it loses its redness and begins to brown. Sprinkle with the flour and bubble for 2 minutes, then add the stock and bubble gently for 5 minutes. Stir in the purée, salt, pepper and soy sauce. Put the meat into the casserole.

Peel the potatoes, cut them into quarters and put them in a pan containing sufficient boiling water to cover them. Add a good pinch of salt, bring back to the boil, cover and cook at a steady boil for 15 minutes, or until a piece feels tender when pierced with a thin vegetable knife. Drain the water from the potatoes, return them to the stove in the same pan and shake over gentle heat until all the moisture has evaporated. Add the margarine in small pieces and the seasonings and start whisking either with a balloon whisk or a portable electric-mixer. Continue to whisk on a very low heat until the potatoes lighten in colour and look fluffy. Pile on top of the meat and fork into a design. Bake for 30 minutes in a moderate oven, Gas No. 4 (350°F/180°C), or until golden brown.

SHEPHERD'S PIE

Serves 4–6.
Leftovers keep 2 days under refrigeration.
Freeze 1 month.

This is made with leftover meat, mixed with a savoury sauce. Because the meat is already cooked, the pie is baked for a shorter time at a hotter temperature than the cottage pie.

2 tbsp sunflower oil or olive oil
2 stalks of celery, finely sliced
½ large onion, minced or chopped in the food processor
2 level tbsp flour
15 fl oz (425 ml/2 cups) thin gravy or stock
1 small clove of garlic, crushed
2 teasp chopped parsley
salt
black pepper
1 lb (450 g) (minimum) coarsely minced cooked, braised or roast meat
1 recipe mashed potatoes as in Cottage Pie (above)

Melt the fat and fry the celery and onion gently for 5 minutes. Stir in the flour and cook a further 2 minutes, then add the liquid and garlic and cook until bubbly. Add parsley, salt and black pepper to taste. Stir the sauce into the minced meat. The mixture should be moist but not soggy. Well grease an oven dish approximately 7 x 7 x 2 inches (18 x 18 x 5 cm) and put in the meat mixture. Smooth the potatoes over the top and ridge with a knife into a design. Put in a hot oven, Gas No. 7 (425°F/220°C) for 20 minutes, until crisp and golden.

THE 5-HOUR RAGÚ

Serves 4 with 1 lb (450 g) pasta.
Keeps 5 days under refrigeration.
Freeze 2 months.

Your aim when preparing this superb sauce the Bolognese use on their home-made tagliatelle is to achieve a creamy texture that is just thick enough to cling to the pasta without either sinking in to it or sitting heavily on top. No starchy thickener is used, just a gentle reduction of the liquid content as it is absorbed by the particles of meat. The long, slow cooking is also essential: it produces a flavour that cannot be replicated in a food factory. Serve it with (preferably fresh) tagliatelle (broad noodles), tortellini (curved ravioli), rigatoni (short-cut tubular pasta) or in lasagne.

2 tbsp olive oil
1 tbsp margarine
1 medium onion, finely chopped
1 carrot, finely chopped
2 stalks of celery, finely chopped
1 medium green pepper, finely chopped
2 cloves of garlic, finely chopped
1 lb (450 g) extra-lean raw minced beef

1 large chicken liver, koshered (see p. 134), cut in 8
4 fl oz (125 ml/½ cup) red wine
5 fl oz (150 ml/⅔ cup) chicken stock
1 x 15 oz (425 g) can chopped tomatoes
2 level tbsp tomato purée
1 bay leaf
1 teasp dried Italian herbs
1 teasp brown sugar
1 teasp salt
15 grinds of black pepper

Select a fairly deep (rather than wide) earthenware or enamelled steel casserole (this is to prevent the mixture drying out during the long cooking period).

Heat the oil and fat, add the chopped vegetables, cover and sauté for 10 minutes, then uncover and cook until a rich golden brown. Add the meat and liver and continue to cook until both have lost their redness. Add the wine and bubble 2 minutes, then stir in the remaining ingredients. The meat should be barely covered with liquid; if not, add a little more wine. Cover and cook very, very slowly, either on top of the stove or in the oven, Gas No. 2 (300°F/150°C), for 5 hours. Your aim is to keep the mixture steaming, with bubbles breaking the surface only occasionally.

SPAGHETTI ALLA NAPOLITANA

Serves 4–5.
Keeps 4 days under refrigeration.
Freeze 3 months.

This southern Italian speciality is made with meatballs which are browned, then cooked in a rich tomato, wine and herb sauce.

1 large onion (8 oz/225 g), chopped
white part of a fat leek and a small handful of parsley, chopped together
1 clove of garlic, crushed to a paste with a little salt
1 teasp dried basil or oregano
2 tbsp extra virgin olive oil
5 oz (150 g/⅔ cup) can or tube of Italian tomato purée
4 fl oz (125 ml/½ cup) red wine and 1 tbsp red wine vinegar or 3 fl oz (75 ml/¾ cup) meat stock plus 2 tbsp red wine vinegar
2 level teasp brown sugar
1 teasp salt
10 fl oz (275 ml/1¼ cups) chicken or meat stock
1 x 14 oz (400 g) can Italian tomatoes
½ recipe Basic Minced Beef Mixture (see p. 142) formed into 'golf balls'
1 lb (450 g/5 cups) cooked long spaghetti, tossed in a little olive oil

Cook the chopped vegetables and herbs in the oil until golden brown, then add all the remaining ingredients (except the meatballs and spaghetti). Simmer very gently, uncovered, for 30 minutes. Then add the meatballs and simmer, covered, a further 45 minutes.

To serve, put a serving of spaghetti on each plate and top with a ladleful of sauce and meatballs.

GEFILTE PAPRIKA
(Stuffed Peppers, Hungarian Style)

Serves 4–6.
Keeps 3 days under refrigeration when cooked.
Freeze 2 months.

You may be offered a dish of stuffed vegetables in any Jewish household eastwards from Austria, for when kosher meat was scarce, particularly during the Middle Ages, it was often 'stretched' by mixing it with a 'filler' of rice or meal and stuffing it into readily available local vegetables. This recipe is a more sophisticated version than usual (note the wine in the sauce), reflecting the *'cuisine soignee'* typical of this part of Europe.

For the sauce
1 medium onion
1 tbsp oil
5 oz (150 g) can tomato purée
10 fl oz (275 ml/1¼ cups) hot water
2 tbsp demerara (brown) sugar
2 tbsp lemon juice
½ teasp mixed spice (piment) or cinnamon
5 fl oz (150 ml/⅔ cup) white wine (optional but nice)

For the peppers and stuffing
4–6 squat red peppers
1 egg
1 onion, grated
1 level teasp salt
½ teasp mustard
1 teasp paprika pepper
1 lb (450 g) lean minced (ground) beef
2 level teasp matzah meal or porridge oats

If peppers are to be stewed on top of the stove, use the same pan to make the sauce. Chop the onion finely, then sauté in the oil until soft and golden. Add all the remaining ingredients. Simmer uncovered for 20 minutes.

Slice off and retain the tops of the peppers and remove the seeds and ribs. Put into a pan and pour over boiling water, then leave for 5 minutes. Beat the egg, grate the onion and add salt, mustard and pepper. Then mix in the meat and meal. Drain the peppers on kitchen paper, then stuff with the meat mixture and cover each pepper with its top. Put into the pan in which the sauce is simmering. Cover with foil, and then with the lid of the pan. Simmer gently for 1 hour, basting twice. When done, the sauce will be thick and the peppers tender. To cook in the oven, simmer at Gas No. 3 (325°F/160°C) for 1½ hours.

To cook in the microwave Mix all the sauce ingredients in a jug and cook uncovered on 100 per cent power for about 5 minutes or until bubbling. Arrange the stuffed peppers in a 5-pint-deep (3-1/12½ cup) lidded casserole large enough to hold the peppers side by side. Pour the sauce round them and cook on 100 per cent power for 10 minutes, or until bubbling, then reduce to 80 per cent power and cook for a further 15 minutes, until the peppers feel tender when pierced with a sharp knife. Stand for 5 minutes before serving.

STUFFED CARROTS, SYRIAN STYLE

Serves 6.
Keeps 3 days under refrigeration when cooked.
Freeze 2 months.

As an Ashkenazi housewife prepares for the Sabbath by making a panful of chicken soup and a dish of chopped liver, so many Sephardi housewives cook a selection of vegetables stuffed with minced (ground) beef. These can be served either hot or cold, and reheat to perfection. Leeks and courgettes (zucchini) can both be treated in the same way as the carrots in this interesting recipe.

12 young carrots
2 tbsp sunflower oil

For the meat stuffing
1 lb (450 g) lean minced (ground) beef or lamb

½ onion, grated
4 level tbsp raw, well-washed short-grain rice
1 level teasp salt
pinch of white pepper
½ level teasp allspice or cinnamon
a little water
1 tbsp ouk (see below) or lemon juice

Mix all the stuffing ingredients together, binding with a little water. Scrape the carrots and hollow out the centre with an apple corer (it is possible to buy a special instrument for the job), leaving a shell ¼ inch (0.5 cm) thick. Stuff the carrots with the minced beef mixture. Sauté slowly in the oil, 5 minutes on each side, until they look slightly glazed and are beginning to soften. Arrange in a baking dish and pour on the frying oil. Add the ouk (or lemon juice) and water to cover. Cover and bake in a moderate oven, Gas No. 4 (350°F/180°C) for 30 minutes, then turn down to Gas No. 3 (325°F/160°C) and simmer for a further 1½ hours, by which time the sauce will be syrupy and the carrots meltingly tender.

VARIATION

STUFFED TOMATOES

Serves 6.
Keeps 3 days under refrigeration.
Freeze 2 months.

12 fat tomatoes
meat stuffing as for carrots (see above)
2 teasp oil
1 tbsp ouk (see below) or lemon juice
2 level teasp sugar
½ level teasp salt
10 grinds of black pepper

Slice a 'lid' off the tomatoes and hollow them out, putting the tomato pulp into an ovenproof dish just wide enough to hold the tomatoes when packed tightly side by side. Salt the tomato shells lightly, then fill them with the meat mixture and replace the lids. Add the oil, ouk (or lemon juice) and seasoning to the tomato pulp in the dish, then arrange the tomatoes in it. Add sufficient water to ensure that the tomatoes are barely covered. Cover the dish with foil and then a lid. Bring to the boil on top of the stove, simmer for 5 minutes, then transfer to the oven and cook at Gas No. 5 (375°F/190°C) for 45 minutes.

OUK

Keeps indefinitely.

This is a flavouring syrup (originally made with pomegranate juice) that gives the characteristic Sephardi flavour to stuffed carrots, cabbage, vine leaves and courgettes.

1 lb (450 g/1⅓ cups) black treacle (molasses)
4 oz (125 g/½ cup) demerara (brown) sugar
2 oz (50 g) citric acid crystals (sour salt)
2 level tbsp salt

Warm all the ingredients together until blended. Store in a jar.

KUCARAS DE BERENCENA
(Aubergines Stuffed Turkish Style in a Sweet-and-Sour Tomato Sauce)

Serves 6–8.
Keeps 3 days under refrigeration.
Freeze 3 months.

3–4 (8 oz/225 g each) boat-shaped aubergines (eggplants)

For the stuffing
1 medium onion, roughly chopped
1 egg
1 level teasp salt
10 grinds of black pepper
3 tbsp sunflower oil
1 large thick slice of bread
1½ lb (675 g) minced (ground) beef

For the sauce
1 small (4 oz/125 g) onion, finely chopped
15 fl oz (425 ml/2 cups) passata (sieved tomatoes) or 1 x 14 oz (400 g) can chopped tomatoes in juice
1 tbsp lemon juice
1–2 tbsp soft brown sugar
½ teasp salt
10 grinds of black pepper

To prepare the filling, purée the onion, egg, seasoning and torn bread in the blender or food processor, then add to the meat and mix well with a fork.

Cut the aubergines in half lengthwise and use a spoon to scoop out the inside, leaving ½ inch (1.25 cm) of flesh all the way round. Finely chop the scooped-out flesh and fry in the oil until soft. Remove from the pan with a slotted spoon, then chop to a pulp and add to the minced-meat mixture.

Divide the meat mixture between the aubergine halves, press down firmly and then fry them gently in the remaining hot oil, on both sides, until a golden brown. (The meat won't stick to the pan if left until the brown crust has formed.)

Arrange in a wide, shallow ovenproof casserole (an enamel one is excellent).

To prepare the sauce, cook the chopped onion in the same oil until golden, then stir in all the remaining ingredients. When the sauce is bubbling, pour it round the aubergines – they should be just submerged. If not, top up with a little chicken stock or water.

Cover the dish and put in a moderate oven, Gas No. 4 (350°F/180°C), for half an hour (until the sauce is bubbling nicely), then turn oven down to Gas No. 2 (300°F/150°C) and cook for a further 2 hours. When the aubergines are ready, they will have absorbed most of the sauce, leaving just enough to pour over each one when it is served. This dish reheats well.

Note For other stuffed vegetable dishes, see 'Sukkot', p. 568.

STUFFED BAKED MARROW WITH FRESH NOODLES AND BASIL

Serves 4–6.
Keeps 2 days under refrigeration.
Do not freeze.

The marrow, a favourite food of an earlier generation of Jewish cooks, has in recent years lost out to the daintier charms of the courgette. Now farmers are growing sweeter, less-coarse varieties of marrow which make a perfect case for fillings of various kinds. One of these marrows, stuffed with savoury mincemeat and baked in the oven, can make a succulent and splendid dish for an economic mid-week meal, with savoury noodles to fill any corners.

Marrows are at their best in mid-summer, when you can buy them at roadside farm shops or even pick your own.

1 medium, very fresh marrow
1 tbsp sunflower oil
1 oz (25 g/2 tbsp) margarine

For the filling
1 medium (5 oz/150 g) onion
1 small clove of garlic
1 tbsp sunflower oil
1 lb (450 g) raw minced (ground) beef
4 oz (125 g/1¼ cups) mushrooms, finely chopped
1 large, thick slice of brown bread (1 oz/25 g)
1 level tbsp tomato purée
1 tbsp chopped parsley
1 teasp dried Italian herbs
½ teasp salt
10 grinds of black pepper
12 stuffed olives (approx. 2 oz/50 g/½ cup)

Use a potato peeler to remove a thin layer of peel from the marrow, then cut a thick lengthwise slice off the top (to form the lid) and scoop out the seeds. Preheat the oven to Gas No. 5 (375°F/190°C).

To make the filling Fry the finely chopped onion and garlic in the hot oil until softened and golden (covering the pan), then add the meat and cook, stirring with a fork, until it starts to brown. Add the finely chopped mushrooms and cook a further 2 or 3 minutes to drive off some of their moisture, then stir in the crumbed bread, tomato purée, herbs, salt, pepper and sliced olives. Lay the marrow shell in a baking dish (just large enough to hold it) and spoon in the meat filling, then cover with the marrow lid. Heat the oil and margarine until well blended and steaming, then pour over the marrow. Bake uncovered for 1½ hours, basting 2 or 3 times. The meat filling will by this time be cooked and the marrow nicely browned.

For the noodles Cook 12 oz (350 g) fresh noodles in a pan of boiling salted water until just tender, then rinse thoroughly under hot water to remove any excess starch. In the same pan heat 1 oz (25 g/2 tbsp) margarine together with a rounded tablespoon each of chopped parsley and shredded fresh basil leaves. Add the well-drained noodles, sprinkle with 10 grinds of black pepper and a few grinds of sea salt, then toss thoroughly together until piping hot. Serve with the slices of marrow.

AUBERGINE MOUSSAKA

Serves 6–8 for a main dish, 10 for an entrée.
The cooked dish keeps 2 days under refrigeration.
Freeze for 2 months.

Moussaka is a splendid dish for a supper party, not the least of its virtues being that it actually benefits from being made a day in advance. This treatment helps to give it the correct consistency to be cut into firm but juicy squares. In Greek-Jewish kitchens a soufflé is often substituted for the traditional custard topping, but I prefer to make a thick sauce based on chicken stock and then lighten it with beaten eggs.

2½ lb (1 kg) medium-sized aubergines (eggplants)
1 medium onion, finely chopped
2 tbsp olive oil
1½ lb (675 g) minced (ground) fresh beef (or lamb)
4 fl oz (125 ml/½ cup) dry red wine or beef stock
1 x 14 oz (400 g) can tomatoes, well drained
1 generous tbsp chopped parsley
2 level teasp dried fines herbes or oregano
2 level teasp salt
few grinds of black pepper
4 oz (125 g/1 cup) fresh breadcrumbs
oil (preferably olive) for grilling the aubergines

For the (parev) Béchamel sauce
scant 2 oz (50 g/½ cup) cornflour (cornstarch)
1¼ pints (725 ml/3 cups) chicken stock
2 oz (50 g/¼ cup) margarine
½ teasp nutmeg
½ teasp salt
10 grinds of black pepper
3 tbsp sherry
2 eggs

Wash the aubergines. Do not peel but cut in long, slanting slices, each ⅓ inch (1 cm) thick, and place in a colander, sprinkling each layer with salt. Leave for 1 hour, then rinse well and dry with paper towels.

To prepare the meat sauce Sauté the finely chopped onion in the oil until soft. Add the raw meat and cook, stirring with a fork, until the meat loses its redness. Add the wine or stock, tomatoes, parsley, herbs, salt and pepper. Half-cover and simmer very gently for 30 minutes. The mixture should be thick and juicy but not wet; if it is, cook uncovered for a few minutes. Add half the breadcrumbs and stir well. While the meat is simmering, brush each side of the aubergine slices with oil and grill on both sides until golden, turning once. Drain thoroughly on crumpled kitchen paper.

To prepare the Béchamel sauce Put the cornflour in a bowl with about 6 tablespoons of the cold stock and mix to a thin cream. Bring the remaining stock to the boil, then pour on to the cornflour, stirring constantly. Return to the pan and bubble 3 minutes, then add the margarine (cut in little pieces) and the seasonings. The sauce should now be thick and shiny. In the cornflour bowl, beat the sherry with the eggs thoroughly, then slowly add the hot sauce, stirring all the time.

To assemble the Moussaka Grease an ovenproof dish approx 9 x 13 x 2 inches (22.5 x 32.5 x 5cm) (or use two foil ones). Scatter with a few of the remaining breadcrumbs. Arrange half the aubergine slices to cover the bottom of the dish, then spread with the meat and tomato mixture. Cover with the remaining aubergines. Finally, pour the sauce over the aubergines to cover them completely, then scatter the remaining breadcrumbs on top. Bake uncovered in a moderate oven, Gas No. 4 (350°F/180°C) for 45 minutes, until golden and bubbly.

To reheat Cover lightly with foil and reheat in a moderate oven for 30 minutes until bubbling again.

A Variety of Meat Stews

Meat cooked in a savoury sauce can be one of the most delectable of dishes if certain rules are followed:

1 Always brown the meat to develop its flavour and to seal it, thus preventing the total escape of the meat juices into the cooking liquid. However, for many recipes, provided the pan is first heated for 2-3 minutes, it need be greased only with oil sprinkled on a thick pad of kitchen paper. When the outside of the meat is brown it will easily come away from the surface of the pan.
2 Use only enough liquid to cover the meat, so that the meaty flavour does not become diluted.
3 Make sure that the liquid never boils, but 'shivers' all the time, so that the cooked meat is soft without being stringy.

Note Meat stews freeze well, but expect the flavour to fade after a month.

SAVOURY GOULASH

Serves 4–5.
Keeps 3 days under refrigeration.
Freeze 3 months.

2 lb (900 g) well-dried stewing or braising steak, cut into 1-inch (2.5-cm) cubes and sprinkled on both sides with 20 grinds of black pepper
1 tbsp sunflower oil or olive oil
2 large onions, sliced wafer-thin
2 teasp brown sugar or granular sweetener added off the heat
1 pint (575 ml/2½cups) water or meat stock
2 bay leaves
2 level teasp salt
2 level tbsp cornflour (cornstarch) dissolved in 4 tbsp cold water

Heat an empty, heavy, lidded frying pan or oven casserole for 3 minutes, then grease with a thick wad of kitchen paper sprinkled with oil. Add the meat, sprinkled with the black pepper, and brown briskly on all sides, then remove to a plate. Add the oil and the onions, sprinkle with the brown sugar and continue to cook until the mixture is a really rich brown. Return the meat to the pan and pour in the water or stock, the bay leaves and the salt. Cover and simmer for 1½ hours on the top of the stove, or 2 hours in a slow oven, Gas No. 2 (300°F/150°C). Adjust the temperature so that the liquid is barely bubbling all the time. Add the dissolved cornflour and continue to cook for a further 3 minutes. Taste and add more seasoning if necessary.

VARIATIONS

Canned tomatoes can be substituted for all the liquid.

Red wine can be substituted for half the liquid.

The bay leaves can be omitted and 2 level teaspoons of paprika sprinkled on the meat as it is browning.

MEAT AND HERB STEW

Serves 6.
Keeps 3 days under refrigeration.
Freeze 3 months.

Simple and savoury.

2lb (900 g) braising or stewing steak, cubed
2 oz (50 g/½ cup) flour
15 grinds of black pepper
1½ teasp salt
2 tbsp sunflower oil or olive oil
1 large (10 oz/275 g) onion, finely chopped
1 clove of garlic, crushed
2 carrots, diced
4 celery stalks, chopped, or a pinch of celery salt
2 teasp brown sugar
1 meat stock-cube and hot water to cover meat
1 level teasp dried Italian seasoning herbs
1 large bay leaf

Dredge the meat in flour seasoned with salt and pepper. Heat the oil and brown the meat, then remove. Add onion, garlic, carrot and celery and continue to cook until the onion is soft and golden, sprinkling with the brown sugar to help the process. Return the meat to the casserole and add any remaining flour. Cook for 1 minute, then add the crumbled stock-cube, Italian seasoning herbs, bay leaf and enough hot water barely to cover the meat. Cook, stirring until thickened. When simmering, cover the casserole and transfer to the oven. Cook at Gas No. 2 (300°F/150°C) for 2 hours, or until meat is tender.

SWEET AND SOUR BEEF

Serves 6.
Keeps 3 days under refrigeration.
Freeze 3 months.

The pineapple gives this delectable stew a refreshingly different flavour.

1 tbsp oil for greasing the pan
2 lb (900 g) braising or stewing steak, cut into 1-inch (2.5-cm) cubes
1 medium onion, coarsely chopped
3 sticks of celery, chopped
1 x 14 oz (400 g) can pineapple chunks
10 fl oz (275 ml/1¼ cups) beef stock made with a bouillon-cube
2 level teasp salt
a few grinds of black pepper
2 level tbsp cornflour (cornstarch)
1 tbsp soy sauce
1 tbsp tomato ketchup
2 tbsp vinegar

Heat the pan for 3 minutes, then grease with a thick wad of kitchen paper sprinkled with oil. Add well-dried meat and brown on all sides. Add the onion and celery and continue to cook for a further 5 minutes, until the vegetables have wilted. Drain the juice from the pineapple and make it up to 10 fl oz (275 ml/1¼ cups) with water. Add with the stock and seasoning to the meat. Bring to the boil, cover and simmer for 2 hours, or until the meat is tender. Blend the cornflour with the soy sauce, ketchup and vinegar, and stir into the meat with the pineapple chunks. Simmer for 3 minutes. Serve piping hot. If preferred, this dish can be transferred to the oven and allowed to simmer (300°F/150°C) for 2½ hours.

CARBONNADE DE BOEUF FLAMANDE
(*Belgian Beef Stew*)

Serves 4–5.
Keeps 3 days under refrigeration.
Freeze 3 months.

The beer in this recipe adds flavour, but it also helps to tenderize the meat.

2 level teasp salt
20 grinds of black pepper
1 oz (25 g/4 tbsp) flour
2 lb (900 g) braising or stewing meat, cut into 1-inch (2.5-cm) cubes
2 tbsp sunflower oil
2 large onions (8–10 oz/225–275 g), thinly sliced
1 clove of garlic, crushed
1 can light beer
1 tbsp dark soy sauce
2 teasp bottled brown sauce (optional)
2 bay leaves
2 lb (900 g) new potatoes
1 tbsp chopped parsley

In a large bowl mix salt, pepper and flour. Toss the cubes of meat in it to coat them. Heat the oil in a heavy casserole, then sauté the onions and garlic for 8 minutes, or until soft. Remove. Put in the meat and brown well on all sides. Add the onions and garlic, then the beer, soy, brown sauce and bay leaves. Bring to the boil, cover and simmer for 2 hours on top of the stove, or in the oven, Gas No. 2 (300°F/150°C). Boil potatoes and toss in parsley. Put stew in dish and serve surrounded by the potatoes.

STUFATO DI MANZO FIORENTINA
(*Beef Stew, Florentine Style*)

Serves 4–6.
Keeps 3 days under refrigeration.
Freeze 3 months.

A full-flavoured, herb-scented dish.

2 cloves of garlic, finely chopped, or 2 teasp garlic purée
1 teasp fresh or dried rosemary, finely chopped
2 tbsp olive oil
2½ lb (1.25 kg) braising steak, cut in 1-inch (2.5-cm) chunks
1 teasp salt
10 grinds of black pepper
2 teasp brown sugar
9 fl oz (250 ml/1 cup plus 2 tbsp) dry red wine
5 fl oz (150 ml/⅔ cup) beef stock
3 tbsp tomato purée
1 teasp dried Italian seasoning herbs
1 tbsp chopped parsley
1 tbsp chopped fresh basil
12 oz (350 g/3 cups) penne or fusilli (short hollow pasta)

Gently sauté the garlic and rosemary in the oil to flavour it. Add the well-dried meat and sauté until it is richly browned all over, sprinkling it with the salt, pepper and sugar. Don't crowd the pan - if necessary, fry the meat in 2 batches. Pour in the wine and bubble fiercely for 3 minutes to concentrate the flavour, then add the stock, purée and dried herbs. Cover and simmer for 2 hours on top of the stove, or 2½ hours in a slow oven, Gas No. 2 (300°F/150°C). The meat should be bathed in a thick sauce. Stir in the parsley and basil. Serve with the pasta, cooked according to packet directions.

A FINE BEEF RAGOUT

Serves 6–7.
Keeps 3 days under refrigeration.
Freeze 3 months.

A French country recipe, simple and succulent. Serve with mashed or plain boiled potatoes or noodles.

For the marinade
5 fl oz (150 ml/$^2/_3$ cup) medium-dry red wine
1 teasp dried herbes de Provence
1$^1/_2$ tbsp red wine vinegar
1 teasp onion salt or 2 teasp dried chopped onion
1 tbsp chopped parsley
1 bay leaf
1 teasp salt
15 grinds of black pepper

For the ragout
2$^1/_2$–3 lb (1.2–2.5 kg) lean stewing beef (well-trimmed brisket, shin beef or top rib)
2 tbsp olive or sunflower oil
1 tbsp margarine
2 large onions, coarsely chopped
2 cloves of garlic, chopped
1 oz flour
1 teasp salt
10 grinds black pepper
1 beef stock cube dissolved in 10 fl oz (275 ml/1$^1/_4$ cups) boiling water
2 bay leaves
12–16 button mushrooms
12–16 shallots or pickling onions, peeled

Early in the day, or overnight, put all the marinade ingredients into a wide, shallow dish, add the beef cut in 1$^1/_2$-inch (4-cm) chunks and leave to marinate overnight, or at room temperature for 3–4 hours. When ready to cook the meat, lift it out of the marinade with a slotted spoon, drain it well and then lay on paper towels to dry. Reserve the marinade.

Heat the fats in a large heatproof casserole, then sauté the chopped onions and the garlic (half-covered) until they are softened and a light gold in colour. Toss the dried meat in the seasoned flour, then add to the pan and cook, stirring frequently, until it is browned on all sides and the onions are golden brown. Add the strained marinade, the stock and enough additional water if necessary barely to cover the meat. Add the bay leaves, then cover and simmer very slowly for 2 hours on top of the stove, or 2$^1/_2$ hours ina slow oven, Gas No. 2 (300°F/150°C). Add the mushrooms and the onions, cover again and cook for a further 30 minutes, by which time the meat will be meltingly tender.

CACEROLA DE CARNE CON VINO Y NARANJAS

(*Beef Cooked in Orange Juice and Red Wine*)

Serves 6.
Keeps 3 days under refrigeration.
Freeze 3 months.

A stew in the Spanish style, with citrus juice and zest adding a refreshing flavour.

2 tbsp olive oil
2$^1/_2$ lb (1.5 kg) topside or top rib of beef, cut in 1$^1/_2$-inch (4-cm) chunks
1 oz (25 g/2 tbsp) margarine
1 large (8 oz/225 g) onion, finely chopped
2 cloves of garlic, finely chopped
juice from 2 large oranges (approx. 6 fl oz/175 ml/$^3/_4$ cup)
10 fl oz (275 ml/1$^1/_4$ cups) hearty red wine
3 strips lemon peel
4 strips orange peel
1 cinnamon stick
1 bay leaf
4 cloves
2 teasp salt
15 grinds of black pepper
4 oz (125 g/1 cup) fat black or green olives
2 teasp cornflour (cornstarch) mixed to a cream with 2 tbsp cold water

For the garnish
2 oranges, segmented

In a flameproof casserole, heat the oil, then add the chunks of beef and brown thoroughly on all sides. Add the margarine and sauté the onion and garlic more gently until golden. Pour in the orange juice and enough wine barely to cover the meat. (You can use half wine and half beef stock if you prefer.) Add the citrus peel, the spices, salt and pepper. Cover and simmer gently for 2 hours on top of the stove, or 2½ hours in a slow oven, Gas No. 2 (300°F/150°C), until the meat is tender. 15 minutes before the end of the cooking time, stir in the olives and the cornflour. Serve straight from the casserole, garnished with the sections of fresh orange.

BEEF AND ROSEMARY RAGOUT

Serves 6–7.
Keeps 3 days under refrigeration.
Freeze 3 months.

In the traditional version of this dish - very similar to Boeuf Bourguignonne but aromatic with the pungent rosemary of Provence, a whole bottle of wine is used for cooking liquid. It is then concentrated by simmering the casserole uncovered for 1 hour. I find so much wine too heavy - not to mention too expensive - for my taste and prefer the lighter recipe I give below.

This kind of rich ragout needs very simple accompaniments. I cook fresh tagliatelle in beef stock rather than water, then toss it with plenty of fresh parsley and black pepper to serve instead of potatoes. No vegetables, but a green salad - perhaps endive, chicory, iceberg lettuce, shredded green pepper - mixed just before serving with a thinly sliced avocado which has been marinated for several hours in a fresh herb vinaigrette (see p. 300).

3 tbsp extra virgin olive oil
1 large (10 oz/275 g) onion, finely chopped
1 large carrot, cut in ½-inch (1-cm) chunks
2 plump cloves of garlic
2½–3 lb (1.25–1.5 kg) braising steak (weight when trimmed) cut in 1-inch (2.5-cm) cubes
2 oz (50 g/½ cup) flour
1 teasp salt
10 grinds of black pepper
½ bottle of a fruity, dry red wine
1 x 14 oz (400 g) can tomatoes
2 oz (50 g) parsley (a good bunch), including the stalks
3 sprigs of fresh rosemary or 1 teasp dried rosemary
2 level teasp salt
20 grinds of black pepper
2 level teasp dark brown sugar

For the garnish
1 tbsp chopped fresh basil

Heat the oil in a heavy frying pan, add the finely chopped vegetables and the garlic and cook until softened and golden - about 10 minutes over moderate heat. Remove with a draining spoon.

Toss the meat in the seasoned flour, then add to the pan and sear over high heat until evenly browned (you may need to do this in 2 batches as overcrowding the pan lowers the temperature of the oil and retards the browning of the meat). Put the meat and vegetables into an ovenproof casserole, then add the wine, stir well and bubble uncovered for 5 minutes to concentrate the flavour. Now add the tomatoes and all the seasonings, pour over the meat and vegetables in the casserole, and transfer to the oven, Gas No. 2 (300°F/150°C) for 30 minutes, or until bubbles are breaking the surface. Then turn down to Gas No. 1 (275°F/140°C) for a further 2 hours, or until the meat is meltingly tender. Remove the sprigs of rosemary and parsley before serving, and stir in the basil.

GUISADO CON CIRUELAS
(*Spanish Beef with Prunes*)

Serves 6.
Keeps 3 days under refrigeration.
Freeze 3 months.

Prunes are the unexpected addition to this delicious dish in which chunky pieces of beef are stewed in spiced white wine.

2 tbsp flour
2 teasp salt
15 grinds of black pepper
$2\frac{1}{2}$ lb (1.25 kg) top rib or good stewing beef, well trimmed, cut in 2-inch (5-cm) chunks
2 tbsp olive oil plus 1 tbsp
1 large onion, finely sliced
1 clove of garlic, finely chopped
1 teasp dark brown sugar
5 fl oz (150 ml/$\frac{2}{3}$ cup) dry white wine
2 level tbsp tomato purée
10 fl oz (275 ml/$1\frac{1}{4}$ cups) boiling water plus 1 meat stock-cube, or 10 fl oz (275 ml/$1\frac{1}{4}$ cups) thin beef gravy
1 teasp paprika
8 oz (225 g/$1\frac{1}{2}$ cups) ready-pitted prunes, or 8 oz (225 g/$1\frac{1}{2}$ cups) regular prunes soaked in strained tea overnight before stoning
1 oz (25 g/$\frac{1}{4}$ cup) toasted pine kernels (optional but delicious)

Preheat the oven to Gas No. 2 (300°F/150°C).

Put the flour, salt and pepper in a plastic bag, add the beef cubes in 2 batches and shake until evenly coated. Brown the meat on all sides in the hot oil, then lift on to a plate lined with paper towels. Add the extra oil to the pan (if necessary), then gently sauté the onion and garlic, covering the pan for 5 minutes and then uncovering and sprinkling with the brown sugar. Continue to cook until a rich golden brown. Add the wine and bubble for 1 or 2 minutes, then add all the remaining ingredients except the pine kernels. Stir and bring to the boil. Put the beef into an ovenproof casserole and pour on the sauce. It should barely cover the meat; if it does not, add a little boiling water. Cover and cook for $2\frac{1}{2}$–3 hours, making sure the liquid is just bubbling. Turn the oven down if the casserole is cooking too quickly. After 2 hours, add a little boiling liquid if necessary – the sauce should be thick but still very juicy. Taste at this point and reseason with salt and pepper if necessary.

Meanwhile, put the pine kernels on a heat-proof dish and leave in the oven until golden brown or toss over direct heat in a non-stick frying pan. Garnish each serving with a sprinkling of the nuts.

AMERICAN DUMPLING STEW DELUXE

Serves 6.
Keeps 3 days under refrigeration.
Freeze 3 months.

A hearty stew for a winter's night. Meat stock can be substituted for the wine if preferred.

2 tbsp oil
$2\frac{1}{2}$ lb (1.25 kg) sliced bola or first-cut shoulder steak, cut in 1-inch (2.5-cm) cubes
2 large onions, sliced
2 level teasp brown sugar
1 large carrot, diced
white part of a fat leek
3 level teasp salt
few grinds of black pepper
2 teasp each flour and dry mustard
1 teasp ground ginger
8 fl oz (225 ml/1 cup) red wine
hot water

For the dumplings

$1\frac{1}{2}$ oz (40 g/3 tbsp) margarine
4 oz (125 g/1 cup) self-raising (all-purpose) flour plus 1 teasp baking powder
2 teasp chopped parsley
$\frac{1}{2}$ teasp salt
10 grinds of black pepper
1 oz (25 g/$\frac{1}{4}$ cup) ground hazelnuts
1 egg
2 tbsp water

Heat the oil in a heavy pan, put in the meat (in 2 or 3 batches) and brown quickly, stirring all the time. Add the sliced onions and brown sugar, the diced carrot and leek, and continue to cook until a rich brown juice flows from the mixture - about 5 minutes. Sprinkle in the salt and pepper, flour, mustard and ginger, stir well, then add the wine and enough hot water barely to cover the mixture. Simmer on top of the stove or in the oven at Gas No. 2 (300°F/150°C) for 2½ hours, making sure that the liquid only shivers rather than bubbles, or until the meat is bite-tender.

Meanwhile, make the dumplings by rubbing the fat into the flour, adding the parsley, salt, pepper and hazelnuts, then mixing to a sticky dough with the egg and water. After the meat has been cooking for 2 hours, using a wet spoon, drop tablespoons of the mixture on to the simmering stew, cover and continue to cook for a further 30 minutes.

Meat Pies and Strudels

A perfect meat pie has to be made with care. The meat must first be simmered till tender, in a succulent sauce, and the crust then baked crisp on the outside, yet within, moist and juicy from the filling.

This crust can be made from either puff or shortcrust pastry, the meat cubed or minced before cooking. But in both cases the filling must be quite cool before it is covered, or the crust will be soggy.

TO MAKE A MEAT PIE WITH A SINGLE CRUST

Serves 6.
Leftovers keep 3 days under refrigeration (but will go a little soggy).

1 recipe Savoury Goulash (see p. 156) or Meat and Herb Stew (see p. 157)
8 oz (225 g) puff pastry or ½ recipe Rough Puff Pastry made with margarine (see p. 403)

Cook the meat mixture according to the recipe, but allow it to cool. Then spoon it into a pie dish 2 inches (5 cm) deep with a ½-inch (1.25-cm) rim all the way round. Roll out the pastry until it is the thickness of a penny and ½ inch (1.25-cm) larger all the way round than the top of the dish. Trim off this extra ½-inch (1.25-cm) and lay it on the dampened rim of the dish. Dampen the strip of pastry in turn, then carefully transfer the remaining pastry to the dish, pressing it down well on to the pastry rim that is already in position. A pie funnel helps the pie crust to keep its shape. Use a fork to crimp the edges of the pie. If you have a little beaten egg, use it to paint the top of the pie; otherwise leave it plain. Bake in a hot oven, Gas No. 8 (450°F/230°C) for 20 minutes.

TO MAKE A MEAT PIE WITH A DOUBLE CRUST

Serves 6.

1 recipe Savoury Goulash (see p. 156) or Carbonnade de Boeuf Flamande (see p. 158)
8 oz (225 g) puff pastry or ½ recipe Rough Puff Pastry made with margarine (see p. 403)

Divide the pastry in half and roll 1 piece to fit the bottom of a 7-inch (18-cm) or 8-inch (20-cm) pie dish. Spoon in the cooled meat mixture. If there is too much gravy, omit it and serve separately. Dampen the edges of the pie, then cover with a second crust rolled from the remainder of the pastry. Crimp the edges with a fork, brush with beaten egg or leave plain, and bake for 10 minutes at Gas No. 8 (450°F/230°C), then for a further 15 minutes at Gas No. 7 (425°F/220°C).

TO MAKE A MEAT PIE WITH A DUMPLING CRUST

Serves 6.

In this recipe the meat must *be hot when the crust is put on, as it needs the steam to cook it.*

1 recipe Savoury Goulash (see p. 156), Meat and Herb Stew (see p. 157) or Carbonnade de Boeuf Flamande (see p. 158)
4 oz (125/1 cup) self-raising flour plus 1 level teasp baking powder, or 4 oz (125 g/1 cup) plain (all-purpose) flour plus 2 level teasp baking powder
½ level teasp salt
2 oz (50 g/¼ cup) margarine
2 teasp chopped parsley
2 tbsp (approx.) cold water

Mix the flour, baking powder and salt, then rub in the margarine until the mixture resembles coarse crumbs. Stir in the chopped parsley and sufficient cold water to make a stiff dough. Gently roll out the dumpling on a floured board to fit the top of the casserole in which the meat is bubbling. 45 minutes before the meat is done, uncover the casserole, top with the dumpling crust, re-cover and continue to cook. By the time the meat is ready, the crust will have become puffy and brown.

MEAT STRUDEL

Makes 2 strudels, each serving 3–4.
Will keep under refrigeration 2 days raw or 3 days cooked.
Freeze raw 2 months.
For best results do not reheat but serve fresh from the oven.

1 lb (450 g) frozen puff pastry, thawed, or 1 recipe Rough Puff Pastry made with margarine (see p. 403)

For the meat mixture

1 tbsp sunflower oil
1 medium onion, finely chopped
1 large green or red pepper, finely chopped
1 lb (450 g) minced (ground) beef
1 heaped tbsp tomato purée or ketchup
salt
pepper
pinch of nutmeg
2 teasp dark soy sauce
2 teasp finely chopped parsley

For the glaze

1 beaten egg or 1 egg yolk plus 1 teasp cold water
1 rounded tbsp sesame seeds

Heat the oil and add the onion and pepper. Cook until the onion softens (about 3 minutes), then add the meat and stir with a fork until it loses its redness and starts to brown. Add purée, seasoning and parsley. Simmer gently for 20 minutes, until thick but still juicy. Allow to cool.

Divide pastry in half and proceed with each half as follows. Roll first half into a rectangle 16 inches (40 cm) by 10 inches (25 cm). It must be so thin that you can see the board through it. Spread half the cooled meat over the pastry, leaving a 1-inch (2.5-cm) margin all the way round. Turn ends in to seal, then roll up like a flattened Swiss roll. Transfer to an ungreased baking sheet, join side down, and brush with beaten egg, then decorate if liked with sesame seeds for crunchiness. Make cuts 2–2½ inches (5–7 cm) apart, through the top layer of pastry to prevent the strudel bursting, and also to make it easy to portion when cooked. Bake in a hot oven, Gas No. 7 (425°F/220°C), for 10 minutes, then at Gas No. 6 (400°F/200°C) for a further 15–20 minutes, until crisp and brown. Serve warm. May be reheated. Delicious for a buffet.

VARIATION

SAVOURY MOROCCAN STRUDEL

The meat strudel can be given a completely new taste and texture by adding some of the spices and dried fruit that are so much used in the cooking of Moroccan Jews – the combination of Moorish and French influences in their cuisine has made Moroccan chefs some of the most popular in Israel.

On a more practical note, I have greatly reduced the amount of fat used in the traditional recipe by substituting extra-lean minced beef for lamb, and by softening the onions mainly with steam, so that only a very little fat is needed. If you have time to chill the cooked meat mixture overnight, even more of the fat can be skimmed off the top next day. This is a great dish for a meat buffet.

1 x 1 lb (450 g) pack puff pastry

For the meat mixture

1 medium onion, finely chopped
1 fat clove of garlic, finely chopped
1 tbsp sunflower oil
1 lb (450 g) extra-lean minced beef
4 oz (125 g/¾ cup) tenderized apricots, quartered
1 teasp ground cumin
1 tbsp chopped parsley
⅛ teasp ground nutmeg
1 teasp cinnamon
½ teasp sea salt
8 grinds of black pepper
4 tbsp meat or chicken stock

For the glaze

1 whole egg, beaten, or 1 egg yolk plus 1 teasp cold water
2 tbsp sesame seed

First prepare the meat filling. In a large sauté or a deep frying pan, cook the onions and the garlic in the oil over moderate heat until soft and golden, keeping the pan covered. Add the finely minced meat. Continue to cook uncovered, breaking the meat up with a fork until it loses its pinkness, then add all the remaining ingredients and bring to the boil. Cover and simmer for 15 minutes until the meat feels tender when tasted. At this stage the mixture should be juicy but with little free liquid. If too wet, continue to cook uncovered until this moisture disappears. Taste and add a little extra salt if necessary, then spread on a flat dish to cool.

To assemble the strudels, proceed as for the Meat Strudel (p. 163) and then bake in the same way.

PASTELES
(*Sephardi-style Meat Pies*)

Makes 24 small pies.
Freeze baked or unbaked pasteles for 2 months.

The minced (ground) beef filling differs from the Ashkenazi mixture in that the meat is browned before use, contains no egg, is seasoned with allspice and contains fried pine kernels, which give it a most unusual texture.

A Sephardi cook will mould the pasteles by hand, sealing the top to the bottom with an intricate edging which it is difficult to describe. Unless you can get a Sephardi cook to demonstrate, it is best to use the simple Western method, as in the recipe below.

For the pastry

12 oz (350 g/3 cups) plain (all-purpose) flour
1 teasp salt
6 oz (175 g/¾ cup) block margarine
2 tbsp sunflower oil
5 tbsp (approx.) warm water

For the meat filling

1 oz (25 g/¼ cup) pine kernels
1 tbsp sunflower oil
1 medium onion (finely chopped)
1 lb (450 g) raw minced (ground) beef (or lamb)
5 tbsp cold water
½ teasp ground cinnamon
½ teasp ground allspice (piment)
1 teasp salt
10 grinds of black pepper

For the glaze

1 egg, beaten
sesame seeds

Fry the pine kernels gently in the oil until brown then drain (they burn easily). Put the chopped onion into the pan and brown gently, then add the meat and continue to cook until it is a uniform brown all over. Barely cover with water, add the seasonings and simmer, uncovered, until the moisture has almost evaporated and the meat looks juicy. Stir in the pine kernels. The filling is now ready.

To make the pastry and shape the pasteles, put flour, salt and margarine, cut into small chunks, into a large bowl and sprinkle with the oil. Now rub the fat into the dry ingredients as for shortcrust pastry. Sprinkle with enough of the water to make a firm but non-sticky dough. Roll out ⅛ inch (0.25 cm) thick on a lightly floured board and, using plain metal pastry-cutters, cut the dough into equal quantities of 3½-inch (8-cm) and 2-inch (5-cm) rounds. There should be enough for about 24 of each.

To shape the cases the Western way, place circles of pastry in 24 patty tins, add a spoonful of cooled meat mixture, and cover with another round, sealing the edges well together.

To shape the cases in the traditional Middle Eastern way, use your fingers to make pleats round the larger circles to form cups ¾ inch (2 cm) deep. Fill with the cooled meat, then put a 2-inch (5-cm) circle on top and twist together into a 'pie-crust' edging. Arrange on ungreased baking sheets about 1 inch (2.5 cm) apart.

Brush the pies with beaten egg and scatter with sesame seeds. Bake in a hot oven, Gas No. 6 (400°F/200°C) for 20–25 minutes, or until a rich brown.

BEEF AND AUBERGINE PIE

Serves 6.
Cooked meat filling or leftover pie keeps 2 days under refrigeration.
Freeze 3 months.

To avoid sogginess, fill and bake pie the same day.

If canned aubergines (eggplants) are not available, use 8 oz cubed fresh aubergines fried in oil for 5 minutes, or omit altogether and use an extra 4 oz (125 g) lean minced (ground) beef.

½ recipe Flaky Pastry made with margarine (see p. 403) or shortcrust pastry made with 8 oz (225 g/2 cups) plain (all-purpose) flour, 5 oz (150 g/⅔ cup) firm margarine, pinch of salt and icy water to mix

For the filling

1 medium onion, finely chopped
1 clove of garlic, crushed
1 tbsp olive oil or sunflower oil
12 oz (350 g) minced (ground) beef
1 tbsp chopped parsley
2 teasp dark soy sauce
1 level teasp salt
10 grinds of black pepper
good pinch of ground mace
1 can (8 oz/225 g) tomato sauce or 2 tbsp tomato purée mixed with 8 fl oz (225 ml/1 cup) stock, and a pinch each of sugar and salt
8 oz (225 g) canned aubergines

Preheat the oven to Gas No. 7 (425°F/220°C) – or Gas No. 5 (375°F/190°C) if shortcrust is used.

Sauté the onion and garlic in the oil until soft and golden – about 5 minutes (keep the pan covered). Add the meat, together with all the remaining ingredients except aubergines, and simmer for 5 minutes, giving the mixture an occasional stir. It will be thick but juicy. Stir in the aubergines. Allow to cool for 5 minutes. Roll out half the pastry to fit an 8–9 inch (20–2.5 cm) pie dish approx. 1 inch (2.5 cm) deep. Spoon in the cooled filling. Top with a lattice of pastry strips, cut ½ inch (1 cm) thick and arranged the same distance apart and sealed to the edge of the dish with cold water (or cover with a lid of pastry cut to fit). Either brush with a little beaten egg or leave plain. Bake for 45 minutes, until golden brown. Serve hot.

Braised Steak

One of the most versatile of meat dishes available to the Jewish cook is braised steak, as braising is the perfect method of tenderizing lean meat that has been koshered (the salt used in the process can have a toughening effect). You will find variations of the following recipes in every Jewish community – I was once served it for lunch in the Jewish Town Hall in Prague, where people had been out of contact with the West for 25 years!

The original 'braising' dish had a shallow lid into which hot charcoal could be placed. This meant that a dish cooked on top of the stove could have both moist and dry heat applied to it, so it developed a flavour quite different from a stew. Today we use a similar dish, but without the charcoal, for the modern oven can supply the all-round heat more efficiently.

The meat One can use either blade steaks or slices of bola (chuck) or first-cut shoulder steak, but in all cases the meat must be at least ¾ inch (2 cm) thick, otherwise it just dissolves into the sauce. If slices of steak are used, cut them into servings before they are cooked.

The braising liquid One can use tomatoes, paprika-flavoured liquid or a variety of vegetables to provide the flavour.

The cooking Always brown the meat quickly but thoroughly to seal the surface. To cut fat to a minimum brush the empty pan with sunflower or, preferably, olive oil, which promotes a better colour, then put over moderate heat until you can feel the heat on the palm of your hand held 2 inches (5 cm) above it. Quickly sear the meat on both sides - when the surface has been sealed the meat comes off the pan easily. Then use just enough liquid barely to cover it - it isn't a stew, remember.

You have a choice of cooking dishes. *Either* do the initial browning in a heavy-based frying pan and then transfer to a pottery or enamelled iron or steel casserole, or use a large diameter, lidded, deep sauté pan (mine is of heavy stainless steel with a thick aluminium base which is suitable for both stove-top and oven cooking).

SWISS STEAK

Serves 4–5 generously.
Keeps 4 days under refrigeration.
Freeze 2 months.

A favourite American dish.

1 oz (25 g/¼ cup) flour
1 level teasp salt
pinch of pepper
1 teasp paprika
1½–2 lb (675 g–1 kg) first-cut shoulder steak ¾ inch (2 cm) thick, trimmed of gristle and cut into individual portions
1 tbsp sunflower oil
1 x 14 oz (400 g) can plum tomatoes in juice
2 onions, finely sliced
2 stalks of celery, diced
1 clove of garlic, crushed
2 teasp bottled brown sauce (optional)

Mix together the flour and seasonings, then, using an old saucer, pound into both sides of the meat using the saucer edge. (This helps to break down the tissues and tenderize the meat.) Heat the fat in a heavy frying pan, quickly brown the pieces of meat on both sides, then put into an oven casserole. Spoon over the remaining ingredients, cover and bake slowly, first at Gas No. 3 (325°F/160°C) for half an hour, then for a further 2 hours at Gas No. 2 (300°F/150°C). If the sauce is too thin, uncover for the last half-hour.

BRAISED STEAK WITH MUSHROOMS

Serves 4–5.
Keeps 4 days under refrigeration.
Freeze 2 months.

2 lb (900 g) bola (chuck) or first-cut shoulder steak, cut ¾ inch (2 cm) thick in 2 slices
2 tbsp flour
1 teasp paprika pepper
2 tbsp sunflower oil
1 large onion, sliced
8 oz (225 ml/2½ cups) button mushrooms
8 fl oz (225 ml/1 cup) leftover gravy or stock-cube plus water
1 clove of garlic, crushed
1 level teasp fines herbes or Italian seasoning
1½ level teasp salt
15 grinds of black pepper

Taking each slice of the meat in turn, pound ¼ of the seasoned flour into each side, using the edge of an old saucer. In a heavy pan or casserole, heat the oil and sear the floured meat on both sides until a rich brown, then drain on kitchen paper. Put the onions in the same fat and cook, covered, until soft and golden. Add the whole mushrooms and cook a further 2 minutes. Pour off any unabsorbed fat (but not the sediment), then return the meat to the pan. Pour on the meat gravy (or stock cube plus water) and add the garlic, herbs, salt and pepper. Bring to the boil, cover and transfer to a very slow oven, Gas No. 2 (300°F/150°C) for 2½ hours, or until the meat is meltingly tender.

STEAK BRAISED IN THE ITALIAN MANNER

Serves 6.
Keeps 4 days under refrigeration.
Freeze 2 months.

2 tbsp extra virgin olive oil
2 lb (900 g) first-cut shoulder steak, trimmed of gristle and cut into individual portions ¾ inch (2 cm) thick
1 oz (25 g/¼ cup) flour
1 level teasp salt
10 grinds of black pepper

For the sauce

1 x 14 oz (400 g) can whole or chopped tomatoes in juice
1 tbsp olive oil
1 plump clove of garlic, finely chopped
1½ level teasp salt
2 level teasp brown sugar
10 grinds of black pepper
1 tbsp each chopped fresh oregano and basil or 1 teasp each dried
1 tbsp chopped parsley
1 bay leaf

To make the sauce, put the tomatoes (chopped coarsely if whole) in a small pan with all the remaining sauce ingredients except the herbs. Simmer uncovered for 10 minutes or until it is as thick as ketchup; stir in the herbs. Meanwhile, heat the 2 tbsp oil and fry the meat (coated in the seasoned flour) until a rich brown on both sides. Put into a casserole and pour over the sauce. Cook at Gas No. 3 (325°F/160°C) until it starts to bubble – about 30 minutes – then turn down to Gas No. 2 (300°F/150°C) for a further 1½ hours, or until tender.

STEAK IN THE HUNGARIAN MANNER

Serves 5–6.
Keeps 4 days under refrigeration.
Freeze 2 months.

The essential ingredient is a well-flavoured paprika pepper - Hungarian, for choice.

6 blade steaks or 2½ lb (1.25 kg) of ¾-inch thick (1.5-cm) shoulder steak, cut in serving portions
2 tbsp olive oil or sunflower oil
1 large onion, sliced
8 oz (225 g/2½ cups) mushrooms, sliced
1 fat red pepper, deseeded and sliced
1 level tbsp tomato purée
1 tbsp paprika
2 level teasp salt
1 teasp brown sugar
10 grinds of black pepper
8 fl oz (225 ml/1 cup) boiling liquid (stock, vegetable water or thin gravy)
2 lb (900 g) thickly-sliced boiling potatoes

Put the well-dried pieces of meat into the hot oil. Cook until a rich brown, turn and cook the other side (do this quickly). Lift from the pan and leave on a plate lined with paper towels. Turn down the heat to moderate and, in the remaining oil, gently cook the onion for 10 minutes (covering the pan for the first 5 minutes) until limp and golden. Add the mushrooms and pepper slices and cook a further 5 minutes, then arrange on the bottom of a casserole and place the meat on top of it. Stir the purée and seasonings into the boiling liquid, then pour on top of the meat. Cover and simmer, either on top of the stove or, preferably, in the oven, Gas No. 2 (300°F/150°C), for 1½ hours. Uncover, add potato slices, then cover and simmer for a further hour.

How to Cook Kosher Steak

Kosher steaks can be grilled (broiled) successfully under a really efficient grill (broiler), but I think they are more satisfactory, particularly for new cooks, when sautéd on top of the stove, either in a heavy-based frying pan large enough to hold the steaks in one layer or in a ridged stove-top iron grill. To ensure tenderness, ask the butcher to cut the steaks from a side of beef that has been hung for 7–10 days.

STEAK SAUTÉ

Serves 4.

4 x 6–8 oz (175–225 g) rib steaks (entrecôtes) ¾–1 inch (2–2.5 cm) thick
black pepper
olive oil

For the sauce

5 fl oz (150 ml/⅔ cup) dry white or red wine or white vermouth, or the same amount of gravy left over from a roast or a braise, or stock made from a beef bouillon-cube
2 teasp dark soy sauce
a few grinds of black pepper
1 level teasp salt
1 tbsp chopped parsley

Take the steaks from the refrigerator 1 hour before cooking. Trim most of the fat from each steak, leaving only a very thin edging. Nick with a sharp knife wherever there is any gristle between the fat and the meat. Dry well with paper towels. Sprinkle with freshly ground black pepper.

Heat the frying pan over a high heat until a sprinkling of water sizzles and evaporates as soon as it hits the surface (it should be very hot). Brush very lightly with olive oil, using a piece of kitchen paper, then put in the steaks. Sear the meat on both sides until a rich brown - 2 minutes on each side (3 minutes for well done – then decrease the heat to moderate and cook for approximately 6–8 minutes, turning the steaks several times so that they brown evenly. Nick one and if it's the right colour in the centre, immediately transfer to a warm plate and keep hot.

Turn the heat down and add the liquid. Swirl this round in the pan to loosen the sediment sticking to the bottom. Allow to simmer for a minute to concentrate the flavour. Add the soy sauce and seasonings. Pour over the steak and sprinkle with chopped parsley.

VARIATION

PEPPERED STEAK

With such a satisfying main course, you can forget about potatoes. Instead, sauté a few thickly sliced mixed peppers (in minimal oil), keeping the lid on to soften them), seasoned with plenty of black pepper and coarse salt.

A simple salad of sliced tomatoes, sprinkled with 3 or 4 thinly sliced spring onions, a few spoons of reduced-calorie French dressing and a few shredded leaves of fresh basil, is the perfect accompaniment.

Quantities given for each rib steak (entrecôte).

1 scant teasp black peppercorns
2 teasp oil
1 teasp brandy
3 tbsp meat stock
2 tbsp red wine (if available)

Take the steaks from the refrigerator 1 hour before cooking. Crush the peppercorns coarsely in a mortar or place them between two sheets of greaseproof paper and crush with a rolling pin. Put them in a tiny screw top jar and sprinkle with the brandy, then shake vigorously and leave for 1 hour. Just before cooking, pat the pepper mixture on each side of the steaks.

Cook the steaks as before. Transfer the cooked steaks to a warmed plate and keep hot. Pour the stock and wine into the pan, swirl it round to incorporate any juices from the meat, season lightly with salt then pour over the steaks and serve pronto.

BISTECCA ALLA PIZZAIOLA
(*Steak with Herb and Tomato Sauce*)

Serves 6.
For steak that isn't quite so tasty or tender, this is an excellent Italian recipe.

6 rib steaks, well dried and sprinkled with freshly milled black pepper

For the sauce
1 x 14 oz (400 g) can tomatoes in tomato juice
1 tbsp tomato purée
1 tbsp extra virgin olive oil
1 level teasp salt
1 level teasp brown sugar
10 grinds of black pepper
1 level teasp mixed dried Italian herbs
2 fat cloves of garlic, peeled and crushed
2 level tbsp shredded fresh basil or coarsely chopped parsley

Simmer all the sauce ingredients together in an uncovered pan until thick but still juicy – about 10 minutes on top of the stove, 5 minutes on 100 per cent power in the microwave. Keep the sauce hot while cooking the steaks.

Use a heavy-lidded frying pan rather than a grill (broiler) to cook the steaks on top of the stove. After they have been thoroughly browned on both sides (as for Steak Sauté, see p. 168), pour over the sauce, cover and simmer gently for 5–7 minutes. Nick a steak to check it has been cooked to the desired 'doneness', otherwise give it 1 or 2 minutes longer.

Serve the steaks coated with the sauce.

MINUTE STEAK

Serves 4–6.
Steaks cut from the forequarters can be used for this delicious 'à la minute' *recipe.*

4–6 'minute' steaks (cut by the butcher
¼ inch/0.5 cm thick from frozen shoulder)
Dijon mustard (for thinly coating steaks)

For the sauce
2 shallots (or 4 spring onion bulbs/scallions), finely chopped
2 teasp olive oil
2 large canned tomatoes, drained, or 2 beefsteak fresh tomatoes, skinned
2 tbsp chopped parsley
1 tbsp dark soy sauce
4 tbsp meat jelly or good gravy, or ½ crumbled bouillon-cube
2 tbsp dry white wine (optional)
salt
black pepper

First prepare the sauce in a small pan. Cook the chopped shallots or spring onions in the oil until soft and golden - about 5 minutes. Add the chopped tomatoes and parsley, then stir in the soy sauce, the jelly, gravy or bouillon-cube (add a little water if the bouillon-cube is used), wine (if used) and seasonings. Leave this mixture to simmer very, very gently while you cook the steaks. As these are generally rather large, you will probably need to do them 2 at a time.

Coat each steak thinly with the mustard and sear on both sides until a rich brown, as described in previous recipes. Remove to a hot platter and fry the remaining steaks. Add the sauce to the frying pan and allow to bubble and blend with the pan juices. Add the fried steaks and mix well, then turn back on to the hot platter and serve at once.

Rib of Beef

BEEF KEBABS, PLAIN AND SIMPLE

Serves 4.

The marinade helps to tenderize the meat as well as imparting succulence and flavour.

1 lb (450 g) boned-out eye of rib, cut into 1-inch (2.5-cm) cubes

For the marinade
4 fl oz (125 ml/½ cup) dry red wine
2 tbsp olive oil
1 tbsp red wine vinegar or cider vinegar
1 tbsp Moutarde de Meaux
1 tbsp dried Herbes de Provence
1 fat clove of garlic, finely chopped
15 grinds of black pepper
½ teasp sugar

Whisk together the ingredients for the marinade until evenly blended. Lay the chunks of meat side by side in a shallow dish, then pour over the marinade. Leave at room temperature for 30 minutes, then pour off the marinade and divide the meat between 4 metal skewers. If you like your meat crunchy all over, leave a little room between each cube.

Grill for 10–12 minutes under or over a hot grill (broiler) until the meat is crispy outside and still pink within, brushing with the marinade and turning the meat 2 or 3 times.

BEEF SATAY WITH PEANUT SAUCE

Serves 4.
Freeze the uncooked steak in marinade and the sauce separately for 3 months.

Satay, the kebab of Indonesia, is more likely to be made with chicken than beef in its native land. But using a marinade based on a dark rather than a light soy sauce is a very successful way to tenderize kosher steak and, as a bonus, adds some wonderful flavour to it as well. You can grill the satay either under a regular oven grill, on an indoor or outdoor barbecue or on a well-greased ridged skillet. Satay makes a really savoury main course, accompanied by plain rice and a green salad.

1 lb (450 g) rib steak

For the marinade
2 tbsp dry sherry
2 tbsp soy sauce
1 tbsp sunflower oil
1 tbsp lemon juice
1 clove of garlic, crushed
1 tbsp sesame seeds

For the sauce
5 fl oz (150 ml/$^2/_3$ cup) chicken stock
2 teasp oil
1 teasp dried onion
1 teasp minced garlic
$^1/_4$ teasp Cayenne pepper
$^1/_2$ teasp salt
1$^1/_2$ teasp medium brown sugar
6 tbsp smooth peanut butter
1 tbsp lemon juice

Mix together the marinade ingredients in a large bowl. Add the steak, cut into $^1/_2$-inch (1-cm) cubes. Turn to coat evenly. Cover and leave to marinate for 3–4 hours or overnight.

To make the peanut sauce, put the chicken stock in a pan and heat through. Add all the reminaing sauce ingredients and heat gently until everything has combined to make a smooth sauce. Remove from the heat and leave to cool.

Thread the pieces of marinated steak on to bamboo skewers. Barbecue, turning frequently, for 10 minutes, or until tender. Serve garnished with salad and accompanied by the peanut sauce.

TO ROAST A STANDING WING RIB

Serves 6–8.
Leftovers keep 3 days under refrigeration.
Freeze 2 months.

A wing rib is the prime roasting cut for the Jewish table, but it is also the most expensive. However, as it is difficult to roast a small joint and keep it succulent, I buy a large one with at least two ribs and serve it only on special occasions. To ensure that it is tender, the meat must be hung for 10–14 days after it is made kosher, so it is wise to order it well in advance. Have the rib bone 'chined', so that the meat will sit evenly in the roasting tin.

A meat thermometer is most helpful in ensuring the meat is done to your liking. I have carefully tested the timings I give below, but to get the correct results the meat must be left at room temperature for 2 hours before cooking begins. The cooked joint will be a rich crusty brown and the meat will be tender and juicy whether it is served hot or cold.

As a general guide allow 10–12 oz (275–350 g) per person of raw meat, including the bone.

approx. 5 lb (2.5 kg) standing rib roast
black pepper
mustard powder
flour
oil
salt
1 large onion, peeled and thinly sliced

For the gravy
1 pint (575 ml/2$^1/_2$ cups) meat stock
(from stock-cube)
2 teasp cornflour (cornstarch) slaked with 2 tbsp
cold water

Take the meat from the refrigerator 2 hours before it is to be cooked, wipe dry with a kitchen towel and sprinkle all over with freshly ground black pepper. Just before cooking, mix together 2 teaspoons each of mustard powder and flour and rub into the meat.

Stand the meat in a roasting tin and pour over it 4 or 5 tablespoons of hot oil, then put in a preheated oven, Gas No. 8 (450°F/230°C), for 15 minutes.

Now sprinkle lightly with salt, add the sliced onion to the tin and pour half a cup of water round the meat. Turn the oven down to Gas No. 6 (400°F/200°C) and then allow a further 20 minutes for each pound (450 g). Thus a 5-lb (2.5-kg) rib will take a total of 1 hour 55 minutes to be cooked to the medium to well-done stage. Baste the meat occasionally and add a little more water as it dries up.

To make the gravy Put the meat on a heatproof plate and leave it on a hotplate, loosely covered with foil, or in the oven with the door ajar for 15–20 minutes - this makes it much easier to carve. Drain as much fat as possible from the roasting tin and remove the onion to eat separately if desired. To the tin add 1 pint (575 ml/2½ cups) meat stock, bubble for 10 minutes until reduced by half, then (if a thicker gravy is preferred), add the cornflour. Bring to the boil, simmer for 3 minutes, then season and serve as required.

VARIATION

If you wish to complete the cooking at a lower temperature, reduce the heat to Gas No. 3 (325°F/160°C) after the initial searing, and allow a further 25 minutes for each pound (450 g). Thus a 5-lb (2.5 kg) rib will take a total of 2 hours 20 minutes.

TO CHECK DONENESS WITH A MEAT THERMOMETER OR PROBE

Temperatures should be read while the meat is still in the oven.

For medium rare to be carved straight from the oven without standing time 60°C.

For medium if 15 minutes' standing time is allowed after cooking 60°C.

For medium to well done if to be carved straight from the oven 65–70°C.

For well done if 15 minutes' standing time is allowed after cooking 70°C.

ROAST RIBS OF BEEF WITH A CRUSHED 3-PEPPER COATING

Serves 8–10, with leftovers.
Leftovers keep 3 days under refrigeration.
Freeze 3 months.

This is a joint for a special family occasion. The natural flavours of a well-hung joint of prime beef should need little embellishment. However, this tricolour combination of peppers does point up the satisfying taste of the meat while at the same time adding a delicious crustiness to each slice. The timing I give produces a roast that's a rich brown on the outside and a pale pink within, resulting in meat that's deliciously juicy and tender when hot, yet equally succulent when cold.

1 x 3-rib first cut joint of beef (7 lb/3.25 kg approx.), usually known as 'wing rib', hung for at least 10 days and with the bones chined (shortened) so that the joint will stand evenly in the roasting tin
2 teasp black peppercorns
1 teasp green peppercorns
½ teasp white peppercorns
1 small sprig of fresh thyme (leaves stripped from stalks)
½ teasp sea salt
2 tbsp (approx.) olive oil

For the garnish

1 lb (450 g) finger carrots, peeled (if necessary) and trimmed
8 oz (225 g) shallots or small onions, peeled

For the sauce

5 fl oz (150 ml/⅔ cup) full-bodied red wine
15 fl oz (425 ml/2 cups) good beef stock

1 tbsp Dijon mustard
2 teasp cornflour (cornstarch) slaked with 2 tbsp cold water

Leave the meat at room temperature for 1 hour. Preheat the oven to its highest temperature.

In a mortar (or a strong small bowl) coarsely crush the peppercorns, thyme and sea salt with the pestle or the end of a rolling pin. Brush the meat lightly with the olive oil, then rub with the pepper mixture. Place in the very hot oven for 30 minutes, then turn down to Gas No. 4 (350°F/180°C) and continue to cook for a further 1 hour 30 minutes (65°C on a meat thermometer). Baste the meat at half-hourly intervals - most easily done with a basting syringe. While the meat is cooking, blanch the carrots in boiling water for 5 minutes and the peeled shallots for 3 minutes (use the same water). As each vegetable is cooked, turn into a colander, drench in cold water, then drain well and pat dry.

20 minutes before the meat is cooked, add the vegetables to the roasting tin, turning them so they are coated with the juices. When the meat has cooked for the necessary time, lift it on to a carving dish, cover lightly with foil and leave in a warm place (either a warming oven or the back of the stove) for 20-30 minutes before carving. Remove the vegetables with a slotted spoon and place in a dish lined with paper towels. Keep hot also.

To make the sauce Skim as much fat as possible from the surface of the roasting tin, place over moderate heat, pour in the wine, then stir well with a wooden spoon to deglaze the pan. When all the delicious extractives have been stirred into the wine, bubble for 2 minutes, then turn into a small saucepan. Add the meat stock and simmer for 5 minutes, then stir in the Dijon mustard and cornflour slaked with the cold water. Bubble for 3 minutes until thickened and glossy. Season to taste with salt and pepper.

Serve the vegetables with the roast.

YORKSHIRE PUDDING

Serves 6.
Freeze 2 months.
Open freeze, pack in plastic bags.
Reheat from frozen at Gas No. 5 (375°F/190°C) for 10 minutes.

As the batter for Yorkshire pudding - the traditional accompaniment to roast beef - must be made with water instead of milk in the Jewish kitchen, it can be enriched instead with a little oil and extra egg. I find it cooks most satisfactorily in individual deep patty tins - the non-stick variety are especially good.

Bake the pudding(s) while the meat is resting before carving.

INDIVIDUAL YORKSHIRE PUDDINGS

2 oz (50 g/½ cup) plain (all-purpose) flour
1 level teasp salt
1 large egg
5 fl oz (150 ml/⅔ cup) water
1 tbsp oil

For greasing tins
3 tbsp oil

Put all the ingredients in the blender or food processor and process for 1 minute.

Turn the oven to Gas No. 7 (425°F/220°C) while the meat is resting in the warming drawer. Put 1 teaspoon of oil into each of 12 patty tins and heat for 5 minutes in the oven, then half fill each patty tin with the batter. Return to the oven and bake for 15 minutes, or until a rich brown.

FOR A TRADITIONAL YORKSHIRE PUDDING COOKED IN A DISH

Serves 6–8.

4 oz (125 g/1 cup) plain (all-purpose) flour
2 level teasp salt
2 large eggs
10 fl oz (275 ml/1¾ cups) water
2 tbsp oil

For greasing tin
3 tbsp oil

Make the batter as before.

Preheat the oven to Gas No. 5 (375°F/190°C). Heat 3 tablespoons of oil in a Yorkshire pudding tin (roasting tin) measuring 10 x 12 x 2 inches (25 x 30 x 5 cm) for 5 minutes. Pour in the batter and bake for 15–20 minutes, or until set. Turn the oven to Gas No. 6 (400°F/200°C) and cook for a further 15–20 minutes, until well risen and brown. Cut into 6–8 pieces and serve at once.

BOEUF DIJONNAISE FOR A DINNER PARTY

Serves 8.
Leftovers keep 3 days under refrigeration.
Freeze 3 months.

This should be prepared with a boned-out wing rib. Because the meat is cooked in 2 stages, this is an excellent method to use when you're not certain when your guests will arrive - the second stage can be completed while drinks are being served. The total cooking time is about 1 hour 15 minutes.

1 x 3 lb (1.5 kg) boned-out joint of eye of rib, seasoned with 20 grinds of black pepper

For the coating
3 level tbsp Dijon mustard
1 tbsp dark soy sauce
1 clove of garlic, peeled and crushed
1 teasp Herbes de Provence
1 teasp salt
2 teasp grated fresh ginger
2 teasp olive oil

2 hours before you intend to start roasting the meat, put all the coating ingredients except the oil into a small bowl and stir to blend, then gradually beat in the oil. Paint this mixture all over the beef with a pastry brush, making sure you cover the underside as well. Place the meat on a rack in a roasting tin, and leave at room temperature for 2 hours.

To roast the meat — first stage This is done early in the day after the meat has been standing for 2 hours. Preheat the oven to Gas No. 6 (400°F/200°C). Cook the meat for 45 minutes. Allow to cool.

Second stage — to complete the cooking Preheat the oven as before and cook for a further 30 minutes at the same temperature. Salt lightly. The meat can now be kept hot while the first course is being eaten for up to 20 minutes in a warming oven, Gas No. ½ (250°F/120°C), or it can be covered with foil and kept on a hot plate or ceramic hob set at 'low'.

Sausages and Other Preserved Meats

While according to legend the Jews learned to fry fish from the ancient Egyptians, it is certain that they learned to salt meat and make sausages from their later masters, the Greeks and the Romans.

As far back as the ninth century BCE, one can read of this early 'convenience food', the sausage, in Homer's *Odyssey*. Later Greek writers wrote frequently of it, and a Sicilian playwright Epicharmus even wrote a play around 500 BCE with the title *Sausage*, or *Orya*.

This term has not survived - though in fourteenth-century France the sausage-maker was still known as *cuisiner-oyer* - some of the recipes, and certainly the name of one variety, salami (the word is derived from *sal*, the Latin word for salt), have not only survived but are used almost unchanged to this very day.

Basically a sausage consists of minced lean meat and fat, flavoured variously with spices and curing salts. The permutations of these mixtures are almost without number. In particular the 'filler', or meat extender, varies according to the period and the locality.

As times grew hard, and the meat content of a sausage decreased, the filler often became the predominant ingredient. Thus gefilte kishke - the homemade sausage of every European Jewish household a generation or so ago - consisted of beef casings stuffed with a meatless mixture of fat, onions and flour, almost identical to the white puddings made by farmworkers in the West Country of England.

However, to most people the spicing is the all-important factor, determining their allegiance and also distinguishing the sausage from any other culinary concoction.

Today the main sausage seasoning is allspice or Jamaica pepper, which has the aroma and properties of pepper, cloves, cinnamon and nutmeg, and which the French most logically call *'quatre épices'*. Basil, sage, pennyroyal and marjoram are the favoured English herbs. As to salami, that which comes from Milan is flavoured with ginger, nutmeg and white wine; that from Sardinia with red pepper; and that from Hungary with garlic, paprika and white wine. Mortadella is flavoured with crushed coriander. All of these sausages can be bought in a kosher version.

The Kosher Varieties of Sausage

Even in Roman times, some sausages were sold uncooked and some were boiled, some were made from fresh meat and some were smoked. Over the centuries, these different varieties have been grouped into three main types.

1 *Fresh sausages* These are made from fresh, uncured meats and are known in the delicatessen as 'frying sausages'. They are highly perishable and should be kept under refrigeration for no more than 1 or 2 days before they are used.
2 *Cooked sausages* These are also made principally from fresh uncured meats, though a little cured meat may be added to the mixture. However, they are always cooked after they have been filled, and are sometimes smoked as well before they are sold. In this category are the liver sausages as well as the bolognas, frankfurters and viennas. These are usually artificially coloured pink.
3 *Dry sausages* This is the category into which all the salamis fit. These sausages have 20 per cent or more of their natural moisture removed when they are dried; the higher percentage the longer their 'shelf life'.

Salami is made with fresh meat and saltpetre, which is then cured for 2 or 3 days. After the sausages have been encased, they are either cooked in a smokehouse at a high temperature and then dried in air (as, for example, the cooked salamis) or they may be dried without smoking (as with the majority of those salamis of Hungarian and German origin). These are the sausages used on the hors-d'oeuvre tray, or as part of the cold table. Some are eaten raw as an appetizer; others, such as the saveloy, are first gently poached, then eaten hot or cold.

Jewish sausages and salamis are unusual in that they are always made with beef or liver, unlike others, which almost invariably contain pork.

Wurst

Perhaps the best-known Jewish sausage is this German version of Italian salami, which is made in countless varieties. Frying wurst is pink and lightly spiced, and makes an excellent addition to a mixed grill or to fried eggs. It will keep for a week under refrigeration, months in the freezer, and makes a most delicious alfresco supper with chips.

WURST PFANNKUCHEN (*Sausage Pancake*)

Serves 3–4.

Eat hot off the pan.

8–12 oz (225–350 g) frying wurst (enough slices to cover the bottom of an 8- or 9-inch/ 20–22.5-cm frying pan)
4 eggs
2 teasp cold water
pinch of salt
few grinds of black pepper

Turn on the grill. Heat the empty pan over medium heat for 3 minutes, then lay the slices of wurst (cut ¼ inch/0.5 cm thick) in it side by side. Cook steadily for several minutes until the slices begin to curl. Meanwhile, whisk the eggs with the water and seasoning until the yolks and whites are evenly blended. As soon as the slices of wurst have curled, turn them over, cook for a further minute, then pour on the egg mixture and cook without stirring for several minutes until the underside is golden brown. Place the pan 6 inches (15 cm) from the grill and cook until the top is set and puffy – about 2 minutes. Slide on to a heated platter or serve straight from the pan, cut in wedges.

WURST FRITTATA

Serves 4.

Eat hot off the pan. A more substantial supper dish than the pfannkuchen.

1 fat red pepper
oil to fry
1 medium onion, finely chopped
1 large potato, raw or cooked, cut in ¼-inch (0.5-cm) cubes
8 oz (225 g) wurst, sliced and cut in strips
2 tomatoes, peeled and chopped, or well-drained canned ones
6 eggs
salt
black pepper

Cut the red pepper in half and remove the bitter seeds and white pith 'ribs', then cut in fine strips. Preheat the grill. In a frying pan about 9 inches (22.5 cm) in diameter, put oil to a depth of ⅛ inch (0.3 cm). Cook the onion and potato until both are soft and golden. (If the potato is raw, do this with the lid on for 5 minutes, then take off to brown the other ingredients.) Add the pepper and the wurst and continue to cook for another 3 or 4 minutes, then stir in the tomatoes and mix well, simmering until they are softened. Beat the eggs with the salt and pepper, then pour over the vegetables. Cook as an omelette, lifting cooked mixture to allow uncooked to flow underneath. Finally put under the grill to brown the top.

WURST AND MEAT PIZZA

Serves 6–8 – makes 2 x 10–11-inch (25–27.5-cm) pizzas

May be frozen just before it is ready for the oven. Defrost overnight in the refrigerator or at room temperature for 2 hours, then bake as though freshly prepared.

Sephardi Jews have been making this very special version of pizza for many centuries. It is made, of course, without cheese and is topped instead with cumin-scented minced beef.

My Sephardi friends make it in miniature as finger food for parties (it's then known as 'lahma bi ajeen') but I find it equally sensational cooked in normal, pizza-style rounds, each serving 3 or 4 good appetites. I've also added an optional extra, curls of wurst. New green cucumbers make ideal partners.

For the dough
1 sachet easy-blend yeast or ½ oz (15 g) fresh yeast
11 oz (300 g) plain (all-purpose) flour
1½ teasp salt
1½ teasp sugar
2 tbsp olive oil
1 egg
5 fl oz (150 ml/⅔ cup) hand-hot water

For the topping
2 medium onions
2 tbsp oil
1 lb (450 g) lean minced beef
1 tbsp tomato purée
1 teasp brown sugar
1 teasp salt
15 grinds of black pepper
1 teasp allspice
1 teasp ground cumin
good pinch of Cayenne pepper
3 tbsp chopped parsley
1 tbsp lemon juice

For the garnish
4 oz (125 g) frying wurst

If easy-blend yeast is used, mix it with the flour, salt and sugar; if fresh yeast is used, dissolve it in the water. In either case, mix all the ingredients together to form a soft but non-sticky ball of dough (add a little extra flour if necessary), then knead by hand or machine until smooth. Put the dough in an oiled mixing bowl, turn it over so that it is coated with the oil, then cover with clingfilm (saranwrap) and leave in the kitchen until double in bulk - about 1 hour.

Meanwhile, make the filling. Cook the finely chopped onions in the oil (lid on the pan) until softened and golden, then mix in a bowl with the remaining filling ingredients, using the hands to make sure the mixture is evenly blended together.

Set the oven at Gas No. 8 (450°F/230°C). Grease 2 baking sheets or 10-11-inch (25-27.5-cm) pizza pans. Divide the risen dough in half, knead each portion for 1 or 2 minutes to distribute the gas bubbles evenly, then roll or press out into 2 10-11-inch (25-27.5-cm) rounds and place on the baking sheets or in the pizza pans. Spread each round with an even layer of the filling, making sure the dough is covered right to the edges, then decorate with the sliced wurst. Bake for 15 minutes, until the meat is a rich brown and the wurst has curled. Serve at once.

Boiling Sausages

Viennas, Frankfurters, Saveloys, 'Hot Dogs'

It is important not to reheat these in water that is bubbling too violently or they may burst.

Simmer in water to cover for 5 minutes, then leave covered in steaming water until required. Drain and serve. Allow 3 cocktail-size hot dogs per person.

Home-pickled Meats

Hot salt beef, sandwiched between Sunday-morning-fresh rye bread, is surely the quintessence of the Jewish cuisine - and the Irish pickle beef in almost exactly the same fashion! The main difference lies in the cut of meat. The Jewish cook uses a thick 'corner' of brisket - that humble but tasty cut; the Irish cook uses a hindquarters' cut such as topside or round.

Many butchers will sell you a piece of their own pickled raw meat to cook at home, but if you want to enjoy the genuine article, with all the nuances of flavour found only in a home pickle, it's worth preparing the pickling solution yourself. It is, however, not worth using a piece of meat smaller than specified. If there is no room in the refrigerator, the meat can be left to pickle in a cool shed or larder - the warmer the temperature, the more quickly will the pickle work. Ideally the temperature should be about 40°F (4°C) - the coldest part of the refrigerator or a cold cellar. At a refrigeration temperature it will take 10-14 days. You can tell when the meat is ready to cook, because it will be pink right through to the centre.

It is sometimes difficult to obtain saltpetre - the chemical that gives the meat its pink appearance - in small amounts. In that case, ask your local butcher for some of the same pickling solution he uses, then add your own spicing.

OLD-FASHIONED PICKLED BRISKET (*Corned Beef*)

Serves 8-10 as a 'cold cut', more in sandwiches.
Keeps 4 days under refrigeration.
Freeze 3 months.

Freshly cooked pickled brisket (called 'corned beef' in America) is delicious with boiled potatoes and quartered hearts of cabbage, or with chipped potatoes or latkes, or served in sandwiches.

Lightly pressed and cold, is superb on a buffet or in white- or rye-bread sandwiches. In the recipe I give what I have found makes a pleasant but not overspiced or over-salty pickle.

2 fat cloves of garlic
3 teasp mixed pickling spice
2 crumbled bay leaves
1 level teasp crushed peppercorns
3 oz (75 g/$^1/_3$ cup) demerara sugar
6 oz (175 g/$^3/_4$ cup) coarse salt
2 level teasp saltpetre
5-6 lb (2.5-3 kg) corner of brisket, not rolled

For the cooking the meat
1 large onion
2 bay leaves

I find it convenient to pickle and cook the meat in the same dish - a cast-iron enamelled casserole, such as one would use to braise a fowl. Otherwise an earthenware dish can be used for the pickling. Put the garlic, pickling spices, bay leaves and peppercorns into a mortar and crush coarsely (or crush with the end of a rolling pin if you do not have a mortar). Put into the chosen dish together with the sugar, salt and saltpetre. Add the meat and turn to coat with the mixture, rubbing it well into all the surfaces of the meat. Finally add cold water to come just to the top of the meat (liquid will also ooze out of it as the days go by). Refrigerate for 10-14 days, or leave in cold larder, turning daily.

To cook Take from the liquid and wash well. Pour out the liquid from the dish and put back the meat. Cover with cold water and bring slowly to the boil on top of the stove. Remove all the scum with a spoon dipped in cold water. Now add the large onion and 2 bay leaves. Cover and simmer very gently for 4 hours. You can do this top of the stove (though I find it easier to keep it at the right temperature in a very slow oven, Gas No. 2 (300°F/150°C), as one would cook soup.

Lift the meat out on to a board. Part of it can now be carved rather thickly and served hot. After dinner, fit the rest into a basin, cover with a plate and several weights. Leave under pressure until quite cold. Foil wrap and refrigerate. Use as required.

VARIATION

PICKLED TONGUE

Serves at least 8-10.
Keeps 4 days under refrigeration.
Freeze 3 months.

Proceed exactly as for the pickled brisket but using 1 x 6-lb (3-kg) or 2 x 3-lb (1.5-kg) tongues. Cook the pickled tongue for 3$^1/_2$ hours either on the hob or in the oven as before, until it feels tender when pierced with a fork. Let the tongue cool in the stock, then remove the root and the skin. Coil the tongue round itself in a tin or casserole into which it will barely fit. Weigh down with a plate and then a weight or brick. Leave until quite cold. Unmould and refrigerate until required.

LAMB AND VEAL

Lamb

Lamb is an all-the-year-round meat because, although we usually associate it with the spring, the more mature lambs of late summer and early autumn make equally good eating. However, geneticists, as well as airfreighting from around the world, have reduced the 'sesonality factor' so that 'spring lamb' is now available all year round!

Prime lamb has pinkish meat, creamy yellow fat and bones tinged faintly purple – flinty white bone means mutton!

ROAST SHOULDER OF LAMB ON THE BONE (*Basic Method*)

Serves 6–8.
Will keep 3 days under refrigeration.
Freeze 3 months.

A thick shoulder of lamb is the prime kosher roasting joint of lamb. Care in the cooking will ensure that the roast has a savoury, crunchy skin while the meat itself is juicy and tender.

4 lb (1.75 kg) thick-cut shoulder of lamb
olive oil
flour
dry mustard
salt
black pepper
1 clove of garlic (optional)
1 large onion, thinly sliced

For the glaze
1 tbsp of any of the following: honey, marmalade, redcurrant or cranberry jelly

Brush the meat all over with a thin layer of olive oil, then sprinkle with a little flour, dry mustard, salt and black pepper. Put a small wire rack in the bottom of a roasting tin just large enough to hold the joint, and place the meat on that (this allows the air to circulate and prevents the meat from getting greasy). If you like garlic, put slivers of the peeled clove in between the bone and the flesh, but don't overdo it or the delicate lamb flavour will be lost. Roast at Gas No. 4 (350°F/180°C) for 30 minutes to the pound (450 g) - 2¼ hours for a 4-lb (1.75 kg) joint. After the meat has been in the oven for 1 hour, slip the sliced onion into the bottom of the roasting tin.

There is no need to baste the meat. 15 minutes before the joint is ready, drain off most of the fat and spread the meat with any of the conserves I have suggested. This will not only add a gorgeous flavour but also help to achieve a really crispy skin.

To make the gravy Lift out the meat and keep warm (a stainless-steel carving dish is ideal for cutting the meat on). Put the cooked onion into a small dish to serve with the meat. Drain off all the fat from the roasting tin and stir 1 teaspoon of flour into the sediment. Then add 1 cup vegetable water or stock made from a cube, and seasoning. Boil vigorously for 2-3 minutes. This makes a thin, meaty gravy which tastes of lamb without being greasy. A fruity gravy can be made by omitting the conserve and instead pouring half a cup of orange juice and (when in season) half a cup of chopped mint over the joint, after the fat has been discarded. Baste several times during the last 15 minutes, then pour the pan juices as gravy.

VARIATIONS

ROAST LAMB WITH ORANGE AND WINE SAUCE

Roast the lamb as described. Half-way through the cooking time, pour over 4 fl oz (125 ml/½ cup) each of orange juice and dry red or white wine. Do not brush the meat with conserve; instead sprinkle the meat with demerara sugar 15 minutes before it is done. Use the pan juices for gravy.

ROAST LAMB WITH REDCURRANT SAUCE

Roast the lamb as described, but omit the conserves. 15 minutes before the lamb is cooked, sprinkle it with demerara sugar. Make this sauce:

Redcurrant Sauce

2 level teasp flour
2 level teasp dry mustard
2 tbsp redcurrant jelly
10 fl oz (275 ml/1¼ cups) meat stock or vegetable water

Put the meat on a dish to keep warm. Pour off all but 2 teaspoons of the fat, then stir the flour into it and the sediment from the roast. Add the mustard, redcurrant jelly and stock. Stir vigorously and allow to bubble until the sauce has become slightly thickened and glossy. Serve with the lamb.

ROAST LAMB DIJONNAISE

The mustard glaze marries well with the more mature flavour of winter lamb.

For the coating

4 level tbsp Dijon mustard
1 tbsp dark soy sauce
1 fat clove of garlic, peeled and crushed
½ teasp dried Herbes de Provence
2 teasp grated fresh ginger or ½ teasp powdered ginger
2 teasp olive oil

2 hours before you intend to start roasting the meat, put all the coating ingredients into a small bowl and stir to blend. Paint this mixture all over the lamb with a pastrybrush, making sure you cover the underside as well. Place the joint on a roasting rack and leave at room temperature for 2 hours.

Roast in a preheated oven, Gas No. 4 (350°F/180°C), for 30 minutes to the pound (450 g), then lift the cooked joint on to a serving dish and leave to stand, loosely covered with foil, for 15 minutes.

Meanwhile, pour off any free fat from the roasting tin, add 10 fl oz (275 ml/1¼ cups) lamb or beef stock, stir thoroughly, then allow to bubble until syrupy. Strain into a sauceboat and serve hot.

Boned Rolled Shoulder of Lamb

This is a compact, easy-to-slice joint that makes a superb main dish for a dinner party.

ROAST SHOULDER OF LAMB STUFFED WITH A PINWHEEL OF FRESH HERBS

Serves 6–8.
Leftovers keep 3 days under refrigeration.
Freeze 3 months.

A 'stuffing' of herbs spread on the inside of a boned shoulder of lamb will permeate the roast meat with the most delightful summery fragrance, and when the meat is carved, the pinwheel of green in the centre of each slice looks fresh and inviting on the plate. If preferred, the coating used for Roast Lamb Dijonnaise (see p. 180) can be substituted for the one in the recipe.

3½ lb (1.75 kg) boned shoulder of lamb
1 onion

For the herb mixture

4 tbsp finely snipped chives
2 tbsp chopped parsley
2 tbsp chopped fresh basil or 2 teasp dried basil
2 teasp finely chopped rosemary spikes or ½ teasp dried rosemary
1 teasp grated lemon rind
½ teasp salt
10 grinds of black pepper
1 tbsp olive oil

To coat the lamb

1 teasp dry mustard
1 tbsp oil
2 tbsp demerara sugar

For the gravy

2 teasp fat from the roasting tin
2 level teasp cornflour (cornstarch)
10 fl oz (275 ml/1¼ cups) cold water
1 crumbled beef stock-cube
salt
black pepper

About 3 hours before you intend to roast the meat, mix all the herb ingredients and the lemon rind together in a small bowl. Lay the meat, skin down, on a board, cut out any lumps of fat, then cover with a piece of greaseproof paper and pound to a fairly even thickness with a cutlet bat or the end of a rolling pin. Remove the paper and lightly sprinkle the meat with salt and pepper, then spread the herb mixture all over the surface. Roll the meat up tightly and secure it in 2 or 3 places with string. Leave until you are ready to roast it, then place the lamb on a rack in a roasting tin, rub all over with a teaspoon each of flour and dry mustard, and sprinkle with the oil.

Preheat the oven to Gas No. 4 (350°F/180°C). Roast the meat for half an hour, then baste it well, sprinkle with the demerara sugar and slip a sliced onion under it to brown and flavour the juices. Roast for a further 1½ hours, basting once, or until the meat is a rich brown. Lift the meat on to a dish and leave it to stand (loosely covered with foil) in a warming oven or in the regular oven turned down to its lowest setting. Skim off all but two teaspoons of fat from the tin, remove the onion, add the cornflour mixed to a smooth consistency with the water, the stock-cube and a pinch of salt and black pepper, and bubble on top of the stove until thick and glossy - about 3 minutes. Serve with the sliced meat. It is also delicious cold.

ROAST STUFFED SHOULDER OF LAMB

Serves 6–8.
Leftovers keep 3 days under refrigeration.
Freeze 1 month raw.

This method produces a particularly succulent joint which is equally delicious cold. A dish for the special picnic.

Ask the butcher to bone the meat, if possible leaving a pocket for the stuffing. If this is not possible, the boned meat can be spread with the stuffing then rolled before roasting.

3½–4 lb (1.5–1.75 kg) shoulder of lamb, boned and pocketed, or boned and left flat

For the mint stuffing
2 oz (50 g/¼ cup) margarine
1 small onion, finely chopped
6 oz (175 g/2⅔ cups) fresh breadcrumbs
2 teasp each finely chopped mint and parsley
1 level teasp salt
¼ teasp black pepper
1 egg

For the apricot stuffing
2 oz (50 g/¼ cup) margarine
1 small onion, finely chopped
4 oz (125 g) dried apricots, soaked overnight in cold water to cover, then drained and roughly chopped
grated rind of ½ lemon
½ level teasp salt
pinch of white pepper
4 oz (125 g/1⅓ cups) fresh breadcrumbs
1 egg

For the coating
1 teasp salt
10 grinds of black pepper
dusting of flour
2 tbsp oil
1 tbsp demerara (brown) sugar

For the gravy
2 teasp fat from the roasting tin
10 fl oz (275 ml/1¼ cups) cold water
2 level teasp cornflour (cornstarch)
1 crumbled beef stock-cube
salt and pepper to taste

To make either stuffing Melt the fat in a small frying pan and cook the onion gently until softened and golden. Put all the other ingredients into a bowl, then mix in the onion and fat until well blended. Moisten with the beaten egg. The mixture should just cling together.

To stuff a pocketed shoulder Just pack the stuffing lightly into the pocket and sew it up into a firm, compact shape.

To stuff and roll a shoulder Lay the meat, skin-side down, on a board and cut out any lumps of fat. Spread the stuffing evenly over the meat, pushing it into any little folds. Roll up neatly and sew into a compact shape, or skewer closed if this is possible.

To roast the meat Preheat the oven to Gas No. 4 (350°F/180°C). Put a rack in a roasting tin and lay the meat on top. Sprinkle with the salt and pepper, and dust lightly with flour, then pour over the oil. Roast the meat for 2 hours, then sprinkle with the sugar and increase the heat to Gas No. 6 (400°F/200°C). Cook for a further 20–30 minutes until a rich brown. Leave in a warm place (or in the oven turned down to Gas No. ¼ 225°F/110°C) for 15 minutes before carving.

To make the gravy Pour off all but 2 teaspoons of fat from the roasting tin. Mix the cold water and cornflour to a smooth consistency, then pour into the roasting tin and add the crumbled stock-cube. Bring to the boil, stirring well, then season to taste with salt and pepper.

LE GIGOT QUI PLEURE, KOSHER STYLE

(Boned and Rolled Shoulder of Lamb Spiked with Rosemary and Garlic)

Serves 6–8.
Leftovers keep 3 days under refrigeration.
Freeze 3 months.

Maybe it's because rosemary is a member of the mint family that the flavour of this pungent herb marries so well with roast lamb. And unlike more tender varieties, such as basil and dill, it's tough enough to stand up to a couple of hours in the oven without losing its wonderful aroma. In this recipe the aroma is intensified by spiking the lamb with the herbs several hours before cooking it.

As the meat roasts, some of the juices will ooze out through the spike holes, giving a superb flavour to the vegetables cooking below. For 10 people use a 4½–5-lb (2-2.25-kg) joint and cook it for 30 minutes longer.

3½ lb (1.75 kg) boned and rolled shoulder of lamb
2 sprigs of rosemary
2 peeled and slivered medium cloves of garlic

To coat the lamb
freshly ground black pepper
olive oil
1 teasp dry mustard
1 tbsp flour
2 tbsp demerara sugar

To cook beneath the lamb
2½ lb (1 kg) small new potatoes
1 lb (450 g) shallots
1 pint (575 ml/2½ cups) meat stock

For the sauce
juices from the roasting tin, made up to 10 fl oz (275 ml/1¼ cups) with hot water
3½ fl oz (90 ml/⅓ cup plus 1 tbsp) red wine mixed with 3 teasp cornflour

Preheat the oven to Gas No. 4 (350°F/180°C).

Several hours in advance, or even overnight, use a small pointed knife to pierce the lamb at 2-inch (5-cm) intervals, and in each incision insert a tiny sprig of rosemary and a sliver of garlic. When ready to cook, sprinkle the lamb with 20 grinds of black pepper, brush all over with a thin layer of olive oil and sprinkle with the mixed mustard and flour, then arrange on a rack that will fit 2 inches (5 cm) above a roasting tin.

Put the scrubbed but unpeeled new potatoes into a pan of cold water, add 1 teaspoon of salt and bring to the boil. Lift out with a slotted spoon and arrange in the roasting tin. In the same water, bring the shallots to the boil, then turn into a sieve and drench with cold water. The skins can now be easily removed. Arrange with the potatoes in the roasting tin. Make the stock with boiling water, then pour over and around the potatoes and shallots. Lay the meat on its rack on top of the vegetables, put in the oven and cook for 2¼ hours. After 1 hour, take out the roasting tin and lift off the meat on its rack so that you can stir the vegetables. Replace the meat, sprinkle with the brown sugar and return to the oven. Check after half an hour, and if the stock seems to be drying up, add a little more hot water.

Lift the meat out on to a dish and leave it to stand, loosely covered with foil or in the regular oven turned to its lowest setting. Lift out the vegetables with a slotted spoon and put into a dish. Cover and keep warm.

To make the sauce Put the roasting tin on the stove and add the boiling water, then stir well to release all the delicious sediment. Mix the cornflour to a smooth cream with the wine and add to the pan. Bubble for 3 minutes, stirring well, and taste and reseason if necessary. (At this stage you may wish to transfer the sauce to a small pan to keep hot.)

Allow the meat to stand for 20 minutes before slicing and serving.

Chops and Boned Shoulder Meat

HERBED LAMB CHOPS

Serves 4.

This is the basic method for grilling first-cut chops (also known as cutlets or best end of neck). The herbs can be omitted, but they do give added piquancy to the meat.

1 tbsp extra virgin olive oil
1 cut clove of garlic
1 level teasp each of dried basil and rosemary or 1 tbsp each of the chopped fresh herbs
1 tbsp lemon juice
black pepper
8 first-cut lamb chops (¾ inch/2 cm) thick and trimmed of all but a thin layer of fat

1 hour before the chops are to be grilled, put the oil in a shallow dish wide enough to hold them in a single layer. Add the garlic, herbs and lemon juice. Grind a dusting of black pepper on both sides of the chops, then put them into the dish and turn to coat them with the oil. Leave for 1 hour, turning once or twice during this time, so that they are well and truly steeped in it.

15 minutes before serving time, heat the grill for 3 minutes. Arrange the chops on a rack in the grill pan. Put the grill pan 4 inches (10 cm) below the source of heat and grill the chops for 5 minutes on each side, or until they are a rich brown. Season with freshly ground sea salt.

VARIATION

Omit the basil and rosemary and use 1 tablespoon of mustard with tarragon and 2 tablespoons of fresh tarragon (or 2 teaspoons of the dried herb) instead.

LAMB CHOPS GLAZED WITH MOUTARDE DE MEAUX

Serves 4.

Meaux is one of the most flavoursome of mustards: the traditional recipe contains fresh tarragon, cardamom, fennel, cinnamon and cloves, in addition to the black mustard seeds which are partly crushed and partly ground to give the characteristic crunchy texture. It gives a rich brown colour as well as a delicious flavour to the chops. There is no need to use any oil in the glaze.

8 first-cut lamb cutlets
black pepper
salt

For the coating
2 tbsp Meaux mustard
1 teasp soft brown sugar
a good pinch of powdered ginger or 2 teasp grated fresh ginger root

Preheat the grill. Mix the coating ingredients in a small basin. Trim the chops of all but a thin edging of fat, season well with black pepper, then arrange side by side on the rack of the grill pan. Cook 4 inches (10 cm) from the heat for 5 minutes, then turn over, salt lightly, spread with the coating and cook for a further 5 minutes, until a rich brown. Serve at once.

CUMBERLAND CUTLETS

Serves 6–8.
Leftovers keep 3 days under refrigeration.
Do not freeze.

This is the best way I know to serve lamb cutlets for a dinner party without filling the house with the fumes from the grill. The coated chops are braised in a fruity sauce which gradually reduces in the oven to a delicious syrupy glaze.

12–16 best-end chops (cutlets) of lamb, chined if desired
salt
pepper
2 eggs, beaten
dry breadcrumbs or matzah meal

For the sauce
8 fl oz (225 ml/1 cup) chicken stock
4 rounded tbsp redcurrant jelly (about half a 12 oz/350 g jar)
juice and rind of 3 large oranges (about 8 fl oz/225 ml/1 cup)
3 teasp lemon juice

Grease a roasting tin large enough to hold the cutlets side by side. If preferred, they can first be chined by removing the rib-bone, then formed into a neat roll and kept in shape with a cocktail stick. Otherwise simply trim off all the fat. Salt and pepper the meat, then dip in egg and fine dry breadcrumbs or matzah meal. Arrange side by side in the roasting tin.

To make the sauce, heat all the ingredients together until the jelly melts, then pour half over and round the cutlets. Put in a quick oven, Gas No. 6 (400°F/200°C), for 30 minutes, then add the remainder of the sauce.

Turn down the heat to Gas No. 4 (350°F/180°C) and continue to cook for a further 25 minutes, until the cutlets are a rich golden brown and the sauce is syrupy.

VARIATION

LAMB CUTLETS IN A HONEY GLAZE

Serves 4.
Keeps 3 days under refrigeration, but best eaten the same day. Do not freeze.

6–8 first-cut lamb cutlets, trimmed of all fat
salt
black pepper
2 eggs, beaten
dry breadcrumbs

For the sauce
4 tbsp clear honey
4 tbsp medium brown sugar
3 tbsp concentrated orange juice
3 tbsp red wine vinegar
2 tbsp rich soy sauce
1 tbsp tomato ketchup
1 teasp Dijon mustard

For the garnish
1 orange, peeled, pith removed and segmented
chopped parsley

Egg and crumb the cutlets as before (you will need only 1 egg). Arrange them side by side in a roasting tin. Cook uncovered at Gas No. 6 (400°F/200°C) for 30 minutes.

Bring the sauce ingredients to the boil in a small pan, then pour over the chops. Reduce heat to Gas No. 4 (350°F/180°C) and cook for a further 20 minutes, until the sauce is syrupy and the cutlets are richly glazed.

Serve garnished with the orange segments and a scatter of parsley.

ARNI SOUVLAKIA (*Greek-style Lamb Kebabs*)

Serves 8.
Eat hot off the grill.

Archetypically Balkan, kebabs can range from a simple presentation of lamb brushed with oil and lemon juice to - as in this recipe - a sophisticated dish of lamb marinated in a fragrant liquid which is also brushed on a vivid mélange of vegetables that are skewered together with the meat to provide a feast for the eyes as well as the palate. Serve warm, with pitta bread to mop up the juices.

For the marinade

3 fl oz (75 ml/⅓ cup) fresh lemon juice
3 fl oz (75 ml/⅓ cup) dry red wine
2 tbsp chopped fresh rosemary leaves or 2 teasp dried rosemary
2 tbsp chopped fresh oregano or 2 teasp dried oregano
1 fat clove of garlic, finely chopped
1 teasp salt
15 grinds of black pepper
3½ fl oz (100 ml/⅓ cup + 1 tbsp) extra virgin olive oil
3 lb (1.5 kg) boned-out shoulder of lamb, trimmed of fat and cut in 1½-inch (4-cm) cubes
3 x 8 oz (225 g) courgettes, quartered lengthwise, then cut crosswise into 1½-inch (4-cm) pieces and cooked until barely tender
3 yellow peppers deseeded and cut into 1½-inch (4-cm) pieces
3 small onions, each cut into 8 pieces
1 lb (450 g) cherry tomatoes

At least 6 but preferably 12 hours before cooking, whisk together the lemon juice, wine, rosemary, oregano, garlic, salt and black pepper in a large bowl. Add the oil in a stream, whisking until the marinade thickens as it emulsifies. Add the chunks of lamb. Turn to coat them thoroughly with the marinade, then cover and chill, turning occasionally.

In a shallow dish, let 16 10-inch (25-cm) wooden skewers soak in water to cover for 1 hour (or use 8 flat metal ones). Drain the lamb, reserving the marinade, thread the skewers with the courgettes, peppers, lamb, onions and tomatoes, then brush with some of the reserved marinade. Grill the kebabs on an oiled rack set 5-6 inches (12.5-15 cm) above glowing coals, basting them often with some of the reserved marinade, and turning them, for 15-18 minutes (for medium-rare meat).

Alternatively, grill for 12-15 minutes about 4 inches (10 cm) from a very hot grill, basting and turning as before. Or thermal grill (according to directions) in a fan- or forced-air oven.

LAMB EN CASSEROLE

Boned-out cubed lamb shoulder and shoulder chops both make a superb basis for casseroles, simple and sophisticated, as the meat is sweet and tender. It's a good idea to give the butcher specific instructions as to the size of cubes - if they're too small they can melt into the cooking liquid.

NAVARIN OF LAMB WITH COINTREAU

Serves 6.
Keeps 3 days under refrigeration.
Freezes 3 months.

This sophisticated yet good-tempered dish - lamb braised in a refreshing liqueur-flavoured orange sauce - is excellent for an informal supper as it can be kept hot without spoiling for up to 1 hour. It also makes a splendid family meal using stock instead of the wine and liqueur. Serve with new potatoes.

2½ lb (1 kg) boneless shoulder of lamb cut in 2 x 1 inch (5 x 2.5 cm) chunks
2 tbsp flour
1 teasp salt
10 grinds of black pepper
2 tbsp olive oil

1 medium onion, finely chopped
8 oz (225 g) shallots, peeled
2 teasp medium brown sugar
8 oz (225 ml/1 cup) dry white wine
10 fl oz (275 ml/1¼ cups) chicken stock
zest of 1 orange
3 large navel oranges, sectioned (reserve 12 sections for garnish)
2 teasp cornflour mixed with 2 tbsp cold water
4 tbsp Cointreau or other orange-flavoured liqueur

For the garnish
1 tbsp chopped coriander (or parsley)
reserved orange slices
2 oz (50 g/½ cup) toasted broken cashews

Preheat the oven to Gas No. 2 (300°F/150°C). The meat can be cooked completely in an oven-to-table casserole, or sautéd in a pan first. It can be served from the casserole or arranged on a large platter.

Shake the meat with the seasoned flour in a large plastic bag, pat off any excess, then lightly sauté in the oil in 2 batches. When the meat is a rich brown, lift out on to a plate using a slotted spoon and add the onion to the pan, together with the shallots. Sprinkle with the brown sugar and continue to cook over medium heat until the onion is golden brown.

Add the wine to the pan, stir well to incorporate any bits on the bottom, then bubble for 3 minutes to concentrate the wine flavour. Add the meat and the hot stock and bring slowly to the boil.

Meanwhile, with a zester remove shreds of peel from an orange, then peel all the oranges, removing all the pith. Cut between the sections to release the fruit, then reserve 12 sections for garnish. Add the remaining sections to the meat, together with any juice that can be squeezed out of the orange 'skeleton' and the orange shreds.

When the casserole is bubbling, cover it and transfer to the oven, then cook until the meat is very tender - about 1½ hours. Stir in the dissolved cornflour and the liqueur, stir well, then simmer in the oven, covered, for a further 20 minutes. Just before serving, sprinkle with the chopped herbs and garnish with the orange sections and the nuts.

PATLICAN KEBABI
(Turkish Spiced Lamb and Aubergine Casserole)

Serves 6–8.
Keeps 2 days under refrigeration.
Freeze 3 months.

Lamb chops from the shoulder are meaty and flavourful, and though not quite tender enough to grill, they melt in the mouth when braised in a savoury sauce. This dish from Turkey uses for the sauce a most delicious combination of spices which marries particularly well with the aubergine (eggplants) to make a really succulent dish either for a buffet or an informal dinner. A tip from a Turkish friend: aubergines take up far less fat if deep-fried - the surface is sealed immediately, so the oil cannot penetrate as it does with shallow-frying. 2½–3 lb (1.25–1.5 kg) boned-out lamb cut in 1½ inch (4-cm) cubes can be substituted for the chops.

1½ lb (675 g) aubergines
8–10 lamb shoulder chops, approx. 6 oz (175 g) each in weight
½ teasp salt
5 grinds of black pepper
2 tbsp oil
1 large (10 oz/275 g) onion
1 fat clove of garlic, chopped
17½ fl oz (500 ml/2 cups) vegetable stock
2 level tbsp tomato purée
2 teasp brown sugar
1 teasp ground cumin
1½ teasp ground cinnamon

Cut the unpeeled aubergines in 1-inch (2.5-cm) cubes, then leave covered with water plus 3 teaspoons of salt for 30 minutes. Meanwhile, lightly season the chops with salt and pepper, then in a large frying pan brown quickly on both sides in the oil. Lift out with a slotted spoon and drain on paper towels. In the same oil, cook the finely chopped onion over moderate heat until a rich golden brown, then add all the remaining ingredients (except the aubergines), stir well and bring to the boil. Simmer uncovered for 5 minutes.

Put the meat in an oven-to-table casserole, pour over the bubbling sauce and cook in a slow oven, Gas No. 2 (300°F/150°C), for 1½ hours. Meanwhile, squeeze as much moisture as possible from the aubergines and dry with paper towels. Deep-fry in 2 batches at 170°C (medium setting) for 5 minutes, then lift out on to paper towels. (If no deep-fryer is available, fry in 4 tablespoons oil in a covered frying pan for 10–15 minutes, or until soft and golden.) Add the aubergine cubes to the casserole, re-cover and cook for a further 30 minutes.

Serve from the casserole with rice or bulgur (cracked wheat).

LAMB FRICASSEE WITH VEGETABLES
(Lamb with Fresh Whole Beans)

Serves 6–8.
Keeps 3 days under refrigeration.
Freeze 3 months.

This Graeco-Jewish casserole is by tradition cooked on top of the stove. If you're around the house, it's quite pleasant to do it this way, giving the pot a stir every now and again – it doesn't take more than 1 hour. If it's more convenient to cook it in the oven, it will take 1½–2 hours. But whichever way you choose, let the meat cook gently. The beans will not keep their bright colour when cooked this way, but they will have absorbed all the delicious flavours of the sauce. If preferred, use 8 oz (225 g) frozen peas instead, added only 10 minutes before the end of the cooking time.

8–10 lamb neck steaks, approx. 6 oz (175 g) each, or 2½–3 lb (1.25–1.5 kg) boned-out shoulder of lamb cut in 1½-inch (3-cm) cubes
2 oz (50 g/½ cup) flour
1½ teasp salt
20 grinds of black pepper
2 tbsp dried mint
2 tbsp olive oil or sunflower oil
1 large (10 oz/275 g) onion, finely chopped
2 cloves of garlic, finely chopped
8 fl oz (225ml/1 cup) dry white wine or chicken stock plus 1 tbsp lemon juice
2 teasp sugar
8 oz (225 g) tiny button mushrooms
8 oz (225 g) whole green beans (haricots verts or bobo beans)

Coat the lamb with flour seasoned with the salt, pepper and half the dried mint. Heat the oil and sauté the onion and garlic until a pale gold. Add the meat and sauté until a rich brown. Add the wine or chicken stock and lemon juice and bubble for 3 minutes to concentrate the flavour, then add the sugar and mushrooms. Simmer for 1 hour on top of the stove or 1½ hours in a slow moderate oven, Gas No. 3 (325°F/160°C). About 20 minutes before the end of the cooking time add the raw beans, stir well, and continue to cook until beans and meat are tender.

Serve with new potatoes cooked in their skins or with boiled Basmati rice which you have flavoured as it cooks with 2 cardamom pods. The casserole reheats well.

LAMB IN THE PROVENÇALE FASHION

Serves 6.
Keeps 3 days under refrigeration.
Freeze 2 months.

The use of olive oil, garlic and herbs places the origins of this recipe firmly in Provence. If you do not wish to use wine, substitute an equal quantity of extra chicken stock.

2 tbsp olive oil
$2\frac{1}{2}$ lb (1.25 kg) boned lamb, cut in $1\frac{1}{2}$-inch (3-cm) cubes
1 medium onion, cut in $\frac{3}{8}$-inch (1-cm) cubes
1 large carrot, cut in $\frac{3}{8}$-inch (1-cm) cubes
1 fat clove of garlic, crushed
2 teasp brown sugar
10 fl oz (275 ml/$1\frac{1}{4}$ cups) chicken stock
5 fl oz (150 ml/$\frac{2}{3}$ cup) dry white wine
1 tbsp tomato purée
1 tbsp chopped parsley
1 teasp dried Herbes de Provence
$\frac{1}{4}$ teasp ground nutmeg
1 teasp salt
15 grinds of black pepper
4 oz (125 g/1 cup) button mushrooms, stalks removed

If possible, use a stove-to-table casserole. Heat the oil until you can feel the heat on your hand held 2 inches (5 cm) above it. Add half the well-dried meat and cook briskly until it is brown on all sides, then remove to a plate and fry the second portion of meat in the same way. Cook the onion, carrot and garlic in the same fat until they are softened and golden, sprinkling with the sugar to hasten the process.

Put the meat back on top of the vegetables and add the chicken stock, wine, tomato purée and seasonings. Bring to the boil, then cover and simmer gently, stirring occasionally, for $1\frac{1}{2}$ hours. (Alternatively, cook in the oven at Gas No. 2/300°F/150°C for 2 hours.) Add the mushrooms during the last half-hour.

When the meat feels tender, uncover the dish and simmer for 5 minutes until the sauce is reduced to a coating consistency. If you prefer to thicken it even further, stir in 2 teaspoons of cornflour (cornstarch) mixed with 2 tablespoons of cold water to a smooth consistency and then simmer for a further 3 minutes.

Serve with new potatoes.

Lamb Plus

TAGINE MALSOUKA (*Tunisian Lamb and Apricot Pie*)

Serves 8–10.
Freeze (raw) 2 months.

Cumin adds zing to the mild flavour of the lamb used in this succulent filo pastry pie. The pie can be prepared and refrigerated uncooked for 1 day in advance, but it's best to serve it freshly baked while the golden layers of pastry are at their flaky best. The pie should be served warm rather than hot - 10–15 minutes after it has come out of the oven - but never cold. It can be reheated to crispen the pastry or kept warm for 30 minutes in a very low oven.

For the meat filling

2 large onions, finely chopped
2 tbsp sunflower oil
3 fat cloves of garlic, finely chopped
3 lb (1.5 kg) minced (ground) lean raw lamb (or beef if preferred)
6 oz (175 g/1 cup) plus 2 tbsp) tenderized dried apricots
3 teasp ground cumin
2 tbsp finely chopped fresh coriander or parsley
1 teasp ground nutmeg
1 teasp ground cinnamon
2 teasp sea salt
15 grinds of black pepper
10 fl oz (275 ml/$1\frac{1}{4}$ cups) chicken stock

For the pastry

4–5 oz (125–150 g/$\frac{1}{2}$–$\frac{2}{3}$ cup) melted margarine (approx.)
1 x 1 lb (450 g) pack filo pastry
2–3 tbsp fine semolina

To make the meat filling In an 8-inch (20-cm) heavy-based saucepan, cook the onions in the oil, covered, over a moderate heat until softened and golden - about 10 minutes. Add the chopped garlic and sauté for a further 2 minutes. Add the minced meat and cook, breaking it up and turning with a fork until it loses its pinkness. Add the quartered apricots, spices, seasoning and stock, bring to the boil, then cover and simmer for 15 minutes, until the meat is tender. If there is a lot of free liquid, boil uncovered for 2-3 minutes. Turn on to a flat dish and allow to cool.

To assemble the pie Preheat the oven to Gas No. 3 (325°F/160°C). Divide the pastry sheets in 2 portions of 6-7 sheets each and leave under a cloth - this stops the pastry drying out.

Take a rectangular baking dish approximately 13 x 8 x 2 inches (33 x 20 x 5 cm) and grease lightly with the melted fat. Brush each sheet of pastry lightly with the melted fat, then stack on top of each other. Fit half the sheets into the dish so that the sides as well as the bottom are covered; overlap sheets if necessary. Sprinkle thinly with semolina. Pour in the cooled meat filling, then lay the remaining sheets of pastry on top, trimming any excess so that the pastry is level with the rim of the dish. Grease this top layer of pastry, then use a sharp knife to cut through the layers, marking out 12 squares, or more traditionally lozenges. Bake for 45 minutes, then turn up the oven to Gas No. 6 (400°F/200°C) and cook for a further 15 minutes, until richly browned and crisp.

BARBECUED KOFTA KEBABS IN PITTA POCKETS

Serve fresh.

For the meatballs

small bunch of parsley (about 1½ oz/40 g)
1 clove of garlic
1½ lb (675 g) lean lamb
1 large thick slice (2 oz/50 g) white or brown bread, torn up
1 medium onion, quartered
1½ teasp dried mint
1 teasp ground coriander
1 teasp cumin
1 teasp salt
10 grinds of black pepper

For the salad

8 oz (225 g) cabbage
1 carrot
1 red pepper
1 teasp sweet chilli sauce
6 pitta breads
12 thinly sliced onion rings

To make the meatballs, put the parsley and garlic in the food processor and process until finely chopped. Add all the remaining ingredients, then pulse until the meat is finely chopped and the mixture just clings together. Knead well with the hands to make a smooth, plastic mixture. Shape it into 12 ovals, thread each on to a flat metal skewer, then squeeze firmly round the skewer until about 6 inches (15 cm) long and fairly flat. Chill for at least 2 hours, or overnight.

Shred the cabbage finely, grate the carrot coarsely and cut the pepper in fine strips, then mix all 3 together with the chilli sauce.

Cook the kebabs on the barbecue for 10 minutes, turning frequently. Dip the pitta breads briefly into cold water and cook on the barbecue for about 30 seconds on each side, or until puffed. Slit each bread open lengthwise and spoon some of the salad inside. Slide the kebabs off the skewers and put 2 inside each pitta. Serve with a few onion rings.

Veal

Now that one can be confident that veal is produced in a humane manner, as laid down by British Government Regulations and supported by similar European Union legislation, it can be eaten without qualms.

High-quality veal is always expensive in relation to beef and lamb because it must come from an animal between 16 and 24 weeks old. Coming from an immature animal, it does not have any great depth of flavour. However, cooked correctly in an aromatic liquid, it can be meltingly tender with a fat content lower than any other kind of meat.

The shoulder can be boned out and pocketed, or rolled with a well-flavoured stuffing, then braised, to keep it moist and juicy. Or it can be cut into chops which can be slowly browned with whole shallots and sliced mushrooms, then cooked covered in their juice until tender - this usually takes about half an hour. Cubed veal is for casseroles. Schnitzels are expensive, but a little (about 4 oz/125 g per person) goes a long way, and they are a very special treat. As for minced veal - it's the best way of enjoying meatballs on a low-fat diet.

Braised Joints

STUFFED SHOULDER OF VEAL, BRAISED IN VERMOUTH

Serves 8, or 4 with a hot and a cold meal.
Leftovers keep 3 days under refrigeration.
Freeze 2 months.

The fruited nutty stuffing imparts a delicate flavour to the meat.

1 x 4 lb (1.75 kg) shoulder of veal (blade end), boned and pocketed
2 tbsp oil
1 medium onion, finely chopped
2 carrots, finely chopped
5 fl oz (150 ml/$^2/_3$ cup) dry white vermouth or other white wine, or chicken stock
salt
black pepper
2 bay leaves

For the stuffing

2 oz (50 g/$^1/_4$ cup) margarine
4 oz (125 g) shallots or large bunch spring onion bulbs (scallions), finely chopped
2 cloves of garlic, finely chopped
6 oz (175 g/6 cups) fresh brown or white breadcrumbs
grated rind of 1 lime
grated rind of $^1/_2$ orange
1 tbsp lime juice
1 tbsp orange juice
2 oz (50 g/$^1/_2$ cup) pistachios, blanched and chopped
2 oz (50 g/$^1/_2$ cup) pine kernels, toasted
2 tbsp mixed herbs - parsley, lemon grass, coriander, tarragon - chopped, or 2 tbsp parsley plus 1 teasp dried Herbes de Provence
1 egg, beaten

For the sauce

8 fl oz (225 ml/1 cup) meat stock
1 teasp cornflour mixed with 2 tbsp vermouth

To make the stuffing, melt the fat and sauté the shallots and garlic until golden - about 5 minutes. Mix all the other ingredients (except the egg) in a basin and season with 1 teaspoon of salt and 10 grinds of black pepper. Pour the shallots and garlic on to the breadcrumbs and stir in enough beaten egg to make a moist mixture that just clings together.

To stuff the veal, lay it on a board and stuff the pocket loosely. If there is no pocket, lay the meat flat and spread evenly with the stuffing, then roll up into a neat shape. Sew or skewer closed. Dab the surface dry with paper towels. The meat can be refrigerated overnight at this point, then left at room temperature for 1 hour before cooking.

To cook the veal, preheat the oven to Gas No. 4 (350°F/180°C) and heat the oil in a heavy casserole. Brown the meat thoroughly on all sides - this may take 15 minutes. Remove the meat to a plate and sauté the vegetables in the same fat until soft and golden. Add the vermouth, wine or stock, and bubble until it has almost evaporated.

Lay the meat on top of the vegetables in the casserole, season with 1 teaspoon of salt and 15 grinds of black pepper, and tuck the bay leaves down the side. Cover and cook in the preheated oven for 2 hours. The veal is ready when it feels soft to the touch and is a mahogany brown in colour. Lift the meat on to a serving plate and cover loosely. It may now be kept hot for up to 30 minutes at Gas No. ¼ (225°F/110°C).

To make the sauce, skim off as much fat as possible from the casserole liquid, pour in the stock and the cornflour liquid, stir well, then simmer until thickened. Purée the contents of the casserole in a blender or food processor, then leave in a small pan ready to reheat just before serving.

The meat may be carved in the dining room or sliced thickly then arranged on a heated platter and coated with the sauce in the kitchen.

To press remainder of the veal When sufficient veal to serve hot has been sliced, force the remainder of the joint into a small basin, covering it first with a saucer and then with a 2-lb (1-kg) weight. When cold it can be turned out and will slice thinly.

VARIATION

STUFFED BREAST OF VEAL

Flatten the breast with a cutlet bat or saucer, and spread with stuffing. Roll up and tie in 4 places. Brown and braise as above.

Veal Casseroles

VEAL BRAISED IN THE ITALIAN STYLE

Serves 6.
Keeps 3 days under refrigeration.
Freeze 3 months.

The cubes of veal are simmered in a richly flavoured herb-and-tomato sauce.

5 fl oz (150 ml/⅔ cup) hot beef stock or gravy
1 x 14 oz (400 g) can peeled Italian plum tomatoes
1 level teasp salt
10 grinds of black pepper
2 level teasp brown sugar
1 clove of garlic, crushed
1 bay leaf
2 level teasp dried basil
2 tbsp olive oil
2½ lb (1.25 kg) cubed veal
1 tbsp chopped parsley

Put the stock (or gravy), tomatoes, salt, pepper, sugar, crushed garlic, bay leaf and basil into a small pan and simmer gently until almost as thick as ketchup. Heat the oil in a heavy casserole and brown the meat on all sides (1 teaspoon of brown sugar sprinkled in as it cooks will hasten the process). As it browns, sprinkle the meat with a further level teaspoon of salt and a few grinds of pepper. When a rich brown, add the tomato sauce. Cook very gently in a slow oven for 2 hours, Gas No. 2 (300°F/150°C), or until absolutely tender. If the sauce seems a little too thin, take the lid off for the last 10 minutes. Just before serving, sprinkle in 1 tablespoon of chopped parsley.

TENDRONS DE VEAU À LA GARDIANE

Serves 6–8.
Keeps 2 days under refrigeration.
Freezes 1 month.

'From being forbidden by their usages to mingle butter with meat for any meal, the Jews have oil much used in their cookery of fish, meat and vegetables.' Thus speaks Eliza Acton, one of the most famous of all Victorian cookery writers, in a chapter entitled 'Foreign and Jewish Cookery' in her 1875 book *Modern Cookery*. Having acquired a copy, I was amazed to find a chapter on Jewish cooking, as this predates almost all published Jewish cookery books.

While the emphasis is on oriental Jewish cooking - the majority of Jews in England at the time being Sephardi - there are also some delicious Ashkenazi dishes, including this Tendrons de Veau.

With more veal in the kosher butchers, it may be possible to remain faithful to the original recipe. But if veal is difficult to obtain, the dish is equally good using thin-sliced ball of the rib. This is a really succulent casserole which freezes and reheats to perfection. Add the olives only on the day it is to be served. It is delicious on a bed of noodles.

4 tbsp olive oil
2–2½ lb (900–1.25 kg) boneless breast or shoulder of veal or rib steak, cut into 5-oz (150-g) slices
1 lb (450 g) pickling onions, peeled
1 tbsp tomato purée
3 cloves of garlic, finely chopped
1 sprig of thyme
8 oz (225 g/2½ cups) button mushrooms
5 fl oz (150 ml/⅔ cup) white wine or chicken or beef stock
1½ teasp salt
20 grinds of black pepper
12 black olives, stoned
12 green olives, stoned

Put the olive oil in a wide, shallow casserole. When the oil is hot put in the slices of meat and cook them on both sides until well browned. Remove the meat. Using the same oil, brown the onions. When these have taken colour, add the tomato purée and then, a few moments later, return the meat to the casserole, together with the garlic, thyme and mushrooms. Pour over the white wine or stock and season with the salt and pepper. Increase the heat. As soon as the liquid begins to boil, cover the pot, reduce the heat, and allow the stew to simmer for 1½ hours on the top or 2 hours in the stove at Gas No. 3 (325°F/160°C), stirring from time to time with a spatula to prevent sticking. Add the olives 15 minutes before the end.

SAUTÉ DE VEAU MARENGO

Serves 10–12.
Leftovers keep 3 days under refrigeration.
Freezes 2 months.

A rich and subtly flavoured casserole for a supper party. Ask the butcher to bone and cut the veal into 2-inch (5-cm) squares.

4½ lb (2 kg) veal
5 fl oz (150 ml/⅔ cup) olive oil
3 large onions, finely chopped
2 tbsp flour
15 fl oz (425 ml/2 cups) dry white wine
1½ pints (850 ml/3¾ cups) chicken soup or stock from cubes
3 cloves of garlic, crushed
large sprig of parsley
1 level tbsp salt
black pepper
1 x 28 oz (800 g) can of tomatoes, drained
1 tbsp sugar
12 oz (350 g) white baby mushrooms, sliced

You may find it easier to fry the meat in 2 pans, then combine it in a single casserole for the actual cooking. Heat the oil in a heavy frying pan and put in the veal, a quarter at a time, cooking quickly until brown. Half-way through, add the onions and continue cooking. Sprinkle with flour and cook until it browns a little, then add the wine and bubble for 3 minutes to concentrate the flavour. Put into a large casserole. Add the remaining ingredients (except mushrooms) to the frying pan, and scrape it well to get any delicious sediment into the sauce, then bring to the boil. Pour over the meat, cover and simmer until tender (about 1½ hours) in the oven, Gas No. 2 (300°F/150°C). 20 minutes before the end of the cooking time, remove the lid and add the raw mushrooms. The sauce should be creamy; if a little too thin, leave uncovered for the remainder of the cooking time.

Chops and Escalopes

CÔTE DE VEAU AUX HERBES (*Veal Chops with Fresh Herbs*)

Serves 4–6.
Keeps 2 days under refrigeration.
Freeze 2 months.

The richly flavoured, large flat mushrooms now widely available in most supermarkets combine with the wine to make a superb sauce for the veal. Serve with creamy mashed potatoes and lightly steamed broccoli.

4–6 rib or shoulder chops of veal, each 1–1¼ inches (2.5–3 cm) thick
black pepper
2 tbsp flour
1 teasp salt
3 tbsp olive oil or sunflower oil
6 large (3–4 inches/7.5–10 cm) mushrooms, thickly sliced
6 oz (175 g) shallots or mild onion, finely chopped
5 fl oz (150 ml/⅔ cup) dry white wine or vermouth, or chicken stock
2 tbsp chopped fresh herbs – a mixture of rosemary and marjoram is good

Have the chops trimmed of excess bone so that they will lie flat. If they have been refrigerated, leave at room temperature for 1 hour, then dry well with kitchen paper and sprinkle generously on both sides with the freshly ground black pepper before coating with the seasoned flour. Pat off any excess.

In a lidded frying pan, cook the chops in the hot oil at a gentle sizzle for 3–4 minutes on each side, or until the surface is golden brown. Cover and cook gently for a further 15–20 minutes, turning once, until the juices run clear when the meat is pierced with a small pointed knife. Remove to a warm plate, cover lightly with foil and leave in a low oven. Add the mushrooms and shallots to the pan and sauté briskly for 3–4 minutes, until they are softened and lightly coloured, then add the wine or stock and stir vigorously with a wooden spoon to incorporate any crusty bits sticking to the base. Add the herbs and bubble until the sauce is syrupy. Taste and add salt and pepper if necessary. Spoon the mushroom sauce over the chops and serve at once.

Veal Escalopes or Schnitzels

These make extremely speedy (if expensive) main dishes, so it is useful to have a stock of frozen escalopes in the freezer.

A true escalope is cut from the leg of veal, but as this is not usually available as a kosher cut, it should be cut from the boned-out shoulder or from the eye of the chop instead. It's advisable to beat them out gently, using a cutlet bat or the end of a rolling pin to help tenderize them.

Escalopes of turkey or chicken can be substituted for the veal.

ESCALOPES DE VEAU BASQUAISE (*Escalopes of Veal on a Bed of Ratatouille*)

Serves 6–8.
Leftovers keep 3 days under refrigeration.
Do not freeze.

Thin slices of veal are simmered in white wine and then served on a juicy vegetable ragout. The dish can be prepared early in the day and then gently reheated just before dinner.

6–8 escalopes, cut ⅜ inch (1 cm) thick
2 oz (50 g/½ cup) flour, seasoned with 1 teasp salt and 10 grinds black pepper
sunflower oil for frying
5 fl oz (150 ml/⅔ cup) each dry white wine and chicken stock, or 10 fl oz (275 ml/1¼ cups) chicken stock alone

For the ratatouille
3 tbsp olive oil
2 medium (5 oz/150 g) onions, thinly sliced
1 tbsp brown sugar
1 lb (450 g) aubergines (eggplants), unpeeled and cut in 1½-inch (4-cm) cubes
2 large green peppers, halved, seeded and cut in strips ½ inch (1.25 cm) wide
2 medium courgettes (zucchini), unpeeled, cut in slices 1 inch (2.5·cm) thick
1 x 14 oz (400 g) can tomatoes, drained
1 large clove of garlic, peeled and crushed
2 teasp salt
15 grinds of black pepper
1 tbsp wine vinegar
1 tbsp lemon juice
4 oz (125 g/1 cup) black olives

For the garnish
1 tbsp chopped parsley

To prepare the ratatouille Heat the oil in a heavy frying pan, add the onions, sprinkle with the sugar, then cover and cook until soft and golden - about 10 minutes. Add the aubergines, peppers, courgettes and tomatoes with the garlic, salt and black pepper, stirring well. Cover and simmer for 30–40 minutes, stirring occasionally, until the vegetables are tender but not mushy, and the ragout is thick and juicy. If there is too much liquid in the pan, boil it away. Stir in the vinegar and lemon juice together with the olives. The ratatouille can now be left in the covered pan until required.

To cook the escalopes Cover each escalope with a piece of greasesproof (waxed) paper, beat it out with a cutlet bat or the end of a rolling pin until as thin as possible, then dip in the seasoned flour. Heat enough oil in a heavy frying pan to come to a depth of ¼ inch (0.5 cm) and cook the escalopes in it until they are a golden brown on both sides, removing them to a plate as they are ready. Pour off any oil remaining in the pan, add the white wine (if used) and stock and stir well, then simmer until syrupy. Return the escalopes to the pan, cover and simmer very gently for 15 minutes until they feel tender when cut with a knife. Leave until required.

To serve the dish Reheat the ratatouille until bubbly, either on top of the stove or in the microwave. Bring the meat to simmering point in the sauce but do not allow it to boil as this would toughen it. Arrange the ragout round the edge of a large dish, put the escalopes in the centre and spoon over the sauce. Sprinkle with the chopped parsley and serve.

WIENER SCHNITZEL

Serves 6–8.
Leftovers keep 2 days under refrigeration.
Ready-to-fry breaded schnitzels keep 1 day under refrigeration.
Freeze 1 month.

The origins of the Wiener Schnitzel are somewhat obscure, if fascinating. One version credits its invention to a Turkish cook taken prisoner after the siege of Vienna in 1683, while others claim that the Spanish troops of Charles V were the first to take it to Italy (as in Scaloppe Milanese) and then to Vienna. Certainly, in Vienna any self-respecting housewife always ensures that her schnitzel completely covers the diner's plate.

Serve hot off the pan with boiled new potatoes or Kasha Varnishkes (see p. 278), or at room temperature with a potato salad and a corn and green bean salad.

6–8 ready-cut veal schnitzels, about 1½ lb (675 g) in total
2 tbsp lemon juice
1 teasp salt
15 grinds of black pepper

For the coating
1 heaped tbsp plain flour
2 eggs
5–6 oz matzah meal or fine dry breadcrumbs
½ teasp sea salt
15 grinds of black pepper
good pinch each of garlic powder and paprika
1 tbsp cold water

For frying
6 tbsp sunflower oil

For the garnish
wedges of lime or lemon
sprigs of parsley

Lay each schnitzel between 2 pieces of greaseproof paper and pound with a cutlet bat or the end of a rolling pin until half the original thickness. (Be careful not to tear the delicate meat.) Put the lemon juice, salt and pepper into a shallow dish, turn the schnitzels in it to coat on both sides, then leave in the dish for 30 minutes, turning once.

Meanwhile, put the flour, beaten egg and crumbs (mixed with the seasonings) into separate shallow dishes placed side by side. Toss each schnitzel lightly in the flour, patting off any excess with the hands then brush with a thin layer of beaten egg and water and turn in the seasoned crumbs, patting them on firmly. Leave the schnitzels side by side on a board for 30 minutes to set the coating (longer will do no harm but do refrigerate them meanwhile).

In a large heavy frying pan, heat the oil until you can feel it comfortably warm on your hand held 2 inches (5 cm) above the surface. Put in the schnitzels (don't crowd the pan) and cook them steadily for 5 minutes on each side, or until crisp and brown. As they are cooked, lay them side by side on a tray in a slow oven, Gas No. 1 (275°F/140°C), to keep hot without drying out.

Garnish with the wedges of fruit.

Note Chicken or turkey breast schnitzels can be treated in exactly the same way.

VEAL ESCALOPES WITH VERMOUTH
(*Scaloppine alla Vermouth*)

Serve 6.
Leftovers keep 2 days under refrigeration.
Freeze 2 months.

4–6 escalopes, pounded thin, or the equivalent in scallopine – little bits of escalope veal
seasoned flour
2–3 tbsp sunflower oil or olive oil
1 onion, finely chopped
3 fl oz (75 ml/⅓ cup) sweet vermouth
1 teasp tomato purée
pinch of mace
½ teasp salt
8 grinds of black pepper

Roll the thin pieces of veal in seasoned flour. In the oil cook the finely chopped onion until soft and golden, then brown the meat in the same pan. Lift meat on to a plate and to the pan juices add the vermouth, tomato purée, mace and salt and pepper. Simmer to reduce until syrupy - about 3 minutes - then return the meat to the pan and heat through in the sauce. Serve from the pan.

VEAL SCALLOPS WITH CHICKEN LIVERS

Serves 6.
Keeps 2 days under refrigeration.
Freeze 2 months.

Scallops can be the trimmings from the piece of veal from which schnitzels have been cut, or they can be the eye of the veal chop, thinly sliced. With this dish the best result is achieved when there is some gravy left over from a pot roast. Otherwise use a combination of white wine and strong bouillon or consommé. The dish can be completed just before dinner, then either kept hot on a low heat or reheated.

1½–2 lb (675–900 g) veal scallops
2 tbsp olive oil or sunflower oil
seasoned flour
1 lb (450 g) koshered chicken livers, each cut in 3
1 clove of garlic, chopped
8 fl oz (225 ml/1 cup) rich gravy (e.g. from pot roast or roast chicken), or 5 fl oz (150 ml/⅔ cup) dry white wine plus 5 fl oz (150 ml/⅔ cup) beef stock
2 teasp tomato purée
½ teasp salt
15 grinds of black pepper

For the garnish
chopped parsley

Have the veal cut as thinly as possible, then beat out until paper-thin with a cutlet bat.

Heat the oil gently in a lidded sauté or frying pan. Dip the scallops in and out of the seasoned flour, then fry at a fairly brisk bubble until golden brown on both sides. Add the chicken livers and all the remaining ingredients. Cover and simmer very gently for 10 minutes. Serve sprinkled with the parsley on a bed of noodles.

Veal Plus

VEAL IN WINE SAUCE

Serves 6.

Cold roast veal has an almost chicken-like texture that takes kindly to careful reheating in a well-seasoned sauce. Serve with a pilaff of rice, flavoured with crushed cardamom seeds.

2 tbsp sunflower oil
1 medium onion, finely chopped
4 oz (125 g/2 cups) mushrooms
10 oz (275 g) flour
5 fl oz (150 ml/⅔ cup) white wine
10 fl oz (275 ml/1¼ cups) chicken or veal stock (made with leftover gravy jelly if possible, or use stock-cube)
salt
pepper
1 egg yolk
2 cups leftover roast veal, diced
1 packet (8 oz/225 g) frozen peas, cooked

For the pilaff
½ large onion
2 oz (50 g/¼ cup) margarine
12 oz (350 g/1¾ cups) Basmati rice, well rinsed in cold water
1¼ pints (725 ml/3 cups) chicken stock
6 crushed cardamom seeds
1 bay leaf
1 teasp paprika

Heat the oil, add the onion and cook until golden. Add the sliced mushrooms to the hot oil and cook for 2 minutes. Stir in the flour, then bubble for a further minute. Add wine and cook for 2 minutes, then take off heat and whisk in hot stock. Return to heat to cook for 2-3 minutes. Season with salt and pepper if necessary. Pour sauce on to egg yolk and stir well, then blend in veal and cooked peas. Keep hot in top of double saucepan until needed, or leave in low oven.

To make the pilaff Fry onion until golden in the margarine, add rice and continue to cook for 3 minutes. Add hot stock and seasonings. Cover and cook either at Gas No. 4 (350°F/180°C) or over low heat on top of the stove for 18 minutes.

JOSE LEVENE'S DUTCH-STYLE VEAL BALLS IN AN EGG AND LEMON SAUCE

Serves 3–4.
Leftovers keep 24 hours under refrigeration.
Freeze meatballs and stock (not sauce) 3 months.

This recipe comes from a family with Dutch Sephardi connections. It has a strong affinity with the Greek Sephardi dish Ternera y Espinaca Avgolemono (veal and spinach in an egg and lemon sauce). As *Ternera* is the Spanish word for veal, it suggests a Spanish or even Moorish origin. Rice makes an excellent accompaniment.

For the meatballs
1 lb (450 g) minced fresh veal
1 tbsp chopped parsley
1 medium onion, finely chopped
finely grated zest of 1 medium lemon
1 egg, beaten to blend
½ teasp salt
speck of white pepper
1 oz (25 g/4 tbsp) matzah meal or 1 oz (25 g/½ cup) fresh breadcrumbs

For the stewing liquid
1 large onion, peeled and sliced
approx. 10 fl oz (275 ml/1¼ cups) boiling water
½ teasp salt
speck of white pepper
1 bay leaf

For the sauce
2 teasp cornflour (or potato flour for Pesach use)
4 tbsp lemon juice
2 teasp sugar or granular sweetener
8 fl oz (225 ml/1 cup) stewing liquid
2 eggs

Mix all the meatball ingredients together with a fork, then leave to stand for half an hour. Roll into balls the size of a walnut.

Bring the ingredients for the stewing liquid to the boil in an 8-inch (20-cm) pan, then add the meatballs - they should be barely covered by the liquid; if not, add a little extra boiling water. Bring to the boil, then reduce the heat until the liquid is barely bubbling. Cover and simmer for 45 minutes. Discard the bay leaf, then lift out the meatballs and onion slices with a slotted spoon and set aside. Bubble the liquid until it is reduced to 8 fl oz (225 ml/1 cup). Pour into a jug and rinse out the pan.

Put the cornflour into a bowl and gradually stir in the lemon juice, then whisk in the eggs, sugar and poaching liquid until smooth (or process for 10 seconds in a food processor).

Return to the pan and stir with a wooden spoon over low heat until the sauce thickens enough to coat the back of the spoon, then return the meatballs and onion slices to the pan and heat through until steaming - do not let it come to the boil or it may curdle, though the odd bubble is all right.

To cook the sauce in the microwave, mix the sauce ingredients in a microwave-safe jug. Cook on 50 per cent power for 2 minutes, stir well and cook for a further 2–3 minutes, until thickened to coating consistency. Return to the pan, add the meatballs and onion slices and reheat until steaming.

Taste and add a little more sugar if the sauce is too acid.

POULTRY

Poultry is a weekend regular in almost every Jewish household, particularly with those families who came originally from Eastern Europe, where fowls were often raised in the backyard. This was a habit many immigrants tried to continue when they came to Britain at the end of the nineteenth century. But the East End of London is no village, and most of the immigrants lived in tenements without gardens or yards. So the chicken would share the kitchen with the family until it was time for it to be taken to the *shohet* (slaughterer) and killed. Cleaning and koshering the bird used to be one of the more onerous jobs involved in preparing for the Sabbath but nowadays most birds come ready-koshered, scalded and trussed.

The roaster, in one form or another, has now replaced the traditional 'hen' as the most popular bird. Older birds - or portions of them - are still considered necessary to the flavour of chicken soup, but the main-course bird is now likely to be roasted or casseroled without first having to give its all to the soup.

Joints of chicken and the breast meat of both chicken and turkey are extremely popular for mid-week meals because they can be so quickly and easily prepared. Many poulterers also prepare chicken and turkey schnitzels, as well as the boneless turkey 'roasts' which are ideal for today's busy lifestyle. As a lean white meat, chicken is also enjoying popularity as a low-fat food. Chicken fat – *schmaltz* in Yiddish – on the other hand, has largely been superseded by vegetable oils and margarines, although if it is used in only small quantities, it still has an essential part to play in flavouring certain traditional foods, such as Knaidlach (see p. 51) and Chopped Liver (see p. 4).

When the great debate on saturated *vs* polyunsaturated fat was at its height a few years ago, it was assumed – at least in Jewish households – that chicken fat, like other animal fats, was a bad thing because of its high proportion of saturated fat - which is generally considered an important risk factor in coronary disease.

However, the following puts the matter into perspective. Chicken fat has, in fact, a lower proportion of saturated fat than that to be found in beef fat (33 per cent compared to 50 per cent). In addition it is also richer in the polyunsaturates that are regarded as important in a healthy diet. (21 per cent in chicken compared to 2 per cent in beef fat). This compares with 23 per cent in rapeseed oil, 30 per cent in ground nut oil and up to 50 per cent in some of the vegetable oils that are the highest in polyunsaturates. In addition, like olive oil, it also contains useful amounts of monounsaturated fat - which is now considered an essential part of a healthy diet.

Broadly speaking, therefore, nutritionists rate chicken fat somewhere between the heavily saturated dairy and animal fats, on the one hand, and the vegetable fats which are particularly high in polyunsaturates on the other, as a desirable part of the total intake of fat.

However, people with special dietary prohibitions on medical grounds should seek expert advice before eating it.

About All Kinds of Poultry

Most birds are now sold made kosher and are ready to cook, but fresh birds are to be preferred to frozen as their texture and flavour are both definitely superior. If necessary, see 'How to Make Meat and Poultry Kosher', p. 133

Fowls are specially bred for the Jewish market, unlike non-kosher 'boilers' or 'steam roasters', which are often only mature laying hens. A fowl should weigh between 4½ and 5lb (2.25-2.5 kg) dressed weight. Prepacked birds are sold without either feet or livers for reasons of kashrut.

Roasting chickens to serve 4-6 should weigh between 4 and 5 lb (2-2.5 kg), although birds weighing more than 6 lb (2.75 kg) are also available. For jointing into 4, use a smaller bird weighing about 3½ lb (1.75 kg). Many butchers will bone and stuff whole birds ready for the oven.

Chickens for grilling should weigh between 2½ and 3 lb (1.25-1.5 kg) and are usually split or spatchcocked - that is, flattened for even cooking without actually cutting in 2.

Poussins should weigh between 1¼ and 1½ lb (550-675 g) and will serve 2 if split down the back.

Chicken breasts can be bought on or off the bone or part-boned (with the wing but without most of the rib-cage), while boned and skinned breast meat is sold by the pound (450 g) or cut for schnitzels, kebabs or salads.

Ducks weigh between 4 and 6 lb (2-3 kg).

Turkeys vary in weight between 8 and 20 lb (4-9 kg), though birds weighing as much as 30-40 lb (13-18 kg) are used by the butcher for schnitzels, rolls, roasts and goulash, as well as for smoking and sausage-making.

Game birds are rarely available, though there is no reason why they cannot be used, provided they have been slaughtered in the ritual manner.

If you do have to buy frozen birds, here is a guide to *thawing times*. The bird is completely thawed when it feels cool (but not icy) to the touch and the legs feel pliable. The body cavity should be completely free from particles of ice.

Weight	*At room temperature*	*In the refrigerator*
2 lb (1 kg)	8 hours	28 hours
3 lb (1.5 kg)	9 hours	32 hours
4 lb (2 kg)	10 hours	38 hours
5 lb (2.5 kg)	12 hours	44 hours
6 lb (2.75 kg)	14 hours	50 hours

If you need to thaw a chicken urgently and do not have a microwave, immerse it completely (still in its wrapper) in a bowl of cold water, changing the water several times until the bird is thawed - after 4 or 5 hours for a medium-sized bird.

To thaw a turkey, allow between 24 and 48 hours in a cool larder, according to size.

Treat all thawed birds as fresh, and cook immediately or refrigerate until required.

Be Fair to the Fowl

A fowl, or 'steam roaster' as it is sometimes called, is about 12 months old, mature enough to make excellent soup, yet still young enough to be tender and flavoursome in a casserole. A top-quality bird should have a full, round breast and white skin, and if it is to be braised rather than boiled, it should be free of excessive subcutaneous fat. However, the slow cooking in liquid that is necessary to make a good pot of soup will tenderize even an over-fat grandmother hen. Fowls should weigh between 4½ and 6 lb (2.25–3 kg) ready-dressed and, besides the main dish, will provide such 'extras' as Chicken Soup (see p. 28) Gefilte Helzel (see p. 48) and Chopped Liver (see p. 4) - the true 'package' meal!

TO RENDER CHICKEN FAT

Refrigerate for up to 3 months.
Freeze 6 months.

Before a fowl is boiled or casseroled, the excess fat and the fat-impregnated skin at the back should be removed so that it can be rendered down for use in dishes such as Chopped Liver (see p. 4) and Knaidlach (see p. 51). The fat that solidifies on chilled chicken soup can also be skimmed off and used.

chicken fat
fat-impregnated skin
1 onion, roughly chopped

Cut up the fat with the skin in 1-inch (2.5-cm) squares and add the onion. Put into a small earthenware dish - add no water - and leave in a low oven until the fat has melted (this may take 1 or 2 hours). Strain and store in the refrigerator.

TO BOIL A FOWL

Follow the instructions for boiling a fowl for Chicken Soup (see p. 28).

TO BROWN A BOILED FOWL

If you wish to cook the bird in the soup but prefer to have it hot and brown rather than cold and boiled, proceed as follows:

Cut the legs off the raw fowl before boiling - this makes the bird easier to handle. Cook the bird and legs in the soup until barely tender (about 2 hours), or when the flesh of the leg feels soft when prodded with a fork. Lift the bird from the soup and leave covered until needed.

Next day place the bird and legs in a casserole. Skim the fat off the soup, put it in a frying pan and cook a large sliced onion in it until soft and golden. Sprinkle the bird with a light dusting of paprika and flour, then pour over it the fried onions and the fat in which they were cooked. Cover and cook for 40 minutes at Gas No. 5 (375°F/190°C) until the bird looks brown and juicy. Uncover and add half a cup of the chicken soup. Cover and reheat for a further 10 minutes. Serve the bird in joints with the pan juices.

TO CASSEROLE A FOWL - HAIMISCHE STYLE

Serves 4–8, depending on the size of the bird.
Leftovers keep 3 days under refrigeration.
Freeze 3 months.

A fine plump fowl has, perhaps, more flavour than any other kind of bird. However, as its flesh tends to be dry, it must be cooked in gentle, moist heat. The best way is to braise it slowly on a bed of lightly fried vegetables, in a covered casserole just large enough to contain it.The bird can be whole or jointed, stuffed (with helzel or breadcrumb mixture) or left plain. The vegetables used can be varied with the season, but the basic method is always the same. I prefer to refrigerate a casseroled bird overnight so that all the fat can be skimmed off the gravy before it is gently reheated (see below).

1 level teasp salt
10 grinds of black pepper
2 level teasp flour
2 level teasp paprika
1 fowl, 4½–6 lb (2.25–3 kg) net weight, made kosher and scalded
1 tbsp oil
1 large onion, thinly sliced
1 clove of garlic, crushed
1 bay leaf
1 carrot, thinly sliced
2 soft tomatoes or 2 tbsp tomato purée
any or all of the following if they are available:
½ red or yellow pepper, seeded and cut into strips,
3 stalks of celery, diced
4 oz (125 g/1¼ cups) mushrooms, sliced
4 fl oz (125 ml/½ cup) chicken soup or chicken stock made with a cube

Turn the oven to Gas No. 4 (350°F/180°C). Mix together the salt, pepper, flour and paprika, then rub into the skin of the bird. In a heavy casserole, heat the oil and fry the onion and garlic until soft and golden, then add the bay leaf and all the remaining vegetables and stir over gentle heat, until they have absorbed most of the fat. Put the bird in and turn it in the hot fat until it goes pale gold. Pour the stock or soup down the side of the casserole. Cover and transfer to the oven. After 15 minutes, turn the oven down to Gas No. 3 (325°F/160°C) and cook for 3 hours, or until the bird is a rich golden brown and the leg can be moved easily in its socket. During cooking, the liquid should be bubbling very gently. If bubbling is too violent, turn the oven down to Gas No. 2 (300°F/150°C). Baste twice with the pan juices. If dinner is delayed, the oven can be turned down to a 'keep hot' or minimum setting, and the bird will come to no harm.

To serve, lift the bird on to a warm platter. Skim off as much fat as possible. Blend or process the vegetables and liquid until absolutely smooth - this produces a naturally thickened gravy. Bring to the boil, taste and reseason if necessary, then serve.

To reheat a casseroled fowl Remove some of the jelly in which it will be resting and put this in the soup to enrich it. Put the bird, still covered in the casserole, in a moderate oven, Gas No. 4 (350°F/180°C), for 30 minutes, or until piping hot.

HELZEL STUFFING

Use this to stuff a casseroled bird; it will not cook sufficiently in one that is roasted.

3 oz (75 g/¾ cup) flour
1 oz (25 g/3 tbsp) semolina or fine matzah meal
3 tbsp raw chicken fat, finely chopped
½ medium onion, coarsely grated
½ level teasp salt
pinch of white pepper

Mix all the ingredients together with a fork. (If raw fat is not available, use 3 rounded tablespoons of rendered fat. Use this to cook the onion gently for 2 minutes, then pour on to the dry ingredients and blend well). The mixture should look slightly moist in appearance - add a little fat if too dry; if too moist add a little more semolina or meal. Stuff lightly into the body cavity of the bird.

To Roast a Chicken

The following four ways of roasting a chicken have each in turn been my favourite method, but I can't honestly say that one is vastly superior to the others as they all produce succulent birds of excellent flavour. It's worth trying them all. The common denominator is that they all use olive oil for brushing the bird, as this produces the richest brown.

If you want the bird to absorb the minimum of fat, then roast it on a rack set in the roasting tin. In addition, for anyone on a low-fat diet it's important to discard the skin, however tempting, as this contains a great deal of fat, even after roasting - chicken without the skin also contains *half* the calories of chicken with.

A sliced onion laid beneath the bird will give a good colour to the juices from which the *gravy* can then be made.

A syringe-type baster is essential if you wish to baste the bird without a hassle.

Whatever method is used, the bird is fully cooked when it is a rich golden brown and the juices run clear when the leg is pierced with a skewer.

Always *rest* the bird in a warm place, lightly covered with foil, for 15 minutes before carving it. This allows the meat to 'settle' and makes it much easier to carve.

Poultry shears are indispensable for portioning small cooked birds.

TO ROAST A BIRD TO BE SERVED COLD

Serves 4-6.
Produces approx. $1\frac{1}{2}$ lb (675 g) cooked flesh off the bone.
Keeps 3 days under refrigeration.
Freeze 3 months.

The bird is foil-wrapped and roasted at a very high temperature for a shorter time. Cooked this way, the bird is particularly succulent when cold.

$3\frac{1}{2}$-$4\frac{1}{2}$ lb (1.75-2.25 kg) roaster
$\frac{1}{2}$ orange or $\frac{1}{2}$ lemon
olive oil
salt
pepper

In the body cavity of the bird put the orange or lemon, then brush the whole of the carcase (especially the legs) with a thin layer of olive oil. Season well with salt and pepper and wrap loosely in foil. Put in a very hot oven, Gas No. 8 (450°F/230°C), for 1 hour. After 45 minutes open the fcil parcel and allow the bird to brown.

TO ROAST A BIRD TO BE SERVED HOT (*Simplest Method*)

Serves 4-6.
Leftovers keep 3 days under refrigeration.

This method is perfect for dieters.

$3\frac{1}{2}$-$4\frac{1}{2}$ (1.75-2.25 kg) chicken
salt
black pepper
bunch of parsley
1 clove of garlic, peeled and halved
olive oil

Preheat the oven to Gas No. 5 (375°F/190°C). Salt and pepper the cavity of the bird, then insert a bunch of parsley. Brush all over with a thin coating of olive oil, then sprinkle with freshly ground black pepper and sea salt. Nick the bird where the leg joins the body and insert the halves of garlic.

Put the bird, breast-side down, in the roasting tin (or on a rack if preferred) and cook without basting but turning every 30 minutes, allowing 20 minutes to the pound (450 g) plus an extra 20 minutes.

Lift the bird on to a carving dish and keep warm for 15 minutes to make carving easier. Run off any fat that has collected in the roasting tin, deglaze over medium heat with

10 fl oz (175 ml/1¼ cups) chicken stock, stirring well to loosen any of the delicious sediment in the bottom of the tin, then transfer to a small pan and simmer to concentrate the flavour (taste it). If preferred, the juices can be thickened with 2 teaspoons of cornflour (cornstarch) mixed to a cream with 2 tablespoons of water, wine or sherry, then bubbled for a further 3 minutes.

ROAST CHICKEN IN THE FRENCH STYLE

Serves 4–5.
Leftovers keep 3 days under refrigeration.
Freeze 3 months.

Roasting a chicken means it is crisp and golden; casseroling it produces succulent flesh. Trust the canny French to combine these two methods, surrounding the uncovered bird with a steaming bath of stock. Gradually this stock evaporates so all that is left is the fat, which can be poured away, and the delicious juices from the bird, which can be used for the gravy. In a forced-air or fan-assisted oven, the stock may evaporate before the bird is cooked, so add a little extra liquid if necessary at about half-time.

raw chicken fat from inside the bird
4 lb (2 kg) roaster
a small bunch of parsley
1 eating apple
1 medium carrot
1 medium onion
1 pint (575 ml/2½ cups) hot chicken stock
sea salt
2 teasp cornflour (cornstarch)
2 tbsp cold water or Amontillado sherry

Preheat the oven to Gas No. 5 (375°F/190°C).

Remove any chicken fat from the cavity and insert the bunch of parsley and the quartered apple. Place the bird in a roasting tin just large enough to hold it, and strew the finely sliced carrot and onion around it. Make up the stock with boiling water (or use home-made), then pour it around the bird – it should half fill the roasting tin. Sprinkle the bird lightly with coarse sea salt and lay the chicken fat on top of the breast. Allow 20 minutes to the pound (450 g) plus 20 minutes – that is, 1 hour 40 minutes for a 4-lb (2 kg) bird. If, however, the bird is stuffed, allow 20 minutes' extra roasting time. Roast the chicken, basting it with the stock every 20 minutes. At the end of the cooking time, the bird should be a rich brown and the liquid should have evaporated, leaving only fat and the thickened juices with the browned vegetables in the tin. Transfer the bird to a serving dish and keep hot. Pour off all the fat – it will be pure chicken fat. Put the roasting tin over medium heat and deglaze it with 10 fl oz (275 ml/1¼ cups) of hot water, stirring it well to release the concentrated juices clinging to the bottom. In a small pan have ready the cornflour mixed to a liquid with either the cold water or sherry. Pour the contents of the roasting tin through a sieve on to this liquid, pressing down well to get all the juices from the vegetables. Bubble this gravy for 3 minutes, taste and add salt and pepper only if necessary – remember, it is made up of concentrated stock. The bird is equally good served hot or cold.

SAVOURY BREAD STUFFING

Sufficient for a 4-lb (2 kg) bird.

4 oz (125 g/1¾ cups) stale breadcrumbs (put in food processor or pulled out of crust with a fork)
pinch each of salt, paprika, black pepper and dried oregano
2 tbsp finely chopped parsley
3 oz (75 g/⅓ cup) margarine
2 teasp olive oil
1 small onion, finely chopped

Put the crumbs and the seasonings and herbs into a bowl. Heat the margarine with the oil in a small frying pan, and add the finely chopped onion. Cook gently until the onion is soft and golden, then pour the contents of the pan on to the seasoned crumbs. Toss lightly until all the crumbs are coated with fat. Stuff lightly into the salted cavity of the bird.

VARIATION

STUFFING ENGLISH STYLE

Fry the onion in 2 oz (50 g/¼ cup) margarine and 2 teaspoons of olive oil. Moisten the fat and breadcrumb mixture with a small beaten egg. This makes a firmer stuffing.

ROAST CHICKEN WITH TARRAGON WINE SAUCE

Serves 8.
Keeps 3 days under refrigeration.
Freeze 3 months.

Using this recipe the roast chicken turns a mahogany brown, yet even after 2½ hours in the oven remains fragrant and juicy. The secret: a special herb and wine mixture spread *under* the skin of the breast. The unctuous tarragon and wine sauce provides the perfect complement to the delicate flavour of the bird.

For the herb mixture
4 tbsp finely chopped shallots
3 tbsp dry white wine
1 tbsp white wine vinegar
leaves from 2 stalks of fresh tarragon
(1 tbsp chopped) or 1 teasp dried tarragon
2 oz (50 g/¼ cup) margarine

To roast the bird
6-8 lb (2.5-3.5 kg) chicken (net weight)
plus giblets
salt
pepper
1 small onion, halved
bunch of parsley
olive oil
sea salt
black pepper
1 medium onion (5 oz/150 g) thinly sliced

For the sauce
6 fl oz (175 ml/¾ cup) dry white wine
15 fl oz (425 ml/2 cups) chicken stock
1 level tbsp cornflour (cornstarch) slaked with a little wine
3 teasp chopped fresh tarragon

First make the herb and wine mixture. In a small pan, simmer the shallots, wine, wine vinegar and dried tarragon (if used) until the liquid has evaporated. Cool a little, then beat into the soft fat, together with the chopped fresh tarragon (if used).

Wash the bird inside and out, dry thoroughly and season inside with a sprinkle of salt and a few grinds of pepper. Gently tease the skin away from the breast by slipping your fingers between them, but taking care not to tear the skin. Spread the herb and wine mixture evenly all over the breast under the skin, then pat the skin back in place. Put the onion and parsley in the cavity of the bird, then tie the legs together and arrange on a rack in a roasting tin. Paint the skin of the bird with olive oil and sprinkle with sea salt and black pepper.

Roast for 30 minutes in a quick oven, Gas No. 6 (400°F/200°C), then put the sliced onion and the reserved giblets on to the roasting tin and turn the oven down to Gas No. 3 (325°F/160°C). Potatoes for roasting can be put in at this stage. Continue to roast for 1½-2 hours longer, basting every 30 minutes (the shorter time for the smaller bird), until the juices run clear when the thickest part of the thigh is pierced with a skewer. Transfer the bird to a warm platter and leave it in the warming drawer or the oven turned down to Gas No. ¼ (225°F/110°C) for 20-30 minutes - as convenient. This makes it easier to carve and also conserves the juices.

Pour off all the fat from the roasting tin, then pour in the wine and stir with a wooden spoon to loosen the delicious sediment from the bottom. Bubble until the liquid is reduced by half. Add the chicken stock and bring slowly to simmering point. Slake the cornflour with a little extra wine, then pour into the pan and bubble for 3 minutes to cook the starch. Leave to simmer with the tarragon and reduce to a thin coating consistency, adding salt and pepper if necessary.

CHICKEN WITH PINE KERNELS

Serves 6.
Keeps 3 days under refrigeration.
Freeze 3 months.

Strewing the breast of the bird with fresh herbs and adding a crunch of pine kernels to the gravy quite transforms plain roast chicken into a dinner-party dish.

4-4½ lb (2-2.25 kg) roasting chicken
2 tbsp fresh lemon juice
1 eating apple
olive oil
sea salt
black pepper
12 shallots, peeled
2 tbsp chopped fresh mixed herbs
4 tbsp pine kernels
4 fl oz (125 ml/½ cup) each of dry white wine and chicken stock, or 8 fl oz (225 ml/1 cup) stock alone
2 teasp cornflour (cornstarch) mixed with 2 tbsp cold water
1 small bunch of parsley

Preheat the oven to Gas No. 5 (375°F/190°C). Pat the cavity of the bird dry, squeeze the lemon juice into it, insert the unpeeled quartered apple and carefully transfer the bird to a rack standing in a roasting tin, placing it breast-side down. Brush lightly with olive oil and sprinkle with ground sea salt and about 10 grinds of black pepper. Roast for 1 hour 20 minutes, basting every 20 minutes. Turn the bird over, breast-side up, and slip the shallots underneath the rack. Brush the breast lightly with olive oil, season again and strew with the chopped herbs. Roast for a further 40 minutes, basting once, until the chicken is a rich golden brown, and the juices run clear when the leg is pierced with a skewer. Lift the bird on to a carving dish and leave in a warm place. Remove the shallots with a slotted spoon and keep hot. Put the roasting tin on top of the stove and add the pine kernels, having sautéd them gently until golden brown. Drain off the fat from the dish and add the wine and stock with the cornflour. Bubble for 3 minutes, taste and reseason if necessary. Stir in the parsley. (Add a pinch of sugar if too acid.)

Portion or carve the bird and serve with the pine kernels and sauce. The golden-brown shallots can be served with the other vegetables.

VARIATION

CHICKEN WITH PINE KERNELS ON A BED OF NEW POTATOES AND SHALLOTS

2 lb (900 g) new potatoes, scrubbed
12 oz (350 g) shallots

Put the new potatoes in cold water to cover, add 1 teaspoon of salt and bring to the boil. Cook for 10 minutes, until barely tender. In the same water boil the shallots for 2 minutes. When cool enough to handle, strip off skin from the vegetables. 40 minutes before the chicken is ready, lift it off roasting dish and add vegetables. Put chicken back and continue roasting as described.

Put chicken on carving dish and keep hot, covered with foil. Put vegetables in a heatproof serving dish and leave to continue browning in the oven. Then brown pine kernels and make gravy as described above.

Chicken with Herbs and Spices

CHICKEN WITH A MANGO SAUCE

Serves 8. For 4–5 use 1 bird and half the quantity of sauce, but cook for the same length of time.
Leftovers keep 3 days under refrigeration.
Freeze 2 months.

The chicken is braised in a lightly spiced mango sauce.

2 x 3½–4 lb (1.75–2 kg) chickens
2 tbsp flour
½ teasp salt
½ teasp ground ginger
1 fat lemon
4 tbsp oil
nut of margarine
4 shallots
2 cloves of garlic
1 teasp freshly ground cumin
1-inch (2.5-cm) piece root ginger, finely chopped
10 fl oz (275 ml/1¼ cups) white wine
10 fl oz (275 ml/1¼ cups) chicken stock
1–2 mangoes (1–1¼ lb/450–575 g in total)
½ teasp salt
10 grinds of black pepper

For the garnish
1 medium mango
coriander or parsley

Dust the birds all over with the flour seasoned with the salt and ginger and insert the lemon cut in 8 pieces. Tie the birds' legs together. Fry over moderate heat in the hot oil until golden brown on all sides – about 15 minutes. Remove to a roasting tin large enough to hold the birds side by side. To the oil add a nut of margarine and cook the finely chopped shallots and garlic until soft and golden. Stir in the cumin, ginger, wine, stock and the peeled and coarsely chopped mangoes. Add the salt and pepper, stir well and bring to the boil, then pour around the chickens. Cover with foil and cook in a moderate oven, Gas No. 3 (325°F/160°C), for 2 hours, until a leg can be easily moved in the socket. Lift the birds from the tin and keep hot in a low oven.

Purée the contents of the roasting tin in a blender or food processor, thin with a little chicken stock if necessary, then reheat until bubbly and pour into a jug. Arrange the birds on a flat dish, garnish with the peeled and sliced mango and sprigs of herb, and serve with the sauce.

MARINATED CHICKEN GRILLED WITH PROVENÇALE HERBS

Serves 8 (for 4, use ½ quantities but same cooking time).
Keeps 3 days under refrigeration.
Freeze 3 months.

Serve hot or at room temperature.

This method produces wonderfully juicy birds. The combination of part-grilling and part-baking ensures that the chicken is thoroughly cooked.

2 x 3 lb (1.5 kg) chickens
3 cloves of garlic, crushed
2 teasp dried Herbes de Provence
5 tbsp fruity olive oil
salt
black pepper
8 shallots, peeled
4 juicy lemons, 2 sliced, 2 juiced
1 pack mixed herbs, chopped
2 tbsp chopped parsley
2 tbsp chopped fresh oregano
} *or 2–3 oz (50–75 g) fresh garden herbs*

5 hours in advance, stand each chicken on its back on a board and split in half down the backbone, using a long kitchen knife, then make a parallel cut and remove the bone altogether.

Flatten each half of the bird with the hand, then use a cutlet bat to beat it gently into an even layer. (Don't squash it *too* much.)

Mix the crushed garlic with the dried herbs and the oil. Season the birds on both sides with salt and black pepper. Halve the shallots and arrange in a roasting tin or grill pan large enough to hold the birds side by side. Brush each bird all over with a tablespoon of the flavoured oil, then cover with the lemon slices. Cover loosely with foil and leave in a cool place (if in the refrigerator, bring out 1 hour before cooking).

When ready to cook, preheat the grill at its highest setting. If you have a separate oven, heat it to Gas No. 10 (500°F/250°C) at the same time. Remove the lemon slices and reserve. Grill the chickens until golden - about 10 minutes - then turn and brush each one with a further tablespoon of oil. Continue to grill until the second side is golden brown. (If grill is in the oven, turn off and turn oven to highest setting or put on thermal grill.) Baste with the pan juices, then roast the chickens, breast up, in the oven for a further 15 minutes. Sprinkle with the chopped herbs and then the lemon juice and cover with the sliced lemons. Cook for a further 10-15 minutes, or until the birds are a rich brown and no pink can be seen when the thigh is nicked.

Cut each chicken in 4 (poultry shears make it easy). Arrange on a platter and spoon over the cooking juices and the shallots.

OVEN FRIED CHICKEN

Serves 6.
Freeze 3 months (cooked or raw).

These crunchy portions of chicken are coated with a mixture of crumbs and herbs and are equally delicious hot or cold. They are cooked with only 4 tablespoons of oil, yet are as crisp as if they had been deep-fried. They make excellent 'freezer-fillers' because they can be frozen either cooked or ready-coated and raw.

4 tbsp lemon juice
6 chicken portions or boneless breasts, skinned

For the coating
6 heaped tbsp coating crumbs or medium matzah meal
1 egg
4 tbsp sunflower oil
1 teasp salt
20 grinds of black pepper
3 teasp dried mixed herbs or Herbes de Provence (optional)
1 teasp paprika
¼ teasp garlic salt or ½ teasp garlic granules
rind of 1 lemon, finely grated

To marinate the chicken, 1 hour before cooking put the lemon juice into a flat dish, turn the chicken pieces in it, then leave. Turn once or twice during the hour.

Set the oven at Gas No. 6 (400°F/200°C). If matzah meal is used to coat the chicken, or if the coating crumbs are very pale in colour, spread them out on a baking sheet, put in the oven as it heats up and toast until they are golden brown (this gives a better colour to the cooked chicken).

Whisk the egg and oil together with the salt and pepper until well blended and then put in a shallow dish large enough to hold a portion of chicken. Mix the coating crumbs, herbs and seasonings in a dish of a similar size. Have ready a lightly greased oven tray large enough to hold the portions, well spaced, side by side. Lay each chicken joint in the egg mixture, using a pastry brush to coat it evenly, then roll it in the crumb mixture, again to coat evenly. Pat off any excess with the hands. Arrange on the baking sheet and cook for 40 minutes (30 minutes for the boneless breasts), until a rich brown. There is no need to turn the chicken as it will brown evenly on all sides. The chicken can be kept hot and crisp for up to 30 minutes in a warm oven, Gas No. ½ (250°F/120°C).

VARIATION

SESAME CHICKEN

Mix 6 heaped tablespoons of sesame seeds with the coating crumbs or meal.

MUSHROOM AND WINE SAUCE

Serves 6.
Leftovers can be refrigerated for 2 days.
Do not freeze.

This is an excellent sauce to serve with the Oven-fried or Poached Chicken.

1 oz (25 g/2 tbsp) margarine
4 shallots or the bulbs of 4 large spring onions (scallions), finely chopped
8 oz (225 g/2 cups) white button mushrooms, thinly sliced
4 tbsp medium-dry sherry
6 tbsp white wine
5 fl oz (150 ml/⅔ cup) chicken stock
2 teasp cornflour (cornstarch)
good pinch of salt
good pinch of nutmeg
good pinch of white pepper
juices from the chicken

Over moderate heat, melt the margarine in a medium-sized pan, add the shallots and cook, stirring once or twice, for 5 minutes, until they are softened and starting to turn colour. Add the sliced mushrooms and continue to cook until they too have softened, then add 3 tbsp of the sherry and cook until there is only 1 tablespoon of liquid left in the pan. Add the white wine and simmer gently, uncovered, for a further 10 minutes, then stir in the stock mixed with the cornflour (cornstarch) and seasonings. Simmer for 3 minutes, then add the rest of the sherry.

Chicken by the Joint

Dishes in which the chicken is jointed before it is cooked are especially convenient to serve, as no carving is required at the table. It is also useful to double quantities and freeze half in the sauce which always accompanies this type of dish. All chicken dishes with sauce reheat well. In fact, their flavour is often improved after 24 hours' refrigeration. However, the flavours do fade in the freezer.

Note All chicken casseroles can be reheated from cold in the microwave as follows: put in a microwave-safe dish, cover and cook on 80 per cent power for 8 minutes until bubbling.

CHICKEN PORTIONS EN CASSEROLE

It is useful to have a large, shallow, flameproof casserole or sauté pan in which the joints can first be browned, then cooked in the oven side by side. For large quantities, the portions can first be fried in the sauté pan and then transferred to a very large roasting tin, which can then be covered with foil.

Do not crowd the portions in the sauté pan or it will be difficult to brown them evenly on all sides, as they will give off too much steam.

Wine gives a mellow flavour to a sauce, but chicken stock can be used instead if preferred.

When *reheating* a casserole, bring it only to simmering point before serving, as recooking may cause the flesh to become dry or to fall apart.

For a low-fat diet remove the skin from the chicken joints, then arrange side by side in a lidded dish, season lightly with salt and black pepper, then cover with the sauce. Cover and cook as directed in the recipe.

CHICKEN HAWAII

Serves 4–6.
Keeps 2 days under refrigeration.
Freeze 2 months.

1 tbsp flour
2 teasp salt
pinch of white pepper
4–6 chicken joints, skinned
2 tbsp olive oil

For the sauce
1 medium onion, finely chopped
1 large yellow pepper, seeded, pith removed and cut in ½-inch (1.25-cm) squares
juice and fruit from 15½ oz (430 g) can unsweetened pineapple cubes or rings
9 fl oz (250 ml/1 cup plus 2 tbsp) strong chicken stock
pinch of salt
4 grinds of black pepper
½ teasp lemon juice
2 teasp cornflour (cornstarch) mixed to a cream with 2 tbsp chicken stock

Put seasoned flour in a bag and shake the chicken joints in it one at a time to coat. Fry them in the oil until a rich brown on both sides. Transfer to a casserole, cover and cook for 45 minutes at Gas No. 4 (350°F/180°C) in own juices. Meanwhile, make the sauce in the same pan. Sauté the onion and pepper in the remaining oil. When well softened – after about 5 minutes – add all the remaining ingredients. Simmer for 3 minutes, until thick and clear, then pour over the joints in the casserole. Cook a further 10 minutes, until the chicken is quite tender.

POULET SAUTÉ MARENGO

Serves 4–6.
Keeps 2 days under refrigeration.
Freeze 2 months.

2 tbsp flour
2 teasp salt
10 grinds of black pepper
4–6 chicken joints, skinned
2 tbsp olive oil
1 medium (5 oz/150 g) onion, finely chopped
4 fl oz (125 ml/½ cup) dry white wine
1 tbsp tomato purée
8 fl oz (225 ml/1 cup) chicken stock
1 clove of garlic, crushed
1 bay leaf
1 level teasp brown sugar
1 level teasp salt
10 grinds of black pepper
8 oz (225 g/2½ cups) tiny button mushrooms

Put the seasoned flour in a plastic bag. One at a time, shake each chicken portion in the flour until it has an even coating clinging to it. Heat the oil in a heavy frying pan and fry the coated chicken on all sides over moderate heat until it is golden brown. Lift out. In the same fat, fry the onion gently until golden brown. Add all the remaining ingredients (except the mushrooms) and bring gently to the boil. Transfer to an oven-to-table casserole and add the browned joints. Cook in a moderate oven, Gas No. 4 (350°F/180°C), for no more than 45 minutes, by which time the chicken will be tender but still moist. If the chicken must be kept hot, simply turn the oven down to its lowest temperature and turn up again 5 minutes before serving. 10 minutes before the chicken is cooked, add the raw sliced mushrooms.

POULET PAYSANNE

Serves 4–6.
Keeps 2 days under refrigeration.
Leftovers freeze for 3 months.

French country cooks have a marvellous way of braising chicken legs on a bed of potatoes – and as the dark meat works out at around 25 per cent cheaper than breasts, it makes a fairly economical as well as an easy mid-week meal.

Have the legs divided into the drumstick and the thigh so that they'll fit snugly into a flameproof casserole. Old potatoes can be used instead of new but they'll need cutting in 1-inch (2.5-cm) cubes before cooking.

4–6 chicken legs
3 tbsp olive oil
1 teasp salt
15 grinds of black pepper
1½ lb (675 g) small new potatoes
2 teasp salt
1 rounded tbsp margarine
2 teasp olive oil
1 medium onion
1 bay leaf
1 teasp cornflour
5 fl oz (150 ml/⅔ cup) chicken stock or leftover gravy
3 teasp chopped fresh tarragon or parsley

Preheat the oven to Gas No. 4 (350°F/180°C). Dry the joints well, then sauté in the olive oil until golden brown on all sides. Remove from the pan and drain on paper towels, then sprinkle with the salt and black pepper. Cover the potatoes with cold water, add 2 teaspoons salt, bring slowly to the boil and simmer for 2 minutes, then drain well. Meanwhile, to the oil remaining in the sauté pan add the margarine and the extra 2 teaspoons of olive oil. Sauté the finely chopped onion and the potatoes until golden, keeping them moving in the pan so that they brown evenly. Lightly salt the potatoes then lay the chicken joints on top, tuck in the bay leaf, cover and transfer to the oven. Cook for 30–35 minutes, until the juices run clear when a joint is pierced. Lift out the chicken on to a dish and surround with the potatoes, then keep hot in the oven turned down to Gas No. 1 (275°F/140°C). Add the cornflour mixed with the stock or gravy to the juices in the dish and bubble until slightly thickened. Stir in the chopped herbs and pour over the joints.

CHICKEN IZMIR STYLE

Serves 6–8.
Keeps 2 days under refrigeration.
Freeze 3 months.

The sautéd aubergines (eggplants) give this sauce its distinctive rich, smooth flavour - a perfect dish for a spring dinner party.

1 lb (450 g) aubergines, unpeeled and cut in ¾-inch (2-cm) cubes
1 tbsp salt
6 tbsp sunflower oil
6–8 chicken joints, skinned
1 heaped tbsp flour
½ teasp salt
10 grinds of black pepper
1 tbsp olive oil
1 large onion, chopped
1 clove of garlic, chopped
1 pint (575 ml/2½ cups) vegetable stock
3 level tbsp tomato purée
1 teasp salt
2 teasp brown sugar
10 grinds of black pepper
½ teasp each of cinnamon, cumin and ground coriander

Preheat the oven to Gas No. 3 (325°F/160°C).

Place the aubergine cubes in a bowl, cover with cold water and add 1 tablespoon of salt. Leave for half an hour and then squeeze out as much moisture as possible, or use a salad spinner. Put the 6 tablespoons of oil in a large frying pan and heat for 3 minutes. Add the aubergine, cover and sauté on all sides until golden brown. Lift out and drain on kitchen paper.

Dry the chicken joints well and coat with the seasoned flour. In an oven-to-table casserole or sauté pan, fry the portions in the hot olive oil until they are a rich brown on all sides, then lift out and drain on paper towels to remove any surface fat.

In the same oil, gently sauté the chopped onion and garlic until they turn a rich brown. Keep the pan lid on for 5 minutes to soften them in the steam, then remove it to finish the browning. Add the stock, tomato purée and seasonings. Stir well to release any tasty crispy bits adhering to the base of the dish, then lay the chicken on top and surround with the fried aubergines. Bring to simmering point.

Immediately cover and transfer to the oven. Bake for 50 minutes.

WINTER BARBECUED CHICKEN

Serves 6–8.
Keeps 2 days under refrigeration.
Freeze 3 months.

The chicken is cooked in a tangy sweet-and-sour tomato sauce.

6–8 chicken joints
3 tbsp olive oil or sunflower oil
1 onion, finely chopped
2 level teasp salt
¼ teasp freshly ground black pepper
2–3 level tbsp fine brown sugar (Barbados is nice)
2 teasp prepared mustard
2–3 teasp light soy sauce
juice of ½ large lemon (about 2 tbsp)
1 x 5 oz (150 g) can tomato purée, diluted with 2 cans water and a chicken stock-cube.

Dry the chicken joints well, then fry in the hot oil until golden all over. Remove to a casserole.

Sauté the onion in the remaining fat until soft and golden, then add all the remaining ingredients. Simmer for 5 minutes, then pour over the chicken. Cover and bake in a moderate oven, Gas No. 4 (350°F/180°C), for 1 hour.

This dish is better if refrigerated overnight then heated through until bubbly in a moderate oven.

CHICKEN SAUTÉ IN WHITE WINE AND MUSHROOM SAUCE

Serves 4–5.
Keeps 3 days under refrigeration.
Freeze 3 months.

A simple dish that gains much of its flavour from the fruitiness of the wine.

4 lb (2 kg) chicken, cut into 6–8 medium or 4–5 large joints
3 tbsp sunflower oil or olive oil
1 very large (10 oz/275 g) onion, finely chopped
8 oz (225 g/2½ cups) button mushrooms
1 level tbsp flour
½ bottle fruity dry white wine
salt
pepper
1 tbsp oil

Joint then skin the bird and dry well. In a large, heavy frying pan or casserole (it must be very wide), heat the oil, add the onion and cook uncovered for 10 minutes, until soft and really golden brown. Add the mushrooms (cut in 4 if larger than a mouthful) and mix well to coat with onion and fat, then add the chicken joints. Turn well in the mixture and cook for 10–15 minutes, until a golden brown on both sides. Sprinkle with the flour and blend in well, then add the wine. Bring to the boil, season well with salt and black pepper, stir sauce, cover and simmer until chicken is tender. This will probably take about 45 minutes (1 hour in the oven at Gas No. 3/325°F/160°C). However, the dish reheats very easily.

Note Before serving, the chicken can be lifted out and the sauce thickened by bubbling for a few moments.

POLLO IN PEPITORIA
(*Chicken with White Wine and Ground Almond Sauce*)

Serves 6–8.
Keeps 2 days under refrigeration.
Do not freeze.
Best reheated in the microwave.

The use of ground almonds as a thickener was much used in medieval times, before the invention of a roux thickener. It was probably introduced into Spanish cuisine by the Moors. Penelope Casas, the authority on Spanish food, claims that a kosher bird (a mature fowl) makes the best pepitoria - that is, a chicken dish in which eggs have been used.

2 oz (50 g) flour
1 teasp salt
15 grinds of black pepper
6–8 chicken breasts, skinned but with wing attached
3 tbsp light olive oil or sunflower oil
1 large (8 oz/225 g) onion, finely chopped
1 bay leaf
10 fl oz (275 ml/1¼ cups) dry white wine plus
10 fl oz (275 ml/1¼ cups) good chicken stock, or
1 pint (575 ml/2½ cups) chicken stock
2½ oz (65 g/⅓ cup) ground almonds
2 hard-boiled egg yolks
1 fat clove of garlic, halved
¼ teasp turmeric or powdered saffron

For the garnish
1 oz (25 g/¼ cup) slivered or flaked almonds, toasted
1 hard-boiled egg, grated and mixed with 1 tbsp chopped parsley

The chicken can be fried and the sauce prepared 1½ hours before serving if wished.

Put the flour, salt and pepper into a plastic bag and shake the breasts in it, one at a time, until evenly coated.

Fry them in the hot oil until a rich golden brown. Drain on kitchen paper and transfer to a baking tin large enough to hold them in a single layer.

To make the sauce, sauté the onion in the same oil, covering the pan, until a rich gold and beginning to 'melt'. Add the bay leaf and wine and bubble uncovered for 3 minutes to concentrate the flavour. Then add the stock, cover and leave to simmer gently for 15 minutes.

Put the ground almonds, hard-boiled egg yolks, garlic and turmeric or saffron in the bowl of a food processor. Process until pasty, then gradually add the simmering liquid, discarding the bay leaf, and process until a smooth, creamy sauce is formed. Return to the sauce pan, stir well and leave covered until just before serving.

To complete the cooking, preheat the oven to Gas No. 5 (375°F/190°C) and bake the chicken, uncovered, for 20 minutes. Reheat the sauce gently until simmering. Arrange the chicken breasts on a heated platter and coat with the hot sauce. Scatter with the toasted almonds and the egg and parsley mixture.

BIBLICAL CHICKEN

Serves 6–8.
Keeps 2 days under refrigeration.
Freeze 2 months.

After closer acquaintance with the superb boneless chicken breasts that are so easy to find, I have discovered that the briefer the cooking period the better. So to produce a tender yet juicy breast I fry it lightly on both sides and then, after deglazing the pan, simply leave it to soak in the sauce for 1 or 2 hours. It then needs only bringing slowly back to simmering point in the sauce before serving - what could be more convenient for a dinner party? To cut almonds into slivers, first soften the blanched nuts for 10 minutes in boiling water, then dry well before cutting into strips and toasting or sautéing until golden.

6–8 part-boned chicken breasts, trimmed of rib-cage and skinned
2 tbsp flour
1 teasp salt
10 grinds of black pepper
2 oz (50 g/¼ cup) margarine and 1 tbsp sunflower oil or olive oil
3 oz (75 g/¾ cup) slivered almonds

For the sauce
10 fl oz (275 ml/1¼ cups) fairly dry white wine plus 5 fl oz (150 ml/⅔ cup) good chicken stock, or 15 fl oz (425 ml/2 cups) chicken stock
5 fl oz (150 ml/⅔ cup) orange juice
2 teasp grated lemon rind
1 level tbsp liquid honey
3 tbsp raisins (preferably muscatel)
3-inch (7.5-cm) cinnamon stick
2 teasp cornflour slaked with 1 tbsp cold water or chicken stock
2 small oranges, peel and pith removed then cut in sections

Take each breast in turn and flatten it gently between the hands then coat with the seasoned flour. In a large sauté pan, heat the fats until the foam subsides, then immediately add the almond slivers and cook gently until golden brown. Drain on a paper towel. Add the chicken breasts to the hot fats - probably in 2 batches if the pan is small - and cook on each side for about 3 minutes, or until a golden colour. Remove from the pan and pour away any excess fat without discarding the savoury brown bits at the bottom.

Now add the wine to the pan, stirring well, and bubble for 3 minutes to intensify the flavour, then add the stock, orange juice, lemon rind, honey, raisins and cinnamon stick. Bring the sauce to the boil, add the chicken breasts in a single layer, spoon the liquid over them, then cover the pan and take it off the heat. Just before serving, bring the sauce slowly back to the simmer, add the slaked cornflour and bubble for 3 minutes. Nick a breast to check that there's no sign of pinkness; if there is, bubble 3 more minutes. Lift the breasts out and arrange on a warm plate. Add salt and pepper if necessary, then spoon the sauce over the breasts and decorate the dish with the orange sections and the toasted almonds. Serve accompanied by plain boiled Basmati rice or new potatoes.

Note If the pan won't hold all the chicken breasts in a single layer, arrange them side by side in a roasting tin, pour over the hot sauce and leave covered with foil. To reheat, cook covered at Gas No. 4 (350°F/180°C) for 25 minutes, or until bubbly.

CHICKEN BREASTS IN A HERBED TOMATO SAUCE

Serves 4.
Keeps 2 days under refrigeration.
Freezes 2 months.

A handful of herbs and seasonings, a can of tomatoes and some boneless chicken breasts can be transformed into this deliciously scented low-fat main course in barely 15 minutes. Don't stint on the herbs or the garlic

– they give what is really a simple dish its very special flavour. The wine isn't essential, but if you've the bottom of a bottle nestling at the back of the fridge do tip it into the pan – it will give the sauce an extra depth of flavour.

1 tbsp extra virgin olive oil
½ medium onion
3 cloves of garlic
1 x 14 oz (400 g) can tomatoes in tomato juice
4 fl oz (125 g/⅔ cup) dry white wine or chicken stock
½ teasp sea salt
15 grinds of black pepper
1 tbsp each chopped fresh basil and oregano (or marjoram)
2 tbsp chopped parsley
4 boned and skinned chicken breasts

In an 8-inch (20-cm) lidded sauté pan, put the oil, finely chopped onion and garlic, cover and cook over moderate heat until softened and golden. Add the coarsely chopped tomatoes with their juice, the wine, seasonings and herbs, stir well and then simmer uncovered for 3–4 minutes to concentrate the flavours. Add the breasts, cover and simmer very gently for 5 minutes, then turn and simmer for 5 minutes more. Nick with a knife and check that all pinkness has disappeared. If the sauce is at all watery, lift out the breasts and keep warm, then simmer the sauce until of coating consistency. Serve accompanied by rice or pasta.

POULET VALLÉE D'AUGE

Serves 6–8.
Keeps 2 days under refrigeration.
Freeze 3 months.

A marvellous combination of sweet and tender chicken with tangy Cox's apples that elevates a chicken casserole to dinner-party status. The Calvados can be omitted, but it does impart a superb flavour.

6–8 part-boned chicken breasts, skinned
2 heaped tbsp flour seasoned with 1 teasp salt and ¼ teasp white pepper
1 oz (25 g/2 tbsp) margarine
1 tbsp sunflower oil
4 oz (125 g) shallots or large spring onion bulbs (scallions), finely chopped
4 tbsp Calvados
20 fl oz (575 ml/2½ cups) strong dry cider
10 fl oz (275 ml/1¼ cups) good chicken stock
3 Cox's Orange Pippins, peeled, cored and roughly chopped
1 large sprig of parsley
1 small bay leaf
1 tbsp light brown soft sugar

For the garnish
2 Cox's Orange Pippins
1 oz (25 g/2 tbsp) margarine
2 teasp caster sugar

Preheat the oven to Gas No. 2 (300°F/150°C). Skin the breasts and remove all visible fat, then toss them 1 at a time in a plastic bag holding the seasoned flour. In a large sauté or frying pan, sauté the breasts in the hot fats over moderate heat until golden brown on all sides – don't crowd the pan or the breasts will steam rather than brown. As each joint turns colour, drain it on a paper towel. Add the shallots as the last breasts are browning, cooking until they are softened and golden.

Return all the breasts to the pan. Put the Calvados in a small pan and heat for 2 or 3 minutes, ignite with a match, pour over the joints, then partially cover the pan so that all the alcohol doesn't evaporate. Add the cider, stock and chopped apples to the pan, together with the parsley, bay leaf and brown sugar. Bring to simmering point, then cover and transfer to the oven. Cook for 35 minutes, or until the joints feel very tender. Lift the chicken out on to an oval serving dish, cover with foil and keep hot in the oven turned down to Gas No. 1 (275°F/140°C) for up to 30 minutes.

Purée half the sauce – both solids and liquids – in a food processor or blender, then return to the remainder in the pan and simmer until the flavour intensifies and the sauce thickens to coating consistency. Just before serving, spoon over the joints, coating them completely, and garnish with the apple slices.

To prepare the garnish This can be prepared earlier and reheated. Peel, core and cut each apple into 8 equal segments. In the microwave, arrange in a shallow dish, dot with the fat and sprinkle with the sugar. Cook on 100 per cent power for 3 minutes, turn over and cook another 1-2 minutes, until the slices are tender. Alternatively, sauté the apples in the fat until tender, sprinkling with the sugar as they cook.

PAELLA VALENCIANA

Serves 4.
Keeps 2 days under refrigeration.
Freeze 3 months.

Paella, the national dish of Spain, is usually a 'no-go' area for Jewish cooks as it traditionally contains shellfish. But in this version, which comes from Valencia, on the east coast of Spain, I have substituted stuffed green olives to give extra piquancy. The correct condition of the rice - every grain separate yet creamy rather than dry - is achieved by using either a true Valencia rice or the Italian risotto rice, which is sometimes called Arborio. Sunflower oil may be used instead of olive oil, but the latter gives a fine and most authentic flavour.

In Spain paella is cooked in great twin-handled steel pans, which can measure 16 inches (40 cm) across, but a large, heavy frying pan is equally efficient if not as stylish.

5 tbsp olive oil
4 bone-in chicken breasts (2 lb/900 g total weight)
1 medium red pepper
2 cloves of garlic
1 'beef' tomato or 2 large canned tomatoes
2 pints (1.25 l/5 cups) weak chicken stock
½ teasp turmeric or powdered saffron
12 oz (350 g/2 cups) rice
8 oz (225 g) frozen peas
4 oz (125 g/1 cup) or small jar pimento-stuffed olives
1 teasp salt
15 grinds of black pepper

Heat the oil in a paella pan or 10-inch (25 cm) frying pan, then add the well-dried chicken breasts and cook over moderate heat for 5 minutes, turning so that they cook to an even gold. Add the finely diced, deseeded pepper and the crushed garlic and cook for a further 5 minutes, until they take on a little colour. Then add the peeled and diced tomatoes and cook, stirring, for a further 3 minutes. Pour in the stock with the saffron or turmeric and simmer for 15 minutes, turning the chicken once or twice. Add the rice to the pan and mix gently with the contents, then cook rather more quickly for 10 minutes, stirring occasionally. Add the peas for a further 5 minutes. Just before serving, stir in the whole stuffed olives and adjust seasoning. The dish can be kept hot (in the pan from which it is served) in a slow moderate oven, Gas No. 3 (325°F/160°C), for up to 20 minutes.

SIRKE PAPRIKASH
(*Paprika Chicken*)

Serves 6-8.
Keeps 3 days under refrigeration.
Freezes 2 months.

This is the true Hungarian recipe. The quality of the paprika is the deciding factor in this simple but wonderfully flavoursome dish, so buy the best quality you can find. If you go into a shop in Budapest look for 'kulonleges' (special) paprika, which is the finest in quality and also the most finely ground. Its colour is an intense red, it is pleasantly spicy without being pungent and it has virtually no sharpness in its nature - that depends on the ratio of peppery seeds to sweet flesh used to produce the powder.

2 x 3½ lb (1.5 kg) chickens, backbone removed and each cut in 4, or 8 chicken portions on the bone, lightly salted
3 tbsp sunflower oil
2 medium onions, finely chopped
4 tbsp Hungarian paprika (preferably 'kulonleges')
10 fl oz (275 ml/1¼ cups) chicken stock
4 medium green or red peppers cut into fine (¼-inch/0.5 cm) strips
1 x 14 oz (400 g) can chopped tomatoes
2 teasp cornflour slaked with 2 tbsp cold water
1 teasp salt
10 grinds of black pepper

Dry the chicken pieces with paper towels, then sauté in the hot oil until golden. Remove. In the remaining oil, gently cook the onion (covered) for 10–15 minutes, until softened and golden. Stir in the paprika and chicken stock and cook for a further 2 minutes. Add the chicken (and any juices), the pepper strips and the tomatoes. Cover and cook very gently for 25–30 minutes, until the chicken is cooked through – there will be no sign of pinkness when a piece is nicked with a sharp knife. Lift the chicken pieces on to a warm platter. Add the cornflour mixed with water to the pan. Simmer for 3 minutes, or until thickened to a coating consistency, add the salt and pepper, taste and adjust the seasoning if necessary. Spoon the sauce over the chicken and serve.

Boneless Chicken Breast

KHORESH PORTAGAL
(*Chicken in a Persian Fruited Sauce*)

Serves 6.
Keeps 2 days under refrigeration.
Do not freeze.

Gently does it when cooking this exquisite dish (adapted from the medieval Persian cuisine) in which cubes of chicken-breast meat are simmered in a lightly spiced orange sauce on the lowest possible light until they are meltingly tender. Serve the 'khoresh' for a luncheon or supper party piled on a platter atop the wonderful Chello Rice (see p. 218). It is equally delicious served at room temperature.

3 tbsp olive oil or sunflower oil
1½–2 lb (675 g–1 kg) well-dried chicken-breast meat, cut in 1-inch (2.5 cm) cubes
1½ teasp paprika
1½ teasp cinnamon
¼ teasp nutmeg
½ teasp salt
8 grinds of black pepper
10 fl oz (275 ml/1¼ cups) chicken stock
1 oz (25 g/2 tbsp) margarine
1 teasp oil
1 large (8 oz/225 g) onion, finely sliced
3 very large or 5 medium oranges, peeled and cut in pith-free segments
3 oz (75 g/⅓ cup) granulated sugar
4 tbsp white wine vinegar or cider vinegar
1½ teasp cornflour (cornstarch) mixed to a cream with 1 tbsp water (optional)

Heat the oil and fry the chicken over medium heat in a lidded sauté pan to seal it – it will turn white on all sides. Sprinkle on the spices and seasonings, mix well, cook a further 2 minutes and then add enough stock barely to cover the chicken. Cover and cook on the lowest possible light (with the stock just bubbling) until tender and white all the way through – about 10 minutes. Meanwhile, slowly sauté the onion in the margarine and oil until a rich deep gold (don't over-brown as it will impair the flavour). Put the oranges in another small pan, sprinkle with the sugar and vinegar and cook gently (uncovered) until the fruit is sitting in a thick syrup. Arrange the onion and its juices on top of the chicken, followed by the oranges and their syrup. Reheat very gently, covered, for 10 minutes. If the sauce seems thin, stir in cornflour mix and simmer till clear – a further 3 minutes. May be reheated.

CHELLO RICE

Serves 6–8.
Keeps 3 days under refrigeration.
Freeze for 3 months.

12 oz (350 g/2 cups) Basmati rice
2 tbsp salt
2 tbsp oil plus 2 tbsp extra
1 tbsp water

Soak the rice in cold water for 30 minutes, then strain and rinse thoroughly under the tap until the water runs clear. Bring a large heavy pan or casserole of water to the boil with the salt. Add the rice and cook uncovered, bubbling steadily, for 7 minutes, or until a grain feels almost tender but still has a little resistance at the centre when chewed. Turn the rice into the strainer and rinse thoroughly under the hot tap, then drain well (this removes excess salt).

Put the first quantity of oil into the pan with the water and heat until it steams, then spoon in the rice and cover with the second amount of oil. Finally cover the rice, first with a dry tea-towel (tucking it in well) and then with the lid. Allow the rice to steam over a very low heat for 20 minutes.

Spoon the rice on to a warm platter, then loosen the crisp layer sticking to the bottom of the pan and stir that into the rice.

CHICKEN SATAY

Serves 4–6.
Keeps 2 days under refrigeration.
Do not freeze.

Only 1 tablespoonful of oil for 4 people is needed to cook these Indonesian-style chicken kebabs. The secret lies in the spicy marinade which keeps each chunk of chicken juicy as it grills to an appetizing golden brown. The delicious peanut sauce is traditional but for a low-fat diet a squeeze of lemon juice can be used instead.

1½–2 lb (675 g–2 kg) boned and skinned chicken-breast meat

For the marinade
1 teasp minced dried onion
1 crushed clove of garlic
2 tbsp light soy sauce
pinch of Cayenne pepper
1 teasp ground coriander
1 teasp ground ginger
1 tbsp lemon juice
1 tbsp sunflower oil

For the sauce
2 teasp oil
1 clove of garlic
2 shallots or ¼ onion
¼ teasp Cayenne pepper
½ teasp salt
10 fl oz (275 ml/1¼ cups) water
4 oz (125 g/½ cup) smooth peanut butter
1 tbsp lemon juice
1½ teasp medium brown sugar

At least 2 hours (or the night before), whisk all the marinade ingredients together and pour over the chicken, which should be cut in roughly 1-inch (2.5-cm) cubes and arranged in a shallow dish. Leave at room temperature for 2 hours, basting once or twice. (Refrigerate at this point if not to be cooked at once.)

When ready to cook, heat the grill and divide the chicken pieces between 8–10 skewers, each about 8 inches (20 cm) long. Grill the kebabs for 6–7 minutes, turning once or twice, or until just cooked through. (Test by cutting a chunk of chicken in half – there should be no sign of pinkness.) They can also be thermal-grilled in the oven for about the same time.

While the kebabs are cooking make the sauce as follows. Put the oil in a small pan and add the garlic and roughly chopped onion (put through a garlic crusher), the Cayenne and salt. Fry for about 30 seconds to bring out the flavour, then add the water all at once and bring to the boil. Add the peanut butter, lemon juice and sugar, stir well and continue to boil and stir for 3-4 minutes, until the sauce is thickened to a coating consistency. Taste and add salt if necessary.

Serve the grilled satay on a bed of rice and coat with the sauce.

CERKES TAVUGU
(*Circassian Chicken in Pastry Cases*)

Serves 6–8.
Filling keeps 2 days under refrigeration.
Freeze raw pastry or ready-to-bake cases 1 month, baked cases 2 months.

This Turkish dish (made originally by Circassian slaves of the Ottoman Empire) has an interesting sauce which uses the old Moorish thickener of bread and nuts. It is traditionally served on a bed of rice, but it makes a delicious filling for pastry cases, served either as a starter or on a cold buffet.

For the pastry boats
8 oz (225 g/2 cups) plain (all-purpose) flour
pinch of salt
2 teasp icing sugar
5 oz (150 g/⅔ cup) firm margarine cut in 1-inch (2.5-cm) chunks
3 tbsp cold water (4 if mixed by hand)

For the chicken filling
8 oz (225 g) wings or giblets
water to cover contents of pan (about 1¼ pints/725 ml/3 cups)
2 stalks of celery, sliced
1 medium carrot, sliced
½ onion
1 teasp salt
10 grinds of black pepper
1 lb (450 g) skinned chicken-breast meat

For the sauce
2 slices from a large white loaf plus a little stock to moisten
6–8 fl oz (150–200 ml/¾–1 cup) chicken stock
4 oz (125 g/1 cup) shelled walnut halves
1 small clove of garlic

For the salad garnish
2 medium carrots
1 small piece of mouli (white radish)
sweetened vinegar dressing (see below)

For the garnish
2 teasp walnut oil
¼ teasp paprika
6–8 Cape gooseberries

To make the pastry boats By hand, make as for shortcrust pastry. With a food processor, process all the dry ingredients and the fat until no pieces larger than a small pea can be seen on the surface. Add the water and process only until dry ingredients look slightly moist. Turn out into a bowl, gather into a ball, knead gently until smooth, then flatten until 1 inch (2.5 cm) thick. Wrap in clingfilm (saranwrap) and chill for 1 hour.

Roll out to fit 16 small or 8 large boat-shaped or tart cases. Prick thoroughly all over, then refreeze for 15 minutes. Bake in a quick oven, Gas No. 7 (425°F/220°C), for 8 minutes, then reprick if puffy and bake for a further 5 minutes, until golden brown. Allow to cool.

To cook the chicken Put the wings or giblets into a pan with the vegetables, herbs and seasonings, add the water and bring to the boil, then cover and simmer for 30 minutes. Add the chicken breasts, and simmer, covered, for a further 10 minutes, until the centre of the chicken has lost any sign of pinkness. Leave to cool in the stock for 30 minutes, then lift out and reduce the stock to 10 fl oz (275 ml/1¼ cups) and strain, discarding the vegetables. Cut the chicken into strips about 2 x ½ inches (5 x 1 cm), and put in a bowl.

To make the sauce Put the decrusted bread in a bowl and just cover with stock. Put the walnuts in the food processor with the well-squeezed bread and the garlic and process until it becomes a smooth paste. Gradually add enough of the remaining stock to produce a thick coating sauce. Season with salt and pepper if necessary. Stir the sauce into the chicken to coat it evenly. Leave until required.

To make the salad garnish Grate the vegetables and moisten with a dressing made by dissolving 1 tablespoon of caster sugar in 1 tablespoon of boiling water, then stir in 2 tablespoons of white wine vinegar, a pinch of salt and 5 grinds of black pepper. Refrigerate the garnish for several hours.

To serve Divide the chicken salad between the pastry cases and sprinkle each with a few drops of walnut oil and dust with a little paprika. Serve with a little heap of the salad and garnish with a Cape gooseberry.

What's Sauce for the Chicken

A variety of interesting and satisfying dishes can be made from a savoury mixture of cooked chicken combined with a well-seasoned sauce (turkey can be used in exactly the same way). These include Chicken Feuilleté, Chicken Plate pie and Chicken Blintzes (see below and p. 221).

CHICKEN AND MUSHROOM FILLING

Keeps 1 day under refrigeration.
Do not freeze.

8 oz (225 g) tiny button mushrooms, stalks removed
4 oz (125 g) haricots verts (optional)
2 teasp sesame oil
1 tbsp sunflower oil
½ teasp salt
8 grinds of black pepper
12 oz (350 g) cooked chicken, cut in bite-sized pieces
2 shallots or 4 spring onion bulbs (scallions), finely chopped
1 oz (25 g/2 tbsp) margarine
2 tbsp flour
5 fl oz (150 ml/⅔ cup) each strong chicken stock and dry white wine
good pinch of nutmeg
⅛ teasp white pepper
½ teasp salt
1 tbsp chopped fresh parsley

Stir-fry the mushrooms and haricots verts in the oils for 3–4 minutes, or until barely tender. Season with the first ½ teaspoon of salt and the black pepper, then turn into a bowl with the chicken.

Sauté the onion in the fat until soft and golden, then stir in the flour, followed by the stock, wine, nutmeg, white pepper and the other ½ teaspoon of salt, whisking constantly until thickened. Bubble for 3 minutes, then add the parsley and mix with the chicken, stirring gently. Allow to cool.

CHICKEN FEUILLETÉ

Serves 6.
Serve freshly baked.

A slice of the feuilleton makes a delicious informal starter. Serve it on a long narrow plate and portion at the table.

1 lb (450 g) puff pastry
1 recipe Chicken and Mushroom filling (see above)
1 egg yolk mixed with 1 teasp water
2 tbsp sesame seeds

Divide the pastry into 2 and roll each half into a rectangle measuring approximately 14 x 8 inches (35 x 20 cm). The pastry should be thin. Lay 1 rectangle on a baking tray and spread with the filling, leaving 1 inch (2.5 cm) of pastry clear all the way round. Dampen this margin with cold water, then lay the second rectangle carefully on top. Seal the pastry all the way round by pressing down on it with the side of the hand, then flake the edges with the back of a knife blade. Make cuts through the top layer at 2-inch (5-cm) intervals to allow steam to escape. Chill until ready to bake. (The feuilleton can now be refrigerated for up to 6 hours.)

Preheat the oven to Gas No. 8 (450°F/230°C). Paint the egg yolk and water glaze all over the top of the feuilleton and scatter with the sesame seeds. Bake for 15 minutes, then turn the temperature down to Gas No. 6 (400°F/200°C) for a further 15–20 minutes, when the feuilleton should be well risen, crisp to the touch and richly browned. Serve in slices.

CHICKEN PLATE PIE

Serves 4–5.
Leftovers keep 1 day under refrigeration.

This is a family version of the feuilleton.

8 oz (225 g) pack frozen puff pastry
1 recipe Chicken and Mushroom Filling (see p. 220)
beaten egg

Thaw the pastry and cut in half, then roll out to fit the base of a 9-inch (23-cm) shallow pie plate. Roll the second half slightly larger to fit the top. Spoon the chicken filling into the crust and cover with the pastry lid, pressing the edges firmly together. A little beaten egg (or yolk) brushed on the top will give a beautiful glaze. Bake the pie in a hot oven, Gas No. 8 (450°F/230°C), for 20 minutes. Serve hot.

CHICKEN BLINTZES

Makes 12; serves 6.
Empty crêpes freeze 3 months.
Do not freeze filled blintzes as sauce may separate, but they can be refrigerated ready for frying for up to 24 hours.

For the batter

4 oz (125 g/1 cup) plain (all-purpose) flour
2 level teasp salt
2 eggs
2 tbsp sunflower oil
8 fl oz (225 ml/1 cup) water

For the filling

1 recipe Chicken and Mushroom filling (see p. 220)

To make the batter By blender or food processor, process all the ingredients together for 30 seconds. Use after 10 minutes.

By hand, sift the flour and salt into a bowl. Make a well. Drop in the eggs and start stirring in the surrounding flour. Add the oil and water gradually, to make a smooth batter. When mixture is thin, beat with a rotary whisk until covered with tiny bubbles. Put aside for 1 hour.

To cook the crêpes Heat a 7-inch (17.5-cm) crêpe or omelette pan with a teaspoon of oil until you can feel the heat on your hand held 2 inches (5 cm) above the pan. Wipe out the pan using a pad of kitchen paper. Put the batter in a jug. Pour a thin coating into the frying pan, then immediately pour the excess back into the jug – there should be just a thin layer in the pan. Cook over moderate heat until sides curl from the pan, the top surface is dry and the underneath is golden. Turn out on to greaseproof or silicone paper. Smear the pan again with oil and repeat frying until all the batter is used. Don't stack pancakes on top of each other until they have stopped steaming, then stack and cover with foil until needed.

To fill the blintzes Have ready the cooked chicken and mushroom filling. Take a crêpe with the brown side uppermost. Put a spoonful of filling on it, fold over the bottom and then the two sides like a parcel, and roll it over, sealing it with the edge at the bottom. 10 minutes before dinner, fry the pancakes until golden brown in a pan covered to a depth of ¼ inch (0.5 cm) with hot oil.

Note To avoid last-minute frying when cooking a larger quantity for a crowd, set oven at Gas No. 7 (425°F/220°C), and arrange blintzes side by side on greased trays, leaving ½ inch (1 cm) between them. Pour over 3 fl oz (75 ml/⅓ cup) of hot oil and bake until crisp and golden brown - 10-15 minutes.

CRÊPES PRINCESSE

Makes 12 crepes; serves 6-8.
Complete dish keeps 1 day under refrigeration.
Freeze 1 week.

A problem that so often faces the Jewish cook when converting a recipe from the general cuisine - how to make a 'creamy' sauce without milk - is solved rather neatly in this splendid recipe by using egg yolks to lighten a sauce made with chicken stock alone. What's more, the extra chicken flavour makes for a richer-tasting sauce with which to coat pancakes stuffed with a juicy mixture of tarragon-flavoured chicken and mushrooms. Serve the crêpes either as a first course before a cold main dish or as a light main course for a buffet or supper party. The completed dish can be prepared up to 24 hours in advance and then only needs a short time in a hot oven to bring it to bubbling point.

For the crêpe batter
4 oz (125 g/1 cup) plain (all-purpose) flour
2 eggs
1 oz (25 g/2 tbsp) margarine, melted, or 2 tbsp sunflower oil
½ teasp salt
8 fl oz (225 ml/1 cup) water
1 tbsp finely snipped chives

For the chicken filling
2 shallots or bulbs from a very small bunch of spring onions (scallions), finely chopped
1 oz (25 g/2 tbsp) sunflower oil, margarine or chicken-flavoured vegetable fat
1 lb (450 g) brown cap mushrooms, sliced
4 tbsp Amontillado sherry
½ teasp salt
speck of white pepper
2 teasp chopped fresh tarragon
10 oz (275 g) cooked chicken breast fillets (approx. 1 lb/450 g raw)

For the sauce
1½ oz (40 g/3 tbsp) margarine
1½ oz 40 g/6 tbsp) flour
1 pint (575 ml/2½ cups) good chicken stock
½ teasp salt
speck of white pepper
½ teasp ground nutmeg
2 egg yolks

For the topping
2 tbsp each of fairly coarse dried breadcrumbs and flaked hazelnuts, mixed together
1 oz (25 g/2 tbsp) margarine

To make the crêpes Process all the ingredients in a blender or food processor until smooth and covered with tiny bubbles - about 30 seconds. Pour into a jug and leave to settle for 10 minutes.

To cook the crêpes Heat a 7-inch (17.5-cm) crêpe or omelette pan with a teaspoon of oil until you can feel the heat on your hand held 2 inches (5 cm) above the pan, then wipe out the pan with kitchen paper. Spoon approximately ⅓ of a ladle of batter into the pan and swirl it around to cover the bottom in a thin, even layer. Cook over moderate heat until golden brown underneath. Turn and cook the second side until golden. Turn on to a board covered with silicone or greaseproof paper. Repeat with the remaining batter, regreasing as necessary.

To make the filling Sauté the shallots or spring onions gently in the fat until softened and golden (keep the lid on at first), then add the mushrooms, cover and cook for 5 minutes. Uncover, add the sherry, salt and pepper, and bubble until only a tablespoon of free liquid remains. Stir in the tarragon. Turn into a bowl.

Add the chicken cut into bite-sized strips (Chinese style) and mix together.

Note To poach the chicken in the microwave, cover with 15 fl oz (425 ml/2 cups) of boiling chicken stock (home-made or use a stock-cube), cover the dish and cook on 100 per cent power for 5 minutes, then allow to cool. Alternatively, the breasts can be simmered in the stock on top of the stove for 10 minutes, turning once. This enriched stock can now be used in the sauce.

Divide the chicken stuffing between each of the 12 crêpes, then roll each of them up into a cylinder and lay side by side in a greased gratin dish.

Put all the sauce ingredients (except the egg yolks) into a thick pan and heat gently, using a balloon whisk constantly until the sauce is thickened. Bubble for 3 minutes, then drop in the yolks and whisk vigorously until evenly blended. Spoon over the crêpes, top with the breadcrumb and nut mixture and dot with the fat. The dish can be refrigerated at this point but should be left at room temperature for 1 hour before reheating.

To serve Bake the crêpes in a very hot oven, Gas No. 8 (450°F/230°C), for 10 minutes, then put under a hot grill until golden and bubbly. Alternatively, grill 6 inches (15 cm) away from the heat for the same time.

Chicken and Rice

CHICKEN PILAFF FOR A PARTY

Serves 6–8.
Leftovers keep 2 days under refrigeration.
Freeze 3 months.

Really fresh and fragrant spices and a well-flavoured stock are the essential ingredients that can transform a mundane Monday dish such as pilaff into a party sparkler. In this version, a blend of wild and long-grain rice (now available in ready-mixed packs) adds extra crunch. You can use leftover chicken (or turkey), but flesh from a freshly poached chicken is particularly tasty and juicy. All the separate parts of this richly satisfying dish can be prepared in advance, then put together in 5 or 6 minutes, just before serving.

4 lb (2 kg) chicken, quartered
(1½–2 lb/675 g–1 kg cooked flesh, cut into strips
1 pint (575 ml/2½ cups) water
1 onion
1 teasp salt
15 grinds of black pepper
large sprig of parsley
9 oz (250 g/1¼ cups) American mixed long-grain and wild rice
1 bay leaf
1 pint (575 ml/2½ cups) chicken stock (see below)
2 oz (50 g/½ cup) toasted flaked almonds
2 tbsp virgin olive oil
½ teasp sea salt
fresh coriander leaves or parsley, chopped

For the sauce
8 fl oz (225 ml/1 cup) strong chicken stock
1 teasp cumin
2 teasp ground coriander seeds (preferably freshly ground)
1 teasp freshly grated root ginger
1 clove of garlic, crushed with a little sea salt
16 grinds of freshly ground black pepper

To cook the bird Put it in a pan with the water, onion, salt, pepper and parsley. Cover with foil and then a lid to keep in the steam and simmer very gently for 1 hour, until absolutely tender. Lift out the chicken, skin and bone and cut the meat into strips. Boil the stock if necessary down to 1 pint (575 ml/2½ cups), pour through a sieve and reserve.

To cook the rice Put it in a heavy-based saucepan with the bay leaf and 1 pint (575 ml/2½ cups) stock, cover and bring to the boil over a moderate heat. Stir well, reduce the heat and simmer for 20 minutes, or until the liquid has been absorbed and the rice is cooked but still has a nice bite to it. Discard the bay leaf. Set aside.

To make the sauce Put the stock in a small saucepan over a moderate heat and stir in the cumin, coriander, ginger, garlic and seasoning. Simmer for 5 minutes, remove from the heat and set aside.

Just before serving, gently heat the olive oil in a large frying pan and tip in the cooked rice, toasted nuts and sea salt with enough of the reheated sauce to moisten. Turn the mixture around in the oil until heated through. Meanwhile, gently reheat the chicken either in a steamer lined with oiled foil or for 3 minutes, covered, in the microwave.

Arrange the chicken and rice on a large warmed serving dish, moisten with the sauce and scatter over the coriander or parsley. Serve, handing round any extra sauce separately.

MOROCCAN CHICKEN PILAFF WITH FRUIT AND NUTS

Serves 6–8.
Keeps 3 days under refrigeration.
Freeze for 3 months.

The pilaff can be cooked well ahead, then reheated in the microwave or a moderate oven, but the chicken does need to be stir-fried just before serving - it toughens when reheated.

1 x 5 oz (125 g) pack wild and brown rice
11 oz (300 g/2 cups) white Basmati rice
2 tbsp salt
2 tbsp sunflower oil
1 bunch spring onion bulbs (scallions), finely chopped
4 oz (125 g) ready-to-eat dried apricots, chopped with scissors
2 oz (50 g/½ cup) shelled pistachios
2 oz (50 g/½ cup) pine kernels
1½ tbsp cinnamon
1 teasp cumin
1 teasp salt
15 grinds of black pepper
1½ lb (675 g) chicken-breast meat, cut in 3 x ½ inch (7.5 x 1 cm) strips
salt and pepper to season the chicken
2 tbsp lemon juice
1½ tbsp sunflower oil
2 teasp cinnamon

To cook the rice, soak both sorts in cold water to cover for 30 minutes. Strain and rinse thoroughly under the tap until the water runs clear. Bring a large heavy pan of water to the boil with 2 tbsp salt. Add the rice and cook uncovered, bubbling steadily for 7 minutes, or until a grain feels almost tender when bitten. Turn into a strainer and rinse thoroughly under the hot tap, then drain well. Coat the bottom of the pan with 1 tablespoon of the oil, then add the rice. Finally cover the lid with a tea-towel and place in position on the pan, tucking inside to seal. Steam over the lowest heat for 20 minutes.

Meanwhile, put a further tablespoon of the oil into a medium sauté pan and cook the onions briskly until golden, then add the apricots, pistachios and pine kernels, sprinkling them with the larger portion of the cinnamon and cumin as they cook. Using a slotted spoon, remove this mixture from the pan and stir into the cooked rice, together with the salt and pepper. Set aside in a microwave-safe dish. Season the chicken and sprinkle with the lemon juice. Set aside.

Just before serving reheat the rice in the microwave, covered, on 100 per cent power for 4 minutes. Stir-fry the chicken strips in the very hot 1½ tablespoons of oil for 3 minutes, sprinkling them with the 2 teaspoons of cinnamon, then stir into the reheated rice. Arrange on a shallow platter.

CHICKEN LIVER RISOTTO

Serves 4.
Leftovers keep 2 days under refrigeration.
Freeze 2 months.

This has no pretensions as a party dish. It's just quick and delicious - and uses ingredients you're most likely to have in the house. It's particularly good made with Basmati rice.

1 medium onion
4 oz (125 g/1¼ cups) sliced mushrooms
8 oz (225 g) koshered chicken livers (see p. 134)
2 tbsp oil
7 oz (200 g/1 cup) Basmati rice, rinsed in a sieve under cold water
1 clove of garlic, crushed
4 fl oz (125 ml/½ cup) red wine or 1 tbsp red wine vinegar and 4 fl oz (125 ml/½ cup) chicken stock
1 rounded tbsp tomato purée
2 teasp brown sugar
16 fl oz (450 ml/2 cups) hot chicken stock

Chop the onion finely. Slice the mushrooms, halve the livers. Heat the oil over moderate heat for 2-3 minutes (preferably in a lidded sauté pan). Add the onion and sauté for 5 minutes, until softened and golden. Add the rice and turn in the onion for 3 minutes to cook the starchy coating and allow it to absorb some of the oniony flavourings. Add the liver, mushrooms and garlic and cook for a further 3-4 minutes, then add the wine, tomato purée, sugar and stock. Bring to the boil, cover and cook over low heat for 20 minutes on top of the stove or in the oven, Gas No. 6 (400°F/200°C), for the same length of time. Fluff up with a fork and serve with hearts of lettuce in a vinaigrette dressing.

LOW-FAT CHICKEN LIVER SAUTÉ

Serves 4-5.
Keeps 3 days under refrigeration.
Freeze for 3 months.

For the finest flavour cook several hours in advance, then reheat gently on top of the stove or in a microwave-safe serving dish. A 1-lb (450-g) pack of ready-koshered chicken livers or 1 lb of home-koshered ones (see p. 134) makes a wonderful last-minute sauce to serve over pasta. This recipe needs only 1 tablespoon of oil and is thickened with tomato purée rather than with cornflour. It's particularly good with tagliatelle - the broad lokshen that can now be bought fresh rather than in the less tasty packeted form. It's also excellent served with plain boiled new potatoes, baked potatoes or savoury rice.

Leftover sauce freezes well and can make a second appearance as the filling for a plain omelette, served with challah or black bread and a crisp green salad.

1 clove of garlic
4 oz (125 g/1¼ cups) mushrooms
1 tbsp oil
1 lb (450 g) koshered chicken livers
2 tbsp minced dried onion or 1 teasp onion salt
1 tbsp chopped parsley
2 teasp paprika
15 grinds of black pepper
1 red and 1 yellow pepper
4 rounded tbsp tomato purée
115 fl oz (425 ml/2 cups) chicken stock
1 tbsp wine vinegar

In a large lidded frying pan, gently sauté the chopped garlic and sliced mushrooms (covered) in the oil until golden, then uncover and bubble until the liquid has disappeared. Add all the remaining ingredients (the livers cut in 4, and the peppers deseeded and cut into small squares), and bring to the boil. Cover, then simmer very gently for 30 minutes, stirring occasionally. Uncover, taste and add salt if necessary. If the sauce seems watery, bubble for a further few minutes.

Chicken Salads

A salad using leftover roast chicken (or turkey) makes an excellent mid-week family meal. However, for a party meal, the chicken is juicier if it is poached fresh or roasted in foil. Boneless breast meat is the easiest to handle as it does not need skinning or boning, but many people prefer a mixture of light and dark meat cooked on the bone, in which case joints or a whole bird should be used.

For a salad to serve 8, 1½ lb (675 g) cooked flesh is required - a 4 lb (2 kg) bird will produce that amount when cooked. There are several methods of cooking the bird, all producing tender, juicy chicken. Use whichever is the most convenient.

TO POACH CHICKEN AND TURKEY BREAST FILLETS

IN THE MICROWAVE

The chicken or turkey can be cooked covered without liquid but the flavour is improved by the addition of a little chicken stock. A sprig of tarragon can also be added. When 2 or more breasts are to be cooked, arrange like spokes of a wheel with the thicker part to the outside.

Always test by cutting through a portion of chicken to ensure all pinkness has disappeared and the flesh is an even white. If not, cook for an extra 30 seconds at a time, then retest. Season if necessary *after* cooking.

The chicken is cooked on 100 per cent power unless different instructions are given.

To cook chicken breast meat off the bone:

4 oz (125 g) (1 serving)	*2½ minutes, covered and steamed in 4 tbsp chicken stock*
8 oz (225 g)	*3½ minutes, covered and steamed in 4 tbsp chicken stock*
12 oz (350 g)	*4 minutes, covered and steamed in 4 tbsp chicken stock*
1 lb (450 g)	*6 minutes, covered and steamed in 4 tbsp chicken stock*
1½ lb (675 g)	*7 minutes, covered and steamed in 4 tbsp chicken stock*
2 lb (900 g)	*8 minutes, covered and steamed in 4 tbsp chicken stock*

To cook chicken breasts on the bone

1 breast portion	*3 minutes, covered and steamed in 4 tbsp chicken stock*
2 breast portions	*4 minutes, covered and steamed in 4 tbsp chicken stock*
3 breast portions	*6 minutes, covered and steamed in 4 tbsp chicken stock*
4 breast portions	*7½ minutes, covered and steamed in 4 tbsp chicken stock*

To cook chicken legs

1 whole leg (or thigh and drumstick)	*5 minutes, covered and steamed in 4 tbsp chicken stock*
2 whole legs (or thighs and drumsticks)	*7½ minutes, covered and steamed in 4 tbsp chicken stock*
4 whole legs (or thighs and drumsticks)	*12 minutes, covered and steamed in 4 tbsp chicken stock*

To poach or casserole whole birds Cut into 4 or 6 portions. This works better than trying to poach the bird whole. It is also more economical than buying ready-cut portions (most butchers will portion the bird for you). The liquid can be chicken stock or the flavoured sauce of a casserole.

3½ lb (1.75 kg) bird, cut into 4 or 6 portions	*10 minutes at 100 per cent, 10 minutes at 50 per cent power*	*covered and cooked with 15 fl oz (425 ml/2 cups) liquid, alone or with vegetables*

4 lb (2 kg) bird	*12 minutes at 100 per cent, 10 minutes at 50 per cent power*	*covered and cooked with 15 fl oz (425 ml/2 cups) liquid, alone or with vegetables*

Approximate yield of chicken meat by cupfuls
1 x 4 lb bird (12 kg) gives 1½ lb (675 g) chicken meat, 4½ cupfuls of cubed meat.
2 breast portions (on or off the bone) give approx. 1½ cups cooked meat in cubes or slivers.
3 breast portions (on or off the bone) give approx. 2¼ cups cooked meat in cubes or slivers.
4 breast portions (on or off the bone) give approx. 3 cups cooked meat in cubes or slivers.

Note I have taken the weight of 1 chicken breast portion, skinned and boned, to be 4-5 oz (125-150 g). It will naturally weigh more on the bone but will yield a similar amount of meat.

ON TOP OF THE STOVE

Put the stock in a wide, lidded frying pan, add the chicken pieces in a single layer, cover and simmer at barely a bubble for 5 minutes. Turn and repeat with the second side. Cut through the thickest piece and check it is cooked - there will be no sign of pinkness. Take off the light and leave covered for 30 minutes.

With either method, sprinkle the cooked chicken lightly with salt and white pepper, then drain on paper towels. (Keep the cooking liquid for another purpose.)

TO COOK A 4 LB (2 KG) WHOLE BIRD FOR A SALAD

TO ROAST IN FOIL

Squeeze the juice from half a lemon into the body cavity, then brush the whole bird with olive oil and sprinkle with sea salt and black pepper. Wrap loosely but securely in foil, then cook at Gas No. 8 (450°F/230°C) for 1 hour. Open the foil parcel and allow to brown for a further 15 minutes.

TO COOK IN LIQUID (*Excellent for a Fowl*)

Cut off the legs to make it easier to fit the bird in a soup pan. Barely cover with water, add 1 whole medium (5 oz/150 g) onion, 2 sliced carrots, the leaves and top 2 inches (5 cm) from a head of celery, a sprig of parsley, 2 teaspoons of salt and ¼ teaspoon of white pepper.

Bring to the boil, cover and simmer until the leg feels very tender when prodded with a fork - 2½ hours for a fowl, 1½ hours for a chicken. Lift the bird from the stock and allow to cool.

FRUITED CHICKEN SALAD

Serves 8.
Salad keeps 1 day under refrigeration.
Do not freeze.

Come the winter, fruits such as mangoes, strawberries and grapes, grown in countries still basking in sunshine, are doubly welcome, both for the colour and variety they add to meals and also because of the high proportion of Vitamin C they contain - so essential in helping to ward off winter ills as well as being a pick-me-up for those who've been nursing coughs and colds through December.

When you combine these fruits with cooked chicken in a pleasantly tart dressing, with plenty of crusty bread or with a rice or bulgur salad on the side and a good rib-sticking soup beforehand, you have the makings of a delicious winter meal. And how about a good old-fashioned apple crumble to follow?

For the dressing

2 tbsp olive oil
4 tbsp sunflower oil
2 tbsp fresh lime juice
1 teasp each wholegrain and Dijon mustard
1 teasp salt
1 teasp caster sugar
15 grinds of black pepper
small handful (half a ½ oz/15 g pack) fresh coriander or parsley
4 rounded dessertspoons mild mayonnaise

For the salad

1½ lb (675 g) freshly cooked chicken-breast meat, cut in ½-inch (1.25-cm) wide strips (leftover cooked chicken or turkey can be substituted)
5 fl oz (150 ml/⅔ cup) chicken stock
heart of a celery, finely sliced
1 large or two mini-cucumbers
6 oz (175 g/1¼ cups) seedless black grapes
2 medium mangoes, sliced and cut in ½-inch (1-cm) pieces
8 oz (225 g/1½ cups) strawberries, thickly sliced

To make the dressing Shake all the ingredients (except the mayonnaise) in a screw-top jar until a thick emulsion is formed. Put the mayonnaise in a large bowl, then gradually stir in the emulsion. Set aside.

To assemble the salad Put the chicken strips and all the remaining ingredients in the bowl with the dressing and stir well to blend.

Turn into a salad bowl and chill until served.

A LIGHTLY CURRIED CHICKEN AND AVOCADO SALAD

Serves 6–8.
Leftovers keep 1 day under refrigeration.
Do not freeze.

A superb main dish salad for a cold supper or meat buffet. Slices of peeled mango can be substituted for the avocado if preferred (in which case omit the lemon juice).

1½ lb (675 g) meat from a 4 lb (2 kg) roast or poached chicken
1 large or 2 medium, ripe avocados or mangoes
2 tbsp fresh lemon juice
10 fl oz (275 ml/1¼ cups) mild mayonnaise
1 tbsp medium-strength curry powder
2 rounded tbsp mango chutney
1 teasp grated fresh ginger root

For the rice salad

8 oz (225 g/1⅓ cups) Basmati rice
15 fl oz (425 ml/2 cups) chicken stock
4 tbsp vinaigrette dressing (see p. 300)
1 large red pepper, seeded and finely diced
3 rounded tbsp seedless raisins
2 oz (50 g/½ cup) dry-roasted peanuts, chopped

For the garnish

2 fresh grapefruit, peeled and sectioned
1 bunch watercress

Remove any skin from the chicken and cut the flesh into 2 x 1 inch (5 x 2.5 cm) strips.

Peel, halve and stone the avocado (or mango), cut it into thick slices and, if using avocado, mix gently with the lemon juice.

In a large bowl mix the mayonnaise, curry powder, chutney and fresh ginger, then gently stir in the chicken and avocado or mango, cover and chill until required.

To make the rice salad, cook the rice (covered) in the chicken stock for 15 minutes. Remove from the heat but leave covered to steam for a further 15 minutes. Fluff up with a fork. Put the hot rice into a bowl and mix gently with the vinaigrette, using a large fork and spoon. Stir in the red pepper, raisins and nuts, then refrigerate in a covered container for several hours.

To serve, spoon the rice salad round the edge of an oval platter and pile the chicken salad in the centre. Just before serving, decorate with the grapefruit segments and sprigs of watercress.

POLYNESIAN CHICKEN SALAD

Serves 4.
Leftovers keep 1 days under refrigeration.
Do not freeze.

A simple, tasty salad.

2 oz (50 g/½ cup) blanched almonds, toasted
1 tbsp oil
small can of pineapple titbits
4 spring onions (scallions) sliced in ¼-inch (0.5-cm) lengths
4 sticks from the heart of a celery, finely sliced
2 cups of cubed cooked chicken (flesh from ½ x 4 lb/2 kg bird)
4 fl oz (125 ml/½ cup) mayonnaise
1 teasp light soy sauce
good pinch of salt
crisp salad greens, including watercress

Fry the almonds in 1 tbsp oil for 3 or 4 minutes, then drain on kitchen paper, split when cool and lightly salt them. Drain the pineapple, saving 2 tablespoons of the syrup. In a large bowl toss together the almonds, pineapple, spring onions, celery and chicken. Blend together the mayonnaise, pineapple syrup, soy sauce and salt, then stir in the salad. Toss lightly and mound into a shallow salad bowl or gratin dish lined with the crisp greens.

ORIENTAL CHICKEN AND RICE SALAD

Serves 4 as a main course, 6–8 for a buffet.
Leftovers keep 2 days under refrigeration.
Do not freeze.

The rice adds body to this simple but tasty salad. For the finest flavour stir the dressing into the rice while it is hot.

4 level tbsp raisins
nut of margarine
7 oz (200 g/1 cup) long-grain rice, cooked (3 cups when cooked) (see p. 273)
1 medium red pepper, seeded and finely sliced
4 level tbsp walnuts, roughly chopped
12 oz (350 g/3 cups) cooked chicken
1 tbsp mayonnaise

For the dressing
4 tbsp olive oil
2 tbsp wine vinegar
1 cut clove of garlic
1 level teasp salt
10 grinds of black pepper
lettuce leaves for serving

Sauté the raisins in the margarine until plump and glossy (about 5 minutes). This greatly enhances their flavour. Whisk the dressing ingredients together in a bowl while the rice is cooking. When the rice is cooked, discard the garlic, add the hot rice and coat with the dressing, then stir in all the remaining ingredients. Leave in a cool place for several hours to intensify the flavour. Line a shallow bowl with crisp lettuce leaves and spoon the salad into the centre.

TURKEY CELEBRATION SALAD

Serves 6–8.
Keeps 1 day under refrigeration.

Freshly cooked turkey-breast meat makes a wonderfully juicy addition to this elegant and colourful but low-calorie main-dish salad. Roast turkey is almost as good, but of course it's just that little bit drier. However, if it is marinated in the vinaigrette dressing for a while, some of the juiciness is restored. With the salad as part of a meat buffet, I would serve a hot meatball casserole and both a rice and a green salad to give a good balance. The combination of sunflower and walnut oil in the dressing gives a superb flavour, while the wholegrain mustard helps to thicken it to a creamy consistency.

1 small Galia melon
2 oz (50 g/½ cup) almonds or cashews
1 tbsp oil
sea salt
2 celery hearts, finely sliced
1 red and 1 yellow or orange pepper, cut in thin strips
1½ lb (675 g) roast turkey or freshly cooked turkey meat (see p. 234), cut in ½-inch (1.25-cm) strips
4 oz (125 g/¾ cup) each of seedless black and green grapes (or seeded and cut in half)

For the dressing
2 tbsp walnut oil
4 tbsp sunflower oil
2 tbsp raspberry vinegar or white wine vinegar
1 teasp wholegrain mustard
1 teasp salt
1 teasp caster sugar or granular sweetener
10 grinds of black pepper
1 shallot, finely chopped
1 tbsp fresh tarragon, finely chopped

First make the dressing by shaking all the ingredients together in a screw-top jar until a thick emulsion is formed. Set aside.

Make balls from the melon, put in a sieve and allow to drain while you are preparing the other ingredients.

Fry the nuts over medium heat in oil until golden brown. Drain on crumpled kitchen paper and sprinkle with a little sea salt.

In a bowl put the celery hearts, pepper strips, warm turkey (if freshly cooked) and grapes, and add enough of the dressing to moisten thoroughly. Just before serving, stir in the melon balls.

Pile the salad in the centre of a fairly shallow dish and top with the nuts.

Roast Duck

There are very few recipes that I know of for duck in Jewish cuisine - goose and hen have mostly been the favoured fowl. However, as they are now more readily available, both as whole birds and in portions, ducks make a pleasant change from chicken for a special meal.

As the duckling has a higher ratio of bone to flesh than a chicken, a bird weighing 4–5½ lb (2–2.75 kg) oven-ready weight will serve only 4. You may prefer to serve smaller (4 lb/2 kg) birds, which will each serve 2. However, by using the 2-stage method below, the portioning of the birds can be done well ahead, which avoids wrestling with 2 birds at the table. Alternatively, you can use duck joints and avoid the hassle. Both methods are given below.

TO ROAST A DUCK (OR PORTIONS) — 2-STAGE METHOD

Serves 6–8.
Leftovers keep 3 days under refrigeration.
Freeze 1 month.

This is the ideal method when cooking duck for a dinner party. The bird is given a preliminary cooking earlier in the day and then divided into serving portions and put back in the cleaned roasting tin. Shortly before serving it is briefly recrisped. The result is crispy brown duck with succulent flesh.

3 x 4 lb (2 kg) ducks (for 6) or 2 x 5½ lb (2.75 kg) ducks (for 8), or 6–8 duck portions

Stage 1 In the morning, dry the ducks thoroughly inside and out with paper towels, then wrap in fresh towels and leave 30 minutes. Remove the towels, prick all over with a fork, and arrange side by side on a rack over a greased roasting tin. Sprinkle with salt then roast, breast-side down, in a quick oven, Gas No. 6 (400°F/200°C), for 1¼ hours (45 minutes for portions), or until the juices run only faintly pink when a leg is pierced. Pour off the fat.

To section the whole ducks, with poultry shears take out the backbone. Trim off the winglets and remove the breast-cage with a sharp boning knife. Replace on the rack in the cleaned roasting dish. Set aside (if for more than 3 hours, refrigerate, but leave at room temperature for 1 hour before stage 2).

Stage 2 15 minutes before serving, sprinkle the ducks again with a little salt and recrisp in a hot oven, Gas No. 7 (425°F/220°C), for 15 minutes.

TO MAKE DUCK STOCK FOR SAUCE

Keeps 3 days under refrigeration.
Freeze 3 months.

15 fl oz (425 ml/2 cups) chicken stock
giblets from the duck(s)
1 sliced carrot
1 whole onion, peeled
large sprig of parsley

While the ducks are roasting during stage 1, simmer all the stock ingredients together in a covered pan for 1 hour, then strain out the vegetables and bubble uncovered until only 15 fl oz (425 ml/2 cups) of liquid remains. The stock can, of course, be made the day before.

Note If preferred, a strong chicken stock can be used instead when giblets are unavailable (as with portions).

A Quartet of Duck Sauces

All the sauces can be made the day before if convenient. Reheat just before serving.

A SIMPLE FRUIT SAUCE

Serves 6–8.
Keep 3 days under refrigeration.
Freeze 3 months.

1½ tbsp duck fat
1½ tbsp flour
15 fl oz (425 ml/2 cups) duck or chicken stock
1½ tbsp Morello (sour cherry) or apricot conserve
pinch of salt
5 grinds of black pepper

Pour off all but 1 tablespoon of fat from the roasting tin, then stir in the flour and cook for 2 minutes, until the flour begins to brown. Now add the stock, stirring well to incorporate any juices that have congealed on the bottom of the pan. Tip the sauce from the roasting pan into a saucepan, add the jam and bubble until reduced to a syrupy consistency. Season and serve.

AN APPLE AND DRAMBUIE LIQUEUR SAUCE

Serves 8.

1½ lb (675 g) Bramley cooking apples, peeled, cored and thinly sliced
2 oz (50 g/¼ cup) light brown sugar
2 tbsp lime juice
1 teasp grated fresh ginger
5 tbsp Drambuie liqueur
8 grinds of black pepper

Put the prepared apples, sugar and lime juice into a covered pan or microwave-safe casserole. Simmer on top of the stove until pulpy, or cook on 100 per cent power in the microwave for 6 minutes. Turn the mixture into a bowl and whisk in all the remaining ingredients until smooth. Just before serving, reheat until steaming (boiling will cause the alcohol to evaporate).

VARIATION

Substitute Calvados for the Drambuie.

DAMSON, PORT AND RED WINE SAUCE

Serves 4.
A rich fruity sauce with an intense flavour.

10 fl oz (275 ml/1¼ cups) duck stock
10 fl oz (275 ml/1¼ cups) red wine such as Pinot Noir
1 lb (450 g) damsons (frozen can be used) or 1 x 25 oz (700 g) jar Morello cherries plus 4 fl oz (225 ml/½ cup) of the syrup
2 tbsp port or red Kiddush wine
4 tbsp (50 g/¼ cup) sugar to taste

Put the duck stock and the 10 fl oz of wine in a pan and bring to the boil. Bubble gently until the mixture is syrupy and reduced by half. Meanwhile, cook the damsons in another pan until tender with a little water and 4 tbsp sugar (5 minutes in the microwave). Purée the damsons, removing any stones, then add the stock and wine mixture. (If cherries are used, purée them with the measured juice.) Add the port and a little more sugar if required - but keep the mixture quite tart.

Shortly before serving, reheat the sauce, adjust the seasoning and add a little stock if necessary to bring to a pouring consistency.

Place a duck portion on each plate and surround with a pool of the lovely red sauce.

A CHESTNUT AND WINE SAUCE

The combination of chestnuts and red wine produces a richly coloured, subtly flavoured sauce. This is especially good with duck portions.

1 medium onion, finely chopped
1 large clove of garlic, crushed
2 tbsp duck or chicken fat, or light olive oil
½ x 15 oz (425 g) can of natural chestnut purée (freeze the remainder)
5 fl oz (150 ml/⅔ cup) well-flavoured red wine
10 fl oz (275 ml/1¼ cups) well-flavoured duck or chicken stock
3 teasp dark soy sauce
black pepper

For the garnish
freshly cooked or canned whole chestnuts

Sauté the chopped onion and the garlic in the fat over gentle heat until soft and golden. Break up the chestnut purée into roughly 1-inch (2.5-cm) chunks and put into the food processor with the wine, processing until smooth and creamy in texture. Gradually add the stock, the soy sauce and the sautéd onion and garlic, then pour into a small pan. Just before the duck is cooked, reheat the sauce and season to taste - if necessary bubble 2-3 minutes to produce a thin coating consistency.

Spoon some of the sauce on to a hot serving

dish and arrange the duck or portions on top. Garnish with the chestnuts. Have the remaining sauce on the table. Serve with new potatoes and minted petit pois.

DUCK BREASTS WITH A HONEY AND GINGER GLAZE

Serves 6–8.
Leftovers keep 3 days under refrigeration.
Freeze 2 months.

This produces a duck in the Chinese style with a mahogany brown, crunchy skin. No sauce is necessary, but a fruity salad (such as Orange, Chicory and Toasted Sesame Salad, see p. 285) makes a refreshing accompaniment.

6–8 large duck breasts
fresh root ginger
freshly ground black pepper
juice of 1 small orange
2 tbsp runny honey
2 teasp soy sauce
pinch of salt

Remove any lumps of fat from the duck joints and prick all over, piercing only the skin, not the flesh. Peel, then finely chop enough of the ginger to make 2 rounded tablespoons.

Lay the duck joints side by side in a large dish, scatter with the ginger and sprinkle with the black pepper, rubbing in well. Pour over the orange juice, then turn the joints to make sure they are evenly moistened on all sides. Cover and set aside for several hours or overnight (in a cool place or the refrigerator).

To cook the duck breasts, preheat the oven to Gas No. 6 (400°F/200°C). Drain the marinade from the duck and scrape off the ginger, then mix together and reserve.

Arrange the breasts on the rack and roast for 45 minutes. Mix the honey (or firm honey heated until runny) with the marinade and stir in the soy sauce and salt.

Pour off all the fat that has collected under the duck, then paint the portions all over with the glaze. Roast for another 20 minutes, basting once.

At the end of this time the duck should be a mahogany brown and deliciously tender. If it seems to be browning too quickly, cover loosely with a tent of foil.

Turkey Plus

The turkey, a relative newcomer to the Jewish menu, makes an excellent alternative to casseroled fowls or roast chickens for a Yomtov menu, or for a large family for the Sabbath.

How Big Should It Be?

Allow ¾–1 lb (350–450 g) per serving, the higher figure referring to the smaller bird (to allow for the higher ratio of bone to flesh). Thus an 8 lb (4 kg) bird will provide 8 to 9 servings, a 12 lb (5.5 kg) bird about 16. From a 12 lb (5.5 kg) bird, a family of 4 adults and 4 children could well get a hot meal, a cold meal and a rechauffé dish such as turkey pie or blintzes.

But, wait a moment! Will the chosen bird fit your oven? Too large a bird in too small an oven produces uneven browning. There should be 1-inch (2.5-cm) clearance of the sides when the roasting tin is put in position.

A fresh bird is infinitely preferable to a frozen one, because both the texture and the flavour are vastly superior. However, if the only available bird is frozen, it is important to allow sufficient time for it to thaw before cooking. This is essential for the interior to reach a temperature high enough to kill bacteria such as salmonella. For the same reason, I now prefer to cook the stuffing outside the bird - the *neck* end (crop) can be stuffed with confidence and this does help to keep the bird a good shape with a nice plump breast.

How to Thaw

A large bird - 15 lb (7 kg) or over - may take up to 48 hours in a cool larder or outhouse; a smaller bird - up to 12 lb (5.5 kg) - will take 20–30 hours. If the bird thaws before it is time to cook it, refrigerate and treat as a fresh bird.

ROAST TURKEY WITH A MINEOLA (OR ORANGE) AND VERMOUTH SAUCE

Serves 11–12.

I have tried every method of cooking a turkey, both with and without some kind of protection. I have found that a bird that is completely covered with butter muslin (cheesecloth) or a similar material soaked in oil is the easiest to handle during the cooking period and turns a wonderful mahogany brown with succulent flesh. However, it is necessary to use a syringe-type baster.

The timing I give is for a 15 lb (7 kg) bird, which will serve 11–12 with half the bird left for later use. This is based on an initial 15 minutes at a high temperature plus 12 minutes to the pound (450 g), plus 30 minutes' standing time to allow it to settle before carving. For a smaller bird allow 15 minutes plus 15 minutes to the pound (450 g).

15 lb (7 kg) turkey

For the turkey stock

the giblets
1 large carrot, cut in 4
1 medium onion
3 pints (1¾ l/7¼ cups) water
1 teasp black peppercorns
1 bay leaf
1 teasp salt

For the stuffing

salt
pepper
8 oz (225 g) dry weight any preferred stuffing for the crop (e.g. Helzel, see p. 48)
large bunch of parsley
1 large apple, cut in 8, to cook inside bird
olive oil for brushing bird

For the basting sauce

4 fl oz (225 ml/1 cup) sunflower oil
4 oz (225 g/½ cup) margarine
4 fl oz (225 ml/½ cup) mineola (or orange) juice
2 tbsp fresh lemon juice

For the gravy

1½ tbsp cornflour
3 fl oz (75 ml/⅓ cup) dry vermouth (optional)
1 pint (575 ml/2½ cups) strained turkey stock (see below)
salt
black pepper
2 oz (50 g/½ cup) toasted pine kernels (optional)

To make the stock, the day before the turkey is to be cooked put the giblets (except for the liver) into a pan with the vegetables, water and seasonings. Simmer uncovered for 2 hours on a very low light, skimming occasionally. (In the microwave, use 1¼ pints (725 ml/3 cups) water and cook covered on 100 per cent power for 15 minutes - until bubbling - then cook on 50 per cent power for a further 20 minutes.) Strain stock and chill overnight then remove any fat.

The night before, pat the bird dry inside and out, lightly season the body cavity with salt and pepper and put in the parsley and apple sections. Stuff the neck loosely with the stuffing and sew it closed. Tie the drumsticks together. Brush the bird all over with a thin layer of olive oil.

Meanwhile, put the oil and melted fat for the basting sauce into a bowl and in it moisten a piece of butter muslin or a large-size J-cloth (or 2) big enough to cover the bird. Cover the turkey completely with the fat-soaked cloth, tucking it well in all the way round so no flesh is exposed. Refrigerate or leave in a cool place overnight.

Next day, assuming you want to serve the

turkey at 2 pm, take it from the refrigerator at 9.45 am and turn the oven to Gas No. 7 (425°F/220°C).

At 10 am set the bird on a rack in a roasting tin and roast for 15 minutes.

Turn the oven down to Gas No. 3 (325°F/160°C) and cook for a further 3 hours, basting with a syringe baster every 30 minutes so that the cloth remains moist at all times. One hour before the bird is ready, pour the mineola or orange and lemon juice over it and baste thoroughly as before.

At 1.30 pm the bird should be cooked - the juices should run clear if the fleshy part of the thigh is pricked with a skewer. Uncover the bird - it will be a rich mahogany brown - and discard the cloth, then lift it on to a carving dish, cover loosely with foil and leave in a warm place for 30 minutes before carving.

Note For a smaller bird, cook for the first 15 minutes as before, then cook for 15 minutes to the pound (450 g); for a larger bird, allow 12 minutes to the pound (450 g).

To make the gravy Mix the cornflour with the vermouth to a smooth cream. Pour the fat from the roasting tin into a basin, reserving the juices. To these add a cupful of the measured stock, and put over a low light, stirring well to release any brown bits sticking to the bottom of the tin. Pour into an 8-inch (20-cm) pan, bring to the boil and then add the remaining stock and the cornflour liquid. Bring to the boil again, stirring well. Leave to simmer, uncovered, stirring occasionally for a further 10 minutes, until slightly thickened. Taste and season with salt and black pepper. Stir in the pine kernels.

ROAST TURKEY OR CHICKEN WITH A FRUITED BULGUR STUFFING

Serves 8–10.
Leftovers keep 3 days under refrigeration.
Freeze 3 months.

A glaze of lemon and honey gives a glorious golden-brown sheen to a roast bird. Treated in this way, either an outsize chicken or a small turkey makes a superb main course for a special dinner for 8. Put a little of the unusual bulgur stuffing inside the bird to keep it moist, but cook the rest separately during the last half-hour - you don't need to serve potatoes as well, but if your family insist, let it be a dish of plain boiled new ones.

7–8 lb (3.5–4 kg) chicken or young turkey

For the stuffing
4 oz (125 g) each of dried apricots and dried pears
4 tbsp olive oil
1 medium onion
1 large clove of garlic
1 tbsp chopped fresh ginger
12 oz (350 g/2 cups) bulgur (cracked wheat)
3 pints (1.75 l/7 cups) good chicken stock
2 oz (50 g/½ cup) pine kernels, lightly toasted
½ teasp nutmeg
finely grated rind of 2 lemons
1 teasp salt
15 grinds of black pepper

For the glaze
2 level tbsp liquid honey
2 tbsp fresh lemon juice

First prepare the stuffing. Cover the dried fruit with boiling water and leave to plump up for 30 minutes. In the microwave, cover the fruit with 4 tbsp hot water, cover and cook on 100 per cent power for 3 minutes, then leave until required.

Heat half the olive oil in a lidded sauté pan and cook the chopped onion and garlic for 5 minutes, until a rich gold. Stir in the chopped fresh ginger and cook for a further minute, then add the bulgur, coating it well with the oil. Add 2 pints of the hot stock and the coarsely chopped dried fruit, cover and cook over very low heat for about 10 minutes, or until the liquid has been absorbed. Stir in the pine kernels, nutmeg, lemon rind, salt and pepper. Set to one side.

When ready to roast the bird, preheat the oven to Gas No. 8 (450°F/230°C). Fill the cavity of the bird loosely with some of the stuffing, then tie the legs together to make it a compact shape. Oil a roasting tin and set a rack in it, then arrange the bird on top and brush all over with the remaining oil. Put the remaining stuffing in a casserole and cover tightly, ready for reheating during the last 30 minutes of roasting time. Put the bird in the oven and immediately turn the temperature down to Gas No. 5 (375°F/190°C). Roast the bird, allowing 20 minutes to the pound (450 g - weight unstuffed). While the bird is roasting, mix together the honey and lemon juice. 30 minutes before the bird is done, brush all over with glaze and put the dish with the bulgur in the oven. After a further 15 minutes, brush again with the glaze, and yet again when the bird is cooked, by which time it should be a rich, shiny golden brown. Put on a warm dish to rest while the gravy is made.

Pour the remaining 1 pint of stock into the pan and stir well over moderate heat to release the crusty bits, then pour the liquid through a sieve into a small pan. Skim off as much fat as possible, then boil down until it is smooth and well seasoned. Serve with the sliced bird.

TURKEY HELZEL STUFFING

Sufficient for a 10–15 lb (5–7 kg) bird.
Do not freeze raw.

This makes a firm, savoury and easily sliced stuffing for the crop. To prevent the helzel drying out during the long cooking time, protect the crop area of the turkey with foil before covering the whole bird with the oil-soaked cloth (see Roast Turkey recipe preceding).

5 oz (150 g/1¼ cup) plain (all-purpose) flour
1 oz (25 g/¼ cup) fine matzah meal or semolina
4½ rounded tbsp raw chicken or turkey fat or 3 oz (75 g/⅓ cup) firm margarine, cut or chopped in tiny pieces
½ teasp salt
good pinch white pepper
1 medium onion, finely grated

Mix all the ingredients together with a fork. The mixture should look slightly moist, neither 'cloggy' (if so, it needs more flour) nor crumbly (if so, add a little more fat). Stuff the mixture loosely into the crop of the turkey, and be sure to push it well down so that the breast is plumped up nicely. Sew the neck skin to the backbone.

BAKED CHESTNUT STUFFING

Serves 10–12.
Leftovers keep 3 days under refrigeration.
Do not store uncooked except in freezer.
Freezes well, cooked or uncooked, for 3 months.

2 lb (900 g) chestnuts or 2 x 15 oz (425 g) cans whole chestnuts (each can giving 285 g/10 oz drained weight)
chicken stock
4 oz (225 g/½ cup) melted margarine
1 medium onion, finely chopped

6 oz (175 g/3 cups) fresh breadcrumbs
2 tbsp chopped parsley
2 teasp salt
¼ teasp white pepper
2 large eggs

To prepare chestnuts For the fresh nuts, with a small, very sharp knife, cut through the skin right round. Drop into boiling water. As soon as the cut widens to show the flesh, take out a nut at a time and remove the inner and outer skin. Put in a pan and just cover with chicken stock. Simmer gently until tender when tested - about 30 minutes.

Drain canned chestnuts.

To make the stuffing Melt the fat without colouring it and in it simmer the chopped onion until soft and golden. Meanwhile, coarsely chop the chestnuts and put in a bowl with the bread, parsley and seasonings. Pour on the fat and onion and mix well. Finally mix in the beaten eggs, stirring with a fork until the ingredients are evenly dampened. Spoon into an ovenproof casserole. When the turkey is 'resting', turn up the oven to Gas No. 5 (375°F/190°C) and cook the stuffing uncovered for 20-25 minutes, until crunchy and brown on top. Serve from the casserole or spoon into a decorative serving dish.

PARSLEY STUFFING

Serves 8-10 - enough for a 10-12 lb (5-6 kg) bird. Freeze 3 months, cooked or uncooked.

A fluffy, light stuffing for the body cavity.

8 oz (225 g/4 cups) breadcrumbs
1 level teasp dried mixed herbs or Italian herb mixture
2 level tbsp finely chopped parsley and celery
2 level teasp salt
¼ level teasp white pepper
4 oz (125 g/½ cup) margarine
1 large onion, finely chopped

Put the breadcrumbs in a bowl and blend with the herbs and seasoning. Melt the margarine in a large frying pan, add the onion and simmer until tender. Add the seasoned breadcrumbs to the pan and stir thoroughly to moisten. If the breadcrumbs appear dry, add another 2 oz (50 g/¼ cup) margarine at the side of the pan, melt and stir in.

HOW TO CARVE A TURKEY

1 Cut off the legs and wings.
2 Separate the drumstick from the leg, using poultry shears or the point of a knife.
3 Carve slices of meat from the legs, beginning at the bony end.
4 Carve slices of meat from the breast, starting at the neck end. Wrap leftover turkey in foil and refrigerate.

VEGETABLES

VEGETABLES AND MAIN DISH ACCOMPANIMENTS

Vegetables in a Hurry

You used to be able to tell the geographical origins of Jewish families by the way they prepared their vegetables. Ashkenazi Jews whose origins lay in Eastern Europe - in particular Russia, Poland and the Baltic states - had a limited repertoire of dishes as the main vegetable crops in that part of the world are root vegetables and cabbages. As you moved into warmer climates, peppers and aubergines (eggplants) appeared on the menu, while in Sephardi households hailing from the Mediterranean countries and the Middle East exotica such as vine leaves, okra, chick peas and artichokes, not to mention spinach, courgettes, tomatoes and cucumbers, were everyday fare.

In a generation all that has changed. Whatever the season, every supermarket now offers a positive cornucopia of fresh vegetables, picked in their prime and then airlifted from Israel, North and South America and Africa, or rushed by road from our native growers or the fields of continental Europe. And many of them come ready for the pot - even trimmed and destalked, shaped, shredded and sliced if you're prepared to pay the price. Then there are the so-called 'designer' vegetables - miniaturized vegetables that have all the flavour of the mature traditional varieties, potatoes bred for specific purposes, such as baking, boiling, salads and gratins - and I haven't yet looked into the frozen food cabinet!

Frozen vegetables - the luxury foods of the 1950s and 1960s - have gradually descended the gastronomic ladder so that today they are mostly kept for emergency use, and only petit pois and possibly leaf spinach and corn on the cob can stand comparison with fresh produce.

Cooking methods too have changed. For many people, the microwave or the steamer has replaced the traditional boiling method, while others prefer to cut their vegetables small and stir-fry them.

What pack of vegetables you choose and how you decide to cook it are very much matters of personal choice - and the particular needs of the moment. For example, although it might well be extravagant to buy a pack of ready-for-the-pot mixed vegetables for everyday use, it would be worth it in time and labour saved if preparing for a dinner party. Similarly, it would pay to buy loose baking potatoes even of slightly varying sizes for a large family, while it would be policy to buy a more expensive ready-washed and size-selected pack of 4 or 6 when cooking for 1 or 2.

So in this chapter I will be giving what I've found to be the best technique for the different methods of basic vegetable cookery, as well as some of the traditional Jewish dishes - in particular those for potatoes, for rice and other grains and for pasta that have stood the test of time.

To Cook Fresh Green Vegetables

To conserve their colour and food value, all green vegetables should be cooked as rapidly as possible, then served as soon as they are barely tender.

General Preparation

See specific recipes for preparing more unusual varieties.

Brussels Sprouts Remove any discoloured outer leaves and examine each sprout closely for insects. If any are seen, discard the sprout. Make 2 little nicks in the stalk end (to hasten the cooking), then leave in water to cover plus 1 level teaspoon of salt, for half an hour. Rinse well and cook by preferred method (see below).

Cauliflower Cut the flowerets free from the stalk end. Soak as above and cook by preferred method (see below).

Spring cabbage Remove the coarse outer leaves and discard. Rinse the tender inner leaves under the cold tap, 1 at a time. Put on a chopping board and shred finely. Cook by preferred method (see below). When tender, drain well, put on board and chop till fine. Mix with a nut of butter or margarine.

White cabbage Cut in quarters and remove the stalk. Cut each quarter into thin shreds and soak in salted water as for sprouts. Cook in boiling water on stove top (see below). When the cabbage is tender, strain, turn on to a board and chop until fine.

Young green cabbage *(usually in season in July)* Quarter the cabbage head then shred finely, discarding any tough outer leaves and the stalk. Half-fill a bowl with cold water and add 2 level teaspoons of salt. Put in the cabbage and leave for half an hour. For cooking method see p. 245.

French beans *(string beans)* Remove strings, rinse under cold tap, cut in diagonal slices and cook by preferred method (see below).

Broad beans *(kidney or shell beans)* Shell and cook by preferred method (see below).

Mangetout or sugar snap peas Top and tail, and string if necessary. Cook by preferred method (see below) but only until barely tender - after 2-5 minutes.

Stove-Top Methods

Boiling Water

Prepare the vegetables according to the variety (see above). Have ready a heavy-based saucepan with a tight-fitting lid in which is boiling 5 fl oz (150 ml/⅔ cup) of water seasoned with 1 level teaspoon of salt. Put in the prepared vegetables, then boil rapidly until they feel barely tender when pierced with a slim knife. Pour off any liquid that is left and use it in soups and gravies as it will be rich in mineral salts.

Steaming

Vegetables take about as long to steam as when cooked by the boiling-water method. However, as all their natural salts are retained (they don't leach out as when cooked in water), no additional salt needs to be added before serving, so it's an excellent method for those on a low-salt or salt-free diet.

For a large family it may be worthwhile to buy an electric steamer. For the smaller family a collapsible steaming basket - they are made in metal, plastic or bamboo - can be used in an ordinary pan.

Steaming a Small Quantity in an Ordinary Pan

This is my favourite method when catering for 1 or 2. It is essential to have a heavy-based pan with a close-fitting lid - I use a stainless steel pan with a cast aluminium base. Put only enough water in the bottom to create steam - it should be about ¼ inch (1 cm) in depth. Bring to the boil, add the vegetables in the steaming basket, then put on the lid and cook until tender.

Stir-Frying

It is essential to cut the vegetables into pieces of uniform size so that they all cook in the very brief time involved in this method. This might be time-consuming, but the vegetables do keep their colour and crunch, and vitamin and mineral loss is kept to a minimum.

A STIR-FRY OF BABY VEGETABLES

Serves 6–8.

This delicious vegetable *mélange* can be prepared either with small, fresh 'designer' vegetables or a pack of pre-cut mixed 'stir-fry' ones from the chill counter.

2 x 8 oz (225 g) pack (approx.) sugar snap peas or mangetout
1 x 8 oz (225 g) pack (approx.) broccoli florets
1 x 8 oz (225 g) pack (approx.) miniature asparagus, halved lengthwise

For the stir-frying
1½ tbsp sunflower oil
1 peeled clove of garlic, cut in tiny slivers
1 inch (2.5 cm) piece peeled fresh ginger, cut in tiny slivers
2 teasp light soy sauce
10 grinds of black pepper
½ teasp salt

Early in the day, cook each kind of vegetable separately in boiling salted water until barely tender. Drench with cold water and allow to drain thoroughly.

Just before serving, heat the oil with the garlic and ginger slivers in a wok or wide frying pan over high heat for 3 minutes. Add all the vegetables and toss over high heat until steaming - about 3 minutes. Sprinkle with the soy sauce and the seasonings, toss well and serve at once. (May be done just before dinner then reheated.)

Using the Microwave

All times given are based on using a 650-watt oven. Adjust accordingly for ovens with a different power output (see p. *xx*).

Vegetables thrive in the microwave - it cooks them to just the right degree of 'doneness', while keeping their colour and nutrients intact. If necessary, it can also reheat them in their serving dish without any loss of colour or flavour. For this reason, it is sensible to cook vegetables before other microwaved dishes which have a longer cooking period.

As with other food, the more similar in size the pieces of vegetable, the more quickly and evenly they will cook. It is particularly important to stir the vegetables half-way through the cooking period so that those in the centre of the dish are repositioned near the edge and get their full share of the microwave energy. Most vegetables need to stand 2 or 3 minutes after cooking to complete the transference of heat to the centre of the dish. So resist the temptation to give them extra time. Even if they seem a little firm in texture at the end of the given cooking time, they will soften further by the time they are served.

Note For cooking all vegetables with the exception of high-bulk ones such as cabbage, I use a shallow-lidded casserole large enough to hold the pieces in an even layer. All vegetables, even potatoes, need no more than a few tablespoons of water as a cooking medium. As this water heats up and vaporizes, the vegetables are effectively steamed with the minimum loss of water-soluble nutrients. I prefer to cook new potatoes, mangetout, sugar snap peas and all types of green beans on top of the stove using either the boiling or the steaming methods, as I think this gives a more succulent result.

Asparagus

Fresh Unless you have an asparagus pan - a tall double-boiler - in which the fibrous stalks are cooked in water while the tender heads are steamed, the microwave is undoubtedly the preferred method of cooking this delectable vegetable to the correct *'al dente'* stage. Choose a green-stemmed variety with tight heads (avoid those with a large portion of woody stalk). Bundles of asparagus contain stalks of even thickness, but if you are buying it loose you will have to do this selection for yourself to ensure all the spears cook to an even tenderness. To prepare, trim off any woody part of the stalk, wash thoroughly in a bowl of cold water, then gently shake dry.

To cook 1 lb (450 g) asparagus, arrange the stalks side by side in a lasagne-type oblong dish, with the tender tips to the centre. Sprinkle with 4 tablespoons of water, cover and cook on 100 per cent power for 4 minutes, then rearrange by bringing the outer stalks to the middle and vice versa. Re-cover and cook a further 4-6 minutes, or until a stalk is just tender when pierced with a sharp knife. Drain and serve with melted butter or Hollandaise Sauce (see p. 77).

Frozen This will already have been trimmed and blanched, so the cooking time will be much shorter than for fresh. However, arrange and re-arrange the stalks in the dish as for the fresh vegetable but for the time recommended on the pack.

Aubergine

Baked This is a quick and easy way to cook aubergine (eggplant) if it is to be puréed. Use medium (8 oz/225 g) aubergines to ensure even cooking. Cut off the spiny calyx, prick all over with a fork, then arrange on a double thickness of paper towelling. Cook on 100 per cent power for the minimum cooking time and then test for 'done-ness' by piercing with a skewer. If not completely tender (the vegetable will also look slightly 'collapsed'), cook for a further 2 minutes. (See Aubergine and Tahina Purée p. 23.)

8 oz (225 g) take 6 minutes
1 lb (450 g) takes 10 minutes
1½ lb (675 g) take 15 minutes

Allow to cool before halving and removing the pulp.

Sliced for a casserole This is an excellent way to cook aubergine for dishes such as Moussaka (see p. 155), using very little oil. However, don't expect them to be as golden brown as when sautéd. Peel the aubergines (the skin toughens in the microwave), then cut in ½-inch (1-cm) slices and arrange in layers in a colander or salad spinner, sprinkling each layer lightly with cooking salt. Leave for 30 minutes, rinse and dry, then in a 3½–4 pint (2-l /9–10-cup) casserole or bowl toss to coat on all sides with 2–3 tablespoons of oil. Cook, covered, on 100 per cent power, stirring gently half-way to rearrange the slices, until tender when pierced with a sharp knife, then treat as sautéd.

1–1¼ lb (450–600 g) take 8 minutes
1½ lb (675 g) take 10 minutes
2 lb (900 g) take 14 minutes

Beans, Whole Green

(Including String, Kenyan and Bobo Beans)

To prepare and cook Remove strings if necessary, top and tail, then arrange in one layer in a shallow-lidded casserole. Add 4 tablespoons of water, cover and cook on 100 per cent power. Cooking times are based on very fresh beans; older or more mature ones will take a little longer. Drain well and season with sea salt and black pepper.

4 oz (125 g) take 4 minutes
8 oz (225 g) take 4½ minutes
1 lb (450 g) takes 6–9 minutes

Broccoli

To prepare and cook The brilliant green that fades so quickly in a pan of boiling water is miraculously retained in the microwave, provided the vegetable is prepared so that the florets and stalks can become tender at the same time. However, the broccoli must be completely fresh, with no sign of yellowing. Cut off and discard any thick, tough stalks, then divide the broccoli into florets. Cut off the slimmer stalks and slice them thinly. Put both in a microwave-safe serving dish, arranging the stalks to the outside with the heads in the centre. Add 3 tablespoons of water, cover and cook on 100 per cent power until the stalks are just tender when pierced with a slim, sharp knife. For immediate use, drain, salt lightly and serve or coat with a sauce. For later use, put in a colander and drench with cold water to set the colour. Season and reheat as required.

8–10 oz (225–275 g) take 5–6 minutes
1 lb (450 g) takes 7–9 minutes (according to variety)

Brussels Sprouts

To prepare and cook Choose very green, very tight sprouts as even in size as possible (to ensure even cooking). Trim the stalk end, then arrange in a single layer in a shallow-lidded casserole. Add 4 tablespoons of water, cover and cook on 100 per cent power until just tender when pierced with a slim, sharp knife – time will vary according to size and maturity. Drain, season and serve.

8 oz (225 g) take 4–5 minutes
12 oz (350 g) take 6–6½ minutes
1 lb (450 g) takes 7–8 minutes

Cabbage

To cook There's no saving of time when cabbage is cooked in the microwave, but there's a big advantage – it can be done in the serving dish. The only kind worth cooking this way is the hearted green cabbage of late summer and early autumn.

To cook 1 lb (450 g) of finely shredded cabbage, put in an oven-to-table microwave-safe dish, add 3 tablespoons of water, cover and cook on 100 per cent power, stirring once, for 8–10 minutes, or until bite-tender. Drain thoroughly, salt and pepper lightly and serve plain or with a sprinkle of caraway seeds.

Carrots

To cook Avoid fibrous old carrots as they will never get really tender. Peel (or scrape if young), then slice in thin rings or in julienne strips. Put in an even layer in a shallow-lidded casserole, add 3 tablespoons of water, cover and cook on 100 per cent power, stirring once, until *'al dente'*.

8 oz (225 g) take 6½–7 minutes
lb (450 g) takes 10–12 minutes

Cauliflower

To cook Use only a very fresh, very white cauliflower and cook it if possible on the day of purchase - even slightly stale cauliflower develops an 'off' flavour in the microwave. Don't attempt to cook a whole head as it's too big a mass to cook evenly, but florets can be cooked to perfection. Cut them away from their stalk - each floret should be about 2 inches (5 cm) in diameter (or use a prepack of florets); 1 lb (450 g) is the equivalent of a medium head of cauliflower. Arrange in a single layer in a shallow-lidded round casserole or serving dish. Add 3 tablespoons of water, cover and cook on 100 per cent power, stirring once to reposition the florets. Test by piercing with a slim, sharp knife, or nibble a piece - it should be tender but still crisp. Drain, then season with salt, pepper and a pinch of nutmeg.

8 oz (225 g) take 6–7 minutes
1 lb (450 g) takes 10–12 minutes

Courgettes

To cook These retain their colour and texture superbly well and cook in their own juices without added liquid. Choose firm ones with shiny, unblemished skins. Tiny ones the size of a finger can be cooked whole; when more mature slice or halve lengthwise, then quarter. Rinse the courgettes and arrange in an even layer in the dish. Cover and cook on 100 per cent power, then stand covered for 3 minutes before seasoning and serving with a sprinkle of fresh herbs such as shredded fresh basil leaves or chopped parsley.

8 oz (225 g) take 8–9 minutes
1 lb (450 g) takes 10–12 minutes

Mushrooms

They cook extremely well in the microwave. To cook *without* fat heat 5 fl oz (150 ml/⅔ cup) vegetable or chicken stock in a wide, lidded casserole for 1 minute. Add 8 oz (225 g/2½ cups) thickly sliced closed cup mushrooms, cover and cook on 100 per cent power for 2 minutes, stirring once. Remove the mushrooms with a slotted spoon and serve, reserving the stock for a soup or sauce.

To cook mushrooms in a *flavoured butter*, put 1 oz (25 g/2 tbsp) butter or margarine and 1 crushed clove of garlic or 1 teaspoon of chopped fresh herbs into a wide-lidded casserole and cook on 100 per cent power for 1 minute. Add 8 oz (225 g/2½ cups) button mushrooms, turning them in the melted fat until well coated. Cover and cook on 100 per cent power for 2 minutes, then season with sea salt and black pepper. This makes an ideal quick snack or starter for 1 or a vegetable accompaniment for 2. For 4 simply double the quantity of mushrooms and the cooking time.

Onions, Pickling or Shallots

To remove the skins quickly and without tears, cut off the root and top end, put in a casserole with 3 tablespoons of water, then cover and cook on 100 per cent power until the skins are softened - about 3-4 minutes according to the weight of onions. The skins will then slip off easily.

Parsnips

To cook completely Trim 1 lb (450 g) parsnips at either end, then peel and cut into 1-inch (2.5-cm) chunks. Lay the chunks in an even layer in a shallow-lidded casserole, add 4 tablespoons of hot water, then cover and cook on 100 per cent power for 9 minutes, stirring once, until absolutely tender when pierced with a slim, pointed knife. Drain, re-cover and allow to stand for 3 minutes. Mash with a little butter or margarine, or purée.

To parcook for roasting Leave small parsnips whole. Cut larger ones in half lengthwise, then cook as above, but for only 4 minutes. Drain well and add to ¼ inch (1 cm) deep hot fat, then roast for 30-40 minutes until golden brown and tender.

Potatoes

To boil (eg for mashing) Peel and cut into 1-inch (2.5-cm) chunks. Arrange in 1 layer in a wide-lidded casserole. Add 4 tablespoons of hot water, cover and cook on 100 per cent power until there is no resistance when the potatoes are pierced with a slim, sharp knife. Leave covered for 2 minutes, then drain and cover lightly with a paper towel to absorb excess moisture. Use as required.

1 lb (450 g) potatoes takes 8–10 minutes
1½ lb (675 g) take 10–12 minutes
2 lb (900 g) take 12–14 minutes

To parboil for roasting Parboiling before roasting ensures that the potatoes are tender and fluffy inside, with a really crunchy brown outside. Use a good roasting potato such as Desiree, King Edward or Pentland Dell. Peel the potatoes and cut into 1-1½-inch-thick (2.5-4-cm) wedges. Put in a shallow casserole with 2 tablespoons of water, cover and cook on 100 per cent power for 5 minutes, then drain and stand covered with a paper towel for 5 minutes to dry off.

1 lb (450 g) takes 5 minutes (serves 2–3)
2 lb (900 g) take 8 minutes (serves 4–5)

To bake Although the flesh of a potato is particularly fluffy when cooked in the microwave, the skin will not be crisp unless a combination oven is used. You can achieve a certain degree of crispness, however, by grilling (broiling) the potatoes after they come out of the microwave. If you do have a combination setting on your microwave, you can achieve both a crisp skin and a fluffy flesh in about half the conventional cooking time.

Choose a prepacked baking potato or use a good baking variety such as Maris Piper or King Edward. If not prepacked, wash and dry the potatoes. Prick them all over to prevent them bursting. Arrange in a circle (if several are cooked together) on a piece of kitchen paper and cook on 100 per cent power, turning over once.

Cooking times for 5 oz (150 g) potatoes are as follows:

1 potato takes 5 minutes
2 potatoes take 6–8 minutes
3 potatoes take 9–10 minutes
4 potatoes take 10–11 minutes

Cooking times for 8 oz (225 g) potatoes are as follows:

1 potato takes 6 minutes
2 potatoes take 12 minutes
3 potatoes take 17 minutes
4 potatoes take 20 minutes

To Cook Vegetables for a Party

Because it is impossible to gauge the exact moment at which green vegetables are to be served at a dinner party, it is wiser to follow the French method of precooking vegetables by first blanching them in a large amount of boiling water and then drenching them with cold water to set the colour. This ensures not only that the vegetables are cooked *'à point'* until tender but still firm, but also that the colour remains a brilliant green. After this preliminary treatment, the vegetables can be reheated either on top of the stove or in their serving dish in the microwave, in butter, margarine or a sauce, and will taste freshly cooked. This method is not suitable for regular use as the food value is not as good as when vegetables are cooked by the conventional 'short boil' method in a minimum of water.

Blanching

Earlier in the day, half-fill a large pan with water and bring to the boil on top of the stove. Add a teaspoon of salt and the chosen vegetable. Cook at a vigorous boil with the lid only partly on (to preserve the colour) until the vegetables are still slightly chewy. Immediately drain through a colander, then hold under the cold tap until steaming stops. Allow to drain thoroughly (this can be done by spinning in a salad basket). If the vegetables are to be reheated in the microwave, arrange in a serving dish and refrigerate until an hour before serving, then leave at room temperature. Reheat in the microwave, season and serve.

An ABC of Vegetables

Aubergines

The aubergine (eggplant) is a favourite vegetable of the Sephardi Jews who came originally from the Middle East via the Iberian Peninsula, as well as Ashkenazi Jews from the Balkan States. Today it is widely grown, and eaten, in Israel. Many of the best recipes are of Turkish, Romanian or Hungarian origin. A choice aubergine may be either egg-shaped or elongated, but it should always be glossy, plump and firm, for shrinkage, dullness and softness herald decay. For stuffing, the boat-shaped kind are best and for cubing, the egg-shaped; unless it is to be cooked whole, the flesh should first be salted, as this reduces by 50 per cent the amount of oil needed to sauté it. Deep-frying also allows a minimum of oil to penetrate the flesh. If slices of aubergine are to be used in a dish, the amount of oil needed can be drastically reduced by *brushing* each side with oil and grilling (broiling) until golden instead of sautéing. With this method, pre-salting is not necessary.

It is inadvisable to freeze raw aubergine as it goes watery and bitter. However, stuffed or stewed aubergine will freeze well.

A fresh aubergine can be stored in the refrigerator for up to a week without deteriorating in any way.

AUBERGINE SAUTÉ

Serves 4 generously.
Prepare and eat the same day.

This is the best way to taste the characteristic flavour in its simplest form, and a good recipe to serve with grilled steaks or chops.

2 large plump aubergines (eggplants) – 1½ lb (675 g) total weight
coarse salt
4 tbsp sunflower or extra virgin olive oil

1 clove of garlic, crushed
1 level tbsp parsley
2 level teasp dried leaf oregano or 2 tbsp chopped fresh oregano
10 grinds of black pepper

Peel then cut the aubergines into ½-inch (1.25-cm) cubes. Put into a colander or salad spinner, sprinkle with coarse salt, cover with a plate and a weight and leave for 30 minutes for the juices to drain away. Rinse with cold water, then dab dry with paper towels or spin. Heat the oil in a heavy frying pan - it should be ⅛ inch (0.3 cm) deep - put in the cubes and cook gently, shaking the pan occasionally until they are meltingly tender - about 15 minutes. After 10 minutes, add the crushed garlic. Just before serving, add the parsley and oregano and sprinkle with the black pepper. The dish can be reheated and comes to no harm if made early and left to stand.

AUBERGINE MEUNIÈRE

Serves 6–8.
Eat immediately.
Do not freeze.

The aubergines need to be freshly cooked or the coating may go soggy. They can be kept hot in a shallow dish for 15 minutes at Gas No. 4 (350°F/180°C).

1½–2 lb (800–900 g) aubergines (eggplants)
salt
4 tbsp flour
6 tbsp extra virgin olive oil
2 tbsp chopped parsley
15 grinds of black pepper

Cut the unpeeled aubergines in ½-inch (1.25-cm) thick slices, discarding the hard stalk ends. Put into a colander or salad spinner, sprinkle with salt, cover with a plate and a weight, and leave for 30 minutes for the bitter juices to run out. Rinse thoroughly with cold water, then dry on paper towels or spin dry. Put the flour in a plastic bag and drop in the slices a few at a time. Shake them until evenly coated, brushing off excess flour before frying them 1 layer at a time in the hot fat - which should come to a depth of ¼ inch (0.5 cm) in the frying pan. As they brown and become tender, transfer the slices to a shallow tin in a warm oven. When all of them are fried, transfer to a shallow dish and sprinkle with parsley and black pepper. Serve at once.

AUBERGINES STUFFED IN THE MEDITERRANEAN FASHION

Serves 6.
Leftovers keep 2 days under refrigeration.

These stuffed aubergines are used as an accompaniment rather than as a dish in their own right, as when stuffed with meat or chicken livers. They make an excellent accompaniment to hot fried or grilled fillets of sole or plaice.

6 small or 3 plump aubergines (eggplants)
coarse salt
3 tbsp extra virgin olive oil
½ oz (15 g/1 tbsp) butter or margarine
1 large onion, finely chopped
½ large red or yellow pepper
1 x 14 oz (400 g) can peeled plum totatoes in juice, well drained
2 level teasp dried oregano
1 tbsp chopped parsley
1 clove of garlic, crushed
salt
pepper
pinch of sugar

For the topping
3 tbsp dry breadcrumbs
2 tbsp melted butter or margarine
1 tbsp grated cheese

Cut aubergines in half lengthwise, make deep criss-cross cuts into the flesh, and sprinkle lightly with coarse salt. After half an hour, rinse off the surface and dry well, squeezing out any free juice. Heat oil gently, put aubergines in pan face-down and fry gently on both sides until flesh feels soft. Remove and allow to cool, then scrape out the flesh, leaving a ½-inch (1.25-cm) lining. Put the skins in an oven-proof casserole dish. Meanwhole, sauté the chopped onion in butter in a covered pan until soft and golden, then add the pepper and tomatoes and cook for a few minutes longer. Add mashed or chopped aubergine flesh, herbs, garlic, seasonings and sugar, and simmer all together until mixture is thick but still juicy. Divide the mixture evenly between the skins, mix the crumbs with the melted butter and then the cheese, and sprinkle on the aubergines. Put under a moderate grill (broiler) for 5 or 6 minutes, or bake in a quick, moderate oven, Gas No. 6 (400°F/200°C), for 15 minutes.

STIR-FRIED WHOLE GREEN BEANS AND MUSHROOMS

Serves 6–8.
Leftovers keep 1 day under refrigeration.
Do not freeze.

A quick yet subtly flavoured dish that can be prepared early in the day.

12 oz–1 lb (350–450 g) whole green Kenya (French) beans or sugar snap peas
1½ tbsp sunflower or extra virgin olive oil
1 clove of garlic
1 inch (2½ cm) fresh ginger
12 oz (350 g/4 cups) white mushrooms
1 teasp light soy sauce
½ teasp salt
10 grinds of black pepper

Early in the day, top and tail the beans, then cook, uncovered, in a large pan of boiling salted water until barely tender - about 4 minutes. Turn into a colander and drench with cold water. Drain well, then chill.

Heat the oil in a large frying pan for 3 minutes with the peeled garlic and slivered ginger, then add the thinly sliced mushrooms and stir-fry briskly for 4 minutes. Leave in the pan. Just before serving, add the beans and toss over high heat until steaming - about 3 minutes. Sprinkle with the soy sauce and seasonings and serve piping hot.

A SAUTÉ OF GREEN BEANS AND ALMONDS

Serves 6.
Leftovers keep 3 days under refrigeration.
Do not freeze.

This is an excellent vegetable dish for a special occasion, as most of the preparation can be done early in the day. The split almonds can be toasted in a moderate oven, under the grill (broiler) or in the microwave (4 minutes on 100 per cent power, stirring once or twice).

1 lb (450 g) thin French beans
2 teasp salt
1 oz (25 g/2 tbsp) butter or margarine
2 oz (50 g/½ cup) blanched almonds, split and toasted
½ teasp sea salt
10 grinds of black pepper

Earlier in the day, top and tail the beans if necessary. Bring a large pan of water to the boil with 2 teaspoons of salt. Add the beans slowly, bring back to the boil (half-covering the pan to hasten the process), then boil for 5 or 6 minutes, or until just bite-tender. Turn into a colander and drench with cold water to stop the beans cooking and to set the colour. Drain well, then refrigerate.

Just before the meal, melt the butter or margarine in a heavy pan until it turns a light hazelnut brown. Add the almonds and the beans, and toss thoroughly over a low heat, seasoning with sea salt and black pepper. When steaming hot, turn into a dish and serve at once (they can be kept hot in a low oven for not longer than 30 minutes).

VARIATION

GREEN BEANS WITH GARLIC BUTTER

Omit the almonds and add a good pinch of garlic granules to the melted fat instead.

TO COOK WHITE- OR GREEN-HEARTED CABBAGE

Serves 6–8.
This is better cooked fresh and in the minimum amount of water.

1 medium cabbage (1½–2 lb/675–900 g)
2 level teasp salt
1 oz (25 g/2 tbsp) butter or margarine
salt
black pepper

Quarter the cabbage head, then shred finely (if possible in a food processor), first discarding any tough outer leaves and the stalk. Half-fill a large bowl with cold water and add 2 teaspoons of salt. Put in the cabbage and leave for half an hour.

Melt the fat in a heavy-based 8-inch (20-cm) saucepan. Lift the cabbage from the water and, without drying it, put into the saucepan. Add a sprinkle of salt and a few grinds of pepper. Cover and simmer in the fat and juices, shaking occasionally, until the cabbage is bite-tender – 10–15 minutes. Uncover and leave over a low heat to remove any excess moisture. Turn into a dish. If you need to keep it hot for 10–15 minutes, cover and put in a warm oven, Gas No. ½ (250°F/120°C), or just before serving give it 1 minute on 100 per cent power in the microwave.

BRAISED RED CABBAGE IN THE VIENNESE STYLE

Serves 6–8.
Keeps 4 days under refrigeration.
Freeze 3 months.

Jewish cooks with a German and Austrian background make wonderful variations on the theme of red cabbage, using apples, dried fruit, fruit jelly, vinegar and wine in different permutations to create the sweet and sour effect that's characteristic of this luscious dish. Serve the cabbage with meat casseroles and pies, cold roast or pickled meats, or as part of a mixed vegetable platter for a vegetarian meal.

2 lb (900 g) red cabbage
2 oz (50 g/¼ cup) butter or margarine
1 large onion, finely chopped
1 oz (25 g/2 tbsp) brown sugar or granular sweetener (optional)
2 generous tbsp crabapple or redcurrant jelly *(see pp. 496, 497)*
2 tbsp cider vinegar
1 tbsp water
2 teasp salt
¼ teasp white pepper
1 large bay leaf

Quarter the cabbage (remove the stalk section and discard), then shred finely by hand or machine. Rinse in cold water and drain well.

Melt the fat in a heavy pan large enough to hold the cabbage. Add the finely chopped onion and cook for 5 minutes until golden brown. Add the sugar (if used) and stir until it begins to caramelize. Now add the cabbage and all the remaining ingredients, stirring well to blend, until bubbling. Transfer to an oven casserole – a covered roaster or an enamelled steel dish are both excellent. Cook in a preheated oven, Gas No. 5 (375°F/190°C), for 45 minutes to 1 hour. Stir twice. Taste and add more sugar if necesary – the cabbage should have an equal balance of sour and sweet. It should also have a little bite left when it is ready. It can then be kept hot at Gas No. 1

(275°F/140°C) for as long as required. It also reheats extremely well, covered, in the microwave on 100 per cent power for 4 minutes, or until steaming.

The Capsicum (or Sweet Peppers)

The pepper needs sun and warmth to mature and sweeten it. Israel, Spain, Hungary and Italy grow it with great success, but it is also produced under glass elsewhere in Europe. It is much used in the cuisine of Jewish families with a Hungarian, Romanian and Austrian background (for Stuffed Peppers, see p. 152).

It is a most useful vegetable to have in stock, for even a quarter will add flavour to a stew or salad, and the remainder can be wrapped in clingfilm (saranwrap) or foil and refrigerated for up to a week. I used to think there was little to choose in flavour between red, yellow or green peppers, but more recent varieties of red, yellow and orange ones are definitely sweeter and less acid. In the great market in Budapest you will see peppers that are so 'hot' they take away your breath, but among the rainbow of colours, there isn't a dark green one to be seen.

Whatever the colour, the vegetable should be glossy and firm and quite free from bruises. Before it is used, every scrap of the white ribs and bitter seeds needs to be discarded.

FRIED PEPPERS

Serves 4.

This is the simplest - and one of the most delicious - ways to cook peppers.

4 large glossy peppers of any colour
2 tbsp extra virgin olive oil
small clove of garlic, crushed with salt
1 tbsp chopped fresh or 1 teasp dried marjoram or oregano
1 level teasp salt
10 grinds of black pepper

Cut the peppers in half and remove the seeds and ribs. Wash and then slice in strips, 3 to each half. Heat the oil gently, then add the peppers and cook quickly for a few minutes, until beginning to soften, stirring frequently. Add the garlic, cover, reduce heat to the minimum and cook slowly for 15-20 minutes, until tender. Add the herbs and seasonings.

These are best eaten hot off the pan as they tend to go soggy if reheated.

PEPERONATA

Serves 6–8.
Keeps 3 days under refrigeration.
Freeze 3 months.

A juicier dish altogether, which can be served either hot as a vegetable or cold as a starter. Use green peppers if red are not available.

6 fine peppers
3 tbsp extra virgin olive oil
1 medium onion
1 teasp brown sugar or granular sweetener
1 clove of garlic, crushed
1 x 14 oz (400 g) can tomatoes, drained, or 8 peeled and chopped fresh tomatoes
1 teasp dried Herbes de Provence
1 tbsp fresh chopped parsley
10 grinds of black pepper
½ teasp sea salt

Halve the peppers, remove seeds and core, then cut in 1-inch (2.5-cm) strips. Put the oil in a deep, wide frying pan and heat gently. Peel the onion, halve, then slice as thinly as possible and cook in the oil until limp and pale gold, sprinkling on the sugar to hasten the process - about 5 minutes. Add the peppers and continue to cook gently for 15 minutes, turning in the oil. Add the garlic, the tomatoes, herbs and seasonings and continue to bubble until the mixture is like a thick stew - another 10 minutes. The peppers should be soft but not soggy. Taste and add more seasoning if necessary.

Ratatouille

This kind of vegetable 'stew' is made all over the Mediterranean, and is particularly popular with Jews who came from the former Ottoman Empire. If aubergines (eggplants) are out of season, use a 10-inch-long (25-cm) vegetable marrow, or extra courgettes (zucchini). Serve with roast veal, grilled steak or roast chicken, or at room temperature as a starter with brown or rye bread.

RATATOUILLE NIÇOISE

Serves 6.
Keeps 3 days under refrigeration.
Freeze 3 months.

2 long or 1 fat egg-shaped aubergine
(approx. 1 lb/450 g total weight)
2 large green peppers
1 large onion
2 courgettes (optional)
smallest size can tomatoes, without juice, or
6 fresh tomatoes
1 clove of garlic, crushed
5 tbsp extra virgin olive oil
salt
pepper
1 teasp brown sugar or granular sweetener
1 tbsp wine vinegar
1 tbsp lemon juice

First prepare the vegetables. Peel and cube the aubergines; seed, slice, then dice the peppers; slice the onion thinly; scrub and slice the courgettes (if used); peel and quarter tomatoes if fresh. Crush the garlic with a little salt. Put the oil in a heavy-lidded frying pan and cook the onion gently, covered, until soft, then add the remaining vegetables. Season with salt and pepper, sprinkle with the sugar, cover and cook for 1 hour. If the mixture starts to stick, add a little hot water. It should be thick but juicy; if too runny, remove lid and allow to thicken. Just before serving, add the wine vinegar and lemon juice.

VARIATION

RATATOUILLE WITHOUT OIL

Serves 4–6.
Keeps 3 days under refrigeration.
Freeze 3 months.

This may not be *'classique'* but it is a very delicious dish in its own right. It makes an ideal accompaniment to grilled steak, beefburgers or roast chicken, or it can be served as a starter with coarse brown bread.

6 fresh 'beef' tomatoes, peeled and chopped, or
1 x 15 oz (425 g) can tomatoes, plus juice
1 tbsp tomato purée
5 fl oz (150 ml/⅔ cup) vegetable stock
(made from a cube or 1 teasp vegetable paste)
1 fat clove of garlic, peeled and crushed
1 teasp salt
10 grinds of black pepper
1 teasp brown sugar or granular sweetener
1 tbsp dried minced onion
3 medium-sized peppers, seeds removed,
sliced ¼ inch (1 cm) wide
2 medium-sized green peppers, seeds removed,
sliced ⅜ inch (1 cm) wide
1½ lb (675 g) aubergines (eggplants) unpeeled,
sliced ⅜ inch (1 cm) thick
12 oz (350 g) courgettes (zucchini) unpeeled, sliced
⅜ inch (1 cm) thick
1 teasp dried Herbes de Provence
1 tbsp parsley or fresh basil
2 tbsp lemon juice
2 oz (50 g/½ cup) black olives (optional)

Put the tomatoes, tomato purée, stock, garlic salt, pepper, sugar and onion into a fairly wide pan and bring to the boil. Add the peppers and aubergines, cover and simmer for 20 minutes. Add the courgettes and herbs, half-cover and simmer for a further 5-10 minutes, until they are just tender. If the mixture is watery, uncover and bubble for 5 minutes, or until it is thick but still juicy. Stir in the lemon juice and olives (if used). This dish may be reheated.

GLAZED CARROTS

Serves 6.
Keeps 2 days under refrigeration.
Freeze 1 month.

1½ lb (675 g) new carrots
good nut of margarine or butter
1 teasp peeled and chopped fresh ginger
1 level tbsp mild honey
2 teasp grated orange rind
1 level teasp salt

Scrape the carrots, then slice as thinly as possible. Put in a deep narrow pan, add fat and sprinkle with the other ingredients. Cover completely with water, then bring to the boil. Simmer uncovered until the water has evaporated and the carrots are tender and coated in a shiny glaze - about 30 minutes.

For a party, the carrots can be cooked until almost dry earlier in the day. They can be reheated for 1 or 2 minutes to drive off the remaining liquid while the meat is being sliced between courses. Or they can be cooked completely then arranged in a serving dish and reheated in the microwave. Carrots cooked in this way can also be mixed with peas and make a most delicious and colourful vegetable dish.

MINTED CARROT PURÉE

Serves 6–8.
Keeps 3 days under refrigeration.
Freeze 1 month.

2 lb (900 g) carrots, peeled and cut in 1-inch (2.5-cm) pieces
1 teasp dried mint or 1 tbsp fresh in season
2 oz (50 g/¼ cup) soft butter or margarine
1 teasp sugar or granular sweetener
1 teasp salt
¼ teasp white pepper

Cook the vegetables in a large pan of boiling, salted water until tender - about 20 minutes. Drain well and reserve some of the liquid. Purée the vegetables in a food processor or put through a food mill, then return to the pan, add the remaining ingredients and use a balloon whisk to incorporate evenly. Add a little of the hot cooking liquid if necessary to make a creamy consistency.

Reheats well in the microwave.

CARROT AND CORIANDER PURÉE

Serves 6.
Keeps 3 days under refrigeration.
Freeze 1 month.

2 lb (900 g) carrots
1 bunch spring onions (scallions)
1 tbsp freshly ground coriander
1½ teasp sugar or granular sweetener
1½ teasp salt
20 grinds of black pepper
2 oz (50 g/¼ cup) margarine or butter

In a saucepan combine the thinly sliced carrots, the trimmed spring onions cut in 2-inch (5-cm) lengths, the coriander, sugar, salt and pepper and enough hot water to barely cover the vegetables. Bring to the boil, then cover and simmer for 25 minutes, or until the carrots are very tender. Strain through a sieve, reserving about ½ cup of the cooking liquid. Purée the carrots in a food processor, adding enough of the liquid to make a thick, slightly moist purée, then pulse in the margarine. Taste and reseason if necessary. The purée may be made ahead, then reheated either over a low light on top of the stove or in a covered dish in the microwave on 100 per cent power for about 3 minutes.

Reheats well in the microwave.

CAULIFLOWER AU GRATIN

Serves 8–10.
Keep oven-ready dish 2 days, cooked leftovers 1 day, under refrigeration.
Do not freeze.

A most delicious dish when it is made with really fresh cauliflower cooked until tender but still slightly firm.

2 x 8-inch (20-cm) cauliflowers, tough stalk removed and divided into florets, or 2 x 1 lb (450 g) ready-to-eat florets

For the Sauce Mornay
1½ pints (850 ml/3¾ cups) milk
2 oz (50 g/¼ cup) butter or margarine
2 oz (50 g/½ cup) flour
½ level teasp salt
4 oz (125 g/1 cup) sharp cheese, coarsely grated
pinch of nutmeg
pinch of Cayenne pepper

For the topping
3 tbsp fine dry crumbs
3 tbsp grated cheese
2 oz (50 g/¼ cup) melted butter or margarine

Plunge half the washed cauliflower florets into a large pan, three-quarters full of boiling water, with 3 level teaspoons of salt. Boil steadily, uncovered, for 6–8 minutes, or until the stalk feels just tender when pierced with a sharp knife – it's safest to taste a piece. Lift carefully from the water to prevent crushing and put into a colander. Plunge into a basin of cold water. Leave for 3 minutes, then lift out and allow to drain. Repeat with the remaining cauliflower. It is now ready for the sauce.

Put the cold milk, butter and flour into a heavy-based 7–8-inch (17.5–20-cm) saucepan and cook over moderate heat, whisking constantly with a balloon whisk until smooth, thick and bubbling. Add the cheese and seasonings and allow to simmer for 3 minutes (to cook the starch), stirring particularly well round the bottom edge of the pan with a wooden spoon.

Have ready a buttered gratin dish approximately 11 inches (27.5 cm) in diameter and 2 inches (5 cm) deep (or use a rectangular dish of similar depth). Lightly cover the bottom with sauce, then arrange the cauliflower on top. Mask completely with the remainder of the sauce. Mix the dry crumbs and cheese and sprinkle evenly on top. Finally pour over the melted butter. Leave loosely covered with greaseproof paper until ready to bake.

Cook in a moderately hot oven, Gas No. 5 (375°F/190°C), for 30 minutes, until bubbly and golden brown. Keep hot at Gas No. 2 (300°F/150°C) until required. Or heat through in the microwave on 100 per cent power for 4–5 minutes until bubbling, then brown under the grill (broiler).

Courgettes

Some would say this vegetable lacks flavour – it certainly has a very high water content. However, crisply sautéd or stewed in a savoury sauce, it has much to commend it. Always choose shiny skinned, small or medium-size specimens (the larger, coarser ones are fine for soup – see p. 31 and resist the temptation to overcook them, because they can become very flabby in texture. To prepare, cut off ¼ inch (0.5 cm) from both ends and wash well. There is no need to peel good-quality ones.

A SIMPLE LOW-FAT SAUTÉ OF COURGETTES

Serves 4–6.
Keeps 1 day under refrigeration.
Do not freeze.

The courgettes are cooked in their own juices with just a little fat to add flavour.

1½ lb (675 g) courgettes (zucchini)
nut of butter or margarine, or 1 tbsp extra virgin olive oil
1 clove of garlic, chopped
½ teasp salt
10 grinds of black pepper
1 tbsp chopped fresh or 1 teasp dried oregano or marjoram
Herbes de Provence

Slice the unpeeled courgettes 1 inch (2.5 cm) thick. In a heavy 8–9 inch (20–22.5 cm) frying or sauté pan, heat the fat and garlic for 1 minute, then add the courgettes. Sprinkle with the salt and pepper, cover and cook over medium heat, shaking the pan occasionally until browned and just tender (taste one!). Sprinkle with the herbs and serve.

COURGETTES IN A TOMATO AND HERB SAUCE

Serves 6–8.
Keeps 3 days under refrigeration.
Freeze 2 months.

This can be served hot or cold.

1½–2 lb (675–900 g) courgettes (zucchini)
2 tbsp extra virgin olive oil
2 medium onions, thinly sliced or chopped
1 x 15 oz (425 g) can of whole tomatoes
1 tbsp snipped fresh or 1 teasp dried basil
1 bay leaf
1 teasp salt
1 teasp brown sugar or granular sweetener
15 grinds of black pepper
1 clove of garlic, crushed

Cut the unpeeled courgettes into 1-inch (2.5-cm) slices. Heat the oil gently and sauté the onions until they are pale gold, limp and transparent – 5–10 minutes. Add all the remaining ingredients except the courgettes and simmer, uncovered, for 5 minutes. Add the courgettes, cover and simmer until tender when pierced with a sharp knife – about 10 minutes. If the sauce is too runny, simmer a minute or so to thicken it.

VARIATION

COURGETTES NIÇOISE

Prepare as above but with the addition of 1 tablespoon of chopped parsley and 12 stoned and roughly cut-up black olives.

COURGETTE CRISPS

Serves 6–8.
Eat immediately.

These crispy 'chips' are quite delicious – and so easy to make with an automatic deep-fryer (they can be made in a chip pan one-third full of oil, but I don't think they're then worth the effort!).

Serve them with grilled chops or steak, with veal or turkey escalopes, or even – instead of potato chips – with cold cuts or wurst.

1½–2 lb (675–900 g) courgettes (zucchini), unpeeled
salt
flour
oil for deep frying

Cut each courgette lengthwise into slices ¼ inch (0.5 cm) thick, then cut across into 'chips' about 1½ inches (4 cm) long. Put them in a colander and sprinkle with salt. Leave for 1 hour, then dry well with paper or a tea-towel.

Put 2 tablespoons of flour into a plastic bag and toss the chips in it until they are lightly coated.

Heat a deep-fryer to 375°F (190°C) - chip-frying temperature. Put in the floured courgettes in 2 batches, cooking until golden brown and crisp - about 3-4 minutes for each batch. Keep hot at Gas No. 6 (400°F/200°C) until all are done. If there is a delay, they can be kept hot at Gas No. 1 (275°F/140°C) for up to 20 minutes.

LIME-SCENTED COURGETTE RIBBONS WITH SESAME SEEDS

Serves 6–8.

This is a particularly pretty dish for a dinner party, though it does need to be stir-fried shortly before dinner. The courgettes can then be reheated, uncovered, until steaming, on top of the stove or in the microwave just before serving.

2 lb (900 g) courgettes, about 1 inch (2.5 cm) in diameter, topped and tailed
1½ oz (40 g/3 tbsp) butter or margarine, or 2 tbsp extra virgin olive oil
2 teasp caster sugar or granular sweetener
½ teasp salt
1 teasp ground coriander
zest of a lime cut into fine strips
1½ tbsp lime juice
1 tbsp fresh chopped parsley or coriander
2 tbsp toasted sesame seeds (optional)

Use a swivel-bladed potato peeler to cut the unpeeled courgettes into ribbons by drawing the peeler down the length of the courgette - hence the need for a fairly thick courgette. This can be done early in the day.

When ready to cook, heat the butter or margarine in a wok or wide sauté pan until sizzling (if oil is used, until you can feel the heat on your hand held 2 inches (5 cm) above the pan). Add the courgettes (don't worry if the pan looks crowded - they will shrink dramatically) and sprinkle with the sugar, salt and ground coriander.

Using 2 large spoons, toss over high heat, until softened and glazed, then add the lime rind and juice. Toss again until steaming, then serve scattered with the chopped herbs and sesame seeds.

GRATIN OF COURGETTES

Serves 6–8.
Keeps 2 days under refrigeration, uncooked or as leftovers.

This is a splendid dish for a dairy or fish dinner party as it can be assembled well in advance, or as a main dish for vegetarians. It is important to blanch the vegetables very briefly or their texture will be ruined.

2 lb (900 g) courgettes

For the béchamel sauce
15 fl oz (425 ml/2 cups) milk
1 oz (25 g/2 tbsp) butter or margarine
1 oz (25 g/¼ cup) flour
½ teasp salt
pinch of white pepper
pinch of nutmeg
2 oz (50 g/½ cup) Gruyère cheese
2 oz (50 g/½ cup) Parmesan or another sharp grated cheese
5 fl oz (150 ml/⅔ cup) whipping cream
1 large egg, beaten
1 tbsp snipped chives

For the topping
3 tbsp extra Gruyère
¼ teasp paprika

Top and tail the courgettes and cut them into ⅜-inch-thick (1-cm) diagonal slices. Bring a pan of salted water to the boil, then put in the slices, bring back to the boil for 1 minute, then turn into a colander and drench with cold water. Allow to drain thoroughly.

To make the sauce, put the cold milk, butter and flour into a thick-based pan and whisk with a balloon whisk over moderate heat until smooth and bubbly. Add the seasonings, then simmer for 3 minutes, stirring with a wooden spoon. Add the cheese, cream, egg and chives, and stir well together.

Arrange the courgettes in even layers in a buttered gratin dish measuring approximately 15½ x 8½ x 2½ inches (39 x 22 x 6 cm) rim to rim. Pour over the sauce, scatter with the extra Gruyère, and dust with the paprika.

Bake at Gas No. 7 (425°F/220°C) for 25 minutes, until golden brown and bubbling at the edges. The dish can be prepared in advance and then cooked until bubbling on 100 per cent power in the microwave - after about 6 minutes - then browned under the grill (broiler).

Mushrooms

Mushrooms were much prized by the Jewish communities of Eastern Europe - but only in their dried form. According to Edouard de Pomiane, the French chef who studied the cookery of the Polish Jews before the Second World War, these were of the variety *Boletus edulis,* known to the French as *'cèpes'* and the Italians as *'porcini'*.

In her book *A Taste of Russia,* Darra Goldstein explains how they were dried. The mushrooms were freshly gathered from the woods and fields (none was cultivated as today), then well wiped and the stalks removed. They were laid out on brown paper to dry in the sun for 2 to 3 days, covered with muslin to protect them from insects, and brought in at night as soon as it began to grow damp. Once they were dry, they were threaded on twine and hung in the sun or in a well-ventilated room until they were completely dried out, then stored in airtight jars. Before use they were reconstituted by soaking for 30 minutes in warm water.

According to a legend in the family, when my great grandmother came on a visit from Russia to England in the early years of this century, the present she brought was a string of these dried mushrooms which were mainly used in 'krupnik' - a superb barley soup.

Being grown in the dark and therefore quite independent of the vagaries of the weather, the mushroom is the one vegetable that is in prime season all the year round. And because it includes such useful nutrients as protein, iron, potassium and a range of the B vitamins (including B12, which is particularly important for the vegetarian), yet contains virtually no fat and less than 30 calories per 4 oz (125 g/1¼ cups), it's one of the few gourmet foods that can be enjoyed without a dietetic qualm. However, if you are watching your weight, it is best to eat mushrooms raw, baked, micro-waved, poached, casseroled or grilled, as frying will increase the calorie content tremendously.

Which Mushroom?

Some 98 per cent of all the cultivated mushrooms sold in this country are of the variety *Agaricus bisporus.* They are sold as 'buttons', 'cups' and 'open flats' or 'breakfast mushrooms'. These terms refer to the stages of growth of the mushrooms on picking, *not* to specific mushroom varieties.

These cultivated mushrooms are grown in sterilized compost so that they do not need to be peeled. If the stalks are used, discard only the last ¼ inch (0.5 cm) of tip, but use all the rest. Rinse only briefly (or wipe with a damp cloth) and dry before use. A truly fresh mushroom is plump and clean with a sweet smell, and its gills, whatever the size of the cap, should be a pinky beige and never a murky brown.

Buttons are small, white and tightly closed. They have a delicate flavour and because of their pale colour are suitable for sauces. They are decorative for garnishing and can be used whole, sliced or quartered and added to salads, cooked dishes and used fresh as *crudités* for dips.

Cups (which are allowed to grow on the mushroom bed for a further 12-24 hours) are slightly more mature, with a fuller flavour. Closed (when the skin is closed beneath the cup) or open cups (the fine white skin drawn away from the stalk to reveal the pink gills) are very versatile and may be used in place of buttons and flats in most recipes. They can be sliced, quartered or chopped. They're ideal in casseroles, soups, stuffings and for frying and baking, and as a vegetable.

Opens, flats or 'breakfast' mushrooms are fully mature with a rich flavour - at this stage the darkened gills are completely exposed. They're usually sold prepacked to prevent bruising. These are best for grilling and frying. Their deeper flavour makes them good accompaniments to robust foods such as chops and steaks.

Eaten raw, mushrooms will retain most of their vitamins, although if they are to be marinated, covering them with clingfilm (saranwrap) will prevent damage to the vitamins from exposure to the air.

Since the advent of the shrink-wrapped prepack, the lifespan of the cultivated mushroom stored in the domestic refrigerator has been extended from 24 hours to 5 days. This is because they're protected from the air and warm atmospheres, both of which make them discolour and curl up at the edges. So if you do buy mushrooms loose, store them in an airtight container in the refrigerator, as tightly packed as possible to enclose the minimum of air. For the finest taste and texture, all mushrooms are best eaten as soon as possible after purchase.

Cooking means the loss of some of the B group vitamins into the juice, but since the liquid is generally consumed with the mushrooms in a soup or casserole, the vitamins stay in the dish.

When frying, choose the closed-cup mushrooms and always cook them quickly to retain their goodness.

Using a microwave oven, cook 1 lb (450 g/5 cups) of button mushrooms with a little butter, margarine or stock on 100 per cent power for about 4 minutes.

For freezing, sauté 1 lb (450 g/5 cups) of sliced cup mushrooms in 2 oz (50 g/¼ cup) butter or margarine and 1 teaspoon of lemon juice for 1-2 minutes. Cool and store in freezer bags for up to 3 months.

Two new varieties of cultivated mushrooms are now widely available, and need to be handled and used rather differently from the familiar *Agaricus bisporus.*

Oyster mushrooms, named for their resemblance to the oyster shell, have a distinctive light-coloured flesh and creamy gills. Eaten raw, the texture is crisp and the flavour mildly 'woody'. When cooked, the texture softens but remains firm.

To prepare, cut off the lowest part of the stalk only. Depending on size, halve or quarter for use. Try them raw, thinly sliced with fresh herbs, yoghurt, soured cream, fromage frais and lemon juice. Chop into salads. Fry with a little butter and lemon juice until lightly browned. Bake in foil with butter and lemon at Gas No. 6 (400°F/200°C) for 5-10 minutes depending on size. Perfect as a side dish for a dairy meal.

Shitake mushrooms, which are sometimes called 'forest mushrooms' or 'black mushrooms' in oriental recipes, may vary in colour from creamy brown to a very dark chestnut. Cultivated on sawdust or cut logs, the flavour of the shitake mushroom is far more pronounced than other varieties, with 'meaty' or 'garlicky' overtones, and the flesh is significantly softer. Prepare and cook like oyster mushrooms, but do not remove the majority of the stalk. Do *not* boil or shitake will lose their aroma and become tough. Ideal in oriental recipes, omelettes, stews and casseroles.

MUSHROOMS FRIED IN BUTTER

Serves 3–4.
Keeps 1 day under refrigeration.
Freeze 3 months.

Mushrooms are very porous, so as soon as they are put into a frying pan they appear to absorb all the fat. However, do not be tempted to add more; simply keep shaking the pan so that they cook evenly and in 2 or 3 minutes your patience will be rewarded and the fat will reappear on the surface of each mushroom. After 2 or 3 more minutes (keep tossing them in the pan) they will have browned to perfection and be cooked. The mushrooms make a superb omelette filling.

8 oz (225 g/2½ cups) open-cup mushrooms
1 oz (25 g/2 tbsp) butter or margarine
2 teasp flavourless oil – eg sunflower oil
½ teasp fine sea salt
10 grinds of black pepper
good pinch of nutmeg

Trim the stalks off at the cup. If the mushrooms are small, leave whole, otherwise cut into quarters. Heat the butter and oil in a 9–10-inch (22.5–25-cm) frying pan large enough to hold the mushrooms in 1 layer, with the fine sea salt, black pepper and nutmeg. The butter will foam, and as soon as this subsides, immediately put the mushrooms into it. Cook steadily for 5 minutes, tossing them lightly until they are evenly browned.

VARIATION

MUSHROOMS SAUTÉD WITH GARLIC AND PARSLEY

These are superb with grilled beefburgers, chops or steaks.

8 oz (225 g/2½ cups) 'opens', 'flats' or open-cup mushrooms
1½ tbsp extra virgin olive oil
1 clove of garlic, peeled and finely chopped
½ teasp fine sea salt
10 grinds of black pepper
1 tbsp finely chopped parsley

Prepare as above. Heat the oil for 2 minutes, then add the garlic and mushrooms and cook as before. Season with sea salt and black pepper, then stir in the chopped parsley just before serving.

GRILLED MUSHROOMS

Keeps 1 day under refrigeration.
Do not freeze.

Remove the stalks from open cups or 'flats' (refrigerate for other use). Brush the mushrooms all over with melted butter or extra virgin olive oil and arrange hollow side up on a grill (broiler) pan. Sprinkle with salt and pepper and grill under moderate heat for 5 minutes. Turn, brush lightly with fat and grill for a further 5 minutes on the other side. Season when cooked. Use as a garnish or serve on toast.

MUSHROOMS IN SOURED CREAM, CREAMED SMETANA OR FROMAGE FRAIS

Serves 6–8.
Keeps 1 day under refrigeration.
Do not freeze.

This is a delicious and unusual accompaniment to grilled, fried or baked fish. The sauce should just coat the mushrooms.

1 lb (450 g/5 cups) mushrooms
2 oz (50 g) mild onion, shallots or the bulbs of a small bunch of spring onions (scallions)
1 oz (25 g/2 tbsp) butter
1 tbsp olive oil
1 clove of garlic, crushed

½ teasp salt
¼ teasp nutmeg or ground mace
speck of white pepper
1 tbsp lemon juice
5 fl oz (150 ml/⅔ cup) soured cream, creamed smetana or 8% fromage frais

Trim the mushroom stalks level with the cups. Chop the onion finely and sauté in the butter and oil until soft and golden - about 3 or 4 minutes. Add the mushrooms, toss to coat them well, then cook briskly, shaking the pan and sprinkling the vegetables with the seasonings and lemon juice as they cook. After 5 minutes they will have absorbed the butter and be tender. Continue to cook until most of the liquid from the mushrooms has evaporated, then pour on the cream, smetana or fromage frais and heat until steaming, but do not allow to boil. The mushrooms can be cooked in advance and then reheated for 3 or 4 minutes and the cream added just before serving.

GINGERED PARSNIP PURÉE

Serves 6-8.
Keeps 3 days under refrigeration.
Freeze 3 months.

A superb 'extra vegetable' to serve with a roast. Reheats well, preferably in the microwave (4 minutes on 100 per cent power) or 30 minutes in a moderate oven.

1½ lb (675 g) parsnips
2 medium potatoes (12 oz/350 g)
2 teasp ground ginger
2 oz (50 g/¼ cup) margarine
1 teasp salt
speck of white pepper
1 rounded tbsp mild honey

Peel the parsnips and cut in 1-inch (2.5-cm) cubes. Peel and quarter the potatoes. Cook the vegetables together in a large pan of boiling, salted water until tender - about 20 minutes - or in the microwave (see p. 247). Drain well. Purée the vegetables through a food mill or ricer, return to the pan, add the remaining ingredients and use a balloon whisk to incorporate evenly. Alternatively, purée the cooked vegetables and all the other ingredients in the food processor. Reheat if necessary over a low light or in the microwave.

PARSNIP AND WALNUT PURÉE

Serves 6-8.
Keeps 3 days under refrigeration.
Freeze 3 months.

Delicious with turkey. May be reheated.

3½-4 oz (100-125 g ⅞-1 cup) walnut halves
2½ lb (1.25 kg) parsnips
3 tbsp walnut oil
1 teasp salt
15 grinds of black pepper
¼ teasp nutmeg

Lightly toast and then roughly chop the walnuts.

Peel the parsnips and remove any woody core, then cut into even-sized chunks. Cook in salted water until very soft when pierced with a pointed knife (or in the microwave, see p. 247), then drain and put into the food processor (or put through a food mill). Add the oil and seasonings and process or beat until smooth - the mixture should be the consistency of creamy mashed potatoes. Pulse in the walnuts, then turn into a serving dish and decorate the surface with a fork or knife blade. To reheat, cover and cook in the microwave on 100 per cent power for 4 minutes, or for 30 minutes in a moderate oven, Gas No. 4 (350°F/180°C).

FRESH GARDEN PEAS FOR A PARTY
(*in the French manner*)

Serves 8–10.
Leftovers keep 1 day under refrigration.
Do not freeze.

From mid-June to October, fresh peas are available from the garden or certain greengrocers. However, unless they are small and prime, it's better to use frozen petit pois. The preliminary blanching can be done early in the day, then finished just before serving. However, with a microwave oven the entire cooking process can be completed in advance and the peas reheated in their serving dish.

3 lb (1.5 kg) fresh green peas
(approx. 2 lb/900 g shelled weight)

For finishing
1 level teasp caster sugar or granular sweetener
pinch of white pepper
2 oz (50 g/$\frac{1}{4}$ cup) softened butter or margarine
1 tbsp fresh chopped mint

Drop the peas into a gallon (5-l/20-cup) pan, three-quarters full of water salted with 3 level teaspoons of salt. Boil for 7 minutes, or until almost tender but still a little chewy, then stand them in a colander or salad spinner in cold water for 2 minutes to set the colour. Drain well.

About 10 minutes before serving, put the peas in a pan over gentle heat to evaporate any moisture, then add the sugar, pepper, butter and mint. Put on the lid and allow to steam through for 10 minutes to finish the cooking (3 minutes in the microwave on 100 per cent power). Serve as soon as possible.

Winter Squashes

These are some of the most decorative and delicious of vegetables, with such charming names as 'Acorn', 'Golden Nugget', 'Chayote' and 'Spaghetti', and a shape that may resemble a banana, an onion, or even a handbell! And despite their sweet flavour, they contain only 25 calories per 3$\frac{1}{2}$ oz (100 g). A good-quality specimen will feel hard and be free of soft spots or cracks, and if it feels heavy for its size, it will have a high proportion of edible flesh to skin. Apart from the spaghetti squash (which needs refrigerating), all the other varieties will keep in good condition for up to 6 months provided they're stored in a cool dry place – hanging in a net bag is ideal.

One of the most interesting varieties in both appearance and flavour is the 'Butternut', which has a pinky-beige skin and a cylindrical shape that grows bulbous at one end. Once you've cut through the very tough skin with a bread knife, the flesh inside is a rich orange in colour. In many ways it is a little like a marrow (you can stuff it with mincemeat in the same way), except for the taste, which is even richer and sweeter than a sweet potato.

For a first-time taste, it's particularly good as a purée, cooked either in the microwave or the regular oven and served with roast meat or chicken or with grilled fish. It can be reheated after several hours without any change in flavour. 'Buttercup' or 'Hubbard' squash can also be cooked in the same way – indeed, though the outside may be very different, the inside of most varieties of squash is much the same.

A PURÉE OF BUTTERNUT SQUASH

Serves 4–6.
Keeps 3 days under refrigeration.
Freeze 3 months.

approx. 2$\frac{1}{2}$ lb (1.25 kg) butternut squash
nut of butter or margarine
2 level tbsp soft light brown sugar or granular sweetener
$\frac{1}{2}$ teasp salt
10 grinds of black pepper
1 rounded tbsp chopped pecans or walnuts

Cut the unpeeled squash in half and remove the seeds and fibrous pulp. To microwave, cover each half tightly with clingfilm (saranwrap) and cook on 100 per cent power for 12–14 minutes. To cook in a conventional oven, arrange the halves cut side down in a small roasting tin or casserole. Cook at Gas No. 6 (400°F/200°C) for 45 minutes–1 hour. In either case, after the minimum cooking time has elapsed, test by piercing the flesh with a slim, sharp knife. If not completely tender, cook a further 2 minutes in the microwave, 10 minutes in the oven.

Allow the squash to cool for 5 minutes, then scoop out the flesh and place in a food processor. Add the fat and sugar (or substitute) with the seasoning and process until puréed and creamy - about 10 seconds. Pile into a heatproof dish and scatter with the nuts. Reheat for 2 minutes in the microwave and 10 minutes in the oven, then serve from the dish.

Sweet Potatoes

Sweet potatoes can be baked and fried just like ordinary potatoes. Or you can bake 2¼ lb (1 kg) of them with 12 oz (350 g) of ordinary potatoes, then mash them together to make a delicious purée. Prick the potatoes, then bake them either in a conventional oven at Gas No. 6 (400°F/200°C) for 1½ hours, or in the microwave (25 minutes on 100 per cent power, then rest for 5 minutes). Put the skinned cooked potatoes in a warm bowl and beat in 2 oz (50 g/¼ cup) of butter or margarine, 2 egg yolks, 2 teaspoons of salt and ⅛ teaspoon of white pepper.

But this vegetable really comes into its own when combined with apple - the fruit's touch of acidity contrasts with the natural sweetness of the potato. Paradoxically, a little added sweetness - in the shape of brown sugar - is needed to balance the flavours.

However, as the flavour is more exotic than a dish made with ordinary potatoes, count it as an extra vegetable rather than a substitute.

SWEET POTATO AND SPICED APPLE CASSEROLE

Serves 6–7.
Keeps 2 days under refrigeration.
Do not freeze.

3 lb (1.5 kg) sweet potatoes
3 Granny Smith apples
2 oz (50 g/¼ cup) butter or margarine
3 oz (75 g/⅓ cup) light brown or demerara sugar
1 teasp cinnamon
2 oz (50 g/⅔ cup) tenderized, coarsely chopped pitted prunes
2 teasp lemon juice
1 teasp salt

In a large saucepan cover the unpeeled sweet potatoes with cold water, bring to the boil and simmer covered for 20 minutes, or until they feel just tender when pierced with a small, sharp knife. Meanwhile, peel, core and cut each apple into 16 slices. In an 8-inch (20-cm) frying pan, gently sauté the apple slices in the fat until softened - about 3 minutes - then sprinkle with the sugar, cinnamon, chopped prunes and lemon juice, and cook for a further 2 minutes, turning them over gently until they are glazed and golden.

Drain the potatoes and leave on a plate until cold enough to handle, then strip off the skin and cut into ½-inch (1.25-cm) slices. Arrange the slices overlapping slightly in a greased gratin or other shallow casserole (measuring approximately 12 x 7 x 2 inches/30 x 17.5 x 5 cm) and sprinkle with the salt. Spoon the apple and prune mixture on top of the sweet potatoes and drizzle over them any glaze remaining in the pan.

Bake at Gas No. 5 (375°F/190°C) for 20 minutes, until bubbly and golden brown. In the microwave, reheat uncovered for 4 minutes on 100 per cent power, or until bubbling.

SWEET POTATOES DUCHESSE

Serves 6–8.
Keeps 2 days under refrigeration.
Do not freeze.

A lovely vegetable presentation for a dinner party.

2¼ lb (1 kg) sweet potatoes
12 oz (350 g) Maris Piper or other mashing potatoes
3 oz (75 g/⅓ cup) butter or margarine
4 egg yolks
2 teasp salt
⅛ teasp white pepper

Wash the potatoes, prick all over and bake at Gas No. 6 (400°F/200°C) for 1 hour, or until tender. Alternatively, bake in the microwave for 25 minutes on 100 per cent power, then rest for 5 minutes. Skin when cool enough to handle. Scoop the potato into a warm bowl and, using an electric whisk or a large balloon whisk, beat in all the remaining ingredients (reserving half a yolk for glaze). (Potatoes mashed in the food processor become gluey.) The mixture should be smooth enough to pipe.

Grease 2 oven trays and pipe the mixture into 2-inch (5-cm) mounds using a coarse rose tube. Allow to go cold, then brush all over with egg wash made by adding a little water to the remaining half yolk.

Bake in a preheated oven, Gas No. 7 (425°F/220°C), for 15 minutes, or until a rich golden colour.

SWEET POTATO AND APPLE PURÉE

Serves 6–8.
Keeps 2 days under refrigeration.

Lovely with grilled herrings or mackerel or (using margarine) with chicken, turkey or duck.

3 lb (1.5 kg) sweet potatoes
12 oz (350 g) baking apples
2 oz (50 g/4 tbsp) butter or margarine
1½ teasp salt
10 grinds of black pepper

To cook the potatoes, cover with cold water, bring to the boil and cook covered for 25 minutes, until they feel absolutely tender when pierced with a fork, then drain. Alternatively, prick all over and cook on 100 per cent power for 25 minutes in a microwave, then allow to rest for 5 minutes. Meanwhile, peel, core and cut the apples in tiny cubes, put in a pan with half the fat, cover and cook gently until tender. In the microwave, cook covered on 100 per cent power for 4 minutes, stirring once.

Strip off the skin from the potatoes and put them in a warm bowl with the apples. Using a hand-held electric whisk or a balloon whisk, cream the mixture until it is fluffy, beating in the remaining fat and seasonings. Pile into a dish and serve. May be reheated either in the microwave, or, covered, in a moderate oven, Gas No. 4 (350°F/180°C), for 15 minutes.

SWEET POTATO AND ORANGE GRATIN

Serves 8.
Keeps 2 days under refrigeration.
Do not freeze.

An excellent dish for a vegetarian meal.

3 lb (1.5 kg) large sweet potatoes
salt
2 large navel oranges, sliced
2 rounded tbsp brown sugar
4 fl oz (125 ml/½ cup) orange juice
1½ oz (40 g/3 tbsp) butter or margarine
2 oz (50 g/½ cup) walnuts

In a large saucepan cover the unpeeled potatoes with cold water, bring to the boil and simmer covered for 20 minutes, until they feel just tender when pierced with a pointed knife. Drain, then take off the heat but cover with a tea-towel and leave to steam for 10 minutes. When cool enough to handle, peel and cut in ½-inch-thick (1.25-cm) slices. Arrange half the slices in a greased gratin dish measuring approximately 12 x 7 x 2 (30 x 17.5 x 5 cm) and sprinkle lightly with salt. Top with half the orange slices and brown sugar then repeat with a second layer. Mix the orange juice with the melted fat and drizzle over the top, then sprinkle with the chopped nuts. Bake at Gas No. 3 (325°F/160°C) for 45 minutes, basting half-way through, until golden and bubbly. Can be kept hot, covered, in a warm oven if necessary. Reheat in the microwave, uncovered, on 100 per cent power for 4 minutes.

SWEETCORN FRITTERS WITH AUBERGINE, INDONESIAN STYLE

Serves 6–8.
Keeps 3 days under refrigeration.
Freeze 1 month.
Serve hot off the pan or at room temperature.

Corn fritters in a *parev* version are generally tasteless and not worth the effort - which can't be said for this delicious recipe, which I have adapted from Sri Owen's wonderful book on Indonesian food and cooking. They also make very interesting finger food for a drinks party.

1 medium aubergine
salt
7 tbsp sunflower oil
4 medium shallots, peeled and finely chopped
½ teasp chilli powder
2 cloves of garlic, finely chopped
1 teasp ground coriander
½ teasp salt
1 x 11½ oz (325 g) can sweetcorn
1 egg, beaten
3 tbsp plain flour
1 teasp baking powder
2 tbsp chopped spring onions (scallions) including 4 inches (10 cm) of the green part

Peel the aubergine and cut in ⅜-inch (1-cm) dice, then put in a colander or salad spinner and sprinkle with salt. Leave for 30–40 minutes, then rinse and squeeze as dry as possible. In a heavy sauté or frying pan, heat the 2 tablespoons of oil and stir-fry the shallots, chilli powder and garlic for 2 minutes, add the aubergine cubes, stir well and season with the ground coriander and salt. Simmer together for 4 minutes, until the aubergine is tender, then set aside to cool.

Put the drained corn in a bowl. Add the aubergine mixture and all the remaining ingredients apart from the 5 tablespoons of oil and mix well. Reseason if necessary. Heat the oil in the sauté pan and drop the mixture by heaped tablespoons into it, flattening each fritter with the back of a fork. Cook over moderate heat for 3 minutes on each side. Serve hot or at room temperature. You can keep fritters hot at Gas No. ½ (250°F/120°C) for up to 30 minutes.

Note Cold fritters can be gently reheated under the grill (broiler).

Tomatoes in the Provençale Style

The tomato - that ubiquitous ingredient of almost every self-respecting salad - has recently achieved 'designer' status as supermarkets vie with each other to offer an ever-increasing number of named varieties, each with its own shape, flavour and recommended usage. Even the season has been manipulated so that English-grown tomatoes can be in the shops as early as March.

Imported tomatoes offer an enormous choice - cherry tomatoes from Spain (for garnishing and low-calorie nibbling), 'beef' tomatoes from Portugal (for slicing into salads and starters) and the fat deep-red French tomatoes, which have a special 'sun-kissed' flavour because they're allowed to ripen on the vine. These are ideal for those simple Italian- and French-style salads that need dressing only with a little vinegar and a good-quality olive oil mixed with plenty of chopped fresh herbs. Optional extras might be slices of Mozzarella or cubes of Feta cheese, sections of Israeli avocado or grilled and skinned red and yellow peppers. And because they keep their shape even when heated, they're magnificent grilled.

TOMATES PROVENÇALES

Serves 6.
Leftovers keep 1 day under refrigeration.

The flavour of this simple but aromatic dish depends on using well-flavoured tomatoes - Ferline and Marmande are ideal varieties for this purpose. Treated in this way, they go particularly well with grilled chops, steak or chicken, as well as with grilled mackerel. For a low-fat meal, simply brush the tomatoes with olive oil, then sprinkle with the other filling ingredients, omitting the breadcrumbs. If they are not a really deep red when you buy them, leave the tomatoes at room temperature for a couple of days.

3 sun-ripened tomatoes, each about 3 inches (7.5 cm) in diameter
fine sea salt
15 grinds of black pepper

For the filling

4 tbsp extra virgin olive oil
3 tbsp chopped shallots or spring onions (scallions)
1 fat clove of garlic, crushed
4 tbsp fresh chopped parsley
1 teasp dried Herbes de Provence
6 large basil leaves, torn or shredded, or 1 teasp dried basil
1½ oz (40 g/½ cup) coarse dry breadcrumbs or matzah meal
½ teasp fine sea salt
10 grinds of black pepper

Cut the tomatoes in half and gently squeeze out the juice and seeds. Sprinkle lightly with salt and pepper and turn upside down on to kitchen paper to drain.

To prepare the filling, gently heat 3 tablespoons of the oil and sauté the shallots until soft and golden. Add all the remaining ingredients and mix well.

Spoon the filling into the tomatoes. Sprinkle with a few drops of the remaining olive oil, then arrange on a heatproof platter or dish. The tomatoes can be refrigerated for up to 6 hours at this point.

Grill (broil) gently for 10 minutes, until softened and golden, or bake in a preheated oven, Gas No. 6 (400°F/200°C), for 15 minutes, until they are tender but still hold their shape. Serve hot or cold.

Perfect Potatoes

When you consider the calories in a potato, it's got to be well cooked to be worth the expenditure! However, eaten in moderation potatoes are very valuable as an inexpensive source of carbohydrates and Vitamin C, as well as being a useful source of protein, iron, thiamin, niacin and dietary fibre. The recipes in this section are limited but really good. They're not dishes to 'fill up the gaps' but ones to add real eating pleasure to a meal.

BAKED POTATOES

This method conserves all the nourishment which lies under the skin and is usually discarded with the potato peelings.

Good baking varieties include Cara, Pentland Dell, Pentland Square and Romano.

1 medium potato per person
butter or margarine

Set the oven at Gas No. 6 (400°F/200°C). Choose potatoes of an even size so that they will be ready at the same time. Scrub thoroughly with a nylon pan scrub kept for the purpose, then remove any eyes with a potato peeler. Dry thoroughly and prick all over with a fork (to stop the potato bursting). Arrange on a baking tin. Cook for 1-1½ hours, depending on size, until the potato feels tender when it is gently squeezed.

To serve, squeeze the skin to break it and allow some of the steam to escape from inside. This makes the potato floury and light. Serve in an uncovered dish to prevent the skin going soggy. Hand round the butter or margarine, salt and a pepper mill.

Soured cream or low-fat fromage frais flavoured with 2 teaspoons of snipped chives makes an excellent accompaniment.

Note Potatoes so-called 'baked' in an ordinary microwave oven are really steamed. However, with a 'combination' oven, a really crisp result can be achieved in half to two-thirds the normal cooking time.

MASHED POTATOES

Serves 4–6.
Eat the same day.

No packeted potato can match the perfection of home-made mashed potatoes cooked by the method described below. But don't keep them hot for more than 15 minutes - they lose their flavour and much of their nourishment.

Good varieties include Desiree, Maris Piper and Cara.

2–3 lb (900 g–1.5 kg) potatoes
2 level teasp salt
4 fl oz (125 ml/½ cup) hot milk
2 oz (50 g/¼ cup) butter or margarine
¼ level teasp white pepper

Peel the potatoes, cut them into quarters and put them in a pan containing sufficient boiling water to cover them. Add the salt, bring back to the boil, cover and cook at a steady boil for 15 minutes, or until a piece feels absolutely tender when pierced with a thin vegetable knife. (Do not boil vigorously, or the potatoes may become 'soupy'.) Drain the water from the potatoes, return them to the stove in the same pan and shake over a gentle heat until all the moisture has evaporated. Pour the milk down the side of the pan and when it starts to steam, add the butter and white pepper, then start whisking together with the potatoes, using either a small balloon whisk or a portable electric mixer. Continue to whisk on a very low heat until the potatoes lighten in colour and look fluffy. Add more milk if the mixture seems too dry - the texture is a matter of preference. Taste and add more salt if necessary. Pile into a warm vegetable dish and serve immediately.

VARIATIONS

FOR A MEAT MEAL

Omit the milk and butter. Substitute two rounded tablespoons of chicken fat or 3 oz (75 g/⅓ cup) margarine. The mixture won't be as creamy, but will be equally tasty.

DUCHESSE

Mash the boiled potatoes with 2 fl oz (50 ml/¼ cup) milk, 1 oz (25 g/2 tbsp) butter and 1 egg yolk. Put into a piping bag fitted with coarse rose tube. Pipe on to greased trays and bake at Gas No. 6 (400°F/200°C) until golden brown - about 10 minutes. Serves 4–5.

POTATO PUFF BALLS

Mix 3 oz (75 g/1 cup) finely grated cheese with a good pinch of dry mustard. Shape the duchesse potato mixture into balls the size of an egg. Roll in the cheese mixture. Arrange on a greased tray and bake at Gas No. 6 (400°F/200°C) for 10 minutes, until golden brown. Alternatively, brown under the grill (broiler). Serves 4–5.

ROAST POTATOES

Serves 4–6.
Eat immediately.

If the potatoes are parboiled before roasting rather than put in the oven raw, they develop a crisp yet tender crust and a deliciously soft inside.

Good varieties include Desiree, Maris Piper, Cara, Pentland Square and Romano (all available September–May).

2–3 lb (900 g/1.5 kg) potatoes
salt
oil
margarine

Peel the potatoes and cut them (if large) into slices 1 inch (2.5 cm) thick. Put in a pan half-full of boiling water, add 1 level teaspoon salt and bring slowly back to the boil. Cook until the potatoes are almost but not quite tender – they will feel slightly hard when pierced with a slim vegetable knife. This will take about 15–20 minutes. Drain the potatoes, then return them to the empty pan and shake over a low heat until they look absolutely dry. Meanwhile, put in the oven a shallow roasting tin (just large enough to hold the potato slices in one layer) which has a thin layer of oil covering the bottom. The oven can be set at any of the temperatures I give below (whichever is most convenient for the main dish cooking at the same time).

Put the tin of hot oil on the cooker, add a nut of margarine, then carefully lay the potatoes in it and immediately turn them over so that they are coated with the hot fat. Sprinkle lightly with the salt and roast, turning once or twice, for the time given below.

Temperature	*Cook for*
Gas No. 3 (325°F/160°C)	1¾ hours
Gas No. 4 (350°F/180°C)	1½ hours
Gas No. 5 (375°F/190°C)	1½ hours
Gas No. 6 (400°F/200°C)	1¼ hours
Gas No. 7 (425°F/220°C)	1¼ hours

FRIED POTATOES

Serves 4–5.
Eat immediately.

This is a dish for *very* occasional use as it has a high fat content. To achieve a really crisp, flavourful result, the potatoes should be fried slowly at first to absorb the fat, and then more quickly when they are almost ready, to make them crisp. Cold leftover potatoes can be used, but the finest results are achieved with potatoes freshly cooked in their skins.

Good frying potatoes include Wilja, Estima, Desiree, Maris Piper, Cara and Pentland Squire.

2 lb (900 g) potatoes
salt
2 tbsp flavourless oil such as sunflower
2 oz (50 g/¼ cup) butter or margarine
black pepper

Scrub the potatoes, then cook them whole in their skins, covered with boiling salted water, for 25–40 minutes, depending on their size. Drain the potatoes and return to the empty pan to dry off on a low heat. Leave until cool enough to handle, then skin and cut into thick slices or cubes.

To fry, put the oil and butter in a heavy frying pan. When the butter starts to foam, put in the potatoes and cook very gently, shaking the pan occasionally so that the potatoes absorb the fat rather than fry in it. This will take about 15 minutes. When the potatoes are golden all over, increase the heat to make them crisp. Drain from the fat (there should be very little, if any, left), put in a dish and sprinkle with salt and black pepper.

GOLDEN NEW POTATOES
(*Pommes de Terre Château*)

Serves 6.
Eat the same day.

These make a beautiful garnish for a special meal. Use small new potatoes measuring about 2 x 1 inch (5 x 2.5 cm). The waxier they are the better. Good varieties include Belle de Fontenay, Charlotte and Jersey Royal.

2 lb (900 g) new potatoes
1½ oz (40 g/3 tbsp) butter or margarine
1 tbsp sunflower oil
salt
3 teasp chopped parsley for serving

Scrape the potatoes and dry thoroughly in a towel. Put the butter and oil in a 9-inch (22.5-cm) lidded frying pan and melt it over moderate heat. The minute the fat starts to foam, add the potatoes and shake them gently until they are well coated in fat on all sides. Cover and cook very gently until tender when pierced with a sharp knife - about 25 minutes. If required the vegetables can be kept hot on a tiny light for up to 30 minutes, then recrisped just before serving.

To serve, lift from the pan and sprinkle with the chopped herbs.

OVEN-CRISP POTATOES, LYONNAISE STYLE

Serves 6–8.
Keeps 1 day partly cooked under refrigeration.
Do not freeze.

This is an excellent dish for a dinner party as you can achieve the effect of a sauté of potatoes without having to hover over a frying pan at the last minute. The trick is to *partly* fry the potatoes beforehand - even the day before - and then recrisp and brown them in a hot oven half an hour before the meal. This method produces the most delicious golden-brown potatoes, which are given added flavour by the fried onions and chopped parsley. Use any of the potatoes varieties for frying mentioned on p. 268.

3 lb (1.5 kg) potatoes
1 teasp salt
3 oz (75 g/⅓ cup) butter or margarine plus 3 tbsp sunflower oil, or 6 tbsp sunflower oil
2 medium onions, finely chopped or thinly sliced

For the garnish
a little sea salt
15 grinds of black pepper
1 tbsp chopped parsley

Scrub the potatoes, then cook them whole in their skins, covered with boiling salted water, until tender - 25–40 minutes (test with the point of a sharp knife). Drain off the water, then return the pan to the heat and dry the potatoes off. Leave until they are cool enough to handle, then skin and cut into ⅜-inch-thick (1-cm) slices or cubes.

To sauté the onions and potatoes, put the chosen fat(s) into a frying pan and heat until the warmth can be felt on the hand held 2 inches (5 cm) above it. Add the chopped onion (for cubed potatoes) or the sliced onion (for sliced potatoes) and cook gently until soft and golden - about 10 minutes. Remove to an oven tray wide enough to hold the onions and the potatoes in 1 layer - a roulade tin measuring about 14 x 10 x 2 inches (35 x 25 x 5 cm) is ideal. Put the potatoes in the frying pan, stirring frequently until they are a light-golden colour - they should slowly absorb the fat rather than fry in it. Turn into the tin and mix well with the onions. Leave until 40 minutes before serving.

To crisp the potatoes, preheat the oven to Gas No. 7 (425°F/220°C). A slightly lower temperature can be used to suit other dishes cooking in the oven, but the potatoes will then take longer to brown. Put the dish with the potatoes and onions into the oven and cook for 30–40 minutes, until crisp and golden, shaking occasionally. The potatoes can be kept hot for up to 20 minutes in a moderate oven, Gas No. 4 (350°F/180°C).

Turn into a serving dish, season with a few shakes of sea salt and black pepper and sprinkle with the parsley. Serve piping hot.

GRATIN OF POTATOES À LA DAUPHINOISE

Serves 4–6.
Eat the same day.

For the special fish or dairy meal, this is the perfect potato dish for flavour, appearance and convenience - and you can even take the dish out of the oven for a while and then reheat or brown it just before serving.

1½–2 lb (675–900 g) baking potatoes
(the oval Estima variety is superb)
⅛ teasp nutmeg
½ teasp salt
10 grinds of black pepper
1 crushed clove of garlic (optional)
10 fl oz (275 ml/1¼ cups) whipping cream
4 oz (125 g/1 cup) grated Gruyère cheese
1–2 oz (25–50 g/¼–½ cup) Parmesan or
other finely grated mature cheese
1½ oz (40 g/3 tbsp) butter, melted

Peel and then finely slice the potatoes (most easily done in a food processor) and soak in cold water for 5 minutes, then spin dry. Add the nutmeg, salt, pepper and garlic to the cream, mixing well. Lightly butter a gratin dish approximately 1½ inches (4 cm) deep. Arrange a layer of the potatoes in overlapping rows on the bottom of the dish and season lightly with salt, then spoon over a quarter of the seasoned cream, a quarter of the mixed cheeses and a quarter of the butter. Repeat 3 times, ending with a layer of cheese and the remaining butter. Cover lightly with silicone paper and bake for 1¼–1½ hours in a preheated oven, Gas No. 4 (350°F/180°C), until the potatoes are tender when pierced with a sharp knife. Remove the paper and brown under the grill (broiler) if necessary, or turn up the oven to Gas No. 7 (425°F/220°C) for 10 minutes. The potatoes may be kept hot in a low oven, Gas No. 2 (300°F/150°C), for 30 minutes.

Using a microwave, layer the ingredients as described above in a microwave-safe dish, cover with a lid or pierced clingfilm (saran-wrap) and cook on 100 per cent power for 30 minutes. Leave to stand for 5 minutes, then uncover and brown under a hot grill until golden.

VARIATION

GRATIN OF POTATOES FOR A MEAT MEAL

Use margarine instead of butter. Substitute dry cider or chicken stock for the cream and omit the cheese. Layer and cook as before.

Chips (French Fries)

For an occasional treat there's nothing quite like a dish of crisply fried chips, unless it's a similar dish of latkes! Success depends on the correct combination of potato variety and oil temperature, and many packs of potatoes now indicate which are best for what purpose. Here is the list of 'chippers' recommended by the British Potato Marketing Board.

August–March Wilja, Estima
September–May Desiree, Maris Piper, Cara, Pentland Dell, Pentland Squire, Romano

There are also many imported varieties to fill in the seasonal gaps.

For frying, I strongly recommend an automatic deep-fat-fryer, preferably plugged in near the back door so that any fumes not absorbed by the built-in filter can be wafted out of the kitchen. However, I give instructions for using a chip pan and basket as well.

To achieve really crisp chips with a soft interior, the chips are best cooked by the French method as follows.

CRISP CHIPS

Serves 4–6.
Eat immediately.

4 large potatoes (approx. 1½ lb/675 g) when peeled

Peel the potatoes, cut them into slices 3/8 inch (1 cm) thick, then cut the slices into chips 3/8 inch (1 cm) wide. Result: chips that are of equal width and depth (this is important for even cooking). If you are great chip-eaters you can, of course, invest in a chipper. Soak the chips in cold water for half an hour - this will dissolve excess surface starch. Drain and dry thoroughly on a tea-towel.

To fry in a deep-fat-fryer, heat the oil (any flavourless variety) to the chip-frying temperature recommended by the manufacturers (usually 190°C/375°F). Put the raw chips in the basket and cook for 3-4 minutes, until they feel tender when pierced with a slim pointed knife. Lift the basket from the oil and allow any unabsorbed oil to drain back into the pan.

This preliminary process is called 'blanching' and can be done at any time before a meal. When the chips are required, reheat the oil to its former temperature, put the chips back in and fry for a further 1 minute, until crisp and golden. Shake gently to remove excess oil and serve in a hot dish at once.

Note It is better to do the final crisping in small batches, for if the frying basket is too full, the oil will be cooled and the chips will take much longer to brown.

To fry in an open chip pan, you will be frying in exactly the same way as for the deep-fryer, but need to heat the oil and test for correct temperature as follows. Fill the chip pan one-third full of flavourless oil and heat. To test the temperature of the oil either

1. use an oil thermometer,
2. drop in a 1-inch (2.5-cm) square of day-old bread, which should brown in 40 seconds, or
3. gently drop in a dry chip, which should rise to the surface of the oil a few seconds after being dropped in.

Put the chips in a frying basket and lower into the oil.

VARIATIONS

CHIPS FOR 2

For a small number of chips good results can be obtained by frying only once in a large saucepan.

2 large potatoes

Fill the pan (it can be a saucepan or deep frying pan) one-third full of oil and heat to 375°F/190°C, or until a dry chip sizzles gently when put into it.

Carefully lower the remainder of the chips into the oil and cook at a steady but busy bubble for 7-10 minutes, or until they look a rich, crisp brown. Lift out with a slotted spoon, drain briefly on crumpled tissue paper and serve at once.

CRISPS

Peel small potatoes and cut into paper-thin slices with a mandoline (vegetable cutter) or the finest slicing blade of a food processor. Soak for half an hour, dry thoroughly and then fry for 5-6 minutes.

POTATO KUGEL
(*Potato Cake or Pudding*)

Serves 6.
Keeps 3 days under refrigeration.
Freeze 3 months.

Strong men grow weak at the knees just at the thought of this dish from *'der heim'*. It probably packs in more calories per cubic inch than any other dish and really cannot be justified on any grounds other than 'tradition'. However, in the poorly heated homes of the Pale of Settlement, it did provide a very efficient personal form of central heating!

4 large potatoes
(15 fl oz/425 ml/2 cups when grated)
2 oz (50 g/¼ cup) margarine or 2 tbsp chicken fat or substitute
2 eggs
2 oz (50 g/½ cup) self-raising flour or 2 oz (50 g/½ cup) plain (all-purpose) flour and ½ level teasp baking powder
1 level teasp salt
1 medium onion, grated

Grate the potatoes finely and put in a sieve to drain for 10 minutes. Set the oven at Gas No. 8 (450°F/230°C) and put the fat in a casserole to melt and heat in it.

Whisk the eggs until fluffy, then add the well-drained potatoes, flour, salt and onion. Swirl the hot fat round the baking dish to coat the sides (this ensures a crisp outside for the kugel), then pour into the potato mixture. Blend thoroughly and return to the dish. Bake for 15 minutes, then turn the oven down to Gas No. 4 (350°F/180°C) for a further hour, or until crisp, well risen and golden brown.

Rice and Other Grains

Rice is one of the most ancient of foods - the first record of its cultivation dates from the reign of the Chinese Emperor Shen Nung about 3,000 BCE. Yet it is still popular, not only in those Eastern countries where it is the staple food, but all over the Western world. Sephardi Jews are great rice cooks, using it both as a main dish accompaniment and as an ingredient in many of their most delicious recipes.

Until a generation ago, most rice came in hessian sacks, with a full quota of stones, dirt and rubbish - the 'picking over' of rice to remove these impurities used to be a traditional chore of Sephardi Jewish housewives before Pesach. The cooking quality of the grain also varied from country to country, and indeed from crop to crop, so a major part of the preparation of rice for cooking used to be the cleansing. Meanwhile, the cooking process itself had to be varied according to the rice's quality and country of origin.

Today it is a very different story. Most of the rice sold in the Western world is precleaned and prepacketed. The quality is standardized and so, therefore, is the cooking method. If you cannot buy packeted rice, then the best advice I can give is to cook it according to the traditional method of the country where it has been grown.

Although botanists have recorded no less than 7,000 different varieties, to most Western cooks buying rice has meant shopping by name for but 3 of them: 'Carolina' for puddings, and 'Patna' or 'Basmati' for curries, pilaffs and other savoury dishes. Rice sold under these names has often been grown from seed descended from the original varieties and is now successfully cultivated in many other parts of the world. In addition, small quantities of 'wild' rice are marketed alone or in a pack containing brown rice, and in the Po valley of Italy is grown the 'risotto' or Arborio rice which cooks creamily while still retaining its chewiness.

You can cook rice according to the customs of the Chinese, Persians and Turks, the Egyptians, the Sephardim or indeed the English and, if you've the time and the patience, you will get consistently good results.

Basmati rice is my favourite for all savoury

dishes, except when making the creamier kind, such as risotto, for which the Italian round-grain rice is definitely the best. It is wise to buy brown rice in a packet rather than from a sack, as it is of a much more consistent quality than the bulk variety, which can often take an interminable time to become tender. Ordinary boiled or steamed rice acquires a whole new image when it's cooked with a few cardamom pods and 1 or 2 tablespoons of sultanas (white raisins).

To refrigerate rice Store in an airtight container for up to a week if it has been cooked in water, for up to 3 days if cooked in stock.

To freeze rice Pack in plastic bags or containers for up to 6 months.

To defrost rice in a covered container Either leave overnight in the refrigerator or cook in the microwave on 50 per cent power for 4–5 minutes until steaming, stirring half-way through with a fork.

To reheat rice in a covered container First sprinkle lightly with water (to create steam), then either cook covered in the microwave on 100 per cent power for 2–3 minutes until steaming, stirring half-way through with a fork, or cover and reheat in a moderate oven, Gas No. 4 (350°F/180°C), or over moderate heat on top of the stove, for 15 minutes.

Note Never stir rice with a spoon, as it crushes the grains together. Always fluff it up with a fork.

I cook savoury rice in any of the following 3 ways, according to time and mood.

1 On top of the stove or in the oven, in a measured amount of liquid.
2 In the microwave in a measured amount of liquid. This doesn't save cooking time but it does mean the rice can be cooked and served in the same dish and requires no attention.

Both these methods are quick and easy and the rice becomes fluffy and separate and does not need draining.

3 The 'chilau' (steamed, Persian style) method, which is particularly suitable for a large quantity. This involves a brief boiling and then steaming and results in particularly fluffy grains of rice.

Note As rice freezes well, it's very convenient to cook extra since it takes no longer (except in the microwave).

PLAIN BOILED RICE

Serves 4–5.
Keeps 3 days under refrigeration.
Freeze 6 months.

A simple method for salad or to accompany a main dish.

7–8 oz (200–225 g/1–1⅓ cups) brown or white long-grain (Patna or Basmati) rice
2 cups hot water or chicken stock
1 teasp salt

Rinse the rice in a sieve under the cold tap until the water runs clear (this removes excess starch). Bring the water and salt to the boil, add the rice and stir well. When the water is boiling again, cover pan tightly and simmer for 20 minutes for white rice, 30 minutes for brown, until the liquid has been absorbed and the rice is tender. (Or cook at Gas No. 6/400°F/200°C for the same time, or Gas No. 4/350°F/180°C for 30 minutes for white rice, 40 minutes for brown.) At the end of the cooking period, leave the rice to steam on the lowest possible light for 10 minutes. Fluff up with a fork and serve.

RICE PILAFF

Serves 6–8.
Keeps 3 days under refrigeration.
Freeze 3 months.

This gives a rather more savoury result, but does involve sautéing both the onion and the rice.

12 oz (350 g/2 cups) Patna or Basmati rice
2 tbsp oil
1 medium onion, finely chopped
1¼ pints (725 ml/3 cups) hot chicken stock
2 level teasp salt
15 grinds of black pepper

Rinse the rice carefully in a sieve under the cold tap until the water runs clear.

In a heavy-based pan heat the oil for 2–3 minutes, add the onion and cook for 5 minutes, until softened and golden. Add the well-washed rice and turn in the onion and fat for 3 minutes. Add the hot stock, salt and pepper and stir well. Bring to the boil, then cover tightly and cook for 20 minutes over a low heat, either on top of the stove, in a quick oven, Gas No. 6 (400°F/200°C), or Gas No. 4 (350°F/180°C), whichever is the most convenient.

If it is to be served hot, fluff up the rice with a fork.

VARIATION

TURKISH PILAFF

Serves 6.
Keeps 3 days under refrigeration.
Freeze 6 months.

A superbly flavoured dish to serve with roast chicken or chops.

10 oz (275 g/1⅔ cups) Basmati rice
1 heaped tbsp margarine
1 medium onion, finely chopped
1 pint (575 ml/2½ cups) hot chicken stock
¼ teasp turmeric
½ teasp salt
½ teasp mixed sweet spice
2 oz (50 g/⅓ cup) sultanas (white raisins)
2 oz (50 g/⅓ cup) natural pistachios, blanched and halved, or 2 oz (50 g/½ cup) cashew nuts, toasted

Make in exactly the same way as the Rice Pilaff, adding all the seasoning and the sultanas with the hot liquid. Stir in the nuts with a fork just before serving.

SAVOURY RICE COOKED IN THE MICROWAVE

Serves 6.

Rice takes the same time to cook in the microwave as it does by conventional methods, but it can be cooked and served in the same dish and requires no watching.

10 oz (275 g/1⅔ cups) Patna or Basmati rice
2 tbsp oil
1½ tbsp minced dried onion
1 pint (575 ml/2½ cups) hot chicken or vegetable stock
1½ level teasp salt
10 grinds of black pepper

Turn the rice into a sieve and hold under the cold tap until the water runs clear (this will remove excess starch). Put the drained rice into a 3-pint (1½-l/8-cup) lidded casserole or bowl.

Mix all the ingredients except the rice in a large jug, then add to the rice and stir well. Cover and cook on 100 per cent power for 5 minutes, or until bubbling, then cook on 80 per cent power for a further 10 minutes.

Allow to stand covered for 5 minutes, then fluff up with a fork.

To reheat, sprinkle the surface with a little cold water, cover and cook on 100 per cent power for 3–4 minutes, or until steaming. Fluff up with a fork and serve as freshly cooked.

RICE FOR THE FREEZER (*Chilau Method*)

The days of the freezer 'cook-in' - exhausting hours over a hot stove and only egg and chips for supper that night to show for it - are fortunately no more. Most of us find it's more sensible, and fits better into today's lifestyle, to double or treble a recipe, then eat some and freeze the rest for another day. Rice lends itself to this technique because it freezes well and then is easy to bring back to life in the microwave. The chilau (Persian) method of cooking rice is particularly suitable for these large quantities and can be infinitely varied by the addition of different flavourings either before or after freezing. I give quantities of rice for 16 servings, but it can be divided or multiplied as you wish - the cooking times remain the same. However, you will need a very large (1-gallon/5-l/20-cup) pan for the full amount.

PERFECT STEAMED RICE

Serves 16.
Keeps 2 days in the refrigerator.
Freezes 3 months.

1½ lb (675 g/4 cups) Basmati rice
2 tbsp salt
4 tbsp sunflower oil
1 tbsp water
10 cardamom pods

Soak the rice in cold water to cover for 30 minutes. Strain and rinse thoroughly under the cold tap until the water runs clear. Bring a large heavy pan of water to the boil with the salt. Add the rice and cook uncovered, bubbling steadily, for 7 minutes, or until a grain feels almost tender when bitten. Turn into a strainer and rinse thoroughly under the hot tap, then drain well.

Put half the oil and the tablespoon of water into the pan and heat until it steams, then add half the rice, the cardamom pods and the remaining oil. Add the rest of the rice. Cover the lid of the pan with a tea-towel, then place it firmly into position so that you have a perfect seal. Leave on the lowest heat for 20 minutes. The result is perfect, fluffy rice. And the crunchy layer that forms on the base of the pan is particularly prized.

To vary the rice, add any of the following mixtures (quantities sufficient for half the cooked rice) either when freshly cooked or when reheated. Reheat covered when required, either in a moderate oven for 20 minutes or for 3-4 minutes on 100 per cent power in the microwave.

VARIATIONS

MUSHROOM PILAU

Serves 6–8.

Half-quantity of cooked rice (see above)
1 onion
2 tbsp sunflower oil
6 tbsp currants
8 oz (22 g/2½ cups) mushrooms (brown cap if possible)

Sauté the finely chopped onion in the oil until softened and golden, then add the currants and the thinly sliced mushrooms. Sauté briskly until no free liquid remains in the pan. Add to the rice, taste and add salt and pepper if necessary.

GOLDEN CARROT RICE

Serves 6–8.

Half-quantity of cooked rice (see above)
1 onion
1 tbsp sunflower oil
12 oz (350 g) carrots
2 teasp light brown sugar
1 teasp salt
1 teasp cinnamon

In a heavy-lidded pan, sauté the finely chopped onion in the oil until golden, then add the grated carrot and the sugar. Cover and cook in their own juices until tender and golden - about 15 minutes - stirring occasionally. Stir in the salt and cinnamon, then blend carefully into the rice.

NUTTY RICE

Serves 6–8.

Half-quantity of cooked rice
(see p. 275)
2 oz (50 g/½ cup) blanched almonds
2 oz (50 g/½ cup) pine kernels
1 tbsp olive oil
1 teasp whole cumin seeds

Coarsely chop the nuts and sauté in the oil over moderate heat until golden. Stir in the rice. To serve, pile in a dome shape on a platter and top with the cumin seeds, lightly crushed in a mortar or with the end of a rolling pin.

CHINESE FRIED RICE

Serves 4.
Eat the same day.

A lovely way to flavour leftover rice.

1 onion, finely chopped
2 tbsp sunflower oil
4 oz (125 g/2 cups) button mushrooms, coarsely chopped
1 medium green or red pepper
3–4 cups cooked rice (about 7 oz/200 g/1 cup raw)
3 teasp light soy sauce
salt
pepper
1 level tbsp snipped chives or chopped parsley

Fry the onion in the oil until soft and golden, together with the mushrooms and the deseeded and slivered pepper. Add the cold rice and heat gently, stirring the rice until brown. Stir in the soy sauce, salt and pepper to taste and the herbs. Serve very hot.

KOREAN SPICED RICE

Serves 6–8.
Keeps 3 days under refrigeration.
Freeze 3 months.

The addition of a little minced meat simmered in wine gives this rich casserole extra body and flavour. It is a perfect dish to serve at a buffet supper party with cold meat or poultry.

6 tbsp sesame seeds
1 tbsp sunflower oil
1 medium onion, finely chopped
8 oz (225 g) raw minced (ground) beef
12 oz (350 g/3 cups) Basmati or other long-grain rice
10 fl oz (275 ml/1¼ cups) full red wine
1 tbsp dark soy sauce
1 level teasp paprika
2 level teasp salt
1 pint (575 ml/2½ cups) beef stock

Set the oven at Gas No. 4 (350°F/180°C). Put the sesame seeds on a baking tray and toast in the oven for 10–15 minutes, or until golden brown. Remove.

Meanwhile, gently heat the oil and sauté the onion until soft and golden. Add the meat and cook until it loses its redness and begins to brown, stirring with a fork. Now add the rice and cook until it loses its glassy appearance, stirring well. Pour in the wine and bubble fiercely until its volume is reduced by half. Add the seasonings and stock and bring to a full boil. Stir well and transfer to the oven. Cook, covered, for 30 minutes, until the rice is tender and has absorbed all the liquid. Stir in the toasted sesame seeds.

The dish can be kept hot in a low oven, Gas No. 2 (300°F/150°C), for half an hour. To reheat, sprinkle the surface lightly with water, cover, then put in a moderate oven, Gas No. 4 (350°F/180°C), for 15 minutes, or until warm. In the microwave, cook covered on 100 per cent power for 4 minutes.

Bulgur (Cracked Wheat)

Bulgur is a very ancient wheat product – the *'Arusah'* of the Bible, it is the 'alien corn' mentioned in the story of Ruth. Today it is often called 'cracked wheat' in the West, but it's also sold under the names of pourgouri, bourghoul and, of course, bulgur.

Packeted bulgur has been partially boiled before sale and is usually marked 'semi-boiled', 'precooked' or 'parched', so it needs very little cooking.

BULGUR PILAFF

Serves 8.
Keeps 2 days under refrigeration.
Freeze 3 months.

This can be served hot as a light and savoury accompaniment or at room temperature with a cold buffet, whichever is most convenient. It is equally tasty either way.

1 large onion, finely chopped
3 tbsp oil
12 oz (350 g/2 cups) bulgur (cracked wheat)
2 teasp finely grated orange rind
6 tbsp raisins
1½ pints (850 ml/3¾ cups) chicken stock
salt
pepper
2 oz (50 g/½ cup) pine kernels, toasted
2 oz (50 g) chopped parsley (enough to 'green' the pilaff)
1 small bunch spring onions (scallions), finely sliced

In an 8–9-inch (20–22.5-cm) heavy-based saucepan or sauté pan, sauté the onion in the oil over moderate heat, stirring until it is softened. Stir in the bulgur and the orange rind and cook the mixture, stirring, for 1 minute. Add the raisins, the stock and salt and pepper to taste, bring the liquid to the boil and cook, covered, over low heat for 10 minutes, or until the liquid is absorbed.

To serve hot, fluff the pilaff with a fork and stir in the pine kernels, parsley and spring onions. To serve cold, allow the pilaff to cool for 15 minutes before stirring in the remaining ingredients.

It reheats well in the microwave – allow 3 minutes in a covered dish on 100 per cent power or until piping hot.

VARIATION

TO COOK BULGUR IN THE MICROWAVE

For 4–5 Put 1 cup of bulgur, 2 teaspoons of minced dried onion and 2 cups of boiling chicken or vegetable stock into a 2½-pint (1.5-l/6-cup) deep-lidded casserole. Stir in the 1 tablespoon of oil, cover and cook on 100 per cent power for 5 minutes, or until bubbling. Turn down to 50 per cent power for a further 4 minutes, then leave to stand, covered, for 5 minutes. Fluff up with a fork and serve.

For 8–10 Double all quantities, but cook on 100 per cent power for 7 minutes, or until bubbling, then cook exactly as directed for the smaller amount.

COUSCOUS TO SERVE WITH STEW, NORTH AFRICAN STYLE

Serves 4.
Keeps 2 days under refrigeration.
Freeze 3 months.

2 cups couscous
3 tbsp sunflower oil
1 tbsp salt
lukewarm water

Put couscous and oil in a bowl and add the salt. Add lukewarm water to twice the depth of the couscous, stir well for 1 minute, then drain in a sieve.

For a small quantity leave in sieve and steam, covered, over boiling water for 10 minutes, until fluffy and separate.

For a larger quantity, line the top of a steamer with a light-coloured non-woven kitchen cloth, add the drained couscous, cover and steam for 10 minutes. In the microwave, reheat covered on 100 per cent power for 2 minutes.

Kasha (Roasted Buckwheat)

Today's interest in 'natural' foods should surely place kasha - a favourite *'heimische'* food of an earlier generation - high on any list of healthy, nutritious dishes. Kasha, which is sold in this country (usually in health food shops) as 'roasted buckwheat', is positively crammed full with nature's nutritional goodies. These include a high proportion of vegetable protein and iron as well as almost the entire range of B complex vitamins, not to mention calcium, phosphorus and rutic acid - which is used in homoeopathic medicine for a variety of circulatory problems.

More important, perhaps, the groats have a delicious nutty flavour which makes them very good companions for meat and chicken dishes. And if you add half a pound of cooked 'farfalle' (noodles shaped like bow-ties) just before serving, you have made 'kasha varnishkes' - a traditional Hanukkah dish in many families whose origins lie in the shtetls of the Pale of Settlement. The finest flavoured kasha casserole is made using a little rendered chicken fat. However, a polyunsaturated margarine can be used instead.

KASHA COOKED IN THE TRADITIONAL MANNER

Serves 6.
Keeps 3 days under refrigeration.
Freezes for 3 months.

8 oz (225 g/1⅓ cups) roasted buckwheat
1 beaten egg
16 fl oz (450 ml/2 cups) boiling water
2 teasp paprika
1 teasp salt
10 grinds of black pepper
1 large onion, finely chopped
3 level tbsp chicken fat or margarine
3–4 tbsp leftover beef or chicken gravy (optional)

Put the kasha into a large sauté pan and add the beaten egg. Mix well and cook over medium heat for 5 minutes, stirring occasionally until the groats look puffy and dry. Add the boiling water and the seasonings, cover and simmer for 15 minutes, until the liquid is absorbed. Meanwhile, gently sauté the onion in the fat in a covered pan until soft and golden, then add to the cooked kasha, stirring well. Stir in the gravy, if used, and reheat until steaming. May be reheated.

MILLET RISOTTO

Serves 4.
Keeps 2 days under refrigeration.
Freeze 2 months.

This seed isn't just for the birds! It's a marvellous dish with a nutty flavour to serve as part of a vegetarian meal.

8 oz (225 g/1⅓ cups) millet
2 onions, finely chopped
2 tbsp sunflower oil
4 oz (125 g/1¼ cups) mushrooms, thinly sliced
1 large carrot, finely diced
1 teasp salt
10 grinds of black pepper
½ teasp ground coriander
35 fl oz (1l/4½ cups) vegetable stock

Preheat the oven to Gas No. 4 (350°F/180°C). Heat a heavy flame-proof casserole or frying pan for 2 minutes over medium heat, then add the millet and toast without fat, stirring until it turns a golden brown. Remove it to a dish, then sauté the onions in the oil until golden brown. Add the mushrooms and continue to cook for a further 3 or 4 minutes, then return the millet to the caserole, together with the carrot, seasonings and stock. Cover and bake in the oven for 30–40 minutes, until the millet is tender. The risotto may be kept hot in a low oven, Gas No. 2 (300°F/150°C), or reheated.

Pasta (Lokshen)

I have an early memory of my late grandmother cutting the lokshen (the word is derived from the Turkish *'laktsche'*) for the Sabbath meals, her hand with the knife moving so surely and swiftly that it appeared as no more than a blur to my child's eye. Then she would hang the fine ribbons over a wooden clothes-horse draped with snowy tea-towels to dry, ready to be put into the chicken soup or made into a savoury or sweet lokshen kugel (see pp. 280, 306).

This was a chore that had to be done each week in every Ashkenazi Jewish household until the advent of factory-made packeted lokshen. Those who can remember, tell me that the texture and taste of the home-made variety was incomparably superior, but I had to wait for many years before I could judge for myself.

It was in a humble trattoria in Florence that I tasted my definitive pasta. It was a dish of cannelloni, each forkful light and melting on the tongue, and a thousand gastronomic miles distant from any I had eaten before.

At the time - more than a decade ago - the words *'fatti in casa'* on the menu meant nothing to me, but later Italian friends explained that this phrase was the key to it all - the pasta was home-made, it was fresh, and had never seen the inside of a packet.

It's only recently, however, that the true secret of this delicate pasta has been revealed to me, as the sale of *'fatti in casa'*, tagliatelle, fusilli, ravioli and cappelletti has become commonplace in this country. For to be home-made is not enough; to be melt-in-the-mouth, it must also be *fresh*, protected from the atmosphere from the very moment it ribbons out of the pasta machine. It should then be used within 24 hours, though it may be carefully wrapped and frozen for up to 2 months. This fresh pasta takes 1-3 minutes to cook, and no Italian cook worthy of the name would dream of leaving the kitchen once the pasta has gone into the pot, for once it's overcooked - *'scotta'* - as they say in Italy - you might as well throw it away.

Now, the fact that all the major supermarkets and delicatessens are offering this wonderful fresh pasta is not to belittle the *dry* variety, which is particularly useful to serve with a hearty sauce. Here the pasta is allowed to dry until it feels brittle - you may have seen it festooned over clothes-lines in the back streets of Naples. The drying process extends its life, and also the cooking time, which may be anything from 3 to 15 minutes, depending on quality and size. But even with dried pasta there are differing degrees of excellence. Look for the words 'durum wheat' or 'durum semolina' on the packet; they are your guarantee that the pasta will cook to perfection and still have a little 'bite' left in it.

Dry or fresh, the pasta must be able to *swim* in the pan, which means using one that can hold 1 gallon (5-1/20 cups) if you are cooking 1 lb (450 g) of pasta. Don't be tempted to break long strands of pasta to get them into the pan. Instead, lower them gently into the boiling water, and as they soften they will coil round on themselves, fitting the pan to perfection. A few drops of olive oil added to the cooking water will avoid any danger of sticking.

For recipe for home-made lokshen, see p. 49.

PARSLEYED NOODLES

Serves 6.
Leftovers keep 2 days under refrigeration.
Freeze 6 weeks.

1 lb (450 g) broad noodles (tagliatelle)
3 tbsp extra virgin olive oil
generous tbsp chopped parsley
several grinds of black pepper

Cook the broad noodles in boiling salted water. Rinse with cold water to remove excess starch. Put the oil in a heavy pan or oven-proof casserole and add the parsley and black pepper. Add the noodles and toss thoroughly until well coated with the herb and steaming hot.

SAVOURY LOKSHEN (*Noodles*)

Serves 4–5.
Keeps 2 days under refrigeration.
Freeze 2 months.

Serve with grilled steaks and chops.

1½ pints (850 ml/3¾ cups) boiling water
1 chicken or beef stock-cube
8 oz (225 g/1½ cups) broad egg noodles
nut of margarine
1 tbsp chopped parsley
black pepper

Bring the water to the boil, add the stock-cube and the noodles, partially cover and simmer for 10 minutes. While the noodles are cooking, put the margarine in the serving dish in a warm oven. Drain the noodles (reserving the stock for other use), and add to the margarine with the parsley and black pepper. Toss well, then serve piping hot.

VARIATION

For a milk meal, boil the noodles in water. Heat 2 oz (50 g/¼ cup) butter in the serving dish, then blend with the noodles, parsley and black pepper.

NOODLES WITH FRESH BASIL

Serves 6–8.
Leftovers keep 2 days under refrigeration.
Freeze 2 months.

These savoury noodles go well with a braised joint of veal or with veal chops.

12 oz (350 g) fresh tagliatelle
meat stock or salted water
3 oz (75 g/⅓ cup) margarine or butter
2 tbsp parsley
2 tbsp fresh basil leaves
plenty of black pepper

Cook the tagliatelle according to the packet instructions, in water or stock. Turn into a colander and drench with cold water to remove any excess starch. Drain thoroughly.

In the same pan, melt the fat and add the parsley, basil and pepper. Add the tagliatelle and continue to heat over a low light, tossing thoroughly until the tagliatelle is well coated with the herbs and is piping hot. The dish may be kept hot, covered, for up to 30 minutes, either on top of the stove or in a low oven, Gas No. 1 (275°F/140°C). In the microwave, reheat covered on 100 per cent power for 3–4 minutes, or until steaming.

SAVOURY LOKSHEN KUGEL (*Noodle Pudding*)

Serves 4–5.
Keeps 2 days under refrigeration.
Freeze 1 month.

This can be served as a soup accompaniment (to make a more substantial meal on the Eve of the Day of Atonement - Erev Yom Kippur), or in place of potatoes with a main course. The flavour is best when rendered chicken fat is used as well as 'grebenes' - the crackling from the rendered fat!

I give the original recipe for tradition's sake, but would find it difficult to justify in these cholesterol-conscious days. See pp. 199–200 for fat analysis of chicken fat.

4 oz (125 g/1½ cups) medium egg noodles
4 level tbsp rendered chicken fat or margarine
1 large egg
2 level tbsp of grebenes (optional)
salt
pepper

Turn the oven to Gas No. 2 (300°F/150°C). Half-fill an 8-inch-diameter (20-cm) pan with cold water, add 1 level teaspoon salt and bring to the boil. Then add the noodles, stir until the water comes back to the boil, half-cover the pan and allow to boil steadily for 8 minutes. (Do not cover tightly, or the water will froth over the side of the pan.) Taste a piece of noodle. It should be bite-tender. Turn the noodles into a metal sieve, but do not rinse under the cold tap because the starch on the outside of the noodles helps to 'set' the pudding. Allow the noodles to drain completely.

Put the chicken fat or margarine into a 2-pint (1.25-l/5-cup) casserole and leave in the oven for a few minutes. Meanwhile, beat the egg, add the grebenes (if used), a pinch of salt and pepper and the drained noodles. Take the hot dish out of the oven, swirl the fat to coat the sides, then pour it on to the noodle mixture. Stir well, then spoon into the casserole.

Bake for 1½ hours, or until crisp on top and set within. Lokshen kugel can be cooked in a Gas No. ¼ (225°F/110°C) oven overnight, but double the quantity must be used if the dish is not to be dry.

SALADS AND THEIR DRESSINGS

In our grandparents' time in the early years of the twentieth century, a salad meant little more than a piece of cucumber, a few spring onions (scallions) and a handful of radishes (*'rettach'*) dressed with vinegar or soured cream. These were the only vegetables in common use then in most of Eastern Europe, and indeed in the late 1980s that self-same salad was still being served when I had lunch at the Jewish Town Hall in Prague. Romanian Jews, coming from a more favourable climate, did prepare interesting relish salads using aubergines (eggplants) and peppers, but it is to the German, Hungarian and Austrian Jews in particular that we owe a lot of the new interest and expertise in salad-making that has characterized much Jewish catering in recent years. American, Syrian, Egyptian and Israeli cooks have also added new recipes to our salad repertoire, in particular those using the more exotic fruit and vegetables. My years in California gave me great affection for the salad in all its manifestations and I hope this is expressed in the recipes and advice that follows. Properly dressed and prepared with a careful regard for the texture, colour and flavour combination, the salad is one of the best of the modern Jewish food fashions.

The Green Salad

There is a bewildering variety of green salad ingredients now available all the year round, many in washed and trimmed ready-to-eat packs. These are a good buy either for the small family or if you want to base a green salad on a mix of several different greens, or indeed when time is of the essence.

Otherwise, leaves should be washed in plenty of cold water and spun dry in a salad spinner. I find that if they are then put in a bowl which has been lined with either kitchen paper or a tea-towel and refrigerated, the salad will be beautifully crisp and dry. If the greens need tearing into bite-sized pieces, this is best done just before the salad is dressed so that the crispness is retained. Mixing the salad greens offers the opportunity for limitless permutations of flavour and texture, and that's before you even start mixing the dressing.

I prefer to mix herbs with the greens rather than with the dressing, so fresh basil, parsley and chives should be scissored (rather than chopped) into the salad bowl.

As a green salad must always be dressed at the table and a dressing that has been matured for an hour has a deeper flavour than one mixed at the last moment, leave the prepared dressing in a screw-top jar which can be shaken just before it is spooned through the salad at the table.

A SHORT GUIDE TO SALAD GREENS

Chicory To the British the oval bulb of white leaves fringed with green (called 'endive' or 'witloof' by the French). Its slightly bitter taste can add a pleasing astringency when combined with gentler flavours.

Curly endive, endive, frisée A large flat lettuce with a heart of tightly packed, pale-green, crinkly leaves and an outer layer of inedible, tough, dark ones. Where available it's just as cost-effective to buy the prepacked edible centre, usually labelled *frisée*. The crisp, frilly fronds contrast particularly well with the softer leaves of the ordinary garden lettuce.

Little Gem A crisp dwarf variety of the more familiar nutty-flavoured long *Cos* or *Romaine* lettuce. Only the hearts are sold, so there is no waste from the discarded outer leaves. It's particularly good halved and served with a blue cheese or mayonnaise-based dressing such as Green Goddess (see p. 299).

Lamb's Lettuce Also known as *Corn Salad* or *Mâche* in France, this has small velvety leaves with a delicate flavour. It makes a pretty garnish, lightly dressed with a walnut oil vinaigrette, for a first-course mousse or fish pâté, or it can be combined with crisp lettuce varieties such as *Batavia, Iceberg,* or *Webb.*

Radicchio This is actually a rosy-leaved chicory, very pretty with its white veins and curly shape. Slightly bitter, like its green relation, and excellent as part of a mixed salad to accompany a hearty main course.

Oak Leaf Also known in France as *Feuille de Chêne,* this variety, named for obvious reasons, and the dimple-leaved *Quattro Stagione* add a decorative touch to salads or starters.

Rocket Called *Arugola* or *Rucola* in Italy, this has intense green dandelion-like leaves and a pungent flavour – a little makes a good companion to softer, milder-flavoured lettuces.

Watercress The prepacked leaves trimmed of the coarser stalks keep crisp and green for longer than bunches, and require no preparation before adding their distinctive taste and texture to green or fruited salads.

Fresh herbs These are a relatively new concept in Jewish cookery. Middle Eastern Jews have long used mint in salads such as tabbouleh (see p. 295) and in Eastern Europe dill and 'knobl' (garlic) were widely used in the pickle for cucumbers. And that was the end of the story.

These days Israel is one of the main sources of fresh herbs now available all the year round. I also recommend a small herb bed as one of the most pleasurable forms of gardening. However, herbs grown in a temperate climate lack the zing that comes from ripening under a Mediterranean sun – the flavouring oils in varieties such as oregano, rosemary and thyme are less intense in flavour.

Little bouquets of herbs can be treated like any other leaf and added to the salad bowl to great effect on both the appearance and the flavour.

The easiest herbs to grow in the domestic garden are mint, parsley, chives, rosemary, thyme, oregano, marjoram and lovage. The more delicate herbs, such as tarragon, dill and basil, can be started off in a greenhouse or propagating frame, or bought as young plants which are hardy enough to be grown outdoors when the weather is warm enough.

In the salads that follow I have suggested combinations of salad greens that I've found work well together. However, none of these recipes need to be followed to the letter – half the pleasure in salad-making lies in experimentation.

A SALAD OF SPRING LEAVES WITH A NUT-OIL DRESSING

Serves 6–8.

A light and refreshing all-green salad with a high 'crunch' factor to serve with a steak or grilled chops.

'Two veg' are rarely served with meat on the Continent nowadays. More often the vitamin and texture elements are provided by a really interesting salad served either as a starter or garnished with fruit and nuts as a palate freshener after a hearty main course.

1 Batavia lettuce
1 Cos lettuce
1 bunch watercress, leaves only
1 fine bulb of fennel, trimmed
1 tbsp fresh lemon juice
8 oz (225 g) small courgettes (zucchini)
1 small handful of parsley

For the dressing
3 fl oz (75 ml/$^1/_3$ cup) sunflower oil
1 fl oz (25 ml/2 tbsp) walnut or hazelnut (filbert) oil
1 fl oz (25 ml/2 tbsp) white wine vinegar or cider vinegar
1 teasp lemon juice
1 teasp caster (superfine) sugar or granular sweetener
1 teasp wholegrain mustard
$^1/_2$ teasp sea salt
5 grinds of black pepper
1 small clove of garlic, peeled and halved

To make the dressing, put all the ingredients in a large screw-top jar and shake well until thickened. Leave in the refrigerator to mature for several hours.

Wash, spin-dry, then wrap the lettuces and watercress in a dry tea-towel and leave in the refrigerator to crisp for at least 2 hours. Slice the fennel (discarding the tough base) and leave in a bowl sprinkled with the lemon juice – this prevents browning and also lessens the strong flavour of aniseed. Top, tail and very thinly slice the courgettes and divide the parsley into tiny sprigs.

An hour before the meal, tear the lettuce into bite-sized pieces and arrange with all the remaining ingredients in a salad bowl large and wide enough to allow the contents to be later tossed with the dressing. Cover and refrigerate again until required.

Just before serving, shake the dressing well and pour over the salad, tossing until all the ingredients are glistening.

CHICORY SALAD IN THE FRENCH MANNER

Serves 6.
Undressed leaves keep 1 day, whole chicory 3 days, under refrigeration.

An excellent salad for late winter when lettuces are in poor supply.

6 small heads of chicory

For the dressing
3 tbsp extra virgin olive oil
1 tbsp white wine vinegar or cider vinegar
1 level teasp salt
1 level teasp caster (superfine) sugar or granular sweetener
plenty of fresh ground black pepper
1 level tbsp finely chopped parsley
1 level teasp freeze-dried fines herbes
1 small clove of garlic, crushed

Cut off the base of the chicory so that the leaves can be removed whole. Put these in a colander and rinse under the cold tap, then dry well. Put in a salad bowl, cover with clingfilm (saranwrap) and refrigerate for a few hours until required. Make the dressing by shaking all the ingredients together in a screw-top jar until they thicken (about 2 minutes), then refrigerate as well. Just before serving, pour the dressing over the chicory, toss thoroughly until all the leaves are coated with the dressing and serve at once.

CHICORY AND FRISÉE SALAD WITH BLUE CHEESE AND TOASTED PECANS

Serves 8.

An excellent 'starter' salad, or to serve after a fish or dairy main course.

4 fl oz (125 ml/½ cup) extra virgin olive oil
2 fat cloves of garlic, finely sliced
4 thick slices bread, cut in ½-inch (1.25 cm) cubes
2 oz (50 g/½ cup) pecan halves
2 tbsp fresh lemon juice
3 teasp white wine vinegar
½ teasp each salt and caster sugar
10 grinds of black pepper
2 packs of frisée
6 small heads of chicory, cut lengthwise into 4
3 oz (75 g/⅔ cup) crumbled blue cheese

Flavour the olive oil with the garlic by leaving them together for 2 hours, then strain out the garlic. Arrange the bread cubes in a shallow ovenproof tray, drizzle them with 2 tablespoons of the oil and season with a little salt. Toss well to coat evenly, then bake for 15–18 minutes at Gas No. 5 (375°F/190°C), until golden brown. Put the pecan halves in a small baking tin, then crisp at the same time (check colour half-way through. Allow to cool.

To make the dressing, into a screw-top jar put the lemon juice and vinegar together with the remaining garlic oil, the salt, sugar and black pepper. Shake until slightly thickened.

An hour before serving combine the frisée, chicory, pecans and cheese in a large bowl. Add the dressing and toss until all the ingredients are evenly coated. Turn into a salad bowl and scatter with the croûtons.

ORANGE, CHICORY AND TOASTED SESAME SALAD

Serves 6–8.
Eat the same day.

A refreshing salad to serve with roast duck or cold meats.

12 oz (350 g) chicory (4–5 very small heads)
3 large thin-skinned oranges
(seedless navels if possible)
3 tbsp toasted white sesame seeds or 1 oz
(25 g/¼ cup) toasted pine kernels

For the dressing
2 tbsp walnut or sunflower oil
1 tbsp lemon juice
2 teasp chopped fresh mint
1 teasp caster (superfine) sugar or granular sweetener
½ teasp salt
speck of white pepper
juice from orange 'skeleton'

Cut the ends off the chicory, then separate the leaves. Peel the oranges as you would an apple, removing the pith as well, and section them. Add any free orange juice to the dressing ingredients and whisk well to form a slightly thickened emulsion. Arrange the chicory (you can use watercress if you prefer) and the orange sections in a salad bowl – a glass one for the prettiest effect. Toss in the dressing. Just before serving, scatter with the sesame seeds or pine kernels.

SALADE MENTON

Serves 6–8.
Eat the same day.

I found this exquisite salad in Holland. It uses Israeli kumquats marinated in a piquant dressing to spark up a green salad. Arrange in a wide, preferably glass, salad bowl. You will find, then, that it looks as superb as it tastes.

6 oz (175 g) kumquats or peeled orange sections out of season
2 oz (50 g/½ cup) toasted pine kernels
fine sea salt
1 lb (450 g) chicory
1 pack frisée or the pale-green centre of the whole lettuce

For the dressing
3 fl oz (75 ml/⅓ cup) sunflower oil
1 fl oz (25 ml/2 tbsp walnut or hazelnut (filbert) oil
1 fl oz (25 ml/2 tbsp) raspberry vinegar
1 teasp fresh lemon juice
2 teasp sugar or granular sweetener
½ teasp wholegrain mustard
½ teasp salt
5 grinds of black pepper
3 teasp chopped parsley

Several hours in advance, make the dressing by shaking all the ingredients together in a large screw-top jar until thickened, then add the topped, tailed and quartered kumquats (or orange sections), cover and refrigerate. Toast the pine kernels by tossing in a hot frying pan until golden, then sprinkle lightly with the fine sea salt.

Cut the stems from the chicory and discard any damaged outer leaves. Separate the leaves, then wash and spin dry. Arrange in a wide, shallow salad bowl with the sprigs of frisée, cover and chill.

Just before dinner, cut the chicory leaves, if necessary, into bite-sized pieces. Shake the dressing again, then pour on to the salad with the kumquats and toss until the leaves are well coated and glistening. Sprinkle with the pine kernels.

INSALATA SICILIANA

Serves 6–8.
Enough croûtons for 2 salads.

A green salad is enlivened with herb-and-cheese-flavoured croûtons and an anchovy-flavoured dressing.

mixed greens such as 'Little Gem', frisée, radicchio or shredded Iceberg, or 2 packs ready-to-serve mixed salad greens
small pack cherry tomatoes (halved if necessary)

For the croûtons
1 large clove of garlic, cut in half lengthwise
1 teasp dried Italian seasoning
1 teasp fines herbes
½ teasp sea salt
20 grinds of black pepper
2 fl oz extra virgin olive oil
8 large slices brown or white bread, cut in ¾-inch (2-cm) cubes (challah is also excellent)
2 rounded tbsp finely grated Parmesan or other sharp cheese (optional)

For the dressing
3 teasp anchovy essence or purée
2 tbsp red wine vinegar
7 tbsp extra virgin olive oil
10 grinds of black pepper
1 teasp caster (superfine) sugar or granular sweetener

First prepare the croûtons. In a small pan combine the garlic, herbs, salt, pepper and oil and simmer for 5 minutes, then remove from the heat. Leave to infuse for 15 minutes, then discard the garlic. Mix with the bread cubes in a shallow baking tin (eg a roulade tin), then bake at Gas No. 5 (375°F/190°C) for 10 minutes. Stir well, then sprinkle with the cheese (if used) and bake for a further 8 minutes, until golden brown. Add a little more salt if necessary. When quite cold, store in an airtight tin.

Several hours in advance, make the dressing by shaking all the ingredients together in a screw-top jar until thickened, then refrigerate. If necessary, rinse the greens, spin them dry and then wrap in a tea-towel and allow to crispen in the refrigerator. Then, tear them into bite-sized pieces and put in a large bowl together with the tomatoes and the croutons. Just before serving, add the dressing and toss thoroughly.

ISRAELI FRUITED WINTER SALAD

Serves 6–8.
Eat the same day.

A refreshing green salad to serve either as a starter or for a buffet supper.

2 oz (50 g/½ cup) blanched split almonds
1 Iceberg lettuce, shredded
4-inch (10-cm) piece of Chinese leaves, finely sliced, or any preferred salad greens
8 oz (225 g) black grapes

For the dressing

3 fl oz (75 ml/⅓ cup) sunflower oil
1 fl oz (25 ml/2 tbsp) extra virgin olive oil
1 tbsp wine vinegar or raspberry vinegar
1 tbsp fresh lemon juice
1 teasp caster (superfine) sugar or granular sweetener
½ teasp whole-grain mustard
½ teasp sea salt
8 grinds of black pepper

Shake all the dressing ingredients together in a screw-top jar until slightly thickened, then chill for several hours.

Toast and lightly salt the blanched almonds.

Arrange the finely shredded lettuce and Chinese leaves (or other greens) in a wide salad bowl, cover and refrigerate. Shortly before serving add the halved and de-pipped grapes and the almonds and toss with the dressing.

Relish Salads

The salads in this section all add piquancy to blander foods and are therefore more in the Jewish tradition than the green salads. They are especially suitable for a cold buffet.

THREE PEPPER SALADS

Serves 6–8.
Keeps 48 hours under refrigeration.

This succulent and very decorative roasted-pepper salad is made all over the Mediterranean, where it is served either as a starter with very fresh, coarse brown bread or warm pitta, or as part of a summer luncheon to accompany cold chicken and meats. It can be made with fresh peppers alone, but I find a combination that includes some canned pimentos is excellent and certainly saves a great deal of preparation time.

1 large green pepper
1 large yellow pepper
2 x 14 oz (400 g) cans red pimentos in brine
6 oz (175 g/1½ cups) fine black olives

For the dressing

6 tbsp extra virgin olive oil
1 large clove of garlic, crushed
2 tbsp finely chopped fresh coriander or parsley
1 tbsp chopped fresh or 1 teasp dried mint
1½ tbsp lemon juice
10 grinds of black pepper
1 teasp sea salt

Grill (broil) the fresh peppers under or over fierce heat until the skin has blackened and feels papery all over - 10–15 minutes. Leave covered with a paper towel until cool enough to handle, then rub off the skin and remove the seeds and white pith.

Drain the canned pimentos, then cut them and the peppers into strips ½ inch (1.25 cm) wide and place in a shallow dish with the olives.

Whisk the dressing ingredients together in a small bowl, then spoon over the peppers. Cover and refrigerate, if possible for several hours or overnight.

PIQUANT STRING BEANS

Serves 6–8.
Keeps 2 days under refrigeration.

An excellent relish to serve with fried and grilled fish or cold meats.

12–16 oz (350–450 g) packet frozen whole green beans
1 x 11½ oz (325 g) can corn with red pepper
½ small onion or 3 fat spring onions (scallions), finely chopped

For the dressing
3 tbsp sunflower oil
4 tbsp white wine vinegar or cider vinegar
2 teasp sugar or granular sweetener
½ teasp salt
8 grinds of black pepper
1 tbsp finely snipped chives

Cook the beans in boiling salted water for 4–5 minutes, or until barely tender. Alternatively, microwave on 100 per cent power with 3 tablespoons of water for the same time. Rinse under the cold tap to set the colour, then drain and put in a bowl with the well-drained corn and chopped onion.

Shake all the dressing ingredients together in a screw-top jar until slightly thickened, then blend with the vegetables. Spoon into a fairly shallow dish, cover and refrigerate for several hours.

BEAN, RED PEPPER AND HEARTS OF ARTICHOKE SALAD

Serves 6–8, or 10 for a buffet.
Keeps 3 days under refrigeration.

The pesto adds an intriguing flavour to the dressing. However, it can be omitted and 1 tablespoon of finely shredded fresh basil added to the dressing instead.

1 x 15 oz (425 g) can red kidney beans, drained
1 x 15 oz (425 g) can cannellini (haricot) beans, drained
1 red pepper
1 x 15 oz (425 g) can artichoke hearts
small bunch of spring onions (scallions)

For the dressing
4 tbsp olive oil
3 teasp pesto (optional)
2 tbsp red wine vinegar
½ teasp salt
10 grinds of black pepper

For the garnish
8 oz (225 g) cherry tomatoes

Drain the beans thoroughly and put into a bowl with the red pepper cut in ⅜-inch (1-cm) dice, the drained artichoke hearts sliced in 4 and the spring onions with their green trimmed 2 inches (5 cm) in length and finely sliced.

To make the dressing, put the oil in a small bowl and whisk in the pesto (if used), followed by the remaining ingredients. Pour over the salad ingredients, toss gently, then chill for at least 2 hours. Just before serving, toss gently again and arrange in an entrée dish. Cut the tomatoes in half and arrange around the edge of the salad.

CACIK
(Cucumbers in a Creamy Minted Dressing)

Serves 6–8.
Keeps 1 day under refrigeration.

A dish popular all over the Middle East, this version, with its garnish of mint, comes from Turkey. Yoghurt is more authentic, soured cream more satisfying. Strained Greek style yoghurt or 8% fromage frais is as thick and creamy as soured cream but has a lower fat content. This is a good dish to serve with salmon, whether poached or grilled.

1 large cucumber, unpeeled and sliced
1 tbsp salt

For the dressing
10 oz (275 g/1¼ cup) strained Greek-style yoghurt
3 teasp white wine vinegar
2 teasp caster (superfine) sugar
½ teasp salt
10 grinds of black pepper
1 small clove of garlic, crushed
1 tbsp fresh chopped mint leaves or
1 teasp dried mint

For the garnish
tiny sprigs of fresh mint

Several hours before the meal put all the dressing ingredients into a large basin and whisk lightly together. Refrigerate.

Put the slices of cucumber in a salad spinner or colander, sprinkle with the salt and leave for 30 minutes, then rinse and dry.

Add the cucumber to the dressing and turn to coat, using 2 spoons. Transfer to a shallow dish, such as a pottery quiche dish, and garnish with the mint springs.

VARIATION

CACIK WITH CUCUMBER JULIENNES

This produces a better texture if the Cacik is to be served as a sauce (rather than a salad) to accompany a hot salmon dish.

½ a cucumber
dressing ingredients as before

Cut the cucumber into 1-inch (2.5-cm) lengths, then cut each of them into ¼-inch-wide (0.5-cm) strips, holding the cucumber together with finger and thumb. Cut ¼-inch (0.5-cm) strips at right angles to first ones and you will have produced juliennes. Salt them, then add to the dressing as before.

DANISH CUCUMBER SALAD

Serves 6–8.
Keeps 3 days under refrigeration.

A light and refreshing salad to serve with grilled or cold poached salmon. The dressing must be both sweet and sour.

1 fat cucumber
coarse salt

For the dressing
2 level tbsp caster (superfine) sugar or 2 tbsp granular sweetener
2 tbsp boiling water (or cold water if sweetener is used)
4 tbsp wine vinegar
plenty of black pepper
1 tbsp finely cut chives

Thinly slice the unpeeled cucumber with a mandolin or in the food processor. Put the slices on a soup plate, sprinkle with the salt, cover with an upturned plate and a 1-lb (450-g) weight, and leave for 30 minutes. (This salting process can be omitted if the salad is made less than an hour before serving.) Pour off any liquid.

Dissolve the sugar in the boiling water or the granular sweetener in cold water, then add all the remaining dressing ingredients. Pour on to cucumber slices arranged in a shallow dish.

VARIATIONS

CUCUMBER AND STRAWBERRY SALAD

Keeps 1 day under refrigeration.

Arrange the cucumber slices in concentric circles alternately with 8 oz (225 g) thickly sliced strawberries. Add 1 tablespoon of snipped dill to the dressing instead of chives, and use 2 tablespoons each of wine vinegar and raspberry vinegar. Do not add the dressing until half an hour before serving as it tends to bleach the strawberries.

CUCUMBER AND ORANGE SALAD

Keeps 1 day under refrigeration.

Arrange the cucumber slices in concentric circles with sections cut from 4 navel oranges. Use chopped mint or dill instead of chives in the dressing.

HUNGARIAN CUCUMBER SALAD

Serves 6–8.
Keeps 2 days under refrigeration.

An excellent salad for a low-fat diet as no oil is used in the dressing.

1 fat cucumber
1 lb (450 g) small tomatoes
1 large red pepper
3 teasp cooking salt

For the dressing
2 level teasp caster (superfine) sugar or granular sweetener
1 tbsp hot water
4 tbsp wine vinegar
15 grinds of black pepper
1 teasp salt
1 tbsp fresh snipped dill, chives or chopped mint

Make the salad at least 2 or 3 hours before serving to allow the flavour to develop. Slice the unpeeled cucumber as thinly as possible. Cut the tomatoes in halves or quarters according to size. Halve, deseed and remove the white pith from the pepper, then cut the flesh in thin strips. Put the cucumber slices and tomatoes in a basin, sprinkle with cooking salt and leave for an hour.

Put the sugar in a basin, pour on the hot water, stir well, then add all the remaining dressing ingredients. (If using granular sweetener, dissolve in cold water.) Lift out the tomatoes and cucumber slices with a slotted spoon and discard the liquid that has come out of them, then return to the bowl and add to the peppers. Pour over the dressing. Turn into a serving dish and refrigerate until required.

COLESLAW

Serves 6–8.
Keeps 3 days under refrigeration.

Commercial coleslaw is widely available, but it rarely compares with the home-made version, which is quickly made using the shredding attachment of a food processor. Allow the salad to mature for several hours, by which time it will have softened and improved in flavour.

1 white winter cabbage ($1\frac{1}{2}$ lb/675 g)
1 large carrot, grated
1 red pepper, thinly sliced

Optional
2 oz (50 g/$\frac{1}{3}$ cup) sultanas (white raisins)
1 oz (25 g/$\frac{1}{4}$ cup) dry roasted peanuts

For the dressing
5 fl oz (150 ml/$\frac{2}{3}$ cup) mild mayonnaise
1 level tbsp malt vinegar
1 level tbsp caster (superfine) sugar or granular sweetener
1 level teasp dry mustard

Discard any discoloured leaves, quarter the cabbage and remove the white core. Shred very finely with a knife, electric shredder or food processor. If the cabbage has a strong smell, soak it in a bowl of cold water (to cover) with 2 level teaspoons of salt for 1 hour, then drain well and dry thoroughly. In either case mix well with the grated carrot, the pepper and the sultanas (if used).

Blend all the dressing seasonings with the mayonnaise in a large mixing bowl. Add the salad ingredients and turn with a spoon and fork until well coated. Chill until required. Put into a serving bowl and top with the nuts (if used).

SPICED MUSHROOMS

Serves 4–6 as a starter, 6–8 as part of an hors d'oeuvre.
Keeps 3–4 days under refrigeration.

A superb relish that improves with time.

1 lb (450 g/5 cups) tiny button mushrooms
squeeze of lemon juice
1 tbsp extra virgin olive oil
1 tbsp sunflower oil
2 tbsp wine vinegar
1 level teasp salt
2 teasp grated onion
1 clove of garlic, crushed
½ teasp ground cumin
10 grinds of black pepper
1 level tbsp chopped parsley

Remove the mushroom stalks, then simmer the mushrooms in a squeeze of lemon juice and enough salted water to cover for 5 minutes. Drain well and mix with the dressing ingredients, which have been shaken together in a screw-top jar to form an emulsion. Cover and leave until quite cold.

PIMENTO, BLACK OLIVE AND ORANGE SALAD

Serves 8–10.

A good one for the buffet table, this is also delicious served with grilled steak or chops instead of a vegetable. The crisp frisée acts as a counterbalance to the other softer ingredients.

1 x 8 oz (225 g) can whole roasted pimentos in salt water
32 black or green olives (stoned weight about 8 oz/225 g/2 cups)
2 mild salad onions
3 navel oranges
2 packs frisée
1 pack watercress

For the dressing
2 tbsp olive oil
4 tbsp sunflower oil
2 tbsp raspberry or other fruity white wine vinegar
1 fat clove of garlic, crushed
10 grinds of sea salt
1 teasp Dijon mustard
2 teasp sugar
2 teasp fresh snipped tarragon

Drain and slice pimentos, slice olives away from the stone, peel and finely slice the onions and peel and section oranges, discarding pith and membrane. Line a wooden salad bowl with the frisée and arrange the remaining ingredients on top. Shake the dressing ingredients together in a screw-top jar until thickened.

Chill both the salad and the dressing. Just before serving, toss together until all the ingredients are lightly but evenly coated with the dressing.

PERFECT POTATO SALAD

Serves 6–8.
Keeps 2 days under refrigeration.

The kidney-shaped waxy yellow potato is ideal for salads as it keeps its shape when cooked and absorbs flavourings well. Some recommended varieties are Desiree, Golden Wonder, Maris Peer, Wilja, Red Craigs Royal. However, if you cook an ordinary new potato with special care, add the oil and vinegar when the potatoes are hot and the mayonnaise when they are cold, I am sure you will agree that this is the best potato salad you have ever tasted.

1½ lb (675 g) waxy or new potatoes
4 tbsp prepared French dressing (see p. 300)
or 3 tbsp oil and 1 tbsp vinegar, ½ teasp salt, pinch of pepper, pinch each of sugar and mustard
1 level tbsp finely chopped onion or shallot
1 tbsp scissored chives
1 tbsp finely chopped parsley
5 fl oz (150 ml/⅔ cup) mild mayonnaise
1 level teasp Dijon mustard
1 tbsp boiling water
1 tbsp lemon juice

For the garnish
chopped parsley

Boil potatoes in their skins until almost tender. Drain, return to the heat covered with a tea-towel, then steam gently for a further 3 or 4 minutes until tender and absolutely dry (they will be firm). Spread on a cloth and leave until cool enough to handle, then skin and dice or slice into a bowl. Mix the dressing with onion and herbs, then stir gently through the potatoes. Heap into a shallow bowl. Blend together the mayonnaise, mustard, boiling water and lemon juice. Spoon on top of the potatoes. Leave in a cool place for at least an hour. Just before serving mix the mayonnaise through the salad and garnish with more parsley. Always serve the salad at room temperature.

CYPRUS TOMATO SALAD

Serves 6–8.
Keeps 1 day under refrigeration.

The traditional Greek-Cypriot accompaniment to grilled lamb.

1 medium cucumber
4 large tomatoes
1 large green or yellow pepper
12 little sprigs of parsley

For the dressing
4 tbsp olive oil
2 tbsp lemon juice
1 teasp salt
1 teasp sugar
10 grinds of black pepper
1 clove of garlic, crushed
1 tbsp snipped fresh basil

For the garnish
about 4 oz (125 g/1 cup) black Calamata (Greek-style) olives

Peel the cucumber, cut in ½-inch (1.25-cm) dice and put in a salad spinner or colander. Sprinkle lightly with salt and leave for 30 minutes, then rinse and dry. Cube the tomatoes and deseed, then dice the pepper.

Shake all the dressing ingredients together in a screw-top jar until well blended. Arrange the tomatoes, cucumber and pepper in a shallow bowl and garnish with the sprigs of parsley. Just before serving, sprinkle on the dressing and toss well. Top with the black olives.

KIBBUTZ SALAD

Serves 6–8.
Eat the same day.

This is the archetypal Israeli salad, made with greater or less finesse depending on where you are. But whether it's prepared for 200 kibbutzniks or by street vendors who spoon it into your pitta bread along with their freshly fried felafel balls, it's always made with cubes of vegetables - cucumber, tomato and pepper, cut large or small, according to the patience of the cook. It makes a refreshing foil for grilled dishes, whether meat or fish, but it's equally good with cold poultry and meats. All the salad ingredients and the dressing can be prepared a day ahead, but to retain the characteristic crispness, they are best combined an hour before serving.

1 red pepper
1 green pepper
1 long, fat and straight cucumber, unpeeled
4 large firm but ripe tomatoes

For the dressing
3 tbsp sunflower oil
1 tbsp fruity olive oil
1 tbsp wine vinegar
1 tbsp lemon juice
1 fat clove of garlic, peeled and crushed
1 level teasp salt
10 grinds of black pepper
1 teasp caster (superfine) sugar
1 tbsp finely snipped fresh or 1 teasp dried mint
2 tbsp chopped parsley

Halve and deseed the peppers and remove the white pith. Cut each of the vegetables into even ¾-inch (1.25-cm) cubes or squares, then put the tomatoes and peppers into separate bowls, cover and refrigerate. Put the cucumber cubes into a salad spinner or sieve, sprinkle with 1 teaspoon of coarse salt and leave for 30 minutes, then spin or drain and refrigerate. In a screw-top jar, shake together until thickened all the dressing ingredients except the fresh herbs. Add the dried mint (if used) then leave for several hours to mature in flavour.

Put the cucumber, pepper and tomato cubes into a large bowl, then stir in the chopped parsley and mint, together with the dressing, and mix well, using 2 spoons. Arrange the salad in a fairly shallow dish - it looks particularly effective against black or white. Serve cool but not chilled.

PROVENÇALE TOMATO SALAD

Serves 6.
Keeps 24 hours under refrigeration, but best when freshly prepared.

A rich-tasting salad ideal to serve with grilled chicken, steak or chops instead of a green vegetable. The secret of the flavour is to use very ripe, well-flavoured tomatoes marinated in a salted dressing (this draws out excess liquid) which is then discarded.

1½ lb (675 g) large ripe tomatoes
the bulbs and 4 inches (10 cm) of stalk from a small bunch of spring onions (scallions)
3 teasp fine salt
10 grinds of black pepper
4 tbsp wine vinegar
2 tbsp extra virgin olive oil
1 fat yellow pepper

To add just before serving
1 tbsp extra virgin olive oil
1 tbsp finely shredded fresh basil leaves or chopped parsley

Start the preparation 2–3 hours in advance. Cut each of the washed tomatoes into 8 sections and put in a bowl (smaller tomatoes can be cut in half or quartered). Add the finely sliced onions, sprinkle with the salt, black pepper, wine vinegar and olive oil, stir gently to coat with this mixture and then leave at room temperature for 2–3 hours, stirring occasionally. Shortly before serving, drain the tomatoes in a colander and throw away the liquid. Arrange in a shallow dish with ½-inch (1.25-cm) strips of the deseeded pepper and sprinkle with the remaining tablespoon of olive oil and the herbs. Gently stir together then serve.

VARIATION

Serves 8–10.

Add to the tomatoes before salting 1 medium cucumber, cut in 'sticks' 1 inch (2.5 cm) long and ⅜ inch (1.25 cm) wide.

MELON AND CHERRY TOMATO SALAD

Serves 8–10 for a buffet.
Keeps 1 day under refrigeration.

A very decorative salad to serve with cold salmon.

1 large ripe Galia or Ogen melon
1 lb (450 g) Gardeners' Delight or other cherry tomatoes

For the dressing
3 tbsp sunflower oil
1 tbsp walnut oil
1½ tbsp raspberry vinegar
½ teasp salt
pinch caster (superfine) sugar
speck of white pepper
2 tbsp mayonnaise
1 tbsp finely chopped mint

For the garnish
a few sprigs of mint

Use a melon-baller to scoop out the melon flesh. If tomatoes are too large for a mouthful, cut in half. Put all the salad dressing ingredients into a screw-top jar and shake together until thickened - about 2 minutes. An hour before serving, combine the tomatoes and melon and mix gently with the dressing. Arrange in a bowl and chill. Garnish with the mint leaves just before setting on the table.

A SALAD OF TOMATOES, MOZZARELLA AND AVOCADO

Serves 6–8.
Eat the same day.

To reproduce faithfully the flavours of this salad from the sun, it's essential to use tomatoes that have been picked only when fully ripe (these are now widely available) and a really herby dressing. If kosher Mozzarella is not available, Gouda can be used instead.

Sun-dried tomatoes (*pomodori secchi*) have been used for centuries in Calabria in southern Italy. Plum tomatoes are split with a knife, sprinkled with salt, then laid out in the sun to dry. This treatment concentrates their flavour, making them a marvellous ingredient - usually mixed with olive oil, in either strips or purée form - to enhance the flavour of dressings and rice dishes, or as a topping for canapés of all kinds.

8 oz (225 g) Mozzarella, chilled well
1¼ lb (575 g) fully ripe salad tomatoes
2 fat ripe avocados (not squashy)

For the dressing
3 tbsp virgin olive oil
3 tbsp sunflower oil
2 tbsp sundried tomato purée or 1 extra tbsp each olive oil and vinegar and 1 teasp tomato purée
1½ tbsp wine vinegar or lemon juice
1 tbsp snipped chives
1 tbsp chopped parsley
1 tbsp finely shredded fresh basil
1 medium clove of garlic, finely chopped
15 grinds of black pepper
½ teasp sea salt

For the garnish
sprigs of fresh herbs

About 2 hours before serving, slice the chilled Mozzarella and the tomatoes ¼ inch (0.5 cm) thick. Halve, peel and stone the avocados and cut into slices ¼ inch (0.5 cm) thick also, then arrange all these slices overlapping on 1 large dish or 6–8 individual dishes.

Shake all the dressing ingredients together until thickened, then drizzle over the salad, making sure the avocado slices are coated. Just before serving, garnish with the fresh herbs and serve with granary or other brown bread.

WALDORF SALAD DELUXE

Serves 6–8.
Keeps 1 day under refrigeration.

The original concept of this salad was developed by Oscar Tschirky, the maître d'hotel of the Waldorf Astoria Hotel in New York. A recipe for it is given in the *Settlement Cookbook*, an early twentieth-century American cookbook written mainly for young immigrant Jewish women which gives both kosher and non-kosher recipes. (My 1926 edition is the fifteenth, but I don't know the original date of publication.)

Tschirky's recipe called only for celery and apple, bound with mayonnaise, but each generation has added a little more excitement.

8 large stalks celery
2 small red-skinned apples
4 oz (125 g/⅔ cup) fresh dates
4 oz (125 g/¾ cup) seedless grapes
2 oz (50 g/⅓ cup) seedless raisins

For the dressing
1 tbsp orange juice
1 tbsp lemon juice
1 teasp fine brown sugar
5 fl oz (150 ml/⅔ cup) mild mayonnaise

For the garnish
2 oz (50 g/½ cup) chopped walnuts or salted peanuts (optional)

Cut the celery in ¼-inch (0.5-cm) cubes. Quarter the apples, then core and cut into ¾-inch (1-cm) cubes. Stone and roughly chop the dates. Put in a bowl with the raisins and grapes. Stir the dressing ingredients together, then mix with the salad ingredients, stirring well. Refrigerate several hours. Turn into a bowl and garnish with the chopped nuts (if used).

A GOOD RICE SALAD

Serves 6–8.
Keeps 2 days under refrigeration.

This simple but savoury salad can stand in its own right on a buffet table. But it's most useful as a basis for chicken or turkey salads. It's important to add the vinaigrette to the *hot* rice, which then absorbs it more readily than it would when cold.

1¼ pints (725 ml/3 cups) chicken stock
12 oz (350 g/2 cups) Basmati (long-grain Indian) rice
1 large yellow or orange pepper
1 x 8 oz (225 g) can sweet pimentos
3 rounded tbsp seedless raisins
6 tbsp vinaigrette dressing *(see p. 300)*

Bring the chicken stock to the boil and add the rice. Cover and simmer for 15 minutes, then take off the heat and leave covered to steam for a further 10 minutes. Uncover – the rice will have absorbed all the liquid and can be fluffed up with a fork. Put into a bowl and add the deseeded, finely diced pepper, pimentos and raisins. Sprinkle with the vinaigrette and mix gently with a fork. Refrigerate in a covered container for several hours.

TABBOULEH

Serves 8.
Keeps 4 days under refrigeration.

Innumerable versions of this salad are made by Jews from all over the Middle East, and especially Lebanon. In Israel it is often used as a stuffing for pitta bread. For the finest flavour, mix the cracked wheat (usually sold as 'bulgur', 'pourgouri' or 'bourghoul') with the dressing and leave overnight. It will look very green from all the herbs. If preferred, the tomato and cucumber slices can be replaced by tiny dice and folded in shortly before serving rather than used as garnish.

8 oz (225 g/1 cup) cracked wheat
1 teasp salt
12 fl oz (350 ml/1½ cups) boiling water

For the dressing
6 tbsp olive oil
4 tbsp lemon juice
1 small bunch of spring onion (scallion) bulbs
2 teasp salt
20 grinds of black pepper
2 tbsp chopped fresh mint leaves
1 cup finely chopped parsley (about 2 oz
50 g of the whole herb)

For the garnish
black olives
tomato and cucumber slices

Put the cracked wheat with the salt into a heatproof bowl, cover with the boiling water and leave for 20 minutes for the water to be absorbed. Stir in all the dressing ingredients, mixing thoroughly to blend the flavours. Taste and add more salt or lemon juice if necessary – it should be tart but not sour. Chill overnight.

Serve the chilled tabbouleh piled in an oval gratin or decorative dish and garnish just before serving.

Salad Dressings

To our Jewish grandmothers, dressing a salad meant sprinkling it with a little salt and vinegar. Mayonnaise and what is generally known as 'French dressing' (vinaigrette) were completely unknown. Yet when serving salads in the modern manner, the dressing is an integral part of the whole.

SALAD OILS

I use 4 oils in my salad dressings – sunflower, olive, walnut (huile de noix) and hazelnut (huile de noisette). I have only specified a particular oil where its flavour is essential to the recipe.

Sunflower oil Light in texture, tasteless and relatively cheap. I use it as an all-purpose oil or mixed in varying proportions with the other more assertively flavoured and expensive oils.

Safflower oil, *grapeseed* oil and *nut* (refined peanut) oil are alternatives.

Olive oil The finest 'extra virgin' quality (made from the first pressing of the ripe olive pulp) is now widely available, some even made from the olives of a single village only – rather like wine produced from the grapes of a named vineyard. It's interesting to note that some of the finest olive oil is sold by wine merchants who stock wines from areas where the olive oil is produced.

The finer the oil, the lower its acidity, and the smoother the flavour. Check the label against these legal definitions of quality:

Extra Virgin Olive Oil Perfect flavour, perfect aroma, perfect colour (light yellow to green), maximum acidity of 1 per cent.

Fine Virgin Olive Oil The same qualities as extra virgin, but it has a maximum acidity of 1½ per cent.

Pure Olive Oil The one you're likely to find on supermarket shelves, it has a good flavour, good aroma, good colour (light yellow), maximum acidity 1½ per cent.

As olive oil is principally used in salads to give a fruity flavour to the dressing, it is worth buying the best. 'Pure' olive is, however, perfectly suitable as a frying medium, except for a dish to be served cold (such as vegetable ragout), in which case I would use a better grade for its superior aroma.

As with wine, the flavour of even the finest olive oil varies – in this case according to the variety of olives used and the kind of soil in which the olive trees are grown. It all comes down to personal experiment and choice.

Walnut oil Made from shelled and pulped walnuts which are first heated in a cauldron to a temperature of 325°–350°F (160°–180°C) and then pressed rather like olives. Unroasted walnut oil, like unroasted coffee beans, has no smell or taste. It has been roasted and used in the kitchen only since the nineteenth century; before then it was used as a varnish – for example, on Stradivarius violins.

The nutty flavour of this topaz-coloured oil marries particularly well with that of the avocado and is also excellent in certain green salads which contain fruit or have a nutty garnish.

Hazelnut Oil Produced only since 1978, it has a particularly penetrating smell but a more delicate, subtle flavour than walnut oil.

Hazelnut oil is used in a similar way to walnut oil. However, because of their intense flavours both should be used sparingly, usually in conjunction with a flavourless oil such as sunflower.

Olive oil, walnut oil and hazelnut oil should be protected from light, which can affect their flavour. In addition, both the nut oils quickly become rancid at room temperature so they should always be stored in the refrigerator.

VINEGAR

It's important to have a vinegar in salad dressings that is not too acid, otherwise it will destroy the balance of flavour. So malt and spirit vinegars are best kept for pickling. Beyond that the choice is enormous, ranging from vinegars made from white and red wines and champagne, sherry and cider, to those flavoured with fruit (such as cherry or raspberry) or herbs (such as tarragon or basil). Beware of cheap and nasty fruit vinegars which have been over-flavoured with a 'natural' essence rather than fruit. Price is usually the best guide to quality.

Kosher wine vinegars are now available.

Balsamic vinegar is much more complicated than ordinary wine vinegar. It's made from the reduced must of grapes added to wine vinegar and can be aged in wooden barrels for up to 100 years. Good-quality balsamic vinegar is very dark brown to black in colour, sweet and fruity, with a good balance of acidity and a lovely aroma.

MAYONNAISE

Excellent factory-made mayonnaise can now be bought, and for everyday use a good-quality calorie-reduced mayonnaise (with a lower oil content than average) can be very acceptable. However, for special dishes a 'custom-made' variety is definitely superior in flavour and texture. The blender and the food processor have both demystified the art of making mayonnaise so that it's easy to achieve an emulsion without fear of curdling.

Always add the mustard to the eggs before adding any oil, as this helps to produce a good emulsion. If the mayonnaise seems too thick for your taste, add 1 or 2 teaspoons of boiling water to lighten it.

Note that 6 fl oz (175 ml/¾ cup) is the maximum quantity of oil that 1 egg yolk can absorb (10 fl oz/275 ml/1¼ cups if whole eggs are used in a blender or food processor).

Note Before using raw eggs in uncooked dressings, it is as well to check on the latest authoritative advice on the current micro-biological situation.

TRADITIONAL MAYONNAISE

Makes 15 fl oz (425 ml/2 cups).
Keeps 1 month under refrigeration.
Do not freeze.

This is a thick, yellow mayonnaise. It can be made with either a rotary hand whisk, an electric whisk, or a blender or food processor. If you are using a rotary hand whisk, this method demands the most patience and takes the longest time.

2 egg yolks
1 level teasp dry mustard
2 level teasp Dijon mustard
1 level teasp salt
1 level teasp sugar
pinch of Cayenne pepper
2 teasp lemon juice
12 fl oz (350 ml/1½ cups) oil (half olive, half sunflower is good)
2 teasp wine vinegar or cider vinegar
1–2 tbsp boiling water

If you are using a rotary hand whisk, mix the mayonnaise in a pint measure. With a mixer, use a bowl with the smallest diameter into which the beaters can fit. Have the oil and eggs at room temperature (but not too hot or the mixture will not thicken – in summer, chill the oil for an hour before use).

Beat the yolks until creamy, then beat in the seasonings and a teaspoon of the lemon juice. Now start adding the oil. I find that the best method with an electric mixer, blender or food processor is to dribble it down the side of the bowl so that it can be absorbed gradually. With a rotary hand mixer, it is a little more tedious, adding it drop by drop, but as soon as the sauce 'takes' – that is, thickens to the consistency of double (heavy) cream – the oil can be added in a steady stream, thinning the mixture down in between with the remaining lemon juice and the vinegar. Finally, whisk in the boiling water.

Store in a screw-top jar in the bottom of the refrigerator.

PROCESSOR OR BLENDER MAYONNAISE

Makes 12 fl oz (350 ml/1½ cups).
Keeps 1 month under refrigeration.
Do not freeze.

This is my preferred method for making a moderate quantity of the sauce – it's easy, quick and produces a thick and creamy but lightly textured mayonnaise every time.

1 egg
2 teasp mustard powder
1 teasp caster (superfine) sugar
1 teasp sea salt
10 grinds of black pepper
good pinch of Cayenne pepper
1 tbsp lemon juice
8 fl oz (225 ml/1 cup) sunflower or other light, flavourless oil
2 fl oz (50 ml/¼ cup) extra virgin olive oil
1 teasp wine vinegar

Put the egg and the seasonings into the blender or food processor and process for 30 seconds, then add the lemon juice and process for a further 5 seconds. Put the oils into a jug and, with the motor running, pour a thin but steady stream on to the egg mixture – it should lighten in colour and become creamy and thick. Finally process in the wine vinegar. Taste and reseason if necessary, then store in an airtight container in the refrigerator until required.

VARIATION

GREEN HERB MAYONNAISE

This is a wonderful sauce to serve with any poached or fried fish.

Add 1 tablespoon of roughly cut-up chives, a small handful of parsley (no stalks) and a small, peeled clove of garlic to the egg and seasonings. Proceed as before.

MUSTARD MAYONNAISE SAUCE

Serves 6–8.
Keeps 1 month under refrigeration.
Do not freeze.

A Danish version that is excellent with hot or cold fried fish.

8 fl oz (225 ml/1 cup) mayonnaise
1 tbsp Dijon mustard
1 bulb finely chopped spring onion (scallion)
2 teasp finely chopped parsley
2 teasp lemon juice

Beat all the ingredients together.

TUNA MAYONNAISE

Serves 8.
Keeps 3 days under refrigeration.

This is delicious served as a coating for hard-boiled eggs on a fish buffet. It can also be used as a dip for raw vegetable sticks. A good commercial mayonnaise is perfectly adequate.

10 fl oz (275 ml/1¼ cups) mayonnaise
1 x 7 oz (200 g) can tuna, well drained
3 tbsp fresh lemon juice
1 can anchovy fillets, drained
10 grinds of black pepper
pinch of Cayenne pepper or mild chilli powder

Put all the ingredients into the food processor (reserving 4 anchovy fillets for garnish if desired). Process until absolutely smooth – the mixture will feel silky rather than grainy on the tongue. Store in an airtight container in the refrigerator.

GREEN GODDESS DRESSING

Serves 6.
Keeps 4 days under refrigeration.
Do not freeze.

A Californian speciality, usually served on quarters of lettuce hearts or halved Little Gem hearts (see p. 283). I often serve it with fried fish or poached salmon, or blend it with cold flaked fish for a quick starter.

8 fl oz (225 ml/1 cup) mayonnaise
6 anchovy fillets, finely chopped, or 2 teasp anchovy essence (extract) or purée
1 tbsp chopped spring onions (scallions)
1 tbsp chopped chives
2 tbsp chopped parsley
2 tbsp chopped tarragon
a pinch of salt
a pinch of dry mustard
2 teasp lemon juice
5 fl oz (150 ml/⅔ cup) soured cream, 8% fromage frais or Greek-style yoghurt

Blend all the flavourings into the mayonnaise and leave to mature for several hours.

SAUCE TARTARE

Serves 10–12.
Keeps 2 weeks under refrigeration.

A piquant sauce to serve with grilled, poached or fried fish such as lemon sole, haddock, plaice or halibut.

10 fl oz (275 ml/1¼ cups) mild mayonnaise
1 tbsp lemon juice
1 tbsp natural yoghurt or fromage frais
1 small pickled cucumber (about 2 inches/5 cm), finely chopped
2 teasp each of chives, tarragon and parsley, spring onion (scallion) bulb or shallot
a pinch of Cayenne pepper
6 chopped stuffed olives (optional)

Mix all the ingredients together. Refrigerate for several hours to allow the flavours to blend.

French Dressings and Vinaigrettes

This covers a wide variety of salad dressings, many of which the French would vigorously repudiate. Basically they consist of some form of acid - lemon juice, wine vinegar or cider vinegar - in which seasonings are dissolved - shaken into an emulsion usually with the help of a little mustard with varying proportions of oil (corn, peanut, sunflower, olive or nut).

To store, leave in a screw-top jar in the bottom of the refrigerator, where it keeps almost indefinitely. Perishable flavourings such as herbs and onions should be added on the day of use.

JUDI'S VINAIGRETTE

Makes 10 fl oz (275 ml/1¼ cups) - sufficient to dress 2 green salads, each serving 6–8.
Keeps indefinitely under refrigeration.

A gently flavoured dressing which can be varied by the addition of different herbs, oil, vinegars and seasonings. Add fresh herbs on the day of use; otherwise the vinegar and lemon juice will bleach out their colour (see also other variations in specific recipes).

6 fl oz (175 ml/¾ cup) sunflower oil
2 fl oz (50 ml/¼ cup) extra virgin olive oil
2 fl oz (50 ml/¼ cup) wine vinegar or cider vinegar
2 teasp lemon juice
2 teasp caster sugar or granular sweetener
1 teasp wholegrain mustard
1 teasp sea salt
10 grinds of black pepper
1 medium clove of garlic, halved (optional)
½ small onion or 2 spring onion (scallion) bulbs or shallots, finely chopped

Put all the ingredients in a screw-top jar and shake well until thickened. Leave in the refrigerator to mature for several hours. Remove garlic before use.

SAUCE VINAIGRETTE

Serves 6–8.
Refrigerate and use within 2 days.

A sharper dressing suitable for bland vegetables such as tomatoes, French beans or artichoke hearts. This is the dressing to serve with avocado on the half-shell or chilled artichokes, or to dress a hearty mixed salad such as Salade Niçoise.

4 tbsp white wine vinegar or cider vinegar
2 tbsp lemon juice
4 fl oz (125 ml/½ cup) sunflower oil
2 tbsp walnut oil or olive oil
1 fat clove of garlic, peeled and crushed
2 level teasp caster (superfine) sugar
1 teasp Dijon mustard
2 tbsp very finely chopped shallots or spring onion (scallion) bulbs
2 tbsp chopped fresh mixed herbs - parsley, chives, tarragon
1 level teasp salt
20 grinds of black pepper

Put all the ingredients into a screw-top jar and shake together until thoroughly blended and thickened - about 1 minute. Leave at room temperature until required.

A FRUITY VINAIGRETTE

Serves 6–8.
Use on day of preparation.

For citrus fruit salads and fruit cups served as appetizers.

3 tbsp sunflower oil
1 tbsp walnut or hazelnut oil
2 tbsp orange juice
1 tbsp lemon juice
1 teasp bottled or fresh mint sauce, or 2 teasp chopped fresh mint leaves
1 teasp sugar or liquid honey
½ teasp sea salt
10 grinds of black pepper

Shake all the ingredients together in a screw-top jar until thickened.

A PAREV CREAMY VINAIGRETTE

Serves 6–8.
Keeps 2 days under refrigeration.

Useful with fruity chicken and turkey salads, or as an alternative to the Fruity Vinaigrette.

2 rounded tbsp of a lemony mayonnaise
3 tbsp sunflower oil
1 tbsp walnut oil
1 tbsp raspberry vinegar
½ teasp salt
10 grinds of black pepper
1 tbsp fresh dill, snipped

About 4 hours before the meal, put all the ingredients into a screw-top jar and shake until thickened, then refrigerate.

BLUE CHEESE AND MUSTARD DRESSING FOR GREEN SALADS

Serves 6–8.
Keeps 1 day under refrigeration.

A tangy dressing to serve on a salad of mixed green leaves or quartered hearts of Iceberg or Little Gem lettuce.

3 fl oz (75 ml/⅓ cup) sunflower oil
1 fl oz (25 ml/2 tbsp) extra virgin olive oil
1 fl oz (25 ml/2 tbsp) wine vinegar or cider vinegar
1 teasp lemon juice
1 teasp Meaux mustard
½ teasp fine sea salt
5 grinds of black pepper
1 small clove of garlic, halved
1 tbsp chopped parsley
3 oz (75 g/¾ cup) Stilton or other vegetarian blue cheese

Several hours in advance, shake the dressing ingredients (except for the cheese) in a screw-top jar until slightly thickened.

Just before serving, add the crumbled cheese and shake again. Toss with mixed leaves or spoon over sections of hearted lettuce.

DESSERTS

HOT DESSERTS

Hot Desserts in a Hurry

Bread and Butter Pudding	(see p. 308)	Washington Apple Crisp and Variation	(see p. 312)
Eve's Pudding and Variations	(see p. 310)	Barbecued Fruit Kebabs	(see p. 319)

The repertoire of traditional hot desserts is strictly limited to those of the 'shalet' variety (fruit and pastry, layered and baked) or sweet versions of lokshen (noodle) and rice kugel (pudding). In the early years of this century, however, Jewish immigrant mothers were quick to see in the pudding recipes of their adopted countries a cheap means of satisfying their many hungry children. Now the pendulum is swinging the other way, and lighter, fruitier recipes are more in favour - when the sweet course is not restricted to fresh fruit alone. However, young families do enjoy their 'afters' and the recipes that follow are all hot and delicious.

Traditional Puddings

LOKSHEN PUDDINGS

A generation or so ago, a large dish of lokshen pudding was made every Friday in Ashkenazi households and cooked overnight with the cholent (see p. 136) for serving hot on the Sabbath. As with many traditional dishes, the origins of lokshen kugel are lost in the mists of time, but although it was certainly one of the favourite dishes of the Eastern European immigrants of the late nineteenth century, it actually appears in what is believed to be the first *English* Jewish cookbook, published in 1846. *The Jewish Manual* is said on the cover to be 'By a lady' but social historian Chaim Raphael identifies her as Lady Judith Montefiore, who, though married to the famous Sephardi leader Moses Montefiore, came from a German Ashkenazi background. So her recipes for a 'Luction', which is very similar to the recipe below, suggests that the dish might well date from the Middle Ages, when a large proportion of Ashkenazi Jews lived in and around Germany. It has to be admitted that though exceedingly delicious, it packs a powerful calorific punch! It is little wonder, then, that according to many memoirs of Jewish life in the East End of London in the early twentieth century, after consuming a Sabbath meal including lokshen kugel there was no alternative but to have a good *'shlof'* (sleep).

LOKSHEN KUGEL

Serves 6.
Keeps 3 days under refrigeration.
Freeze 3 months.

This is a good-tempered dish that can be cooked at any convenient temperature. To achieve the crusty lining which is the best part of a kugel, the fat is first heated in the cooking dish, then swirled round the sides to coat them.

2 oz (50 g/¼ cup) margarine
8 oz (225 g) egg noodles, broad or narrow as preferred (but no broader than ¼ inch/0.5 cm)
2 eggs
4 oz (125 g/½ cup) caster (superfine) sugar
pinch of cinnamon
pinch of salt
grated rind of ½ lemon
2 oz (50 g/6 tbsp) raisins
2 oz (50 g/¼ cup) chopped glacé (candied) fruit (optional)

Preheat the oven to the preferred temperature (see below) and put in a 2-inch-deep (5-cm) oven-to-table casserole measuring approximately 10 x 8 inches (25 x 20 cm) - it should have a liquid capacity of 2½ pints (1.5 l/6¼ cups) - or a round 7-8-inch (17.5-20-cm) dish (such as a soufflé dish or a glazed earthenware dish or '*teppel*') together with the margarine.

Meanwhile, boil the noodles according to packet directions, then drain well. Whisk the eggs and the sugar to blend, then stir in the flavourings and the raisins (and glacé fruit if used). Finally stir in the noodles and the hot fat which has been swirled round the baking dish to coat the sides.

Bake either at Gas No. 5 (375°F/190°C) for 45 minutes or at Gas No. 2 (300°F/150°C) for 1½ hours. In either case it should be set inside and crisp and brown on top.

FAYE'S NEW-STYLE LOKSHEN PUDDING

Serves 6-8.
Leftovers keep 3 days under refrigeration.
Freeze 3 months.

This is a fruitier version, sweetened by a little honey instead of a lot of sugar. It does not have the crustiness of the original but is altogether lighter in texture.

8 oz (225 g/1½ cups) broad egg noodles
2 eating apples
4 oz (125 g/½ cup) glacé (candied) cherries
2 oz (50 g/¼ cup) margarine
4 oz (125 g/¾ cup) sultanas (white raisins)
4 oz (125 g/¾ cup) raisins
1 egg
1 level teasp allspice
2 tbsp orange juice
1 rounded tbsp mild honey

Break the noodles into small pieces and boil until tender. Peel, core and grate the apples, wash and slice the cherries, melt the margarine. Mix all the ingredients gently but firmly together, then turn into a greased 2-pint (1.25-l/5-cup) pudding basin. Cover with foil and steam for 1½ hours or bake at Gas No. 2 (300°F/150°C) for 1½ hours. Turn out and serve plain or with fresh strawberries.

HELEN SELIGSON'S RICE KUGEL

Serves 6.
Keeps 2 days under refrigeration.

This recipe was given to me by a superb traditional Jewish cook of Russian origin. This is exactly how her family made the dish in the years before the Second World War. By today's standards it is very rich, but I have included it because it would be wrong to break this culinary link with our past.

6 oz (175 g/¾ cup) Carolina
(short-grain or pudding) rice
3 oz (75 g/⅓ cup) butter
2 eggs
4 oz (125 g/½ cup) caster (superfine) sugar
4 oz (125 g/1 cup) raisins or sultanas
(white raisins)
½ teasp vanilla essence
½ level teasp cinnamon

Cook the rice in a large pan of boiling salted water until very tender (about 20 minutes), then strain and allow to cool. Meanwhile, set the oven at Gas No. 3 (325°F/160°C) and put the butter in an oven casserole about 3 inches (7.5 cm) deep (eg a soufflé dish) to melt it. Whisk the eggs, add the sugar and carry on whisking to a creamy consistency. Mix in the raisins, flavourings and rice. Swirl the butter round the casserole to coat the sides, then pour the surplus into the rice mixture. Stir until thoroughly blended, then pour into the casserole. Bake for 1 hour, until golden brown. Serve plain or with melted syrup.

Family Sponge Puddings

There is no necessity to cream fat and sugar for a family pudding: the 1-bowl method works to perfection, as in the recipes that follow.

Note I don't recommend cooking this sponge in the microwave – the mixture rises so much that a 2-pint (1.25-l/5-cup) basin can accommodate only half the amount. However, leftovers can be reheated in the microwave.

STEAMED SPONGE PUDDING

Serves 6.
Keeps 3 days under refrigeration.
Freeze 3 months.

4 oz (125 g/½ cup) soft margarine
4 oz (125 g/½ cup) caster (superfine) sugar
4 oz (125 g/1 cup) self-raising flour or
4 oz (125 g/1 cup) plain (all-purpose) flour plus
1 teasp baking powder
2 large eggs
grated rind of ½ lemon

For the topping

2 tbsp golden (corn) syrup, marmalade, raspberry jam or stewed apple

Put a pan half-full of water on to boil, with a steamer on top. If you have no steamer, the pudding should be 'boiled' – that is, stood on a metal trivet or a folded cloth in the bottom of the pan with water coming half-way up the sides.

Put the margarine, sugar, flour, eggs and lemon rind into a bowl and beat until smooth and creamy (3 minutes by hand, 2 minutes by electric mixer, 20 seconds by food processor, scraping the sides down half-way with a rubber spatula). Turn into a greased pudding basin in which you have first put the topping. There should be a 1-inch (2.5-cm) gap between the top of the pudding mixture and that of the basin. Cover with foil. Steam or boil for 2 hours. Turn out on to a warm dish and serve.

VARIATIONS

APPLE BUTTERSCOTCH PUDDING

Lavishly spread the inside of the pudding basin with butter or margarine and smear thickly with golden (corn) syrup. Put 2 tablespoons of stewed apples or 2 baking apples, finely sliced and mixed with 1 oz (25 g/2 tbsp) sugar, in the bottom. Make the sponge pudding as in the recipe above and cook as directed. Serve with warm golden syrup or custard.

APRICOT-TOP PUDDING

Put 3 tablespoons of apricot conserve in the bottom of the basin and fold 1 tablespoon of conserve into the pudding mixture. Proceed as before.

BREAD AND BUTTER PUDDING

Serves 4–6.
Keeps 3 days under refrigeration.

A simple, comforting family pudding.

demerara (brown) sugar
6 thin slices buttered white bread or bun loaf
3 tbsp currants or mixed dried fruit
2 level tbsp custard powder (vanilla pudding mix)
2 level tbsp caster (superfine) sugar
1 pint (575 ml/2½ cups) milk

Butter a casserole and sprinkle it with brown sugar. Cut the bread into fingers and arrange in layers, sprinkling demerara sugar and dried fruit between the layers. Make custard with the powder, 2 tablespoons of sugar and the milk (it should be a thin pouring custard). Pour slowly into the dish down the sides. Allow to stand half an hour for the custard to be absorbed. Bake in a preheated oven, Gas No. 3 (325°F/160°C), for 1½ hours, increasing the heat at the end if necessary to brown the top. Sprinkle with demerara sugar.

BREAD AND BUTTER PUDDING DELUXE

Serves 8–10 or 4–5.
Keeps 2 days under refrigeration.

It was that master chef extraordinaire, Anton Mosimann, who elevated the bread and butter pudding to *haute cuisine* by suggesting that the custard which is the foundation of the dish should be enriched with double cream, and that soft rolls should be used instead of any old bread. This is my version, using a light buttering kuchen and rather less cream. It's a memorable dish! If you intend to make the bigger size, do check that you have a large enough baking tin to act as a bain marie.

The pudding is exquisite by itself, but an accompaniment of poached peaches or apricots makes a pleasing contrast.

For 8–10
2 oz (50 g/¼ cup) melted butter
4 oz (125 g/¾ cup) sultanas (white raisins)
2 tbsp brandy, whisky or orange juice
21 fl oz (600 ml/2¾ cups) milk
15 fl oz (425 ml/2 cups) double (heavy) cream
1 vanilla pod
pinch of salt
6 eggs
9 oz (250 g/1¼ cups) vanilla sugar (see below)
7 oz (200 g) light buttering kuchen or soft-topped bread rolls
2 heaped tbsp apricot jam

For 4–5
1 oz (25 g/2 tbsp) melted butter
2 oz (50 g/6 tbsp) sultanas (white raisins)
1 tbsp brandy, whisky or orange juice
10 fl oz (275 ml/1¼ cups) milk
8 fl oz (225 ml/1 cup) double (heavy) cream
1 vanilla pod
pinch of salt
3 eggs
4½ oz (140 g/½ cup plus 1 tbsp) vanilla sugar (see below)
3½ oz (90 g) light buttering kuchen or soft-topped bread rolls
1 heaped tbsp apricot jam

The best flavour is achieved if the sugar used comes from a container in which several vanilla pods have been buried for a few days. Otherwise use 2 ½–¾ oz (15–20 g) packets of vanilla sugar and reduce the ordinary sugar to 8 oz (225 g/1 cup) for the larger version, 1 packet vanilla sugar, ordinary sugar reduced to 4 oz (125 g/½ cup) for the smaller.

Use a little of the melted butter to grease a large oval gratin dish approximately 11 x 9 x 2 inches (27.5 x 22.5 x 5 cm) with a capacity of 5-5½ pints (2¾-3 1/2-2¼ cups) for the larger version, or a pie dish 2 inches (5 cm) deep for the smaller.

Put the sultanas in a small basin, sprinkle

with the spirit or juice, cover and microwave on 100 per cent power, $1\frac{1}{2}$ minutes for the larger, 1 minute for the smaller amount. Bring the milk, cream, vanilla pod and salt slowly to the boil. Meanwhile, whisk the eggs and sugar until creamy, then remove the vanilla pod and whisk in the hot milk and cream, stirring constantly. (This operation is most easily done in a large food processor.)

Slice the rolls or the kuchen and brush with the melted butter, then arrange in the chosen dish. Place this dish on a thick wad of newspaper in the dish that is to act as a bain marie. Sprinkle with the sultanas and then gently pour in the egg and cream mixture - the bread will float to the top. The dish can now be left for an hour or so, or cooked right away, as preferred.

Preheat the oven to Gas No. 3 (325°F/160°C).

Boil a kettle, then pour enough hot water into the bain marie to come half-way up the sides of the dish. Cook for 45 minutes - the pudding should tremble very slightly. Heat the jam until liquid (most easily done for 40 seconds on 100 per cent power in the microwave), then brush over the pudding. Serve plain or sprinkled with icing sugar.

CREAMY RICE PUDDING

Serves 4.
Keeps 2 days under refrigeration.

This is an excellent version of the traditional pudding which my mother and her classmates were taught to make at the Jews' School in Manchester before the First World War. It was hoped that by learning how to cook English dishes, these children of immigrant parents would fit more easily - and inconspicuously - into the British way of life and thus avoid causing embarrassment because of their 'foreign' ways to the local Jewish community, which had been established in the city for over 100 years.

bare 2 oz (50 g/$\frac{1}{3}$ cup) Carolina
(short-grain or pudding) rice
1 oz (25 g/2 tbsp) butter
1 pint (575 ml/$2\frac{1}{2}$ cups) whole milk
pinch of salt
1 oz (25 g/2 tbsp) light brown or white sugar
pinch of nutmeg

Wash the rice in cold water and drain well. Use half the butter to grease a 1-pint (575-ml/$2\frac{1}{2}$-cup) pudding dish. Put the milk, salt and the rice in the dish and leave for 1 hour to soften. Preheat the oven to Gas No. 2 (300°F/150°C). Stir the sugar into the rice and add the remaining butter cut into tiny pieces. Scatter with the nutmeg. Bake for at least 2 hours, stirring occasionally for the first hour, then leave to allow a golden-brown topping to form.

Fruit Puddings

EVE'S PUDDING

Serves 6.
Keeps 3 days under refrigeration.
Freeze 2 months.

A light, quickly mixed apple sponge, ideal for a mid-week meal.

3 oz (75 g/⅓ cup) very soft butter or margarine
3 oz (75 g/⅓ cup) caster (superfine) sugar
5 oz (150 g/1¼ cups) self-raising flour or 5 oz (150 g/1¼ cups) plain (all-purpose) flour plus 1 level teasp baking powder
pinch of extra baking powder
2 eggs
1 tbsp milk or water (for a meat meal)

For the fruit mixture
4 large baking apples (1¾–2 lb/800–900 g weight unpeeled)
4 tbsp orange juice
1 tbsp lemon juice
pinch of cinnamon
2 oz golden granulated sugar

Peel, core and slice the apples ⅛ inch (0.3 cm) thick and arrange in a wide buttered casserole 12 x 8 x 2 inches (30 x 20 x 5 cm) in size. Pour over the orange and lemon juice and sprinkle with the cinnamon and sugar.

Put all the pudding ingredients into a bowl and beat together untii smooth and glossy (3 minutes by hand, 2 minutes by electric mixer, 20 seconds by food processor), scraping down the sides half-way with a rubber spatula. Spoon on top of the apples and bake in a preheated oven. Gas No. 4 (350°F/180°C), for 45–50 minutes, until golden brown and firm to the touch. Serve plain for a meat meal or with hot custard for a milk meal.

VARIATION

PLUM OR DAMSON PUDDING

Bring to the boil the contents of a medium can of Victoria plums or damsons or 1 lb (450 g) fresh fruit stewed in syrup. Pour into an ovenproof casserole as above. Top at once with the pudding mixture and bake in the same way.

DUTCH APPLE SPONGE

Makes 12 good-sized squares.
Keeps 2 days under refrigeration.
Freeze 3 months.

On a bitterly cold winter's night, how good to come home to a nice, comforting hot pud. And it doesn't have to be unhealthy either. With lots of fruit and brown sugar and a sponge made with wheatmeal flour, it can be nutritious as well as warming and delicious.

Good eating habits apart, the more fruit you can cram into the topping the better as this delicious apple sponge needs a high ratio of topping to sponge to avoid stodginess. English eating apples are better than baking apples as they give out much less liquid in the oven and require less sugar. And if there is any left over, it doubles as a very acceptable cake.

9 oz (250 g/2¼ cups) wheatmeal or white self-raising flour, or 9 oz (250 g/2¼ cups) plain (all-purpose) flour plus 2 teasp baking powder
1 level teasp baking powder
4 oz (125 g/½ cup) light brown sugar
3 eggs
4 fl oz (125 ml/½ cup) water
3 oz (75 g/⅓ cup) soft margarine
1 teasp grated lemon rind

For the topping
2 lb (900 g) large eating apples (Cox's preferably)
2 tbsp lemon juice
2 oz (50 g/¼ cup) melted margarine
4 oz (125 g/½ cup) soft brown sugar
1½ teasp cinnamon

Preheat the oven to Gas No. 6 (400°F/200°C). Grease a shallow tin approximately 12 x 8 inches (30 x 20 cm). Place all the cake ingredients in a bowl and mix until smooth (3 minutes by hand, 2 minutes by electric mixer, 20 seconds by food processor), scraping down the sides half-way with a rubber spatula. Spoon into the tin and smooth level with a knife.

Peel, core and slice the apples ⅛ inch (0.3 cm) thick. Toss the apples in a bowl with the lemon juice, then arrange in tightly packed overlapping rows on top of the cake mixture, covering it completely. Drizzle the melted margarine on top, and sprinkle evenly with the sugar and cinnamon mixed together. Bake for around 45 minutes, until the cake is a rich brown and the apples are tender. Serve warm or at room temperature with *parev* or dairy ice-cream, custard or natural yoghurt sweetened with honey.

PINEAPPLE UPSIDE-DOWN PUDDING

Serves 4–5.
Keeps 3 days under refrigeration.
Freeze 3 months.

Other fruit (such as apricots) can be used, but I don't think they equal the flavour of the pineapple version bathed in a butterscotch glaze.

2 oz (50 g/¼ cup) butter or margarine
2 oz (50 g/¼ cup) light muscovado sugar
2 level tbsp golden (corn) syrup
1 x 15 oz (425 g) can pineapple rings, spears or chunks
a few walnut or pecan halves

For the pudding mixture
4 oz (125 g/½ cup) butter or margarine
4 oz (125 g/½ cup) caster (superfine) sugar
4 oz (125 g/1 cup) self-raising flour or
4 oz (125 g/1 cup) plain (all-purpose) flour plus
1 teasp baking powder
1 teasp vanilla essence
2 eggs

For the pineapple sauce
3 teasp cornflour (cornstarch)
2 tbsp caster (superfine) sugar
1 tbsp lemon juice
2 tbsp orange juice
enough pineapple syrup to make 8 fl oz (225 ml/1 cup) liquid in all

Grease an 8-inch-round (20-cm) solid-based cake tin. Melt the fat in a heavy saucepan. Add the brown sugar and golden syrup and simmer together until the sugar is dissolved in the butter and the mixture is a rich brown – about 3 minutes. Pour into the cake tin. Arrange the well-drained pineapple and nuts in a design on top.

To make the pudding mixture, put the soft fat and the other ingredients into a bowl and beat together until smooth and glossy (3 minutes by hand, 2 minutes by electric mixer, 20 seconds by food processor), scraping down the sides half-way with a rubber spatula. Spoon on to the fruit and nuts and level with a knife. Bake in a preheated oven, Gas No. 5 (375°F/190°C), for 35–40 minutes, or until the pudding is golden brown and firm to the touch. Reverse on to a serving dish and leave for 5 minutes. Lift off the cake tin. Serve plain, with custard, or with the pineapple sauce.

To make the sauce, mix the cornflour and sugar in a small pan, then stir in the juices and syrup. Bring to the boil and simmer for 3 minutes.

VARIATION

PINEAPPLE UPSIDE-DOWN PUDDING – MICROWAVE METHOD

This is a pudding that does extremely well in the microwave, so I give the method in full. The ingredients are identical.

Select a soufflé dish or round microwave-safe plastic or glass container about 7–8 inches (18–20 cm) across and 2 inches (5 cm) deep.

Melt the fat in a small bowl lightly covered

with a paper towel on 100 per cent power for 1 minute. Use a little to grease the chosen container. To the remainder of the butter or margarine add the golden syrup and sugar, stir, then cook uncovered on 100 per cent power for 1 minute, stir and cook a further 1 minute. Pour this butterscotch into the chosen dish.

Drain the pineapple, reserving the juice, and arrange in a pattern on the glaze with the nuts.

Beat all the cake ingredients together by hand or machine until smooth and glossy. Spoon over the fruit and cook on 100 per cent power for 5½ minutes, or until a cocktail stick comes out clean from the centre. If still moist, give it another minute (there may still be areas of dampness on the surface that will disappear during the resting time). Allow to rest for 5 minutes, then turn out on to a serving dish.

To make the sauce, in the serving jug mix the cornflour and sugar thoroughly, then stir in the liquids. Microwave on 100 per cent power for 1½ minutes, stir and cook for a further 2½ minutes, until bubbling and clear. Serve hot. May be reheated on 80 per cent power for 2 minutes.

WASHINGTON APPLE CRISP

Serves 6.
Keeps 3 days under refrigeration.
Freeze 3 months.

This is the original American recipe dating back to the early 1940s. It is simple to make, uncomplicated in flavour and utterly delicious to eat!

4 large baking apples (Bramley's if possible)
2 oz (50 g/¼ cup) white or brown sugar, mixed with ½ level teasp cinnamon
1 tbsp lemon juice
3 fl oz (75 ml/6 tbsp) water

For the topping

3 oz (75 g/¾ cup) flour
1 oz (25 g/3 level tbsp) porridge oats
4 oz (125 g/½ cup) soft brown sugar
3 oz (75 g/⅓ cup) margarine or butter

Peel, core and slice the baking apples into a shallow baking or gratin dish approximately 11 x 8 x 1½ inches (27.5 x 20 x 4 cm) deep. Sprinkle them with the mixed sugar and cinnamon followed by the lemon juice and water.

For the topping, combine the flour, oats and brown sugar, then gently rub in the fat until the mixture is crumbly. Sprinkle in an even layer over the apples. Bake in a preheated oven, Gas No. 5 (375°F/190°C), for 1 hour, or until crunchy and golden brown. Serve plain or with custard or yoghurt.

VARIATION

DAMSON CRUNCH

Arrange the fruit from a can of damsons over the base of the dish. Spoon on enough of the juice to cover the bottom to a depth of ¼ inch (0.5 cm). Top with the crunch and bake as before. A little stewed apple may be mixed with the damsons to add body.

GINGERED FRESH PEACH, AMARETTO AND HAZELNUT CRUMBLE

Serves 6–8.
Keeps 3 days under refrigeration.
Freeze 1 month.

This is a 'deluxe' version with a luscious peach filling to serve for a special meal – it's just as delicious in a *parev* version. If there are no fresh peaches around substitute 2 large cans of sliced peaches and use only 1 oz (25 g/2 tbsp) of brown sugar in the fruit mixture.

For the fruit

2½ lb (1.1 kg) peaches or nectarines
2 oz (50 g/¼ cup) soft light brown sugar
2 tbsp Amaretto or other almond-flavoured liqueur (optional)
2 teasp cornflour
¼ teasp ground nutmeg
2 oz (50 g/¼ cup) crystallized (candied) ginger (optional)
2 tbsp fresh lemon juice

For the topping

4 oz (125 g/1 cup) plain (all-purpose) flour
pinch of salt
4 oz (125 g/½ cup) light brown sugar
4 oz (125 g/1 cup) coarsely ground hazelnuts (filberts)
4 oz (125 g/½ cup) butter or margarine, cut in roughly 1-inch (2.5-cm) chunks

Put the peeled, stoned and thickly sliced peaches or nectarines in a large bowl, toss with the mixed sugar, Amaretto, cornflour, nutmeg and ginger, then sprinkle with the lemon juice. Turn into a lightly greased oven-to-table dish measuring approximately 11 x 8 inches (27.5 x 20 cm) such as a gratin or lasagne-type dish.

To make the topping, put all the ingredients into a bowl and rub lightly to a moist crumble. Sprinkle evenly over the fruit and bake at Gas No. 5 (375°F/190°C) for 40–45 minutes, or until a rich brown and bubbling round the edges. Leave to cool for 10 minutes before serving.

In the microwave, cook uncovered on 100 per cent power for 11 minutes, then crisp under the grill (broiler) for 3 minutes. Leave to stand for 10 minutes.

Serve plain or with yoghurt, smetana or fromage frais.

PEAR AND BRANDY CRUNCH PUDDING

Serves 6.
Keeps 3 days under refrigeration.
Serve warm rather than hot.

An unfamiliar variety of pear, the Passecran, which has recently appeared on supermarket shelves, has firm but juicy flesh which makes it ideal for this superb baked pudding. As the pears don't soften in the cooking, buy them a few days in advance to ensure they're fully ripe. They should 'give' all over - rather like an avocado - when cradled in the hand. (Comice or Beurre Hardy pears could be substituted.)

In this delicious hot pudding, which would make an ideal dinner party finale after a light main dish, the marinated pears are topped with a particularly light and crunchy crumble. The mango is optional but does add an exotic flavour. For a family meal substitute 4 tablespoons of orange juice for the brandy. The hazelnuts are nicest ground in the food processor until they are the consistency of coarse sand, but you can use ready-ground ones if this is more convenient.

2 lb (900 g) firm but ripe Passecran pears
1 ripe mango (optional)
1 tbsp granulated sugar
2 tbsp fresh lemon juice
4 tbsp brandy

For the topping

4 oz (125 g/1⅓ cups) porridge oats
1 oz (25 g/¼ cups) wholemeal (wholewheat) or wheatmeal flour
2 oz (50 g/½ cup) coarsely ground hazelnuts (filberts)
5 oz (150 g/⅔ cup) light Muscovado sugar
1 teasp cinnamon
½ teasp ground ginger
¼ teasp ground nutmeg
4 oz (125 g/½ cup) butter or firm margarine

Preheat the oven to Gas No. 4 (350°F/180°C). Lightly grease a gratin dish or shallow oval casserole dish about 12-14 inches (30-35 cm) long.

Peel, halve and core the pears and mango (if used), then slice ½ inch (1.25 cm) thick and mix in a bowl with the granulated sugar, lemon juice and brandy (or orange juice). Leave for 30 minutes, basting once or twice, then arrange in an even layer in the dish.

Mix the dry ingredients in a large bowl. Add the fat cut in small chunks and rub it in lightly until the mixture is crumbly. Spread the crumble evenly on top of the fruit. Bake for 45 minutes, or until the top is a rich brown and crunchy.

Perfect Baked Apples

You can't really spoil a baked apple however you cook it - though you can cause it to burst if the oven is too hot - but you can turn it into a dinner party dish if you cook it with sufficient care. The basic method is easy. Even-sized cooking apples (preferably Bramley's) are first cored and then slit through the skin around their 'equator' - this stops the flesh exploding. The core cavity is then filled with brown or white sugar, dried fruits or jam, and the apples are set side by side in a buttered baking dish about 2 inches (5 cm) deep. The bottom of this dish is covered with water to a depth of ⅜ inch (1 cm) and sugar (1 tablespoonful for each apple used) is scattered on top. The apples are then cooked in a slow oven, Gas No. 2 (300°F/150°C), for 2 hours, with frequent bastings of the syrupy juices.

You can cook the baked apples in the microwave in a fraction of the time, but although the flesh will be creamy, the skin will be tough and inedible.

Other flavour suggestions include filling the cavity with granulated sugar flavoured with a pinch of cinnamon or nutmeg; or with brown sugar blended with a few chopped walnuts and a nut of butter (or margarine); or mixed dried fruit, topped with sugar, with additional dried fruit scattered round to enrich the syrup. If you want to be more ambitious, you can try the following.

CALIFORNIA BAKED APPLES

Serves 6.
Keeps 3 days under refrigeration.

6 medium Bramley's (tart cooking apples)
2 oz (50 g/½ cup) raisins
3 tbsp lemon juice
2 oz (50 g/½ cup) chopped walnuts or pecans
6 teasp brown sugar
4 generous tbsp golden (corn) syrup
juice of a medium orange

Core the apples and nick the skin around the centre. Arrange in a buttered baking dish. Mix the raisins, lemon juice and walnuts and use to fill the centre of each apple. Top each apple with 1 teaspoon of brown sugar. Dribble the syrup over the apples. Add enough water to cover the bottom of the dish to a depth of ¼ inch (0.5 cm), then add the orange juice. Bake at Gas No. 2 (300°F/150°C) for 2 hours, basting several times.

BAKED APPLES IN ORANGE SYRUP

Serves 4-5.
Keeps 3 days under refrigeration.

4 or 5 baking apples
brown sugar
currants
butter (or margarine for a meat meal)
5 fl oz (150 ml/⅔ cup) orange juice (2 oranges)

Core the apples and make a cut round the circumference, then arrange side by side in a buttered baking dish. In each cavity put 1 teaspoon of soft brown sugar, a few currants, a pea-sized piece of butter or margarine and finally top with a further teaspoonful of sugar. Scatter more currants in the dish and pour over them the orange juice. Scatter another 2 or 3 tablespoons brown sugar on to the juice. Bake at Gas No. 2 (300°F/150°C) for 2 hours, or until absolutely tender, basting with the syrup 2 or 3 times.

Pancakes Plus

French Dessert Crêpes

The French crêpe or pancake is richer than an English pancake (because it contains more eggs) and more 'cakey' than a blintze (because it contains more fat and sugar.) The secret of making successful crêpes lies in the pan, which should have a solid base that sits evenly on the heat source. It should be 6-7 inches (15-17.5 cm) in diameter and a good non-stick lining is a bonus.

Pancakes can be kept ready for service in 2 ways. Either they can be laid 1 on top of the other on the back of a plate over a pan of boiling water and kept covered with a pan lid until needed. Or they can be laid overlapping on a greased dish, covered with foil, and reheated in a moderate oven, Gas No. 4 (350°F/180°C), for 20 minutes (this is the best way to reheat defrosted frozen pancakes). See also individual recipes. Filled and rolled pancakes can be reheated, covered, in the serving dish for 2-2½ minutes on 100 per cent power in the microwave.

To freeze or refrigerate crêpes, allow to stop steaming, then pile on top of each other. Wrap in clingfilm (saranwrap) and then in foil, making an airtight package.

BASIC CRÊPE MIXTURE

Makes 12 crêpes; serves 6-8.
Keeps 3 days under refrigeration.
Refrigerate raw batter up to 24 hours.
Freeze cooked but unfilled crêpes 3 months.

2 oz (50 g/¼ cup) butter
4 oz (125 g/1 cup) plain (all-purpose) flour
pinch of salt
2 eggs
8 fl oz (225 ml/1 cup) milk
1½ level tbsp caster sugar

Warm the butter in a small pan until it turns a pale fawn, then process all the ingredients in a blender or food processor until smooth and covered with tiny bubbles - about 30 seconds. Pour into a jug and leave to settle for 10 minutes.

To cook the crêpes, heat a 6-7 inch (15-17.5 cm) crêpe or omelette pan with a teaspoon of oil until you can feel the heat on your hand held 2 inches (5 cm) above the pan, then wipe out the pan with kitchen paper. Spoon approximately one-third of a ladle of batter into the pan and swirl it round to cover the bottom in a thin, even layer.

Cook over moderate heat until golden brown underneath, turn and cook the second side until golden. Turn on to a board covered with silicone or greaseproof paper. Repeat with the remaining batter, regreasing as necessary.

Pancakes in the English Fashion

As the crêpes are cooked, toss them on to a piece of greaseproof paper thickly covered with caster (superfine) sugar. Turn over, sprinkle with lemon juice and roll up. Keep hot in a warm oven, Gas No. 1 (275°F/140°C), until all the pancakes are ready.

CRÊPES NORMANDES

Serves 6.

1 recipe Basic Crêpe Mixture (see p. 315)

For the filling
1 oz (25 g/2 tbsp) butter
12 oz (350 g) baking apples
pinch of cinnamon
3 oz (75 g/⅓ cup) soft light-brown sugar

Melt the butter in a heavy pan. Add the finely sliced apples, cinnamon and sugar. Cover and cook until pulped (4 minutes, stirring halfway, on 100 per cent power in the microwave). As each crêpe is cooked, spread it with the apple purée, roll up, lay side by side and keep hot in a moderate oven, Gas No. 4 (350°F/ 180°C).

To serve, sprinkle with caster (superfine) sugar and put under the grill (broiler) for 1 minute.

APRICOT AND PINEAPPLE PANCAKES

Serves 6.

1 recipe Basic Crêpe Mixture (see p. 315)

For the filling
2 tbsp apricot jam
1 x 12 oz (350 g) can pineapple titbits plus juice
squeeze of lemon juice

Put the jam in a saucepan. Add the pineapple and enough juice to make a thick, creamy mixture. Add a squeeze of lemon juice and heat until bubbling. Use to spread on each crêpe. This mixture can be flavoured with 1 tablespoon of brandy or kirsch.

GALETTE NORMANDE FLAMBÉE AU CALVADOS

Serves 6–9.
Best eaten fresh.

A stunning presentation with a superb flavour. The crêpes and filling can be made in advance, but the galette should be assembled and served on the same day.

1 recipe Basic Crêpe Mixture (see p. 315)

For the filling
2 lb (900 g) crisp Bramley's (tart cooking apples) (weight when peeled)
2 tbsp lemon juice
3 rounded tbsp apricot jam
4 oz (125 g/½ cup) medium brown sugar
2 tbsp Calvados (or brandy or rum)
4 oz (125 g) macaroons (6 macaroons) or 1 x 85 g (3 oz) pack ratafia biscuits, crushed to crumbs

For the topping
1 oz (25 g/2 tbsp) melted butter
2 tbsp granulated sugar
2 oz (50 g/½ cup) pecans, chopped and toasted

To flame the galette
5 tbsp Calvados (brandy or rum)

Make and cook the crêpes as described.

To make the filling, core and peel the apples, then quarter and chop them roughly. Cook in a covered pan with the lemon juice and jam over a low heat for about 20 minutes, stirring occasionally, until apples are tender. Alternatively, cook, covered, in the microwave on 100 per cent power for 9 minutes, stirring once. Uncover, add sugar, raise heat and boil, stirring, for 5 minutes or more (3 minutes in the microwave). The apple sauce should reduce and be thick enough to hold itself in a fairly solid mass in the spoon. Stir in the Calvados (or brandy or rum).

Centre a crêpe in the base of a lightly

buttered oven-to-table lipped ovenproof dish (eg a quiche dish). Spread a layer of apples over it and sprinkle with a bare tablespoon of the crushed macaroons. Continue with layers of crêpe, apples and macaroons, ending with a crêpe. The galette will now look like a many-layered cake. Spoon over the melted butter (or margarine) and sprinkle with the sugar mixed with the pecans.

About 30 minutes before serving, place in the upper part of a preheated oven, Gas No. 5 (375°F/190°C), to heat through thoroughly. The sugar on top of the galette should almost begin to caramelize. (Can be kept hot at Gas No. ¼ (225°F/110°C) for up to an hour.)

To flame the galette, just before serving heat the Calvados (brandy or rum) till steaming in a small pan, set alight, then pour over the hot galette. Spoon the flaming liqueur over the galette until the flame subsides, then cut portions as you would from a cake.

TOLTOTT PALACSINTA
(*Crêpes with Morello Cherry Wine Filling*)

Serves 6.
Freeze filled crêpes 1 month, unfilled crêpes 3 months.

The classic Hungarian dish, simple in concept but very sophisticated in flavour.

1 recipe Basic Crêpe Mixture (see p. 315)

For the filling
1 x 16 oz (450 g) can pitted Morello cherries
5 fl oz (150 ml/⅔ cup) fruity red wine
1 level tbsp cornflour (cornstarch)
1 cinnamon stick
approx. 2 level tbsp caster (superfine) sugar

For brushing on the crêpes
1 oz (25 g/2 tbsp) melted butter
caster sugar

Make the crêpes as described on p. 315.

Drain the cherries. Put the liquid from the fruit and the wine into a measuring jug - there should be 10 fl oz (275 ml/2½ cups). If not, add a little water. Put the cornflour into a small bowl and stir to a cream with a little of the liquid. Bring the remaining liquid to the boil, with the cinnamon stick, then stir in the cornflour mixture. Bring to the boil again and simmer for 3 minutes, then add half the sugar, taste and add the rest if necessary - it will depend on what wine you use. Remove the cinnamon stick. This mixture can also be made the day before, but it must be reheated before use.

To assemble the crêpes, fill each with a spoonful of filling, roll up, and lay side by side in a heatproof dish. Brush with a little melted butter then sprinkle with caster sugar. When required, reheat at Gas No. 6 (400°F/200°C), until golden and piping hot - about 10-15 minutes.

OMELETTE SOUFFLÉ AUX CERISES
(*Cherry Soufflé Omelette*)

Serves 4.
Eat freshly made.

This quite delectable dessert works best with quantities for 4, so it's ideal for a special family meal or as the ending to an informal supper with close friends. As they linger over the cheese, this delicate soufflé can be rising dramatically in the oven - it takes only 10 minutes. It's a good dish for using up excess egg whites. The filling can be any lightly sugared fresh fruit in season - sliced mangoes, berries or pineapple - or a slightly thickened compôte of fruits such as stewed apricots, peaches or the cherries given in the recipe.

For the omelette

3 egg yolks
grated rind of ½ lemon
½ teasp vanilla essence
6 egg whites
4 oz (125 g/½ cup) caster sugar
1½ oz (40 g/6 tbsp) flour
1½ oz (40 g/3 tbsp butter, melted
1 oz (25 g/2 tbsp) butter (for frying the omelette)
2 tbsp best-quality apricot conserve
1 tbsp Cointreau

For the filling

1 x 15 oz (425 g) can morello (sour) cherries
1 tbsp cornflour
1 tbsp light brown sugar
sifted icing (confectioners') sugar

Just before dinner, mix the egg yolks, rind and vanilla essence in a large bowl. Put the egg whites in another large bowl and leave at room temperature. Weigh out all the other ingredients, preheat the oven to Gas No. 6 (400°F/200°C) and select an 8-inch (20-cm) omelette pan with a heatproof handle (or cover a wooden one with foil). Plug in an electric whisk.

Make the filling as follows. Mix the juice from the cherries (made up with orange juice or water if necessary to 8 fl oz) with the cornflour and brown sugar, then bring to the boil, stirring, and bubble for 3 minutes.

To make the omelette, after the main course has been eaten, whisk the whites until they hold stiff peaks, then whisk in the sugar a tablespoon at a time, whisking until stiff after each addition. Carefully fold the meringue into the yolk mixture, using a rubber spatula to avoid beating out the air. Sift the flour over this mixture, then fold in, followed by the melted butter. Melt the 1 oz butter in the frying pan, then immediately spoon in the soufflé mixture, smoothing the top with the rubber spatula. Leave for 2 minutes over moderate heat, then put in the oven for 10 minutes. Meanwhile, mix the apricot conserve with the Cointreau. Take the omelette from the oven, make a slight dent across the centre to make it easier to fold in half, spread with the conserve and arrange the rewarmed fruit filling on 1 side, then cover it with the other.

Slide on to a serving dish, dust with icing sugar and serve immediately.

VARIATION

OMELETTE SOUFFLÉ AUX ANANAS
(*Pineapple Soufflé Omelette*)

Make exactly as for Omelette Soufflé aux Cerises, but with this filling.

2 tbsp best-quality apricot conserve
3 slices fresh pineapple, peeled, cored and cut in ½-inch (1.25-cm) sections
1 tbsp kirsch
icing (confectioners') sugar for dusting the omelette

While the soufflé is in the oven, prepare the filling. Warm the apricot conserve, the pineapple and the liqueur together until steaming but not bubbling. (This can be done most easily in the microwave.) Take the omelette from the oven, make a slight dent across the centre to make it easier to fold in half, arrange the fruit on 1 side and cover it with the other.

Slide on to a serving dish, dust with icing sugar and serve immediately.

BARBECUED FRUIT KEBABS

Serves 6.
Leftovers keep 1 day under refrigeration.

Besides the varieties mentioned, any assortment of fruit in season - pineapple, banana, nectarine - can be used, provided it is cut in chunky pieces.

2 oranges
2 dessert apples
2 firm pears
3 tbsp lemon juice (1 large lemon)
2 fresh peaches or 1 can peach halves, well drained
4-6 fat black grapes

For the basting sauce
3 oz butter (or margarine for a meat meal)
1 tbsp dark soft brown sugar
1 teasp ground cinnamon
good pinch of freshly-grated nutmeg
1 tbsp apple or orange juice

Peel the oranges with a serrated knife, making sure all the pith has been removed, and divide each of them into 6 wedges. Cut each apple into 6 sections and remove any core. Cut the pears in quarters, remove the cores, then cut each quarter into 3 chunks. Dip the apple sections and pear chunks in the lemon juice to prevent them discolouring. Cut the fresh peaches in half and remove the stones. Cut each fresh or canned half into 3 pieces.

Thread all the fruits on 6 flat metal skewers, mixing the varieties.

To make the sauce, melt the fat in a small saucepan, then stir in the sugar, cinnamon, nutmeg and fruit juice. Heat gently, stirring until well blended.

When the coals have reached the white ash stage, place the skewers on the barbecue grill (broiler) and baste with the sauce. Grill, turning the skewers frequently, for about 5 minutes, until the sugar coating begins to caramelize. Serve warm within 10 minutes of cooking.

COLD DESSERTS

With a few exceptions, I cannot claim that there is any influence of the traditional Jewish cuisine to be found in the recipes that follow, unless it be the large number of fruited desserts that are permissible to serve after both a meat and a milk meal. Rather, these are the results of years of travel and study of international cuisine. When I started experimenting with desserts, an electric mixer was a rarity and the blender and food processor quite unknown. Now these electrical 'kitchen maids' make it possible for even the inexperienced cook to produce elaborate sweets with ease and speed.

All the recipes are explicit as to methods; the only general advice I can give is to ensure that the finest quality ingredients are used. Many of the recipes depend for their success on the simple but careful preparation of superb raw ingredients. Without them, they are nothing.

Where recipes include orange or citrus blossom water, you will find these available either at a chemist's or a Cypriot or Greek delicatessen.

Creaminess in many guises

When the first edition of this book went to press in the mid-1970s *cholesterol* and *saturated fats* were not part of the cook's vocabulary. Nor were products such as fromage frais or Greek-style strained cows' milk yoghurt sitting on the supermarket shelves. The choice for creaminess lay between double (heavy), whipping and single (light) cream, with soured cream and smetana available only at ethnic delicatessens.

Each of these new dairy products has special characteristics - their taste and fat content vary enormously and so does their role in the kitchen. Below I list their fat content - the taste is a subjective matter you will have to assess yourself. However, the only ones that can be *whipped* are double, whipping and non-dairy creams. If you wish to achieve a similar texture and volume with the other products, then you will need to use twice as much by volume to achieve a similar result: for example, 5 oz (150 ml/⅔ cup) whipping cream = 10 fl oz (275 ml/1¼ cups) by volume when whipped; therefore it will need 10 fl oz (275 ml/1¼ cups) of, say, fromage frais to replace it satisfactorily.

Product	*Approx. Fat Content* (check exact percentage on nutritional label)
clotted cream	55%
double cream	48%
whipping cream	40%
single cream	18–35%
soured cream	18–20%
crème fraîche (single cream cultured with bacteria to give it the texture of whipped cream)	18–35%
smetana	10%
Greek-style strained cow's-milk yoghurt	10%
fromage frais – creamy	8%
fromage frais – low fat	trace
low- and very low-fat yoghurts	these vary in fat content – check the label

Fruit Compôtes

A compôte is a dish of fresh or dried fruit that is stewed in a sugar syrup to ensure that it keeps its shape and texture.

FRESH APRICOT COMPÔTE

Serves 6.
Keeps 3 days under refrigeration.
Freeze 6 months but expect some change in texture.

This fragrant compôte is delicious served plain or with pouring cream or ice-cream. With the addition of drained pineapple titbits and sliced bananas it becomes a fruit salad. Alternatively, the fruit can be halved and stoned before poaching, then drained when cooked and used to fill a flan case.

4 oz (125 g/½ cup) sugar
10 fl oz (275 ml/1¼ cups) water
1½ lb (675 g) fresh or frozen apricots
juice of ½ lemon

In a wide, shallow, lidded pan dissolve the sugar in the water over gentle heat, then bring to the boil and simmer until syrupy – about 5 minutes. Put in the whole fruit in 1 layer, cover and simmer very, very gently until almost fork tender – about 10 minutes. Add the lemon juice and leave covered to complete the cooking, then chill well.

MORELLO OR OTHER CHERRIES COOKED IN THEIR OWN JUICES

Serves 4–5.
Keeps 3 days under refrigeration.
Freeze 6 months.

Sugar is used to draw out the natural juice from the fruit, as it cooks slowly in the oven.

1½ lb (675 g) Morello (sour red) or other cherries (not stoned)
4 oz (125 g/½ cup) demerara (brown sugar) or 8 oz (225 g/1 cup) if Morello cherries are used
juice of a large lemon

Put cherries in a fairly shallow ovenproof dish. Sprinkle with the sugar and pour over the lemon juice. Cover and cook at Gas No. 4 (350°F/180°C) for 35 minutes, or until cherries are tender, swimming in juice. Serve warm or cold.

FIGS IN RED WINE WITH FRESH ORANGE SECTIONS, RASPBERRIES AND HONEYED GREEK YOGHURT

Serves 6–7.
Keeps 3 days under refrigeration.
Do not freeze.

A wonderful blend of flavours. Serve without the yoghurt after a meat meal.

5 fl oz (150 ml/⅔ cup) fruity red wine
3 tbsp brown sugar (or to taste)
2 cinnamon sticks
6 whole cloves
1 lb (450 g) dried dessert figs
water to cover the fruit
1 tbsp lemon juice
1 tbsp citrus blossom water (if available)
3 large oranges, skin and pith removed and cut into segments
8 oz (225 g) raspberries
1 carton Greek cow's-milk yoghurt
1 tbsp liquid honey

Put the wine and sugar into a pan and heat gently until the sugar is dissolved. Add the spices and the figs, then top up with water until the fruit is barely covered. Cover the pan and simmer until the figs feel absolutely tender when pierced with a sharp, slim knife. Uncover the pan and boil the liquid down until it is syrupy and tastes pleasantly sweet – there should be just enough left to bathe the figs. Stir in the lemon juice and citrus blossom water.

Chill the mixture for 1 or 2 hours, then arrange either on a rimmed glass plate or on a decorative entrée dish. Surround with orange segments and raspberries and any juice that has come out of the fruit. Stir the honey into the yoghurt and serve separately.

COMPÔTE OF FRESH PEACHES

Serves 6–8.
Keeps 3 days under refrigeration.
Freeze 6 months.

A wonderfuly fragrant compôte to serve plain or with fromage frais or ice-cream.

4 level tbsp apricot jam
1 teasp grated orange rind
2 tbsp lemon juice
3 level tbsp sugar
8 fl oz (225 g/1 cup) water
6–8 large peaches or nectarines

Put jam, orange rind, lemon juice, sugar and water in a wide saucepan. Stir over gentle heat until sugar dissolves, then cook gently for about 3 minutes, until mixture looks syrupy. Leave fruit whole, or cut in half if freestone peach variety and remove stones. Drop fruit into syrup, cover and cook very gently until just tender – 5–7 minutes – basting once or twice. Now lift off skins and discard. Serve very cold.

VARIATION

COMPÔTE OF PEACHES AND RASPBERRIES WITH A FRESH MANGO SAUCE

Serves 6–8.

This superb dish makes a light contrast to a traditional apple pie or strudel. Nectarines may be substituted for the peaches.

For the sauce

2 large mangoes (approx. 1½ lb/675 g)
3 oz (75 g/⅓ cup) caster (superfine) sugar
3 tbsp lemon juice
4 tbsp orange juice

For the garnish

1 oz (25 g/¼ cup) toasted flaked almonds

Poach the peaches as before and when quite cold stir in 8 oz (225 g) fresh or frozen raspberries.

To make the sauce, peel the mangoes, cut the flesh away from the stone, then purée with all the other ingredients in a food processor or blender. Chill overnight.

To serve, arrange a peach and a little of the juice on each plate and spoon some of the mango sauce at the side, then scatter with the toasted almonds.

AUTUMN PEACH AND ORANGE COMPÔTE

Serves 6–8.
Keeps 2 days under refrigeration.
Freeze peaches only 6 months.

A beautiful presentation, excellent for using the last of the peaches.

6–8 peaches
3–4 large oranges
sprigs of mint

For the syrup

3 tbsp smooth apricot jam
1 teasp each grated orange and lemon rind
3 level tbsp granulated sugar
8 fl oz (225 ml/1 cup) water
2 teasp arrowroot or cornflour
3 tbsp lemon juice
2 tbsp apricot brandy or other liqueur

Put the jam, rinds, sugar and water into a wide saucepan or lidded frying pan. Stir over gentle heat until the sugar dissolves. Put in the halved, stoned peaches, cover and cook very gently until just tender when pierced with a knife. Lift off skin and discard, then arrange in a wide dish about ½–1 inch (1.25–2.5 cm) deep (eg a gratin dish).

Mix the cornflour or arrowroot with the lemon juice then stir into the syrup. Bring to the boil and simmer until clear and thickened. Stir in the liqueur. Pour over the peaches.

Prepare the oranges by peeling them like an apple (removing all the white pith), then cut into segments, discarding the pith. Leave on a dish covered with clingfilm (saranwrap). About 2 hours before serving, arrange the segments in between the peach halves. Chill well. Just before serving, arrange tiny sprigs of fresh mint in between the fruit.

PEACHES IN RED WINE WITH PASSION FRUIT AND PINE KERNELS

Serves 8.
Serve after 24 hours.
May be refrigerated for up to 4 days.

A beautiful dinner party dessert – the passion fruit seeds give a wonderful fillip to the flavour.

8–10 large choice peaches or nectarines

For the poaching syrup

4 oz (125 g/½ cup) golden granulated sugar
5 fl oz (150 ml/⅔ cup) water
10 fl oz (275 ml/1¼ cups) red wine
1 stick cinnamon

For the garnish

seeds from 2 passion fruit
4 tbsp (2 oz/50 g approx.) pine kernels, lightly toasted in a non-stick frying pan

The day before, poach the peaches as follows. In a shallow lidded pan wide enough to hold the peaches in 1 layer add the sugar, water, wine and cinnamon stick. Bring to the boil stirring constantly, then add the washed fruit, baste with the liquid, cover and poach for 5–8 minutes, or until barely tender when pierced with a slim knife (do *not* overcook). Cover and leave off the heat to steam for 15 minutes, then lift off the skins and discard.

Lift the peaches out singly with a slotted spoon and place in a wide lidded container. Bring the syrup back to the boil and simmer for 5 minutes, or until the flavour has intensified. Pour over and around the fruit, cover and chill overnight, turning the fruit once or twice.

To serve, remove the cinnamon stick and arrange the peaches on a large serving dish or in individual serving bowls or plates. Divide the syrup between them, then halve the passion fruit and spoon the seeds over the peaches. Finally scatter with the pine kernels.

OVEN-BAKED RHUBARB COMPÔTE

Serves 4–5.
Keeps 3 days under refrigeration.

Rhubarb cooked in this manner will keep its shape and colour and make its own rich syrup. The diced flesh of a small pineapple or 3 sectioned oranges can be added just before serving. This is an excellent dish for Passover use.

1 lb (450 g) forced (pink) rhubarb
5 oz (150 g/⅔ cup) sugar
1 tbsp water

Put half rhubarb, cut in 1-inch (2.5-cm) pieces, into a casserole. Sprinkle with half the sugar. Add the remaining rhubarb and sugar and sprinkle with the water. Cover and bake at Gas No. 5 (375°F/190°C) for 40 minutes, stirring once.

Alternatively, cook in the microwave by preparing as before but layering with *caster* (superfine) sugar. Add no water. Cover and cook on 100 per cent power for 5 minutes, stirring carefully but thoroughly half-way. Leave covered until steaming stops.

MIRKATAN

Serves 6–8.
Keeps 4 days under refrigeration.
Do not freeze.

In this ancient Armenian recipe, plump and juicy dried fruits mixed with nuts and sections of orange are macerated in a delicately spiced wine syrup. The compôte can be served either warm or cold, plain or accompanied in the traditional manner by rosewater-scented whipped cream or, as I prefer it, with Greek-style yoghurt lightly sweetened with Hymettus honey.

8 oz (225 g) pitted prunes
8 oz (225 g) dried apricots
8 oz (225 g) dried peaches or pears
freshly brewed tea to cover the dried fruit
3 oz (75 g) walnut halves
water
5 fl oz (150 ml/⅔ cup) fruity red wine
3 strips of orange zest
1 cinnamon stick
3 oz (75 g/⅓ cup) caster (superfine) sugar
1 tbsp fresh lemon juice
1 tbsp citrus blossom water
2 navel oranges, peeled and sectioned

The day before, put the dried fruit in a bowl and pour the strained tea over it. Cover and leave overnight.

Next day, strain into a bowl (reserving the liquid) and insert the walnut halves into the prunes. Make up the reserved tea with water, if necessary, to 8 fl oz (225 ml/1 cup). Put in a wide pan together with the wine, orange zest, cinnamon stick and sugar. Bring to the boil and simmer uncovered for 3 minutes.

Add the dried fruit, cover and simmer for 20 minutes, until the fruit is tender and the syrup has thickened. Stir in the lemon juice, citrus blossom water and orange sections. Serve hot or cold.

Fruit Salads

Sugar, be it scattered over the raw fruit or combined with water and fruit juice to make a syrup, helps to draw the natural juices from cut-up fruit, intensifying the flavour of the fruit salad. However, for a sugar-free diet an equivalent bulk (spoon for spoon) of granular sweetener can be used instead. Do not heat it, as this destroys the sweetness.

A DECORATIVE ICE BOWL FOR FRUIT SALAD OR ICE-CREAM

I first saw this dramatic presentation at Myrtle Allen's lovely Ballymaloe House Hotel in Eire. Like so many innovative ideas, it's actually very easy when you know how, and the effect of the fruit or ice-cream in its shimmering bowl is tremendous.

Take 2 bowls, one about double the capacity of the other. Do not use aluminium. Half-fill the big bowl with cold water, then place the second bowl inside. Weight it down with water until the rims are level. Then adjust so that the smaller bowl stays in a central position by securing the two together with 5 or 6 pieces of parcel tape. The water should come to within ½ inch (1.25 cm) of the top. Put bowls in the freezer.

After 24 hours turn out as follows. Remove the tape, then twist and shake the small bowl free of the ice bowl. Dip the big bowl for a second or so in tepid water, or leave at room temperature for half an hour. Twist and shake the ice bowl free of the larger bowl and turn it out carefully. If the ice bowl should split, press it together firmly and put it back in the big bowl to refreeze for 15 minutes. Serve at once on a folded serviette to absorb moisture, filled with fruit salad, berries or ice cream. Wiped clean with a damp cloth after use, and put back in the freezer, it can be used 2 or 3 times before it begins to look worn.

To make a flower- or herb-decorated bowl, fill the big bowl only one-third full. Position the smaller bowl as before, then arrange flower heads in the water. Freeze. Add another layer of flowers, freeze again, then top up so that the water comes to within ½ inch (1.25 cm) of the top of the big bowl. Freeze, then proceed as described.

AUTUMN FRUIT SALAD

Serves 6–8.
Keeps 2 days under refrigeration.
Do not freeze.

A lovely dish to serve at Rosh Hashanah (New Year), when melons and peaches are both in season.

For the syrup

4 oz (125 g/½ cup) sugar
3 tbsp water
juice of 1 lemon and any juice from the fruit
2 tbsp raspberry jam

For the fruit

2 large oranges, peeled and sliced
2 large peaches, peeled and sliced
2 large Comice pears, peeled and sliced
4 dessert plums, cut up
1 small, very ripe melon, cubed
12 oz (350 g) seedless or pipped grapes

Dissolve the sugar in the water, simmer for 3 minutes, then add the lemon juice and raspberry jam and any fruit juice from cut-up oranges, etc.

Put all the fruit except the grapes in a bowl and pour over the hot syrup. Leave in a cool place. Just before serving add the grapes.

SCARLET FRUIT SALAD FOR WINTER

Serves 6–8.
Keeps 1 day under refrigeration.
Do not freeze.

This has the beauty of utter simplicity. The flavour of the fruit, enhanced by the wine, speaks for itself.

For the syrup
4 fl oz (125 ml/½ cup) fruity red wine
4 oz (125 g/½ cup) caster (superfine) sugar

For the fruit
8 oz (225 g) frozen redcurrants
8 oz (225 g) frozen raspberries or loganberries
1 lb (450 g) frozen cherries

Heat the syrup ingredients together until the sugar has melted. Bring to the boil, then cool and pour over the frozen fruit.

Allow the fruit to stand at room temperature, stirring once or twice, until it has defrosted and the wine syrup has started to draw out some of the fruit juices. Refrigerate until required.

Note If frozen cherries are not available, drain a can – preferably of Morello (sour red) cherries – and use the fruit only, reserving the syrup for some other use.

MULLED-WINE FRUIT SALAD

Serves 6–8.
Keeps 2 days under refrigeration.
Do not freeze.

The bottom of the bottle of any red wine, lightly sweetened and spiced, makes a superb base for a winter fruit salad with a difference. The wine is first simmered to concentrate its flavour, then used as a catalyst to draw out the natural juices from a selection of fresh fruit. For an unusual presentation, arrange the mixture in a wide, fairly shallow bowl and top with toasted nuts. Serve a slice of sponge cake or a crisp biscuit on the side.

12 oz (350 g) choice black or green grapes, seedless or pipped
6 clementines, peeled and sectioned
1 large, ripe mango, peeled and thinly sliced
1 x 15 oz (425 g) can lychees plus juice
2 Kiwi fruit, sliced
2 large, ripe bananas, sliced
2 oz (50 g/½ cup) pecans or walnuts, shelled
2 oz (50 g/½ cup) Brazil nuts, shelled

For the syrup
5 fl oz (150 ml/⅔ cup) fruity red wine
5 fl oz (150 ml/⅔ cup) lychee juice
3 tbsp light-brown sugar
1 tbsp lemon juice
8 cloves
1 cinnamon stick or a good pinch of cinnamon

Put the fruit in a bowl. Pour the wine, juice, sugar, lemon juice and spices into a pan and simmer for 5 minutes. Cool, then pour over the fruit and refrigerate. Coarsely chop the nuts, toast until golden under the grill (broiler) or arrange on a flat dish and cook in the microwave on 100 per cent power for 8 minutes, stirring twice.

FOUR-FRUIT SALAD

Serves 8.
Eat the same day.

1 large (approx. 1 lb/450 g) mango
1 large Ogen or Galia melon
1 lb (450 g) fresh or frozen raspberries or fresh strawberries
12 oz (350 g) seedless black grapes

For the syrup
juice of 1 large lemon (3–4 tbsp)

2–3 tbsp caster (superfine) sugar
(lesser amount if liqueur is used)
6 mint leaves, finely chopped, or 2 tbsp Cointreau

Peel the mango, then cut away from the stone in ½-inch-thick (1.25-cm) slices and cut these in turn into wedges. Put in a bowl. Heat the lemon juice and sugar in a pan until the sugar has dissolved, then pour over the mango. Halve the melon, remove and discard the pips and scoop the flesh out with a melon-baller. Leave the balls in a sieve to drain so that excess juice can be discarded. If strawberries are used, do not hull and slice until the day of use. Cover all the fruit with clingfilm (saran-wrap) and refrigerate until required.

Several hours beforehand, combine all the fruit and syrup in a large bowl. Add the chopped mint or the liqueur and mix gently together. Leave at room temperature for 1 hour, stirring once or twice, then chill until required. Serve with ice-cream and/or Greek-style yoghurt or fromage frais.

VARIATION

Use 3 large, ripe nectarines instead of the mango. Plunge into boiling water for 30 seconds, then strip off the skin. Cut away from the stone in ½-inch-thick (1.25-cm) slices and marinate like the mango in the lemon syrup.

RASPBERRY AND REDCURRANT MÉLANGE

Serves 4–6.
Keeps 1 day under refrigeration.
Do not freeze.

Simple but superb!

8 oz (225 g) fresh or frozen raspberries
8 oz (225 g) fresh or frozen redcurrants
2 tbsp caster (superfine) sugar or
granular sweetener
2 tbsp Liqueur de Framboise (optional)

Gently mix the fruit with the sugar and the liqueur (if used). Stand at room temperature until the fruit has defrosted, then stir gently. Transfer to a serving dish and chill until required.

PERSIAN HONEYED FRUITS

Serves 6–8.
Keeps 2 days under refrigeration.
Do not freeze.

If a recipe calls for the rind of an orange as well as the juice, then it's sensible to squeeze the juice yourself from the whole fruit. Otherwise it's just as economical and much more labour-saving to buy a commercial pack. In this recipe the fresh juice is used to marinate the fruit, helping to draw out its own natural juice and creating a wonderfully refreshing *parev* dessert.

2 large ripe mangoes
1 medium pineapple
6 fl oz (175 ml/¾ cup) fresh orange juice
3 tbsp mild honey, caster (superfine) sugar or
granular sweetener
2 tbsp fresh lemon juice
4 oz (125 g/½ cup) crystallized ginger,
finely chopped

Peel the mangoes, then cut away the stone in ½-inch-thick (1.25-cm) slices. Cut the pineapple into slices the same thickness, trim away the peel and cut out the core, then cut each slice into ½-inch-wide (1.25-cm) segments. Warm the orange juice with the honey or sugar until it has dissolved, then put in a bowl with the lemon juice. (Stir in the sugar substitute, if used, at this point.) Add the prepared fruit and the ginger, stir gently to blend, then cover and leave at room temperature for 1 hour before refrigerating until required.

STRAWBERRIES IN THE VENETIAN MANNER

Serves 8–10 for a buffet or supper.
Leftovers keep 1 day under refrigeration.

This is the way to treat really superb young strawberries that are fully ripe.

2½–3 lb (2.2–1.5 kg) strawberries
juice of 2 lemons or small oranges
caster (superfine) sugar
pouring cream

Arrange the hulled strawberries in a fairly shallow dish. Chill for half an hour. At the table pour over orange juice (for slightly tart fruit) or lemon juice (for very sweet fruit) and offer caster sugar and pouring cream.

STRAWBERRIES IN A RASPBERRY SAUCE

Serves 6.
Eat the same day.

This treatment can be given to any of the summer fruits. Thus a strawberry sauce can be spooned over sliced ripe peaches, or a blackberry sauce gently mixed with sections of fresh mango. In each case the fruit for the sauce is whirled with a little sugar in the food processor or blender until it thickens naturally. The sauce can then be thinned to a coating consistency if necessary with orange or lemon juice, a little sweet dessert wine or a fruit-flavoured liqueur.

1½ lb (675 g) choice strawberries
2 ripe bananas
8 oz (225 g) raspberries
2 oz (50 g/¼ cup) caster (superfine) sugar
1 tbsp orange juice
1 tbsp lemon juice

For the garnish
a few toasted slivered or nibbed almonds

Slice the strawberries, then divide between 6 wine glasses or small fruit bowls. Push the raspberries through a sieve (to remove the pips), then purée with the sugar in the food processor or blender for 2 minutes until thickened. Blend in the orange and lemon juices. Chill well but leave the strawberry mixture at room temperature. Shortly before serving, slice the bananas on top of the strawberries, spoon the sauce over the fruit and sprinkle with the toasted almonds.

VARIATION

AN EXOTIC FRUIT SALAD WITH A STRAWBERRY LIME SAUCE

Serves 8.
Fruit salad keeps 1 day under refrigeration, but bananas should be added only an hour before serving.

Here the fruit sauce is used to coat a fruit salad. If granular sweetener is used in the sauce, this is an excellent sugar-free dessert (though the sauce won't be as thick).

For the sauce
3 tbsp fresh lime or lemon juice
3 tbsp caster (superfine) sugar
8 oz (225 g) strawberries, fresh or frozen without sugar

For the fruit salad
1 large pineapple
4 Kiwi fruit
1 large ripe mango
4 bananas

Process the juice, sugar and half the strawberries in a blender or food processor for 2 minutes, then chill. Peel the pineapple and cut into lengthwise fingers, discarding the centre core, then cut each finger across into ½-inch (1-cm) pieces. Put these in a bowl together with the peeled and sliced Kiwi fruit and the peeled and sliced mango. Allow to stand at room temperature for 1 hour, then stir gently, cover and refrigerate.

An hour before serving, add the sliced bananas and divide between 8 glasses. Top with the strawberry lime sauce.

SUMMER PUDDING

Serves 8.
Keeps 3 days under refrigeration.
Freeze 4 months.

This classic English midsummer dessert is at its best when prepared with bread made from a Jewish challah mixture! A pudding basin is lined with strips of this rich bread and then filled brimful with sugared soft fruit. After the pudding has been left under a weight overnight, the juice permeates the bread, giving it a sponge-like texture. This is delicious served with thick natural yoghurt.

8 slices from a challah baked in a 2-lb (900-g) loaf tin (also known as 'best bread'), preferably machine sliced by the baker and at least 24 hours old, or 8 slices from a large best-quality white sliced loaf
2 lb (900 g) mixed summer fruits – eg strawberries, raspberries, blackberries, redcurrants, bilberries, or 2 x 1 lb (450 g) packs frozen summer fruits (very convenient)
8 oz (225 g) caster (superfine) sugar
4 tbsp any fruit juice or syrup (not necessary if fruit is frozen)

Select a pudding basin with a 2-pint (1.25-1/5-cup) capacity (fill it with water to make sure). Cut a small disc of silicone paper to fit the base of the basin. If unsliced, decrust the challah and cut it in ⅜-inch (1-cm) slices. Decrust the sliced bread, then cut each slice into wedges about 1 inch (2.5 cm) wide, which can then be fitted tightly together round the sides of the basin, meeting at the bottom and covering it – it is important that there are no gaps in the bread lining to let the juices escape. Alternatively, each slice of bread can be cut into rectangles, which are then arranged overlapping each other.

Pick over but do not wash fresh fruit. Put into a bowl and mix thoroughly with the sugar and fruit juice (if used). (If the fruit looks rather dry, cook it lightly with the sugar until the juices flow. If, on the other hand, it is very juicy, as frozen fruit often is when defrosted, the additional fruit juice can be omitted and only sugar added.)

Spoon the prepared fruit into the bread-lined basin, pressing it down gently with the back of a wooden spoon so that the juices begin to penetrate the bread. Cut slices of bread to make a 'lid' on top. To weight the pudding, press down firmly with your hands, cover it with clingfilm (saranwrap) or foil, put a small pan that just fits on top, and on top of that put either a 2-lb (900-g) weight or bag of sugar. Refrigerate the pudding for at least 24 hours, sitting on a plate to collect any juice that may overflow.

Don't unmould the pudding until you are ready to serve it, as the case may collapse. Have ready a pie or flan dish about ½ inch (1.25 cm) deep. Carefully run a knife round the inside of the bowl to make sure the lining will come away, then reverse on to the serving plate. Any juice that has overflowed can be spooned on top.

Fruit with Alcohol

The judicious addition of a small amount of liqueur or wine can greatly enhance a simple fruit dish. Do not be overlavish, however, or the delicate flavour of the fruits will be masked.

ORANGES IN CURAÇAO SYRUP

Serves 6–8.
Keeps 1 day (without bananas) under refrigeration.

It is worth the trouble to candy the cut orange peel in a syrup, as the flavour of the dish is greatly enhanced. Any orange-flavoured liqueur can be used if Curaçao is not available.

6 large oranges
4 oz (125 g/½ cup) sugar
8 fl oz (225 ml/1 cup) water
juice of 1 lemon
3 tbsp Curaçao
3 large bananas
8 oz (225 g) black grapes (optional)

Using a blade-type potato peeler, shave off the peel of 1 orange. Cut it in 1-inch (2.5-cm) matchsticks. Dissolve the sugar in the water, add the peel and simmer, half-covered, for 30 minutes, or until the peel looks translucent. Add the lemon juice. Peel oranges, using a sharp, serrated knife, and cut in segments. Put in a serving dish with any juice that comes out in the preparation. Pour on the peel, syrup and liqueur, cover and leave several hours or overnight. Just before serving, slice in the bananas and pipped grapes.

VARIATION

PINEAPPLE PYRAMIDS

Prepare the syrup as directed but omit the liqueur. Peel, then slice the oranges across and soak in the syrup.

To serve, allow 1 thick slice of fresh pineapple per person, the core cut out and the slice trimmed, 1 thick slice of soaked orange and 3 or 4 black grapes. Put a slice of pineapple on each plate and top with a slice of orange and a little of the syrup. Garnish with the black grapes. Chill for 1 hour before serving and pass a bottle of Kirsch round for the guests to sprinkle on their own serving.

WHOLE ORANGES IN COINTREAU SYRUP

Serves 6.
Keeps 1 day under refrigeration.

6 oranges
8 oz (225 g/1 cup) sugar
5 fl oz (150 ml/⅔ cup) water
1 tbsp apricot jam
3 tbsp lemon juice
2 tbsp Cointreau or other orange-flavoured liqueur
6 slices fresh or canned pineapple
few black grapes

Peel the oranges, using a small, serrated knife, removing all the pith. Cut a tiny slice off the base so that they will sit straight on the dish. Slice each of them crosswise into 4–6 slices, then reassemble into shape and arrange in a shallow casserole. Make a very thick syrup by dissolving the sugar in the water and adding the apricot jam. Simmer for 3 minutes, then remove from the heat, and add the lemon juice and the liqueur. Pour this syrup over the oranges. Put the dish in the refrigerator and chill for several hours, basting the fruit with the syrup 3 or 4 times.

To serve, arrange a slice of fresh or canned pineapple on each serving plate. On it stand a glazed orange and pour over a little of the syrup. Spear pipped black grapes on to a cocktail stick and stick in the top of each orange.

ORANGE AND GINGER SALAD

Serves 6.
Keeps 1 day without bananas under refrigeration.

4 large navel oranges
3 pieces bottled or preserved ginger
2 tbsp ginger syrup
2 tbsp cherry brandy, Curaçao or Cointreau
2 peeled and sliced bananas

With a sharp, serrated knife, peel the oranges, removing the pith at the same time. Cut each half-segment into fan-shaped pieces. Put into a bowl with any juice that has dripped from them. Add the ginger sliced into slivers with the syrup and liqueur. Mix gently together, then refrigerate for 2 hours. Just before serving, add the bananas. Serve plain or with yoghurt, fromage frais or cold custard.

ORANGES VENETIENNES

Make and serve the same day.

This recipe was given to me by a waiter who used to prepare oranges in this manner for Winston Churchill, when he wintered in Marrakesh. It is simple but refreshing after a heavy meal. I often serve it at a Chanukkah dinner.

For each serving
1 very large juicy orange, chilled
caster (superfine) sugar
Grenadine (pomegranate-flavoured) or any other fruit syrup
Kirsch or any fruit brandy such as Eau de Poires, or lemon juice

Take each orange in turn and cut a thin slice off the base so that it will sit evenly on the plate. Cut a lid off the orange about two-thirds of the way up, where the fruit begins to narrow. Prepare the fruit itself as if it were a grapefruit, loosening the segments and removing the core with a special grapefruit knife. Fill the core cavity with caster sugar and saturate it with the fruit syrup. Sprinkle the surface of the orange pulp with the lemon juice, Kirsch or fruit brandy. Replace the lid and leave at room temperature for at least an hour.

The sugar will draw out the natural juices of the fruit.

Serve with a grapefruit spoon.

PÊCHES CARDINALE

Serves 8.
Poached fruit and raspberry purée keeps 3 days under refrigeration.

It's useful to have plastic cups of sweetened berry purée in the freezer for just such a dish (see p. 328). This classic dessert has a most refreshing blend of flavours. Out-of-season it can be made with choice canned whole or halves of peaches.

8 oz (225 g/1 cup) granulated sugar
$1\frac{1}{4}$ pints (725 ml/2 cups) water
8 ripe fresh peaches
12 oz (350 g) fresh raspberries
4 oz (125 g/$\frac{1}{2}$ cup) granulated sugar
2 tbsp Cointreau or Curaçao
mint leaves or toasted almonds

Put the 8 oz sugar and water into a pan and stir until the sugar has dissolved. Add the unpeeled peaches, bring to simmering point, and allow to stand, covered, in the hot syrup (which should be barely bubbling) for 8 minutes. Take the pan off the stove, keep covered and leave for 20 minutes. (The syrup can be used again for another dish.) Drain peaches on a cake rack. Peel while warm (the skin will slip off easily) and arrange in an oval entrée dish.

Sieve the raspberries to remove the pips then place the purée in the blender with the

4 oz sugar. Cover and blend at top speed for about 2 minutes, until thickened to a coating consistency. Add the liqueur to the sauce. Chill. Pour chilled sauce over chilled fruit and leave in the refrigerator until needed. Decorate either with mint leaves or toasted almonds.

SCENTED STRAWBERRIES WITH AN ORANGE-LIQUEUR CREAM

Serves 6–8.
Eat the same day.

As so many people now say 'No, thank you' to rich desserts, a sophisticated fruit salad should have a place on every dinner party menu. This one brings out the superb flavour of home-grown strawberries but adds an exotic touch with orange or citrus blossom water. An excellent Muscat wine is now imported from Israel. It can, however, be omitted and the same amount of orange or mango juice be used instead.

2 oz (25 g/2 tbsp) caster (superfine) sugar
1 glass (3½ fl oz/90 ml) Muscat wine (pudding wine)
1 tbsp lemon juice
2 tbsp orange or citrus blossom water
1 lb (450 g) fresh strawberries
6 oz (175 g) kumquats, quartered
2 ripe bananas
2 oz (50 g/½ cup) pistachios

For the orange cream
1 large egg, separated
2 level tbsp caster (superfine) sugar
2 tbsp orange liqueur
10 fl oz (275 ml/1¼ cups) 8% creamy fromage frais or Greek-style strained cow's-milk yoghurt
grated rind of 1 orange

Over moderate heat, dissolve the sugar in the wine, then boil rapidly for 1 minute. Stir in the lemon juice and orange or citrus blossom water and chill.

Leaving a few strawberries with their leaves on for garnish, hull the remainder, then cut in half. Put in a decorative glass bowl with the quartered kumquats and pour over the cold syrup. Refrigerate until an hour before dinner, then add the sliced bananas and the skinned and slivered pistachios and leave at room temperature. Serve plain or with the orange cream.

To make the orange cream, whisk the egg white until it holds soft peaks, then whisk in the sugar a teaspoonful at a time. Stir in the egg yolk until the colour is even. Gently stir the liqueur into the fromage frais or yoghurt then fold into the egg mixture with the orange rind. Pile into a serving dish or sauce boat. Refrigerate for up to 2 hours. If more convenient, freeze then defrost in the fridge for 1 hour.

VARIATION

BRANDIED ORANGES

Serves 6.
Prepare and serve the same day.

6 large oranges
juice of 1 large lemon
caster (superfine) sugar

For the brandy liqueur cream
as before but substitute brandy for the orange liqueur

For the garnish
1 oz (25 g/¼ cup) toasted slivered almonds

Finely grate the rind from 1 orange and reserve for the sauce, then peel it with the other oranges, section and put into a bowl. Pour over the lemon juice, then sprinkle lightly with the caster sugar. Leave in a cool place (*not* the refrigerator) to allow the juices to flow from the fruit. This will take about 2 hours. Chill.

Make the cream as before.

About 30 minutes before serving, divide the fruit and juice between 6 large wine glasses. Top with a spoonful of the liqueur cream and a scatter of almonds.

MARINATED STRAWBERRIES WITH A WEINCHADEAU

Serves 6–8.

Not perhaps for a formal dinner party, but one for close friends who will appreciate this superb dessert and talk among themselves while you spend 5-6 minutes in the kitchen whipping up the glorious wine cream.

It is best to sugar the strawberries not more than 2 hours before dinner - long enough to draw out some of the natural juices without breaking down the structure. The weinchadeau can be whisked to blend before dinner, and then 5 minutes' whisking over a pan of simmering water is all that is necessary to transform it into a golden fluff.

1½–2 lb (675–900 g) strawberries, cut lengthwise in quarters
a generous 1 oz (25 g/2 tbsp) caster (superfine) sugar
2 tbsp Cointreau or Grand Marnier
1 small packet of Amaretti (dry Italian macaroons)

For the weinchadeau
4 egg yolks
3 oz (75 g/⅓ cup) caster (superfine) sugar
1 teasp cornflour (cornstarch) or arrowroot
6 fl oz (175 ml/¾ cup) medium-dry, fairly fruity white wine
2 tbsp Cointreau or Grand Marnier

Allow the sliced strawberries to macerate with the sugar and liqueur for up to 2 hours, then divide between fairly large glass serving dishes - large brandy balloons are superb. Sprinkle with 1 or 2 teaspoons of the coarsely crushed Amaretti and chill during the meal. Just before the meal, select a mixing bowl that will fit comfortably over a pan which should be left half-full of gently simmering water. Using a hand-held electric whisk, whisk together the egg yolks and sugar until pale and mousse-like, then whisk in the cornflour, wine and liqueur, whisking until well blended. Leave away from the heat during dinner.

To prepare the weinchadeau, after the final course before dessert, put the bowl over the simmering water and whisk until the mixture can be softly mounded - about 5 minutes. Divide between the bowls of strawberries, sprinkle with a few more Amaretti crumbs and serve immediately.

ZABAGLIONE CON MANGO E FRAGOLE *(Sicilian Wine Sauce with Mango and Strawberry Compôte)*

Serves 6–8.

2 fine ripe mangoes
3 tbsp caster (superfine) sugar, warmed until dissolved in 3 tbsp fresh lemon juice
1 lb (450 g) strawberries

For the zabaglione
5 egg yolks
5 level tbsp caster (superfine) sugar
10 tbsp Marsala 'fine' or 'all uovo', or medium-dry Amontillado sherry

Up to 24 hours before the meal, peel the mango, cut away in large sections from the stone, then slice into a container, cover with half the syrup and refrigerate until required. About 2 hours before serving, pour the remaining syrup over the strawberries. Leave at room temperature for 1 hour, then mix gently with the mango compôte and divide between 6–8 glass bowls or very large brandy balloons. Chill until required.

An hour or so before the meal, put the yolks and sugar into a heavy basin that can be suspended over a saucepan half-filled with water without the base actually touching the water. Whisk (away from the water) with a hand-held electric whisk or balloon whisk until thickened and creamy, then set aside. Just before dinner, set the pan half-full of water to simmer in readiness. When ready to serve the dessert, place the bowl with the egg mixture on top of the simmering water and add the Marsala gradually, whisking constantly. Continue to whisk until the mixture more than doubles in volume and has the consistency of softly whipped cream. Spoon the zabaglione on top of the compôte and serve at once.

Mere Trifles

The trifle is said to have originated in Spain, where the native sherry was poured over a sponge cake, which in turn was covered with a rich custard. Sephardi Jews, who were expelled from Spain in 1492 by Ferdinand and Isabella, still refer to a sponge cake as a 'Pan de Espana'. However, its English origins go back to the Middle Ages. Hannah Glasse (1741) gives recipes for it, as does Lady Judith Montefiore (1846). Certainly it has been enthusiastically taken into the cuisine of British Jews – trifle has become a traditional dish at Chanukkah in many households (see p. 587).

Recipes are legion. Here are just 2 made in our family.

STRAWBERRY TRIFLE

Serves 8.
Keeps 2 days under refrigeration.

4 oz (125 g) sponge fingers (boudoir biscuits) or the equivalent in slightly dry sponge cake
strawberry or raspberry conserve – home-made for preference (see pp. 443–5)
4 fl oz (125 ml/½ cup) wine (port-type or sweet sherry)
10 fl oz (275 ml/1¼ cup) double (heavy) cream or 15 fl oz (425 ml/2 cups) 8% creamy fromage frais, plain or fruited
2 level teasp caster (superfine) sugar
1½ lb (675 g) fine whole dessert strawberries
candied angelica
toasted almonds

For the custard

4 egg yolks
2 oz (50 g/¼ cup) caster (superfine) sugar
1 level teasp cornflour (cornstarch)
15 fl oz (425 ml/2 cups) milk
few drops vanilla essence (extract)

Spread the sponge fingers with the conserve and cover the bottom of a fairly deep glass bowl. Pour over the wine or sherry and leave for an hour to soak in well.

To make the custard, whisk the egg yolks, sugar and cornflour until creamy (easiest in a food processor). Heat the milk until it steams, then gradually pour on to the egg mixture, whisking constantly or processing. Put in the top of a double saucepan or in a bowl over a pan of simmering water and cook gently, stirring all the time, until the custard thickens and coats the back of a wooden spoon. Stand at once in a bowl of cold water to stop further cooking. Stir in the vanilla essence.

Pour the hot custard over the sponge cake and allow to set. Whisk the cream with the caster sugar until it holds soft peaks then spread all over the custard, or spoon over the fromage frais. Stud the entire surface with the strawberries and decorate with small strips of angelica and almond. Serve very cold, in small portions.

RASPBERRY AND BANANA TRIFLE

Serves 8.
Keeps 2 days under refrigeration.

This trifle has a layer of fruited jelly in between the cake and the custard.

4 oz (125 g) sponge fingers (boudoir biscuits) or the equivalent in slightly stale sponge cake
raspberry jam
$3\frac{1}{2}$ oz (85 g) packet ratafia biscuits or crunchy macaroons
4 fl oz (125 ml/$\frac{1}{2}$ cup) sherry
1 kosher jelly (gelatin mix), lemon or raspberry flavour
8 oz (225 g) fresh or frozen raspberries or mixed berries, sprinkled with 1 tbsp caster (superfine) sugar
2 large ripe bananas, thinly sliced
1 pint (575 ml/$2\frac{1}{2}$ cups) custard (see recipe above)
5 fl oz (150 ml/$\frac{2}{3}$ cup) double (heavy) cream
1 egg white
1 tbsp orange-flavoured liqueur
2 teasp caster (superfine) sugar
chopped toasted hazelnuts

Spread the sponge fingers with jam and cut in 4. Coarsely crush the biscuits. Arrange in the bottom of a glass dish. Spoon over the sherry. Make the jelly - nicest with 4 fl oz (125 ml/$\frac{2}{3}$ cup) fruit juice substituted for part of the water - and put in the refrigerator or freezer until as thick as unbeaten egg whites.

Arrange the raspberries and bananas on top of the sponge, then spoon over the jelly and leave to set. Pour on the cooled custard. Finally, whip the cream and egg white until thickening, then whisk in the liqueur and sugar. Spoon or pipe over the custard and decorate with toasted nuts. Chill thoroughly, preferably for several hours.

SAVARIN AU KIRSCH

Makes 2 savarins each serving 6–8, or
1 large savarin serving 12–16.
To make 1 small savarin, simply halve the ingredients.
Keeps 2 days under refrigeration.
Freeze 3 months.

A savarin is a ring of rich, light yeast sponge soaked with an alcoholic syrup, then garnished with fruit and cream. It can also be served without cream but with a fruit compôte. It is particularly successful when frozen, then reheated and treated as freshly baked. This means that only the soaking and garnishing need be done on the day it is to be served.

1 x $\frac{1}{4}$ oz (7 g) packet easy-blend yeast
8 oz (225 g/2 cups) strong white bread flour
$\frac{1}{2}$ level teasp salt
1 oz (25 g/2 tbsp) caster (superfine) sugar
6 tbsp milk, heated till hand-hot
4 eggs, beaten to blend
4 oz (125 g/$\frac{1}{2}$ cup) soft butter or margarine

For the syrup

(quantities given are for each small savarin; double up for 1 large savarin)
6 oz (175 g/$\frac{3}{4}$ cup) granulated sugar
8 fl oz (225 ml/1 cup) water
5 tbsp Kirsch or rum
2 tbsp smooth apricot jam, warmed until liquid

Mix the yeast with the dry ingredients, then add all the remaining ingredients and beat until the mixture does not stick to the spoon or mixer (5 minutes by hand or 3 by electric mixer).

Divide the mixture between 2 $1\frac{1}{4}$-pint (700-ml/$3\frac{1}{4}$-cup) or 1 $2\frac{1}{2}$-pint (1.5-l/$6\frac{1}{4}$-cup) ring tin(s). Slip into a plastic bag and leave until the mixture reaches the top - 20–30 minutes. Bake in a preheated oven, Gas No. 6 (400°F/200°C), for 25 minutes, or until toast brown. Leave 5 minutes, then turn out. Can be frozen, if desired, as soon as cold. To use, defrost, then reheat in the tin until lukewarm at Gas No. 2 (300°F/150°C) or in the microwave.

While the savarin is cooking, make the syrup by dissolving the sugar in the water. Bring to the boil, then simmer for 3 minutes. Stir in the Kirsch or rum. Leave the cooked savarin in the tin for 5 minutes, then turn out and place, puffy side up, in a shallow round casserole. Pour the warmed syrup all over, then leave until it has absorbed it completely, basting if necessary.

To serve, turn right side up on a serving dish and brush with the warm apricot glaze. Fill the centre with whipped cream or slightly sweetened Greek-style yoghurt topped with sweetened raspberry, strawberry or blackberry purée (see p. 328) or any fresh or stewed fruit in season.

Fruits and Creams

These sweets all depend for their charm on the blending of fruit with sweet or soured cream. This type of sweet should be chilled for several hours before use to allow it to develop its flavours to the full.

GOOSEBERRY FOOL

Serves 6.
Keeps 2 days under refrigeration.
Freeze 3 months.

The purée given in this recipe can be made in bulk (most easily in the oven), and stored in plastic cups in the freezer for winter use.

1½ lb (675 g) green gooseberries
6 oz (175 g/¾ cup) sugar
3 fl oz (75 ml/⅓ cup) water
green colouring (optional)
5 fl oz (150 ml/⅔ cup) cream (more does no harm)
or 10 fl oz (275 ml/1¼ cups) creamy fromage frais
or Greek-style strained cow's-milk yoghurt

For the custard
10 fl oz (275 ml/1¼ cups) milk
2 level tbsp custard powder (vanilla pudding mix)
3 level tbsp sugar

Make the custard and leave to cool, covered with damp greaseproof paper.

Stew the fruit with the sugar and water until soft. Sieve and leave to go cold. Whip the cream.

When the custard and the fruit purée are both cold, blend together, then fold in the cream. Turn into individual glasses and leave to go cold.

A judicious few drops of green colouring greatly add to the appearance of the dish.

APRICOT CLOUD

Serves 6–8.
Keeps 2 days under refrigeration.
Freeze 1 month.

This is my interpretation of a dish from Sonia Wezian's *Cuisine of Armenia*. Although it contains neither jelly nor potato flour, this fruit and liqueur-flavoured cream sets overnight to a mousse-like consistency. It can either be served in glasses like a syllabub (as I suggest below) or used as a filling for a 4-egg Pavlova (see p. 344). It keeps 2 days under refrigeration and freezes for 1 month.

3 oz (75 g/⅓ cup) caster (superfine) sugar
8 fl oz (225 ml/1 cup) water
8–9 oz (225–250 g) tenderized apricots
1 tbsp lemon juice
½ teasp vanilla essence
3 tbsp apricot liqueur or apricot brandy
10 fl oz (275 ml/1¼ cups) double
(or non-dairy) cream
flavoured apricot syrup (see below)
2 oz (50 g/½ cup) toasted pine kernels or
almond nibs

For the garnish
sprigs of fresh mint

Bring the sugar and water to the boil in an 8-inch (20-cm) saucepan, add the apricots, then cover and simmer for 15 minutes, until tender but not mushy. Take off heat and stir in the lemon juice, vanilla essence and apricot liqueur. Refrigerate for about 40 minutes.

Put the cream into a bowl with the syrup drained from the apricots. Whip until it stands in stiff peaks, then fold in the apricots, cut in small cubes, reserving some cubes for garnish. Fold in almost all the pine kernels.

Divide the flavoured cream between individual flutes or glass bowls and decorate with the remaining fruit and pine kernels. Chill until required.

Just before serving, garnish with sprigs of fresh mint.

BANANA FOOL

Serves 6–8.
Keeps 2 days under refrigeration.
Do not freeze.

The secret of a successful fool is to ensure that the fruit purée, the custard and the cream are of a similar consistency when they are folded together, for unlike a mousse no jelly (gelatin) is used in this type of sweet.

10 fl oz (275 ml/1¼ cups) milk
2 level tbsp custard powder (vanilla pudding mix)
2 level tbsp sugar
juice of 1 large lemon
2 tbsp damson jam
5 large bananas
8 fl oz (225 ml/1 cup) cream (some can be soured) or 15 fl oz (425 ml/2 cups) creamy (8%) fromage frais
2 teasp sugar
1 teasp vanilla essence (extract)
12 little meringues, roughly crushed (optional)

Make the custard in the usual way, using the first 3 ingredients. Allow to go cold. Put the lemon juice and jam in the blender or food processor for 10 seconds. Add the bananas in chunks and blend until smooth, then add the cooled custard and blend a further 15 seconds.

Turn into a bowl and fold in the whipped cream or fromage frais (save some for decoration), flavoured with the sugar and vanilla essence – taste to see if more sugar is required. Gently fold in the meringues. Divide into 6 or 8 glasses. Decorate with cream and chill thoroughly.

DULCE ZACATECANO
(*Bananas with Sherried Cream*)

Serves 6.
Keeps 1 day under refrigeration.

A delicious Mexican way with bananas – the cooked bananas change their texture and combine extremely well with the creamy topping.

6–8 stubby green-tipped bananas cut in half lengthwise
3 oz (75 g/⅓ cup) butter
3 oz (75 g/⅓ cup) soft brown light Muscovado sugar
8 fl oz (225 g/1 cup) whipping or double (heavy) cream
2 level teasp caster (superfine) sugar
3 tbsp sherry

For the garnish
toasted almonds or lightly browned coconut

Peel the bananas. Melt the butter and stir in the brown sugar. Keep stirring until the sugar has melted and mixture is smooth, then add the bananas and cook, turning them in the butterscotch until they are softened – about 5 minutes. Lift out and arrange in a shallow serving dish.

Whip the cream, sugar and sherry until the mixture stands in peaks, then spoon over the bananas, covering them completely. Chill for several hours. Serve garnished with the almonds or coconut.

A MULLED WEINCHADEAU CUP

Serves 6–8.
Keeps 2 days under refrigeration.
Freeze 1 month.

The only difficult thing about this delicious confection is to remember to allow 24 hours for the spices to infuse in the wine. As the flavours are so deep, non-dairy cream can be used with great success.

For the syllabub

8 fl oz (225ml/1 cup) red wine
6 tbsp caster (superfine) sugar
4-inch (10-cm) cinnamon stick
8–10 whole cloves
zest of 1 lemon
zest of 1 tangerine
15 fl oz (425 ml/2 cups) double cream or
11 fl oz (300 ml/1⅓ cups) non-dairy cream

For the sponge base

4 trifle sponges
3 fl oz (75 ml/⅓ cup) tangerine juice
1 fl oz (25 ml/1 tbsp) lemon juice
2 tbsp Cointreau
8 oz (225 g) redcurrants, raspberries or loganberries

Put the wine, sugar, cinnamon, cloves and lemon and tangerine zests into a saucepan and bring to the boil. Take off the heat and set aside for 24 hours to infuse.

Next day cut the sponge fingers in ½-inch (1.25-cm) cubes and divide between 8 glasses (or lay in the base of a glass bowl). Moisten with the mixed juices and liqueur and arrange a little fruit on top. Save a few berries for garnish.

To make the syllabub, whip the cream until it hangs on the whisk, then gradually whisk in the strained wine, whipping continuously until the mixture holds soft peaks. Pipe on top of the fruit and chill for at least 1½–2 hours. Garnish with the remaining berries. Serve with little sponge biscuits or any dessert biscuit.

SUMMER FRUITS WITH CREAM AND CRUNCH

Serves 8.
Keeps 2 days under refrigeration.
Do not freeze.

The Danes delight in a dessert that combines layers of stewed apples and crispy fried breadcrumbs with a 'veil' of whipped cream on top. Borrowing their theme of soft *v.* crunchy, I've used a more interesting fruit compôte and an exotic crumble, and substituted the less rich but equally delicious fromage frais (or Greek yoghurt) for the cream. The result is the perfect dessert to put together when you're running out of time – the crunch can be stored in an airtight container for a week and the dessert then 'assembled' in minutes. A carton of ready-to-serve compôte of summer fruits cuts the preparation time even further. Margarine and whipped non-dairy cream can be used for a *parev* version.

1 lb(450 g) fresh or frozen mixed berries
1 tbsp cornflour (cornstarch)
4 tbsp water
4 tbsp sugar
1 large banana
2 tbsp fruity liqueur – preferably Crème de Framboise or Crème de Fraise (optional)
1 x 8–10 oz (225–275 g) carton creamy fromage frais or Greek strained yoghurt

For the crunch

1½ oz (40 g/3 tbsp) unsalted butter or margarine
4 rounded tbsp soft medium brown sugar
½ teasp cinnamon
pinch of salt
2 teasp finely grated orange rind
6 tbsp desiccated coconut
3 oz (75 g/1 cup) porridge oats
2 oz crushed macaroons
2 oz (50 g /⅓ cup) ready-toasted flaked almonds

Put the berries into a pan. Mix the cornflour to a cream with the water, then add to the pan and bring to the boil. Keep the mixture just bubbling, stirring gently, then add the sugar. Allow to go cold, then stir in the sliced banana.

To make the crunch, in a heavy frying pan melt the fat then add the brown sugar and cook, stirring, until it has melted in. Add all the remaining ingredients, and continue to cook over moderate heat, stirring constantly until the mixture is a rich chestnut brown. Turn out of the pan and allow to go cold and crisp.

To assemble, have ready 8 glasses - the bowl-shaped Paris goblets are ideal. Swirl the liqueur through the fromage frais to marble it, then arrange layers in each glass as follows: fruit compôte, fromage frais, crunch, fruit and finally crunch. Chill thoroughly before serving. (Can be made 1 day and served the next.)

Note For the crispest effect, the top layer of crunch can be sprinkled on 30 minutes before serving.

SUMMER FRUIT AND FROMAGE FRAIS BOWL

Serves 8.
Eat the same day.

Simple but succulent. The fruit can be varied as the season demands.

2 large peaches
2 fat bananas, peeled
1 lb (450 g) choice strawberries
1 tbsp lemon juice
2 tbsp grenadine or other bottled fruit syrup, or fruity liqueur such as Crème de Framboise or Crème de Cassis
10 fl oz (275 ml/1¼ cups) fruity fromage frais or Greek-style strained yoghurt

Slice the peaches (no need to peel), bananas and strawberries, sprinkle with sugar, then with the lemon juice and grenadine or liqueur. Leave in a cool place for the juices to flow for 2 hours. Drain off the juice, then fold it gently into the fromage frais or yoghurt to give a marbled effect. Blend fruit in gently, then chill thoroughly for 1 hour.

MARBLED STRAWBERRY CREAM

Serves 6.
Keeps 2 days under refrigeration.

A simple sweet that looks beautiful. The soured cream brings out the flavour of the strawberries in a most subtle manner.

1 strawberry jelly (gelatin mix)
juice of ½ lemon
1 lb (450 g) sliced strawberries, lightly sugared
10 fl oz (275 ml/1¼ cups) soured cream, fromage frais or Greek-style strained cow's-milk yoghurt

Make the jelly up to 1 pint (575 ml/2½ cups), then stir in the lemon juice. Allow to chill until syrupy, then stir in sugared strawberries and soured cream - it should have a marbled effect. Leave to chill until set in a glass dish.

A BRILLIANT BRÛLÉE

Serves 6–8.
Eat the same day.

This is a new and simplified - and slightly more economical - version of the luscious classic Crème Brûlée. Instead of using a pint of cream and eggs, this uses only a half-pint and a little custard powder. Also, since it is notoriously difficult to get the burnt sugar just right when done the traditional way under the grill (broiler), this has a little caramel poured on top of the vanilla-scented cream.

8 oz (225 g) raspberries
8 oz (225 g) blackberries
3 tbsp Crème de Framboise or other fruit-flavoured liqueur

For the flavoured cream
8 fl oz (225 ml/1 cup) milk
1 oz (25 g/2 tbsp) sugar
1 oz (25 g/2 tbsp) custard powder
8 fl oz (225 ml/1 cup) whipping cream
1 teasp vanilla essence (extract)

For the caramel
8 oz (225 ml/1 cup) granulated sugar
2–3 tbsp water

Put the fruit in a bowl and sprinkle with the liqueur. Leave at room temperature for at least 2 hours. Make a custard with the milk, sugar and custard powder and chill thoroughly.

Whisk the cream with the vanilla essence until it holds stiff peaks. Whisk the cold custard in the food processor until creamy (about 30 seconds), then fold into the cream. Divide the fruit and juice between 6–8 small soufflé dishes. Cover fruit with custard cream and chill while preparing the caramel.

Have ready in the sink a large bowl of cold water. Put the sugar in a heavy pan with enough water to moisten it. Heat sugar and water, stirring until clear, then boil until a rich brown caramel. Immediately plunge the base of the pan into the bowl of cold water to stop further cooking. Take the soufflé dishes from the refrigerator and cover the chilled creams with a thin layer of caramel. Chill until required.

VARIATION

PÊCHES BRÛLÉES

Serves 6–8.
Eat the same day.

flavoured cream and caramel as before
6 peaches
2 level tbsp caster (superfine) sugar
2 tbsp orange liqueur
1 tbsp lemon juice

Drop each peach into boiling water for 1 minute, then remove its skin. Slice the peaches into a bowl and sprinkle with the sugar, liqueur and lemon juice. Allow to stand for 2 hours, then divide between 6–8 small soufflé dishes. Cover with the cream, and then proceed as before.

LEMON DAINTY

Serves 6–8.
Eat the same day.
Leftovers keep 1 day under refrigeration.

This wondrous pudding has stood the test of several decades, and with its superb balance of sweet and tart, creamy and spongy, can still surprise and charm at the end of a dairy meal. However, I have now cut down the sugar content and increased the lemon juice. With the aid of a food processor it can be put together in a fraction of the time taken by the traditional method.

The pudding can be served either 1 or 2 hours after baking at room temperature or well chilled. As it separates into a creamy sauce topped with a light sponge, it's essential to use a dish of the right size - one that's too wide and shallow will result in a dry pudding.

This is delicious served with a sweetened fruit purée such as strawberry, blackberry, mango, or, for a dinner party, with the apricot sauce given below.

1 oz (25 g/2 tbsp) soft butter
4 oz (125 g/½ cup) plus 2 oz (25 g/¼ cup) caster (superfine) sugar
grated rind and juice of 2 lemons (5 tbsp juice)
3 large eggs, separated
1½ oz (40 g/⅓ cup) self-raising flour or 1½ oz (40 g/⅓ cup) plain (all-purpose) flour plus ⅓ teasp baking powder
12 fl oz (350 ml/1½ cups) milk

For the apricot sauce

3 oz (75 g/⅓ cup) granulated sugar
4 fl oz (125 g/½ cup) water
1 lb (450 g) fresh apricots, halved
1 tbsp lemon juice
1 tbsp apricot brandy

Grease an oven-to-table casserole at least 2 inches (5 cm) deep and of 3-pint (1.75 l/8-cup) capacity. Half-fill a roasting tin with boiling water, put it in the oven, and preheat to Gas No. 4 (375°F/180°C).

Put the butter, 4 oz caster sugar, lemon rind and juice, egg yolks and flour into a food processor or blender and process until creamy. With the motor running, add the milk through the feed tube and process until evenly mixed.

In a large bowl whisk the egg whites until they hold soft peaks, then whisk in the remaining sugar, a teaspoon at a time. Gradually pour the yolk mixture on to the meringue, folding the 2 together with a rubber spatula until evenly blended. Gently pour into the prepared dish and place in the tin of hot water. Bake for 35–40 minutes, until golden brown and firm to gentle touch. Serve at room temperature or well chilled.

To make the sauce, simmer the sugar and water in a wide-lidded pan until slightly syrupy, then add the apricots. Simmer until absolutely tender. Purée the contents of the pan in a blender or food processor with the lemon juice and apricot brandy. Chill thoroughly.

VARIATION

Divide the mixture between 6–8 small soufflé dishes or cocottes. Cook in the same way for the same amount of time.

Rich and Creamy

CHESTNUT PAVÉ

Serves 8–10.
Keeps 3 days under refrigeration.
Freeze 2 months.

A delectable dessert that can be made and frozen in advance, or refrigerated for several days before use.

4 oz (125 g) plain (semi-sweet) chocolate
4 oz (125 g/½ cup) butter
1 x 17 oz (475 g) can sweetened chestnut purée
5 fl oz (150 ml/⅔ cup) whipping or double (heavy) cream
2 level teasp caster (superfine) sugar
1 additional tbsp liqueur
27–30 crisp sponge fingers – about 2 packets (also known as boudoir biscuits)
5 fl oz (150 ml/⅔ cup) strong hot coffee (made with 4 level teasp instant coffee) flavoured with 1 tbsp rum, brandy or Tia Maria liqueur (optional)

Put the broken-up chocolate in a basin standing over a pan of very hot water and leave to melt (or microwave, uncovered on 100 per cent power for 1½ minutes). Cream the butter, then beat in the soft chocolate followed by the chestnut purée. Have ready a 2-lb (900-g) loaf tin, approximately 9 x 5 x 3 inches (22.5 x 12.5 x 7.5 cm) or an 8-inch (20-cm) round tin about 3 inches (7.5 cm) deep. Lightly grease the tin and then line the bottom with silicone paper.

Whip the cream, sweeten with the caster sugar and stir in the additional tablespoon of liqueur.

To assemble, divide the sponge fingers into 3 groups. Dip the unsugared side of the first group quickly in and out of the hot flavoured coffee, then lay on the bottom of the chosen tin. Spread with half the chestnut cream. Repeat with the second portion of biscuits and cream, and finally lay the remaining soaked biscuits on top.

This mixture must now be refrigerated for at least 12 hours.

To serve, run a knife round the tin to loosen the filling, then turn the cake out on to a serving dish. Mask with the flavoured whipped cream and decorate as required.

ISRAELI ICEBOX CAKE

Serves 12.
Keeps 3 days under refrigeration.
Freeze 2 months.

Like many modern Israeli recipes, I suspect this is really of American origin. However, it was brought back from Israel and the name has stuck. It is utterly delicious for a party, or half can be eaten and half frozen - it really is not worth making a smaller quantity than that specified.

6 oz (175 g) dessert (semi-sweet) chocolate
2 tbsp water
3 tbsp caster (superfine) sugar
16 fl oz (450 ml/2 cups) double (heavy) cream
5 fl oz (150 ml/$\frac{2}{3}$ cup) hot water with
2 level teasp instant coffee
30 crisp sponge fingers - about 2 packets
(also known as boudoir biscuits)
1 tbsp rum
2 oz (50 g/$\frac{1}{2}$ cup) toasted, skinned and chopped hazelnuts, walnuts or toasted almonds

The day before, put the chocolate, water and sugar into a pan over low heat. When smooth, add 6 fl oz (175 ml/$\frac{3}{4}$ cup) of the cream and bring to the boil. Immediately remove from the heat and refrigerate. Next day, put the chocolate mixture into a bowl, add 1 tablespoon of rum and beat or whisk until fluffy. Make the hot coffee.

To assemble, have ready a 2-lb (900-g) loaf tin, approximately 9 x 5 x 3 inches (22.5 x 12.5 x 7.5 cm) or an 8-inch (20-cm) round tin about 3 inches (7.5 cm) deep. Lightly grease the chosen tin, then line with silicone paper.

Divide the biscuits into 3. Take the first group, dip the unsugared side into the hot coffee, then place side by side, sugared side down, on the base of the tin. Spread with half the chocolate cream. Repeat with the second layer, the remaining chocolate and finally the third layer of biscuits.

The cake should now be refrigerated, then left a minimum of 12 hours before turning out.

To serve, run a knife round the tin to loosen the filling, then turn the cake out on to a serving dish. Whisk the remaining 10 fl oz (275 ml/1$\frac{1}{4}$ cups) cream with the tablespoon of rum until it holds soft peaks, then pipe or swirl over the cake. Scatter with the chopped nuts.

CHOCOLATE MOUSSE

Serves 4–6.
Keeps 4 days under refrigeration.
Freeze 3 months.

This recipe uses chocolate rather than jelly (gelatin) to achieve a mousse-like texture. It is particularly useful as it contains no dairy products and can therefore be served after a meat meal.

4 oz (125 g) plain dessert (semi-sweet) chocolate
4 large eggs, separated
2 teasp instant coffee dissolved in 3 teasp hot water
1$\frac{1}{2}$ tbsp Tia Maria or other coffee-, chocolate- or orange-flavoured liqueur
3 teasp caster (superfine) sugar

Break up the chocolate and stand in a basin over very hot (not boiling) water. Heat gently until melted, then remove from the heat (or melt, uncovered, for 1$\frac{1}{2}$ minutes on 100 per cent power in the microwave). Immediately drop in the egg yolks and beat vigorously until the mixture begins to thicken. Stir in the coffee and the liqueur. Allow to go quite cold. Beat the whites until they just hold soft peaks, then beat in the caster sugar. Pour the chocolate mixture into the bowl containing the egg whites and blend together. Spoon into 8 individual cups or a small soufflé dish. Leave to chill overnight.

IRISH LIQUEUR CHEESECAKE

Serves 8–10.
Keeps 3 days under refrigeration.
Freeze 3 months.

Chef Patron Peter Haden of Gregan's Castle Hotel in Eire actually serves individual cheese-cakes, rather cleverly using disposable plastic cups as individual timbale moulds. If you wish to emulate him, you will need to double the crumb mixture as given in the recipe. The whiskey reinforces the flavour of that in the liqueur but Peter Haden does advise caution – taste before you exceed the stated dose!

7 oz (200 g) digestive or oatcrumb biscuits, crushed to crumbs
2½ oz (65 g/5 tbsp) melted butter
¾ oz (20 g) powdered kosher gelatine
1½ lb (675 g/3 cups) cream cheese
5 fl oz (150 ml/⅔ cup) Irish Cream Liqueur
9 fl oz less 2 tbsp (250 ml/1 cup plus 2 tbsp) whipping cream
1 tbsp whiskey (preferably Irish)
2 egg whites
4 oz (125 g/½ cup) caster (superfine) sugar

For the garnish
a few frozen redcurrants or fresh Cape gooseberries

Crush the biscuits to fine crumbs either with a rolling pin or in the food processor and mix evenly with the melted butter. Pat evenly on the base of an 8-inch (20-cm) cake tin approximately 2 inches (5 cm) deep.

Put 3 tablespoons of cold water in a bowl, sprinkle on the gelatine, stir well, then heat over hot water until it clears (40 seconds on 100 per cent power in the microwave).

Put the dissolved gelatine, cheese and liqueur into the food processor and process until evenly blended – about 5 seconds (this can also be done by hand or with an electric mixer). Turn into a bowl. Whisk the cream with the whiskey until it holds soft peaks, then fold into the cream cheese mixture. Whisk the egg whites until they too hold soft peaks, then add the sugar a tablespoon at a time, whisking until very firm peaks are formed. Fold into the cream mixture. Spoon the mixture on top of the crumb crust and chill for at least 4 hours, or overnight. Run a sharp knife round the edge of the tin, then carefully turn out the cheesecake on to a serving platter. Garnish with the fruit.

Note For other cheesecakes, see 'Cakes' and 'Shavuot' chapters.

INDIVIDUAL CRÈME CARAMEL

Serves 5–6.
Keeps 2 days under refrigeration.
Do not freeze.

These luscious custards are made in the same way as the classic French sweet, but cooled in individual cocottes with the caramel sauce spooned over the *unmoulded* custards. Served topped with pouring cream, they make a marvellously delicate dessert.

For the custard

1½ oz (40 g/3 tbsp) caster (superfine) sugar
2 whole eggs plus 2 yolks
½ teasp vanilla essence (extract)
15 fl oz (425 ml/2 cups) full-cream milk

For the caramel sauce

6 oz (175 g/¾ cup) sugar
3 tbsp cold water
4–5 tbsp hot water

Preheat the oven to Gas No. 4 (350°F/180°C).

Put the sugar in a bowl and gradually whisk in the whole eggs, the egg yolks and the vanilla essence until evenly blended, using a balloon whisk (or blend in the food processor).

Heat the milk until steaming, then very slowly add to the eggs, whisking only until homogeneous - do not overwhisk or the custards will be full of holes.

Put 6 individual soufflé dishes or cocottes on a pad of newspaper in a roasting tin and fill with the custard. Half-fill the tin with very hot water, then place in the oven. Immediately turn down to Gas No. 3 (325°F/160°C) and leave for 40 minutes. Test by inserting a knife in the centre - it should come out almost clean and a custard will 'tremble' slightly when gently shaken. The custard will set completely as it cools. Chill thoroughly.

To make the sauce, mix the sugar and cold water in a heavy-based 8-inch (20-cm) saucepan or frying pan, put on the lid and cook over moderate heat for 3 minutes. Uncover, stir well to ensure the sugar has dissolved, then continue to cook, stirring occasionally, until a rich chestnut-brown caramel has formed. Cover the arm holding the pan with a tea-towel (to avoid splashes of the boiling mixture), then pour in the hot water.

Stir over moderate heat until the mixture is smooth and homogeneous, then chill until required.

To serve, pour a little chilled sauce on top of each custard and top, if you like, with pouring cream or creamy fromage frais.

Pavlovas and Torten

PAVLOVAS

Serves 8–10. Makes 2 x 9 inch (22.5 cm) layers.
Keeps 3 days under refrigeration.
Freeze 3 months.

Pavlovas, or 'schaum torten' as they are known on the Continent, are meringue sweets with a difference as they combine a crisp outer crust with an inside which has the texture of marshmallow. They can be baked as cake layers or piped into the shape of small or large cases for their filling of fruit and cream. Once baked and filled, they freeze extremely well. Unlike conventional meringues, they do not go soft once they are filled; in fact the texture and flavour are vastly improved after several hours under refrigeration.

As the meringues expand slightly in the oven, do not pipe shapes too close together. A selection of fillings follows the basic recipe.

2 level teasp cornflour (cornstarch)
8 oz (225 g/1 cup) caster (superfine) sugar
4 large egg whites
¼ teasp cream of tartar or 1 teasp vinegar
1 teasp vanilla essence (extract)

Mix the cornflour and the sugar in a bowl. Separate the eggs. Put the yolks into an airtight plastic container and refrigerate at once for another use within 24 hours. Put the whites into a large mixing bowl and add the cream of tartar (if used). Otherwise add a pinch of salt. Start whisking at low speed until the mixture is frothy, then increase the speed and whisk until the mixture stands in stiff but glossy peaks. Now start adding the cornflour/sugar mixture a rounded tablespoon at a time, beating until stiff after each addition. When all the sugar has been added and the mixture is a solid meringue, beat in the vanilla. Finally beat in the vinegar (if used). The mixture is now ready to shape.

Draw 2 8-inch (20-cm) circles on greaseproof paper, then lay each piece of paper on a flat baking tin and very lightly grease (or use silicone paper that does not need greasing). Pipe or spoon the meringue into 2 rounds, making sure that the round to be used for the top of the cake is neat and even.

Have the oven heated to Gas No. 2 (300°F/150°C). Turn down to Gas No. 1 (275°F/140°C). Put in the cakes and bake for 45 minutes–1 hour, changing the position of the layers at half-time. They are ready when the top feels really firm and crisp to the touch and the meringues come away easily from the paper when a spatula is slipped underneath.

To serve 12–16
6 egg whites
12 oz (350 g/1½ cups) sugar
3 level teasp cornflour (cornstarch)
generous ¼ teasp cream of tartar or 1½ teasp vinegar

Pipe into 2 10-inch (25-cm) circles.

LEMON PAVLOVA

Serves 8–10.
Keeps 3 days under refrigeration.
Freeze 3 months.

This is perhaps the most refreshing of all the variations. The sweet and sour filling makes a perfect contrast to the very sweet meringue and, conveniently, makes use of the egg yolks as well.

4 egg yolks
4 oz (125 g/½ cup) caster (superfine) sugar
5 tbsp lemon juice
finely grated rind of 1 lemon
10 fl oz (275 ml/1¼ cups) double (heavy) cream or
8 fl oz (225 ml/1 cup) non-dairy cream
2 layers Pavlova (4 egg white size)

Traditional method Put the yolks and sugar into a small thick-bottomed pan and beat with a wooden spoon until creamy. Stir in the juice and rind. Put over gentle heat and cook, stirring constantly, until the mixture thickens to the consistency of lemon curd. Do not boil. Take off the heat and keep on stirring for 1 or 2 minutes. It will keep on thickening with the heat of the pan. Turn into a bowl.

Microwave method Process the yolks, sugar, juice and rind for 30 seconds in the food processor or blender. Pour into a 2-pint (1.25-l/5-cup) jug or bowl and cook on 100 per cent power for 2 minutes, stirring well half-way. Cook for a further 30 seconds and stir well again – the mixture should resemble a thick custard. If not, cook for a further 30 seconds. Take out and stir for 30 seconds – it will then continue to thicken even more.

Chill in the freezer or refrigerator until completely cold – 30–40 minutes. Whip the cream until it holds firm peaks, then gently whisk in the lemon custard a tablespoon at a time. Use to fill the layers. Freeze until 20 minutes before serving, then leave at room temperature – the filling will be the consistency of soft ice-cream when it is served.

BERRY PARTY PAVLOVA

Serves 10–12.
Keeps 3 days under refrigeration.
Freeze 3 months.

juice (3 tbsp) and grated rind of 1 lemon
4 tbsp water
2 level tbsp sugar
1 lb (450 g) thickly sliced fresh or frozen berries – strawberries, raspberries, loganberries, tayberries
2 tbsp Crème de Framboise or orange-flavoured liqueur (optional)
10 fl oz (275 ml/1¼ cups) whipping or double (heavy) cream
2 Pavlova layers (6-egg-white size)

Put lemon juice and rind, water and sugar into a small pan and bring to the boil. Immediately pour over the fruit and leave for 1 hour.

Drain the syrup into a bowl and add the liqueur if used and the cream. Whisk until thick as whipped cream. Fold in the fruit and use the mixture to sandwich the Pavlova layers. Chill thoroughly.

SWISS CHOCOLATE PAVLOVA

Serves 8–10.
Keeps 3 days under refrigeration.
Freeze 1 month.

Another filling that makes use of the egg yolks left over from the Pavlova.

3 tbsp water
1 level tbsp instant coffee
8 oz (225 g) plain dessert (semi-sweet) chocolate
4 egg yolks
10 fl oz (275 ml/1¼ cups) double (heavy) cream or 8 fl oz (225 ml/1 cup) non-dairy cream
1 level tbsp caster (superfine) sugar
1 teasp vanilla essence (extract)
2 Pavlova layers (4-egg-white size)
toasted almonds

Bring to the boil, stirring constantly, the water and the coffee, remove from the heat and add the chocolate broken into bits. Stir until smooth, then beat in the egg yolks 1 at a time, and cool. Fold in the whipped cream, sweetened with the sugar and flavoured with vanilla. Use to fill the Pavlova layers and chill overnight. Serve sprinkled with toasted almonds.

PINEAPPLE AND KIRSCH PAVLOVA

Serves 8–10.
Keeps under refrigeration 3 days.
Freeze 1 month.

3 large slices fresh pineapple
2 level tbsp caster (superfine) sugar
2 tbsp Kirsch
10 fl oz (275 ml/1¼ cups) double (heavy) cream
2 Pavlova layers (4-egg-white size)

Cut the fresh pineapple into pieces, sprinkle with sugar and Kirsch and leave for 2 hours for the juices to flow. Put the cream into a bowl and whisk until it begins to thicken. Whisk in the fresh pineapple syrup. Fold in the fruit and spoon between the layers. Chill for at least an hour, but preferably overnight.

PISCHINGERTORTE

Serves 10.
Keeps 4 days under refrigeration.
Do not freeze.

One of my Viennese-born friends first introduced me to this unusual gateau. It consists of several large (about 8–10 inches/20–30 cm in diameter) wafers, sandwiched with a delicate nut cream. According to Gretel Beer, the Viennese food authority, Pischinger was the name of the firm that made these distinctive wafers (which are rather like a superior kind of ice-cream wafer), but I've also read that he was a famous Viennese patissier - perhaps he had a cottage industry! Certainly you can't make the cake without them - they're usually to be found in shops specializing in unusual continental foods.

1 packet Karlsbader Oblaten wafers or similar

For the filling
4 oz (125 g/½ cup) unsalted butter or soft margarine
4 oz (125 g/½ cup) granulated sugar
6 tbsp cold water
2 egg yolks
4 oz (125 g) plain (semi-sweet) chocolate, melted
2 tbsp chocolate flavoured liqueur
3 oz (75 g/¾ cup) ground hazelnuts

For the topping
2 oz (50 g/¼ cup) butter
4 oz (125 g) plain (semi-sweet) chocolate
1 tbsp chocolate-flavoured liqueur

To make the filling, have the soft fat ready in a bowl. In a small heavy-based pan, dissolve the sugar in the water, stirring until no grains of sugar can be seen. Boil rapidly without stirring until the mixture forms a short thread - 6 minutes at a fast boil. To test, lift a few drops of the syrup on a teaspoon, moisten the index finger and thumb with cold water and take a small pinch of syrup from the spoon; a short thread should be formed when the thumb and finger are opened and closed rapidly (syrup at this stage is heavier than thick canned-fruit syrup).

Whisk the egg yolks well, then whisk in the syrup gradually until the mixture cools and becomes thick and creamy. Beat this into the soft fat, together with the melted chocolate, liqueur and hazelnuts. Chill for half an hour, or until thick enough to spread.

To make the topping, melt the butter and chocolate together, either over hot water or in the microwave (1½ minutes on 100 per cent power). Stir well and add the liqueur.

Assemble the torte on a baking sheet lined with silicone paper. Using 5 wafer layers, sandwich them with filling, leaving the top one uncovered. Pour over the topping evenly, so that it covers the top and sides. Leave for 5 minutes, then mark into 10 even sections like the spokes of a wheel. Decorate with a few hazelnuts.

COFFEE PRALINE TORTE

Serves 8–10.
Keeps 3 days under refrigeration.
Freeze 1 week uncovered, 3 months wrapped in foil.

A superb combination of textures and flavours.

10 fl oz (275 ml/1¼ cups) whipping cream or 8 fl oz (225 ml/1 cup) non-dairy cream
3 teasp boiling water
3 teasp caster (superfine) sugar
1 tbsp Tia Maria or Sabra liqueur
2 Pavlova layers (4-egg-white size) piped into 2 12 x 7 inch (30 x 17.5 cm) rectangles and baked as before

For the praline
4 oz (125 g/½ cup) granulated sugar
2 oz (50 g/½ cup) slivered almonds

To make the praline, line a small tin with silicone paper. Put the sugar and nuts into a wide frying pan or heavy-based saucepan and cook without stirring over moderate heat (shaking the pan occasionally) until the sugar and nuts are chestnut in colour. Pour at once on to the paper and leave to set - about 15 minutes. Then break in pieces and crush, either in a food processor or with a rolling pin, until like coarse sand.

Whip the cream until it hangs on the whisk, then add the cooled coffee, the sugar and the liqueur and whisk until thick. Stir in the praline. Lay 1 rectangle of meringue on a serving dish (a small tray is good), spread with the filling, then carefully position the second rectangle on top. Freeze until required. Bring out and leave at room temperature 20 minutes before serving.

LIME AND AVOCADO SCHAUM TORTE

Serves 8–10.
Keeps 4 days under refrigeration.
Freeze 1 week unwrapped, 4 weeks wrapped in foil.

2 Pavlova layers (4-egg-white size)

For the filling
2 medium very ripe avocados
2 tbsp lemon juice
1 teasp grated lemon rind
10 fl oz (275 ml/1¼ cups) double (heavy) cream or
8 fl oz (225 ml/1 cup) non-dairy cream
3 level tbsp icing (confectioners') sugar
6 tbsp best-quality lime cordial
2 oz (50 g/½ cup) blanched pistachios, coarsely chopped

Make Pavlova layers as directed, but pipe or spoon on to 2 rectangles 12 x 7 inches (30 x 17.5 cm) marked on the silicone paper. Bake and allow to go cold as directed.

To make the filling, purée the peeled and stoned avocados with the lemon juice and rind, using a blender or food processor. Whisk the cream until it is softly whipped, add the sugar and lime cordial and continue to whisk until it stands in peaks. Fold into the purée and then fold in the pistachios.

If the torte is to be frozen for more than a week, have ready a sheet of foil large enough to enfold it completely. Otherwise it can be assembled directly on to a serving tray or dish and does not need wrapping for the freezer. Put 1 piece of meringue on the foil or dish, gently spoon the filling in an even layer on top. Cover with the other piece. Freeze. Remove from the freezer 20 minutes before serving, when the filling will be like soft ice-cream.

RASPBERRY ICE-CREAM PAVLOVA

Serves 8–10.
Keeps 3 days under refrigeration.
Freeze 1 month.

8 oz (225 g) sweetened semi-thawed frozen raspberries
1 small packet vanilla ice-cream (250 ml)
5 fl oz (150 ml/⅔ cup) double (heavy) cream
2 teasp lemon juice
2 Pavlova layers (4-egg-white size)

Have the raspberries half-thawed and the ice-cream as soft as cream. Whip the double cream with the lemon juice until it holds its shape, then fold in the ice-cream and raspberries. Use to fill the layers and put in the freezing compartment of the refrigerator. Take it out 10 minutes before you intend to serve it. Cut in wedges like a cake.

KUMQUAT BLITZ TORTE

Serves 10–12.
Keeps 3 days under refrigeration.
Complete cake freezes 1 month.

For this 'showstopper' of a dessert, alternate layers of smooth sponge and crisp meringue are sandwiched with a luscious filling of glazed Israeli kumquats. Do be sure to use a special fine or sponge self-raising flour as it's essential for the melt-in-the-mouth texture. An alternative filling would be slightly sweetened frozen raspberries, using their juice and 3 tablespoons of Crème de Framboise raspberry liqueur to beat into the cream. This makes a very large torte. For a smaller version serving 6–8, use 8½-inch (22-cm) tins and the same amount of filling, but 4 oz (125 g/½ cup) fat, 4 oz (125 g/½ cup) sugar, 4 egg yolks, 2 tbsp liquid and 4 oz (125 g/1 cup) flour to make the cake layers; for the meringue use 4 egg whites and 6½ oz (¾ cup plus 1 tbsp) caster (superfine) sugar.

For the cake
5 oz (150 g/⅔ cup) soft butter or margarine
5 oz (150 ml/⅔ cup) caster (superfine) sugar
pinch of salt
5 egg yolks
2 tbsp milk or water
4 oz (125 g/1 cup) sponge self-raising flour or 4 oz (125 g/1 cup) cake flour plus 1 teasp baking powder

For the meringue
5 egg whites
7½ oz (215 g/1 cup) caster (superfine) sugar
2 oz (50 g/½ cup) flaked almonds
2 teasp sugar mixed with ½ teasp cinnamon

For the filling
4 oz (125 g/½ cup) granulated sugar
7 fl oz (200 ml/¾ cup plus 2 tbsp) water
8 oz (225 g) kumquats or sections of satsuma
10 fl oz (275 ml/1¼ cups) whipping cream or 8-9 fl oz (225-250 ml/1 cup plus 2 tbsp) non-dairy cream
3 tbsp Cointreau
1 tbsp lemon juice

To make the cake, preheat the oven to Gas No. 4 (350°F/180°C). Grease 2 x 9½-inch (24-cm) sandwich or springform tins, and line with circles of silicone paper. Cream the butter, sugar and salt until fluffy. Add the yolks and milk or water, then fold in the flour. Divide between the prepared tins and smooth level.

For the meringue, whisk the whites until they hold floppy peaks, then add the sugar gradually, whisking until stiff peaks are formed. Spread half over each layer of cake mixture, scatter with almonds and then the cinnamon sugar. Bake for 30 minutes, or until the meringue is nicely browned. Cool for a few minutes, then ease on to wire racks. When cold, freeze or cover with paper until the next day.

To glaze the kumquats, dissolve the sugar and water in a wide pan, then add the sliced kumquats in 1 layer. Cook uncovered until the fruit is softened and glazed and the syrup is thick. (Don't allow it to caramelize or the fresh flavour will be lost.) Partly whip the cream, then beat in the kumquat syrup, liqueur and lemon juice until thick and fold in the fruit.

To serve, several hours in advance, lay 1 layer, meringue side down, on a plate, spread with the fruit and cream and top with the other cake, meringue side up. Chill before serving.

The Chilled Soufflé or Bavaroise

With the proliferation of 'creamy' ready-to-serve desserts based on cultured milk products such as yoghurt and fromage frais in all their various manifestations, this is not so popular now as it was in the 1970s and 1980s. However, the Bavaroise recipes that follow have such a superb flavour that they can hold their own on any sweet trolley. As they each have a very intense flavour, non-dairy cream can be used in them for serving after a meat meal.

The aim is to use just enough 'gel' to hold together a blend of fruit, custard, meringue and (when used) whipped cream, and still preserve a finished texture that resembles fluffy, flavoured whipped cream rather than jelly (gelatin). This is most easily achieved when the fruit purée, cream and meringue are all of a similar texture, so that they can be folded together easily.

This type of sweet can be presented in a collared soufflé dish or set in individual cups; or it may be poured into a loose-bottomed cake tin, previously side-lined with soft sponge fingers, from which it can be eased just before serving.

Curiously, Bavaroises of varying quality appear on almost every restaurant menu in Israel - usually as 'Bavarian Cream'!

BANANA BAVAROISE WITH AN ORANGE SALAD

Serves 12–16. For 6–8, halve the quantities and set in a 6-inch (15-cm) tin or in individual glass dishes.
Keeps 3 days under refrigeration.
Freeze 3 months.

4 eggs, separated
2 oz (50 g/¼ cup) caster (superfine) sugar
2 tbsp lemon juice
4 tbsp orange juice
2 teasp each grated orange and lemon rind
1 level tbsp (½ oz/15 g) kosher gelatine or 1 orange jelly (gelatin mix)
1½ lb (675 g) ripe bananas weighed in their skins (5 large)
1 pint (575 ml/2½ cups) whipping cream or non-dairy cream, or 10 fl oz (175 ml/1¼ cups) each of double (heavy) and single (light) cream, chilled
2 tbsp orange liqueur (Cointreau, Curaçao or Grand Marnier)
2 teasp caster (superfine) sugar
approx. 30 sponge fingers – about 2 packets (also known as boudoir biscuits) (optional)

For the orange salad
6 large oranges
2 oz (50 g/¼ cup) caster (superfine) sugar
1 tbsp lemon juice

For the garnish
toasted almonds

In the blender or food processor, put the egg yolks, sugar, fruit juices, rind and gelatine (if used) and blend for 40 seconds, then add the peeled bananas cut in chunks and blend for a further 30 seconds, or until absolutely smooth. Turn into a pan with a thick base and stir over gentle heat until the mixture is steaming (do not let it boil) and is thick enough to coat the back of the spoon like a custard. Add the jelly (gelatin mix) if used and stir until dissolved. Remove from the heat, turn into a bowl or plastic container and stir until it stops steaming.

Put the chilled cream into a bowl and whisk until it is thick enough to hang on the whisk. Take out a fifth and put into a smaller bowl, then continue to whisk it until it holds stiff peaks. Cover and refrigerate until needed for decoration. To the remaining four-fifths gradually add the liqueur, whisking until it holds floppy peaks only. Rinse the beaters thoroughly, then whisk the egg whites until they hold very floppy peaks. Add the caster sugar and continue to whisk until they hold soft peaks (they won't stand up straight).

Using a metal spoon, fold the liqueur cream into the chilled banana mixture, followed by the whites. The mixture can now be spooned into a soufflé dish or serving bowl, or moulded as follows. Select a 9-inch (22.5-cm) cake tin with a loose bottom. Take the sponge fingers (if used) and stick then side by side all round the inside. To do this most easily, moisten the sugary side of each biscuit with a dab of apricot jam and stick it to the tin. When all the biscuits are in place, gently pour in the banana mixture.

Now make the orange salad by removing the peel and pith from each orange using a sharp, serrated knife. Cut out the sections and put into a container. Scatter with the sugar and pour over the lemon juice. Cover and refrigerate with the Bavaroise.

To serve, if a tin has been used, stand it on 1 of smaller diameter and pull down the sides, then put the sweet (still standing on the base of the tin) on to a round plate or silver tray. Decorate the Bavaroise with some of the orange sections and the reserved cream. Scatter with toasted almonds. Serve in slices with a spoonful of orange salad.

LEMON BAVAROISE

Serves 12.
Keeps 3 days under refrigeration.
Freeze 3 months.

This has a delectable fresh lemon flavour

which makes it especially refreshing. It is equally successful with non-dairy cream.

3 eggs, separated
6 oz (175 g/¾ cup) caster (superfine) sugar
3 fl oz (75 ml/⅓ cup) lemon juice
2 teasp grated lemon rind
2 level teasp gelatine or 1 lemon jelly (gelatin mix)
3 fl oz (75 ml/⅓ cup) water
15 fl oz (425 ml/2 cups) whipping cream or non-dairy cream
26–28 sponge fingers or packet of trifle sponges

With an electric beater whisk the yolks until thickened, then whisk in the sugar. Whisk in the juice and rind until mousse-like. If gelatine is used, soak in the water for 5 minutes, then place over hot water until clear (40 seconds on 100 per cent power in the microwave). If jelly is used, heat with the water until dissolved. Add to the first mixture, then put in the freezer until the consistency of unbeaten egg white - about 15 minutes (longer in the refrigerator). Take out and whisk until smooth again.

Whisk the cream until it hangs on the whisk, then add almost all to the egg mixture (save about a quarter for decoration).

Whisk the egg whites until they hold soft peaks, then fold them in. Have ready a loose-bottomed 9-inch (22.5-cm) tin which has been greased and then lined, sides and bottom, with sponge fingers (see Banana Bavaroise above for the method). Pour in the mixture, top with any remaining sponge fingers. Chill overnight.

To serve, run a knife round the sides of the tin, then ease the cake out by standing on a tin of smaller diameter. Put on a serving dish, still on the cake-tin base. Decorate with the remaining whipped cream and some fruit - for example, sliced bananas or sugared soft fruit.

VARIATION

LIME BAVAROISE

Replace the lemon rind and juice with the same quantity of fresh lime. Or use 3 fl oz (75 ml/⅓ cup) best-quality lime cordial and reduce the caster sugar to 4 oz (125 g/½ cup).

ORANGE AND STRAWBERRY BAVAROISE

Serves 12.
Keeps 2 days under refrigeration.
Freeze 3 months without strawberries.

The gentle flavour of oranges is notoriously difficult to capture in a cold sweet as it is easily masked by that of eggs and cream. In this recipe I have used concentrated orange juice to solve the problem. The result is a wonderfully refreshing Bavaroise which marries well with fresh berries. It can be set in a ring of sponge fingers like the Lemon Bavaroise, in a crystal bowl, in demi-tasse cups or small soufflé dishes.

3 whole eggs
2 egg yolks
3 oz (75 g/⅓ cup) caster (superfine) sugar
juice and grated rind of ½ large lemon
6 fl oz (175 ml/¾ cup) concentrated frozen orange juice, left at room temperature for ½ hour
½ oz (15 g) kosher gelatine or 1 lemon jelly (gelatin mix) dissolved in 4 tbsp water
8 fl oz (225 ml/1 cup) whipping or non-dairy cream
2 tbsp Cointreau or other orange-flavoured liqueur
1 lb (450 g) small strawberries

For the garnish
tiny sprigs of mint

Put the whole eggs and egg yolks into a basin and beat until frothy, preferably with an electric whisk. Gradually add the sugar and continue to whisk until the mixture becomes thick and mousse-like, and a little of the mixture dropped from the whisk remains on the surface for a few seconds.

Gradually add the lemon juice and grated rind and the undiluted orange juice to the egg mixture, whisking all the time. Finally add the gelatine or melted jelly.

Whisk the cream and liqueur until thick enough to hold its shape. Gradually fold the egg mixture into the cream using a rubber spatula. Slice the strawberries thinly and fold into the orange mixture.

Spoon into whatever dish is being used and chill for at least 4 hours. Garnish with sprigs of mint.

BERRY LIQUEUR MOUSSE

Serves 8.
Keeps 2 days under refrigeration.
Freeze 2 months.

This has a marvellous fruit flavour and is especially good served half-frozen.

5 oz (150 ml/⅔ cup) water
1 kosher lemon jelly (gelatin) mix
1 lb (450 g) fresh strawberries, fresh or frozen raspberries or mixed berries
caster (superfine) sugar to taste
2 egg whites
2 teasp caster sugar
10 fl oz (275 ml/1¼ cups) whipping cream
4 sponge fingers (boudoir biscuits)
3 tbsp Curaçao, Cointreau or Kirsch

Put the water and jelly into a saucepan and heat gently until jelly dissolves (or 1½ minutes on 100 per cent power in the microwave). Sieve or blend the fruit until smooth (raspberries will need to be sieved). Add to jelly. Measure and if necessary add a little sugar and enough water to make mixture up to 15 fl oz (425 ml/2 cups). Chill until the mixture is the consistency of unbeaten egg white.

Whisk the egg whites until they form stiff peaks, then whisk in the 2 teaspoons of caster sugar. Whisk the cream until it is thick enough to hang on the whisk, reserving a quarter to decorate the mousse. Fold the remaining cream into the fruit mixture, followed by the meringue. Crumble the sponge fingers and sprinkle with the liqueur, then fold into the fruit mixture. Spoon into a glass bowl, a soufflé dish or into 8 wine glasses, and chill for several hours. Decorate with a few strawberries or raspberries coated in caster sugar and the remaining cream.

CHRISTINE'S GÂTEAU A LA CHÂTAIGNE, SAUCE CARAMEL BLOND (*Chestnut Liqueur Slice*)

Serves 10–12.
Keeps 3 days under refrigeration.
Freeze 2 months.

This unusual cake (perhaps better described as a baked, chilled soufflé), which is a speciality of a noted woman chef from the Ardèche area of France, is served on a delicate caramel sauce. Start preparations 1 or 2 days early.

7 oz (200 g/¾ cup plus 2 tbsp) butter
4 eggs, separated
1 x 18 oz (500 g) can sweetened chestnut purée

For the sauce

8 oz (225 g/1 cup) granulated sugar
3 fl oz (75 ml/⅓ cup) water
15 fl oz (425 ml/2 cups) whipping cream
4 tbsp Greek yoghurt or creamy (8%) fromage frais

For the garnish

2 oz (25 g/¼ cup) toasted flaked almonds or sliced preserved chestnuts

Have ready a long slim 2-lb (900-g) loaf tin, 11 x 5 x 3 inches (27.5 x 12.5 x 7.5 cm), greased lightly with oil.

Melt the butter over very low heat (3 minutes, covered with a paper towel on 80 per cent power in the microwave). Off the heat, stir in the egg yolks and add chestnut purée. Whisk the whites until they hold stiff glossy peaks, then carefully fold them into the chestnut mixture. Spoon into the tin and level off. Cover tightly with foil and place in a roasting tin half-full of hot water. Bake in a moderate oven, Gas No. 4 (350°F/180°C), for 45–50 minutes, or until a skewer comes out clean from the centre.

Chill overnight. To unmould, loosen cake from sides of tin, then plunge into a bowl of very hot water for 20 seconds. Remove the foil, then turn out on to a long dish.

To make the sauce, dissolve the sugar in the water in an 8-inch (20-cm) heavy-based pan, stirring continuously, then allow to boil until syrupy and a golden chestnut in colour. Plunge the base of the pan in a bowl of cold water to stop it cooking. Meanwhile, heat the cream until steaming (3 minutes on 100 per cent power in the microwave), then *gradually* add to caramel. (Keep your arm covered in case of splattering.) Whisk until smooth, then whisk in the yoghurt or fromage frais.

Serve the cake whole, sprinkled with almonds, or spoon a thin layer of sauce over each dessert plate, arrange a slice of cake on top and decorate with almonds or preserved chestnuts.

FROZEN DESSERTS

Frozen Desserts in a Hurry

Poires Belle Hélène	(see p. 361)	with Florida Orange Sauce	(see p. 366)
Ice cream with Fudge Sauce	(see p. 366)	with Pineapple Sauce	(see p. 366)
		with Fresh Raspberry Sauce	(see p. 366)

With the help of the freezer and (if possible) one of the new generation of domestic-size sorbetières, it is now quite simple to make ice-creams and sorbets at home.

Home-made ice-creams and sorbets are a rare delight. By using choice ingredients, one can achieve glorious flavours and textures without the addition of any additives or synthetic flavourings.

It is also possible to create superb *parev* frozen desserts, using non-dairy cream combined with definite flavourings such as coffee, chocolate or caramel.

THE INGREDIENTS

Fruit purée The fruit for purées must be fully ripe and of a deep flavour. An electric blender purées soft fruit very quickly, but fruits with seeds (raspberries, blackberries, etc.) must in addition be pressed through a fine sieve or mouli. Harder fruits, such as blackcurrants, need to be softened by cooking before they can be sieved. If possible leave sweetened fruit purées to mature in flavour overnight.

Purées freeze well. When using a frozen purée, thaw it overnight in the refrigerator, or allow 20–30 minutes at room temperature. You can hurry it up by standing the container in hot water, or defrosting in a microwave.

Sugar When added to a hot mixture any kind of sugar will dissolve and is therefore suitable. But when added to a cold mixture, as in a frozen mousse, icing (confectioners') sugar or caster (superfine) sugar are the only kinds that will dissolve. The proportion of sugar in an ice-cream is important for the texture as well as the flavour. The ice-cream will taste less sweet when frozen than when liquid.

Cream Cream should be whisked until light and thick but not stiff and buttery, otherwise it becomes difficult to incorporate smoothly into the ice-cream mixture. Whipping cream (35% butterfat) is ideal, otherwise use equal amounts of double (heavy) and single (light) cream (48% and 18% butterfat respectively). Cream whips more readily if cold, so keep in the refrigerator until needed. Provided the ice-cream is well flavoured, non-dairy (vegetarian) cream may be used.

Storage Time

Ice-cream can be stored in the freezer for 3 months. For storage time in the ice-making compartment of a refrigerator, consult the instruction book. Never refreeze ice-cream as the texture will be ruined and there is a danger of food poisoning, particularly with egg-based mixtures.

Serving Suggestions for Ice-cream and Sorbets

Ice-cream can be scooped, piped or turned out of a mould. This can be done several hours before dinner and the ice-cream or sorbet can then be left in the freezer until it is time to transfer it to the refrigerator shortly before serving, when the final garnish of fruit, nuts or cream can be added.

A bombe is frozen in a special metal mould or in a mixing bowl, then turned out and either surrounded with a ribbon of fruit sauce, or masked with it.

Scoops of the ice can be piled up in a bowl and decorated with little sprigs of fresh currants or berries in season.

An ice-cream slice is frozen in a long loaf tin, then turned out on a narrow plate and decorated with small clusters of toasted nuts or with a complementary fruit.

Coffee demi-tasses or little porcelain pots make charming containers for ice-cream. They can be decorated with shavings of chocolate or with sugared fresh fruit.

Sorbets can be frozen until they are the consistency of whipped cream, then piped in whirls on a tray. The whirls are quickly refrozen and then arranged just before serving in wineglasses or on individual glass plates and decorated with slices of exotic fruit.

Several scoops of different sorbets look spectacular in long-stemmed glasses with wide, shallow bowls.

A solid metal ice-cream scoop is a useful investment. Otherwise use a spoon with a round bowl, dipped in a jug of boiling water.

Ice-Cream Parfaits Plus

All the ice-creams in this section are based on a meringue into which is folded icing (confectioners') sugar, egg yolk, whipped cream and flavouring. (Non-dairy cream may be substituted if desired.) This mixture produces an exceptionally smooth ice-cream simply by freezing in an ordinary domestic freezer. It has a 'soft scoop' texture, so it can be taken straight from the freezer to the table. As the ice-cream will freeze well for up to 3 months, I have given relatively large amounts, sufficient for 8–10.

Note Contaminated raw eggs can cause food poisoning. Before making any of the ice-creams that use uncooked egg yolks, it is advisable to seek advice from public health authorities on the current health situation.

VANILLA PARFAIT

Serves 8–10.
Freeze 3 months.

3 large eggs, separated
salt
3 oz (75 g/¾ cup) icing (confectioners') sugar
10 fl oz (275 ml/1¼ cups) double (heavy), whipping or non-dairy cream
2 teasp good-quality vanilla essence (extract)

Put the whites into a bowl, then add a pinch of salt. Whisk until they hold stiff peaks when the beaters are withdrawn, then add the icing (confectioners') sugar a tablespoon at a time, whisking after each addition. Gently whisk in the yolks until the colour is even.

Put the cream and the vanilla essence into a

bowl and whip until it hangs on the whisk when lifted from the bowl. (Don't overwhip or the cream will turn buttery.) Carefully fold into the meringue mixture. Turn into a plastic container (which can also be used for storage) and leave to freeze for about 6 hours.

VARIATIONS

COFFEE PARFAIT

Proceed as above but instead of vanilla, flavour with 3 tablespoons of instant coffee dissolved in a tablespoon of boiling water and then cooled. An optional extra is to add 1 tablespoon of coffee-flavoured liqueur or 2 oz (50 g/½ cup) chopped walnuts lightly fried in a nut of butter or margarine.

LIQUEUR PARFAIT

This can be made with Kirsch (to serve with stewed cherries) or with Cointreau or Curaçao (to serve with peaches or raspberries). Proceed as for Vanilla Parfait, but add 2 tablespoons of the chosen liqueur to the egg yolks instead of the vanilla.

RUM AND RAISIN PARFAIT

The preparation must be started 48 hours in advance, when 4 oz (125 g/¾ cup) seedless raisins are put into a small container, covered with 3 tablespoons of rum, and the container closed.

Make as for Vanilla Parfait, but whisk any unabsorbed rum with a strong cold coffee solution - 1 tablespoon of instant coffee dissolved in 1 tablespoon of boiling water - into the cream. Fold the raisins into the mixture at the end.

CHOCOLATE PARFAIT

Melt 4 oz (125 g) plain (semi-sweet) chocolate in a basin standing in a pan of simmering water or in the microwave. Stir into the meringue mixture after the yolks, with the vanilla essence, then proceed as directed.

IRISH COFFEE PARFAIT

This is excellent served with slices from a choice pineapple.

Extra ingredients:

2 tbsp instant coffee dissolved in 1 tbsp boiling water then cooled
4 tbsp Irish cream liqueur

Proceed as with Vanilla Parfait. As you are whipping the cream until it thickens, whisk in 2 tablespoons of instant coffee that has been dissolved in 1 tablespoon of boiling water and then cooled, together with 4 tablespoons of Irish cream liqueur. Keep whisking until the cream hangs on the whisk when it is lifted from the bowl. Continue as before.

FROZEN GINGER PARFAIT

Serves 8–10.
Freeze 3 months.

This luscious dessert is a speciality of the superb Croque en Bouche restaurant at Malvern Wells in Worcestershire. I have taken some liberties with chef Marion Jones's inspired recipe to 'domesticate' it. The flavour vastly improves after 48 hours in the freezer.

For the meringue

3 egg whites
½ teasp cream of tartar
6 oz (175 g/¾ cup) caster (superfine) sugar
1 teasp cornflour (cornstarch)

For the syrup

1 tbsp instant coffee
2 teasp sugar
2 teasp boiling water

For the parfait

15 fl oz (425 ml/2 cups) double (heavy) cream or 12 fl oz (275 ml/1½ cups) parev (non-dairy) cream

1 tbsp coffee liqueur
3 pieces stem ginger, finely chopped
3 teasp of the ginger syrup

For the garnish
2 Cape gooseberries per serving

First make the meringues. Put the egg whites into a mixing bowl and add the cream of tartar. Mix the sugar and cornflour together. Whisk the whites until they hold floppy peaks, then add the sugar mixture a tablespoon at a time, whisking until stiff after each addition. Spoon or pipe meringues on to sheets lined with silicone paper, leaving 2 inches (5 cm) between them. Preheat the oven to Gas No. 2 (300°F/150°C). Bake for 1 hour, until crisp to the touch and easy to lift off the paper. Allow to go quite cold, then break into roughly 1-inch (2.5-cm) pieces.

Make the coffee syrup by mixing all the ingredients until they dissolve. Chill well.

Whip the cream to the soft-peak stage, then whisk in the liqueur and half the coffee syrup. Fold in the ginger, meringues and ginger syrup. Marble the mixture with the remaining coffee syrup.

Spoon either into individual timbale moulds, petit pots or little soufflé dishes, or into a 2-lb (900-g) loaf tin lined with silicone paper. Freeze for at least 24 hours, and preferably 48, before serving straight from the freezer.

Garnish with the Cape gooseberries.

LUSCIOUS LEMON PARFAIT

Serves 8–10.
Freeze 3 months.

A creamy ice-cream with a beautiful sharp lemon flavour.

grated rind of 1 lemon
juice of 2 large lemons (6 tbsp)
3 large eggs, separated
salt
3 oz (75 g/⅓ cup) and 1 oz (25 g/2 tbsp) caster (superfine) sugar
10 fl oz (275 ml/1¼ cup) double (heavy) or non-dairy cream

Grate the lemon rind very finely, juice the 2 lemons and leave together in a basin. Put the whites into a bowl and add a pinch of salt. Whisk until they hold stiff peaks when the beaters are withdrawn, then add the 3 oz sugar a tablespoon at a time, beating after each addition. Gently whisk in the yolks until the colour is even.

Put the cream and the lemon juice and rind into a bowl with the further 1 oz sugar and immediately whisk until it is thick. (Don't leave standing or the lemon juice may curdle the cream.) Once the cream is thick enough to hang on the whisk when lifted from the bowl, carefully fold the mixture into the meringue.

Turn into a plastic container (6 x 4 inches/15 x 10 cm) and freeze for about 6 hours. Leave in the refrigerator half an hour to soften just before serving.

VARIATIONS

FROZEN LEMON SLICE

For the crumb crust
10 digestive biscuits (graham crackers), crumbed
2 oz (50 g/¼ cup) melted butter or margarine
pinch of cinnamon
1 level tbsp icing (confectioners') sugar

Line a deep ice-tray or a long plastic container measuring about 11 x 4 x 1½ inches (27.5 x 10 x 4 cm) with a strip of greased greaseproof paper, extending it above the top of the container. Combine all crust ingredients. Sprinkle two-thirds of this mixture on to the greaseproof paper, then cover with the lemon ice-cream mixture. Cover with the remaining crumbs. Freeze until firm (about 2–3 hours).

To serve, knife round the edge of the tin, put a long serving plate on top, then carefully reverse and turn out the lemon slice. Remove the greaseproof paper.

ICE-CREAM CUPS

Divide unfrozen lemon ice-cream mixture between 8–10 coffee cups. Freeze. Garnish with chopped nuts or crushed macaroons.

NUT CRUNCH PARFAIT

Serves 12–15.
Freeze 3 months.

This has a glorious butterscotch flavour – very appealing to teenage palates.

For the nut crunch
2 rounded tbsp golden (corn) syrup
1½ oz (40 g/3 tbsp) butter or margarine
scant 4 oz (125 g/½ cup) light brown sugar
scant 4 oz (125 g/1 cup) chopped mixed nuts

For the ice-cream
4 eggs, separated
4 level tbsp icing (confectioners') sugar
10 fl oz (275 ml/1¼ cups) whipping cream or 8–9 fl oz (225–250 ml/1 cup–1 cup plus 2 tbsp) non-dairy cream
1½ teasp vanilla essence (extract)

Line a small baking tin with silicone paper. In a heavy saucepan put the golden syrup, butter and sugar and stir over gentle heat until melted, then add the nuts, turn up the heat and continue stirring until the mixture is a rich golden brown (but stop before it turns chestnut colour, by which time it will have caramelized). Immediately pour on to the tin and leave to set while you prepare the ice-cream.

Whisk the whites until they hold soft peaks, then whisk in the icing sugar a tablespoon at a time, whisking until stiff after each addition. Whisk in the yolks until just blended. Whisk the cream and vanilla until the mixture holds soft peaks, then fold it into the meringue. Leave in the bowl and put in the freezer.

As soon as the toffee is set hard, break it up into approximately 1-inch (2.5-cm) chunks and process in the food processor until a coarse powder. After the ice-cream has been in the freezer for 30 minutes, take it out and carefully stir in the toffee. Pour into a large loaf tin or put in a bowl (for a bombe) or in a large plastic container, and return to the freezer. Leave 24 hours before serving (this allows the flavour to develop fully, the ice-cream will actually freeze in 6 hours).

VARIATION

ICED CHOCOLATE AND CARAMELIZED WALNUT TERRINE

Make the Nut Crunch Parfait above using chopped walnuts (or pecans) instead of the mixed nuts. While it is freezing for 30 minutes put 10 chocolate digestive biscuits in the freezer as well.

Line the base and narrow sides of a deep ice-tray or a long plastic container or loaf tin measuring about 11 x 4 x 1½ inches (27.5 x 10 x 4 cm) with a strip of silicone or greaseproof paper.

After 30 minutes take out the biscuits and crush to crumbs (most easily done in the food processor), then mix with 2 oz (50 g/¼ cup) melted butter or margarine.

Sprinkle two-thirds of this mixture on the lining paper. Take out the ice-cream and stir in the powdered toffee, then spoon over the remaining crumbs, patting down well. Freeze until firm (2–3 hours).

To serve, run a knife round the edge of the tin, put a long serving plate on top then carefully reverse and turn out the terrine. Remove the lining paper. Refreeze until required.

Just before serving, decorate with clusters of seasonal fruits such as redcurrants or tiny seedless grapes.

BISCUIT TORTONI

Serves 8–10.
Freeze 3 months.

The almond flavour of the liqueur is reinforced by that of the crunchy little biscuits which are folded through the ice-cream. It is superb for a party sweet as it is always frozen in individual containers.

3 eggs, separated
pinch of salt
2½ oz (65 g/½ cup) icing (confectioners') sugar
10 fl oz (275 ml/1¼ cups) whipping cream or
8 fl oz (225 ml/1 cup) non-dairy cream
2 tbsp Amaretto di Saronno or other almond-flavoured liqueur
½ teasp vanilla essence (extract)
1 x 3½ oz (85 g) packet of Amaretti or ratafia biscuits
2 oz (50 g/½ cup) toasted almond nibs
autumn fruits

Whisk the egg whites with a pinch of salt until they hold stiff peaks, then whisk in the icing sugar a tablespoon at a time, whisking until stiff after each addition. Whisk in the yolks just enough to blend the colours evenly.

Whisk the cream with the liqueur and essence until it holds soft peaks. Crush the biscuits to a coarse powder. Mix the biscuit crumbs and the toasted almonds together and reserve a rounded tablespoon for garnish.

Fold the whipped cream into the meringue, together with the almond and biscuit mixture. Divide between individual containers - demi-tasses, petits pots or little soufflé dishes. Sprinkle the tops evenly with the reserved nut mixture.

Freeze for at least 12 hours before serving. The Tortoni does not need softening but can be served straight from the freezer, garnished with the fruit.

HALVA AND PISTACHIO ICE-CREAM

Serves 8–10.
Freeze 3 months.

Halva gives both a delectable taste and a very smooth texture to this ice-cream. And the recipe works successfully whether it's made with dairy or non-dairy cream.

For a dinner party, it looks splendid in a loaf shape with the bright green of the pistachio nuts revealed as each slice is cut. As the mixture is rather rich, it's a good idea to balance it with a garnish of delicately flavoured fruit such as sliced strawberries, lightly sugared redcurrants or poached fresh peaches.

The texture is soft enough to serve straight from the freezer.

2 oz (50 g/½ cup) shelled pistachio nuts
6 oz (175 g) halva
10 fl oz (275 ml/1¼ cups) whipping cream or non-dairy cream
3 eggs
2 oz (50 g/¼ cup) caster (superfine) sugar

Blanch the pistachio nuts by covering them with boiling water, cooking on 100 per cent power for 1 minute in the microwave, or bubbling for the same time on top of the stove. Drain well, then slip off the skins. Chop 1 oz in half and set them aside to dry on a plate. Crumble the halva until it looks like coarse sand.

Whisk the cream until it holds soft peaks, then gently fold in the halva. Without washing the beaters, whisk the eggs and sugar until pale cream in colour and greatly increased in volume - this takes about 5 minutes using an electric whisk.

Fold the eggs gently into the cream mixture, together with the halved pistachio nuts. Spoon the mixture into a loaf tin measuring approximately 12 x 5 inches (20 x 12.5 cm), or if you prefer to serve in scoops, into a large plastic container. Freeze for 1 hour, then stir gently to redistribute the nuts. Leave undisturbed for at least another 3 hours, though it's preferable to leave it overnight so the flavour can ripen. Before dinner, turn out on to a serving plate and return to the freezer.

Serve garnished with the remaining nuts and accompany with the chosen fruit.

PLOMBIERE ALLA TORINESE (*Chestnut Ice-cream*)

Serves 6–8.
Freeze 3 months.

2 eggs
10 fl oz (275 ml/1¼ cups) creamy milk (or light cream)
2 oz (50 g/¼ cup) caster (superfine) sugar
1 can (8½ oz/240 g) unsweetened chestnut purée
1 tbsp brandy or rum
5 fl oz (150 ml/⅔ cup) double (heavy) cream

For the garnish
Chestnuts canned in syrup

Process eggs until well blended in the food processor or blender. Heat the milk until bubbling around the edges, then add to beaten eggs, processing until evenly blended. Cook in a heavy-based pan over moderate heat, stirring constantly until the mixture is thick enough to coat the back of a wooden spoon (the bubbles on the surface will disappear as the custard 'takes'). Take off the heat at once and stir in the sugar. Chill well.

Turn the chestnut purée into a bowl, then stir in the rum or brandy followed by the cooled custard. Fold in the whipped cream, then freeze in a sorbetière according to the instructions. Transfer to the freezer until required. Without a sorbetière, freeze 2 hours, then stir vigorously and leave to freeze.

NESSELRODE PUDDING

Serves 8–10.
Freeze 3 months.

A rich custard-based chestnut ice-cream, studded with sultanas (white raisins) and cherries. Freeze in a loaf tin to make a beautiful dinner party presentation.

10 fl oz (275 ml/1¼ cups) single (light) cream
4 egg yolks
5 oz (150 g/⅔ cup) sugar flavoured with vanilla pod or 4½ oz (135 g/½ cup) sugar and ½ oz (15 g/1 tbsp) packet vanilla sugar
4 oz (125 g/½ cup) unsweetened chestnut purée
2 oz (50 g/⅓ cup) sultanas (white raisins)
4 fl oz (125 ml/½ cup) Amontillado (medium) sherry or Marsala
2 oz (50 g/⅓ cup) chopped glacé (candied) cherries
10 fl oz (275 ml/1¼ cups) double (heavy) cream

For the garnish
chocolate squares

Heat the single cream until steaming, pour on to the yolks and sugar in a blender or food processor and blend for 30 seconds. Cook in a heavy-based pan over very gentle heat, stirring constantly until thick enough to coat the back of a wooden spoon. Do *not* allow to come to the boil (it is thick enough when bubbles on the surface disappear – for peace of mind, cook the custard in a double saucepan. Stir into the chestnut purée and chill.

Put the sultanas in a small bowl and pour over the sherry or Marsala. Microwave on 100 per cent power, covered, for 1½ minutes. Leave to cool, then stir into the custard with the glacé cherries.

Whip the double cream until it hangs on the whisk, then fold into the custard. Freeze in a sorbetière according to the instructions. Alternatively, freeze until almost solid, then turn sides to centre and stir very well. Turn into a narrow 2-lb (900-g) loaf tin and freeze solid. Turn out on to a long dish and decorate with chocolate squares.

PEACH COUPE, CHERRIES JUBILEE

Serves 6.

This is superb made with fresh poached peaches or fat nectarines (see Compôte of Fresh Peaches, p. 322). With canned fruit it's another story.

1 large can or jar of Morello (sour red) cherries or 1 lb (450 g) stewed cherries
2 level tbsp caster (superfine) sugar (more if cherries are very sour)
1 level tbsp cornflour (cornstarch)
1 tbsp lemon juice
1 piece (3 inches/7.5 cm) lemon peel
2 tbsp cherry brandy
6 poached peaches or nectarines
1 recipe Vanilla Parfait (p. 355)

Drain and stone the cherries, reserving the juice (there should be about 8 fl oz/225 ml/1 cup). If using fresh cherries, use stewing syrup. Mix sugar and cornflour, then stir in cherry juice and lemon juice and strip of peel. Cook gently until thick and clear - about 3 minutes. Take off heat, remove the peel and stir in the cherry brandy and fruit. Leave to go cold in a dish suitable for heating up (either in the oven or on top of the stove).

To serve, put a whole peach or 2 halves in each sundae glass and top with ice-cream. Pour over the hot cherry sauce and serve at once.

POIRES BELLE HÉLÈNE

Serves 8.

A bed of ice-cream scoops, arranged in a shallow entrée dish, is topped with choice William pears, poached in syrup. Mask each serving with this wonderful bitter-sweet chocolate sauce.

8 oz (225 g) plain (semi-sweet) chocolate, broken up
2 level teasp instant coffee made up with 4 fl oz (125 ml/$\frac{1}{2}$ cup) hot water
1 oz (25 g/2 tbsp) caster (superfine) sugar
nut of butter or margarine
2 teasp rum or brandy

Put all the ingredients except the rum or brandy in a bowl and microwave, uncovered, on 100 per cent power for $2\frac{1}{2}$ minutes, then stir and if not completely liquid, microwave for a further 30 seconds.

Alternatively, put the hot coffee in a small thick-bottomed pan. Add the broken chocolate and sugar, then stir over gentle heat until mixture is smooth and of coating consistency.

Remove from heat and add the rum and fat. Serve warm.

To serve later, store in an airtight container under refrigeration (keeps for weeks). To reheat, put in a serving bowl and stand it in a pan of simmering water. Reheat, stirring until warm.

Fruit Sorbets

Water-ices always used to be featured in the formal banquets of the nineteenth and early twentieth centuries to 'refresh' the palate half-way through the traditional 12-course meals - those menus which have survived from the Jewish weddings of the period almost always feature a lemon-flavoured 'ice'.

In Jewish households today sorbets have won renewed popularity as a refreshing finale to a meat meal, though they can also play a similar role in a dairy meal which has perhaps featured a rich and creamy dessert.

Freezing a sorbet in a sorbetière This is really child's play - one simply switches on and pours the cold mixture into the machine. The stirring paddle and the cold do the rest. After 20 or 30 minutes, the sorbet has been smoothly frozen. It will have a soft, almost ice-cream-like texture and can then be transferred to the freezer to firm up.

Freezing a sorbet without a sorbetière Without the automatic stirrer built in to a sorbetière, if the sorbet is to be smooth rather than crystalline on the tongue, it is essential to whisk the mixture several times during the freezing process in order to ensure that the ice crystals that form will be as small as possible. This is the procedure. An hour before preparing the sorbet mixture, set the freezer to 'fast freeze'. Freeze the cooled sorbet mixture in a fairly shallow dish until semi-frozen - after about 3 hours. Turn into the food processor and process for 45 seconds, until the mixture looks creamy and lighter in colour (or use a balloon whisk or electric whisk). Freeze again until semi-frozen, then process the sorbet again as before. Finally, pulse in the whisked egg whites if used. Freeze again until required.

Note An hour before serving, check the consistency of the sorbet - if 'soft-scoop', leave in the freezer. If very hard, remove to the refrigerator just before dinner. If, however, you have already arranged it in scoops in a serving bowl, there should be no need to remove from the freezer until just before serving.

If you are using wine in a sorbet recipe, you will find that the alcohol slows down the freezing process.

THREE-FRUIT SORBET

Serves 6–10 (according to use).
Freeze 3 months.

This has a particularly refreshing flavour. If an electric sorbetière is used, add the whisked egg white with the sweetened juices at the beginning and freeze together. This sorbet should be just the right texture even when taken straight from the freezer.

rinds and juices of 1 large orange, 1 large lemon, 1 ripe lime
extra orange juice (see below)
5 oz (150 g/$\frac{2}{3}$ cup) granulated sugar
8 fl oz (225 ml/1 cup) water
1 egg white

Put the finely grated fruit rinds and the juices into a measuring jug and make up to 12 fl oz (350 ml/1$\frac{1}{2}$ cups) with additional orange juice. Put aside to allow the juices to absorb the flavouring from the rinds. In a small pan stir the sugar and water over moderate heat. When the sugar dissolves, boil steadily but gently for 8 minutes, then cool until the syrup stops steaming. Mix with the juice and rind, and chill thoroughly for several hours.

With a sorbetière, freeze according to the maker's instructions. Without a sorbetière, put into a plastic container and fast-freeze for 3 hours, until semi-frozen. Break up into chunks if necessary, then process in a food processor for 45 seconds - this can be done with an electric whisk, but it is an important stage in making a creamy sorbet. Return to the container and freeze again until semi-firm. Whisk the egg white until it holds soft peaks, process the sorbet for a further 45 seconds and then pulse in the egg white until it disappears. Freeze until firm - a further 5 hours.

VARIATION

FOUR-FRUIT SORBET

This time use the rinds and juices of 1 large orange, 1 large lemon, 1 tangerine or satsuma and 2 tablespoons of lime cordial, and proceed as before.

MORELLO CHERRY SORBET

Serves 6–8.
Freeze 3 months.

A very simple sorbet which depends on the use of well-flavoured cherries.

1 lb (450 g) Morello (sour red) or other tart fresh or frozen cherries
approx. 5 oz (150 g/⅔ cup) caster (superfine) sugar

Stone the cherries, then put in a blender or the food processor together with the sugar and blend until absolutely smooth. Put in the sorbetière and freeze for 20 minutes (or follow instructions for freezing without a sorbetière, p. 362).

Remove from the machine and pile into a glass or other dish. Freeze until required. Does not freeze rock hard.

Note With sweet cherries use 1 lb (450 g) frozen cherries, 2 tablespoons of water, 4 oz (125 g/½ cup) sugar and 1-2 tablespoons of lemon juice.

ELDERFLOWER SORBET

Serves 6–8.
Freeze 3 months.

This has a delicate lemon flavour with a background scent of muscatel. Quite delectable! Gather the flowers in late June–early July. Smell them to make sure they have a gorgeous muscat perfume, then put into a bag and refrigerate as quickly as possible. To use, make sure they are not bug-infested - they must not be washed - then trim each cluster down to 2 inches of the green stalk. Use the clusters whole.

8 oz (225 g/1 cup) sugar
1 pint (575 ml/2½ cups) water
8 clusters of elderflower
thinly pared rind of 2 fat lemons
3 fl oz (75 g/⅓ cup) fresh lemon juice

Dissolve the sugar in the water over moderate heat, stirring, then bring to the boil and bubble fiercely for 7 minutes. Remove from the heat, add the clusters of elderflower and the lemon rind, cover and leave to infuse for 3 hours. Strain the syrup into a jug and stir in the lemon juice. Chill well. Freeze in a sorbetière (or follow instructions for freezing without a sorbetière, p. 362).

Leave in the refrigerator for 30 minutes before serving.

MANGO AND GINGER SORBET WITH A COMPÔTE OF MANGOES, STRAWBERRIES AND KUMQUATS

Serves 8–10.
This dessert will freeze for 2 months.

No sugar syrup is used in this delicately flavoured sorbet, so the perfume of the mangoes comes through strong and clear.

For the sorbet
2 large ripe mangoes, each 10–12 oz (275–350 g)
6 tbsp fresh orange juice
3 tbsp fresh lemon juice
1 teasp grated lemon rind
½ teasp ground ginger
5 oz (150 g/⅔ cup) caster (superfine) sugar
1 egg white (optional, see below)

For the compôte
2 large, ripe mangoes
8 oz (225 g) kumquats, washed and sliced
3 tbsp caster sugar dissolved in 3 tbsp lemon juice
1 lb (450 g) choice strawberries

Set the freezer to 'fast freeze'. Peel the mangoes for the sorbet. Cut the flesh away from the stone, then cut it all in rough 1-inch (2.5-cm) chunks. Purée with the juices, rind, ginger and sugar (using either a blender or a food processor) until the sugar has dissolved - about 1 minute.

The mixture can now be put into an electric sorbetière and frozen according to directions.

Otherwise turn the purée into a plastic container and freeze 3 hours. Have the egg white ready, whisked until it holds stiff peaks. Whisk the purée by hand or machine until it lightens in colour - 45 seconds in the food processor or blender, 1 minute with an electric whisk - then immediately fold in the egg white, return to the container and refreeze until solid - for at least 6 hours.

Start making the compôte - the day before if you like. Peel the mangoes, then slice the flesh neatly and arrange in a shallow serving dish with the sliced kumquats. Sprinkle with the lemon syrup, cover with clingfilm (saranwrap) and refrigerate.

To serve, about 2 hours before, arrange the strawberries, thickly sliced, on a plate and spoon over some of the lemon syrup. Re-cover and leave at room temperature until ready to serve, then add to the other fruit. At the beginning of the meal, transfer the sorbet to the refrigerator to soften. Serve in scoops with the fresh fruit compôte.

RASPBERRY AND REDCURRANT SORBET

Serves 6–8 moderate servings.
Freeze 3 months.

A sorbet with a rich, deep flavour. If you make it for a special occasion, it's a good idea to pipe or spoon it into glasses when it comes out of the sorbetière or when it's frozen to a thick whipped cream consistency. In any case give the sorbet in glasses 10 minutes, the bulk-frozen sorbet 30 minutes, at room temperature before serving.

6 oz (175 g/¾ cup) sugar
2½ fl oz (65 ml/⅓ cup) water
4 oz (125 g) fresh or frozen redcurrants
2 tbsp lemon juice
2 fl oz (50 ml/¼ cup) orange juice
1 lb (450 g) fresh or frozen raspberries

Dissolve the sugar in the water, stirring over moderate heat, then bubble 3 minutes and set aside.

Heat the redcurrants until the juices run (3 minutes on 100 per cent power in the microwave), then beat down with a wooden spoon and add the fruit juices.

If the raspberries are frozen, defrost slightly, then purée in the food processor. Put through the finest sieve of a food mill, together with the redcurrant mixture. Stir in the syrup. Chill for several hours or overnight. (If frozen fruits have been used, the mixture will be chilled enough after an hour.)

If using a sorbetière, freeze for 25 minutes, then spoon into glasses (see above) or freeze in a covered plastic container.

Using the freezer, turn into a shallow container and freeze for 3–4 hours until softly frozen. Turn into the food processor for 1 minute, refreeze and repeat. Freeze until firm - 3 hours or overnight.

WHITE MOSS GEWÜRZTRAMINER SORBET

Serves 10.
Freeze 2 months.

The characteristic spiciness of the wine comes through strong and clear in this superb recipe, a speciality of Peter Dixon, chef at White Moss House, in the Lake District.

10 oz (275 g/1¼ cups) sugar
14 fl oz (400 ml/1¾ cups) water
3 fl oz (75 ml/⅓ cup) orange juice
4 tbsp lemon juice
9 fl oz (250 ml/1 cup plus 2 tbsp) Gewürztraminer
2 egg whites

Dissolve the sugar in the water. Simmer, uncovered, for 10 minutes, then leave to go cold. Strain the fruit juices, then mix together with the wine and the sugar syrup. Put in the chilled sorbetière. When the sorbet mixture is slushy (after about 20 minutes), beat the egg whites until they hold glossy, slightly floppy peaks, then add to the mixture in the machine and continue to freeze until firm (it never goes hard). Remove to the freezer.

Without a sorbetière, freeze as for the Muscat Sorbet (see this page).

LAMBRUSCO AND RASPBERRY SORBET

Serves 8.
Freeze 3 months.

This is the perfect in-between-course sorbet, refreshing and not too sweet. However, if you prefer, it can be served at the end of the meal with a fruit salad of fresh mixed berries which have been allowed to stand for several hours in a syrup made from 3 tablespoons of fresh lemon juice and sugar, warmed together until dissolved.

5 oz (150 g/⅔ cup) granulated sugar
1 pint (575 ml/2½ cups) Lambrusco or other 'frizzante' (semi-sparkling) young red wine
grated rind of 1 bright-skinned orange
6 small sprigs of mint
8 oz (225 g) fresh or frozen raspberries

Several hours before you intend to make the sorbet, dissolve the sugar in the wine over medium heat, then add the orange rind and mint leaves and bubble for 2 minutes. Add the raspberries, crushing them into the syrup with a fork, then cool and refrigerate until quite cold. Lift out and discard the mint, then push the contents of the pan through a fine sieve or the finest mesh of a mouli.

Freeze for 30 minutes in a sorbetière, put in the freezer (still in its container) until an hour before serving, then reprocess in the sorbetière for 5 minutes, or until creamy. Spoon or pile into small glasses or 1 large bowl and put back in the freezer until needed.

Without a sorbetière, freeze the wine and syrup mixture until semi-frozen, then whizz in a food processor for 45 seconds twice at 2-hour intervals, or until smooth and creamy.

MUSCAT SORBET

Serves 6–8.
Freeze 3 months.

The luscious muscatel flavour of the wine is faithfully preserved in this light and refreshing sorbet. Contrary to custom, I like to serve it at the end rather than in the middle of the meal, in place of the glass of pudding wine that I find too often overwhelms the dish it is meant to partner.

Small brandy glasses make elegant containers of just the right capacity for the sorbet.

9 oz (250 g/1¼ cups) granulated sugar
11 oz (300 ml/1⅓ cups) water
zest of a lemon (removed with a potato peeler)
½ bottle (13 fl oz/375 ml/1½ cups plus 2 tbsp) Muscat or similar sweet white dessert wine
4 tbsp fresh lemon juice
5 tbsp orange juice
1 egg white
2 teasp sugar

Put the sugar and water into an 8-inch (20-cm) pan, bring to the boil, stirring until the sugar is dissolved, then simmer for 5 minutes to make a syrup. Turn into a bowl, add the lemon zest, leave to go absolutely cold, then remove the zest and mix the syrup with the wine and fruit juices.

To freeze in a sorbetière, freeze for 20 minutes until slushy, then whisk the egg white until frothy, whisk in the sugar until peaky, then add gradually to the sorbet (a teaspoon is helpful for this job when using a domestic-sized machine with a small aperture). Freeze for another 10 minutes (it will still be very soft), then turn into a plastic container and leave in the freezer overnight.

To freeze in a domestic freezer, turn into a shallow container or ice-cube tray and freeze down as quickly as possible (on fast-freeze) until semi-frozen - about 5 hours. Turn into the food processor and process for 45 seconds (or use a balloon whisk). Add the stiffly whisked egg white and sugar and continue to freeze for several hours, or overnight.

To serve, arrange small scoops of the sorbet in wine-glasses and return to the freezer until required. Serve at once as the sorbet melts very quickly.

ICE-CREAM SAUCES

These are ideal for an 'ice-cream bar' for a children's party - serve them over vanilla or a matching flavour of ice-cream. All these sauces keep under refrigeration for 4 days and freeze 6 months.

FUDGE SAUCE

Serves 8.

A scrumptious sauce - it thickens as it cools.

3 oz (75 g/⅓ cup) brown sugar
2 rounded tbsp golden (corn) syrup
2 oz (50 g/¼ cup) butter
1 x approx. 6 oz (170 g) can evaporated milk

Place all the ingredients in a small, strong saucepan and heat gently, stirring constantly, for about 5 minutes, until they are well blended. *Do not boil.* Serve hot or cold.

FLORIDA ORANGE SAUCE

Serves 8.

4 oz (125 g/½ cup) butter (preferably unsalted)
4 oz (125 g/½ cup) caster (superfine) sugar
3 tbsp orange juice
2 teasp grated lemon rind
2 oz (50 g/⅓ cup) seedless raisins

Melt the butter and sugar in a saucepan and bring to the boil slowly. Stir in orange juice, lemon rind and raisins. Serve hot. Can be reheated.

PINEAPPLE SAUCE

Serves 6.

2 level tbsp sugar
1 level tbsp cornflour (cornstarch)
rind and juice of 1 orange
2 teasp lemon juice
juice strained from 1 x 15 oz (425 g) can of pineapple to make 10 fl oz (275 ml/1¼ cups) with the orange and lemon juices (add a little orange or pineapple cordial if necessary)
finely cut-up pineapple from the can
2 tbsp Curaçao or Cointreau (optional)

Mix together the sugar and cornflour, then add the juices and rind, blending smoothly. Bring to the boil, simmer for 3 minutes, then add the finely cut-up pineapple and the liqueur (if used). Leave until cold.

FRESH RASPBERRY SAUCE

Serves 8.

The perfect 'melba' sauce for serving with fresh poached peaches and vanilla ice-cream. It freezes remarkably well and can be kept for a week under refrigeration. It can also be used to flavour milk shakes.

1 lb (450 g) ripe raspberries
5 oz (150 g/⅔ cup) granulated sugar

Push the fresh fruit through a sieve, then put into the food processor or blender with the sugar. Process for 3 minutes, or until the sauce has thickened and no sugar can be felt.

VARIATION

FRESH STRAWBERRY SAUCE

Use only 3 oz (75 g/⅓ cup) sugar to 1 lb (450 g) fruit, but add with 2 tablespoons lemon juice. There is no need to sieve the fruit; put it straight into the blender with the sugar.

BAKING

PASTRY

Pastry in a Hurry

Pastry, whether it is made with oil, margarine or butter, is an integral part of the Jewish culinary scene all over the world, mainly because when made with a *parev* (neutral) fat it provides the most satisfying dessert that can be served after a meat meal.

The Austrian, Hungarian and German Jews make a sweet and caky 'muerbteig' pastry; the Sephardim the multi-layered filo pastry; the English a shortcrust; the Americans their own version of flaky pastry for pies; the Danes a superb flan pastry; and the French the meltingly tender pâté sucrée. Meanwhile, every Jewish housewife, wherever she may live, makes some kind of strudel paste, whether it is made with oil or butter, and stretched, pulled or rolled.

In this chapter I give what I consider to be, from long years of experiment, the optimum recipes to use for various kinds of sweet pastry dishes (for savoury ones see index). With the increased awareness of the dangers of a diet that contains too high a proportion of fat, the use of pastry in the Jewish kitchen has decreased dramatically. However, there are many occasions - for entertaining, celebrating and rejoicing in the Festival traditions of the past - when it seems appropriate to serve pastry-based dishes. You will find them in this chapter in all their different delicious manifestations.

The Basic Principles of Pastry-making

The complimentary phrase 'a light hand with the pastry' means just what it says; over-vigorous addition of fat to flour (especially with rubbed-in pastry) can result in a heavy, dry texture. While I give explicit directions for making the different types of pastry within the recipe itself, there are certain basic principles common to all kinds.

The well-balanced pastry recipe has a high ratio of fat to flour (the fat never weighing less than half the weight of the flour). It is the fat content that makes pastry tender, and too high a proportion of flour that can make it tough. Too much liquid makes pastry hard, while too little makes it crumbly and dry, so just sufficient liquid to bind the dry ingredients together needs to be used.

All pastries, unbaked or baked, freeze well. The exception is *baked* filo pastry, which tends to crumble when frozen.

The oven temperature must be high enough to cause the starch grains in the flour to burst and so enable it to absorb the fat before it melts and leaks out of the dough.

The detailed method and ingredients for each type of pastry are given in its particular section or in individual recipes.

NOTES ON THE INGREDIENTS

Flour Unless otherwise specified, always use plain (all-purpose) rather than self-raising flour - the pastry will be crisper and go stale less quickly. Self-raising flour is used only in some of the more cake-like pastries. Wheatmeal (81 per cent extraction) flour - which is a compromise between the 100 per cent wholemeal flour that contains all the bran and nutriments of the wheat and the regular white flour (70 per cent extraction) from which they have been mostly removed - makes excellent pastry, both sweet and savoury. It can be used as a direct replacement for the white flour specified.

Sugar Only caster (superfine) and icing (confectioners') sugar should be used to mix pastry. Granulated will overbrown and spot the pastry as it does not dissolve so readily.

Fats I have specified the fat I consider appropriate for each pastry. Margarine may be substituted for butter, though if it is the soft variety the pastry will be more difficult to handle. (Try freezing the carton of margarine beforehand.)

Equipment Electric food processors and mixers do not necessarily make better pastry, but they do make it more quickly and easily, as well as making the even addition of the liquid much more simple. However, it is essential to make sure that the fat is not rubbed in too far, otherwise the pastry will not take up enough water and will be both difficult to roll and crumbly to eat.

A rolling pin about 16 inches (40 cm) long and without handles is superior to a shorter one with handles, as it is much easier to roll the pastry into an even layer. Metal and enamel flan and pie tins help pastry to brown more evenly than heatproof pottery or ceramic. This difficulty can be partly overcome by baking the dish on a metal tray which has been put in the oven as it heats up (this is unnecessary with a fan-assisted or forced-air oven).

Batch baking and freezing Nothing is more time-saving than a stock of ready-to-roll-or-bake frozen raw pastry. This can be stored in 1-inch-thick (2.5-cm) blocks or rounds, or rolled and moulded into pie and flan dishes. Ready-to-fill part-baked flan cases are also extremely useful.

To freeze pastry Wrap in clingfilm (saranwrap) or foil, then put in a plastic freezer bag.

To defrost Allow 1-inch-thick (2.5-cm), 8-oz (225-g) blocks of pastry 2–3 hours to thaw out at room temperatures. Then treat as freshly made.

It is equally possible to freeze 2-crust pies raw or cooked, whichever is convenient (see recipes for detailed instructions).

Freeze fruit pies and unfilled pastry cases for up to 3 months.

Fruit Pies

SHORTCRUST PASTRY FOR FRUIT PIES

Sufficient for a 2-crust plate pie 10 inches (25 cm) in diameter or an 8–9 inch (20–22.5-cm) pie 1 inch (2.5 cm) deep.
Freeze 3 months.
Keeps 2 days under refrigeration.

This recipe produces a short but slightly flaky pastry with a fine flavour that keeps fresh for 2–3 days under refrigeration.

8 oz (225 g/2 cups) plain flour
pinch of salt
2 level tbsp icing (confectioners') sugar
4 oz (125 g/½ cup) butter or margarine
1 oz (25 g/2 tbsp) white fat
1 egg yolk
juice of ½ lemon (1½ tbsp)
1–2 tbsp icy water
1 egg white and granulated sugar for glaze (if used)

To mix by hand or machine Into a large mixing bowl sift the flour, salt and icing sugar. Cut the fats in 1-inch (2.5-cm) cubes, then rub gently into the flour mixture with the tips of the fingers of both hands. (An electric mixer at low speed can be successfully used provided the whisk is used, as paddle-type beaters tend to crush the fat). When the fat has been rubbed in enough, the mixture will resemble floury, coarse crumbs, with no particle larger than a small pea. Do not over rub beyond this stage or the mixture will become sticky, and as it will not be able to absorb the correct amount of liquid, the baked pastry will be crumbly and dry.

Beat together the egg yolk, lemon juice and 1 tablespoon of icy water. Sprinkle this liquid into the bowl, using a cupped hand to turn the mixture over and over, until all the particles are moistened but not wet. Add a little more water if necessary. Gather the dampened mixture together and lightly mould it into a ball.

To mix by food processor To make successful pastry with a food processor, it is best to process both the dry and the liquid ingredients at the same time and to stop processing at the moist 'crumb' stage. This prevents the fat being rubbed in too finely, which makes it very difficult to roll out. The method below produces a lovely short pastry that is easy to roll out.

Use the metal blade and put the dry ingredients and the well-chilled fat (cut into 1-inch/2.5-cm chunks) into the bowl. Mix the liquid ingredients to blend (including eggs if used), then turn on the machine and pour them down the feed tube, pulsing only until the mixture looks like a moist crumble, then tip it into a bowl and gather together into a dough.

With both methods, turn the pastry on to a board or counter-top sprinkled with a very light layer of flour. Knead it gently with the finger-tips to remove any cracks. Divide it into 2 portions, flatten each into a 1-inch-thick (2.5-cm) disc, wrap in foil or clingfilm (saranwrap), and put in the refrigerator for at least half an hour. (At this stage it can be frozen, or refrigerated for 2 days.)

To finish the pie, get ready a 10-inch (25-cm) pie plate or an 8–9 inch (20–22.5-cm) pie dish, 1 inch (2.5 cm) deep. Have the required filling ready in a bowl. Put 1 of the portions of pastry on a lightly floured pastry board. Lightly flour a rolling pin and, using short, sharp strokes, start rolling the pastry into a circle about 11 inches (28 cm) across. Keep making quarter-turns of the pastry, so that the circle is kept even and does not stick to the board. Do not turn the pastry over as raw flour would then be rolled into both sides and the pastry would be toughened. Carefully ease the pastry circle on to the back of the rolling pin, then lay it gently into position in the pie dish.

Spoon in the filling. Lift up the filled dish in one hand and, holding a sharp knife vertically with the other, cut off the overhanging pastry all the way round. Knead these remains into the second portion of pastry and roll that out in exactly the same way, to fit the top of the pie. With a pastry brush, dampen the edge of the bottom crust all the way round and then gently transfer the top crust via the rolling pin to fit the top. With the side of the index finger press the 2 crusts together. Use a dull-bladed knife to nick them together all the way round, making 'cuts' every ⅛ inch (0.3 cm). Alternatively, you can 'scallop' the edges together by pinching with the fingers and thumb.

To glaze the pie Whisk the white of an egg until it is frothy. Make 6 cuts in the centre of the top crust (to allow steam to escape), then paint the egg white evenly over the top. Scatter a thin layer of granulated sugar over the pie and bake as directed. (A sheet of foil on the shelf below is good insurance against any dripping, hot fruit juice.)

PERFECT APPLE PIE

Serves 6 generously.
Cooked pie will keep 4 days under refrigeration.
Freeze cooked pie 3 months.

This produces a very juicy filling in which the slices of cooked apple swim in a cinnamon-sugar sauce. Reheats well.

1 recipe Shortcrust Pastry for Fruit Pies (see above)

For the filling
4 large baking apples – Bramley's for preference (about 1½ lb/675 g weight, unpeeled)
3 oz (75 g/⅓ cup) granulated or medium brown sugar
2 level teasp cornflour (cornstarch)
1 level teasp cinnamon
grating of nutmeg
2 tbsp raisins (optional)

Peel, core and quarter the apples and cut into slices ⅛ inch (0.3 cm) thick. Put them in a bowl and mix well with all the remaining ingredients. Choose a pie dish 8 inches (20 cm) in diameter and 1 inch (2.5 cm) deep. Fill the bottom crust with the apple mixture, mounding it into the centre. Cover with the top crust and glaze with egg white and sugar as directed above.

Put in a hot oven, Gas No. 7 (425°F/220°C), for 10 minutes, then reduce the heat to Gas No. 5 (375°F/190°C) and bake for a further 40 minutes, or until the apple feels tender when the pie is pierced with a slim, pointed knife, and the pastry is a rich golden brown.

SPICY APPLE PIE

Serves 6 generously.
Cooked pie will keep 4 days under refrigeration.
Freeze 3 months.

The apples are bathed in a spicy butterscotch sauce.

1 recipe Shortcrust Pastry for Fruit Pies (see p. 371)

For the filling
1½ lb (675 g) cooking apples (weight unpeeled)
2 tbsp lemon juice
3 oz (75 g/⅓ cup) soft brown sugar
½ level teasp cinnamon
½ level teasp ground nutmeg
2 level tbsp sultanas (white raisins) or currants
2 teasp cornflour (cornstarch)
½ oz (15 g/1 tbsp) butter or margarine

Choose a pie dish 8 inches (20 cm) in diameter and 1 inch (2.5 cm) deep. Peel, core and quarter the apples and cut in slices ⅛ inch (0.3 cm) thick. Arrange in the lined pie dish and sprinkle them with the lemon juice. Mix the sugar, spices, raisins and cornflour and scatter on top. Dot with the butter or margarine. If the apples are dry (particularly at the end of the season) sprinkle over 3 tablespoons water or orange juice. Put on the top crust and glaze with egg white as directed above.

Put in a hot oven, Gas No. 7 (425°F/220°C), for 10 minutes, then reduce to Gas No. 5 (375°F/190°C) and bake for a further 40 minutes, or until the apple feels tender when the pie is pierced with a knife and the pastry is a rich golden brown. Serve warm.

RUM AND RAISIN DEEP-DISH APPLE PIE

Serves 8. Makes 1 9-inch (22.5-cm) pie.
Keeps 3 days under refrigeration.
Freeze for 3 months.

This deluxe pie has a juicy apple filling enlivened with rum-soaked raisins and toasted pecans. It can be served warm or at room temperature but *never* hot. For a dairy meal serve with custard or fromage frais.

For the pastry

10 oz (275 g/2½ cups) plain (all-purpose) flour
6 oz (175 g/¾ cup) firm butter or margarine
2½ level tbsp icing (confectioners') sugar
pinch of salt
1 egg yolk
2 teasp wine vinegar or cider vinegar
3 tbsp icy water
1 egg white and granulated sugar

For the filling

2 oz (50 g/⅓ cup) raisins
2 tbsp rum
2 oz (50 g/½ cup) toasted pecans (or walnuts)
2½ lb (1.1 kg) baking apples (weight unpeeled)
4 oz (125 g/½ cup) soft light brown sugar
1 oz (25 g/¼ cup) plain (all-purpose) flour
1 teasp cinnamon
pinch of grated nutmeg
½ teasp grated lemon rind
pinch of salt
2 teasp lemon juice
1 oz (25 g/2 tbsp) butter or margarine

Make the shortcrust pastry as directed on p. 371.

To make the filling, cover the raisins with the rum and bring to simmering point on top of the stove or in the microwave (1 minute on 100 per cent power). Leave to cool while the rest of the filling is prepared.

Preheat the oven to Gas No. 7 (425°F/220°C). Immediately put the coarsely chopped nuts (on a baking tray) into the oven and leave for 10 minutes to crisp and lightly brown.

Core and peel the apples and slice about ⅜ inch (1 cm) thick - this can be done in the food processor). Put in a bowl and add the sugar, flour, spices, rind, salt and the soaked raisins and stir gently but thoroughly. Sprinkle with the lemon juice.

Roll out 1 portion of pastry and line a 9-10-inch (22.5-25-cm) pie or flan dish, 1½ inches (4 cm) deep. Spoon the apple mixture evenly on top of the pastry, scatter with the toasted nuts and dot with the fat. Roll the remaining pastry large enough to cover the filling. Moisten the edges of the lower pastry with cold water, then gently position the rolled-out pastry on top. Seal the 2 layers of pastry together by pressing with the side of the hand, then crimp the edge with the thumb and forefinger.

Whisk the egg white with a fork until frothy, then paint evenly all over the top of the pie. Scatter with about 2 teaspoons of granulated sugar.

Bake at Gas No. 7 (425°F/220°C) for 30 minutes, then reduce the heat to Gas No. 5 (375°F/190°C) for a further 20 minutes, or until the pie is a rich brown and a skewer goes through the apple filling easily. If the pie is well browned but the apples are still not tender, cover the top loosely with foil and continue to cook for a further 10 minutes before testing again.

BILBERRY TART

Serves 6.
Cooked pie will keep 4 days under refrigeration.
Freeze cooked pie 3 months.

Bilberries are also known as blueberries or whinberries. The bushes grow wild on moorland and the fruit ripens towards the end of August, but you need a great deal of persistence to pick enough for a pie. Fortunately you can buy them fresh or frozen - either will do for this scrumptious pie. Choose a shallow pie plate 10 inches (25 cm) in diameter.

1 recipe Shortcrust Pastry for Fruit Pies (see p. 371)

For the filling
12 oz (350 g) bilberries (blueberries)
4 oz (125 g/½ cup) granulated sugar
2 tbsp lemon juice

Mix the fruit, sugar and lemon juice. Mound into the lined pie plate. Put on the top crust and glaze with egg white as directed (see p. 372).

Preheat the oven to Gas No. 6 (400°F/200°C). Put in the pie, then immediately turn down to Gas No. 5 (375°F/190°C) and bake for 35 minutes until golden brown. Serve warm, plain or with cream or custard.

SPICY DAMSON PIE

Serves 6–8.
Cooked pie keeps 4 days under refrigeration.
Freeze cooked pie 3 months.

Cooked damsons have a wonderfully tart yet sweet flavour. However, it's impossible to remove the stones beforehand so be sure to warn your guests to take care. Raw damsons freeze very well so, as they have a short season, it's worth buying a few pounds for winter use.

1 recipe Shortcrust Pastry for Fruit Pies (see p. 371)

For the filling
2 lb (900 g) fresh or frozen damsons
juice of ½ large lemon (2 tbsp)
5 oz (175 g/⅔ cup) granulated sugar
2 level teasp cornflour (cornstarch)
½ level teasp cinnamon
½ level teasp nutmeg
1 oz (25 g/2 tbsp) butter or margarine

Choose a pie dish 8–9 inches (20–22.5 cm) in diameter and 1 inch (2.5 cm) deep. Put the damsons into a bowl and sprinkle with the lemon juice. Mix together the sugar, cornflour and spices and stir into the plums. Mound into the pastry-lined dish and dot with the fat. Put on the top crust and glaze with egg white as directed (see p. 372).

Preheat the oven to Gas No. 6 (400°F/200°C) and bake for 45 minutes, or until the crust is golden and crunchy. Serve slightly warm, not hot.

GOOSEBERRY TART

Serves 6.
Cooked tart keeps 4 days under refrigeration.
Freeze cooked pie 3 months.

This is most flavourful when sour green gooseberries are used – hence the large amount of sugar!

1 recipe Shortcrust Pastry for Fruit Pies (see p. 371)

For the filling
1½ lb (675 g) green gooseberries, topped and tailed
6 oz (175 g/¾ cup) granulated sugar
1 level tbsp cornflour (cornstarch)
3 tbsp water

Choose a shallow pie plate 9–10 inches (22.5–25 cm) in diameter. Mix together the gooseberries, sugar and cornflour, then mound into the lined pie plate. Sprinkle with the water. Put on the top crust and glaze with egg white as directed (see p. 372).

Preheat the oven to Gas No. 6 (400°F/200°C). Put in the pie, then immediately turn the oven down to Gas No. 5 (375°F/190°C) and bake for 35 minutes until golden brown. Serve warm, plain or with fromage frais, yoghurt or custard.

OLD-FASHIONED PEACH PIE

Serves 6.
Cooked pie keeps 4 days under refrigeration.
Freeze cooked pie 3 months.

An American recipe, best made with freestone, cling or Hale peaches.

1 recipe Shortcrust Pastry for Fruit Pies (see p. 371)

For the filling
4–5 peaches
juice of 1 lemon
4 oz (125 g/½ cup) light brown soft sugar
2 level tbsp flour
½ level teasp cinnamon

Choose a shallow pie plate, 9 inches (22.5 cm) in diameter. Immerse the peaches in a pan of boiling water for 1 minute, then turn into a bowl of cold water. Lift off the skin with a knife. Slice them thickly into a bowl and sprinkle with the lemon juice. Mix the sugar, flour and cinnamon, then gently stir into the peaches. Spoon the peach filling in the pastry-lined plate. Put on the top crust and glaze with egg white as directed (see p. 372).

Preheat the oven to Gas No. 7 (425°F/220°C) and bake pie for 15 minutes, then turn to Gas No. 5 (375°F/190°C) for a further 20 minutes, or until golden brown. Serve warm, plain or with ice-cream or fromage frais.

RAISIN PIE

Serves 6.
Cooked pie keeps 4 days under refrigeration.
Freeze cooked pie 3 months.

A favourite of the fishermen along the Columbia River in Washington State, USA – it's a real rib-sticker which helps to keep out the cold.

1 recipe Shortcrust Pastry for Fruit Pies (see p. 371)

For the filling
15 fl oz (425 g/2 cups) water
8 oz (225 g/1½ cups) raisins
3 oz (75 g/⅓ cup) brown sugar
3 level teasp cornflour (cornstarch)
½ level teasp cinnamon
½ level teasp ground nutmeg
1 oz (25 g/2 tbsp) butter or margarine

Choose a pie dish 8 inches (20 cm) in diameter and 1 inch (2.5 cm) deep. Bring the water to the boil in a small pan, then add the raisins and simmer uncovered for 5 minutes. Mix together the sugar, cornflour and spices. Stir into the raisins over low heat and bubble until thickened and clear – about 3 minutes. Stir in the butter or margarine and leave to cool. Pour the cold filling into the pastry-lined pie dish. Put on the top crust and glaze with egg white as directed (see p. 372).

Preheat oven to Gas No. 7 (425°F/220°C) and bake the pie for 30 minutes. Serve warm, plain or with custard or ice-cream.

RHUBARB PIE

Serves 6.
Cooked pie keeps 4 days under refrigeration.
Freeze cooked pie 3 months.

This pie has the prettiest colour and the most delicate flavour when it is made with forced spring rhubarb, grown under cover.

1 recipe Shortcrust Pastry for Fruit Pies (see p. 371)

For the filling
1½ lb (675 g) rhubarb
6 oz (175 g/¾ cup) granulated sugar
2 level teasp cornflour (cornstarch)
½ oz (15 g/1 tbsp) butter or margarine

Choose a pie dish 8 inches (20 cm) in diameter and 1 inch (2.5 cm) deep. Cut off the heel from each stick of rhubarb but do not peel the fruit. Cut into 1-inch (2.5-cm) lengths and put into a bowl with the sugar and cornflour, then stir well. Spoon into the pastry-lined pie dish and dot with the fat. Put on the top crust and glaze with egg white as directed (see p. 372).

Preheat the oven to Gas No. 7 (425°F/220°C) and bake pie for 10 minutes, then turn down to Gas No. 5 (375°F/190°C) for a further 30 minutes, until golden brown. Serve warm or cold, plain or with custard.

APPLE MARZIPAN PIE

Serves 8.
Keeps 3 days under refrigeration.
Freeze 3 months.

The marzipan adds a new flavour dimension to this apple pie.

For the pastry

10 oz (275 g/2½ cups) plain (all-purpose) flour
pinch of salt
6½ oz (190 g/¾ cup plus 1 tbsp) firm butter or block margarine
2 tbsp caster (superfine) sugar
1 egg
2 teasp cold water

For the filling

4 oz (125 g) ready-to-use marzipan, chilled then coarsely grated
4 oz (125 g/½ cup) soft butter or margarine
2 oz (50 g/¼ cup) caster (superfine) sugar
2 large eggs, separated
4 Bramley cooking aples (1½ lb/675 g weight unpeeled), peeled and coarsely grated

For the glaze

1 egg white
granulated sugar

Make by either of the methods given for Shortcrust Pastry for Fruit Pies on p. 371. Knead lightly to remove the cracks, then divide in 2 pieces, 1 slightly larger than the other. Wrap in foil, flatten into a block and chill for at least 1 hour.

Preheat the oven to Gas No. 7 (425°F/220°C). On a floured board roll out the larger piece of pastry ⅛ inch (0.3 cm) thick and line the base and sides of a 10-inch (25-cm) heatproof flan dish. Grate the marzipan in an even layer over it.

To make the filling, cream the butter and sugar until fluffy, then beat in the egg yolks. Stir in the grated apples, then fold in the egg whites whisked until they hold glossy peaks. Spoon the filling into the pastry.

Roll out the remaining pastry ¼ inch (0.5 cm) thick, then cut in ½-inch-wide (1-cm) strips and arrange in a lattice pattern on top of the filling, pressing the ends firmly to the rim of the flan dish. Paint all over with the egg white whisked until foamy and scatter with the granulated sugar. Bake for 35–40 minutes, until golden brown. Serve warm.

To reheat, cover loosely with foil and leave in a moderate oven, Gas No. 4 (350°F/180°C), for 20–25 minutes, or until warm to the touch.

The Continental Touch

ZWETSCHKEN PLUM TART

Serves 6.
Cooked pie keeps 4 days under refrigeration.
Freeze cooked pie 3 months.

The zwetschken plum – black, sweet and freestone – grows all over the part of Europe which once comprised the Austro-Hungarian Empire. Here were developed some of the finest dishes of the Western Europe cuisine. These plums are sometimes made into a superb conserve called 'povidl' and sometimes used as a topping for a yeast kuchen. In this delicious recipe they are used as the filling for a 1-crust tart made with 'muerbteig', the sweet caky shortcrust common to German and Austrian cooking. (*Muerbe* is the German word for 'crumbly' and in fact this pastry has a lot in common with the French pâté sablée – literally 'sandy' pastry.)

Because of the high proportion of sugar in this pastry, the pie is cooked at a lower temperature than the preceding fruit pies. This pastry is much used by Jewish cooks of German and Austrian origin.

For the pastry

3 oz (75 g/⅓ cup) caster (superfine) sugar
6 oz (175 g/1½ cups) plain (all-purpose) flour
3 oz (75 g/⅓ cup) butter or margarine
1 egg yolk
1 teasp lemon juice
ice water if needed

For the filling

1½ lb (675 g) zwetschken plums
3 oz (75 g/⅓ cup) caster (superfine) sugar
1 level teasp cinnamon
2 teasp lemon juice
1 oz (25 g/2 tbsp) butter or margarine

To make the pastry, mix the sugar and flour, then rub in the butter or margarine and mix to a dough with the egg yolk, lemon juice and ice water (if required). (See p. 371 for detailed instructions.) Form the dough into a ball, foil-wrap and chill for at least 30 minutes. Roll out to fit a 9-inch (2.5-cm) shallow pie plate or sandwich tin, and flute the edges with the fingers.

Halve and stone the washed plums, then arrange, cut side up, on the pastry in a series of concentric circles. Mix together the caster sugar and the cinnamon, then sprinkle half of it in an even layer over the fruit. Pour over the lemon juice and dot with the fat. Bake in a moderate oven, Gas No. 4 (350°F/180°C), until the pastry is a golden brown – about 30 minutes. Take from the oven and sprinkle with the remaining sugar. Serve warm or cold.

PFLAUMEN KUCHEN
(*Plum Dessert*)

Serves 8 generously.
Keeps 3 days under refrigeration.
Freeze leftovers 1 month.

This delicious dish consists of a plum and apple filling in an almond pastry case, topped with a 'streusel' or crumble. The rich pastry keeps well, and is a favourite Rosh Hashanah dish of Jews of German origin.

For the pastry

22 oz (50 g/½ cup) ground almonds
4 oz (125 g/½ cup) fine brown sugar
8 oz (225 g/2 cups) self-raising flour or 8 oz (225 g/2 cups) plain (all-purpose) flour plus
2 teasp baking powder
6 oz (175 g/¾ cup) butter or margarine
squeeze of lemon juice
1 beaten egg

For the filling

1 lb (450 g) cooking apples (weight peeled and cored)
1½ lb (675 g) zwetschken (freestone) plums, halved and stoned
4 oz (125 g/½ cup) granulated sugar
little extra ground almonds

For the streusel topping

2 oz (50 g/½ cup) plain flour
2 oz (50 g/¼ cup) butter or margarine
5 oz (150 g/⅔ cup) fine brown sugar

To make the pastry, mix together the ground almonds, brown sugar and flour. Rub in the fat gently, then mix to a soft dough with the squeeze of lemon juice and all but 1 tablespoon of the egg. (See p. 371 for detailed technique.) Chill for 1 hour, wrapped in foil or clingfilm (saranwrap).

To make the filling, peel, core and slice the apples very thinly (this can be done in the food processor). Put in a bowl and mix them with the plums. Mix with the sugar just before the fruit is needed or the juices will run and make the pastry soggy.

To make the streusel, mix all the ingredients with the fingers until a crumbly mass forms.

Roll the chilled pastry to fit the bottom and sides of a 9-inch (22.5-cm) loose-bottomed tin or a springform tin that opens at the side. If the pastry breaks, don't worry; just patch it up, as it is very short. Sprinkle the bottom of the pastry with a thin layer of ground almonds (to absorb excess juice), add the sugared fruit, squeeze a little lemon juice over the top and finally cover with an even layer of the crumble.

Bake in a moderate oven, Gas No. 4 (350°F/180°C), for 1-1¼ hours, or until the crumble is a golden brown and the filling feels absolutely soft when pierced with a knife. Serve warm or cold.

If zwetschken plums are not available and juicy plums are used, mix 2 level teaspoons of cornflour with the sugar when sweetening the fruit so as to thicken the juice.

LA TARTE TATIN
(*French Caramelized Apple Tart*)

Serves 10.
Keeps 3 days. Do not freeze.

Imagine closely packed layers of caramelized apples resting on a fragile disc of pastry and you will begin to understand why this dish has become a star of the classic French cuisine, even though it was originally devised by two elderly sisters living deep in French apple country. Although it's very simple to make, you do need a dish that can go both on top of the stove (to make the caramel) and then into the oven to cook the apples and pastry. The French chef from whom I learned the technique used a copper cocotte, but I find a heavy frying pan works just as well (a handle that is not heatproof can be covered in foil). It's important to use the full quantity of apples as they shrink in the cooking. The tarte can be made in both a dairy and a *parev* version. Fortunately it can be made early and reheated on top of the stove just before dinner.

For the pastry
4 oz (125 g/1 cup) plain (all-purpose) flour
3 oz (75 g/⅓ cup) butter or block margarine
1 teasp caster (superfine) sugar
pinch of salt
2 tbsp cold water

For the caramel and apple filling
1½ oz (40 g/3 tbsp) butter or margarine
2 oz (50 g/¼ cup) granulated sugar
3 teasp fresh lemon juice
1 oz (25 g/¼ cup) slivered blanched almonds
4 lb (2 kg) dessert apples (Golden Delicious or Cox's)
4 fl oz (125 ml/½ cup) water

To put on top of the apples under the pastry
½ oz (15 g/1 tbsp) butter or margarine
3 tbsp granulated sugar

To sprinkle on the pastry
2 teasp granulated sugar

Make the pastry by the shortcrust method (see p. 371) and chill.

To prepare the filling, peel the apples and thinly slice half of them. Set aside. Core the remaining apples and cut in sixths. (A special metal apple-corer and divider is ideal for the job.) Preheat the oven to Gas No. 6 (400°F/200°C).

In a heavy 8½-9-inch (21-22.5-cm) frying pan (preferably non-stick), melt the butter or margarine and sugar, then sprinkle with the lemon juice and cook over moderate heat, tilting the pan so it cooks evenly until the caramel is a rich chestnut brown - 3-4 minutes. Add the slivered almonds, cook for a further 20 seconds, then remove from the heat and arrange the thick sections of apple in 1 concentric layer on the butterscotch. Cover these with the apple *slices*, add the water, bring to the boil, cover with a lid and cook for 10 minutes, or until the apples are tender. Uncover and bubble for a further 8 minutes, until most of the liquid has evaporated. Remove from the heat. Dot the surface of the apples with the ½ oz (15 g) of fat and sprinkle with the 3 tablespoons of sugar. Roll out the pastry until it is slightly larger in diameter than the top of the pan, then lay it carefully on top, tucking the edges well in to fit. Sprinkle with the 2 teaspoons of sugar and bake for 45 minutes, until the pastry is golden brown.

Serve warm (not hot), inverted on a large platter, apple side up.

TO MAKE A SHAPELY SWEET-PASTRY CASE

Too often a flan case that goes into the oven looking perfectly shaped comes out shrunken and misformed. Here's how to produce a shapely case every time.

Roll out the pastry on a lightly floured board, starting with a ball-shaped piece of dough for a round case, a square block for a square or rectangular one.

Give the pastry a quarter of a turn after each roll so that it doesn't stick to the board. To avoid overstretching the dough (a main cause of shrinkage), put all the pressure on the forward rather than the backward rolling action.

When the dough is approximately the right size and thickness, lay the rolling pin on top, then gently roll the pastry loosely round it. Gently unroll it on to the tin, then ease into place.

Now for the important part. Make a little 'tuck' in the pastry all the way round the bottom edge of the tin so that the case is slightly thicker at the bottom than the top (this prevents the sides shrinking back on themselves).

Roll the rolling pin over the top of the tin to cut off any excess pastry (you may prefer to do this with the side of your thumb).

To bake 'blind', without filling, prick the bottom and the sides of the pastry with a fork held at a slight angle to prevent making holes through which the filling might ooze, then press a large piece of foil into its shape, completely covering the bottom and sides. If possible freeze for an hour before baking according to the recipe.

FRESH APRICOT AND FRANGIPANE FLAN

Serves 8–10.
Keeps 2 days under refrigeration.
Leftovers freeze 1 month.

Ready-to-use almond paste makes an unusual filling for this luscious fresh fruit flan. It's equally good in the dairy or the *parev* version.

For the pastry

2 egg yolks
2 oz (50 g/⅓ cup) icing (confectioners') sugar
5 oz (150 g/⅔ cup) butter or firm margarine, cut in 1-inch (2.5-cm) cubes
1 teasp grated lemon rind
8 oz (225 g/2 cups) plain (all-purpose) flour
pinch of salt

For the filling

9 oz (250 g) block white marzipan
4 oz (125 g/½ cup) unsalted butter or margarine, softened
3 level tbsp flour
2 x size 2 eggs
10 fresh apricots, halved and stoned, or 2 x 16 oz (450 g) cans choice apricots
¾ cup (6 oz/175 g approx.) smooth apricot jam or sieved conserve
2 tbsp lemon juice

For the garnish

toasted almond flakes or strips

Make the pastry by either method given on p. 371. Roll out the chilled dough ⅛ inch (0.3 cm) thick and carefully ease into a 10–11-inch (25–27.5-cm) loose-bottomed flan tin, taking a little 'tuck' in it all the way round the bottom edge of the tin so that the case is slightly thicker near the bottom than it is at the top (this is to prevent shrinkage). Roll the rolling pin over the top edge of the case to remove excess pastry.

Prick the bottom and the sides of the case with a fork, then press a large piece of foil into its shape, completely covering the bottom and sides of the pastry. Freeze for 1 hour.

Preheat the oven to Gas No. 4 (350°F/180°C). Bake for 15 minutes, then carefully remove the foil, reprick the case if it looks puffy and return to the oven for a further 15 minutes, or until a pale gold in colour. Cool on a rack.

To make the filling, break up the marzipan into 1-inch (2.5-cm) chunks and put in the food processor with the soft butter, the flour and the eggs. Process until absolutely smooth. Spread the mixture on the bottom of the shell and arrange the apricot halves, cut sides down, over it. Bring the jam to the boil with the lemon juice in a small saucepan, stirring until it is melted (1-2 minutes on 100 per cent power in the microwave). Brush the flan with half the glaze and bake for a further 30-40 minutes until the filling is puffed and set. Let the tart cool on a rack, then brush with the reheated reserved jam. Place on a serving dish and scatter with the almonds.

Serve plain or with fromage frais, whipped cream or dairy ice-cream.

CREAMY CUSTARD TART

Serves 6-8.
Keeps 1 day under refrigeration.

Melt-in-the-mouth pastry with a rich creamy custard filling.

For the pastry

6 oz (175 g/1½ cups) self-raising flour or 6 oz (175 g/1½ cups) plain (all-purpose) flour plus 1½ teasp baking powder
3½ oz (90 g/7 tbsp) butter
1½ oz (40 g/3 tbsp) icy water
1½ oz (40 g/6 tbsp) icing (confectioners') sugar
1 whole egg plus 2 tbsp water

For the filling

1 pint (575 ml/2½ cups) milk
1 vanilla pod or ½ teasp vanilla essence (extract)
2 eggs plus 2 egg yolks
3 oz (75 g/⅓ cup) caster (superfine) sugar

For sprinkling on the tart

ground nutmeg

Make the pastry as directed for Shortcrust Pastry for Fruit Pies (see p. 371). The dough will be quite soft but not sticky. Chill for an hour, then roll out ¼ inch (0.5 cm) thick to fit a 10-inch (25-cm) flan case (most convenient is the china kind). Prick all over, then line with foil, which should also protect the edges from overbrowning (see p. 379). Bake at Gas No. 5 (375°F/190°C) for 15 minutes, then remove the foil. If the pastry looks damp, bake a further 5 minutes. If it is set but pale, add the filling.

To make the filling, put the milk and vanilla pod in a pan and heat gently until steaming - do not boil. Whisk the yolks, eggs and sugar together, then whisk in the hot milk (removing vanilla pod or adding the essence at this point) - this is very easy to do in the food processor. When the flan is ready, carefully pour in the custard and sprinkle with the ground nutmeg. Return to the oven and bake at Gas No. 5 (375°F/190°C) for 5 minutes, then turn oven to Gas No. 2 (300°F/150°C) and bake for a further 30 minutes, or until the top of the flan is a pale gold and it seems set when gently shaken. Another 5 minutes will do no harm if you are uncertain.

Remove from the oven and allow to cool completely before cutting.

PECAN PIE

Serves 6-8.
Keeps 2 days under refrigeration.
Do not freeze.

I make this traditional American pie with the superb pecan nuts produced in Israel.

For the pastry
8 oz (225 g/2 cups) plain (all-purpose) flour
4 oz (125 g/½ cup) butter or margarine
1 oz (25 g/2 tbsp) white fat
2 level tbsp icing (confectioners') sugar
pinch of salt
1 egg yolk
juice of ½ lemon (1½ tbsp)
2 tbsp icy water

For the filling
3 eggs
4 oz (125 g/½ cup) soft light brown sugar
5 fl oz (150 ml/⅔ cup) golden (corn) syrup
2 oz (50 g/¼ cup) soft butter or margarine
½ teasp vanilla essence (extract)
1 tbsp rum or milk
6 oz (175 g/1½ cups) pecan nuts or halved walnuts

For the accompaniment
5 fl oz (150 ml/⅔ cup) soured cream, smetana or Greek-style yoghurt

Make the pastry by either method given on p. 371. Gather into a ball, flatten and chill for 30 minutes. On a lightly floured surface roll out into a 12-inch (30-cm) circle and carefully ease into a 9-inch (22.5-cm) pie dish 1 inch (2.5 cm) deep. Fold under the edge of the crust and press into an upright rim, then crimp between the finger and thumb. Freeze while you prepare the filling.

Whisk the eggs to blend. Boil the sugar and syrup together in a saucepan for 3 minutes. Slowly pour on to the beaten eggs and stir in the butter, vanilla and rum or milk. Use half the nuts to cover the base of the pastry case, spoon the syrup mixture over and cover with the remaining nuts.

Bake in a preheated oven, Gas No. 7 (425°F/220°C), for 10 minutes. Reduce heat to Gas No. 3 (325°F/160°C) and cook for a further 35 minutes, until the filling is set like a custard. Allow to cool and serve in wedges either plain or with the soured cream, smetana or Greek yoghurt.

TARTE AU CITRON

Serves 8–10. Makes 1 9½-inch (24-cm) tarte 1¼ (3 cm) inches deep.
Keeps 2 days under refrigeration.
Freeze leftovers 1 month.

The sharp and refreshing filling makes a superb contrast to the crisp, melt-in-the-mouth pastry.

For the pastry
8 oz (225 g/2 cups) plain (all-purpose) flour
pinch of salt
5 oz (150 g/⅔ cup) butter, cut in 1-inch (2.5 cm) chunks
2 oz (50 g/⅓ cup) icing (confectioners') sugar
2 egg yolks

For the filling
finely grated rind and juice of 2 large lemons (4 fl oz/125 ml/½ cup juice altogether)
4 eggs
6 oz (175 g/1 cup) caster (superfine) sugar
5 fl oz (150 ml/⅔ cup) double (heavy) cream

For the glazed lemons (optional garnish)
4 oz (125 g/½ cup) granulated sugar
7 fl oz (200 ml/1 cup minus 2 tbsp) water
2 fine lemons, each sliced into 10

Make the pastry by either method described on p. 371. Flatten, cover with foil and chill for at least 30 minutes, then roll out to fit the flan tin and prick the base. Lay a piece of foil over the pastry, then carefully mould into its shape (see p. 379). If possible, freeze for 30 minutes. (Leftover pastry can be frozen.)

Bake at Gas No. 5 (375°F/190°C) for 10 minutes, then remove the foil, carefully reprick the base of the pastry if necessary and dry off for a further 10 minutes at the same temperature – it should be a pale gold in colour. Remove from the oven and allow to cool. (This can be done at any time beforehand and the part-baked case refrigerated or frozen.)

To complete the tarte, preheat the oven to Gas No. 4 (350°F/180°C).

Mix the lemon juice and rind together. Whisk the eggs and sugar until slightly thickened (don't overbeat or the custard will get holes in it when set). Whisk the cream until it hangs on the whisk, then fold it into the egg mixture, followed by the lemon juice and rind. Put the part-baked tarte (still in the tin) on to a baking sheet and carefully pour in the filling. Put into the oven and bake for 20-25 minutes, or until firm round the edges (the middle may stay a little soft). Leave on a cooling tray until cool, then refrigerate for several hours.

To make the glazed lemons, dissolve the sugar in the water in a large-diameter frying pan, then lay the lemon slices in the syrup side by side and simmer uncovered (turning them occasionally) until they are softened and glazed and the syrup is beginning to froth. (Don't let it turn colour or the fresh lemon flavour will be lost). Allow to go cool.

Remove the sides of the tarte tin and place the tarte on a serving dish, then sprinkle thickly with icing sugar. Serve in sections, each garnished with 2 of the glazed lemon slices.

TARTE AUX FRUITS À L'ALSACIENNE

Serves 6-8. Makes one 9-10-inch (22.5-25-cm) tarte.
The pastry case can be frozen baked or unbaked for up to a month.
Do not freeze with the fruit filling.

Alsace has provided a home for Jews ever since Roman times - they continued to live there even when excluded from the rest of France in the fourteenth century and, according to the historian Nicholas de Lange, the Yiddish-speaking Ashkenazim of Alsace-Lorraine made up the largest Jewish community in France, greater even than that of Paris. This is not to say that they have not been subject to harassment at times during the turbulent history of the area. However, the community - much of it strictly Orthodox - has survived to this day.

In her book *Gastronomie Juive* Suzanne Roukhomovsky lists many dishes of the Alsatian Jewish cuisine, such as Cervelles Ziss-sauer (sweet and sour brains) and Anisbrodchen (aniseed biscuits), which reveal the strong German connections of the Jews of this border area, whereas others, such as Tarte à l'Oignon and this Tarte aux Fruits - in which the seasonal fruits are baked in a rich custard - are simply traditional dishes of the region which have been absorbed into the local Jewish cuisine.

For the pâté sablée
(shortbread-like pastry)
5 oz (150 g/$\frac{2}{3}$ cup) butter or margarine, cut in 1-inch (2.5-cm) chunks
2 oz (50 g/$\frac{1}{4}$ cup) caster (superfine) sugar
1 egg plus 2 teasp water
8 oz (225 g/2 cups) plain (all-purpose) flour
pinch of baking powder
1 oz (25 g/$\frac{1}{4}$ cup) ground almonds

For the filling
6 large, fairly ripe (but not soft) nectarines, peaches or fresh apricots (1$\frac{3}{4}$ lb/800 g total weight)
1 oz (25 g/$\frac{1}{4}$ cup) ground almonds
3$\frac{1}{2}$ oz (100 g/$\frac{1}{2}$ cup) caster (superfine) sugar
2 eggs
$\frac{1}{2}$ teasp vanilla essence (extract)
8 fl oz (225 ml/1 cup) double (heavy) cream

Have ready a metal flan tin 9-10 inches (22.5-25 cm) in diameter and 1$\frac{1}{4}$ inches (3 cm) deep. With a food processor work the butter into the sugar, followed by the beaten egg, then pulse in the flour, baking powder, salt and ground almonds until the mixture begins to cling together in little balls. Tip into a bowl, then gather into a ball. (Or make in the traditional way as for shortbread, see p. 449). Take roughly a heaped tablespoon of the dough at a time and use the palm of the hand to press it into a long 'smear'. Scoop up from the board with a spatula and as each portion of dough is treated, add it to the rest, then gently knead into a block about 1 inch (2.5 cm) thick. This makes it very short. Wrap in clingfilm (saranwrap) and chill 1½ hours, or overnight.

Roll the chilled pastry to fit the flan tin, prick all over, line with foil and bake for 15 minutes at Gas No. 4 (350°F/180°C). Remove foil and bake a further 10 minutes at the same temperature, or until golden.

To make and bake the filling, preheat the oven to Gas No. 4 (350°F/180°C) and place a large baking sheet in the oven. Put the nectarines or peaches into a big pan, cover with boiling water and simmer for 1 minute, then pour off the hot water, cover with cold water and drain well. The skins will now slip off easily. Set aside. (Apricots have a more tender skin, which can be left on.)

Sprinkle the base of the cooked flan case with the ground almonds. If using apricots, halve then arrange with the rounded side uppermost in the flan. If using peaches or nectarines, slice each fruit away from the stone in 1-inch-thick (2.5-cm) sections and pack as tightly as possible into the case in concentric circles.

Whisk together the sugar and the eggs until thick and creamy, then stir in the essence and the cream. Put the flan case on the hot baking sheet, then carefully fill up with the custard - it should come to the top edge of the case. Do not overfill it or it will spill over and make the flan difficult to remove from the case.

Bake for 35–40 minutes, until the flan is a pale gold on top and a knife inserted into the centre of the custard comes out clean or with only a little liquid adhering - the custard will completely set as it cools.

Remove to a cooling tray and when cool enough to handle, carefully remove from the tin (but leave on the base) and arrange on a round serving platter. Serve at room temperature.

VARIATIONS

Use 1½ lb (675 g) green gooseberries, topped and tailed. Increase sugar in filling to 4 oz (125 g/½ cup).

Alternatively, peel, core and slice 1 inch (2.5 cm) thick 2 lb (900 g) best crisp eating apples such as Cox's. Sauté carefully in 2 oz (50 g/¼ cup) butter until softened but not mushy, then arrange in the case as before.

TARTE AUX POIRES À L'ALSACIENNE

Serves 8. Makes 1 x 9-inch (22.5-cm) tarte, 1½ inches (4 cm) deep or 1 x 10-inch (25-cm) tarte, 1 inch (2.5 cm) deep.
Leftovers keep 2 days under refrigeration.
Baked or unbaked pastry case freezes 3 months.

Choice pears are set in an unusual soured cream custard flavoured with fruit brandy. The tarte is at its best on the day it is cooked.

For the pastry

8 oz (225 g/2 cups) plain (all-purpose) flour
pinch of salt
5 oz (150 g/⅔ cup) butter, cut in 1-inch (2.5-cm) chunks
2 oz (50 g/⅓ cup) icing (confectioners') sugar
1 whole egg
½ an egg shell of cold water
1 teasp wine vinegar

For the filling

4–5 choice ripe pears (Packham, Beurre Hardy or William) (1½ lb/675 g total weight, peeled and cored)
2 tbsp caster (superfine) sugar
2 tbsp fresh lemon juice
2 whole eggs
1 egg yolk
5 fl oz (150 ml/⅔ cup) soured cream
2 tbsp Eau de Vie de Poire or other fruit brandy
1 oz (25 g/2 tbsp) caster (superfine) sugar
grated rind of ½ lemon
½ teasp vanilla essence (extract)

For the topping

3 oz (75 g/¾ cup) flaked almonds
1 egg white, whisked to floppy peaks
2 oz (50 g/¼ cup) caster (superfine) sugar

Make the pastry by either method given on p. 371. Roll the chilled pastry to fit the tarte case, prick the bottom and sides with a fork, carefully line with foil moulded into the shape of the tarte and bake in a quick oven, Gas No. 6 (400°F/200°C), for 8 minutes, or until the sides have set. Remove the foil, prick any air bubbles with the fork, then bake a further 6 minutes or until a pale gold in colour. Leave to cool.

Meanwhile, if the pears are underripe, put them in a dish, sprinkle with the sugar and the lemon juice, cover and cook in the microwave for 5-6 minutes on 100 per cent power until just tender. Allow to cool a little, then slice into fans and arrange on the bottom of the cooled flan case. In a bowl whisk together the eggs, egg yolk, soured cream, Eau de Vie, sugar, lemon rind and vanilla (easiest in the food processor). Ladle carefully over the pears and bake in a moderate oven, Gas No. 4 (350°F/180°C), for 20 minutes, or until the custard is barely set in the centre. Lift out on to a rack. In a bowl combine the almonds, egg white and sugar and stir until the almonds are coated with the egg white mixture. Spoon over the top of the custard, smoothing it even, then return to the oven for 15 minutes, or until a pale gold.

Serve the same day, warm or at room temperature.

TARTE MAISON

Serves 9–10.
Eat freshly baked.
Leftovers keep 2 days under refrigeration.
Freeze baked or unbaked pastry cases 3 months.

Queues form early on Sunday mornings in the towns and villages of France as the locals come to buy these magnificent foot-wide open tarts, glistening with the fruits of the season nestling on a luscious pastry cream.

The French prefer to leave their making to the local patissier, but there's a great satisfaction in producing one '*à la maison*' – taken stage by stage it's far from difficult.

The pastry case and the pastry cream can be prepared in advance, and then it's only an assembly job on the day.

Use any soft fruit in season – frozen berries (other than strawberries, which go flabby) can be used out of season. Plums, apricots, nectarines, peaches and pears will need poaching very gently in a sugar syrup so that they keep their shape. To achieve this, proceed as follows.

Prepare the fruit according to type (stoned, halved and sliced if large; pears peeled, halved and cored). In a wide, shallow pan dissolve 5 oz (150 g/⅔ cup) granulated sugar in 8 fl oz (225 ml/1 cup) water. Bubble uncovered for 3 minutes, then add 2 lb (900 g) of the prepared fruit, cover and simmer until *almost* tender. (The time will vary according to the ripeness of the fruit – test with a small, pointed knife.) Take off the heat, cover and leave for 20 minutes to allow the fruit to steam to complete tenderness. Lift out and drain on a rack, then use to fill the tarte. The poaching syrup can be kept in the refrigerator for several weeks for use another time.

For the fruit filling

2 lb (900 g) poached fruit (see above) or
2 lb (900 g) any berries in season

For the biscuit pastry

8 oz (225 g/2 cups) plain (all-purpose) flour
pinch of salt
5 oz (150 g/⅔ cup) butter or margarine
2 level tbsp caster (superfine) sugar
1 egg
½ eggshell of cold water
2 teasp vinegar

For the pastry cream

8 fl oz (225 ml/1 cup) milk
1 oz (25 g/¼ cup) custard powder (vanilla pudding mix)
1 tbsp caster (superfine) sugar
8 fl oz (225 ml/1 cup) double (heavy) cream, whipped
2 tbsp any fruit-flavoured liqueur or Amaretto (optional)

For the glaze
8 oz (225 g) redcurrant jelly
2 level tbsp granulated sugar
2 tbsp lemon juice

Make the pastry by either method given on p. 371. Roll out the chilled pastry $\frac{1}{8}$ inch (0.3 cm) thick on a lightly floured board, lift it over the rolling pin and carefully ease it into the flan tin. To prevent the pastry from shrinking, take a little 'tuck' in it all the way round the bottom edge of the tin so that the case is slightly thicker near the bottom than it is at the top. Roll the rolling pin over the top of the tin to cut off any excess pastry. Prick the bottom and the sides of the case with a fork and press a large piece of foil into its shape, completely covering the bottom and sides of the pastry. Put in the freezer for 1 hour.

To bake the flan case, preheat the oven to Gas No. 6 (400°F/200°C). Bake for 15 minutes, then carefully remove the foil, prick the base again if it looks puffy, turn the oven down to Gas No. 5 (375°F/190°C) and cook for a further 15-18 minutes, until an even golden brown. If the sides start to brown before the base, lay a piece of foil lightly over the top. Put the cooked flan on a cooling rack, and when quite cold carefully ease out of the tin and put on a flat tray or serving dish. The flan is now ready to fill.

For the pastry cream, make a custard according to packet instructions with the milk, custard powder and sugar, either on top of the stove or in the microwave. Put in the freezer to chill for 20 minutes. Whisk the chilled cream until it holds soft peaks, then whisk in the liqueur. Take the chilled custard from the freezer and process or blend for 1 minute, until it looks smooth and creamy. Fold it gradually into the whipped cream, then spoon the mixture into the flan case and smooth level. Chill until required - it can be left overnight at this stage.

To make the glaze, heat all the glaze ingredients together, stirring, then boil rapidly until sticky drops of jam-like consistency fall from the spoon - about 5 minutes. Cool slightly.

To assemble the flan, arrange the fruit on top of the pastry cream, tightly packed together, then spoon the tepid glaze over the fruit and allow to set. Chill until required.

TARTE MONTMORENCY

Serves 10-12.
If possible, eat the same day.
Leftovers keep 2 days under refrigeration.
Freeze 3 months.

A study in contrasts - crisp, meltingly tender pastry, tart fruit and sweet and spongy almond topping. A slice makes a refreshing dessert, particularly after a meat meal.

For the pastry
8 oz (225 g/2 cups) self-raising flour or
8 oz (225 g/2 cups) plain (all-purpose) flour plus
2 teasp baking powder
pinch of salt
5 oz (150 g/$\frac{2}{3}$ cup) butter or margarine
2 oz (50 g/$\frac{1}{4}$ cup) caster (superfine) sugar
1 egg

For the filling
1 oz (25 g/3 tbsp) icing (confectioners') sugar
2 lb (900 g) raw pitted Morello (sour red) or black cherries, or well-drained canned cherries sufficient to cover base of flan in 1 layer (1$\frac{1}{2}$-2 cans)

For the almond sponge
4 oz (125 g/$\frac{1}{2}$ cup) soft butter or margarine
4 oz (125 g/$\frac{1}{2}$ cup) caster (superfine) sugar
2 eggs
few drops almond essence (extract)
4 oz (125 g/1 cup) ground almonds
3 level tbsp flour

Make pastry by rubbing-in or by the food-processor method, see p. 371. Chill for 1 hour, then roll out to fit an 11-12-inch (27.5-30-cm) flan case. Prick the base all over and sprinkle with the icing sugar. Arrange the cherries in a single layer, very close together.

Make the almond sponge by beating together the soft butter or margarine, sugar, eggs, almond essence, ground almonds and flour until smooth (10 seconds in the food processor). Spread evenly over cherries. Bake at Gas No.5 (375°F/190°C) for 15 minutes, then at Gas No. 4 (350°F/180°C) for 30 minutes, or until the topping has set into a sponge that feels springy to the touch.

The flan may be iced with glace icing or it can be served dusted with sifted icing sugar. Alternatively it can be dusted thickly with icing sugar, then put back in the oven at Gas No. 8 (450°F/230°C) until the icing sugar melts into a golden brown glaze. Watch it!

VARIATION

Instead of cherries use 1½ lb (675 g) fresh or frozen raspberries, tayberries or loganberries.

TRANCHE DE FRAISES PROVENÇALE

Serves 10–12.
Leftovers keep 1 day under refrigeration. Freeze tranche without fruit topping 2 months.
Eat the same day the fruit topping is added.

This looks stunning in a long narrow or square flan tin. The filling is very light and delicate.

For the pastry

1 egg
3 oz (75 g/⅓ cup) caster (superfine) sugar
5½ oz (165 g/¾ cup) firm butter or block margarine, cut in 1-inch (2.5-cm) cubes
4 oz (125 g/1 cup) each plain and self-raising flour or 8 oz (225 g/2 cups) plain (all-purpose) flour plus
1 teasp baking powder

For the filling

4 oz (125 g/½ cup) caster (superfine) sugar
4 oz (125 g/1 cup) ground almonds
3 eggs
1 teasp vanilla essence (extract)
1 tbsp citrus blossom water (optional)
1 oz (25 g/¼ cup) potato flour or cornflour (cornstarch)
½ teasp baking powder
pinch of salt
3 oz (75 g/⅓ cup) butter or margarine, melted

For the fruit topping

1 jar (5 oz/150 g) redcurrant jelly
2 tbsp lemon juice
2 lb (900 g) fine, even-sized strawberries

Make pastry by rubbing-in or by the food-processor method, see p. 371. Chill for 20 minutes.

To make the filling, mix the sugar and ground almonds, then whisk in the eggs, vanilla and citrus blossom water if used until smooth. Mix the potato flour (or cornflour), baking powder and salt in a small bowl, then gently stir into the first mixture, together with the melted butter.

To assemble, roll out the chilled pastry to fit a 14 x 4-inch (35 x 10-cm) rectangular or a 9-inch (22.5-cm) square or round tarte case with a loose bottom. Pour in the almond mixture, smooth level and bake at Gas No. 5 (375°F/190°C) for 30 minutes, until golden brown and firm to the touch. (May be refrigerated or frozen at this point.)

Unmould on to a serving dish. Brush the surface lightly with the redcurrant jelly, warmed until liquid with the lemon juice (easiest in the microwave), then cover with the strawberries, halved and overlapping each other. Finally brush with the remaining redcurrant jelly. Leave to set for 1 hour.

LA PIGNOLA

Serves 10–12.
The tarte will freeze for 2 months or keep 1 week under refrigeration, but is at its best freshly cooked.

This wonderful tarte from Provence has an orange-scented almond filling similar to that used in the Tranche de Fraises Provençale, but instead of fruit it is covered with a luxurious layer of crunchy pine kernels. It can be served plain or with a summer fruits compôte or a Mango Sauce (see p. 322–3).

Note that the topping is heavier if made with margarine.

1 recipe pastry for Tranche de Fraises (see p. 386)

For the filling

1 oz (25 g/2 tbsp) unsalted butter or margarine, melted
6 oz (175 g/1½ cups) pine kernels
4 oz (125 g/1 cup) ground almonds
4 oz (125 g/½ cup) caster (superfine) sugar
3 eggs
1 oz (25 g/4 tbsp) potato flour or cornflour (cornstarch)
½ teasp baking powder
pinch of salt
grated rind of 1 orange
2 teasp citrus blossom water
3 oz (75 g/⅓ cup) unsalted butter, melted
2 tbsp apricot conserve

To make the filling, melt the 1 oz butter or margarine in a small frying pan and lightly brown the pine kernels. Drain on crumpled kitchen paper, then set aside.

In a large bowl mix the almonds and sugar, then beat in the eggs 1 at a time, whisking until smooth and creamy.

Mix the potato flour, baking powder and salt in a small basin, then gently stir into the first mixture, together with the grated rind, citrus blossom water and the 3 oz butter.

To assemble the tart, preheat the oven to Gas No. 5 (375°F/190°C) and roll out the chilled dough to fit a 9-inch (22.5-cm) round or square loose-bottomed flan tin 1½ inches (4 cm) deep. Spread the pastry with the apricot conserve, then spoon in the almond mixture. Smooth level and bake for 10 minutes. Take out and quickly cover the surface with the pine kernels. Return to the oven and bake for a further 20 minutes, until the pastry is a golden brown and the pine kernels are a chestnut colour.

Serve in thin wedges or diamond shapes with the compôte or sauce.

TARTE NORMANDE FLAMBÉE AU CALVADOS

Serves 8.
Leftovers keep 2 days under refrigeration.

I found this glorious version of the famous Normandy apple pie in the heart of Calvados country in northern France. The farmer's wife who made it for me insisted it should be flamed with the local apple brandy, but it's no less delicious if you use ordinary brandy or Armagnac – or even no alcohol at all!

This particular recipe produces a meltingly tender tart filled with fluffy slices of apple bathed in a golden caramel. It is at its most delicious served 15 minutes after baking, but it can also be gently reheated. Do not freeze, as the apples then lose their texture. (Margarine may be substituted for butter for a meat meal.)

My French friend uses her own puff pastry for the tarte case. I find filo pastry works far better than commercial puff pastry. Or you could use Quick Flaky Pastry (see p. 403).

6 sheets filo pastry
1½ oz (40 g/3 tbsp) melted butter or margarine
6 large crisp eating apples – eg Cox's or Granny Smith's (3–3½ lb/1.5–1.75 kg unpeeled weight)

For the glaze

5 oz caster sugar
1 x ½–¾ oz (15–20 g) pack vanilla sugar
2 whole eggs, beaten until frothy
2 oz ((50 g/¼ cup) melted butter or margarine

To flame the tarte

4 tbsp Calvados or other brandy

Lay each sheet of pastry in turn on the table and brush with the melted fat then overlap them lengthways (see diagram p. 388). Place in an 11-inch (27.5-cm) ceramic flan dish and crumple the edges of the pastry with the fingers, trimming off any excess. Brush the edges with the remaining fat.

STACKING THE SHEETS FOR THE PASTRY CASE

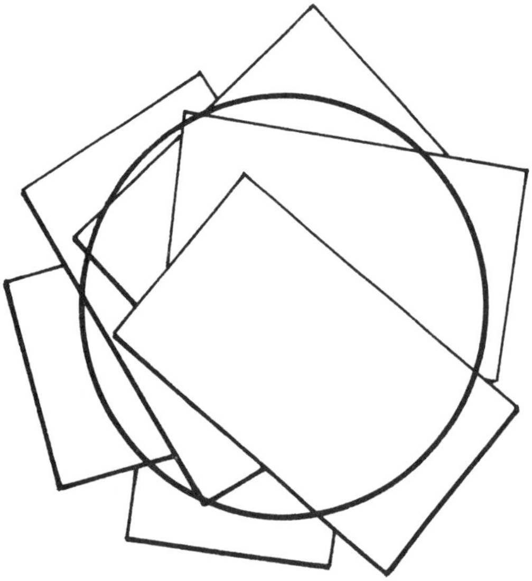

Peel, core and slice the apples ¾ inch (2 cm) thick (an apple corer/sectioner is ideal) and arrange on top of the pastry in a spiral pattern. For the glaze, whisk the sugars and eggs together until foaming, then blend with the melted fat and spoon or brush over the apples, making sure all the surfaces of the fruit are lightly coated. (At this stage the tarte can be left for 1 hour.)

Preheat the oven to Gas No. 6 (400°F/200°C). Bake the tarte for 45 minutes, cool for 10.

To flame, just before serving heat the Calvados until steaming in a small pan, set alight and then pour over the flan. Serve the tarte plain or accompanied by crème fraîche or fromage frais.

The Strudel Saga

The fragile rolypoly that is strudel represents perhaps the greatest triumph of culinary skill over the exigencies of domestic economics. A strudel dough, whether it be stretched or rolled, prepared with yeast, oil or puff pastry, is extravagant only in the time needed to make it, for the filling may be as humble as apple, or as exotic as morello (sour red) cherries or Turkish delight.

As to the feathery flaky pastry used in the true Viennese Apfelstrudel (allegedly invented, by the way, by the Hungarians), whatever its antecedents, no one can dispute that the combination of buttery apples and featherlight pastry is irresistible. The authentic method I give was taught me by a Viennese - a natural cook whose graceful yet powerful hands moved in an almost primitive rhythm as she kneaded the puddingy mess of flour and water into the silken dough that is the first step in strudel-making.

My Austrian friends fondly remember the Friday morning strudel-making sessions when their mother would rise at 5 am to stretch, roll and fill strudels as long as the kitchen table which were then cut and baked to satisfy the family's appetite for the entire weekend.

Note that in Vienna special flour known as 'glattes mehl' is used. This is high in gluten content and so can be stretched without tearing. Here you must use plain household or bread flour and knead well to develop the gluten as much as possible.

I must admit, though, that nowadays I rarely make stretched strudel dough myself. Instead I tend to rely on the widely available commercial strudel or filo pastry.

Since the first edition of this book was published in the mid-1970s, the strudel scene has changed radically as factory-made filo/strudel pastry of excellent quality has become easily available. We have also become more familiar with handling and using it. For example, because it is almost fat-free, it dries out if left exposed to the air; to prevent this the pack should not be opened until just before use. In addition, because of its low fat content, it needs 'feeding' with a thin brushing of fat, as explained below - the first time I made a strudel with commercial pastry, I didn't realize this and ended up with a mound of stewed apples and tissue paper on the baking tray. Although the final effect in taste and texture is very similar to those obtained with puff pastry, filo pastry contains only half the fat. If the particular pack of filo you buy is frozen, it should be allowed to defrost unopened at room temperature for 2 hours before use (or overnight in the refrigerator). Packs of strudel vary in the width of the sheets. On p. 390 I suggest the way of using 1½ sheets to produce a finished strudel of 16–18 inches (40–45 cm) in width. Of course, if the sheets you buy are already 20 inches (50 cm) wide (allowing a 1-inch/2.5-cm turning at either side), they can be used as they are.

What I give on p. 390, then, is my definitive version of strudel made with commercial filo pastry which I have evolved after much discussion with continental strudel experts and my own experiments on a domestic scale. Even so, there are almost as many versions of strudel as there are cooks, so if you have a good family recipe, then cherish and use it.

APFELSTRUDEL MADE WITH STRETCHED STRUDEL DOUGH

Makes 18 slices.
Keeps 3 days under refrigeration.
Freeze cooked 1 month.

8 oz (225 g/2 cups) plain (all-purpose) flour
2 level teasp sugar
1½ tbsp sunflower or other tasteless oil
1 egg
approx. 4 fl oz (125 ml/½ cup) water

For the filling

3 lb (1.5 kg) baking apples
about 4 oz (125 g/1 cup) dried breadcrumbs
6–8 oz (175–225 g/¾–1 cup) sugar, depending on tartness of apples
6 oz (175 g/¾ cup) melted unsalted butter, margarine or oil

Put the flour on the table or a large pastry board and make a hollow in the centre. Into this put the sugar, oil and egg and mix with a knife to draw in some of the surrounding flour. Add enough tepid water to make a slightly sticky dough - like a scone dough. Knead the dough with the palm of the hand until it is silky and smooth. Brush lightly with oil, then cover with an inverted mixing bowl and leave to rest for half an hour while the filling is prepared.

Peel, core and quarter the apples, then cut into blade-thin slivers and set aside.

Cover the table with a white cloth or extra-large tea-towel and rub in a little flour. Roll the dough into a 15-inch (37.5-cm) circle and brush with a little oil or melted unsalted butter. Lift the dough and lay it on to the back of the hands, then pull it a little. Put back on the table and start walking round, pulling the dough from underneath with the knuckles until it is as thin as tissue paper.

To assemble the strudel, sprinkle half the pastry with the dry breadcrumbs, then cover with the apples in an even layer. Dredge with most of the sugar, then sprinkle with almost all the fat. At the far end of the strudel, where there are no apples, brush with the fat and sprinkle with remaining sugar. Turn in the edges of the strudel and roll up, holding on to the cloth to facilitate the process. Carefully ease on to a baking sheet join-side down, and curve into a horseshoe shape to fit. Brush with the remaining butter. Bake at Gas No. 6 (400°F/200°C) for 30 minutes, turning the heat down to Gas No. 5 (375°F/190°C) after 15 minutes if the pastry seems to be browning too quickly. Serve warm in slanting 2-inch-thick (5-cm) slices.

APFELSTRUDEL WITH FILO PASTRY

Serves 8–9.
The cooked strudel will keep 3–4 days under refrigeration.
Freeze cooked 1 month.

6 sheets filo pastry (defrosted if necessary)
2–3 oz (50–75 g/¼–⅓ cup) unsalted butter or margarine, melted

For the filling

1½ oz (40 g/3 tbsp) unsalted butter or margarine
2 oz (50 g/1 cup) fresh breadcrumbs
2 oz (175 g/½ cup) walnuts, finely chopped (optional)
4 oz (125 g/½ cup) granulated sugar
1 teasp ground cinnamon
juice and finely grated rind of ½ lemon
1½ lb (675 g) baking apples, cored, peeled and coarsely grated or thinly sliced
3 oz (75 g/½ cup) raisins, sultanas (white raisins) or chopped dates

Preheat the oven to Gas No. 5 (375°F/190°C). Melt the 1½ oz fat in a baking tin, then add the breadcrumbs and nuts (if used). Stir well, then allow to crisp and brown in the oven for 10–15 minutes, stirring once, then remove and cool for 20 minutes.

Grease a large baking sheet with a little of the melted butter. In a large basin mix together the sugar, cinnamon, lemon juice and rind, then mix in the apples, dried fruit and nuts coating them with the cinnamon and sugar (this is best done just before the filling is required, otherwise juice may ooze out of the fruit and make the pastry soggy).

Melt the 2–3 oz fat in a small basin and set

TO ENLARGE BOUGHT SHEETS OF FILO (FOR STRUDEL)

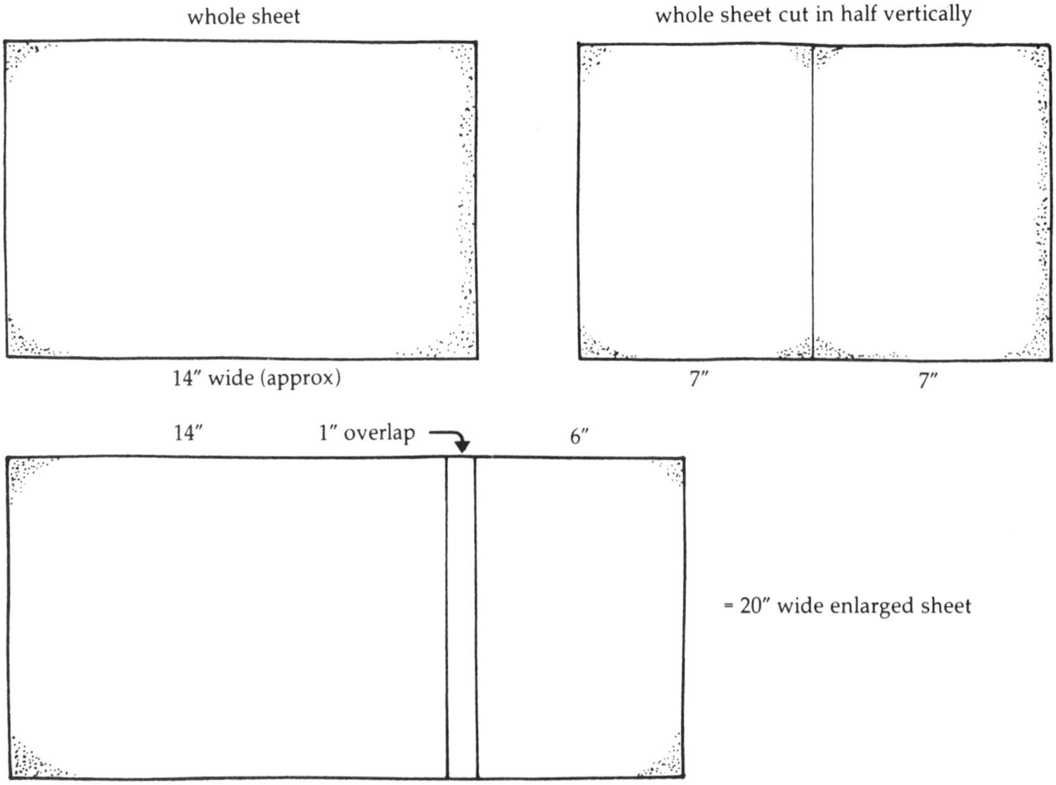

aside. (This can be done in the microwave - 1½ minutes at 100 per cent power, covered with a paper towel to avoid spattering.) Count out 6 sheets of filo pastry, then reseal the packet and return to the refrigerator or freezer, according to packet directions. Cut 2 of the sheets in half vertically. Use these to overlap each full sheet in turn, to widen the strudel.

Lay 1½ sheets (as described on p. 389) on a tea-towel and brush evenly with the melted fat, then scatter with a quarter of the crumb mixture, and repeat with the remaining 3 sheets and crumb mixture. Arrange the apple mixture over the half of pastry nearest to you, leaving a 1-inch (2.5-cm) border free on the bottom and sides. Fold in the left and right sides of the pastry, then with the help of the tea-towel roll up the pastry and filling into a strudel with the join-side under. Carefully transfer the strudel to the baking sheet and brush it all over with a thin layer of the remaining fat (too much may stop it browning evenly). Make 8–9 diagonal slashes, about 2 inches (5 cm) apart, through the top layers of pastry.

Lay a piece of silicone or greaseproof paper on top, then bake for 35–40 minutes, until the strudel is crisp and golden brown and a small knife pushed through one of the slits will go right through the filling - if it doesn't feel absolutely tender, give it another 5 minutes. Lift (using 2 spatulas) on to a cooling tray. Just before serving, sprinkle thickly with icing (confectioners') sugar. May be reheated until warm to the touch. Do not reheat in the microwave (unless it is a combination oven) as the strudel tends to go soggy.

A TOASTED NUT AND WILD BERRY STRUDEL

Makes 1 strudel, serving 8.
Keeps 2 days under refrigeration.
Freeze 1 month.

The frozen packs of mixed berries now available, some with cherries, make a refreshing and unusual filling for a strudel.

Depending on your preference, it is possible to omit the sugar in the filling and instead sprinkle a little sugar or granular sweetener on top for those who want it.

6 sheets filo pastry
3 oz (75 g/⅓ cup) melted unsalted butter or margarine
2 oz (50 g/¼ cup) granulated sugar

For the filling

1½ oz (40 g/3 tbsp) butter or margarine
2 oz (50 g/1 cup) fresh brown or white breadcrumbs
2 oz (50 g/½ cup) chopped almonds
1 lb (450 g) mixed fresh or frozen berries
2 tbsp Crème de Framboise or other fruity liqueur (optional)

Set the oven at Gas No. 5 (375°F/190°C). Melt the 1½ oz fat in a baking tin, add the breadcrumbs and almonds and stir well. Allow to crisp and brown for a further 10–15 minutes, then remove and cool for 10 minutes.

Put the fruit straight from the freezer into a bowl and sprinkle with the liqueur.

Melt the 3 oz fat in a small basin and set aside. Take 6 sheets of filo pastry, then reseal the packet and return to the refrigerator or freezer, according to packet directions. Cut 2 of the sheets in half vertically. Use these to overlap each full sheet in turn, to widen the strudel.

On a tea-towel lay the 4 enlarged, buttered sheets of filo on top of each other as in the Apfelstrudel recipe on p. 390, sprinkling each layer with the nut and crumb mixture. Arrange the fruit in a 2½-inch-wide (6-cm) band 2 inches (5 cm) from the lower end and leave 1 inch (2.5 cm) clear at either side. Scatter with sugar. Turn in the sides, then roll up with the help of the tea-towel into a strudel with the join underneath.

Carefully transfer the strudel to the baking sheet and brush it all over with a thin layer of the remaining fat. Make 8-9 diagonal slashes about 2 inches (5 cm) apart through the top layer of pastry. Bake for 35-40 minutes, until crisp and golden brown. To serve, sprinkle thickly with icing (confectioners') sugar or granular sweetener. Serve plain or with a fruited fromage frais.

VARIATION

If there is a diabetic in the party, you can make a sugarless version by omitting the sugar from the filling and using 2 tablespoons of orange juice instead of the fruit liqueur. When the strudel is baked, omit the icing sugar, but sprinkle with granular sweetener. A sugar sifter can be passed round the table for sugar-eaters.

KIRSCHENSTRUDEL
(*Cherry Strudel*)

Makes 1 strudel, serving 8.
Keeps 2 days under refrigeration.
Freeze 1 month.

Fresh morello (sour red) cherries produce a strudel with a superb sweet and sour flavour. There are, however, some excellent bottled and canned cherries from Eastern Europe - pitted ones for preference - which can be bought instead.

3 oz (75 g/⅓ cup) unsalted butter or block margarine, melted
6 sheets filo pastry

For the filling

2 lb (900 g) fresh Morello cherries, pitted or 1 x 1 lb 12 oz (750 g) can or bottle cherries
4 oz (125 g/½ cup) light brown sugar or 2 oz (50 g/¼ cup) if canned cherries used
2 tbsp lemon juice
2 tbsp cherry brandy (optional)
1½ oz (40 g/3 tbsp) butter or margarine
3 oz (75 g/1½ cups) fresh brown or white breadcrumbs
2 oz chopped almonds

Put the fruit into a bowl and sprinkle with the brown sugar, lemon juice and cherry brandy. Allow to marinate for at least 30 minutes.

Set the oven at Gas No. 6 (400°F/200°C). Melt the 1½ oz fat in a baking tin, add the breadcrumbs and almonds and stir well. Allow to crisp and brown in the oven for 10-15 minutes, stirring once, then remove and cool for a further 10 minutes.

Melt the 3 oz butter in a small basin and set aside. Count out 6 sheets of filo pastry, then reseal the packet and return to the refrigerator or freezer, according to packet directions. Cut 2 of the sheets in half vertically. Use these to overlap each full sheet in turn to widen the strudel (it should then be approximately 18 inches/45 cm wide).

On a tea-towel lay the 4 enlarged buttered sheets of filo on top of each other as in the Apfelstrudel recipe (see pp. 390-91), sprinkling each layer with a little of the nut and crumb mixture but reserving a rounded tablespoon to scatter on the fruit. Life the cherries out of the marinade with a slotted spoon and arrange in a 2-inch-wide (5-cm) band about 3 inches (7.5 cm) from the edge of the pastry nearest to you, leaving 1 inch (2.5 cm) of pastry clear of fruit at either side. Spoon a tablespoon of the remaining marinade on top of the fruit and scatter with the remaining nut and crumb mixture.

Turn the sides of the pastry in to seal in the juices and then, with the help of the tea-towel, roll up into a strudel, and place on a shallow greased baking tray, join-side down. Brush the top of the strudel with an even layer of the remaining fat. Make 8 diagonal slashes about 2 inches (5 cm) apart through the top layer of pastry. Bake for 25-30 minutes, until crisp and golden brown. To serve, sprinkle thickly with icing (confectioners') sugar. Serve plain or with thick yoghurt, smetana or soured cream.

PFIRSICHSTRUDEL
(*Fresh Peach and Macaroon Strudel*)

Makes 1 strudel, serving 8.
The strudel will keep 2 days under refrigeration.
Freeze 1 month.

Almond biscuits and liqueur combine to make a superb 'marriage' of flavours with the peaches. 2 large cans of peach halves (well drained) can be used out of season, but the sugar in the marinade should then be reduced to 2 tablespoons.

3 oz (75 g/⅓ cup) unsalted butter or block margarine, melted
6 sheets filo pastry

For the filling
6 large firm peaches (total weight approximately 1¾ lb/800 g)
4 tbsp caster sugar
2 teasp fresh lemon juice
4 tbsp Amaretto (almond-flavoured liqueur) or brandy
1 x 3½ oz (85 g) packet of macaroons (ratafia biscuits) or Amaretti, crumbled
generous 1 oz (25 g) of dry toasted breadcrumbs
6 tbsp granulated sugar

Cut the unpeeled fruit away from the stone in slices ½ inch (1 cm) thick or slice canned peach halves. Place in a bowl and sprinkle with the caster sugar, lemon juice and the liqueur or brandy. Allow to stand for at least 30 minutes to soak up the juices.

Preheat the oven to Gas No. 5 (375°F/190°C). Crush the biscuits with a rolling pin until like coarse sand, then mix with the breadcrumbs and sugar.

Melt the fat in a small basin and set aside. Count out 6 sheets of filo pastry, then reseal the packet and return to the refrigerator or freezer, according to packet directions. Cut 2 overlap each of the 4 full sheets in turn, to widen the strudel.

On a tea-towel lay the 4 enlarged buttered sheets on top of each other as in the Apfelstrudel recipe (see pp. 390–91), sprinkling each layer with nut and crumb mixture, but leaving a tablespoon or so to scatter over the fruit. Lift the peach slices out of the marinade with a slotted spoon and arrange in a line about 3 inches (7.5 cm) from the edge of the pastry nearest to you and leaving 1 inch (2.5 cm) of pastry clear of fruit at either side. Spoon a tablespoon of the remaining marinade on top of the fruit and scatter with the rest of the nut and crumb mixture. (Any marinade left can be used as the basis for a fruit salad.)

Turn in the sides of the pastry to seal in the juices, then with the help of the tea-towel roll up into a strudel and place on a shallow greased baking tray, join-side down. Brush the top of the strudel with an even layer of the remaining fat. Make 8 diagonal slashes about 2 inches (5 cm) apart through the top layer of pastry. Bake for 35 minutes, until crisp and golden brown.

To serve, sprinkle thickly with icing (confectioners') sugar. Serve plain or with Greek-style yoghurt or smetana.

CHANA'S NUSSESTRUDEL

Makes 2 strudels, 10 slices in each.
Cooked strudel keeps 3 days at room temperature in an airtight container.
Freeze 3 months.

A wonderful pastry for the nut-lover – there's an interesting texture contrast between the crunchy filling and the flaky pastry that enfolds it. It's important to use best-quality walnuts – halves are generally better than broken pieces – and avoid any packs with nut 'dust'.

1 recipe Cream-cheese Flaky Pastry (see p. 402)

For the filling
8 oz (225 g/2 cups) walnuts, finely chopped
1 egg white
3 oz (75 g/⅓ cup) granulated sugar
1 rounded tbsp thin honey or golden (corn) syrup
2 teasp finely grated lemon rind
½ teasp vanilla essence (extract)

For spreading on the dough
2–3 tbsp apricot (or cherry) conserve

For the glaze
1 egg yolk mixed with 1 teasp water

For dredging the cooked strudels
sifted icing (confectioners') sugar

The day before, make the pastry and also the filling – this allows it time to mature in flavour. Toss the nuts in a non-stick frying pan over moderate heat or put under the grill (broiler) until they smell 'toasty' (watch them as they burn easily), then chop finely (most easily done in the food processor). Whisk the egg white until it holds floppy peaks, then fold in the sugar. Add the remaining filling ingredients and mix well. Cover and refrigerate.

To assemble the strudel the next day, remove the pastry from the refrigerator and divide into 2 portions. On a lightly floured board, roll 1 portion into a rectangle approximately 12 x 7 inches (30 x 17.5 cm), then neaten the edges with a knife. Spread the dough with a thin layer of half the conserve, leaving clear a ½-inch (1-cm) border all the way round, then spread with half the filling. Turn in the short ends to enclose the filling, then roll up into a long cylinder. Repeat with the other portion of pastry and filling.

Arrange the strudels side by side on an ungreased baking sheet. (The raw strudels may be frozen at this point.)

Preheat the oven to Gas No. 8 (450°F/230°C) and brush the strudels all over with the egg glaze. Prick decoratively with a fork or tweezers: this prevents the pastry bursting in the oven and makes it easier for the icing sugar to cling to the surface after baking. Bake for 5 minutes, then turn the heat down to Gas No. 5 (375°F/190°C) for a further 20 minutes, until the strudels are a rich brown.

To serve, have the strudels at room temperature. Dredge thickly with icing sugar, then cut in diagonal slices 1½ inches (4 cm) wide. Serve plain with tea or coffee, or for dessert accompanied by a fruit compôte.

FEUILLETÉ AUX POMMES (*Apple Slice*)

Serves 6.
Eat freshly baked.
Leftover keep 2 days under refrigeration.

A feuilleté is akin to a strudel in that a fruit filling is enclosed within layers of pastry. However, as puff or flaky pastry is used rather than filo, I find it stays crisper if shaped into a 'sandwich' rather than rolled like a strudel.

approx. 12–14 oz (350–400 g) fresh or frozen puff pastry (see p. 403)

For the filling
1 oz (25 g/2 tbsp) butter or margarine
1½ lb (675 g) cooking apples (weight after peeling and coring)
4–6 level tbsp brown sugar
grated rind and juice of ½ lemon (1½ tbsp)
1 tbsp apricot jam (optional)

Melt the fat in a wide frying pan or 8-inch (20-cm) saucepan, then add the apples (cut in thick slices – about 8 to the apple) alternately with the sugar. Pour over the rind and juice and sprinkle with the jam. Cover and cook very gently for about 15 minutes, until the apples are tender but still whole, or arrange in a 10–11-inch (25–27.5-cm) lidded dish and microwave on 100 per cent power for 7 minutes, stirring once. Leave to stand for 5 minutes. Allow to go quite cold before using.

Divide the pastry in 2 and roll each half into a very thin rectangle measuring 14 x 8 inches (35 x 20 cm). Place 1 piece of pastry on a wet, ungreased baking sheet (this keeps the pastry in shape), then pile on the cooled apples, leaving a ¾-inch (2-cm) margin all the way round. Dampen this margin with water. Take the second sheet of pastry, fold it lengthwise and make slanting slits down the centre, then unfold and lay in position on top of the filling. Press the edges together all the way round, then gently rub the blunt side of a knife blade across, thus sealing them without crushing the pastry layers.

Bake in a very hot oven, Gas No. 8 (450°F/230°C), for 15 minutes. Take out and sprinkle with caster (superfine) sugar, then reduce the heat to Gas No. 6 (400°F/200°C) and continue to bake for a further 10-15 minutes, until golden brown. Serve warm in slices.

VARIATIONS

FEUILLETÉ AUX ABRICOTS

(Apricot Slice)

For the filling

3 tbsp apricot conserve
1½ lb (675 g) fresh apricots or nectarines, halved and stoned, or 1 large can choice apricot halves, well drained, or 8 oz (225 g) tenderized ready-to-eat dried apricots
2 tbsp lemon juice
3 oz (75 g/⅓ cup) golden granulated sugar (for fresh fruit only)
1 oz (25 g/¼ cup) toasted almond flakes (optional)

Spread the bottom layer of pastry with the apricot conserve to within ¾ inch (2 cm) of the edge all the way round. Mix the filling ingredients together, then arrange on top of the conserve. Proceed as before.

FEUILLETÉ AUX CERISES

(Cherry Slice)

For the filling

1 can best-quality cherry pie filling, or large can pitted black or Morello (sour red) cherries
3 level tbsp cornflour (cornstarch)
1 tbsp lemon juice
1-3 tbsp granulated sugar (more if morellos are used)

Drain the cherries, reserving the juice. Mix the cornflour, lemon juice and sugar, then stir in the juice. Bring to the boil and simmer for 3 minutes, or mix in a jug and microwave uncovered on 100 per cent power for 1½ minutes. Stir and cook for a further 2½ minutes, until bubbling and clear. Allow to go cold.

Spread the filling on the bottom layer of pastry to within ¾ inch (2 cm) of the edge all the way round. Proceed as before.

DANISH APPLE BRAID

Serves 8.
Raw braid will freeze 1 month, baked ready-to-serve 1 week.

Not even the Danes bake their famous pastries at home, they're so tricky to make. But you can produce a very passable and quite delicious facsimile, using puff pastry instead of the authentic yeast dough.

The trick is to paint the pastry with apricot jam the moment it comes out of the oven, and then to spread a lemon icing on top so that the flavours mingle and sink into the filling. This recipe serves 8 as either cake or dessert.

1 x 14–16 oz (400–450 g) packet puff pastry

For the filling
1¼ lb (575 g) cooking apples or well-flavoured eating apples
nut of butter or margarine
3–4 tbsp soft brown sugar
rind and juice of ½ lemon
1 tbsp orange juice
1 tbsp apricot jam
½ teasp ground cinnamon

For the topping
1 tbsp lemon juice
3 oz (75 g/½ cup) sifted icing (confectioners') sugar
2 tbsp apricot jam
12 toasted chopped almonds

Preheat the oven to Gas No. 8 (450°F/230°C). Cut the peeled and cored apples into ½-inch (1-cm) slices. Put them with the fat, sugar, juices, jam and cinnamon into a shallow pan, then cover and simmer gently until they are tender but unbroken - around 15 minutes (or 6 minutes on 100 per cent power in the microwave). Allow to cool completely.

Prepare a large ungreased baking tray, sprinkle lightly with cold water, then roll the pastry into a rectangle approximately 14 x 12 inches (35 x 30 cm). Leaving a centre panel 6 inches (15 cm) wide intact to form the base of

TO MAKE A BRAID

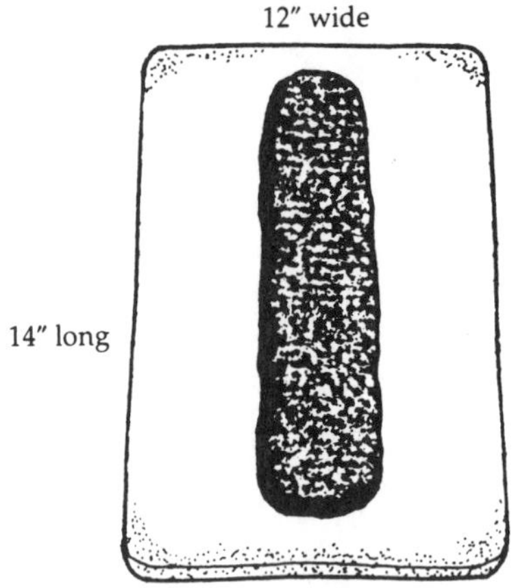

Arrange filling down centre of pastry

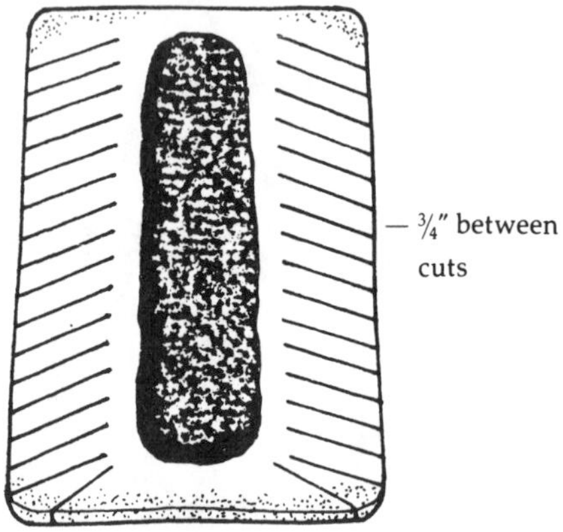

Make diagonal cuts

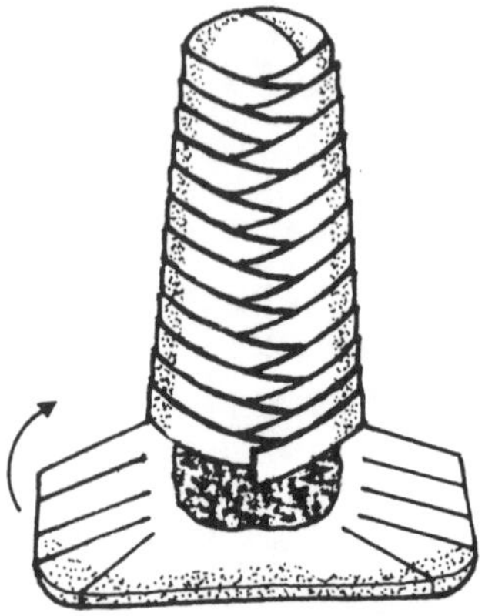
Fold in top of pastry and overlap strips to form a braid

the slice, make slanting cuts downwards from each side of the panel ¾ inch (2 cm) apart. Leave ½ inch (1 cm) uncut on each side of the panel. Lift the apple out of the dish with a slotted spoon and arrange on the base section of the slice. Turn the pastry in at the top and the bottom, then cross over strips from either side, giving a plaited effect. Ensure the filling is well sealed, then bake for 30-40 minutes, or until brown and readily crisp to the touch.

While the slice is in the oven, mix enough lemon juice with the icing sugar to make a thick coating consistency. As soon as the pastry comes out of the oven, brush the top thoroughly first with the apricot jam and then with the icing. Scatter with nuts.

VARIATION

BRANDIED MINCEMEAT AND ALMOND BRAID

Serves 10-12.
Raw braid will freeze 1 month, ready-to-serve cooked braid 1 week.

This elegant confection is assembled in the same way as the Danish Apple Braid but the filling is altogether richer and more luxurious, so a small slice will suffice. It is undoubtedly at its best when freshly baked.

1 lb (450 g) puff pastry
2 rounded tbsp apricot conserve

For the almond filling
2 oz (50 g/¼ cup) butter or margarine
2 oz (50 g/¼ cup) caster (superfine) sugar
1 egg
½ teasp vanilla essence (extract)
4 oz (125 g/1 cup) ground almonds
1 tbsp flour
1 oz (25 g/¼ cup) almond nibs, toasted

For the mincemeat filling
12 oz (350 g) mincemeat
1 tbsp brandy
1 tbsp ground almonds

For the icing
3 teasp orange juice
3 teasp Cointreau
5 oz (150 g/¾ cup) icing (confectioners') sugar
1 oz (25 g/¼ cup) toasted almonds

To make the almond filling, put all the ingredients into a bowl and beat until creamy - about 2 minutes.

Preheat the oven to Gas No. 8 (450°F/230°C) and roll the pastry into a rectangle measuring 14 x 9 inches (35 x 22.5 cm) when well trimmed. Arrange the almond filling in a strip 2½ inches (6 cm) wide down the length of the pastry, leaving 1 inch (2.5 cm) clear at either end.

Mix the mincemeat filling ingredients in a bowl, then spoon this on top of the almond filling.

Leaving ½ inch (1 cm) of uncut pastry on either side of the filling, cut the pastry into ¾-inch-wide (2-cm) diagonal strips - about 15 on each side. Criss-cross the strips of pastry over the filling, covering it almost completely. Finally turn the ends under and pinch to seal. Lift the braid carefully on to a silicone-lined baking sheet and cook for 30 minutes, until crisp and brown.

Meanwhile, mix the icing ingredients into a smooth thick paste. As soon as the braid comes from the oven, carefully brush over with the apricot conserve, followed by half the icing. Cool for 20 minutes, then apply a further coat of icing and decorate with almonds. Serve in 1-inch (2.5-cm) slices.

Small Pastries

APFELSCHNITTEN
(*Apple Slices*)

Serves 6–8 as a dessert.
Makes 20–24 little squares to serve with coffee.
Raw pastry will freeze 1 month.
Do not freeze when cooked as it goes soggy.

I first came across this magical almond pastry in Gretel Beer's seminal *Austrian Cooking*, published in the austere days of 1954. Since then it has become a favourite of both my Jewish and non-Jewish readers - it's also a superb pastry for mincepies.

As it's so very tender, I always found it difficult to roll out in 1 piece for the top of the Schnitten, but I now *freeze* the top portion and then grate it over the filling. It then bakes to a crunchy textured topping (it doesn't matter if you have to patch the bottom layer). For a *parev* version, use a whole egg to mix the pastry and omit the cream. The texture will be rather crisper.

For the almond pastry
9 oz (250 g/2¼ cups) plain (all-purpose) flour
pinch of salt
1 oz (25 g/¼ cup) ground almonds or hazelnuts
3 oz (75 g/⅓ cup) caster (superfine) sugar
grated rind of ½ lemon
6 oz (175 g/¾ cup) butter or firm margarine, cut in 1-inch (2.5-cm) chunks
1 egg yolk
2 tbsp single (light) cream or evaporated milk

For the filling
2 lb (900 g) baking apples (approx. 1½ lb/675 g when peeled and cored)
4 oz (125 g/½ cup) granulated sugar
1 teasp ground cinnamon
3 tbsp raisins or sultanas (white raisins)
2 oz (50 g/½ cup) walnuts, coarsely chopped
2 tbsp lemon juice

For sprinkling on top
golden granulated or demerara sugar

To make the pastry, put the flour, salt, nuts, sugar and lemon rind into a bowl. Add the chunks of butter and rub in gently until the mixture resembles dry breadcrumbs. Mix the egg yolk and the cream, then sprinkle on the dry ingredients and mix to a dough. (Alternatively make by the food-processor method, see p. 371.)

Divide the dough in 2 and knead each piece gently on a floured board until smooth. Flatten each piece until 1 inch (2.5 cm) thick. Wrap in foil, chill 1 and freeze the other for 1 hour.

Preheat the oven to Gas No. 5 (375°F/190°C) and have ready a shallow tin approximately 12 x 8 x ¾ inch (30 x 20 x 2 cm). Roll the chilled piece of pastry to fit the tin, then gently ease into place and trim the edges level.

Assemble the pastry and filling just before baking, or the juicy apples may make the base soggy. Coarsely grate or finely slice the apples and mix with all the other filling ingredients. Immediately spread in an even layer over the pastry, then coarsely grate the frozen pastry over the top. Sprinkle with the sugar, then bake for 45 minutes until golden brown.

Serve warm or at room temperature, accompanied by a cinnamon cream made by mixing together 9 oz (250 g) of fromage frais with 2 teaspoons each of caster sugar and cinnamon.

PFIRSICHSCHNITTEN
(*Peach and Almond Slice*)

Serves 8 generously.
Keeps 2 days under refrigeration.
Freeze leftovers 3 months.

This looks particularly effective baked in a rectangular or square loose-bottomed flan tin, then unmoulded on to a serving dish. However, it can be baked in an ordinary baking tin about 12 x 8 x 1 inches (30 x 20 x 2.5 cm), but it will then need to be cut into portions in the tin. The non-dairy version makes a refreshing dessert to serve after a meat meal.

1 recipe Almond Pastry (see p. 398)

For the filling

1 oz (25 g/¼ cup) ground almonds (or hazelnuts)
3 oz (75 g/⅓ cup) granulated sugar
1 tbsp cornflour (cornstarch)
2 teasp finely grated lemon rind
1½–2 lb (675–900 g) (about 6 large) ripe peaches or nectarines
1 tbsp lemon juice

For the topping

1 tbsp golden granulated sugar
2 tbsp chopped pecans or walnuts

About 1 or 2 hours in advance, make the almond pastry. Knead lightly until smooth, then divide in 2 squares about 1 inch (2.5 cm) thick. Wrap separately in clingfilm (saranwrap), chill 1 portion and put the other in the freezer for 1 hour, or until frozen almost solid.

Preheat the oven to Gas No. 5 (375°F/190°C), putting in a baking sheet to heat at the same time (unnecessary with a fan-assisted oven). Roll out the unfrozen pastry to fit the chosen tin and sprinkle with the ground nuts. Mix the sugar, cornflour and lemon rind in a bowl, add the sliced fruit (cut away from the stone), then mix to coat with the sugar mixture. Sprinkle with the lemon juice and turn into the pastry case. Coarsely grate the frozen pastry in an even layer on top, then sprinkle with the sugar and nuts. Bake for 40–45 minutes, until a rich golden brown. Serve warm or at room temperature. May be reheated.

RUM AND MINCEMEAT SQUARES

Makes 20–24 small squares.
Keeps 1 week at room temperature in an airtight container.
Freeze 3 months.

An Anglo-Jewish interpretation.

1 recipe Almond Pastry (see p. 398)

For the filling

2 lb (900 g) vegetarian or home-made mincemeat (see p. 500)
2 rounded tbsp apricot conserve
3 tbsp rum, brandy or orange juice
2 oz (50 g/½ cup) fine biscuit crumbs or ground hazelnuts

For the topping

1 tbsp golden granulated sugar

Make the almond pastry, then divide into 2, chilling 1 portion and freezing the other.

Mix all the filling ingredients together. If too wet (it should be moist and spreadable), firm up with a few more crumbs or ground nuts.

Roll out the pastry, spread with the filling and top with the grated pastry as described for Apfelschnitten (see p. 398) and sugar. Bake at Gas No. 5 (375°F/190°C) for 40–45 minutes, until a rich golden brown. Cut into small squares when cool. Serve slightly warm. Reheats well.

STUFFED MONKEY

Makes 24 2-inch (5-cm) squares.
Keeps under refrigeration for several weeks.
Freeze 3 months.

The saga relating to the origin of the name of this unusual pastry unfolded in the pages of the *Jewish Chronicle* over many years, with all the clues leading to a Dutch origin. One recipe I was sent came from a family with strong Dutch connections and the method is very reminiscent of that for Dutch Boterkoek. It was first introduced to Britain early this century by a Jewish baker called Monnickendam, who had a famous cake shop in the East End of London. In his *Children of the Ghetto*, Israel Zangwill wrote of Wentworth Street (in the East End) and its confectioners' shops crammed with stuffed monkey and 'fat women all washing down the luscious spicy compound with cups of hot chocolate'.

The most plausible suggestion for the name is that with popular usage Monnickendam's became Monnike's from where it's a small step to 'monkey' and then but a whisker to 'stuffed monkey' - in any case, a not illogical name for a sweetmeat that's made with a brown-sugar pastry.

Whatever the derivation of its name, it is a delicious confection, sandwiching a luscious cinnamon-scented filling between layers of meltingly tender brown-sugar pastry.

For the brown-sugar pastry

8 oz (225 g/2 cups) plain (all-purpose) flour
5 oz (150 g/⅔ cup) butter or margarine
4 oz (125 g/½ cup) soft brown sugar
1 small egg or ½ large one
1 level teasp cinnamon

For the filling

3 oz (75 g/⅓ cup) butter or margarine
4 oz (125 g/1 cup) ground almonds
2 oz (50 g/⅓ cup) caster (superfine) sugar
4 oz (125 g/¾ cup) orange or citron candied peel
1 egg yolk
few drops vanilla essence (extract)
grated rind of ½ lemon

For the topping

1 egg white
golden granulated sugar

Make the pastry by either method on p. 371. Knead well and divide into 2. Roll half of it to fit a shallow lined tray 12 x 8 x ¾ inches (30 x 20 x 2 cm).

To make filling, put soft fat and all remaining filling ingredients in a bowl and beat until creamy. Spread over the pastry base. Cover with the remaining pastry, rolled out to fit. Mark into small squares.

Beat egg white until frothy, paint over dough and sprinkle with golden granulated sugar. Bake at No. 5 (375°F/190°C) for 30 minutes, until firm to touch. Serve cold, cut into squares.

GINGER SLICES

Makes 24–30 small squares.
Keeps for 1 month at room temperature in an airtight container.
Freeze 3 months.

The original recipe, which was very popular in Jewish homes in Britain between the wars, called for a jar of preserved ginger. However, I've found a good-quality ginger preserve or marmalade works extremely well and makes a fruity contrast to the crunchy pastry. The same pastry is used as for the Stuffed Monkey (see this page), and as that recipe is definitely of Dutch origin I believe this one also originated in the Netherlands, but was so good that it was taken up by the general Anglo-Jewish community.

1 recipe brown-sugar pastry (see this page)

For the filling

1 lb (450 g) jar best-quality ginger preserve

For the topping

milk or beaten egg
3 tbsp flaked almonds
2 tbsp demerara or golden granulated sugar

Preheat the oven to Gas No. 5 (375°F/190°C). Get ready an ungreased, shallow baking tin measuring approximately 12 x 8 x ¾ inches (30 x 20 x 2 cm). Roll out 1 portion of the dough on a floured board until it is the size of the tin. Carefully transfer to the tin and trim level with the rim. Spoon the ginger preserve evenly all over the dough. Roll out the remainder of the dough and carefully lay on top. Again, trim level with the sides, then press with the tines of a fork to seal to the edge of the tin. Brush the top of the pastry with the milk or beaten egg, then scatter evenly with the flaked almonds, mixed with the sugar.

Bake for 40 minutes, or until golden-brown and firm to gentle touch. Leave for 15 minutes, then mark into 24 or 30 small squares. When quite cold, lift from the tin.

ENGLISH VARIATION

RHUBARB SLICE

Cooked squares keep 2 days under refrigeration. Do not freeze.

For the filling
1½ lb (675 g) forced rhubarb cut in 1-inch (2.5-cm) pieces
6 oz (175 g/¾ cup) granulated sugar
1 level tbsp cornflour (cornstarch)

Make and bake exactly as before, but use the rhubarb filling instead.

SWEET TARTLET CASES

Makes about 40 tartlets.
Keeps 3 weeks at room temperature in an airtight container.
Freeze empty cases 3 months.

The icing (confectioners') sugar in the pastry gives it a very crisp texture and the egg yolks a pleasing fragility which makes it literally melt-in-the-mouth. When the tartlets are baked 'blind', there is no need to line them with foil - simply prick with a fork and they will keep their shape to perfection. Unlike many other rich pastries, they retain their crispness for several hours even after they've been filled - for example, with soft fruits.

8 oz (225 g/2 cups) plain (all-purpose) flour
pinch of salt
5 oz (150 ml/⅔ cup) soft butter
3 oz (75 g/½ cup) icing (confectioners') sugar
2 egg yolks

Make by the food-processor method (see p. 371) or the traditional shortbread method (see p. 449). Chill for at least 1 hour. Roll out on a board sprinkled with icing sugar instead of flour to a thickness of ⅛ inch (0.3 cm). Cut to fit patty tins and prick well.

Preheat the oven to Gas No. 4 (350°F/180°C) and bake the tartlet cases for 15-20 minutes, until a pale gold in colour.

DANISH STRAWBERRY TARTS

Makes 20.
Eat the same day.

½ recipe Sweet Tartlet Cases (see this page)

For the filling
redcurrant jelly
1 tbsp lemon juice
2 teasp maraschino or grenadine syrup
5 fl oz (150 ml/⅔ cup) creamy (8%) fromage frais
1½ lb (675 g) strawberries

In the bottom of each cooled shell put a little chopped redcurrant jelly. Melt 4 tbsp more redcurrant jelly with the lemon juice until liquid (easiest in the microwave). Gently stir the syrup through the fromage frais, creating a marbled effect.

Arrange 3 strawberries in each tartlet and glaze with the redcurrant jelly. When set, decorate with a blob of the creamy topping. Chill until required.

BERRY AND CREAM-CHEESE TARTLETS

Makes 20.
Eat the same day.

½ recipe Sweet Tartlet Cases *(see p. 401)*

For the filling
1 oz (25 g/2 tbsp) butter
1 oz (25 g/2 tbsp) caster (superfine) sugar
6 oz (175 g/¾ cup) cream cheese
1 tbsp yoghurt or fromage frais
few drops vanilla essence (extract)
1 lb (450 g) whole strawberries, raspberries, tayberries, loganberries or blackberries
4 tbsp redcurrant jelly
1 tbsp lemon juice

Cream the soft butter and sugar until fluffy, then beat in the cheese, yoghurt or fromage frais and the vanilla. Line each tartlet with some of the filling. Arrange a layer of berries on top and coat with the redcurrant jelly and lemon juice, which have been warmed together until liquid. Chill until required.

CREAM-CHEESE FLAKY PASTRY
(*Topfenblaetterteig*)

Freeze 3 months.

This is a delicious continental pastry that makes a perfect base for pizzas or quiches. It can also be used for sweet or savoury turnovers in place of rough puff pastry (see p. 403) or quick flaky pastry (see p. 403). Because of its richness, it should be chilled for several hours, or overnight, and it is then very easy to roll out.

4 oz (125 g/½ cup) firm butter
4 oz (125 g/½ cup) dry curd or sieved cottage cheese
4 oz (125 g/1 cup) self-raising flour or 4 oz (125 g/1 cup) plain (all-purpose) flour with a pinch of salt and 1 level teasp baking powder

Cream the butter and cheese until well blended. Stir in the flour (and baking powder and salt if used), mixing to a dough. Foil wrap and chill in the refrigerator for at least 1 hour.

VARIATION

SAVOURY CHEESE PASTRY

Add 3 oz (75 g/¾ cup) finely grated dry cheese and 2 level teaspoons of dry mustard to the flour before stirring it into the butter and curd cheese.

JAM PUFFS
(*Polster Zipfel*)

Makes about 24.
Keeps 4 days at room temperature in an airtight container.
Freeze 3 months.

A Viennese speciality. My Austrian-born friends make these the authentic way – from squares of pastry folded into triangles to enclose the jam – but it's easier to get a uniform shape, and much quicker, using a biscuit cutter.

1 recipe Cream-cheese Flaky Pastry (see this page)
a slightly tart jam such as 'Povidl' (dark plum jam)
a little beaten egg
caster (superfine) sugar

Roll out the chilled pastry to the thickness of a knife blade, then cut into 2½-inch (6-cm) circles with a pastry cutter. Put a tiny spoonful of jam in the centre, dampen the edges with water and fold over to seal into a half moon. Brush with the egg and bake in a preheated oven, Gas No. 7 (425°F/220°C), for 15 minutes or until golden brown. Sprinkle with caster sugar while warm.

ROUGH PUFF PASTRY

Keeps 3 days (raw) under refrigeration.
Freeze 3 months.

This is the easiest kind of puff pastry for the home cook to make. I give this recipe for reference as few of us make either rough puff or puff pastry, except for special occasions. Making true puff pastry is a specialized skill which demands a great deal of practice. This is an excellent and far simpler alternative and can be used in any recipe calling for puff pastry.

Pointers to success Use a 'strong' (bread) flour and a firm, plastic (as opposed to soft and greasy) butter or margarine. Soft fats will not incorporate properly with the flour.

7 oz (200 g/1 cup minus 2 tbsp) butter or margarine
8 oz (225 g/2 cups) plain (all-purpose) flour
1 level teasp salt
7 tbsp cold water
1 tbsp wine or wine vinegar

Cut the fat into 15 x ½-inch (1.25-cm) cubes. Put the flour and salt into a bowl, then add the butter or margarine and mix very gently to coat with the flour. Add the water and wine gradually, stirring with a spoon until the mixture leaves the sides of the bowl clean and no dampened flour remains. Gather into a ball.

Roll into a rectangle 6 x 8 inches (15 x 20 cm), using sharp, firm rolls rather than long, squashing ones. Fold the bottom third of the pastry over, cover with the top third and seal on all sides by pressing the edges firmly with a rolling pin. Make a one-quarter turn of the pastry and repeat the exercise.

Wrap in clingfilm (saranwrap) or foil, and chill for at least half an hour, or until firm. Repeat the rolling and turning process 4 times. Chill covered until required, or freeze for later use.

QUICK FLAKY PASTRY

Freeze raw 3 months.

Traditional flaky pastry is made by a similar method to rough puff, but the butter is incorporated in flakes rather than in cubes. It is rather tedious. This recipe achieves very similar results with much less effort.

10 oz (275 g/1½ cups) butter or firm margarine
6 fl oz (150 ml/¾ cup) boiling water
1 lb (450 g/4 cups) plain (all-purpose) flour

Cut the butter into small pieces and put into a bowl. Pour over the boiling water. Stir until dissolved. Add flour, mix to a dough and chill overnight. Use as for flaky pastry, cooking at Gas No. 7 (425°F/220°C).

ECCLES CAKES

Makes 16.
Keeps 3 days at room temperature in an airtight container.
Freeze cooked pastries 3 months.

This is the kind of very 'English' cake that my mother and the children of other Jewish immigrants were taught at the Manchester Jews' School in the early years of this century, as part of a concerted effort to teach them the ways of their new country. By teaching the children, the leaders of the established community hoped they in turn would teach their foreign-born parents. In this way my grandmother was able to add rice pudding and roast beef and Yorkshire pudding to her repertoire of Eastern European dishes such as kuchen and tsimmes.

This is a traditional Lancashire recipe consisting of a buttery dried-fruit filling encased in flaky pastry. It is best made with butter pastry. For speed, vegetarian mincemeat can be substituted for the filling. I give a recipe for a large quantity so that part can be frozen.

1 recipe Quick Flaky Pastry, chilled (see p. 403)

For the filling
4 oz (125 g/½ cup) butter
8 oz (225 g/2 cups) currants
4 oz (125 g/½ cup) soft brown sugar
4 oz (125 g/¾ cup) chopped mixed candied peel

For the topping
1 egg white
caster (superfine) sugar

Melt the butter in a small pan, then stir in the currants, sugar and peel. Mix well together and leave to cool in a basin. Divide the pastry in 2 and work on each half as follows. Roll the pastry to a rectangle measuring 12 x 6 inches (30 x 15 cm). Trim the edges to make them quite straight, then cut down the centre so that each piece measures 12 x 3 inches (30 x 7.5 cm). Divide each section into 4 3-inch (7.5 cm) squares. Put a little filling on each square, dampen the edges with water, then draw them together to enclose the filling, and seal well with the fingers. Turn the filled pastries over and gently press them into a round measuring 3 inches (7.5 cm) in diameter, using the rolling pin. Make 3 slashes across the top to allow steam to escape during the baking, then arrange on dampened baking sheets. Leave in the refrigerator for 20 minutes.

Bake at Gas No. 7 (425°F/200°C) for 15 minutes. Take out, brush with the egg white (whisked until foamy) and then scatter with caster sugar. Bake for a further 5 minutes, until the glaze is set and golden brown. Leave to cool on a wire tray. Serve fresh or reheat until warm when required.

LEBANESE FILO PASTRIES WITH A 3-NUT FILLING

Makes 20–22.
Keeps 2 weeks in an airtight container in a cool cupboard.
Freeze 3 months.

These luscious little pastries with their distinctive filling – it's the sesame seeds that indicate their Lebanese origin – should be served with strong black coffee to counteract their sweetness. They make a superb finale to a special meal. They are similar in taste to a baklava (see pp. 578–9) but are more quickly put together and deal in smaller amounts of ingredients.

4 oz (125 g/½ cup) unsalted butter or margarine
8 sheets of filo pastry (about 8 oz/225 g)

For the filling
2 oz (50 g/½ cup) white sesame seeds
4 oz (125 g/1 cup) almond nibs
1 oz (25 g/2 tbsp) butter or margarine
2 oz (50 g/½ cup) pistachios (blanched to remove the skins), chopped as finely as the almond nibs
½ teasp mixed sweet spice
3 teasp citrus blossom water
1 egg white
1½ oz (40 g/3 tbsps) caster sugar

For the syrup
8 oz (225 g/1 cup) granulated sugar
6 fl oz (175 ml/¾ cup) water
1 tbsp lemon juice
1 tbsp citrus blossom water
2 teasp rosewater

For the garnish
1 tbsp skinned pistachios, coarsely chopped

Grease a roulade or Swiss roll tin about 12 x 8 x 1 inch (30 x 20 x 2.5 cm) with melted fat. Preheat the oven to Gas No. 5 (375°F/190°C).

Sauté the sesame seeds and the almond nibs in the 1 oz (25 g) fat until golden. Turn into a bowl and stir in the pistachios, spice and citrus blossom water. Whisk the egg white until it holds stiff peaks, then whisk in the sugar a teaspoon at a time. Add to the nut mixture and mix well.

Melt the butter or margarine (in the microwave 1½ minutes on 100 per cent full power, covered with a paper towel). Open the packet of filo and take out 8 sheets, reseal the packet then refrigerate or refreeze, according to packet directions. Brush the top surface of each piece of filo in turn with the melted fat, laying them on top of each other until you have a stack of 8 sheets. Spread three-quarters of the top of this pastry stack with the filling, leaving the quarter of pastry furthest away from you quite bare. Roll up into a tight Swiss roll, finishing with the join underneath. Lightly brush this roll all over with fat. Cut the roll into 20–22 slices, each rather more than ½ inch (1.25 cm) thick, then lay the slices side by side in the tin but without touching. Brush the tops and sides lightly with the remaining fat. Bake for 30 minutes, or until the slices are golden brown.

Meanwhile, prepare the syrup. Put the sugar and water into a 6–7-inch (15–17.5-cm) pan and heat, stirring until the sugar has dissolved. Add the lemon juice and bubble for about 12 minutes, or until the syrup will thickly coat the back of a wooden spoon, then stir in the citrus blossom and rosewater and leave – as it cools the syrup will thicken to the consistency of thin honey. If too thick, add a little boiling water, stirring well. When the pastries come out of the oven, leave them in the tin to cool for 5 minutes, then pour the syrup over them and allow it to soak in for 2 hours, basting once or twice.

Serve at room temperature with the bottom of each roll to the top, each one lightly scattered with the chopped pistachios.

MA'AMOULES
(*Syrian Date Pastries*)

Makes 24.
Keeps 1 week at room temperature in an airtight tin.
Freeze 3 months.

These elegant little pastries with their luscious filling are a speciality of Sephardi cooks. Like so many Middle Eastern recipes, they are extremely labour-intensive, as each pastry case is moulded by hand rather than shaped with a cutter in the Western way. For this reason the dough must have a plastic rather than a short texture. This recipe comes from my Masterclass partner Sula Leon, who is from an Ashkenazi background but learned it from her Egyptian-born mother-in-law – a good example of the cross-fertilization of ideas from different food cultures that makes Jewish cooking so fascinating and enduring.

For the pastry

10 oz (275 g/1¼ cups) butter, cut in 1-inch (2.5 cm) chunks
1 lb (450 g/4 cups) plain (all-purpose) flour
2–3 tbsp cold water
1 tbsp citrus blossom water

For the filling

1 lb (450 g) stoneless dates
2 tbsp apricot conserve
grated rind of 1 lemon
4 tbsp cold water
½ teasp ground cinnamon
4 oz (125 g/1 cup) walnuts, finely chopped

To coat

4 oz (125 g/⅔ cup) icing (confectioners') sugar, sifted

To make the pastry, rub the fat into the flour until the mixture resembles coarse crumbs. Mix the water and citrus blossom water, scatter on the dry mixture and work to a dough using a fork. Chill.

To make the filling, separate the dates and put in a thick-bottomed pan with all the other ingredients, except the walnuts. Cook, stirring, until a smooth paste is formed, then stir in the nuts and allow to cool.

Divide the dough in half and roll each piece into a rope 12 inches (30 cm) long, then cut into 1-inch (2.5-cm) lengths – 24 pieces altogether. Take each piece in turn and place in the palm of the hand, then with the fingers of the other hand shape into a little cup. Spoon in a teaspoon of the filling and pinch the pastry together to enclose it completely. Turn over and place on an ungreased baking sheet. Repeat with the remaining dough and filling.

Pinch the surface of each ma'amoule with

little pastry tweezers or roughen with a fork (this makes it easier for the icing sugar to cling to the surface after the biscuits have been baked).

Preheat the oven to Gas No. 5 (375°F/190°C) for 25 minutes, until set but uncoloured. Remove to a cooling tray and leave for 15 minutes, then dredge thickly with the icing sugar. When quite cold, store in an airtight tin.

VARIATION

DATE ROLL FROM DAMASCUS

Makes about 30 pastries.
Keeps 1 week at room temperature in an airtight container.
Freeze 3 months.

This is a simplified and anglicized version given to me by Mrs Marie Nahum, the legendary *grande dame* of South Manchester Jewry, who was born in Damascus but educated at Manchester High School for Girls, a very 'English' girls' public day school. These might not look as spectacular as the original ma'amoules, but they can be made in a fraction of the time.

For the pastry
6 oz (175 g/¾ cup) butter
12 oz (350 g/3 cups) self-raising flour
4–5 tbsp icy water

For the filling
12 oz (350 g/2 cups) stoned dates
1 tbsp water
½ oz (15 g/1 tbsp) butter
2 level teasp cinnamon
squeeze of lemon juice

Make pastry as before.

Mix the dates with the water and butter over gentle heat and stir until a smooth paste results. Add a little more water if necessary. Stir in the cinnamon and lemon juice and cool.

Divide the dough into 3 balls and roll each of them into a rectangle approximately 10 x 8 inches (25 x 20 cm). Spread the filling to within ½ inch (1.25 cm) of the edge. Roll the pastry over twice as for a flat strudel. Cut into 1-inch-thick (2.5-cm) diagonal slices. Arrange on ungreased tins and bake in a preheated oven, Gas No. 6 (400°F/200°C), for 20 minutes, or until risen and slightly golden. Cool 15 minutes, then dredge with icing (confectioners') sugar.

CAKES AND ICINGS

Cakes and Icings in a Hurry

Ginger cakes, sponge cakes, butter cakes and yeast cakes - these are the traditional 'cut and come again' varieties of the Jewish kitchen, which every good 'balabusta' (housewife) worthy of the name would keep ready in the cake tin for the unexpected guest or the hungry child. Now that even the most delicate or perishable cake can be stored, ready for use, or leftover sections safely kept for another day in the freezer, besides the familiar family-type cakes in this chapter you will find more elaborate gateaux and fruit-and-cream cakes, as well as 1-bowl cakes for immediate use and very rich cakes which are best matured at room temperature. However, it has to be said that with greater awareness of the need for moderation in the consumption of fats and sugars - and the ever-increasing standard of commercial cakes - cake-baking is no longer as central to Jewish cooking as it was even a decade or so ago.

Storage All cakes need air-tight storage as this retards staling. In addition, cream cakes should be refrigerated, covered in some way to prevent the absorption of 'foreign' flavours from other foods.

Freezing All cakes freeze exceptionally well, provided they are tightly enclosed in foil or plastic. Iced or cream-topped cakes should first be frozen uncovered until the topping is solid, and then wrapped as usual. Although cakes won't go 'off' in the freezer, both their flavour and texture will deteriorate with time. That is why I have suggested a maximum of 3 months' storage (less in special cases, which are detailed in individual recipes). Uncooked cake batter can be frozen for a maximum of 14 days, but this is advisable only in an emergency as there will be some loss of lightness in the cake when it is finally baked.

Preparing the tin Unless the tin has a non-stick coating, it must be prepared in some way to prevent the baked cake from sticking to it. Unless specified otherwise in the individual recipe, the tin should always be lightly but thoroughly brushed with a thin coating of oil - butter and margarine may cause the mixture to stick. Richer cakes will also need to be either bottom-lined with a piece of silicone paper or oiled greaseproof paper or, if they are to spend longer than 1½ hours in the oven, completely lined, sides as well.

Cooling the cake Set the cake on a metal cooling rack for 5-10 minutes to allow it to set, then gently ease out of the tin. A spatula may be necessary to loosen the cake from the sides. Gently turn the cake over so that it is right side up. The easiest way to do this is to transfer it on to a second cooling rack. To remove a cake from a tin with a loose bottom, stand the cake on a canister of smaller diameter, then gently ease down the sides of the cake tin. Use a spatula to transfer the cake (still on the base) from the canister to a cooling rack. Remove the base when the cake is cool enough to handle. This method is recommended for fragile cakes or heavy fruit cakes which might not take kindly to being turned upside down to release them.

Baking temperatures and timing These are given in individual recipes. However, when using a forced-air or fan-assisted oven, these will need to be adjusted according to manufacturer's instructions - and your own experience.

THE FOOD PROCESSOR *vs.* THE ELECTRIC MIXER

The classic method of mixing a rich cake - by creaming together the sugar and butter until the first has dissolved into the second - can be tedious and time-consuming. So when the '1-stage' method was introduced - with all the ingredients being simply beaten together until smooth and creamy - it was welcomed. With the advent of the food processor, this new method proved even faster, though there was a niggling doubt about the texture of the finished cakes. More recently, I have developed a food-processor method which offers a better result: the eggs and sugar are processed together for 1 minute until the sugar has dissolved in the liquid, then the fat is pulsed in, followed by the dry ingredients and any other liquid.

Each of these methods has something to commend it but, as in most things, there are horses for courses.

To my mind, when there is time to employ it, and in every case when texture is all-important, the traditional creaming method is best used. This will give a fine-textured cake of excellent volume. (See method for Family Favourite Cake, p. 409)

When texture is still important but time is of the essence, the food-processor method that involves processing the eggs and sugar together gives a similar, if slightly less perfect, result.

When time is so short that there is a fine balance between making or buying a cake for family eating, then the 1-stage method, using either a wooden spoon and electric mixer or a food processor can be used, though do not expect a cake of as large a volume.

Within each recipe I have indicated my first choice of method, as much depends on the ratio of the different ingredients to each other.

FOOD-PROCESSOR METHOD 1

This gives a similar result to the creamed method.

Put the unbeaten eggs and the sugar in the bowl of the processor and process for 1 minute, scraping the sides down once with a rubber spatula. Take off the lid and drop the soft fat by spoonfuls on top of this mixture, together with any flavouring (eg vanilla or grated rind), then pulse until it disappears - the mixture will now resemble mayonnaise. Add the liquid and all the dry ingredients, cover and pulse until the mixture is smooth in texture and (if chocolate or cocoa has been added) even in colour - scrape the sides down with a rubber spatula if necessary. The mixture is now ready to go into the prepared tin.

FOOD-PROCESSOR METHOD 2

This gives a similar result to the 1-stage method using a wooden spoon or electric mixer. However, the volume of the baked cake will be less.

Put all the ingredients into the bowl and process for 10 seconds (count to 10 slowly). Take off the cover, scrape down the sides of the bowl with a rubber spatula, then replace the cover and process for a further 5 seconds. The mixture is now ready to go into the prepared tin.

Note Over-processing will toughen the cake as the metal blade of the food processor has a kneading rather than a mixing action.

SUGAR

Brown, unrefined sugars contain significant amounts of important minerals and trace elements. However, they must be the genuine article and not white sugar which has had colouring and flavouring added without the nutrients. Many supermarkets now sell unrefined sugars with a special recognition symbol.

Moderate amounts of the right variety of unrefined sugar also make good culinary sense.

Golden granulated Can be substituted for ordinary granulated.

Demerara Excellent in fruit crumbles and sprinkled on breakfast cereals, porridge and muesli.

Light muscovado Has a soft texture and mild flavour, making it interchangeable with caster (superfine) sugar.

Dark muscovado Has a mild, toffee-like flavour which makes it ideal for ginger and fruit cakes.

Molasses Tastes just like treacle toffee and is best when used in already highly-flavoured dishes, such as barbecue sauce, chutney and pickles.

Cake-cupboard Insurance

These 'cut and come again' cakes will keep moist in an airtight tin for 7 days, longer if wrapped in foil as well. Take care not to overbake as this is a primary cause of dryness. (See individual recipes for specific baking instructions.)

FAMILY FAVOURITE CAKE

Keeps 1 week at room temperature in an airtight container.
Freeze 3 months.

A superb basic cake mixture, tender and moist, which can easily be varied to suit individual tastes.

3 oz (75 g/⅓ cup) soft butter
3 oz (75 g/⅓ cup) soft margarine
7 oz (200 g/1 cup) caster (superfine) sugar
1 teasp vanilla essence (extract)
3 eggs
8 oz (225 g/2 cups) plain (all-purpose) flour
1½ level teasp baking powder
3 tbsp hot water

Bake the cake in a 9–10-inch (22.5–25-cm) oiled ring tin or an 8-inch (20-cm) loose-bottomed cake tin, 3 inches (7.5 cm) deep, which has been oiled and bottom-lined with silicone paper.

By hand or electric mixer, cream the 2 fats until they resemble mayonnaise, then add the sugar a tablespoonful at a time, beating thoroughly after each addition, until the mixture has lightened in colour and is fluffy in texture. Beat the essence into the creamed mixture (the fat helps to spread flavourings evenly right through the cake). Whisk the eggs to blend the yolks and whites, then beat in a spoonful at a time. Have the flour and baking powder sifted together, then *stir* into the creamed mixture in 3 portions, alternating with the hot water. The mixture is now ready to be flavoured and baked as required (see below).

Alternative: use Food-processor method 1 (see p. 408).

MARBLE CAKE

To make a Marble Cake, use half the mixture to fill any of the tins, dropping it by spoonfuls - with gaps in between - to leave room for the other half. To the remaining cake mixture add 2 level tablespoonfuls of cocoa, 4 level tablespoons of drinking chocolate and 1 tablespoon of hot water. Mix thoroughly until the colour is even, then drop this mixture into the gaps left. Pull a knife horizontally through the centre of the cake mixture, then smooth the top of the cake level.

SULTANA (WHITE RAISIN) CAKE

Omit the vanilla essence and instead beat in the grated rind of half a lemon. Plump 8 oz (225 g/1½ cups) of sultanas by standing them in boiling water for 5 minutes (in the microwave, add 4 tablespoons of water, cover and cook on 100 per cent power for 2½ minutes), then drain and dab dry with a tea-towel. Stir into the cake mixture with the flour.

COCONUT CAKE

Omit the vanilla and instead fold 2 oz (50 g/½ cup) of desiccated coconut and the grated rind of a lemon into the cake with the flour.

ALMOND CAKE

Omit the vanilla and instead add 8 drops of almond essence (extract). Substitute 2 oz (50 g/½ cup) of ground almonds for 2 oz (50 g/½ cup) of the flour.

MADEIRA CAKE

Leave the cake mixture plain, as in the basic recipe. Bake the cake in a 7-inch-diameter (17.5-cm) cake tin. After half an hour of cooking time, open the oven, lay a 3-inch-long (7.5-cm) sliver of candied orange or lemon peel over the cake and close the oven door again.

If you do not wish to ice the cakes, proceed as follows.

Before the cake is baked, paint the uncooked top of the cake with milk and scatter with a thin, even layer of caster (superfine) sugar. (This is unnecessary in a ring tin, as the top of the cake will become the underside when it is cooked.)

To bake the cakes In a 9-inch-square (22.5-cm) or ring tin (kugelhopf tin) bake at Gas No. 4 (350°F/180°C) for 45 minutes. In a round, deep tin bake for 1 hour, Gas No. 4 (350°F/180°C), then reduce the heat to Gas No. 3 (325°F/160°C) for a further 15 minutes, if necessary.

To test whether done Open the oven and gently press the centre of the cake with the top of the forefinger. If it is ready, the cake will spring back at once. If not, a faint impression will remain, and in that case give it a little longer. The sides of the cake will have shrunk slightly from the sides of the tin. When the cake is cooked, remove it from the oven and stand it in the tin on a metal cooling tray. Leave for 5 minutes. If it is in a ring tin, reverse the tin on to a second cooling tray. If it is in a loose-bottomed tin, stand it on a canister of smaller diameter and gently ease down the sides. When the cake is quite cool, remove the loose bottom. If it is in a square, solid-bottomed tin, reverse on to a second cooling tray.

When the cakes are quite cool, wrap in foil and store in an airtight cake tin.

ALMOND FEATHER CAKE

Keeps 1 week at room temperature in an airtight container.
Freeze 3 months.

Fluffy yet moist, this is a truly delectable cake, at its best when baked in a ring tin, a fluted one for the prettiest effect.

8 oz (225 g/1 cup) soft butter
8 oz (225 g/1 cup) caster (superfine) sugar
few drops almond essence (extract)
4 large eggs
5 oz (150 g/1¼ cups) self-raising flour or 5 oz (150 g/1¼ cups) plain (all-purpose) flour plus 1 teasp baking powder
3 oz (75 g/¾ cup) ground almonds

Cream the butter until it resembles mayonnaise, then beat in the sugar and almond essence and continue beating until the consistency of whipped cream. Add the eggs 1 at a time, beating vigorously after each of them, and adding a tablespoonful of flour with each egg. Finally fold in the sifted flour and almonds. Spoon into a greased 9–10-inch (22.5–25-cm) ring tin, or an 8-inch (20-cm) square tin. Bake in the middle of a preheated oven, Gas No. 4 (350°F/180°C), for approximately 1 hour, or until the cake has shrunk from the sides of the tin and the centre springs back when gently pressed.

The top can be covered with a thin layer of Lemon Glacé Icing (see p. 435) or painted with milk and sprinkled with caster (superfine) sugar before it goes into the oven.

RICH ALMOND CAKE

Keeps moist 1 week in an airtight container.
Freeze 3 months.

Small portions only are needed – the cake is delicious served with a fruit compôte.

4 oz (125 g/½ cup) butter or soft margarine
5 oz (150 g/⅔ cup) caster (superfine) sugar
2-3 drops almond essence (extract)
3 eggs
3 oz (75 g/⅓ cup) ground almonds
1½ oz (40 g/3 tbsp) plain (all-purpose) flour
a little caster (superfine) sugar for sprinkling on top

Grease a 7-inch-diameter (17.5-cm) tin 1½ inches (4 cm) deep and cover the base with a disc of silicone or greaseproof paper. Preheat oven to Gas No. 4 (350°F/180°C).

To preserve maximum volume Using butter and an electric mixer or wooden spoon, cream the butter and sugar until soft and light, then beat in the essence. Add the eggs 1 at a time, each with a third of the ground almonds, beating until fluffy. Fold in the flour.

Using soft margarine and a food processor Follow food-processor method 1 (see p. 408).

Turn the mixture into the prepared tin and bake for 45–50 minutes, or until a skewer inserted in the centre comes out clean. Turn out on to a cooling tray and when cold sprinkle with the caster sugar.

SPONGE CHERRY CAKE

Keeps 1 week at room temperature in an airtight container. Freeze 3 months.

Light yet fruity, this cake is improved by a covering of glacé icing (see pp. 435–6).

3 oz (75 g/⅓ cup) soft white vegetable fat or margarine
3 oz (75 g/⅓ cup) soft butter
6 oz (175 g/¾ cup) caster (superfine) sugar
3 eggs beaten to blend
4 oz (125 g/1 cup) each self-raising and plain (all-purpose) flour or 8 oz (225 g/2 cups) plain (all-purpose) flour plus 1 teasp baking powder
grated rind of 1 lemon
2 tbsp boiling water
6 oz (175 g/¾ cup) glacé (candied) cherries

By hand or electric mixer (or use food-processor method 1, see p. 408) cream the fats until like mayonnaise, then beat in the sugar until fluffy. Beat in the eggs, 1 at a time, adding a little flour with the last egg. Stir in the lemon rind. Beat in the boiling water, beating till the mixture resembles whipped cream. Cut the cherries in half, then mix with the flour. Add the sifted flour and cherries to the mixture, stirring rather than beating, until the mixture is smooth and homogeneous. Spoon into the chosen tin.

Bake in an oiled 9-inch (22.5-cm) ring tin at Gas No. 5 (375°F/190°C) for 20 minutes, and then at Gas No. 4 (350°F/180°C) for 30 minutes, or in a 7–8-inch (17.5–20-cm) tin at Gas No. 4 (350°F/180°C) for 1 hour.

MOTHER'S ORANGE CAKE

Keeps 1 week at room temperature in an airtight container.
Freeze 3 months.

A lovely cake for a family tea-party.

4 oz (125 g/½ cup) butter
5 oz (150 g/⅔ cup) caster (superfine) sugar
2 teasp finely grated orange rind
2 large eggs, beaten to blend
6 oz (175 g/1½ cups) self-raising flour or
6 oz (175 g/1½ cups) plain (all-purpose) flour plus 1½ teasp baking powder
2 tbsp hot water

Cream the butter until it is like mayonnaise. Beat in the caster sugar and the orange rind, then the eggs. Finally fold in the flour and add the water.

Bake in an oiled 8-inch-diameter (20-cm) sandwich tin 2 inches (5 cm) deep at Gas No. 4 (350°F/180°C) for 45 minutes, or until golden brown. When quite cold, ice with Orange Glacé Icing (see p. 436) and decorate with candied orange and lemon slices.

Alternative: use food-processor method 1, see p. 408.

ORANGE RING CAKE

Keeps 1 week at room temperature in an airtight container.
Freeze 3 months.

A moist fruity cake which bakes best in a 9-inch (22.5-cm) ring tin (such as a kugelhopf tin) with a loose bottom.

9 oz (250 g/1⅛ cups) butter
9 oz (250 g/1⅛ cups) caster (superfine) sugar
grated rind of ½ orange and ½ lemon
4 large eggs
1 tbsp boiling water
3 tbsp orange juice (approx. 1 small orange)
9 oz (250 g/2¼ cups) plain (all-purpose) flour
1 level teasp baking powder

Preheat the oven to Gas No. 4 (350°F/180°C).

Cream the butter until it resembles mayonnaise, then beat in the sugar until the mixture looks like whipped cream. Add the rinds, then the egg yolks 1 at a time. Finally beat in the boiling water and orange juice.

Whip the whites until they form floppy peaks. Sift the flour with the baking powder, then sift on to the creamed mixture. Lay the whites on top then fold the whole thing together - it should be of a soft, dropping consistency; if not, add a little more water. Turn into an oiled 9-inch (22.5-cm) ring tin. Bake for 45 minutes. Allow to cool 5 minutes in tin, then turn out. When quite cold, either sift with icing (confectioners') sugar or coat with Glacé Icing (see p. 435), or with Orange-flavoured Butter Icing (see p. 438).

Alternative: use food-processor method 1, see p. 408.

Six Favourite Chocolate Cakes

Each of the 6 cakes that follow has a true chocolate flavour but a different texture. Block chocolate should always be melted *over* hot water rather than in a pan set directly on the stove top, as overheating will prevent it becoming liquid. To melt in the microwave, break the chocolate up into a basin and cook, uncovered, on 100 per cent full power as follows:

2 oz (50 g) takes approx. 1 minute
4 oz (125 g) takes approx. 1½ minutes
6 oz (175 g) takes approx. 2½ minutes

Note Chocolate plus liquid takes a shorter time - cook for 30 seconds less.

MILK CHOCOLATE CAKE

Keeps 1 week at room temperature in an airtight container.
Freeze 3 months.

A soft and scrumptious cake.

4 oz (125 g/½ cup) soft butter or margarine
4 oz (125 g/½ cup) caster (superfine) sugar
1 teasp vanilla essence (extract)
2 eggs
5 oz (150 g/1¼ cups) self-raising flour or
5 oz (150 g/1¼ cups) plain (all-purpose) flour plus
1¼ teasp baking powder
2 oz (50 g/½ cup) ground almonds
3 oz (75 g/¾ cup) drinking (instant) chocolate
1 tbsp cocoa
2 tbsp milk
2 tbsp hot water

Cream the butter and sugar until fluffy, add the vanilla, then gradually beat in the eggs. Add flour, nuts, drinking chocolate and cocoa, alternating with the milk and water, stirring thoroughly until evenly mixed. Bake in an 8-inch (20-cm) loose-bottomed cake tin for 35–40 minutes at Gas No. 4 (350°15F/180°C). Ice when cold with Milk Chocolate Icing (see p. 436).

Alternative: use food-processor method 1, see p. 408.

MOCHA FUDGE GÂTEAU

Keeps 1 week at room temperature in an airtight container.
Freeze 3 months.

The basic cake is similar to the Milk Chocolate Cake (though without the ground almonds) but is filled and topped with a luscious frosting.

4 oz (125 g/½ cup) butter or soft margarine
4 oz (125 g/½ cup) caster (superfine) sugar
1 teasp vanilla essence (extract)
2 eggs, beaten to blend
2 tbsp hot water
5 oz (150 g/1¼ cups) self-raising flour or 5 oz (150 g/1¼ cups) plain (all-purpose) flour plus 1¼ teasp baking powder
2 level tbsp cocoa
3 oz (75 g/¾ cup) drinking (instant) chocolate
2 tbsp cold milk

For the filling
1 recipe Mocha Fudge Frosting (see p. 438)
2 oz (50 g/¼ cup) glacé (candied) cherries
2 oz (50 g/½ cup) chopped walnuts

Cream the fat until soft, then beat in the sugar a tablespoonful at a time until the mixture looks fluffy. Beat in the vanilla and the slightly beaten eggs, then beat in the hot water. Finally, stir in the flour (which has been mixed with the cocoa and drinking chocolate), alternating with the cold milk.

Spoon into a loaf tin approximately 9 x 5 x 3 inches (22.5 x 12.5 x 7.5 cm) which has been oiled and bottom-lined with silicone paper or oiled greaseproof paper. Level with a spatula. Bake at Gas No. 4 (350°F/180°C) for 50-60 minutes, or until firm to the touch. Leave to cool for 5 minutes, then gently turn out on to a wire cooling tray.

Alternative: use food-processor method 1, see p. 408.

To make the filling, add the coarsely chopped walnuts and glacé cherries to half the Mocha Fudge Frosting.

Split the cold cake in 2 and sandwich together with the cherry and walnut mixture. Spread the top with the remaining plain frosting, rough up with a fork into a decorative design and arrange halved cherries and walnuts in a pattern on the top. To keep the icing fresh, store this cake in an airtight tin in the refrigerator. Leave at room temperature for 45 minutes before serving.

For another excellent chocolate cake, see 1-bowl Cakes, p. 418).

YOMTOV CHOCOLATE CAKE WITH TOBLERONE TOPPING

Keeps 1 week at room temperature in an airtight container.
Freeze 3 months.

This is a larger cake suitable for a family tea-party. Both the cake and its icing can be made in a *parev* version.

6 oz (175 g/¾ cup) soft light brown sugar
3 eggs
6 oz (175 g/¾ cup) soft margarine or butter
2 teasp instant coffee dissolved in 4 tbsp hot water
2 teasp vanilla essence (extract)
8 oz (225 g/2 cups) self-raising flour or 8 oz (225 g/2 cups) plain (all-purpose) flour plus 2 level teasp baking powder
4 oz (125 g/1 cup) drinking (instant) chocolate
2 level tbsp cocoa

For the icing
2½ oz (65 g/5 tbsp) soft margarine or butter
4 tbsp strong coffee or single (light) cream or evaporated milk
3 tbsp cocoa
8 oz (225 g/2 cups) icing (confectioners') sugar, sifted
1 teasp vanilla essence (extract)
3 oz (75 g/¾ cup) finely chopped blanched almonds, toasted under the grill (broiler) or browned in the oven as it heats up

Preheat the oven to Gas No. 4 (350°F/180°C). Grease a 9-inch (22.5-cm) loose-bottomed cake tin 2 inches (5 cm) deep or (preferably) a 'moule à manqué' (sloping-sided round tin) of the same size, and line the bottom with silicone or greaseproof paper.

Either make by the food-processor method 2 (see p. 409), adding the coffee with the vanilla essence and the cocoa and drinking chocolate sifted with the flour, or mix by hand or electric mixer by putting all the ingredients in a bowl and beating until smooth and creamy - about 3 minutes.

Spoon the cake mixture into the prepared tin and smooth level. Bake for 40–45 minutes, until springy to the touch. Turn on to a cooling rack and leave to go cold.

To ice the cake, melt the fat in the liquid, either in a small pan on top of the stove or in a bowl in the microwave (covered with a paper towel, for 1 minute on 100 per cent power). Put the cocoa, icing sugar and essence into a bowl, then pour on the hot liquid and beat until smooth - about 2 minutes. Stir in the toasted nuts. Place a plate beneath the cooling rack to catch any drips, then gently pour the icing on top of the cake so that it flows over the sides, coating it completely. Leave to set.

A WINE AND CHOCOLATE GATEAU WITH A CAPPUCINO FROSTING

Keeps 1 week at room temperature in an airtight container.
Freeze 3 months.

A special-occasion cake with a light, moist texture and an intriguing but gentle flavour offset by the rich coffee frosting.

4 eggs
7 oz (200 g/1 cup) caster (superfine) sugar
9 oz (250 g/1⅛ cups) soft butter or margarine
1 teasp vanilla essence (extract)
1 teasp each cinnamon and cocoa
9 oz (250 g/2¼ cups) self-raising flour or
9 oz (250 g/2¼ cups) plain (all-purpose) flour plus
2½ teasp baking powder
3½ oz (100 g) bar plain (semi-sweet) chocolate
4 fl oz (125 ml/½ cup) fairly dry red wine

For the icing
8 oz (225 g/2 cups) sifted icing (confectioners') sugar
2 teasp dark-roast instant coffee
4 tbsp (approx.) boiling water

Grease and bottom-line a 10-inch (25-cm) springform tin. Preheat the oven to Gas No. 3 (325°F/160°C).

In the food processor, process the eggs and sugar for 1 minute, then add the margarine in spoonfuls down the feed tube, processing constantly. Don't worry if it begins to curdle. Add the vanilla essence, cinnamon and cocoa, then take off the lid and add the flour, coarsely grated chocolate and wine. Pulse about 4 times, until the consistency is even, scraping down the sides of the bowl once if necessary. (Or make by the creaming method.)

Turn the fluffy mixture into the tin, smooth level, then bake for 1 hour, until firm to gentle touch and a skewer comes out clean from the centre. Cool on a rack, then gently remove from the tin.

To make the icing, sieve the sugar into a small pan and add the coffee dissolved in 2 tablespoons of the water. Heat *very* gently for 3 or 4 minutes, stirring constantly, to remove the raw sugar taste, adding the extra water if necessary; the icing should be of a coating consistency that will flow off the spoon.

Put a plate beneath the cake rack, then pour the icing over the cake, coaxing it down the sides with a knife dipped in hot water. Leave plain or decorate with chocolate 'shot' or a little grated chocolate.

FRENCH CHOCOLATE CAKE WITH A COGNAC FROSTING (*Known in France as Gâteau Reine de Saba*)

Keeps 1 week at room temperature in an airtight tin.
Freeze 3 months.

A rich, tender cake that keeps fresh for days. The use of potato flour makes it especially soft and the large amount of chocolate gives it a rich, dark colour and pronounced chocolate flavour. It can be served plain with a dusting of icing sugar or with the icing given below - the top of the cake is rather crusty, so I find it best to ice the bottom.

4 oz (125 g/½ cup) unsalted butter
4 oz (125 g/½ cup) caster (superfine) sugar
1 x ½-¾ oz packet (15-20 g) vanilla sugar
6 oz (175 g) plain (semi-sweet) chocolate
4 egg yolks
1 teasp baking powder
2 oz (50 g/⅓ cup) potato flour
4 egg whites
pinch of salt

For the frosting
2 oz (50 g/¼ cup) unsalted butter
4 oz (125 g) plain (semi-sweet) chocolate
1 tbsp cognac (or brandy)

Preheat the oven to Gas No. 4 (350°F/180°C). Grease the inside of an 8-inch (20-cm) round, loose-bottomed cake tin or an 8-inch (20-cm) 'moule à manqué' (French-style tin with sloping sides), and line the bottom with a circle of silicone paper.

In a small pan, melt the butter, then add the sugar, vanilla sugar and broken chocolate, and melt gently together until smooth (or cook in a small basin for 2 minutes on 100 per cent power in the microwave, stirring once). Stir in the egg yolks, the baking powder and the potato flour. Put the whites into a large bowl with the pinch of salt and whisk until they hold stiff, glossy peaks, then use a rubber spatula to fold them gently but thoroughly into the chocolate mixture. When the colour is even, pour the cake mixture into the prepared tin and bake for 40-45 minutes, or until firm to gentle touch. Leave the cake, still in the tin, on a cooling rack for 5 minutes, then carefully ease out and leave until cold.

To make the frosting, melt the butter and broken chocolate with the brandy, either in a small pan on top of the stove or in the microwave (approximately 1½ minutes on 100 per cent power), then stir well together until quite smooth. The mixture should be thick enough to coat the back of a wooden spoon. If it is too liquid, chill for about 10 minutes until it thickens slightly. Pour over the top and sides of the cake and allow to set.

A CHOCOLATE AND NUT TORTE FROM LITHUANIA

Keeps 1 week in an airtight container under refrigeration.
Freeze 3 months.

This kind of flour-free cake is made all over the Baltic States and the countries of the former Austro-Hungarian Empire. It is moist yet light in texture, worthy of a special occasion.

3½ oz (100 g/¾ cup plus 2 tbsp) ground almonds
3 level tbsp fine dry bread or rusk crumbs
3½ oz (100 g) plain (semi-sweet) chocolate, grated
3 x size 2 eggs, separated
4 oz (125 g/½ cup) caster (superfine) sugar
1 tbsp lemon juice

For the coating
1 tbsp strong coffee or 2 teasp instant coffee dissolved in 1 tbsp hot water
1 tbsp Tia Maria
2 rounded tbsp drinking (instant) chocolate
3 oz (75 g/⅓ cup) butter, softened
3 oz (75 g/¾ cup) icing (confectioners') sugar

For the garnish
8 whole blanched almonds, toasted

Preheat the oven to Gas No. 4 (350°F/180°C). Have ready an 8-inch (20-cm) loose-bottomed tin, greased and lined with silicone or oiled greaseproof paper.

Mix the ground almonds, crumbs and the grated chocolate. Whisk the egg whites until they hold stiff peaks, then add the sugar a tablespoon at a time, whisking until stiff after each addition. Fold in the yolks, followed by the dry ingredients. Finally, stir in the lemon juice. Spoon the mixture into the tin and level off.

Bake for 45 minutes, until golden brown and firm to gentle touch - a skewer should come out clean. Leave on a cooling tray until cold, then carefully turn out.

To make the icing, put the coffee, liqueur and chocolate in a bowl and mix well. Stir in the butter and icing sugar and beat until smooth. Coat the cake with the icing and decorate with toasted almonds.

One-bowl Cakes

These cakes were first developed in the early 1940s in the United States for use with soft white fats. As such shortenings had air introduced during manufacture, it was found that to produce a light-textured cake it was unnecessary to cream them with sugar in the conventional manner. Later, the same method was adapted for soft margarines and I have found that results are equally good with soft (but not with waxy) butters. Extra baking powder also helps to lighten this type of cake. Speed is the main advantage of this method. Most recipes can be adapted, but while the fresh product is excellent, staling is more rapid than with the creamed method. However, it's a very practical method for family use or for quickly mixing up a cake for the unexpected guest.

ONE-BOWL SANDWICH CAKE

Keeps 5 days at room temperature in an airtight container.
Freeze 3 months.

4 oz (125 g/½ cup) soft butter or margarine
4 oz (125 g/½ cup) caster (superfine) sugar
5 oz (150 g/1¼ cups) self-raising flour sifted with 1 level teasp baking powder or 5 oz (150 g/1¼ cups) plain (all-purpose) flour with 2 level teasp baking powder
2 eggs
jam for filling

For decoration
icing (confectioners') or caster (superfine) sugar

Place all the ingredients into a mixing bowl and beat with a wooden spoon or electric mixer until smooth - about 2–3 minutes. Place in an 8-inch (20-cm) or 2 7-inch (17.5-cm) sandwich tins which have been oiled and then lined with silicone or oiled greaseproof paper. Smooth the surface level. Bake in a preheated oven, Gas No. 3 (325°F/160°C), until spongy to the touch. Bake the 8-inch (20-cm) cake for 35–45 minutes, the 2 smaller cakes for 25–35 minutes. Turn out on to a cooling tray. When quite cold, split the larger cake to make 2 layers. Sandwich the cakes with jam, lemon curd or jam and whipped cream. Sprinkle the top with icing or caster sugar.

Alternative: use food-processor method 2 (see p. 409).

ONE-BOWL CHOCOLATE CAKE

Keeps 1 week at room temperature in an airtight container.
Freeze 3 months.

This is much loved by small boys!

4 oz (125 g/½ cup) soft butter or margarine
4 oz (125 g/½ cup) caster (superfine) sugar
4 oz (125 g/1 cup) self-raising flour or
4 oz (125 g/1 cup) plain (all-purpose) flour plus
1 teasp baking powder
2 eggs
2 level tbsp drinking (instant) chocolate
1 level teasp baking powder
2 level tbsp cocoa
1 tbsp cold milk
1 teasp vanilla essence (extract)

Preheat the oven to Gas No. 4 (350°F/180°C).

Lightly grease 2 7-inch (17.5-cm) sandwich tins or a deeper, 8-inch (20-cm) round tin. Put all the ingredients into a bowl and beat by mixer or wooden spoon until smooth and creamy - about 3 minutes. Divide the mixture between the 2 smaller tins or place in the larger tin and smooth level with a spatula. Bake the sandwiches for 25-30 minutes, the larger cake for 35-40 minutes, until springy to the touch. Turn on to a cooling tray. When quite cold, sandwich together with Milk Chocolate Icing (see p. 436) and then spread the remainder on top. The larger cake can be split and filled, or you can smooth all the icing on the top. Decorate with grated chocolate.

Alternative: use food-processor method 1 or 2, see pp. 408, 409.

CHOCOLATE CUPCAKES

Makes 20-24.
Keeps 5 days in an airtight container.
Freeze 6 months.

These moist and more-ish little cupcakes are very popular at children's parties.

4 oz (125 g/½ cup) soft margarine
4 oz (125 g/½ cup) medium brown sugar
2 eggs
4½ oz (140 g/1 cup plus 2 tbsp) self-raising flour or 4½ oz (140 g/1 cup plus 2 tbsp) plain (all-purpose) flour plus 1 teasp baking powder
2 level tbsp drinking (instant) chocolate
½ level teasp baking powder
2 level tbsp cocoa
1 tbsp cold milk
1 teasp vanilla essence (extract)

Put 24 paper baking cases on a flat tray or in patty tins. Set the oven to Gas No. 5 (375°F/190°C).

Put all the ingredients into a bowl and beat by mixer or hand until smooth and creamy - about 3 minutes. With a food processor, put all the ingredients (except the flour) into the bowl and process until blended. Add the flour and pulse just until blended (do not overbeat as this toughens the cake).

Fill the cases two-thirds full with the mixture and bake for 15 minutes, until spongy to the touch. Serve plain, sprinkled with icing (confectioners') sugar or topped with any chocolate icing.

FEATHERLIGHT FAIRY CAKES

Makes 18.
Keeps 5 days at room temperature in an airtight container.
Freeze 4 months.

The children's favourite.

5 oz (150 g/⅔ cup) caster (superfine) sugar
2 eggs
grated rind of ½ lemon or orange
4 oz (125 g/½ cup) soft margarine
6 oz (175 g/1½ cups) self-raising flour or

6 oz (175 g/1½ cups) plain (all-purpose) flour plus
1½ level teasp baking powder
2 rounded tbsp raisins (optional)

For decoration
Orange or Lemon Glacé Icing (see pp. 435, 436)

Preheat the oven to Gas No. 6 (400°F/200°C). Arrange 18 paper cases in patty tins.

Make by food-processor method 1, or place all ingredients in a mixing bowl and beat with a wooden spoon until well mixed and smooth in texture - 2-3 minutes. Half-fill the cake cases with the mixture, then bake for 15 minutes, until golden brown and spongy to gentle touch. Cool on a wire tray.

To decorate, place teaspoons of the icing on top of each cake and spread evenly. The cakes can also be left plain.

LUSCIOUS LEMON CAKE

Keeps 1 week under refrigeration in an airtight container.
Freeze 3 months.

This delicate sponge, moistened with a tart lemon syrup, must be the all-time family favourite, and is the star of a thousand coffee-morning cake stalls! This cake will keep moist for as long as any of it remains uneaten!

4 oz (125 g/½ cup) soft butter or margarine
6 oz (175 g/¾ cup) caster (superfine) sugar
6 oz (175 g/1½ cups) self-raising flour or 6 oz (175 g/1½ cups) plain (all-purpose) flour and 1½ level teasp baking powder
4 tbsp milk (3 tbsp if food processor is used)
grated rind of 1 lemon
2 large eggs
pinch of salt

For the lemon syrup
3 oz (75 g/¾ cup) icing (confectioners') sugar
juice of 1½ large lemons (4 tbsp)

Well oil a 2-lb (900-g) loaf tin, 9 x 5 x 3 inches (22.5 x 12.5 x 7.5-cm), or a 6-inch (15-cm) square tin and line the bottom with silicone or oiled greaseproof paper (this is important). Put all the cake ingredients into a bowl and beat by mixer or wooden spoon until smooth - about 3 minutes. Turn into the cake tin and smooth level. Bake for 45 minutes at Gas No. 4 (350°F/180°C). Remove from the oven and stand the cake, still in the tin, on a cooling tray. Gently heat the sugar and lemon juice until a clear syrup is formed. Prick the warm cake all over with a fork, then gently pour the syrup over it, spooning it from the sides until it has been completely absorbed. Leave until the cake is cold, then carefully turn out. Serve sprinkled with icing (confectioners') sugar.

Alternative: use food-processor method 1, see p. 408.

DUTCH APPLE CAKE

Serves 6-8 as a pudding, 12 as a cake.
Keeps 3 days under refrigeration in an airtight container.
Freeze 1 month.

This can be served hot as a pudding or cold as a cake. During the baking, the melted butter and sugar form a beautiful glaze over the apples.

6 oz (175 g/1½ cups) self-raising flour or
6 oz (175 g/1½ cups) plain (all-purpose) flour plus
1½ teasp baking powder
3 oz (75 g/⅓ cup) caster (superfine) sugar
1 egg
4 fl oz (125 ml/½ cup) milk
1½ oz (40 g/3 tbsp) melted butter

For the topping
1 oz (25 g/2 tbsp) melted butter
1 lb (450 g) baking apples
3 oz (75 g/⅓ cup) granulated sugar
1 level teasp cinnamon

Grease a baking tin 12 x 7 x 1 inch (30 x 17.5 x 2.5 cm) with oil or line with silicone paper using a strip that covers the base and the short sides. Put the flour, baking powder and sugar into a bowl and add the egg, milk and 1½ oz melted butter. Mix to a smooth batter, then pour into the tin. Smooth the top level, then brush with the 1 oz (25 g/2 tbsp) melted butter.

Peel and core the apples and cut into quarters, then into slices about ¼ inch (0.5 cm) thick. Lay the slices in overlapping rows on the cake batter to cover it completely. Mix the sugar and cinnamon and sprinkle evenly over the top. Bake at Gas No. 6 (400°F/200°C) on a shelf slightly above the centre of the oven for 35 minutes. Cut into squares.

Alternative: use food-processor method 2, see p. 409.

A HEALTHY NUT AND FRUIT CAKE

Keeps 2 weeks at room temperature in an airtight container.
Freeze 3 months.

This *parev* family fruit cake made with brown flour, dried fruits and walnuts has a high nutritional value as well as a moist and tender texture and a rich flavour - and it takes just 15 seconds to mix in a food processor! The nuts can be chopped in the food processor, using a pulse action, but should then be removed and only added again at the end (as indicated in the recipe), to prevent them being chopped too finely.

6 oz (175 g/1¼ cups) soft margarine
6 oz (175 g/1¼ cups) light or medium brown Muscovado sugar
3 eggs
1 rounded tbsp golden (corn) syrup
2 tbsp water
4 oz (125 g/1 cup) 85% wheatmeal self-raising flour or 4 oz (125 g/1 cup) 81% wheatmeal stoneground plain (all-purpose) flour plus 1 teasp baking powder
4 oz (125 g/1 cup) plain (all-purpose) white flour
2 teasp mixed sweet spice
12 oz (350 g/2¼ cups) mixed dried fruit
4 oz (125 g/1 cup) chopped walnuts

For the glaze
water
golden granulated sugar

Preheat the oven to Gas No. 4 (350°F/180°C). Lightly oil and line a 7-inch (17.5-cm) loose-bottomed cake tin. Put all the ingredients (except the dried fruit and nuts) into a bowl and mix until very well blended - 3 minutes by hand, 2 minutes by electric mixer, 15 seconds with a food processor. Stir or pulse in the fruit and nuts just to blend. Spoon into the tin and smooth level. Brush lightly with the water and scatter lightly with the golden granulated sugar.

Bake for half an hour, then turn down to Gas No. 3 (325°F/160°C) and bake for a further hour (50 minutes in a forced-air oven), until the cake is a rich brown and a skewer plunged into the centre comes out clean. Stand on a cooling tray for 30 minutes, then ease out of the tin and store.

Whisked Sponges, Plain and Fancy

The whisked sponge is surely the archetypal Jewish cake, served with a glass of wine after the synagogue or for Saturday afternoon tea. Old family recipes (such as the Plava given below) usually contain no fat, and though very light and tender when freshly baked, they tend to stale quickly. Modern recipes are often enriched with oil or melted butter, which help to keep the cake moister longer and also to give it a slightly firmer texture.

The success of any recipe depends mainly on the correct incorporation of the eggs with the sugar - the stage at which the air needed to leaven the cake is beaten in. By hand, this means a long and tedious job, but with an electric mixer the mixture can be beaten to the correct mousse-like thickness swiftly and efficiently. Once this stage has been reached, it is important to fold in the flour and any liquids with a rubber spatula, or the lightening air will be beaten out and the cake will be small and close in texture.

If an electric mixer is not available, use a stainless steel rotary hand whisk or a balloon whisk and speed the thickening process by standing the mixing bowl over a pan of steaming water (this is, however, extremely tedious!). There are several methods of beating the sugar and eggs together, and despite exhaustive experimentation I cannot recommend one more than another. In the recipes that follow, the method suggested gives the best results for each particular cake.

PLAVA

Keeps 5 days at room temperature in an airtight container.
Freeze 4 months.

The traditional name of this most typical of Jewish sponge cakes would seem to derive from the Russian *plava*, meaning that which swims or floats in water. Translate *plava* as sponge (in the aquatic sense) and you have a fair description of this light, open-textured cake. This is a cake with a sugary crust and a soft, satisfying texture that makes it particularly suitable to serve unadorned by either filling or icing.

5 eggs, separated
10 oz (275 g/1⅓ cups) caster (superfine) sugar
1 tbsp orange flower water or lemon juice
pinch of salt
6 oz (175 g/1½ cups) plain (all-purpose) flour

Preheat the oven to Gas No. 4 (350°F/180°C).

Put 5 oz sugar into a bowl with the egg yolks, then whisk with an electric beater until white and thick. If no electric beater is available, stand the eggs and sugar in a bowl over a pan of very hot but not boiling water and whisk until thick and white. Add the orange flower water or lemon juice. In another bowl, whisk the whites and salt until they hold firm peaks. Gradually beat in the sugar until a firm meringue is formed, then fold into the first mixture. Finally fold in the sifted flour. Put into a deep, loose-bottomed 9-inch (22.5-cm) round tin, which has been oiled and lightly sprinkled with sugar. Sprinkle a thin layer of caster sugar over the surface of the cake mixture.

Bake for 1 hour, 10 minutes. Leave in the tin until cold, then remove. Store wrapped in foil.

The cake can also be baked in a 12 x 10 x 2 inch (30 x 25 x 5 cm) baking tin and will take approximately 50 minutes, when the top will be firm to very gentle pressure and the cake will have shrunk slightly from the sides.

HOT MILK SPONGE

Keeps 5 days at room temperature in an airtight container.
Freeze 3 months.

This is a recipe which takes the traditional Plava of the Russian Jewish cuisine and Americanizes it with a method developed in the United States in the 1940s. The result is a sponge of meltingly tender texture, which is extremely good for filling and icing. In the United States, high-ratio cake flour is used; other countries with a stronger flour can get a similar result by using a mixture of flour and cornflour.

3 eggs, separated
pinch of salt
6 oz (175 g/¾ cup) caster (superfine) sugar
3 fl oz (75 ml/⅓ cup) hot milk
3 oz (75 g/¾ cup) plain (all-purpose) flour
1 oz (25 g/¼ cup) cornflour (cornstarch)
1 level teasp baking powder
grated rind of ½ lemon

Preheat the oven to Gas No. 6 (400°F/200°C). Prepare an 8-inch (20-cm) cake tin by brushing it with oil, then fitting a round of greaseproof paper into the bottom and oiling that, or by using a round of silicone paper. Mix 2 teaspoons each of caster sugar and flour and shake all over the tin to form a fine coating, discarding any excess.

Drop the whites into a mixing bowl, add a pinch of salt and whisk until they hold stiff but glossy peaks. Now start adding the sugar a little at a time, whisking well between each addition, until all has been added. Then gently whisk in the egg yolks - the mixture should be pale and mousse-like.

Have the milk ready in a saucepan, heated until the edges of the milk bubble. Have ready also the flour, cornflour and baking powder, sifted on to paper, with the lemon rind added. Now sift the flour on to the eggs and pour the milk gently down the side, immediately folding the mixture over and over with a rubber spatula, until no flour can be seen. Pour into the cake tin and sprinkle the surface with granulated sugar.

Put the cake into the oven and immediately turn it down to Gas No. 4 (350°F/180°C). Bake for 45 minutes, until the surface of the cake is firm to gentle touch and the mixture has begun to shrink from the sides of the tin. Leave in the tin for 10 minutes on a cooling rack before turning out carefully away from any draught.

CHIFFON SPONGE

Keeps 1 week at room temperature in an airtight container.
Freeze 3 months.

The main virtue of this cake lies in its easy mixing and surprisingly tender texture. It also keeps extremely well because of its oil content. A good cake to choose if an electric mixer is not available.

3 oz (75 g/¾ cup) plain (all-purpose) flour plus 1 oz (25 g/4 tbsp) cornflour (cornstarch), 1 level teasp baking powder or 3 oz (75 g/¾ cup) self-raising flour plus 1 oz (25 g/4 tbsp) cornflour (cornstarch), ½ level teasp baking powder
5 oz (150 g/⅔ cup) caster (superfine) sugar
3 tbsp sunflower or other flavourless oil
3 eggs, separated
2 tbsp orange juice
grated rind of 1 orange or ½ lemon
¼ teasp cream of tartar

Preheat the oven to Gas No. 3 (325°F/160°C).

Into a mixing bowl put the sifted flour, cornflour, sugar, baking powder and, if plain flour is used, a pinch of salt. Make a well in this mixture and add the oil, unbeaten yolks, orange juice and the rind. Beat until smooth. In a large bowl put the whites and the cream of tartar and whisk together until the meringue holds stiff peaks and is so solid that it will stay in the bowl when turned upside down. Pour the yolk mixture on to the meringue and, using a rubber spatula, cut and fold the 2 together until the mixture is evenly creamy in colour.

Have ready a large ring tin or a deep 9-inch (22.5-cm) round cake tin or a deep 8-inch (20-cm) square cake tin, but do not grease them. Pour the mixture into the cake tin and bake for 45 minutes, or until firm to the touch. Leave the tin upside down on a cooling tray. When quite cold, run a knife round the inside edges of the tin and the cake will fall out. Serve the cake plain, as an accompaniment to fruit or ice-cream, or split it and fill with fruit and cream.

SOUTH AFRICAN SPONGE LAYERS

Keeps 1 week under refrigeration in an airtight container.
Freeze 3 months.
Leftover cake should be refrigerated either in an airtight container or covered with a bowl.

This recipe produces a cake with a fine texture that makes it perfect for filling with fruit and cream, jam and cream, or buttercream. It can be baked either in 2 separate shallow tins or in the deeper 'moule à manqué' (the sloping-sided French cake tin), which produces a cake well shaped for easy icing.

3 eggs, separated
pinch of salt
4 oz (125 g/½ cup) caster (superfine) sugar
4 oz (125 g/1 cup) self-raising flour or
4 oz (125 g/1 cup) plain (all-purpose) flour plus
1 teasp baking powder
½ oz (15 g/1 tbsp) butter, melted in 3 tbsp boiling water
grated rind of ½ lemon

Preheat the oven to Gas No. 5 (375°F/190°C).

Whisk the whites with a pinch of salt until they form stiff, glossy peaks, then whisk in the sugar a tablespoonful at a time, until a stiff meringue is formed. Whisk in the yolks until the colour is an even gold. Sift the flour over the surface of the mixture, then gently fold it through and through, using a metal spoon or rubber spatula. Finally stir the butter into the boiling water until it melts, add the grated rind and pour it down the side of the bowl. Fold the liquid into the flour mixture until both are completely amalgamated.

Divide the mixture between 2 lightly oiled 7- or 8-inch (17.5- or 20-cm) sandwich tins which have been bottom-lined with silicone or oiled greaseproof paper, or spoon into an 8-inch (20-cm) 'moule à manqué' prepared in the same way. Bake the sandwich tins for 20 minutes. For the 'moule à manqué' (which is deeper), turn the oven down to Gas No. 3 (325°F/160°C) and bake for 40 minutes. In both cases, the cake is ready when the surface springs back after gentle finger pressure and the cake has shrunk slightly from the sides of the tin. After 5 minutes, turn the cakes out on to a wire cooling tray. Fill when quite cold.

To fill with jam and cream Whisk 5 fl oz (150 ml/⅔ cup) of whipping cream with 2 tablespoons of caster (superfine) sugar and ½ teaspoon of vanilla essence (extract) until it holds its shape. Spread 1 sandwich cake (or the bottom half of the split deeper cake) with raspberry, strawberry or apricot jam, then top with the cream and the remaining layer or half-cake.

To fill with berries and cream Leave 8 oz (225 g) of raspberries or strawberries lightly sprinkled with sugar at room temperature for half an hour. Whisk 5 fl oz (150 ml/⅔) of whipping cream with 1 unbeaten egg white and 2 teaspoons of caster (superfine) sugar until the mixture forms soft peaks. Whisk in any juice from the sugared fruit. Fold in the fruit.

Other fruit fillings 8 oz (225 g) sliced bananas, tossed in lemon juice, 3 rings canned or sweetened fresh pineapple or 4–5 stewed fresh apricots. Spoon on to the bottom sandwich or layer of the cake and top with the cream mixture.

To assemble either cake With a sharp knife cut the second sandwich or the top half of the split cake into 6 or 8 even segments, then reassemble into shape on top of the filling (this makes serving easy). Sift icing (confectioners') sugar evenly over the top. Leave at the bottom of the refrigerator until required.

CINNAMON SPONGE LAYERS

Keep cream-filled cake 2 days under refrigeration. Freeze unfilled 3 months.

A light sponge with a delicately spiced flavour. The hot milk gives a particularly smooth texture.

3 eggs, separated
pinch of salt
6 oz (175 g/¾ cup) caster (superfine) sugar
3 tbsp hot milk
3 oz (75 g/¾ cup) plain (all-purpose) flour
1 oz (25 g/4 tbsp) cornflour (cornstarch)
1 level teasp baking powder
2 level teasp cinnamon
2 level teasp cocoa

Preheat the oven to Gas No. 6 (400°F/200°C). Prepare an 8-inch (20-cm) cake tin 2–3 inches (5–7.5 cm) deep or 2 8-inch (20-cm) sandwich tins by brushing the tins with oil, then fitting a round of silicone or oiled greaseproof paper in the bottom. Mix 2 teaspoons of caster sugar and flour and shake over the tin to form a fine coating, discarding any excess.

Drop the whites into a mixing bowl, add a pinch of salt and whisk until they hold firm but glossy peaks. Now start adding the sugar a little at a time, whisking well between each addition, then gently fold in the yolks - the mixture will be pale and mousse-like. Have the milk ready in a saucepan, heated until the edges of the milk bubble. Have ready the flour, cornflour, baking powder, cinnamon and cocoa sieved on to paper. Sift the flour mixture on to the egg mixture and pour the milk gently down the side. Immediately fold the mixture over and over with a rubber spatula until no flour can be seen. Pour into the cake tin and sprinkle with granulated sugar. Put the cake or cakes in the oven and immediately turn it down to Gas No. 4 (350°F/180°C). Bake layers for 30 minutes, the deep cake for 45 minutes, or until the surface of the cake is firm to gentle touch and the mixture has begun to shrink from the sides of the tin. Leave in the tin for 10 minutes before turning out carefully, away from any draught. Fill the layers (or split and fill the larger cake) with 5 fl oz (50 ml/⅔ cup) of slightly sweetened whipped cream or 10 fl oz (275 ml/1¼ cups) fruited fromage frais.

CHOCOLATE SPONGE LAYERS

Cream-filled cake keeps 2 days under refrigeration. Freeze 3 months.

An excellent chocolate sponge to fill with French whipped cream - a subtle combination of cream and fromage frais.

2 tbsp hot water
nut of butter
3 oz (75 g/¾ cup) self-raising flour or
3 oz (75 g/¾ cup) plain (all-purpose) flour plus
¾ level teasp baking powder
2 level tbsp cocoa
3 eggs, separated
4 oz (125 g/½ cup) caster (superfine) sugar
½ teasp vanilla essence (extract)

For the filling
5 fl oz (150 ml/⅔ cup) whipping cream, whipped
5 fl oz (150 g/¼) 8% fromage frais

Preheat the oven to Gas No. 5 (375°F/190°C) and put the water and butter to melt in it. Sift the flour and cocoa mixture. Whisk the whites until they form stiff peaks, then whisk in each yolk and a third of the sugar, whisking until thick again after each addition. By the time all have gone in, the mixture should be mousse-like and hold its shape. Fold in the sifted flour mixture. Finally dribble the water, butter and vanilla down the side of the sponge, folding it in carefully with a rubber spatula. Have ready a 7- or 8-inch (17.5- or 20-cm) loose-bottomed deep sandwich tin lined with silicone or greaseproof paper. Spoon in the mixture and level.

Bake for 25 minutes, or until firm to the touch. Cool for 10 minutes, then turn out. When cold split and fill with whipped cream or 8% fromage frais and dust the top layer with icing (confectioners') sugar.

A BUTTERING GINGERBREAD

Keeps 2 weeks wrapped in foil at room temperature in an airtight container.
Freeze 1 month.

Gingerbread was originally just that – a gingered bread. According to Meg Pybus, an authority on its history, the original gingerbread or 'melitates' was first baked on the island of Rhodes. When it was made more cake-like by adding more fat, sweetening and eggs, extra spicing was added to disguise the taste of the chemical residue left by the crude raising agents of the day.

It is a favourite cake in the Jewish family, most notably the honeyed Lekach (see pp. 559–62). This version is firm textured and closer to a tea loaf than a cake. It really needs to mature for 3 days before use. It can then be thinly sliced and buttered or spread with cream cheese.

1 lb (450 g/4 cups) plain (all-purpose) flour
2 level teasp mixed sweet spice
2 level tbsp ground ginger
2 level teasp bicarbonate of soda (baking soda)
8 oz (225 g/1 cup) margarine
8 oz (225 g/1 cup) soft brown sugar
8 oz (225 g/⅔ cup) golden (corn) syrup
8 oz (225 g/⅔ cup) treacle (molasses)
8 oz (225 g/1½ cup) sultanas (white raisins) (optional)
4 oz (125 g/1 cup) ground almonds (optional but nice)
4 eggs
5 fl oz (150 ml/⅔ cup) milk

Preheat the oven to Gas No. 3 (325°F/160°C).

Line a tin approximately 12 x 9 x 2 inches (30 x 22.5 x 5 cm) with silicone or oiled greaseproof paper. Sift together the flour, spices and soda. Put into a pan the margarine, sugar, syrup and treacle and heat until liquid, then stir into the dry ingredients together with the well-beaten eggs and the milk. Mix thoroughly, then pour into the prepared tin. Bake for 1½ hours, or until firm to the touch. Serve sliced and buttered.

A SPONGE GINGERBREAD

Keeps 2 weeks foil-wrapped at room temperature in an airtight container.
Freeze 1 month.

This is a lovely 'cut and come again' cake for a winter's tea. It's superb (if a little hard on the digestion) served hot from the oven. But the texture becomes moister – and the spicing intensifies – if it's stored for a few days.

8 oz (225 g/1 cup) butter
8 oz (225 g/1 cup) soft brown sugar
8 oz (225 g/¾ cup) treacle (molasses)
12 oz (350 g/3 cups) plain (all-purpose) flour
1 level teasp cinnamon
1 generous tbsp ginger
2 eggs, beaten to blend
10 fl oz (275 ml/1¼ cups) milk
2 level teasp bicarbonate of soda (baking soda)

Preheat the oven to Gas No. 2 (300°F/150°C).

Melt the butter, sugar and treacle over low heat, then allow to cool a little. Sift the flour, cinnamon and ginger together, add the butter mixture and stir in the eggs. Warm the milk until steaming and pour on to the bicarbonate of soda, then add to the flour mixture. Mix thoroughly - the batter will be thin. Pour into a rectangular tin approximately 12 x 9 x 2 inches (30 x 22.5 x 5 cm) which has been greased then bottom-lined with silicone or oiled greaseproof paper.

Bake for 1½-2 hours, depending on the size of the tin. Test after 1½ hours. If it springs back when lightly touched with a finger, it is ready. Turn out on to a cooling rack. When cold, wrap in foil and store in the washed tin.

MOIST GINGER CAKE

Keeps 2 weeks wrapped in foil at room temperature in an airtight container.
Freeze 2 months.

This is a good family cake. You can vary the flavour by substituting treacle (molasses) for half the syrup.

5 oz (150 g/⅔ cup) margarine
6 oz (175 g/1 cup) golden (corn) syrup (measured in an oiled measuring cup)
4 oz (125 g/½ cup) soft brown sugar
7 oz (200 g/1¾ cups) self-raising flour or 7 oz (200 g/1¾ cups) plain (all-purpose) flour and 2 level teasp baking powder
2 level teasp ground ginger
1 level teasp mixed sweet spice
2 eggs
rind and juice of 1 lemon
2 oz (50 g/⅓ cup) chopped crystallized (candied) ginger (optional)

Preheat the oven to Gas No. 4 (350°F/180°C).

Warm the margarine, syrup and sugar together over gentle heat. When smooth and melted, pour on to the sifted dry ingredients, followed by the beaten eggs, the lemon rind and juice, and the crystallized ginger (if used). Beat until smooth. Pour into a greased 8- or 9-inch (20- or 23-cm) round tin or a 2-lb (900-g) loaf tin measuring approximately 9 x 5 x 3 inches (22.5 x 12.5 x 7.5 cm). Bake for 40 minutes, or until firm to the touch. Turn out on to a cooling tray and when quite cold wrap in foil.

Bake Now, Eat Later

The texture and flavour of certain rich creamed cakes is actually improved if they are allowed to mature in a tightly sealed container before they are eaten. This ripening period varies with the recipe, but generally the fruitier the cake, the longer it takes to reach perfection. To store during this maturing period, first allow the cake to cool completely, then wrap it tightly in foil and put it in an airtight tin or plastic container. (For a storage period of more than a month, seal the container itself with adhesive tape.) Do not refrigerate or freeze the cake until it is mature, as very cold temperatures delay the ripening process. Minimum storage times are given with individual recipes.

SHERRIED SULTANA CAKE

Keeps 2 weeks at room temperature in an airtight container.
Freeze 3 months.

8 oz (225 g/1½ cups) sultanas (white raisins)
3 tbsp medium-dry sherry
3 oz (75 g/⅓ cup) soft butter
3 oz (75 g/⅓ cup) soft margarine
6 oz (175 g/¾ cup) caster (superfine) sugar
grated rind of ½ lemon
3 large eggs
9 oz (250 g/2¼ cups) sifted self-raising flour or 9 oz (250 g/2¼ cups) plain (all-purpose) flour plus 2 teasp baking powder

To glaze and decorate the cake
milk
granulated sugar
1 oz (25 g/¼ cup) slivered almonds

Preheat the oven to Gas No. 4 (350°F/180°C).

Put the sultanas in a small bowl, pour over the sherry and cover. Either leave overnight or cook on 100 per cent power in the microwave for 2½ minutes, then leave to cool. Grease a 2-lb (900-g) loaf tin 9 x 5 x 3 inches (22.5 x 12.5 x 7.5 cm) and line the bottom with a strip of silicone or oiled greaseproof paper, or use an 8-inch (20-cm) loose-bottomed cake tin. Cream the fats until as soft as mayonnaise, add the sugar gradually, beating until like whipped cream, then add the lemon rind. Beat the eggs until thick, then beat into the creamed mixture a spoonful at a time, adding a little flour if the mixture starts to curdle. Finally fold in the fruit and any unabsorbed sherry alternately with the flour. Spoon into the prepared tin and level the top. Paint the top lightly with milk and sprinkle with granulated sugar, then scatter with the almonds.

Bake for 45 minutes, then turn the oven down to Gas No. 3 (325°F/160°C) for a further half hour, or until the cake is a rich golden brown. Leave in the tin for 10 minutes, then turn out on to a cooling tray.

Store for 3 days before use.

ALMOND CHERRY CAKE

Keeps 2 weeks at room temperature in an airtight container.
Freeze 3 months.

A rich, moist cake in the English tradition.

4 eggs
8 oz (225 g/1¼ cups) glacé (candied) cherries
2 oz (50 g/⅓ cup) angelica or candied lemon peel, finely chopped (optional)
4 oz (125 g/1 cup) ground almonds
8 oz (225 g/1 cup) soft butter
8 oz (225 g/1 cup) caster (superfine) sugar
grated rind of 1 lemon
8 oz (225 g/2 cups) plain (all-purpose) flour
1 level teasp baking powder
juice of 1 lemon
milk
flaked almonds
granulated sugar

Preheat the oven to Gas No. 4 (350°F/180°C).

Put the eggs into a small bowl and beat until fluffy. Quarter the cherries and mix with the chopped peel and the ground almonds. Beat the butter until like mayonnaise, then beat in the caster sugar a tablespoonful at a time and continue to beat until like whipped cream. Add the eggs a little at a time, beating until like cream again after each addition. Beat in the lemon rind. Stir in the flour sifted with the baking powder, then stir in the lemon juice and finally the cherry and almond mixture. Spoon into an 8-inch-diameter (20-cm) deep cake tin which has been lined sides and bottom with silicone or oiled greaseproof paper. Level off the top. Paint with a little milk and scatter with a few flaked almonds and a very little granulated sugar. Bake in the middle of the oven for 45 minutes, then turn to Gas No. 3 (325°F/160°C) for a further 45 minutes, or until the cake is firm to the touch and has shrunk slightly from the sides.

Store for 1 week before use.

CHERRY AND GINGER RING

Keeps 2 weeks at room temperature in an airtight container.
Freeze 3 months.

A lightly fruited cake with a rich flavour. It looks decorative when baked in a shallow ring tin, though a 9-inch (22.5-cm) round cake tin can also be used.

4 oz (125 g/½ cup) butter
2 oz (50 g/¼ cup) soft margarine
6 oz (175 g/¾ cup) caster (superfine) sugar
grated rind of ½ lemon
3 large eggs
7 oz (200 g/1¾ cups) self-raising flour or 7 oz (200 g/1¾ cups) plain (all-purpose) flour plus 2 teasp baking powder
4 oz (125 g/⅔ cup) quartered glacé (candied) cherries
2 oz (50 g/⅓ cup) finely sliced crystallized (candied) ginger
2 fl oz (50 ml/4 tbsp) milk
2 oz (50 g/½ cup) ground almonds

Preheat the oven to Gas No. 4 (350°F/180°C).

Cream butter, margarine and sugar until like whipped cream, stir in the lemon rind and then beat in the eggs (which have been whisked to blend) a tablespoonful at a time, together with a little of the sifted flour. Mix the cherries and ginger with a tablespoonful of the flour. Add a third of the flour to the creamed mixture, then half the milk, then the fruit and another third of the flour, the remaining milk and finally the remaining flour, mixed with the ground almonds. Turn into a shallow oiled ring tin 10 inches (25 cm) in diameter. Bake for 40 minutes. In an ordinary 9-inch (22.5-cm) tin, bake for 1-1¼ hours, or until firm to the touch.

Store 3 days before use.

TRADITIONAL FRUIT CAKE

Makes 1 x 9-10-inch (22.5-25-cm) cake.
Keeps 1 year wrapped in foil at room temperature in an airtight container.

This is the dark fruit cake that usually graces a wedding table. This recipe makes a moist, tender cake. While still warm, it can be enriched with spirits by pouring 3 tablespoons of brandy, rum or whisky slowly over the base of the cake.

10 oz (275 g/1¼ cups) butter
10 oz (275 g/1¼ cups) light, soft brown sugar
grated rind of 1 orange
6 eggs
8 oz (225 g/1½ cups) currants
8 oz (225 g/1½ cups) seedless raisins
1 lb (450 g/3 cups) sultanas (white raisins)
4 oz (125 g/⅔ cup) candied peel
2 oz (50 g/⅓ cup) chopped angelica (if available)
2 oz (50 g/⅓ cup) glacé (candied) pineapple
4 oz (125 g/1 cup) ground almonds
12 oz (350 g/3 cups) plain (all-purpose) flour
2 level teasp mixed spice
pinch of salt

Preheat the oven to Gas No. 2 (300°F/150°C).

Cream the butter and sugar until like mayonnaise, then beat in the orange rind and the lightly whisked eggs a tablespoonful at a time, until the mixture is fluffy in texture. Add all the fruits and ground almonds alternately with the flour, spice and salt. Stir very thoroughly. Put into a brown-paper-lined 9-10-inch (22.5-25-cm) cake tin. Bake for 3-3½ hours. The cake is done when a skewer or knitting needle comes out clean from the centre.

Store at least 2 weeks before use.

WHISKY AND GINGER CAKE

Keeps 3 months at room temperature in an airtight tin.

This is the alternative cake for those who do not like a very rich fruit cake. It has a lighter texture than the traditional fruit cake but in 10 days it will develop a wonderfully moist texture, as well as a truly magnificent flavour, thanks to the whisky which is used to plump the dried fruit before baking and also to inject into the cake afterwards. This is a suitable cake for weddings, engagements or barmitzvahs, as it is firm enough to decorate with royal icing.

4 tbsp whisky plus additional 4 tbsp whisky to pour over cake
1 lb (450 g) mixed dried fruit
8 oz (225 g/1 cup) butter or soft margarine
10 oz (275 g/2½ cups) plain (all-purpose) flour
2 oz (50 g/½ cup) ground almonds
1 level teasp mixed sweet spice
1 level teasp baking powder
8 oz (225 g/1 cup) soft, light brown sugar
rind of 1 orange and 1 lemon, finely grated
5 eggs, whisked to blend
1 tbsp lemon juice
4 oz (125 g/½ cup) glacé (candied) cherries, quartered
4 oz (125 g/½ cup) crystallized (candied) ginger, chopped
4 oz (125 g/1 cup) walnuts, coarsely chopped

For the decoration (optional)
4 tbsp smooth apricot jam
4 tbsp sugar
4 tbsp water
juice of 1 lemon
selection of glacé (candied) fruits

Preheat the oven to Gas No. 3 (325°F/160°C).

Pour whisky over the dried fruit and leave for at least 1 hour, or until absorbed (or cook covered in the microwave on 100 per cent power for 3 minutes).

Have the butter or margarine at room temperature. Grease a 9-inch (22.5-cm) tin, 3 inches (7.5 cm) deep, and line the bottom and sides with silicone or oiled greaseproof paper. Sift together the flour, ground almonds, spice and baking powder.

Cream the butter or margarine until it is like mayonnaise, then gradually beat in the sugar until the mixture is fluffy. Add the orange and lemon rinds, then beat in the eggs a little at a time, followed by the lemon juice, adding a little of the sifted flour mixture after each addition to prevent curdling. Fold in the flour, soaked fruit, cherries, ginger and walnuts.

Turn into the prepared tin, level off, then bake for 1 hour. Turn the heat down to Gas No. 2 (300°F/150°C) and continue to bake for a further 30 minutes (20 minutes in a forced-air or fan-assisted oven), or until the top springs back when gently touched with the finger and a skewer comes out cleanly from the centre.

Take the cake out and put on a cooling-rack. When quite cold remove from the tin and turn over so that the base is uppermost. Put a plate under the rack, then prick the cake all over with a skewer and gradually spoon over the remaining 4 tablespoons of whisky. Wrap in foil and keep in an airtight tin.

The cake can be left plain or glazed and decorated with glacé fruit. Put the jam, sugar, water and lemon juice in a pan and bring to the boil gently, stirring until smooth and slightly thickened. Cool a little, then brush all over the top of the cake. Arrange the glacé fruit in an attractive pattern on the cake, then brush with the remaining apricot mixture.

Allow the cake to mature for 2 weeks before cutting.

Cheesecakes

These delicacies have been among the glories of Jewish cookery for many centuries. Indeed, as cheesecakes are known to have been made in Greece as far back as 350 BCE, it is not fanciful to conjecture that they have been part of Jewish cuisine since the Greek occupation of Palestine in the second century BCE.

The best of the early Greek cheesecakes were reputedly made on the Aegean island of Samos – Pythagoras's birthplace. You can find some of the recipes in *The Deipnosophists*, an anthology of gastronomic writings compiled by the Egyptian philosopher Athenaeus in the third century of this era.

Jews of the pre-Christian era also made some form of cheesecake to celebrate Shavuot, for they saw in the whiteness of milk cheese a symbol of the purity of the Mosaic Code. But at a time when ordinary flour was as coarse as oatmeal and baked as brown as gingerbread, it's not surprising that the pale and delicately textured cheesecake was so often made to mark a special occasion. What is a little surprising is that it has remained in fashion ever since.

Today there are as many cheesecakes as there are cookery books, though they are almost all a variation on the original Greek recipe - curd cheese, sweetenings and eggs, baked in some form of protective crust. Polish cheesecakes are thickened with ground almonds, Swiss ones with semolina, while in America it is usual to thicken the mixture with cornflour instead. In Italy the cheese mixture is blended with glacé (candied) fruits or cinnamon, while in Germany brandy or rum is the favoured flavouring.

The Jews who came to England from Russia and Poland at the end of the nineteenth century continued to make their traditional cheesecake in a rich shortcrust case flavoured with lemon rind and studded with sultanas, quite unaware that the country of their adoption had a long tradition of cheesecake-making itself. For instance, in the East Riding of Yorkshire they used to make 'Chissicks' - curd blended with butter, cream and brandy; in Melton Mowbray currants, ginger and lemon peel were preferred; while in the Derbyshire Dales, the curd made from the 'beestings' - the first milk of a cow after calving - is so rich that only sugar and currants needed to be added to make perhaps the most delicious traditional English cheese-cake of all.

Nearly 60 years ago, my Lithuanian grand-mother made her own cheese for the cakes she made with a rich yeast dough. Today I usually buy my curd cheese - technically known as 'low- or medium-fat soft cheese with a 10–20% butter fat content' - to make the delectable cheesecakes which I describe below.

To freeze any cheesecake recipe Cheesecakes freeze extremely well with no loss of flavour. Allow the cake to cool in the tin, standing on a cooling-rack, then put it, uncovered and still in the tin, into the freezer and leave until solid. Ease out of the tin, foil-wrap and label. To defrost, take from the freezer, unwrap and put on a serving dish. Refrigerate until required - it takes about 3 hours to defrost in the refrigerator.

THE BASE FOR A CHEESECAKE

There are 3 main varieties of crust for a baked cheesecake: sponge, crushed biscuit and pastry. The choice is mainly a matter of taste, and the amount of time you have available.

SPONGE BASE

This is made of enough ½-inch-thick (1-cm) slices of slightly stale sponge to cover the bottom of the chosen tin. Use either bought trifle sponges or leftover home-made or baker's whisked sponge.

CRUMB CRUST

Sufficient to cover the base of an 8- or 9-inch (20- or 22.5-cm) loose-bottomed round tin.

4 oz (125 g) Digestive biscuits (graham crackers)
1 level tbsp caster (superfine) sugar
½ level teasp cinnamon
2 oz (50 g/½ cup) melted butter

Make crumbs from the biscuits in the food processor or blender, or by putting the biscuits in a plastic bag and crushing to crumbs with a rolling pin. Then add the sugar and cinnamon, and stir in the butter until the crumbs are evenly moistened. Press on to the base of an oiled tin.

PASTRY CRUST

Keep under refrigeration for up to 2 days.
Freeze 3 months.
Sufficient for a 9–10-inch (22.5–25-cm) loose-bottomed flan tin about 1¼ inches (3 cm) deep or an 8-inch (20-cm) tin with sloping sides about 2 inches (5 cm) deep.

6 oz (175 g/1½ cups) self-raising flour or 6 oz (175 g/1½ cups) plain (all-purpose) flour plus
1½ teasp baking powder
4 oz (125 g/½ cup) butter or margarine
2 oz (50 g/½ cup) icing (confectioners') sugar
1 egg yolk (reserve the white)
1 tablespoon water

Put all the ingredients into a bowl and work together until a dough is formed. Chill for 30 minutes. Roll out the pastry on a lightly floured board to fit the chosen tin, easing it in gently so as not to stretch it. Chill again while you prepare the filling.

TRADITIONAL CHEESECAKE

Serves 10.
Keeps 3 days under refrigeration.
Freeze 2 months.

This is an updated version of the traditional cheesecake from Eastern Europe which used to be made with home-made 'kaese' (soft cheese, see p. 106) and baked in a pastry case (for Kaesekuchen Baked on a Sweetened Yeast Dough, see p. 476). It is rather more luxurious than older recipes, but as most of us only make this cake on special occasions, I think it is worth putting in the finest ingredients and making it in a size to serve a crowd. Home-made kaese (which was always used in the past) has much more tang than the bland factory-made soft cheese of today, so I have added extra flavourings such as lemon juice and vanilla to compensate. Always serve at room temperature or slightly warm, but never chilled as this affects the texture.

1 recipe Cheesecake Pastry Crust (see this page)

For the filling

3 eggs, separated
12 oz (350 g/1½ cups) low- or medium-fat soft cheese
2 oz (50 g/½ cup) ground almonds
1 oz (25 g/2 tbsp) soft butter
2 oz (50 g/½ cup) caster (superfine) sugar
2 tbsp lemon juice
grated rind of ½ lemon
½ teasp vanilla essence (extract)
5 tbsp sultanas (white raisins)

For decoration

1 tbsp granulated sugar
1 oz (25 g/¼ cup) flaked almonds

Preheat the oven to Gas No. 4 (350°F/180°C).

Put the egg yolks and all the remaining ingredients (except the sultanas) into a bowl and mix until thoroughly blended. Whisk the whites with a pinch of salt until they hold floppy peaks, then carefully fold into the cheese mixture. Stir in the sultanas, then pour into the unbaked flan case.

Take the egg white left over from the pastry and whisk with a fork until frothy. Paint it over the cheese mixture, then sprinkle with the granulated sugar. Scatter the almonds. Bake the larger flan for 40 minutes, the smaller, deeper flan for 20 minutes, then turn the oven down to Gas No. 3 (325°F/160°C) and bake for a further 30 minutes. In either case, the cheesecake is ready when it is a pale gold colour and firm to gentle touch round the edges. (The filling continues to set as it cools.)

VELVET CHEESECAKE

Serves 10.
Keeps 3 days under refrigeration.
Freeze 2 months.

I permutated 30 different recipes from as many different sources in both the United States and Europe before I arrived at what I consider the best 'modern' home-made cheesecake of all. This version is creamy, light and smooth on the tongue. Its success depends on a short baking period (which prevents the overheating of the cheese which often causes the cake to fall on cooling) and the use of a fairly dry curd rather than a rich cream cheese.

For the base, any of the 3 crusts given (see above) can be used, but I personally like the sponge base. Use to line a 7-inch (17.5-cm) square tin or an 8-inch (20-cm) loose-bottomed sandwich tin not less than 2 inches (5 cm) deep. Leftover pastry can be frozen.

For the filling

2 eggs, separated
1 lb (450 g/2 cups) curd cheese
½ teasp vanilla essence (extract)
juice and rind of ½ lemon
2 oz (50 g/¼ cup) melted butter
2 oz (50 g/¼ cup) caster (superfine) sugar
2 level tbsp cornflour (cornstarch)
5 fl oz (150 ml/⅔ cup) soured cream or 8% fromage frais

Keep the egg whites in a separate bowl. Put all the other ingredients into a bowl in the order given and beat until smooth and thick. Whisk the whites until they form stiff glossy peaks, then whisk in 2 teaspoons of caster sugar. Fold this meringue into the mixture in the bowl and then into the tin, previously lined with the chosen base. Smooth level.

Preheat the oven to Gas No. 4 (350°F/180°C). With a sponge or crumb lining allow 25 minutes, with a pastry lining 40 minutes. The cake is done when the inch (2.5 cm) of filling adjacent to the rim of the tin feels firm to the touch. Cheesecakes continue to set as they cool. Leave to cool in a draught-free place. When cold, refrigerate until required. Serve plain or topped with sugared soft fruit.

VARIATIONS

WITH A SOURED CREAM TOPPING

Make the Velvet Cheesecake but omit the soured cream from the filling. Instead add 2 tablespoons of single or soured cream or fromage frais. For the topping, stir 10 fl oz (275 ml/1¼ cups) of soured cream or 8% fromage frais with 1 level tablespoon of caster (superfine) sugar and a few drops of vanilla essence (extract). When the cake has cooked, remove from the oven and leave for 10 minutes. Turn the oven up to Gas No. 6 (400°F/200°C). Spread the soured cream topping over the cake. Return to the oven for 8 minutes to set the topping. When cold, foil-cover and refrigerate until thoroughly chilled.

WITH A FRUIT GLAZE

Make the Velvet Cheesecake and allow to go quite cold. Drain a can of black or morello cherries, sliced peaches, pineapple rings or apricots, measuring 8 fl oz (225 ml/1 cup) of syrup from the can. In a small saucepan put 1 level tablespoon of cornflour (cornstarch) and 2 oz (50 g/¼ cup) of granulated sugar, then gradually stir in the fruit-juice syrup. Bring to the boil and simmer for 3 minutes. Taste and add the juice of half or a whole lemon according to personal preference. Arrange the fruit in a design on the cheesecake, spoon over the cooled glaze and leave under refrigeration until set.

WITH A MANGO SAUCE

1 large, very ripe mango
1½ oz (40 g/3 tbsp) caster (superfine) sugar
3 tbsp lemon juice

Peel the mango with a potato peeler, then cut all the flesh away from the stone and process or blend with the sugar and juice until absolutely smooth – about 1 minute. Turn into a bowl and chill with the cake. When ready to serve, cut the cheesecake into 8–10 sections and arrange on a flat glass platter with a bowl of sauce at one end. Spoon some sauce over each slice of cake as it is served.

LIME CHEESECAKE WITH A FRESH STRAWBERRY SAUCE

Serves 8 as a dessert, 10 with coffee or tea.
Keeps 3 days under refrigeration.
Cheesecake freezes 4 months, sauce for a year.

This magnificent cake must be chilled for at least 12 hours, during which time its texture changes dramatically, becoming richer and creamier to eat, with a superb fresh lime flavour. The combination of colours makes this as decorative as it is delicious.

For the crust

4 oz (125 g) ginger biscuits (12 x 2½ inches/5 cm)
generous 1 oz (25 g/2 tbsp) melted butter
2 level tbsp caster (superfine) sugar
or
enough sponge slices cut ⅜ inch (1 cm) thick to cover the base of the cooking container (about 4 trifle sponges)

For the filling

1 lb (450 g/2 cups) low- or medium-fat curd cheese
2 oz (50 g/¼ cup) caster (superfine) sugar
1 oz (25 g/2 tbsp) very soft butter
2 level tbsp cornflour
grated rind of 1 fresh lime
1 tbsp fresh lime juice (½ lime)
2 tbsp proprietary-brand lime cordial
3 eggs

For the topping

1½ x 5 oz (150 g/⅔ cup) cartons soured cream or 8 oz (225 ml/1 cup) Greek-style yoghurt
2 teasp caster (superfine) sugar
1 teasp lime cordial

For the sauce

8 oz (225 g) strawberries
2 oz (50 g/¼ cup) caster (superfine) sugar
2 teasp fresh lime juice

Preheat the oven to Gas No. 3 (325°F/160°C). Crush the biscuits to fine crumbs either in the food processor or with a rolling pin, then mix thoroughly with the butter and sugar. Press evenly on the bottom and part-way up the sides of an 8-inch (20-cm) loose-bottomed or springform tin not less than 1½ inches (3.5 cm) deep.

Using an electric mixer, cream the cheese with the sugar and soft butter in a large bowl, then whisk in the cornflour followed by the rind and juice, the cordial and the eggs. Whisk this mixture until really smooth (don't use a food processor as it breaks down the cheese too much). Turn into the tin, smooth level and bake for 45 minutes, or until the cake is set about 1 inch (2.5 cm) round the edge.

Mix the soured cream with the sugar and cordial, then gently spoon over the hot cake, spreading it well to the edges. Bake for a further 8 minutes, until just set. Place the cake on a cooling rack and leave until it is cold, then refrigerate.

To make the strawberry sauce, purée all the ingredients for 1 minute in the food processor or blender until smooth. Turn into a bowl or jug and refrigerate – it will thicken on standing.

To serve, run a sharp knife around the edges of the cake, then carefully release it from the tin and place on a serving tray. Serve wedges of the chilled cheesecake plain or coated with the sauce.

TUTTI FRUTTI CHEESECAKE

Serves 10 for a snack or 6 for a dinner sweet.
Keeps 3 days under refrigeration.
Freeze 3 months.

The chilled cheesecake, set with gelatine or jelly instead of oven heat, is an American invention - it is really a cold soufflé. The flavour is best if gelatine is used (you can occasionally buy kosher gelatine in granular form), otherwise a kosher lemon jelly (gelatine mix) gives a very acceptable result. (If you find a whole jelly makes too stiff a texture for your taste, use half or three-quarters until you get the correct set - this cheesecake should be just firm enough to cut into portions, but not at all jelly-ish.)

2 eggs, separated
pinch of salt
1 lemon jelly (gelatine mix) or 1 level tbsp powdered kosher vegetarian gelatine
2 oz (50 g/¼ cup) sugar
juice and rind of 1 large lemon (3 tbsp)
6 tbsp fresh orange juice
5 fl oz (150 ml/⅔ cup) double (heavy) cream
2 tbsp caster (superfine) sugar
12 oz (350 g/1½ cups) cream cheese
1 teasp vanilla essence (extract)
4 Digestive biscuits (graham crackers), crushed
½ oz (15 g/1 tbsp) melted butter
pinch of cinnamon

For decoration
a few lightly sugared raspberries, strawberries or redcurrants, or thin slices of banana

Whisk together the egg yolks, salt, gelatine (if used) and 2 oz sugar, then gradually add the lemon and orange juices (most quickly and effectively done in the food processor). Cook in a double saucepan over boiling water (or in a basin standing in a pan of water) until the mixture becomes a thin custard that coats the back of the spoon. If using a jelly add at this stage and dissolve. Leave to cool. Whisk the cream until it thickens and hangs on the whisk when it is withdrawn. Whisk the egg whites until they hold stiff peaks, then whisk in the 2 tablespoons of caster sugar. Now stir the cooled custard into the cheese, followed by the cream, the vanilla and finally the meringue. Spoon the mixture into an 8-inch (20-cm) loose-bottomed sandwich tin. Mix the crushed crumbs with the melted butter and cinnamon and sprinkle round the top edge. Chill for several hours, preferably overnight.

To serve, run a knife around the edge of the cake to loosen it, then lift out, still on the base. Put on a serving dish and decorate just before serving with the sugared soft fruits or sliced banana. Chill until needed.

VARIATION

Top either with Morello (sour red) cherry conserve or this glaze.

1 can (14 oz/400 g) Morello (sour red) cherries
juice of ½ lemon
2 oz (50 g/¼ cup) caster (superfine) sugar
1 level tbsp cornflour (cornstarch)
juice strained from fruit

Arrange drained fruit in a design on top of the cheesecake. Mix all remaining ingredients, boil for 3 minutes, then cool until lukewarm and spoon over fruit. Chill.

PINEAPPLE CREAM CHEESE TORTE

Serves 6–8.
Keeps 3 days under refrigeration.
Freeze 3 months.

The sweetness of the pineapple is counteracted by the slight acidity of the soured cream used instead of sweet cream. However, if it is more convenient, whipped sweet cream can be used and a little more lemon juice added to the cheese mixture. Double the recipe for a 10- or

12-inch (25- or 30-cm) cake suitable for a celebration.

Do *not* use fresh pineapple as the enzyme it contains will prevent the torte setting.

3 oz (75 g/⅓ cup) sugar
¾ lemon jelly (gelatine mix) or 1 level tbsp powdered kosher vegetarian gelatine
pinch of salt
1 egg, separated
4 fl oz (125 ml/½ cup) juice drained from a medium can of pineapple chunks in pineapple juice
12 oz (350 g/1½ cups) cream cheese
juice of ½ lemon (2 tbsp)
½ teasp vanilla essence (extract)
5 fl oz (150 ml/⅔ cup) soured cream, 8% creamy fromage frais or Greek-style yoghurt

For the topping

3 Digestive biscuits (graham crackers), crushed
1 oz (25 g/2 tbsp) melted butter
2 level teasp caster (superfine) sugar
¼ level teasp mixed sweet spice

For decoration

a few glacé (candied) cherries or glacé pineapple cut in thin slices

In the top of a double saucepan or bowl standing in a pan of boiling water put sugar, gelatine (if used) and salt. Stir in the egg yolk, blended with the pineapple syrup. Cook until the mixture thickens enough to coat the back of a wooden spoon. Add jelly (if used) at this stage and stir until dissolved. Leave to cool while you put the cheese into a bowl and stir in the lemon juice and essence. Whisk the egg white until it holds stiff, glossy peaks. Now fold into the cheese first the cooled custard, then the soured cream and the whisked egg white. Finally fold in two-thirds of the pineapple, cut in bite-sized pieces. Spoon this mixture into an 8-inch (20-cm) loose-bottomed sandwich tin. Crush the Digestive biscuits to fine breadcrumbs and mix with the melted butter, sugar and spice. Sprinkle the topping in an even band ¾ inch (2 cm) wide round the edge of the cake. Chill, foil-covered, overnight.

To serve, loosen the torte from the sides of the tin with a sharp knife, then pull down the sides, leaving the torte on the base. Place on a serving plate. Decorate with the remaining pineapple and a few glacé cherries or pineapple pieces. Refrigerate until required.

Cake Icings, Toppings and Fillings

True cake decoration is the province of the professional. The recipes that follow lend themselves to more homely use and have been developed in most cases to go with specific cake recipes. They are easy to prepare and delicious to eat, and give the maximum effect with the minimum of effort. For more specialized advice, it is better to go to a book devoted to this craft alone.

GLACÉ ICING

This is a simple icing that gives a smooth, flat finish suitable for decorating with glacé fruits or nuts.

8 oz (225 g/2 cups) sifted icing (confectioners') sugar
squeeze of lemon juice
2-2½ tbsp water

Put the icing sugar into a small saucepan, stainless steel or enamel-lined if possible, as aluminium may turn white icing grey. Add the lemon juice and 2 tablespoons of the water. Beat well with a wooden spoon while warming over very gentle heat. Avoid too much heat as it may cause the icing to crack or dull on the cake - the base of the pan should never be too hot to touch with the fingers. To test the consistency of the icing, dip the wooden spoon into it - it should thickly coat the spoon before running off. If it is too thick, add the further ½ tablespoon of water and reheat. It is impossible to be specific about the exact amount of liquid required as some sugars absorb more liquid than others. However, it is generally better to have the icing too thick than too thin, as a thick icing can always be eased over the cake with a hot palette knife, whereas icing that is too thin will run straight down the sides, leaving the top naked and forlorn.

This quantity will ice the tops of 2 7-inch (17.5-cm) cakes or the top and sides of 1 8-inch (20-cm) cake.

To ice the cake Have ready any decorations such as nuts, glacé (candied) fruit or chocolate shot, as these must be applied immediately the icing has been poured on to the cake. Stand the cake on a cooling rack or plate where it can be left until it has set. If using a rack, put a plate underneath to catch the drips. Pour the icing over the cake, helping it to spread, if necessary, with a palette knife. Arrange the decoration and leave to set.

To coat the top and sides, allow the icing to run down the sides, helping it to spread smoothly by tilting the cake or smoothing the icing with a palette knife.

VARIATIONS

ORANGE GLACÉ ICING

8 oz (225 g/2 cups) sifted icing (confectioners') sugar
2–2½ tbsp strained orange juice
a few drops of food colouring

COFFEE GLACÉ ICING

8 oz (225 g/2 cups) sifted icing (confectioners') sugar
2 level teasp instant coffee dissolved in 2–2½ tbsp hot water

CHOCOLATE GLACÉ ICING

Ideal for chocolate eclairs.

4 oz (125 g) plain (semi-sweet) chocolate
½ oz (15 g/1 tbsp) butter or margarine
2 tbsp water
8 oz (225 g/2 cups) sifted icing (confectioners') sugar

Grate or shred the chocolate with a knife and put it into a small thick-bottomed pan with the butter. Add the water and warm over very gentle heat, stirring with a wooden spoon until a smooth cream is formed. (Alternatively, break the chocolate into small pieces and put with water in a small bowl. Cook, uncovered, in the microwave on 100 per cent power for 1½ minutes, then stir well.)

Gradually stir in the icing sugar, adding a little more hot water if necessary, to produce a coating consistency.

MILK CHOCOLATE ICING

This sets to give a topping the consistency of a bar of chocolate.
Sufficient to ice a cake 7–9 inches (17.5–22.5 cm) in diameter, depending on the thickness required.
Half the quantity will thinly ice a 7-inch (17.5 cm) cake.

4 oz (125 g) milk chocolate
2 fl oz (50 g/¼ cup) butter

Grate or shave the chocolate with a knife and put into a small thick-bottomed pan with the butter. Heat very gently until smooth (or break the chocolate into bits and cook uncovered in the microwave on 100 per cent power for 1½ minutes), then pour over the cake.

VARIATION

FRENCH MOCHA ICING

4 oz (125 g) plain dessert (semi-sweet) chocolate
2 oz (50 g/¼ cup) butter
1 tbsp rum
1 level teasp instant coffee

Heat very gently until smooth as before, then stir in rum and coffee. Pour over the cake. This amount will ice the same size cake as the Milk Chocolate Icing (p. 436).

ONE-STAGE FROSTING

This makes an ideal topping for a family cake. Although it does not have the fine texture of a creamed icing, it has just as much flavour - and it is made in minutes. Soft margarine can be used if the cake is to be served after a meat meal.

8 oz (225 g/2 cups) sifted icing (confectioners') sugar
3 oz (75 g/⅓ cup) soft butter or margarine
1 tbsp single (light) cream, fromage frais or fruit juice (orange, lemon or blackcurrant)

Put all the ingredients into a bowl and beat by machine or hand until creamy. This makes sufficient to fill and ice the top of an 8-inch (20-cm) sandwich cake.

ONE-BOWL MILK CHOCOLATE FROSTING

3 oz (75 g/⅓ cup) soft butter
4 oz (125 g/1 cup) sifted icing (confectioners') sugar
2 level tbsp drinking (instant) chocolate
2 teasp fromage frais or strong black coffee
½ teasp vanilla essence (extract)

Put all the ingredients into a bowl and beat until smooth and fluffy. Use to decorate the top of the 1-bowl Chocolate Cake (see p. 418).

BUTTER CREAMS

This kind of mixture lends itself to both icing and filling a cake, and to simple piped decorations or designs made with a fork or palette knife. The use of butter accentuates the flavour of ingredients such as chocolate, rum or liqueur. It can be mixed either by hand or by machine. To make the addition of the icing (confectioners') sugar easy, cream the butter first until it resembles mayonnaise, and only then beat in the icing sugar in several portions. All the recipes in this section will fill and frost 2 8-inch (20-cm) layers or 1 8-inch (20-cm) cake split in 2. To spread the icing on the cake use a palette knife or a piping bag and tube following manufacturers' directions.

VELVET BUTTER CREAM

This makes a rather yellow icing, but it has a delicious flavour and silken texture. Excellent for piping decorations as it holds its shape well.

4 oz (125 g/½ cup) butter
1 egg yolk
8 oz (225 g/2 cups) sifted icing (confectioners') sugar
1 teasp orange flower water
1 teasp rosewater or 2 teasp orange, lemon juice or other fruit syrup

Cream the butter, then beat in the egg yolk. Beat in the icing sugar, a third at a time, alternating with liquids.

MOCHA BUTTER CREAM

3 oz (75 g/⅓ cup) butter
1 egg yolk
6 oz (175 g/1½ cups) icing (confectioners') sugar
1½ tbsp cocoa
1½ tbsp strong coffee made with 2 level teasp instant coffee and 1½ tbsp hot water

Cream the butter until like mayonnaise, then beat in the egg yolk. Sift together the sugar and cocoa and beat into the butter, alternating with the coffee, until the icing is smooth and easy to spread.

ORANGE AND LEMON BUTTER CREAM

The juices and rinds are soaked together to draw out the flavouring oils from the rinds, which are then discarded.

1 level tbsp grated orange rind
2 level teasp grated lemon rind
1 tbsp lemon juice
2 tbsp orange juice
4 oz (125 g)½ cup) butter
1 egg yolk
10 oz (275 g/2½ cups) sifted icing (confectioners') sugar

Leave the rinds and juices to stand for 30 minutes, then strain. Beat the butter until creamy, then beat in the egg yolk. Add a little of the sifted icing sugar, then some of the strained juice. Continue beating, adding icing sugar and juice alternately, until smooth.

MOCHA FUDGE FROSTING

This is a cross between glacé icing and butter cream, creamier than the former but not as rich as the latter.

8 oz (225 g/2 cups) icing (confectioners') sugar
2 oz (50 g/¼ cup) butter
1 level teasp instant coffee
1 tbsp hot water 1 tbsp top milk or single (light) cream

Sift icing sugar into a bowl. Put butter, coffee, water and milk into a small pan and heat slowly without boiling until the butter melts (or microwave for 1 minute on 100 per cent power, covered, with a paper towel to stop splashing). Allow to cool until steaming stops, then pour over the icing sugar. Beat well. Spread on top of chocolate cake, or use to fill and frost it if preferred.

TO ICE A RICH FRUIT CAKE WITH ROYAL ICING AND ALMOND PASTE

Unless you are an expert, my advice is to bake the fruit cake for a special occasion, such as a wedding or barmitzvah, and have a professional pastrycook apply the almond paste and the decoration of royal icing. If, however, a simple finish only is required, perhaps for Chanukkah or another festival, a very acceptable result can be achieved at home with little more than a great deal of patience! Below I give the basic instructions for finishing a cake in this way.

The cake should be made at least 8 weeks before it is required, to allow it to mature. Storing instructions are given with the recipe.

At least 10 days before it is required, put the almond paste on the cake. It must have time (48 hours is the minimum) to dry out before the icing is put on, or the almond oil may seep through. If you intend to cover the sides as well as the top of the cake, double these quantities.

ALMOND PASTE

For a 7-inch (17.5-cm) cake
4 oz (125 g/1 cup) ground almonds
2 oz (50 g/¼ cup) caster (superfine) sugar
2 oz (50 g/½ cup) icing (confectioners') sugar
few drops almond and vanilla essence (extract)
1 egg yolk

For a 9-inch (22.5-cm) cake
6 oz (175 g/1½ cups) ground almonds
3 oz (75 g/⅓ cup) caster (superfine) sugar
3 oz (75 g/¾ cup) icing (confectioners') sugar
few drops almond and vanilla essence (extract)
1½ egg yolks or 1 large yolk

For brushing either cake
1 unbeaten egg white or 2–3 tbsp smooth apricot jam, warmed until spreadable

Mix the dry ingredients, then knead with the yolk and essence until the mixture forms a ball. Don't squeeze too hard or the paste will be oily. Using the bottom of the cake tin as a guide, roll the paste into a round on a sugared board. Brush the cake to remove any crumbs, then brush again with unbeaten egg white or warm apricot jam. Lay the round of almond paste on top and roll gently to smooth it. If you wish to cover the sides, roll 2 strips the depth and half the circumference of the cake. Press gently into place, then even up by rolling a jam jar round the cake, pressing the paste into place. With a spatula and your hand, make a right angle of the join between top and sides. Now cut a strong strip of paper long enough to go under the cake and come above the sides. Lay the cake on this and use it as a 'sling' to lift the cake into the tin and out again later. Leave the cake uncovered, for 48 hours at least, to dry out the paste.

Icing the cake You can do this any time from 48 hours after the almond pasting up to 1 or 2 days before it is needed. I advise you to get it done when your nervous system is still unfrazzled!

ROYAL ICING

For a 7-inch (17.5-cm) cake
top only
8 oz (225 g/2 cups) icing (confectioners') sugar
1 egg white

top and sides
1½ lb (675 g/6 cups) icing (confectioners') sugar
2½ egg whites (2½ fl oz/65 ml/5 tbsp)

For a 9-inch (22.5-cm) cake
top only
12 oz (350 g/3 cups) icing (confectioners') sugar
1½ egg whites (1½ fl oz/40 ml/3 tbsp)

top and sides
2 lb (900 g/8 cups) icing (confectioners') sugar
4 egg whites

Both sizes will need a few drops of acetic acid or a squeeze of lemon juice. Sift icing sugar thoroughly. Beat the whites until they are foamy. Make a well in the centre of the sugar, stir in most of the egg white and the acid or lemon juice, then beat until the icing is thick, pliable and glossy – at least 15 minutes (this can be done with an electric mixer).

Keep the icing covered with a damp cloth as you work, then any that is left over can be kept for 1 or 2 days in a plastic container for final decorations. Stand the cake on an upturned plate or special cake turntable and swirl the icing over the top and sides (if they're to be covered). Then, using a deep jug of boiling water, dip a spatula in this, shake dry and smooth the icing. If you want a snow scene, pull the icing up into little peaks. Drawing the spatula right across the top in a sweeping movement is the quickest way of getting a smooth finish. Now put the cake away, covered, to dry thoroughly overnight, before you apply the decorations.

For piping, your icing may need a little more beating to make it really stiff. Tint it if you will, but go easy!

Decide on the outline of your design and prick it out on the top of the cake. For inspiration look in high-class confectioners' and buy one of the booklets put out by the icing-tube manufacturers.

If all this sounds too intimidating, and if you've made a plain rather than a fruit cake, decorate the cake with 7-minute Icing that follows. It peaks beautifully and is soft on the tongue. However, don't make it more than 2 days before it is needed, otherwise it gets rather dry.

SEVEN-MINUTE ICING

2 egg whites
11 oz (300 g/1½ cups) granulated sugar
4 tbsp cold water
a pinch of cream of tartar
1 teasp vanilla esence (extract)

Combine all the ingredients in a double boiler. Beat over boiling water, using a hand or electric mixer, for 7 minutes, until the icing forms peaks. Remove from the heat and beat until thick enough to spread.

BISCUITS

Biscuits in a Hurry

The biscuit (cookie) or 'kichel' served to the visitor with a glass of schnapps or wine is a very old tradition in Jewish hospitality. Before the days of *parev* margarine, the biscuit would always be made with cooking oil so that it could be offered to a visitor after either a milk or a meat meal. These oil biscuits or 'kichels' are still delicious, even to modern palates, but increasingly butter or margarine is being used for biscuit-making, and the traditional repertoire has been enriched by biscuit recipes from all over the world.

While biscuits are more time-consuming to make than cakes, their flavour cannot be duplicated in the factory, so provided the finest ingredients only are used, they are well worth making at home.

Most of these biscuits are very quickly made: dropped from a teaspoon, rolled into balls or crescents, cut into fingers, frozen and sliced, or pressed into a tin - anything to avoid rolling them out on a board! I've suggested that kind of time-consuming operation only if the result is a biscuit that's very special indeed. If you follow my guidelines for easier biscuit-making, however, even that kind of hard work will be minimized.

THE INGREDIENTS

It is false economy to use any but the best butter - cheaper ones do not produce the melt-in-the-mouth texture you should expect. Caster (superfine) sugar will give a finer texture than granulated, and icing (confectioners') sugar makes the crispest, shortest biscuit of all.

MIXING THE BISCUITS

Although biscuits can be made successfully either by hand or with an electric mixer, I generally use a food processor because a batch of even the most delicate biscuit dough can be prepared in it in little more than 1 minute. Specific mixing instructions are given with each recipe, but there is an important point to bear in mind: if you are preparing a dough that needs to be rolled, process the mixture only until it begins to form tiny balls, then tip these into a bowl and gather them up into a dough by hand. If the mixture is processed until it forms a big ball, it becomes very soft and difficult to handle.

BAKING THE BISCUITS

Bake the biscuits on heavy, flat tins kept specially for the purpose - pressed aluminium is ideal as it does not become distorted even with constant use, so the biscuits cook evenly. To save the chore of washing greasy tins after use, I line them with silicone paper, but if you don't have any, use a flavourless oil (such as sunflower) for greasing rather than butter or margarine, which may cause the biscuits to stick.

FREEZING

Almost all biscuits freeze well. Fragile biscuits should be stored in a plastic container which has been sealed with freezer tape. As many biscuits as are required can be taken out, the container resealed and put back in the freezer. Firmer varieties can be stored in plastic bags. Biscuits take about 30 minutes to defrost.

REHEATING

If biscuits have gone soggy in the freezer, put them on an ungreased tray and leave in a preheated moderate oven, Gas No. 4 (350°F/180°C), for 10 minutes. Take out and treat as though freshly baked.

It's a Tradition

Traditional Ashkenazi Jewish biscuits are made either with oil or with butter and are really sweetened pastry of the kind used in strudels (see pp. 388-94) or Hamantaschen (see pp. 590-596).

TRADITIONAL KICHELS

Makes about 50, depending on size.
Keeps 2 weeks in an airtight container.
Freeze 3 months.

These are a favourite biscuit for all kinds of occasions because they do not include any dairy products and so are suitable to serve before, with or after either a meat or a dairy meal. Use only the minimum amount of flour needed to achieve a rollable dough and the 'kichels' will be light and crisp.

2 large eggs
5 oz (150 g/$^2/_3$ cup) caster (superfine) sugar
4 fl oz (125 ml/$^1/_2$ cup) sunflower or other flavourless oil
rind of 1 orange
1 teasp vanilla essence (extract)
11-12 oz (300-350 g/3 cups) flour (use half plain (all-purpose) and half self-raising) or all plain (all-purpose) plus 3 teasp baking powder

Whisk the eggs until thick, then gradually whisk in the sugar, followed by the oil, the orange rind and the essence. Finally stir in enough flour to make a rollable, non-sticky dough. Knead until smooth, then roll out $^3/_8$ inch (1 cm) thick on a floured board. Sprinkle the dough with caster sugar, then roll lightly to press in the sugar. Cut into shapes with biscuit-cutters and arrange on oiled or silicone-paper-lined trays, leaving room for the biscuits to spread. Bake in a moderate oven, Gas No. 4 (350°F/180°C), for 20-25 minutes, or until a pale gold in colour.

QUICK KICHLACH

Makes 36.
Keeps 2 weeks in an airtight container.
Freeze 3 months.

Featherweight biscuits which are ideal to serve with stewed fruit or morning coffee. They have the same flavour as Traditional Kichels (see above), but are lighter in texture and far quicker to make - rolling and cutting can be so tedious.

2 eggs
5 fl oz (150 ml/$^2/_3$ cup) oil
2 small teasp vanilla essence (extract)

1 teasp grated lemon rind
5 oz (150 g/⅔ cup) caster (superfine) sugar
8 oz (225 g/2 cups) self-raising flour or 8 oz (225 g/2 cups) plain (all-purpose) flour plus 2 teasp baking powder
pinch of salt
almond nibs

Beat eggs with a fork until well blended. Stir in the oil, vanilla and lemon rind. Blend in the sugar until the mixture thickens, then add the flour and a pinch of salt (the dough will be soft). Drop rounded teaspoons on to an ungreased biscuit tin, 2 inches (5 cm) apart. Using the bottom of a glass which has been dipped in oil and then in sugar, flatten each biscuit into a round. Decorate with almond nibs. Bake in a quick oven, Gas No. 6 (400°F/200°C), for 8–10 minutes, or until golden.

VARIATION

ALMOND KICHLACH

Makes 36.
Keeps 1 week at room temperature in an airtight container.
Freeze 6 months.

A roll-and-cut version, rather quicker to shape. The texture is similar to shortbread.

1 recipe Vanilla Kipferl dough *(see p. 445)*

For the glaze
1 egg white
1 teasp water
1 oz (25 g/¼ cup) flaked almonds
1 tbsp caster (superfine) sugar

Roll out the dough ¼ inch (0.5 cm) thick and cut into crescents with a 2½-inch (6-cm) cutter. Arrange on ungreased baking sheets, 1 inch (2.5 cm) apart.

Whisk egg white with the water until frothy, then brush over the biscuits. Scatter with the flaked almonds mixed with the caster sugar. Bake at Gas No. 3 (325°F/160°C) for 15–18 minutes, or until a pale gold.

Allow to mature for 24 hours in an airtight container.

TRADITIONAL BUTTER BISCUITS

Makes about 40.
Keeps 2 weeks in an airtight container.
Freeze 3 months.

These should be very thin and very crisp.

8 oz (225 g/2 cups) plain (all-purpose) flour
½ level teasp baking powder
5 oz (150 g/⅔ cup) butter
3 oz (75 g/⅓ cup) caster (superfine) sugar
2 tbsp beaten egg (taken from 1 whole egg)

For the topping
the reserved egg
4 level tbsp caster (superfine) sugar
½ level teasp cinnamon
2 level tbsp chopped almonds

To mix the dough by hand or electric mixer, sift together the flour and baking powder, then rub in the butter until the mixture resembles breadcrumbs. Stir in the sugar and add enough of the egg to make a soft, non-sticky dough.

To mix by food processor, process the dry ingredients and the butter (cut in 1-inch (2.5-cm) chunks) for 5 seconds, then drop in the vanilla essence and egg and process for 3 seconds, or until little balls of dough are beginning to form. Tip the mixture into a bowl and knead by hand into a dough.

Chill for half an hour, then on a lightly-floured board roll out the dough to a thickness of ⅛ inch (0.3 cm). Stamp out into rounds or crescents using a floured cutter. Brush with the reserved egg, diluted with a teaspoonful of water. Decorate with the topping ingredients mixed together. Bake in a preheated oven, Gas No. 6 (400°F/200°C), for 8–9 minutes, or until golden brown.

GRANDMA'S VANILLA BISCUITS

Makes about 60.
Keeps 2 weeks in an airtight container.
Freeze 3 months.

The use of icing (confectioners') sugar and the high proportion of butter give these biscuits a meltingly tender texture. They keep well.

10 oz (275 g/2½ cups) plain (all-purpose) flour
pinch of salt
4 oz (125 g/1 cup) sifted icing (confectioners') sugar
8 oz (225 g/1 cup) butter
1 egg
2 teasp vanilla essence (extract)

For the decoration
1 oz (25 g/¼ cup) finely chopped nuts
1 oz (25 g/2 tbsp) caster (superfine) sugar

By hand or mixer, mix together the flour, salt and sugar. Rub in the butter until the mixture resembles coarse crumbs, then mix to a dough with 2 tablespoons of the beaten egg and the vanilla essence.

By food processor, make exactly as for the Traditional Butter Biscuits (see p. 443).

Wrap in foil and chill for 30 minutes. Roll out ⅛ (0.3 cm) thick on a lightly floured board and cut into shapes with a floured cutter. Transfer to ungreased baking sheets. Paint with the remaining egg and sprinkle with the mixed sugar and nuts. Bake in a preheated oven, Gas No. 5 (375°F/190°C), for 7 minutes, or until golden.

JUDEBROD - JEWISH CAKES
(*Danish Cardamom Biscuits*)

Makes approximately 60.
Keeps 1 week in an airtight container.
Freeze 6 weeks.

Cardamom - that wonderfully aromatic spice which gives authentic Danish pastries their unique flavour - magically transforms these quickly made, melt-in-the-mouth biscuits into very special petits fours to serve with a compôte of summer fruits or ice-cream. Danish friends tell me that, as its name implies, this recipe is originally of Jewish origin. It calls for the kind of coarse white sugar crystals which make a particularly crunchy topping on sugar buns, but demerara sugar can be used (if not quite as effectively) instead. For the freshest flavour cardamom seeds should be pulverized in a nut- or coffee-grinder, although the ground spice can be bought from a health-food shop or some supermarkets.

4 oz (125 g/½ cup) butter, cut in roughly 1-inch (2.5-cm) chunks
4 oz (125 g/½ cup) light muscovado sugar
1 teasp ground cinnamon
1 teasp freshly pounded or ready-ground cardamom seeds
1 egg
1 teasp baking powder
9 oz (250 g/2¼ cups) plain (all-purpose) flour

For the decoration
1 oz (25 g/2 tbsp) brown or white coarse sugar
1 oz (25 g/¼ cup) almond nibs

By hand or electric mixer, work together until a dough is formed.

By food processor, put all the ingredients in and process until little moist balls of dough are beginning to form. Tip out into a bowl and knead into a dough. Flatten into a block 1 inch (2.5 cm) thick, then chill for several hours or overnight.

Preheat the oven to Gas No. 5 (375°F/190°C). Mix the coarse sugar and almond nibs together.

Roll out the dough ⅛ inch (0.3 cm) thick and stamp out 2-inch (5-cm) rounds with a cutter. Brush them with water, then dip them into the sugar and almond mixture.

Place the biscuits on silicone-paper-lined or

greased baking sheets and bake for 10–12 minutes, or until firm to the touch. Leave on wire racks until cold.

VANILLA KIPFERL

Makes 36.
Keeps 2 weeks at room temperature in an airtight container.
Freeze 3 months.

The pride and joy of every Jewish cook of Austro-Hungarian origin, this is one of the great biscuits of the world. It has been served in the *konditorei* (coffee houses) of Vienna and Budapest since the seventeenth century. A good kipferl should be barely coloured and literally melt in the mouth.

7 oz (200 g/¾ cup plus 2 tbsp) butter at room temperature
2½ oz (65 g/¼ cup plus 1 tbsp) caster (superfine) sugar
1 oz (25 g) (2 small packets) vanilla sugar
2 egg yolks
10 oz (275 g/2¼ cups) plain (all-purpose) flour
2 oz (50 g/½ cup) ground almonds or hazelnuts, or half and half
pinch of salt

For coating the biscuits
sieved icing (confectioners') or caster (superfine) sugar

The biscuits can be made on the board like shortbread or in the mixer or food processor, but in the latter case care must be taken not to overmix the sugar and butter.

In the mixer or food processor, cut the soft butter into chunks then work in the sugar and vanilla sugar until absorbed. Work in the egg yolks. Gradually add the flour, ground nuts and salt, until the dough leaves the side of the bowl clean.

To make on the board by the traditional method, put the mixed salt, flour and nuts on the board, make a well in the centre and put in the butter (cut into roughly 1-inch/2.5-cm chunks) and the sugar. Work these together with the fingers, blend in the egg yolks, then gradually work in the surrounding dry ingredients until a dough is formed. Chill for 1 hour.

In shaping the biscuits, try not to use any flour on the board as this will toughen the biscuits. Pinch off pieces of dough the size of a walnut and roll between the palms into small balls. Roll each ball into a 'pencil' about ½ inch (1.25 cm) thick and 4 inches (10 cm) long, then bend into a crescent.

Arrange on ungreased baking sheets, leaving about 1 inch (2.5 cm) between each biscuit, as they do spread a little. Bake in a preheated oven, Gas No. 3 (325°F/160°C), for 18 minutes, or until a pale-gold colour.

Carefully lift on to a cooling tray and leave for 3 minutes to firm up, then dip into a bowl of icing or caster sugar. Dip again when completely cold. Allow to mature 24 hours in an airtight container.

NUSSKIPFERL

Makes about 50.
Keeps 2 weeks under refrigeration.
Freeze 3 months.

A variation on the Vanilla Kipferl (see above) theme, using chopped walnuts instead of ground almonds.

8 oz (225 g/1 cup) butter
bare 3 oz (75 g/⅓ cup) caster (superfine) sugar
2 teasp hot water
2 small teasp vanilla essence (extract)
8 oz (225 g/2 cups) sifted plain (all-purpose) flour
pinch of salt
2 oz (50 g/½ cup) chopped walnuts

For coating the biscuits
sieved icing (confectioners') sugar

Cream the butter thoroughly and add the sugar gradually. Then add the water and essence and beat again. Finally stir in the flour, salt and nuts. Wrap the dough in clingfilm (saranwrap) and leave to harden for 1 hour. Shape pieces of dough into pencils, then curve into 3-inch (7.5-cm) crescents. Arrange on ungreased sheets, leaving room to swell. Bake in a preheated oven, Gas No. 3 (325°F/160°C), for 15 minutes, until firm but still pale. Cool 5 minutes, then dip in icing sugar.

GEREYBES
(*Sephardi-style shortbread*)

Makes about 36.
Keeps 2 weeks at room temperature in an airtight container.
Freezes 3 months.

The baking of the Sephardim, particularly those from communities in the Middle East, is of a delicacy and refinement rarely equalled in Western cooking. Craft plays a great part in shaping the many different kinds of pastries of which this delicate butter biscuit is typical. Gereybes are of a similar texture to the Greek 'kourabiedes' and the Arabic 'ghorayebah' - 'lovers' pastries' - but the typical bracelet shape of this biscuit is of Syrian origin. This recipe comes from a family with roots in the Damascus of the late nineteenth century.

8 oz (225 g/1 cup) unsalted butter
(at room temperature)
5 oz (150 g/⅔ cup) caster (superfine) sugar
12 oz (350 g/3 cups) plain (all-purpose) flour
2 oz (50 g/½ cup) split blanched almonds

Preheat the oven to Gas No. 3 (325°F/160°C).

Using an electric mixer, cream the butter until like mayonnaise, then add the sugar gradually, beating until the mixture is almost white. Add the flour a little at a time, beating after each addition. When enough flour has been added, the dough will come away from the edges of the bowl.

Turn out on to a lightly floured board and knead gently but thoroughly until the dough is quite smooth. Take a piece of the dough and roll into a salami shape about 1 inch (2.5 cm) in diameter, then cut across at ½-inch (1-cm) intervals. Roll each of these pieces in turn into a pencil shape about 5 inches (12.5 cm) long. Form into a 'bracelet' and put a split almond over the join. Repeat with the remaining dough.

Arrange on ungreased trays leaving 1 inch (2.5 cm) between each biscuit. Bake for 20 minutes, or until the biscuits are barely coloured and just firm to the touch - do not overbrown or the delicate flavour will be compromised. Leave on the trays until cold.

Store in an airtight container.

Frivolities

VANILJEKRANSE

Makes about 48.
Keeps 1 week in an airtight container.
Freeze 3 months.

Another wonderful Danish biscuit to serve with ice-cream or a cold sweet.

8 oz (225 g/1 cup) butter
3 oz (75 g/½ cup) caster (superfine) sugar
about 2 tbsp beaten egg
½ teasp vanilla essence (extract)
8 oz (225 g/2 cups) plain (all-purpose) flour
½ level teasp baking powder
3 oz (75 g/¾ cup) ground almonds

For the garnish
almond flakes or nibs

Cream the butter until like mayonnaise, then beat in the sugar. Add the egg and vanilla essence, then beat in the flour, baking powder and ground almonds. Beat well - the mixture should be the consistency of butter icing. If it is too solid, beat in a little more egg. Place in a forcing bag with a medium star tube, or put in a biscuit press. Pipe into rings or into sticks on a slightly greased or silicone-paper-lined baking sheet. Scatter with almond flakes or nibs. Bake in a preheated oven, Gas No. 5 (375°F/190°C), for 10–12 minutes.

SPRITZ BISCUITS

Makes 40.
Keeps 2 weeks in an airtight container.
Freeze 3 months.

Vanilla sugar, usually sold in $\frac{1}{2}$ or $\frac{3}{4}$ oz (15 or 20 g) packs, gives the best flavour to these delicate little biscuits. However, if you keep a vanilla pod in the caster (superfine) sugar you use for cooking, a tablespoon of that makes a reasonable substitute.

3 oz (75 g/$\frac{1}{3}$ cup) caster sugar
2 x $\frac{1}{2}$–$\frac{3}{4}$ oz (15–20 g) packets vanilla sugar
6 oz (175 g/$\frac{3}{4}$ cup) softened butter
1 egg yolk, beaten
8 oz (225 g/2 cups) plain (all-purpose) flour
pinch of salt
1 teasp water, if necessary

Chill 2 ungreased baking trays until needed. In a large bowl or the food processor work together the sugars, butter and egg. When smooth and fluffy, work in the flour sifted with the salt. If the mixture seems too stiff to pipe, add the teaspoon of water. Put into a large piping bag fitted with a coarse rose tube, and pipe out into small biscuits about $\frac{3}{4}$ inch (2 cm) in diameter, leaving $1\frac{1}{2}$ inches (4 cm) between each of them. Bake for 10 minutes at Gas No. 5 (375°F/190°C), until a pale golden brown.

Alternatively, the mixture may be taken by the teaspoon and dropped into a bowl of chopped walnuts or slightly crushed sugared cornflakes, then formed lightly into a flattened disc and baked the same way.

TUILES

Makes 24.
Keeps 1 week in a dry atmosphere in an airtight container.
Do not freeze, as they go limp.

A special-occasion French biscuit to serve with ice-cream or a fruit mousse. These do need all your attention but are worth the effort.

5 oz (150 g/$\frac{2}{3}$ cup) caster (superfine) sugar
2 egg whites
pinch of salt
3 oz (75 g/6 tbsp) unsalted butter, melted and cooled until lukewarm
2 tbsp sunflower or other flavourless oil
2 oz (50 g/$\frac{1}{2}$ cup) plain (all-purpose) flour
2 oz (50 g/$\frac{1}{2}$ cup) finely chopped almonds or almond nibs

Beat the sugar, egg whites and salt with a wooden spoon or electric beater until the sugar has dissolved and the mixture has thickened. Add the butter and oil and blend well, then stir in the flour and almonds. Drop rounded teaspoons of the mixture on to silicone-paper-lined baking sheets, leaving plenty of room in between. Spread the mixture thinly into a round about 3 inches (7.5 cm) in diameter with a fork – it doesn't matter how thin as it will join up in the cooking.

Bake in a preheated oven, Gas No. 4 (350°F/180°C), for 12 minutes, or until golden brown. Take from the oven, cool for 30 seconds then lift off and mould over a rolling pin. When set, put on a cooling tray. Store when quite cold.

BRANDY (GINGER) SNAPS

Makes 48.
Keeps 2 weeks at room temperature in an airtight container.
Freeze 6 months.
Brandy snaps can be frozen empty, or filled with whipped cream, or the uncooked mixture can be frozen.

The factory-made version cannot equal the delicate taste and texture of these admittedly 'tricky' biscuits. However, you will find the mixture very easy to handle and shape if you chill it and then roll it into even-sized balls as described, rather than dropping it from a teaspoon in the conventional manner. My husband made me a 'brandy-snap' machine by sticking 4 pieces of ½-inch (1-cm) dowelling into a connecting piece of wood at 4-inch (10-cm) intervals.

Children love brandy snaps plain; more sophisticated palates will relish them filled with brandy-flavoured whipped cream. (Do not fill more than 1 or 2 hours before serving or the biscuit may lose its snap.)

4 oz (125 g/½ cup) butter
3 oz (75 g/⅓ cup) caster (superfine) sugar
4 oz (125 g/5 tbsp) golden (corn) syrup
3½ oz (100 g/⅞ cup) plain (all-purpose) flour
1 teasp ground ginger
1 teasp grated lemon rind

Weigh all the ingredients very carefully. Put the butter into a thick-bottomed pan and heat gently until it is just melted, then stir in the sugar and syrup and continue heating and stirring until smooth. Do not allow to boil. Stir in remaining ingredients. Cool for 10 minutes, until the mixture is the consistency of putty. Form into balls the size of a large marble by rolling a little of the mixture between the palms, then arrange 3 inches (7.5 cm) apart on lightly oiled baking trays.

Bake at Gas No. 3 (325°F/160°C) for 10 minutes, until golden brown. Leave to cool for 1 minute, or until the snaps can be lifted off the tray with a flexible spatula. Roll each in turn round a wooden spoon handle, and when firm enough to hold its shape, slide off and leave to harden on a cooling tray. If they become too brittle before they can be rolled, return to the oven for 1 minute to soften again.

Serve plain or filled with brandy cream made as follows. Whip 5 fl oz (150 ml/⅔ cup) of whipping cream until it hangs on the whisk, then stir in 1 teaspoon each of brandy and sugar, and continue to whip carefully until it will just hold its shape in a peak when the whisk is withdrawn.

MERINGUE KISSES

Makes about 36, depending on size.
Keeps 2 weeks at room temperature in an airtight container.
Freeze 3 months.

This recipe is easier to make than the traditional meringue. It produces a crisp outside with a marshmallow interior. As all the sugar must be beaten in, it should not be attempted without some form of electric mixer.

1 level teasp cornflour (cornstarch)
¼ teasp cream of tartar
6 oz (175 g/¾ cup) caster (superfine) sugar
1 teasp vanilla essence (extract)
3 egg whites

Make sure there is no trace of grease in the mixing bowl or mixers and no trace of yolk in the whites, or the mixture will not achieve its true volume. Mix the cornflour, cream of tartar and sugar and put the essence into an egg cup. Whisk the whites until they hold stiff, glossy peaks, then start adding the sugar/cornflour mixture a spoonful at a time, beating until stiff again after each addition. When all the sugar has been added and the mixture is solid, beat in the vanilla essence. Have ready baking sheets covered with silicone paper. Either pipe the mixture on to the tray, using a coarse rose tube, or drop from a teaspoon in little blobs. Bake in a preheated oven, Gas No. 1 (275°F/140°C), for about 40 minutes, or until the meringues feel crisp and lift off the tray without difficulty. Use either as a petit four or sandwich together with cream.

Shortbread and Variations

Traditional Scottish shortbread is made on a pastry board the same way as the French pâté sucrée, of which it is a lineal descendant - the chefs who came from France with Mary Queen of Scots introduced this biscuit to Scotland. However, it also has an affinity with the Traditional Butter Biscuit (see p. 443).

For speed, it can be made by creaming or rubbing the butter and sugar together, but the texture is not quite as delicate on the tongue. However, life is short, so I give both methods. Shortbread can be made with all flour, with flour and cornflour (cornstarch), or with flour and rice flour (to achieve a more crumbly texture); and it can be mixed without liquid, with egg yolk or with cream. All the methods have something to commend them and I can only suggest you try them for yourself.

Shortbread burns easily, so it must be baked carefully and only long enough to colour it lightly.

PERFECT SHORTBREAD
(Traditional Method)

Makes about 30 fingers, 40 biscuits or 3 rounds.
Keeps 2 weeks in an airtight container.
Freeze 3 months.

12 oz (350 g/3 cups) plain (all-purpose) flour or
10 oz (275 g/2½ cups) plain (all-purpose) flour and 2 oz (50 g/½ cup) cornflour (cornstarch), or
10 oz (275 g/2½ cups) plain (all-purpose) flour and 2 oz (50 g/½ cup) rice flour or fine semolina
pinch of salt
5 oz (125 g/⅔ cup) caster (superfine) sugar
8 oz (225 g/1 cup) waxy butter
1 tbsp double (heavy) cream or 2 egg yolks

Sift the flours and salt on to a pastry board and make a 'clearing' in the centre. Into this put the sugar and on top place the butter, which should be neither too hard nor too oily. On top of the butter, scatter a handful of flour, then start kneading it into the butter and sugar, adding flour until all but about a cupful has been used. Flatten the dough with the heel of the hand and spread it either with the cream or with the yolks. Fold the dough over to enclose the liquid, then add the remaining flour and knead until the dough is quite smooth and free from cracks. Chill for half an hour to allow the mixture to firm up.

Sprinkle the pastry board with caster sugar (not flour) and roll the dough to a thickness of ½ inch (1 cm). It can then be cut with fancy biscuit-cutters or, using a sharp knife, into rectangular fingers. Another method is to cut it to fit a shallow sponge tin, lined with silicone or greaseproof paper. The traditional 'edging' for fingers or rounds of shortbread is the same as for piecrust - pinching the dough between the thumb and forefinger of one hand and the forefinger of the other. Rounds of shortbread should then be lightly marked into sections like the spokes of a wheel. All shapes must be pricked with a fork or skewer at ¼-inch (0.5-cm) intervals to prevent the dough from puffing up when it is cooked.

Bake the shortbread in a preheated oven, Gas No. 3 (325°F/160°C), until a pale golden brown. Biscuits will take about 20 minutes, rounds (protected by the tin) about 35 minutes. Immediately the shortbread comes from the oven, place on cooling trays and scatter with caster (superfine) sugar.

VARIATION

Divide the dough into 3. Leave 1 plain, work 2 oz (50 g/⅓ cup) of chopped glacé (candied) cherries into another and 2 oz (50 g/½ cup) of chopped almonds or walnuts into the third.

TOFFEE SHORTBREAD

Makes about 20.
Keeps 2 weeks in an airtight container.
Freeze 3 months.

Half the master recipe can be used for these delectable biscuits, or a batch made from scratch. Children especially enjoy this confection.

For the base
4 oz (125 g/½ cup) butter
6 oz (175 g/1½ cups) plain (all-purpose) flour
2 oz (50 g/¼ cup) caster (superfine) sugar

For the toffee
4 oz (125 g/½ cup) butter
4 oz (125 g/½ cup) soft medium brown sugar
2 level tbsp golden (corn) syrup
1 x 6 fl oz (175 ml/¾ cup) tin sweetened condensed milk
½ teasp vanilla essence (extract)

For the topping
4 oz (125 g) coating milk chocolate

Use a tin either 11 x 7 x 1 inches (27.5 x 17.5 x 2.5 cm) or with a similar area. Rub the butter into the flour and sugar until like breadcrumbs, then knead into a dough. Roll on a sugared board to the size of the tin. Lift off and arrange in the base, trimming the sides even. Prick all over. Bake at Gas No. 4 (350°F/180°C) for 20 minutes, or until pale gold in colour. Allow to cool.

Put all the toffee ingredients (except the essence) into a thick-bottomed pan and heat, stirring until the sugar has dissolved. Bring to the boil and cook, stirring every once in a while, for 7 minutes, by which time the mixture will be a golden-brown toffee colour. Take from the heat, add the vanilla essence and beat for 1 minute. Pour the toffee mixture on to the cooled shortbread base. Leave until cold.

Melt the chocolate over hot water (1½ minutes in the microwave, uncovered, on 100 per cent power) and as soon as it is liquid, pour over the toffee. When almost set, mark lightly into squares.

HAZELNUT SHORTBREAD

Makes 24 2-inch (5-cm) squares.
Keeps 2 weeks in an airtight container.
Freeze 3 months.

Buttery squares with a superb nutty flavour. The 'short-cut' method given below avoids the need to roll out the dough and can be used for any of the previous recipes.

Leave 2 days before eating to allow the flavours to develop.

3½–4 oz (100–125 g/¾–1 cup)white hazelnuts (already skinned for convenience)
8 oz (225 g/1 cup) mild chilled butter, cut in roughly 1-inch (2.5-cm) chunks
4 oz (125 g/½ cup) caster (superfine) sugar
8 oz (225 g/2 cups) plain (all-purpose) flour
½ teasp salt

To sprinkle on biscuits
2 tbsp granulated sugar

Have ready a tin approximately 12 x 8 x 1½ inches (30 x 20 x 4 cm). Preheat the oven to Gas No. 3 (325°F/160°C).

Toast the hazelnuts until a rich gold, either under a moderate grill (broiler) or at Gas No. 4 (350°F/180°C) for 15 minutes. (If the nuts haven't been skinned before purchase, the papery covering will have to be rubbed off in a tea-towel – buying the 'white' hazelnuts avoids this.)

Put the cooled nuts in the food processor and grind until almost as fine as commercial ground almonds. Add all the remaining biscuit ingredients and pulse until the mixture looks like fine crumbs. Spoon into the tin and use the back of a fork to press into an even layer, then prick all over (to prevent the mixture rising in the oven) and sprinkle with 1 tablespoon of the granulated sugar. Bake for 30–35 minutes, until the surface is firm and the mixture is a light gold.

Put the tin of shortbread on to a cooling rack and leave to firm up for 10 minutes, then sprinkle with the remaining sugar and cut into 2-inch (5-cm) squares.

Biscuits in a Hurry

These biscuits can be made literally in minutes, as the most time-consuming operation - rolling and cutting - has been side-stepped altogether. Instead, the mixture is either dropped from a spoon or rolled into balls which form into perfect biscuits in the heat of the oven.

Note When the shortening is to be melted, use only butter or oil. Margarine is less successful used in this way.

BUTTER CRUNCHIES

Makes approximately 48.
Keeps 1 week at room temperature in an airtight container.
Freeze 3 months.

Simple but delicious.

4 oz (125 g/½ cup) soft butter
4 oz (125 g/½ cup) caster (superfine) sugar
1 egg
grated rind of ½ lemon
8 oz (225 g/2 cups) self-raising flour
granulated sugar for rolling

Put all the ingredients in a bowl and beat until a dough is formed. Roll into walnut-sized balls between wetted palms, then roll in granulated sugar. Arrange on buttered trays. Bake in a preheated oven, Gas No. 5 (375°F/190°C), for 18 minutes, until golden brown.

CINNAMON BITES

Makes 36–40.
Keeps 2 weeks under refrigeration.
Freeze 3 months.

These have an exotic flavour and a moist yet light texture.

8 oz (225 g/1 cup) waxy butter
4 oz (125 g/12 cup) caster (superfine) sugar
2 egg yolks
1 teasp vanilla essence (extract)
5 oz (150 g/1⅔ cups) desiccated coconut
8 oz (225 g/2 cups) plain (all-purpose) flour
1 teasp ground cinnamon
½ teasp baking powder
½ teasp salt

To coat the biscuits
1 teasp ground cinnamon
2 oz (50 g/½ cup) icing (confectioners') sugar

Use the food processor. If the butter is hard, first soften it for 30 seconds in the microwave. Cut into 1-inch (2.5-cm) chunks. Process until creamy, then add the sugar, yolks and vanilla essence and process until just absorbed. Add the coconut and process for 2 seconds, then add the flour sifted with the cinnamon, baking powder and salt, and process until a rough dough is formed.

Turn on to a floured board and divide in 2, then knead each portion gently until smooth and pliable. Add a little flour as you go if the dough is sticky. Wrap the dough in clingfilm (saranwrap) and chill in the refrigerator for 20 minutes, then pinch off pieces the size of a walnut and roll into balls. Arrange 2 inches (5 cm) apart on greased trays.

Bake in a preheated oven, Gas No. 3 (325°F/160°C), until firm to gentle touch but only lightly coloured - about 18 minutes. Leave for 5 minutes on the trays, then gently dip each biscuit into the mixed cinnamon and icing sugar. When the biscuits are quite cold, dip again, then arrange in layers in a container and sprinkle with any remaining sugar.

COUNTRY CRUNCH BISCUITS

Makes 48.
Keeps 1 week in an airtight container.
Freeze 3 months.

A delicious after-school biscuit, with very nutritious ingredients.

3 oz (75 g/¾ cup) plain (all-purpose) flour
8 oz (225 g/1 cup) soft light brown sugar
3 oz (75 g/1 cup) desiccated coconut
4 oz (125 g/1⅓ cup) rolled or porridge oats
1 oz (25 g/¼ cup) toasted slivered almonds, sesame seeds or sunflower seeds
4 oz (125 g/½ cup) butter or margarine
1 tbsp golden (corn) syrup
1 teasp bicarbonate of soda (baking powder)
2 tbsp warm water

Mix the dry ingredients except the bicarbonate in a bowl, melt the fat and syrup together (1 minute on 100 per cent power in the microwave), then add the bicarbonate mixed with the warm water. Pour on to the dry ingredients and mix very thoroughly with a wooden spoon or electric mixer, then leave for 10 minutes to firm up. Roll into balls the size of walnuts and place 2 inches (5 cm) apart on greased silicone-paper-lined trays. Bake at Gas No. 4 (350°F/180°C) for 10-12 minutes, until a rich brown. Remove from the tray when firm.

CHOCOLATE BUTTERBALLS

Makes about 40.
Keeps 2 weeks in an airtight container.
Freeze 3

The combination of both chocolate and cocoa gives these biscuits a particularly rich flavour.

8 oz (225 g/1 cup) butter or firm margarine
4 oz (125 g/½ cup) dark brown sugar
1 teasp vanilla essence (extract)
1 egg
8 oz (225 g/2 cups) plain (all-purpose) flour
½ teasp salt
2 oz (50 g/½ cup) cocoa
4 oz (125 g) plain chocolate or chocolate dots

Use the food processor. Process the soft fat until creamy, then add the brown sugar, vanilla and egg and process until just absorbed. Pulse in the flour, salt and cocoa, then pulse in the chocolate cut into tiny bits or the chocolate dots. Tip on to a board and form into a rough ball. Chill for 20 minutes, then with damp palms roll rounded teaspoonfuls of the mixture into balls 1 inch (2.5 cm) in diameter. Arrange 1 inch (2.5 cm) apart on baking trays covered with silicone paper, bake in a moderate oven, Gas No. 4 (350°F/180°C), for 20 minutes, then immediately remove to a cooling tray. Store in an airtight container when cold.

CHOCOLATE AND WALNUT SHORTBREADS

Makes about 30.
Keeps 2 weeks at room temperature in an airtight container.
Freeze 3 months.

These crunchy fork biscuits have a rich chocolate flavour. They are very quickly made with a food processor.

3 oz (75 g/¾ cup) walnuts
7 oz (200 g/¾ cup plus 2 tbsp) soft butter
1 egg yolk
7 oz (200 g/1 cup) light brown sugar
2 teasp vanilla essence (extract)
8 oz (225 g/2 cups) plain (all-purpose) flour
½ teasp baking powder
3 tbsp cocoa

For the coating
1 egg white, lightly whisked
1 oz (25 g/2 tbsp) caster (superfine) sugar

Chop all the walnuts finely in the food processor, then divide into 2 oz and 1 oz portions. Cut the butter into roughly 1-inch (2.5-cm) chunks, then process for 5 seconds until creamy. Add the egg yolk, sugar and vanilla essence and process until absorbed. Add the flour mixed with the baking powder, cocoa and 2 oz portion of walnuts and pulse until a rough dough begins to form. Turn out on to a floured board, divide in 2 and knead lightly until smooth. Flatten each portion into a 1-inch-thick (2.5-cm) block, then wrap in clingfilm (saranwrap) and chill for at least 30 minutes. Pinch off walnut-sized pieces of dough and roll into small balls. Arrange 2 inches (5 cm) apart on greased or silicone-paper-lined trays and press down firmly with a wet fork to form biscuits about ⅜ inch (1 cm) thick. Paint each biscuit with some of the whisked egg and sprinkle with the sugar mixed with the 1 oz of walnuts.

Bake in a moderate oven, Gas No. 4 (350°F/180°C), for 15 minutes, or until firm to gentle touch. Leave for 2 or 3 minutes on the tray, then leave till cold on a cooling rack. Store in an airtight container and leave at room temperature for a day for the flavours to develop.

DANISH NUT CRISPS

Makes 40.
Keeps 1 week in an airtight container.
Freeze 3 months.

Some of my best-ever yet simplest biscuits, with an irresistible flavour and light-as-air texture.

7 oz (200 g/¾ cup plus 2 tbsp) butter
6 oz (175 g/¾ cup) caster (superfine) sugar
1 x ¾ oz (20 g) packet vanilla sugar or
1 teasp vanilla essence (extract)
8 oz (225 g/2 cups) self-raising flour or 8 oz (225 g/2 cups) plain (all-purpose) flour and 2 teasp baking powder
1 level teasp bicarbonate of soda (baking soda)
2 oz (50 g/½ cup) nibbed or flaked almonds

Work the butter into the sugar using a wooden spoon, mixer or food processor. When the sugar has been absorbed, add the vanilla flavouring and the flour sifted with the bicarbonate of soda. Mix to a dough - don't overwork.

Roll into balls the size of a large cherry and arrange on ungreased trays, leaving room for the biscuits to flatten and spread. Top each with a split almond. Alternatively, dip the balls in a bowl of nibbed almonds before arranging on trays.

Bake in a preheated oven, Gas No. 4 (350°F/180°C), for 15 minutes, or until golden brown.

FLAPJACKS

Makes 48.
Keeps 2 weeks at room temperature in an airtight container.
Freeze 3 months.

An old-fashioned recipe that still tastes good today.

4 oz (125 g/½ cup) butter
4 oz (125 g/½ cup) moist brown sugar
8 oz (225 g/⅔ cup) golden (corn) syrup
8 oz (225 g/2⅔ cups) breakfast oats or rolled oats

Melt the butter in a pan, then add the sugar and syrup and warm together. Stir in the oats and mix well. Spoon into a large, greased baking tin 14 x 9 x 1 inches (35 x 22 x 2.5 cm), flattening into a layer 1/4 inch (0.5 cm) thick with wetted fingers. Bake in a preheated oven, Gas No. 3 (325°F/160°C), for 30–40 minutes, until a rich brown. Cut into fingers while warm. Remove from the tin when cold.

VARIATION

NUTTY FLAPJACKS

Replace 3 oz (75 g/1 cup) of the breakfast oats with 1½ oz (40 g/⅓ cup) chopped walnuts and 1½ oz (40 g/½ cup) desiccated coconut.

GOLDEN BUTTONS

Makes 30.
Keeps 1 week at room temperature in an airtight container.
Freeze 3 months.

Crunchy little biscuits with a delicious butterscotch flavour.

3 oz (75 g/¾ cup) self-raising flour or 3 oz (75 g/¾ cup) plain (all-purpose) flour plus ¾ teasp baking powder
3 oz (75 g/1 cup) porridge oats
3 oz (75 g/½ cup) caster (superfine) sugar
3 oz (75 g/6 tbsp) butter
1 level tbsp golden (corn) syrup
½ level teasp bicarbonate of soda (baking soda)
1 tbsp milk

Put flour and oats into a bowl. Bring sugar, butter and syrup slowly to bubbling point, stirring all the time to dissolve the sugar. Immediately add the mixed bicarbonate of soda and milk, then pour on to the dry ingredients and mix well. Leave for 10 minutes. Roll into ¾-inch (2-cm) balls and arrange well apart on greased trays. Bake in a preheated oven, Gas No. 5 (375°F/190°C), for 10–12 minutes, or until golden brown.

ORANGE CRISPS

Makes 20.
Keeps 1 week at room temperature in an airtight container.
Freeze 3 months.

Crisp and tender biscuits with a marvellous scent of oranges. Some of the best of my collection!

5 oz (150 g/1¼ cups) self-raising flour
2 oz (50 g/¼ cup) caster (superfine) sugar
finely grated rind of 1 orange
4 oz (125 g/½ cup) butter cut in 1-inch (2.5-cm) chunks

Put the flour, sugar and rind in a bowl, add butter and rub in by hand or machine until a dough is formed which can be gathered into a ball. Pinch off pieces the size of a small walnut and roll between the palms into little balls. Arrange 2 inches (5 cm) apart on ungreased trays. Take a large fork, dip it into cold water and then press it down gently on the balls to form biscuits about ⅜ inch (1 cm) thick.

Bake in a preheated oven, Gas No. 4 (350°F/180°C), for 15 minutes, until a pale gold in colour. Remove from the oven and immediately sprinkle with caster sugar.

Child's Play

Any of these delicious biscuits can be made by a child of 8 or 9 with only minimal adult supervision. Use a large breakfast cup (8 fl oz/225 ml) as a measure when necessary.

CHOCOLATE PEANUT CLUSTERS

Makes about 24.
Keeps 1 week under refrigeration.
Freeze 1 month.

The roasted peanuts add greatly to the flavour of these biscuits but can be omitted for young children - or if you haven't the patience to skin the nuts!

4 oz (125 g/1 cup) peanuts
8 oz (225 g) packet milk chocolate for dipping
3 cups Rice Crispies or similar cereal

Toast the peanuts in a moderate oven, Gas No. 4 (350°F/180°C), until golden brown - about 15 minutes - then rub in a tea-towel to remove skins. Melt the chocolate in a bowl standing in a pan of simmering water. (In the microwave, cook on 100 per cent power for 3 minutes.) When melted, stir in nuts and Rice Krispies. Spoon into little paper cases and allow to set.

CEREAL MACAROONS

Makes approximately 24.
Keeps 1 week in an airtight container.
They tend to dry out in the freezer.

2 egg whites
pinch of salt
1 cup caster (superfine) sugar
1 teasp vanilla essence (extract)
1 cup shredded coconut
2 cups cornflakes or Rice Krispies

For decoration
8 glacé (candied) cherries

Whisk the whites with a pinch of salt until they form stiff, glossy peaks. Carefully fold in the sugar, using a metal spoon so that the air is not expelled. Fold in the vanilla, coconut and cereal. Drop in little heaps on to a greased baking sheet and decorate with a piece of glacé cherry. Bake in a preheated oven, Gas No. 4 (350°F/180°C), for 10-15 minutes, or until golden brown. Remove immediately to a cooling tray.

GORDON'S FANCY

Makes about 30.
Keeps 1 week in an airtight container.
Do not freeze.

Some kind of electric mixer is essential to beat these biscuits, as it is too laborious by hand. They have a delicious marshmallow inside with a crispy outside.

4 egg whites
9 oz (250 g/2¼ cups) icing (confectioners') sugar
few drops of peppermint essence (extract)
approx. 8 oz (225 g/3 cups) desiccated coconut
few drops of green food colouring

Whisk the whites and icing sugar in an electric mixer at high speed until they hold peaks. Stir in the essence and enough coconut to make a mixture which, though moist, will just hold its shape in a little pile. Finally stir in enough green colouring to tint the mixture a delicate shade. Fill little paper cases two-thirds full of the mixture. Bake in a pre-heated oven, Gas No. 4 (350°F/180°C), for about 20 minutes, until crisp and pale brown on top though creamy within.

BREAD, ROLLS AND YEAST KUCHENS

Kuchens and Scones in a Hurry

Every Thursday evening, from teatime to dawn, a dwindling band of Jewish Master Bakers mixes, shapes and bakes the challahs, twists and tin loaves of 'best' bread which have been part of every Jewish Sabbath for close on 3,000 years.

Into the dough (now mixed and divided by machine but in many cases still shaped by hand), these craftsmen put oil, salt and sugar according to the recipe developed for their famous 'Cappadocian' bread by the Macedonian bakers of Perseus II, and leaven it with yeast, whose miraculous raising powers were first discovered in Egypt at about the same period as their ancestors were the slaves of Pharaoh. They even scatter the loaves with poppy seeds by the method described in the third century of this era by gastronomic historian Athenaeus.

But even when bread was made from the unleavened flour and water mixture described in Genesis 18, it was a food highly regarded by the Jews. Indeed, since Sarah mixed her meal-and-water hearth cakes for the visiting angels, it has been the privilege of the Jewish mother to bake this staple food and offer it as a mark of hospitality to family guests. Until the Second World War, it was still the custom for Jewish housewives (particularly in the East End of London) to take their unbaked loaves to be baked in the more even heat of the professional baker's oven. The early immigrants from Eastern Europe rarely had ovens in their tenement flats, so they laid their risen loaves on a tray, covered them with a white cloth and took them to the local baker, just as they had done in *'der heim'*.

Today, very few women make bread themselves, and it is left to a tiny band of professionals to shape the loaves according to the season. By tradition a bread for the Sabbath is made in the shape of a plait so that pieces can be broken off by hand without the aid of a knife, which symbolizes violence rather than the peace that should surround the household at that time. For Rosh Hashanah it is round, to symbolize the fullness of the year ahead, while on the Eve of Yom Kippur a ladder sits on top, or a dove - a *'feigele'* - to carry one's prayer up to heaven. Comes Hashanah Rabbah and the loaf is shaped like a key, while Purim is marked by a raisin bread Kalischbrod (see p. 594), which is a descendant of the *'artologanus'* or cake bread the Romans used to bake.

Until the beginning of this century, white or 'best' bread was reserved for the Sabbath and festivals alone, while at other times black or brown bread, solid and satisfying with its characteristic sour dough flavour, was the rule. While the recipe for Jewish bread is almost universal, the names and shapes of the loaves made from the dough vary between communities, and when it comes to rolls, one would need to be an expert in linguistics to distinguish between 'bulkes', 'barches', 'bobkes' and 'bundes'. For one man's 'zemmel pampalik' (onion roll) is another man's 'tzibbele bonde' and the 'plaetzel' of one country is the 'mohn kichel' (poppy-seed roll) of another.

Which brings us, inevitably, to the bagel - one name and shape which remains the same wherever it is eaten. Elaborate attempts have been made to establish the etymology of the word, and to date its origins to the defeat of the Turks before Vienna in 1683. Some food historians trace its origins back to the 'buegels' or stirrup-shaped rolls baked on that occasion in honour of the victorious King of Poland, and suggest that the word was corrupted to 'byegel' and 'bagel' by Galician Jews. I myself think fifteenth-century France rather than seventeenth-century Vienna saw the birth of this inimitable confection and that the bagel is a lineal descendant of the *'pain échaude'* (boiled bread) of medieval French bakery.

Perhaps the best policy would be to forget the whole matter and be content to buy one's bagels from the baker's on Sunday morning. Then again, you could follow my superb recipe and make your very own!

To Freeze Bread Rolls and Bagels

BAKED BREAD

All baked bread, bought or home-baked, freezes well, provided it is frozen when freshly baked, but length of storage time varies with the type of bread.

To freeze Wrap in polythene freezer bags.

Storage times

White and brown bread Keep well for up to 4 weeks.

Enriched bread and rolls (milk, fruit, malt loaves and soft rolls) Keep up to 6 weeks.

Crisp-crusted loaves and rolls Have a limited storage time as the crusts begin to 'shell off' after 1 week. Vienna-type loaves and rolls keep for 3 days only.

To thaw

Loaves Leave in packaging at room temperature for 2–3 hours depending on the size of loaf *or* leave overnight in the refrigerator, *or* defrost in the microwave as follows: stand uncovered on a paper towel and heat on defrost for 2 minutes then leave for 5 minutes, then slice and leave 2–3 minutes until completely defrosted.

Toast Sliced bread can be toasted while frozen. Separate slices carefully with a knife before toasting.

Rolls Leave in packaging at room temperature for 1½ hours or place frozen rolls wrapped in foil in a hot oven, Gas No. 8 (450°F/230°C), for 15 minutes.

Note Crusty loaves and rolls thawed at room temperature should be refreshed before serving. Place unwrapped loaves or rolls in a hot oven, Gas No. 6 (400°F/200°C), for 5–10 minutes, until crust is crisp.

BREAD DOUGHS

All doughs can be frozen but the storage times vary with the type of dough, plain or enriched, and also whether it is frozen risen or unrisen. All standard bread recipes can be frozen but the best results are obtained from doughs made with 50 per cent more yeast than is given in the standard recipes - ie ½ oz (15 g/1 cake) yeast should be increased to ¾ oz (20 g/1½ cakes). Freeze dough in quantities you are most likely to use - ie 1 lb 2 oz (500 g) dough for a 1-lb (450-g) loaf tin. Heavy-duty polythene bags, lightly greased, are best. They must be tightly sealed as any air left inside causes skinning on the dough surface, which will crack during handling and gives the baked dough crumb a streaky appearance. If there is a chance of the dough rising a little before freezing, leave 1 inch (2.5 cm) of space above the dough.

UNRISEN DOUGH

To freeze
After kneading, form dough into a ball. Place in a large, lightly greased polythene bag, seal tightly and freeze immediately.

Storage times
Plain white and brown doughs keep up to 4 weeks. Enriched dough keeps up to 12 weeks.

To thaw
Unseal polythene bag and then tie loosely at the top to allow space for rising. Leave for 5–6 hours at room temperature, *or* overnight in the refrigerator. Complete rise, then knock back, shape, rise and bake.

RISEN DOUGH

To freeze
Place dough in a large, lightly greased polythene bag, tie loosely at the top and put to rise. Turn risen dough on to a lightly floured surface, flatten firmly with knuckles to knock out air bubbles, then knead until firm. Replace in polythene bag, tightly seal and freeze immediately.

Storage time
Plain and enriched white and brown doughs keep up to 2 weeks. Dough kept longer than these times gives poor results.

To thaw
See unrisen dough instructions. After thawing, knock back if required, shape, rise and bake.

PART-BAKED ROLLS AND LOAVES

Both home-baked white and wheatmeal rolls can be frozen partly baked. This is a very successful way of freezing rolls as the frozen rolls can be put straight from the freezer into the oven to finish baking. It is the best method of freezing rolls to serve for breakfast. Loaves are not so successful as rolls because during part-baking the crust becomes well formed and coloured before the centre of the loaf is set. Part-baked loaves and rolls available in shops freeze well.

To part-bake rolls
Place shaped and risen rolls in a slow oven, Gas No. 2 (300°F/150°C), for about 20 minutes. The rolls must be set but still pale in colour. Cool.

To freeze
Pack cooled rolls in usable quantities in freezer bags. Seal and freeze. As the sides of the rolls are still slightly soft, care must be taken when packing to avoid squashing.

Storage time
Up to 4 months.

To thaw and finish baking
Unwrap and place frozen rolls in oven to thaw and complete baking. Bake white rolls at Gas No. 6 (400°F/200°C), brown rolls at Gas No. 8 (450°F/230°C) for 20 minutes.

To freeze
Freeze immediately after purchasing. Leave loaves in polythene bags in which they were sold. Pack rolls in polythene bags and seal.

Storage time
Up to 4 months.

Note Many commercial part-baked rolls and bread can be stored at room temperature. Follow instructions on the pack.

The Ingredients for Breads and Kuchens

ALL ABOUT YEAST

Many very experienced cooks associate yeast cookery with mystery and mumbo-jumbo, and when they see the word in a recipe they immediately turn the page. The trouble arises because, as yeast is a living organism, it will flourish - and so make dough rise - only if it is treated with understanding and care. Fortunately, both fresh and dried yeast are now of a much more consistent quality and need far less attention that what was in use even 20 years ago. I trust this will be evident in the recipes that follow.

Fresh yeast is now available almost everywhere, usually at the local health-food shop. If it is tightly wrapped in foil it will keep in excellent condition, sweet-smelling, slightly moist and pale in colour, for up to 1 month in the refrigerator. It can only be *frozen* successfully for up to 6 weeks, although yeast doughs can be frozen for up to 3 months.

There is now a new kind of 'easy-blend' **dried yeast** that is as simple to use as baking powder. It is even mixed with the dry ingredients in exactly the same way. The new-style dried yeast, which I prefer to the more familiar granular kind, is very finely powdered and hyperactive, so that a tiny sachet weighing ¼ oz (6 or 7 g) can replace 1 oz (28 g) of fresh yeast. Its shelf life is limited to 6-12 months, but it has a 'use-by' date on the packet.

BREAD FLOUR

The 'whiteness' or 'brownness' of a flour depends on the proportions it contains of the 3 main constituents of the wheat grain: the starchy inner endosperm, the bran and the vitamin-rich germ. The flour itself can be produced either by roller-milling the wheat or by grinding it between stones - the method used from earliest times until roller-milling was invented in the nineteenth century. Stoneground flour is now enjoying an enormous revival with the great interest in foods produced by traditional methods.

The more of its 3 main constituents a particular flour contains, the higher its *extraction rate* is said to be.

Wholewheat flour (also known as *wholemeal* or *graham* flour) has a 100 per cent extraction rate; it contains all the nourishment of the original grain.

Wheatmeal flour with an extraction rate of between 80 and 90 per cent, hasn't got as much of the bran and wheatgerm as wholemeal flour has, but it has enough to make a positive contribution to the diet.

Wheaten flour is wheatmeal flour with extra pieces of whole wheat grain.

Granary flour has malted wheat and rye

grains added to wheatmeal flour.

White flour, with an extraction rate of approximately 70 per cent, is milled only from the starchy endosperm - it contains none of the bran or the wheatgerm. In Britain, however, some of the vitamins and minerals have to be put back into the flour by law.

The best bread is made from a *strong flour,* which is usually labelled 'bread flour' on the packet. Bread made from wholewheat flour has a coarse, close texture; if it is made with wheatmeal flour it is much spongier. Many people prefer a bread made from a mixture of brown and white flours. It is worth experimenting to find the mixture of flours you like the best.

Sweet (enriched) yeast doughs can be made either with a white bread flour or with the plain white (all-purpose) flour normally used for cakes and biscuits.

SALT

This is essential to give flavour to the dough, and also to prevent the yeast fermenting too quickly. However, too much will kill the yeast so do not use more than stated.

FAT

This greatly improves the flavour of the dough and the softness and colour of the crumb. It also keeps the bread fresh longer.

MIXING AND KNEADING THE DOUGH

Kneading is essential to strengthen the dough so that there is a good 'rise'.

In the old days you had 2 ways of mixing a yeast dough. You beat the softer doughs with a wooden spoon and you kneaded the firmer doughs with your hand. Then came the electric mixer with its beater and dough hook for performing the same functions mechanically, and now there's also the food processor.

With the standard-size processor you can mix a bread dough based on 1 lb (450 g/4 cups) of flour and a kuchen (enriched) dough based on 12 oz (350 g/3 cups). With a large food processor, however, you can mix a bread dough based on 2 lb (900 g/8 cups) of flour and a kuchen dough based on 1½ lb (675 g/6 cups). The kneading is done by the metal knife and takes only 1-1½ minutes to produce a smooth and silky dough (see pp. 472-3 for full details).

However, a sticky dough may cause the machine to 'labour' and the engine to cut out. If a food processor dough looks too wet, immediately add 1 or 2 tablespoons of flour so that the mixture comes together into a soft ball round the metal blade.

Traditional Loaves and Rolls

PLAITED BREADS

The best way to learn how to plait bread is by example - watching someone demonstrate it to you. However, as this is not always possible, I have tried to put the method into words, with the help of a diagram for a 4-strand plait that illustrates the general principle.

The real secret of following a plaiting sequence is that you must always count the strands *as you see them on the board.* Don't try to remember what their original positions were when you started to plait them (this becomes very clear once you actually begin). I have found it helpful to practise for the first time using strands of plasticine instead of dough.

Before you begin to plait, always prepare the strands of dough on the board as follows.

1. Start with dough that has had 1 rising. Divide it into as many pieces as you require strands, then shape each piece into a ball.
2. Roll each ball with your hands into a strand about 12 inches (30 cm) long that tapers slightly at each end.

3 Fan out the strands evenly on the board, then pinch them firmly together at the top end - you may find it helpful to weigh this end down with a heavy knife (the exception is the 7-strand herringbone plait, which starts differently - see below).
4 Count the strands from left to right as you see them on the board. Remember that when you have moved a strand according to your chosen sequence, you count all the strands as you *now* see them on the board. In other words, the 'number' of each strand changes from its 'starting number' as the plaiting proceeds.
5 Now follow the plaiting sequence of your choice.

PLAITED BREAD

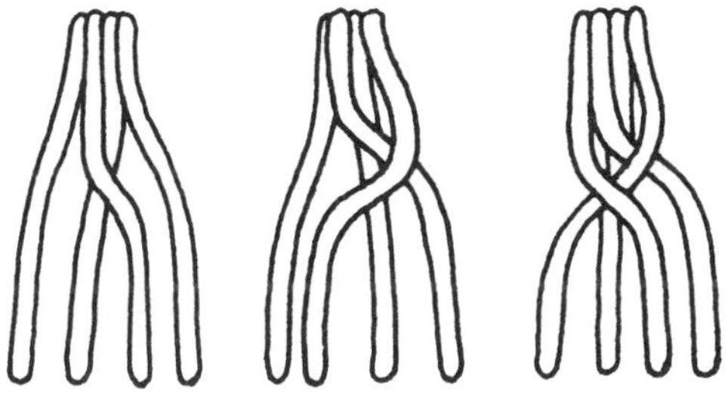

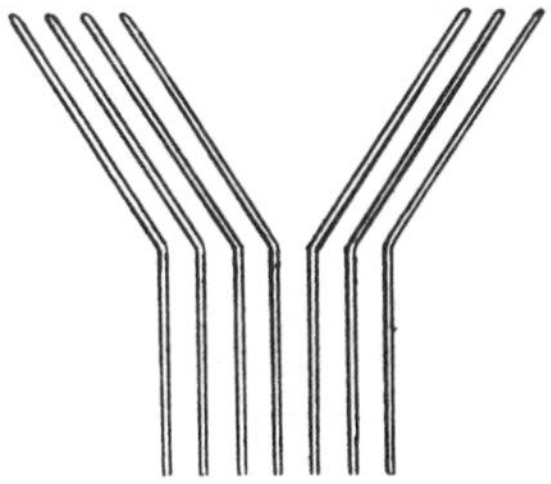

3 strands Bring alternate outer strands between the remaining 2 and repeat until the ends of the strands are reached.

4 strands Prepare as usual then plait as follows:

strand 2 over strand 3,
strand 4 over strand 2;
strand 1 over strand 3.

Repeat until the ends of the strands are reached.

5 strands Prepare as usual, then plait as follows:

strand 2 over strand 3,
strand 5 over strand 2,
strand 1 over strand 3.

Repeat until the ends of the strands are reached.

6 strands Prepare as usual, then plait as follows:

preliminary move (not repeated) - strand 6 over strand 1,
then,
strand 2 over strand 6,
strand 1 over strand 3,
strand 5 over strand 1,
strand 6 over strand 4.

Repeat the last 4 moves until the ends of the strands are reached.

8 strands Prepare as usual, then plait as follows:

preliminary move (not repeated) - strand 8 under strand 7 and over strand 1,
then,
strand 2 under strand 3 and over strand 8,
strand 1 over strand 4,
strand 7 under strand 6 and over strand 1,
strand 8 over strand 5.

Repeat the last 4 moves until the ends of the strands are reached.

7 strands (herringbone) Arrange the strands side by side, then divide the bottom half with 4 strands on 1 side and 3 on the other (see diagram). Bring the outside strands alternately to the centre, starting from the side with 4 strands. Join the ends and turn the top half towards you, then divide this other half with 4 strands on 1 side and 3 on the other (see diagram). Bring the outside strands alternately to the centre, starting from the side with 4 strands. After all the strands of dough have been plaited their full length, pinch all the free ends together, sealing them firmly. Turn the completed plait over on its side, then roll it gently to improve its shape.

CHALLAH

'Challah' is used today as the generic term for the rich and slightly sweetened white bread, usually, though not always, plaited, that is eaten on the Sabbath. The Hebrew root of the word actually means 'round', but depending on the context 'challah' itself is sometimes translated as 'cake' as in the Bible, or as 'dough' as in the Talmud. In both the Bible and the Talmud, however, 'challah' is used to refer to the small portion of the risen dough from a Sabbath bread that the Jews of the Temple period gave as a weekly offering to the kohanim - the priests of the Temple.

The origin of this *mitzvah* (pious deed or divine command) is to be found in the Bible, Numbers, Chapter 15, which is translated from the Hebrew as: 'Of the first of your dough, ye shall set apart a cake (challah) for a gift . . . of the first of your dough ye shall give unto the Lord a portion for a gift throughout your generations.' It was laid down in Jewish law that only the finest flour made from wheat, barley, spelt, oats or rye could be used for this gift - rather than 'inferior' ones such as rice, millet or pea.

To ensure that the bread was ritually pure enough for the priests to eat, the dough had to be mixed with running, rather than still water. If this was not available, beaten eggs had to be used instead. Thus, challah shares with matzah the distinction of being one of the only two Jewish dishes whose ingredients are laid down in religious law! As you will see from the recipe below, even though the religious reason for the use of eggs has disappeared, it has remained a 'minhag' (custom) right down to this day.

After the destruction of the Temple, the bread offering to the priests ceased, but to commemorate this ancient law Jews still take off a small portion of dough - about 27 g or the weight of a large olive - and burn it. This separation of the portion of dough is by custom delegated to the woman of the house as a remembrance of things past.

PERFECT CHALLAH

Makes 2 large plaited loaves, each 12-15 inches (30-37½ cm) long or 2 medium tin loaves.
Keeps 3-4 days at room temperature in a bread container.
Freeze baked 3 months or shaped and ready for baking 2 weeks.

11 fl oz (300 ml/1⅓ cups) warm water
1½ lb (675 g/6 cups) white strong (bread) flour
1 oz (25 g/2 cakes) fresh yeast or 1 sachet easy-blend yeast
2 oz (50 g/¼ cup) sugar or 2 rounded tbsp honey (this can be reduced to 1 tbsp if preferred)
1½ teasp salt
3 tbsp sunflower or other flavourless oil
2 large eggs

For the glaze

1 egg yolk
1 teasp water
good pinch of salt
poppy seeds or sesame seeds

If using fresh yeast, attach the dough hook to the mixer, then put the water into the mixing bowl, followed by a third of the flour, the crumbled yeast and the sugar or honey. Mix until smooth - about 2 minutes - then cover with a tea-towel and leave for 10 or 15 minutes, until it has frothed up. Add all the remaining ingredients for the dough.

If using easy-blend yeast, omit the preliminary mixing and rising. Mix the yeast thoroughly with the other dry ingredients, then add all the remaining ingredients to the bowl.

Now mix at low speed until a sticky ball begins to form, then turn to medium speed, and knead for 4 or 5 minutes, until the dough is slapping against the edges of the bowl, leaving it clean as it goes round. If it looks sticky after this time, work in a further 1 or 2 tablespoons of flour.

Tip the dough on to a floured board and knead with the hands for a further minute, until it is tight and springy with a silky feel - as smooth as a baby's cheek! Grease a large bowl with oil, turn the dough in it to coat it (this stops the surface drying out), cover with clingfilm (saranwrap) and leave to rise in the refrigerator. If it rises before you have time to deal with it (it takes from 9 to 12 hours but can be left for up to 24 hours), punch it down and leave it to rise again.

To shape the loaves, take the risen dough from the refrigerator and leave it to come to room temperature in the kitchen - about 1 hour. (Or put it in the defrost cycle of the microwave oven for 2 minutes, until warm to the touch.) Divide the dough in 2 and work on each half (to make 1 large loaf) as follows. Knead the dough by hand or machine to break down any large bubbles of gas, then leave for 5 minutes to tighten up under a cloth.

To make a 3-strand plait Divide the piece of dough into 3. Flatten each piece with a fist, then roll up into a little 'Swiss roll'. Flatten again, roll up as before, then shape into a ball - this greatly improves the texture of the loaf. Roll each ball into a 12-inch (30-cm) strand that tapers slightly at each end. Join the 3 strands firmly together at 1 end, then fan them out on the board. Plait in the usual way. Arrange on a greased tray. For more elaborate plaits, see pp. 460-62.

To make a tin loaf Lightly grease a 2-lb (900-g) loaf tin measuring approximately 9 x 5 x 3 inches (about 22.5 x 12.5 x 7.5 cm). Divide the remaining dough into 3 and flatten each piece with the fist, then roll up into a little 'Swiss roll', flatten, roll up again, then finally roll into a ball. Arrange 2 of the balls side by side in the middle of the tin. Divide the third ball in 2 and shape into two smaller balls, then place 1 on either side of the centre balls. Brush with the glaze and scatter with poppy or sesame seeds.

To prove either the plait or the tin loaf Slip the tray or the loaf tin into a large plastic bag and leave in the kitchen or airing cupboard for 45 minutes to 1 hour, or until puffy again. (This creates a miniature 'greenhouse' atmosphere - damp and free from draughts - which the dough needs to rise.) Remove from the bag.

To bake the bread Preheat the oven to Gas No. 8 (450°F/230°C). Put the bread in the oven and immediately turn the temperature down to Gas No. 6 (400°F/200°C). Bake the plait for 25-30 minutes or until crusty and brown; bake the loaf for 30-40 minutes, or until the bottom sounds hollow when tapped.

BROWN CHALLAH OR TRADITIONAL TIN LOAF

4 fl oz (125 ml/½ cup) boiling water made up to 12 fl oz (350 ml/1½ cups) with cold water
1 tbsp dark brown sugar or honey
1 oz (25 g/2 cakes) fresh yeast or 2 sachets easy-blend dried yeast
6 oz (175 g/1½ cups) strong white (bread) flour plus 18 oz (500 g/4½ cups) wholemeal flour, or 1½ lb (675 g/6 cups) wheatmeal or wholemeal flour
3 teasp salt
3 tbsp any flavourless oil
2 eggs, beaten (saving 2 tbsp for the glaze)

For the glaze
2 tbsp reserved egg
2 tbsp poppy or sesame seeds

Make exactly as for Perfect Challah but with the above ingredients.

TO SHAPE A VARIETY OF ROLLS

The risen dough can be used to make approximately 20 rolls, depending on the size (2 oz/50 g dough produces an average-sized roll). When at room temperature divide into 20 pieces.

PLAETZELS (DIMPLE ROLLS)

Take each piece of dough and knead into a ball the size of a small apple. Roll out into a round about ⅜ (1 cm) thick. With 2 fingers press a 'dimple' firmly into the centre of the dough. Brush with salted egg mixture and scatter with poppy or sesame seeds. Put on a floured tray, slip it into a plastic carrier bag and leave to rise until puffy - about 45 minutes, depending on the temperature of the kitchen. Bake in a hot oven, Gas No. 7 (425°F/220°C), for 15 minutes, until a rich brown.

TZIBBELE BONDES (ONION ROLLS)

Top the dimpled rolls with a teaspoon of finely chopped raw onion. Brush with salted egg mixture and bake at Gas No. 5 (375°F/190°C) for 20 minutes.

KNOTS

Roll each piece of dough into a rope 7 inches (17.5 cm) long. Shape into a coil and push 1 end through the centre of the coil to make a knot (also known as a Turk's hat). Leave to rise until puffy. Brush with egg and bake as for the plaetzels.

MINIATURE CHALLAHS

Divide each piece of dough into 3 and roll into a 6-inch (15-cm) rope. Plait as for the challah. Allow to rise until puffy. Brush with salted egg mixture and scatter with poppy seeds. Bake like the plaetzels.

BAGELS

Once you know that they must be boiled before they are baked, it is surprisingly easy to produce professional-looking bagels at home. As you can make 30 bagels from just over 1½ lb (675 g/6 cups) flour, it is worthwhile making a stock for the freezer, particularly if you live far from a Jewish bakery. The method I have developed is adapted from the professional technique used by the craftsmen at a bakery in Manchester, who were my instructors in the art of bagel-making at 2 am one Sunday morning.

The dough This is identical to the dough used for challah, with the exception of the flour. As bagels are much firmer in texture than bread, use 1 lb 11 oz (750 g/6¾ cups) of flour instead of 1½ lb (675 g/6 cups). Mix and refrigerate the dough in exactly the same way as for the challah. The difference in technique starts once the risen dough is taken from the refrigerator.

To shape the bagels Work with the chilled dough direct from the refrigerator. Divide it into 30 pieces. Shape each bagel as follows.

Knead the piece into a ball, then flatten with the palm of the hand and roll into a rope 7 inches (17.5 cm) long and ⅜ inch (1 cm) thick. Wind the rope round the knuckles of your hand, and press on the table to seal the joint. Roll the joint gently on the table to seal it firmly, then slip the bagel off the knuckles on to a floured board. Repeat with all the pieces of dough. Leave to rise for an hour until the bagels have increased slightly in size but are not as puffy as rolls. Have the oven set at Gas No. 10 (500°F/250°C), and a large (soup) pan of boiling water ready on the stove. Put 5 or 6 bagels at a time into the boiling water and boil for 2 minutes, turning them over with a slotted spoon as they rise to the top. Drain from the water and lay on a board. Repeat with the remaining bagels. Put the boiled bagels on a floured tray and put in the oven for 1 minute to dry the top surface, then turn and bake for a further 15 minutes until a rich shiny brown. Makes 30 bagels.

For an alternative method of rising and shaping bagels the same day: let dough rise 2 hours in the kitchen, knock back, roll out ½ inch (1 cm) thick and leave for 20 minutes. Cut with a biscuit-cutter and make a hole in the centre with your finger. Whirl round on your finger into a bagel shape. Leave 10 minutes, then bring water to boil and proceed as in the recipe.

RYE AND CARAWAY BREAD

Makes 3 medium-sized loaves.
Keeps moist for 4–5 days loosely wrapped in a plastic bag.
Freeze 3 months.

I am often asked for a recipe for a 'real old-fashioned rye bread'. But which bread, since there are literally dozens that qualify for that description?

Finally I chose this recipe because the method is simpler than most, yet the result is a light delicious loaf with a moist texture. The inclusion of beer gives the bread the traditional, tangy taste without the complexities of using a sour-dough starter.

I also found, tucked away in Elizabeth David's definitive book on bread, the secret of that crisp, shiny crust you get with a baker's rye loaf - a glaze made with potato flour.

The particular combination of white bread flour and rye flour in this recipe produces a soft, light texture, but if you prefer a denser loaf use wholemeal flour in place of white.

Most of the preparation for the bread is done the day before baking, so you may need to plan ahead.

1 oz (25 g) fresh yeast or 2 sachets easy-blend yeast
5 fl oz (150 ml/⅔ cup) lukewarm water with fresh yeast, boiling water with easy-blend
1 tbsp medium brown sugar
15 fl oz (425 ml/2 cups) beer
1¼ lb (575 g/5 cups) white bread flour
12 oz (350 g/3 cups) rye flour
3 teasp salt
3 teasp caraway seeds

For the glaze
1 teasp hot water
1 teasp brown sugar
or
1 teasp potato flour
1 teasp cold water
4 fl oz (125 ml/½ cup) boiling water

With fresh yeast, crumble the yeast into a large mixing bowl, add the water and brown sugar, stir well and leave for 10 minutes, or until frothy. Add the beer, then, using the K beater (paddle) of the electric mixer, add in the well-mixed flours, salt and 2 teaspoons of the caraway seeds, a cupful at a time, until the dough becomes too thick to continue. Change to the dough hook and add the remaining flour, mixing until it forms a dough.

With easy-blend yeast, fit the dough hook and in the bowl of the food mixer, mix well together the easy-blend yeast, the brown sugar, white and rye flour, salt and 2 teaspoons of the caraway seeds. Add the beer mixed with the boiling water and mix to a dough.

Knead for 3 or 4 minutes, until the dough has a silky, rather limp texture. Turn out on to the table, knead gently into a ball, then put in a well-oiled container large enough to let it expand to 3 times its size. Turn it over to make sure it is lightly coated with oil, cover with a lid or clingfilm (saranwrap) and refrigerate overnight.

Next day, leave the dough (still in the container) in the warm kitchen for 1½ hours, until it has lost its chill (or warm on defrost in the microwave for 1 minute), then turn it out on to a floured board and knead gently but firmly to expel all the gas bubbles. Divide into

3 1-lb (450-g) pieces. Knead each piece into a round or baton and arrange well apart on greased trays.

To glaze, either mix the water and sugar until dissolved, or mix the potato flour and cold water, then pour on the boiling water and mix to a thick clear paste. Brush the 3 loaves with either glaze, scatter with the remaining caraway seeds and make 2 slanting slashes in the top with a sharp, floured knife. Slip each tray into a large plastic carrier and leave until they have almost doubled in size and feel spongy to the touch - after ¾-1 hour.

Meanwhile, preheat the oven to Gas No. 6 (400°F/200°C). Bake the loaves for 35-40 minutes, or until they are a deep chestnut in colour. (If using the potato flour to glaze, brush the loaves again 15 minutes before the end of baking time.) Leave on a cooling tray until cold.

ILSE ETON'S PUMPERNICKEL
(Traditional German Sour-dough Rye Bread)

Makes 2 large loaves.
Keeps fresh 4 days (sour dough keeps in an airtight container in the refrigerator for 4 weeks).
Freeze 6 months.

This superb bread owes its unique flavour to the mixing of fresh and fermented dough. This fermented or sour dough need only be made once. After the initial batch has been made, a piece can be taken off and left in the refrigerator, where it will slowly ferment, to become the sour dough for the next batch of bread (see the recipe).

For the initial sour dough
1 teasp sugar (brown or white)
½ x ¼ oz (7 g) packet easy-blend yeast
4 rounded tbsp wholemeal (wholewheat) flour
2 rounded tbsp rye flour
1 teasp salt
4-6 fl oz (125-175 ml/½-¾ cup) warm water

For the bread dough
2 x ¼ oz (7 g) packets easy-blend yeast
11 oz (300 g/2¾ cups) wholemeal (wholewheat) flour
1 lb 5 oz (600 g/5¼ cups) rye flour
1 level tbsp salt
1 heaped tbsp caraway seeds (optional)
2 tbsp sunflower or other flavourless oil
1 heaped tbsp malt extract
1 heaped tbsp molasses or treacle
approx. 20 fl oz (575 ml/2½ cups) warm water

To make the sour dough, the day before you intend to bake the bread, mix together the dry ingredients, then mix to a firm consistency with the water. Place in a covered basin and leave to stand at room temperature overnight, during which time the dough will ferment.

The following day, mix together the yeast, flours and salt in the bowl of the mixer, then add the sour dough and all the other ingredients and knead with a dough hook for 5 minutes (10 minutes by hand), until smooth and firm. Put in a warm place to rise, covered with a damp tea-towel or clingfilm (saranwrap). Allow to rise for 1-1½ hours, until double in bulk, then use the dough hook or knead by hand again for a couple of minutes to break down any large bubbles of gas. Remove approximately 12 oz (350 g) of the mixture and place in an air-tight container and refrigerate (this will become the sour dough for the next batch of bread).

Divide the dough in 2 and then, using floured knuckles, flatten into a rectangle 9 inches (22.5 cm) wide. Roll up tightly, then place into 2 warmed 2-lb (900-g) loaf tins. Lightly score the top of each loaf with a floured knife (to help prevent uneven rising and blistering of the bread), then allow to rise for another hour in a warm place, either covered with a cloth or placed in a plastic carrier bag. After an hour (the centre of the loaf should peep over the sides of the tin and the sides will be ¼ inch (0.5 cm) from the top), brush with a solution of 3 tablespoons of water and 1 teaspoon of salt, and put on the middle shelf of a preheated oven at Gas No. 6 (400°F/200°C). Place a basin with water in the bottom of the oven, as this improves the bread. Bake for 30 minutes, then turn the loaves out of the tins, place on a baking tray and continue to bake at a lower temperature-Gas No. 5 (375°F/190°C) - for a further 30 minutes. Allow to cool before storing.

Variety Breads

TWO LOVELY BROWN LOAVES

Keeps moist 4-5 days loosely wrapped in a plastic bag in a bread drawer or container.
Freeze 6 weeks.

This is a flavoursome, straightforward bread for daily use - it's similar to Hovis. You can vary the texture with different flours. If you go for *all* wholemeal flour, the dough may need an extra fl oz (25 ml) or so of water and the texture will be denser than when white flour is used.

1 pint (575 ml/2½ cups) warm water (blood heat) for fresh yeast or hand-hot for easy-blend dried yeast
1½ level tbsp soft brown sugar
1 oz (25 g/2 cakes) fresh yeast or 2 x ¼ oz (7 g) sachets easy-blend dried yeast
1 lb (450 g/4 cups) each white bread flour and wholemeal (wheatmeal) flour, or 2 lb (900 g/8 cups) brown (wheatmeal) flour of your choice
3 teasp fine sea salt
2 tbsp sunflower or other flavourless oil

To glaze the loaves
½ teasp fine salt dissolved in 2 teasp hot water

Put the water, sugar and the crumbled fresh yeast (if used) into a large mixing bowl and add about a quarter (8 oz/225 g/2 cups) of the flour. Mix to a smooth batter, cover with a tea-towel and leave for 15 minutes until frothy. Uncover and add the salt, oil and remaining flour and mix to a spongy scone-like dough. (If you use 1 of the easy-blend dried yeasts, it must be added to the dry ingredients *not* the liquid, and the dough can then be mixed in 1 stage). Knead the dough until it loses its stickiness and feels silky smooth - 1½ minutes with the steel blade of a food processor, about 4 minutes with a dough hook, 10 minutes by hand. Turn the machine-kneaded dough on to a floured board and knead by hand for 30 seconds. Grease the mixing bowl with oil, put the dough back and immediately turn it over so that the top is covered with a film of oil (to stop it drying out). Cover the bowl with clingfilm (saranwrap) and leave to rise until it is double in bulk and will spring back when lightly prodded with a finger. Choose the time and method for rising the dough that suits you best. It will take 45-60 minutes in an airing cupboard, 1½-2 hours in a pleasantly warm kitchen, 8-12 hours in a cold larder and 12-24 hours in the refrigerator. Remember, though, that dough risen in the refrigerator needs to be brought back to room temperature before shaping. This takes 1 hour in the kitchen or 2 minutes on defrost in the microwave.

To shape the loaves, knead the risen dough again to get rid of the bubbles - 2 minutes - then divide in 2 and shape each piece into a loaf as follows. Using floured knuckles, flatten into a rectangle 9 inches (22.5 cm) wide, then roll up tightly and place, join down, in an oiled tin measuring 9 x 5 x 3 inches (22.5 x 12.5 x 7.5 cm). Cover and leave a further 25 minutes, until risen to the top of the tin, then brush with 2 tablespoons of water mixed with 1 teaspoon of salt (for crustiness) and scatter with dry muesli, crushed cornflakes or granary flour.

Bake at Gas No. 8 (450°F/230°C) for 20 minutes, then at Gas No. 6 (400°F/200°C) for a further 20 minutes, or until the loaf sounds hollow when the base is tapped. Leave to cool on a wire rack.

VARIATION

GRANARY COBS OR BATONS

Use exactly the same ingredients except for the flour: 1½ lb (675 g/6 cups) granary bread flour and 8 oz (225 g/2 cups) strong plain bread flour.

Instead of shaping into a rectangle, form each half either into a round 6 inches (15 cm) in diameter (to make a cob), or into an elongated oval about 6 inches (15 cm) long and 4 inches (10 cm) wide (to make a baton) and flatten slightly with the hands. Put on 2 greased, floured baking trays and slip each tray into a plastic carrier bag. Leave in the kitchen until puffy - about 30 minutes. Take out of the bags. On the top surface of the cob, make 2 deep cuts at right angles to each other, using a sharp knife dipped in flour. On the top of the baton make 2 slanting cuts, parallel to each other, in the same way. Brush with salt water and scatter with buckwheat, oats or muesli. Bake in a hot oven, Gas No. 7 (425°F/220°C) for 35 minutes, until browned and loaves sound hollow when tapped with the knuckles on the underside. Leave to cool on a wire rack.

MIXED-GRAIN BREAD

Makes 2 1-lb (450-g) loaves.
Keeps moist for 3–4 days loosely wrapped in a plastic bag.
Freeze baked loaves 3 months.

Oats, wheat and rye have each in their day been the grain most favoured to make the flour for our daily bread. Wheat flour became the eventual favourite because it produces the lightest loaf - rye and oats are both very low in gluten (the protein in flour that gives bread its stretch and rise), so when they are used by themselves they produce a dense and heavy dough. If, however, you mix them with some wholewheat flour, you get all the benefit of their varied flavours and nutriments, and a much more palatable loaf.

The mixed-grain bread made from this recipe has a nutty flavour and a moist yet firm texture, quite different from ordinary wholemeal (wheatmeal) bread. Provided that half the flour used to make the dough is wholemeal, you can juggle the proportions of the other 3 flours to suit your own taste - granary flour is wheatmeal flour with malted wheat and rye flakes added to produce the distinctive taste and texture.

12 oz (350 g/3 cups) wholemeal (wheatmeal) flour
6 oz (175 g/1½ cups) rye flour
2 oz (50 g/½ cup) granary flour
4 oz (125 g/1⅓ cups) medium oatmeal (or porridge oats processed in food processor for 15 seconds)
3 teasp salt
1 tbsp soft brown sugar
1 x ¼ oz (7 g) sachet easy-blend yeast
2 tbsp sunflower oil
5 fl oz (150 ml/⅔ cup) boiling water made up to 15 fl oz (425 ml/2 cups) with cold water
a little extra wholemeal flour (if necessary)

For the glaze
½ teasp salt dissolved in 2 teasp very hot water
2 teasp caraway or sesame seeds

In the bowl of the food mixer (or a large food processor) mix all the dry ingredients. Add the oil and water and process to a dough using either the dough hook for 4 minutes or the metal blade of the food processor for 1 minute, until a soft but non-sticky dough is formed that leaves the sides of the bowl clean. Turn out on to the board and knead for 30 seconds until smooth (add an extra tablespoon of wholemeal flour if necessary).

Turn into a large, lightly oiled bowl, roll the ball over to coat with the oil, cover with clingfilm (saranwrap) and leave to rise until double in bulk. This will take about 1½ hours in the kitchen. (If you have a microwave, you can cut the rising time to 50 minutes - see p. 469.)

Divide the dough in 2 and knead each portion for a minute to get rid of any large gas bubbles. Oil 2 x 1-lb (450-g) bread tins and line with a strip of silicone paper.

Shape each half into a loaf as follows. On a lightly floured board roll into a rectangle the width of a 1-lb (450-g) loaf tin. Roll up tightly like a Swiss roll then place in the greased tin, join side at the bottom. Paint with the glaze. Slip the 2 loaves into a large plastic carrier bag. Leave in a warm place until spongy to the touch - about 25 minutes. Meanwhile, turn the oven as high as it will go. When the bread is spongy, remove from the bag and place in the oven. Turn the oven down to Gas No. 7 (425°F/220°C) and bake for 30 minutes, until well risen and a rich brown. To test, turn out of the tin and tap the base, which should sound hollow. If the sound is muffled, leave in the oven but out of the tin for a further 5 minutes. Serve thinly sliced and buttered.

WALNUT GRANARY BREAD

Makes 2 1-lb (450-g) loaves or 20 'knots' (rolls). Keeps moist for 3 days in bread container or drawer. Freeze 3 months.

A natural flavouring essence, the delectable walnut oil - which imparts the delicate taste of crushed walnuts - is a useful addition to the good cook's repertoire. This oil, which is pressed from choice walnuts, is much more expensive than olive oil but fortunately the flavour is very intense, so only a little need be used. Combined with chopped walnuts, it makes a loaf with a mouthwatering flavour that uses granary flour plus a small amount of white flour to soften the texture. This is a superb bread to serve with a vegetable starter such as Salade Provençale (see p. 24), Champignons à la Grecque (see p. 23) or Individual Salade Niçoise (see pp. 24-5). The crusty rolls make an excellent accompaniment to a smooth soup such as Tomato and Basil Soup (see p. 33) or Crème Forestière (see p. 43).

1¼ lb (575 g/5 cups) granary flour
4 oz (125 g/1 cup) strong white bread flour
1 x ¼ oz (7 g) sachet easy-blend yeast
3 level teasp salt
1 tbsp brown sugar or 1 rounded tbsp honey
3 tbsp walnut oil
5 fl oz (150 ml/⅔ cup) boiling water made up to 15 fl oz (425 ml/2 cups) with cold water (14 fl oz/400 ml/1¾ cups if using food processor)
3½-4 oz (100-125 g/⅞ cup) walnuts, finely chopped

For the glaze
1 teasp salt dissolved in 1 tbsp boiling water

In the bowl of the food mixer (or a large food processor) mix all the dry ingredients (except the nuts). Add the oil and water and, if using a food mixer, all but 2 tablespoons of the walnuts (keep these for garnish). Process to a dough using either the dough hook for 4 minutes or the metal blade of the food processor for 1 minute, until a soft but non-sticky dough is formed that leaves the sides of the bowl clean. With a food processor, now pulse in the nuts.

Turn into a large, lightly oiled bowl, roll the ball over to coat with the oil, cover with clingfilm (saranwrap) and leave to rise until double in bulk. This will take about 1½ hours in the kitchen.

If you have a microwave, you can cut the rising time to 50-55 minutes as follows. Put in the dough on defrost for 1 minute. Leave for 10 minutes. Cook for a further 20 seconds, and after 10 more minutes another 20 seconds. Leave till very spongy and double in bulk - about 30-35 minutes.

Divide the dough in 2 and knead each portion for 1 minute to get rid of any large gas bubbles. Shape each half into a loaf as follows. On a lightly floured board roll into a rectangle the width of a 1-lb (450-g) loaf tin. Roll up tightly like a Swiss roll, then place in the greased tin, join side at the bottom. Paint with a glaze of 1 tablespoon of boiling water and 1 teaspoon of salt. Sprinkle with the reserved walnuts.

Slip the 2 loaves into large plastic carrier bags. Leave in a warm place until springy to the touch - about 25 minutes. Meanwhile, turn the oven as high as it will go. When the bread is spongy, remove from the bags and place in the oven. Turn the oven down to Gas No. 7 (425°F/220°C) and bake for 30 minutes, until well risen and a rich brown. To test, turn out of the tin and tap the base, which should sound hollow. If the sound is muffled, leave in the oven but out of the tin for a further 5 minutes. Serve thinly sliced and buttered.

To make the knots Divide the dough into 20 pieces - each will weigh 2 oz (50 g). Roll each piece into a little ball, then into a 7-inch-long (17.5-cm) rope. Tie into a knot (it should resemble a turban).

Arrange the rolls 2 inches (5 cm) apart on trays lined with silicone paper. Brush with a mixture of 2 tablespoons of boiling water and 2 teaspoons of salt. Slip each tray in a large plastic bag and leave until spongy again - about 25 minutes. Sprinkle evenly with the reserved nuts. Bake at Gas No. 8 (450°F/230°C) for 15-18 minutes, until a rich brown.

HONEY AND HAZELNUT GRANARY ROLLS

Makes 16-18.
Freshly baked rolls should be eaten the same day.
Freeze baked rolls 3 months, shaped but unbaked rolls 3 weeks.

Chewy and full of flavour, these rolls are good to serve with cream soups, main dish salads or savoury tartes as part of a vegetarian menu.

12 oz (350 g/3 cups) strong white bread flour
12 oz (350 g/3 cups) granary flour
1 x ¼ oz (7 g) sachet easy-blend yeast or 1 oz (25 g/2 cakes) fresh yeast
3 teasp salt
15 fl oz (425 ml/2 cups of comfortably hand-hot water (for fresh yeast 15 fl oz/425 ml/2 cups of lukewarm water)
1 rounded tbsp honey
2 oz (50 g/¼ cup) soft butter or 3 tbsp hazelnut oil
2 oz (50 g/½ cup) chopped hazelnuts

For the topping
1 egg
1-2 tbsp flaked hazelnuts

Mix together the flours, easy-blend yeast and salt in a bowl. Put the liquid in the bowl of the mixer with the honey and stir until dissolved. Crumble in the fresh yeast if used, then leave 5 minutes to dissolve. Now add the soft fat or the oil and a third of the flour mixture and beat until smooth - by hand or mixer, about 2 minutes. Add a further cupful of flour, beating all the time. Now gradually beat or work in the remaining flour and the nuts, mixing well until a smooth, elastic, scone-like dough that leaves the sides of the bowl clean is formed. Turn on to a floured board and knead until smooth - about 20 seconds. (Add a little extra flour if the dough is still sticky.) Place in an oiled bowl, then turn over to coat with the oil. Cover with clingfilm (saranwrap) and leave to rise until spongy and double in bulk. Punch the dough down and either shape at once or refrigerate for up to 3 days, punching down each day. Be sure to keep the dough tightly covered.

To shape and bake the rolls, divide the dough in half and shape each half into a 8-9-inch-long (20-22.5-cm) roll. Cut into 8 or 9 slices, then roll each slice into a 6-inch-long (15-cm) strip. Twist into a loose knot or roll into a ball. (At this point the uncooked rolls may be frozen.) Brush with beaten egg and arrange the rolls 2 inches (5 cm) apart on a greased baking tray. Slip into a large plastic bag and leave to rise again until spongy - about 30 minutes. Brush the rolls again with the beaten egg and sprinkle with the nuts. Bake in a hot oven, Gas No. 8 (450°F/230°C), for 15 minutes, until well risen and brown.

Serve fresh-baked or reheated in a moderate

oven in a foil parcel, or in the microwave. Raw frozen rolls should be defrosted until soft, allowed to rise until spongy again, then glazed and baked as above.

GREEK OLIVE BREAD
(*Elioti*)

Makes 2 medium loaves.
Freeze for 2 months.

These moist and flavoursome loaves keep fresh in the breadbin for up to 5 days - if you can hide them from the midnight-snackers.

If olives are not your favourite food, add 4 oz (125 g/1 cup) chopped walnuts and an extra teaspoon of salt instead and use walnut oil instead of olive oil.

9 oz (250 g/2¼ cups) each granary or wholemeal (wholewheat) flour and strong white bread flour
1 teasp salt
1 teasp sugar
1 x ¼ oz (7 g) sachet easy-blend yeast
3 tbsp extra virgin olive oil
1 egg, beaten (save 2 tbsp for glaze)
9 fl oz (250 ml/2 cups plus 2 tbsp) hand-hot water
8 oz (225 g/2 cups) black olives, stoned and halved

Put all the dry ingredients into the bowl of the mixer or food processor, mix briefly to blend, then add all the remaining ingredients except for the olives. Beat until the mixture leaves the bowl almost clean - 1 minute in the food processor, 4 minutes in the mixer. It should be a scone-like dough. If too wet, add a further 1 or 2 tablespoons of flour until the mixture can be gathered into a soft ball. Turn on to a floured board and knead for 30 seconds, or until smooth on the underside. Lightly oil a large bowl, put in the dough, then turn it over so that it is coated on all sides. Cover with clingfilm (saranwrap) and leave to rise until doubled in bulk. (Giving the covered dough 1 minute on defrost in the microwave before putting it to rise will help speed the process.)

Turn the risen dough on to the board, knead lightly to remove any large bubbles of air, then work in the chopped olives, adding a little flour if at all sticky. Divide in 2 equal portions and knead each into a ball, then flatten into a baton shape. Arrange well apart on a tray (or trays) lined with silicone paper and brush with the reserved egg. Slip the tray with the balls of dough into a large plastic carrier and leave until spongy and puffy - a further ¾-1 hour. Brush again with the egg.

Bake in a quick oven, Gas No. 6 (400°F/200°C), for 35-40 minutes, or until a rich brown and hollow when tapped underneath.

Kuchens of Many Kinds

Translated literally, kuchen means 'cake', but it is also the generic term for the vast range of yeast-raised confectionery that was the main kind of sweet mixture baked by European Jewish women until after the First World War. Its main virtue lay in its economy, for few eggs and little sugar or fat were required to make a whole kitchenful of rolls, cakes and fruited desserts. Today we value it mainly for the wonderful taste and texture you get with a yeast-raised cake, but also because of the relatively low fat and sugar content of many varieties. Recipes are legion, ranging from the economical Russian to the prodigal Hungarian ones. Excellent kuchens can be bought from any Jewish baker, but there is a unique pleasure to be gained from making them occasionally at home.

Below I give 2 methods for making basic kuchen doughs. In each the dough can be baked the same day or safely left to rise slowly overnight. Both methods can be used in all the recipes that follow.

To freeze kuchens of any kind
For best results, bake, then freeze.

To freeze
Wrap in foil or polythene bags.

Storage time
Up to 6 weeks (icings tend to crumble after 1 or 2 weeks).

To thaw
Leave in packaging at room temperature for 2–3 hours or, if undecorated, place foil-wrapped in moderate oven, Gas No. 4 (350°F/180°C), for 15–20 minutes. In the microwave heat on defrost for 30 seconds to 2 minutes, according to size.

In the past, kuchen dough, which is softer than a bread dough, had to be beaten by hand or with a wooden spoon - a process rather more laborious than kneading the firmer bread dough. Then the advent of the electric mixer - particularly the sort with a flat, paddle-shaped beater - did the job equally efficiently and without any of the hard work.

Several years ago I developed a method using a food processor, which was equally efficient and even quicker. It is also useful if you don't have a powerful electric mixer.

As these techniques differ in several respects, I give them both in full. However, once the dough is ready for shaping, the technique is exactly the same.

KUCHEN DOUGH MADE WITH A FOOD PROCESSOR

Makes 2 large loaves.
Keeps fresh 3 days under refrigeration.
Freeze cooked kuchen 3 months, unrisen dough 3 months, shaped but unbaked kuchens 2 weeks.

If you are shy of yeast cookery - particularly the kneading of the dough - this is a marvellous way to gain confidence, and to produce kuchens of professional standard from the start. This amount of mixture can be processed either in a large food processor - 5-pint (2.75-l/12-cup) bowl capacity - or in a regular-sized one fitted with a special dough dome. Or half the mixture can be processed at a time, on a regular-sized - 3 pint (1.75 l/8 cups) - machine, the 2 balls made into 1 and then risen and shaped together as in the recipe. Rather less liquid is used in this dough than in one kneaded with a dough hook, as it is distributed so much more quickly and evenly by the food processor. If the dough does not form a ball immediately after all the liquid has been added, do not process it any further but add an extra 1 or 2 tablespoons of flour and then continue to process until a ball is formed.

The dough can be risen and shaped the same day or left to rise overnight. Or the shaped kuchens can be frozen and then defrosted in the refrigerator overnight, or on 'defrost' in the microwave for 1 minute, or until the dough feels slightly warm again to the touch. It is then left to rise until spongy, as described in the recipe.

2 eggs
3 fl oz (75 ml/⅓ cup) milk
1 oz (25 g/2 cakes) fresh yeast or 2 x ¼ oz (7 g) sachets easy-blend dried yeast
1 lb (450 g/4 cups) plain (all-purpose) white flour or bread flour
1 level teasp salt
3 oz (75 g/⅓ cup) soft butter or margarine
3 oz (75 g/⅓ cup) caster (superfine) sugar

Break the eggs into a measuring jug, add cold milk, whisk to blend, then make up to 9 fl oz (250 ml/1 cup plus 2 tbsp) with *very* hot water (the liquid should now be pleasantly warm). Dissolve the fresh yeast, if used, in this liquid (don't add easy-blend yeast at this stage, however). Put the flour, salt, butter or margarine and sugar (and easy-blend yeast if used) into the bowl of the food processor and process for 2 seconds to rub in the fat, then add the liquid through the feed tube and process until a soft ball of dough is formed round the knife. Add the extra flour if necessary, then process for a further 40 seconds to knead the dough.

Lift out the knife, leaving the dough in the bowl, then flour your hands and lift out the dough. Knead for 30 seconds on a floured board, then put in a large, lightly oiled bowl and turn over to coat with the oil. Cover the bowl with clingfilm (saranwrap).

To rise and shape the same day Leave the dough in the kitchen for 1 hour, or until it has doubled in bulk, then put back in the food processor and process for 30 seconds (or knead by hand for 2 minutes). Put the dough back into the bowl, re-cover and leave to rise for a further 30 minutes - this second rising gives the dough a very fine texture and it is now ready to shape into the kuchen.

To rise overnight Leave in the least cold part of the refrigerator. Next day, allow the dough to come back to room temperature - after about 2 hours - or put in the microwave on defrost for 1 minute, or until slightly warm to the touch.

KUCHEN DOUGH MADE BY HAND OR MIXER

Makes 2 large loaves.
Keeps fresh 2 days under refrigeration.
Freeze unrisen dough 3 months, shaped but unbaked cakes 2 weeks, baked cakes 3 months.

2 eggs
3 fl oz (75 ml/$\frac{1}{3}$ cup) cold milk
1 oz (25 g/2 cakes) fresh yeast or 2 x $\frac{1}{4}$ oz (7 g) sachet easy-blend dried yeast
1 lb (450 g/4 cups) plain white (all-purpose) flour
1 level teasp salt
3 oz (75 g/$\frac{1}{3}$ cup) soft butter or margarine
rind of 1 lemon, grated
3 oz (75 g/$\frac{1}{3}$ cup) caster (superfine) sugar

Break the eggs into a measuring cup, add the cold milk, whisk to blend, then make up to 10 fl oz (275 ml/$1\frac{1}{4}$ cups) with hot water. Add the fresh yeast (if used) and stir until dissolved. (If you are using easy-blend dried yeast, mix it with the dry ingredients *before* adding them to the eggs and liquid in the bowl.) Put the flour, salt and sugar into the mixer bowl and mix thoroughly. Add the liquid, the soft butter and the lemon rind and beat for about 5 minutes, until the dough is smooth and stretchy and leaves the bowl and the beater clean when pulled away. If too sticky, add a further 1 or 2 tablespoons of flour - the dough should be firm enough to form into a soft ball.

To use at once Turn the dough on to a pastry board and knead for a few seconds - you will now have a satiny ball of dough. Grease a mixing bowl very lightly with oil, turn the ball of dough in it to coat it, then leave in the bowl and cover with clingfilm (saranwrap). It will take about $1\frac{1}{2}$ hours in the kitchen to double in bulk. Then press the dough down, turn it over and knead it in the bowl for 1 or 2 minutes - this distributes the gas bubbles that have formed in the dough evenly throughout its mass.

To rise overnight Slip the dough into a greased polythene bag large enough to allow it to double in volume. Tie loosely and put on the bottom shelf of the refrigerator. Before using it next day, bring it out into the kitchen for 1 hour so that it returns to room temperature. (If you have a microwave you can hasten the process by putting it on defrost for 2 minutes.) Knead the dough for a further 1 or 2 minutes, as directed for the dough that has risen in the kitchen. In either case, leave the dough while you prepare the fillings for your chosen cakes.

BUTTERING KUCHEN WITH DATE FILLING

Makes 1 large loaf.
Keeps fresh 2 days under refrigeration.
Freeze cooked kuchen 3 months, unrisen dough 3 months, shaped but uncooked kuchen 2 weeks.

This is delicious when sliced and spread with butter, margarine or cream cheese. It is also good to eat if toasted when it begins to dry out after a few days.

½ recipe risen Kuchen Dough (see pp. 472–3)

For the date filling
8 oz (225 g/1⅓ cups) stoned dried dates, chopped
½ oz (15 g/1 tbsp) butter or margarine
1½ level teasp cinnamon
3 tbsp sultanas (white raisins)

For the icing
2 oz (50 g/½ cup) sifted icing (confectioners') sugar
2 teasp (approx.) lemon or orange juice
1 oz (25 g/¼ cup) chopped walnuts

To make the filling, put all the ingredients into a small pan, cover and simmer, stirring occasionally until the mixture forms a thick juicy paste. Allow to cool.

Grease a 2-lb (900-g) loaf tin measuring about 9 x 5 x 3 inches (22.5 x 12.5 x 7.5 cm). Roll out the dough into a rectangle 1 inch (2.5 cm) wider than the base of the loaf tin and ½ inch (1 cm) thick. Spread with the filling to within ½ inch (1 cm) of either side, then turn these sides over the filling to seal it in, and roll up tightly into a Swiss roll. Lay in the tin, join side down. Put the tin into a large plastic bag and leave until the kuchen looks puffy and feels spongy to the touch - 30–40 minutes.

Meanwhile, preheat the oven to Gas No. 4 (350°F/180°C). Bake the kuchen for 35-40 minutes, until golden brown and firm to gentle touch. Turn on to a cooling rack and, while still warm, spread with the icing made by adding enough fruit juice to the icing sugar to make a thick coating consistency. Decorate with the nuts.

VARIATIONS

CINNAMON RAISIN FILLING

1 oz (25 g/2 tbsp) butter or margarine
2 oz (50 g/¼ cup) soft light brown sugar
1 teasp cinnamon
2 oz (50 g/⅓ cup) sultanas (white raisins)
2 oz (50 g/½ cup) flaked hazelnuts (filberts) (optional)

Mix all the ingredients together until spreadable.

POPPY-SEED FILLING

4 oz (125 g/1 cup) whole or ready-ground poppy seeds
4 fl oz (125 ml/½ cup) water
1 oz (25 g/2 tbsp) margarine
2 oz (50 g/¼ cup) sugar
1 rounded tbsp golden (corn) syrup or honey
2 oz (50 g/⅓ cup) raisins
1 teasp vanilla essence (extract)

Grind the whole poppy seeds in a nut- or coffee-mill until they are of the consistency of ground almonds (they can also be bought ready-ground). Put into a pan with all the remaining ingredients and simmer for 5 minutes, stirring all the time, until a thick paste is formed. Leave to go cold.

SCHNECKEN WITH BUTTERSCOTCH GLAZE

Makes 12.
Keeps fresh 2 days under refrigeration.
Freeze 3 months.

These luscious little pinwheels were always known in my family as 'milchike' - presumably because the dough was made with butter and milk. I have seen identical yeast buns in the patisseries of Alsace. Is it fanciful to imagine that my forebears lived there in the late Middle Ages before moving on towards Lithuania and the Baltic States?

These are nicest either freshly baked or reheated in the microwave or in a moderate oven, Gas No. 4 (350°F/180°C) - 15 minutes in a foil parcel.

½ recipe risen Kuchen Dough (see pp. 472–3)

For the glaze
1 oz (25 g/2 tbsp) butter
1 oz (25 g/2 tbsp) brown sugar
1 oz (25 g/2 tbsp) golden (corn) syrup

For the filling
1 oz (25 g/2 tbsp) soft butter
2 oz (50 g/¼ cup) caster (superfine) sugar
1 level teasp cinnamon
2 oz (50 g/⅓ cup) raisins
1 oz (25 g/¼ cup) chopped walnuts

Put glaze ingredients in a pan and simmer for 1 minute, or until a rich golden brown. Divide between 12 greased bun tins.

For the filling, put the soft butter in a bowl and beat in the sugar and cinnamon, followed by the raisins and walnuts. Roll out the dough ⅜ inch (1 cm) thick into a rectangle measuring 12 x 6 inches (30 x 15 cm). Spread all over with the filling. Roll up lengthwise into a tight roll, then cut into 12 1-inch (2.5-cm) slices. Arrange these, cut-side up, in the bun tins. Slip the tray of tins into a plastic carrier bag and leave until puffy - 30–40 minutes.

Bake in a preheated oven, Gas No. 6 (400°F/200°C), for 15–20 minutes, or until a rich brown. Allow 5 minutes for the glaze to set a little, then remove the Schnecken from the tins and leave them, with the glaze on top, on a cooling tray.

APFELKUCHEN

Keeps 2 days under refrigeration.
Freeze 3 months.

This is delicious served warm or at room temperature with fromage frais or Greek-style yoghurt. Apricots, peaches and plums can be used in season.

½ recipe risen Kuchen Dough (see pp. 472–3)

For the filling
4 large cooking apples
plum jam or ginger marmalade (preserve)
4 oz (125 g/½ cup) caster (superfine) sugar
1 level teasp cinnamon

Peel, core and slice the apples ¼ inch (0.5 cm) thick (easiest in the food processor).

Roll the dough to a thickness of ⅜ inch (1 cm) and use to line a Swiss roll tin measuring 14 x 10 inches (35 x 25 cm), lightly greased. Allow the dough to rise again for 30 minutes, then spread with jam (or marmalade) and arrange the apple slices in overlapping rows on top. Mix sugar and cinnamon together and sprinkle over the top. Leave for 10 minutes. Bake in a moderate oven, Gas No. 4 (350°F/180°C), for 40 minutes. Serve warm or cold.

KAESE (CHEESE) KUCHEN

Keeps fresh 2 days under refrigeration.
Freeze 3 months.

My grandmother made this using her own tart home-made kaese. Alas, we must make do with the bland factory-produced version. However, you can add extra flavour by mixing a tablespoon of natural yoghurt with the cheese.

½ recipe risen Kuchen Dough (see pp. 472–3)

For the filling
12 oz (350 g/1½ cups) curd or other low- or medium-fat soft cheese
1 egg
2 oz (50 g/¼ cup) sugar
pinch of salt
2 level teasp flour
grated rind of ½ lemon
½ teasp vanilla essence (extract)

For glazing the kuchen
milk or beaten egg

Blend all the filling ingredients together until smooth. A few sultanas can also be added.

Grease a round, loose-bottomed 9-inch (22.5-cm) tin about 2½ inches (6 cm) deep. Roll out a circle of the risen dough 1 inch (2.5 cm) thick and ease into the tin. Allow to rise for 10 minutes, then spoon the cheese filling on top. Roll some of the dough into strips and make a latticework to cover the filling partly. Leave to rise for 30 minutes, then brush with milk or a little beaten egg. Bake in a moderate oven, Gas No. 4 (350°F/180°C), for 40 minutes.

STREUSEL KUCHEN

Keeps fresh 2 days under refrigeration.
Freeze 3 months.

The spongy dough is topped with a spicy crumble.

½ recipe risen Kuchen Dough (see p. 472–3)

For the streusel
2 oz (50 g/½ cup) butter
2 oz (50 g/½ cup) flour
5 oz (150 g/⅔ cup) soft brown sugar
1 level teasp cinnamon
2 oz (50 g/½ cup) chopped walnuts (optional)

Melt the butter, then stir it into the flour mixed with the sugar, cinnamon and walnuts (if used). Mix to a crumble with the fingertips. Roll out the risen dough to fit a tin approximately 14 x 10 inches (35 x 25 cm) which has been lightly greased. Allow the dough to rise for 30 minutes, then brush with the melted butter and sprinkle evenly with the streusel. Leave for a further 10 minutes, then bake in a preheated oven, Gas No. 5 (375°F/190°C), for 25 minutes, or until a rich brown. Serve in squares.

GERMAN STOLLEN

Keeps fresh 2 days under refrigeration.
Freeze 3 months.

The dough is enriched with dried fruits and nuts. The stollen is sliced and served plain or buttered.

½ recipe risen Kuchen Dough (see pp. 472–3)
2 oz (50 g/½ cup) chopped walnuts or toasted chopped almonds
4 oz (125 g/¾ cup) mixed dried fruit
rind of 1 lemon, grated
2 oz (50 g/¼ cup) glacé (candied) cherries, quartered
1½ oz (40 g/3 tbsp) very soft butter

Turn the risen dough on to a floured board and knead in the nuts, fruit mixture (but not the cherries) and lemon rind. Roll into a 10-inch (25-cm) circle, spread with 1 oz (25 g/2 tbsp) of the soft butter, then lay the cherries in a line down the centre. Fold the dough into 3 rather like an omelette, covering the cherries and pressing gently to seal the top layer to the bottom. Put on a greased tray and brush with the remaining butter.

Slip into a plastic bag and leave to prove until light and spongy to the touch - about 40 minutes. Bake at Gas No. 6 (400°F/200°C) for 30 minutes, until brown. When cold, dredge thickly with icing (confectioners') sugar.

KOLACKY

Makes about 8.
Keeps fresh 2 days under refrigeration.
Freeze 3 months.

These Polish-style sweet buns are also known as Kolatchen in Bohemia.

A soft yeast dough is refrigerated overnight, then topped with an apple or cream cheese mixture. Use the Kuchen Dough made by hand or mixer (see p. 473) - it's too sticky to make in the food processor - but with 5 fl oz (150 ml/⅔ cup) instead of 3 fl oz (75 ml/⅓ cup) of milk and make the liquid (including eggs) up to 12 fl oz (350 ml/1½ cups). Allow to firm up in the refrigerator overnight, then leave at room temperature for 1 hour, or until it is spongy like a scone dough.

For the cheese filling
(for ½ the dough)
8 oz (225 g/1 cup) curd or other soft white cheese
1 egg
1 level tbsp caster (superfine) sugar
a few drops vanilla essence (extract)
2 teasp lemon juice
½ oz (15 g/1 tbsp) butter

For the apple filling
(for ½ the dough)
nut of butter
8 oz (225 g) eating apples
1 heaped tbsp brown sugar
squeeze of lemon juice

For the glaze
1 egg, beaten to blend

To make the cheese filling, beat all the ingredients together until smooth.

To make the apple filling, melt the butter, add the peeled apples cut into ¾-inch (2-cm) cubes, simmer with the lid on for 15 minutes (or 4 minutes on 100 per cent power in the microwave) or until tender, then stir in the sugar and lemon juice. Allow to go cold.

To shape, on a floured board roll out the dough ½ inch (1 cm) thick and cut into 3-inch (7.5-cm) rounds. Put these rounds on to greased trays, leaving 2 inches (5 cm) between each round. Put the trays in plastic carrier bags and leave in a warm place (eg the warming-drawer of the cooker). When the dough has risen to double its size - about 45 minutes - make a deep impression in the centre with a floured finger, paint all over with the beaten egg, and put in a spoonful of filling.

Bake the kolacky for 15 minutes in a preheated oven, Gas No. 6 (400°F/200°C), or until golden brown.

Serve in wedges that day or refrigerate until the next. Alternatively, pack in plastic bags and freeze.

KERSTOL
(*Dutch Bread*)

Makes 1 2-lb (900-g) loaf.
Keeps fresh 2 days under refrigeration.
Freeze 3 months.

This luscious loaf is crammed with good things like currants, raisins and glacé (candied) fruit, and - best of all - it has a layer of marzipan hidden inside. Serve it plain or buttered as you prefer.

For the marzipan

3 oz (75g/¾ cup) ground almonds
1½ oz (40 g/3 tbsp) caster (superfine) sugar
1½ oz (40 g/5 tbsp) icing (confectioners') sugar
2 drops almond essence (extract) or ¼ teasp vanilla essence (extract)
½ teasp lemon juice
1 egg yolk

For the dough

5 fl oz (150 ml/⅔ cup) warm milk
2 oz (50 g/¼ cup) caster (superfine) sugar
bare 1 oz (25 g/2 cakes) fresh yeast
12 oz (350 g/3 cups) plain (all-purpose) flour
1½ teasp mixed sweet spice
1 teasp salt
1 egg, beaten, to blend
3 oz (75 g/⅓ cup) soft butter
2 teasp grated lemon rind
4 oz (125 g/¾ cup) currants
4 oz (125 g/¾ cup) raisins
3 oz (75 g/⅓ cup) ready-chopped mixed glacé (candied) fruit

For the glaze

1 oz (25 g/2 tbsp) caster (superfine) sugar, dissolved in 1 tbsp milk

Mix all the marzipan ingredients together to form a smooth paste.

Warm the milk to blood heat (50 seconds on 100 per cent full power in the microwave), then stir in a teaspoon of sugar and the yeast and set aside. Mix the flour, sugar, spice and salt in a mixing bowl and make a well in the centre. Stir the yeast mixture with the beaten egg until smooth, then add to the flour and mix to a dough first with a wooden spoon and then with your hands. Turn out on to a floured board and knead until smooth and silky - about 3 or 4 minutes by hand. (Add a little flour if the dough sticks to the board.)

Lightly oil a large bowl, put in the ball of dough, then turn it over so that it is coated with the oil. Cover with clingfilm (saranwrap) and leave to rise for 30 minutes in a warm place (the oven heated to its lowest temperature then turned off is ideal).

Now beat in the butter and lemon rind and work in the dried and glacé fruit with well-floured hands until the dough is smooth again.

Grease and bottom-line with silicone paper a 2-lb (900-g) loaf tin measuring 9 x 5 x 3 inches (22.5 x 12.5 x 7.5 cm). On a floured board pat the dough into a rectangle the length of the tin, then arrange the marzipan in a 1-inch (2.5-cm) strip down the centre. Work the dough round the marzipan, sealing it well and shaping it to fit the tin. Place join side down in the tin and slip it into a large plastic bag.

Leave in a warm place until the dough reaches the top of the tin and feels puffy to the touch. Bake in a preheated oven, Gas No. 7 (425°F/220°C), for 10 minutes, then at Gas No. 4 (350°F/180°C) for a further 45 minutes, until richly browned. Carefully loosen from the tin and turn out on to a cooling tray. Turn right side up and spread with the glaze while hot.

KRINGLE MED MANDELFYLLNING
(*Swedish Almond Ring*)

Keeps fresh 2 days under refrigeration.
Freeze 3 months.

The luscious almond filling makes a creamy contrast to the fluffy kuchen. It is sliced and served plain or buttered as preferred.

½ recipe risen Kuchen Dough *(see pp. 472–3)*

For the filling

3 oz (75 g/¾ cup) ground almonds or hazelnuts (filberts)
finely grated rind of ½ orange
3 oz (75 g/⅓ cup) caster (superfine) sugar
1 egg yolk
½ teasp vanilla essence (extract)

For the glaze

3 oz (75 g/¾ cup) icing (confectioners') sugar
1 tbsp orange juice
few toasted almond flakes

Mix the filling ingredients together to form a spreadable paste, adding a little cold water if necessary.

Roll the dough into a rectangle measuring about 11 x 6 inches (22 x 15 cm). Spread all over with the almond paste, leaving ½ inch (1 cm) clear along each short side. Roll up lengthwise into a tight roll, then twist round to form a circle, sealing it well. Place on a greased tray. Using kitchen scissors, make cuts two-thirds of the way through the ring at intervals of 1½ inches (4 cm). Slip the tray into a plastic bag and leave to rise until puffy - about 30 minutes.

Bake in a preheated oven, Gas No. 6 (400°F/200°C), for 25 minutes, or until golden-brown. Mix the sugar and juice to form an icing that will coat the back of the spoon. When the ring has cooled for 10 minutes, brush on the icing using a pastry brush and scatter with the almonds.

Quick Kuchens, Teabreads and Scones

People have been eating some form of cake for almost as long as they have been eating bread. The first rudimentary cakes were in fact a form of bread, sweetened with honey and highly flavoured with spices.

Quick kuchens, teabreads and scones are all closely related to these primitive 'cake-breads' but instead of being leavened with yeast, they rely on chemical reagents to produce the gases which lighten them. Bakers began to experiment with chemical leavening in the late Middle Ages, but the chemicals that were used (such as pearlash and alum) left a distasteful residue even though they helped to lighten the cakes. It was only with the advent of baking powder and self-raising flour in the middle of the nineteenth century that the baking of pleasant-tasting, economical cakes that did not rely on the leavening power of either yeast or beaten eggs became universally popular.

All the recipes in this section freeze extremely well.

QUICK KUCHENS

'Quick kuchen' is a general term to cover a wide range of cakes that can be topped either with sweet crumbles (usually called streusels) or with an assortment of seasonal fruits. These cakes do not have the same flavour or texture as a yeast-raised kuchen but they are quite delicious in their own right. The cake mixture itself is economical, containing a low ratio of eggs and butter to flour, but a high proportion of baking powder. The resulting cake is light and, when freshly baked, can also be served as a dessert. This basic cake mixture can be used for both streusel and fruit kuchens.

To reheat any of the Quick Kuchens that follow, leave in either a moderate oven, Gas No. 4 (350°F/180°C), or a microwave oven until warm to the touch.

QUICK KUCHEN MIXTURE

8 oz (225 g/2 cups) self-raising flour and 1 level teasp baking powder or 8 oz (225 g/2 cups) plain (all-purpose) flour, a pinch of salt and 3 level teasp baking powder
3 oz (75 g/⅓ cup) soft butter
4 oz (125 g/⅔ cup) caster (superfine) sugar
1 large egg
5 fl oz (150 ml/⅔ cup) milk (4 fl oz/125 ml/½ cup if mixing in a food processor)

Put all the ingredients into a bowl and mix by hand or machine until a thick, smooth batter is formed - 15 seconds by food processor, 2 or 3 minutes by hand or electric mixer.

Oil either a rectangular cake tin measuring 12 x 9 x 2 inches (30 x 22.5 x 5 cm) or a 9-inch (22.5-cm) round or square tin of a similar depth. Spoon the batter into the chosen tin and smooth level. The kuchen is now ready to be used as the basis for any of the Quick Kuchens that follow.

STREUSEL KUCHEN

Serves 12.
Freeze 3 months.

This kuchen is soft and tender for 3 days after it has been baked. When it begins to stale, it can be sliced and buttered like a teabread. When really stale it is delicious toasted and buttered.

1 recipe Quick Kuchen Mixture (see above)

For the topping
2 oz (50 g/½ cup) flour
2 level teasp ground cinnamon
5 oz (150 g/⅔ cup) light brown sugar
2 oz (50 g/¼ cup) butter

Mix the flour, cinnamon and sugar. Melt the butter, then pour on to the dry ingredients and blend with a fork until evenly moistened.

Turn the kuchen batter into an oiled tin measuring 12 x 9 x 2 inches (30 x 22.5 x 5 cm). Sprinkle the crumble over the unbaked kuchen. Bake at Gas No. 5 (375°F/190°C) for 40–45 minutes, or until well risen and golden brown.

VARIATIONS

APPLE KUCHEN

Serves 12.
Freeze 3 months.

This is delicious served hot or cold. A layer of thinly sliced apple is sandwiched between the kuchen mixture and the streusel.

1 recipe Quick Kuchen Mixture (see this page)
2 lb (900 g) baking apples (weight before peeling)

Evenly spread the kuchen dough in a greased tin measuring 12 x 9 x 2 inches (30 x 22.5 x 5 cm).

Peel, core and quarter the apples, then cut into slices ⅛ inch (0.3 cm) thick. Arrange the apple slices in overlapping rows so that the kuchen batter is completely covered. Cover with the streusel as before.

Bake in a preheated oven, Gas No. 5 (375°F/190°C) for 40 minutes, or until the cake has shrunk from the sides of the tin, the apples feel tender when pierced with a knife and the streusel is golden brown.

PEACH KUCHEN

Serves 12.
Freeze 3 months.

Peel 6 large peaches (by plunging for 1 minute into boiling water, then cold water and skinning). Slice and use to cover the kuchen instead of the apples.

CHERRY KUCHEN

Serves 12.
Freeze 3 months.

Morello (sour red) cherries are ideal for this recipe. Their tartness combines with the fruit and cream custard to make a sweet-sour topping.

1 recipe Quick Kuchen Mixture (see p. 480)
2 oz (50 g/½ cup) ground almonds

For the topping
at least 2 lb (900 g) Morello (sour red) cherries (weight before stoning)
2 egg yolks
8 oz (225 g/1 cup) light brown sugar
3 fl oz (75 ml/⅓ cup) double (heavy) cream
juice from cherries when stoned

Evenly spread the kuchen mixture in a greased tin measuring 12 x 9 x 2 inches (30 x 22.5 x 5 cm). Sprinkle with a thin layer of ground almonds. Cover the surface with the stoned cherries.

Beat together all the remaining ingredients, then pour over the fruit. Bake at Gas No. 5 (375°F/190°C) for 40–45 minutes, or until golden brown.

PLUM KUCHEN

Serves 12.
Freeze 3 months.

A true Viennese speciality. Use the black freestone (zwetschken) plums that usually come from Hungary, Poland or Italy. Serve warm or cold, if possible with thick cream.

1 recipe Quick Kuchen Mixture (see p. 480)

For the topping
1 oz (25 g/2 tbsp) melted butter
2 lb (900 g) plums (weight before stoning)
6 oz (175 g/¾ cup) granulated sugar mixed with 1 level teasp cinnamon

Evenly spread the kuchen mixture in a greased tin measuring 12 x 9 x 2 inches (30 x 22.5 x 5 cm).

Brush the batter with the melted butter. Arrange the stoned and halved plums, flesh-side up, all over the surface. Sprinkle with half the sugar. Bake in a preheated oven, Gas No. 5 (375°F/190°C), for 40 minutes, until well risen. Take out of the oven and sprinkle with the remaining sugar. Allow to cool in the tin.

BANANA STREUSEL KUCHEN WITH APRICOT FROMAGE FRAIS

Makes about 12 servings.
Keeps 3 days under refrigeration if tightly foil-wrapped.
Do not freeze.

1 recipe Quick Kuchen Mixture (see p. 480)

For the topping
3 large bananas
2 tbsp lemon juice
scant 2 oz (50 g/½ cup) flour
2 level teasp ground cinnamon
2 oz (50 g/¼ cup) butter, cut in bits
4 oz (125 g/½ cup) light brown sugar

For the apricot fromage frais
4 oz (125 g/¾ cup) ready-to-eat tenderized dried apricots, chopped
1 oz (25 g/¼ cup) pine kernels, toasted
1 x 9 oz (250 g) carton creamy fromage frais

Evenly spread the kuchen mixture in a greased tin measuring 12 x 9 x 2 inches (30 x 22.5 x 5 cm).

Peel and slice the bananas about ⅜ inch (1 cm) thick. Arrange the sliced bananas on top of the batter and sprinkle evenly with the lemon juice. Rub the flour, spice, butter and sugar gently together until they form a crumble. Sprinkle this evenly over the bananas. Bake for 40–45 minutes, or until golden brown.

To make the apricot fromage frais, gently stir the chopped apricots and toasted pine kernels into the fromage frais and chill until required.

TEABREADS

These are very like the first bread-cakes, but baking powder has been substituted for yeast as a leavening agent. They originated in farmhouse kitchens as an economical way of providing something sweet for the farm-workers. They are best stored for at least a day before cutting, as they tend to crumble when fresh.

WHOLEMEAL (WHOLEWHEAT) BANANA TEABREAD

Makes 1 2-lb (900-g) loaf.
Keeps 1 week under refrigeration.
Goes heavy when frozen.

A wonderfully moist, flavourful loaf of American origin, which can be served plain, buttered or spread with honey, lemon curd or cream cheese. It will keep moist for a week in an airtight tin. Store in a cool place or refrigerator because of the fruit content.

1 lb (450 g) bananas (unpeeled weight)
2 eggs
6 oz soft, medium brown sugar
1 teasp vanilla essence (extract)
grated rind of 1 orange
4 oz (125 g/½ cup) soft margarine
8 oz (225 g/2 cups) 100% fine-milled wholemeal (wholewheat) flour
1 teasp baking powder
½ teasp bicarbonate of soda (baking soda)

Preheat the oven to Gas No. 4 (350°F/180°C). Lightly grease a 2-lb (900-g) loaf tin and line the bottom and short sides with silicone or greaseproof paper.

With a food processor, peel bananas and cut in roughly 1-inch (2.5-cm) chunks, then process until puréed. Add the eggs and sugar and process for 1 minute. Through the feed tube with the machine running add, in turn, the vanilla, orange rind and heaped teaspoonsful of the soft margarine. Process for 10 seconds, or until the mixture looks like mayonnaise. Remove the lid and add the flour sifted with the baking powder and bicarbonate of soda. Cover and pulse (using an on-off action) until the flour disappears - about 5 seconds - scraping down the sides half-way with a rubber spatula.

By hand or electric mixer, mash the peeled bananas well, then put in a bowl with all the remaining ingredients and beat until smooth and creamy - 2–3 minutes. The volume will be less than if put in a food processor.

Spoon the mixture into the tin and level the top with a spatula. Bake for 50 minutes. The loaf will have shrunk slightly from the sides of the tin, the top of the cake will be springy to gentle touch and a skewer should come out clean from the centre. Place the tin on a cooling rack and leave for 10 minutes, then gently ease out. Allow to cool completely, then wrap in foil to store. Leave overnight before cutting.

VARIATION

CHERRY, WALNUT AND BANANA TEABREAD

A more luxurious version. Make exactly as the Wholemeal Banana Teabread but with the ingredients below. Pulse in the walnuts and cherries with the flour.

8 oz (225 g/2 cups) self-raising flour plus 1 level teasp baking powder or 8 oz (225 g/2 cups) plain (all-purpose) flour plus 3 teasp baking powder
½ teasp bicarbonate of soda (baking soda)
4 oz (125 g/½ cup) butter
5 oz (150 g/½ cup) caster (superfine) sugar
2 eggs
1 lb (450 g) bananas, unpeeled weight
2 oz (50 g/½ cup) chopped walnuts
2 oz (50 g/⅓ cup) chopped glacé (candied) cherries
grated rind of ½ orange or lemon

WHOLEMEAL FRUIT LOAF

Makes 1 2-lb (900-g) loaf.
Keeps moist 1 week.
Freeze 3 months.

This contains no fat except for a couple of spoonfuls of peanut butter, so it makes a healthy snack for after school. Cut in fairly thick fingers and serve plain or spread with soft white cheese or honey.

10 oz (275 g/2½ cups) mixed dried fruit
6 oz (175 g/¾ cup) soft brown sugar
10 fl oz (275 ml/1¼ cups) strained hot tea
1 egg
2 tbsp crunchy peanut butter
12 oz (350 g/3 cups) fine-milled wholemeal self-raising flour, or 85% extraction wheatmeal self-raising flour, or 12 oz (350 g/3 cups) wholemeal (wheatmeal) plain (all-purpose) flour plus 3 teasp baking powder
1 teasp cinnamon

For sprinkling on top
1 tbsp demerara sugar

1 hour in advance (or the night before if more convenient) put the dried fruit and sugar in a large bowl and strain the tea over it. Mix well and leave for the fruit to swell and the tea to go cold.

Preheat the oven to Gas No. 4 (350°F/180°C). Grease and bottom-line a loaf tin measuring 9 x 5 x 3 inches (22.5 x 12.5 x 7.5 cm). Whisk the egg, then stir it into the fruit mixture, followed by the peanut butter and the flour sifted with the cinnamon. Mix thoroughly together, then turn into the prepared tin and smooth the top. Sprinkle with the demerara sugar and bake for 1 hour, or until firm to the touch and a skewer comes out clean from the centre. If it is still a little sticky, turn the oven down to Gas No. 3 (325°F/160°C) and cook for a further 10–15 minutes.

Leave for 10 minutes to cool, then turn out on to a rack.

MOTHER'S FRUIT LOAF

Makes 1 2-lb (900-g) loaf.
Store in an airtight container.

This is *completely* fat-free and yet is very moist.

5 fl oz (150 ml/⅔ cup) hot strained tea
8 oz (225 g/1½ cups) mixed dried fruit
4 oz (125 g/½ cup) brown sugar
1 egg
1 rounded tbsp ginger or orange marmalade
8 oz (225 g/2 cups) self-raising flour or
8 oz (225 g/2 cups) plain (all-purpose) flour and
2 level teasp baking powder

Pour the strained tea over the fruit and sugar in a large basin. Leave overnight. Next day stir in the beaten egg, the marmalade and sifted flour and the baking powder (if used). Mix well, then spoon into a greased 2-lb (900-g) loaf tin.

Bake in a preheated oven, Gas No. 3 (325°F/160°C), for 1¼ hours, or until firm. Turn out, allow to cool completely, then wrap in foil. Use after 2–3 days, sliced and buttered.

DATE AND WALNUT LOAF

Makes 1 2-lb (900-g) loaf.
Keeps 1 week at room temperature in an airtight container.
Freeze 3 months.

A moist and more-ish tea loaf to slice and butter.

8 oz (225 g/1⅓ cups) chopped stoned dates
6 oz (175 g/¾ cup) soft brown sugar
1 oz (25 g/2 tbsp) butter
1 level teasp bicarbonate of soda (baking soda)
8 fl oz (225 ml/1 cup) boiling water
1 large egg
1 teasp vanilla essence (extract)
2 oz (50 g/½ cup) chopped walnuts
8 oz (225 g/2 cups) self-raising flour or
8 oz (225 g/2 cups) plain (all-purpose) flour plus
2 teasp baking powder

Put dates, sugar and butter into a basin, sprinkle with the bicarbonate of soda and pour on the boiling water. Leave until steaming stops, then add the beaten egg, vanilla essence, walnuts and flour. Pour into a 2-lb (900-g) loaf tin, greased and bottom-lined with silicone or greaseproof paper.

Bake in a preheated oven, Gas No. 4 (350°F/180°C), for 1–1¼ hours, depending on the depth of the tin. When done, the loaf will spring back when lightly pressed with a finger. Leave overnight before slicing.

SCONES

Scones are what the Americans call 'biscuits'. But it's not that simple – the word is also used to describe the slightly sweetened cakes cooked on a girdle (called a griddle across the Atlantic) that the Americans call 'hot cakes'. This produces a certain amount of confusion in the minds of cooks on both sides of the Atlantic! But however you bake it, and whatever you call it, this kind of mixture always contains very little fat and a great deal of raising agent. This may be baking powder or, in the Scottish fashion, a mixture of cream of tartar and bicarbonate of soda. The liquid may be water, sweet or sour milk, cream or yoghurt. An unsweetened scone mixture can be moulded into a loaf or shaped into rolls that relate to yeast breads in the same way that quick kuchens relate to yeast kuchens. Scones and their ilk are not traditional in the Jewish kitchen but they have been made by many Jewish housewives, particularly in America, since the beginning of this century, and they are now extremely popular everywhere. All scones should be served the day they are made, though they can be toasted when stale. They freeze extremely well.

OVEN SCONES

Makes 10.
Serve freshly baked or place on kitchen paper and reheat from frozen in the microwave.
Freeze 3 months.

The best scones – with a light, fluffy texture – are achieved by adding the liquid all at once to the dry ingredients and mixing swiftly to a springy, non-sticky dough. A very hot oven is essential to activate the large amount of chemical raising agent they contain. As there really is nothing to compete with a freshly baked scone, it is convenient to double the amounts given and store the remainder in a screw-top jar or plastic container, where it will keep under refrigeration for many weeks. It will then only need liquid to turn it into an instant scone dough.

8 oz (225 g/2 cups) self-raising flour and 1 level teasp baking powder, or 8 oz (225 g/2 cups) plain (all-purpose) flour and 3 level teasp baking powder, or 8 oz (225 g/2 cups) plain (all-purpose) flour and 1 level teasp bicarbonate of soda (baking soda) and 2 level teasp cream of tartar

1 oz (25 g/2 tbsp) sugar
½ level teasp salt
1½ oz (40 g/3 tbsp) butter
5 fl oz (125 ml/⅔ cup) sweet or sour milk

For the glaze
milk
granulated sugar

Mix together the dry ingredients, then rub in the fat until the mixture resembles fine crumbs. With a food processor, process the dry ingredients to the fine crumb stage, then tip into a bowl and mix with the liquid (as directed below).

Make a well in the centre, pour in the liquid and mix to a soft but non-sticky dough with a round knife, cutting through and through the dry ingredients to moisten them equally. Turn out on to a lightly floured board and knead for 30 seconds, or until no cracks remain on the underside. Roll the dough ¾ inch (2 cm) thick. Cut into circles 2 inches (5 cm) in diameter and place on greased trays. Brush with milk then sprinkle with granulated sugar.

Bake at Gas No. 8 (450°F/230°C) for 12–15 minutes, or until golden brown. When cool, split and butter and serve plain, or with jam and unsweetened whipped cream.

VARIATIONS

SULTANA (WHITE RAISIN) SCONES

Add 1 oz (25 g/3 tbsp) of sultanas or other dried fruit before mixing with the liquid.

BROWN SCONES

Use 5 oz (150 g/1¼ cups of wholemeal (wholewheat) flour and 3 oz (75 g/¾ cup) of white plain (all-purpose) flour instead of the 8 oz (225 g/2 cups) of white flour.

CHEESE SCONES

Makes 12–15 scones.

Omit the sugar but add 2 oz (50 g/½ cup) of finely grated mature cheese, 1 level teaspoon of salt and a pinch of dry mustard with the dry ingredients. Mix to a dough with an egg beaten with 4 tablespoons of cold water. (Save a little of the liquid for brushing the scones.) Roll out ½ inch (1 cm) thick and cut into 2-inch (5-cm) rounds. Brush with the egg mixture and put on greased trays.

Bake at Gas No. 7 (425°F/220°C) for 10–15 minutes. Split and butter when cool. Serve plain or with any savoury spread such as cream cheese, Liptauer Cheese (see p. 528), cheese and chives, or Egg and Olive Butter (see p. 526).

FLUFFY YOGHURT SCONES

Makes 10–12 scones.
Serve fresh on the day.
Freeze 3 months.

As an alternative to butter or jam, these can be spread with a low-fat curd cheese or with honey. The yoghurt gives them a particularly soft texture.

8 oz (225 g/2 cups) white (all-purpose) flour or fine wholemeal (wheatmeal) flour
3 teasp baking powder
¼ teasp salt
1 oz (25 g/2 tbsp) golden granulated sugar
2 oz (50 g/¼ cup) butter, cut into small pieces
3 oz (75 g/½ cup) sultanas (white raisins) (optional)
4–5 fl oz (125-150 ml/¾ cup) natural yoghurt or smetana

For the glaze
a little of the smetana or yoghurt
golden granulated sugar

Preheat the oven to Gas No. 7 (425°F/220°C). Line a baking sheet with silicone paper.

Sift together the flour, baking powder, salt

and sugar. Rub in the butter until the mixture resembles coarse crumbs. (This can be done using the pulse action in a food processor, or in a mixer.) Turn into a bowl, stir in the sultanas, make a well and add the liquid, then mix with a knife to a soft non-sticky dough. Turn it out on to a lightly floured board and knead gently for 30 seconds to smooth the underside. Roll out the dough ½ inch (1.25 cm) thick and cut it into 10–12 rounds with a pastry-cutter.

Place the scones on the baking sheet and brush with yoghurt or smetana. Scatter with sugar and bake for 12–15 minutes, until they begin to brown on the top. Cool and then eat or freeze.

GIRDLE (GRIDDLE) SCONES

Serve fresh on the day.
Freeze 3 months.

If a girdle (or griddle as it is sometimes known) is not available, use the base of a heavy frying pan, a solid electric hot plate or an electric skillet. The girdle was the traditional Scottish utensil for scone- and bread-making and until recent times it was always part of the equipment of the Scottish soldier. Scones cooked on a girdle are especially soft and tender. Baking powder can be used, as in the Oven Scone micture, but the traditional Scottish recipe is as follows.

8 oz (225 g/2 cups) plain (all-purpose) flour
½ level teasp salt
1 level teasp bicarbonate of soda (baking soda)
2 level teasp cream of tartar
1 oz (25 g/2 tbsp) butter
1 oz (25 g/2 tbsp) sugar
5 fl oz (150 ml/⅔) milk

Sift the flour, salt, bicarbonate of soda and cream of tartar into a basin. Rub in the butter and stir in the sugar. Mix to a soft but non-sticky dough with the milk, then knead for 30 seconds, or until smooth. Heat the oiled girdle, frying pan or electric skillet until the heat can be felt with the hand held 2 inches (5 cm) above it. (Another good test is to drop a teaspoon of cold water on to the hot girdle. When it is the right temperature the water will immediately form tiny droplets and 'skitter' across the surface before evaporating.)

Divide the dough into 2 portions, and roll each into a circle ¼ inch (0.5 cm) thick. Divide each circle into 6 triangular segments. Cook on the girdle until golden brown – about 5 minutes – then turn and cook the other side. When cool, split and butter.

DROP SCONES
(*Scotch Pancakes*)

These light and tender hot cakes are at their best served split and buttered as soon as they are cooked, with honey, jam or golden (corn) syrup.

8 oz (225 g/2 cups) plain (all-purpose) flour
½ level teasp salt
1 level teasp bicarbonate of soda (baking soda)
2 level teasp cream of tartar
or
8 oz (225 g/2 cups) self-raising flour
2 level teasp baking powder
or
8 oz (225 g/2 cups) plain (all-purpose) flour
plus 4 teasp baking powder
1 level tbsp caster (superfine) sugar
1 egg
3 teasp golden (corn) syrup
6 fl oz (175 ml/¾ cup) milk

Sift the flour, salt and raising agents into a bowl and add the sugar. Beat the egg then stir in the syrup and the milk. Add to the dry ingredients and mix quickly to a thick batter that will just flow in a thick stream from the spoon. Drop the mixture from the point of a tablespoon on to a greased girdle heated as described for Girdle Scones (see p. 486). When the bubbles on the surface of each scone start to break and the underside is a pale gold, turn it over with a palette knife. As each pancake is cooked, slip it inside a folded tea-towel - the steam will keep the surface soft. Serve buttered.

SUGAR AND SPICE RINGS

Makes 12.
Freeze 6 months.

These are a quick version of the Schnecken on p. 474.

For the scone dough

8 oz (225 g/2 cups) self-raising flour plus 2 level teasp baking powder
1 oz (225 g/2 tbsp) caster or soft brown sugar
1½ oz (40 g/3 tbsp) butter
5 fl oz (150 ml/⅔ cup) milk

For the filling

1 oz (25 g/2 tbsp) soft or melted butter
1 level teasp cinnamon
2 oz (50 g/¼ cup) caster sugar
about 4 tbsp raisins (enough to cover the dough in a thin layer)

For the glaze

1 oz (25 g/2 tbsp) melted butter
1 oz (25 g/2 tbsp) light brown sugar
1 rounded tbsp golden (corn) syrup

To make the scone dough, sift the dry ingredients, then rub in the fat by hand or machine until the mixture resembles coarse crumbs. Make a well in the centre, pour in the milk and mix to a soft but non-sticky dough with a round-ended knife, cutting through and through the dry ingredients to moisten them evenly.

Turn out on to a lightly floured board and knead for about 30 seconds, or until no cracks remain on the underside of the dough. Roll out into a rectangle about 12 inches (30 cm) long and 7 inches (17.5 cm) wide. Spread with the 1 oz (25 g/2 tbsp) of butter, and sprinkle with the cinnamon, sugar and raisins, leaving 1 inch (2.5 cm) clear all the way round. Turn in the sides. Roll up tightly like a Swiss roll, then cut into slices 1 inch (2.5 cm) wide. In a small pan bubble the glaze ingredients together until a rich caramel colour, then divide between each of 12 lightly oiled patty tins and top with a slice, cut-side up.

Bake at Gas No. 7 (425°F/220°C) for 15 minutes, or until a rich brown. Immediately turn out on to a cooling rack. These are nicest when fresh or slightly warmed. Reheat in a foil parcel in a moderate oven, Gas No. 4 (350°F/180°C), until just warm to the touch - about 15 minutes (or in the microwave).

PRESERVES

JAMS, JELLIES AND PICKLES

Spending a few back-breaking hours at the local fruit farm each summer may evoke a half-forgotten folk memory from *'der heim'*, but picking a harvest of berries and currants to freeze, purée and jam is well worth it come the long, cold winter.

For earlier generations, jamming and pickling were essential household skills if a family was to enjoy fruits and vegetables beyond their natural growing period in a climate as extreme as that of Eastern Europe. My mother's generation – English-born but of immigrant parents – continued the tradition, often using copper preserving pans their mothers had brought with them, but added English preserves such as lemon curd and blackcurrant and strawberry jams. Much of this activity centred on preparations for the different festivals and this is a tradition that still survives today in many Jewish homes. Rosh Hashanah is not complete without home-pickled cucumber, and Pesach means stirring great pans of 'eingemacht'. In former days these luscious conserves of fruits suspended in a thick syrup were eaten with a spoon, accompanied by a glass of scalding-hot Russian tea, but today they are more likely to be treated as jam and used as a spread for buttered matzah or as a filling for a sponge cake.

I don't want to break the link in the chain, so I have tried to simplify the process by using modern kitchen technology – preserving some of the jams by freezing rather than by boiling and others by cooking in the microwave. My husband (for his part) still follows the old family recipe for pickling cucumbers but extends their 'shelf life' by refrigerating them at their peak.

Alas, I doubt whether these ancient skills will be considered worthy of preserving by future generations. Who needs a sugary food such as jam, and pickled cucumbers can be bought at any supermarket!

However, it would be tragic if domestic arts which have been practised and perfected by countless generations of Jewish women - and men - should be lost for ever, so for this chapter I have chosen just a small selection of jams, jellies and pickles that fit into our present way of living. Other recipes can be found in the Pesach chapter (see pp. 602–7).

Jams

For the occasional jam-maker it is better to make only small batches at a time. The process is less lengthy and success seems easier. Indeed, if you grow your own fruit, it is better to jam it as it ripens, pound by pound, when it is in the optimum condition.

THE EQUIPMENT

A preserving pan of cast aluminium or stainless steel, wide-based and heavy, or a pressure cooker of similar dimensions (copper pans destroy the vitamin C). Too small a pan is useless, even for small quantities, as the sugar and fruit mixture may froth up to 3 times its own height and will boil over. The pan should only be a third full when the sugar and fruit are in it.

A large wooden spoon.

A soup ladle approximately 3 inches (7.5 cm) in diameter and *a metal jam funnel* to make it easy to spoon the hot jam into jars. A heatproof jug is another option, but the funnel avoids any possibility of drips down the side of the jar.

A wooden board on which to set the warm jars to be filled, to prevent any possibility of cracking.

Jars with rubber rings integral to the screw lids. You can reuse them many times and they do give a super seal without the fuss involved in using other types of closure - for example, cellophane and rubber rings.

At the beginning of the jam-making season (usually the end of June, when raspberries, strawberries, loganberries, gooseberries, red and blackcurrants start to ripen), sort out your stock of empty jars. Put them all to soak in very hot detergent. When the water is hand-hot, rinse the jars thoroughly in clear hot water and leave them to drain and dry, then store them in a dust-free cupboard. When it is time to make the jam, put the required number of jars into a cool oven, Gas No. 1 (275°F/140°C), and leave them to heat through while the jam is boiling. By the time the jam is ready, the jars will be well heated and the boiling jam can be poured into them without any danger of cracking the glass.

The jars can also be heated in the microwave. This is a useful method when making a small quantity of jam, or on a hot summer's day when you don't want to light the oven. Fill each jar one-third full with water and leave on 100 per cent power until bubbling - 1½-2½ minutes - then drain upside down on a paper towel.

A sugar thermometer is optional but useful. If the fruit is in the right condition and the proportions of the recipe are correct, the jam will set at exactly 200°F (104°C). The use of the thermometer wil therefore cut out all guess-work from the most uncertain part of making jam - testing for the set. However, it's only worth using if you are seriously into jam-making.

THE INGREDIENTS

The fruit Whether it is from the garden or the greengrocer, the fruit should be slightly under-rather than overripe. Its pectin and acid content - both vital to the successful setting of the jam - will then be at their optimum.

The sugar Preserving sugar is specially prepared for making jam. The sugar is in the form of large white crystals, which prevent the sugar settling in a dense layer on the bottom of the pan, as is the case with ordinary granulated sugar. This sugar also produces very little froth, so that it is unnecessary to skim the jam (which is rather wasteful) or to butter the pan. If preserving sugar is not available, granulated sugar can be successfully substituted but care must be taken to prevent the jam from burning or from frothing over.

A jam sugar already containing the natural jelling agent, pectin, is particularly useful for making jellies - follow the packet instructions for use.

Testing for a set With any of the recipes that follow, you can be sure the jam has set when the temperature on a sugar thermometer reaches 200°F (104°C). There are also 2 rule of thumb methods - the saucer test and the flake test.

The saucer test Before starting to make the jam put 3 little saucers into the freezer to chill thoroughly. When the correct cooking time has elapsed, take out 1 saucer and put a teaspoonful of jam on it. Return it to the cold for 2 or 3 minutes, and meanwhile take the pan of bubbling jam off the heat. To test for a set, push the chilled jam back with the finger. If the jam is set, the surface will form a thin skin and wrinkle slightly. If not, continue to boil and test on another saucer.

The flake test Catch a little jam in the bowl of the wooden spoon, lift it above the pan, and allow it to cool for a minute. Turn the spoon so that the jam drops from the edge. If the jam has reached the setting point, the drops of jam will run together to form a flake which breaks off cleanly and sharply from the spoon. Jam that needs further boiling will run off in a liquid stream or separate droplets.

Potting and Storing the Jam Place the required number of clean hot jars on a heatproof surface and use a ladle to fill the jars to the top through a jam funnel. Immediately cover the hot surface with a greaseproof-paper or silicone-paper disc. (If the jam is to be used within 3 months I now omit the paper disc and screw down the lid while the jam is hot.) When quite cold, screw on the lid or cover with a circle of cellophane held in place with a rubber band. Label with the variety and year.

Keep in a cool cupboard away from the light or (if there is room) at the back of the refrigerator.

All jams (other than uncooked jams) and jellies will keep at least a year in a cool, well-ventilated cupboard.

BLACKCURRANT JAM

Makes 5 lb (2.5 kg).
Keeps 1 year in a cool, well-ventilated cupboard.

A tart, refreshing jam. If you don't grow your own fruit, you can still make the jam with bought blackcurrants, provided you choose fruit which is plump and glossy, never shrivelled or dusty-looking. You may find the skins are tougher than with garden fruit (as the fruit is bound to be slightly less fresh), so it will be necessary to simmer the currants longer. This initial simmering is most important, for once the sugar has been added the fruit will not soften, however long it is cooked, and the tough skins will remain in the finished jam. This quantity will do nicely in a large thick saucepan or pressure cooker.

2 lb (900 g/4 cups) blackcurrants
$1\frac{1}{2}$ pints (850 ml/$3\frac{3}{4}$ cups) water
3 lb (1.5 kg/7 cups) granulated or preserving sugar

Remove all stalks and wash the fruit. Put into the pan with the water and simmer gently, uncovered, for 30 minutes, or until the liquid has reduced by a quarter and a berry rubbed between the fingers is absolutely soft. Have the sugar warming in a bowl, together with the jam jars, in a low oven, Gas No. 1 (275°F/140°C). Tip the sugar on to the fruit and stir with a wooden spoon until it is boiling vigorously, then allow it to bubble without stirring. After 2 minutes, start testing (see 'Testing for a Set', p. 492). If the jam has not set, boil another minute and retest. (As black-currant jam sets easily, I usually keep testing it with a wooden spoon, and when I think it is set, then I put a little in the saucer for confirmation.) Stand the warm jars on a heatproof surface and, using a soup ladle, spoon in the jam up to the top of the jars. Immediately put a wax disc on each. Allow to go cold before covering, labelling and storing (see this page).

RASPBERRY OR LOGANBERRY JAM

Makes approx 2 lb (900 g).
Keeps at least 1 year in a cool, well-ventilated cupboard.

This recipe is ideal for jamming each day's crop as it ripens in the garden. If you are making a larger quantity, to save time heat the sugar in a bowl in the oven while the fruit is simmering; for a small quantity, this is not necessary. The short cooking time gives this jam a marvellous fresh-fruit flavour. If the fruit is not freshly picked, simmer it until it is tender, then add the sugar. After the fruit and sugar have come back to the boil, it will probably take 3 minutes to reach setting point.

1 lb (450 g/2¾ cups) freshly picked fruit
(raspberries, loganberries, or a mixture of both)
1 lb (450 g/2¼ cups) sugar

Put the fruit in a heavy pan and mash it with a potato-masher or large fork to extract some of the juice. Bring to the boil, then tip in the sugar and stir until it has dissolved. Bring back to a fierce boil - that is, one that cannot be 'stirred out' with the wooden spoon. *Immediately* take the pan off the heat. Ladle the jam into warm jars and cover at once with wax discs. Allow to go cold before covering, labelling and storing (see p. 493).

WHOLE-FRUIT STRAWBERRY JAM WITH LIQUID PECTIN

Makes 5 lb (2.5 kg).
Keeps at least 1 year in a cool, well-ventilated cupboard.

This is an ideal recipe if the strawberries have been bought and need to be washed. The jam has a delicious fresh flavour and colour, with the whole fruit in a lightly set jelly.

2¼ lb (1 kg/7 cups) small strawberries
3 tbsp lemon juice (1 large lemon)
3 lb (1.5 kg/7 cups) sugar
½ x 8 fl oz (125 ml/½ cup) bottle liquid pectin
nut of butter

Hull the fruit and wash quickly if necessary. Put in a pan with the lemon juice and sugar. Stand for 1 hour, stirring occasionally. When the sugar has dissolved, add a small nut of butter to reduce foaming. Bring to a full, rolling boil, and boil rapidly for 4 minutes, stirring from time to time. Remove from the heat, add the pectin and stir very well. Cool for at least 20 minutes, or until a skin begins to form on top (this stops the fruit floating to the top of the jar). Ladle the jam into warm jars and cover at once with wax discs. Allow to go cold before covering, labelling and storing (see p. 493).

ECONOMICAL RASPBERRY JAM

Makes 10 lb (4.5 kg).
Keeps at least 1 year in a cool, well-ventilated cupboard.

This uses commercial pectin to 'extend' the jam - particularly useful if the fruit has to be purchased. It makes an excellent jam.

4 lb (2 kg/13 cups) raspberries
5½ lb (2.75 kg/12 cups) sugar
1 x 8 fl oz (225 ml/1 cup) bottle liquid pectin

Crush the berries. Add the sugar and heat slowly until dissolved, stirring continually. Bring to a full, rolling boil quickly and boil hard for 2 minutes. Remove from the heat, add the pectin and stir very well. Cool for 20 minutes, until a skin begins to form on top (this prevents the fruit rising to the top of the jar). Ladle the jam into warm jars and cover at once with wax discs. Allow to go cold before covering, labelling and storing (see p. 493).

Note When making half the quantity, boiling the fruit and sugar for 1 minute is enough.

UNCOOKED STRAWBERRY JAM

Makes about 6 lb (3 kg).
Refrigerate for up to 3 months.
Freeze 2 years.

I must confess that the only way I ever make strawberry jam today is in this *uncooked* version. This method avoids any guesswork about the setting point, there's no sticky pan to clean, the vitamin C content is undiminished and it tastes exactly like the newly picked fruit. Children will love it in brown bread sandwiches spread with cream cheese. Adults will enjoy it on scones or buttering kuchen. And you can stir a spoonful of it into a winter fruit salad or natural yoghurt or fromage frais to give it the taste of summer.

This is a new, improved version with a lovely wobbly jell. Allow to defrost for about half an hour before using.

2½ lb (1.25 kg/8 cups) firm strawberries
3 lb 12 oz (1.7 kg/8¼ cups) caster sugar
4 tbsp lemon juice
1 x 8 fl oz (225 ml/1 cup) bottle liquid pectin

Whirl the strawberries for 4 seconds in a food processor or crush with a potato-masher to a rough pulp, then turn into a very large glass or plastic basin (don't use metal) and stir in the sugar and lemon juice. Leave until the sugar dissolves completely in the strawberry juice, stirring occasionally - about 2 hours. Stir in the pectin, mixing thoroughly but gently. Divide between ½-lb (225-g) jam jars or plastic cups - it doesn't set so well in 1-lb (450-g) jars - then cover with a lid or foil and leave on a window ledge for 2-4 days, or until lightly set when tested with a spoon (sunshine hastens the process). It will be a *soft* set, more like a conserve than a jam. Freeze or refrigerate.

VARIATION

UNCOOKED RASPBERRY JAM

Make exactly as before but use 2½ lb (1.25 kg/8 cups) of raspberries. The flavour is quite magnificent.

MORELLO CONSERVE
(Spiced Cherry Jam)

Makes 5-6 lb (2.5-3 kg) (depending on juiciness of the cherries).
Keeps 1 year in a cool, well-ventilated cupboard.

This was a favourite conserve of the immigrant Jews from Eastern Europe, where the Morello (sour red) cherry flourishes. The cherries were also used to make 'vishnik' - a very potent cherry brandy.

I make this superb conserve with Morellos from a tree in the garden which is still bearing fruit after 30 years. You can buy Morello cherries or other tart cherries, but I don't advise using a sweet variety as the flavour tends to be insipid.

Over the years I have gradually reduced the amount of sugar in the conserve, so it's now got a wonderful sweet and sour flavour - it's very tart when freshly made but *softens* after a few days. It is worth investing in a really efficient cherry-stoner, preferably one with a plunger rather than a pincer action (the latter is tediously slow).

3 lb (1.5 kg/7 cups) granulated or preserving sugar
4 lb (2 kg/ 3 cups) Morello cherries
(3 lb/1.5 kg/6 cups when stoned)
juice of 1 large lemon (3 tbsp), or 1 teasp tartaric acid (sour salt) crystals, or 1 teasp citric acid crystals
½ level teasp ground cinnamon
½ level teasp mixed spice
1 x 8 fl oz (225 ml/1 cup) bottle liquid pectin

Wash the jars thoroughly, then put in a low oven, Gas No. 1 (275°F/140°C), to dry and warm while making the jam. Weigh the sugar and put that in the oven at the same time. Stone the cherries, reserving the juice.

Put the cherries and juice into the pan, bring to the boil, then simmer for 5 minutes, or until a cherry feels tender when rubbed between the thumb and forefinger (this preliminary cooking can be omitted if cherries are very ripe and the skins tender). Add the sugar and the lemon juice or acid, stir until the sugar is dissolved, then add the spices. Bring to a full, rolling boil that cannot be stirred out. Boil hard for 3 minutes, stir in the pectin and continue to boil for a further 3-5 minutes, or until the jam falls off the wooden spoon in flakes rather than in droplets. Leave in the pan until a skin begins to form on the surface - about 15-20 minutes. Take the hot jars from the oven. Put on a heatproof surface, then fill with the conserve. Cover the jars immediately with a wax disc and lid when cold (see p. 493).

VARIATION

FRENCH MORELLO CHERRY AND VANILLA CONSERVE

Proceed exactly as above but omit the spices. Add a vanilla pod to the pan once the sugar is dissolved. Remove the pod just before potting the conserve (it can be washed, dried and used again).

Jellies

REDCURRANT AND PORT JELLY

Makes 5 small jars.
Keeps at least 1 year in a cool, well-ventilated cupboard.

Add a little Kiddush (port-type) wine to the traditional recipe and you get 5 small jars of shimmering ruby jelly from just 3 lb (1.5 kg) of the fresh fruit. Redcurrants are so high in natural pectin - the enzyme which helps jams and jellies to set - that the recipe works equally well with frozen fruit. Redcurrant jelly is invaluable for both sweet and savoury dishes. It can be used to glaze fruit flans, to add shine to a lamb roast or sauce, or to mix with orange juice, lemon juice and a little cornflour for a Cumberland sauce to serve with cold poultry.

3 lb (1.5 kg) redcurrants
approx. 1 pint (575 ml/2½ cups) cold water
1½ lb (675 g/3¼ cups) preserving sugar
4 tbsp Kiddush (port-type) wine

Strip the berries from their stalks using a fork, then put them into a preserving pan and add water to barely cover the fruit. Simmer, uncovered, until the fruit is absolutely tender and reduced to a thick pulp - about 20 minutes. Pour into a scalded jelly bag or butter-muslin bag, and allow to drip overnight without squeezing or pushing the fruit through - I suspend the bag over an upturned stool and place a large bowl underneath to catch the juice. Next day, measure the liquid. There should be about 1½ pints (850 ml/3¾ cups) but if not, make it up with a little water, then return to the pan and add the sugar and the wine. Heat gently until the sugar dissolves, then boil vigorously until the jelly sets - usually in 5-6 minutes. Carefully skim the scum from the surface with a spoon dipped in boiling water, then pour the jelly into jars which have been sterilized by heating in a low oven, Gas No. 1 (275°/140°C), for 10 minutes or in the microwave (see p. 492). Cover and, when quite cold, store in a dark cupboard.

APPLE MINT JELLY

Makes about $3\frac{1}{2}$ lb (1.75 kg).
Keeps in a cool cupboard up to 2 years.

Every time I would wait until the crab-apples were ripe in September to make mint jelly - by which time the mint was flowering and way past its prime. Recently, I've given the mint priority and used ordinary baking apples instead. The result is a superbly flavoured jelly, deliciously tart and minty, and equally good with lamb or cold cuts, as a dressing for new potatoes or to whisk in by the teaspoonful to flavour vinaigrette. I've also tried using special 'jam' sugar containing pectin (see p. 492), which ensures a perfect set.

You will need a jelly bag, suspended on a stand or an upturned stool.

For the apple juice

3 lb (1.5 kg) Bramley's (baking) apples
$1\frac{1}{4}$ pints (725 ml/3 cups) water
1 big bunch of mint
1 pint (575 ml/$2\frac{1}{2}$ cups) cider vinegar

For the jelly

the strained apple juice (approx. 2 pints/$1\frac{1}{4}$ l/5 cups)
2 lb (900 g/$4\frac{1}{2}$ cups) jam sugar with pectin or granulated sugar if unavailable
6 tbsp ($1\frac{1}{2}$ oz/40 g) chopped apple mint or spearmint

Quarter the washed apples, then put them in a preserving pan with the water and the washed and bruised bunch of mint (bash with a rolling pin). Cover and cook until the apples have fallen and are absolutely soft. Add the vinegar and boil gently, half-covered, for 10 minutes. Turn into the dampened jelly bag and allow to drip overnight - the thick pulp will miraculously produce a cloudy liquid. Discard the apple pulp and mint.

Next day, to hasten the making of the jelly, put the liquid in the preserving pan to heat up and the sugar (in a heatproof bowl) either into a moderate oven, Gas No. 4 (350°F/180°C), for 10 minutes or in the microwave on 100 per cent power for 4 minutes until it feels warm to the touch (*not* in a plastic container as the heat of the sugar may melt it). Add to the liquid and bring to the boil, stirring until the sugar has completely dissolved. Bring to a fast boil and cook uncovered for about 15 minutes, or until the jelly falls off the spoon in large globules rather than drops. Skim off the white froth with a perforated spoon dipped in hot water, then leave for 15 minutes to cool. When a skin is beginning to form on the top, stir in the mint. Spoon into small hot jars, cover with a disc of paper and allow to go quite cold, then cover with a screw-top lid with a rubber inset.

Store in a cool cupboard or at the back of the refrigerator.

CRAB-APPLE JELLY

Makes $1\frac{1}{2}$ lb (675 g/3 cups).
Keeps 1 year in a cool, well-ventilated cupboard.

If you intend to make jelly every year, then it's worth buying a proper jelly bag, which ensures that clear rather than cloudy juice is extracted from the fruit. Otherwise you will have to improvise a bag with a double thickness of butter-muslin (cheesecloth).

Pick the fruit when it is barely ripe as that is when it has the highest content of pectin - the natural jelling agent which helps to set the jelly. For the same reason do not peel or core the fruit, as the peel and the core section are both rich in pectin.

For the crab-apple juice

2 lb (900 g) crab-apples
1 pint (575 ml/$2\frac{1}{2}$ cups) cold water, or just enough to cover the fruit

For the jelly

1 pint (575 ml/$2\frac{1}{2}$ cups) crab-apple juice
juice and grated rind of $\frac{1}{2}$ large lemon
1 lb (450 g/2 cups) preserving or granulated sugar

Remove the stalks from the crab-apples but

leave the fruit whole. Wash them in cold water and drain in a colander, then place in a preserving pan, cover with the water and bring to the boil. Reduce the heat, then simmer very gently, stirring and crushing the fruit occasionally, until it is absolutely tender - this will take about an hour.

Dampen the jelly bag, then suspend it over a large bowl - an easy way to do this is to fix the loops over the legs of an upturned stool. Turn the fruit pulp into the bag and leave it to drip through overnight - do not press the juice through the bag or the jelly will be cloudy.

Next day, measure the juice - there should be about 1 pint. If it is short of the amount by only 1 or 2 tablespoons, make up the quantity with water; otherwise use proportionately less sugar. Set the oven to Gas No. 1 (275°F/140°C). Wash 4 small glass jars (each with a capacity of approximately 6 fl oz (175 ml/¾ cup), rinse them in hot water, then stand them upside down on an oven shelf to dry and heat through. Put the crab-apple juice, lemon juice and lemon rind into the preserving pan and add the sugar, then cook, stirring, until the sugar has dissolved. Bring to the boil and cook without stirring until it will set (see pp. 492-3) - about 8-10 minutes. Remove any scum from the surface with a wet metal spoon. Pour into the hot jars and cover each jar with a waxed disc. Cover with cellophane or lids when cold.

Frozen Fruit Purées

It's useful to freeze these purées in plastic cups covered with foil. Then, come winter, they can be defrosted and used as a sauce for ice-cream or sorbets, spooned over sliced peaches or nectarines, mixed into yoghurt or used with an equal amount of fromage frais as a topping for a fresh or dried fruit salad, or served with cheesecake or fruit mousse.

STRAWBERRY PURÉE

Whirl 3 oz (75 g/⅓ cup) of caster (superfine) sugar and 2 teaspoons of lemon juice to every 1 lb (450 g) of fruit for 2 minutes in the food processor - the mixture thickens naturally on standing. You can use 6 level tablespoons of granular sweetener instead of the sugar, but the purée won't thicken in the same way.

RASPBERRY PURÉE

Sieve the fruit to remove the pips, then process as for the strawberry purée, using 4 oz (125 g/½ cup) of sugar per 1 lb (450 g) of fruit.

BLACKCURRANT PURÉE

For each 1 lb (450 g) of fruit, dissolve 5 oz (150 g/⅔ cup) of granulated sugar in 8 fl oz (225 ml/1 cup) of water, then simmer the fruit in this syrup in a covered pan until tender - about 10 minutes. Push through a mouli or sieve, then freeze as before.

Special Preserves

OLIVIA'S POMERANTZEN
(*Glacé candied citrus peels*)

Keeps 1 year in an airtight container in the refrigerator or a well-ventilated cupboard.

These delectable 'frivolities' are cooked in the microwave - it doesn't shorten the cooking time dramatically, but it does avoid a lot of tedious pan-watching. However, it is important to use a microwave-safe ceramic dish - the sugar gets too hot for plastic or even heatproof glass. Otherwise, simmer the peel in the syrup on top of the stove.

As fruit is eaten, the *skins* should be collected and stored in a polythene bag or plastic container and kept tightly closed in the refrigerator - they keep about 5 days.

This recipe does demand patience but I think the delicious result is well worth the effort. To gild the lily, dip the glacé peel (unsugared) in melted chocolate. Pomerantzen are a favourite sweetmeat of Jews of German extraction.

peel of 3 grapefruit, 3 oranges, 2 lemons, 2 limes
4 tbsp salt
1 gallon water (4½/20 cups)

For the syrup
2 lb (900 g/4½ cups) golden granulated sugar
15 fl oz (425 ml/2 cups) water
3 heaped tbsp golden (corn) syrup

Leave the peel to soak in the salted water overnight, covered with a large plate. Put a weight on top of the plate to ensure all the fruit is submerged.

The following morning, pour off the water and rinse the peels thoroughly. Put them in a large pan and cover with unsalted cold water. Bring to the boil and simmer for a few minutes. Repeat 3 times, using fresh cold water each time to remove the bitterness from the peels.

Cool the peels, then remove all the white pith, using a serrated grapefruit spoon or a sharp, serrated, pointed paring knife. Work from the centre of the peel towards the edge. Leave to drain in a colander.

While the peel is draining, prepare the syrup. Put all the ingredients in a large pan over medium heat or in the microwave, and stir every 5 minutes until syrup and sugar have dissolved and liquid is simmering - 15-20 minutes.

Divide the peels into 2 batches and, using a serrated knife, cut into strips about ⅜ inch (1 cm) wide. Put each batch in a microwave-safe bowl and cover with half the syrup.

Cook a batch at a time in the microwave, starting on 100 per cent power and producing a heat that keeps the syrup simmering. When the peel is transparent - about 25 minutes - remove from the syrup with a slotted spoon and drain in a colander until the excess syrup has drained off. Repeat with the second batch.

Cover a cake rack with silicone or greaseproof paper and place the peel on it. Sift a little granulated sugar on to the strips of peel and turn a few times during the drying, which will take 2 days in all. Pack in airtight containers - jam jars, for example - and keep in the refrigerator or a well-ventilated cupboard.

CUMBERLAND RUM BUTTER

Makes approx. 1¼ lb (575 g).
Keeps 6 months in the refrigerator.

There is no vestige of Jewish influence in this recipe. It was given to me by a friend from Cumberland and I can only say it's absolutely delicious spread on hot toast or scones or with a steamed Chanukkah pudding.

8 oz (225 g/1 cup) butter
12 oz (350 g/1½ cups) caster (superfine) sugar
½ teasp nutmeg
½ teasp cinnamon
3 fl oz (75 ml/⅓ cup) rum

Warm the butter until it is of a thick pouring consistency (not hot) - about 30 seconds on defrost in the microwave. Pour gradually on to the caster sugar, which has been mixed with the spices. Beat thoroughly until smooth and free from sugar crystals. Add the rum and beat well again. Pour into little glass dishes. When set, dredge with caster sugar.

MINCEMEAT

Makes 2½ lb (1.25 kg).
Keeps 6 months in the refrigerator, 3 weeks in the larder.

This is a flavourful mixture quickly made and always available for making into Brandied Mincemeat and Almond Braid (see p. 397) or as a filling for baked apples or little tarts. It's made with butter or margarine instead of the suet traditional in the English recipe, so that it not only has a superb flavour but can also be served cold if desired.

1½ lb (675 g/5 cups) mixed dried fruit
10 oz (275 g) apples, grated coarsely
4 oz (125 g/1 cup) walnuts, chopped coarsely
2 oz (50 g/⅜ cup) glacé (candied) cherries, chopped coarsely
2 tbsp ginger marmalade
2 tbsp warm golden (corn) syrup
2 oz (50 g/¼ cup) soft brown sugar
1 teasp cinnamon
½ teasp mixed spice
¼ teasp ground nutmeg
rind and juice of a medium lemon (3 tbsp)
2 tbsp each brandy and Kiddush (port-type) wine
2 oz (50 g/¼ cup) melted butter or margarine

Combine all the ingredients in a large mixing bowl in the order given. Leave in the bowl for 2 days before potting.

Note 8 oz (225 g) mincemeat will fill 12 mincepies.

Pickles Plus

HAIMISCHE PICKLED CUCUMBERS

Makes 10 lb (5 kg).
Keeps 4–6 weeks under refrigeration.

This is the most delicious version of the pickle that I know, traditional to my husband's family (which originated from Lithuania), and always prepared by the male members of it. I've only ever come across a similar taste once - in the Nasch Market in Vienna - and those cucumbers (*'Ugekes'* in Yiddish) were fished out of a big black barrel. Maybe they don't take kindly to the modern pickle-factory production line!

The refinement of refrigeration has been added in this generation, and it does maintain the cucumbers at their peak for a far longer period than in the past. The cucumbers are usually pickled a month before the New Year, so that they provide a very special treat for the holiday.

Although the recipe must have developed through folk knowledge and experience passed on from generation to generation, the method is absolutely correct when measured against today's knowledge of the scientific principles involved - for example, we now know that the initial scrubbing of the cucumbers is essential to remove surface moulds and yeast, which although invisible to the eye would cause spoilage if not removed in this way.

2 gallons (10 l/40 cups) water
1 lb (450 g) coarse cooking or koshering salt
10 lb (5 kg) firm green gherkins or ridge cucumbers (4–6 inches/10–15 cm long)

For the spices
4 medium pieces dried root ginger
6 red pickling peppers
6 cloves garlic, peeled
1 level tbsp mixed pickling spice
6 bay leaves
2 teasp (33%) acetic acid

Put the water into a large pan and add the salt and all the ingredients except the cucumbers. Bring to the boil, stirring until the salt has dissolved. Boil rapidly for 5 minutes. Take off the heat and leave until absolutely cold. Scrub the cucumbers thoroughly with a small soft-bristle nailbrush (kept especially for the purpose), discarding any that have soft or diseased parts. Rinse them in cold water, then use them to fill a plastic or enamel bucket to within 3 inches (7.5 cm) of the top. As each layer is put in the bucket, scatter on it some of the spices strained from the liquid. Cover the cucumbers with a large, upturned plate, then weigh it down with a heavy weight such as a clean brick sealed in a plastic bag. Pour the cold pickling solution down the side of the bucket until it covers the plate to the depth of 1 inch (2.5 cm). Cover with a muslin cloth or thin tea-towel and leave in a cool place, such as an outhouse, for 10 days, After 10 days, skim off the froth that will have appeared on the surface. Cover again and leave for a further week. Skim again, and test by slicing into a cucumber. If the taste is not right, leave them for a further week, or until ready (the speed of the pickling depends on the ambient temperature). When the cucumbers are ready, skim again, pack into large plastic or glass containers and fill up with the pickling liquid until the cucumbers are completely submerged. Store in the refrigerator.

NEW GREEN CUCUMBERS

Makes 2 x 2-pint (1.25-l) jars of cucumbers.

We Jews have long had a special talent for the art of pickling. In the villages of Eastern Europe herrings, cabbage, beetroot and even white fish were 'gipikilte' in their season, to add a little spice to a diet that was all too often lacking in flavour. It is interesting to note that the medieval English word 'pykyll' is similar to the Yiddish *'gipikilte'*, which in turn is derived from the old Dutch and German *'pekel'*.

Perhaps such linguistic similarities are not so surprising, as pickling, one of the oldest methods of food preservation, is practised in every part of the world. The Chinese have their pickled vegetables, the British their pickled walnuts, the Indians their chutneys, the Americans their pickled watermelon. The major Jewish contribution is undoubtedly the pickled cucumber, and in particular the small ridge cucumbers or gherkins that come into season in August, just in time for putting down for the High Holy Days. However, always in season, equally delicious and far less complicated to prepare are New Green Cucumbers, which take only about 5 minutes to prepare and 4 days to mature in the refrigerator. Since I cannot find a recipe for these in any of my English or American Jewish cookery books, this suggests they are a fairly recent invention that is simply handed down from one generation of a family to the other. All the recipes I've found seem to originate in London and come from cooks whose families originated in Romania.

2 large fine cucumbers
2 tbsp (33%) acetic acid
2 level tbsp cooking salt
1 level tbsp granulated sugar or granular sweetener

For the spices
4 level teasp mixed pickling spice
4 chillies
2 level teasp black peppercorns
2 cloves of peeled and chopped garlic

Wash and rinse 2 x 2-pint (1.25-l) jars (as used for commercial pickled cucumbers). Wash the cucumbers, cut each in half crosswise, then in 4 lengthwise and then into 3-inch (7.5-cm) lengths (some people prefer them much smaller). Divide the pieces of cucumber between the jars. Put the acid, salt and sugar into a 2-pint (1.25-l/5-cup) measure, then fill up to the top with cold water. Stir well to dissolve the salt and sugar, then divide the mixture between the 2 jars. Put half the spices into each jar, screw on the lid tightly and then turn upside down to distribute evenly. Leave in the refrigerator for 4 days, turning each day. (You can start tasting after 2 days.) They keep as long as your family let them.

A Trio of Spiced Fruits

A sweet spiced vinegar not only acts as a preservative for fresh fruit but also permeates the flesh with a wonderful sweet and sour flavour. These 3 pickles are excellent with all cold meats and poultry. I find it best to keep them in the refrigerator, as they are not sterilized before storage. The damsons and kumquats can be kept in this way for a year; the peaches are best used within a week as they tend to go flabby if kept for a longer period.

SPICED DAMSONS

Makes 2 lb (900 g).
Keeps up to 1 year in the refrigerator.

This richly spiced pickle, which can be made from either fresh or frozen fruit, is cooked in the oven to prevent the skin of the fruit from bursting. Keep 1 week before using. It's delicious with roast poultry (especially duck) and lamb.

2 lb (900 g) ripe damsons
1 lb (450 g/2½ cups) soft light brown sugar
2 teasp lemon rind, finely grated
¼ teasp ground cloves
¼ teasp allspice
¼ teasp ground ginger
½ teasp ground cinnamon
½ pint (275 ml/1¼ cups) white vinegar

Preheat the oven to Gas No. 4 (350°F/180°C). Leave the damsons whole but prick each one all over with a fork. Put the sugar, lemon rind, spices and vinegar into a pan and heat until all the sugar has dissolved, stirring constantly. Arrange the damsons in 1 layer in a lidded heatproof casserole and pour the hot vinegar syrup over them. Cover and cook in the oven for 35 minutes, or until the damsons are tender but unbroken.

Meanwhile, wash and rinse 2 1-lb (450-g) jars with lids. Put in the oven to heat through after the damsons have been cooking for 30 minutes. Spoon the damsons with the vinegar into the hot jars and cover tightly. When cold, refrigerate for 1 week before serving.

SPICED KUMQUATS

Makes 1 lb (450 g).
Keeps at least 3 months under refrigeration.

As the pickle matures, the unpeeled fruit become translucent and tender. The flavour is superb. Keep for 3 weeks before using.

1 lb (450 g) kumquats
1 lb (450 g/2¼ cups) granulated sugar
1 stick cinnamon
6 cloves
3 blades mace
2 cardamom pods
8 fl oz (225 ml/1 cup) cider vinegar

Place the kumquats in a saucepan, barely cover with water and simmer covered for 10 minutes. Meanwhile, dissolve the sugar with the spices in the vinegar. Bring to the boil and cook for 5 minutes. Drain the kumquats and reserve the cooking liquid. Place them in the syrup and if necessary add some of the reserved liquid so that the fruit is barely covered. Simmer, covered, for 30 minutes. Remove from the heat and leave uncovered for 24 hours, turning in the syrup once or twice. Next day bring back to the boil, drain the fruit and pack in jars heated as for jam (see p. 492). Bring the syrup back to the boil and boil hard to thicken slightly. Pour over the kumquats with the spices. Cover and refrigerate.

SPICED PEACHES

A simple but delicious sweet-sour relish, very quickly made. It's particularly good with cold turkey. Make the day beforehand to allow the flavours to permeate the peaches.

2 large cans peach halves (16 halves)
whole cloves
8 fl oz (225 ml/1 cup) peach syrup from can
8 fl oz (225 ml/1 cup) malt or cider vinegar
3-inch (7.5-cm) stick cinnamon or pinch ground cinnamon
4 oz (125 g/½ cup) granulated sugar

Stud each peach half with 3 cloves. Simmer the remaining ingredients uncovered for 3-4 minutes, then add the peach halves. Cool, then turn the peaches and syrup into a screw-top jar and store overnight. Serve the drained halves with meat or fish.

BALLYMALOE TOMATO CHUTNEY

Keeps 1 year under refrigeration.

Irish hotelier Myrtle Allen makes this superb chutney from the last small but ripe tomatoes left on the tomato plants at the end of the season. It's lovely with curries or cold meats, but she also uses it to spark up her Cheese Fondue (see p. 111).

3 lb (1.5 kg) ripe tomatoes
8 oz (225 g) shallots or onions
1 lb (450 g/2¼ cups) granulated sugar
4 oz (125 g/¾ cup) sultanas (white raisins)
1 tbsp salt
1 teasp white pepper
3 level teasp mustard seed
½ teasp allspice
1½ pints (900 ml/3¾ cups) vinegar

Skin the tomatoes and roughly chop the shallots or onions. Put all the other ingredients into a heavy-based pan and bring to the boil. Add the tomatoes and onions and simmer slowly without a lid until thick. Pot and keep like jam.

APPLE AND MINT SAUCE

Serves 6–8.
Keeps 2 days under refrigeration.

This is a very refreshing version - the apple softens the tartness of the lemon juice or vinegar. It can be made in the food processor, provided the apple is added last and not over-chopped. A Granny Smith apple is best as it retains its good colour.

6 good sprigs of mint
2 tbsp caster (superfine) sugar
juice of 2 lemons, made up to 5 fl oz (150 ml/ ⅔ cup) with wine vinegar or cider vinegar
1 Granny Smith apple

Remove the leaves of the mint from the stalks. Chop very finely with the sugar, then add to the lemon juice, wine vinegar and finely chopped apple. Leave to stand in order to dissolve the sugar, stirring from time to time. It may be found necessary to use more sugar, according to taste.

COOKING FOR A CROWD

ENTERTAINING

The tradition of hospitality to 'the stranger within the gates' has been part of the Jewish way of family life from the very dawn of our recorded history.

Indeed, from the famous occasion when Abraham ordered Sarah to 'make ready 3 measures of fine meal, knead it and make cakes' for 3 strangers he saw coming out of the desert, it has been the custom even in the most humble of households and in the most difficult of circumstances to welcome guests to the family table.

It was when times were particularly troublesome that the necessity for the *mitzvah* (pious deed or divine command) of hospitality was most urgent. An interesting picture of the way European Jews in the early Middle Ages kept open doors for their persecuted co-religionists can be found in *The Rabbi of Bacharach* by Heinrich Heine. In that story, a place at the family's Passover table was always kept for the fellow Jew who might be pursued by 'blood libel' persecutors, and the tradition was continued all through those centuries when the Jews lived in tight little isolated communities surrounded by a hostile population. The manner of offering hospitality to both family and friends has, of course, been constantly reinterpreted according to the customs of the host country. In Russia, the samovar was always kept ready to offer a glass of lemon tea, accompanied by a 'kichel' or a slice of 'plava' or 'lekach'. In the countries of the Austro-Hungarian Empire there would be a glass of schnapps or a cup of coffee with kuchen or strudel. In Germany, it might be cheesecake or kugelhopf and a glass of beer (Jews were great brewers until driven from the craft). In the Sephardi communities, trays of baklava and delicate buttery gereybes, or melt in the mouth filo boreks filled with cheese were offered with a cup of Turkish-style coffee flavoured with cardamom. American Jews who took the customs of *'der heim'* to the New World were soon quick to adopt more modern modes of entertaining, such as the brunch, the dinner party or the buffet supper.

It is interesting to trace the new trends in Jewish hospitality that have developed since the end of the Second World War. Immediately after the war, particularly in the United Kingdom, the warmth of one's welcome was equated with the amount of (rationed) sugar-rich confections that could be crammed on to the table. But a later, more diet-conscious generation took up with enthusiasm the concept of the dinner and supper party. This was an innovation in the pattern of Jewish entertaining customs, for in the nineteenth century, though guests were often invited to join the family table - particularly on the Sabbath and Holy Days - they were never invited to a meal that had been specifically prepared for them, unless there was a wedding or a barmitzvah to be celebrated.

Today the Jewish hostess has to face entirely new situations. No longer do we live and move in the limited social circles - usually family-centred - of earlier generations, but we find our friends in ever widening spheres. And at the moment in our history when careers after marriage and increasing involvement in community life and social welfare leave even less time for 'ancillary' activities, the Jewish woman is expected to entertain in a more sophisticated fashion than ever before, paying attention to the flowers, the décor and the table accoutrements as well as to the food that she sets before her guests.

Now, however, as we approach the end of the twentieth century, new trends towards easier, less formal entertaining are developing in every Jewish community. No longer is the warmth of hospitality judged by the labour the hostess has expended on preparation. The kosher food factory or specialized deli can offer a huge variety of ready-to-serve food, *almost* as good as mama used to make! However, the most successful ploy is to combine these foods with home-made ones, however simple, and this is particularly successful when composing a demi-deli lunch or a same-day invitation for lunch or supper. There are, of course, times when a more formal meal better suits the occasion, or when there is cause to celebrate a special happening with a drinks party. Suggestions for all these different scenarios are given in this chapter, but using every resource of modern food and food-preparation machine technology. Sarah, I'm sure, would have welcomed a food processor when she had to make those 'short order' cakes for the angels!

The Dinner Party

The dinner party is perhaps the most satisfying way of entertaining a fairly small group of people. Carefully chosen and cooked food is served in the maximum of comfort in a pleasing setting, so that conditions are perfect for relaxation and conversation. However, don't put all your effort into the food – I reckon it contributes only about 50 per cent to a successful evening. The rest is up to the guests.

The number of guests In the average home, a maximum of 10 guests is perhaps the most that can be seated round a table and served a hot meal in comfort, though 6–8 is probably the best number to sustain a single animated conversation. More guests can be accommodated if smaller tables are used, but this then becomes a more formal occasion.

The setting An imaginatively set table adds excitement to a meal as much as the quality of the food. Indeed, some of the most successful hostesses I know have built their reputation on serving simple but beautifully presented food at a table set with carefully chosen linen, flowers and accessories.

The service Unless this is a formal dinner party, it is usual for the hostess to serve, assisted by a member of the family (husband, or teenage son or daughter) or by a waitress. The hostess usually serves the main course (preferably from a hot plate set on a sideboard or serving trolley), and the guests help themselves to vegetables and salads. It is usual to have the first course on the table before the guests sit down (unles it is a hot soup), and the dessert laid on a trolley or sideboard for service by the hostess.

The food Today it is fashionable to serve no more than 3 courses or 4 on special occasions. It is important to contrast hot food with cold, crisp with soft, and spicy with bland. Colour is also vital, as a monochrome meal can be excessively dull. In planning the menu, consider also practical details. If there is no one to dish up in the kitchen, have only 1 (or at the most 2) hot courses, and those chosen to need no last-minute attention. Choose recipes that can be kept hot without spoiling, as guests are not always as prompt as they might be. In general, plan the menu round seasonal food, as it will then be in its prime. Do not serve too many exotic or unusual dishes in the same menu or they will cancel each other out.

Pre-preparation Even the working hostess can

serve a superb dinner party if she plans the menu so that the preparation can be staggered over several cooking sessions. Freeze as much as possible - for example, pastry cases, sauces, dessert components - though avoid a completely frozen menu as this can be deadly dull. Use the refrigerator also to store those foods, particularly soups, casseroles and desserts, which improve overnight.

Once the menu has been planned, compile a master shopping list and then divide it into different types of food - greengrocer, grocery, delicatessen, etc. Make sure there is room cleared in the refrigerator and freezer for all the food that will be required.

Make a rough timetable, both for shopping and preparation of the different components of the meal, such as sauces, salad dressing, fruit and vegetable preparation. As these are checked off the list, it's most reassuring and avoids last-minute panics. Check all the items that are necessary for the table-setting, so that these can be washed and, if necessary, polished well beforehand and the table set early in the day. It is best to buy flowers the day before and soak them overnight, then arrange them early on the day, otherwise you won't have either time or patience to do the job later on.

Unless you have staff to do most of the preparation (and certainly the cooking), I do not think it is practical for the working hostess to plan a dinner party on a weekday - the ad hoc supper (see p. 515) or demi-deli meal (see p. 514) is much less stressful.

Drinks before dinner A maximum of 2 drinks before dinner ensures that the guests will still be able to appreciate the nuances of flavour in the food - more will certainly dull the palate. I do not believe in serving elaborate canapés or appetizers unless these are planned as a first course in themselves. Rather serve appetite-provoking foods such as pickled cucumbers, olives or savoury dips. For a hot meal I think it is also wise to be specific as to the time at which dinner is to be served. The best formula is to state 'come at 8 for 8.30', allowing 30 minutes' leeway for guests to arrive, meet their fellow guests and relax over a drink.

Drinks during the meal This is always the province of the host, who pours the wine himself. For non-wine drinkers it is wise to have a selection of chilled alcohol-free wines or fruit juices and spring water at hand.

Coffee after the meal The tray for coffee should be prepared beforehand, and the coffee pot itself left to warm during the meal. It is a matter of preference whether the coffee is served at the table or in the living room, though if conversation is flourishing round the table it is best not to interrupt it by moving to another room. (Do make sure your chairs are comfortable enough to stand up to 3 hours' sitting down on them!) With the coffee, serve petits fours or sweetmeats such as nougat, bitter chocolate, mints, crystallized ginger or Turkish Delight, which will round off the meal rather than overload it.

I have served in my own home all the menus that follow. They have been chosen because they represent my philosophy of dinner-party planning as set out above. Further dinner party menus can be found in the 'Festival Foods' sections (see p. 555).

Menus

MENU 1 BEEF

Fresh Peach and Avocado Salad (see p. 19)
matzah crackers or fingers of challah
Roast Ribs of Beef with a 3-pepper Coating (see p. 172)
Individual Yorkshire Puddings (see p. 173)
Roast Potatoes (see p. 268)
Parsnip and Walnut Purée (see p. 261)
Fresh Apricot and Franzipane Flan (see p. 379)
Cherries Cooked in Their Own Juices (see p. 321)

This is a wonderful menu for a family celebration. The magnificent rib roast can be borne in to the dining room to be admired before being carved discreetly in the kitchen (an electric knife makes short work of the job). The extras that accompany a roast do require some last-minute attention, but this can all be given in the essential 'resting' time before the meat is carved, when the oven can be turned up to crisp the roast potatoes and cook the Yorkshire Pudding. The parsnip purée can be cooked (or frozen) in advance - it reheats well in the regular oven or the microwave. The cherries can be poached up to 3 days in advance; the tartes are best made on the day - otherwise reheat them gently just before dinner to recrisp the pastry.

MENU 2 LAMB

Avocado aux Anchois (see p. 18)
Honey and Hazelnut Rolls (see p. 470)
Patlican Kebabi (Lamb and Aubergine Braise) (see p. 187)
Bulgur Pilaff (see p. 277)
A Sauté of Green Beans and Almonds (see p. 250)
Apple Marzipan Pie (see p. 376)
Orange and Ginger Salad (see p. 331)

Hazelnut oil goes well with avocados, so use it in the dressing as well as in the delicious, slightly chewy rolls. The lamb is a famous Turkish dish, simple but luscious in flavour - how convenient, too, that it improves with reheating! It marries very well with the light texture of the pilaff. The richness of the marzipan in the stunning pie is offset by the refreshing simplicity of the fruit salad.

MENU 3 VEAL

Butternut Squash Soup with Ginger and Lime (see p. 41)
Stuffed Shoulder of Veal Braised in Vermouth (see p. 191)
Oven-crisp Potatoes, Lyonnaise Style (see p. 269)
Lime-scented Courgette Ribbons with Sesame Seeds (see p. 257)
A Toasted Nut and Wild Berry Strudel (see p. 391)
Raspberry and Redcurrant Sorbet (see p. 364)

Now that you can be confident that veal is produced humanely, a boned and roast shoulder can be reinstated as a premier dinner-party dish - good-tempered (it doesn't spoil if kept waiting), always tender and, when braised in an aromatic liquid, full of flavour. The fruitiness of the elegant strudel is emphasized by partnering it with a matching sorbet.

MENU 4 CHICKEN

Tomato Soup with Fresh Basil and Croûtons (for a meat soup) (see p. 33)
Poulet Vallée d'Auge (Chicken in an Apple-scented Sauce) (see p. 215)
Gratin of Potatoes for a Meat Meal (see p. 270)
Stir-fried Whole Green Beans and Mushrooms (see p. 250)
La Tarte Montmorency (see p. 385)
Autumn Peach and Orange Compôte (see p. 323)

The chicken dish at the heart of this menu has a sauce that's wonderfully rich and fruity yet light. Together with the vegetables, it's best cooked on the day, but the soup and both the desserts take kindly to refrigeration overnight. The soup can also be frozen but without the basil, which should be added during the reheating process.

MENU 5
FRESH SALMON

Curried Cream of Broccoli Soup (see p. 44)
Walnut Granary Bread (see p. 469)
Fillets of Salmon under a Crushed Pecan Crust, garnished with miniature asparagus (see p. 79)
Gratin of Potatoes Dauphinois (see p. 270)
Minted petit pois
Chicory Salad in the French Manner (see p. 284)
Stilton and grapes
Frozen Ginger Parfait garnished with Cape Gooseberries (see p. 356)
Vanilla Kipferl (see p. 445)

A crunchy topping of finely chopped nuts, bound together with a little herbed butter, creates a superb 'crust' under which the salmon stays moist and creamy as it is briefly baked. The luscious gratin of potatoes can be left in a low oven or warm spot in the kitchen and should stay hot for those few minutes, but can always be briefly flashed under the grill (broiler) while the salmon cools a little before serving. The soup, bread and dessert all freeze well.

MENU 6 LEMON SOLE

Chilled Ogen or Galia Melon on the Half-Shell (see p. 15)
Fillets of Sole in Herbed Pastry Envelopes (see p. 85)
Golden New Potatoes (see p. 268)
Gratin of Courgettes (see p. 257)
Salade Menton (see p. 286)
Summer Fruits with Cream and Crunch (see p. 338)
White Moss Gewürztraminer Sorbet (see p. 364)

A simple but sophisticated meal, perfect for a lovely evening in spring or summer, with a magnificent presentation of sole and smoked salmon wrapped in herb-flavoured pastry being the only time-consuming part of the menu.

MENU 7
FISH KEBABS, TURKISH STYLE

Caponata alla siciliana (see p. 95)
Granary Bread (see p. 468)
Samak Kebab (see p. 81)
Tomates Provençales (see p. 265)
Grilled Mushrooms (see p. 260)
New potatoes boiled in their skins
Halva and Pistachio Ice-cream (see p. 359)
Fresh Apricot Compôte (see p. 321)

A light – and light-hearted – meal with a main dish of white fish kebabs marinated in a wondrous marinade that quite transforms even everyday fish such as cod and haddock into something rich and rare. The starter and dessert are both made well in advance, which leaves only a grilling session for the main course on the day. The many and varied flavours of the vegetable ragoût do need 24–48 hours in the refrigerator to meld; the apricot compôte also deepens in flavour if treated in the same way.

MENU 8
VEGETARIAN WITH A BROWN-PASTRY TOURTE

Caved Katsis Tsimchoni (Aubergine Pâté)
(see p. 94)
Ilse Eton's Pumpernickel (see p. 466)
Tourte Forestière (Mushroom Flan) (see p. 127)
Bean, Red Pepper and Hearts of Artichoke Salad
(see p. 288)
Tabbouleh (see p. 295)
Scented Strawberries with an Orange Liqueur
Cream (see p. 332)
Chana's Nussestrudel (see p. 393)

Whole foods of many kinds, including an abundance of colourful grains, nuts, fresh vegetables and fruits, make this dinner a feast for the eye as well as the palate.

The tourte reheats well, so it can be made the day before, together with the richly flavoured vegetable pâté and the salads. The nussestrudel and the wonderful sour-dough bread can be frozen whenever convenient.

MENU 9
VEGETARIAN WITH PASTA

Basque Sweet Pepper and Rice Soup (see p. 41)
Mixed Grain Bread (see p. 468)
Pesto Lasagne (see p. 113)
A Salad of Spring Leaves with a Nut-oil Dressing
(see p. 284)
Melon and Cherry Tomato Salad (see p. 294)
Gingered Fresh Peach, Amaretto and Hazelnut
Crumble (see p. 312)
Honeyed Greek-style yoghurt

The vegetarian version of the delectable soup with the 4-grain bread is almost a meal in itself. However, there are even more satisfying flavours to come in the elegant lasagne and the trio of salads. The unusual crumble can happily share the oven with the lasagne, making this a very convenient menu.

The Buffet Lunch or Supper

This is one of my favourite ways of entertaining any number of friends from 6–12 and upwards. It's more informal than a dinner party and often more satisfying socially for close friends than a cocktail or drinks party. It's also a convenient way of simplifying the preparations that are inevitably involved in cooking and serving meals for friends.

The set-up The cold food is placed on 1 table, the hot food on a hotplate (preferably on a sideboard or serving table), the sweets on a trolley – or they can be part of the table decorations. Guests help themselves and then sit informally at 1 or more tables according to numbers. These can be set with the cutlery or it can be collected with the food and plates at the table.

The menu and service Usually the food consists of hot casseroles or savoury pastries, with salads and rice or pasta accompaniment, followed by a selection of desserts. A 'hold-in-the-hand' first course – usually a dip or a spread – is offered with the pre-dinner drinks (see p. 509), or it could be a hot or cold soup served after drinks.

Guest serve themselves with the main course, and then the dessert trolley is wheeled round to them, together with the coffee. Accompanying drinks are served by the host as they eat (see pp. 520–21) for ideas on punches and other mixed drinks).

Pre-preparations This kind of entertaining lends itself particularly well to freezing in advance. Only salads and fresh fruit desserts needs to be made on the day of the party. (These do-ahead jobs are given with each menu.)

Meat, fish and dairy menus can be used successfully, though 1 hot dish at least should always be included in the menu for variety. Equally important is to contrast crunchy foods with smooth ones, bland flavours with highly spiced mixtures. While a supper-party menu can be similar in form to a dinner party - with informal service making the main distinction - it can also be based much more simply on pizzas or savoury quiches, or indeed on a variety of cheese, cheese dips and pickled and spiced fish, followed by a simple dessert, or Danish pastries and fruit.

The menus that follow are only suggestions. You can, of course, mix and match them with your own tried and trusted recipes.

Menus

MENU 1
CHICKEN AND MEAT

Pasteles (see p. 164)
Nutty Rice (see p. 276)
Crêpe Princesse (see p. 222)
Israeli Fruited Winter Salad (see p. 287)
Piquant String Beans (see p. 288)
Swiss Chocolate Pavlova (with non-dairy cream) (see p. 346)
Persian Honeyed Fruits (see p. 327)

Plan your timetable carefully and this becomes an easy-to-manage supper, with all the dishes ready in advance in the fridge or freezer, needing only the finishing touches on the day. The only exception is the Winter Salad, the ingredients for which should be combined shortly before serving.

MENU 2
WITH TURKEY AND MEAT

Chicken Soup with Hobene Gropen (see p. 36)
Turkey Celebration Salad (see p. 230)
Savoury Moroccan Strudel (see p. 163)
A Good Rice Salad (see p. 295)
Orange, Chicory and Toasted Sesame Salad (see p. 285)
A Mulled Weinchadeau Cup (with parev *cream) (see p. 338)*
Lebanese Filo Pastries with a 3-nut Filling (see p. 404)

The wonderfully satisfying soup with its 'creamy' texture makes an unusual start to the meal. (It can be kept on a hotplate, with guests helping themselves.) Be sure to leave time for the wine and spices to macerate together for the Weinchadeau Cup. The luscious little pastries (they keep fresh at room temperature for several weeks) provide an exotic finale to the meal. Serve them with plenty of strong black coffee to counteract their sweetness.

MENU 3
WITH FISH IN PASTRY

Hummus b'Tahina with Toasted Pine Kernels (see p. 528)
Chatzilim (see p. 22)
Warm brown pitta bread
Salmon Kulebiaka with Dilled Fromage Frais (see p. 86)
Pimento, Black Olive and Orange Salad (see p. 291)
Chicory Salad in the French Manner (see p. 284)
Hot Herb Bread (see p. 544)
Tranche de Fraises Provençale (see p. 386)
Liqueur Parfait (see p. 356)

The dips can be part of the buffet or offered with drinks before this innovative menu, which needs very little last-minute attention. The wonderful strawberry slice will look spectacular on the table.

MENU 4 TRADITIONAL FISH DISHES

Carrot, Orange and Coriander Soup (see p. 40)
Buttered Croûtons (see p. 53)
Chopped Fried Fish with Chrane (pink horseradish sauce) (see p. 65)
or
Terrine of Gefilte Fish with a Pink Mayonnaise Sauce (see p. 68)
New Green Cucumbers (see p. 501)
Gefilte Fish in Egg and Lemon Sauce (see p. 640)
Baked Potatoes (see p. 266)
Spiced Mushrooms (see p. 291)
Provençale Tomato Salad (see p. 293)
Bread and Butter Pudding Deluxe (see p. 308)
Whole Oranges in Cointreau Syrup (see p. 330)

Even the most sophisticated guest will relish these traditional dishes which are so rarely made today except on special occasions. The baked potatoes make a pleasing contrast with the highly seasoned salad. As there's nothing else to go in the oven, the pudding in its large water bath can have the space all to itself - it will need it!

MENU 5 VEGETARIAN WITH MINIATURE PIZZAS

Petites Pissaladières (see p. 124)
Salade Menton (see p. 286)
Bean and Pasta Salad (see p. 116)
English farmhouse cheeses, grape clusters and celery
Greek Walnut Bread (see p. 471)
A Brilliant Brûlée (see p. 340)
Mango and Ginger Sorbet (see p. 363)

Follow the recipe carefully and the Pissaladières will be very easy to time, even with their yeast base. The mango sorbet is particularly quick to make, but there are excellent varieties to buy if you prefer.

MENU 6 VEGETARIAN WITH A FILO-PASTRY STRUDEL

Asparagus Strudel with a Minted Cucumber Sauce (see p. 117)
Badinjan Kuku (Baked Aubergine Omelette) (see p. 162)
A Salad of Tomatoes, Mozzarella and Avocado (see p. 294)
Danish Cucumber Salad (see p. 289)
4-fruit Salad (in an Ice Bowl) (see pp. 326, 325)
Kumquat Blitz Torte (see p. 348)

The wonderful desserts are the stars of this menu - the fruit salad in its glittering bowl and the spectacular many-layered torte, the simple 'construction' of which belies its sophisticated appearance.

The Demi-Deli Brunch or Supper

If you augment the Sunday bagel with a careful trawl through the deli-counter's more interesting titbits, you're well on your way to a hassle-free Sunday lunch. And the same formula can be used in the evening, adding perhaps a spectacular home-made dessert.

Besides roast and pickled poultry, meats and salamis, fried, smoked and marinated fish, delis can provide salads and dips such as chopped herring, hummus and taramasalata, not to mention vegetable kibbes and samosas. Look out for canned exotica such as vineleaves stuffed with rice and 'patlican dolmasi' - a delicious ragout of aubergines (eggplants) stuffed with rice, pine kernels and currants in a tomato sauce.

For a dairy meal there's now a huge choice of kosher cheeses. A good cheeseboard might include an English farmhouse, a blue and a creamy one. To make a light main course, cubes of Israeli feta can be added to a simple cucumber and tomato salad or slices of mozzarella alternated with tomato and avocado, then topped with a herby vinaigrette. And if you decide to pick up a strudel to serve with coffee, recrisp it in the oven and then 'customize' it by serving with it fromage frais (the 8% creamy variety) sweetened with a spoonful of liquid honey, and a scattering of ready-toasted flaked or nibbed almonds.

If you can persuade someone else to do the shopping, it will give you time to add the 'home-made' touch. This might be a steaming bowl of a home-made soup (check whether you have one in the freezer) or a trio of unusual mezzes whizzed up in the food processor - the home-made versions are superior in taste and texture to most of those you can buy, so give them a whirl. It's only worth making your own, though, if you can do so a day or so in advance, to give the flavours a chance to develop.

Menus

Suggestions for the home-made contribution.

MENU 1
A FISH OR DAIRY MEAL

From the freezer
Spinach and Green Pea Soup with Fresh Mint (see p. 42)

From the refrigerator
(made in minutes by food processor)
Provençale Tuna Pâté (see p. 529)
Liptauer Cheese (see p. 528)
Aubergine and Yoghurt Mezze (see p. 326)

An instant dessert
Strawberries in the Venetian Manner with honeyed yoghurt, (see p. 328), with bought sponge cake

MENU 2
A MEAT MEAL

From the freezer
Hungarian Goulash Soup (see p. 38)

From the refrigerator
Egg and Spring Onion Forspeise (see p. 6)
Chatzilim (see p. 22)

An instant dessert
Strawberries (or other fruits in season) in a Raspberry Sauce (see p. 328)

The Ad Hoc Meal

Setting another place at the table was once the hospitality norm in the Jewish household. The dishes people cooked in those days - meatballs, tsimmes, chopped and fried fish - made it easy to accommodate an 'elastic' number of guests at short notice.

But that all seemed too '*haimishe*' for the post-war generation. The 1950s was the decade of the 'evening', when hostesses vied with each other to load the table with the largest variety of cakes they could concoct from their sugar ration as well as great platters of savoury 'bunnies' (bridge rolls).

In the 1960s, bridge rolls were banished in favour of the supper party: cold cuts and hot dogs followed by *parev* chocolate mousse and fruit salad - a formula which culminated in the late 1970s with the quiche and savoury dip.

The 1980s were the era of the dinner party - the more elaborate the better - with butchers working overtime to bone and trim, stuff and roll so that Carré d'Agneau and Beef Wellington could appear on even the most kosher of tables.

Now it's all become too much hassle, even with modern gadgets. A new and welcome trend in entertaining is the same-day invitation: 'Would you like to pop round for something to eat - nothing special. How about this evening?'

Both hostess and guest know this is a coded message which means: 'We'd love to see you but we haven't the time/energy/desire to go in for a full-scale dinner party.'

So let's plan for a relaxed meal for a few close friends that can be put together in under an hour and requires the minimum of shopping.

If you want to make a habit of this kind of impromptu entertaining, you will need a good stock of 'et ceteras', such as coating crumbs or matzah meal, ready-grated frozen cheese, raw, (preferably) home-frozen fish, good-quality pasta, tuna and nuts. I also like to keep a small stock of interesting fruits and vegetables in the fridge.

Menus

All the food can be prepared on the day with the minimum of time spent in the kitchen. Besides foods from 'stock', allow time the day before to pick up meat or fish (if not in the freezer) and any special fruit and vegetables.

MENU 1
A FISH MEAL

Drinks and bought nibbles
Fillets of Trout under a Cheese Crust (see p. 82)
or
Tagliatelle al Tonno (see p. 90)
A Salad of Spring Leaves (see p. 284)
(use a prepacked mixture)
Assorted cheeses with grapes and celery
Part-baked Ciabatta (Italian-style) rolls
Scarlet Fruits (see below) and bought sorbet

For a superb aperitif, combine one part Crème de Pêche with four parts of a fruity white wine.

Liven up the usual nuts and crisps with these savoury mouthfuls: halve and de-pip 3-4 cherry tomatoes per person, spread each half thickly with bought pesto, then sandwich with a tiny cube of feta cheese and spear with a toothpick.

For the dessert, dissolve 3 tablespoons of sugar or granular sweetener in the juice of a large lemon, stir in 2 tablespoons of raspberry or orange liqueur (or non-alcoholic grenadine), then pour over a mixture of soft red fruits as available - you will need 2 lb (900 kg) in all. Serve with scoops of bought passion-fruit sorbet.

MENU 2
A MEAT MEAL

Drinks and bought nibbles
Lamb Chops Glazed with Moutarde de Meaux
(see p. 184)
Noodles with Fresh Basil (see p. 280)
Sugar snap peas
Pear and Brandy Crunch Pudding (see p. 313)
Bowl of clementines

A chilled fino sherry makes a perfect aperitif to sharpen the appetite. A small pot of liver pâté from the freezer spread on fingers of challah marries well with it.

The mustard gives a rich glaze to the chops; tarragon mustard is even better than plain Dijon.

Frozen noodles reheat well in the microwave (reheat for 3-4 minutes on 100 per cent power in a covered dish, or until steaming).

For the crumble use soft *parev* margarine instead of butter. If you can't find a fresh mango, forget it.

MENU 3
A VEGETARIAN MEAL

Taratour (see p. 47) with a brown loaf (see p. 467)
from the freezer or granary bread from the baker
Lovage Soufflé (see p. 108)
Kibbutz Salad (see p. 292)
Feuilleton aux Abricots with Ice-cream (see p. 394)
A bowl of fresh lychees

The splendid bread can be eaten throughout the meal, to accompany both the no-cook herb-scented soup and the soufflé. The sauce base of the soufflé can be made early in the day (dot the surface with a little butter to stop a skin forming). Just before baking (make sure the oven is well and truly heated to temperature), heat the sauce until lukewarm to the touch, then *fold* in the egg white and bake.

The feuilleton is quickly put together with bought puff pastry.

Join Us for Drinks

Although it's far from traditional in the Jewish canon of entertaining, the informal drinks party can be a very pleasant - and practical - way of entertaining a large group of friends, particularly if one moves in several 'worlds' and wants to have the opportunity of mixing them.

The Time Morning from 11 am–1 pm (12–2 pm if you are providing a 'fork' meal) or evenings from 6–8 pm is probably the best. Two hours seems to me the maximum time that one can comfortably stand and chat. After that the party can sink under waves of guest-exhaustion!

The Help This depends on the formality of the occasion. The drinks must be the concern of at least one person - either a professional barman or a son or daughter of the house. The food can be either passed round by waitresses or scattered on tables with easy access, with young members of the family passing round the hot food. For more than 50 guests it is useful to have some help both in the preparation of the food before the guests arrive and to ensure a regular supply of hot-from-the-oven food as it is required - you will enjoy the party much more and have time to socialize. Many freelance waitresses will help with both food preparation and service; they will also advise you on the number of staff you require and on quantities to provide, according to the size of the guest list.

Ambience Part of the charm of a drinks party lies in the fact that it is easy to pass from one group to another. So the room should be as clear of furniture as possible, with chairs and sofas pushed into the corners for those who want to have a brief sit-down. Don't ask more guests than the room will hold - while it is essential to have enough guests to fill the room comfortably, there must also be enough space for them to move around from one group to another.

As a change from 'straight' wine and to add sparkle to a party, there's nothing to equal a champagne cocktail, made using one of the many excellent bubbly alternatives reinforced with brandy, or a Buck's Fizz, made with equal quantities of orange juice and wine. Equally good as an ice-breaker is a Kir, together with its various relations, made with either still or sparkling wine. This type of drink consists of a sweet fruit liqueur such as Crème de Cassis (as in the original), Framboise (raspberry), Fraise (strawberry) or Pêche (peach). The drill is to put 1 or 2 tablespoons of the chosen liqueur in a wine glass, then, as the guests arrive, fill up with a well-chilled, fairly dry white wine or a sparkling one.

For larger numbers, there are the fruit cups or punches - mixtures of fruit and wine pepped up with a spirit such as brandy or rum and/or liqueur that can be made more or less alcoholic depending on the proportions of wine used. You can even use lemonade as a mixer if you prefer. There are also some delicious drinks completely without alcohol - sparkling grape and apple juice are particularly good options.

Menus

In this section of the book there is a wide selection of drinks, dips and spreads, rolled sandwiches and hot titbits suitable for a drinks party, together with quantities to allow and other background information.

The menus below have proved their worth at actual parties, but are only given as a 'kick-start' to your own ideas.

MENU 1
FISH AND VEGETABLE

Courgette Pâté on biscuits (see p. 94)
La Tapenade on biscuits (see p. 529)
Savoury Bites with Mushroom Filling (see p. 533)
Cocktail Fish Balls (see p. 536) with lightly curried natural yoghurt
Stilton and Walnut Slice (see p. 534)
Satsumas
Coffee Praline Meringue Cups (see p. 547)

MENU 2
FISH AND VEGETABLE

Low-fat Smoked-mackerel Mousse (see p. 13) with crisps and crudités
Cherry Tomato Mezze (see p. 25)
Asparagus Rolls (see p. 530)
Smoked Salmon Rolls (see p. 530)
Smoked Boreks (hot) (see p. 533)
Individual Party Pizza (hot) (see p. 532)
Strawberries with a Raspberry Sauce (see p. 328) for dipping
Slices of Date Roll from Damascus (see p. 406)
or
Rum and Mincemeat Squares (see p. 399)

MENU 3
VEGETARIAN

On slices of brown French stick:
Avocado and Coriander Dip (see p. 527)
Pineapple and Cream Cheese Spread (see p. 525)
or
Walnut and Cream Cheese Spread (see p. 526)
Babâ Ghanoush with triangles of pitta bread (see p. 23)
Cheese and Olive Tartlets (see p. 531)
Savoury Sephardi Cheesecakes (see p. 534)
Bowls of black and green grapes
Chana's Nussestrudel (see p. 393)

FOOD — A GUIDE TO QUANTITIES

As with the drink, it is impossible to give precise quantities for this kind of party. However, from experience I have worked out the following rule of thumb. For each guest allow:

4-5 canapés and closed sandwiches and 2 small rolled sandwiches
2-3 hot snacks (depending on size) as well as assorted dips and nibbles
2-3 biscuits or pastries (depending on size)

Remember that almost all freshly made food can be frozen if extra to requirements.

THE FOLLOWING INFORMATION MAY BE HELPFUL

1 long French stick (18 inches/45 cm) cuts into 50-60 slices.
1 x 7 oz (200 g) packet of savoury crackers contains 40-50.
1 large sliced loaf contains approx. 25-30 slices, according to thickness
A spread containing 6-8 oz (175-225 g) of cream cheese, minced fish or liver is enough for 40-50 canapés.
8-12 oz (225-350 g) of sliced meat or poultry and 1 large sliced loaf make approx. 50 tiny closed sandwiches (quarter of a large slice).

TO MAKE CANAPÉS AND SANDWICHES IN ADVANCE

Always cover tightly with clingfilm (saranwrap) or foil and refrigerate or leave in a cool place.

Open French bread canapés Make up to 4 hours in advance.

Closed sandwiches Make up to 4 hours in advance.

Savoury cracker or toast canapés Make up to 1 hour in advance.

Rolled sandwiches Make not less than 2 hours but up to 12 hours in advance (in which case cover with foil).

DRINK — A GUIDE TO QUANTITIES

If possible, arrange to have the drinks on a sale or return basis - many wine merchants will do this if the quantity is large enough - so that you can always have a comfortable reserve. The quantity drunk will depend on many different factors - the time of year, the temperature of the room, the kind of food served and the age of the guests. However, as a rough guide, allow half to one-third of a bottle of wine per person.

Here is a guide I have found reliable for a party of 50, serving a sparkling wine cocktail or white, red or rosé wine as the main drink.

For champagne or sparkling wine cocktails

15–18 bottles
1 bottle 3 star brandy
1 bottle Angostura bitters
1 lb (450 g) sugar lumps
1 jar (8 oz/225 g) maraschino cherries
6 oranges (for garnish)

Red, white or rosé wine

18–20 bottles
The price, as well as personal preference, will probably guide your choice.

General drinks

1 bottle whisky
1 bottle gin
1 bottle vodka
1 bottle brandy
12 bottles ginger ale
12 bottles bitter lemon
6 bottles tonic water
6 cans beer
2 bottles cordial
2 x 1 litre cans tomato juice
soda water
2 x 1 litre packs each orange juice and exotic fruit juice
1 x 1 litre pack apple juice
(Note *Pasteurized juice in cartons has a refrigerator life of approx. 10 days.)*
4 litres spring water

Et ceteras

100 cocktail sticks (extra as needed for food on sticks)
8 dozen cocktail-size paper napkins
large pack each oval dish papers and doilies
7 dozen champagne flutes (borrow from wine merchant)
assorted glasses for short and long drinks

HOT PUNCH
(*Gluhwein*)

Serves 25.

During the winter months, perhaps the best drink to serve is that wonderful hot and spicy punch Gluhwein. And as the only way to get the flavour just right is to taste as you go along, it'll be as popular with the host as with his guests. It is an excellent replacement for shorts.

You'll need your largest soup pan, and if possible an electric hotplate to keep the drink hot. The exact spicing is a matter of personal preference, so keep on tasting! It is sometimes possible to buy a special Gluhwein Spice pack at wine merchants or department stores.

1 teasp cinnamon or 2 cinnamon sticks
1¾ pints (1 l/4½ cups) water
4–8 oz (125–225 g/1½–1 cup) sugar (see below)
12 cloves
¼ teasp ground nutmeg
peel of 1 large orange
1 lemon, sliced
4 litres any moderately priced fruity red wine
5 fl oz (150 ml/⅔ cup) Cointreau or other orange-flavoured liqueur

Over moderate heat, dissolve the minimum quantity of sugar in the water with the spices, peel and sliced lemon. Simmer 5 minutes, then add the wine. Taste and keep on adding extra sugar until the taste is right. (This will depend on the dryness of the wine.) Cover and leave at steaming point (*do not boil*) for about an hour. Shortly before serving, bring back to steaming point and add Cointreau.

CLASSIC CHAMPAGNE COCKTAIL

Serves 30 (2 wine glasses each).

Perfect for a drinks party.

sugar lumps
Angostura bitters
1 bottle brandy (an inexpensive one, eg grape brandy, is fine)
8 bottles sparkling white wine (preferably 'Méthode Champenoise')

Put a sugar lump into each glass and add 3 drops of bitters to each. Add at least 1 tablespoon brandy and top up with wine immediately before serving. (Optional: add 1 slice frozen lemon to each glass.)

MYER'S FRUIT PUNCH

Serves approx. 10–12.

A juicy, fruity punch – a splendid ice-breaker before a supper party.

½ bottle orange and pineapple cordial
¼ bottle lime juice cordial
1 tbsp Angostura bitters
4 fl oz (125 ml/½ cup) gin
1 small liqueur glass (3 fl oz/75 ml/⅓ cup) any liqueur
approx. 4 x 1 litre bottles fizzy lemonade

For the garnish
orange and lemon slices
cucumber slices
fresh mint sprigs (if available)
8 oz (225 g) seedless green grapes

Pour the liquid ingredients (except lemonade) in order given into very large bowl. When ready to serve, decant into jugs and dilute to taste with the chilled lemonade. Garnish with orange, lemon, cucumber, mint and grapes.

SANGRIA BLANCA

Serves 4–6.

Truly a peach of a drink to serve before a dinner party.

1 small lemon, thinly sliced
1 small orange, thinly sliced
3 tbsp caster sugar
1 peach, peeled and thinly sliced
2 fl oz (50 ml/$^1/_4$ cup) peach brandy, schnapps or other peach-flavoured liqueur
1 x 75 cl bottle dry white wine, chilled

In a large bowl combine the lemon, orange, sugar, peach, liqueur and wine and stir until the sugar is dissolved. Chill for at least 1 hour. Strain the sangria into wine glasses and put several pieces of the fruit into each glass.

MINTY ORANGE FROST

Serves 6.

A delicious non-alcoholic 'cocktail' or pick-me-up. The fruit sugar in the orange juice gives instant energy.

juice of 6–7 large oranges or 25 fl oz (725 ml/3 cups) frozen or bottled juice
3 sprigs of mint
12 ice-cubes
3 teasp grenadine
3 teasp lemon juice

Liquidize until smooth. Serve at once.

TROPICAL WINE COCKTAIL

Serves 10–12 (2 wine glasses each).

A very refreshing drink – with a sting in the tail!

2 bottles white wine such as a Riesling or hock
1 litre apple juice or cider
2 limes, peeled like an apple but with the peel left anchored at the bottom of the fruit
1 small can pineapple titbits
1 small glass each (3 fl oz/75 ml) vodka and orange liqueur

Stir together all the ingredients, floating the limes in the liquid. Serve well chilled.

Cooking for a Crowd

There are many occasions when it is necessary to produce food in quantity, whether it be for community or fund-raising functions or for family celebrations. Provided one has reliable recipes and quantities, there are only a couple of major points to keep in mind.

First, large-scale cooking requires not only more ingredients but also more time – for bringing a large pan of water to the boil, for sautéing quantities of meat or poultry, and so on. It is essential to remember this when organizing preparation time and calculating the number of helpers that will be required. If plenty of time is allowed for a planning session, when recipes are chosen, shopping lists prepared and the timetable planned, the actual cooking will be most enjoyable – rather like playing in an orchestra instead of performing solo!

Second, correct equipment will greatly speed the preparation. This means that large enough pans and baking dishes should be borrowed or bought, and that knives should be well sharpened beforehand.

Below I give a selection of simple but useful recipes for use when catering for 50 people. They can be prepared by any proficient home cook. In addition, there are other recipes for varying numbers of people that I have found worked extremely well – with useful notes that I made at the time.

This kind of catering for large numbers cannot be an exact science - not that that would necessarily be a good thing, as each occasion has different guests with differing expectations. These recipes have proved their worth for occasions as varied as wine tastings, charity luncheons, family celebrations and International Wine and Food Society 'self-catering' functions. For all these occasions, the quality, and quantity, of the food has been all-important. Even with charity functions you have to gain a reputation for serving only the best, even if it's as simple as a ploughman's lunch, if you hope to sell tickets to the same people again.

You will find that my quantities are rather on the generous side - unlike with professional caterers, portion control is *not* the name of the game! However, if you take the precaution of having a supply of foil containers and plastic bags, it's usually very easy to sell, give away or freeze any supplies that remain at the end.

QUANTITIES

In the Table of Quantities that follows I give recommended individual servings and the actual quantities to buy. However, if the same group or committee is doing the catering, they will already have built up a rule of thumb - how many servings of salad from that bowl, how much fish can be cooked in that tray, how many portions it will produce, and so on.

I would recommend every organization to keep their own diary, making a note of the disasters as well as the triumphs.

Remember also that if you offer a choice of, for example, 3 salads, you don't have to allow 3 full servings per guest. They will take smaller servings that will work out at the equivalent of 1½ normal servings. So 50 people = 75 servings = 25 servings of each of the 3 salads, plus a little extra for good luck!

TABLE OF QUANTITIES TO SERVE 50

Food	*Serving per person*	*To order*
Bread and rolls		
crisp rolls	1-1½	4½-6½ dozen
large loaf	1-2 slices	2-3 loaves
Drinks		
cocoa	8 fl oz (225 ml/1 cup)	8 oz (225 g/2½ cups)
coffee (ground)	6½ fl oz (190 ml/¾ cup)	1-1¼ lb (450-600 g/4-5 cups)
coffee (instant)	6½ fl oz (190 ml/¾ cup) (1 teasp per cup)	2½ oz (65 g/⅔ cup) note: 1 x 100 g jar = 70 teasp
tea (amount will vary with quality and blend)	8 fl oz (225 ml/1 cup)	6 oz (150 g/2 cups)
tomato juice	3 fl oz (75 ml/⅓ cup)	7½ pints (3.75 l/18 cups)
Rice and Pasta		
noodles	5 oz (150 g/½ cup) (cooked)	4 lb (2 kg/24 cups)
macaroni or spaghetti	5 oz (150 g/½ cup) (cooked)	4-5 lb (2-2.5 kg/20-25 cups)
rice	5 cups (150 g/¼ cup) (cooked)	3 lb (1.5 kg/7 cups)

Food	*Serving per person*		*To order*
Dairy products			
butter for table	1-1½ pats		1-1½ lb (450-675 g/2-3 cups)
butter for sandwiches	2 teasp		1 lb (450 g/2 cups)
cream (non dairy creamer) for coffee	1 tbsp		1½ pints (850 ml/3¾ cups)
cream, whipping (for garnish)	1 tbsp		*¾ pint (425 ml/2 cups)*
cottage cheese	scant 3 oz (75 g/⅓ cup)		*10 lb (5 kg/20 cups)*
cheese for sandwiches	1¼ oz (35 g/¼ cup)		*4 lb (2 kg/8 cups)*
eggs	1-2		*50–100*
ice-cream, bulk	1 scoop		1½ gallons
ice-cream, brick	about ⅐ brick		7-8 family bricks
milk (for tea)	approx. 1 tbsp		3 pints (1.75 l/7¾ cups)
milk (for coffee)	*⅓ cup*		5 pints (2.5 l/12½ cups)
Fruit			
prunes	3 oz (75 g) (cooked)		5½ lb (2.75 kg)
apples (stewed)	3 oz (75 g) (raw)		15 lb (7.5 kg)
apples (for 8-inch/20 cm pie)	6-7 servings per pie		15 lb (7.5 kg)
canned fruit	4 oz (125 g)		2 x A10 cans
fruit juice (canned)	4 fl oz (125 ml/½ cup)		4 x 46 fl oz (1.15 l) cans
Meats	**cooked weight**	**raw weight**	
chuck or bola (braised)	3 oz (75 g)	5 oz (150 g)	20–22 lb (10–11 kg)
minced (ground) meat for patties	3½ oz (90 g)	4 oz (125 g)	14 lb (7 kg)
standing rib roast	3 oz (75 g)	8 oz (225 g)	25–28 lb (12.5–14 kg)
stew with vegetables	5½ oz (165 g)		15 lb (7.5 kg)
braising steak, sliced	3½ oz (90 g)	5 oz (150 g)	16 lb (8 kg)
veal chops (3 to lb/450 g)	1 each		17 lb (8.5 kg)
lamb chops (4 to lb/450 g)	2 each		25 lb (12.5 kg)
salami	2 oz (50 g)		6½ lb (3 kg)
saveloys (12 to lb/450 g)	2 each		8-10 lb (4-5 kg)
Poultry			
chicken, casseroled	¼ chicken		40 lb (20 kg) (8 hens, 5-6 lb/ 2.5-3.5 kg each, 12 chickens approx. 3½ lb/5 kg each)
chicken, fried	¼-½ chicken		13-25 fryers, 2½-3 lb (1-1.5 kg) each
turkey, roast	3 oz (75 g)		35-40 lb (17-20 kg)
Fish	**raw weight**		
fish fillets	4 oz (125 g)		12½ lb (6 kg)
fish steaks	6 oz (175 g)		20 lb (9 kg)
whole salmon (including head)	8 oz (225 g)		25 lb (12.5 kg)

Food	*Serving per person*	*To order*
Vegetables		
canned	4 oz (125 g)	2 x A10 cans
frozen	2½-3 oz (65-75 g)	7½-10 lb (3.5-5 kg)
lettuce for salad	1½-2 oz (40-50 g)	8-10 heads
lettuce for garnish		4-5 heads
potatoes, baked	6 oz (175 g)	20 lb (10 kg)
potatoes, mashed	6 oz (175 g)	20 lb (10 kg)
potatoes, roasted	6 oz (175 g)	20 lb (10 kg)
potatoes, chipped (french fries)	about 4½ oz (140 g)	12-15 lb (6-7.5 kg)
potato crisps (chips)	¾-1 oz (20-25 g)	2½-3 lb (1.25-1.5 kg)
tomatoes, sliced	3 oz (75 g)	10-12 lb (5-6 kg)
Miscellaneous		
mixed nuts		1½ lb (675 g/6 cups)
honey	2 tbsp	5 lb (2.5 kg/7½ cups)
jam	2 tbsp	5 lb (2.5 kg/7½ cups)
sugar, lump	1-2 cubes	1½ lb (675 g/5 cups)
sugar, granulated	2 teasp	1 lb (450 g/2 cups)
sugar, brown	2 teasp	1 lb (450 g/2 cups)
Desserts		
cakes	2½ oz (65 g)	2 tins, each approx. 12 x 10 inches (30 x 25 cm) - 25 pieces from each
fruit cake	2½ oz (65 g)	8 lb (4 kg)
pies, 8-inch (20-cm)		
pastry (2 crust) 12 oz (300 g) per pie		6 lb (3 kg)
pastry (1 crust) 6½ oz (165 g) per pie		3¼ lb (1.5 kg)
Salads		
vegetable (eg coleslaw)	5 fl oz (150 ml)	1½ gallons (6 l/30 cups)
potato	4 fl oz (125 ml)	1¼ gallons (5 l/25 cups)
Soups		
cream soup	5 fl oz (150 ml)	1½ gallons (6 l/30 cups)
clear soup	8 fl oz (225 ml)	2¼ gallons (9 l/45 cups)
gravy	3-4 tbsp	5-6½ pints (2½ l/12½-17½ cups)
sauce, thickened for meat	2 tbsp	2½ pints (1.25 l/6¼ cups)
mayonnaise	1½ tbsp	2 pints (1.1 l/5 cups)

COFFEE

Freshly brewed coffee for a large number is usually made in an automatic coffee-maker of one kind or another - filter or drip. Follow the maker's instructions for quantities.

However, a premium grade of freeze-dried coffee from a freshly opened jar is equally acceptable. Allow 1 teaspoon per person. A standard 100 g (3½ oz) jar contains 70 teaspoonsfuls.

Either put a teaspoon of coffee in each cup and fill up with very hot water (just off the boil for the finest flavour) *or* use large jugs with the appropriate number of teaspoonsful.

Allow 1 lb (450 g/2 cups) of demerara sugar (you will certainly have some over).

CANAPÉS

Serve canapés on crisp crackers (not cheese-flavoured) or tiny rounds of crisp French bread, well buttered. Cracker canapés should not be made more than an hour in advance as they quickly go soggy, but canapés on bread can be made up to 4 hours beforehand, provided trays or dishes are carefully wrapped in clingfilm (saranwrap) to prevent them drying out. Make each kind of canapé at a time and put on flat trays, then arrange on large platters using a variety to make an attractive pattern.

Have ready an assortment of garnishes - cucumber and tomato slices, sliced black olives, anchovies, radish slices, pickled cucumber and gherkin slices, canned pimento, chopped parsley, paprika pepper, cress.

For 50 allow 6 x 8 oz (225 g) packets of crisp crackers or 2 packets of crackers plus 4 French loaves.

LEMON BUTTER SPREAD

This is a light and low-calorie spread, excellent for use on canapés or rolled sandwiches.

4 oz (125 g/½ cup) soft butter or margarine
3 teasp fresh lemon juice
3 teasp boiling water
1 teasp grated lemon rind
pinch of salt
10 grinds of black pepper

Beat together until light.

All the following will be sufficient to spread on 40–50 rounds of French bread or crackers.

SMOKED SALMON WITH LEMON

Serve within 1 hour of preparation.

Sprinkle slices of smoked salmon with lemon juice and a little black pepper. Cut to fit crackers or bread slices. Garnish with thin sections of lemon or sliced fresh cucumber. Allow 1½ lb (675 g) salmon.

PINEAPPLE AND CREAM CHEESE

Keeps 2 days under refrigeration.
Do not freeze.

Use 8 oz (225 g/1 cup) of cream cheese blended with 1 small can of drained, crushed pineapple and 1-2 tablespoons of mayonnaise.

WALNUT AND CREAM CHEESE

Keeps 4 days under refrigeration.
Do not freeze.

Use 8 oz (225 g/1 cup) of cream cheese blended with 2 oz (50 g/½ cup) of finely chopped walnuts and 2 tablespoons of mayonnaise.

GAFFELBITTER, TOMATO AND CUCUMBER

Serve within 1 hour of preparation.

Allow 3 cans of gaffelbitter. On each biscuit place first a slice of fresh cucumber, then tomato and finally 1 drained piece of gaffelbitter.

CHOPPED HERRING SALAD

Keeps 3 days under refrigeration.
Do not freeze.

Double the quantity of recipe on p. 10. Serve on buttered black bread. Garnish with finely grated hard-boiled egg (allow 1 2-lb (900-g) black bread, plus 2 hard-boiled eggs for garnish).

EGG AND OLIVE BUTTER

Keeps 3 days under refrigeration.
Do not freeze.

Mash 6 hard-boiled eggs with 1 oz (25 g/2 tbsp) of butter, 2 tablespoons of mayonnaise and 2 oz (50 g/½ cup) of finely chopped stuffed olives. Garnish with anchovies.

DIPS AND SPREADS

All the following can be used either for dipping or for spreading as preferred. When several dips are on offer, allow 1 serving per person in total. Thus if you make 3 dips each serving 16 people, the total of all the dips will actually serve *50* people.

Serve canapés on crisp crackers (not cheese-flavoured) or crackers and buttered French bread slices.

AUBERGINE AND YOGHURT MEZZE

Serves 14–16 as a dip, 8 as a starter, 50 with 2 other dips.
Keeps 1 week under refrigeration.
Do not freeze.

Give it time to develop its cool yet spicy flavours by preparing the mixture 6 hours to 2 days ahead. Arrange in a pottery dish and serve with pitta bread, crackers or crudités.

1½ lb (675 g) oval aubergines (eggplants)
1 medium green pepper
2 large, firm tomatoes
1–2 cloves of garlic
2 tbsp extra virgin olive oil
2 tbsp lemon juice
½ teasp cumin
½ teasp salt
10 grinds of black pepper
4 rounded tbsp Greek style yoghurt or low-fat fromage frais or smetana

Prick the aubergines all over, then grill (broil) under high heat with the pepper and the whole tomatoes until the skins are charred and they look collapsed. (The aubergines will take the longest time.) Wrap in paper towels. When cool enough to handle, halve the aubergines and scoop out the flesh, strip the skin from the pepper and remove the seeds, skin the tomatoes.

Purée the vegetables in the food processor with the peeled and halved garlic, then add the olive oil, lemon juice, cumin, salt and pepper, processing until smooth and creamy. Finally, pulse in the yoghurt, fromage frais or smetana. (Without a processor use a *'hackmesser'* to purée and mix the ingredients.) Cover and chill until required.

AVOCADO DIP

Serves 16, 50 with 2 other dips.
Keeps 2 days under refrigeration.
Freeze 1 month.

This has a most distinctive flavour.

¼ onion
½ green pepper
2 medium or 1 large avocado, peeled, skinned and cut in chunks
8 oz (225 g/1 cup) low- or medium-fat soft white cheese
1 level teasp salt
20 grinds of black pepper
2 tbsp lemon juice
1 teasp snipped chives
1 teasp chopped parsley

Process all the ingredients in the food processor until absolutely smooth - texture should be like soft cream cheese.

VARIATION

AVOCADO DIP WITH SMOKED FISH

Stir in at the end 4-6 oz (125-175 g) of skinned and flaked smoked mackerel or shreds of smoked salmon.

AVOCADO AND CORIANDER DIP

Serves 10-12, 35 with 2 other dips.
Keeps 3 days under refrigeration.
Freeze 1 month.

This is lighter and spicier than the avocado and cream cheese mixture.

1 large or 2 medium, very ripe avocados
2 canned tomatoes, drained, or 2 large, peeled fresh tomatoes
¼ medium onion or ½ teasp onion salt
½ clove of garlic
1 tbsp extra virgin olive oil
1-2 tbsp lemon juice
1 teasp ground coriander
salt to taste
10 grinds of black pepper

Buy the avocados 2-3 days beforehand so that they can ripen at room temperature until they feel tender all over under gentle pressure. Halve them and remove the stones, then scoop out the flesh and cut it into rough chunks. Put it into the food processor together with all the remaining ingredients and process until smooth - about 30 seconds. Taste and adjust seasoning if necessary. Spoon into a decorative bowl and sprinkle the surface sparingly with lemon juice, which helps to retard the loss of the green colour. Cover tightly with clingfilm (saranwrap) and chill for at least 3 hours. If the surface has discoloured through oxidization, give the mixture a stir just before serving.

BLUE CHEESE DIP

Serves 6-8, 25 with 2 other dips.
Keeps 3 days under refrigeration.

5 fl oz (150 ml/⅔ cup) fromage frais (8% fat)
3 oz (75 /¾ cup) blue cheese
1 spring onion (scallion)
1 tbsp reduced-calorie mayonnaise
¼ teasp freshly ground black pepper

For the garnish
finely chopped spring onions (scallions) or chives

By hand or processor, slowly beat the fromage frais into the crumbled cheese together with the spring onion, mayonnaise and black pepper. Spoon into a dish and garnish.

HUMMUS B'TAHINA WITH TOASTED PINE KERNELS

Serves 9, 30 with 2 other dips
Keeps 3 days under refrigeration.

12 oz (350 g) good-quality ready-made hummus
2 rounded tbsp tahina
1 tbsp lemon juice
½ teasp ground cumin (if necessary)

For the garnish
small bunch parsley
1½ tbsp virgin olive oil
3 tbsp toasted pine kernels

Process the parsley with the oil in the food processor until the oil is bright green and the parsley finely chopped. Put in a small bowl. Process the other ingredients (except the nuts) till evenly blended (taste for seasoning, adding extra lemon juice if not tangy enough). Spoon into a fairly shallow dish. Just before serving, drizzle with the herbed oil and sprinkle with the pine kernels.

LIPTAUER CHEESE

Sufficient to top 60 savoury biscuits or slices of French bread.
Keeps 1 week under refrigeration.
Do not freeze.

The wonderful Viennese recipe.

10 oz (275 g/1¼ cups) low-fat soft cheese
2 teasp anchovy paste
1 level tbsp chopped capers
2 teasp prepared mustard
3 teasp paprika
pepper
celery salt
1 tbsp snipped chives

Beat all ingredients together and leave for several hours to develop flavour.

SMOKED MACKEREL SPREAD

Enough for topping 60 savoury biscuits or rolled sandwiches (see p. 530).
Keeps 4 days under refrigeration.
Freeze 6 weeks.

8 oz (225 g) smoked mackerel fillets, skinned
2 oz (50 g/¼ cup) very soft butter
2 tbsp lemon juice
10 grinds of black pepper
2 teasp horseradish relish
8 tbsp creamy 8% fromage frais or Greek-style yoghurt

Put all the ingredients except the fromage frais in the food processor or blender and process until absolutely smooth. Turn into a container and fold in the fromage frais. Taste and add more pepper if necessary.

Chill for several hours, well covered, to allow the flavours to blend. If frozen, allow 4 hours to defrost in the refrigerator.

MEXICAN CHEESE

Serves 16, 50 with 2 other dips.
Keeps 1 week under refrigeration.
Do not freeze.

A crunchy, tangy mixture that is universally popular. Make at least 24 hours before required.

green part of 2 spring onions (scallions) or 2 tbsp chives
sprig of parsley
1 tbsp mayonnaise
1 tbsp vinaigrette dressing (see p. 300)
½ teasp salt

1 tbsp natural yoghurt or fromage frais
2 oz (50 g/¼ cup) soft butter
8 oz (225 g/1 cup) low- or medium-fat soft white cheese
6 cocktail gherkins
½ large red pepper

Put the onions, parsley, mayonnaise, vinaigrette, salt and yoghurt in the food processor and process until smooth and creamy. Add butter and cream cheese and blend until smooth. Add sliced gherkins and pepper. Process until gherkins are finely chopped but still visible.

PROVENÇALE TUNA PÂTÉ

Serves 6–8.
Keeps 3 days under refrigeration.

A tongue-tingling flavour - 2 cans of sardines can be used if preferred.

large sprig parsley
1 x 7 oz (200 g) can tuna in oil, drained
6 oz (175 g/¾ cup) low-fat soft cheese
2 fat spring onion (scallion) bulbs plus 4 inches (10 cm) of the green
10 plump black olives, stoned
½ teasp mild chilli powder
½ teasp salt
8 grinds of white pepper
2 teasp wine vinegar

Put all the ingredients into the food processor and process until smooth. Turn into a small bowl, cover with clingfilm (saranwrap) and refrigerate for several hours.

SMOKED SALMON MOUSSE

Serves 10–12.
Keeps 4 days under refrigeration.
Freeze 6 weeks.

Enough for topping 60 savoury biscuits or rolled sandwiches.

8 oz (225 g) medium-priced (eg Pacific) smoked salmon
1½ oz (40 g/3 tbsp) unsalted butter or soft margarine
1½ teasp creamed horseradish
1½ teasp lemon juice
15 grinds of black pepper
10 fl oz (275 ml/1¼ cups) Greek yoghurt or 8% fromage frais

Process the salmon, fat and seasonings, then pulse in the yoghurt or fromage frais until evenly blended. Pack in a container, cover and refrigerate for several hours to allow the flavour to develop.

LA TAPENADE

Serves 12–15 with other dips.
Keeps 5 days under refrigeration.
Do not freeze (it goes very *salty).*

Serve as a dip with crudités and crackers, as a spread on crackers or toast fingers, or in home-made or bought miniature pastry cases. It has a wonderful, almost primitive flavour.

1 x 2oz (50 g) can anchovies in olive oil, drained
3 oz (75 g) whitemeat tuna, drained
24 Calamata or other large black olives, stones removed
1 small (2½ oz/65g) jar capers (about 2 heaped tbsp), drained
1 small clove of garlic
2 teasp lemon juice
1 level teasp whole grain mustard (Moutarde de Meaux)
3 teasp brandy (optional but nice)
4 hard-boiled eggs
3 fl oz (75 ml/⅓ cup) extra virgin olive oil

Purée all the ingredients (except for the oil) in the food processor until absolutely smooth, then add the olive oil through the feed tube in a slow stream as for mayonnaise. Pile into a bowl and leave several hours or overnight.

VARIATION

EGGS STUFFED WITH TAPENADE

Serve with drinks or on a cold buffet.

8 hard-boiled eggs
1 recipe Tapenade

Halve the eggs and use the yolks in the tapenade. Chill the tapenade thoroughly, then spoon or pipe into the halves of egg just before serving. Garnish with salad.

Rolled Sandwiches

These delicious mouthfuls consist of a fine-textured brown bread spread with a savoury filling, then rolled and cut in 3. They are particularly convenient to make as they must be prepared well ahead of time in order to 'set'.

ASPARAGUS ROLLS

Makes 60 tiny rolls.
Serves 30 as part of a mixed assortment of sandwiches and canapés.
Keeps 12 hours under refrigeration.
Freeze 1 month.

1 large, sliced, fine-textured brown loaf
5 oz (150 g/$^2/_3$ cup) butter
salad cream
1 x 12 oz (340 g) can asparagus tips
salt

Decrust the bread, then roll each slice with a rolling pin to make the texture more compact and so facilitate rolling.

Butter, then spread thinly with salad cream. Lay 1 or 1½ asparagus tips (according to length) along the long edge of each slice, then roll up and place join-side down on a tray. Repeat until all are completed, packing the rolls tightly together to stop them unrolling. Cover with clingfilm (saranwrap) and chill for not less than 2 hours, though they can be left for up to 12 hours (in which case cover with foil as well).

When ready to arrange, cut each roll into 2 or 3 and arrange standing on end in an entrée or similar dish about 1½ inches (4 cm) deep.

VARIATIONS

EGG AND OLIVE ROLLS

Keeps 12 hours under refrigeration.
Freeze 1 month.

Make the Egg and Olive butter on p. 526. Use to spread on each slice of bread. Roll up and cut as before.

SMOKED SALMON OR MACKEREL ROLLS

Keep 1 day under refrigeration.
Freeze 1 month.

Use either the Smoked Mackerel Spread (see p. 528) or the Smoked Salmon Mousse (see p. 529).

Butter the bread, then spread each slice generously with the chilled fish mixture. Lay 1 or 2 long strips of pickled cucumber - about ¼ inch (0.5 cm) wide - down the long side of the bread in place of the asparagus. Roll and cut as before.

SMOKED SALMON ROLLS USING SLICES OF FISH

Serves 30.
Keeps 1 day under refrigeration.
Freeze 1 month.

These are extravagant but quite superb for the special occasion.

1 very large, fresh white tin loaf, sliced
5 oz (150 g/⅔ cup) softened butter
1 tbsp lemon juice
1 level tbsp chopped parsley
10–12 oz (275–350 g) smoked salmon, very thinly sliced

Decrust the bread, then roll each slice with a rolling pin to facilitate rolling.

Beat together the butter, lemon juice and parsley, then use to butter the bread. Arrange very thin slices of salmon to cover each slice. Roll up and place each roll on a tray, join-side down. Cover with clingfilm (saranwrap) and chill for up to 12 hours, but not less than 2 hours. When ready to arrange, cut each roll into 2 or 3 and arrange standing up side by side in a dish about 1½ inches (4 cm) deep.

To freeze Pack the rolls in a rigid container with greaseproof paper or foil between the layers.

To defrost Loosen lid and thaw at room temperature for 4 hours.

For half-quantity Use 1 small loaf, 3 oz (75 g/¾ cup) of butter, 2 teaspoons of lemon juice, 2 teaspoons of chopped parsley, 6 oz (175 g) of smoked salmon.

Hot Titbits

CHEESE AND OLIVE TARTLETS

Makes 24.
Keeps 2 days under refrigeration.
Freeze pastry 3 months, baked tartlets with filling 1 month.

For the pastry
8 oz (225 g/2 cups) plain (all-purpose) flour
5 oz (150 g/⅔ cup) butter or firm margarine
pinch of salt
2 level teasp icing (confectioners') sugar
5 tbsp iced water

For the filling
1 oz (25 g/2 tbsp) butter
2 shallots or ½ small onion, finely chopped
1 tbsp cornflour (cornstarch)
10 fl oz (275 ml/1¼ cups) milk
3 eggs
1 teasp Dijon mustard
pinch of salt
10 grinds of black pepper
pinch of Cayenne pepper
6 oz (175 g/1¼ cups) grated sharp cheese (Cheddar or Lancashire)
4 oz (125 g/1 cup) stuffed olives, sliced
6 anchovy fillets cut in ¼-inch (0.5-cm) pieces (optional)

Make the pastry by either method on p. 371. Chill it for 30 minutes, then roll out to fit 24 patty tins. At this stage the cases can be chilled overnight or frozen. (There's no need to defrost them before filling or baking). Preheat the oven to Gas No. 6 (400°F/200°C).

To make the filling, melt the butter and gently sauté the shallots until soft and golden. Put the cornflour into a bowl and gradually add the milk, stirring to blend evenly. Add the eggs, mustard, salt and peppers, then whisk to blend. Finally stir in the cheese, olives and anchovies (if used). Divide the mixture between the tartlets. Bake for 20 minutes, until golden or puffed. Serve warm or cold. They may be reheated in a moderate oven, Gas No. 4 (350°F/180°C), until warm to the touch.

CHEESE FEUILLETÉ

Serves 50 (9 individual feuilletés).
Make and bake the same day
Freeze 3 months.
Thaw before baking.

9 x 12–14 oz (350–400 g) packets puff pastry
3½ lb (1.75 kg) Cheddar cheese, grated
4½ lb (2 kg) low- or medium-fat soft cheese (curd or Quark)
9 eggs
8 oz (225 g/2 cups) blue cheese – Stilton or Danish Blue
1 tbsp plus 1 teasp paprika
9 tbsp (2 oz/50 g) chopped parsley
4½ tbsp (1 oz/25 g) chopped fresh or 1 tbsp dried marjoram or oregano
9 tbsp (2 oz/50 g) snipped chives

For the glaze
3 eggs, beaten to blend
4½ tbsp sesame seeds

Follow instructions on p. 394.

INDIVIDUAL PARTY PIZZAS

Makes 50.

Double the recipe for Party Pizza on p. 123, but roll out the pastry and cut to fill 48 tartlet cases. Prick well, bake at Gas No. 7 (425°F/220°C) for 12 minutes, or until set and coloured, then freeze or store in a tin for up to a week. Fill and top as directed and bake at the same temperature for 15 minutes. Alternatively, the filling and topping can be arranged in well-pricked, unbaked cases and then baked at the same temperature for 20 minutes.

PETITES QUICHES LORRAINES, KOSHER STYLE

Makes 5.
Serve immediately.
Freeze unbaked cases 6 months.

The creamy filling contrasts well with the crisp and tender shortcrust pastry.

For the savoury shortcrust pastry
1 lb 2 oz (500 g/4½ cups) plain (all-purpose) flour
½ teasp salt
12 oz (350 g/1½ cups) butter or margarine
3 level teasps icing (confectioners') sugar
5 fl oz (150 ml/⅔ cup) water

For the filling
4 eggs
6 oz (175 g/1½ cups) finely grated mature Cheddar or tasty Lancashire cheese
1 tbsp cornflour (cornstarch)
good pinch of salt
20 grinds of black pepper
2 level tbsp chives
10 fl oz (275 ml/1¼ cups) single (light) cream
4 oz (125 g/½ cup) butter

Make pastry by either method on p. 371. Roll chilled pastry to fit 48 patty tins. Prick well. Beat eggs thoroughly, then add cheese, cornflour, seasonings and cream. (At this stage tartlets which have been frozen can be taken out of the freezer and pricked.) When ready to bake, place a small nut of butter in the bottom of each pastry case. Three-quarters fill with the cheese mixture. Bake in a preheated oven, Gas No. 6 (400°F/200°C), for 10–15 minutes, or until pastry is golden and filling is puffed.

SAVOURY BITES

Makes 72–80.
Raw bites keep 3 days under refrigeration.
Freeze raw 3 months.
Do not reheat.

These can be made with a cheese, mushroom, or herb filling.

2 lb (900 g) bought puff or home-made rough puff pastry (double the recipe on p. 403)

Roll out the pastry to the thickness of a knife blade. Cut into 2-inch diameter (5-cm) rounds. Put a teaspoon of filling (see below) in the centre, fold over and seal into a crescent. This can be done 2 days beforehand, provided the puffs are then foil-covered and refrigerated - most conveniently on the ungreased baking trays - or the puffs can be frozen uncooked. Brush with beaten egg and scatter with sesame seeds just before baking in a hot oven, Gas No. 8 (450°F/230°C), for 15 minutes. Serve warm.

CHEESE FILLING

1 lb (450 g/4 cups) sharp cheese, finely grated
3 large eggs (save ½ egg for gilding puffs)

Blend thoroughly together to make a firm but moist paste.

MUSHROOM FILLING

1 lb (450 g/5 cups) mushrooms
3 fl oz (75 ml/⅓ cup) water
juice of 1 lemon
nut of butter
1 pint (575 ml/2½ cups) milk
salt
white pepper
pinch of powdered mace or nutmeg
2 tbsp dry sherry
2 oz (50 g/¼ cup) butter
2 oz (50 g/½ cup) flour

Chop the rinsed mushrooms coarsely. Add to a pan containing the water, lemon juice and nut of butter. Cover and simmer for 3 minutes. Uncover and cook to evaporate most of the liquid.

Bring the milk to the boil, then pour into a measuring jug. Rinse out the pan and melt the butter. Stir in the flour and cook for a minute, then add the hot milk all at once off the heat and whisk until smooth. Return to the heat and bubble for 3 minutes. Season with salt, pepper and mace, then stir in the mushrooms and sherry. Allow to cool to lukewarm before using.

HERB FILLING

12 oz (350 g/1½ cups) curd cheese
8 oz (225 g/2 cups) grated hard cheese
2 large eggs (save some for gilding the puffs)
1 tbsp very finely chopped spring onion (scallion)
1 crushed clove of garlic or a pinch of ready-chopped garlic
2 level tbsp finely chopped parsley
salt and black pepper to taste

For the glaze

a little beaten egg
sesame seeds

Mix the cheeses together. In another bowl beat the eggs and add the spring onion, garlic and parsley and seasonings. Combine the two - the resulting mixture should be the consistency of a thick moist paste. Glaze with egg and sprinkle with the sesame seeds.

VARIATION

SAVOURY BOREKS

Makes 24.
Raw and cooked triangles keep 3 days under refrigeration (raw triangles brushed lightly with fat) and tightly covered with foil.
Freeze raw 3 months.

The same fillings can be used with filo pastry in the traditional Sephardi manner as follows.

8 sheets of filo pastry (about 8 oz/225 g)

Cut each sheet of filo pastry into 3 long strips, each 5 inches (12.5 cm) wide. Brush very lightly but evenly with the melted fat, then fold in half lengthwise and brush with fat again. Put 1 heaped teaspoon of the chosen filling at the bottom of a strip about 1 inch (2.5 cm) from the shorter edge and fold as illustrated.

SAVOURY BOREKS

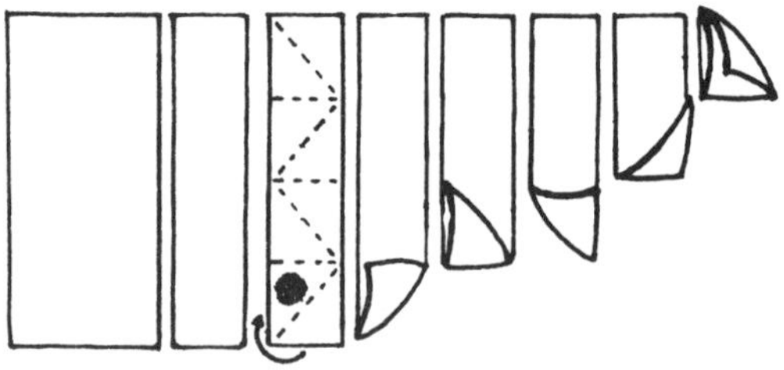

Put pastries on 2 oiled baking trays and brush again with melted fat. Bake for 20-25 minutes until crisp and golden at Gas No. 6 (400°F/200°C). Serve at room temperature. May be briefly reheated.

SAVOURY SEPHARDI CHEESECAKES

50 servings of 2 puffs per person.
Make and bake the same day.
Do not reheat.

These delicious little puffs can be served as a main course for a dairy lunch or with drinks.

2 lb (900 g/8 cups) mature Cheddar cheese, finely grated
4 large eggs
1 level teasp salt
2½ lb (1.5 kg) puff pastry

For sprinkling on the puffs
white sesame seeds

To grate cheese in the food processor, cut into pieces that will fit into the feed tube, then freeze for 1 hour. This stops the cheese from melting and gumming up the mechanism. Grate using fine grater disc, then put in a large bowl.

Whisk the eggs to blend and reserve 2 tablespoons for gilding the puffs. Add the remainder of the eggs and the salt to the cheese and mix to a sticky paste.

Roll the pastry to the thickness of a knife blade, then cut with 2½-inch (6-cm) plain cutters into approximately 100 rounds. Damp the edges of each round, place a teaspoon of filling in the centre and fold over to form a half moon. Arrange on baking trays lined with silicone paper. Just before cooking, brush with the beaten egg and dip in the sesame seeds. Bake in a hot oven, Gas No. 7 (425°F/220°C), for 10–15 minutes. Serve warm.

STILTON AND WALNUT SLICE

Makes 2 14 x 4½ inch (35 x 11 cm) rectangular or 2 9-inch (22.5-cm) round tins.
Serves 50 for cocktails, 25 on a buffet.
Pastry keeps 3 days under refrigeration and freezes 3 months.

A mouthwatering combination of flaky pastry and creamy/crunchy filling. The pastry can be frozen ahead or rolled out and used to line the tin and then baked blind. Put in the filling and freeze raw. Bake from frozen, allowing an extra 10 minutes' baking time.

For the cream cheese pastry
6 oz (175 g/¾ cups) cold butter, cut in 1-inch (2.5-cm) pieces
4 oz (125 g/½ cup) each Ricotta and herb cream cheese, or 8 oz (225 g/1 cup) Ricotta alone, or other low-fat soft white cheese
8 oz (225 g/2 cups) plain (all-purpose) flour
1 level teasp salt

For the filling

3 oz (75 g/¾ cup) walnut halves, toasted (reserve 2 oz/50 g/½ cup for the topping)
10 oz (275 g/1¼ cups) double (heavy) cream
6 oz (175 g/1½ cups) Stilton or other kosher blue cheese, crumbled
1 tbsp snipped chives
3 eggs, beaten to blend
15 grinds of black pepper
salt if necessary

For the topping

2 oz (50 g/½ cup) walnuts, toasted and chopped coarsely
2 tbsp Parmesan or other finely grated mature cheese
5 grinds of sea salt

For the garnish

1 packet watercress

First make and bake the pastry shells blind as follows. In a food processor blend the butter, cheeses, flour and salt, pulsing the motor until the dough just begins to cling together. Turn out, gather into a ball, knead lightly until smooth and then flatten into a 1-inch (2.5-cm) disc. Chill for 1 hour or leave overnight.

Chop or process the 3 oz of walnuts until very fine but still with a little texture left. Set aside. Divide the pastry in half and roll each portion to fit the chosen tins. Trim the edges well and prick lightly with a fork, then press the ground walnuts into the surface. Line with foil, pressing it into the shape of the tins, then bake in a preheated oven, Gas No. 7 (425°F/220°C), for 10 minutes. Remove the foil carefully, then bake the shells for a further 5–6 minutes, until they are golden. Let them cool on a rack.

In a saucepan combine the cream and the Stilton. Bring to the boil and stir until the cheese has just melted and the mixture is smooth. Stir in the chives. Pour on to the beaten eggs, mixing constantly. Taste and add the black pepper and a little salt if necessary. Pour into the part-baked pastry shells and bake in a quick oven, Gas No. 5 (375°F190°C), for 30-35 minutes, or until a knife inserted in the custard ½ an inch (1 cm) from the edge comes out clean. (The centre will set later.) After 15 minutes in the oven, when the tarte has begun to form a skin, sprinkle with the topping ingredients, mixed together, and continue to cook as described.

Let the tartes cool to room temperature. To serve, arrange on a platter with the watercress, or cut into neat pieces.

Fish and Cheese Dishes

NOODLE AND KAESE CASSEROLE

Serves 50.
Leftovers keep 2 days under refrigeration.
Do not freeze.

This delicious entrée can be served with salad or to accompany fish. If large, shallow baking tins approximately 1 inch (5 cm) deep are not available, use foil containers instead.

4 lb (2 kg/24 cups) broad egg noodles
4 pints (2.25 l/10 cups) soured cream
4 lb (2 kg/8 cups) curd (medium-fat) cheese
2 dozen eggs, separated
8 level tbsp chopped fresh chives or parsley
1 tbsp salt
1 level teasp black pepper
1 lb (450 g/2 cups) butter

Boil the noodles according to packet directions and drain. Pour hot water over them to remove any excess starch. Drain again and mix with the soured cream, cheese, beaten yolks, herbs and seasonings. Fold in the egg whites, beaten until they hold stiff, glossy peaks. Melt the butter. Pour half into the bottom of a shallow container approximately 24 x 20 inches (60 x 50 cm) or 2 smaller containers. Add noodle mixture. Pour remaining butter over the top. Bake in a preheated oven, Gas No. 5 (375°F/190°C), for 45 minutes, or until puffed and golden. Cut into squares.

FRIED FISH PATTIES
(*Gefilte Fish*)

50 portions of 1 patty each.
Fried fish keeps 2 days under refrigeration.
Freeze raw or cooked patties 3 months.

Follow method for Gefilte Fish Mix on p. 64 but use the following quantities.

4 lb (1 kg) haddock fillet
4 lb (2 kg) cod fillet
8 large eggs
2 large onions
2 level tbsp salt
1 level teasp white pepper
2 level tbsp sugar
4 tbsp sunflower or other flavourless oil
8 oz (225 g/2 cups) medium matzah meal

Note If blender or food processor is used for egg, onion and seasonings, add no extra water. If onion is minced, add approximately 8 fl oz (225 ml/1 cup) of water, sufficient to make the mixture soft enough to shape into patties. Fry in oil that almost covers patties. However, if the equipment is available, deep-fry for speed.

COCKTAIL FISH BALLS

Serves 50. Makes 200 small balls.
Keeps 1 day under refrigeration.
Freeze 3 months.

Prepare Gefilte Fish Mix as on p. 64 but with these ingredients.

6 lb (2.75 kg) fish
6 large eggs
3 medium onions
1½ tbsp salt
¾ teasp pepper
1½ tbsp sugar
3 tbsp sunflower or other flavourless oil
6 oz (175 g/1½ cups) medium matzah meal

The total 'wet mix' will go into a very large food processor. Use half at a time with a standard-size machine. The fish mix is most easily mixed in a large plastic bowl. Use a large vegetable piping bag without a pipe. Fill with some of the mix, then pipe out in blobs the size of a walnut. Roll between the palms into little balls. Put about 20 balls at a time into a plastic bag containing 2 tablespoons of flour. Shake until the balls are evenly coated. Fry in deep, hot fat (360°F/180°C), or hot enough to brown a 1-inch (2.5-cm) cube of bread in 40 seconds. Fry quickly until golden brown, then drain on crumpled tissue. Repeat until all the balls are fried. When the balls are quite cold, put into plastic bags and freeze until required.

To serve, spread the frozen balls on to an oven tray and heat at Gas No. 4 (350°F/180°C) until crisp to the touch - about 5 minutes. Serve warm or cold, plain speared on cocktail sticks or with double the Tartare Sauce recipe (see p. 299).

GEFILTE FISH PROVENÇALE

50 portions of 1 patty each.
Cooked fish will keep 2 days under refrigeration.
Freeze 3 months.

Follow method for Gefilte Fish Provençale on p. 67). Use same quantities of mixture as for Fried Fish Patties (see this page) and use the following quantities of sauce.

30 fl oz (12 rounded tbsp) canned or tubed tomato purée
3 pints (1.75 l/7½ cups) hot water
6 rounded tbsp tomato ketchup
6 tbsp olive or sunflower oil
5 red or yellow peppers, seeded and thinly sliced
6 medium onions, finely chopped
1½ level tbsp salt
1½ level tbsp sugar
1½ tbsp dried Herbes de Provence
1 level teasp ground black pepper

FISH PIE

Serves 50.
Keeps 2 days under refrigeration.
Do not freeze.

Make it in foil containers or in heatproof dishes that measure approximately 13 x 8½ x 2 inches (35 x 21 x 5 cm) - any deeper and the potatoes may burn.

A very hearty fish dish.

12 lb (5.5 kg) smoked haddock fillet
7½ pints (4.25 l/19 cups) milk
15 oz (425 g/1¾ cups) butter
15 oz (425 g/3¾ cups) plain (all-purpose) flour
black pepper
white pepper
1 tbsp mace
1 tbsp mild curry powder (or to taste)
4 tbsp dry mustard
1¼ lb (675 g/2¼ cups) grated cheese
15 rounded tbsp double (heavy) cream or 5 small cans evaporated milk
15 hard-boiled eggs

For the topping

15 lb (7 kg) boiled potatoes
approx. 1¼ pints (725 ml/3 cups) milk
12 oz (350 g/1½ cups) butter
2½ tbsp salt
1 teasp white pepper

Cover fish with cold water. After bringing to the boil, discard the water. Put fish in 2 oven dishes, cover with milk and leave in moderate oven, Gas No. 4 (350°F/180°C), for 20 minutes. Drain fish. Put milk in 2 pans (too much to handle in 1). Add to each pan half the butter, flour and seasonings. Whisk with balloon whisk until thickened, then stir with wooden spoon, constantly stirring bottom and sides to prevent burning. Bubble 3 minutes, then add cheese and cream and stir until smooth. Flake the fish with a fork (watching for bones) and divide between pans of sauce, mixing well. Add quartered hard-boiled eggs. Divide between the chosen dishes (I used a dish 10 x 14 x 2½ inches (25 x 35 x 6 cm) and another 10 x 16 x 3½ inches (25 x 40 x 9 cm).

Cook potatoes in 2 batches, watching that they don't fall to bits. Drain thoroughly. Mash with potato-masher, adding hot milk, butter and seasonings, then beat until fluffy in an electric mixer using the flat beater (probably in 3 batches).

Pipe the potatoes over the fish mixture. Refrigerate until 3 hours before the pies are to be cooked. Leave to come to room temperature. Bake at Gas No. 5 (375°F/190°C) for 2-2½ hours, until brown on top and bubbling underneath.

SALMON MAYONNAISE

Serves 50.
Keeps 1 day under refrigeration.

8 lb (3.75 kg) cooked salmon or salmon trout fillet or 13 lb (6 kg) whole fish with head
2 large cucumbers, cut in ⅜-inch (1-cm) dice
2 lb (900 g/4 cups) mild mayonnaise
4 tbsp wine vinegar or cider vinegar
1 tbsp Dijon mustard
4 dozen hard-boiled eggs
2 lb (900 g) cherry tomatoes

For the garnish

chives or parsley

To cook the salmon in the oven, see p. 74.

Dice the cucumber, sprinkle with salt and leave in a colander or salad spinner for 15 minutes, then rinse and dry. Skin and bone the salmon if necessary, then flake roughly with a fork. Put the mayonnaise into a bowl and add the vinegar and mustard. Stir three-quarters of it into the salmon, mixed with the cucumber. Mixture should be moist but not wet.

Pile into centre of round platters. Surround with stuffed hard-boiled eggs (see p. 538) and halved cherry tomatoes. Spoon the remaining mayonnaise over the centre and garnish with snipped chives or parsley.

For the egg stuffing Mix together the hard-boiled yolks plus about 4 oz (125 g/½ cup) of butter or margarine, 5 oz (150 ml/⅔ cup) of mayonnaise, pepper, salt and 2 teaspoons of curry paste (or to taste). The consistency should be of soft cream cheese. Pile back into hard-boiled whites.

TUNA LASAGNE

Serves 50.
Makes 4 lasagne, each approximately 15 x 9 inches (37.5 x 22.5 cm), serving 12–13.
Keeps 2 days under refrigeration.
Do not freeze.

It's best to make this in 4 dishes, each with the following ingredients.

18 strips par-cooked lasagne
large onion, chopped
1½ large red peppers
3 x 7 oz (200 g) cans coarsely flaked tuna
5 hard-boiled eggs
4 oz (125 g/½ cup) butter
4 oz (125 g/1 cup) plain (all-purpose) flour
2½ pints (1.5 l/6¼ cups) milk
1½ teasp dry mustard
¼ teasp nutmeg
2 teasp salt
8 oz (225 g/2 cups) mature Cheddar, grated
1 tbsp chopped parsley
½ x 6 oz (175 g) can of evaporated milk or single (light) cream

To make the sauce, finely chop the onion and the peppers. Flake the tuna and slice the eggs. Melt the butter and cook the onion in a covered pan for 5 minutes, until softened, then add the peppers, cover and cook a further 3 or 4 minutes. Uncover, stir in the flour, followed by the milk and the seasonings. Whisk until bubbly, simmer 3 minutes, then stir in three-quarters of the cheese, and all the evaporated milk, parsley, tuna and hard-boiled eggs.

To assemble the lasagne, butter the dish and put a thin layer of sauce on the bottom, cover with 6 strips of lasagne, then sauce. Repeat twice, ending with a thin layer of sauce. Cover with the remaining cheese.

It is convenient to par-cook the dishes of lasagne the day before serving, at Gas No. 5 (375°F/190°C). When set but still pale - after about 30 minutes - take out, cool, cover with foil and refrigerate.

Next day, reheat, covered, at Gas No. 4 (350°F/180°C), or until bubbling. Before serving remove the foil and grill (broil) or cook in the turned-up oven, Gas No. 8 (450°F/230°C) until crusty and brown. Cool for 10 minutes before cutting in squares to serve.

Meat and Chicken Dishes

HOLISHKES
(*Meat-stuffed Cabbage Rolls*)

Serves 50, 2 holishkes each.
Keeps 2–3 days under refrigeration.
Freeze 3 months.

Can be prepared 2 days before and reheated.

8 firm heads white cabbage
5 large onions
8 oz (225 g/1 cup) margarine
1 lb (450 g/2⅔ cups) Basmati rice
1½ pints (850 ml/3¾ cups) chicken stock
8 lb (4 kg) lean minced (ground) beef
2 level tbsp salt
½ teasp ground black pepper

For the sauce
2½ lb (1.25 kg) tomato purée
1 tbsp salt
½ teasp black pepper
1 level teasp citric or tartaric acid (sour salt)
4 pints hot water

Follow recipe on p. 570. Allow an extra hour's cooking time for this quantity.

MEATBALLS IN TOMATO SAUCE

Serves 50.
Keeps 3 days under refrigeration.
Freeze 3 months.

5 medium onions
10 eggs
1½ tbsp salt
1 teasp white pepper
10 lb (5 kg) minced shoulder steak (ground beef)
10 oz (275 g/1¼ cups) medium matzah meal

For the tomato sauce
3 large onions, sliced
5 tbsp sunflower oil
3 x 28 oz (800 g) cans tomatoes in tomato juice
15 oz (425 g) can tomato purée
3 level tbsp brown sugar
1 teasp white pepper
3 bay leaves
1 pint (575 ml/2½ cups) water
4 beef stock-cubes
2 level tbsp salt
juice of 2 lemons

To make the meatballs, process onions, eggs and seasonings in blender or food processor until smooth. Alternatively grate onions and add to eggs beaten with seasoning. Add the meat and the meal and blend thoroughly, either by hand or electric mixer at low speed. Leave for 1 hour, then form into balls with wetted hands.

To make the sauce, put the onions into cold oil, then heat gently and cook, covered, until softened and transparent. Uncover and cook until pale gold in colour. Add sieved or liquidized tomatoes and all the remaining ingredients. Bring to the boil.

Drop in the meatballs, cover and simmer for 1 hour. Serve with 3 lb (1.5 kg) of plain boiled rice.

BEEF AND WINE CASSEROLE

Serves 50.
Leftovers keep 3 days under refrigeration.
Freeze 3 months.

A really savoury dish that can also be used with a top crust or with dumplings.

12–15 lb (6–7.5 kg) lean beef (such as shoulder steak or top rib), cut into 1½-inch (4-cm) cubes
½ level teasp black pepper
6 tbsp sunflower or other flavourless oil
3 oz (75 g/6 tbsp) margarine
4 large onions, finely chopped
4 large carrots, peeled and cubed
1 head of celery, sliced
4 cloves of garlic
5 oz (150 g/1¼ cups) plain (all-purpose) flour
2½ pints (1.5 l/6¼ cups) beef stock
2½ level tbsp salt
1½ bottles dry red wine
1 small can (5 oz/150 g) tomato purée
bunch of parsley
4 large bay leaves

Sprinkle the meat with the pepper. Heat the oil in a heavy frying or sauté pan and brown the meat quickly in batches on all sides (don't over-crowd the pan or the meat won't brown quickly because of the steam - if possible use 2 pans simultaneously). In another pan, heat the margarine and gently sauté the onion, carrots, celery and garlic, covered, until golden brown.

Carefully drain both the meat and vegetables and arrange either in oven dishes 2 inches (5 cm) deep or in 1 or 2 large pans. Put the remaining fat together in a large (1-gallon/5 l/24-cup) pan and stir in the flour. Bubble for 2 or 3 minutes, then add the salt, beef stock and wine, followed by the remaining ingredients, and bring to the boil. Pour over the meat mixture, dividing it equally between the 2 pans (if used). Cover and simmer very slowly for 2½ hours on top of the stove, or in a slow oven, Gas No. 2 (300°F/150°C), for 3 hours.

HUNGARIAN GOULASH

Serves 50.
Leftovers keep 3 days under refrigeration.
Freeze 3 months.

12–15 lb (6–7.5 kg) braising or stewing steak, cubed
3 large onions, chopped
6 fl oz (175 ml/¾ cup) sunflower or other flavourless oil
1 level tbsp dry mustard
4 level tbsp paprika
4 level tbsp salt
5 oz (150 g/⅔ cup) brown sugar
5 fl oz (150 ml/⅔ cup) dark soy sauce
2 tbsp vinegar
1½ pints (850 ml/3¾ cups) tomato ketchup
5 pints (2.5 l/12½ cups) water
8 oz (225 g/2 cups) cornflour (cornstarch), mixed with 1½ pints (850 ml/3¾ cups) water

Brown the beef and the onion in the fat. Add all the remaining ingredients except the thickening and bring to the boil. Simmer in a covered container for 2½–3 hours, or until meat is tender. Stir in cornflour mixture, bring back to boil and simmer for 3 minutes. Serve over cooked noodles.

SWEET AND SOUR BEEF

Serves 50.
Keeps 2 days under refrigeration.
Freeze 3 months.

This is an excellent dish for a crowd as the meat mixture can be frozen ahead. On the day it is to be served, add the vinegar and pineapple mixture and bring to the boil to thicken. Alternatively, the meat can be cooked and refrigerated overnight, then thickened the next day.

6 onions
1 head of celery
6 oz (175 g/¾ cup) margarine
6 fl oz (175 ml/¾ cup) sunflower or other flavourless oil
5 x 20 oz (575 g) cans pineapple titbits
16 lb (8 kg) braising steak
4 level tbsp salt
1 level teasp black pepper
6 tbsp dark soy sauce
4 pints (2 l/10 cups) beef stock (5–6 cubes)
8 tbsp tomato ketchup
8 fl oz (225 ml/1 cup) any vinegar
5 oz (150 g/⅔ cup) cornflour (cornstarch)
pineapple juice made up to 4 pints (2.25 l/10 cups) with water

Follow directions for Sweet and Sour Beef on p. 157.

CHICKEN BREASTS IN BARBECUE SAUCE

Serves 50.
Cooked chicken keeps 2 days under refrigeration.
Freeze 3 months.

50 part-boned chicken breasts, skinned
sunflower oil to cover pan to depth of ¼ inch (0.5 cm) to fry chicken breasts
7 fl oz (200 ml/¾ cup plus 2 tbsp) sunflower or olive oil
8 medium onions, finely chopped
4 x 10 oz (275 g) jars tomato purée
4 pints (2.25 l/10 cups) hot water
4 tbsp salt
1 teasp black pepper
6 oz (175 g/¾ cup) brown sugar
4 tbsp soy sauce
3 tbsp prepared mustard
6 tbsp lemon juice (add gradually and taste)

Dry the skinned joints well, then fry in the hot oil until golden all over. Drain on paper kitchen towels, then remove to 2–3 baking dishes just large enough to go in the oven.

Use at least a 6-pint (3.5-l/15½-cup) capacity

pan to make the sauce. Sauté the onion, covered, until softened, then uncover and cook until golden. Add all the remaining ingredients. Simmer for 5 minutes.

Pour over the chicken, cover with foil and cook at Gas No. 4 (350°F/180°C) for 45 minutes, or until chicken joints feel tender. Keep hot until required. Alternatively, refrigerate the cooked joints and reheat. It may well take 1½ hours in a moderate oven, Gas No. 4 (350°F/180°C) until heated through and bubbly.

CHICKEN TAJ MAHAL

Serves 25-30 or 50 (for larger quantity, double ingredients).
Keeps 2 days under refrigeration.
Do not freeze.

A superb main dish salad.

For 25-30
4½ lb (2.25 kg) chicken breast meat, poached (see below)
1½ lb (675 g/3 cups) mayonnaise
3 tbsp curry powder
6 rounded tbsp mango chutney
3 teasp grated peeled fresh ginger

For the salad
2 pints (1.25 l/5 cups) chicken stock
1¼ lb (575 g/3¼ cups) rice
1 can pimentos
6 rounded tbsp raisins
6 fl oz (175 g/¾ cup) vinaigrette (see p. 300)

For the garnish
paprika

To poach the chicken, lay the breasts side by side in a large baking dish. Season. Add 10 fl oz (275 ml/1¼ cups) of white wine. Cover with foil and cook at Gas No. 4 (350°F/180°C), with a pan of hot water beside them (to stop them drying out), for 35 minutes.

In the microwave, cook 2 lb (900 g) at a time, with 4 tablespoons of chicken stock. Cover and cook on 100 per cent power for 8 minutes.

Cut the flesh into bite sized pieces (the stock can be used to cook the rice). In a large bowl mix together the mayonnaise, curry powder, chutney and fresh ginger. Stir in the chicken and leave covered until required. This can be done at any time of the day, but allow enough time for the salad to stand for at least 30 minutes, to let the flavours develop.

To make the rice salad, bring the chicken stock to the boil and add the rice. Cover and bring to the boil, then simmer for 15 minutes. Take off the heat and leave covered to steam for a further 5 minutes. Uncover - the rice will have absorbed all the liquid and can be fluffed up with a fork. Put into a bowl and add the pimentos (drained and cut in thin strips) and the raisins. Sprinkle with the vinaigrette and mix gently with a fork or spoon. Refrigerate in a covered container for several hours.

To assemble the salad, spoon the rice on to an oval platter, and pile the chicken salad on top. Just before serving, dust with paprika.

Potatoes, Salads and Bread

LATKES

50 servings
Freeze 4 months.

If there is help in the kitchen these can be made most successfully for a crowd. Another option is to fry and then freeze them ahead and reheat in a hot oven (see below). Freshly fried latkes can be kept hot and crisp for up to 15 minutes in a warm oven, Gas No. 2 (300°F/150°C).

6 pints (3.5 l/15 cups) grated potatoes
(about 24 large)
2 large onions
1 dozen eggs
12 oz (350 g/3 cups) self-raising flour or
12 oz (350 g/3 cups) plain (all-purpose) flour plus
3 teasp baking powder
2 level tbsp salt
½ teasp white pepper

Cut the potato into chunks and grate finely in a food processor. Drain in a sieve or colander for 10 minutes, pressing down well on the potato pulp. Put the onion, egg, flour and seasonings into the bowl and process until purèed. Blend with the grated potato. The mixture should be like a thick batter. If too thin, add a little more flour.

The latkes are most quickly cooked in a deep-fryer, dropping large teaspoons of the mixture into fat heated to 375°F (190°C). A batch will take about 4 minutes. The latkes should be crunchy and crisp on the outside and creamy inside. Drain on crumpled kitchen paper and serve at once on cocktail sticks.

To freeze Cook the latkes but only until they are a pale brown. Drain thoroughly, then open-freeze. When firm, put into plastic bags.

To reheat Defrost the latkes for 1 hour on a foil-covered baking sheet, then reheat at Gas No. 8 (450°F/230°C) for 7–8 minutes, until crisp and brown.

CREAMED POTATOES IN THE FRENCH STYLE

Serves 45–50.
Eat freshly made.

16 lb (8 kg) potatoes
2 tbsp salt
1 lb (450 g)1 cup) butter or margarine
8 eggs
1 tbsp pepper
1 tbsp nutmeg
15 fl oz (425 ml/2 cups) milk or
single (light) cream

Use method on p. 267. Allow plenty of time for the potatoes to come to the boil.

MIXED GREEN SALAD

Serves 50.
Undressed salad keeps 1 day under refrigeration.

10 large lettuces (eg Cos, Batavia, etc.)
5 bunches watercress
2 large cucumbers
5 red or yellow peppers
3 lb (1.5 kg) cherry tomatoes, halved

For the dressing
12 fl oz (350 ml/1½ cups) sunflower oil
4 fl oz (125 ml/½ cup) extra virgin olive oil
4 fl oz (125 ml/½ cup) wine vinegar
1 tbsp lemon juice
1 tbsp caster sugar or granular sweetener
2 teasp prepared wholegrain mustard
2 teasp sea salt
20 grinds of black pepper
3 medium cloves of garlic, halved (optional)
4 tbsp parsley, chopped (½ oz/15 g)

Put all the dressing ingredients (except the parsley) in a large screw-top jar or bowl and shake or whisk until well thickened. Leave in the refrigerator to mature for several hours. Add parsley on the day, as it is bleached by the vinegar if put in too early.

To serve, discard garlic cloves from dressing, toss prepared salad greens with dressing in a very large bowl and then transfer to smaller ones to serve.

EASY COLESLAW

Serves 50.
Keeps 2 days under refrigeration.

For a large quantity it is often more time-saving to buy prepared coleslaw and add extra ingredients.

7 x 12 oz (350 g) cartons coleslaw
2 small heads celery, sliced across in ¼-inch (0.5-cm) slices
2 green or red peppers, halved deseeded and cut in very thin strips
2 red apples, cored and cut into ½-inch (1-cm) cubes
8 oz (225 g/2 cups) sultanas (white raisins)

Mix all ingredients together thoroughly.

CELERY, APPLE, MELON AND GRAPE SALAD

Serves 50 (the recipe can be doubled, trebled or quadrupled easily to serve 100, 150 or 200).
Keeps 1 day under refrigeration.

For 50
(2 large bowls)
4 medium Canteloupe-type melons (Galia or Ogen)
4 hearts of celery (about 32 stalks)
8 red apples
2 lb (900 g) seedless grapes

For the dressing
1 lb (450 g) mayonnaise
1 tbsp orange juice
2 tbsp lemon juice

Stir together all the dressing ingredients, then put aside. Halve the melons, remove the seeds, then scoop out the flesh using a melon-ball cutter. Leave in sieves to drain. Cut the celery in ⅜-inch (1-cm) cubes. Core and then quarter the apples and cut into cubes of the same size. Put in a bowl with the grapes and mix with the dressing. Chill for several hours.

Half an hour before serving, stir in the melon.

CORN SALAD

Serves 50.
Keeps 2 days under refrigeration.

8 fl oz (225 ml/1 cup) vinaigrette dressing (see p. 300)
6 level tbsp chopped parsley (generous 1 oz/25 g)
1 large salad (mild) onion, finely chopped
12 x 11 oz (300 g) cans sweetcorn with peppers
8 fl oz (225 ml/1 cup) mayonnaise

Blend the vinaigrette with the parsley and chopped onion. Stir into the well-drained corn. Refrigerate for at least an hour. Just before serving, blend with mayonnaise.

POTATO SALAD

Serves 50.
Keeps 1 day under refrigeration.

12 x 19 oz (525 g) cans new potatoes
1 pint (575 ml/2½ cups) vinaigrette (see p. 300)
2 pints (1.25/5 cups) mayonnaise
2 bunches spring onions (scallions), finely chopped
10 tbsp parsley, chopped (2 oz/50 g)

Drain potatoes and cube. Put into the vinaigrette and leave half an hour. Drain off remaining dressing and blend into mayonnaise, together with spring onions and most of the parsley. Fold in the potatoes. Chill for at least an hour. Serve garnished with the remaining parsley.

CYPRUS TOMATO SALAD

Serves 50.
Keeps 1 day under refrigeration.

Make according to the recipe on p. 292 but use the following ingredients.

6 large cucumbers
6 lb (3 kg) firm tomatoes
8 large green or yellow peppers
6 tbsp parsley, chopped (generous 1 oz/25 g)
1½ lb (850 g/3¾ cups) black olives for garnish (optional)

For the dressing
15 fl oz (425 ml/2 cups) olive oil
8 fl oz (225 ml/1 cup) lemon juice (3–4 large lemons)
2 level tbsp salt
2 level tbsp caster (superfine) sugar
1 level teasp black pepper
1 level teasp garlic salt
6 tbsp snipped fresh basil

TOMATO AND BASIL SALAD

Serves 25 or 50 (for larger quantity double the ingredients).

For 25
4 lb (2 kg) ripe, well-flavoured tomatoes
2 bunches spring onions (scallions), trimmed leaving 4 inches of the green, then thinly sliced
3 handfuls basil, finely snipped, or 3 tbsp chopped parsley plus 3 teasp dried basil
8 fl oz (225 ml/1 cup) vinaigrette (see p. 300)

Thinly slice the tomatoes and arrange, overlapping, in a shallow dish (eg a gratin or quiche dish). Scatter with the finely sliced spring onion. Finally add the herbs to the vinaigrette and spoon over the top. Leave in a cool place but do not refrigerate as the flavour is better at room temperature.

HERB BREAD

Serves 25 or 50 (for larger quantity double the ingredients).
Keeps 3 days under refrigeration.
Freeze in foil 2 weeks.

For 25
6 10-inch-long (25-cm) French sticks
2 handfuls (2 oz/50 g) fresh mixed herbs – chives, tarragon, dill, thyme
3 teasp dried Herbes de Provence (freeze-dried if possible)
3 cloves of garlic or 1½ tbsp garlic granules
30 grinds of black pepper
12 oz (350 g/1½ cups) softened butter or margarine
3 teasp lemon juice

Cut the bread into slanting slices about ½ inch 1.25 cm) thick but stop at the base so that the loaf is left intact. Beat together all the ingredients until creamy.

Butter *each side* of each slice thickly, then lay the loaves on a piece of foil large enough to enclose them. Spread the top crust with any remaining herb butter, then seal tightly. Refrigerate or freeze until required.

Preheat the oven to Gas No. 6 (400°F/200°C). Bake the loaves for 20 minutes (30 minutes if frozen), then turn back the foil and allow to go brown for 5 minutes. Cool for 5 minutes before serving on a long platter.

Fruit Desserts

APPLE CRUMBLE FOR A CROWD

Serves 25 or 150–60.

This is an excellent dish to prepare in the synagogue kitchen, to serve in winter after a cold main dish. It's better, of course, to use fresh baking apples, but this isn't practical for a larger number. I used apples canned in water instead.

If mixture is baked one day and served the next it will go a little watery as apple juice is drawn out by sugar. Reheat in a moderate oven until bubbly - about 45 minutes.

3 helpers took 1 hour to prepare crumble ready for oven.

Note We had 2 lb (900 g) of crumble left over, but this might not have been the case if we had used wider containers.

For 25

1 x 6 lb (3 kg) can apples in water or 20 medium baking apples
12 fl oz (350 ml/1½ cups) water (only with fresh fruit)
8 oz (225 g/2 cups) granulated sugar
2 teasp cinnamon
4 tbsp lemon juice

For 150–60

6 x 6 lb (3 kg) can apples in water or 40 lb (20 kg) baking apples
15 fl oz (425 ml/2 cups) lemon juice
3½ pints (2 l/9 cups) water (only with fresh fruit)
3 lb (1.5 kg/6¾ cups) granulated sugar
3 tbsp cinnamon

For the topping
For 25

12 oz (350 g/3 cups) white or 81% flour
4 oz (125 g/1⅓ cups) porridge oats
1 lb (450 g/2¼ cups) soft brown sugar
12 oz (350 g/1½ cups) margarine

For 150–60

4½ lb (2 kg/18 cups) white or 81% flour
1½ lb (675 g/8 cups) porridge oats
6 lb (2.75 kg/13½ cups) soft brown sugar
4½ lb (2 kg/9 cups) margarine

Drain the apples and divide between the dishes available. (Best way is to get a collection of large dishes, about 2–3 inches (5–7.5 cm) deep, and estimate how many will be needed to provide the desired number of portions.) The apple should be about 2 inches (5 cm) deep. Scatter with the granulated sugar mixed with the cinnamon and sprinkle with the lemon juice.

The topping for 25 can be done at 1 time in a regular Kenwood, so weigh out 6 lots for 150. Put all topping ingredients in the mixer - margarine in 1-inch (2.5-cm) chunks - and rub together until crumbly. As each batch is mixed, put in an extra-large plastic bowl and finish rubbing in the fat by hand in case there are any lumps left. Divide this crumble between the dishes, putting a thick layer on each and patting it down well.

Bake at Gas No. 4 (350°F/180°C) for 1 hour, until the crumble is a rich brown and crisp to the touch.

FRUIT SALAD

Serves 50.
Leftovers keep 1 day under refrigeration.

3 lb (1.5 kg) crisp apples, peeled and sliced
3 x 28 oz (800 g) cans pears in juice or syrup
2 x 28 oz (800 g) cans sliced peaches in juice or syrup
2 x 28 oz (800 g) cans pineapple pieces in juice or syrup or 2 large fresh pineapples
2 x 15 oz (425 g) cans black cherries
10 oranges
12 bananas

For the syrup
juice or syrup strained from cans
1½ lb (675 g) apricot jam
juice of 4 lemons

To make the syrup, simmer juice from cans with apricot jam until smooth, then stir in lemon juice and any juice from fruit preparation. Add the prepared fruit. Leave for several hours.

SPICED WINE FRUIT SALAD

Serves 45–50.
Syrup keeps 2 days under refrigeration.

Prepare and serve fruit salad same day.

12 oz (350 g/3 cups) pecans or walnuts
12 oz (350 g/3 cups) Brazil nuts
4 lb (2 kg) green seedless grapes
3 lb (1.5 kg) black grapes, seedless if possible
20 oranges, peeled and segmented
3 large cans lychees
20 bananas, peeled and sliced

For the syrup
1 litre (4½ cups) any fruity red wine
1 pint (575 ml/2½ cups) lychee juice from cans
6 tbsp lemon juice
10 oz (275 g/1¼ cups) brown sugar
21 cloves
6 sticks cinnamon

Toast the nuts for 10 minutes in a moderate oven, Gas No. 4 (350°F/180°C), until golden.

Prepare the fruit and put into a large bowl.

Put the wine, juices, sugar and spices into a pan and simmer for 5 minutes, until the flavour has concentrated. Allow to go cold. Pour over the fruit, except for the bananas, which are added half an hour before serving. Refrigerate. Add the nuts with the bananas.

STRAWBERRY AND MANGO COMPÔTE

Serves 25 or 50.
Leftovers keep 1 day under refrigeration.
Do not freeze.

For 25
9 level tbsp caster (superfine) sugar
6 fl oz (175 ml/¾ cup) fresh lemon juice
5 mangoes
5 lb (2.25 kg) strawberries

For 50
9 oz (250 g/1⅓ cups) caster (superfine) sugar
8 fl oz (200 ml/2 cups) fresh lemon juice
9 mangoes
9 lb (4.5 kg) strawberries

The day before, warm sugar and lemon juice until sugar has dissolved. Peel and slice the mangoes into bite-size pieces and leave to marinate in half the lemon syrup.

Remove the calyx from the strawberries, slice in half if large and refrigerate in a covered container. About 2 hours before serving, pour the remaining syrup over the strawberries.

Mix the mango and strawberries gently together 1 hour before serving and chill until required.

For 25, serve with 1½ pints (850 ml/3¾ cups) of whipping cream, whipped and flavoured as wished, or 2 lb (900 g) Greek yoghurt slightly sweetened. For 50, double these quantities.

LEMON PAVLOVA

Serves 50.
*Makes 3 Pavlovas, each 10 inches (25 cm) in diameter (**see p. 344**).*
Keeps 2 days under refrigeration.

For the filling
(do all 3 together)
18 egg yolks
18 oz (500 g/2½ cups) caster (superfine) sugar
12 fl oz (350 ml/1½ cups) lemon juice (about 6 lemons)
grated rind of 4 lemons
2 pints (1.25 l/5 cups) whipping cream

Whisk the yolks and sugar together in a food processor until creamy, then add lemon juice and rinds. Turn into a heavy-based pan and cook gently until thick as mayonnaise, stirring constantly (do *not* allow to boil). Take off the heat and continue to stir for a minute - it will continue to cook with the heat of the pan. Allow to go quite cold.

Whip the cream until it holds stiff peaks, then gradually whisk in the lemon mixture, 2 tablespoons at a time. It should now resemble lemon-coloured whipped cream. Use to fill the 3 Pavlovas. May be frozen.

Note For 25 (small) servings, use 9 eggs and pipe into a rectangle 15 x 10 inches (37.5 x 25 cm).

For 25-30 larger portions, use 12 eggs in 2 6-egg rectangles approximately 12 x 7 inches (30 x 17.5 cm). Use a 12-yolk filling with 1½ pints (850 ml/3¾ cups) cream.

MERINGUE CUPS

Individual meringue cups filled with a fluffy, subtly flavoured mixture look stunning on a buffet table, and though they take longer to shape they are easier to serve to a crowd than a round Pavlova. If, however, you wish to make round Pavlovas, use the same amount of filling, but you will need to make a meringue based on 18 egg whites (see Lemon Pavlova for 50, this page).

Empty cups will keep 2 weeks at room temperature in an airtight container.

Open-freeze the filled cups, then pack in plastic containers or lay on trays and cover with another tray upside down.

COFFEE PRALINE MERINGUE CUPS

Serves 50-60.
Keep 2 days under refrigeration.
Freeze filled cups 3 months.

12 egg whites
¾ teasp cream of tartar
6 level teasp cornflour (cornstarch) or potato flour
1½ lb (675 g/3¼ cups) caster (superfine) sugar

For the filling
8 oz (225 g/2 cups) nut brittle
3 level tbsp dark roast instant coffee - eg Espresso
2 tbsp hot water
2 pints (1.25 l/5 cups) whipping cream or 1¾ pints (1 l/4½ cups) non-dairy cream
2 tbsp caster (superfine) sugar
4 tbsp Tia Maria or Sabra liqueur (optional)

Preheat the oven to Gas No. 2 (300°F/150°C).

For convenience, I suggest doing 2 half-quantities of meringue in a large Kenwood, rather than trying to do the full amount at once.

Using silicone paper for the best results, line 4 baking trays. Whisk the whites with the cream of tartar until they hold stiff peaks. Mix the cornflour with the caster sugar, then add a tablespoon at a time, whisking until stiff after each addition. Put a ½-inch (1-cm) plain or coarse rose pipe into a large piping bag, fill two-thirds full with the meringue and, starting from the centre of the base, pipe out little cups about 2½ inches (6 cm) across. The cups will expand in the oven, so leave 2 inches (5 cm) between them.

Put the trays of meringues into the oven and then turn it down to Gas No. 1 (275°F/140°C). Bake for 1 hour, or until the cups feel crisp to the touch and lift off the tray easily. Put on cooling trays.

To make the filling, crush the nut brittle to a praline powder in the food processor - it should be like coarse sand - or crush with a rolling pin. Dissolve the coffee in the hot water and allow to cool. Whisk the cream until thick enough to hang on the whisk, then whisk in the coffee, sugar and liqueur. (Don't use boiling hot coffee or it may curdle the cream.) Fold in the praline, reserving some for garnish. Pipe or spoon the cream into the cups, building it up well. Refrigerate or freeze until required.

Just before serving, sprinkle each cup with a teaspoon of the praline.

Note Defrost at room temperature for 20 minutes before serving.

LEMON MERINGUE CUPS

Serves 50.

For the meringue cups

see Coffee Praline Meringue Cups above, p. 547

For the filling

12 oz (350 g/1½ cups) sugar
12 egg yolks
8 fl oz (225 ml/1 cup) lemon juice (about 4 lemons)
grated rind of 3 lemons
2 pints (1.25 l/5 cups) whipping cream

Make the meringue cups as directed.
Make the filling as for the Lemon Pavlova for 50 (see p. 547).

STRAWBERRY MERINGUE CUPS

Serves 50.

For the meringue cups

see Coffee Praline Meringue Cups, p. 547

For the filling

4 level tbsp caster (superfine) sugar
4 tbsp lemon juice
2 pints (1.25 l/5 cups) whipping cream
5 lb (2.25 kg) sliced strawberries

Make the meringue cups as directed.

To make the filling, put the sugar, lemon juice and cream into a bowl and whisk until stiff, then fold in the strawberries. Use to fill the meringues.

If refrigerator space is limited, the best thing is to chill the filling very thoroughly, then lay individual meringue cups on trays and fill just before they are served.

DESSERT SQUARES

For service on a large scale, it is convenient to bake pies and puddings in rectangular tins. It is then easy to portion them correctly.

All the recipes below are baked in tins approximately 12 x 10 x 1 inches (30 x 25 x 2.5 cm). This gives a yield of 25 portions. To make 50 portions simply double the recipe and use 2 tins of the same size.

All these desserts can be frozen in advance.

CANADIAN APPLE SLICE

Serves 25.
Keeps 2 days under refrigeration.
Freeze 3 months.

For the pastry
2 large eggs
1 lb (450 g/4 cups) self-raising flour or 1 lb (450 g/4 cups) plain (all-purpose) flour and 4 level teasp baking powder
9 oz (250 g/1 cup plus 1 tbsp) margarine
juice of 1 lemon (3 tbsp)
2 oz (50 g/⅓ cup) icing sugar

For the filling
3 lb (1.5 kg) apples
8 oz (225 g/1 cup) sugar
2 level teasp cinnamon

Reserve 1 egg white for glazing the top. Make the pastry by either of the methods for shortcrust for fruit pies on p. 371. Divide into 2 balls, foil-wrap and chill while the filling is being prepared. Then roll out first ball to fit a tin 12 x 10 x 1 inches (30 x 25 x 2.5 cm).

Peel and core the apples and grate into a bowl, then stir in the sugar and cinnamon. Immediately spread on to the pastry and cover with another layer of pastry, rolled to fit, from the second ball. Press gently down on to apples and lightly mark into 25 squares. Beat the reserved egg white until frothy, then paint all over the top. Sprinkle with a thin layer of granulated sugar.

Bake in a preheated oven, Gas No. 5 (375°F/190°C), for 45 minutes, or until golden brown and crisp. Cut into squares. Serve warm or cold. May be reheated.

PEACH SLICE

Serves 25.
Keeps 2 days under refrigeration.
Freeze 3 months.

For the pastry
10 oz (275 g/2½ cups) plain (all-purpose) flour
6 oz (175 g/¾ cup) butter or half butter and half margarine
3 oz (75 g/⅓ cup) caster (superfine) sugar
1 oz (25 g/¼ cup) ground almonds
grated rind of ½ lemon
3 tbsp single (light) cream or milk top
1 egg yolk
1 egg white for glazing

For the filling
6 large peaches (about 2 lb/900 g)
juice of 1 lemon
5 oz (150 g/⅔ cup) soft light brown sugar
1 level tbsp cornflour (cornstarch)
1 level teasp cinnamon

Make the pastry by either of the methods on p. 371. Knead into a ball and divide in 2 balls, 1 slightly larger than the other. Flatten each ball so that it is 1 inch (2.5 cm) thick, then wrap in clingfilm (saranwrap). Chill the smaller piece 1 hour in the refrigerator and freeze the larger piece.

Leave each peach in a pan of boiling water for 1 minute. Lift out with a slotted spoon and plunge into cold water, then peel when cold enough to handle. Halve, then slice ⅛ inch (0.3 cm) thick, put in bowl and blend with lemon juice. In another bowl mix the sugar, cornflour and cinnamon.

Roll the smaller piece of pastry to fit a tin approximately 12 x 10 x 1 inches (30 x 25 x 2.5 cm). Blend the sugar mixture with the peaches, then spoon evenly into the tin. Grate the frozen pastry in an even layer on to the fruit filling and scatter with golden granulated sugar.

FARMHOUSE FRUIT CAKE SQUARES

Serves 25.
Keeps moist 1 week at room temperature in an airtight container.
Freeze 3 months.

12 oz (350 g/1½ cups) soft margarine
12 oz (350 g/1½ cups) soft medium brown sugar
6 eggs
2 tbsp golden (corn) syrup
1½ lb (675 g) mixed dried fruit
4 oz (125 g/1 cup) coarsely chopped walnuts (optional)
1 lb (450 g/4 cups) plain (all-purpose) flour
2 teasp baking powder
1 tbsp mixed sweet spice

For the glaze
milk (or water for a parev *cake)*
demerara sugar

Grease a tin 12 x 10 x 2 inches (30 x 25 x 5 cm). Put all the ingredients into a bowl and blend until smooth and creamy - about 3 minutes. Turn into the tin and smooth level. Brush with milk (or water) and scatter with the sugar.

Bake in a preheated oven, Gas No. 4 (350°F/180°C), for 45-60 minutes, or until golden brown and firm to gentle pressure. When cold, cut into 25 squares.

ICE-CREAM WITH SAUCE

This is an economical sweet for serving to a large number. Allow 1½ gallons (6 l/30 cups) of ice-cream for 50 portions.

CHOCOLATE SAUCE

Keeps 3 days under refrigeration.
Freeze 6 months.

12 oz (350 g/1½ cups) butter
2 lb (900 g/5 cups) sieved icing (confectioners') sugar
12 oz (350 g/3 cups) cocoa
24 fl oz (700 ml/3 cups) evaporated milk

Melt the butter in a large saucepan, then add the sugar and cocoa. Mix thoroughly, adding a little of the milk if the mixture is very stiff. Add the remaining milk gradually, beating well until the mixture is smooth. Bring to the boil, stirring constantly. Continue to stir and simmer gently for 2-3 minutes. Serve warm.

PINEAPPLE SAUCE

Keeps 3 days under refrigeration.
Do not freeze.

5 oz (150 ml/⅔ cup) brown sugar
5 level tbsp cornflour (cornstarch)
12 fl oz (350 ml/1½ cups) orange cordial
3 tbsp lemon juice
4 x 20 oz (575 g) cans pineapple, finely chopped

Mix together the sugar and cornflour (cornstarch), then blend with the cordial, lemon juice and syrup strained from the fruit. Bring to the boil, stirring constantly, then simmer for 3 minutes. Add the finely chopped pineapple. Leave to go cold.

BUTTERSCOTCH SAUCE

Serves 50.
Keeps 3 days under refrigeration.
Do not freeze.

8 oz (225 g/1 cup) butter
1½ pints (850 ml/3¼ cups) unsweetened evaporated milk
1½ lb (675 g) soft medium brown sugar
12 oz (350 g/1¼ cups) golden (corn) syrup

Place all the ingredients in a heavy-bottomed pan. Heat gently, stirring constantly, until a smooth sauce is formed. Do not boil or it will go grainy.

CHOCOLATE MOUSSE

Serves 50.
Keeps 4 days under refrigeration.
Freeze 3 months.

An excellent *parev* sweet. Set in paper cases or serve by the spoonful with fruit salad. Make exactly as for Chocolate Mousse on p. 342 with the following quantities.

2 lb (900 g) plain (semi-sweet) chocolate
30 eggs
4 level tbsp instant coffee, dissolved in
6 tbsp hot water
6 fl oz (175 ml/¾ cup) rum, Crème de Menthe, brandy, Cointreau or orange juice
5 tbsp caster (superfine) sugar

For the garnish
8 oz (225 g/2 cups) toasted almonds or chopped walnuts

FESTIVALS

THE JEWISH YEAR

Rosh Hashanah (New Year)	1 and 2 Tishri (September/October)
Yom Kippur (Day of Atonement)	10 Tishri (September/October)
Sukkot (Tabernacles)	15 Tishri (September/October)
Simchat Torah (The Rejoicing of the Law)	23 Tishri (September/October)
Chanukkah (Feast of Lights)	25 Kislev (December)
Purim (Feast of Lots)	14 Adar (February/March)
Pesach (Passover)	15 Nissan (March/April)
Shavuot (Pentecost or Feast of Weeks)	6 Sivan (May/June)

FESTIVAL FOODS

The tapestry of festivals that is woven through the Jewish year is probably the strongest link we have with our heritage. To prepare the house and table for each festival as it occurs in its turn is one of the most pleasurable responsibilities involved in running a Jewish household.

Although it is permitted to cook on a festival, it is not permitted to *create* a flame. If you have a gas stove with a pilot light, it is permissible to light the oven and also to use an electric oven on a time switch. Most women prefer to get all the special cooking and baking done in advance, so that they too can enjoy the holiday spirit. In earlier generations this meant a great deal of hard work, for every single food had to be made at home, without any mechanical or electrical assistance. Fish had to be chopped by hand, after being carried home in the early morning from the local fish market. Then there was special enriched bread to be kneaded, intricately plaited and gilded with a goosefeather dipped in egg. The fowl had to be plucked and drawn, herrings skinned and filleted, kreplach rolled and boiled, and beetroots hand-chopped for borscht.

Today, frozen gefilte-fish mix can be bought at the supermarket; the baker labours over the bread; the fowl comes ready-scalded and koshered; borscht comes ready to be poured from a bottle; and kreplach comes ready to turn out of a tin. All of which is very labour-saving, but just a little sad. I do hope that the tradition of making at home those dishes which recall great moments in our history (and at the same time provide a unique social commentary on Jewish life-styles over the past 3,500 years) will not die out completely. That is why, in the pages that follow, I have modernized the method of making these delicacies while trying to retain the essential flavour of the dish.

For each festival I give a selection of special recipes. For other dishes traditionally associated with the occasion, recipes will be found in other sections of the book.

ROSH HASHANAH (NEW YEAR)

Ever since the return from Babylon (where the art of sugar cookery is thought to have originated), Jewish housewives have made all kinds of sweet foods at this festival as a symbol of the sweetness they hope for in the year ahead.

This sweetness is often introduced into dishes by using dried fruits or honey, as in the Ashkenazi Pflaumen Tsimmes, a long-simmered prune and carrot casserole, and the Lekach, a honey cake for which there are innumerable recipes. In Morocco, it's customary at this season to make a lamb or chicken tagine (stew) sweetened with both dried fruits and honey, while in Syrian Jewish homes there will be a dish of okra (ladies' fingers) containing both dried prunes and apricots.

While all kinds of fruit are served at Rosh Hashanah, the apple is the symbolic fruit of the season, expressing in both its sweetness and its round shape the hope for a satisfying and sweet New Year. Besides being used in all kinds of pies, cakes and strudels, it is also served in both Ashkenazi and Sephardi households spread with honey after Kiddush (the prayer of sanctification) has been made on the eve of the festival. On the second night, it is usual to serve an additional fruit such as pineapple or pomegranate to justify the recitation of the 'Shehechiyanu' blessing, which is always recited over a new and fresh food.

As at every other festival, no Rosh Hashanah is complete in Ashkenazi homes without a platter of poached and fried gefilte fish. In Sephardi households it is also customary to eat fish dishes, such as the Italian Pesce all' Ebraica and the Moroccan fish stuffed with dates, which symbolize fruitfulness and fertility in their culture, as do dishes with seeds such as the Turkish Pollo con Susam (Chicken with Sesame Seeds).

Even the familiar challah (enriched bread) takes on a new shape at this season, for it is baked in a special round shape by Jews everywhere to signify that the year has gone full cycle and there is a new and hopefully better one about to commence. The Ashkenazi custom is to enrich this spiral-shaped bread with extra egg and sugar, and in some cases with raisins. A particularly delicious Sephardi bread baked at New Year is the round 'Khubz', containing both sesame seeds and aniseed.

Menus for Rosh Hashanah

MENU 1
A CHICKEN MEAL

A blend of the traditional and newer, lighter dishes, with a strong emphasis on fruits of the season. Everything (except the chicken, which should be cooked early in the day - see recipe) can be prepared over several days, leaving only the final 'assembly job' on the day.

Slices of apple spread with honey (see p. 556)
A Challah for Rosh Hashanah (see p. 558)
Chicken Liver Pâté with Marinated Tarragon Pears (see p. 5)
Chicken Soup with Lokshen and Knaidlach (see pp. 28, 49, 51)
Biblical Chicken with Honey, Almonds and Raisins (see p. 213)
Tsimmes with (optional) Dumpling (see p. 563)
Sweet Potato and Apple Purée (see p. 264)
Biscuit Tortoni (with parev *cream) (see p. 359)*
Peaches in Red Wine with Passion Fruit and Pine Kernels (see p. 323)

MENU 2
A FISH MEAL

The filleting of the whole fish by the fishmonger makes it very easy to portion at the table. A light yet luscious menu.

Slices of apple spread with honey (see p. 556)
A Challah for Rosh Hashanah (see p. 558)
Crème Forestière (see p. 48)
A Whole Filleted Salmon with a Lime and Watercress Sauce (see p. 75)
Perfect Potato Salad (see p. 292)
A Melon and Cherry Tomato Salad (see p. 294)
Salade Menton (see p. 286)
Pfirsichschnitten (Peach slice) with Peach-flavoured Fromage Frais (see p. 398)
4-fruit Salad (see p. 326)

SUGGESTED BAKING FOR ROSH HASHANAH

If any of the cakes or biscuits are to be served for tea after a meat meal, substitute a *parev* block margarine for the butter.

Wine and Spice Cake (see p. 562)
Lekach with Cognac (see p. 561)
Yom Tov Chocolate Cake with Toblerone Topping (see p. 414)
Danish Nut Crisps (see p. 453)
Traditional Butter Biscuits (see p. 443)
Judebrod (see p. 444)
Nusskipferl (see p. 445)
German Stollen (see p. 476)

CHALLAH FOR ROSH HASHANAH

Makes 2 medium loaves.
Keeps 3 days at room temperature in a bread container.
Freeze baked 3 months, or shaped and ready for baking for 2 weeks.

It's a great *mitzvah* - and a special pleasure - to make your own challot for this Festival, shaped not in the usual plait but wound into a spiral, reaching symbolically towards heaven, carrying our hopes and prayers for a happy New Year.

In the 'old' days it would take 20 minutes to knead the dough by hand until it became like a springy, silken ball. Today it takes just 5 minutes with a dough hook, and the bread will have the same fine texture - almost like that of cake. The dough seems to make the very best bread if it can be left to rise slowly overnight, as described in the recipe, but if time is short it can be allowed to rise in a warm kitchen, where it will take about 2 hours. Alternatively, the bread can be shaped ready for the oven and then frozen; in this case, once it is defrosted, bake it as though it were newly prepared.

11 fl oz (300 ml/1⅓ cups) warm water
1½ lb (675 g/6 cups) white strong (bread) flour
1 oz (25 g/2 cakes) fresh yeast or 1 sachet easy-blend yeast
2 oz (50 g/¼ cup) sugar or 2 rounded tbsp honey
1½ teasp salt
5 tbsp oil
2 large eggs

For the glaze
1 egg yolk
1 teasp water
good pinch of salt
poppy seeds or sesame seeds

Attach the dough hook to the mixer, then put the water into the mixing bowl followed by a third of the flour, the crumbled yeast and the sugar or honey. Mix until smooth, about 2 minutes, then cover with a tea-towel and leave for 10 or 15 minutes, until it has frothed up. Add all the remaining ingredients for the dough.

If you use easy-blend yeast, omit the preliminary mixing and rising. Mix the yeast thoroughly with the other dry ingredients, then add all the remaining ingredients to the bowl.

Now mix at low speed until a sticky ball begins to form, then turn to medium speed and knead for 4 or 5 minutes, until the dough is slapping against the edges of the bowl, leaving it clean as it goes round. If it looks sticky after this time, work in a further 1 or 2 tablespoons of flour.

Tip the dough on to a floured board and knead with the hands for a further minute, until it is tight and springy with a silky feel. Grease a large bowl with oil, turn the dough in it to coat it (this stops the surface from drying out), cover with clingfilm (saranwrap) and leave to rise in the refrigerator. If it rises before you have time to deal with it (it takes from 9 to 12 hours but can be left for up to 24 hours, punch it down and leave it to rise again.

To shape the loaves Take the risen dough from the refrigerator and leave it to come to room temperature in the kitchen - about 1 hour. (Or put it on the Defrost cycle of the microwave oven for 2 minutes, until warm to the touch.) Divide the dough into 2 pieces and work on each half (to make 1 loaf) as follows. Knead the dough by hand or machine for 2 minutes to break down any large bubbles of gas, then leave for 5 minutes to tighten up again under a cloth. Roll into a 'snake' about 18 inches (45 cm) long and 1½ inches (4 cm) in diameter. Take the left-hand end of the 'snake' and start coiling it round on itself, making a spiral, so that when all the dough has been wound, the end you started with will be on top and the right-hand end can be tucked underneath. Repeat with the second piece of dough.

To glaze Mix together the yolk, water and salt for the glaze, then paint the mixture all over the risen loaves and scatter with the seeds.

A ROUND CHALLAH FOR ROSH HASHANAH

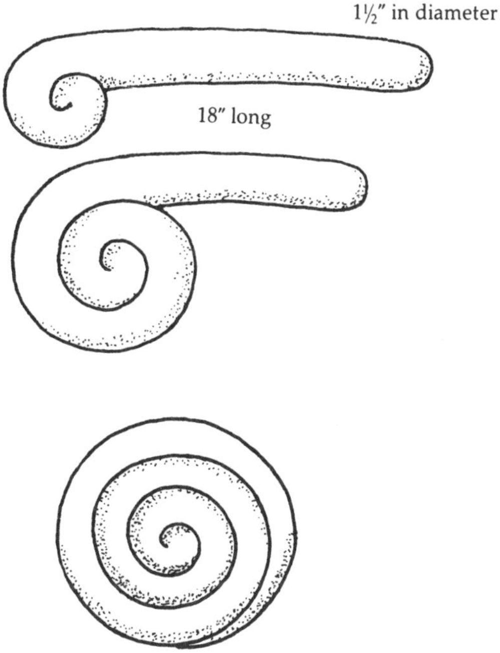

To prove and bake the loaves Arrange the loaves on 1 large or 2 smaller lightly greased trays, then slip the tray(s) into a large plastic bag and leave until the loaves have almost doubled in size, feel light and spongy to the touch and spring back immediately when lightly dented with a finger. This takes 30 or 40 minutes. Meanwhile, preheat the oven to Gas No. 7 (425°F/220°C). Bake for 25 minutes, then turn the oven down to Gas No. 6 (400°F/200°C) for a further 10–15 minutes, or until the bread is a rich brown. Lift the loaves off the tray and tap the bottom. If the bread sounds hollow, take them out. Otherwise leave them in the oven for another 5 minutes and tap the bottom again. When done, remove to a cooling tray.

A Quintet of Lekachs

Lekach is the cake most closely associated with Rosh Hashanah in Ashkenazi households. Although it is generally thought of as a honey cake, in many communities a lekach can be any kind of sweet and spicy cake that is made for a special occasion, whether it be a festival or a family celebration.

The lekach has perhaps the longest pedigree of any traditional Jewish cake, probably dating back to the Middle Ages, when most cakes had to be spiced to mask the flavour of the crude chemicals used as raising agents and honey was actually a cheaper sweetener than sugar. (As the first printed Jewish cookbook did not appear until around 1811, one can only set an approximate date by looking for similar cakes in general cookbooks of the period.)

Recipes for lekach are infinite in their variety, each shtetl of the Pale of Settlement having its own version that was passed around by word of mouth. Honey was the chosen sweetener because cheap refined sugar was not widely available until the end of the nineteenth century (golden/corn syrup is essentially an Anglo-Jewish ingredient), while the oil with which this cake is traditionally mixed makes it *parev*, so that it could be eaten after either a meat or milk meal. Most honey cakes need to mature for a week in a tightly closed tin or foil container and after a month kept at room temperature can be frozen, but the spices do tend to lose some of their flavour.

AN ANGLO-JEWISH LEKACH

Keeps 2 weeks at room temperature in an airtight container.
Freeze 3 months.

This is the archetypal lekach made by many Jewish cooks in Britain. Like all cakes raised by the action of bicarbonate of soda with an acid ingredient such as coffee, fruit juice, honey or golden (corn) syrup, it will go into the oven as a thin batter and come out a spongy moist cake several times its uncooked volume. So it's important to get the alkaline-acid balance correct by measuring all the ingredients very carefully, and also to use the size of tin recommended in the recipe to allow the cake room to rise without overflowing into the oven.

6 oz (175 g/1½ cups) plain (all-purpose) flour
3 oz (75 g/⅓ cup) caster (superfine) sugar
½ teasp ground ginger
½ teasp ground cinnamon
1 level teasp mixed spice
8 oz (225 g/¾ cup) clear honey
4 tbsp sunflower oil
2 eggs
1 level teasp bicarbonate of soda (baking soda) dissolved in 3 fl oz (125 ml/½ cup) orange juice and the grated rind of the orange
2 oz (50 g/½ cup) chopped walnuts

Mix together the flour, sugar and spices. Make a well in the centre, then add the honey, oil, rind and eggs. Beat well together until smooth. Dissolve the bicarbonate of soda in the orange juice and add the nuts. Stir into the flour mixture. Pour into a greaseproof- or silicone-paper lined tin approx. 10 x 8 x 2 inches (25 x 20 x 5 cm).

Bake at Gas No. 4 (350°F/180°C) for 50–55 minutes, or until firm to the touch. Remove from the oven and leave to cool. When quite cold, foil-wrap and leave at room temperature if possible for 4–5 days before using. Improves with keeping.

VARIATION

COFFEE AND SPICE HONEY CAKE

Use 2 level teaspoons each cinnamon and ginger. Dissolve bicarbonate of soda in 4 fl oz (125 ml/½ cup) hot coffee instead of orange juice.

AMERICAN-STYLE LEKACH

Makes 2 x 2 lb (900 g) loaf cakes.
Keep at room temperature wrapped in foil for several days before using.
Will keep 1 month in an airtight container.
Freeze for 3 months (the spices tend to lose their flavour after that).

Twentieth-century American-style lekachs often include ingredients such as orange juice, brandy and coffee, that are not usually found in Anglo-Jewish versions. This recipe actually uses frozen concentrated orange juice *and* coffee, which produces a richly flavoured cake with a spongy texture that becomes deliciously moist after 4 or 5 days.

Because it's so light, this cake would be ideal to serve with that first cup of tea after the Yom Kippur Fast.

10 oz (275 g/2½ cups) plain white flour and 4 oz (125 g/1 cup) wholemeal flour or 14 oz (400 g/3½ cups) white flour
1 teasp ground cinnamon
1 teasp mixed spice
⅛ teasp salt
1½ teasp baking powder
2 teasp bicarbonate of soda (baking soda)
4 eggs
3 fl oz (150 ml/⅓ cup) sunflower or other vegetable oil
7 oz (200 g/1 cup) medium brown soft sugar
bare 11 oz (300 g/1 cup) honey
1 tbsp instant coffee granules
8 fl oz (225 ml/1 cup) warm water
6 fl oz (175 ml/¾ cup) frozen concentrated orange juice, thawed but not diluted

Grease 2 x 2-lb (900 g) loaf tins measuring approximately 9 x 5 x 3 inches (22.5 x 12.5 x 7.5 cm) and line the bottom and the shorter side of each tin with a strip of silicone paper. Preheat the oven to Gas No. 3 (325°F/160°C). Mix together well the flour, spices and raising agents. In a large mixing bowl, use an electric mixer at medium speed to beat together the eggs, oil, sugar and honey until completely combined. Dissolve the instant coffee granules in the water and add with the remaining ingredients. Beat, scraping the bowl occasionally, for 3 minutes, or until the batter is very smooth. This can also be done in a large food processor, but pulse in the flour only until it disappears.

Divide the mixture between the 2 tins evenly. Bake for 1 hour 10 minutes, or until a toothpick inserted in the centre of each cake comes out clean. Cool in the tins on a wire rack for 45 minutes. Run a knife around the edge of each cake to loosen it, then turn out of its tin and peel the silicone paper from the bottom. Invert the cakes so the tops are facing upwards. Cool completely on the wire racks, then wrap in foil for storage.

A LEKACH WITH COGNAC

Keeps 2 weeks at room temperature in an airtight container.
Freeze 3 months.

This recipe uses dark brown sugar for extra moistness and cognac for extra flavour.

1 teasp dark coffee granules
3 fl oz (75 ml/⅓ cup) boiling water
9 oz (250 g/⅓ cup plus 1 tbsp) runny honey
1 tbsp cognac (optional)
2 eggs
5 tbsp sunflower oil
5 oz (150 g/⅔ cup) dark brown sugar
7 oz (200 g/1¾ cups) plain (all-purpose) flour
pinch of salt
1 teasp bicarbonate of soda (baking soda)
½ teasp ground cinnamon
½ teasp ground ginger
¼ teasp ground nutmeg

Preheat the oven to Gas No. 4 (350°F/180°C). Grease a tin measuring 8–8½ inches (20–21 cm) square and 2 inches (5 cm) deep (a little larger will do no harm, but a smaller one may cause the mixture to overflow in the oven). Line the bottom and 2 sides of the tin with a strip of silicone paper. Melt the coffee granules in the boiling water then pour on to the honey, stir until smooth, then stir in the brandy.

In a large bowl, whisk the eggs until frothy, then whisk in the oil and brown sugar. Sieve all the dry ingredients into another bowl, then gradually add to the egg mixture, alternately with the honey mixture, stirring until absolutely smooth – it will be very thin.

Pour into the tin and bake for 50–55 minutes, or until firm to gentle touch on the surface. Stand on a cooling tray for 5 minutes, then turn out carefully and foil-wrap when absolutely cold.

INDIVIDUAL LEKACH

Makes 24.
Keeps 2 weeks at room temperature in an airtight container.
Freeze 3 months.

If you've not had time to mature a large lekach in advance of the festival, try these individual ones, which are deliciously moist as soon as they are baked.

4 oz (125 g/½ cup) soft margarine
4 oz (125 g/½ cup) soft brown sugar
6 oz (175 g/½ cup plus 2 tbsp) honey or golden (corn) syrup
1 egg
8 oz (225 g/2 cups) plain flour
2 level teasp ground ginger
½ level teasp mixed sweet spice
4 fl oz (125 ml/½ cup) warm water
½ teasp bicarbonate of soda (baking soda) dissolved in the warm water

Preheat the oven to Gas No. 5 (375°F/190°C). Arrange 24 greaseproof baking cases in patty tins.

Put the margarine, sugar, honey or syrup and egg into a bowl or food processor. Beat until smooth. Finally, add the flour sifted with the spices alternately with the bicarbonate of soda dissolved in the water. The batter will be thin. Put a level tablespoon of the mixture into each case.

Bake for 20 minutes until a rich brown and spongy to gentle touch.

A WINE AND SPICE CAKE

Keeps 2 weeks at room temperature wrapped in foil in an airtight container or the baking tin.
Freeze 1 month (spicing fades if frozen longer).

This is a most unusual cake, light as a feather yet with a pleasing moistness. The spicing is delicate - add a little more if you find it too mild. It can be eaten fresh.

1 lb (450 g/1⅓ cups) golden (corn) syrup
10 fl oz (275 ml/1¼ cups) cold water
7 oz (200 g/1 cup) granulated sugar
8 fl oz (225 ml/1 cup) flavourless oil (eg sunflower)
3 eggs
1 lb (450 g/4 cups) self-raising flour or 1 lb (450 g/4 cups) plain (all-purpose) flour with 4 level teasp baking powder
1 level teasp each of ground ginger, cinnamon and mixed sweet spice
1 level teasp baking powder
1 level teasp bicarbonate of soda
2 tbsp plus 2 teasp (50 ml) port-type (eg Kiddush) red wine

Preheat the oven to Gas No. 6 (400°F/200°C). Lightly brush with oil a baking tin measuring 12 x 9 x 2 inches (30 x 23 x 5 cm) and line the base and short sides with a piece of silicone paper. Heat the syrup, water, sugar and oil over gentle heat, stirring until the mixture is smooth and the sugar has dissolved. In a large bowl, whisk the eggs together until creamy and frothy, then gradually add the syrup mixture, mixing with a wooden spoon or balloon whisk all the time.

Finally, stir in all the dry ingredients, which have been sifted together, and the bicarbonate of soda dissolved in the wine. Make sure the mixture is smooth and even in colour. Pour into the tin and then put into the oven. Immediately turn the heat down to Gas No. 2 (300°F/150°C) and bake for 1¼-1½ hours, or until firm to the touch and a rich brown. Turn the tin over on to a cooling tray. After 5 minutes remove the tin and turn the cake the right side up on to another cooling tray. When quite cold return to the washed tin and cover with foil. Cut in squares to serve.

CIDER APPLE CAKE

Makes 24 fingers.
Keeps 3 days under refrigeration.
Freeze 3 months.

A wonderful flavour permeates this light and tender cake as well as its filling. It's quickly made, *parev*, and it cuts into 24 generous pieces. It can also be served as a dessert, slightly warm and accompanied by a fruit compôte after a meat meal, or soured cream or honeyed yoghurt after a dairy one.

2 medium baking apples, peeled, cored and very thinly sliced

For the nut mixture
3½ oz (100 g/⅞ cup) packet shelled pecans, finely chopped
3 oz (75 g/⅓ cup) granulated sugar

For the cake mixture
4 oz (125 g/½ cup) soft margarine
5 oz (150 g/⅔ cup) caster (superfine) sugar
3 eggs
8 oz (225 g/2 cups) plain (all-purpose) flour or fine-milled brown flour
1 teasp baking powder
1 teasp bicarbonate of soda
1 teasp cinnamon
½ teasp mixed spice
5 fl oz (150 ml/⅔ cup) dry cider or apple juice

Chop the nuts coarsely (most easily done in a food processor), then put with the sugar in a small bowl. Put the apples in another. Grease a tin approximately 12 x 8 x 2 inches (30 x 20 x 5 cm) and preheat the oven to Gas No. 5 (375°F/190°C).

If you are preparing the cake mixture in a mixer, cream the fat and sugar until fluffy, beat in the eggs 1 at a time, then stir in the flour (sifted with the spices and raising agents) alternately with the liquid. Or use Food Processor Method 1 (see p. 408).

Pour half the mixture into the prepared tin, arrange the sliced apples in an even layer on top and sprinkle with half the nut mixture. Smooth the remaining cake mixture on top and sprinkle with the remaining nut mixture. Bake for 35 minutes, until spongy to the touch and a toothpick comes out clean from the centre.

Serve at room temperature cut in fingers.

TSIMMES WITH DUMPLING

Serves 6 as a main course, 8 as a side dish – but you can never *make enough tsimmes to satisfy everyone.*

A 'tsimmes' might be called a Jewish hotpot, for its flavour depends on long, slow cooking during which the sweet elements in it – be they carrots, dried fruits, sweet potatoes, squash, honey or golden (corn) syrup – slowly caramelize, giving rise to a glorious aroma. Some tsimmes recipes are purely vegetarian, but the inclusion of brisket – either as a joint or in cubes – gives added richness. The dumpling (halke) was always a special feature of the dish, but as it boosts the calorie content considerably, it is usually omitted today.

2 lb (900 g) slice of brisket
3 lb (1½ kg) carrots
4 slightly rounded tbsp golden (corn) syrup
¼ teasp white pepper
2 teasp salt
1 tbsp cornflour (cornstarch)
1½ lb (675 g) potatoes

For the dumpling (optional)
3 oz (75 g/⅓ cup) margarine
6 oz (175 g/1½ cups) self-raising flour or 6 oz (175 g/1½ cups) plain (all-purpose) flour plus 1½ teasp baking powder
½ teasp salt
3–4 tbsp water to mix

Trim excess fat off the meat, leaving a thin edging, then cut into 1½-inch (4-cm) chunks. Peel the carrots and cut into ½-inch (1.25-cm) cubes. Put the carrots and meat into a pan, barely cover with hot water, add 2 tablespoons of the syrup, the pepper and ½ teaspoon of salt, bring to the boil, and simmer for 2 hours either on top of the stove or in a slow oven. Skim, or if possible, chill overnight, so that most of the fat can be removed.

4 hours before you want to serve the tsimmes, make the dumpling by rubbing the margarine into the flour and salt. Mix to a soft dough with the water. Put the dumpling in the middle of a large oval earthenware, enamel or enamelled-iron casserole. Lift the meat and carrots from their cooking liquid with a perforated spoon and arrange round it. (Without a dumpling, simply put the carrots and potatoes into the casserole.) Mix the cornflour with enough water to make a smooth cream, then stir into the stock from the carrots and meat. Bring to the boil and pour over the carrots and meat. Peel and cut the potatoes into large cubes and arrange on top, adding extra boiling water if necessary so that they are just submerged. Sprinkle with the remaining 1½ teaspoons of salt and 2 tablespoons of syrup. Cover and bring to the boil on top of the stove, then transfer to a slow oven, Gas No. 2 (300°F/150°C), for 3½ hours. Uncover and taste, adding a little more syrup if necessary. Allow to brown for a further half an hour, then serve. The potatoes and the dumpling should be slightly brown and the sauce slightly thickened.

VARIATION

PFLAUMEN TSIMMES

Add 8 oz (225 g) tenderized prunes and/or 8 oz (225 g) dried apricots when the dish is cooked for the second time. American recipes also include 2 large sweet potatoes, peeled and cubed, as well as ordinary ones.

MOROCCAN CHICKEN AND PRUNE TAGINE

Serves 6–8.
Keeps 2 days under refrigeration.
Freeze 2 months.

Any dish containing a black food – be it prunes or olives – is never served on the Eve of Rosh Hashanah in Moroccan Jewish households for fear it would dim the lightness and brightness of the first day of the festival. But on the second night a tagine (the name refers to the traditional earthenware pot in which the dish is cooked) made with either chicken or lamb is eaten, because of the sweet ingredients – the dried fruit and honey it contains. A similar dish, Poyo kon Prounes, is also to be found in the Graeco-Jewish cuisine.

4 oz (125 g) prunes, preferably tenderized
4 oz (125 g) dried apricots, preferably tenderized
2 oz (50 g/½ cup) toasted split almonds
3 tbsp extra virgin olive oil
6–8 chicken portions
1 teasp salt
20 grinds of black pepper
1 large onion
2 cloves of garlic
1 teasp ground turmeric
3 cardamom pods
1 teasp ground ginger
2 teasp ground cinnamon
20 fl oz (575 ml/2½ cups) chicken stock or half stock and half white wine
1 tbsp honey
2 teasp cornflour (cornstarch)
2 teasp lemon juice or water

Several hours in advance or overnight, soak the dried fruit (if necessary) in water to cover. Preheat the oven to Gas No. 2 (300°F/150°C). Fry the almonds in the hot oil over moderate heat until golden brown, then drain on paper towels and reserve. Remove the skin and any visible fat from the chicken portions, thoroughly dry them, then season with the salt and pepper. Fry the chicken in the hot oil until rich brown on all sides, then lift out and drain on paper towels to remove any surplus fat. Lay the pieces side by side in a lidded casserole and surround with the drained fruit.

In the same oil gently sauté the finely chopped onion and garlic until they turn a rich golden brown (keep the pan lid on for 5 minutes to soften them in the steam, then remove it to finish the browning). Add the spices and stock (and wine if used) and honey. Stir well to release any crispy bits adhering to the base of the pan, then bring to the boil and simmer for 5 minutes. Stir in the cornflour mixed with the lemon juice (or water, if wine has been used). Pour over the chicken. Cover and bake for 1 hour, or until tender when pierced with a sharp knife. Do not overcook as the chicken will soften during the reheating.

Garnish the dish with the almonds.

YOM KIPPUR (DAY OF ATONEMENT)

Although Yom Kippur is a Fast Day, the main preparations from the cook's point of view are concerned with making 2 special meals - that before the Fast on Kol Nidre, and that eaten 25 hours later, when it has ended. The *minhag* (custom) that governs the menu before and after the Fast leaves very little room or desire for innovation. Simple, soothing food that is satisfying without being thirst-making is essential for Kol Nidre night. Chicken soup with kreplach or matzah balls, followed by an uncomplicated roast or braised bird, and a fruity dessert, followed by a large glass of lemon tea, is the general Ashkenazi pattern throughout the world - what food can bring us closer to our roots on that day?

In Sephardi households chicken in both soup and casserole is also on the Kol Nidre menu, although Algerian Jews prefer a meaty couscous. A green or vegetable salad accompanies the main course, with dishes of okra and rice, followed by a refreshing fruit such as watermelon or nut-filled pastries ('cigares'). A charming Algerian custom is the baking of sweet rolls (petits pains) filled with almonds and raisins and baked in the shape of the initials of the family! It is customary for small children to be given a small loaf with an egg in its shell baked in the centre to eat while the adults are abstaining from food. The Ashkenazi *'feigele'* challah is shaped like a little bird to carry our prayers up to Heaven!

After the meal, the table is cleared and then reset with the cloth and candles. A special *yahrzeit* candle is lit if any one in the household has lost a parent and then the woman of the house lights the festival candles and the Fast has commenced.

The meal should be prepared in good time as it must be eaten much earlier than usual (usually between 5 and 6 pm, according to the calendar), as immediately afterwards the family leave for the synagogue and the Kol Nidre service. To avoid this many Dutch Sephardim prefer to have a 2-course main meal at lunchtime, followed by a light meal just before they leave for the service - this seems to me an eminently sensible arrangement and kinder on the digestion.

After the Fast in Ashkenazi households there are only minor variations from the sequence that goes: a glass of Kiddush wine, then a piece of buttered kuchen or plain cake, with several cups of tea and some kind of smoked or pickled fish - some say it's to restore mineral salts lost by the body during the day, but most people enjoy the way a spicy food tickles the fasting palate - then to the table for a fish meal and a not-too-demanding dessert.

In Sephardi communities, a host of dishes are traditional for breaking the Fast. According to Gilda Angel in her fascinating *Sephardic Holiday Cooking,* these can vary from the 'pipitada' (melon-seed milk) of the Greek and Turkish Jews, to the 'sutlac' (cold rice pudding) from Izmir (Smyrna), to the 'pannekoeken' (pancakes) of the Dutch Jews, to the 'hojaldres de queso o berenja' (cheese and aubergine filo pastries) of the Jews of Rhodes.

Menus for the Eve of the Fast

MENU 1
A CHICKEN MEAL

A quickly prepared, easy-to-digest meal that won't provoke thirst. You may prefer to use chicken breasts instead of the legs; the potatoes are cooked with the chicken.

Chicken Soup with Kreplach (see pp. 28, 50)
Poulet Paysanne (see p. 211)
Special mixed vegetables (frozen)
Washington Apple Crisp (see p. 312)
Melon and Grape Cocktail (see p. 16)
Lemon tea

MENU 2
A FISH MEAL

Winter Cream of Vegetable Soup with Croûtons (see pp. 39, 53)
Stove-top Fish Casserole (includes new potatoes and peas) (see p. 70)
Baked Apples in Orange Syrup (see p. 314)
Yogurt, Custard or Vanilla Parfait (see p. 355)
Tea

ALTERNATIVE VEGETARIAN MAIN COURSE

Eggs in Corn and Cheese Sauce (see p. 105)

Menus for after the Fast

First stimulate the tastebuds with the traditional *'forspeise'*, then satisfy thirst – and hunger – with tea and simple cake and kuchen. Finally, sit down to enjoy a meal that needs only a brief reheating of the comforting soup and the cauliflower.

WITH A GLASS OF KIDDUSH WINE ON RETURNING HOME

Smoked Salmon or Pickled Herring on buttered challah (see pp. 7, 10)

WITH COPIOUS CUPS OF TEA

Lekach, American Style, or Buttering Kuchen (can be bought from the baker) (see pp. 560, 474)

Soup au Cresson, served hot, with Croûtons (see pp. 48, 53)
Chopped and Fried Fish (see p. 65)
Fried Steaks or Fillets of Plaice with chrane (pink horseradish sauce) (see p. 61)
Cauliflower au Gratin, reheated in microwave or very hot oven (see p. 255)
Spiced Mushrooms (see p. 291)
Cherry tomatoes
Frozen Lemon Slice with Strawberry Sauce (see pp. 357, 366)
More tea

ALTERNATIVE VEGETARIAN MAIN COURSE

Lancashire Cheese Tart with Garden Herbs (see p. 126)

SUKKOT (TABERNACLES)

Sukkot, the week-long autumn harvest festival commemorating the years that the Jews had to wander in the wilderness, living out their days in makeshift huts, is a particularly happy occasion in the Jewish calendar. Many families make their own Sukkah or Tabernacle, where they eat their meals, and every house is sweet with the fragrance of fruit and flowers.

Immediately after the end of the Yom Kippur Fast, it is the custom in many communities for the men to construct a Sukkah in the grounds of the synagogue, then line its roof (which must be partly open to the sky) with greenery. Then the women get to work decorating it with fruit and vegetables - these are usually sent to hospitals and old peoples' homes at the end of the festival. At the end of each service, the congregation moves into the Sukkah for Kiddush (benediction) and a slice of a traditional cake or biscuit.

The synagogue itself is decorated with autumn fruits and flowers (donated by the members) and during the service every member is given the opportunity to make the blessing over the *etrog* - a particularly fragrant citrus fruit - and the *lulav* - a sheaf composed of 2 willow branches, a palm branch and 3 myrtle branches. During the prayer the *lulav* is shaken according to a laid-down ritual. Many people can be seen holding the *etrog* up to their noses so that its exquisite perfume can be savoured. During the service, the *etrog* and *lulav* are carried round the synagogue but on the last day - Hoshana Rabbah - it is carried round 7 times!

To symbolize the richness of the harvest (for Sukkot is one of the 3 harvest festivals that used to be celebrated by pilgrimages to the Temple in Jerusalem) stuffed foods of all kinds are served as both savouries and sweets. Cabbages, vine leaves, tomatoes, aubergines (eggplant) and peppers are stuffed with lean minced (ground) beef and braised in a sweet-and-sour tomato or meat sauce. Holishkes and gevikelte kraut are the most popular in the West, but in Israel stuffed aubergines ('chatzilim') and peppers ('pilpel mimulad') are making a new tradition. For dessert, strudels are stuffed with apples and dried fruits, and melons of all kinds are served in the Sukkah.

Menus for Sukkot

Stuffed vegetables from different Jewish food cultures make up this traditional meal, preceded by an elegant soup that uses one of the vegetables of this season in an innovative way.

MENU 1
A MEAT MEAL

Aubergine and Coriander Soup (meat version) (see p. 40)
Assorted stuffed vegetables
Holishkes (see p. 570)
Stuffed Aubergines (see p. 248)
Gefilte Paprika (see p. 152)
or
Bstilla (Chicken Pie) (see p. 572)
Golden Carrot Rice (see p. 275)
Mulled Wine Fruit Salad with Toasted Nuts (see p. 326)
Millie Livshin's Sukkot Strudel (see p. 574)

MENU 2
A FISH MEAL

The fish improves vastly after at least 24 hours in the refrigerator. The microwave version is particularly quick and easy with a rich flavour. The superb bread freezes well, so make it in advance.

Baba Ghanoush with warm pitta bread (see p. 23)
Gefilte Fish Provençale (see p. 67)
Insalata Siciliana (see p. 286)
Rye and Caraway Bread and butter (see p. 465)
Cheese board (Lancashire, Stilton, Gruyère) with sections of satsumas
Feuilleton aux Pommes, with Greek-style yoghurt (see p. 394)

ALTERNATIVE VEGETARIAN MAIN COURSE

A Strudel of Stir-fried Vegetables with Mayonnaise Chantilly (see p. 118)

SUGGESTED BAKING FOR SUKKOT
(*Home or Synagogue*)

Alex Baron's Baklava (see p. 578)
Puff Pastry Strudel (see p. 573)
Romanian Turkish Delight Strudel (see p. 577)
Apfelschnitten (see p. 398)
Ginger Slices (see p. 400)
Chocolate Cupcakes (see p. 418)
Farmhouse Fruitcake Squares (see p. 550)

ON STUFFED CABBAGE LEAVES FOR SUKKOT

The Romanian connection in our family call them 'holishkes', the Moscow one 'gevikelte cabbage', and we have friends to whom they're definitely 'praakes' or 'galuptzi'. However, the dish of meat-stuffed cabbage is delectable in any language – though the sauce may be a sweet-and-sour tomato or one based on beef stock, it all comes down to celebrating Sukkot with the good things of the earth. A very modern tip: instead of that tedious job, blanching the cabbage, and the even worse one of peeling off the leaves, *freeze* the cabbage for 24 hours then defrost at room temperature overnight (or for 30 minutes on Defrost in the microwave). The leaves will peel off like a dream.

HOLISHKES
(*Meat-stuffed Cabbage Leaves, Braised in a Sweet-and-Sour Sauce*)

Serves 6 for an entrée, 4 for a main course.

The holishkes will taste better if they can be kept in the refrigerator for 2–3 days before using. Freeze leftovers for up to 3 months.

1 firm head of white cabbage
1 onion
2 tbsp chicken-flavoured fat, sunflower oil or margarine
4 tbsp long-grain rice
4 fl oz (125 ml/½ cup) chicken stock
1 lb (450 g) lean minced (ground) beef
1 teasp salt
10 grinds of black pepper

For the sauce
5 oz (150 g/⅔ cup) tomato purée
½ teasp salt
black pepper
4 tbsp brown sugar
juice of 1 large lemon
10 fl oz (275 ml/2¼ cups) water

Freeze and defrost cabbage as described on p. 569. Use a knife to detach at least 12 leaves from the defrosted cabbage stalk. Cook the finely chopped onion in the oil or fat until golden and tender, then add the rice and cook for 3 minutes, until opaque. Add the stock and cook gently until absorbed, then stir into the meat together with the seasonings.

Lay the cabbage leaves on a board, put 1 tablespoon of filling on each and fold in the edges to enclose the filling. Roll up to make parcels, then squeeze gently between the palms to seal. Pack closely in a large casserole dish.

Preheat the oven to Gas No. 2 (300°F/150°C). Mix the sauce ingredients together with the water and pour over the cabbage parcels. Cover the casserole and cook the holishkes for 2½ hours, then uncover, baste well and turn up the oven to Gas No. 4 (350°F/180°C) for a further 30 minutes to brown the holishkes and thicken the sauce.

GEVIKELTE KRAUT

Serves 6 for an entrée, 4 for a main course.
Keeps 3 days under refrigeration.
Freeze leftovers 3 months.

This is the version favoured by Jews of Russian origin. It has a sweet-and-sour meat sauce, and tastes better if it can be left under refrigeration for 2 days before it is served either hot or cold.

Follow the instructions for freezing and defrosting the cabbage (see Holishkes above) so that the leaves can easily be removed.

1 firm head of white cabbage

For the stuffing
1 lb (450 g) minced raw steak (ground beef)
2 leve tbsp medium matzah meal
1 level teasp salt
pinch of white pepper
1 beaten egg
½ onion, grated

For the sauce
2 tbsp wine vinegar or cider vinegar
2 generous tbsp golden (corn) syrup
1 bay leaf and 5 peppercorns
1 level teasp salt
beef stock or thin gravy barely to cover the cabbage

Mix all the stuffing ingredients together.

Detach 12 large leaves from the defrosted cabbage. Stuff each leaf, one at a time, by placing a tablespoonful of the stuffing in the centre, turning in the sides and rolling up into a bundle. Lift each bundle and give a gentle squeeze with the palm of the hand to seal it. Lay the bundles side by side in a wide, shallow casserole and add sufficient stock (or thin gravy) barely to cover them. Spoon the remaining sauce ingredients over the top.

Put in a moderate oven, Gas No. 4 (350°F/180°C), for half an hour. Then, when the sauce is simmering, turn the oven down to Gas No. 2 (300°F/150°C) for a further 2 hours. 15 minutes before the dish is cooked, uncover it and turn the heat back to brown the tops of the cabbage bundles and thicken the sauce.

STUFFED AUBERGINES

Serves 6.
Keeps 3 days under refrigeration.
Freeze 3 months.

This is the way Egyptian Jews prepare stuffed aubergines (eggplants). It is one of my favourite stuffed vegetable recipes. The dish reheats well.

3 oval aubergines, each weighing approx. 8 oz/225 g
approx. 4 tbsp sunflower oil for frying (add extra if required)
flour for coating

For the stuffing
1 lb (450 g) raw minced (ground) beef
1 beaten egg
1 level teasp salt
10 grinds of black pepper
1 level teasp paprika
4 level tbsp uncooked rice
fried aubergine flesh (see below)

For the sauce
½ onion, finely chopped
1 x 15 oz (400 g) can Italian tomatoes, sieved
3 level tbsp brown sugar
juice of 1 large lemon (3 tbsp)
½ level teasp salt
pinch of white pepper
a little chicken stock or water if necessary

Cut the aubergines in half and scoop out the flesh, leaving a good ¼ inch (0.5 cm) of aubergine all the way round. Roughly chop the scooped-out aubergine flesh, then fry until soft in a little oil. Add to the meat, together with all the remaining stuffing ingredients, and mix well. Mound the meat mixture into each aubergine, pressing it well in.

Dip each stuffed aubergine in flour, then brown it quickly on both sides in a little hot oil. Arrange the browned aubergines in an oven-proof casserole. In the same oil, cook the chopped onion until golden, then stir in all the remaining ingredients for the sauce. When the sauce is bubbling, pour it round the aubergines - they should be just submerged. If not, top up with a little chicken stock or water.

Cover the dish and put in a preheated oven, Gas No. 4 (350°F/180°C) for half an hour (until the sauce is bubbling nicely), then turn the oven down to Gas No. 2 (300°F/150°C) and cook for a further 2 hours. When the aubergines are ready, they will have absorbed most of the sauce, leaving just enough to pour over each aubergine when it is served.

PEPPER RAGU

Serves 6–7.
Keeps 4 days under refrigeration.
Do not freeze.

All the scents and flavours of the Sukkah are encapsulated in this wonderful vegetable starter that combines the sweetness of grilled peppers with the tang of olives and anchovies. If the anchovies are omitted, this makes a superb Sukkot dish for vegetarians. After a day in the fridge to allow the flavours to blend, it can be served in little pots with challah or rye bread, or spooned into a gratin dish as part of a fish buffet.

6 large mixed-colour peppers
1 large onion
1 fat clove of garlic
3 tbsp extra virgin olive oil
½ teasp salt
15 grinds of black pepper
1 vegetable stock-cube
2 tbsp red wine vinegar or cider vinegar
2 tbsp chopped fresh oregano or
1½ teasp dried oregano
1 teasp sugar or granular sweetener
16 black olives
6 anchovy fillets (optional)
1½ tbsp capers

Put the whole peppers under a fierce grill, turning them until the skin is black on all sides. Put them in a plastic bag, close it and leave them to 'steam' for 30 minutes - the skin can then be easily peeled off with the fingers. Cut the peppers into quarters, remove the core, seeds and membranes, then cut in ½-inch-wide (1.25-cm) wide strips.

Put the finely sliced onion, chopped garlic and the oil into an 8-inch (20-cm) sauté pan or deep saucepan, sprinkle with the salt and pepper and 2 tablespoons of water, then cook gently, covered, until the onion is meltingly soft. Uncover and continue to cook until the onion turns golden. Add the peppers, the crumbled stock-cube, the vinegar, herbs and sugar.

Cook, uncovered, on a very low light for half an hour, stirring occasionally (add a couple of tbsp of hot water if the mixture seems to be drying out). Add the flesh cut from the olives, the anchovies cut in ½-inch (1.25-cm) lengths (if used) and the capers, well rinsed, and continue to cook for a further 10 minutes, until you have a rich sauce.

BSTILLA
(*Moroccan Chicken and Filo Pie*)

Serves 6–8.
Ready-to-cook pie keeps 1 day under refrigeration.
Leftovers keep 3 days under refrigeration.
Do not freeze.

This wondrous sweet and savoury pie is served at most Moroccan Jewish celebrations, but it is specially appropriate for Sukkot, because it is stuffed with good things such as chicken, almonds, eggs and spices. In some versions the eggs used in the filling are scrambled, but I prefer Claudia Roden's method, which produces a creamier sauce.

In Morocco, tin-lined copper round trays called t'bseel are used; in the West some cooks use a wok or a paella or pizza pan. I have simplified the construction by using a rectangular lasagne-type dish.

In North Africa, cooks use a home-made filo-type dough called *'warka'* (also transliterated as *'ovarka'*), but commercial filo pastry will do very well.

1 large (4 lb/2 kg) chicken
1 large onion, finely chopped or grated
salt
black pepper
½ teasp ground ginger
½ teasp ground cinnamon
½ teasp mixed spice or ground allspice
1 tbsp finely chopped parsley
10 fl oz (275 ml/1¼ cups) stock from the chicken
7 eggs

4 oz (125 g/1 cup) blanched almonds
5 oz (150 g/$^2/_3$ cup) margarine, melted
16 sheets filo pastry (1 x 14 oz/400 g packet)
1 tbsp sugar
$^1/_4$ teasp ground cinnamon

For the garnish
a little cinnamon and sugar

Wash the bird. Quarter and simmer with the giblets in 10 fl oz (275 ml/1$^1/_4$ cups) water, onion, seasonings and parsley for about 1 hour, or until the bird is absolutely tender (cover the pan with foil and then the lid to keep in the steam). When cooked, drain off the stock and reserve. Skin and bone the cooked chicken and cut the meat into bite-sized pieces.

Take 8 fl oz (225 ml/1 cup) of the stock and blend it with the eggs in the food processor. Pour into a small pan and stir over low heat until the mixture becomes creamy - do not allow to boil. Take off the heat and continue to stir until it stops steaming. The savoury custard and the chicken constitute the filling of the pie. Allow to cool.

Dry-fry the chopped almonds until golden (2 minutes on 100 per cent power in the microwave).

Brush a rectangular overproof dish about 13 x 9 inches (35 x 22.5 cm) and 1$^1/_2$-2 inches (4-5 cm) deep with melted fat (a lasagne dish is ideal). Fit a sheet of filo in the dish so that the sides are also covered. Lay 6 sheets on top of each other, brushing melted fat evenly on each sheet and up the sides. Sprinkle the top layer with sugar, cinnamon and almonds. Spread rather more than half of the cooled egg mixture over this and sprinkle with a little of the remaining stock. Cover with another 4 sheets of filo, each brushed with fat as before. Lay the boned pieces of chicken neatly on top and cover with the rest of the egg mixture. Sprinkle with a little more chicken stock. Cover with the remaining sheets of filo, brushing each one with fat. Trim the filo sheets level with the edges of the dish and then turn the top $^1/_2$ inch (1.25 cm) in and seal to the edge.

Paint the top with the remaining fat and bake in a preheated oven, Gas No. 4 (350°F/180°C) for the first 40 minutes, then raise the temperature to Gas No. 6 (400°F/200°C) and bake for a further 15 minutes, until the pastry is crisp and the top is deep golden in colour. Cool for 10 minutes.

Serve sprinkled with sugar and cinnamon and cut in squares or lozenges. May be assembled one day and cooked the next. May also be reheated until warm to the touch.

STRUDELS STUFFED WITH DRIED FRUITS

Unlike the stretched strudel dough, this type of strudel is extremely easy to prepare and keeps well in a tin. It is served for afternoon tea rather than as a dessert.

PUFF PASTRY STRUDEL

Makes 2 strudels, cutting into approximately 18 slices.
Keeps 1 week under refrigeration.
Freeze 3 months.

To be successful the pastry must be rolled to the thickness of a knife blade. It's nicest served warm and can be reheated.

8 oz (225 g) packet puff pastry

For the filling
12 oz (350 g/2$^1/_4$ cups) mixed dried fruit or
same amount of currants and raisins
2-3 tbsp thick stewed apple (drain off any juice)
3 oz (75 g/$^1/_3$ cup) sugar
1 teasp cinnamon
raspberry, blackcurrant or damson (plum) jam
1 egg white or milk

Roll out the pastry as thinly as possible. Cut in 2. Each half should measure 7 x 12 inches (18 x 30 cm); if not, roll again until the right size.

Mix together the dried fruit, stewed apple, sugar and cinnamon.

To make each strudel, spread the jam generously on the pastry, leaving 1 inch (2.5 cm) clear all the way round. Arrange half the filling down the centre. Dampen the long edges of the rectangle and bring to the centre, one side overlapping the other. The strudel should now be 12 inches (30 cm) long and about 3 inches (7.5 cm) wide. Turn over and carefully lift on to a silicone-paper-lined tray. (This makes it easier to remove if the jam boils out.) Seal the ends of the strudel and mark into slices 1 inch (2.5 cm) wide, cutting through the top layer of pastry only. Brush with slightly beaten egg white. If inconvenient, use milk. Sprinkle with granulated sugar.

Bake at Gas No. 7 (425°F/220°C) for 10 minutes, then reduce to Gas No. 5 (375°F/190°C) for 15 minutes, or until crisply brown.

MILLIE LIVSHIN'S SUKKOT STRUDEL
(Also known as Stuffed Monkey or Geviklte)

Makes 5 x 9-inch (22.5-cm) strudels (40–50 slices).
Keeps 1 month in an airtight container in the refrigerator.
Freeze 3 months.

This biscuity pastry makes a delicious contrast to the juicy filling in this recipe. Mrs Livshin makes this large quantity as she has a host of visitors to serve in the family's Sukkah.

For the filling

1 lb (450 g/3 cups) each sultanas (white raisins), raisins, currants
4 oz (125 g/½ cup) glacé (candied) cherries, coarsely chopped
4 oz (125 g/½ cup) candied peel, coarsely chopped
1 dessert apple, grated
4 oz (125 g/½ cup) sugar
1 teasp cinnamon
2–3 tbsp seedless jam (eg apricot)
2 tbsp desiccated coconut

For the pastry

1 lb (450 g/4 cups) self-raising flour or
1 lb (450 g/4 cups) plain (all-purpose) flour plus 4 teasp baking powder
3 oz (75 g/⅓ cup) caster (superfine) sugar
8 oz (225 g/1 cup) block margarine or butter
1 oz (25 g/2 tbsp) white cooking fat
2 eggs
2–3 tbsp granulated sugar

To make the filling Cover the dried fruit with cold water, bring to the boil and simmer for 4 minutes, then drain thoroughly and pat dry with paper towels. Put in a large bowl. Add the cherries, peel, apple, sugar and cinnamon and mix well. Leave to cool.

To make the pastry Mix the flour and sugar. Cut the fats into roughly 1-inch (2.5-cm) cubes, then rub in by hand or machine to form the texture of breadcrumbs. Mix in 1 whole egg and 1 yolk, plus 3–4 tbsp water and gather into a non-sticky dough. Knead lightly until smooth. (Or make by Food Processor Method, p. 371.) Chill for 30 minutes.

Preheat the oven to Gas No. 5 (375°F/190°C).

Divide the pastry into 5 balls and work on each as follows. Roll out thinly to a 7 x 11 inch (18 x 28 cm) rectangle, spread sparingly with jam and then thickly with the fruit mixture, leaving a 1-inch (2.5 cm) border. Sprinkle lightly with the desiccated coconut, turn in the short sides, then roll up widthways.

Glaze with the reserved lightly whisked egg white. Place on a baking tray with the join underneath. Sprinkle with a thin layer of granulated sugar. Make slanting cuts ¾ inch (2 cm) apart through the top layer of strudel – this prevents cracking.

Bake for 30 minutes until golden. Cool and serve in slices.

DIABETIC STRUDEL

Makes 3 strudels, each containing approximately 32 g carbohydrate. Weigh ingredients in grams for accuracy.
Average serving 11 g carbohydrate.
Keeps 1 week under refrigeration.

1 x 250 g pack puff pastry
120 g diabetic or low-sugar jam
120 g unsweetened coconut

Roll out the pastry paper-thin, making a rectangle 15 x 17 inches (37.5 x 42.5 cm). Divide this into 3 narrow rectangles, each measuring 5 x 17 inches (12.5 x 42.5 cm).

Working on each rectangle in turn, spread 40 g of the jam in a narrow band the length of the piece of pastry, leaving ½ inch (1.25 cm) clear at either end. Sprinkle the jam with 40 g of the coconut, then roll up into a strudel. Bake in a hot oven, Gas No. 7 (425°F/220°C), for 10 to 15 minutes, until a rich brown.

APPLE BUWELE

Serves 6.
Keeps 3 days under refrigeration.
Freeze until required.

Wrapped in tender yeast dough, a cinnamon-scented apple filling is the heart of a famous South German Jewish dish that by tradition was served at Sukkot. Sometimes it was called 'schalet' but more often – and more endearingly – 'apfel buwele', or little apple boy. In her delicious book on Yomtov specialities, Joan Nathan describes how, in her family, it was cooked in a big black pot so that the spicy juices that oozed out as it baked could be used to baste the cake and glaze it.

In my version, the apples are tightly enclosed by the dough, keeping it deliciously moist, perfect to serve in thin slices for afternoon tea or with a glass of wine in the Sukkah. An easy-blend yeast makes a splendid light cake, but fresh yeast can be used if preferred. In that case it should be mixed with some of the lukewarm liquid before adding to the dry ingredients.

For the yeast pastry

1 lb (450 g/4 cups) plain (all-purpose) flour
½ teasp salt
1 sachet easy-blend yeast or 1 oz (25 g/2 cakes) fresh yeast
3 oz (75 g/⅓ cup) caster (superfine) sugar
2 eggs plus 5 fl oz (150 ml/⅔ cup) milk or water, making 9 fl oz (250 ml/1 cup plus 2 tbsp) liquid in all
3 oz (75 g/⅓ cup) butter or margarine, or 6 tbsp oil

For the apple filling

1½ lb (675 g) Bramley cooking apples
1 oz (25 g/2 tbsp) butter or margarine
3 oz (75 g/⅓ cup) light brown soft sugar
1 tbsp lemon juice
2 rounded tbsp raisins or sultanas

For the icing

3 oz (75 g/¾ cup) icing (confectioners') sugar
1 tbsp lemon juice
a few flaked almonds

To make the pastry, put the flour, salt, yeast and sugar into the mixer bowl and stir thoroughly. Put the eggs into a measuring jug and add hand-hot milk or water, whisking well, to make up the liquid. Add to the dry ingredients, together with the soft fat or oil, and mix with a beater or dough hook for about 5 minutes, until it forms a soft shiny ball that leaves the sides of the bowl clean. If too soft to gather into a ball, add a little more flour. Turn on to a floured board, knead for 30 seconds, then put into an oiled bowl and turn it over to coat it with the oil. Cover with clingfilm (saranwrap). It can now be given 3 bursts of 100 per cent power for 20 seconds each, at 5 minute intervals, in the microwave. This will almost halve the rising time. Otherwise, leave it in the kitchen until double in bulk – about 1½ hours. Knead it for 1–2 minutes then leave for a further 10 minutes.

While the dough is rising the first time, prepare the filling by peeling, coring and thinly slicing the apples, then putting them into a pan with all the remaining ingredients and cooking gently until softened but not mushy (this will take about 5 minutes in a microwave on full power). Allow to go quite cold.

To shape the strudel, roll the dough into a large rectangle about 3/8 inch (1 cm) thick, spread with the apple filling, turn in the sides and roll up like a strudel. Lay on a greased tin in a horseshoe shape. Put into a large plastic carrier bag and leave until puffy - about 30 minutes.

Remove the tray from the bag and bake in a quick oven, Gas No. 6 (400°F/200°C), for 35-40 minutes until a rich brown. Take out and cool for 5 minutes, then brush with the icing made by mixing together the sugar and juice. Sprinkle with the almonds and allow to go cold.

SIMCHAT TORAH (THE REJOICING OF THE LAW)

The festival of 'The Rejoicing of the Law', when the last portion of the Torah - the Five Books of Moses - is read in the synagogue and the readings from the Sefer Torah - the Scroll of the Law - start all over again with a passage from Genesis, concludes the month of High Holy Days. All the Scrolls of the Law are taken from the Ark and paraded round the synagogue with much singing and dancing, in which the whole congregation joins. The children take advantage of the lack of the usual decorum to wave flags and pelt the readers with sweets - which they immediately scramble to pick up.

A special reception is held after the service either to honour the 'Bridegrooms of the Law', who have read the 2 portions of the Law, or only the 'Chatan Torah', while the other - the 'Chatan Bereshit' - is honoured on the following Saturday, 'Shabbat Bereshit'. Either way, everyone enjoys delicious vegetable dips and luscious cakes - perhaps the most luxurious being the stretched dough strudels of the Ashkenazi and the baklava of the Sephardim.

STRETCHED STRUDELS FOR SIMCHAT TORAH

The pastry that is called *'strudelteig'* in Vienna changes its name to 'filo' as you travel east. As far as I can tell, they are identical, and must be credited in the first place to the chefs of the Ottoman Empire. As the Turks engulfed huge areas of the Balkans and the Middle East, their cooking went with them, and you can see a reminder of this Turkish occupation in the wonderful Turkish Delight strudel that is traditional at Simchat Torah in Jewish households with a Romanian background.

Further east, the pastry is the same but the filling and the technique are different for the wondrous baklava that is made in many Sephardi households for this festival.

Commercial filo/strudel pastry is very easy to handle if you remember that it dries out quickly (so don't open the packet until you're quite ready to use it) and coat it evenly with fat. Each recipe gives exact instructions so you just can't go wrong.

ROMANIAN TURKISH DELIGHT STRUDEL

Makes 2 strudels, each cutting into 10–12 slices.
Keeps at least 1 week in an airtight container at room temperature.
Freeze raw with the tops of the strudels well greased. Allow to defrost either in the refrigerator or for 2 hours at room temperature before baking.

This is delicious for afternoon tea or to serve as a petit four with after-dinner coffee. The baked strudel can be frozen, although the pastry tends to crumble a little.

Remember, though, that genuine Turkish Delight (Rahat Lokum, to give its real name) does not contain gelatine - check the label for kashrut.

1 box (12 oz/350 g) rosewater and lemon Turkish Delight
2 oz (50 g/¼ cup) caster (superfine) sugar
icing (confectioners') sugar from box of Turkish Delight
8 oz (225 g/2 cups) walnuts, finely chopped
4 oz (125 g/1 cup) ground almonds
1 tbsp lemon juice
grated rind of 1 lemon
1½ tbsp citrus blossom water
6 sheets of filo pastry (about 6–8 oz/175–225 g)
4 oz (125 g/½ cup) melted unsalted butter or margarine
extra icing (confectioners') sugar for dusting the baked strudel

Cut the Turkish Delight with scissors into approximately ½-inch (1.25-cm) cubes. Put into a bowl and gently mix with the caster and icing sugar, walnuts, 2 oz (50 g/½ cup) of the ground almonds, the lemon rind and juice and the citrus blossom water.

Divide the remaining ground almonds in half. Lay 1 sheet of pastry on a lightly floured board and brush evenly with melted fat; scatter with 1 portion of the ground almonds. Lay another sheet on top and repeat. Lay a third sheet on top, brush with fat and scatter the top half of the pastry furthest from you with 1 tbsp ground almonds. Arrange half the filling evenly over the half of the pastry nearest to you, leaving ½ inch (1 cm) clear all the way round. Fold in the sides of the pastry to cover the filling, then roll up from the side nearest to you and arrange join-side down on a tray lined with silicone or oiled greaseproof paper. Butter the top and sides of the strudel. Repeat with a further 3 sheets of pastry and the remaining ingredients.

Bake the strudels in a preheated oven, Gas No. 5 (375°F/190°C), for 25 minutes, or until a rich golden brown. Take out and, when cool, put on a cooling rack. Just before serving, dust thickly with the icing sugar and cut in 1-inch (2.5-cm) slices. Serve plain or with half-whipped cream.

Baklava

The chefs of the Ottoman Empire are generally credited with devising baklava – the glorious many-layered pastry stuffed with nuts and soaked in a rose-scented syrup that is one of the supreme achievements of Middle Eastern cuisine. According to Claudia Roden, the authority on Middle Eastern food, there is no mention of it in either Arab or Persian medieval works that predate the founding of the Turkish Empire in the early thirteenth century, and certainly it is those Jews from communities that once formed part of the Ottoman Empire – Syria, Iraq, Egypt and Israel – who make it with such expertise. Like so many Sephardi dishes, it demands great deftness and skill on the part of the cook. In many Sephardi homes, there is always a supply of baklava and other delicacies, such as mamoules and gereybes, ready for guests, but it is particularly prepared at Sukkot, when Ashkenazis cook their version of stuffed pastry – the strudel.

This particular recipe comes from a superb Sephardi cook whose family came to England from Syria as cotton merchants in the early years of the twentieth century. Like most Sephardi recipes, it is made in a size sufficient to feed a large family and a very wide circle of friends! Fortunately, baklava keeps well even without freezing, or you could team up with a friend – share the work and the results. There is more than enough for 2 1990s-sized households.

ALEX BARON'S BAKLAVA

Makes 80 pieces.
Keep uncooked pastries 3 days under refrigeration.
Cooked baklava will keep in the tin in a cool larder for 2 weeks.
Freeze 3 months.

1 lb (450 g) filo pastry
10 oz (275 g/1¼ cups) unsalted butter

For the filling

12 oz (350 g/3 cups) walnuts
12 oz (350 g/3 cups) blanched almonds
good pinch of cinnamon
5 oz (150 g/$^{2}/_{3}$ cup) granulated sugar
1 tbsp each rosewater and orange flower water
(or to taste – the strengths vary)

For the syrup

1 lb (450 g/$2^{1}/_{4}$ cups) granulated sugar
10 fl oz (275 ml/$1^{1}/_{4}$ cups) water
2 teasp lemon juice
1 teasp each rosewater and orange flower water
(or to taste)

Mince the nuts through the coarsest cutter – this is important as the oil produced in the mincing process helps the filling to cling together and stay moist and succulent. Mix with the cinnamon, sugar, rosewater and orange flower water. It should be a tacky mixture.

Have ready a tin measuring 11 x 16 x 1 inches (27.5 x 40 x 2.5 cm). Melt the butter without allowing it to change colour.

Brush the tin with butter. Open the pack of pastry only when ready to assemble the baklava (this prevents it from drying out) and unfold the sheets. Take 1 sheet of pastry and lay it in the tin. Fold any overlap back on to this sheet. Brush with melted butter. Repeat with another 5 layers of pastry, folding in any excess as before and brushing each layer in turn with butter. Now tip the nut mixture on to the pastry and spread it evenly. Cover with 10 more layers of pastry, brushing each with butter as before. With a sharp pointed knife make diagonal cuts $1^{1}/_{2}$ inches (4 cm) apart right through the pastry in 2 directions to form diamonds. Brush with the remaining butter, then bake in a preheated oven, Gas No. 4 (350°F/180°C) for 45 minutes–1 hour, or until crisp and golden brown.

While the baklava is cooking, prepare the syrup. In a 7–8 inch (17.5–20 cm) saucepan heat the sugar and water, stirring to prevent it from boiling until the sugar dissolves. Add the lemon juice, then bubble very gently for 25 minutes, or until the syrup is thick enough to coat the back of a metal spoon. Add the rosewater and orange flower water.

Take the cooked baklava out of the oven and allow it to cool for 15 minutes before pouring over the warm syrup – both syrup and baklava should be the same temperature. Leave in tin and store in a cool cupboard.

CHANUKKAH (FEAST OF LIGHTS)

The famous defeat of the Greeks in the second century BCE by Judas Maccabaeus (in Hebrew Yehuda HaMaccabee) and his followers is celebrated during the 8 days of Channukah with parties and presents - particularly for the children. According to tradition, after Yehuda's family - the Hasmoneans - inspired by their father, Mattathias the High Priest, had defeated the tyrant Antiochus IV, who had desecrated the Temple in Jerusalem with pagan rites, there was only enough pure, undefiled oil for the sacred Menorah (candelabra) to allow it to burn for 24 hours. However, by a miracle the Menorah stayed alight for 8 days and nights, until more pure oil could be obtained. So in every Jewish home, an extra candle is lit in the Chanukkiah (the 8-branched candelabra) on each of the 8 nights of the festival, and the family and their friends gather round to sing the famous hymn of praise, 'Maoz Tsur' ('Rock of Ages').

So it's not surprising that foods cooked in oil have become traditional at this festival, as well as rich and sweet foods such as trifles and fruit cakes and puddings steamed with wine sauces.

Another culinary thread in the Chanukkah story comes from the tale, told in the Apocrypha, of Judith, a Jewish heroine. She entertained the Greek general Holofernes at a notorious gathering - he ate too much saity cheese, was overcome by thirst, drank deeply to quench that thirst and ended up being beheaded (by Judith), and his soldiers fled so that her town was saved! So in many communities cheese dishes such as 'rugelach' (cream cheese pastries) and latkes made with cheese are eaten as well.

Menus for Chanukkah

MENU 1
A CHICKEN MEAL, ASHKENAZI STYLE

A wonderful combination of flavours true to the spirit of Chanukkah without the heaviness! Freeze the cooked latkes ahead, then briefly reheat as described in the recipe.

Egg and Spring Onion Forspeise, spread on fingers of challah (see p. 6)
A Pâte of Chicken Livers and Stuffed Olives, spread on fingers of challah (see p. 5)
Tomato and Rice Soup (see p. 32)
Roast Chicken (or Turkey) with a Tarragon Wine Sauce (see p. 205)
Latkes (see p. 581)
A Purée of Butternut Squash (see p. 262)
Chanukkah Pudding No. 2 (see p. 586)
Russian Wine Sauce (see p. 587)
Oranges Vénétienne (see p. 331)

ALTERNATIVE VEGETARIAN FIRST AND SECOND COURSES

Champignons à la Grecque (let the mushrooms soak in their sauce for at least 24 hours) with Mixed-Grain Bread (see pp. 23, 468)
Israeli Cheese Pancakes (as symbolic of this festival as Latkes) (see p. 107)

MENU 2
A MEAT MEAL, SEPHARDI STYLE

A menu with the flavours of several different cuisines happily blended together.

Hummus b'Tahina with Toasted Pine Kernels, with warm pitta bread (see p. 528)
Chanukkah Kibbeh (Kibbeh bil Seniyah) (see p. 582)
Turkish Pilaff (see p. 274)
Bimuelos de Chanukkah (see p. 585)
Mishmishya (dried apricot sweetmeats) (see p. 588)
Turkish or other rich and strong coffee

ALTERNATIVE MAIN COURSE

Badinjan Kuki (baked aubergine omelette) (see p. 102)

POTATO LATKES

Serves 4–6.
Keeps 2 days under refrigeration.
Freeze 4 months.
Best served hot off the pan.

Latkes are fritters which were originally made with cream cheese in honour of Judith, whose heroism is said to have inspired the Maccabees in their rebellion. As Chanukkah falls in December, when milk was scarce, the Jews of Eastern Europe substituted potatoes for cheese to make these delectable latkes. It is important to allow the grated potato to drain well before use. Latkes may be served straight off the pan as a special treat; but they are also delicious instead of chips (French fries) with cold meats or poultry.

Before the advent of the food processor, the potatoes always had to be painfully grated by hand on a *'rebeizin'* (metal grater) - this onerous job was usually delegated to the men of the household while the women hovered over the frying pan. However, it is possible to make excellent latkes in the food processor and also to freeze them ahead. Many people insist that the old ways were the best - and it's a fact that you can *never* cook them fast enough to keep up with the consumption that makes latkes at Chanukkah so special. I give both methods for tradition's sake.

4 large potatoes, peeled (weight about 1½ lb/675 g) - enough to fill a pint (575 ml/2½ cup) measure when grated
½ a medium (5 oz/150 g) onion, peeled and cut in 1-inch (2.5-cm) chunks
2 eggs
1 level teasp salt
speck of white pepper
4 level tbsp self-raising flour or 4 level tbsp plain (all-purpose) flour plus a pinch of baking powder
any flavourless oil for frying

Traditional Method Grate potatoes so finely that they are almost a pulp. Leave in a sieve to drain for 10 minutes. Put in a bowl and add the remaining ingredients. In a heavy frying pan put enough oil to come to a depth of ½ inch (1.25 cm). When it is hot, put in tablespoons of mixture, flattening each latke with the back of the spoon. Cook over steady moderate heat, 5 minutes on each side, until a rich brown. Drain on crumpled kitchen paper, then serve as soon as possible, or keep hot in a moderate oven, Gas No. 4 (350°F/180°C), for up to 15 minutes.

Food Processor Method With many grating discs the potato pulp will be too coarse, so it's advisable to pulse it briefly as well, using the metal blade. The potatoes should be grated only 15 minutes before you cook them, otherwise they tend to go an unattractive brown.

Cut the potatoes to fit the feed tube, then grate through the grating disc. Turn into a metal sieve and press down firmly with a spoon to remove as much moisture as possible. Leave to drain.

Put the onion, eggs, seasonings and flour into the bowl and process with the metal blade until smooth - about 5 seconds. Add the drained potatoes and *pulse* for 3 or 4 seconds, until the potatoes are much finer and are almost reduced to a coarse pulp. Put oil ½ inch (1.25 cm) deep into a 9-inch (22.5-cm) heavy frying pan (skillet). Shape and fry as in the traditional method.

To freeze Cook the latkes, but only until they are a pale brown. Drain thoroughly, then open-freeze. When firm put into plastic bags.

To reheat Either put the frozen latkes into hot deep fat and fry for 2 or 3 minutes until a rich brown, or fry in shallow fat for 2 or 3 minutes on each side until a rich brown. Drain on paper towels. Or reheat in the oven, preheated to Gas No. 8 (450°F/230°C), for 7 or 8 minutes, until crisp and brown.

To cook latkes for a party The latkes are most quickly cooked in a deep-fryer, dropping large teaspoons of the mixture into fat heated to 375°F (190°C). A batch will take about 4 minutes and they can then be speared on cocktail sticks to serve.

To reheat a large number of latkes for a party Defrost the latkes for 1 hour on a foil-covered baking sheet, then reheat at Gas No. 8 (450°F/230°C) for 7 or 8 minutes, until crisp and brown.

CHANUKKAH KIBBEH

Serves 8.
Keeps 3 days under refrigeration.
Freeze 2 months.

To those of us whose family traditions originated in Eastern Europe, the food that spells Chanukkah is potato latkes. To a new generation, doughnuts are the Chanukkah staple, but in other Jewish communities it is more often bulgur, or cracked wheat, that appears in one form or another on the family menu.

This recipe, using bulgur, is an easy-to-make, layered version of the famous torpedo-shaped kibbeh widely sold in Israel. It can be served hot or cold and is particularly delicious cut in tiny triangles as a cocktail titbit.

It is usually made with minced (ground) lamb, but beef is equally delicious - and often less fatty. It is important to use fine bulgur.

For 4, use half-quantities and cook in a dish approximately 8 x 6 inches (20 x 15 cm).

For the crust

1 large onion, finely grated
1½ lb (675 g) minced beef or lamb
12 oz (350 g/2 cups) fine bulgur (cracked wheat)
½ teasp salt
10 grinds of black pepper
2 tbsp cold water

For the meat filling

1 large (8–10 oz/225–275 g) onion, finely chopped
2 tbsp oil
1 lb (450 g) raw minced beef or lamb
1 egg
2 tbsp water
1 teasp cinnamon
1 teasp salt
10 grinds of black pepper
2 oz (50 g/½ cup) pine kernels, toasted
3 oz (75 g/⅓ cup) margarine, melted

To make the crust Mix the grated onion and meat, kneading until smooth. Put the bulgur into a sieve and rinse with cold water. Squeeze out the moisture and add to the meat mixture with the salt, pepper and cold water. Mix to a very smooth paste.

To make the filling Sauté the chopped onion in the oil until golden, then add the meat and stir with a fork until the meat loses its redness and starts to turn brown. Beat the egg with the water, then add to the meat mixture, together with the seasoning and the pine kernels. (To toast pine kernels, either toss them over moderate heat in an ungreased frying pan until golden, or microwave on 100 per cent power for 4 minutes, stirring twice.)

Grease a fairly shallow baking tin measuring about 9 x 13 inches (22.5 x 32.5 cm) and spread half the crust mixture smoothly on the bottom. Cover with the meat mixture and spread the remaining dough on top. Score the top crust into diamonds with the point of a sharp knife, then drizzle the melted margarine over the top. Bake at Gas No. 6 (400°F/200°C) for 30 minutes, until the top is brown and crisp.

DOUGHNUTS FOR CHANUKKAH

Makes 12.
Best eaten the same day.
Freeze 3 months.

'Please can we have a recipe for our Chanukkah doughnut cook-in?' said the children from my synagogue's religion classes. 'Only if you promise to fry them in an electric deep-fryer and with plenty of adult supervision,' I said - open pans of oil and junior cooks should be kept well apart. Here's the easy-to-follow recipe I gave them, using baking powder instead of the more temperamental yeast. Expect these doughnuts to go faster than the proverbial hot cakes!

6 oz (175 g/1¼ cups) flour
½ teasp salt
1 teasp baking powder
2 oz (125 g/¼ cup) margarine
1 oz (25 g/2 tbsp) sugar
1 egg
2 tbsp milk
a little raspberry jam
extra sugar for dusting
cinnamon
oil for frying

Sieve flour, salt and baking powder. Cut and rub in margarine and add sugar, mixing to a light dough with beaten egg and milk.

Turn mixture on to a floured board and roll out ¼ inch (0.5 cm) thick. Cut into small rounds. Put a little raspberry jam on half these circles. Brush the other half with milk and put 2 together, pinching carefully round the edges to fasten securely. Fry in oil heated to 360°F (170°C) - preferably in an electric deep-fryer - for 6-8 minutes. Toss in sugar or a mixture of sugar and ground cinnamon.

SUFGANIYOT
(*Israeli-style Doughnuts*)

Makes 24.
Keeps 2 days under refrigeration.
Freeze raw 1 month, cooked 3 months.

These jam-filled doughnuts are sold in the streets of Israel during Chanukkah. As the Sufganiyot freeze extremely well, it's worth making a large batch. Otherwise, simply halve all the ingredients but still use 1 oz (25 g/2 cakes) fresh yeast. Eat some of the Sufganiyot on the day they are made - although they stay quite fresh for up to 2 days in the refrigerator. Alternatively, take them from the freezer as they are required, and reheat either in the microwave or uncovered in a moderate oven.

1 oz (25 g/2 cakes) fresh yeast or 2 sachets easy-blend yeast
10 fl oz (275 ml/1¼ cups) warm milk
1 teasp sugar
4 egg yolks
1 oz (25 g/2 tbsp) caster (superfine) sugar
1 lb (450 g/4 cups) plain white (all-purpose) flour
pinch of salt
4 oz (125 g/½ cup) very soft butter

oil for deep frying
tart jam such as apricot or blackcurrant
caster (superfine) sugar for coating the doughnuts

Put the fresh yeast (if used), 2 fl oz (50 ml/¼ cup) of the warm milk and the 1 teaspoon of sugar into a bowl, stir well, then leave to rise for 10 minutes. Put into the mixer bowl with all the remaining ingredients (except oil, jam and sugar for coating).

If you use easy-blend yeast omit the preliminary rising. Mix the yeast thoroughly with the other dry ingredients, then add all the remaining ingredients (except oil, jam, coating sugar) to the bowl.

Now beat everything together for 5 minutes, until the very soft dough looks smooth, shiny and elastic, and will leave the sides of the bowl and the beater clean - this can be done with a wooden spoon or your hand, but it's hard work! Leave in the bowl, covered with clingfilm (saranwrap), and allow to rise until double in bulk - about 1½ hours.

Turn out on to a floured board and if the dough is at all sticky, work in a little more flour so that it is soft but easily rolled out. Roll out this dough to ⅜ inch (1 cm) thick and cut into rounds about 2 inches (5 cm) across. Leave the rounds on the board, covered with a tea-towel, and let them rise until puffy - about 20 minutes.

Have ready a pan one-third full of oil, or a deep-fryer heated to 360°F (170°C) - when a cube of bread browns in 40 seconds (it should not be quite as hot as for fried fish.) Fry the doughnuts in batches, leaving room for them to swell. They should be covered until the first side has browned - about 4 minutes. Then uncover, turn them over and allow the second side to brown. Lift them out and drain well on kitchen paper. Make a little slit in each doughnut and insert a teaspoon of the jam, then roll in the caster sugar.

A PINEAPPLE AND PECAN FRUIT CAKE FOR CHANUKKAH

Leave for 10–14 days before cutting.
Keeps 3 months at room temperature in an airtight container.

This is a beauty of a cake. Although it's only lightly fruited, in the 14 days it will develop a wonderfully moist texture as well as a truly magnificent flavour - thanks to the brandy which is used to plump the dried fruit before baking and is also 'injected' into the cake afterwards.

8 oz (225 g/1 cup) butter or soft margarine
8 oz (225 g/1 cup) soft light brown sugar
rind of 1 orange, finely grated
rind of 1 lemon, finely grated
5 eggs, whisked to blend
1 tbsp lemon juice
10 oz (275 g/2½ cups) plain (all-purpose) flour
½ teasp salt
2 oz (50 g/½ cup) ground almonds
1 level teasp baking powder
1 level teasp mixed sweet spice
4 tbsp brandy
additional 4 tbsp brandy to pour over cake
4 oz (125 g/½ cup) crystallized (candied) pineapple, chopped
8 oz (225 g/1½ cups) sultanas (white raisins)
4 oz (125 g/½ cup) glacé (candied) cherries, quartered
4 oz (125 g/1 cup) pecans, coarsely chopped

Using these ingredients, make in exactly the same way as the Whisky and Ginger Cake on p. 428, substituting brandy for the whisky.

BIMUELOS DE CHANUKKAH
(*Fritters Soaked in Syrup*)

Serves 8–10.
Serve immediately.

Latkes hot off the pan may spell Chanukkah to Jews with their roots in Eastern Europe, but the Sephardim have other foods to fry! For after all, it is the oil that is the common symbol of the festival, whether it is Ukrainian latkes, Romanian fried lokshen pudding or bimuelos de Chanukkah - the Ladino name for these exquisite little puffs soaked in a scented syrup which bear more than a passing resemblance to the famous Greek loukmades.

Coincidentally, it is the belief in Greek Jewish communities that these fried cakes were being made in Palestine at the time of the Maccabean victory over the Seleucid Greeks. As both Sephardi and Greek Jews are quick to point out, it couldn't have been potato latkes - potatoes weren't discovered until the sixteenth century.

Whatever their provenance, these little pastries are quite delicious and, with the aid of a food processor or a strong right arm, they are also simple to make. Serve them cold, piled into a pyramid, either as a dessert, or as a special Chanukkah treat with coffee or tea.

For the batter

8 oz (225 g/2 cups) strong white bread flour
half a packet (1 level teasp) easy-blend yeast
4 fl oz (125 ml/½ cup) boiling water
5 fl oz (150 ml/⅔ cup) cold milk

For the syrup

1 lb (450 g/2 cups) sugar
10 fl oz (275 ml/1¼ cups) water
2 tbsp lemon juice
1 tbsp orange flower water
1 tbsp rosewater

To make the batter Mix the flour and yeast thoroughly. Add the liquids and process for 1 minute or beat by hand for 5 minutes - the mixture should be the consistency of a thick batter. Leave to rise for 1 hour, or until puffy, giving a 30-second beating (2 minutes by hand) twice during the hour. The mixture should now be elastic and stringy.

Meanwhile, put the sugar and water into a thick-based pan and stir over moderate heat until the sugar is dissolved. Bring to the boil and bubble gently for around 10 minutes, until the syrup is thick enough to coat the back of a wooden spoon. Stir in the lemon juice and flavoured waters, simmer for 2 minutes more, then allow to cool and chill until required.

To complete the fritters Heat oil in a deep fryer or pan one-third full until it reaches 375°F (190°C) - a cube of bread will brown in 40 seconds. Dip a teaspoon in cold water, take a teaspoonful of the batter and push it into the hot oil with another wet teaspoon, forming a ball shape. Repeat, dipping the spoon in cold water to prevent the batter from sticking, and cook over moderate heat until golden brown, but don't overcrowd the pan. Remove and drain on absorbent paper, then dip fritters into the cold syrup and lift on to a serving dish. Cook the remaining batter, piling dipped fritters into a pyramid.

CHANUKKAH PUDDING (1)

Makes 1 x 7-inch-diameter (17.5-cm) pudding.
Serves 10–12.
Keeps in a cool cupboard at least 1 year.

This rich, fruited, steamed 'plum' pudding has become a Chanukkah tradition for British Jews in the last 150 years - there is a recipe for a plum pudding not dissimilar to the one I give below in Lady Judith Montefiore's *The Jewish Manual*, published in 1846. This recipe is lighter and less rich than a traditional English pudding, but its main advantage is that, though its keeping qualities are good, it can be eaten a few days after being made. The secret of a dark pudding lies in the long steaming period.

4 oz (125 g/½ cup) margarine
4 oz (125 g/½ cup) soft brown sugar
4 oz (125 g/1 cup) plain (all-purpose) flour
pinch of salt
pinch of nutmeg
pinch of mixed spice
2 beaten eggs
grated rind and juice of 1 orange
2 tbsp brandy
4 tbsp Guinness (stout) or ale
1 small apple, peeled, cored and grated
4 oz (125 g/1⅓ cups) fresh white breadcrumbs
2 oz (50 g/½ cup) blanched and chopped almonds
2 oz (50 g/⅓ cup) cut mixed peel
8 oz (225 g/1½ cups) currants
8 oz (225 g/1½ cups) sultanas (white raisins)

Melt the margarine and sugar together and sift the flour with the salt and spices. Place all ingredients in a bowl and beat with a spoon until thoroughly mixed (about 3 minutes). Place mixture in a greased 7-inch (17.5-cm) pudding basin. Cover with a double thickness of greaseproof or silicone paper and then with foil. Steam for 6 hours.

To reheat on the day, steam or boil for a further 4 hours.

CHANUKKAH PUDDING (2)

Makes 1 x 7–8-inch (17.5–20-cm) diameter pudding.
Serves 10–12.
Keeps in a cool cupboard at least 1 year.

A richer, more traditional 'plum' pudding containing an interesting mixture of dried fruits. The long cooking periods ensure that this pudding can be made even as late as a week before use and will still be a rich dark colour with a superb flavour and moist texture. Serve with a double quantity of Russian Wine Sauce (see below).

4 oz (125 g/¾ cup) stoned and tenderized dried prunes
4 oz (125 g/¾ cup) dried dates
1 lb (450 g/3 cups) mixed dried fruit
5 fl oz (150 ml/⅔ cup) Guinness or other stout or ale
3 oz (75 g/¾ cup) self-raising flour or
3 oz (75 g/¾ cup) plain (all-purpose) flour plus
¾ teasp baking powder
scant teasp of salt
¾ level teasp ground nutmeg
¾ level teasp ground cinnamon
¾ level teasp ground mixed spice
finely grated rind of 1 orange
finely grated rind of 1 lemon
2 oz (50 g/½ cup) ground almonds
8 oz (225 g/1 cup) polyunsaturated white cooking fat
6 oz (175 g/3 cups) fine fresh breadcrumbs
6 oz (175 g/¾ cup) soft brown sugar
4 large eggs

To pour over when cold
3 tbsp brandy or rum

Chop the prunes and dates finely and put in a basin with the mixed dried fruits.

Pour over the Guinness or ale. Cover with clingfilm (saranwrap) and cook on 100 per cent power for 4 minutes in the microwave, then allow to stand, covered, until cold.

When ready to mix the pudding, put the flour, salt, spices, grated rinds, ground almonds, white fat, breadcrumbs and sugar into a very large (10-inch/25-cm) mixing bowl. Add the soaked fruits and mix very thoroughly. Whisk the eggs until slightly thickened, then add to the mixture and stir well. Spoon into the greased pudding basin and cover first with silicone paper and then with foil. Refrigerate overnight or for several hours.

Steam for 6 hours or put in a pan two-thirds full of boiling water and boil for the same time, topping up with more boiling water from the kettle from time to time. Remove from the heat, allow to cool and then uncover and spoon over the brandy or rum. Re-cover with fresh silicone and foil and store in a cool place.

Just before serving steam or boil for a further 4 hours.

RUSSIAN WINE SAUCE

Serves 8.
This is an old family recipe. The sauce is a delicate pink.

2 egg yolks
2 oz (50 g/¼ cup) caster (superfine) sugar
2 level teasp cornflour (cornstarch)
8 fl oz (225 ml/1 cup) kosher Kiddush wine, port or port-type
1–2 tbsp brandy or orange-flavoured liqueur

Using a hand-held electric whisk, whisk together the yolks and sugar in a heatproof bowl or the top of a double saucepan, until pale, then beat in the cornflour, wine and the brandy or liqueur. Cook over boiling water, whisking until thickened. Can be left standing in warm water and then reheated just before using.

WEINCHADEAU

Serves 8.
Another delicious sauce to serve with the Chanukkah Pudding.

3 egg yolks
3 oz (75 g/¾ cup) caster (superfine) sugar
1½ teasp cornflour (cornstarch)
5 fl oz (150 ml/⅔ cup) Amontillado sherry

Put the egg yolks and sugar into a basin or the top of a double saucepan and whisk by hand or electric whisk until pale and mousse-like. Whisk in the cornflour and sherry. Stand the basin (or pan) over a pan of simmering water and whisk constantly until the mixture becomes thick and foamy - about 3–4 minutes. Serve at once or leave over warm water and rewhisk just before serving.

CHANUKKAH TRIFLE

Keeps 2 days under refrigeration.
Do not freeze.
A delicious trifle that uses Kiddush (port-type) wine to provide its special flavour.

1 pint (575 ml/2½ cups) custard (choose from 2 recipes below)
1 jam Swiss roll (jelly roll)
4 tbsp Kiddush (port-type) wine
5 fl oz (150 ml/⅔ cup) double (heavy) cream or 10 fl oz (275 ml/1¼ cups) creamy (8%) fromage frais, plain or fruity
4 tbsp fruity syrup from any canned fruit
1 cupful (approx.) fresh or canned fruit salad

1 For powder custard
1 pint (575 ml/2½ cups) milk
2 level tbsp custard powder (vanilla pudding mix)
2 level tbsp caster (superfine) sugar
1 egg yolk

2 For egg custard
15 fl oz (425 ml/2 cups) full-cream milk
1½ oz (40 g/3 tbsp) sugar
2 whole eggs plus 2 egg yolks
½ teasp vanilla essence (extract)

Make the powder custard according to packet instructions. If making egg custard, heat the milk until it steams. In blender goblet or food processor put the hot milk, sugar, eggs and egg yolks and blend for 10 seconds (or whisk by hand). Cook very gently over boiling water until thick enough to coat the back of a wooden spoon, or whisk over gentle heat, without allowing to come to bubbling point. Add the vanilla then leave to cool.

Slice the Swiss roll ½ inch (1.25 cm) thick and use to line the bottom of a glass bowl.

Sprinkle with the wine. Pour the custard over the cake and leave to cool. Whisk the cream until it starts to thicken, then add the fruit syrup gradually, whisking again until thick (this stage should be omitted if fromage frais is used). Fold the fruit into the cream mixture or fromage frais and spoon over the top. Freeze for 1 hour to chill thoroughly, or leave in the coldest part of the refrigerator overnight.

MISHMISHYA

Makes 48.
Keeps 4–6 weeks under refrigeration.

These apricot petit fours are a favourite Sephardi Chanukkah dish.

1 lb (450 g) tenderized dried apricots
3½ lb (1.75 kg/7¾ cups) granulated sugar, plus extra for coating
2 oz (50 g/½ cup) blanched pistachios

Put the apricots and sugar into the food processor and process until a smooth paste is formed. Turn into a bowl, then form into 1-inch (2.5-cm) balls and roll in the granulated sugar. Press a whole pistachio into the top of each ball. Leave uncovered at room temperature for 2 days to allow the surface to dry out. Serve in tiny paper cases.

PURIM (FEAST OF LOTS)

Purim occurs exactly 1 month before Passover. It commemorates the downfall of Haman, the vizier of King Ahasuerus (Artaxerxes II), who in the fifth century BCE formulated his own 'Final Solution' by planning the massacre of the entire Jewish population of Persia. Haman ended up on the gallows he had prepared for his enemies, and his name is perpetuated in a variety of unusual cakes and sweetmeats. By tradition, these are three-cornered - some say like Haman's ears, others like his purse, which he planned to fill with Jewish gold, represented in many of the dishes by *'mohn'*, poppy seeds. There are Hamantaschen - Haman's purses - and Orejas de Haman - sugared fritters which translate as Haman's ears - Mohne Torten (poppy-seed cakes), Mohn Kichlach (poppy-seed biscuits/cookies), Sambusak (Iraqi-style yeast pastry turnovers stuffed with minced meat or chicken and chickpeas) and Little Hamens (gingerbread men) made by Jews in Holland and Scandinavia - and many more.

Purim, like Chanukkah, is not a full festival but a working day. However, late in the afternoon a special meal, Purim Seudah, is eaten. Kreplach (see p. 50) are often served and a magnificent semi-sweet raisin bread, Kalisch-brod, symbolizing the rope used to hang Haman, is used to make the traditional blessing. Because this is a folk festival, complete with a beautiful queen (Esther) and a wicked queen (Vashti), every community has its own *minhag* (custom), but children take part in 'Purim *spiels*' (joky plays) and one has to watch out for 'spoof' articles in Jewish magazines and papers, written to hoodwink the unwary, rather as on April Fool's Day.

Common to all is a happy, carefree atmosphere. Purim is the one time in the year when Jews are actually encouraged to drink to excess so that one cannot distinguish between the name of Mordechai (the hero of the Purim story) and Haman (the villain). During the reading of the Megillah - the scroll that contains the story of Purim - many synagogues keep whisky and wine handy, the usual decorum is abandoned and there is singing and dancing in the aisles!

Two charming customs are associated with the festival: children receive 'Purim *gelt*' (money) from their parents and grandparents, and many people perform the *mitzvah* (divine command) of *'shlach monos'* ('sending portions' in English, *'mish loach manot'* in Hebrew) - gifts of Purim foods exchanged between friends or given to the poor or needy.

Menus for Purim

PURIM TURKEY SCHNITZELS, ISRAELI STYLE

Serves 6–8.
Serve hot off the pan with boiled new potatoes or kasha varnishkes (see p. 278), or at room temperature with a potato salad and a corn and green bean salad.

The Israelis don't have the time – or the patience – to wait for the hundreds of years it usually takes to establish new food traditions for festivals. Here's how they've established turkey for Purim in less than a generation!

The literal translation of *'tarnegol hodu'* – the modern Hebrew word for turkey – means 'cock of India'. King Ahasuerus was said to 'reign from India unto Ethiopia'. The turkey is credited with being the most foolish of fowl, while Esther's king was also not known for good judgement. The Israelis have a thriving turkey industry. Ergo, let's make turkey schnitzels a (newly) traditional Israeli Purim dish! A less demanding dish can be made using slices of Israeli smoked turkey breast, alternating with crescents of juicy melon for a superb starter.

1½ lb (675 g) raw turkey breast or 6–8 ready-cut turkey schnitzels
2 tbsp lemon juice
1 teasp salt
15 grinds of black pepper

For the coating
1 heaped tbsp plain (all-purpose) flour
2 eggs beaten to blend with 1 tbsp cold water
5–6 oz (150–175 g/1¼–1½ cups) matzah meal or fine dry breadcrumbs
½ teasp sea salt
15 grinds of black pepper
good pinch of garlic powder
good pinch of paprika

For frying
6 tbsp sunflower oil

For the garnish
wedges of lime or lemon
sprigs of parsley

Ask the butcher to cut the breast into thin fillets. Lay each fillet between 2 pieces of greaseproof paper and pound with a cutlet bat or the end of a rolling pin until half the original thickness (be careful not to tear the delicate meat). Put the lemon juice, salt and pepper into a shallow dish, turn the fillets in it to coat on both sides, then leave in the dish for 30 minutes, turning once.

Meanwhile, put the flour, eggs beaten with water and crumbs (mixed with the seasonings) into 3 separate shallow dishes placed side by side. Toss each fillet lightly in the flour, patting off any excess with the hands, then brush with a thin layer of beaten egg and water, and turn in the seasoned crumbs, patting them on firmly. Leave the schnitzels side by side on a board for 30 minutes to set the coating (longer will do no harm, but do refrigerate them meanwhile).

In a large heavy frying pan, heat the oil until you can feel it comfortably warm on your hand held 2 inches (5 cm) above the surface. Put in the schnitzels (don't crowd the pan) and cook them steadily for 5 minutes on each side, or until crisp and brown. As they are cooked, lay them side by side on a tray in a slow oven, Gas No. 1 (275°F/140°C), to keep hot without drying out.

Garnish with the wedges of fruit and the parsley.

HAMANTASCHEN

Hamantaschen can be made with a yeast dough, a soured cream dough, a rich shortcrust or a kichel (biscuit) dough. Each variety is delicious in its own way.

However, they are always made in a tricorn

shape and have various traditional stuffings – sweetened ground poppy seeds, cream cheese, fruit compôtes or dried fruit and nut mixtures. They can be bite size (usually made with a pastry or kichel dough) or large enough to slice and butter (made with a yeast dough).

In earlier days, women living in the shtetls of the Pale of Settlement in Eastern Europe would get together for a Purim 'bake-in' – a custom still followed in many synagogues. However, most people today buy their yeast hamantaschen from the local Jewish baker. But there is a special pleasure in baking them at home and filling the house with the glorious smell – perfume even. So I give recipes for every kind.

MELT-IN-THE-MOUTH PASTRY HAMANTASCHEN

Makes 20 hamantaschen filled with either fruit or poppy seeds.
Keeps 1 week at room temperature in an airtight container.
Freeze 3 months.

These are made with a meltingly tender short pastry which is especially easy to handle. This is the pastry that Sephardi cooks use to make their wonderful moulded biscuits, such as 'ma'moules'. When they're filled with a traditional Ashkenazi filling such as spiced apples and raisins or poppy seeds, a bite of one of these hamantaschen is a *'mechia'* (special delight) if ever I tasted one.

For the pastry

5 oz (150 g/⅔ cup) butter or firm margarine
8 oz (225 g/2 cups) plain (all-purpose) flour
pinch of salt
2 tbsp cold water
1 tbsp citrus blossom water or 2 teasp lemon juice and 2 teasp extra water

For the fruit filling

6 oz (175 g/1 cup plus 2 tbsp) raisins
1 x 8 oz (225 g) baking apple, peeled, cored and cut in ½-inch (1.25-cm) cubes
3 tbsp finely chopped walnuts
1 oz (25 g/2 tbsp) butter or margarine
1 teasp ground cinnamon
2 oz (50 g/¼ cup) soft brown sugar
1 tbsp lemon juice
1 dessertspoon apricot conserve

For the poppy-seed filling

4 oz (125 g/1 cup) ground poppy seeds
4 fl oz (125 ml/½ cup) milk or water
1 oz (25 g/2 tbsp) butter or margarine
2 oz (50 g/¼ cup) granulated sugar
1 level tbsp golden (corn) syrup
2 tbsp sultanas or raisins
2 oz (50 g/1 cup) cake crumbs
1 teasp vanilla essence

For coating the pastries

2 tbsp icing (confectioners') sugar
2 tbsp caster (superfine) sugar

First make the chosen filling, then allow it to cool. For the fruit filling simmer all the ingredients together until the apple is just tender (4 minutes covered on 100 per cent microwave power). For the poppy-seed filling, grind the poppy seeds in a nut- or coffee-grinder, then heat gently with all the other ingredients (except the crumbs and vanilla), stirring constantly until a thick paste is formed. Stir in the crumbs and vanilla.

To make the pastry, rub the fat into the flour and salt until the mixture looks like breadcrumbs, then sprinkle with the liquids and mix to a dough. (Or follow Food Processor method, p. 371.) Knead lightly until smooth – it will have a plasticine-like texture. Chill until the filling is cold, then roll out ⅛ inch (0.3 cm) thick on a lightly floured board. Cut out into 20 x 3-inch (7.5-cm) circles (an empty 7-oz (200-g) well-washed tuna can makes an ideal cutter).

Put a heaped teaspoon of filling in the centre of each circle, then bring the edges together to form a triangle, pinching them with the fingers to ensure a tight seal but leaving a gap in the centre to allow steam to escape (see the diagram on p. 593).

Bake in a preheated oven (Gas No. 5/375°F/190°C) for 25 minutes, until firm to gentle touch but uncoloured. Leave on a cooling tray for 10 minutes, then sprinkle with the mixed sugars using a teaspoon. When quite cold, coat again with the sugars. Store in an airtight container.

KICHEL HAMANTASCHEN

Makes 24.
Keeps fresh 4 days in an airtight container.
Freeze 3 months.

This recipe produces a caky pastry which contrasts well with a fruit filling.

For the pastry

2 eggs (reserve a little for glazing)
5 oz (125 g/⅔ cup) caster (superfine) sugar
4 fl oz (125 ml/½ cup) sunflower oil
1 teasp vanilla essence (extract)
grated rind of ½ orange
12 oz (350 g/3 cups) flour (half plain, half self-raising) or 12 oz (350 g/3 cups) plain (all-purpose) flour and 1½ level teasp baking powder

For the apple filling

1 lb (450 g) peeled, cored and sliced eating apples
3 oz (75 g/⅓ cup) sugar
juice and rind of 1 small lemon

For the apricot filling

8 oz (225 g/1½ cups) tenderized dried apricots
½ cup (150 g) honey
2 teasp grated orange rind
juice of ½ orange

For the prune filling

8 oz (225 g/1½ cups) tenderized prunes
3 oz (75 g/½ cup) raisins
2 oz (50 g/½ cup) walnuts
juice and rind of 1 lemon
4 oz (125 g/½ cup) sugar

To make the apple filling, put apples, sugar, juice and rind in layers in a pan, cover and cook gently until apples are tender. Uncover and cook a little longer to drive off any free liquid. Cool. Alternatively, in the microwave cook covered on 100 per cent power for 3 minutes. Uncover and cook a further 2 minutes. Cool.

To make the apricot filling, coarsely chop the apricots in the food processor or put through the coarse blade of the mincer. Add the rest of the ingredients and stir well together.

To make the prune filling, prepare in exactly the same way as the apricot filling.

For the pastry, whisk eggs until thick, then whisk in the sugar, oil and flavourings. Finally, stir in enough of the flour to make a rollable dough. Roll out ¼ inch (0.3 cm) thick on a floured board, and cut into 3-inch (7.5-cm) rounds. Place a spoonful of filling in the centre, then draw up 3 sides to form a triangle and pinch the edges firmly together (see diagram p. 593). Brush the tops with a little beaten egg. Bake in a preheated oven, Gas No. 4 (350°F/180°C) for half an hour, until golden brown.

WINE-AND-WALNUT-FILLED HAMANTASCHEN - ROMANIAN STYLE

Makes 30.
Keeps fresh for 4 days in an airtight container.
Freeze 3 months.

Here a typical continental-style shortcrust or '*muerbteig*' is used. If possible, leave the filling to mature for 2 days at room temperature. Refresh the pastries, if necessary, by heating until warm to the touch in a moderate oven or very briefly in the microwave.

For the filling
12 oz (425 g/2¼ cups) mixed dried fruit
1 apple (5 oz/150 g), peeled and grated
2 oz (50 g/¼ cup) walnuts, coarsely chopped
1 oz (25 g/2 tbsp) soft brown sugar
1 tbsp ginger marmalade (ginger preserve)
1 tbsp warm golden (corn) syrup
½ teasp cinnamon
½ teasp mixed spice
pinch of ground nutmeg
grated rind and juice of ½ lemon
1 tbsp brandy
1 tbsp Kiddush (port-type) wine
1½ oz (40 g/3 tbsp) melted butter or margarine

For the pastry
3 oz (75 g/⅓ cup) butter or margarine
2 oz (50 g/¼ cup) white fat
4 oz (125 g/1 cup) self-raising flour or
4 oz (125 g/1 cup) plain (all-purpose) flour plus
1 teasp baking powder
4 oz (125 g/1 cup) plain (all-purpose) flour
1 level tbsp icing (confectioners') sugar
1 egg yolk
2 tbsp water

For the glaze
1 egg white
granulated sugar

To make the filling, combine all the ingredients in the order given. Leave in a covered bowl for 1 day to mature.

To make the pastry, cut the fats into 1-inch (2.5-cm) cubes. By hand or machine, rub them into the flour until the mixture looks like breadcrumbs, add the sugar, then mix to a dough with the yolk blended with the water. Knead lightly until smooth, then chill for 30 minutes.

To shape and bake the Hamantaschen, preheat the oven to Gas No. 6 (400°F/200°C). Have ready 2 ungreased oven trays. Roll the pastry out ¼ inch (0.5 cm) thick on a board lightly dusted with icing sugar and cut into 3-inch (7.5-cm) circles, gathering up the trimmings and rerolling and cutting until all the pastry has been used. Put a spoonful of filling on each circle and draw up to form a triangle, pinching the edges firmly together in the shape of a tricorn hat (see diagram). Arrange on the trays.

HAMANTASCHEN

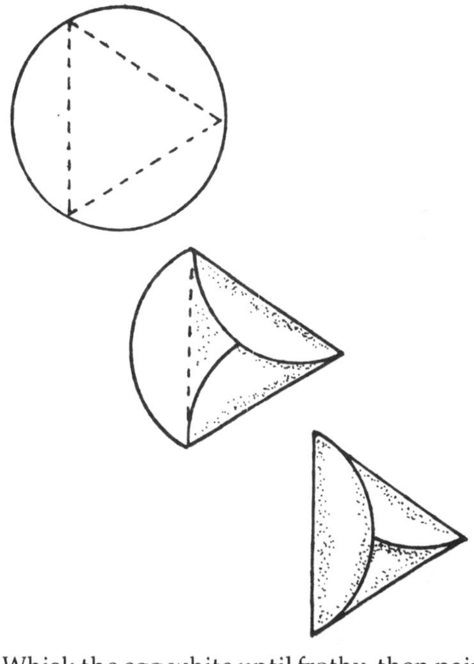

Whisk the egg white until frothy, then paint all over the Hamantaschen and sprinkle with granulated sugar. Bake for 20 minutes, or until golden brown. Allow to cool.

Kalischbrod

Kalischbrod (from the Russian 'Kulich', Easter bread) - or Purim bread, as it is colloquially known - is a rich, slightly sweetened, raisin bread, probably a direct 'descendant' of the Artolaganus or cake bread baked in ancient Rome. It is used to make the traditional 'Hamotzi' (blessing for bread) at the festive meal, the Purim Seudah, and as this is usually a meal with meat or poultry it is important that the dough is parev - containing no dairy ingredients.

Purim bread is magnificent to behold. In some communities it takes the form of a plait 6 feet in length! A friend who was born in Bukovina (part of the old Austro-Hungarian Empire) remembers his mother making a 12-strand plait with a 5-strand plait on top. Then it was borne through the streets (covered with a white cloth) to be put in the baker's oven. The recipe that follows is for a bread probably a quarter of the size.

PAREV DOUGH FOR KALISCHBROD AND HAMANTASCHEN

Shiphra Grosskopf, a Manchester friend and an outstanding traditional Jewish cook, gave me this superb recipe for *parev* dough, which can be made into magnificent Purim bread and also Hamantaschen.

The quantities given below will make a medium-size Purim bread and 6 large Hamantaschen. If you want a very large loaf - and your oven can accommodate it - use the whole quantity of dough for the bread. Bread and Hamantaschen will keep fresh 2 days under refrigeration and freeze 3 months.

For a large family or for entertaining, you could double up on quantities and make a large loaf and 12 large Hamantaschen. If you prefer, fill with mixed fruit or cheese.

1½ lb (675 g/6 cups) plain (all-purpose) flour
1½ teasp salt
1½ oz (40 g/3 cakes) fresh yeast
3 oz (75 g/⅓ cup) caster (superfine) sugar
2 eggs
9 fl oz (250 ml/1 cup plus 2 tbsp) warm water
3 oz (75 g/⅓ cup) lukewarm melted margarine

For the bread
2 oz (50 g/6 tbsp) raisins

For the bread glaze
1 egg yolk
1 teasp water
2 tbsp poppy or sesame seeds

For the Hamantaschen filling
4 oz (125 g/1 cup) poppy seeds
4 fl oz (125 ml/½ cup) water
1 oz (25 g/2 tbsp) margarine
2 oz (50 g/¼ cup) sugar
1 rounded tbsp golden (corn) syrup or honey
2 oz (50 g/6 tbsp) raisins
1 teasp vanilla essence (extract)

For the Hamantaschen glaze
warmed honey or golden (corn) syrup

To make the bread Using the dough hook on the mixer, place flour and salt in the mixer bowl. Make a well in the centre and crumble in the yeast, then cover it with a tablespoon of the surrounding flour. Sprinkle the sugar on top and the unbeaten eggs at the side. Turn on mixer, adding water alternately with the margarine. Continue kneading with the dough hook until the dough leaves the sides of the bowl and looks smooth and shiny (about 4 minutes).

Turn dough on to a floured board and knead by hand for 30 seconds. Place dough in a large, lightly oiled bowl and turn to coat with a thin film of oil. Cover the bowl with clingfilm (saranwrap) and refrigerate for at least 3 hours (it may be left overnight), during which time the dough will double in size. While the dough is rising, cover the raisins with boiling water and leave to plump.

To shape the Kalischbrod (Purim) bread, turn the risen dough on to a floured board and knead for 1 minute. Cut in half, then take 1 piece (the remaining half is for Hamantaschen) and knead in the well-drained raisins. Divide equally into 4. Flatten each piece with the fist, then roll up into a little Swiss roll. Flatten and roll up again, then form into a ball - this isn't essential but improves the texture. Repeat for all 4 quarters.

Take each ball and roll into a 12-inch (30-cm) strand that tapers slightly at each end. Join the 4 strands of dough at one end, then fan them out on the board (see diagram p. 461). To make the plait, bring 2 over 3, then 4 over 2, and 1 over 3. Repeat until the strands of dough have been plaited. Seal the end, then roll the plait over on its side to improve the shape. Arrange on a greased oven tray, then slip loaf and tray inside a large plastic bag and leave in the warm kitchen for 1 hour, or until spongy to the touch. Remove from the bag, brush with the yolk and water glaze, scatter with poppy or sesame seeds and bake for 30 minutes at Gas No. 5 (375°F/190°C), until a dark brown.

To make the Hamantaschen The filling can be made while the dough is being refrigerated and rising, as it must be cold when it is used.

Grind the poppy seeds in a grinder or coffee-mill to the consistency of ground almonds. Place in a pan with the remaining filling ingredients and simmer for 5 minutes, stirring all the time, until a thick paste is formed. Leave to go cold.

To shape the Hamantaschen, divide the second half of the dough into 6 equal pieces and knead each piece into a ball. Roll each ball into a circle ¼ inch (0.3 cm) thick, then spread with the filling. Fold the edges of the circle together to form a triangle (see diagram). Seal at the centre, then arrange, well apart, on a greased tray. Place the tray inside a plastic bag leave for 1 hour. Remove from the bag and bake at Gas No. 5 (375°F/190°C) for 25 minutes. Brush hot Hamantaschen with a thin coating of golden (corn) syrup or honey. Serve in slices, plain or buttered.

SOURED CREAM HAMANTASCHEN

Makes 8 large Hamantaschen.
Keeps 3 days under refrigeration.
Freeze 3 months.

This is a delicious yeast dough, extremely easily made even if you are inexperienced at yeast cookery. The dough is allowed to rise slowly in the refrigerator overnight, which makes it easy to handle and also gives a splendid texture.

For the dough

1 oz (25 g/2 cakes) fresh yeast
4 fl oz (125 ml/½ cup) lukewarm milk
1 lb (450 g/4 cups) plain bread flour
1 level teasp salt
2 eggs
4 oz (125 g/½ cup) caster (superfine) sugar
4 oz (125 g/½ cup) melted butter or margarine
5 fl oz (150 ml/⅔ cup) soured cream
melted honey or golden (corn) syrup

For the poppy-seed filling

4 oz (125 g/1 cup) ground poppy seeds
4 fl oz (125 ml/½ cup) milk
1 oz (25 g/2 tbsp) butter or margarine
2 oz (50 g/¼ cup) caster (superfine) sugar
2 level tbsp golden (corn) syrup
2 oz (50 g/½ cup) walnuts, chopped
2 oz (50 g/⅓ cup) seedless raisins, chopped
½ teasp vanilla essence (extract) or grated lemon rind

In a small jug crumble the yeast into the milk and leave to dissolve for 5 minutes, sprinkling the top with a pinch of sugar to hasten the process. Put the flour and salt into a large bowl. Make a well in the centre and drop in the eggs, sugar, melted butter and soured cream. Stir the yeast mixture well and add that. Gradually stir in the surrounding flour and beat until a soft dough is formed. Keep on beating until the dough leaves the beater or the fingers clean - about 5 minutes. Tip the mixture into a polythene bag large enough to allow the dough to expand (the bag should be greased beforehand with a few drops of oil). Close loosely and refrigerate overnight.

Next day divide the dough into 8 even pieces (you can weigh them to make sure), then knead each into a ball and roll out into a circle $\frac{1}{4}$ inch (0.3 cm) thick.

Meanwhile, make the filling by grinding the poppy seeds if necessary in a coffee- or nut-mill, then stir in the milk, followed by all the other ingredients (except the vanilla or lemon rind) and cook until thick - about 5 minutes - stirring constantly. Taste and add more sugar if necessary. Add vanilla or lemon rind when cold. Apple, apricot or prune filling can be used instead (see p. 592.)

Put a spoonful of filling in the middle of each of the 8 dough pieces and draw the edges together to make a three-cornered shape (see diagram p. 593.) Arrange on greased baking trays, brush with melted honey or golden syrup and leave in a warm place until double in bulk - about 1 hour. At this stage the Hamantaschen will look puffy and feel spongy when poked with the finger. Bake in a preheated oven, Gas No. 5 (375°F/190°C), for 30 minutes, or until a rich brown.

FIVE-STAR FILLINGS

These alternative new fillings are sufficient to fill 6 large yeast Hamantaschen (see p. 594).
They will keep 2–3 days in a sealed container in the refrigerator and freeze for 3 months.

CHEESE FILLING

1 lb (450 g/2 cups) curd
(low- or medium-fat) cheese
1 egg yolk
bare 3 oz (75 g/$\frac{1}{3}$ cup) caster (superfine) sugar
grated rind of $\frac{1}{2}$ lemon
$\frac{1}{2}$ teasp vanilla essence (extract)
1 level tbsp custard powder (vanilla pudding mix)
or cornflour (cornstarch)
3 oz (75 g/$\frac{1}{2}$ cup) sultanas (white raisins)

Put the cheese into a bowl, then beat in the egg yolk followed by all the remaining ingredients. The mixture should be the consistency of butter icing; if it is too dry, add a little yoghurt or milk. Chill while the Hamantaschen dough is rising.

WALNUT FILLING

8 oz (225 g/2 cups) fine walnuts
3 oz (75 g/$\frac{1}{3}$ cup) soft brown sugar
1 rounded tbsp golden (corn) syrup or honey
1$\frac{1}{2}$ teasp cinnamon
3 oz (75 g/$\frac{1}{2}$ cup) sultanas (white raisins)
3 fl oz (75 ml/$\frac{1}{3}$ cup) hot milk or water

Grind or grate the walnuts coarsely. This can be done using the metal blade of the food processor, but stop before the nuts are as fine as ground almonds. Put them into a bowl and mix thoroughly with the sugar, golden syrup, cinnamon and sultanas. Pour on the hot milk to make a spreadable paste. Set aside.

Shape and fill the Hamantaschen as in the previous recipe.

HAMAN'S EARS

Makes 36–40 (according to size).
Keeps 4 days in an airtight container under refrigeration.

Known as Hamansooren in Holland, Orechie de Aman in Italy and Oznei Haman in Israel; Orejas de Haman or Hojuelos de Haman is the Ladino (Judaeo-Spanish) name. A fritter-like pastry, deep-fried and served sprinkled with icing (confectioners') sugar.

1 egg
pinch of salt
3 teasp sunflower oil
1 tbsp caster (superfine) sugar
3 teasp tepid water or rosewater
½ teasp baking powder
4 oz (125 g/1 cup) plain (all-purpose) flour

To dust the cakes
icing (confectioners') sugar

Beat the egg until fluffy, then add the salt, oil, sugar and water or rosewater, beating well. Stir in the flour mixed with the baking powder to make a soft, slightly sticky dough (the amount of flour may vary a little with the size of the egg). Turn the dough on to a floured board and knead until absolutely smooth - 2–3 minutes. Wrap in clingfilm (saranwrap) and rest for 1 hour. Roll out to the thickness of a knife blade - about $\frac{1}{16}$ inch (0.15 cm) thick - you should be able to see the board through it. Cut into half-moons using a 2-inch (5-cm) round cutter, moving the cutter down the dough to form the crescents. Pinch each crescent in the centre so that it looks like a bow tie with an 'ear' on either side of the centre. Heat a pan of deep oil until it reaches 375°F (190°C) on a fat thermometer or a 1-inch (2.5-cm) cube of bread browns in 40 seconds (or use an automatic deep-fryer, heated to the same temperature). Fry the 'ears' a few at a time (don't crowd the pan as they do puff up a great deal) until golden brown, turning over with a slotted spoon so that they brown evenly. Drain on crumpled tissue paper. Serve hot or cold, well sprinkled with icing (confectioners') sugar.

PURIM POPPY-SEED TREATS

Makes about 30.
Keeps 1 week in an airtight container.
Freeze 2 months.

And now for something completely different - tender little pastry triangles topped with a brown-sugar meringue stuffed with ground poppy seeds (buy them ready-ground or pulverize them yourself in a nut-mill or coffee-grinder). A box of these 'alternative' Hamantaschen would make the perfect gift for '*shlach monos*' (see p. 589).

2 oz (50 g/¼ cup) butter or firm margarine
2 oz (50 g/¼ cup) caster (superfine) sugar
2 egg yolks
1 teasp vanilla essence (extract)
6 oz (175 g/1½ cups) self-raising flour or
6 oz (175 g/1½ cups) plain (all-purpose) flour plus
1½ teasp baking powder
2 egg whites
pinch of cream of tartar
4 oz (125 g/½ cup) medium brown sugar
5 oz (150 g/1¼ cups) poppy seeds, ground

Put the butter or margarine (cut in 1-inch/2.5-cm chunks), caster sugar, egg yolks, vanilla and flour into the food processor and process until like moist crumbs, then press firmly into a greased tin measuring approximately 7 x 11 x 2 inches (127.5 x 27.5 x 5 cm). Beat the egg whites with the cream of tartar until they form soft peaks, then gradually beat in the brown sugar until firm peaks are formed. Fold in the poppy seeds, then spread the meringue evenly over the pastry base. Bake at Gas No. 4 (350°C/180°C) for 30 minutes, until the surface is firm to the touch and lightly browned, then cut in 1½-inch (4-cm) triangles.

RUSSIAN MOHN (POPPY-SEED) TORTE

Makes 1 x 9 inch (22.5-cm) ring cake.
Keeps 4 days in an airtight container.
Freeze 3 months.

This is very similar to a Genoese sponge, with a delicate but satisfying texture.

2 x size 1 or 2 eggs
8 oz (225 g/1 cup) caster (superfine) sugar
1 teasp vanilla essence (extract)
6 oz (175 g/1½ cups) ground poppy seeds
2 teasp finely grated orange rind
4 oz (125 g/1 cup) fine self-raising flour or 4 oz (125 g/1 cup) plain (all-purpose) flour plus 1 teasp baking powder
4 fl oz (125 ml/½ cup) milk
4 oz (125 g/½ cup) unsalted butter, melted and cooled
2 tbsp sunflower oil

For lining the tin

sunflower oil
1 rounded tbsp ground almonds

To dust the cake

icing (confectioners') sugar or orange icing made with 8 oz (225 g/2 cups) sifted icing (confectioners') sugar, mixed to a coating consistency with 2 tbsp hot orange juice

Preheat the oven to Gas No. 4 (350°F/180°C). Grease a 9-inch (22.5-cm) ring tin and dust the inside with the ground almonds.

Beat the eggs, sugar and vanilla essence for 5 minutes with an electric whisk, until the mixture lightens in colour and is as thick as softly whipped cream. Stir in the poppy seeds and orange rind. Gently fold in the sifted flour alternately with the milk, followed by the cooled butter and the oil.

Spoon into the prepared tin and bake for 40–45 minutes, until the surface is firm to gentle touch.

Leave the cake in the tin on a cooling tray for 10 minutes, then run a knife round the edges of the tin and turn the cake out on to the cooling tray. When it is quite cold, dust it thickly with icing sugar, or cover with the orange water icing.

URSULA GROSS'S ISRAELI POPPY-SEED CAKE

Keeps 4 days in an airtight container.
Freeze 3 months.

This is a *parev*, fatless cake, but with an unusual moist texture. It can be served as a dessert, plain or with a fruit sauce or Greek yoghurt (for a dairy meal).

6 eggs
6 rounded tbsp caster (superfine) sugar
2 medium cooking apples, peeled, cored, and coarsely grated
3½ oz (100 g/⅞ cup) ground almonds
3½ oz (100 g/⅞ cup) poppy seeds

For the chocolate icing

4 oz (125 g) semi-sweet dessert chocolate
3 tbsp hot water
2 oz (50 g/¼ cup) soft butter or margarine
icing (confectioners') sugar

With an electric whisk beat the egg yolks and sugar very well until thick. Whisk the egg whites in a separate bowl until they hold together in peaks. Squeeze the juice out of the coarsely grated apples by hand (it is best to leave the grating of the apples as long as you can to avoid their going brown).

Gently fold all the ingredients together with a rubber spatula. Turn into an oiled loose-bottomed round tin approximately 9½x 2½ inches (24 x 6.5 cm), bottom-lined with silicone paper. Bake at Gas No. 4 (350°F/180°C) for 30 minutes, until firm to the touch.

Melt the chocolate with the water, either over direct but gentle heat or in the microwave (approx. 1½ minutes on 100 per cent power). Beat into the soft fat, then add enough icing sugar to make a coating consistency. Pour over the cake and allow to set.

PESACH (PASSOVER)

Each spring, during the 8 days of Passover, the great festival of freedom which commemorates the liberation of the Jews from slavery in Egypt more than 3,500 years ago, the Jewish household takes on an appearance quite different from the one it presents during the rest of the year, or indeed during any other festival.

In the kitchen unfamiliar pots and pans stand on the cooker top and counters; in the cupboards, matzot, matzah meal and other Passover foods are stacked on the freshly covered shelves, and there is no trace anywhere of either bread or flour. Meanwhile, in the dining room dishes are served that do not appear on the table at any other season.

This festival is seen as a time of renewal, a great family occasion, when everyone gathers to enjoy the Seder - the ceremonial meal whose order is laid down in the Haggadah, a text used by Jewry worldwide for centuries past. During the Seder meal, the story of the Exodus from Egypt is read from the Haggadah, and a succession of symbolic foods, displayed on a special plate, are tasted by everyone at the table.

The customs associated with this festival vary from one Jewish community to another - and indeed from one family to the next. The Ashkenazim and the Sephardim both have their separate traditions, and these could fill a book of their own if they were to be fully enumerated. (Details of the many and varied customs associated with Pesach can be found in Jewish cookery books that are devoted solely to the festivals - see the Bibliography.)

However, there are certain interesting differences between Sephardi and Ashkenazi conventions that should be mentioned. For instance, some Sephardim are permitted to use rice (a staple food of Eastern countries) while Ashkenazim are not. However, the rice has first to be picked over with great care to ensure that it does not contain any foreign bodies or 'chometz' (food forbidden at Pesach). Similarly, in Sephardi homes it is customary to eat 'legumes' such as peas and beans. However, Ashkenazim do not eat these *kitniyot* - as they are called in Hebrew - and you will often see on a Passover pack produced in Israel for export the words 'Does not contain *kitniyot*' or '*kitnit*' to reassure customers in the West.

Detailed authoritative guides are available from rabbinical authorities on how to prepare the home, and in particular the kitchen, for this important festival.

In this chapter, I shall attempt to set the scene, albeit according to the *minhag* (custom) of my own family and community.

However, wherever you may be, and whatever particular *minhag* is followed, it is always a magical moment when the house reveals its once-a-year Pesach face, with the traditional plates and dishes that appear only at this time. The kitchen is filled with the wonderful perfume of eingemacht (Passover preserves) and lemon curd, and the cakes and biscuits - the macaroons, sponge cakes and cinnamon balls - whose recipes have been passed down the chain from mother to daughter from early medieval times - ready and waiting for the family's verdict.

In my family, it's become the custom for the Seder plate to be prepared by the men of the house - and that includes preparing the Charoset and tasting the salt water as well.

The Preparation of the Seder

It has to be said that even with the proliferation of ready-to-eat Passover foods, preparing for this festival involves an enormous amount of planning and plain hard work. But the labour does bring with it enormous satisfaction. Each year I still delight in that moment when all the preparations are complete, the white cloth has been laid on the table, the candles are ready and there's a wine glass for each guest, with one for the prophet Elijah in pride of place in the centre.

The Seder meal is unlike any other eaten in a Jewish home, both in the way the table is prepared and in the order of the Haggadah service that precedes it. It is symbolic of the last meal that the Jews ate before the Exodus from Egypt.

Early in the afternoon on the Eve of Passover, the table is laid with a white tablecloth and the freshly polished candlesticks are put on their tray. As it is traditional to invite guests (especially those who might otherwise be alone on this night), there are usually many chairs to be set at the table. A wine glass is placed for each guest. A special large cup for Elijah the Prophet dominates the centre of the table. (As the glasses will be refilled no less than 4 times during the meal, it is a good idea to set each glass on a small plate to avoid spilling wine on the tablecloth.) In our family, it is the custom to leave the table bare of cutlery and crockery until it is time for the meal. The cutlery for each guest is previously rolled in a linen napkin, and all the plates are stacked on a side table or trolley. As soon as the first part of the Seder service is completed, the wine glasses are removed to a place of safety and the table is quickly set. This method also gives the hostess time to organize the first course. The system works well for us, but others may have a completely different tradition in their family.

It is traditional for the men to lean back in comfort during the meal, so cushions should be put on the chairs of the male guests. Near the seat of the host, place a small table containing a basin, jug and hand-towel. Just before the Seder service starts, the jug can be filled with water for the washing of the hands during the service.

THE CEREMONIAL PLATE

On the ceremonial plate, which through the years has offered inspiration to many fine craftsmen in ceramic and metal, are set out the 6 symbolic foods, prepared according to tradition by the father of the family. Details of the correct arrangement of these foods can be found in the Haggadah.

The Shankbone of a lamb usually represented today by a chicken's neck, is roasted until brown under the grill.

The 'roasted' egg a symbolic 'burnt offering' for the festival, is first hard-boiled and then browned under the grill.

The root of horseradish which recalls the bitterness of slavery, is peeled and trimmed, then a 2-inch (5-cm) length is set ready to cut into pieces during the service.

The dish of salt water symbolizing the tears shed by the Israelites in Egypt, is taken from the larger quantity prepared for the Eggs in Salt Water (see p. 602).

The bitter herbs are represented in Ashkenazi households by small sprigs of parsley, and among the Sephardim by lettuce leaves.

The Charoset is evocative in appearance (but certainly not in taste) of the mortar mixed by the Jewish slaves when they were forced to build the Egyptian treasure cities of Pithom and Ramses. It is made according to a recipe using fruit, nuts and wine, which is inspired by 2 verses from the Song of Songs: 'Under the apple tree I awakened thee' and 'I went down into the garden of nuts.' The wine is used as a symbol of the miraculous parting of the Red Sea.

MATZAH

The matzot - 3 pieces of unleavened bread - are set out on the table, but concealed in the folds of a linen napkin or in a special *matzah dekke*. They represent the three hereditary 'orders', dating from Temple times, into which Jews are still divided: the Kohanim (the priests), the Levites (their assistants) and the Israelites (the remainder of the population).

Many people are surprised to find that unleavened bread is actually made from flour, whose use is otherwise not allowed during the Festival. However, this is very special flour whose production has been strictly supervised - in the case of the special *shemura* matzot eaten by the very Orthodox Jews, from the moment that the sheaves of wheat are gathered in the field. This is to ensure that at no stage can either the grain or the flour become damp and ferment, causing the dough to rise, leavening the bread - which is, of course, strictly forbidden.

For the same reason, once water has been mixed with the flour to make the dough, to avoid any possibility of fermentation and therefore leavening of the dough, no more than 18 minutes must elapse before the baked matzot are brought out of the oven. Because of the precise terms of the rules governing its manufacture, the matzah-baking process has barely changed throughout the centuries; in the remains of the matzah bakery attached to the fourteenth-century synagogue at Carpentras in Provence, one can see the remains of utensils that are almost identical to those still in use in some Hassidic communities today. I have watched the members of one such community preparing their own matzot as a special *mitzvah* (good deed), with hordes of little boys happily rolling the dough, each using a length of broom handle as a rolling pin. This community even won a special dispensation from the Clean Air Act to allow the matzot to be baked in a traditional wood-fired oven on the Eve of Pesach!

WINE

The serving of four ritual glasses of wine, as well as the custom of sitting on cushions and reclining to dine, is said to have originated in Graeco-Roman times. Certainly it has persisted to this day.

CHAROSET

Makes 20 ½-teaspoon servings.
Keeps 3 days under refrigeration.

The quantity given will be sufficient for 2 Sedarim, each of 8-10 people. Charoset - which is said to have been invented by Rabbi Hillel, who lived between 60 BCE and 9 CE - is not eaten on any other occasion. This is our family recipe - a similar mixture is prepared in all Ashkenazi Jewish households whose families came originally from Eastern Europe. However, Sephardim achieve a mortar-like mixture by using other fruits such as dates, apples, oranges, bananas and pears. The Turks, Greeks, Moroccans and Egyptians each have their own recipe, although nuts, cinnamon and wine are common to all. A large quantity of Charoset - perhaps for a communal Seder - is most quickly made in the food processor. However, my husband, the family Charoset-maker, insists on a small electric mixer which is used only on this one occasion during the year. Tradition!

3 oz (75 g/¾ cup) walnuts
¼ large cooking apple
kosher wine to moisten
2 level teasp cinnamon
2 level teasp sugar

Mince the walnuts and the apple. Moisten with the kosher wine and flavour with cinnamon and sugar. The consistency should be that of mortar!

EGGS IN SALT WATER

This delicious if unorthodox dish is *never* served except at this time of the year. Whether you give each guest a whole egg and a bowl of the salt water, or slice the egg in the water to make a 'soup', the proportions remain the same. Allow 1 hard-boiled egg per person, with a third of an egg extra for 'seconds', together with ½ teaspoon salt dissolved in 5 fl oz (150 ml/⅔ cup) of cold water for each egg used. Put the salt and water in a very large bowl or tureen, and add the whole shelled eggs, or the sliced eggs, half an hour before the commencement of the Seder. Serve with a soup ladle.

Menus for the Seder

As with all cooking during Pesach, use only packaged foods (including oil) with a '*kosher le Pesach*' label. Lists of these are published in the Jewish press, well before the festival.

Advice on how to keep food hot during the first part of the Seder service is given with each main-course recipe. See also 'How to Cook Vegetables for a Party' (p. 248).

Ashkenazi Sedarim generally commence with Eggs in Salt Water (see above) whatever the subsequent menu. In each meal I have tried to juxtapose the well-loved familiar dishes with some new ones in the spirit of the old.

MENU 1
A CHICKEN MEAL

Slimline Mushroom and Courgette Soup with Knaidlach (see pp. 31, 51)
Poulet au Pommes (fruited chicken casserole) (see p. 631)
New potatoes
Glazed Carrots (see p. 254)
Cinnamon Torte with a Mixed Berry Filling (see p. 641)
Mirkatan (Armenian-style dried fruit compôte) (see p. 324)

ALTERNATIVE VEGETARIAN STARTER AND MAIN DISH

Passover Minestrone (see p. 627)
Twice-baked Cheese Soufflé (see p. 624)
or
Vegetarian Moussaka (see p. 625)

MENU 2
A FISH MEAL

Pecan (or Walnut) Smoked Salmon Roulade with a Salad of Mixed Leaves (see p. 8)
Terrine of Gefilte Fish with a Pink Mayonnaise (see p. 68)
Halibut in an Egg and Lemon Sauce (see p. 628)
New potatoes
Cherry tomatoes
Japonais au Moka (see p. 645)
4-fruit Salad (using Passover liqueur) (see p. 326)

ALTERNATIVE VEGETARIAN STARTER AND MAIN COURSE

Katsis Kishuim (courgette pâté) (see p. 94)
or
Avocado and Egg Pâté (see p. 95)
Aubergine, Tomato and Cheese Casserole (see p. 109)

Jams and Preserves

'Eingemacht' covers a variety of delicious preserves that are made only at this time of the year. People who would never dream of making jam in the summer still get out the treasured family recipe and make enough for their whole extended family – so there is a constant to-ing and fro-ing of little pots!

Eingemachts are not jams in the English sense of the word, but are more like heavy syrups in which a variety of fruits and nuts are suspended. Lemon curd is the exception, coming from a very old English tradition.

LEMON CURD
(*Conventional Method*)

Makes about 2½ lb (1.25 kg).
Keeps 3 months under refrigeration.

This used to be one of the slowest and trickiest preserves to make. Over the years I have gradually simplified the whole procedure, using first the food processor, to reduce the possibility of curdling even when the mixture is cooked on a direct flame (itself a great time-saver over the double-saucepan method) and then - for smaller quantities - using the microwave oven (the microwave method follows this conventional one).

This wonderfully tart and buttery curd is delicious on buttered matzah, and when it's combined with an equal volume of whipped cream it makes a wonderful filling for sponge cakes and meringues.

To get the maximum juice from citrus fruit, put them in the microwave on 100 per cent power for 45 seconds, or until warm to the touch.

juice of 6 or 7 lemons - 12 fl oz (350 ml/1½ cups)
finely grated rind of 6 lemons
1 lb (450 g/2 cups) granulated sugar
6 oz (175 g/¾ cup) unsalted butter
6 whole eggs

Put the juice and the grated rind into a bowl and leave for 2 hours so that the oils in the rind can flavour the juice. Set the oven at Gas No. ½ (250°F/120°C) and put in the sugar and 5 small jars to heat up. Pour the juice and rind through a fine strainer (discard the rind).

Melt the butter over gentle heat in a heavy-based pan, then add the warm sugar and the strained juice. Stir constantly until the sugar has completely dissolved.

Process the eggs in the food processor until thoroughly blended - about 10 seconds - then add a ladleful of the hot sugar mixture, processing all the time.

To mix by hand Whisk the yolks and whites to blend, then add a ladleful of the hot sugar mixture, whisking constantly.

Tip the egg mixture into the pan and stir constantly over gentle heat until the mixture thickens to a pouring custard that will coat the back of a wooden spoon. *Do not allow the mixture to boil* or it will curdle. (You will find that at the point of thickening, any froth on top of the curd disappears.)

Take off the heat and continue to stir for 2 or 3 minutes - it will thicken a little more with the heat from the pan. Pour the curd into the hot jars and cover with wax paper discs. When quite cold, cover with lids and refrigerate until required.

LEMON CURD
(*Microwave Cooking Method*)

Makes approx 1¼ lb (575 g/3 cups).
Keeps 3 months under refrigeration.

This is an excellent method for a smaller quantity - the total cooking time is only 3 minutes!

rind of 3 lemons, finely grated
6 fl oz (175 ml/¾ cup) lemon juice, from about 3 large lemons
3 oz (75 g/⅓ cup) unsalted or lightly salted butter
8 oz (225 g/1 cup) caster (superfine) sugar
3 whole eggs

Have ready 2 washed and rinsed 8 oz (225 g) jars plus a small soufflé or jam dish.

2 hours in advance, leave the rind to soak in the lemon juice in a large microwave-safe jug to extract the flavouring oils. Pour this mixture through a sieve, then discard the rind.

In the same jug, melt the butter at 100 per cent power for 1 minute (cover lightly with a paper towel to prevent spattering). Stir in the lemon juice and sugar and cook uncovered on 100 per cent power for 2 minutes. Then stir again to ensure that the sugar is dissolved in the liquid.

In a food processor or blender, process the eggs to blend for 10 seconds, then slowly add the hot, buttery liquid through the feed tube, processing all the time. Return the mixture to the jug and microwave on 100 per cent power for 2½ minutes, stirring half-way.

Take out and stir vigorously to ensure the curd is even in texture - it should be the consistency of a thick coating custard. If not, cook for a further 30 seconds.

Sterilize the jars as follows. Fill them a quarter full with cold water and heat uncovered on 100 per cent power for about 2 minutes - until the water is boiling. Remove carefully from the oven as they will be very hot. Pour away the water and stand them upside down to drain on a paper towel. Turn them over immediately and fill to the brim with the curd, then cover with a lid with an inset rubber ring. The small amount left can be put in the smaller dish as a 'taster'. Store in the refrigerator.

VARIATIONS

LIME CURD

In the 3-egg quantity of curd use 4-6 limes, depending on size, with their finely grated rind, instead of the 3 lemons.

LEMON AND PASSION FRUIT CURD

Makes approx. 1¼ lb (575 g).
Keeps 3 months under refrigeration.

The passion fruit add a new and intriguing dimension to the familiar lemon flavour.

To the 3-egg recipe add the pulp from 3 passion fruit.

Two hours in advance, leave the rind to soak in the lemon juice to extract the flavouring oil. After two hours add the scooped out passion fruit pulp then pour this mixture through a sieve, pressing down well to extract as much juice as possible. Discard the rind and seeds. Proceed exactly as for Lemon Curd.

APRICOT EINGEMACHT (*Conventional Method*)

Makes 4 lb (2 kg).
Keeps 12 months in a cool ventilated cupboard.

A wonderful conserve. If whole dried apricots are used, divide in 2 before soaking.

1 lb (450 g/3 cups) dried apricots
2 pints (1.25 l/5 cups) cold water
2 lb (1 kg/4 cups) granulated sugar
5 tbsp fresh lemon juice
3 oz (75 g/¾ cup) almonds, blanched and split

The night before you plan to make the conserve, put the fruit in a preserving pan or other heavy pan of half-gallon (2.25-l/10-cup) capacity and cover with the water. (If tenderized apricots are used, omit soaking and use only enough water - approximately 1 pint/575 ml/2½ cups - barely to cover the fruit when cooking it.) The next day, add more water if necessary, to ensure the fruit is barely covered, half-cover the pan, then bring to the boil and simmer until the apricots are absolutely tender - 10-15 minutes. Meanwhile, wash and rinse sufficient jars, and put in a low oven, Gas No. ¼ (225°F/110°C), to dry and warm.

Add the sugar to the tender fruit, stir until it has been dissolved, then add the lemon juice and almonds and boil hard until the jam falls off the spoon in flakes rather than droplets - the liquid will then be a thick and viscous syrup. (Do not overboil or the sugar will begin to caramelize and spoil the delicate flavour of the conserve.) Put into the warm, dry jars and cover at once with wax discs. Leave to cool, then cover each jar with cellophane or a lid with a rubber seal.

APRICOT EINGEMACHT
(Microwave method)

Makes 1½–2 lb (675–900 g)
Keeps 12 months in the refrigerator.

Note: To produce a *diabetic* version of the apricot eingemacht, use exactly the same method but substitute 8 oz (225 g) fructose for the 1 lb (450 g) of granulated sugar used in the regular recipe.

8 oz (225 g) dried apricots
1 pint (575 ml/2½ cups) cold water
3 tbsp lemon juice
1 lb (450 g/2 cups) granulated sugar
2 oz (50 g/½ cup) blanched almonds (optional)

Put the apricots into a lidded casserole, pour on the cold water (it should cover them – if not, add a little more), cover and cook on 100% power in the microwave for 10 minutes, then leave covered for 20 minutes.

Lift the apricots out of the liquid and put in a 4-pint (2.25 litre/10 cup) bowl. Add 5 fl oz (150 ml/⅔ cup) of the liquid, the lemon juice, sugar and almonds (if used) and cook uncovered in the microwave on 100% power for 3 minutes. Then stir well to ensure the sugar is dissolved.

Cook uncovered for a further 15 minutes, until the apricots are bubbling in a syrup which will just coat the back of a wooden spoon (the mixture should have been bubbling fiercely for 10 minutes). Take out of the microwave.

Put 4 tablespoons of cold water in each of 2 clean 1 lb (450 g) jam jars and bring to the boil, uncovered, on 100% power – about 1½ minutes. Then turn upside down to drain and dry on paper towelling.

After 30 seconds turn right-side up, fill with the conserve and seal with the lid.

Note: Using *ready to eat* dried apricots and jam sugar with pectin: cook the apricots in the casserole as before but in 15 fl oz (425 ml/2 cups) water – drain immediately. There is no need to allow them to stand for 20 minutes.

If using *jam sugar with pectin* cook uncovered on 100% power for 10 minutes not 15.

PRUNE EINGEMACHT
(Conventional Method)

Makes 2 lb (900 g).
Keeps for 1 year in a cool cupboard or refrigerator.

The tartness of the lemons counterbalances the sweetness of the prunes - a wonderful conserve.

1 x 9 oz (250 g) packet tenderized prunes (if available) - ideally stoned
1 pint water (575 ml/2½ cups) - if prunes are tenderized omit soaking and use only 10 fl oz (275 ml/1¼ cups) water, sufficient barely to cover the fruit
2 oz (50 g/½ cup) blanched almonds
3 large lemons
1 lb 2 oz (500 g/2½ cups) granulated sugar

If prunes are not tenderized, soak in the pint of water overnight. If they are tenderized, stuff each prune with a split almond.

Have ready 4 small jars washed, rinsed and put in a low oven, Gas No. ¼ (225°F/110°C), to dry and heat. Also have ready 4 wax paper discs and lids or cellophane circles to cover the jars.

Remove the prune stones (if necessary) and replace each with half an almond. Peel the lemons, remove all the pith, then slice and cut each slice in half. Put the prunes and their soaking liquid into a 9-inch (22-5-cm) heavy pan, together with the sugar, lemon slices, juice and remaining almonds. Stir over gentle heat until the sugar dissolves, then cook uncovered at a fast boil until the syrup looks thick and viscous and a little will drop from the spoon in thick globules - it won't fall off in flakes like ordinary jam. (If it boils for too long and goes gluey, stir in a cupful of water, bring back to the boil and cook as before until *just* done.) Turn into the hot jars and cover with the wax paper discs. Cover with the lids when quite cold.

PRUNE EINGEMACHT (*Microwave Method*)

This method avoids soaking non-tenderized prunes overnight.

If prunes are not tenderized put them with 1 pint (575 ml/2½ cups) of water into a lidded casserole (the water should cover them - if not, add a little more), cover and cook on 100 per cent power for 10 minutes, then leave covered until cold enough to handle (30-40 minutes). Remove stones from non-tenderized prunes and replace with a split almond, reshaping each prune.

Put the prunes in a 4-pint (2-1/10-cup) bowl. Add 5 fl oz (150 ml/⅔ cup) of the soaking liquid (water if using tenderized prunes), the lemon sections and sugar, and cook on 100 per cent power for 3 minutes, then stir well to ensure the sugar is dissolved. Cook uncovered for a further 15 minutes, until syrup will just coat the back of a wooden spoon. The mixture should have been bubbling fiercely for 10 minutes.

Put 4 tablespoons of cold water in each of the clean jars and bring to the boil, uncovered, on 100 per cent power - about 1½ minutes - then turn upside-down to drain on paper towelling. Turn right-side up, fill with the conserve and seal with the lid.

LEMON AND WALNUT EINGEMACHT

Makes about 1 lb (450 g).
Keeps at least 1 year in a cool cupboard.

A thick conserve which is traditionally eaten with a spoon, washed down with lemon tea. It is delicious on matzah crackers.

4 oz (125 g/1 cup) walnut halves
5 fl oz (150 ml/⅔ cup) water
2 large lemons
12 oz (350 g/1½ cups) sugar

Put the walnuts into a pan with enough cold water to cover, and bring to the boil. Stand for 1 minute, strain and set aside.

Remove the peel and pith from the lemons and reserve it; cut the lemon flesh into segments, reserving the membranes and pips. Tie up the lemon peel, pith, pips and membranes securely in a square of butter muslin (cheesecloth) or a piece of light-coloured non-woven kitchen cloth.

Put the sugar and water into a large heavy-based pan and heat gently until the sugar has dissolved. Add the scalded walnuts, the lemon segments and the butter-muslin parcel. Boil gently, stirring from time to time, until setting point is reached, when the jam falls off the spoon in thick globules - it won't fall off in flakes like ordinary jam - about 20 minutes. Remove the pan from the heat and take out the parcel. Allow to stand for 10 minutes, then put the preserve into small clean jars, previously warmed in the oven, and cover.

PAM'S BEETROOT EINGEMACHT

Makes nearly 7 lb (3.25 kg).
Keeps 1 year in a cool cupboard or refrigerator.

This traditional beetroot conserve must be cooked until it goes brown - a sign that the sugar in the beets has caramelized, giving the jam its inimitable flavour.

5 lb (2.25 kg) uncooked beets or
4 lb (2 kg) ready-cooked skinned beets
4 lb (2 kg/9 cups) granulated sugar (for uncooked beets) or 3 lb (1.25 kg/6¾ cups) granulated sugar (for cooked beets)
3 large lemons, peeled
6 oz (175 g/1½ cups) split almonds
1-1½ oz (25-40 g) ground ginger

Boil the uncooked beets in water to cover for 1 hour, cool and skin.

Cut the cooked beets in slivers ⅜ inch (1 cm) wide and 1-2 inch (2.5 cm) long (or use the julienne- or chip-cutter on the food processor).

Put in a large bowl with the sugar, mix well, then leave overnight to allow liquid to form.

Next day, put the sugar/beet mixture into a very large, heavy pan, together with the lemons, sectioned like an orange. Bring to the boil, stirring, until the sugar has dissolved, then leave to bubble on a low light, stirring occasionally, for at least 3 hours, until the mixture loses its redness and the beets become translucent and start to turn brown.

Finally add the nuts and the smaller amount of ginger (taste, but be careful - it's hot - and add the extra ½ oz/15 g ginger if you wish). Bubble for a further 15 minutes. The preserve thickens as it cools.

Ladle the hot jam into warm jars which have been heated for 10 minutes in a low oven, Gas No. ½ (250°F/120°C). Cover with wax discs and then with a lid when quite cold.

Cakes

Yes, it is possible to buy Passover cakes, cake mixes and shop biscuits. But despite the inevitable hassle involved in baking these labour-intensive recipes - they almost all date from an earlier, less hurried time - one experiences a very special afterglow when surveying the results of all this labour that I would not wish to forgo.

In many families it is the custom to join forces for Pesach baking - certainly some kind of 'assembly-line' makes it all more pleasurable.

Here are a few pointers to success.

1 Use eggs left at room temperature for 1 hour, not straight from the refrigerator - they will whisk to a much greater volume this way than when chilled.
2 As dampness may cause heaviness, make sure that both matzah meal and potato flour are absolutely dry by leaving the packages in an airing cupboard or warming drawer of the cooker for 24 hours before use.
3 To avoid any chance of cakes sticking in the tins, use silicone lining paper, as the commercial bakers do. Prepare the tins before preparing the cake mixture, as whisked sponges lose volume if allowed to stand before baking.
4 To allow for loss of heat when the oven is opened, preheat it to 1 gas mark (25°F/10°C) higher than is indicated in the recipe. Turn down to the correct temperature when the cake is put in. This is a necessary precaution with a delicately structured cake like a Passover sponge.
5 When whisking egg whites, never leave the electric mixer unattended. Overbeaten whites collapse into a liquid state again and cannot be reconstituted.
6 Always use a metal spoon or a rubber spatula for folding the dry ingredients into the egg mixture. A wooden spoon would crush out the air which has been beaten in.

Note To change medium matzah meal into fine meal, or fine meal into cake meal, put in an electric grinder or liquidizer for 5 seconds. To change medium meal directly into cake meal, grind or liquidize for 10 seconds. The same procedure can be followed to change granular sugar into caster (superfine) sugar.

Several days beforehand, it is wise to plan exactly what confectionery is to be made at home. As some recipes need all whites and others all yolks, if possible select those recipes that will use up an equal quantity of both. Any leftover egg whites can be stored, tightly covered, in the refrigerator for use later in the week, but leftover egg yolks should be refrigerated immediately and used within 24 hours.

WEIGHING WITHOUT SCALES

Measure these foods with a tablespoon as follows:

1 oz (25 g) matzah meal (medium, fine or cake) = 1 heaped tablespoon
1 oz (25 g) potato flour = 1 rounded tablespoon
1 oz (25 g) ground almonds or hazelnuts (filberts) = 1 heaped tablespoon
1 oz (25 g) granulated or caster (superfine) sugar = 1 rounded tablespoon
1 oz (25 g) icing (confectioners') sugar = 2 rounded tablespoons
1 oz (25 g) desiccated (dried and shredded) coconut = 2 rounded tablespoons
1 oz (25 g) cocoa = 4 level tablespoons
1 oz (25 g) grated cheese = 1 heaped tablespoon
5 fl oz of any liquid = 8 tablespoons

To avoid having to duplicate cake tins and casseroles for Passover, use disposable foil sandwich, cake and quiche tins and lidded, foil baking containers.

PASSOVER SPONGE CAKES

The majority of Passover cakes date back before the invention of baking powder (in the middle of the nineteenth century), to the time when the only way to lighten a cake was to use yeast (which is forbidden during this Festival) or entrap air by whisking eggs, usually with sugar. It follows, therefore, that Passover is the time for sponge cakes, variously flavoured and enriched with nuts, cocoa, fruit and various flavourings. In addition, instead of flour, matzah meal ground to different degrees of fineness and potato flour (also known as '*fécule*') are used. However, I have found that when equal quantities of the finest meal (cake meal) and potato flour are substituted for the same total weight of flour, a similar (if slightly coarser) texture can be achieved.

A sponge cake is lightened by the expansion in the oven of the air which is entrapped in the beaten eggs. Whether the whole eggs are whisked together or the yolks and whites are whisked separately, it is essential that they are beaten to the correct stage. This varies according to the specific recipe, but the wording used is always the same.

Stiff, glossy peaks of egg whites Withdraw the beaters – the egg whites will stand up straight without tilting to one side or the other. The texture is shiny. When over-beaten the texture becomes dull and like cotton-wool in appearance.

Thick and white yolks and sugar Lift the beater and allow some of the mixture to fall back on to the surface. This should retain its shape for a few seconds before disappearing. The mixture lightens considerably in appearance. The same test can be applied when the yolks and whites are beaten together with the sugar – whether by electric whisk or by hand over hot water.

To test for doneness Slight pressure of the finger should leave no impression on the surface and there should be no sound of bubbling.

Note All whisked sponges should be left in the baking tin, resting on a wire cooling tray, until completely cold, so that the delicate structure can be set before the cake is turned out.

As before, all eggs are size 3 (standard) unless otherwise stated.

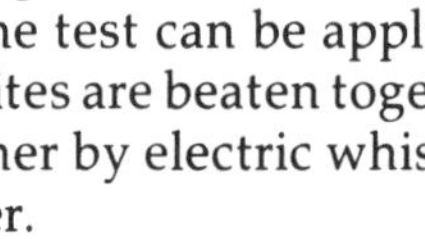

PASSOVER PLAVA

Keeps 1 week at room temperature in an airtight tin. Freeze 3 months.

A family-sized fine-textured sponge which stays moist for several days.

For 1 x 9-inch (22.5-cm) cake or 2 x 7-inch (18-cm) cakes

5 eggs
10 oz (275 g/1⅓ cups) caster (superfine) sugar
1 tbsp lemon juice
3 oz (75 g/⅔ cup) cake meal
3 oz (75 g/½ cup) potato flour

For 1 x 7-inch (18-cm) cake

3 eggs
6 oz (175 g/¾ cup) caster (superfine) sugar
2 teasp lemon juice
2 oz (50 g/½ cup) cake meal
2 oz (50 g/⅓ cup) potato flour

Separate the yolks from the whites. Divide sugar into 2 equal quantities. Put 1 amount of sugar into a bowl with the yolks and whisk until thick and white. (If an electric beater is not available, stand the eggs and sugar in a bowl over a pan of very hot water and whisk until thick and white.) Beat in the juice. In another bowl, whisk whites until they form stiff, glossy peaks, then beat in the other quantity of sugar until a firm meringue is formed. Fold into the first mixture. Finally fold in the sifted meal and potato flour. Spoon into the cake tin, which has been oiled and then sprinkled with sugar. Level the surface. Sprinkle a thin layer of caster sugar over the top.

To bake 9-inch cake at Gas No. 4 (350°F/180°C) for 1 hour 10 minutes; 7-inch at same temperature for 45 minutes.

VARIATIONS

RASPBERRY SPONGE

Make the 7-inch (18-cm) cake, folding in 1 tablespoon of Passover raspberry jam after the meal and flour have been added. Sprinkle the sugared surface of the uncooked cake with 2 level tablespoons of finely chopped blanched almonds. Bake as above.

ALMOND SPONGE

A deliciously moist cake. Make in exactly the same way as the 7-inch (18 cm) plava, folding in 3 oz (75 g/¾ cup) ground almonds with the sifted meal and potato flour.

TRADITIONAL PASSOVER SPONGE

Keeps 1 week at room temperature in an airtight container.
Freeze 3 months.

This recipe is excellent if a more shallow cake is required. If preferred, the sugar quantity can be reduced to 14 oz (375 g/2 cups).

10 eggs
1 lb (450 g/2¼ cups) caster (superfine) sugar
juice of 1 lemon
4 oz (125 g/⅔ cup) potato flour
5 oz (150 g/1¼ cups) cake meal or fine matzah meal

Conventional method Whisk the yolks until they are creamy and light in colour, then add the sugar gradually, whisking until the mixture forms a thick glossy ribbon as it falls back into the bowl from the beaters. Beat in the lemon juice. Sift the potato flour and meal together 3 times. Whisk the whites until they form stiff but still glossy peaks. Carefully fold the meal into the yolk mixture, then cut and fold in the whites using a metal spoon and an 'over-and-over' cutting action, rather than a 'round-and-round' stirring, which tends to press out the air. Spoon the mixture into the prepared tins and sprinkle the surface with 3 teaspoons of caster sugar.

New method This is an easier method for a beginner. Whisk the whites with a pinch of salt until they form stiff, glossy peaks (leave the yolk in each half-shell). Now add the yolks one at a time, alternating with a tablespoon of the sugar, whisking well after each addition. When all the sugar and yolks are in, whisk a little longer until the mixture is thick and mousse-like. Finally whisk in the lemon juice and fold in the potato flour and meal as in the first method.

To bake With both methods, you now have a choice of 3 different ways to proceed:

1 Divide between 2 greaseproof-paper-lined baking tins, each approximately 10 x 7 x 3 inches (25 x 18 x 7.5 cm). Bake at Gas No. 4 (350°F/180°C) for 1 hour.

2 Spoon into 3 8-inch (20-cm) lined cake tins. Bake at Gas No. 4 (350°F/180°C) for half an hour, then at Gas No. 3 (325°F/160°C) for a further 15 minutes.

3 Divide between 2 9-inch (22.5-cm) ring tins. Bake at Gas No. 3 (325°F/160°C) for $1\frac{1}{4}$ hours.

Leave all the cakes in the tin to cool completely before turning out on to a cooling tray. Store in airtight tins. The sponge cakes can be split and filled as follows:

LEMON CURD

Cream 2 oz (50 g/$\frac{1}{4}$ cup) butter with 3 oz (75 g/$\frac{3}{4}$ cup) sifted icing (confectioners') sugar. Beat in 2 tablespoons of lemon curd or fold together equal quantities of curd and whipping cream.

CHOCOLATE BUTTER CREAM

Cream 2 oz (50 g/$\frac{1}{4}$ cup) butter or margarine until soft. Beat in 4 oz (125 g/1 cup) sifted icing (confectioners') sugar, alternating quantities of the sugar with 2 oz (50 g) chocolate which has been melted in 2 tablespoons strong coffee (made with 2 teaspoons of instant coffee).

A CITRUS CHIFFON PLAVA

Keeps 1 week in an airtight container.
Freeze 3 months.

A luscious cake with a light, moist texture to serve plain, with tea or coffee, a glass of wine, or even a fruit compôte.

3 oz (75 g/$\frac{1}{2}$ cup) potato flour
$2\frac{1}{2}$ oz (65 g/$\frac{1}{2}$ cup plus 2 tbsp) cake meal
5 oz (150 g/$\frac{2}{3}$ cup) caster (superfine) sugar
5 egg yolks
2 fl oz (50 ml/$\frac{1}{4}$ cup) oil
2 fl oz (50 ml/$\frac{1}{4}$ cup) orange juice
1 teasp grated lemon rind
1 teasp grated orange rind
5 egg whites
pinch of salt
2 oz (50 g/$\frac{1}{4}$ cup) caster (superfine) sugar

Preheat the oven to Gas No. 3 (325°F/160°C). Grease a 10-inch (25 cm) ring tin, about 3 inches (7.5 cm) deep. Sieve the potato flour, cake meal and 5 oz sugar into a large bowl and mix well.

In a small bowl, mix together the egg yolks, oil, orange juice and the lemon and orange rind. Make a well in the middle of the dry ingredients, pour in the egg-yolk mixture and stir with a wooden spoon until smoothly and evenly mixed. Whisk the egg whites with a pinch of salt until they hold stiff, glossy peaks, then whisk in the 2 oz caster sugar, a tablespoon at a time, whisking after each addition. Spoon $\frac{1}{4}$ of the meringue onto the egg mixture and stir well to lighten the texture then fold in the remainder with a rubber spatula. Spoon into the prepared tin, smooth level, then bake for 1 hour, until firm to gentle touch. Put the cake, in the cake tin, on a cooling rack and leave until it feels cool to the touch. Loosen from the edges of the tin with the tip of a knife and gently ease out. Store in an airtight container.

ORANGE WALNUT TORTE

Keeps 1 week at room temperature in an airtight container.
Freeze 3 months.

A deliciously flavoured cake, which can be served plain, topped with a water icing flavoured with lemon juice or rum, or split and filled with rum-flavoured whipped cream. Half-quantities make 1 7–8 inch (17.5–20 cm) cake.

7 oz (200 g/1 cup) caster (superfine) sugar, divided into 2
6 eggs, separated
grated rind and juice of a small orange
7 oz (200 g/1¾ cups) ground walnuts
5 level tbsp (7 American tbsp) cake meal

Whisk 1 portion of sugar with the yolks until thick and mousse-like. (If no electric beater is available, do this over hot water.) Whisk in the rind and juice. Whisk whites with a pinch of salt until they form stiff, glossy peaks, then beat in the second portion of sugar, a tablespoonful at a time, beating after each addition. Finally fold the meringue into the yolks.

Mix together the ground nuts and meal, then fold into the egg mixture. Spoon into 2 7-inch (18-cm) or 1 9- or 10-inch (22.5- or 25-cm) loose-bottomed cake tin which has been oiled, then sprinkled with meal. Smooth the top of the mixture level, then sprinkle lightly with caster sugar (omit if to be iced).

Bake in a preheated oven, Gas No. 4 (350°F/180°C), for 1 hour 10 minutes, or until firm to the touch and slightly shrunken from the sides. Allow to cool in tin on a cooling rack for 30 minutes, then ease out.

VARIATION

Use ground hazelnuts instead of walnuts and flavour with lemon juice and rind.

ORANGE BLOSSOM CAKE

Makes 1 x 9-inch (22.5-cm) cake.
Keeps moist 1 week at room temperature in an airtight tin.
Freeze 3 months.

This has a moist and tender texture with a delicate but definite orange flavour. It requires no icing. The flavour is best with butter rather than margarine. It doesn't rise very much in the oven.

4 oz (125 g/½ cup) unsalted butter
4 oz (125 g/½ cup) caster (superfine) sugar
3 egg yolks
3 tbsp fresh orange juice
grated rind of 1 orange
4 oz (125 g/1 cup) ground almonds
1 oz (25 g/¼ cup) matzah cake meal
1 oz (25 g/3 tbsp) potato flour
3 egg whites
1 tbsp caster (superfine) sugar

For the decoration
sifted icing (confectioners') sugar

Preheat the oven to Gas No. 4 (350°F/180°C). Lightly oil then dust out with cake meal a 9-inch (22.5-cm) tin at least 1½ inches (4 cm) deep. Melt the butter gently until it is just liquid (1 minute in the microwave at 80 per cent power). Leave to cool. Using a balloon or electric whisk, whisk the sugar and the yolks until creamy and lighter in colour – the mixture will fall from the whisk in a 'ribbon'. Add the juice and rind and whisk a further 2 minutes, until foamy and covered with bubbles. Sift together, then stir in the ground almonds, meal and potato flour.

Whisk the whites with a pinch of salt until they hold peaks that just bend over at the top, then whisk in the tablespoon of sugar. Using a rubber spatula, fold the cooled, melted butter into the cake mixture, leaving any milky residue behind in the bowl. *Stir* a quarter of the meringue into this mixture to lighten its texture, then *fold in* the remainder as delicately as possible, using the spatula. Spoon into the prepared cake tin and level the top.

Bake for 30-35 minutes, or until a pale gold on top and springy to gentle touch. Place the cake tin on a cooling tray and leave for 10 minutes, then run a knife round the edge and turn it gently over so that the cake falls out. Immediately reverse it on to another cooling tray so that the top of the cake isn't marked. When quite cold sprinkle lightly with icing sugar through a paper doily laid on the top - this gives a very pretty pattern effect. Store in an airtight tin.

BANANA NUT CAKE

Keeps 1 week under refrigeration.
Freeze 3 months.

A lovely moist and fruity cake that is also delicious as a dessert served with a dried or fresh fruit compôte.

7 eggs, separated
10 oz (275 g/1⅓ cup) caster (superfine) sugar
2 tbsp lemon juice
4 small or 3 medium bananas
(approx 1 lb–1 lb 2 oz/450–500 g) total weight
½ teasp salt
2 teasp grated orange or lemon rind
4 oz (125 g/1 cup) matzah cake meal
4 oz (125 g/1 cup) ground almonds
2–3 tbsp extra ground almonds for dusting the tin

Preheat the oven to Gas No. 4 (350°F/180°C). Lightly grease with oil then dust out with ground almonds a 9-inch (22.5-cm) ring tin, 3½ inches (9 cm) deep. If the ring tin is only 2½ inches (6.5 cm) deep, prepare in addition a smaller ring tin or a 7-inch (17.5-cm) round tin not less than 2½ inches (6.5 cm) deep.

Whisk the yolks until thick and light in colour, then add the sugar and lemon juice and whisk until the mixture flows in a continuous ribbon when the beaters are lifted. Stir in the bananas, mashed to a purée, the salt, rind, cake meal and almonds. Whisk the egg whites until they hold peaks that bend slightly when the beater is withdrawn. Stir a quarter of this meringue into the first mixture then fold in the remainder very gently, using a rubber spatula. Turn the mixture into the prepared tin(s) and smooth level. (Fill only up to ½ inch (1.5 cm) from the top of the tin.) Bake for 40–45 minutes (35 minutes for the smaller cake) or until a toothpick or skewer comes out clean.

Leave the cake(s) to cool completely on a rack. Run a thin knife round the edge and the tube of the pan. Release it carefully.

UGAT SCHEKADEME
(*Chocolate and Almond Cake*)

Serves 8–10.
Keeps 1 week at room temperature in an airtight container.
Freeze 3 months.

A wonderfully moist cake made with grated chocolate.

3½ oz (100 g/¾ cup plus 2 tbsp) ground almonds
3 level tbsp fine matzah meal
3½ oz (100 g) plain (semi-sweet) chocolate, grated
3 x size 2 (large) eggs, separated
4 oz (125 g/½ cup) caster (superfine) sugar
1 tbsp lemon juice

For the frosting
4 oz (125 g/1 cup) sifted icing (confectioners') sugar
1 tbsp cocoa
2 oz (50 g/¼ cup) soft butter or margarine
1 teasp instant coffee dissolved in 3 teasp boiling water

For the garnish
8 whole blanched almonds, toasted

Preheat the oven to Gas No. 3 (325°F/160°C). Have ready an 8-inch (20-cm) loose-bottomed tin, greased and lined with silicone paper, or a loaf tin measuring approximately $10\frac{1}{2}$ x $4\frac{1}{2}$ x 3 inches (26 x 11 x 7.5 cm).

Mix the almonds, the meal and the grated chocolate. Whisk the egg whites until they hold stiff peaks, then add the sugar a tablespoon at a time, whisking until stiff after each addition. Fold in the yolks, followed by the dry ingredients. Finally stir in the lemon juice. Spoon the mixture into the tin and level off.

Bake for 45 minutes, until golden brown and firm to gentle touch - a skewer should come out clean. Leave on a cooling tray until cold, then carefully turn out.

To make the frosting, put all the ingredients into a bowl and beat until smooth - about 1 minute. Spread on top of the cooled cake, rough up with a fork, and decorate with the almonds.

ALL-IN-ONE VICTORIA SPONGE

Cake keeps 1 week at room temperature in an airtight container.
Freeze 3 months.
Cream-filled cake keeps 2 days under refrigeration.

A very good all-purpose cake which can be eaten plain, filled or iced. It's also good for the base of a trifle.

6 oz (175 g/¾ cup) soft margarine
6 oz (175 g/¾ cup) caster (superfine) sugar
3 eggs
3 oz (75 g/½ cup) potato flour
3 oz (75 g/⅔ cup) cake meal
1½ teasp Passover baking powder
½–¾ oz (15–20 g) packet vanilla sugar
3 tbsp hot water

Preheat the oven to Gas No. 4 (350°F/180°C). Grease and bottom-line an 8- or 9-inch (20- or 22.5-cm) tin about 2 inches (5 cm) deep.

Put all the ingredients into a bowl and beat by hand or machine until a smooth batter is formed (3 minutes by hand, 2 minutes by electric beater, 20 seconds by food processor).

Turn into the prepared tin and bake for 30–40 minutes, until golden brown and firm to gentle touch. Serve plain, dusted with icing (confectioners') or caster (superfine) sugar, or split and fill with jam and/or cream.

Alternatively, top with a citrus frosting made by putting 8 oz (225 g/2 cups) sifted icing (confectioners') sugar in a small pan with 1 tablespoon each of orange and lemon juice and warming together over very gentle heat for 30 seconds. Pour over the cake.

MOCHA GATEAU

Keeps 1 week at room temperature in an airtight container.
Freeze 3 months.

A moist and spongy family-size cake that needs no tedious whisking and can be made in either a dairy or a *parev* version.

For the cake

3 oz (75 g/¾ cup) matzah cake meal
3 oz (75 g/½ cup) potato flour
2 teasp Passover baking powder
9 oz (250 g/1 cup plus 2 tbsp) caster (superfine) sugar
3 tbsp cocoa
2 x ⅔ oz (20 g) packets vanilla sugar
3 eggs
6 fl oz (175 g/¾ cup) oil

For the mocha frosting

2 tbsp cocoa
1 tbsp cognac (optional)
2 teasp instant coffee
1½ tbsp boiling water
4 oz (125 g/½ cup) butter or margarine
8 oz (225 g/2 cups) sifted icing (confectioners') sugar
1 oz (25 g/¼ cup) chopped toasted almonds or a little grated chocolate

Preheat the oven to Gas No. 4 (350°F/180°C). Lightly oil a 9½-inch (24-cm) tin and line the base with a circle of silicone paper. Put all the cake ingredients into a bowl and beat by hand or machine until smooth and creamy - 3 minutes by hand, 2 minutes by electric mixer, 15 seconds by food processor - scraping down the sides half-way through with a rubber spatula. Turn into the prepared tin, level the surface, then bake for 40 minutes until the surface is spongy to gentle touch. Leave 5 minutes, then turn out on to a cooling tray.

To make the frosting Put the cocoa, cognac (if used) and instant coffee into a small bowl and pour on the boiling water, mixing until smooth. Cream the fat until like mayonnaise, then add the icing sugar in two portions alternately with the cocoa mixture, beating until fluffy. When the cake is completely cold, either mix the toasted almonds with the frosting, then spread over the top and sides, or simply spread the cake with the frosting, forking it into a design then grating a little chocolate over the top.

VARIATION

HAZELNUT ICING

1½ oz (40 g/3 tbsp) butter or margarine
1 x 100 g (3½ oz) bar Passover hazelnut chocolate, broken into small pieces

Either melt the fat in a small pan until liquid, then add the chocolate and stir over gentle heat until melted, or put the fat and chocolate into a bowl and cook in microwave on 100 per cent power for 1½ minutes. Stir to blend smoothly, then pour over the cooled cake.

PASSOVER PASTRY

Keeps 1 day raw under refrigeration.
Freeze 3 months.

This makes an excellent shortcrust which is easy to roll out, provided it is allowed to chill overnight.

4 oz (125 g/⅔ cup) potato flour
4 oz (125 g/1 cup) cake or fine meal
5 oz (150 g/⅔ cup) soft margarine or butter
3 oz (75 g/⅓ cup) caster (superfine) sugar
1 egg
1 tbsp lemon juice
1 teasp water

Put all the ingredients into a bowl and work together with an electric mixer or wooden spoon until a dough is formed. Dust the ball of dough thickly with meal, wrap in foil, flatten into a block about 1 inch (2.5 cm) thick and chill in the refrigerator overnight. Use as required.

JAM OR CURD TARTLETS

Keeps 1 week at room temperature in an airtight container.
Freeze 3 months.

Roll out the pastry to fit tartlet cases (foil ones are fine). Add 1 or 2 teaspoons of jam or curd and bake at Gas No. 4 (350°F/180°C) for 15 minutes, or until golden brown.

SPONGY ALMOND SLICES

Makes 24.
Keeps 1 week at room temperature in an airtight container.
Freeze 3 months.

½ Passover Pastry recipe (see above)
apricot eingemacht (see p. 604)

For the topping
4 oz (125 g/½ cup) soft butter or margarine
4 oz (125 g/½ cup) caster (superfine) sugar
2 eggs
4 oz (125 g/1 cup) ground almonds or hazelnuts
½–¾ oz (15–20 g) packet vanilla sugar

Preheat the oven to Gas No. 4 (350°F/180°C).

Roll out the pastry to fit a tin (or foil container) measuring 11 x 7 x 1 inches (27.5 x 18 x 2.5 cm). Spread with an even layer of the apricot eingemacht.

Beat all the topping ingredients together by hand or machine until smooth and creamy, then spread over the jam. Bake for 40 minutes, or until golden brown, then take out and dust with icing or caster sugar. Cool a further 5 minutes, then cut into slices.

COCONUT FINGERS

Makes 24.
Keeps 1 week at room temperature in an airtight container.
Freeze 3 months.

½ Passover Pastry recipe (see p. 614)
Lemon Curd (see p. 603)

For the topping
2 egg whites
4 oz (125 g/½ cup) caster (superfine) sugar
3 oz (75 g/1 cup) desiccated (shredded and dried) coconut
1 teasp finely grated lemon rind

For the garnish
2 tbsp flaked or chopped almonds

Preheat the oven to Gas No. 4 (350°F/180°C).

Roll out the pastry to fit a tin or foil container measuring 11 x 7 x 1 inches (27.5 x 18 x 2.5 cm). Spread with a thin layer of lemon curd.

Whisk the egg whites until they look fluffy and hold a soft peak that tips over slightly when the beater is withdrawn. Now whisk in the caster sugar a tablespoon at a time, whisking until stiff peaks form after each addition. Finally fold in the desiccated coconut and the grated lemon rind.

Spread the coconut mixture on top of the lemon curd and scatter with the flaked almonds.

Bake for 15 minutes, then turn the heat down to Gas No. 3 (325°F/160°C) for a further 10 minutes. When cold cut into strips about 2½ x 1 inches (6 x 2.5 cm).

CHOCOLATE MACAROON TARTLETS

Makes 12.
Keeps 1 week at room temperature in an airtight container.
Freeze 3 months.

Very moist and moreish.

½ recipe Passover Pastry (see p. 614)

For the filling
3 oz (75 g/¾ cup) ground almonds or hazelnuts
4 oz (125 g/½ cup) caster (superfine) sugar
½–¾ oz (15–20 g) packet vanilla sugar
1 egg, beaten
1 oz (25 g) Passover chocolate, melted
a few slivered almonds or chopped walnuts for the top

Preheat the oven to Gas No. 5 (375°F/190°C).

Roll out the pastry as thinly as possible and use some to line 12 patty tins.

Mix the ground nuts and sugars together, then beat in the egg and the melted chocolate. Divide between the pastry cases and sprinkle with the nuts, then bake for 18 minutes, or until firm to gentle touch.

Biscuits

ALMOND MACAROONS

Makes 12 or 13.
Keeps moist 1 week under refrigeration in an airtight container.
Freeze 3 months.

This is my definitive recipe after many years of failure or only partial success. The secret seems to lie in the amount of egg white used - just the right raw texture and the biscuits will bake crisp on the outside and moist and chewy within.

4 oz (125 g/1 cup) ground almonds
1½–2 egg whites (1½–2 fl oz/40–50 ml) broken up with a fork
5 oz (150 g/⅔ cup) caster (superfine) sugar
¾ oz (20 g) packet vanilla sugar
sifted icing (confectioners') sugar
12 or 13 halves of blanched almonds

Preheat the oven to Gas No. 6 (400°F/200°C). Cover a baking tray with silicone paper.

Put the ground almonds into the food processor and process for 15 seconds, or until very fine. (Omit this stage if mixing by hand - it is not strictly necessary, but it does make a biscuit with a finer texture.) Add about half an egg white, and process another 10 seconds. Then add half the caster sugar and the vanilla sugar, and process another 10 seconds. Add another half-egg white and the remaining sugar in the same way. Then add a further half-egg white. The mixture will now be soft but just capable of being formed into balls with the hands. If it is too stiff, add the remaining half-egg white.

Take up pieces of the dough and roll between the hands into balls the size of a large walnut - you should get 12 or 13 balls. If you make more, they're too small and should be rerolled. Put the balls 2 inches (5 cm) apart on the paper and gently flatten with the fingers. Brush all over with cold water then sprinkle with the icing sugar. Lay an almond half on each biscuit, or leave plain, as you prefer.

Bake for 16–17 minutes, or until the tops are just lightly browned. (Over-baking will result in crisp instead of moist macaroons.) Remove from the tray using a spatula. When cold, store in an airtight tin.

CITRUS-SCENTED MACAROONS

Makes 15–20.
Keep 1 week under refrigeration in an airtight container.

The title says it all!

4 oz (125 g/1 cup) ground almonds
4 oz (125 g/1 cup) icing (confectioners') sugar
grated rind ½ large lemon
grated rind ½ large orange
2 egg whites

For coating the biscuits
2 tbsp blanched almonds, chopped
2 tbsp caster (superfine) sugar
1 tbsp reserved egg white

Preheat the oven to Gas No. 6 (400°F/200°C) and line 2 baking sheets with silicone paper.

By hand or machine mix the ground almonds and icing sugar together with the grated fruit rinds. Add most of the egg whites, reserving 1 tablespoonful for coating, and beat or process until a plasticine-like soft dough is formed. Add the remaining egg white only if necessary to achieve the right consistency.

Pinch off pieces the size of a small walnut, then roll in the hands, forming small balls. In a basin mix the reserved egg white with a teaspoonful of cold water and whisk with a fork until frothy. Mix the almonds and sugar together in another bowl. Dip the balls in the egg white, then in the almond and sugar mixture. Arrange on the trays about 2 inches (5 cm) apart.

Bake for 12 minutes, until light gold on top and firm to the touch - inside they will be the texture of macaroons. Remove from the trays and allow to cool.

CINNAMON BALLS

Makes about 22.
Keeps 1 week at room temperature in an airtight container.
Freeze 3 months.

This must be the definitive recipe for this famous Anglo-Jewish biscuit - the inside will stay soft and moist, provided the balls are not overbaked.

2 egg whites
4 oz (125 g/½ cup) caster (superfine) sugar
8 oz (225 g/2 cups) ground almonds
1 level tbsp cinnamon

For coating the biscuits
a small bowl of icing (confectioners') sugar

Beat the whites until they form stiff peaks. Stir in all the remaining ingredients, mixing until even in colour. Form into balls with wetted hands. Bake on a greased tray at Gas No. 3 (325°F/160°C) for 20 minutes, or until just firm to the touch. Roll in icing sugar while warm and then again when cold.

VARIATION

Fold in 2 oz (50 g/½ cup) finely chopped walnuts before forming the balls.

COCONUT PYRAMIDS

Makes about 16–18.
Keeps 1 week at room temperature in an airtight container.
Freeze 3 months.

These should be slightly moist inside, crunchy on the outside. If the mixture seems too soft to hold its shape, stir in a little more coconut.

2 eggs
4 oz (125 g/½ cup) caster (superfine) sugar
juice and rind of ½ lemon
8–9 oz (225–250g/2⅔–3 cups) fine, unsweetened desiccated (dried and shredded) coconut

Beat the eggs and sugar until creamy, then stir in the lemon juice, rind and coconut. Form into pyramids using an egg cup moistened inside with cold water to prevent sticking. Bake at Gas No. 5 (375°F/190°C) for 18-20 minutes, until tinged with golden brown. Don't overcook!

CHOCONUT KISSES

Makes about 20.
Keeps 1 week at room temperature in an airtight container.
Freeze 3 months.

Baking the mixture in little paper cases produces a chocolate-studded 'kiss' with a crisp outside, while the inside stays moist.

2 egg whites
4 oz (125 g/1 cup) icing (confectioners') sugar
4 oz (125 g/1⅓ cups) fine desiccated (dried and shredded) coconut
½–¾ oz (15–20 g) packet vanilla sugar
4 oz (125 g) plain (semi-sweet) or milk chocolate

Whisk the whites until they form stiff peaks, then gradually whisk in the icing sugar, whisking until stiff after each addition. Fold in the coconut, vanilla sugar and the chocolate chopped into bits (roughly ¼-inch/0.5-cm) cubes). Fill the paper cases two-thirds full with the mixture. Bake at Gas No. 4 (350°F/180°C) for 20 minutes, or until crisp to the touch and golden brown.

VARIATION

DATE AND WALNUT KISSES

Instead of the coconut and chocolate use the following:

4 oz (125 g/1 cup) walnuts, roughly chopped
4 oz (125 g/1 cup) blanched almonds, roughly chopped
4 oz (125 g/⅔ cup) dates, roughly chopped

Make and bake as before.

LUSCIOUS CHOCOLATE BROWNIES

Makes 24.
Keeps 1 week in an airtight container.
Freeze 3 months.

Moist in texture, luscious in flavour, they're also easy and quick to make.

3 eggs
4 fl oz (125 ml/½ cup) Passover oil
7 oz (200 g/1 cup) caster (superfine) sugar
½–¾ oz (15–20 g) packet vanilla sugar
scant 2 oz (50 g/½ cup) matzah cake meal made up to 3 oz (75 g/¾ cup) with cocoa
2 oz (50 g/½ cup) coarsely chopped walnuts

For topping no. 1
caster (superfine) sugar

For topping no. 2
3½ oz (100 g) plain (semi-sweet) or milk (sweet) chocolate, vanilla- or coffee-flavoured
2 oz (50 g/¼ cup) butter or margarine
2 teasp Passover liqueur - e.g. Chocolate Mint or cognac (optional)

Preheat the oven to Gas No. 4 (350°F/180°C). Lightly grease a tin or foil container measuring approximately 11 x 7 x 1 inches (27.5 x 18 x 2.5 cm). By hand or machine, whisk together the eggs, oil and sugars until slightly thickened and no grains of undissolved sugar can be felt. Sift together the meal and cocoa and stir into the first mixture, together with the nuts, until smooth and creamy. Spoon into the tin and smooth level, then bake for 25 minutes, or until firm to gentle touch. (Overbaking will ruin the lovely moist texture.)

For topping no. 1, sprinkle an even layer of caster sugar over the top of the cake, then cut into 24 squares.

For topping no. 2, heat together the chocolate, butter and liqueur (if used), either in a small pan over gentle heat or in the microwave (2 minutes on 100 per cent power). Stir well until quite smooth. The mixture should be thick enough to coat the back of a spoon; if not, leave it to thicken for a few moments. Pour over the cake. Cut in squares when cold.

COCONUTTIES
(*Coconut Chocolate Fingers*)

Makes about 30.
Keeps 1 week at room temperature in an airtight container.
Freeze 3 months.

Moist and spongy chocolate-coated coconut biscuits.

4 oz (125 g) plain (semi-sweet) Passover nut chocolate, broken into pieces
3 oz (75 g/⅓ cup) butter
6 oz (175 g/2 cups) desiccated (dried and shredded) coconut
5 oz (150 g/⅔ cup) caster (superfine) sugar
2 eggs, beaten

Preheat the oven to Gas No. 4 (350°F/180°C) and line a Swiss roll or roulade tin measuring 12 x 8 inches (30 x 20 cm) with silicone paper.

Melt the chocolate gently in the roulade tin in the oven and spread out with a palette knife. Refrigerate until set.

Melt the butter and cool until it stops steaming. Put the coconut and sugar into a bowl, then add the melted butter, together with the beaten eggs, mixing well. Spread over the set chocolate using a flexible knife. Bake for 25 minutes or until set. Leave for 15 minutes, then cut in fingers of about 3 x 1 inches (7.5 x 2.5 cm). Chill for 30 minutes (to set the chocolate), then carefully invert on to a board and peel off the silicone paper.

Separate the fingers.

SUGARED ALMOND STICKS

Makes about 36.
Keeps 1 week at room temperature in an airtight container.
Freeze 3 months.

These are very quickly made and have a melt-in-the-mouth texture.

2oz (50 g/⅓ cup) potato flour
3 oz (75 g/¾ cup) ground almonds
2 oz (50 g/½ cup) cake or fine meal
2 oz (50 g/¼ cup) caster (superfine) sugar
½–¾ oz (15–20 g) packet vanilla sugar
4 oz (125 g/½ cup) butter
1 egg, separated

For the topping
1 oz (25 g/¼ cup) flaked almonds
1 oz (25 g/¼ cup) caster (superfine) sugar

Mix together the potato flour, almonds, meal and sugars. Rub in the butter as for pastry, then mix to a dough with the egg yolk. Divide into 6 portions. Roll each portion on a lightly sugared board into a 12-inch-long (30-cm) sausage. Lay the 6 'sausages' side by side and brush the tops generously with the slightly beaten egg white, then sprinkle with the mixed almonds and sugar. Cut across all the strips to make biscuits 1½ inches (4 cm) long. Separate the cut pieces and place on silicone-paper-lined baking sheets. Bake in a preheated oven, Gas No. 4 (350°F/180°C), for 18 minutes, until a light golden brown.

ROSE'S BISCUITS

Makes about 4 dozen.
Keeps 4 days at room temperature in an airtight container.
Freeze 1 month.

What, no ground almonds? A super family biscuit.

2 eggs
6 oz (175 g/¾ cup) caster (superfine) sugar
4 oz (125 g/½ cup) very soft or melted margarine
5 oz (150 g/1¼ cups) cake meal
1 tbsp potato flour
1 teasp grated lemon rind
2 teasp lemon juice
Passover jam

Preheat the oven to Gas No. 5 (375°F/190°C). Line flat baking trays with foil or silicone paper. By hand or machine, mix all the ingredients together until a soft smooth dough is formed. Take pieces of the dough and roll into balls about 1 inch (2.5 cm) in diameter, then arrange 2 inches (5 cm) apart on the trays. Dipping the little finger into some cake meal to prevent sticking, make little indentations in each ball and fill with a little jam. Bake for 20 minutes, until pale gold and set.

PASSOVER CRUNCHIES

Makes 24 or 36, according to method of shaping (see below).
Keeps 1 week at room temperature in an airtight container.
Freeze 3 months.

3 oz (75 g/½ cup) potato flour
3 oz (75 g/¾ cup) cake meal
2 oz (50 g/½ cup) ground almonds
4 oz (125 g/½ cup) caster (superfine) sugar
½–¾ oz (15–20 g) packet vanilla sugar
juice of ½ lemon
6 oz (175 g/¾ cup) soft butter or margarine
2 eggs, separated
desiccated (dried and shredded) coconut, chopped walnuts or toasted almonds (see below)

Beat all the ingredients (except the egg whites, coconut, walnuts or almonds) until they form a smooth, heavy mixture - use either a wooden spoon, an electric mixer (for 2-3 minutes) or a food processor (for 15 seconds). The mixture can then be used in either of the following ways:

1 Beat the 2 whites until foamy. Have ready a bowl of desiccated coconut, chopped walnuts or toasted almonds. Take a tablespoon of the mixture, form into a rough ball, drop into the egg white and then into the chopped nuts. Arrange well apart on silicone-lined baking trays and flatten slightly with the base of a glass. Bake in a preheated oven, Gas No. 4 (350°F/180°C), for 12 minutes. Makes about 24.
2 Put the mixture into a piping bag fitted with a coarse rose tube. Pipe into rosettes, sticks or rings. Scatter with almond nibs. Bake at Gas No. 5 (375°F/190°C) for 8–10 minutes, until golden brown. Makes about 36.

CHOCOLATE AND ALMOND BALLS

Makes 24.
Keeps 1 week at room temperature in an airtight container.
Freeze 3 months.

These have a rich chocolate flavour.

4 oz (125 g/1 cup) ground almonds
4 oz (125 g/1⅓ cups) desiccated (dried and shredded) coconut
7 oz (200 g/1 cup) caster (superfine) sugar
4 level tbsp cocoa
2 teasp honey
2 egg whites

Stir together in a bowl the ground almonds, 3 oz (75 g/1 cup) of the coconut, the caster sugar and the cocoa. Mix to a soft paste with the honey and unbeaten egg whites. With wetted palms, roll into balls the size of a small plum. Dip into the remaining coconut and arrange, 2 inches (5 cm) apart, on silicone-lined baking trays. Bake at Gas No. 6 (400°F/200°C) for 8–10 minutes, until the coconut is lightly browned – the biscuits should still be moist inside. Carefully lift on to a cooling tray and store when quite cold.

CHOCOLATE AND WALNUT SHORTCAKES

Makes 30.
Keeps 1 week at room temperature in an airtight container.
Freeze 3 months.

Quickly made, melt-in-the-mouth biscuits.

3 oz (75 g/¾ cup) walnuts
7 oz (200 g/1 cup plus 2 tbsp) soft butter or margarine
1 egg yolk
6 oz (175 g/¾ cup) caster (superfine) sugar
2 x ¾ oz (20 g) packets vanilla sugar
4 oz (125 g/1 cup) matzah cake meal
4 oz (125 g/⅔ cup) potato flour
½ teasp Passover baking powder
3 tbsp cocoa

For the topping
1 egg white, whisked until frothy
walnuts (see below)
1 oz (25 g/2 tbsp) caster (superfine) sugar

Preheat the oven to Gas No. 4 (350°F/180°C) and line 2 baking sheets with silicone paper.

Chop all the walnuts finely, then set 1 oz 25 g/¼ cup) aside for the topping.

Cut the fat into roughly 1-inch (2.5-cm) chunks, then beat or process until creamy. Work in the egg yolk and sugars, followed by the matzah meal, potato flour, baking powder, cocoa and walnuts. Turn out on to a board dusted with potato flour and knead to a smooth dough. Pinch off walnut-sized pieces of dough and roll into small balls. Arrange 2 inches (5 cm) apart on the trays, then press down firmly with a large wet fork to form biscuits about ⅜ inch (1 cm) thick. Whisk the egg white until frothy, then brush each biscuit in turn with it and sprinkle with the mixed walnuts and sugar.

Bake for 15–18 minutes, or until firm to gentle touch. Leave for 2 or 3 minutes to firm up, then transfer to a cooling rack. Leave for 1 day in an airtight container for the flavours to develop.

LEMON PECAN SPRITZ BISCUITS

Makes 48.
Keeps 1 week at room temperature in an airtight container.
Freeze 3 months.

Tender biscuits with a lovely lemony flavour.

3½–4 oz (100–125 g/⅞–1 cup) shelled pecans or walnuts
4 oz (125 g/1 cup) icing (confectioners') sugar, sifted
8 oz (225 g/1 cup) soft mild butter, cut in 1-inch (2.5-cm) chunks
1 egg yolk
1 tbsp fresh lemon juice
1 teasp grated lemon rind
1 teasp vanilla essence
4 oz (125 g/⅔ cup) potato flour
4 oz (125 g/1 cup) fine meal
½ teasp salt

To coat the biscuits
sifted icing (confectioners') sugar

Preheat the oven to Gas No. 4 (350°F/180°C) and line 2 trays with silicone paper.

Put the nuts in the food processor with half the icing sugar and process until finely ground. Add all the remaining ingredients and process until absolutely smooth and creamy in texture.

Fill a 14-inch (35-cm) piping bag fitted with a 1-inch (2.5-cm) rose nozzle with the mixture and pipe in 2-inch (5-cm) crescents or sticks, leaving 2 inches (5 cm) between the biscuits.

Bake for 12 minutes, or until the biscuits are beginning to colour. Lift on to a cooling tray and after 10 minutes coat thickly with icing sugar. Allow to cool completely before storing.

WALNUT SLICES

Makes 4 dozen.
Keeps 4 days in an airtight container.
Freeze 1 month.

These very thin crisp biscuits are sliced rather than shaped by hand, so it takes only a matter of minutes to bake a fresh batch as required.

4 oz (125 g/½ cup) butter or soft margarine
6 oz (175 g/¾ cup) caster (superfine) sugar
1 egg
2 oz (50 g/½ cup) finely chopped walnuts
rind of ½ lemon
½–¾ oz (15–20 g) packet vanilla sugar (if available)
2 oz (50 g/½ cup) cake meal
2 oz (50 g/⅓ cup) potato flour

Preheat the oven to Gas No. 5 (375°F/190°C). Cream the butter or margarine and sugar until fluffy, then beat in all the remaining ingredients.

Take a piece of greaseproof paper about 12 inches (30 cm) long. Lay the mixture down the centre, then fold over the sides of the paper and form into a roll about 2 inches (5 cm) in diameter. (You can use an empty foil or clingfilm (saranwrap) container to help shape the dough.)

Freeze for 1 hour until firm, or chill overnight, then cut into slices ⅛ inch (0.3 cm) thick. Place well apart on greased or silicone-paper-lined trays. Bake for 10–12 minutes, or until golden brown. Remove carefully with a spatula, then leave to cool and crisp. Store in an airtight container.

BUTTERY NUT CRISPS

Makes 30.
Keeps 2 weeks at room temperature in an airtight container.
Do not freeze.

Measure the ingredients very carefully and you will score a real taste triumph with these biscuits, which I have constantly updated over the years.

3 oz (75 g/¼ cup plus 2 tbsp) butter
3 oz (75 g/⅓ cup) caster (superfine) sugar
3 level teasp double (heavy) cream
4 oz (125 g/1 cup) flaked or slivered almonds

Preheat the oven to Gas No. 4 (350°F/180°C). Lightly grease as many baking sheets as you can fit into the oven at a time, then line them with silicone paper.

Slowly bring the butter, sugar and cream to boiling point, stirring constantly. Add the nuts and cook at a fast boil, stirring for 1 minute, until slightly caramelized (pale gold in colour), then immediately take off the heat. Leave to firm up for 10 minutes.

Use 2 teaspoons to shape the biscuits: scoop up a small amount of the mixture with one and push it off on to the tray in a neat pile with the other, leaving 3 inches (7.5 cm) between the biscuits to allow them room to spread. Bake for 12 minutes, until golden brown. Cool for 2 or 3 minutes, then use a spatula to lift them off the paper and on to a cooling tray. Repeat, using the same silicone paper, until all the mixture has been baked.

PRELATOES

Makes about 24.
Keeps 1 week in an airtight container.
Freeze 1 month.

Light and crisp sponge biscuits, excellent for the base of a trifle.

3 eggs
2½ oz (65 g/¼ cup plus 1 tbsp) caster (superfine) sugar
½–¾ oz (15–20 g) packet vanilla sugar
1½ oz (40 g/¼ cup) potato flour
1½ oz (40 g/¼ cup plus 1 tbsp) cake or fine meal

Separate the eggs and cream together the yolks and sugars until white and fluffy. Whisk the whites until they form stiff, glossy peaks. Sift together potato flour and meal. Stir about a third of the egg white into the yolks and then fold in the flour and meal very gently, using a metal spoon or rubber spatula. Finally fold in the remaining egg white. The mixture should be firm but fluffy.

Using a ½-inch (1.25-cm) plain pipe, pipe into finger lengths or rounds (or drop from a teaspoon in rounds) on a baking tray lined with silicone paper. Dust with caster sugar, tilting the baking tray to remove any surplus.

Bake in a preheated oven, Gas No. 5 (375°F/190°C), for 5-7 minutes, or until a pale golden brown.

BASIL'S TRUFFLES

Makes 16.
Keeps 2 weeks under refrigeration in an airtight container.
Freeze 3 months.

These truffles are rich and rare - and truly mouthwatering.

2 oz raisins, cut in half if large
6 teasp Passover brandy or rum
3½ oz (100 g) bar plain (semi-sweet) Passover chocolate
½ oz (15 g/1 tbsp) butter
1 teasp cream
7 heaped teasp icing (confectioners') sugar, sifted
4 heaped teasp ground almonds

To coat the truffles

Either 2 oz (50 g) plain (semi-sweet) chocolate plus 4 teasp Passover orange-flavoured liqueur (coats 6–8), or sifted icing (confectioners') sugar, or cocoa, or toasted dessicated coconut, or finely chopped walnuts

Put the raisins with 3 teaspoons of the brandy or rum in a small bowl, cover with clingfilm (saranwrap), microwave on 100 per cent power for 20 seconds, then leave to infuse for 30 minutes. (Otherwise leave raisins and spirit to infuse at room temperature for 1 hour.)

The chocolate is most easily melted in the microwave: break it up and put into a basin with the butter. Cook on 100 per cent power for 2 minutes, then stir well. Otherwise, melt the chocolate and fat in a basin over a pan of simmering water. Stir in the remainder of the ingredients (including the soaked raisins and the remaining 3 teaspoons of spirit) and beat together until smooth. Chill for 1 hour until the mixture has the texture of plasticine.

Pinch off pieces of the mixture and shape between the palms into balls the size of large marbles.

To coat some of the truffles with chocolate Melt chocolate as before and stir in the liqueur. Holding truffles with a fork, dip or spread them with the chocolate, using a palate or broad-bladed knife, then arrange on a chilled plate covered with greaseproof or silicone paper.

To coat with the sugar, cocoa or nuts Put some of the chosen coating on a piece of paper and roll the truffles in it.

Put the truffles in tiny petits fours paper cases and arrange in an airtight tin. Refrigerate or freeze.

Defrost frozen truffles for 30 minutes before use. Serve chilled straight from the refrigerator.

Savoury Dishes

MATZAH BREI

Serves 3–4.
Eat hot off the pan.

There are many variations of this Passover 'French toast'. My family likes the soaked matzah just fried in butter without egg – it's a matter of choice.

2 whole matzot
2 eggs
pinch of salt
pinch of pepper
1 oz (25 g/2 tbsp) butter

Break matzah into bite-sized pieces and put in a bowl covered with cold water. Soak for 3 minutes, then squeeze out the excess water. Add the matzah to the beaten, seasoned egg.

Heat the butter in a 7–8 inch (17.5–20 cm) frying pan until it stops foaming, then pour in the mixture and pat into a large pancake shape. Cook over moderate heat until golden brown, then turn and brown the second side. Cut into 3–4 wedge-shaped pieces and serve plain or with a mixture of ground cinnamon (1 teaspoon) and caster (superfine) sugar (2 oz/50 g/¼ cup).

MATZAH MEAL PANCAKES (CHREMSLACH)

Serves 4.
Eat hot off the pan.

These are probably similar to the meal cakes that were offered as a sacrifice in the Temple at Jerusalem.

2 eggs
1 level teasp salt
5 fl oz (150 ml/⅔ cup) warm water
3 oz (75 g/¾ cup) fine matzah meal
1 level tbsp caster (superfine) sugar

For the cinnamon sugar
1 teasp ground cinnamon
2 oz (50 g/¼ cup) caster (superfine) sugar

Beat the eggs, salt and 2 tablespoons of the water until thick. Gradually add the meal and the sugar and enough additional water to make a thick batter that just drops from the spoon. Fry in oil ¼ inch (0.5 cm) deep or a mixture of 2 oz (50 g/¼ cup) butter and 1 tablespoon oil until golden brown and puffy. Turn and cook the other side. Serve hot off the pan, plain or with the mixed cinnamon and sugar.

TWICE-BAKED CHEESE SOUFFLÉS

Makes 8 individual soufflés.

A superb vegetarian main dish. The soufflés are baked earlier in the day then fall, only to rise dramatically again on their second baking under a creamy sauce.

2 oz (50 g/¼ cup) butter
3 level tbsp potato flour
15 fl oz (425 ml/2 cups) milk
1 teasp salt
10 shakes of white pepper
8 oz (225 g/2 cups) grated Cheddar or Lancashire cheese
1 oz (25 g/¼ cup) crumbled blue cheese
6 eggs

For the coating sauce

15 fl oz (425 ml/2 cups) single (pouring) cream or 10 fl oz (275 ml/1¼ cups) double (heavy) cream diluted with 5 fl oz (150 ml/⅔ cup) water
1 tbsp finely snipped chives
pinch of salt
pinch of pepper
1 oz (25 g/¼ cup) grated cheese

Early in the day carefully butter 8 x 8-oz (225-ml/1-cup) teacups and arrange in a 2-inch-deep (5-cm) baking tin. Preheat the oven to Gas No. 5 (375°F/190°C). Boil the kettle. Mix the potato flour to a cream with a little of the measured milk. Heat the remainder until it is steaming, then gradually pour on to the potato flour, stirring vigorously. Return to the pan, add the seasonings and bring slowly to the boil. Add the cheeses, followed by the egg yolks, stirring continuously. Cook gently until the mixture thickens to the consistency of thick custard, then remove from the heat. Whisk the egg whites with a pinch of salt until they hold stiff glossy peaks, then fold into the custard using a rubber spatula. Divide the mixture between the teacups - they should be two-thirds full. Half-fill the baking tin with water from the kettle, then bake for 20 minutes until golden and firm on top. Allow to cool for 30 minutes, then loosen from the edge of the cup with a knife and carefully unmould on to a large buttered gratin dish.

Mix the cream with the seasonings and herbs and set aside.

When ready to serve, preheat the oven to Gas No. 8 (450°F/230°C). Sprinkle a little cheese on the top of each soufflé and coat with the sauce. Bake for 15 minutes until risen and golden. Serve at once, either as an entrée or a main dish with baked potatoes and a selection of salads.

VEGETARIAN MOUSSAKA

Serves 4.
Keeps 2 days under refrigeration.
Do not freeze.

For the vegetarian at the Seder table, I offer this delicious dish, which makes 4 portions and also reheats well. For 8, double all quantities, but be warned that grilling 4 lb (2 kg) of aubergines (eggplants) takes a lot of patience!

2 lb (900 g) aubergines
Passover oil for brushing the aubergines

For the savoury custard topping
1 level tbsp potato flour
6 fl oz (175 ml/¾ cup) milk
1 oz (25 g/2 tbsp) butter or margarine
⅛ teasp ground or grated nutmeg
½ teasp salt
good pinch of white pepper
8 oz (225 g/1 cup) curd cheese or 1 x 7 oz (200 g) pack cream cheese
2 beaten eggs

For the tomato sauce
1½ x 11 oz (300 g) cans Passover tomato and mushroom sauce
1 tbsp tomato purée (if available) or ketchup
½ teasp cinnamon

For the topping
4 oz (125 g/1 cup) Cheddar cheese

Cut the unpeeled aubergines into ½-inch (1.25-cm) slices, then place them in a colander or salad spinner, sprinkling each layer generously with salt. Leave for 30 minutes then rinse, pat dry and arrange in a single layer on a lightly oiled baking tray or trays. Lightly brush the slices with oil and grill 4 inches (10 cm) from the heat for 5 minutes, or until golden. Turn over, brush again with oil, and grill until golden. Transfer to paper towels to drain.

Meanwhile, make the custard. Put the potato flour in a pan and slowly add the milk, mixing until smooth. Then add the butter or margarine, and the seasonings and bring to the boil. Simmer until thickened. Put the curd or cream cheese in a bowl, gradually mix in the beaten eggs, then whisk in the sauce until smooth.

To make the tomato sauce, mix all the ingredients together.

To assemble the dish Spread half the tomato sauce in the bottom of a gratin dish or a foil container measuring approximately 8 x 6 x 2 inches (20 x 15 x 5 cm). Top it with half the aubergine slices and half the grated cheese, then spoon over the remaining tomato sauce and top it with the remaining aubergines. Finally spoon the custard over the top and sprinkle with the remaining cheese. Bake at Gas No. 3 (325°F/160°C) for 35 minutes, or until the top is set. Leave for 20 minutes before serving. (For the Seder, leave in a warming oven until the meal.)

FRITADA DE ESPINACA
(*Sephardi-style Spinach and Mushroom Bake*)

Serves 4–5 as a main dish.
Eat warm or at room temperature.
Keeps 2 days under refrigeration.
Do not freeze.

This is especially creamy in texture when made with a '*kosher le* Pesach' herb cream cheese instead of milk. It can be frozen uncooked. Thaw and bake when required. Serve warm or cold.

8 oz (225 g) pack frozen leaf spinach, thawed
the bulbs and 3 inches (7.5 cm) of stalk from a small bunch of spring onions (scallions), finely sliced
1 oz (25 g/2 tbsp) butter or margarine
4 oz (125 g/1¼ cup) mushrooms, finely sliced
3 eggs
approx. 5 oz (142 g) pack herb cream cheese

6 oz (175 g/1½ cups) grated Lancashire or Cheddar cheese (reserve 3 tbsp for topping)
1 teasp salt
15 grinds of black pepper
1 tbsp chopped parsley

Preheat the oven to Gas No. 5 (375°F/190°C). Butter a rectangular baking dish approximately 12 x 8 x 2 inches (30 x 20 x 5 cm) or a foil container 9-10 inches (22.5-25 cm) square and 2 inches (5 cm) deep.

Put spinach in a sieve and press out as much moisture as possible, then roughly chop. Sauté the onions in the fat until soft and golden, then add the mushrooms and cook until softened. Add the spinach and continue to cook, stirring, until there is no free moisture in the pan - this will take 2-3 minutes.

Whisk the eggs in a small bowl. Put the cream cheese in a larger one and stir in the grated cheese. Add the eggs, sautéd vegetables and seasonings. Pour into the prepared dish and scatter with the reserved cheese. Bake for 30 minutes, or until firm to the touch and golden brown.

CHEESE LATKES

Serves 3-4 (makes 14 latkes).
Eat hot off the pan.
Freeze 4 months.

Potato latkes make a tasty main dish with an intriguing flavour if grated cheese is added to the basic potato mixture.

2 large potatoes
(peeled weight 12-14 oz/350-400 g)
1 large egg
½ teasp salt
pinch of white pepper
½ teasp Passover baking powder
2 tbsp cake meal
6 oz (175 g/1½ cups) very finely grated cheese

Grate the potatoes very finely, by hand or in a food processor, then turn into a sieve and leave to drain for 15 minutes. Whisk the egg with the seasonings, then stir in the rest of the ingredients. In a large frying pan put oil to the depth of ½ inch (1.25 cm). When you can feel a comfortable heat on your hand held 2 inches (5 cm) above it, put tablespoons of the mixture into the oil, flattening each latke with the back of the spoon so it will cook evenly. Fry at a steady bubble until a rich brown, then turn and fry the second side. Do not attempt to turn the latkes too soon or they may stick to the pan - they will come off easily when they are brown and crisp. Drain on paper towels.

TOMATO AND ORANGE SOUP WITH LITTLE KNAIDLACH

Serves 4-5.
Keeps 3 days under refrigeration.
Freeze leftovers 2 months.

A quickly made, superbly flavoured soup. If possible, allow it to mature for several hours before serving.

For the knaidlach

1 oz (25 g/2 tbsp) soft chicken fat or margarine
1 egg
3 oz (75 g/⅔ cup) medium matzah meal
2 tbsp warm water
1 tbsp ground almonds
¼ teasp salt
few shakes of white pepper

For the soup

1 x 3½ oz (100 g) can of tomato purée
2 pints (1.25 l/5 cups) vegetable or chicken stock
3 teasp finely grated onion or 2 teasp dried onion
1 small clove of garlic or 1 teasp garlic granules
2 teasp sugar
2 strips of orange peel
1 bay leaf
½ teasp salt
10 grinds of black pepper
1 tbsp fresh basil leaves (if available)
2 teasp chopped parsley

Make the knaidlach first, to allow them to firm up. Put the soft fat in a mixing bowl, then beat in the remaining ingredients in the order given. Put in the freezer.

Combine all the soup ingredients (except the parsley) in a pan or microwave-safe casserole. Simmer, covered, for 30 minutes on top of the stove, or 8 minutes on 100 per cent power in the microwave. Leave to stand while you roll the knaidlach mixture into marble-sized balls, using wetted palms. Add to the soup, cover and cook for a further 20 minutes on top of the stove, or 5 minutes in the microwave. Stir in the parsley just before serving.

PASSOVER MINESTRONE

Serves 8.
Without lokshen (noodles), keeps 3 days under refrigeration.
Freeze without lokshen 3 months.

An economical but rich-tasting soup that can be made in a milk or meat version.

1 oz (25 g/2 tbsp) butter or margarine (for a meat meal)
1 tbsp sunflower oil
1 medium (5 oz/150 g) onion, finely chopped
8 oz (225 g) hard white cabbage, very finely shredded
white part of a fat leek, finely sliced
4 stalks celery, thinly sliced
1 carrot, grated
1 medium green or red pepper, seeded and cut into ¼-inch (0.5-cm) cubes
3 pints (1.75 l/7½ cups) vegetable or beef stock
1 rounded tbsp tomato purée
2 teasp salt
10 grinds of black pepper
few sprigs of parsley

For the Passover lokshen
3 eggs
3 tbsp cold water
½ teasp salt
3 tbsp matzah cake meal

For the garnish
1 tbsp chopped parsley
grated cheese (if milk meal)

First make the soup Melt the fats, add the onion, cover and simmer 5 minutes until the onion is pale gold. Add the cabbage, leek, celery, carrot and pepper, stir well, then add the stock, tomato purée and salt and pepper and bring to the boil. Cover and simmer for 2 hours. If possible leave overnight.

To make the lokshen Whisk or process all the ingredients together until smooth, then put in a jug. Lightly grease a 7-inch (17.5-cm) round-sided frying pan with oil and heat until a drop of water sizzles when dropped on to its surface. Pour in some of the batter, then tip the pan so that any excess runs back into the jug, leaving a very thin layer behind. Cook this pancake gently until the bottom is a golden brown, then turn and lightly cook the second side until just golden. Turn out on to greaseproof (waxed) paper and repeat with the remaining batter - you will have enough to make 4 pancakes. Allow to cool for 5 minutes, then roll up each pancake and cut in 'noodles' about ⅜ inch (1 cm) wide.

Bring the soup slowly to the boil again, then add the chopped parsley and the lokshen. Serve with grated cheese for a milk meal.

MUSHROOM AND LEEK SOUP

Serves 6–8.
Keeps 2 days under refrigeration.
Freeze 3 months.

A rich and creamy soup to serve at a Seder or Friday night meal.

1 medium onion, finely sliced
2 oz (50 g/¼ cup) butter or margarine

12 oz (350 g/3¾ cups) white mushrooms, finely sliced (reserve 3 oz/75 g/1 cup)
12 oz (350 g) white part of leek, finely sliced
6 fl oz (175 ml/¾ cup) dry white wine (optional)
1½ pints (850 ml/3¾ cups) vegetable stock
2 medium bay leaves
1½ teasp salt
15 grinds of black pepper
¼ teasp ground nutmeg or mace
1 tbsp potato flour
10 fl oz (275 ml/1¼ cups) milk
3 tbsp medium-dry Passover sherry

For the garnish
1 tbsp snipped chives
5 fl oz (150 ml/⅔ cup) single cream (optional)

Sauté the onion in the fat in a covered pan for 5 minutes, uncover and continue to cook, stirring, for a further 5 minutes, until pale and golden. Add the leeks and mushrooms and cook, stirring, for 5 minutes. Pour in the wine (if used) and bubble for 3 minutes to intensify the flavour, then add the stock and seasonings, cover and cook for 15 minutes, until the vegetables are tender.

Purée, preferably in a blender, return to the pan and stir in the potato flour and milk, which have been mixed to a smooth cream. Add the reserved mushrooms, finely sliced, and bring slowly to the boil. Simmer for 3 minutes, then leave to cool. Refrigerate for at least 8 hours.

To serve, stir in the sherry and reheat until barely bubbling, reseasoning if necessary. If using cream, pour it in a small jug and stir in the chives, then spoon a tablespoonful on to each serving.

HALIBUT IN AN EGG AND LEMON SAUCE

Serves 6–8.
Keeps 4 days under refrigeration.
Do not freeze.

This classic Anglo-Jewish Passover dish should be refrigerated for 24 hours to allow the sauce to permeate the fish. Serve at room temperature.

6–8 pieces of halibut on the bone (1½–2 lb/675–900 g total weight)

For poaching the fish
water to cover the fish (approx 15 fl oz/425 ml/2 cups)
1 large onion, thinly sliced
3 level tbsp sugar
2 level teasp salt
pinch of white pepper

For the sauce
8 fl oz (225 ml/1 cup) fish liquor
2 large eggs
4 tbsp fresh lemon juice
2 level teasp potato flour

In a saucepan or lidded frying pan wide enough to hold all the fish in a single layer, bring the water, the onion and the seasonings to the boil (adding the sugar at this stage greatly improves the taste of the fish without noticeably sweetening it). Put in the washed and salted steaks, bring the liquid back to the boil, then lower the heat so that the liquid is barely bubbling. Partially cover the pan and simmer very gently for 20 minutes. Lift out the fish with a slotted spoon or fish slice, draining any liquid back into the pan. Place the fish in an oval entrée dish about 1½ inches (3.75 cm) deep. Remove the skin but leave in the bone, then leave to cool while you make the sauce.

To make the sauce After the fish has been removed from the pan, boil the fish liquor for 3 minutes to concentrate the flavour, then strain it and measure out 8 fl oz (225 ml/1 cup). Beat the eggs thoroughly with a rotary whisk, then whisk in the fish liquor, lemon juice and the potato flour (which has been mixed to a cream with the minimum of cold water). Alternatively, mix all the sauce ingredients for 10 seconds in a blender or food processor – this makes it easier to thicken the sauce without fear of it curdling. Put this liquid into a thick-bottomed saucepan and cook gently over low heat until the sauce thickens to the consistency of a coating custard - you will need to stir it constantly. Do not let it boil or the eggs may curdle.

To cook the sauce in the microwave Cook the blended ingredients, uncovered, in a jug or bowl on 50 per cent power for 2 minutes, whisk well, then cook for a further 2-3 minutes, until thickened to the consistency of a coating custard.

Taste the sauce and add extra lemon juice, if necessary, to make it equally sweet and sour. Pour the sauce over the fish, coating it completely. Leave in the refrigerator overnight, covered with foil. Serve garnished with parsley.

VARIATION

GEFILTE FISH IN EGG AND LEMON SAUCE

Poach 7 large or 14 small patties of Gefilte Fish mix (see p. 64) as above. Then make the sauce and coat the fish in the same way.

BAKED HALIBUT ON A VEGETABLE BED

Serves 4-6.
Leftovers keep 2 days under refrigeration.
Do not freeze.

New potatoes are all that are needed as an accompaniment - the vegetables are already built in!

1½-2 lb (675-900 g) halibut
1 oz (25 g/2 tbsp) butter

For the vegetable bed
1 oz (25 g/2 tbsp) butter
5 spring onions plus 4 inches (10 cm) of the green, finely chopped
4 oz (125 g/1¼ cups) mushrooms
4 large tomatoes, peeled and chopped
4 tbsp white wine or juice of a large lemon
1 level teasp salt
pinch of black pepper
pinch of sugar
½ clove of garlic, crushed
1 level tbsp parsley

For the vegetable bed, melt the butter in a small pan and cook the onion until soft and golden, then add the thinly sliced mushrooms and cook a further 2 minutes. Finally, add tomatoes, wine, salt, pepper, sugar and garlic and cook until a thick sauce is formed. Stir in the parsley and lay sauce down the centre of a buttered 1-inch-deep (2.5-cm) baking dish just large enough to hold the fish. Lay the halibut steaks on top. Rinse out the frying pan and melt a further 1 oz (25 g/2 tbsp) of butter, then paint over the top of the fish. Grill gently for 10-12 minutes, until a rich brown.

FILLETS OF LEMON SOLE IN A SPANISH SAUCE

Serves 8-10.
Serve at room temperature.
Leftovers keep 2 days under refrigeration.
Do not freeze. The dish can be made and refrigerated overnight, but it should be left at room temperature during the first part of the Seder.

A delicious entrée for the Seder, before a hot meat or poultry main course.

1 large or 2 medium fillets of lemon sole per person, skinned

For the sauce
1 tbsp oil
bunch of spring onion bulbs (scallions)
2 x 11 oz (300 g) cans Passover tomato and mushroom sauce
1 tbsp tomato purée

3 tbsp tomato ketchup
1 large red pepper
2 level teasp each salt and sugar
1 tbsp lemon juice
15 grinds of black pepper

For the garnish
1 tbsp chopped parsley
4 oz (125 g/1 cup) sliced stuffed olives

Sprinkle the washed and skinned fillets lightly with salt, then roll or fold (if very thick) and arrange side by side in a heatproof dish. Preheat the oven to Gas No. 6 (400°F/200°C).

To make the sauce, heat the oil gently in a heavy saucepan and sauté the thinly sliced spring onion bulbs until softened (about 3 minutes), then add the tomato and mushroom sauce, purée, ketchup and pepper (halved, seeds removed and cut in fine slivers), with all the seasonings. Bring to the boil, stirring, then pour over the fish. Cover loosely with foil. Bake for 20 minutes, then remove the foil and allow the sauce to bubble for a further 10 minutes. Refrigerate when cold.

2 hours before serving, sprinkle with the parsley, cover with the sliced olives and leave until required.

FISH FILLETS IN A SOURED CREAM SAUCE

Serves 6–8.
Keeps 2 days under refrigeration.

Serve hot or cold. A simple but succulent dish that can be served either as an entrée or a main dish.

5 fl oz (150 ml/$^2/_3$ cup) mild mayonnaise
5 fl oz (150 ml/$^2/_3$ cup) soured cream
4 tbsp dry or medium-dry Passover sherry
$1^1/_2$ tbsp lemon juice
small bunch spring onion bulbs (scallions) or 2 large shallots, thinly sliced
2 lb (900 g) fillets of lemon sole, baby halibut or thick plaice
1 fine lemon, thinly sliced

Preheat the oven to Gas No. 4 (350°F/180°C). In a bowl stir together the mayonnaise, soured cream, sherry and lemon juice. In a baking dish large enough to hold the fish in a single layer sprinkle the onions or shallots, then lay the fish on top (fold the fillets to make an even thickness if necessary). Spoon the sauce evenly over the fish and arrange the halved slices of lemon decoratively on top. Bake uncovered for 25–30 minutes, or until the fish flakes.

POULET AUX POMMES
(Fruity Chicken Casserole)

Serves 8.
Keeps 3 days under refrigeration.
Freeze for up to 3 months.

This can be made and refrigerated up to 48 hours beforehand, or it can be frozen for later. Leave the ready-to-serve casserole in a slow oven, Gas No. 2 (300°F/150°C), during the first part of the Seder service and then as soon as the meal commences, turn the oven up to Gas No. 4 (350°F/180°C) and put in the apple garnish to reheat as well. Both should be covered and the idea is to reheat them to steaming point only, so that they do not overcook.

8 chicken breasts or 2 x 3½ lb (1.75 kg) chickens, jointed
2 oz (50 g/½ cup) cake meal
1 teasp salt
¼ teasp white pepper
2 oz (50 g/¼ cup) margarine
2 tbsp oil
4 oz (125 g) shallots or spring onion bulbs (scallions)
3 large Cox's Orange Pippins or Golden Delicious apples
1 pint (575 ml/2½ cups) good chicken stock
10 fl oz (275 ml/1¼ cups) dry Passover white wine or an extra 10 fl oz (275 ml/1¼ cups) chicken stock
2 teasp lemon juice
large sprig of parsley

For the garnish
2 large apples
1 oz (25 g/2 tbsp) margarine
2 teasp caster (superfine) sugar
1 oz (25 g/¼ cup) toasted flaked almonds

Preheat the oven to Gas No. 5 (375°F/190°C). Skin the chicken joints and toss in a bag with the seasoned cake meal to coat them evenly. Cook until a pale gold all over in the hot margarine and oil, then add the chopped shallots or spring onions to the pan and continue to cook until the chicken is a rich golden brown and the onions are soft and coloured also. (The chicken may need to be cooked in 2 batches.) Transfer to a large casserole or roasting tin in which the chicken pieces can lie side by side. Peel, core and dice the 3 apples roughly, then add to the drippings in the pan, together with the hot chicken stock and the wine, the lemon juice and the parsley sprig. Stir well to incorporate any brown bits on the bottom of the pan, then pour over the chicken joints, cover with a lid or foil, and cook in the oven for 15 minutes, until the sauce is beginning to bubble. Turn down to Gas No. 3 (325°F/160°C) and cook for a further 25 minutes, until the chicken is tender when pierced with a knife.

Lift the chicken on to a heatproof serving dish, put all the cooking liquid into the blender or food processor and process until absolutely smooth (or push through a sieve). Pour into a saucepan and boil rapidly for 2 or 3 minutes, until it is thick enough to coat the back of a spoon, then spoon over the chicken, coating the pieces completely.

To prepare the garnish, peel, core and cut the other 2 apples into 8, then sauté gently in the margarine, sprinkling with the sugar and almonds and cooking until the slices are tender and caramelized. Garnish the chicken with the apples and serve with new potatoes.

CHICKEN IN A HONEYED TOMATO SAUCE

Serves 6–8.
Keeps 3 days under refrigeration.
Freeze 3 months.

Mushrooms and peppers add an extra flavour dimension to this delicious chicken casserole, which can be safely left to reheat during the Seder service. For 12 joints, use 50 per cent more sauce ingredients and cook for 10 minutes longer.

6–8 chicken portions, skinned
2 rounded tbsp cake meal
3 tbsp oil
1 large (7 oz/200 g) onion, peeled and finely chopped
1 medium clove of garlic, peeled and finely chopped
8 oz (225 g/2½ cups) white or brown cap mushrooms, thinly sliced
1 medium red and 1 medium yellow pepper, deseeded and cut in ¾-inch (2-cm) cubes
2 tbsp honey
2 teasp sugar
1 teasp salt
15 grinds of black pepper
1 x 5 oz (150 g) can tomato purée
15 fl oz (425 ml/2 cups) chicken stock
2 teasp lemon juice

Preheat the oven to Gas No. 3 (325°F/160°C). Dry the joints well, then coat with the cake meal. Fry in the hot oil over moderate heat until they are a golden brown all over, then lift out and drain on paper towels to remove any surface fat. Arrange side by side in a large casserole or roasting tin.

In the same oil, gently sauté the onion and garlic until golden. (Keep the pan lid on for the first 5 minutes to soften them in the steam, then remove it to finish the browning.) Add all the remaining ingredients to the pan, stirring well. Simmer for 2 minutes, until really bubbling, then pour over the chicken and cover the dish with a lid or foil. Bake for 50 minutes, basting once.

CHICKEN IN A MUSHROOM AND RED WINE SAUCE

Serves 8.
Keeps 3 days under refrigeration.
Freeze 3 months.

This dish has a deep, rich flavour.

8 chicken joints, skinned
1 heaped tbsp matzah cake meal
1 teasp salt
15 grinds of black pepper
3 tbsp oil
1 large onion
1 clove of garlic
1 x 15 oz (425 g) can tomatoes
2 teasp sugar
1 large red pepper
10 fl oz (275 ml/1¼ cups) chicken stock
5 fl oz (150 ml/⅔ cup) red wine
1 lb (450 g/5 cups) button mushrooms
8 oz (225 g/2 cups) large green olives

Preheat the oven to Gas No. 4 (350°F/180°C). Skin the chicken joints, then coat thinly with the cake meal seasoned with the salt and pepper – most easily done by shaking them together in a plastic bag. Brown 4 of the joints at a time in the hot oil, them remove to a roasting tin. In the remaining oil, gently sauté the finely chopped onion and garlic until golden, then add the tomatoes, sugar and pepper, cut in ½-inch (1.25-cm) squares. Simmer, uncovered, for 15 minutes.

Add the stock and the wine and simmer for a further 5 minutes, then pour this sauce over the chicken joints, so they are half covered. If necessary, add a little more stock. Cook, covered, in the oven for 40 minutes, basting once. Uncover, add the whole mushrooms and the olive flesh (cut away from the stone) and allow to cook for a further 15 minutes.

To reheat Cover and leave in a slow oven, Gas No. 2 (300°F/150°C) during the Seder. Check at the start of the meal. If it is not steaming hot and on the point of bubbling, turn the oven up to Gas No. 3 (325°F/160°C) during the earlier courses.

MINA DE PESAH
(*Layered Chicken and Matzah Casserole*)

Serves 4–5.
Keeps 2 days under refrigeration.
Do not freeze.

A good Sephardi mid-festival dish for Chol Hamoed. The moistened matzot replace the lasagne of the original dish.

12 oz (350 g) cooked chicken (1 lb/450 g raw)
1 bay leaf (optional)
½ medium onion
1 clove of garlic
1 oz (25 g/2 tbsp) margarine
4 oz (125 g/1¼ cups) button mushrooms
6 eggs
10 grinds of black pepper
½ teasp salt
2 tbsp chopped parsley or coriander
10 fl oz (350/1¼ cups) chicken stock
3 tbsp oil
6 sheets matzah

Preheat the oven to Gas No. 5 (375°F/190°C). Have ready a baking dish approximately 10 x 8 x 2 inches (25 x 20 x 5 cm) - a foil one is excellent.

The chicken can be leftover (half a 4 lb/2 kg) bird or chicken-breast meat poached until tender or microwaved on 100 per cent power for 6 minutes covered with 10 fl oz (350 ml/1¼ cups) water and 1 bay leaf. Cut the chicken into strips about ½ x 1½ inches (1 x 4 cm).

Sauté the finely chopped onion and garlic in the fat until soft and golden, then add the thinly sliced mushrooms and sauté until tender - another 5 minutes. Allow to cool while you beat the eggs until blended, then stir in the mushroom and chicken mixture, ½ teaspoon of the salt and the pepper and chopped herbs.

Make up 10 fl oz (275 ml/1¼ cups) of chicken stock or use leftover chicken soup or the poaching liquid.

Heat the oil in a small pan for 3 minutes, then pour 2 teaspoons into the baking dish and swirl it round to coat both the bottom and the sides. Dip 2 of the matzot into the stock (or the chicken poaching liquid) until well moistened, then lay side by side in the baking dish. Spoon half the egg mixture on top, cover with 2 more moistened matzot, then the remaining egg mixture and finally the 2 remaining matzot, also moistened. Pour half the remaining oil over the top and bake for 15 minutes, then sprinkle with the remaining oil and bake a further 10–15 minutes until a rich crisp brown. Cool for 10 minutes, then serve in squares.

MEATBALLS IN A SWEET-SOUR SAUCE

Serves 6.
Keeps 3 days under refrigeration.
Freeze 3 months.

As soaked bread cannot be used to lighten the traditional minced (ground) beef mixture, it is a good idea to add a grated potato instead. The meat mixture can then be used as required, and is especially nice as stuffing for aubergines (eggplants), peppers or tomatoes.

For the meatballs

1½ lb (675 g) minced shoulder steak (ground beef)
½ onion, finely grated
1 level teasp salt
good pinch of white pepper
1 medium potato, grated and drained for 10 minutes
2 level tbsp medium matzah meal
2 beaten eggs
1 tbsp oil for frying

For the sauce

1 onion, finely chopped
1 can Passover tomato and mushroom sauce
juice of ½ lemon
2 level teasp sugar

1 bay leaf
1 crushed clove of garlic
4 tbsp red wine or meat stock

To make the meatballs, mix all the ingredients (except the oil) together - the mixture should be just firm enough to form into balls. Leave for 30 minutes. Form into balls and fry in the oil on both sides until a rich golden brown, shaking the pan so that they brown evenly. Arrange side by side in a shallow casserole.

In the same oil used to fry the meatballs, fry the onion until golden brown. Pour in the tomato and mushroom sauce, lemon juice, sugar, bay leaf and garlic and thin the sauce with the wine or stock.

Note If canned tomato and mushroom sauce is not available, use 8 fl oz (225 ml/1 cup) Passover tomato soup instead.

Alternatively, use the Pizzaiola sauce (see p. 169) using Passover oil instead of olive oil.

Pour the sauce over the meatballs, cover and transfer to the oven, Gas No. 3 (325°F/160°C). Cook for 1½ hours, basting occasionally. If the sauce starts to boil (it should barely bubble), turn the oven down to Gas No. 2 (300°F/150°C). Can be reheated.

STEAK BRAISED IN WINE

Serves 4–6.
Keeps 4 days under refrigeration.
Freeze 2 months.

The wine both tenderizes the meat and flavours the sauce.

2 tbsp oil
1 large onion, thinly sliced
2 lb (900 g) first-cut shoulder steak or top rib, cut ½ inch (1 cm) thick and then cut in portions, or 4–6 slices blade steak
4 fl oz (125 ml/½ cup) red wine (optional) or additional stock
4 fl oz (125 ml/½ cup) thin gravy or meat stock
3 tomatoes, peeled and sliced, or 3 canned tomatoes, well drained
1 clove of garlic, crushed
1 teasp salt
15 grinds of black pepper
1 teasp brown sugar
1 teasp dried herbes de Provence or 1 tbsp chopped fresh oregano or parsley

Heat the oil in a heavy pan or casserole. Put in the sliced onion and cook gently until soft and golden. Remove. In the same fat quickly brown the well-dried meat, then remove to a plate. Put the onion back, then add the wine (if used) and allow to come to the boil. Add the stock, tomatoes, garlic and seasonings. Lay the steaks on top. Put in a slow oven, Gas No. 2 (300°F/150°C), for 2 hours, until the meat is tender and the gravy thickened.

SPANISH BEEF WITH PRUNES

Serves 6.
Keeps 3 days under refrigeration.
Freeze 3 months.

2 tbsp cake meal
2 teasp salt
15 grinds of black pepper
2½ lb (1.25 kg) top rib or good stewing beef, well trimmed and cut in 2-inch (5-cm) chunks
3 tbsp oil
1 large onion, finely sliced
1 clove of garlic, finely chopped
1 teasp brown sugar
5 fl oz (150 ml/⅔ cup) dry white wine plus 10 fl oz (275 ml/1¼ cups) stock, or 15 fl oz (425 ml/2 cups) stock only
2 level tbsp tomato purée
1 teasp cinnamon
8 oz (225 g) ready-pitted prunes or 8 oz (225 g) regular prunes soaked in strained tea overnight before stoning

Preheat the oven to Gas No. 2 (300°F/150°C). Put the seasoned cake meal in a plastic bag, add the beef cubes in 2 portions and shake until evenly coated.

Brown the meat in 2 portions in 2 tablespoons of hot oil until a rich brown on all sides, then lift on to a plate lined with paper towels. Add extra oil to the pan if necessary, then gently sauté the onion and garlic, covering the pan for 5 minutes, then uncovering and sprinkling with the sugar. Continue to cook until a rich golden brown. Add the wine (if used) and bubble for 1 or 2 minutes, then add all the remaining ingredients (except the prunes), stir well and bring to the boil. Put the beef into an ovenproof casserole and pour on the sauce - it should barely cover the meat. If there is not enough liquid, add a little boiling water. Cover and cook for 2½–3 hours, making sure the sauce is barely bubbling - turn the oven down if the casserole is cooking too quickly. After 2 hours add the prunes and a little boiling water if necessary - the sauce should be thick but still very juicy. Taste at this point and reseason with salt and pepper if necessary.

BEEFSTEAK PIE

Serves 6.
Keeps 2 days under refrigeration.
Meat will freeze 3 months.

An enriched mashed-potato topping makes this a perfect mid-week Passover main dish.

2 lb (900 g) braising or stewing steak
2 tbsp oil
2 large onions, finely sliced
(preferably in a food processor)
1 teasp brown sugar
approx. 15 fl oz (425 ml/2 cups) hot beef stock
to cover the meat
1½ level teasp salt
15 grinds of black pepper

For the topping
2½ lb (1.25 kg) mashing potatoes, peeled
and cut in chunks
1 tbsp margarine
salt
pepper
2 eggs, beaten well
1 teasp chopped parsley

Cut the meat into 1-inch (2.5-cm) cubes. Brown in the hot oil on both sides then remove to a plate. Add the onions and sugar to the oil and cook until the onions are brown. Return the meat to the pan and barely cover with the stock. Add the salt and pepper, bring to the boil and simmer, covered, on top of the stove or in the oven at Gas No. 2 (300°F/150°C) until quite tender - about 2 hours.

To make the crust Boil the potatoes until tender, then strain and return to the pan, and mash over a gentle heat with the fat, salt and pepper. Remove from the heat and add the eggs and parsley. Use this mixture to line the bottom and sides of a deep casserole, previously well greased. Pour in the hot stew and smooth the remaining potato mixture on the top. Brush over with a little egg. Put in a quick oven, Gas No. 6 (400°F/200°C), for 15–20 minutes, or until a rich brown.

LAMB WITH ORANGES

Serves 6.
Keeps 3 days under refrigeration.
Freeze 2 months.

The meat from a boned shoulder of lamb - considered by connoisseurs to have the finest flavour - is cooked in a very refreshing orange-flavoured sauce. Good with new potatoes and lightly cooked broccoli.

2½ lb (1.25 kg) boneless lamb,
cut in 1½-inch (4-cm) chunks
2 tbsp cake meal

1 teasp salt
10 grinds of black pepper
2 tbsp oil
1 medium onion, finely chopped
1 teasp sugar
10 fl oz (275 ml/1¼ cups) chicken stock plus
5 fl oz (150 ml/⅔ cup) dry white wine, or
15 fl oz (425 ml/2 cups) chicken stock
½ teasp salt
2 navel oranges
2 teasp potato flour smoothly mixed with
2 tbsp cold water
1 tbsp chopped parsley

Preheat the oven to Gas No. 2 (300°F/150°C). Lightly coat the meat with the seasoned cake meal (patting off any excess), then sauté in the oil (in 2 batches) until it is a rich brown. Lift out on to a plate using a slotted spoon, then add the onion to the same oil, sprinkle with the sugar and continue to cook over medium heat until the onion is golden brown.

Add the wine (if used) to the pan. Stir well to incorporate any bits on the bottom, then bubble for 3 minutes to concentrate the flavour. Add the meat, the half-teaspoon of salt and the hot stock and bring slowly to the boil.

Remove all the pith from the oranges, then cut between the sections to release the fruit. Reserve 6 pieces of orange for garnish. Add the sections to the meat, together with any juice that can be squeezed out of the orange 'skeleton'.

When the casserole is bubbling, cover it and transfer to the oven, then cook until the meat is very tender - about 1½ hours. Add the potato flour dissolved in the water, stir well and then simmer in the oven for a further 20 minutes. Just before serving, sprinkle with the chopped parsley, and garnish with the reserved orange slices.

SHOULDER OF VEAL WITH A PINEAPPLE STUFFING

Serves 8.
Keeps 3 days under refrigeration.
Freeze 3 months.

This is the best method of cooking a joint of veal to keep it moist yet flavoursome. When freshly cooked, it is superb cut in fairly thick slices, but if you press the leftovers into a basin and allow them to go cold, you will be able to cut beautiful thin slices to serve with latkes or chips.

1 x 4 lb (2 kg) shoulder of veal, boned and pocketed
2 tbsp oil
1 medium onion
2 carrots
5 fl oz (150 ml/⅔ cup) white wine or
chicken stock
1 teasp of salt
15 grinds of black pepper
2 bay leaves

For the stuffing
4 matzot
8 oz (225 g) canned or peeled fresh pineapple
2 tbsp syrup from the canned fruit plus 4 fl oz
(125 ml/½ cup) water, or 5 fl oz (150 ml/⅔ cup)
water if using fresh fruit
bunch of spring onion bulbs (scallions)
2 oz (50 g/¼ cup) margarine
grated rind of 1 lemon
2 oz (50 g/½ cup) chopped walnuts
1 level teasp salt
speck of white pepper
1 large egg

For the sauce
8 fl oz (225 ml/1 cup) chicken stock
1 teasp potato flour mixed with 2 teasp water

To make the stuffing Crumble the matzot into a large basin. Drain the canned pineapple (if using) and add the syrup and water (or the water alone) and leave to soften. Meanwhile, cook the finely sliced spring onion bulbs in the margarine until soft and golden. Add the lemon, nuts, seasonings and the beaten egg to the matzot mixture, then add to the onions in the pan and cook gently, stirring until the matzah starts to brown and loses some of its wetness. Stir in the roughly chopped pineapple.

To stuff the veal Lay the meat on a board, skin-side down, and stuff the pocket loosely. If there is no pocket, lay the meat flat and spread evenly with the stuffing, then roll up into a neat shape. In either case, sew or skewer closed. Dab the surface dry with paper towels. The meat can be refrigerated overnight at this point, then left at room temperature for 1 hour before cooking.

To cook the veal Preheat the oven to Gas No. 4 (350°F/180°C). Heat the oil in a heavy casserole or frying pan. Brown the meat thoroughly on all sides - this may take 15 minutes. Remove it to a plate and sauté the finely chopped vegetables in the same fat until soft and golden. Add the wine and bubble until it becomes syrupy.

Lay the meat on top of the vegetables, season with salt and black pepper, and tuck the bay leaves down the side. Cover and cook in the preheated oven for 2 hours. The veal is ready when it feels soft to the touch and is a mahogany brown in colour. Lift the meat on to a serving plate and cover loosely with foil. It may now be kept hot for up to 30 minutes at Gas No. ¼ (225°F/110°C).

To make the sauce Skim off as much fat as possible from the casserole, then pour in the stock and the potato-flour liquid, stir well and then simmer until thickened. Purée the contents of the casserole in a blender or food processor or push through a sieve, then leave in a small pan ready to reheat and reseason if necessary just before serving.

The meat may be carved in the dining room or thickly sliced in the kitchen, arranged on a heated platter and then coated with the sauce.

PASSOVER POTATO LATKES

Serves 4–6.
Serve hot off the pan.
Freeze 4 months.

4 large potatoes, grated
(16 fl oz/450 ml/2 cups when drained)
2 eggs
½ a medium (5 oz/150 g) onion
1 level teasp salt
pinch of white pepper
4 tbsp cake or fine meal plus ½ teasp Passover baking powder

Grate potatoes and onion and leave to drain in a sieve for 15 minutes. Beat eggs with seasonings, then stir in potatoes, onion, baking powder and matzah meal. Fry tablespoonfuls of the batter in ¼-deep (0.5-cm) hot fat until a rich brown on both sides, turning once. When cooked, the outside of the latkes should be crunchy with a soft inside. Drain on crumpled kitchen paper.

See p. 582 for reheating advice.

ROLLS

Makes 12.
Eat the same day or freeze for up to 1 month and then defrost as required.

With a crunchy crust and fluffy inside, these matzah-meal rolls can be filled with hard-boiled eggs, cheese or fish and make eminently 'portable' school or office lunches, or they can be served as a change from matzah at lunch or dinner.

8 oz (225 g/2 cups) medium matzah meal
1 teasp salt
3 teasp sugar
4 fl oz (125 ml/½ cup) oil
8 fl oz (225 ml/1 cup) hot water
4 eggs

Mix the meal with the salt and sugar and set aside. In an 8-inch (20-cm) heavy saucepan bring the oil and water to the boil, then add the meal mixture all at once, stirring vigorously over a low light until the mixture forms a ball that can be rolled around the pan.

Take off the heat and beat in the eggs 1 at a time until the mixture is smooth and thick. Leave until cool enough to handle - about half a hour. Meanwhile, preheat the oven to Gas No. 5 (375°F/190°C). Have ready 2 baking sheets greased or lined with silicone paper. Roll the dough between the palms into 12 balls and place 2 inches (5 cm) apart on the baking sheet. Bake for 50 minutes, until a rich brown.

Desserts

PASSOVER 'PASTRY' FLAN CASE

Keeps 2 days under refrigeration.
Freeze 1 month.

This 'pastry' is made from sponge cake or Prelato crumbs (see p. 622). It is advisable to make and bake any dish using this pastry in an oven-to-table decorative flan dish as it is too delicate to turn out.

bare 3 oz (75 g/⅓ cup) soft butter or margarine
bare 3 oz (75 g/⅓ cup) caster (superfine) sugar
½ teasp cinnamon
4 oz (125 g/1½ cups) sponge cake or prelato crumbs

Cream the butter, sugar and cinnamon then work in the crumbs. Spread over the bottom and sides of a 9-inch (22.5-cm) oven-to-table flan dish. Put in a preheated oven, Gas No. 5 (375°F/190°C), for 10 minutes, or until golden brown. Leave to cool.

A MIXED BERRY FRANGIPANE FLAN

Makes one 9–10 inch (22.5–25 cm) flan. Serves 8.
Keeps 2 days under refrigeration.
Freeze 3 months.

This is a universal favourite. Frozen cherries or well-drained canned apricots can be used instead of the mixed berries.

1 Passover flan case (unbaked, see above) in a 9-inch (22.5-cm) oven-to-table flan dish
Passover jam

For the filling
1 lb (450 g/2¾ cups) unsweetened frozen mixed berries or summer fruits

For the frangipane
3 oz (75 g/⅓ cup) soft butter or margarine
3 oz (75 g/⅓ cup) caster (superfine) sugar
3 oz (75 g/¾ cup) ground almonds
½–¾ oz (15–20 g) packet vanilla sugar
2 eggs
2 level tbsp potato flour

For sifting on top of the baked flan
icing (confectioners') sugar

Preheat the oven to Gas No. 5 (375°F/190°C). Spread a layer of Passover jam on top of the unbaked flan case, then arrange the fruit in an even layer on top.

Put all the frangipane ingredients into a bowl and beat together until creamy (3 minutes by hand, 2 minutes by electric mixer, 15 seconds in the food processor, scraping the sides down half-way). Spoon carefully over the fruit and level off.

Bake for 15 minutes, then turn down to Gas No. 4 (350°F/180°C) for a further 30 minutes, until golden brown and springy to gentle touch. Serve warm, dusted with the icing sugar. Reheats well.

RUM AND APPLE FLAN

Serves 6–8.
Keeps 2 days under refrigeration.
Freeze 1 month.

Simple but with a lovely blend of flavours.

1 Passover flan case (see p. 638)

For the filling
1 oz (25 g/2 tbsp) butter or margarine
2 lb (900 g) baking or eating apples, peeled, cored and thinly sliced
3 oz (75 g/⅓ cup) white or brown sugar (to taste)
2 tbsp lemon juice
2 teasp lemon rind
3 rounded tbsp apricot eingemacht or other Passover jam
2 tbsp Passover rum or brandy (optional)

For the dairy version
5 oz (150 g/⅔ cup) carton fromage frais or
5 oz (150 g/⅔ cup) soured cream
2 tbsp toasted almonds

For the parev version
2 rounded tbsp desiccated (dried and shredded) coconut
4 tbsp macaroon crumbs

Make and bake the flan as described.

To make the filling Melt the fat in a heavy based pan, then add the apple slices, layered with the sugar, lemon rind and juice and the apricot jam. Put on the lid and cook gently until the apples are just tender. Leave covered until cold, when they will be translucent. Stir in the spirit. Spoon on to the baked crust.

For the dairy version Top with the fromage frais or soured cream and nuts.

For the parev version Top with the shredded coconut or macaroon crumbs. Chill well before serving.

LEMON MERINGUE FLAN

Serves 6–8.
Bake and serve the same day.

There is a delicious contrast between the creamy filling and the crisp meringue with its marshmallow texture underneath.

1 Passover flan case (see p. 638)
approx. 12 oz (350 g/1½ cups) lemon curd (see p. 603)

For the meringue
3 egg whites
pinch of salt
6 oz (175 g/¾ cup) caster (superfine) sugar
1 rounded teasp potato flour

Make and bake the flan case as described, cool, then spread the lemon curd carefully over the base.

Whisk the egg whites until stiff with the pinch of salt. Add the sugar and potato flour (blended together) a tablespoonful at a time, whisking after each addition until a solid meringue is formed. Spoon over the lemon curd, sealing the meringue to the edges of the pie.

Bake in a preheated oven, Gas No. 2 (300°F/150°C), for half an hour, or until the meringue is crisp on the surface. Serve cold.

SYBIL SHIELDS'S MATZAH PUDDING

Serves 6.
Leftovers keep 3 days under refrigeration.
Freeze 3 months.

A richly flavoured yet simple dessert that can be served either hot or cold - a great favourite on matzah picnics and rambles.

4 matzot
6 oz (175 g/1 cup plus 2 tbsp) raisins, soaked in boiling water for 5 minutes, then drained

1 cooking apple, peeled and coarsely grated
3 oz (75 g/⅓ cup) caster (superfine) sugar
2 oz (50 g/½ cup) chopped walnuts (optional)
1½ teasp cinnamon
1 rounded tbsp apricot jam or marmalade
juice and grated rind of ½ lemon
3 eggs, whisked until thick
2 level tbsp matzah cake meal
3 oz (75 g/⅓ cup) margarine, melted
1–2 tbsp granulated sugar

Preheat the oven to Gas No. 4 (350°F/180°C). Grease a tin or baking dish about 8 inches (20 cm) square and 2½–3 inches (6–7.5 cm) deep.

Pour *cold* water over the broken-up matzot in a mixing bowl and leave for 10 minutes, then drain well and beat with a fork until smooth. Add all the other ingredients, except the margarine and granulated sugar, to the matzot in the order given, beating well. Stir in half the melted margarine and turn into the chosen baking dish. Drizzle the remaining margarine over the top and sprinkle with the granulated sugar. Bake for about 1 hour, or until a knife inserted in the centre comes out clean.

MENORAH APPLE PUDDING

Serves 8.
Leftovers freeze 3 months.

'Why,' asked one of my favourite rabbis, 'were there no Jewish cookery books written in English before Lady Judith Montefiore's *Jewish Manual* of 1846?' This apple pudding - the recipe for which I got from a friend, who got it from a friend, etc. - is surely the answer. With good friends - or what the social historians call 'the oral tradition' - who needs cookery books?

2 lb (900 g) baking apples
2 oz (50 g/¼ cup) any sugar
1 rounded tbsp apricot eingemacht (optional)
1 tbsp lemon juice
3 tbsp orange juice

For the topping
7 oz (200 g/¾ cup plus 2 tbsp) soft butter or margarine
7 oz (200 g/¾ cup plus 2 tbsp) caster (superfine) sugar
8 oz (225 g/2 cups) ground almonds or hazelnuts
4 eggs
grated rind of 1 lemon

Peel and core the apples and cut into ½-inch-thick (1.25-cm) slices. Stew with the sugar, eingemacht and juices on top of the stove until barely tender (in the microwave cook on 100 per cent power for 7 minutes, stirring once).

Arrange the fruit mixture in a greased gratin or other oven-to-table dish about 10–11 inches (25–27 cm) long and 2 inches (5 cm) deep.

Beat all the topping ingredients together until they form a smooth mixture, then spread evenly on top. Bake at Gas No. 4 (350°F/180°C) for 40 minutes, or until golden and firm to gentle touch. Serve plain or with yoghurt or fromage frais.

BANANA SOUFFLÉ

Serves 6.

A delicious ending to a light meal and especially pleasing served with an orange pineapple fruit salad.

6 large ripe bananas
4 oz (125 g/½ cup) caster (superfine) sugar
juice of 1 orange
2 teasp lemon juice
grated rind of 1 lemon
2 tbsp chopped almonds, fried until golden with nut of butter
3 large egg whites

Preheat the oven to Gas No. 6 (400°F/200°C). Purée the bananas either in a blender or food processor, or press through a sieve, then beat in 3 oz (75 g/3/8 cup) of the sugar, the juices and the rind and the toasted nuts. Whisk the egg whites until they form stiff peaks, then whisk in the remaining amount of sugar a tablespoon at a time. Fold into the banana mixture. Have ready a buttered round dish, approximately 8 inches (20 cm) in diameter and 3-4 inches (7.5-10 cm) deep. Sprinkle with caster (superfine) sugar. Spoon in the soufflé mixture and level off. Turn the oven down to Gas No. 5 (375°F/190°C), put in the soufflé and bake for 30 minutes. Serve at once.

CINNAMON APPLE TORTE

Makes 12-18 squares.
Keeps 3 days under refrigeration.
Freeze 3 months.

A thick and juicy apple filling is sandwiched between layers of light and spongy cake. Equally good served hot or cold, as a dessert or as a cake.

3 oz (75 g/3/4 cup) matzah cake meal
3 oz (75 g/1/2 cup) potato flour
1 1/2 teasp Passover baking powder
4 oz (125 g/1/2 cup) soft margarine
3 oz (75 g/1/3 cup) caster (superfine) sugar
rind of 1/2 lemon
2 eggs
1 1/2 lb (675 g) baking apples, thinly sliced
2 tbsp granulated sugar
1 teasp cinnamon
1 tbsp lemon juice
1 heaped tbsp apricot eingemacht

For the topping

1 oz (25 g/*1/4 cup) hazelnuts, coarsely chopped (optional)*
1 oz (25 g/2 tbsp) demerara sugar

Preheat the oven to Gas No. 4 (350°F/180°C). Grease a tin or foil container measuring approximately 12 x 8 x 1 1/2 inches (30 x 20 x 4 cm).

Put the meal, potato flour, baking powder, margarine, caster sugar, lemon rind and eggs into a bowl and beat by hand, mixer or food processor until smooth. Take two-thirds of the mixture and spread it thickly over the base of the tin. Arrange the sliced apples in an even layer on top, sprinkle with the granulated sugar, cinnamon and lemon juice and dot with the eingemacht. Drop the remaining cake mixture by teaspoonfuls all over the apple filling and put in the oven.

After 10 minutes, open the oven, quickly smooth the blobs of cake mixture over the top of the apples with a large fork, then sprinkle evenly with the mixed coarsely chopped nuts and sugar. Close the oven and bake for a further 30 minutes, or until the cake is golden brown and the apples feel tender when pierced with a sharp knife.

Cut into 2-3 inch (5-7.5 cm) squares to serve.

CINNAMON TORTE WITH A MIXED BERRY FILLING

Serves 6-8.
Cooked torte keeps 1 day under refrigeration.
Leftovers 3 days.
Freeze 1 month.

A modern interpretation of the traditional Passover Almond Sponge Pudding - fruit, frozen without sugar, can be used without a special Passover seal.

8 oz (225 g/1 1/2 cups) each fresh or frozen raspberries and mixed summer berries
2 1/2 oz (65 g/1/2 cup plus 2 tbsp) cake meal
2 1/2 oz (65 g/1/2 cup) potato flour
1 teasp Passover baking powder
5 oz (150 g/2/3 cup) soft margarine
5 oz (150 g/2/3 cup) caster (superfine) sugar
5 oz (150 g/1 1/4 cups) ground almonds
2 eggs

1 teasp ground cinnamon
1 rounded tbsp granulated sugar
2 oz (50 g/½ cup) flaked almonds

For the garnish
1 teasp cinnamon
2 tbsp icing sugar

Preheat the oven to Gas No. 4 (350°F/180°C). Lightly oil an 8½-inch (22-cm) springform cake tin.

Reserve 4 oz (125 g/¾ cup) of the raspberries for garnish and refrigerate.

Mix together the meal, potato flour and baking powder. In a mixing bowl or food processor put the margarine, sugar, almonds, meal mixture, eggs and cinnamon, and process or beat until a smooth but fairly heavy mixture is produced. Spread half the mixture into the tin, using a fork to flatten into an even layer. Mix the remaining fruit together, arrange in an even layer on top of the almond mixture, then sprinkle with the granulated sugar. Drop the remainder of the almond mixture in spoonfuls over the fruit. Bake for 10 minutes, then open the oven and quickly spread the softened cake batter all over the fruit, then sprinkle with the almonds. Continue to cook for another 40–50 minutes, or until the surface is firm to gentle touch.

Serve warm (it may be gently reheated, covered with foil, during the meal), dusted with the cinnamon and icing sugar. Garnish with the reserved fruit.

Note Torte can be baked in a 14 x 4 inch (35 x 10 cm) tin but use all the fruit and leave none for garnish.

BANANAS IN WINE SAUCE

Serves 6–8.
Keeps 1 day under refrigeration.
Do not freeze.

A simple but satisfying dessert.

6–8 stubby under-ripe bananas
4 oz (125 g/½ cup) caster (superfine) or demerara sugar
10 fl oz (275 ml/1¼ cups) fruity red wine
½ teasp cinnamon
1½ tbsp lemon juice
coconut, chopped nuts or cream for decoration

Peel, string and cut the bananas in half, lengthwise. Dissolve the sugar in the wine in a wide frying pan. Add the cinnamon and bring slowly to the boil. Lay the bananas in the wine syrup, side by side, and allow them to simmer for 5 minutes, turning once. Lift out the bananas and arrange in a glass serving dish. Simmer the wine mixture until it is thick and syrupy and the flavour has intensified - about 5 minutes. Stir in the lemon juice. Pour over the bananas and chill thoroughly. To serve for a meat meal, sprinkle with the toasted coconut or chopped nuts; for a milk meal decorate with whipped cream. Serve with sponge cake or biscuits.

LUSCIOUS LEMON SPONGE WITH A STRAWBERRY, FRESH APRICOT OR PEACH AND BRANDY SAUCE

Serves 6–8.
Keeps 1 day under refrigeration.
Refrigerate leftovers 3 days.
Do not freeze.

A creamless and almost fat-free dessert - and positively no ground almonds. Serve well chilled.

1 oz (25 g/2 tbsp) soft butter
4 oz (125 g/1½ cup) granulated sugar
1 oz (25 g/3 tbsp) potato flour
1 oz (25 g/4 tbsp) cake meal
½ teasp Passover baking powder
2 teasp finely grated lemon rind
6 tbsp fresh lemon juice
3 egg yolks
12 fl oz (350 ml/1½ cups) milk
3 egg whites
pinch of salt
2 oz (50 g/¼ cup) caster (superfine) sugar

For the strawberry sauce
1 punnet (8 oz/225 g) fresh strawberries
2 oz (50 g/¼ cup) caster (superfine) sugar
2 teasp lemon juice

For the fresh apricot sauce
3 oz (75 g/⅓ cup) granulated sugar
4 fl oz (25 ml/½ cup) water
1 lb (450 g) fresh apricots, halved
1 tbsp lemon juice
2 tbsp Passover apricot brandy (optional)

For the peach and brandy sauce
1 x 14 oz (425 g) can peaches
1 tbsp lemon juice
2 tbsp Passover peach or apricot brandy

This pudding is most easily mixed in a food processor or blender. Otherwise, melt the butter then combine all the ingredients using a balloon whisk or strong rotary whisk.

Preheat the oven to Gas No. 4 (350°F/180°C). Lightly grease a 3-pint (1.75-l/7-cup) baking dish, 1½–2 inches (4–5 cm) deep, or 8 x 5 oz (150 g/⅔ cup) little soufflé dishes. Boil the kettle.

Process all the ingredients (except the whites, pinch of salt and caster sugar) until the mixture is smooth. Whisk the whites with the salt until they hold soft peaks, then gradually whisk in the caster sugar until the meringue stands in firm glossy peaks. Slowly pour the egg and lemon mixture into the meringue, folding them gently together with a rubber spatula. Pour into the dish, place the dish in a roasting tin, surround with very hot water and bake for 40-45 minutes (30 minutes for small puddings), until a pale gold and spongy to gentle touch. Leave in the refrigerator for several hours to chill.

To make the strawberry sauce Process the strawberries with the sugar and lemon juice for 1 minute until smooth and thickened. Chill.

To make the apricot sauce In a wide lidded pan simmer the sugar and water until slightly syrupy then add the apricots. Simmer until absolutely tender. Purée the contents of the pan in a blender or food processor with the lemon juice and apricot brandy (if used). Chill thoroughly.

To make the peach and brandy sauce Purée the peaches with the sugar and lemon juice for 1 minute until smooth and thickened. Stir in the brandy if using.

Garnish each portion of the pudding with a spoonful of the chosen sauce.

LEMON AND STRAWBERRY MERINGUE BASKETS

Serves 10–12.
Empty meringue cups keep 1 week at room temperature in an airtight container.
Filled cups keep 1 day under refrigeration and freeze 1 month.

This meringue sets with a crisp outside and a marshmallow inside. Any kind of fruit and cream mixture can be used to fill the baskets.

For the meringue
4 egg whites
pinch of salt
8 oz (225 g/1 cup) caster (superfine) sugar
1 teasp potato flour
1 teasp lemon juice

For the filling
5 fl oz (150 ml/⅔ cup) double (heavy) cream
5 fl oz (150 ml/⅔ cup) lemon curd (see p. 603)
8 oz (225 g) punnet fresh strawberries

To make the meringue cups Put the whites into the mixer bowl with a pinch of salt and whisk until the mixture forms stiff peaks. Meanwhile, blend sugar and potato flour, then start adding to the meringue a tablespoon at a time, whisking until stiff after each addition. Finally whisk in the lemon juice. Cover a baking tray with greased greaseproof or silicone paper. Pipe or spoon meringue into cups about 3 inches (7.5 cm) in diameter. Preheat the oven to Gas No. 2 (300°F/150°C), put in the tray of meringues, turn down to Gas No. 1 (275°F/140°C) and leave for 30–40 minutes, or until crisp to the touch and easily lifted from the tin. Remove from the tray and store until needed.

For the filling Whip the cream until it holds soft peaks. Fold together the whipped cream and the lemon curd. Spoon into the cups and top with the sliced berries. Serve chilled.

CARAMEL NUSSTORTE

Serves 10 as a dessert.
Makes 24 smaller bars.
Keeps 1 week in an airtight container under refrigeration.
Freeze 3 months.

Tiny fingers of this torte can be served as petit fours with coffee, or the whole torte can be presented as a Seder dessert after a dairy meal, accompanied by a mango or fresh strawberry purée or a salad of exotic fruits. Either way, the contrast of caramelized nuts set on a meltingly tender pastry is irresistible.

1 recipe Passover pastry (see p. 614)

For the filling
7 oz (200 g/1 cup) granulated sugar
3 tbsp cold water
8 oz (225 g/2 cups) coarsely chopped walnuts
1½ oz (40 g/3 tbsp) butter
5 fl oz (150 ml/⅔ cup) double (heavy) cream
1 rounded tbsp mild honey
½–¾ oz (15–20 g) packet vanilla sugar

For dusting the torte
icing (confectioners') sugar

Make the pastry as described. Flatten into a block about 1 inch (2.5 cm) thick and chill in the refrigerator overnight.

When ready to use, roll out sufficient dough to fit a 9-inch (22.5-cm) round or square flan tin, or a 14 x 4 inch (35 x 10 cm) rectangular tin, about 1½ inches (4 cm) deep. Put in the freezer. Pat the remaining dough into a square and freeze.

To make the filling Put the sugar and water in a heavy 8-inch (20-cm) pan and cook over moderate heat without stirring until the mixture turns a light caramel. Remove from the heat and stand the base of the pan in a bowl of cold water to check further cooking. Stir in the walnuts, butter and cream. Return to the heat and simmer, stirring for 5 minutes, then cool for 5 minutes. Stir in the honey and vanilla sugar and spoon into the frozen crust. Preheat the oven to Gas No. 4 (350°F/180°C). Grate an even layer of the frozen pastry over the filling. Bake for 50 minutes, until the pastry is crisp and golden. When cold, dust thickly with icing sugar.

CHOCOLATE AND WALNUT TORTE WITH BRANDIED COFFEE FILLING

Serves 10–12.
Freeze 3 months.

It's easy to make this spectacular dessert if you choose a quiet time and take it slowly! It can be made well ahead as it is at its best served semi-frozen. After a few days in the freezer the meringue layers soften to an almost macaroon-like texture, making it easy to slice.

4 oz (125 g) plain (semi-sweet) chocolate
4 egg whites
pinch of salt
8 oz (225 g/1 cup) caster (superfine) sugar
1½ teasp potato flour
1 teasp lemon juice
4 oz (125 g/1 cup) walnuts, coarsely chopped

For the filling
15 fl oz (425 ml/2 cups) dairy or non-dairy double (heavy) cream or whipping cream
2 oz (50 g/½ cup) icing (confectioners') sugar
3 teasp strong cooled coffee made with 3 teasp coffee granules
3 tbsp Passover brandy

Melt the broken-up chocolate either in a basin standing over a pan of very hot water or in a microwave on 100 per cent for 1½ minutes, then stir well. Leave to cool a little.

Whisk the egg whites with a pinch of salt until they form peaks, then whisk in the mixed caster sugar and potato flour a tablespoonful at a time, whisking until stiff again after each addition. Whisk in the lemon juice. Stir a quarter of this meringue into the melted chocolate, then fold in the remainder of the meringue, together with the finely chopped nuts.

Have ready 3 baking trays lined with silicone paper. Draw an 8-inch (20-cm) circle on each tray using a round baking tin as a guide. Spoon the meringue on to each circle, smoothing it level, or pipe it on using a ½-inch 1.25-cm) nozzle.

Bake in a preheated oven at Gas No. 2 (300°F/150°C) for 50 minutes, until the top is crisp to the touch and a spatula can easily be inserted between the base and the paper. If in doubt, don't hesitate to give it extra baking time. Allow to go cold and firm on the baking tray. (If the oven won't take all 3 at once, no harm will come to the round that is baked later.)

While the meringue layers are baking, prepare the filling. Whisk the cream until it holds a soft peak, then whisk in the icing sugar, followed by the cooled coffee and the liqueur, whisking until it stiffens up again. Chill until the meringues are cool.

To assemble the torte Have ready a plate or cakeboard large enough to hold the torte. Carefully turn 1 layer on to the serving dish and spread half the cream evenly all over it. Cover with the second meringue and spread with the remaining cream. Cover with the remaining meringue. Take from the freezer and leave at room temperature from the beginning of the meal. It will then be just the right texture to slice and serve for dessert.

JAPONAIS AU MOKA

Serves 16 (or 10, using 2 layers only with Moka cream in between – amounts for 10 given in square brackets)
Keeps 3 days under refrigeration.
Freeze for 3 months.

A luscious macaroon dessert that is equally delicious in the dairy or *parev* version.

For the Japonais mixture

6 egg whites [4]
12 oz (350 g/1½ cups) caster (superfine) sugar [8 oz]
2 x ½–¾ oz (15–20 g) packets vanilla sugar [1]
12 oz (350 g/3 cups) ground hazelnuts (or almonds) [8 oz]

For the Moka cream

1 tbsp coffee granules [3 teasp]
3 tbsp water [2 tbsp]
8 oz (225 g) best plain (semi-sweet) dessert chocolate [6 oz]
4 egg yolks [3]
10 fl oz (275 ml/1¼ cups) double (heavy) dairy cream [8 fl oz] or 8 oz (225 g/1 cup) non-dairy cream [6 fl oz]
2 tbsp Passover coffee or chocolate liqueur [5 teasp]

For decoration

icing (confectioners') sugar

To make the Japonais Mark out 3 [2] circles on silicone paper using the base of a 9½–10-inch (22.5–25 cm) springform tin. Arrange on baking sheets. Preheat the oven to Gas No. 5 (375°F/190°C). Whisk the whites until they hold soft peaks, then whisk in half the sugars, a tablespoon at a time, whisking until stiff after each addition. Fold in the remaining sugar and the ground nuts.

Divide between the paper circles, spreading the mixture as evenly as possible. Bake for 20 minutes until the surface is firm to gentle touch. Carefully remove to cooling trays.

To make the filling Dissolve the coffee in the hot water in a basin, add the broken-up chocolate and microwave on 100 per cent power for 1½–2 minutes, or until liquid (or melt over hot water). Drop in the yolks and beat vigorously until smooth and glossy. Allow to cool for 10 minutes. Whisk the cream with the liqueur until it holds soft peaks, then fold into the chocolate mixture.

Arrange one layer on a large plate or foil-covered cake circle. Spoon half the Moka cream on top and then arrange the second layer on top. Spread with the remaining Moka cream and arrange the third layer on top. [For smaller Japonais, spoon all the Moka cream on the first layer and top with the second layer.] Dust thickly with icing sugar. Chill 24 hours or freeze until required.

MOCHA MOUSSE CUPS WITH PECANS OR WALNUTS

Serves 8–10.
Keeps 4 days under refrigeration.
Freeze 3 months.

A little goes a long way, but with an accompaniment of sliced and lightly sugared strawberries or mangoes, this is an excellent *parev* dessert for the Seder meal.

sufficient crushed Prelatoes (see p. 622) or stale sponge cake crumbs to come to a depth of ½ inch (1 cm) in each cup
2 teasp kosher (port-type) wine for each cup
6 oz (175 g) plain dessert (semi-sweet) chocolate
6 large eggs, separated
3 teasp instant coffee dissolved in 1 tbsp hot water
2 tbsp chocolate- or orange-flavoured Passover liqueur
1 tbsp caster (superfine) sugar
3 oz (75 g/¾ cup) pecans or walnuts, coarsely chopped

Divide the crumbs between 8–10 tiny coffee cups (or use 1 large glass bowl) and sprinkle with the wine.

Break up the chocolate and stand in a basin over a pan of hot water. Heat gently until melted, then remove from the heat (or melt, uncovered, for 1½ minutes on 100 per cent power in the microwave).

Immediately drop the egg yolks in the hot chocolate and beat vigorously until the mixture begins to thicken, then stir in the coffee and liqueur and allow to go cold. Whisk the egg whites until they just hold soft peaks, then whisk in the sugar. Stir a few tablespoons of the meringue into the chocolate mixture, then carefully fold in the rest with a rubber spatula. Finally fold in the nuts, saving about 2 tablespoons for decoration. Spoon the mousse into the chosen container(s), sprinkle with the reserved nuts and leave to chill overnight.

PASSOVER POURING CUSTARD

Serves 6-8 (10 as part of a trifle).
Keeps 2 days under refrigeration.
Do not freeze.

Excellent for trifle or to accompany a compôte of dried fruits.

3 whole eggs or 4 egg yolks
2 oz (50 g/¼ cup) sugar
1 x ½-¾ oz (15-20 g) packet vanilla sugar
1 level tbsp potato flour
1 pint (575 ml/2½ cups) milk

Whisk the eggs, sugars and potato flour until thoroughly blended (15 seconds in the blender or food processor). Heat the milk until it steams, then pour on to the egg mixture. Return to the pan and cook gently, stirring all the time, until the custard will coat the back of the spoon. *Do not* allow the custard to boil.

Serve warm or cold.

MICROWAVE CUSTARD

Serves 4.
Keeps 2 days under refrigeration.
Do not freeze.

2 egg yolks
1 oz (25 g/2 tbsp) caster (superfine) sugar
½-¾ oz (15-20 g) packet vanilla sugar
2 teasp potato flour
10 fl oz (275 ml/1¼ cups) milk

In a medium bowl mix the egg yolks and sugars until creamy. Meanwhile, in another bowl mix until creamy the potato flour and 4 tablespoons of the milk. Add the remainder of the milk, then cook on 100 per cent power for 3 minutes, stirring twice. Add this liquid to the egg mixture. Cook on 50 per cent power for 4 minutes, stirring twice until smoothly thickened.

Pesach for Diabetics

Diabetics can find Passover a particularly trying time as so many traditional recipes are loaded with sugar. Fortunately, fruit sugar (fructose) and other sugar substitutes are approved by the kashrut authorities - it's advisable to consult your local rabbi. Fructose has two pluses for those forbidden normal cane sugar. First, it does not require insulin to convert it into energy for the body, and although weight for weight it contains the same number of calories as sugar, it is twice as sweet, so only half the normal quantity of sweetener need be used. Second, it can be used in baking - Passover biscuits, in particular - but you will need to do your own calculation of total carbohydrate content.

COUNTING THE CALORIES

Carbohydrate and calorie content of matzah products (figures supplied by Rakusen Foods).

Tea biscuits and matzah crackers Each contains 3.8 g carbohydrate and 17 K/cals.

Wheaten crackers Each contains 3.8 g carbohydrate and 17 K/cals.

Superfine (white) and wheaten matzot Each large square of matzah contains approximately 17 g carbohydrate and 70 K/cals.

Matzah meal There are 300 g carbohydrate in a 13 oz (375 g) pack of meal (approx. 23 g per oz/1 heaped tbsp).

PASSOVER DIABETIC JAM

Fructose makes excellent diabetic jam, a teaspoon of which contains negligible carbohydrate - a little spread on 2 matzah crackers makes an excellent snack with only 8 carbohydrate units. The jam can be made on the top of the stove in the usual manner (see p. 604), but for a small amount this microwave method is more convenient and cuts out overnight soaking. The almonds are optional. They contain negligible carbohydrate but because of their high fat content will add 115 calories to each pound of jam.

DIABETIC APRICOT EINGEMACHT

Makes 1½–2 lb (675–900 g).
Keep refrigerated.

8 oz (225 g) dried apricots
1 pint (575 ml/2½ cups) cold water
3 tbsp lemon juice
8 oz (225 g) fructose
2 oz (50 g/½ cup) blanched almonds (optional)

Put the apricots into a lidded casserole, pour on the cold water (it should cover them - if not add a little more), cover and cook on 100 per cent power for 10 minutes, then leave covered for 20 minutes. Lift the apricots out of the liquid, cut each into 4 or 5 pieces and put in a 4-pint (2.25-l/10 cup) bowl. Add 5 fl oz (150 ml/⅔ cup) of the liquid, lemon juice, fructose and almonds (if used) and cook uncovered for 5 minutes. Then stir well to ensure the fructose is dissolved. Cook uncovered for a further 15 minutes, until the apricots are bubbling in a syrup that will just coat the back of a wooden spoon (the mixture should have been bubbling fiercely for 10 minutes). Take out of the oven. Put 4 tablespoons of cold water in each of 2 clean 1-lb (450-g) jam jars and bring to the boil, uncovered, on 100 per cent power - about 1½ minutes. Then turn upside down to drain and dry on paper towelling. After 30 seconds turn right-side up, fill with the conserve and seal with the lid.

DIABETIC PRUNE EINGEMACHT

Makes 1½–2 lb (675–900 g).
Keep refrigerated.

1 x 9 oz (250 g) packet tenderized or regular prunes
1 pint (575 ml/2½ cups) water
3 large lemons
2 oz (50 g/½ cup) blanched almonds (optional)
8 oz (225 g) fructose

If prunes are not tenderized, soak in the water overnight. Have ready 4 small or 2 x 1-lb (450-g) well-washed jam jars.

Put the prunes and water into a lidded casserole (it should cover them - if not, add a little more), cover and cook on 100 per cent power for 10 minutes in the microwave, then leave covered until cold enough to handle (30–40 minutes). Remove stones if necessary and cut each prune into 4. Peel the lemons, remove all the pith, then slice and cut each slice in half.

Put the prunes and almonds into a 4-pint (2.25-l/10-cup) bowl. Add 5 fl oz (150 ml/⅔ cup) of the cooking liquid, the lemon slices and fructose and cook on 100 per cent power for 3 minutes. Then stir well to ensure the fructose is dissolved. Cook uncovered for a further 15 minutes, until the syrup will just coat the back of a wooden spoon. The mixture should have been bubbling fiercely for 10 minutes.

Put 4 tablespoons of cold water in each of the clean jars and bring to the boil, uncovered, on 100 per cent power - about 1½ minutes - then turn upside down to drain on paper towelling. Turn right-side up, fill with the conserve and seal with the lid.

DIABETIC ORANGE AND NUT CAKE

Keeps 1 week at room temperature in an airtight container.
Freeze 3 months.

A light, moist cake delicately scented with orange. When cut into 8, each slice contains 5 g of carbohydrate.

6 oz (175 g/1½ cups) ground almonds or ground hazelnuts
3 eggs, separated
2 oz (50 g/¼ cup) plus 1 teasp fruit sugar or diabetic fructose
grated rind and juice (2½–3 fl oz/60–75 ml/¼–⅓ cup) of 1 medium orange

Preheat the oven to Gas No. 4 (350°F/180°C). Grease then dust with some of the ground nuts the inside of a tin measuring 9 x 5 x 3 inches (22.5 x 12.5 x 7.5 cm) and line the bottom and 2 short sides with a strip of silicone paper.

Whisk the egg whites until they hold soft peaks, then set aside. Whisk the yolks and the fruit sugar (fructose) together until the mixture lightens in colour and thickens so that it shows the marks of the whisk, then whisk in the orange juice and rind. Stir in the ground nuts, then carefully fold in the egg whites. Spoon into the prepared tin and bake for 35 minutes, until the top feels spongy when lightly touched. Turn off the oven and leave the cake inside to cool for 30 minutes. Loosen round the edges, then turn out on to a cooling tray. Leave until cold, then wrap in foil.

MICROWAVE CARROT, ORANGE AND CORIANDER SOUP

Serves 3–4.
Keeps 3 days under refrigeration.
Freeze 1 month.

Total calories: 115; total carbohydrate 30 g. With optional milk add 5 g carbohydrate and 65 calories. Those on calorie-controlled diets can omit the margarine, which adds flavour but a further 113 calories.

A bowl of piping-hot low-carbohydrate vegetable soup will satisfy a hungry diabetic and the rest of the household at the same time. To cook on top of the stove, sauté the onion and garlic (covered) in the fat for 10 minutes, then add all the remaining ingredients and simmer for 20 minutes until absolutely tender. Finish as for microwave method.

nut of margarine
1 medium onion
8 oz (225 g) carrots
small clove of garlic
15 fl oz (425 ml/2 cups) hot water plus 1 vegetable or parev stock-cube
4 fl oz (125 ml/½ cup) orange juice plus 2 strips of peel (1 large orange)
pinch of white pepper
¼ teasp salt
½ teasp ground coriander (optional)
3 fl oz (75 ml/⅓ cup) milk
1 tbsp chopped parsley or fresh coriander

In a 3½-pint (2-1/9-cup) lidded casserole or heatproof bowl melt the margarine on 100 per cent power for 30 seconds, then add the peeled and thinly sliced vegetables and garlic. Stir well, then add 5 fl oz (150 ml/⅔ cup) of the hot stock. Cover and cook for 10 minutes, stirring half-way, until the vegetables feel tender when pierced with a slim pointed knife. Purée in the blender or food processor together with the pepper, salt and ground coriander. Return to the dish and whisk in the orange juice and peel, cover and cook on 100 per cent power for 3 minutes. Uncover, lift out the peel and stir in the milk (if used) and herbs. If possible, leave for several hours or overnight to mature in flavour. To reheat, cover and cook on 100 per cent power for 5 minutes, or until bubbling round the edge.

Pesach for Coeliacs

For sufferers from coeliac disease or those who for whatever reason cannot tolerate gluten, I have tested and found quite excellent a gluten-free recipe for matzah sent to me by Health and Nutrition Counsellor Marilyn Kaye, SRN, HV Cert. Dip. ION. The potato flour and ground almonds used instead of flour in this recipe can also be used in any Passover baking, which opens up the possibility of eating 'normal' biscuits such as cinnamon balls, coconut pyramids, almond macaroons and choconut kisses, as well as potato-flour-based sponge cakes and chocolate cakes.

PASSOVER BISCUITS AND CAKES

Ugat Schekademe (but substitute 3 level tbsp finely crushed coeliac matzah for matzah meal) (see p. 612)
French Chocolate Cake (see p. 416)
Almond Macaroons (see p. 615)
Citrus-scented Macaroons (see p. 616)
Cinnamon Balls (see p. 617)
Coconut Pyramids (see p. 617)
Choconut Kisses (see p. 617)
Date and Walnut Kisses (see p. 617)
Coconutties (see p. 618)
Chocolate and Almond Balls (see p. 620)
Buttery Nut Crisps (see p. 621)
Basil's Truffles (see p. 622)

PASSOVER SOUPS

Passover Minestrone (without the lokshen) (see p. 627)
Tomato and Orange Soup (without the knaidlach) (see p. 626)
Mushroom and Leek Soup (see p. 627)

Gluten-free Passover soups can be made by substituting 1 teaspoon of potato flour for each teaspoon of cornflour (cornstarch) or 2 teaspoons of ordinary flour in the recipe.

SAVOURY DISHES

Twice-baked Cheese Soufflé (see p. 624)
Vegetarian Moussaka (but check list of ingredients on can of tomato and mushroom sauce) (see p. 625)
Fritada de Espinaca (see p. 625)

All the fish dishes, but substitute an equal quantity of ground almonds for matzah meal in the gefilte fish mix.

All the chicken dishes, but instead of coating the chicken in matzah meal before frying, dry the joints very well instead.

All the beef and lamb dishes, but omit meal coating and dry meat well before frying.

Do not eat stuffing in veal shoulder. (If preferred the shoulder can be cooked unstuffed.)

DESSERTS

Banana Soufflé (see p. 640)
Bananas in Wine Sauce (see p. 642)
Lemon and Strawberry Meringue Baskets (see p. 644)
Chocolate and Walnut Torte with Brandied Coffee Filling (see p. 645)
Japonais au Moka (see p. 645)
Mocha Mousse Cups (without soaked crumb base) (see p. 646)
Passover Pouring Custard (see p. 647)
Also
All Pavlovas (see pp. 344–8)
All Ice-cream Parfaits (see pp. 355–8)
All Sorbets (see pp. 361–5)

MATZAH CRISPBREAD
(*For Coeliacs*)

Makes 8–10 crispbread; quantities may be doubled.

Mrs Kaye suggests 4–5 tablespoons of water but I found that only 2–3 were needed.

1½ oz (40 g/⅓ cup) ground almonds
2 pinches salt or salt substitute
2½ oz (65 g/½ cup less 1 level tbsp) potato flour
1 oz (25 g/2 tbsp) soft margarine
2–3 tbsp cold water
more potato flour for rolling out

Preheat the oven to Gas No. 8 (450°F/230°C). Put the ground almonds, salt and potato flour into a mixing bowl. Add the margarine and rub in with the fingers until the mixture resembles fine breadcrumbs. Add 2 tablespoons of the water and mix to a stiff paste with a fork. Add more water if required, then knead gently to a soft dough. Continue to knead until the dough comes clean away from the bowl, sprinkling with extra potato flour if at all sticky. Roll out to the thickness of crispbread or matzah and cut into squares or triangles. Use a spatula to place these on baking sheets covered with silicone paper or foil. Prick evenly all over with a fork. Bake for 8–10 minutes, or until a pale gold in colour. Take off the baking sheets and allow to cool and crisp on a wire rack. Store in an airtight container.

ORANGE TORTE WITH A CITRUS SYLLABUB

Serves 10.
Keeps 5 days under refrigeration; freeze 3 months.
Syllabub keeps 2 days under refrigeration; freeze 1 month.

This delicate completely starchless sponge (it will sink into a flan shape) is soaked with an orange syrup and served either with the fruity syllabub (both dairy and *parev*) versions are excellent) or Mango and Strawberry Compôte (see p. 333).

For the cake
6 eggs, separated
3 oz (75 g/⅓ cup) plus 3 oz (75 g/⅓ cup) caster (superfine) sugar
8 oz (225 g/2 cups) ground almonds

For the syrup
10 fl oz (275 ml/1¼ cups) fresh orange juice (juice of 3 large oranges, or bottled)
4½ oz (140 g/½ cup plus 2 tbsp) granulated sugar
1 fat stick cinnamon
3 tbsp Passover orange liqueur

For the syllabub
juice of ½ medium orange and ½ lemon (3 fl oz/75 ml/⅓ cup) altogether
grated rind of ½ lemon and ½ orange
1 tbsp Passover orange liqueur (1½ tbsp with non-dairy cream)
1 level tbsp caster (superfine) sugar
10 fl oz (275 ml/1¼ cups) double (heavy) cream or 8–9 fl oz (225–250 ml/1 cup–1 cup plus 2 tbsp) non-dairy cream or topping

To make the cake Preheat the oven to Gas No. 4 (350°F/180°C). Lightly oil then bottom-line with silicone paper a 10-inch (25-cm) springform or loose-bottomed cake tin. In a large bowl, whisk until creamy the egg yolks, 3 oz caster sugar and the ground almonds. Whisk the egg whites until they hold soft peaks, then whisk in the remaining 3 oz (75 g/⅓ cup) of sugar a tablespoon at a time, whisking until stiff after each addition.

Stir 2 tablespoons of this meringue into the yolk mixture to lighten it, then gently fold in the remainder with a rubber spatula. Turn into the tin, smooth level, then cook for 1 hour, or until a skewer inserted comes out clean and the top springs back when gently prodded. Leave the tin on a cooling tray until cool. (The cake will fall as it cools, but not to worry.)

To make the syrup Put the orange juice, sugar and cinnamon into a pan and stir until the sugar has melted. Then bubble for 5 minutes to concentrate the flavour. Stir in the liqueur. Arrange the cooled cake on a lipped serving dish and pierce the top all over with a skewer. Pour over the syrup and baste the cake now and again until it has all been absorbed.

To make the syllabub Combine the juices, rinds and liqueur in a medium-sized bowl. Add the sugar and stir to dissolve, then add the cream. Whisk by hand or machine until the mixture stands in soft peaks. Chill for at least 3 hours before serving with the cake.

SHAVUOT (PENTECOST OR FEAST OF WEEKS)

In earlier days, when the Temple still stood in Jerusalem, Shavuot was celebrated as a great agricultural festival, when the start of the wheat harvest was marked by offerings of newly baked bread. Every man brought the first fruits of his crops to the Temple, while his wife ground flour from the new season's wheat and baked special cakes and bread in honour of the occasion. Today we commemorate those early days by decorating the house with flowers and plants and by taking them as gifts to the synagogue.

This festival also celebrates the giving of the Torah - the code of Jewish Law - to Moses on Mount Sinai. In the Torah are set out the dietary laws - the regulations that relate to the preparation and consumption of food in the Jewish community - in which special emphasis is placed on the separation of meat and dairy dishes within the same meal. Another tradition links the custom to the gift of the land 'flowing with milk and honey'. So milk and foods derived from it have become the most famous symbolic foods of this festival.

These dairy ingredients are made into some of the most delicious dishes of Jewish cuisine - such as the cheesecakes, blintzes, kreplach and lokshen casseroles that so enrich Ashkenazi tables at this season.

The same theme of dairy foods is expressed in Sephardi households with dishes such as 'sambusak' and 'boreks' (pastry turnovers filled with various vegetables mixed with 'kashkeval', a soft, dry white cheese), 'spanakopita' (a filo pie with a spinach and cheese filling) and 'pain de miele y yoghurt' (honey and yoghurt bread).

While most of these dairy dishes have a long culinary history, there are others of more recent origin which I am sure will take on the mantle of tradition for future generations - especially those inspired by the heterogeneous population of Israel, which someone has calculated represents 120 different ethnic communities world-wide! It is fascinating to see how these different food cultures are producing their own 'traditional' foods, which are generally more suited to our present way of life.

After the synagogue service on the eve of the festival, the congregation enjoys a light dairy meal, with cheesecakes made by members given pride of place, before sitting down to read long into the night passages from the Bible, the Talmud and various rabbinical writings. The Sephardim call this night-long service or night-watch a *'vilada'*, while Ashkenazim know it as *'tikkun leyl Shavuot'*.

Menu for Shavuot

A very pretty meal to look at and just right for early spring, with its young vegetables and first-of-the-season fruits.

Hideg Meggyleves (Cold Cherry Soup)
(see p. 45)
or

Borscht on the Rocks (see p. 46)
or
Cheese Blintzes with Soured Cream (see this page)
Poached Salmon Steaks with a Tarragon and Lemon Sauce (see p. 77)
Boiled new potatoes tossed in chopped parsley
Chicory and Frisée Salad with Blue Cheese and Toasted Pecans (see p. 285)
Quarksahn Schnitten with Raspberry Filling (see p. 662)
or
Lime Cheesecake with a Fresh Strawberry Sauce (see p. 433)

ALTERNATIVE VEGETARIAN MAIN COURSE

Spanakopita (see p. 657)
or
Mushroom Crescents (see p. 120)

CHEESE BLINTZES

Makes 12 (serves 6–8).
Keep filled but unbrowned blintzes 1 day under refrigeration.
Freeze empty crêpes 3 months, filled blintzes 1 month.

These are one of the glories of Jewish cuisine. A blintze is a paper-thin pancake, which is fried on 1 side only. The Yiddish word for these pancakes is *'bletlach'* – or skeleton leaves – which gives some indication of how thin they should be. After it has been filled, the pancake is fried again on the unbrowned side, and served plain or with soured cream. The secret of the perfect blintze lies first in the batter and then in the special method of frying, which I learned from a Russian cook. Follow the instructions implicitly and you can be certain of success.

To freeze Can be frozen either as pancakes or stuffed and ready for the final browning. Each stuffed blintze can be wrapped in foil and then put with the rest in a plastic bag, or if they are all to be used at once, lay side by side on foil, with a piece of foil between each layer. Make into a firm foil parcel and freeze. Defrost before frying.

For the batter

4 oz (125 g/1 cup) plain (all-purpose) flour
pinch of salt
2 large eggs
2 teasp oil
4 fl oz (125 ml/½ cup) milk
4 fl oz (125 ml/½ cup) water
butter and oil for frying

For the filling

12 oz (350 g/1½ cups) curd cheese or sieved cottage cheese, mixed with 2 tbsp soured cream, yoghurt or fromage frais or an egg yolk (whichever is most convenient)
1 level teasp sugar
pinch of salt

To make the batter with a blender or food processor Blend or process all the ingredients (except the fats for frying) until a smooth batter is formed.

To make the batter by hand or with electric mixer Sift the flour and salt into a bowl. Make a well, drop in eggs and 2 teaspoons of oil and start stirring in the surrounding flour to make a stirrable batter. Gradually add the milk and water until smooth. Beat with a whisk until the surface is covered with tiny bubbles.

Leave the batter for half an hour, though it can be refrigerated overnight if more convenient.

To make the filling Mix all the filling ingredients together and leave until required.

To fry the pancakes Stir the batter well and pour into a jug. It should be the consistency of single cream; if too thick, add a further tablespoonful of water. Use a 6–7-inch-diameter (15–17.5-cm) omelette pan (with rounded sides). Put on medium heat for 3 minutes, then drop in a teaspoonful of oil, and swirl it round the base and sides of the pan. Take a pad of tissue or kitchen paper and wipe out any excess. Using the pad of paper, smear the entire inner surface of the pan very thinly with butter, then pour in a thick layer of batter, swirling it round so that it covers the sides as well as the base of the pan. The heat will immediately set a thin layer, so that the excess can be easily poured back into the jug. By this means you will get a blintze so thin that by the time the sides of the pancake begin to curl from the pan, the bottom will be brown and the top side dry. Turn the pancake out on to a sheet of greaseproof or silicone paper. Rebutter pan and repeat the process until all the pancakes have been made (there should be 12). As each pancake stops steaming, stack one on top of the previous one, browned side up. (At this stage the pancakes can be frozen, refrigerated overnight or stuffed.)

To stuff the pancakes Place a pancake brown-side up on a board or counter. Spread a tablespoon of the filling thinly over the bottom half, turn in the sides and roll up into a long thin roll. Repeat with each pancake. (The blintzes can now be refrigerated overnight or frozen.)

To fry Heat 2 oz (50 g/¼ cup) butter and 2 teaspoons of oil in a wide frying pan. The moment the butter stops foaming, put in the blintzes, join side upwards. Cook gently for 3 minutes, until golden brown, turn and cook the second side.

To bake in the oven Melt 2-3 oz (50-75 g/¼-⅓ cup) butter. Preheat the oven to Gas No. 5 (375°F/190°C). Arrange the blintzes 1 inch (2.5 cm) apart on a tray lined with silicone paper. Brush each blintze thoroughly with the melted butter and bake for 20-25 minutes, until crisp and golden brown.

Baked or fried blintzes may be kept hot for up to 15 minutes at Gas No. 3 (325°F/160°C). Serve with ice-cold soured cream or smetana, usually as a starter.

CHEESE BOREKS

Makes 24 small pastries.
Raw and cooked pastries will keep under refrigeration for 3 days (brushed lightly with fat if raw) and covered tightly with foil.
Freeze raw 3 months.

Borekas de Kezo, boreks, borrekas and Hojaldres de Queso are all similar little triangles or half-moons of cheese-filled pastry which are common to the many different Sephardic communities. The fillings are varied and include potato and cheese, aubergine (eggplant) and cheese, egg and cheese, and spinach and cheese (similar to the spanakopitas). They are all very similar in concept to the Ashkenazi knishes and kreplach, the dough or pastry used distinguishing one from another. Turkish Jews, for instance, use a pastry made with melted margarine, water and oil, while Syrians and Lebanese Jews tend to use filo, as in my recipe below.

8 sheets of filo pastry (about 8 oz/225 g)
2-3 oz (50-75 g/¼-⅓ cup) unsalted butter or margarine, melted
sesame seeds

For the filling
8 oz (225 g/2 cups) medium mature Cheddar cheese
1 large egg, beaten to blend
¼ teasp salt
few grinds of black pepper

Preheat the oven to Gas No. 6 (400°F/200°C). Have ready 2 baking sheets brushed with some of the melted butter.

To make the filling Mix the cheese, egg and seasonings to make a sticky paste.

To shape the pastries Cut each sheet of filo

pastry into 3 long strips, each 5 inches (12.5 cm) wide. Brush very lightly but evenly with the melted fat, then fold in half lengthwise and brush with fat again. Put 1 heaped teaspoon of the filling at the bottom of a strip about 1 inch (2.5 cm) from the shorter edge and fold as illustrated.

CHEESE BOREKS

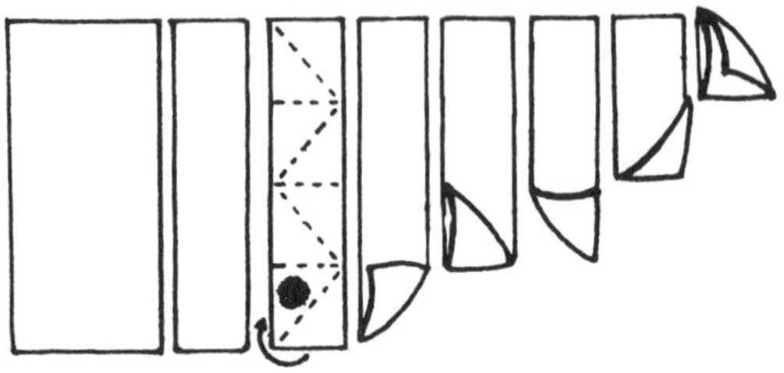

Put pastries on trays and brush again with melted fat, then sprinkle with the sesame seeds. Bake for 20-25 minutes until crisp and golden. Serve at room temperature. May be briefly reheated.

Note If filo pastry is not available, use puff pastry instead, as follows. Preheat the oven to Gas No. 7 (425°F/220°C). Sprinkle 2 oven trays with cold water. Roll out 1 lb (450 g) of puff pastry $\frac{1}{8}$ inch (0.3 cm) thick and cut in circles with a $2\frac{1}{2}$-inch-diameter (6-cm) plain cutter. Put 1 teaspoon of filling in the centre of each circle, then fold over to form a semicircle. Arrange on the trays, brush with beaten egg and scatter with sesame seeds. Bake for 15 minutes until puffed and golden brown. Serve hot. Do not reheat.

CHEESE KNISHES

Makes 24.
Keep 2 days under refrigeration.
Freeze 3 months raw or cooked.

One version of this famous festival dish uses an egg and oil pastry, similar to *'strudelteig'*, another a flaky soured-cream dough, and a third a noodle dough. Although there are many different fillings at Shavuot, one using cheese or a savoury mashed potato is always used. My recipe uses a melt-in-in-the-mouth rich shortcrust which can be made superbly well in the food processor.

For the pastry

8 oz (225 g/2 cups) plain (all-purpose) flour mixed with a pinch of salt
1 teasp icing (confectioners') sugar
5 oz (150 g/$\frac{2}{3}$ cup) firm butter or block margarine
1 egg
1 teasp wine vinegar
1 tbsp icy water
further 1 oz (25 g/2 tbsp) firm butter or margarine

For the filling

nut of butter
2 fat spring onions (scallions), including some of the green
8 oz (225 g/1 cup) medium-fat curd cheese, sieved cottage cheese or Quark
2 tbsp chopped parsley
1 egg, beaten to blend (save 1 tbsp for the glaze)
1 teasp salt
15 grinds of black pepper
little soured cream or natural yoghurt

For the glaze

1 tbsp reserved egg
sesame or poppy seeds

To make the pastry by food processor Put the dry ingredients and the 5 oz (150 g/$\frac{2}{3}$ cup) fat, cut in 1-inch (2.5-cm) cubes, into the bowl. Whisk the egg, vinegar and water to blend, then sprinkle over the surface. Put on the lid, then pulse until the mixture is evenly moistened and looks like a crumble. Tip into a bowl and gather into a ball with lightly floured hands.

To make the pastry by hand or by electric mixer Sift the dry ingredients into a bowl and add the 5 oz (150 g/⅔ cup) fat in cubes, then rub it in until no pieces larger than a small pea come to the surface when the bowl is shaken. Whisk the egg, vinegar and water to blend, sprinkle over the mixture in the bowl, then mix to a dough.

On a floured board, roll the dough mixed by either method into a rectangle about 12 x 6 inches (30 x 15 cm) and spread the top two-thirds with little dabs of the extra 1 oz (25 g/2 tbsp) of fat. Fold in 3, as for flaky pastry, seal the ends and sides with the rolling pin, then gently flatten and roll out again. Fold in 3 once more, seal as before, then chill for at least 1 hour, or overnight. (The dough may also be frozen at this stage.)

To make the filling Heat the nut of butter and quickly sauté the onions until softened but not browned. Combine with all the other ingredients in a bowl and stir well to blend, adding the soured cream or yoghurt only if necessary - the mixture should be moist but thick enough to hold its shape.

To shape and fill the knishes Preheat the oven to Gas No. 7 (425°F/220°C). Have ready 2 ungreased oven trays. Roll out the chilled pastry ¼ inch (0.5 cm) thick and cut into 3-inch (7.5-cm) rounds with a plain cutter. Put a rounded teaspoon of the filling into the centre of each round, then fold into a half-moon and seal the edges. Arrange on the trays and brush with the beaten egg, then scatter with the sesame and poppy seeds. Bake for 15-20 minutes, or until a rich brown. Cool for 15 minutes before serving, or reheat later.

SMETANA AND KAESE BOWL

Serves 6–8.
Keeps 3 days under refrigeration.
Do not freeze.

Cream cheese and soured cream can be served plain as part of a dairy meal, or they can be combined with herbs and seasonings to make a delicious salad bowl, particularly nice with plain digestive biscuits (graham crackers) or fresh brown bread, or as a stuffing for tomatoes.

½ cucumber
1 red or yellow pepper
3 spring onion bulbs (scallions) plus 4 inches (10 cm) of the green stem
1 lb (450 g/2 cups) soft low- or medium-fat cheese
5 fl oz (150 ml/⅔ cup) smetana or fromage frais
1 tbsp low-calorie mayonnaise
1 level teasp salt
1 level tbsp mixed fresh herbs
crisp lettuce

Peel and dice the cucumber, deseed and finely dice the pepper and finely slice the spring onions, then combine with all the other ingredients except the lettuce. Chill, covered, for several hours. Line a wide shallow bowl with the torn lettuce leaves, then spoon the cheese mixture on top.

SPANAKOPITA
Greek Spinach and Cheese Pie

Serves 6–8.
Keeps 2 days under refrigeration.
Freeze raw 1 month.

This can be made in a rectangular dish with the filling sandwiched between layers of filo pastry. But, according to Nicholas Stouroulakis in his *Cookbook of the Jews of Greece*, the Jewish community in Ioannina preferred to spread the filling on layers of pastry, roll it up into a long cylinder and then cut it into 4-inch (10-cm) lengths. Similar Shavuot pastries using a simple Parmesan or Kefotyri cheese filling are called Mourdopita and Frizildik.

In this delicious version the stuffed cylinders are joined together to make a dramatic spiral pastry. However, if preferred, each filled and buttered cylinder can be cut diagonally into 4-inch (10-cm) lengths, scattered with sesame seeds and baked at Gas No. 4 (450°F/180°C) until crisp and golden brown - about 30 minutes.

It is served as a main dish for a dairy meal or as an accompaniment to fish, either plain or with a yoghurt sauce.

12 sheets (approx. 12 oz/350 g) filo pastry
4 oz (125 g/½ cup) unsalted butter, melted

For the filling

2 x 8 oz (225 g) packets frozen leaf spinach or 2 lb (900 g) fresh spinach
1½ oz (40 g/3 tbsp) butter
2 small bunches spring onions (scallions), including 2 inches (5 cm) of the green tops, finely sliced
2 eggs, beaten
8 oz (225 g/2 cups) feta cheese or crumbly Lancashire cheese
3 tbsp fresh chopped dill or 1 tbsp dried dill
½ teasp salt
20 grinds of black pepper
½ teasp grated nutmeg

For scattering on top

2 rounded tbsp sesame seeds

For the sauce

8 oz (225 g/1 cup) Greek-style yoghurt or 8% fromage frais
2 teasp fresh snipped dill or ½ teasp dried dill
½ teasp salt
8 grinds of black pepper

To make the sauce Mix all the ingredients together and chill for several hours.

To make the filling Prepare and cook fresh spinach in the usual way, drain well and chop finely. Defrost frozen spinach, squeeze well in a sieve to remove the moisture, and chop finely. Put in a large mixing bowl.

Heat butter in a frying pan and gently sauté the spring onions until soft - about 5 minutes. Add to the spinach together with the beaten eggs, crumbled cheese, herbs and seasonings. Mix well, then spoon into a 14-inch (35-cm) piping bag fitted with a 1-inch (2.5-cm) plain nozzle.

To assemble Grease an 11-12-inch (27.5-30-cm) pizza pan or the base of a loose-bottomed flan tin, sitting on a baking tray. Stack the sheets of filo on top of each other and cover loosely to prevent them drying out. Place a filo sheet on a board with the long edge towards you and brush lightly all over with melted butter, then cover with a second sheet of filo and brush with butter in the same way. Leaving 1½ inches (4 cm) of the pastry nearest to you clear of filling, pipe a long strip of the filling from one edge of the sheet of pastry to the other. Fold the lower edge of the pastry to enclose this filling, then roll up like a narrow Swiss roll. Repeat with the remaining sheets of filo - there will now be 6 long rolls.

Take 1 roll and brush it lightly all over with butter, then carefully curl it into a spiral and place it in the centre of the baking tin. Take another roll, brush that in the same way, then curl it round the outside of the first spiral. Continue buttering and curling the rolls in the same way, until you have made a giant spiral that completely covers the base of the pan or flan tin. Scatter with sesame seeds. (At this stage it can be frozen or chilled overnight.)

Preheat the oven to Gas No. 5 (375°F/190°C) and bake for 40-45 minutes, or until a rich golden brown.

To serve, transfer to a large glass or pottery plate, leave to cool for 15 minutes, then serve in wedges with the dilled yoghurt.

TOPFENPALATSCHINKEN WITH KIRSCHENSAUCE
(Cream Cheese Pancakes with a Cherry Brandy Sauce)

Serves 6–8.
Keeps 2 days under refrigeration.
Freeze unfilled cooked crêpes 3 months, filled crêpes 1 month.
Sauce keeps 1 week under refrigeration.
Freeze sauce 3 months.

Whereas the origin of cheese blintzes can be found in the native cuisine of Russia, Poland and the Baltic States, these more delicate crêpes are part of the culinary heritage of the former Austro-Hungarian Empire. So the batter is richer, the crêpes are always baked rather than fried and a fruit sauce is served instead of soured cream. They are usually served as a dessert.

batter as for the Blintzes (see p. 654) but using all milk and 1 oz (25 g/2 tbsp) melted butter

For the filling
1 lb (450 g/2 cups) medium-fat curd cheese
1 oz (25 g/2 tbsp) soft butter
3 tbsp caster sugar
1 tbsp lemon juice
1 teasp grated lemon rind
½ teasp vanilla essence (extract)
2 tbsp from an 8 oz (225 g/1 cup) carton Greek-style yoghurt (reserve the remainder to serve with the hot stuffed crêpes)

For the cherry sauce
1 x 15 oz (425 g) can pitted Morello (sour red) cherries and their juice
3 teasp cornflour mixed with 2 tbsp cherry brandy
1 tbsp granulated sugar (if necessary)

To bake the crêpes
1 oz (25 g/2 tbsp) butter, melted

Fry the pancakes as before but cook on the second side also for 30 seconds.

To make the filling Combine all the ingredients and beat until fluffy.

To make the sauce Bring the cherries and their syrup to the boil, stir in the cornflour mixture and allow to bubble for 2 minutes, stirring constantly. Sweeten with sugar if too tart. Pour into a sauce boat and chill.

Lay all the crêpes, pale side up, on a board, and spoon a generous tablespoon of the filling across the lower third of each. Turn the sides and roll up into a cylinder. Arrange side by side on a heatproof platter or gratin dish. The crêpes can be refrigerated at this point for up to 24 hours.

Preheat the oven to Gas No. 5 (375°F/190°C) and brush the surface of the crêpes with the melted butter. Bake for 15 minutes until golden.

Serve accompanied by a spoonful each of cherry sauce and the reserved yoghurt.

YOMTOV CHEESECAKE

Serves 8–10.
Keeps 3 days under refrigeration.
Freeze 3 months.

Serve slightly warm or at room temperature.

A rich, deep cheesecake in the Anglo-Jewish Ashkenazi style, in a lovely tender crust. It can be frozen well in advance.

For the pastry
8 oz (225 g/2 cups) plain (all-purpose) flour
pinch of salt
2 level tbsp icing (confectioners') sugar
5 oz (150 g/⅔ cup) butter
1 egg yolk
1 teasp lemon juice or vinegar
2–3 tbsp icy water

For the filling
4 eggs
2 oz (50 g/¼ cup) caster (superfine) sugar

grated rind of 2 lemons
juice of 1 lemon
8 oz (225 g/1 cup) soft low- or medium-fat cheese
10 fl oz (275 ml/1¼ cups) soured cream
2 level tbsp cornflour (cornstarch)
4 level tbsp sultanas (white raisins)
2 oz (50 g/⅓ cup) chopped mixed candied peel (optional)

To make the pastry by hand or electric mixer Sift together the flour, salt and icing sugar. Cut the butter into 1-inch (2.5-cm) chunks, then rub in gently either by hand or machine until no lumps of mixture larger than a small pea appear on the surface when the bowl is shaken. Beat together the yolk, lemon juice or vinegar, and 2 tablespoons of the water. Sprinkle over the mixture until it is evenly dampened, adding the extra water if necessary. (I usually use my cupped hand at this stage, then gather the dampened mixture together into a dough.)

To make the pastry by food processor Cut the butter into roughly 1-inch (2.5-cm) chunks, then put in the food processor, together with all the other pastry ingredients, and process until the mixture looks like a moist crumble. Tip into a bowl. Gather into a ball.

Using either method, gently knead until smooth and without cracks, flatten into a 1-inch-thick (2.5-cm) disc and chill for at least 45 minutes.

Have ready a round, loose-bottomed flan or cake tin approx 9½ inches (24 cm) in diameter and 2 inches (5 cm) deep. Roll out the pastry ⅛ inch (0.3 cm) thick and carefully lower into the tin, pressing it well in the corners to fit. Cut off the excess from round the rim with a sharp knife. Roll the remaining pastry into a thin round and cut into strips ⅜ inch (1 cm) wide for the lattice top of the cake.

To make the filling, whisk the eggs and sugar until thick, then stir in all the remaining ingredients, ending with the dried fruit. Pour gently into the unbaked pastry base. Moisten the edges of the cake with water, then lay the strips across to form a lattice, sealing well at the edge. Bake in a preheated oven, Gas No. 7 (425°F/220°C), for 15 minutes, then reduce the heat to Gas No. 3 (325°F/160°C) for a further 50 minutes. Turn the oven off and leave the cake to cool in it.

CANADIAN CHEESECAKE

Serves 12.
Keeps 2 days under refrigeration.
Do not freeze.
Best served freshly baked.

Canadian Jewish recipes are a fascinating blend of the *haimische* and the New World. A typical example is this cheesecake - or more correctly, cheese pie - which has a delicious and unusual crust made of cornflakes. Unlike most English cheesecakes, this Canadian one is served hot. Serve squares of it for dessert, accompanied by a luscious cold cherry sauce. It's easy to make the sauce by puréeing a can of cherries and thickening the juice with a little cornflour, or you can use a can of good-quality cherry pie filling, adding a couple of squeezes of lemon juice to offset the sweetness.

The ideal cheese to use is a medium-fat curd cheese (about 12% fat). Otherwise you can use cottage cheese - if it seems rather wet, turn it into a sieve lined with a light-coloured non-woven disposable dishcloth and let it drip for 1 or 2 hours.

For the crust
2 large (8 fl oz/225 ml capacity) cups cornflakes, crushed
4 oz (125 g/1 cup) plain (all-purpose) flour
3 oz (75 g/⅓ cup) brown sugar
½ teasp bicarbonate of soda (baking soda)
4 oz (125 g/½ cup) melted butter

For the filling

2 lb (900 g) curd or other low- or medium-fat soft cheese
4 eggs
5 oz (150 ml/⅔ cup) soured cream
1 tbsp flour
pinch of salt
1 teasp vanilla essence (extract)
grated rind of 1 lemon

Mix all the ingredients for the crust and arrange half the mixture in an even layer in an ovenproof casserole, foil dish or metal baking tray measuring 12 x 7 x 2 inches (30 x 17.5 x 5 cm) - a lasagne-type dish is excellent. Put all the filling ingredients into a mixing bowl in the order given and beat by hand or machine until smooth, then pour on top of the base and cover evenly with the remaining crumb mixture.

An hour before you wish to serve it, bake in a preheated oven, Gas No. 4 (350°F/180°C), for 1 hour.

CREAM CHEESE STRUDEL

Serves 8.
Keep cooked or uncooked strudel 1 day under refrigeration.
Leftovers freeze 2 weeks.

This wonderful strudel is served at room temperature when freshly baked or reheated for 10 minutes in a moderate oven if made overnight. It can be served with tea or coffee, simply dusted with icing (confectioners') sugar. For a dessert, serve it with soured cream or Greek-style yoghurt, plain or lightly sweetened with liquid honey, and mixed with a few chopped toasted almonds or pine kernels or with a fruity fromage frais.

If you cannot obtain filo pastry, use puff pastry rolled paper thin into a rectangle 14 inches (35 cm) wide and 14-16 inches (35-40 cm) long. Bake at Gas No. 8 (450°F/230°C) for 10 minutes, then turn the temperature down to Gas No. 6 (400°F/200°C) for a further 15 minutes, until well browned.

12 oz (350 g/1½ cups) curd or other low- or medium-fat soft cheese
2 oz (50 g/¼ cup) caster (superfine) sugar
1 egg yolk
grated rind of ½ lemon
½ teasp vanilla essence (extract)
1 oz (25 g/2 tbsp) butter
2 oz (50 g/1 cup) fresh breadcrumbs
1 oz (25 g/¼ cup) flaked almonds
6 sheets of filo pastry, defrosted
2-3 oz (50-75 g/¼-⅓ cup) unsalted butter, melted (melt the extra 1 oz/25 g/2 tbsp only if necessary)
little melted butter
1 tbsp granulated sugar, mixed with 1 tbsp flaked almonds

Preheat the oven to Gas No. 5 (375°F/190°C). Have ready a lightly oiled baking sheet.

Mix together the cheese, sugar, egg yolk, lemon rind and vanilla in a bowl. Melt the 1 oz (25 g/2 tbsp) butter in a small frying pan, add the crumbs and almonds and fry gently until golden brown. Allow to cool.

Have ready 6 sheets of pastry, covered with a tea-towel. Lay 1 sheet of pastry on a second tea-towel and, with a pastry brush, paint the top surface very thinly with melted butter. Lay the next sheet on top, brush with butter and repeat for each sheet in turn, stacking them one on top of the other until you have a pile of 6. Leaving 2 inches (5 cm) of pastry bare on the edge nearest to you, spread the third of pastry nearest to you with half the buttered nut and crumb mixture. On top of this mixture lay the cheese filling in a strip about 2 inches (5 cm) wide. Cover with the remaining crumbs.

Now lift up the tea-towel and roll the bare pastry near you on to the filling, then turn in the sides and roll up the strudel. Place it, seam down, on the baking sheet. Paint it all over with a little more melted butter and scatter with the flaked almonds mixed with the granulated sugar. Bake for 20-25 minutes, or until golden-brown.

QUARKSAHN SCHNITTEN (*Cream Cheese Slice*)

Serves 8–10.
Keeps 2 days under refrigeration.
Freeze 1 month.

A true continental torte in the German Jewish style, consisting of a very light sponge filled with a cream-cheese mousse and morello (sour red) cherry or raspberry filling.

A bought fatless sponge can be used, or make the cake described below, which is suitable for any dessert that requires a light and absorbent cake.

1 fatless sponge cake, 9–10 inches (22.5–25 cm) in diameter, frozen for 30 minutes to facilitate slicing
sifted icing sugar
or
3 eggs
3 tbsp cold water
5 oz (150 g/⅔ cup) caster (superfine) sugar
few drops vanilla essence (extract)
2 oz (50 g/½ cup) self-raising flour or 2 oz (50 g/½ cup) plain (all-purpose) flour plus ½ teasp baking powder
2 oz (50 g/½ cup) cornflour (cornstarch)

For the cherry filling
1 x 15 oz (425 g) can morello (sour red) or other tart dessert cherries plus juice
1 tbsp cornflour (cornstarch)
1–2 tbsp Kirsch (optional)

For the raspberry filling
3 oz (75 g/⅓ cup) caster (superfine) sugar
4 fl oz (125 ml/½ cup) water
3 fl oz (75 ml/⅓ cup) orange juice
2 tbsp cornflour (cornstarch)
2 tbsp lemon juice
2 tbsp Crème de Framboises (raspberry liqueur)
1 lb (450 g/2¾ cups) fresh or frozen raspberries

For the cheesecake
½ oz (15 g) kosher gelatine
(or 1 lemon jelly/kosher gelatin mix)
3 tbsp lemon juice
1 lb (450 g/2 cups) curd (medium fat) soft cheese
finely grated rind of ½ lemon
2 oz (50 g/¼ cup) caster (superfine) sugar
½ teasp vanilla essence (extract)
5 fl oz (150 ml/⅔ cup) soured cream or Greek-style yoghurt

To make the cake Whisk the egg whites and water until stiff and fluffy, and then add the sugar and vanilla gradually, whisking until stiff after each addition. Fold in the yolks and then the flour and cornflour (cornstarch). Bake in 2 9-inch (22.5-cm) sandwich tins at Gas No. 4 (350°F/180°C) for about 25 minutes. Then freeze for 30 minutes while you make the fillings.

To make the cherry filling Mix the juice from the cherries made up with orange juice if necessary to 8 fl oz (225 ml/1 cup) with the cornflour (cornstarch). Bring to the boil and bubble for 3 minutes, then stir in the Kirsch (if used). Taste and add sugar if necessary. Add the cherries and allow to go cold.

To make the raspberry filling Dissolve the sugar in the water and orange juice over a moderate heat. Mix the cornflour to a cream with the lemon juice, then stir into the hot syrup, bring to the boil and simmer for 3 minutes until clear. Remove from the heat and stir in the liqueur. Leave to go cold, then stir in the raspberries.

To make the cheesecake Sprinkle the gelatine on to the lemon juice, then heat gently (in the microwave or over hot water) until clear. (If lemon jelly is used, dissolve in the hot lemon juice.)

Put the cheese into a bowl and stir in the dissolved gelatine (or jelly), followed by all the remaining ingredients. Chill while you prepare the tin and cake.

To assemble the cake Have ready a 9–10-inch (22.5–25-cm) loose-bottomed cake tin about 3 inches (7.5 cm) deep. It must be large enough to hold the cake. If using a bought cake, slice in half horizontally and lay the bottom half in the tin. If using the home-made cakes, lay one in the tin in the same way. Spoon the half-set cheesecake on top and cover with the cherry or raspberry filling. Lay the other half or layer of cake lightly on top and refrigerate for at least 6 hours.

To serve Dredge the top of the cake thickly with sifted icing sugar. Stand the tin on a canister or jar of smaller diameter and carefully pull down the sides. Lay the cake, still on the base, on a serving dish. Serve well chilled.

BIBLIOGRAPHY

Allen, Darina, *Simply Delicious*, Gill and Macmillan Ltd, Dublin, 1989.

Allen, Myrtle, *The Ballymaloe Cookbook*, Gill and Macmillan Ltd, Dublin, 1988.

The American Heritage Cookbook, Penguin Books, Harmondsworth, 1967.

Angel, Gilda, *Sephardic Holiday Cooking*, Decalogue Books, Mount Vernon, New York, 1986.

Aresty, Esther B., *The Delectable Past*, Allen and Unwin, London, 1964.

Atrutel, J., *An Easy and Economical Book of Jewish Cookery upon Strictly Orthodox Lines*, London, 1880.

Bahloul, Joelle, *La Culte de la Table Dressée: Rites et Traditions de la Table Juive Algérienne*, Edition A-N Metalie, Paris, 1983.

Ballin, Neville David, *Early Days of Sheffield Jewry: 1760–1900*, Sheffield, 1986.

Bar-David, Molly Lyons, *The Israeli Cookbook*, Crown Publishers Inc, New York, 1964.

——— *Jewish Cooking for Pleasure*, Paul Hamlyn, London, 1965.

Bates, Margaret, *Talking About Cakes*, Pergamon Press, Oxford, 1965.

Batist, Bessie W. (ed), *A Treasure for My Daughter: A Reference Book of Jewish Festivals with Menus and Recipes*, Ethel Epstein Ein Chapter of Hadassah, Montreal, 1950.

Beck, Simone, Louise Bertholle and Julia Child, *Mastering the Art of French Cookery*, Cassell, London, 1964.

Beer, Gretel, *Austrian Cooking*, Andre Deutsch, London, 1954.

Bellin, Mildred Grosberg, *Jewish Cookbook*, Bloch Publishing Co, New York, 1950.

——— *Modern Jewish Meals*, 1952.

Benbassa, Esther and Joelle Bahloul (preface), *Cuisine Judeo-Espagnole: Recettes et Traditions*, Edition du Scribes, 1984.

Berg, Karen, *Danish Home Baking*, Host and Sons Forlag, Copenhagen, 1957.

Blue, Lionel, *Kitchen Blues*, Victor Gollancz, London, 1986.

Boish, Beatrice and Mary Jane Zukin, *From Noodles to Strudels*, Hadassah (Beverley Hills Chapter), Anderson, Ritchie & Simon, Los Angeles, 1972.

Boxer, Arabella, *First Slice Your Cookbook*, Nelson, London, 1965.

Cardella, Antonio, *Sicilia et le Isole in Bocca*, Edizioni Ristampe Siciliana, Palermo, 1986.

Carrier, Robert, *The Robert Carrier Cookery Course*, W. H. Allen, London, 1974.

Casas, Penelope, *The Foods and Wines of Spain*, Penguin Books, Harmondsworth, 1985.

Chamberlain, Narcissa, *The Omelette Book*, Sidgwick & Jackson, London, 1967.

Chamberlain, Samuel, *Bouquet de France*, Hamish Hamilton, London, 1957.

Christensen, Lillian Langseth, *Gourmet's Old Vienna Cookbook*, Gourmet Books Inc., New York, 1959.

Claiborne, Craig, *The New York Times Cook Book*, Paul Hamlyn, London, 1963.

Cornfeld, Lilian, *Israeli and International Cuisine*, G. Cornfeld, Tel Aviv, 1978.

Daniels, Miriam and Hull Friends of Magen David Adom, *Meals Deliciously Appetising*, Hull, 1981.
David, Elizabeth, *French Country Cooking*, Penguin Books, Harmondsworth, 1951.
——— *French Provincial Cookery*, Michael Joseph, London, 1966.
——— *English Bread and Yeast Cookery*, Penguin Books, Harmondsworth, 1977.
Dauzvardis, Josephine J., *Popular Lithuanian Recipes*, Chicago, 1977.
de Lange, Nicholas, *Atlas of the Jewish World*, Equinox, Oxford, 1984.
de Pomiane, Edouarde, *The Jews of Poland: Recollections and Recipes*, Pholiota Press Inc, California, 1985 (1929 in French).
De Quiros, Felipe Torroba Bernaldo, *The Spanish Jews*, Madrid, 1966.
del Conte, Anna, *Secrets from an Italian Kitchen*, Bantam Press, London, 1989.
der Haratounian, Arto, *Sweets and Desserts from the Middle East*, Century, London, 1984.
Dubovsky, Annette and Bloemfontein Women's Zionist League, *Even My Best Friends Have Told Me: Cookery and Cogitations, Recipes and Reminiscences*, Bloemfontein Women's Zionist League, South Africa, 1973.

Eban, Abba, *Heritage - Civilisation and the Jews*, Weidenfeld & Nicolson, London, 1984.
Ellison, J. Audrey, *Patisserie of Scandinavia*, Macdonald Orbis, London, 1989.
Erturk, Ilyas, *Turkish Kitchen Today*, Turkey, 1967.

Fisher, Patty, *Let's Cook with Yeast*, Mills & Boon, London, 1963.
Les Français et la Table, Editions du Réunion des Musées Nationaux, Paris, 1985.
Friedman, Rose and International Jewish Vegetarian Society, *Jewish Vegetarian Cooking: The Finest Traditional Recipes*, Thorsons, Wellingborough, 1984.

General Food Corporation, *All About Baking*, New York, 1935.
Goldstein, Darra, *A Taste of Russia*, Jill Norman, London, 1985.
Greenberg, Florence, *Jewish Cookery*, Penguin Books, Harmondsworth, 1967.
Greenberg, L. J., *Jewish Chronicle Cookery Book*, London, 1934.
Greene, Gloria Kaufer, *Jewish Festival Cookbook*, Robert Hale, London, 1985.
Grossinger, Jennie, *The Art of Jewish Cooking*, Arlington Books, London, 1962 and 1969.
Grossman, Ruth and Bob, *Kosher Cookbook Trilogy*, Galahad Books, New York, 1965.

Hadassah, Naomi Chapter, *Naomi Cookbook*, Toronto, Canada, 1948.
Hartley, Dorothy, *Food in England*, Macdonald, London, 1956.
Hazan, Marcella, *The Classic Italian Cookbook*, Macmillan, London, 1980.
Henry, May and Kate Halford, *Dainty Dinners and Dishes for Jewish Families*, William Lea and Co, London, 1916.
Henry, May and Edith B. Cohen, *The Economical Jewish Cook: A Modern Orthodox Recipe Book for Young Housekeepers - for Schools*, William Lea and Co, London, 1923.
Holt, Geraldene, *French Country Kitchen*, Penguin Books, Harmondsworth, 1987.

Jerome, Helen, *Concerning Cake Making*, Pitman & Sons, London, 1954.

Kander, Simon (Mrs), *Settlement Cook Book*, The Settlement Cook Book Co, Milwaukee, Wis, 1926.
Kasdan, Sara, *Love and Knishes: An Irrepressible Guide to Jewish Cooking*, Vanguard Press, New York, 1956.
Kedourie, Eli (ed), *The Jewish World*, Thames & Hudson, London, 1979.
Kersz, Laurence, *Cuisine de Nos Grand-mères Juives Polonaises*, Editions du Rocher, Paris, 1980.
King, Aileen, *Better Cookery*, Mills & Boon, London, 1957.
Koronyo, V., *Sephardic Cooking Book*, Turkey, 1985.

Leonard, Leah W., *Jewish Cookery: In Accordance with the Jewish Dietary Laws*, Andre Deutsch, London, 1951.

Leventhal, Dennis A. and Hong Kong Jewish Historical Society, *Sino-Judaic Studies: Where and Whither (Kadoorie Memoir), Hong Kong Jewish Chronicle*, 1985.

—— *Faces of the Jewish Experience in China*, Hong Kong Jewish Chronicle, 1990.

Levy, Esther, *Jewish Cookery Book on Principles of Economy Adapted for Jewish Housekeepers*, Pholiota Press Inc, California, 1982 (facsimile; first published in Philadelphia, 1871).

Liebman, Malvina W., *Jewish Cookery from Boston to Baghdad: Customs and Stories*, E. A. Seemann Publishing Inc, Miami, Florida, 1975.

London, Anne and Bertha Kahn Bishov, *Complete American-Jewish Cookbook*, World Publishing Co, Cleveland, Ohio, 1952.

London Beth Din and Evelyn Rose, *Really Jewish Food Guide*, United Synagogue Publications, London, 1992.

Luke, Mark and Judy Ridgway, *Oils, Vinegars and Seasonings*, Mitchell Beazley, London, 1989.

McCall's Cookbook, Random House McCall's, New York, 1963.

McGhee, Harold, *On Food and Cooking*, Allen and Unwin, London, 1984.

Mallos, Tess, *The Tess Mallos Fillo Pastry Cookbook*, A. H. and A. W. Reed, Australia, 1983.

Man, Rosamond, *The Complete Meze Book*, Ebury Press, London, 1986.

Manischewitch, *Traditional Kosher Dishes*, Cincinatti, Ohio, 1930.

Marcovic, Spasenija Pata, *L'Art Culinaire Yugoslave*, Publicisticko-Izdavacki Savod, 1961.

Miner, Viviane Alchech and Linda Krinn, *From My Grandmother's Kitchen: An Exotic Collection of Sephardic Recipes*, Comet, London, 1984.

Montagne, Prosper with the collaboration of Dr Gottschalk, *Larousse Gastronomique*, Paul Hamlyn, London, 1961.

Montefiore, Judith and Chaim Raphael (introduction), *The Jewish Manual, or Practical Information in Jewish and Modern Cookery with a Collection of Valuable Recipes and Hints . . . Edited by a Lady*, Sidgwick & Jackson, London, 1985 (facsimile of the first Jewish cookbook in English, published 1846).

Nicki Morris and Paula Borton (eds), *The Great Fish Book*, Absolute Press, Bath, 1988.

Nahoum, Aldo, *The Art of Israeli Cooking: Original Recipes - Traditional Recipes - All Kosher*, John Gifford Ltd, London, 1970.

Nathan, Joan, *Jewish Holiday Kitchen*, Schocken Books, New York, 1979.

Nathan, Joan and Judy Stacey Goldman, *The Flavour of Jerusalem*, Little, Brown & Co, New York, 1975.

Owen, Sri, *Indonesian Food and Cookery*, Prospect Books, Oxford, 1986.

Pearl, Chaim and Reuben S. Brookes, *A Guide to Jewish Knowledge*, Jewish Chronicle Publications, London, 1958.

Philpot, Rosl, *Viennese Cookery*, Hodder & Stoughton, London, 1967.

Pybus, Meg, *Shropshire's Spicy Secret*, Keith & Meg Pybus, Market Drayton, Shropshire, 1988.

Raphael, Freddy, J. Fisch and J. Koscher, *Recettes de la Table Juive Alsace, Europe de l'Est, Israel, Afrique du Nord*, Librairie Istra, Strasbourg, 1983.

Reider, Frieda, *The Hallah Book: Recipes, History and Traditions*, KTA V Publishing, USA, 1987.

Roden, Claudia, *A New Book of Middle Eastern Food*, Viking, London, 1985.

Romain, Jonathan, *The Jews of England*, Michael Goulston Educational Foundation, London, 1985.

Rose, Evelyn, *The Jewish Home*, Vallentine Mitchell, London, 1969.

——— *Round the Year with Rakusen*, Evelyn Rose and Myer Rose, Manchester, 1981.

——— *The Entertaining Cookbook*, Robson Books, London, 1982 and 1986.

—— (ed), *Cooking for Israel*, Evelyn Rose, Manchester, 1973.

——— *Evelyn Rose Goes Microwave in the*

Jewish Kitchen, Robson Books, London, 1989.

——— *New Jewish Cuisine*, Robson Books, London, 1985 and 1989.

Rose, Evelyn and Magimix, *Magimix Jewish Recipe Book*, ICTC, Isleworth, 1967.

——— *Jewish Cookery with Magimix*, ICTC, Isleworth, 1980.

Ross, Deborah and Manischewitz, *Manischewitz Passover Cookbook*, Walker and Co, New York, 1968.

Rosso, Julee and Sheila Lukins, *The Silver Palate Cookbook*, Ebury Press, London, 1982.

Roukhomovsky, Suzanne, *Gastronomie Juive: Cuisine et Pâtisserie de Russie, d'Alsace, de Roumanie et d'Orient (Tunisie, Egypte)*, Flammarion, Paris, 1968

Scurfield, George and Cecilia, *Home Baked*, Faber & Faber, London, 1956.

Seed, Diana, *The Top 100 Pasta Sauces*, Rosendale Press, London, 1987.

André Simon (ed), *Mushrooms Galore*, Newman Neame, London, 1951.

Sisterhood Temple Beth El (California), *For the Love of Jewish Cooking*, Los Angeles, 1963.

Spry, Constance and Rosemary Hume, *The Constance Spry Cookery Book*, J. M. Dent, London, 1956.

Stobart, Tom, *The Cook's Encyclopaedia*, Batsford Ltd, London, 1970.

State Jewish Museum in Prague, *Tradition of Jewish Cuisine*, State Jewish Museum in Prague, Klausen Synagogue, 1989.

Stavroulakis, Nicholas, *Cookbook of the Jews of Greece*, Lycabettus Press, Greece, 1986.

Sui-Jeung, Chan and Hong Kong Jewish Historical Society, *The Jews in Kaifeng: Reflections on Sino-Judaic History, Hong Kong Jewish Chronicle*, 1986.

Tannahill, Reay, *Food in History*, Penguin Books, Harmondsworth, 1988.

Teubner, Christian and Sybil Grafin Schonfeldt, *Great Desserts*, Paul Hamlyn, London, 1983.

Unterman, Alan, *Dictionary of Jewish Lore and Legend*, Thames & Hudson, London, 1991.

Uvezian, Sonia, *The Cuisine of Armenia*, Harper & Row, New York, 1985.

Viola, Pauline and Knud Ravnkilde, *Cooking with a Danish Flavour*, Elm Tree Books, London, 1978.

White, Florence, *Good Things in England*, The Cookery Book Club, London, 1968.

WIZO (Bowdon and Hale) and Evelyn Rose (foreword), *Our Favourite Recipes*, Bowdon & Hale WIZO, 1961.

WIZO (Hadassah), *Kinnereth Cookbook*, Kinnereth Chapter Hadassah WIZO, Toronto, Canada, 1979.

Wolfert, Paula, *Good Food from Morocco*, John Murray, London, 1989.

Yeshivat Aish Torah WO, *The Kosher for Pesach Cookbook*, Yeshivat Aish HaTorah Women's Organization, Israel, 1978.

Zorica,Herbst and Krausc Peterne, *Magyarorzagi Zsido*, Hungary, 1984.

INDEX